W9-BDH-700

BUSINESS
ESSENTIALS

BUSINESS ESSENTIALS

Ronald J. Ebert
University of Missouri-Columbia

Ricky W. Griffin
Texas A&M University

Frederick A. Starke
University of Manitoba

George Dracopoulos
Vanier College and McGill University

PEARSON

Toronto

Vice-President, Editorial Director: Gary Bennett
Managing Editor: Claudine O'Donnell
Acquisitions Editor: Deana Sigut
Sponsoring Editor: Kathleen McGill
Senior Marketing Manager: Leigh-Anne Graham
Program Manager: Karen Townsend
Project Manager: Rachel Thompson
Developmental Editor: Suzanne Simpson Millar
Media Editor: Nicole Mellow
Media Producer: Daniel Szabo
Production Services: Cenveo® Publisher Services
Permissions Project Manager: Joanne Tang
Photo Permissions Research: Christina Simpson
Text Permissions Research: Sam Bingenheimer
Art Director: Zeneth Denchik
Cover Designer: Miguel Acevedo
Interior Designer: Cenveo Publisher Services
Cover Image: © Jasper James/Stone/Getty

Credits and acknowledgments borrowed from other sources and reproduced, with permission, in this textbook appear on the appropriate page within text.

Original edition published by Pearson Education, Inc., Upper Saddle River, New Jersey, USA. Copyright © 2013, 2011, 2008 Pearson Education, Inc. This edition is authorized for sale only in Canada.

If you purchased this book outside the United States or Canada, you should be aware that it has been imported without the approval of the publisher or the author.

References of company names are not intended to imply any sponsorship, endorsement, authorization, or promotion of Pearson's products by the owners of the company names used, or any relationship between such third parties and Pearson Education, Inc. and/or its affiliates, authors, licensees or distributors.

Copyright © 2015, 2012, 2009, 2006, 2003, 2000, 1997 Pearson Canada Inc. All rights reserved. Manufactured in the United States of America. This publication is protected by copyright and permission should be obtained from the publisher prior to any prohibited reproduction, storage in a retrieval system, or transmission in any form or by any means, electronic, mechanical, photocopying, recording, or likewise. To obtain permission(s) to use material from this work, please submit a written request to Pearson Canada Inc., Permissions Department, 26 Prince Andrew Place, Don Mills, Ontario, M3C 2T8, or fax your request to 416-447-3126, or submit a request to Permissions Requests at **www.pearsoncanada.ca.**

10 9 8 7 6 5 4 3 2 [CKV]

Library and Archives Canada Cataloguing in Publication
Ebert, Ronald J., author
Business essentials / Ronald J. Ebert, Ricky W. Griffin, Frederick A. Starke, George Dracopoulos.—Seventh Canadian edition.
Includes bibliographical references and index.
ISBN 978-0-13-313822-1 (pbk.)
1. Industrial management—Textbooks. 2. Business enterprises—Textbooks. 3. Industrial management—Canada—Textbooks. 4. Business enterprises—Canada—Textbooks. I. Griffin, Ricky W., author II. Starke, Frederick A., 1942-, author III. Dracopoulos, George, 1970-, author IV. Title.

HD70.C3E32 2014 658 C2013-906607-1

ISBN 978-0-13-313822-1

To Fran, for bringing a lifetime of friendship, fun, and love into our family.

—R.J.E.

For Paul and Sherry—Friends for life.

—R.W.G.

To Ann, Eric, and Grant.

—F.A.S.

To Nitsa and Costa Dean.

—G.D.

BRIEF CONTENTS

CONTENTS

PART 1
INTRODUCING THE CONTEMPORARY BUSINESS WORLD 2

04 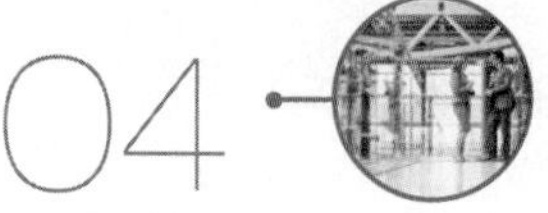

05 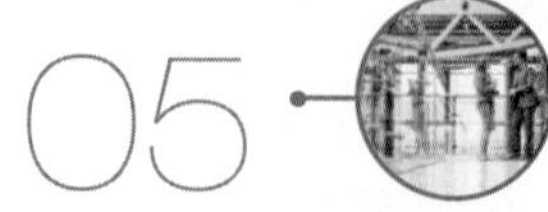

06 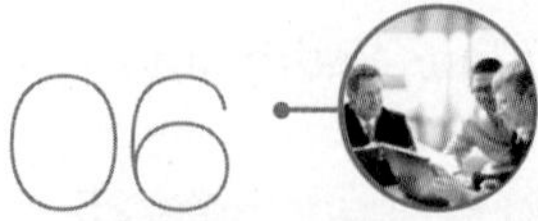

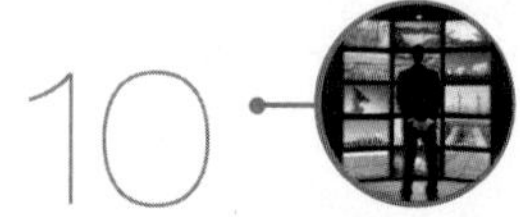

11 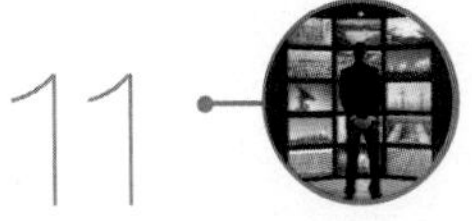

UNDERSTANDING ACCOUNTING 245

PART 4
PRINCIPLES OF MARKETING 278

12 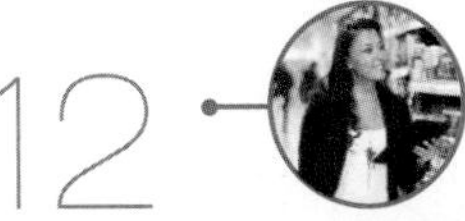

UNDERSTANDING MARKETING PRINCIPLES AND DEVELOPING PRODUCTS 279

13 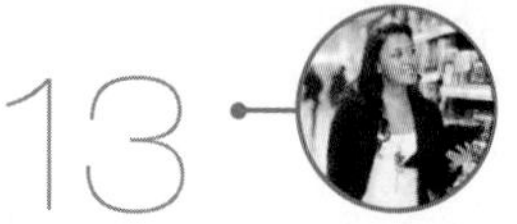

PRICING, PROMOTING, AND DISTRIBUTING PRODUCTS 307

PART 5

MANAGING FINANCIAL ISSUES 334

14 

MONEY AND BANKING 335

15 

FINANCIAL DECISIONS AND RISK MANAGEMENT 359

PREFACE

HELPING STUDENTS BUILD A SOLID BUSINESS KNOWLEDGE FOUNDATION

Welcome to the seventh Canadian edition of *Business Essentials*. In this edition, we continue to emphasize our long-standing principle of "*Doing the Basics Best*." Cutting-edge firsts, up-to-date issues that shape today's business world, and creative pedagogy help students build a solid foundation of business knowledge. This new edition continues with the strengths that made the previous editions so successful—comprehensiveness, accuracy, currency, and readability.

VISUAL WALKTHROUGH

NEW! Interior Design An all-new re-design is clean, bright, and extremely reader-friendly. It will generate a high level of student interest.

UPDATED! Learning Objectives A list of numbered learning objectives is presented at the beginning of each chapter. These objectives—which help students determine what is important in each chapter—are also referenced in the margin opposite the relevant headings in the chapter and in the end-of-chapter summary. Each multiple choice, true/false, and short-answer question in the Test Bank is also identified by Learning Objective.

NEW! Chapter Opening Cases Each chapter begins by describing a situation faced by a real Canadian or global company, which helps students bridge the gap between theory and practice. Topics such as internet entrepreneurs, the NHL lockout, credit-card traps, and others will be of great interest to students. New Questions for Discussion at the end of these opening cases direct student attention to important issues they need to consider.

LO

AFTER READING THIS CHAPTER, YOU SHOULD BE ABLE TO:

LO-1 Define the nature of Canadian *business* and identify its main goals.

LO-2 Describe different types of global *economic systems* according to the means by which they control the *factors of production* through *input* and *output markets*.

LO-3 Describe the interactions between business and government in Canada.

LO-4 Show how *demand* and *supply* affect resource distribution in Canada.

LO-5 Identify the elements of *private enterprise* and explain the various *degrees of competition* in the Canadian economic system.

The Mobile Phone Market: It's Competitive Out There!

The first cell phone call was made in 1973 (with the phone pictured below). Smartphones have come a long way since then and are one of the most successful products ever invented. Beyond the traditional phone call, they

Kathy deWitt/Alamy

AP Photo/Alex Brandon

allow consumers to take pictures, access email, browse the web, and play music. Worldwide, 875 million smartphones were sold in 2013 and that number is expected to increase to 1 billion by 2015. In 2013, Samsung had about 33 percent of the market, Apple about 21 percent.

NEW! There's an APP for that! Each chapter includes a description of several useful apps related to the chapter material. These apps allow students to engage in business concepts in new and dynamic ways.

THERE'S AN APP FOR THAT!

1. **The Economist App** >>> **Platforms:** *Apple, Android, BlackBerry*
   Source: The Economist
   Key Features: Free access to the editor's top 6 must-read articles; access to the full magazine for subscribers
2. **Economics App** >>> **Platforms:** *Apple, Android, BlackBerry*
   Source: WagMob
   Key Features: On-the-go learning—interactive tutorials, quizzes, and flashcards on key economic terms and theories

NEW & UPDATED! Text Boxes on Key Topics Four series of boxed inserts are integrated throughout the text: Managing in Turbulent Times, Entrepreneurship and New Ventures, The Greening of Business, and E-Business and Social Media. Virtually all of the material in these boxed inserts is either new or updated.

ENTREPRENEURSHIP AND NEW VENTURES

Coalition Music: Entrepreneurial Spirit in the Entertainment Industry

Entrepreneurs identify opportunities, access resources, improve on, or build something from scratch. Their creations must provide value that other people can appreciate and support through purchases of goods or services. When you think of that entrepreneurial spirit, you might imagine an old traditional manufacturer or retailer or a new high-tech start-up. However, that entrepreneurial spirit can be found in all types of organizations. The people behind Coalition Music are a prime example.

Eric Lawrence and Rob Lanni founded Coalition Music back in 1990. Today, this organization represents some of the biggest names in Canadian music, such as Simple Plan, Our Lady Peace, and Finger Eleven. For all their hard work, Coalition Music was awarded the honour of Company of the Year at the 2012 Canadian Music and Broadcast Industry Awards. This was a nice acknowledgement,

Success in the music business is not just about numbers, but clearly these statistics point to Eric's and Rob's ability to identify opportunities and manage talent. Dealing with artists requires the skill set to handle egos, provide valuable input, and to manage expectations. After spending over two decades building a wealth of industry knowledge, the two entrepreneurs took their passion to a new level.

Artist Entrepreneur Program

While Coalition Music is a distinct business, they represent music artists who have their own brands, unique identities, fan bases, promotional efforts, etc. In other words, they are in the business of helping each artist manage his or her own distinct business identity. It's the artists' music and their ability to connect with their fans (sell music, tickets, and merchandise) that determines their survival. The second you visit the website and read about the company, this core principle is highlighted—Coalition develops "artist–entrepreneurs" and helps them build long-standing careers in

Simple Plan is one of the great successful acts represented by Coalition Music.

AFP/Getty Images

a classroom. The location has been visited by Drake and MuchMusic.

Do you think you have what it takes to be an artist-entrepreneur? If the answer is yes, you might want to look into this program. If the answer is no (because you lack the raw talent to be a musician) perhaps you might want to reconsider. According to Eric Lawrence, "some of our students have come in dreaming of being a music artist but have

NEW! Video Cases Two video cases appear at the end of each of the five Parts of the text. Nine of the ten video cases are new. The videos can be shown in class to prompt classroom discussion using the questions at the end of the written case. Or, ask students to complete a written assignment based on the questions. This approach to teaching adds a positive dynamic to classes because students will be able to relate text material to actual Canadian business situations. The cases are also available through the MyBizLab for *Business Essentials,* Seventh Canadian Edition.

CBC VIDEO CASE 1-2 CBC

MAKING MONEY BY GOING GREEN?

As concern for the environment increases, more and more Canadian businesses are going green (and trying to make a profit by doing so). Here are three examples.

MARITIME GEOTHERMAL LTD.

Glen Kaye, of Maritime Geothermal Ltd., says that Canadians are starting to become interested in geothermal heat, which is a clean alternative to fossil fuels. Linda Naccarato, a Burlington, Ontario, homeowner, is drilling for this heat in her yard. With it, she can heat her home, swimming pool, and driveway (to melt snow in the winter). This "energy from the ground" produces only one-quarter of the greenhouse gas emissions produced by fossil fuels. The initial installation cost of the system is pretty high, but the system pays for itself within 5 to 7 years. After that, the homeowner gets cheap heat. Electricity is needed to run the heat pump, but the cost of that is only one-quarter of the cost of a traditional furnace burning fossil fuels. Customers using geothermal heat have the added advantage of not having to worry about changes in the price of fossil fuels.

Geothermal heating works because (1) heat travels from something warm to something colder, and (2) a great deal of heat is retained in the falling on the planet. There are two main ways to capture geothermal heat. The most efficient method is used in areas where very hot ground-water is available (usually where tectonic plates come together). This water is pumped directly into radiators to heat homes and offices. This type of heat has been used for many years in Iceland. Thermal water is also used in Boise, Idaho, and Squamish, B.C. Hot water can also be used to run turbines to generate electricity.

The second method involves getting heat from the ground. This is possible because the temperature of the ground three metres below the surface has a fairly stable temperature of about 10 degrees Celsius. Here's how it works: holes are drilled in the ground and small-diameter pipes filled with a mix of water and ethanol are installed in the holes. In the winter, the liquid is colder than the soil, so it absorbs heat from the ground. A heat pump brings the heat to the surface, and fans blow it around. The pipes are connected to a heat exchanger in the home, so no furnace is needed. Once the liquid cools off, it is then pumped back into the ground and the process starts all over again. In summer, when above-ground temperatures exceed 10 degrees, the system is reversed (i.e., the heat pump moves heat from the home or office into the ground where the liquid in the pipes is cooled by the earth and then

NEW! Examples of Business Practice These examples focus on both large and small companies like Beyond the Rack, Netflix, Groupon, Target, Silicon Sisters, Coalition Music, Scotiabank, and Subaru, just to name a few. Some of these examples are brief while others are more detailed, but they all help students better understand important business concepts.

NEW & UPDATED! End-of-Chapter Case Virtually all of the end-of-chapter cases are new or substantially updated.

BUSINESS CASE

IS SUPPLY MANAGEMENT A GOOD IDEA?

Producers in several industries in Canada operate under a system called *supply management*, where domestic production quotas are established for commodities like dairy products, maple syrup, eggs, chickens, and turkeys. Producers of these commodities are not allowed to produce more than the quota they have been granted. To prevent foreign competitors from entering the market, high tariffs are charged on imports of these commodities (e.g., the tariff on butter is 299 percent, on cheese 246 percent, and on milk 241 percent).

David Osborn/Alamy

ARGUMENTS AGAINST SUPPLY MANAGEMENT

The critics of supply management—who have become increasingly vocal during the last decade—argue that supply management leads to higher consumer prices, smuggling, reduced levels of innovation and entrepreneurial activity, and reduced export opportunities.

Higher Consumer Prices By restricting supply, the supply management system provides producers with a more stable environment than companies in other industries have to cope with. As well, companies in supply-management industries don't face much of a threat from foreign competition because such high tariffs are applied to imported products that they are uncompetitive. While this is good for producers, it is not so good for consumers who have to pay higher prices for supply-managed commodities. For example, prices of dairy products in Canada were 115 percent higher than in New Zealand for the entire period between 1983 and 2010, and 23 percent higher than prices in the U.S. The higher prices that result from supply management hurt poor Canadian consumers the most because they spend a larger proportion of their income on food items.

Smuggling and Illegal Purchases One typical outcome of price controls and quotas is smuggling activity, as entrepreneurs see an opportunity to make money by buying a commodity in a low-priced area and selling it in a higher-priced area. The higher the duty that is charged on

They did this because U.S. cheese costs about one-third the price of Canadian cheese. Niagara Regional Police were said to be checking pizza parlours to see if they were using the illegally imported cheese.

There are also some interesting developments in the maple syrup industry. In 2002, the Federation of Quebec Maple Syrup Producers tightened up its supply management system by imposing quotas, which were introduced with the stated goal being to ensure that producers got a "fair" price for their syrup and to reduce volatility in the price of syrup. Producers who exceed their quotas must transfer the excess into the strategic reserve. Inspectors use various techniques to catch syrup bootleggers, just like government agents did during the prohibition era in the 1920s in the U.S. Etienne St. Pierre is one individual who has confronted the Federation about its rules. Because St. Pierre is based in New Brunswick, he says Quebec's quota rules don't apply to him and he can purchase syrup from anyone he pleases. The Federation disagrees, saying he has to buy from accredited suppliers so that the Federation can ensure the high quality of the syrup is maintained, and so the cachet of Quebec's syrup isn't damaged.

Reduced Levels of Innovation and Entrepreneurial Activity The supply management system may create more "order" in an industry, but critics charge that it reduces the innovation and risk-taking that are so important in the development of new products and services. Because companies in supply-managed industries are protected from foreign competition, they have less incentive to innovate and to develop new production methods and new products that consumers want. The Organisation for Economic Cooperation and Development (OECD) praised Canada for eliminating the Wheat Board, but noted that Canada's supply management system is a problem because it distorts production and negatively affects trade.

Lost Export Opportunities Canada is one of the most export-

NEW! Assisted-Graded Writing Assignments Selected end-of-chapter questions, identified by >>>, have been built as assisted-graded assignments within MyBizLab to help assess students' written communication skills. Each question is built with marking rubrics to help facilitate the grading of these assignments.

QUESTIONS AND EXERCISES

QUESTIONS FOR ANALYSIS

1. Why is it important for managers to understand the environment in which their businesses operate?
2. It has been argued that inflation is both good and bad. Explain. Are government efforts to control inflation well-advised? Explain.
3. What are the benefits and risks of outsourcing? What, if anything, should be done about the problem of Canadian companies outsourcing jobs to foreign countries? Defend your answer.

See >>> for Assisted-Graded Writing Assignment

4. >>> Explain how current economic indicators such a and unemployment affect you personally. Explain how managers.
5. At first glance, it might seem as though the goals of e growth and stability are inconsistent with one another. this apparent inconsistency be reconciled?
6. >>> What is the current climate in Canada regarding of business? How might it affect you if you were a ma

APPLICATION EXERCISES

7. Select two businesses you are familiar with. Identify the major elements of their external environments that are most likely to affect them in important and meaningful ways.
8. Assume that you are the owner of an internet pharmacy that sells prescription drugs to U.S. citizens. Analyze the factors in the external environment (economic, technological, political–legal, and socio-cultural) that might facilitate your company's activities. Analyze the factors in the external environment that might threaten your company's activities.
9. >>> Select a technology product, such as the Samsung Galaxy smartphone or Amazon's Kindle e-reader, and research how the various environments of business (economic, technolo cultural, global, political–legal, and general business) a impacting the sales possibilities of the product or serv
10. Interview two business owners or managers. Ask them the following questions: (a) What business functions, i they outsource? (b) Are they focusing more attention process management now than in the past? (c) How applications and the growth of social media changed conduct business?

NEW! Dynamic Study Modules powered by Amplifire Accessed via any computer or mobile device, these Dynamic Study Modules deliver a truly engaging solution that's proven to optimize study times, enhance test scores, boost knowledge acquisition and improve retention.

NEW! Marketing Chapters Condensed Based on reviewer comments, the three marketing chapters in the sixth edition have been reduced to two in the seventh edition. Material has been streamlined and revised to make it more effective for an introduction to business course. Extensive topic coverage of marketing issues continues, but in a more succinct fashion. This change reduces the total number of chapters in the text from 16 to 15.

NEW & UPDATED! Supplemental Content Five supplements are placed at the end of relevant chapters in the text and contain more detailed information about specific topics.

- The first supplement—**A Brief History of Canadian Business in Canada**—is at the end of Chapter 1. The material in this supplement (summarized in the text and included in its entirety online in MyBizLab) describes the development of business activity in Canada over the last 300 years.
- The second supplement—**Business Law**—is found at the end of Chapter 3 and includes key topics such as contracts, the concept of agency, warranties, copyrights and trademarks, and bankruptcy.
- The third supplement—**Information Technology (IT)**—is included at the end of Chapter 11. It focuses on the impact that IT has had on the business world, the IT resources businesses have at their disposal, the threats that information technology poses for businesses, and the ways in which businesses protect themselves from these threats.
- The fourth supplement—**Managing Your Personal Finances**—is at the end of Chapter 14. The material in this supplement (briefly summarized in the text and included in its entirety online in MyBizLab) presents a down-to-earth, hands-on approach that will help students manage their personal finances. Included in the supplement is a worksheet for determining personal net worth, insightful examples demonstrating the time value of money, a method for determining how much money to invest now in order to build a future nest egg of a certain size, suggestions on how to manage credit-card debt, guidelines for purchasing a house, and a personalized worksheet for setting financial goals.
- The fifth supplement—**Insurance as Risk Management**—is found at the end of Chapter 15. It provides information on insurable vs. uninsurable risks, the different types of insurance products that are available, and special forms of business insurance.

CHAPTER SUPPLEMENT 3

Using Technology *to* Manage Information in the Internet and Social Media Era

Throughout the text, we examine how the internet and the emergence of social media have improved communications, revolutionized distribution, augmented human resources practices, revolutionized industries (and threatened others), developed new marketing communication channels, and changed the most basic business systems. In this appendix, we will begin by providing additional information about the internet and social media. We will also examine the evolving role of technology in managing information.

INFORMATION TECHNOLOGY (IT) The various devices for creating, storing, exchanging, and using information in diverse modes, including visual images, voice, multimedia, and business data.

E-COMMERCE Buying and selling processes that make use of electronic technology.

INTERNET MARKETING The promotional efforts of companies to sell their products and services to consumers over the internet.

INTERNET USAGE

Before we look into the specific impact of the Internet on business, let's examine some of the key Canadian internet statistics. In terms of speed, Hong Kong has the fastest internet connections in the world; Canada ranks 13th.[1] However, Canada is ranked 9th among G20 countries in terms of internet contribution to GDP. It is expected to rank 12th by 2016, with Saudi Arabia, Australia and Mexico climbing ahead. There are 25.5 million Canadian internet users and the average time spent online is 41.3 hours per month, which ranks second in the world behind only the United States.[2] In addition, 94 percent of Canadians that live in households with incomes above $85 000 are connected (only 56 percent for households with incomes below $30 000 per year).[3] These figures will continue to increase for the next few years. The federal government has also set its sights on increasing and improving the connectivity in rural settings; it invested in 52 projects worth over $225 million in 2010. At that time, it cost approximately $89 per month for 5Mbps (megabits per second) connections in most rural areas. But consumers could get 10Mbps for about $47 a month in most cities, or get 50 Mbps (a 10 times faster connection) for about the same fee as rural customers paid for only 5Mbps. The improved infrastructure will help increase rural access, build further opportunities for companies wishing to sell to rural Canadian clients, and also provide more incentive and opportunity for small businesses to operate in rural settings.[4]

THE IMPACT OF INFORMATION TECHNOLOGY (IT)

No matter where we go, we can't escape the impact of **information technology (IT)**—the various devices for creating, storing, exchanging, and using information in diverse modes, including visual images, voice, multimedia, and business data. We see ads all the time for the latest smartphones, laptops, iPads and other tablets, and software products, and most of us connect daily to the internet (many of you never disconnect). Email and BlackBerry (BBM) messaging have become staples in business, and even such traditionally "low-tech" businesses as hair salons and garbage collection companies are becoming dependent on the internet, computers, and networks. As consumers, we interact with databases every time we withdraw money from an ATM, order food at McDonald's, use an Apple or Android application to order food or movie tickets, or check on the status of a package at UPS or FedEx.

IT has had an immense effect on businesses—in fact, the growth of IT has changed the very structure of business organizations. Its adoption has altered workforces in many companies, contributed to greater flexibility in dealing with customers, and changed the way that employees interact with each other. E-commerce has created new market relationships around the globe. We begin by looking at how businesses are using IT to bolster productivity, improve operations and processes, create new opportunities, and communicate and work in ways not possible before.

THE IMPACT OF THE INTERNET ON MARKETING

E-commerce refers to buying and selling processes that make use of electronic technology, while **internet marketing** refers to the promotional efforts of companies to sell their products and services to consumers over the internet.[5]

While internet marketing has some obvious advantages for both buyers (access to information, convenience, etc.) and sellers (reach, direct distribution, etc.), it also has weaknesses, including profitability problems (many internet marketers are still unprofitable and the failure rates are high), information overload (consumers may not know what to do with all the information available to them), and somewhat limited markets (consumers who use the web are typically more highly educated). In addition to these weaknesses, internet marketers must also cope with consumer concerns about two security-related issues.

Consumers also object to spyware software, which monitors websites they visit and observes their shopping habits. This software is often implanted on their personal computers as they wander through the web. It then generates advertisements that are targeted to that particular consumer.

WHAT'S NEW IN THE SEVENTH CANADIAN EDITION?

New content has been included in all chapters. An illustrative (but not exhaustive) list is as follows:

Chapter 1—new material on the mobile phone market, the "China effect" on commodity prices, and Canada's supply management system

Chapter 2—new material on Walmart's expansion into South Africa, competitive forces in the Canadian retail market and in the coffee trade, and trends in the economic environment that have led to the growth of discount stores and bargain retailers

Chapter 3—new material on the fair trade movement, ethical models, technological innovations and their impact on ethics, encouraging ethical behaviour in organizations, dilemmas in the green movement, counterfeit brands, whistle-blowers, and sustainability

Chapter 4—new information on the top small- and medium-sized employers in Canada, the role of angel investors, and the activities of business incubators

Chapter 5—new material on the European debt crisis, the BRICS countries, the impact of currency fluctuations on business activity, global adaptation of products, foreign direct investment in Canada, and changes in Europe (a new north vs. south emphasis in contrast to the former east vs. west emphasis)

Chapter 6—new material on goal setting, crisis management, corporate culture, and the overtime pay controversy

Chapter 7—new material on the Occupy Wall Street movement, divisional organization structures, and Kodak's strategy crisis

Chapter 8—new material on the NHL lockout, green careers, employee orientation, workforce diversity, public sector unions, union organizing strategy, and behaviour-based interviewing

Chapter 9—new material on employee satisfaction in the workplace, telecommuting, and employee involvement

Chapter 10—new material on the manufacturing sector in Canada, the production of green energy, production scheduling tools, global productivity comparisons, supply-chain disruptions, and automotive quality rankings

Chapter 11—new material on investigative forensic accounting, ethics in the accounting profession, and progress toward unification of the accounting profession under the Chartered Professional Accountant (CPA) designation

Chapter 12—new material on product values and benefits, green products and services, customer relationship management (CRM), the marketing environment and its impact on marketing strategy, integrated marketing strategy, market segmentation, organizational (B2B) marketing, and extending the product life cycle

Chapter 13—new material on target markets, promotion and its effect on consumer decision processes, the influence of the internet and the power of consumer engagement, mobile media, and supply-chain initiatives

Chapter 14—new material on credit cards, "digital wallets," the Canadian dollar, and the potential mortgage crisis in Canada

Chapter 15—new material on alleged cash "hoarding" by corporations, short selling, mobile investing, and crowdfunding

MyBizLab — Visit the MyBizLab website. This online homework and tutorial system puts you in control of your own learning with study and practice tools directly correlated to this chapter's content.

STUDENT RESOURCES

MyBizLab is an online grading, assessment, and study tool for faculty and students. It engages students and helps them focus on what they need to study. It can help students get a better grade because they are learning in an interactive and focused environment. MyBizLab delivers all classroom resources for instructors and students in one place.

Dynamic Study Modules Break through to a new world of learning with **MyLab's Mobile Dynamic Study Modules**. Accessed via any computer or mobile device, these **Dynamic Study Modules** deliver a truly engaging solution that's proven to optimize study times, enhance test scores, boost knowledge acquisition, and improve retention.

Enhanced eText Available within the online course materials and offline via an iPad app, the enhanced eText allows instructors and students to highlight, bookmark, take notes, and share with one another.

INSTRUCTOR'S RESOURCES

Instructor's Resource Centre Instructor resources are password protected and available for download via **www.pearsoned.ca**. For your convenience, these resources are also available online at **www.pearsoned.ca/mybizlab** in the instructor area.

NEW! Integrated Instructor's Resources eText Useful Teaching Tips and Resources, identified by an apple icon, are easily identified throughout the Pearson eText located within MyBizLab. Instructors will find Chapter Overviews and Outlines, Teaching Tips, Quizzes, Solutions to end-of-chapter exercises, and other valuable resources. Collated versions of this resource can also be downloaded from the Instructor Resources at MyBizLab.com.

NEW & UPDATED! Test Bank This substantially enhanced test bank in Microsoft Word format contains approximately 4000 multiple-choice, true/false, short-answer, and essay questions. **NEW Critical Thinking** multiple-choice questions will help in the assessment of comprehension and application of the concepts. **NEW Bloom's Taxonomy** tagging and textbook page references tied to each question will help in the efficacy of student assessment. This robust test bank is also available in MyTest format (see below).

MyTest Pearson's powerful online assessment-generation program facilitates easy creation and printing of quizzes, tests, and exams, as well as homework or practice handouts. Questions and tests can all be authored online, allowing instructors ultimate flexibility and the ability to efficiently manage assessments at any time, from anywhere.

UPDATED! Instructor's Resource Manual The Instructor's Resource Manual contains chapter synopses, outlines, teaching tips, in-class exercises, case studies, and suggestions on how to use the text effectively. The manual also provides answers to the end-of-chapter questions and cases (including Building Your Business Skills, Exercising Your Ethics, and the CBC Video Cases).

NEW! PowerPoint® Presentations *PowerPoint Presentations* offer an average of 40 PowerPoint slides per chapter, outlining the key points in the text. **NEW** for this edition are improved visuals, unique examples, and quick-check questions. The slides also include lecture notes, summaries, and suggestions for student activities or related questions from the text.

UPDATED! CBC Video Library The CBC Video Library for *Business Essentials*, Seventh Canadian Edition, includes ten segments, nine of which are new to this edition. Drawn from CBC programs such as *The National*, *Dragon's Den*, and *Marketplace*, these videos accompany the video cases found at the end of each part in the text. Business issues from across the country are discussed from a Canadian point of view. The cases can also be viewed online at **www.pearsoned.ca/highered/videocentral**, and answers to the discussion questions are provided in the Instructor's Resource Manual.

NEW! Pearson Introduction to Business CourseConnect CourseConnect is a two-time CODIE-Award winning comprehensive, personalizable, online course built to specific learning outcomes. CourseConnect courses include interactive lesson presentations and a complete, integrated assessment strategy. Our courses are ideal for online and blended environments, in which courses are taught remotely and asynchronously—meaning the instructor and student are not always in the same physical location at the same time. Our courses are built by subject matter experts and credentialled instructional designers, then rigorously evaluated for quality, alignment, and instructional design.

Pearson Custom Publishing Pearson Custom Publishing can provide you and your students with texts, cases, and articles to enhance your course. Choose material from Darden, Ivey, Harvard Business School Publishing, NACRA, and Thunderbird to create your own custom casebook. Contact your Pearson Education Canada sales representative for details.

Online Learning Solutions Pearson Education Canada supports instructors interested in using online course management systems. We provide text-related content in Blackboard/WebCT and Course Compass. To find out more about creating an online course using Pearson content in one of these platforms, contact your Pearson Education Canada sales representative.

Your Pearson Education Canada Sales Representative Your Pearson sales rep is always available to ensure you have everything you need to teach a winning course. Armed with experience, training, and product knowledge, your Pearson rep will support your assessment and adoption of any of the products, services, and technology outlined here to ensure our offerings are tailored to suit your individual needs and the needs of your students. Whether it's getting instructions on TestGen software or specific content files for your new online course, your Pearson sales representative is there to help. Ask your Pearson sales representative for details.

Technology Specialists Pearson's Technology Specialists work with faculty and course designers to ensure that Pearson technology products, assessment tools, and online course materials are tailored to meet your specific needs. This highly qualified team is dedicated to helping schools integrate a variety of instructional materials and media formats. Your local Pearson Education sales representative can provide you with more details on this service program.

CourseSmart CourseSmart is a new way for instructors and students to access textbooks online anytime, from anywhere. With thousands of titles across hundreds of courses, CourseSmart helps instructors choose the best textbook for their class and give their students a new option for buying the assigned textbook as a lower cost eTextbook. For more information, visit www.coursesmart.com.

ACKNOWLEDGMENTS

We owe special thanks to Charlotte Morrison-Reed, copyeditor; Marisa D'Andrea, Production Editor; Kathleen McGill, Sponsoring Editor; Suzanne Simpson Millar, Developmental Editor; and others at Pearson Education Canada who assisted with the production, marketing, and sales of this edition.

We also appreciate the insights and suggestions of the following individuals who provided feedback on the sixth edition or reviewed the manuscript for the new edition:

Bruce Anderson, University of Regina
Charles A. Backman, Grande Prairie Regional College
Bruce Bennett, College of New Caledonia
Maria Blazkiewicz, Dawson College
Katherine Breward, University of Winnipeg
Timothy Hardie, Lakehead University
Steve Janisse, St. Clair College
Gerry La Rocca, Vanier College
Kandy Larden, Langara College
Valerie Miceli, Seneca College of Applied Arts and Technology
Lisa Phillips, Douglas College
Dustin Quirk, Red Deer College
Jeff Short, Humber College Institute of Technology and Advanced Learning
Gordon Spicer, John Abbott College
Foster Stewart, SAIT Polytechnic
Rick Tong, Kwantlen Polytechnic University
Bruce Weir, Kwantlen Polytechnic University

ABOUT THE AUTHORS

Ronald J. Ebert is Emeritus Professor at the University of Missouri-Columbia where he lectures in the Management Department and serves as advisor to students and student organizations. Dr. Ebert draws upon more than 30 years of teaching experience at such schools as Sinclair College, University of Washington, University of Missouri, Lucian Blaga University of Sibiu (Romania), and Consortium International University (Italy). His consulting alliances include such firms as Mobay Corporation, Kraft Foods, Oscar Mayer, Atlas Powder, and John Deere. He has designed and conducted management development programs for such diverse clients as the American Public Power Association, the United States Savings and Loan League, and the Central Missouri Manufacturing Training Consortium.

His experience as a practitioner has fostered an advocacy for integrating concepts with best business practices in business education. The five business books he has written have been translated into Spanish, Chinese, Malaysian, and Romanian. Dr. Ebert has served as the editor of the *Journal of Operations Management*. He is a past-president and fellow of the Decision Sciences Institute. He has served as consultant and external evaluator for *Quantitative Reasoning for Business Studies*, an introduction-to-business project sponsored by the National Science Foundation.

Ricky W. Griffin is Distinguished Professor of Management and holds the Blocker Chair in Business in the Mays School of Business at Texas A&M University. Dr. Griffin currently serves as executive associate dean. He previously served as head of the Department of Management and as director of the Center for Human Resource Management at Texas A&M. His research interests include workplace aggression and violence, executive skills and decision making, and workplace culture. Dr. Griffin's research has been published in such journals as *Academy of Management Review, Academy of Management Journal, Administrative Science Quarterly,* and *Journal of Management.* He has also served as editor of *Journal of Management*. Dr. Griffin has consulted with such organizations as Texas Instruments, Tenneco, Amoco, Compaq Computer, and Continental Airlines.

Dr. Griffin has served the Academy of Management as chair of the organizational behaviour division. He also has served as president of the southwest division of the Academy of Management and on the board of directors of the Southern Management Association. He is a fellow of both the Academy of Management and the Southern Management Association. He is also the author of several successful textbooks, each of which is a market leader. In addition, they are widely used in dozens of countries and have been translated into numerous foreign languages, including Spanish, Polish, Malaysian, and Russian.

Frederick A. Starke is Emeritus Professor of Organizational Behaviour in the Asper School of Business at the University of Manitoba. He began his career at the University of Manitoba in 1968 and has taught courses in organizational behaviour, organization theory, decision making, and marketing. He has served in several administrative positions, including Head of the Department of Business Administration from 1982 to 1987 and from 1989 to 1994, and as Associate Dean of the Asper School of Business from 1996 to 2005.

Dr. Starke earned his BA and MBA from Southern Illinois University and his PhD in Organizational Behaviour from Ohio State University. He has published research articles in such scholarly journals as *Administrative Science Quarterly*, *Journal of Applied Psychology*, *Academy of Management Journal, Journal of Management Studies,* and *Journal of Business Venturing*. He has also written articles for professional journals, such as *Journal of Systems Management, Information Executive*, and *Canadian Journal of Nursing Administration*.

Dr. Starke also writes textbooks that are used by university and community college students in business programs across Canada. These titles include *Organizational Behaviour*, *Business Essentials*, *Management*, and *Business*. Dr. Starke also presents seminars on the topics of decision making and goal setting to practising managers in both the public and private sectors.

George Dracopoulos is a member of the Business Administration department at Vanier College. In the past, he has served as chairman of the department but is now devoting significant energy to his role as the *International Business Exchange Coordinator*. In recent years, George has created links and built bridges with universities and businesses throughout France and Belgium. To date, hundreds of students have benefitted from these initiatives. He is also the co-organizer and co-founder of the national *BDC/Vanier Marketing Case Competition*. George was recently awarded with the distinction as the *Vanier VIP* for his dedication and devotion to the community.

George also serves as a lecturer at McGill University, teaching traditional and online courses. He recently worked on an online broadcast pilot-project and built a prototypical course geared primarily towards aboriginal students. He was recently named as a *"Professor of the Year"* by a McGill University publication for his work in the Desautels Faculty of Management. George earned his MBA at McGill, as well as a graduate Diploma in Education and a Graduate Degree in Applied Management. He earned his BA at Concordia University. Mr. Dracopoulos is an advocate of experiential learning and dedicates a significant amount of class time to hands-on projects. His primary interests are in the fields of marketing and management.

Outside his teaching career, Mr. Dracopoulos has worked in marketing and sales positions. He has been invited to speak and/or provide keynote addresses at major events across North America. While completing his university education, he spent a semester abroad studying management globalization issues in Europe. He has also spent a considerable amount of time coaching high-level sports and organizing events.

In addition to this text, he has worked on many publishing projects providing web content and multimedia material. Recent Pearson publications include *Business in Action*, In-Class Edition, second Canadian edition (2009), co-authored with Courtland L. Bovée and John V. Thill, and *Business,* eighth Canadian edition (2014), co-authored with Ricky Griffin, Ronald J. Ebert, Frederick Starke, and Melanie Lang.

BUSINESS
ESSENTIALS

PART 1 INTRODUCING THE CONTEMPORARY BUSINESS WORLD

Pool/Getty Images

CHAPTER 01

Understanding the Canadian Business System

LO

AFTER READING THIS CHAPTER, YOU SHOULD BE ABLE TO:

LO-1 Define the nature of Canadian *business* and identify its main goals.

LO-2 Describe different types of global *economic systems* according to the means by which they control the *factors of production* through *input* and *output markets*.

LO-3 Describe the interactions between business and government in Canada.

LO-4 Show how *demand* and *supply* affect resource distribution in Canada.

LO-5 Identify the elements of *private enterprise* and explain the various *degrees of competition* in the Canadian economic system.

The Mobile Phone Market: It's Competitive Out There!

The first cell phone call was made in 1973 (with the phone pictured below). Smartphones have come a long way since then and are one of the most successful products ever invented. Beyond the traditional phone call, they allow consumers to take pictures, access email, browse the web, and play music. Worldwide, 875 million smartphones were sold in 2013 and that number is expected to increase to 1 billion by 2015. In 2013, Samsung had about 33 percent of the market, Apple about 21 percent.

Kathy deWitt/Alamy

AP Photo/Alex Brandon

3

Other companies in the top five were China-based ZTE and Huawei Technologies (not to be confused with Taiwan-based HTC). Apple and Samsung currently account for about 99 percent of the profit in the industry, while everyone else is struggling. The market presents huge profit potential for companies that come up with smartphone features that consumers want. However, the market is also characterized by intense competition, a dizzying array of frequent new product introductions, and patent infringement lawsuits. It's competitive out there!

The most publicized new product in the last few years has been Apple's iPhone, but Samsung has become the biggest player in this market with the introduction of its Galaxy S III and S IV smartphones. Other new products include Motorola's Droid, Huawai's Ascend D, BlackBerry's Q10 (with a keyboard) and Z10 (with a touchscreen), Sony's Xperia Z, and ZTE's Grand. About 90 percent of smartphones currently use the Android and iOS operating systems.

Samsung has pulled customers away from Apple in the consumer market and is now taking aim at BlackBerry in the business market. The "sandboxing" trend (separating work functions from the rest of the smartphone for security reasons) means that employees are increasingly using their own phone at work without losing access to other applications like games or social networking. This trend has allowed Samsung to increase its corporate business. BlackBerry used to dominate the business market, but, in 2013, smartphone shipments to companies were dominated by Apple (50 percent) and Samsung (16 percent). BlackBerry had just 10 percent of the business market. Throughout 2013, rumours circulated that BlackBerry would be taken over by another company.

In the first quarter of 2010, BlackBerry was one of the top five mobile phone companies in the world, with a market share of 35.8 percent. By the middle of 2011, it had dropped to just 9 percent. BlackBerry's share price reflects its misfortunes, falling from $70 per share in 2010 to less than $13 per share in mid-2013. BlackBerry lost ground to both Apple and Samsung partly because it didn't have nearly as many apps as they did. For example, Songza—a popular free music app for smartphones—wasn't available for the BlackBerry (the company is now developing one). Apps are very important in the competitive race for sales. There are 775 000 apps available in Apple's App Store and 675 000 apps for Google's Android operating system, but only 90 000 are currently available for the BlackBerry. To fix this problem, BlackBerry is reaching out to app developers by staging events such as the "BlackBerry Jam" developer conferences.

In this industry, no company can relax. For example, in spite of Apple's market success during the past few years, the price of its stock has declined sharply (in early 2013, the price was down 24 percent from its record high of $705 per share in September 2012). Why? Market analysts are concerned about Apple's ability to compete in the rapidly changing smartphone market. Consider what happened to Nokia. Once the top producer of cell phones, it was overtaken by Apple in 2011 and by Samsung in 2012. In 2011, Nokia introduced the Lumia 900 smartphone in an attempt to re-establish itself as an important player in the industry. But Nokia cut more than 10 000 jobs in 2012 and its stock has dropped 70 percent since 2011.

Patent infringement lawsuits abound in this rapidly changing industry, adding another layer of complexity on top of an already highly uncertain situation. In 2012, for example, Apple sued Samsung, claiming that Samsung devices infringed on patents held by Apple. A court ruled in favour of Apple and awarded it $1 billion (the amount was later reduced on appeal). Earlier, BlackBerry was sued by Virginia-based NTP and had to pay that company over $600 million in damages.

It is difficult to predict exactly what will happen in the mobile phone industry or who will be the big winners. The only thing we can be sure of is that competition will remain fierce, new product introductions will continue at a rapid pace, and consumers will eagerly anticipate "the next big thing."

HOW WILL THIS HELP ME?

All businesses are subject to the influences of economic forces. But these same economic forces also provide astute managers and entrepreneurs with opportunities for profits and growth. The ideas presented in this chapter will help you to better understand (1) how *managers* deal with the challenges and opportunities resulting from economic forces, and (2) how *consumers* deal with the challenges and opportunities of price fluctuations.

QUESTIONS FOR DISCUSSION

1. In this chapter, you will read about four different degrees of competition that can be observed in a private enterprise system: perfect competition, monopolistic competition, oligopoly, and monopoly. What degree of competition exists in the smartphone market? Did you have any difficulty deciding on the degree of competition? Explain your reasoning.
2. What is the likely future of the smartphone industry in terms of the number of companies that will exist and the diversity of the products they will offer to consumers? (Hint: Think about what has happened in other industries that grew rapidly when their new products became popular with consumers.)

LO-1 THE IDEA OF BUSINESS AND PROFIT

BUSINESS An organization that seeks to earn profits by providing goods and services.

PROFIT What remains (if anything) after a business's expenses are subtracted from its sales revenues.

NOT-FOR-PROFIT ORGANIZATION An organization that provides goods and services to customers, but does not seek to make a profit while doing so.

The opening case illustrates the dynamic and rapidly changing nature of modern business activity and the evident opportunities and challenges. It also shows how business managers must pay attention to many different things, including the actions of competitors, rapid technological change, new product development, corporate strategy, stock prices, and a host of other variables that you will read about in this book.

Let's begin by asking what you think of when you hear the word *business*. Do you think of large corporations like Shoppers Drug Mart and Walmart or smaller companies like your local supermarket or favourite restaurant? Do you think about successful companies like CN and Samsung or less successful companies like GM Canada? Actually, each of these firms is a **business**—an organization that produces or sells goods or services in an effort to make a profit. Businesses produce most of the goods and services that we consume, and they employ many of the working people in Canada. Taxes that businesses pay help to support governments at all levels. In addition, businesses help support charitable causes and provide community leadership. A 2011 study by *Forbes* magazine ranked Canada No. 1 (out of 134 countries) as the world's top country in which to do business.[1]

Profit is what remains after a business's expenses have been subtracted from its revenues. Profits reward the owners of businesses for taking the risks involved in investing their time and money. Profits can be very large if a company produces something that consumers really like. For example, the four-part film *Hunger Games* will generate large profits for Lions Gate. The first film in the series generated box office receipts of $155 million in just its first week.

Many organizations in Canada do not try to make a profit. These **not-for-profit organizations** use the funds they generate from government grants or the sale of goods or services to provide services to the public. Charities, educational institutions, hospitals, labour unions, and government agencies are examples of not-for-profit organizations. Business principles are helpful to these not-for-profit organizations as they try to achieve their service goals.

LO-2 ECONOMIC SYSTEMS AROUND THE WORLD

A Canadian business is different in many ways from one in China, and both are different from businesses in Japan, France, or Peru. A major determinant of how organizations operate is the kind of economic system that characterizes the country in which they do business. An **economic system** allocates a nation's resources among its citizens. Economic systems differ in terms of who owns and controls these resources, known as the "factors of production."

ECONOMIC SYSTEM The way in which a nation allocates its resources among its citizens.

FACTORS OF PRODUCTION The resources used to produce goods and services: labour, capital, entrepreneurs, and natural resources.

LABOUR The mental and physical training and talents of people; sometimes called human resources.

Factors of Production

The key difference between economic systems is the way in which they manage the **factors of production**—the basic resources that a country's businesses use to produce goods and services. Traditionally, economists have focused on four factors of production: labour, capital, entrepreneurs, and natural resources. Newer perspectives tend to broaden the idea of "natural resources" to include all physical resources. In addition, information resources are often included now.[2]

LABOUR

The people who work for a company represent the first factor of production—**labour**. Sometimes called human resources, labour is the mental and physical capabilities of people. Carrying out the business of a huge company, such as Imperial Oil, requires a labour force with a wide variety of skills ranging from managers to geologists to truck drivers.

CAPITAL The funds needed to operate an enterprise.

ENTREPRENEUR An individual who organizes and manages labour, capital, and natural resources to produce goods and services to earn a profit, but who also runs the risk of failure.

NATURAL RESOURCES Items used in the production of goods and services in their natural state, including land, water, mineral deposits, and trees.

CAPITAL

Capital refers to the funds that are needed to start a business and to keep it operating and growing. For example, Imperial Oil needs capital to pay for its annual drilling costs, which run into the millions of dollars each year. Major sources of capital for businesses are personal investment by owners, the sale of stock to investors, profits from the sale of products and services, and funds borrowed from banks and other lending institutions.

ENTREPRENEURS

Entrepreneurs are people who accept the opportunities and risks involved in creating and operating businesses. Mike Lazaridis (BlackBerry), Sergey Brin and Larry Page (Google), Michael Dell (Dell), and Mark Zuckerberg (Facebook) are well-known entrepreneurs. The boxed insert entitled "Riversong: Innovative Canadian Guitars" describes the activities of one Canadian entrepreneur.

NATURAL RESOURCES

Natural resources include all physical resources such as land, water, mineral deposits, and trees. Imperial Oil makes use of a wide variety of natural resources. It obviously has vast quantities of crude oil to process

ENTREPRENEURSHIP AND NEW VENTURES

Riversong: Innovative Canadian Guitars

Mike Miltimore was born to be an entrepreneur in the music business. He grew up working in a successful family business (Lee's Music stores) in British Columbia. From a young age, he learned how to negotiate and he gained knowledge about the inner workings of musical instruments. At the age of 36, Mike was the General Manager of Lee's Music in Kamloops, B.C., while also earning new entrepreneurial stripes creating Riversong Guitars, a brand built on an innovation in guitar manufacturing. By 2013, Mike's design had already earned significant buzz when he finished second in the Business Development Bank of Canada (BDC) Young Entrepreneurs competition. While the award was a great honour, Mike understood that he had to address two fundamental business issues.

1. How could he build demand for a new brand in an industry dominated by popular names like Gibson, Martin, Taylor, and Godin?
2. Could he supply enough guitars if his aggressive promotional efforts succeeded?

The Product

What makes Riversong Guitars unique? Mike's experience at Lee's Music gave him insight into a recurring problem with acoustic guitars. According to Mike, most guitars have a structural design flaw; they have a joint where the neck meets the body. In addition, manufacturers often used different woods that have different expansion and contraction rates. In time, these weaknesses impact the performance of the instrument. Armed with knowledge earned from years of customer feedback, Mike set out to build a "better mousetrap." After a great deal of trial and error and with the help of a luthier (someone who builds or repairs stringed instruments), the Riversong guitar was born. The joint where the neck met the body was eliminated. Instead, they ran the neck all the way to the base of the guitar. They then created a mechanism that allowed for easy instrument adjustment in less than five minutes. Mike now had a patent-pending design that he was ready to unleash on the music world.

Building Demand

The BDC exposure was a boost and his second place finish also gave him access to $25 000 worth of consulting services. These communications and internet strategy experts helped him create his online store and provided insight on social media strategies. Building on this momentum, Mike went to the National Association of Music Merchants (NAMM) trade show and met important industry players, including current and international dealers.

Managing Supply

Mike Miltimore has big dreams and has made progress in his quest to increase awareness and demand, but if that "tipping point" occurs, if that great contact materializes, can Riversong deliver supply? Mike is working on that problem as well. The typical 100-hour manufacturing process has been cut down to about 24 hours. Riversong uses CNC (Computer Numerical Control) machines to cut

Antony Nettle/Alamy

the profile of the guitars and a custom bending machine for the sides. Mike proudly states that the he recently hired a grade-ten student and, after just two weeks of training, he was making guitar bodies using this process that could not be distinguished from the work of a master luthier. A new facility is part of the plan.

Riversong Guitars is a home-grown brand made of pure Canadian wood, mainly BC Spruce. Long-term success will depend on the entrepreneur's ability to manage supply and demand and build a brand that takes advantage of the innovation while satisfying customer needs for great sound. You can learn more about Riversong at http://riversongguitars.com/.

CRITICAL THINKING QUESTION

1. What else does Mike Miltimore need to do to get his brand noticed in an industry dominated by well-known brands with long and storied histories?

Based on a case written by Christopher Ross, John Molson School of Business, Concordia University, Riversong Guitars, Vanier/BDC Case Competition 2013.

INFORMATION RESOURCES Information such as market forecasts, economic data, and specialized knowledge of employees that is useful to a business and that helps it achieve its goals.

COMMAND ECONOMY An economic system in which government controls all or most factors of production and makes all or most production decisions.

MARKET ECONOMY An economic system in which individuals control all or most factors of production and make all or most production decisions.

COMMUNISM A type of command economy in which the government owns and operates all industries.

each year. But Imperial Oil also needs the land where the oil is located, as well as land for its refineries and pipelines.

INFORMATION RESOURCES

Information resources include the specialized knowledge and expertise of people who work in businesses, as well as information that is found in market forecasts and various other forms of economic data. Information is a key factor of production because unlike land, labour, and capital, information can be shared without it being diminished. For example, if two people exchange apples, they still each have only one apple, but if two people exchange ideas, each person now has two ideas instead of one.[3]

Types of Economic Systems

Different types of economic systems manage the factors of production in different ways. In some systems, ownership is private; in others, the factors of production are owned by the government. Economic systems also differ in the ways decisions are made about production and allocation. A **command economy**, for example, relies on a centralized government to control all or most factors of production and to make all or most production and allocation decisions. In **market economies**, individuals—producers and consumers—make production and allocation decisions through the mechanism of supply and demand.

COMMAND ECONOMIES

The two most basic forms of command economies are communism and socialism. As originally proposed by nineteenth-century German economist Karl Marx, **communism** is a system in which the government owns and operates all sources of production. Marx envisioned a society in which individuals would ultimately contribute according to their abilities and receive economic benefits according to their needs. He also expected government ownership of production factors to be only temporary. But Marx's predictions were faulty. During the last 20 years, most countries have abandoned communism in favour of a more market-based economy. Even countries that still claim to be communist (for example, China, Vietnam, and Cuba) now contain elements of a market-based economy. Whether communism can be maintained alongside a market-based economy remains to be seen.

>>> Starbucks uses various factors of production, including labour (a Starbucks barista), entrepreneurs (CEO Howard Schultz), and natural resources (such as coffee beans).

Tony Karumba/AFP/Getty Images

SOCIALISM A kind of command economy in which the government owns and operates the main industries, while individuals own and operate less crucial industries.

MARKET An exchange process between buyers and sellers of a particular good or service.

INPUT MARKET Firms buy resources that they need in the production of goods and services.

OUTPUT MARKET Firms supply goods and services in response to demand on the part of consumers.

CAPITALISM An economic system in which markets decide what, when, and for whom to produce.

MIXED MARKET ECONOMY An economic system with elements of both a command economy and a market economy; in practice, typical of most nations' economies.

PRIVATIZATION The transfer of activities from the government to the private sector.

NATIONALIZATION The transfer of activities from private firms to the government.

In a less extensive command economic system called **socialism**, the government owns and operates only selected major industries. Smaller businesses such as clothing stores and restaurants may be privately owned. Although workers in socialist countries are usually allowed to choose their occupations or professions, a large proportion generally work for the government. Many government-operated enterprises are inefficient, since management positions are frequently filled based on political considerations rather than ability. Extensive public welfare systems have also resulted in very high taxes. Because of these factors, socialism is generally declining in popularity.[4]

MARKET ECONOMIES

A **market** is a mechanism for exchange between the buyers and sellers of a particular good or service. For example, the internet is a technologically sophisticated market that brings buyers and sellers together through e-commerce. People usually think of e-commerce as being business-to-consumer (B2C) transactions, such as buying books over the internet for personal use. But business-to-business (B2B) transactions are also a very important market. B2B involves businesses joining together to create e-commerce companies that make them more efficient when they purchase the goods and services they need. B2B transactions actually far exceed B2C transactions in dollar value.

In a market economy, B2C and B2B exchanges take place without much government involvement. To understand how a market economy works, consider what happens when a customer goes to a fruit stand to buy apples. Assume that one vendor is selling apples for $1 per kilogram, and another is charging $1.50. Both vendors are free to charge what they want, and customers are free to buy what they choose. If both vendors' apples are of the same quality, the customer will likely buy the cheaper ones. But if the $1.50 apples are fresher, the customer may buy them instead. Both buyers and sellers enjoy freedom of choice (but they also are subject to risks, as the financial meltdown of 2008 demonstrated).

A GlobeScan poll of over 20 000 people in 20 different countries asked people whether they agreed with the following statement: "The free market economy is the best system." Where do you think the highest support for capitalism was found? Not in Canada, the United States, Germany, or Japan, but in *China*, where 74 percent of people polled agreed with the statement.[5] This occurred in spite of the Chinese government's strong support of the communist economic ideology. After China's constitution was amended to permit private enterprise, the private sector has become incredibly productive. It is estimated that China produces 60 percent of all the toys in the world,[6] and China's reputation for being a low-cost producer of goods is legendary. It is also a vast and rapidly growing market for many of the products that Canadian firms produce—chemicals, ores, cereals, and wood products. Changes are also occurring in communist Cuba, where more private initiative is being encouraged, and the role of the state is being reduced in some sectors.[7]

Input and Output Markets A useful model for understanding how the factors of production work in a pure market economy is shown in Figure 1.1.[8] In the **input market**, firms buy resources from households, which then supply those resources. In the **output market**, firms supply goods and services in response to demand on the part of the households. The activities of these two markets create a circular flow. Ford Motor Co., for example, buys labour directly from households, which may also supply capital from accumulated savings in the form of stock purchases. Consumer buying patterns provide information that helps Ford decide which models to produce and which to discontinue. In turn, Ford uses these inputs in various ways and becomes a supplier to households when it designs and produces various kinds of automobiles, trucks, and sport-utility vehicles and offers them for sale to consumers.

Individuals are free to work for Ford or an alternative employer and to invest in Ford stock or alternative forms of saving or consumption. Similarly, Ford can create whatever vehicles it chooses and price them at whatever value it chooses. Consumers are free to buy their next car from Ford, Toyota, BMW, or any other manufacturer. The political basis for the free market economy is called **capitalism**, which allows private ownership of the factors of production and encourages entrepreneurship by offering profits as an incentive. This process contrasts markedly with that of a command economy, in which individuals may be told where they can and cannot work, companies may be told what they can and cannot manufacture, and consumers may have little or no choice as to what they purchase or how much they pay for items.

MIXED MARKET ECONOMIES

Command and market economies are two extremes, or opposites. In reality, most countries rely on some form of **mixed market economy** that features characteristics of both command and market economies. One trend in mixed market economies that began in the 1990s is **privatization**—converting government enterprises into privately owned companies. In Canada, for example, the air traffic control system was privatized, and the federal government sold several other corporations, including Canadian National Railway and Air Canada. The Netherlands privatized its TNT Post Group N.V., and India privatized 18 industries, including iron, steel, machinery, and telecommunications.[9] In 2010, the Organisation for Economic Co-operation and Development (OECD) said that Canada Post's monopoly should be ended and it should be privatized.[10] However, when a worldwide recession began in 2008, the trend slowed. Government bailouts of Chrysler and GM in both Canada and the U.S. meant that government was once again a part-owner of some business firms. A few countries are even pursuing a policy of **nationalization**—converting private firms into government-owned firms. Venezuela, for example, nationalized its telecommunications industry.

OUTPUT MARKETS
Goods
Services

FIRMS
- Supply products in output markets
- Demand resources in input markets

HOUSEHOLDS
- Demand products in output markets
- Supply resources in input markets

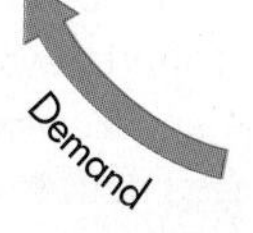

INPUT MARKETS
Labour
Capital
Entrepreneurs
Natural resources
Information resources

<<< **FIGURE 1.1** Circular flow in a market economy

>>> Many former command economies have moved toward a more mixed economic model.

Thierry Roge/Reuters/Landov

Deregulation means a reduction in the number of laws affecting business activity and in the powers of government enforcement agencies. This trend also developed during the 1990s, and deregulation occurred in many industries, including airlines, pipelines, banking, trucking, and communications. But this trend has also slowed (and even reversed in some cases) due to the 2008 recession. For example, there have been calls for a dramatic

DEREGULATION A reduction in the number of laws affecting business activity.

THERE'S AN APP FOR THAT!

1. **The Economist App** >>> **Platforms:** *Apple, Android, BlackBerry*
   Source: *The Economist*
   Key Features: Free access to the editor's top 6 must-read articles; access to the full magazine for subscribers
2. **Economics App** >>> **Platforms:** *Apple, Android, BlackBerry*
   Source: WagMob
   Key Features: On-the-go learning—interactive tutorials, quizzes, and flashcards on key economic terms and theories
3. **IB Smart Economics** >>> **Platforms:** *Apple*
   Source: IB Smart
   Key Features: Fun, interactive games designed to aid learning

APP DISCOVERY EXERCISE

Since APP availability changes, conduct your own search for "Top 3" Economic Statistics APPS and identify the key features.

tightening up of the laws regulating business activity, particularly in the financial sector. The British Petroleum (BP) oil spill in the Gulf of Mexico in 2010 caused the U.S. government to put pressure on BP to reimburse individuals and businesses that were harmed by the spill. Incidents like these have created a dilemma for government policy makers since a 2009 study by the Conference Board of Canada showed that deregulation (in tandem with privatization and increased competition) caused a sharp increase in productivity in sectors like freight and airlines.[11]

As a result of the recession of 2008, mixed market economies are now characterized by more government involvement than was evident just a few years ago. Governments in mixed market economies have intervened in the economic system in an attempt to stabilize it, but this has led to higher deficits (see Chapter 2) and more control of business activity.

LO-3 INTERACTIONS BETWEEN BUSINESS AND GOVERNMENT

CANADIAN RADIO-TELEVISION AND TELECOMMUNICATIONS COMMISSION (CRTC) Regulates and supervises all aspects of the Canadian broadcasting system.

COMPETITION ACT Prohibits a variety of business practices that lessen competition.

In Canada's mixed market economy, there are many important interactions between business and government. The ways in which government influences business and the ways business influences government are described below.

How Government Influences Business

Government plays several key roles in the Canadian economy, and each of these roles influences business activity in some way. The roles government plays are as follows.

GOVERNMENT AS A CUSTOMER

Government buys thousands of different products and services from business firms, including office supplies, office buildings, computers, battleships, helicopters, highways, water treatment plants, and management and engineering consulting services. Many businesses depend on government purchasing, if not for their survival then at least for a certain level of prosperity. Total government expenditures in 2011 were $267.5 billion.[12]

GOVERNMENT AS A COMPETITOR

Government also competes with business through Crown corporations, which are accountable to a minister of parliament for their conduct. Crown corporations like Hydro-Quebec (revenues of $12.7 billion) and Canada Post ($7.4 billion) account for significant economic activity in Canada.[13] Crown corporations exist at both the provincial and federal levels. ex: ICBC & private insurance

GOVERNMENT AS REGULATOR

Federal and provincial governments in Canada regulate many aspects of business activity through administrative boards, tribunals, and commissions. An example is the **Canadian Radio-Television and Telecommunications Commission (CRTC)**, which issues and renews broadcast licences. Provincial boards and commissions also regulate business activity, but different situations exist in different provinces. For example, prior to 2011, the provinces of Quebec and B.C. allowed mixed martial arts events such as the UFC, while Ontario did not (Ontario began allowing these events in 2011).[14] Reasons for regulating business activity include protecting competition, protecting consumers, achieving social goals, and protecting the environment.

Promoting Competition Competition is crucial to a market economy, so government regulates business activity to ensure that healthy competition exists among business firms. Without these restrictions, a large company with vast resources could cut its prices and drive smaller firms out of the market. The guidelines for Canada's competition policy are contained in the **Competition Act**, which prohibits a variety of practices (see Table 1.1). Section 61, for example, prohibits something called resale price maintenance. Labatt Brewing Co. recently pled guilty to resale price maintenance and was fined $250 000 after its sales representatives gave money to store operators who agreed to not lower prices on some brands of beer. This activity meant that customers had to pay higher prices for beer.[15]

The Act prohibits agreements among companies that are designed to reduce competition. Formerly, the government had to prove that such agreements actually reduced competition, but recent changes to the legislation mean that the mere existence of a conspiracy is assumed to be proof that competition has been reduced.[16] Another major change is the dramatically increased fines for misleading marketing practices by corporations (formerly $100 000 for the first offence, now $10 million).[17]

Businesses often complain that the Competition Bureau is too slow in approving or denying merger plans. For example, when Labatt Brewing wanted to take over Lakeport Brewing, it was told that the Competition Bureau would need up to six months to determine whether the takeover would lessen competition. Labatt therefore appealed to the Competition Tribunal to speed up the process. The Tribunal agreed with Labatt, and the merger went ahead sooner than it otherwise would have.[18] In addition to the Competition Bureau delay, the federal industry minister also began an investigation after a Federal Court judge accused the Competition Bureau of providing misleading information in order to get a court order for Labatt's records during its review of the proposed merger.[19]

TABLE 1.1 The Competition Act

Section 45	Prohibits conspiracies and combinations formed for the purpose of unduly lessening competition in the production, transportation, or storage of goods. Persons convicted may be imprisoned for up to five years, fined up to $1 million, or both.
Section 50	Prohibits illegal trade practices. A company may not, for example, cut prices in one region of Canada while selling at a higher price everywhere else if this substantially lessens competition. A company may not sell at "unreasonably low prices" if this substantially lessens competition. (This section does not prohibit credit unions from returning surpluses to their members.)
Section 51	Prohibits giving allowances and rebates to buyers to cover their advertising expenses, unless these allowances are made available proportionally to other purchasers who are in competition with the buyer given the rebate.
Section 52	Prohibits marketing (promotion) activities that are false or misleading. Includes telemarketing activities.
Section 53	Prohibits the deceptive notice that a person has won a prize if the recipient is asked to pay money as a condition of winning the prize.
Section 54	Prohibits charging the higher price when two prices are shown on a product.
Section 55.1	Prohibits pyramid selling (a participant in the plan receives compensation for recruiting other individuals into the plan).
Section 61	Prohibits resale price maintenance. No person who produces or supplies a product can attempt to influence upward, or discourage reduction of, the price of the good in question. It is also illegal for the producer to refuse to supply a product to a reseller simply because the producer believes the reseller will cut the price.
Section 74	Prohibits bait-and-switch selling. No person can advertise a product at a bargain price if there is no supply of the product available to the consumer. (This tactic baits prospects into the store, where salespeople switch them to higher-priced goods.) This section also controls the use of contests to sell goods and prohibits the sale of goods at a price higher than the advertised one.

Protecting Consumers The federal government has initiated many programs that protect consumers. Consumer and Corporate Affairs Canada administers many of these. Important legislation includes the **Tobacco Act** (which prohibits cigarette advertising on billboards and in stores), the **Weights and Measures Act** (which sets standards of accuracy for weighing and measuring devices), the **Consumer Packaging and Labelling Act** (which stipulates labelling requirements for products), the **Textile Labelling Act** (which regulates the labelling, sale, importation, and advertising of consumer textile articles), and the **Food and Drug Act** (which prohibits the sale of food that contains any poisonous or harmful substances). In 2011, the **Canada Consumer Product Safety Act** (which replaced the former Hazardous Products Act) came into force. It requires poisonous, flammable, explosive, or corrosive products to be appropriately labelled. In addition to federal regulations, consumers are also protected by provincial and municipal bylaws (e.g., "no smoking" bylaws).

Achieving Social Goals Social goals, which promote the well-being of Canadian society, include things like universal access to health care, safe workplaces, employment insurance, and decent pensions. All of these goals require the interaction of business firms and the Canadian government. But the decisions of foreign governments—as they pursue their own social goals—can also affect Canadian businesses. For example, when the U.S. government introduced legislation making it difficult for online gambling companies to operate in the U.S., the stock prices of Canadian firms like Cryptologic Inc. and Chartwell Technology dropped.[20]

TOBACCO ACT Prohibits cigarette advertising on billboards and in retail stores and assigns financial penalties to violators.

WEIGHTS AND MEASURES ACT Sets standards of accuracy for weighing and measuring devices.

CONSUMER PACKAGING AND LABELLING ACT States labelling requirements for products

TEXTILE LABELLING ACT Regulates the labelling, sale, importation, and advertising of consumer textile articles.

FOOD AND DRUG ACT Prohibits the sale of food unfit for human consumption and regulates food advertising.

CANADA CONSUMER PRODUCT SAFETY ACT Regulates banned products and products that can be sold but must be labelled as hazardous.

Hazardous products must have warning labels to protect consumers who use them.

Craig Ruttle/AP Photo/CP Images

CANADA WATER ACT Controls water quality in fresh and marine waters of Canada.

FISHERIES ACT Regulates the discharge of harmful substances into water.

ENVIRONMENTAL CONTAMINANTS ACT Establishes regulations for airborne substances that are a danger to human health or to the environment.

REVENUE TAXES Taxes whose main purpose is to fund government services and programs.

PROGRESSIVE REVENUE TAXES Taxes levied at a higher rate on higher-income taxpayers and at a lower rate on lower-income taxpayers.

REGRESSIVE REVENUE TAXES Taxes that cause poorer people to pay a higher percentage of their income than richer people pay.

RESTRICTIVE TAXES Taxes levied to control certain activities that legislators believe should be controlled.

LOBBYIST A person hired by a company or an industry to represent its interests with government officials.

Protecting the Environment Government legislation designed to protect the environment includes the **Canada Water Act** (which controls water quality in fresh and marine waters), the **Fisheries Act** (which controls the discharge of any harmful substance into water), and the **Environmental Contaminants Act** (which establishes regulations for airborne substances that are a danger to human health or the environment).

GOVERNMENT AS A TAXATION AGENT

Taxes are imposed and collected by the federal, provincial, and local governments. **Revenue taxes** (e.g., income taxes) are levied by governments primarily to provide revenue to fund various services and programs. **Progressive revenue taxes** are levied at a higher rate on higher-income taxpayers and at a lower rate on lower-income taxpayers. **Regressive revenue taxes** (e.g., sales tax) are levied at the same rate regardless of a person's income. They cause poorer people to pay a higher percentage of their income for these taxes than rich people pay. **Restrictive taxes** (e.g., taxes on alcohol, tobacco, and gasoline) are levied partially for the revenue they provide, but also because legislative bodies believe that the products in question should be controlled.

GOVERNMENT AS A PROVIDER OF INCENTIVES AND FINANCIAL ASSISTANCE

Federal, provincial, and municipal governments offer incentive programs that attempt to stimulate economic development. The Province of Quebec, for example, has attracted video game companies like Ubisoft by giving them multimillion-dollar subsidies if they locate in the province.[21] The Provinces of Ontario and B.C. have given hundreds of millions of dollars in subsidies to film companies to motivate them to make major films in those provinces.[22]

Industry Canada offers many different programs designed to help small businesses. The Canada Business program, for example, provides information on government programs, services, and regulations in order to improve the start-up and survival rates of small and medium-sized businesses. It also encourages businesses to focus on sound business planning and the effective use of market research. The Department of Foreign Affairs and International Trade (DFAIT) helps Canadian companies doing business internationally by promoting Canada as a good place in which to invest and carry on business activities. It also assists in negotiating and administering trade agreements.

Governments also offer incentives through the many services they provide to business firms through government organizations. Examples include the Export Development Corporation (which assists Canadian exporters by offering export insurance against non-payment by foreign buyers and long-term loans to foreign buyers of Canadian products), Natural Resources Canada (which provides geological maps of Canada's potential mineral-producing areas), and Statistics Canada (which provides data and analysis on almost every aspect of Canadian society). Industry Canada offers many different programs designed to help small businesses.

There are many other government incentive programs, including municipal tax rebates for companies that locate in certain areas, design assistance programs, and remission of tariffs on certain advanced technology production equipment. Government incentive programs may or may not have the desired effect of stimulating the economy. They may also cause difficulties with our trading partners, as we shall see in Chapter 5. Some critics also argue that business firms are too willing to accept government assistance—either in the form of incentives or bailouts—and that managers should put more emphasis on innovation and creativity so business firms can better cope with economic difficulties when they arise, as they did during the 2008 to 2009 recession.

GOVERNMENT AS A PROVIDER OF ESSENTIAL SERVICES

The various levels of government facilitate business activity through the services they supply. The federal government provides highways, the postal service, the minting of money, the armed forces, and statistical data on which to base business decisions. It also tries to maintain stability through fiscal and monetary policy (discussed in Chapter 2). Provincial and municipal governments provide streets, sewage and sanitation systems, police and fire departments, utilities, hospitals, and education. All of these activities create the kind of stability that encourages business activity.

How Business Influences Government

Businesses also try to influence the government through the use of lobbyists, trade associations, and advertising. A **lobbyist** is a person hired by a company or industry to represent that company's interests with government officials. The Canadian Association of Consulting Engineers, for example, regularly lobbies the federal and provincial governments to make use of the skills possessed by private-sector consulting engineers on projects like city water systems. Some business lobbyists have training in the particular industry, public relations experience, or a legal background. A few have served as legislators or government regulators.

The federal Lobbying Act requires lobbyists to register with the Commissioner of Lobbying so it is clear which individuals are being paid for their lobbying activity. It also sets rules for accountability and transparency and requires lobbyists to report detailed information about their communications with what are known as Designated Public Office Holders (DPOHs).[23] For many lobbying efforts, there are opposing points of view. For example, the Canadian Cancer Society and the Tobacco Institute present very different points of view on cigarette smoking and cigarette advertising.

Employees and owners of small businesses that cannot afford lobbyists often join **trade associations**, which may act as an industry lobby to influence legislation. They also conduct training programs relevant to the particular industry, and they arrange trade shows at which members display their products or services to potential customers. Most publish newsletters featuring articles on new products, new companies, changes in ownership, and changes in laws affecting the industry.

Corporations can influence legislation indirectly by influencing voters. A company can, for example, launch an advertising campaign designed to get people to write their MPs, MPPs, or MLAs demanding passage—or rejection—of a particular bill that is before parliament or the provincial legislature.

TRADE ASSOCIATION An organization dedicated to promoting the interests and assisting the members of a particular industry.

LO-4 THE CANADIAN MARKET ECONOMY

Understanding the complex nature of the Canadian economic system is essential to understanding Canadian business. In this section, we will examine the workings of our market economy, including markets, demand, supply, private enterprise, and degrees of competition.

MARKET An exchange process between buyers and sellers of a particular good or service.

DEMAND The willingness and ability of buyers to purchase a product or service.

SUPPLY The willingness and ability of producers to offer a good or service for sale.

LAW OF DEMAND The principle that buyers will purchase (demand) more of a product as price drops.

LAW OF SUPPLY The principle that producers will offer (supply) more of a product as price rises.

DEMAND AND SUPPLY SCHEDULE Assessment of the relationships between different levels of demand and supply at different price levels.

DEMAND CURVE Graph showing how many units of a product will be demanded (bought) at different prices.

SUPPLY CURVE Graph showing how many units of a product will be supplied (offered for sale) at different prices.

MARKET PRICE (EQUILIBRIUM PRICE) Profit-maximizing price at which the quantity of goods demanded and the quantity of goods supplied are equal.

Demand and Supply in a Market Economy

In economic terms, a **market** is not a specific place, like a supermarket, but an exchange process between buyers and sellers. Decisions about production in a market economy are the result of millions of exchanges. How much of what product a company offers for sale and who buys it depends on the laws of demand and supply.

THE LAWS OF SUPPLY AND DEMAND

In a market economy, decisions about what to buy and what to sell are determined primarily by the forces of demand and supply. **Demand** is the willingness and ability of buyers to purchase a product or service. **Supply** is the willingness and ability of producers to offer a good or service for sale. The **law of demand** states that buyers will purchase (demand) more of a product as its price drops. Conversely, the **law of supply** states that producers will offer (supply) more for sale as the price rises.

DEMAND AND SUPPLY SCHEDULES

To appreciate these laws in action, consider the market for pizza in your town. If everyone is willing to pay $25 for a pizza (a relatively high price), the local pizzeria will produce a large supply. If, however, everyone is willing to pay only $5 (a relatively low price), the restaurant will make fewer pizzas. Through careful analysis, we can determine how many pizzas will be sold at different prices. These results, called a **demand and supply schedule**, are obtained from marketing research and other systematic studies of the market. Properly applied, they help managers understand the relationships among different levels of demand and supply at different price levels.

DEMAND AND SUPPLY CURVES

The demand and supply schedule can be used to construct demand and supply curves for pizza. A **demand curve** shows how many products—in this case, pizzas—will be demanded (bought) at different prices. A **supply curve** shows how many pizzas will be supplied (cooked) at different prices.

Figure 1.2 shows the hypothetical demand and supply curves for pizzas in our illustration. As you can see, demand increases as price decreases, and supply increases as price increases. When the demand and supply curves are plotted on the same graph, the point at which they intersect is the **market price**, or **equilibrium price**—the price at which the quantity of goods demanded and the quantity of goods supplied are equal. In Figure 1.2, the equilibrium price for pizzas is $10. At this point, the quantity of pizzas demanded and the quantity of pizzas supplied are the same—1000 pizzas per week.

SURPLUSES AND SHORTAGES

What would happen if the owner tried to increase profits by making more pizzas to sell? Or, what if the owner wanted to reduce overhead,

Canada is the dominant supplier of maple syrup for the world market. But variable weather conditions can create conditions of either surplus or shortage.

Courtesy of Parasuco Jeans Inc.

>>> **FIGURE 1.2** Demand and supply

Source: Adapted from Karl E. Case and Ray C. Fair, *Principles of Economics*, 8th edition, updated (Upper Saddle River, NJ: Prentice Hall, 2007).

SURPLUS Situation in which quantity supplied exceeds quantity demanded.

SHORTAGE Situation in which quantity demanded exceeds quantity supplied.

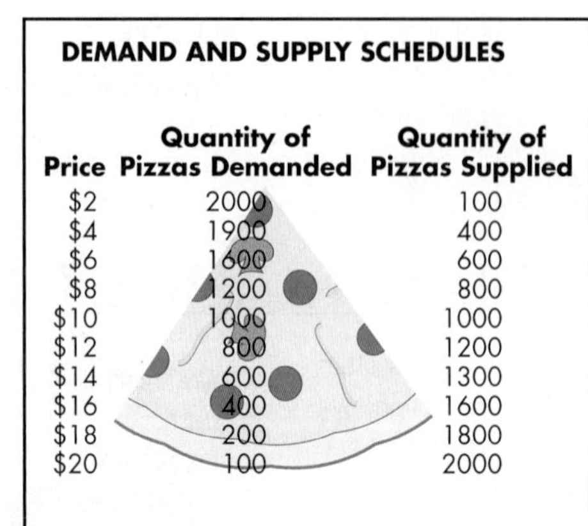

DEMAND AND SUPPLY SCHEDULES

Price	Quantity of Pizzas Demanded	Quantity of Pizzas Supplied
$2	2000	100
$4	1900	400
$6	1600	600
$8	1200	800
$10	1000	1000
$12	800	1200
$14	600	1300
$16	400	1600
$18	200	1800
$20	100	2000

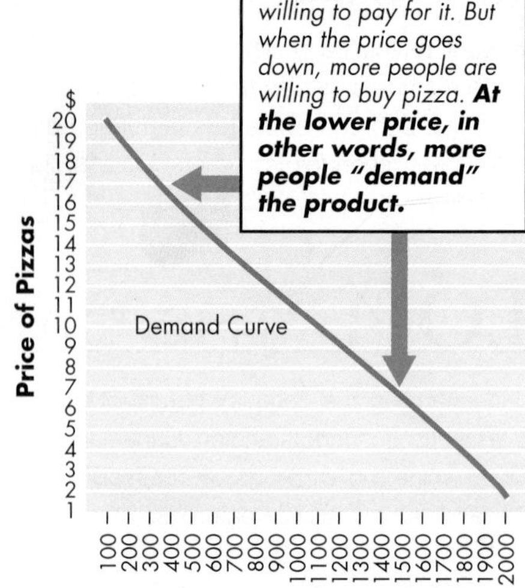
When the price of pizza is high, fewer people are willing to pay for it. But when the price goes down, more people are willing to buy pizza. **At the lower price, in other words, more people "demand" the product.**
Demand Curve
Price of Pizzas
$
20 19 18 17 16 15 14 13 12 11 10 9 8 7 6 5 4 3 2 1
100 200 300 400 500 600 700 800 900 1000 1100 1200 1300 1400 1500 1600 1700 1800 1900 2000
Quantity of Pizzas Demanded

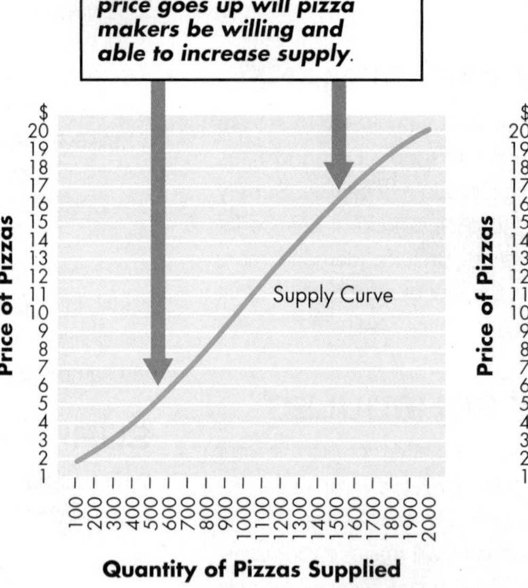
When the price of pizza is low, more people are willing to buy pizza. Pizza makers, however, do not have the money to invest in making pizzas and so they make fewer. Supply, therefore, is limited, and **only when the price goes up will pizza makers be willing and able to increase supply**.
Supply Curve
Price of Pizzas
$
20 19 18 17 16 15 14 13 12 11 10 9 8 7 6 5 4 3 2 1
100 200 300 400 500 600 700 800 900 1000 1100 1200 1300 1400 1500 1600 1700 1800 1900 2000
Quantity of Pizzas Supplied

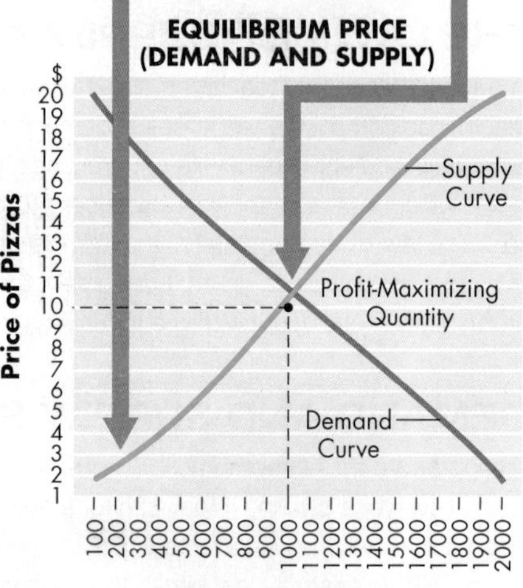
When the pizza makers increase supply in order to satisfy demand, there will be **a point at which the price that suppliers can charge is the same as the price that a maximum number of customers is willing to pay**. That point is the market price, or **equilibrium** price.
EQUILIBRIUM PRICE (DEMAND AND SUPPLY)
Supply Curve
Profit-Maximizing Quantity
Demand Curve
Price of Pizzas
$
20 19 18 17 16 15 14 13 12 11 10 9 8 7 6 5 4 3 2 1
100 200 300 400 500 600 700 800 900 1000 1100 1200 1300 1400 1500 1600 1700 1800 1900 2000
Quantity of Pizzas

cut back on store hours, and reduced the number of pizzas offered for sale? In either case, the result would be an inefficient use of resources. For example, if the restaurant supplies 1200 pizzas and tries to sell them for $10 each, 200 pizzas will not be purchased. The demand schedule clearly shows that only 1000 pizzas will be demanded at this price. The pizza maker will therefore have a **surplus**—a situation in which the quantity supplied exceeds the quantity demanded. The restaurant will thus lose the money that it spent making those extra 200 pizzas.

Conversely, if the pizzeria supplies only 800 pizzas, a **shortage** will result because the quantity demanded will be greater than the quantity supplied. The pizzeria will "lose" the extra money that it could have made by producing 200 more pizzas. Even though consumers may pay more for pizzas because of the shortage, the restaurant will still earn lower profits than it would have if it had made 1000 pizzas. In addition, it may risk angering customers who cannot buy pizzas. To optimize profits, therefore, all businesses must constantly seek the right combination of price charged and quantity supplied. This "right combination" is found at the equilibrium point.

These supply and demand ideas apply to all sorts of commodities, including maple syrup, a quintessential Canadian commodity. We produce 80 percent of the world's supply, but its price fluctuates because weather influences the supply that is available.[24] When prices of commodities fluctuate, there are often unanticipated consequences. For example, as the price of stainless steel and aluminum rose during the last few years, thieves began stealing items such as beer kegs, railway baggage carts, railroad tracks, light poles, and highway guard rails. These items were then sold to scrap yards for cash.[25] The boxed insert entitled "The 'China Effect' on Commodity Prices" provides additional information on how demand influences prices.

LO-5 PRIVATE ENTERPRISE AND COMPETITION

Market economies rely on a **private enterprise** system—one that allows individuals to pursue their own interests with minimal government restriction. Private enterprise requires the presence of four elements: private property rights, freedom of choice, profits, and competition.

- *Private property*. Ownership of the resources used to create wealth is in the hands of individuals.[26]
- *Freedom of choice*. You can sell your labour to any employer you choose. You can also choose which products to buy, and producers can usually choose whom to hire and what to produce.
- *Profits*. The lure of profits (and freedom) leads some people to abandon the security of working for someone else and to assume the risks of entrepreneurship. Anticipated profits also influence individuals' choices of which goods or services to produce.

PRIVATE ENTERPRISE An economic system characterized by private property rights, freedom of choice, profits, and competition.

MANAGING IN TURBULENT TIMES

The "China Effect" on Commodity Prices

During the past decade, the Chinese economy has been growing at a rapid rate, and millions of Chinese are being added every year to the middle class. The increased demand caused by these newly affluent consumers has influenced the prices of a wide range of commodities.

One noticeable area of increased demand is in the so-called "rare earth" metals such as cerium, lanthanum, and neodymium, which are used in products like lasers, ceramics, computers, and wind turbines. China produces about 90 percent of the world's supply, but it has reduced exports because it wants to ensure a reliable supply for domestic production. This action has created concerns about supply shortages in other countries, and has motivated some of them to start developing their own rare earth mines. For example, Vancouver-based Rare Element Resources Ltd. is developing a rare earth mine in the U.S. Chinese demand has also influenced the price of other metals like palladium, which is used in automobile catalytic converters to reduce toxic emissions. From 2010 to 2011, the price of palladium jumped from $400 an ounce to over $900 an ounce. High automobile sales in China are increasing demand for palladium and driving its price higher.

Chinese demand has affected other commodities besides metals. For example, China is the world's largest cotton consumer, and this high level of demand, coupled with the hoarding of supplies, has driven cotton prices to 140-year highs. Many farmers, cotton processors, and the Chinese government are hoarding cotton. The total amount being hoarded is unknown, but it might equal as much as 10 percent of the world's supply. Many countries don't report cotton production, so rumours abound as to how much cotton is (or isn't) available. That uncertainty drives up prices even further.

Yet another commodity that is being affected by demand from China is nuts, such as pistachios, almonds, walnuts, macadamias, cashews, and pecans. Prices on these commodities have risen anywhere from 40 to 70 percent in less than a year. The price of pecans, for example, has soared from $4.25 to $6.50 per pound. Mexico and the U.S.—the world's leading producers of pecans—now export one-quarter of their total crop to China.

CRITICAL THINKING QUESTIONS

1. Most people find it easy to think of negative outcomes that occur because of high prices. Can you think of situations where high prices can lead to positive outcomes? Explain.
2. Consider the following statement: "*The high prices of commodities like rare earth metals and palladium are not really a concern because we do not need metals to survive. The high price of food, however, is a concern because it threatens people's lives. The central governments of the world should therefore coordinate their efforts and put in place rules to ensure that food prices are kept low.*" Do you agree or disagree with this statement? Explain your reasoning.

- *Competition*. **Competition** is evident when two or more businesses vie for the same resources or customers. While profits motivate individuals to *start* businesses, competition motivates them to *operate* their businesses efficiently. Competition forces businesses to make products better and/or cheaper.

Degrees of Competition

Economists have identified four basic degrees of competition within a private enterprise system: perfect competition, monopolistic competition, oligopoly, and monopoly.

PERFECT COMPETITION

In **perfect competition**, all firms in an industry are small, the number of firms in the industry is large, and the products produced by the different firms are virtually identical. Under these conditions, no single firm is powerful enough to influence prices, so they are determined by the market forces of supply and demand. Canadian agriculture is a good example of perfect competition. The wheat produced on one farm is the same as that on another. Both producers and buyers are aware of prevailing market prices. It is relatively easy to start producing wheat and relatively easy to stop when it's no longer profitable.

MONOPOLISTIC COMPETITION

In **monopolistic competition**, there are fewer sellers, but still many buyers. Businesses may be large or small, and small clothing stores can compete successfully with large apparel retailers such as Liz Claiborne and Limited Brands. Whatever their size, sellers try to make their products at least *seem* different from those of competitors, and this product differentiation gives sellers some control over prices. For instance, even though a Sears shirt may look pretty much like a Ralph Lauren Polo shirt, the latter can be priced $20 higher than the Sears shirt. Other differentiating strategies include brand names (Tide and Cheer) and advertising (Coca-Cola and Pepsi).

OLIGOPOLY

When an industry has only a handful of very large sellers, an **oligopoly** exists. Competition is fierce because the actions of any one firm in an oligopolistic market can significantly affect the sales of all other firms.[27] Most oligopolistic firms avoid price competition because it reduces profits. For example, the four major cereal makers (Kellogg, General Mills, General Foods, and Quaker Oats) charge roughly the same price for their cereals. Rather than compete on price, they emphasize advertising, which claims that their cereals are better tasting or more nutritious than the competition's. Entry into an oligopolistic market is difficult because

COMPETITION The vying among businesses in a particular market or industry to best satisfy consumer demands and earn profits.

PERFECT COMPETITION A market or industry characterized by a very large number of small firms producing an identical product so that none of the firms has any ability to influence price.

MONOPOLISTIC COMPETITION A market or industry characterized by a large number of firms supplying products that are similar but distinctive enough from one another to give firms some ability to influence price.

OLIGOPOLY A market or industry characterized by a small number of very large firms that have the power to influence the price of their product and/or resources.

MONOPOLY A market or industry with only one producer, who can set the price of its product and/or resources.

NATURAL MONOPOLY A market or industry in which having only one producer is most efficient because it can meet all of consumers' demand for the product.

large capital investment is usually necessary. Thus, oligopolistic industries (such as the automobile, rubber, and steel industries) tend to stay oligopolistic. As the trend toward globalization continues, it is likely that more global oligopolies will come into being.[28]

MONOPOLY

When an industry or market has only one producer, a **monopoly** exists. Being the only supplier gives a firm complete control over the price of its product. Its only constraint is how much consumer demand will fall as its price rises. For centuries, wine bottles were sealed using natural cork made from tree bark. But a new technology allows wine bottles to be sealed with plastic corks that are cheaper and work just as well. The natural wine cork industry has lost its monopoly.[29] In Canada, laws such as the Competition Act forbid most monopolies. **Natural monopolies**—such as provincial electric utilities—are closely watched by provincial utilities boards, and the assumption that there is such a thing as a natural monopoly is increasingly being challenged. For example, as the volume of mail that Canada Post handles declines,[30] there have been repeated calls to end its monopoly on letters weighing less than 500 grams (competition from companies like FedEx and UPS is allowed for parcels and express mail). During the 10 years after it became a Crown Corporation, Canada Post raised its rates by 41 percent. By contrast, postal rates have dropped in countries where the post office has been privatized (e.g., Germany and the Netherlands).[31]

Consumers often buy products under conditions of monopolistic competition. For example, there are few differences between various brands of toothpaste, cold tablets, detergents, canned goods, and soft drinks.

Photo Researchers, Inc./Science Source

MyBizLab

Visit the MyBizLab website. This online homework and tutorial system puts you in control of your own learning with study and practice tools directly correlated to this chapter's content.

SUMMARY OF LEARNING OBJECTIVES

LO-1 DEFINE THE NATURE OF CANADIAN *BUSINESS* AND IDENTIFY ITS MAIN GOALS.

Businesses are organizations that produce or sell goods or services to make a profit. Profits are the difference between a business's revenues and expenses. The prospect of earning profits encourages individuals and organizations to open and expand businesses. The benefits of business activities also extend to wages paid to workers and to taxes that support government functions.

LO-2 DESCRIBE DIFFERENT TYPES OF GLOBAL *ECONOMIC SYSTEMS* ACCORDING TO THE MEANS BY WHICH THEY CONTROL THE *FACTORS OF PRODUCTION* THROUGH *INPUT* AND *OUTPUT MARKETS*.

An economic system is a nation's system for allocating its resources among its citizens. Economic systems differ in terms of who owns or controls the five basic factors of production: labour, capital, entrepreneurs, physical resources, and information resources. In command economies, the government controls all or most of these factors. In market economies, which are based on the principles of capitalism, individuals and businesses control the factors of production and exchange them through input and output markets. Most countries today have mixed market economies that are dominated by one of these systems, but include elements of the other. The processes of deregulation and privatization are important means by which many of the world's planned economies are moving toward mixed market systems.

LO-3 DESCRIBE THE INTERACTIONS BETWEEN BUSINESS AND GOVERNMENT IN CANADA.

Government plays many important roles within the Canadian economic system, and, in so doing, it influences business firms. Government can play the role of customer, competitor, regulator, taxation agent, provider of incentives, and provider of essential services. Businesses can influence government by lobbying, joining trade associations, and trying to convince voters to support or oppose certain regulations.

LO-4 SHOW HOW *DEMAND* AND *SUPPLY* AFFECT RESOURCE DISTRIBUTION IN CANADA.

The Canadian economy is strongly influenced by markets, demand, and supply. Demand is the willingness and ability of buyers to purchase a good or service. Supply is the willingness and ability of producers to offer goods or services for sale. Demand and supply work together to set a market or equilibrium price—the price at which the quantity of goods demanded and the quantity of goods supplied are equal.

LO-5 IDENTIFY THE ELEMENTS OF *PRIVATE ENTERPRISE* AND EXPLAIN THE VARIOUS *DEGREES OF COMPETITION* IN THE CANADIAN ECONOMIC SYSTEM.

The Canadian economy is founded on the principles of private enterprise, private property rights, freedom of choice, profits, and competition. Degrees of competition vary because not all industries are equally competitive. Under conditions of pure competition, numerous small firms compete in a market governed entirely by demand and supply. In monopolistic competition, there are a smaller number of sellers, and each one tries to make its product seem different from the products of competitors. An oligopoly involves only a handful of sellers who fiercely compete with each other. A monopoly involves only one seller.

QUESTIONS AND EXERCISES

QUESTIONS FOR ANALYSIS

See >>> for Assisted-Graded Writing Assignment in MyBizLab

1. On various occasions, government provides financial incentives to business firms. For example, the Canadian government provided export assistance to Bombardier Inc. with its Technology Transfer Program. Is this consistent with a basically free market system? Explain how this might distort the system.
2. >>> In recent years, many countries have moved from planned economies to market economies. Why do you think this has occurred? Can you envision a situation that would cause a resurgence of planned economies?
3. In your opinion, what industries in Canada should be regulated by the government? Defend your arguments.
4. Familiarize yourself with a product or service that is sold under conditions of pure competition. Explain why it is an example of pure competition and identify the factors that make it so. Then do the same for a product in each of the other three competitive situations described in the chapter (monopolistic competition, oligopoly, and monopoly).
5. Analyze how the factors of production (labour, capital, entrepreneurs, natural resources, and information resources) work together for a product or service of your choice.
6. Government plays a variety of roles in the Canadian mixed economy (customer, regulator, taxation agent, provider of services, etc.). Consider each of the roles discussed in the text and state your view as to whether government involvement in each role is excessive, insufficient, or about right. What criteria did you use to make your assessments?

APPLICATION EXERCISES

7. For a product that is not discussed in Chapter 1, find an example where a surplus led to decreased prices. Then find an example where a shortage led to increased prices. What eventually happened in each case? Why? Is what happened consistent with what economic theory predicts?
8. Choose a locally owned business. Interview the owner to find out (1) how demand and supply affect the business, (2) how the business uses the factors of production, and (3) how the owner acquires each factor of production.
9. Visit a local shopping mall or shopping area. List each store that you see and determine what degree of competition it faces in its immediate environment. For example, if there is only one store in the mall that sells shoes, that store represents a monopoly. Note those businesses with direct competitors (e.g., two jewellery stores) and show how they compete with one another.
10. Pick a specific product that you use. Explain how the factors of production work together to make that product available.

BUILDING YOUR BUSINESS SKILLS

ANALYZING THE PRICE OF DOING E-BUSINESS

GOAL

To encourage students to understand how the competitive environment affects a product's price.

SITUATION

Assume that you own a local business that provides internet access to individuals and businesses in your community. Yours is one of four such businesses in the local market. Each of the four companies charges the same price: $20 per month for unlimited DSL service. Your business also provides users with email service, and two of your competitors also offer email service. One of these same two competitors, plus the third, also provides the individual user with a free, basic personal webpage. One competitor just dropped its price to $15 per month, and the other two have announced their intentions to follow suit. Your break-even price is $10 per customer. You are concerned about getting into a price war that may destroy your business.

METHOD

Divide into groups of four or five people. Each group is to develop a general strategy for handling competitors' price changes. In your discussion, take the following factors into account:

- how the demand for your product is affected by price changes
- the number of competitors selling the same or a similar product
- the methods—other than price—you can use to attract new customers and/or retain current customers

ANALYSIS

Develop specific pricing strategies based on each of the following situations:

- Within a month after dropping the price to $15, one of your competitors raises its price back to $20.
- Two of your competitors drop their prices further—to $12 per month. As a result, your business falls off by 25 percent.
- One of your competitors that has provided customers with a free webpage has indicated that it will start charging an extra $2 per month for this optional service.
- Two of your competitors have announced that they will charge individual users $12 per month, but will charge businesses a higher price (not yet announced).
- All four providers (including you) are charging $12 per month. One goes out of business, and you know that another is in poor financial health.

FOLLOW-UP QUESTIONS

1. Discuss the role that various inducements other than price might play in affecting demand and supply in the market for internet service.
2. Is it always in a company's best interest to feature the lowest prices?
3. Eventually, what form of competition is likely to characterize the market for internet service?

EXERCISING YOUR ETHICS

MAKING THE RIGHT DECISION

THE SITUATION

Hotel S is a large hotel in a Maritime city. The hotel is a franchise operation run by an international hotel chain. The primary source of revenue for the hotel is convention business. A major tropical storm is working its way up the east coast and is about to hit the city. When that happens, heavy flooding is likely.

THE DILEMMA

Because Hotel S is a licensed operation, it must maintain numerous quality standards in order to keep its licence. This licence is important because the international management company handles advertising, reservations, and so on. If it were to lose its licence, it is almost certain that the hotel would have to reduce its staff.

For the past few years, members of the Hotel S team have been lobbying the investors who own the hotel to undertake a major renovation. They fear that without such a renovation, the hotel will lose its licence when it comes up for renewal in a few months. The owners, however, have balked at investing more of their funds in the hotel itself but have indicated that hotel management can use revenues earned above a specified level for upgrades.

The approaching storm has cut off most major transportation avenues and telephone service is also down. The Hotel S staff are unable to reach the general manager, who has been travelling on business. Because the city is full of conventioneers, hotel rooms are in high demand. Unfortunately, because of the disrepair at the hotel, it only has about 50 percent occupancy. Hotel S staff have been discussing what to do and have identified three options:

1. The hotel can reduce room rates in order to help both local citizens and out-of-town visitors. The hotel can also provide meals at reduced rates. A few other hotels are also doing this.
2. The hotel can maintain its present pricing policies. Most of the city's hotels are adopting this course of action.
3. The hotel can raise its rates by approximately 15 percent without attracting too much attention. It can also start charging for certain things it has been providing for free, such as local telephone calls, parking, and morning coffee. The staff members see this option as one way to generate extra profits for the renovation and to protect jobs.

TEAM ACTIVITY

Assemble a group of four students and assign each group member to one of the following roles:

- A member of the hotel staff
- The Hotel S manager
- A customer at the hotel
- A Hotel S investor

ACTION STEPS

1. Before discussing the situation with your group and from the perspective of your assigned role, which of the three options do you think is the best choice? Write down the reasons for your position.
2. Before discussing the situation with your group and from the perspective of your assigned role, what are the underlying ethical issues, if any, in this situation? Write down the issues.
3. Gather your group together and reveal, in turn, each member's comments on the best choice of the three options. Next, reveal the ethical issues listed by each member.
4. Appoint someone to record the main points of agreement and disagreement within the group. How do you explain the results? What accounts for any disagreement?
5. From an ethical standpoint, what does your group conclude is the most appropriate action that should have been taken by the hotel in this situation?
6. Develop a group response to the following question: Can your team identify other solutions that might help satisfy both extreme views?

BUSINESS CASE

IS SUPPLY MANAGEMENT A GOOD IDEA?

Producers in several industries in Canada operate under a system called *supply management*, where domestic production quotas are established for commodities like dairy products, maple syrup, eggs, chickens, and turkeys. Producers of these commodities are not allowed to produce more than the quota they have been granted. To prevent foreign competitors from entering the market, high tariffs are charged on imports of these commodities (e.g., the tariff on butter is 299 percent, on cheese 246 percent, and on milk 241 percent).

David Osborn/Alamy

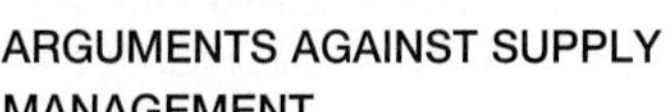

ARGUMENTS AGAINST SUPPLY MANAGEMENT

The critics of supply management—who have become increasingly vocal during the last decade—argue that supply management leads to higher consumer prices, smuggling, reduced levels of innovation and entrepreneurial activity, and reduced export opportunities.

Higher Consumer Prices By restricting supply, the supply management system provides producers with a more stable environment than companies in other industries have to cope with. As well, companies in supply-management industries don't face much of a threat from foreign competition because such high tariffs are applied to imported products that they are uncompetitive. While this is good for producers, it is not so good for consumers who have to pay higher prices for supply-managed commodities. For example, prices of dairy products in Canada were 115 percent higher than in New Zealand for the entire period between 1983 and 2010, and 23 percent higher than prices in the U.S. The higher prices that result from supply management hurt poor Canadian consumers the most because they spend a larger proportion of their income on food items.

Smuggling and Illegal Purchases One typical outcome of price controls and quotas is smuggling activity, as entrepreneurs see an opportunity to make money by buying a commodity in a low-priced area and selling it in a higher-priced area. The higher the duty that is charged on products, the greater the incidence of smuggling that can be expected. In 2012, for example, the CBC reported on a cheese smuggling ring in the Niagara region. The allegation was that pizzerias in the region were importing cheese from the U.S. for which no tariffs had been paid.

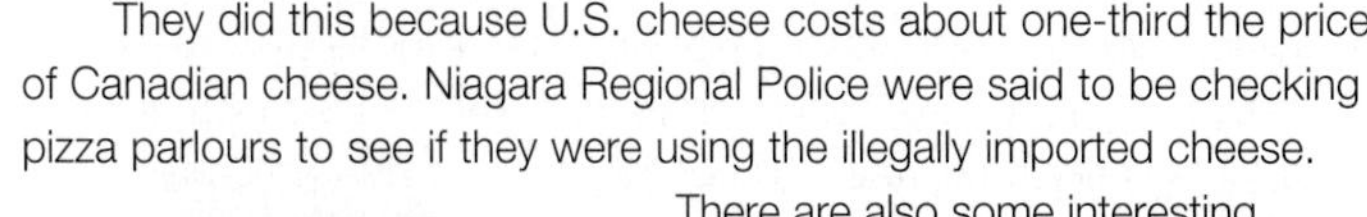

They did this because U.S. cheese costs about one-third the price of Canadian cheese. Niagara Regional Police were said to be checking pizza parlours to see if they were using the illegally imported cheese.

There are also some interesting developments in the maple syrup industry. In 2002, the Federation of Quebec Maple Syrup Producers tightened up its supply management system by imposing quotas, which were introduced with the stated goal being to ensure that producers got a "fair" price for their syrup and to reduce volatility in the price of syrup. Producers who exceed their quotas must transfer the excess into the strategic reserve. Inspectors use various techniques to catch syrup bootleggers, just like government agents did during the prohibition era in the 1920s in the U.S. Etienne St. Pierre is one individual who has confronted the Federation about its rules. Because St. Pierre is based in New Brunswick, he says Quebec's quota rules don't apply to him and he can purchase syrup from anyone he pleases. The Federation disagrees, saying he has to buy from accredited suppliers so that the Federation can ensure the high quality of the syrup is maintained, and so the cachet of Quebec's syrup isn't damaged.

Reduced Levels of Innovation and Entrepreneurial Activity The supply management system may create more "order" in an industry, but critics charge that it reduces the innovation and risk-taking that are so important in the development of new products and services. Because companies in supply-managed industries are protected from foreign competition, they have less incentive to innovate and to develop new production methods and new products that consumers want. The Organisation for Economic Cooperation and Development (OECD) praised Canada for eliminating the Wheat Board, but noted that Canada's supply management system is a problem because it distorts production and negatively affects trade.

Lost Export Opportunities Canada is one of the most export-intensive countries in the world. If we want to sell our commodities to foreign countries, we should assume that they will also want to sell their commodities to us. But the supply management system inhibits imports into Canada because it imposes high tariffs on imports of supply-managed commodities. Professor Colin Carter, a Canadian who works in the U.S., is an expert on global commodity markets. He says that Canadian exports of processed agricultural products to emerging markets are stagnant, and Canada is missing out on export opportunities. For example, the push for a free trade deal with the European Union has been complicated by Canada's supply management system. The EU wants duty-free access to the Canadian market for cheese and dairy products, but high tariffs are in place to protect domestic producers from foreign competition in order to make the supply management system work.

The supply management issue has also affected Canada's acceptance in the Trans-Pacific Partnership (TPP), a Pacific free trade zone that currently includes countries with a total population of 658 million people. Countries participating in the current talks include the U.S., Australia, Chile, Malaysia, New Zealand, Peru, Singapore, Vietnam, and Brunei. Mexico and Canada have recently been invited to join the talks. The TPP may eventually become bigger than NAFTA, and an agreement with the TPP could boost Canadian exports by nearly $16 billion by 2025. One condition of joining the TPP talks is that members must "put everything on the table for negotiation." But the Canadian government has so far insisted that it will not abandon the supply management system. Both Australia and New Zealand have already dismantled their supply management systems, and both countries oppose membership for Canada until it drops its supply management system. Japan has also has expressed an interest in these talks, but it also places high tariffs on agricultural products, so it will have to make changes as well.

A specific example of how the current supply management system can affect international trade can be seen at the Cami International Poultry plant in Welland, Ontario. It can process up to 15 000 chickens a day, most of which are so-called "Hong Kong–dressed" chickens which are marketed to affluent Chinese consumers in Canada and elsewhere. But the Cami plant is closed because owner Jim Lee can't get enough chickens to process. Why can't he get enough chickens? Because in 2012, the chicken marketing boards in Ontario and Quebec sharply curtailed cross-border shipments of live chickens, and Cami's quota was reduced by 70 percent. Lee is now suing the Chicken Farmers of Ontario (CFO) and seeking millions of dollars in damages. He is making the interesting argument that the CFO quota reduction violates his constitutionally protected right to freedom of religion and equality because it restricts the number of chickens that he can make available to religious and cultural minorities. Others have argued—more bluntly—that supply management is completely inconsistent with the free market system because it prevents entrepreneurs from selling products and services that consumers want.

Beyond the situation in specific companies, Canadian businesses in general are losing billions of dollars in lost exports because the Canadian government maintains policies to restrict supply in order to protect domestic producers in certain industries. Critics point out that the current system is indefensible because the value of the lost exports far exceeds the benefits that the producers receive. Chicken and turkey production is growing rapidly in countries that don't have supply management systems, but it is stagnant in Canada. That means that agricultural firms in countries like the U.S., Australia, and New Zealand are better serving the needs of consumers and are increasing their market share.

Supply management problems can also inhibit foreign investment in Canada. Chobani, the yogurt company, wanted to build a plant in Ontario to make Greek yogurt. In Canada, the total amount of yogurt that can be produced is controlled, and, in 2011, new quotas were established. Quebec received 70 percent of the quota, while Ontario got no additional quota at all. Since Ontario is where the Chobani plant was to be located, Chobani had a problem. To date, the plant has not been built (and may never be) because Chobani hasn't been able to get an adequate supply of milk. The Dairy Farmers of Ontario (DFO) did commit to supply milk for the first year of production, but Chobani needed a long-term commitment. Chobani's experience in Canada contrasts sharply with its experience in the state of Idaho, where its plant is getting the milk it needs from U.S. dairy farmers.

ARGUMENTS IN FAVOUR OF SUPPLY MANAGEMENT

Supporters of supply management admit that consumers do pay more for supply-managed products, but they point out that the situation is more complex than it appears at first glance. If we compare our supply management system with different allocation systems in other countries, we see some interesting things. For example, in Europe and the U.S., farmers produce way more milk than they can sell at a profit, so to keep them from going out of business, foreign governments give farmers subsidies. Then farmers dump their artificially cheap products in developing nations, and that threatens the livelihoods of farmers in those nations. Supporters of supply management say that if Canada drops its tariffs, we will be flooded with cheap products from the U.S. and Europe, and our farmers will be driven out of business. They also say that if other countries would stop giving their farmers subsidies, farmers around the world would have a level playing field. Canadian farmers would then be more willing to abandon supply management. Other supporters of supply management say that the *stability* in prices that the system creates is more important than the actual *price*.

The numerous problems with supply management noted above would seem to suggest that there would be a lot of benefit to Canada if the system was dropped. So, why is supply management still so entrenched, given the critics' arguments? One reason (perhaps the main one) is politics. Elected officials are continually pressured by those who support continuation of the supply management system. Yet there don't seem to be many voters in favour of supply management. As well, the number of producers in supply-managed industries has steadily declined over the years. For example, since supply management was introduced in 1971, the number of dairy farms in Canada has declined 91 percent, so there aren't very many votes that would likely sway election results. Perhaps global free trade developments will eventually force Canada to abandon supply management in order to gain access to foreign markets.

QUESTIONS FOR DISCUSSION

1. What are the various roles that government plays in Canada? What role is the government playing as it continues to support supply management for commodities such as dairy products, eggs, and chickens? Explain.
2. Explain the basic ideas of supply, demand, and the price of commodities. What does a supply management system try to achieve with respect to these concepts?
3. Consider the following statement: *Supply management systems are completely inappropriate in a free market economy because they distort prices, inhibit trade, and prevent entrepreneurs from operating their businesses in ways that will best serve consumers' needs.* Do you agree or disagree with the statement? Explain your reasoning.

CHAPTER SUPPLEMENT 01

A Brief History of Business in Canada

In this supplement, we summarize the broad outlines of the development of business activity in Canada. A more detailed discussion of the development of Canadian business activity is found online in MyBizLab.

THE EARLY YEARS

Business activity and profit from commercial fishing were the motivation for the first European involvement in Canada. Beginning in the 1500s, French and British adventurers began trading with the native peoples. The governments of these countries were strong supporters of the mercantilist philosophy, and colonists were expected to export raw materials like beaver pelts and lumber at low prices to the mother country. Attempts to develop industry in Canada were hindered by England and France, which enjoyed large profits from mercantilism.

THE FACTORY SYSTEM AND THE INDUSTRIAL REVOLUTION

British manufacturing took a great leap forward around 1750 with the coming of the **Industrial Revolution**. This revolution was made possible by advances in technology and by the development of the **factory system**. Instead of hundreds of workers turning out items one at a time in their cottages, the factory system brought together in one place all of the materials and workers required to produce items in large quantities, along with newly created machines capable of **mass production**. In spite of British laws against the export of technology and manufacturing to North America, modest manufacturing operations were evident in sawmills, breweries, grist mills for grinding grain, tanneries, woollen mills, shoemakers' shops, and tailors' shops. These operations became so successful that by 1800 exports of manufactured goods were more important than exports of fur.

THE ENTREPRENEURIAL ERA

In the last half of the nineteenth century, entrepreneurs emerged who were willing to take risks in the hope of earning large profits. Some individuals became immensely wealthy through their aggressive business dealings. But the size and economic power of some firms meant that other businesses had difficulty competing against them. At the same time, some business executives decided that it was more profitable to collude than to compete. They decided among themselves to fix prices and divide up markets. Hurt by these actions, Canadian consumers called for more regulation of business.

THE PRODUCTION ERA

Henry Ford's introduction of the moving assembly line in the United States in 1913 ushered in the **production era**. The Scientific Management Movement focused management's attention on production. Increased efficiency via the "one best way" to accomplish tasks became a major management goal. During the production era, less attention was paid to selling and marketing than to technical efficiency when producing goods. The growth of corporations and improved production output resulting from assembly lines sometimes came at the expense of worker freedom. To restore some balance within the overall system, both government and labour had to develop and grow.

THE SALES AND MARKETING ERAS

By the 1930s, business's focus on production had resulted in spectacular increases in the amount of goods and services available for sale. As a result, buyers had more choices and producers faced greater competition in selling their wares. According to the ideas of that time, a business's profits and success depended on hiring the right salespeople, advertising heavily, and making sure products were readily available. In the marketing era (the 1950s and 1960s), businesses increasingly used market research to determine what customers wanted, and then made it for them.

THE FINANCE ERA

In the finance era (the 1980s), there was a sharp increase in mergers and in the buying and selling of business enterprises. Some people now call it the "decade of greed." During the finance era, there was a great deal of financial manipulation of corporate assets by so-called corporate raiders.

THE GLOBAL ERA

During the last two decades, we have witnessed the emergence of the global economy and further dramatic technological advances in production, computer technology, information systems, and communication capabilities. While some Canadian businesses have been hurt by foreign imports, numerous others have profited by exploring new foreign markets themselves. Global and domestic competition has also forced all businesses to work harder than ever to cut costs, increase efficiency, and improve product and service quality.

THE INTERNET ERA

The rapid increase in internet usage has facilitated global business activity. Both large and small businesses are not restricted to thinking only in terms of local markets. Web-based services that are offered through a web browser are helping businesses "go global."

LO

AFTER READING THIS CHAPTER, YOU SHOULD BE ABLE TO:

- LO-1 Explain the concepts of *organizational boundaries* and *multiple organizational environments.*
- LO-2 Explain the importance of the *economic environment* to business and identify the factors used to evaluate the performance of an economic system.
- LO-3 Describe the *technological environment* and its role in business.
- LO-4 Describe the *political–legal environment* and its role in business.
- LO-5 Describe the *socio-cultural environment* and its role in business.
- LO-6 Identify emerging challenges and opportunities in the *business environment.*
- LO-7 Understand recent trends in the *redrawing of corporate boundaries.*

Evolving Models in Video Distribution: Netflix and Beyond

For about two decades, Blockbuster was the premier name in the video rental business. The announcement back in 2011 that the company was going bankrupt was a clear sign of the times.

Blockbuster's troubles turned into a crisis when Hollywood studios called in US$70 million worth of debt. Blockbuster had fallen from a shining star to a victim of technology; it tried to hold on to the past and was slow to evolve. The company announced that it would close its doors, but Dish Network stepped in and acquired Blockbuster for US$320 million. Since then, the decline has continued as the new parent company shuttered 500 stores in 2012 and announced that it would close its last remaining company owned stores in January 2014.

At the time of the original bankruptcy announcement, there was still some short-term profit potential in the Canadian retail DVD market as rentals still accounted for 94 percent of sales in Canada. However, the devastating truth was that this figure had declined to 43 percent in the United States. With the introduction of Netflix (and other services) into Canada, those numbers were declining rapidly as evidenced by the steady closures of retail video spaces across the nation. According to experts like Kaan Yigit, president of Consultancy Solutions Research Group, we had entered the Netflix decade.

Netflix Models: Technological Shocks

Netflix represents the great promise of technology, but is also a perfect example of the challenge of doing business in a technological age. Here is a company that was created only about 15 years ago and yet it has already changed its core business

The Environment *of* Business

CHAPTER 02

model twice. The initial Netflix success story was based on DVD home delivery service in the United States, a novel idea at the time. While competitors like Blockbuster were saddled with big locations and high rental space costs, Netflix was able to provide subscribers with a reliable home delivery service at an economical price. But the initial success would have soon faded if Netflix had not evolved with the times. Netflix quickly jumped on the next game-changing opportunity: the video-on-demand streaming business. At the beginning of 2013, using a dual strategy (online streaming and DVD rentals), they had amassed 33 million subscribers (including 1 million in Canada).

Jacob Wackerhausen/iStockphoto

Competitive Forces

Netflix had become a poster child for online success. It was also a model that new competitors and suppliers quickly copied and/or exploited. One of the reasons for that success was its ability to charge a low monthly flat fee of just US$7.99. As a pioneer, Netflix had negotiated favourable content-rights deals with movie studios and TV show producers. But soon problems began to surface. Canadian customers complained about the limited selection on the Canadian site compared to the U.S. site. In addition, the TV and movie studios had started using Netflix to apply competitive pressure and increase prices charged to TV stations looking to buy content. This meant that Netflix, in turn, also had to pay more. The cost to acquire rights to stream video content increased eight-fold in one year alone. In addition, Netflix had been unsuccessful in renewing certain rights agreements. Netflix also lost its exclusive distribution deal from EPIX, a joint venture company that licenses movies from Paramount, MGM, and Lion's Gate; EPIX licensed the films to Amazon Prime Video. To make matters worse, new threats were coming in many forms:

- Traditional cable and satellite providers like Bell, Videotron, Shaw, and Rogers had launched their own direct video-on-demand services to subscribers.
- Astral Media Inc. possessed exclusive rights to distribute HBO programming in eastern Canada and refused to sell Netflix the rights to its popular shows like *True Blood*. To make matters worse, it launched its own HBO Go streaming service.
- Apple TV was another important threat. The list goes on and on.

Government Regulation

Success is often based on how well a firm plays by the prescribed rules, but rules can be changed. Netflix's competitors were putting pressure on the Canadian Radio-television Telecommunications Commission (CRTC) to create new rules to address the threat of "over-the-top" internet streaming services. The CRTC initially resisted making a ruling that would hurt the likes of Netflix. However, the CRTC also indicated that it will look at this issue on a yearly basis and evaluate its impact on Canadian television with a view to changing the rules if necessary.

External Pressures Lead to New Directions

Netflix had taken advantage of the shift in technology and carved its place in the market, but threats were everywhere. The mounting pressure led company executives to make drastic moves that angered customers and confused investors. First, Netflix announced that it would split the DVD rental and online streaming services; there was also a short-lived attempt to rebrand the DVD rental service under the name Quickster. And then, after it had implemented these policies, it quickly reversed its decision. Based on the trends, Netflix's decision seemed inevitable, although admittedly premature and poorly researched. Customers were not happy; they could no longer get both services for the same price, while there was still strong demand for both. In essence, the subscription price doubled and convenience was sharply reduced, since each entity would require separate login accounts and bills. The result? Within a month, Netflix lost over 1 million subscribers and was forced to reverse their decision.

So where does Netflix go from here? By the beginning of 2013, the company had regained the customers and had 33 million subscribers worldwide. Netflix's initial success had been based on quick manoeuvring, but clearly the moves described above were not in its own best interests. To add to the plot, Netflix invested heavily in creating a show called *House of Cards*—a move that clearly demonstrated their concern about content issues and another sign of their ability to adapt. What direction should Netflix take now? Who or what is the greatest threat to the long-term profitability of the company? Should Netflix consider new affiliations or a potential merger? These are just some of the questions that Netflix executives must answer if they are to continue to grow and survive. One thing is certain, however; the external threats are multiplying.

HOW WILL THIS HELP ME?

By understanding the material in this chapter, you'll be better able to assess (1) the impact that events outside a business can have on its *owners* and *managers*, (2) how environmental change impacts you as a *consumer*, and (3) the challenges and opportunities that environmental change provides to you as an employee or an *investor*.

QUESTIONS FOR DISCUSSION

1. What are the primary external threats for Netflix in the short term? How about in the long term?
2. What do you think of Netflix's latest move—creating new media content? What are the advantages and disadvantages of this strategic move?
3. Form a group with four classmates and identify the new media threats from the perspective of cable providers like Bell and Shaw. How should they react to the changes in the industry?

LO-1 ORGANIZATIONAL BOUNDARIES AND ENVIRONMENTS

EXTERNAL ENVIRONMENT Everything outside an organization's boundaries that might affect it.

ORGANIZATIONAL BOUNDARY That which separates the organization from its environment.

As discussed in the opening case on Netflix, all businesses, regardless of their size, location, or mission, operate within a larger external environment that plays a major role in determining their success or failure. The **external environment** consists of everything outside an organization that might affect it. Managers must understand the key features of the external environment and then strive to operate and compete within it. No single firm can control the environment, but managers should not simply react to changes in the external environment; rather, they should be proactive and at least try to influence their environment.

To better explain the environment of business, we begin by discussing organizational boundaries and multiple organizational environments.

Organizational Boundaries

An **organizational boundary** separates the organization from its environment. Consider the simple case of a neighbourhood grocery store that includes a retail customer area, a storage room, and the owner/manager's office. In many ways, the store's boundary coincides with its physical structure; when you walk through the door, you're crossing the boundary into the business and, when you go back onto the sidewalk, you cross the boundary back into the environment. But this is an oversimplification. During the business day, distributors of soft drinks, snack foods, ice, and bread products may enter the store, inventory their products, and refill coolers and shelves just as if they were employees. These distributors are normally considered part of the environment rather than the organization, but during the time they're inside the store, they are essentially part of the business. Customers may even assume that these distributors are store employees and ask them questions as they restock shelves.

Now consider the case of a large domestic business (such as GM Canada) that is owned by an even larger international corporation (U.S.-based General Motors). The domestic business has a complex network of relationships with other businesses, like Magna International, which conduct research and build components for GM. GM Canada also deals with companies that supply tires, glass, steel, and engines. But GM Canada also functions within the boundaries of its international parent, which has its own network of business relationships, some overlapping and some distinct from GM Canada's network.

<<< Bauer has 52 percent market share of the global hockey equipment market. The company must constantly stay ahead of the technological race with its competitors for products like composite sticks.

Oliver Fantitsch/AP Images

Multiple Organizational Environments

Organizations have multiple environments. Some, like prevailing economic conditions, affect the performance of almost every business. But other dimensions of the environment are much more specific. The neighbourhood grocery store, for example, will be influenced not only by an increase in unemployment in its area, but also by the pricing and other marketing activities of its nearest competitors. Major organizations like Bauer Performance Sports Limited (which owns a 52 percent market share of the global hockey equipment market) must contend with external factors beyond its control, such as competitive actions by companies like Reebok and Easton, as well as stay ahead of the technological race for new composite sticks. However, its success may also be impacted by unexpected issues that can hurt revenues like the 2012 to 2013 hockey lockout.[1]

Figure 2.1 shows the major elements of the external environment: economic conditions, technology, political–legal considerations, social issues, the global environment, issues of ethical and social responsibility, the business environment itself, and emerging challenges and opportunities. We will cover ethical and global issues in detail in Chapters 3 and 5 respectively, so we discuss them here only as they relate directly to the other areas in this chapter.

LO-2 THE ECONOMIC ENVIRONMENT

ECONOMIC ENVIRONMENT Conditions of the economic system in which an organization operates.

The **economic environment** refers to the conditions of the economic system in which an organization operates.[2] In recent years, the economic environment has been characterized by low growth, fairly steady unemployment rates, and low inflation. During periods of rising unemployment, people are less likely to make unnecessary purchases and they may delay the purchase of a new car or new furniture. The fear of potential job loss or an uncertain paycheque is a very powerful enemy of the economy. It's only rational to reduce your spending in tougher times, but this also means that less needs to be produced and this can ultimately lead to more job losses for the economy as a whole. In a positive economic period, momentum pushes unemployment down as consumers spend more.

Despite low overall inflation, rising fuel prices have put economic pressure on businesses in many

>>> The tougher economic times have led to the growth in popularity of the various dollar store retailers across the nation.

Julio Cortez/CP Images

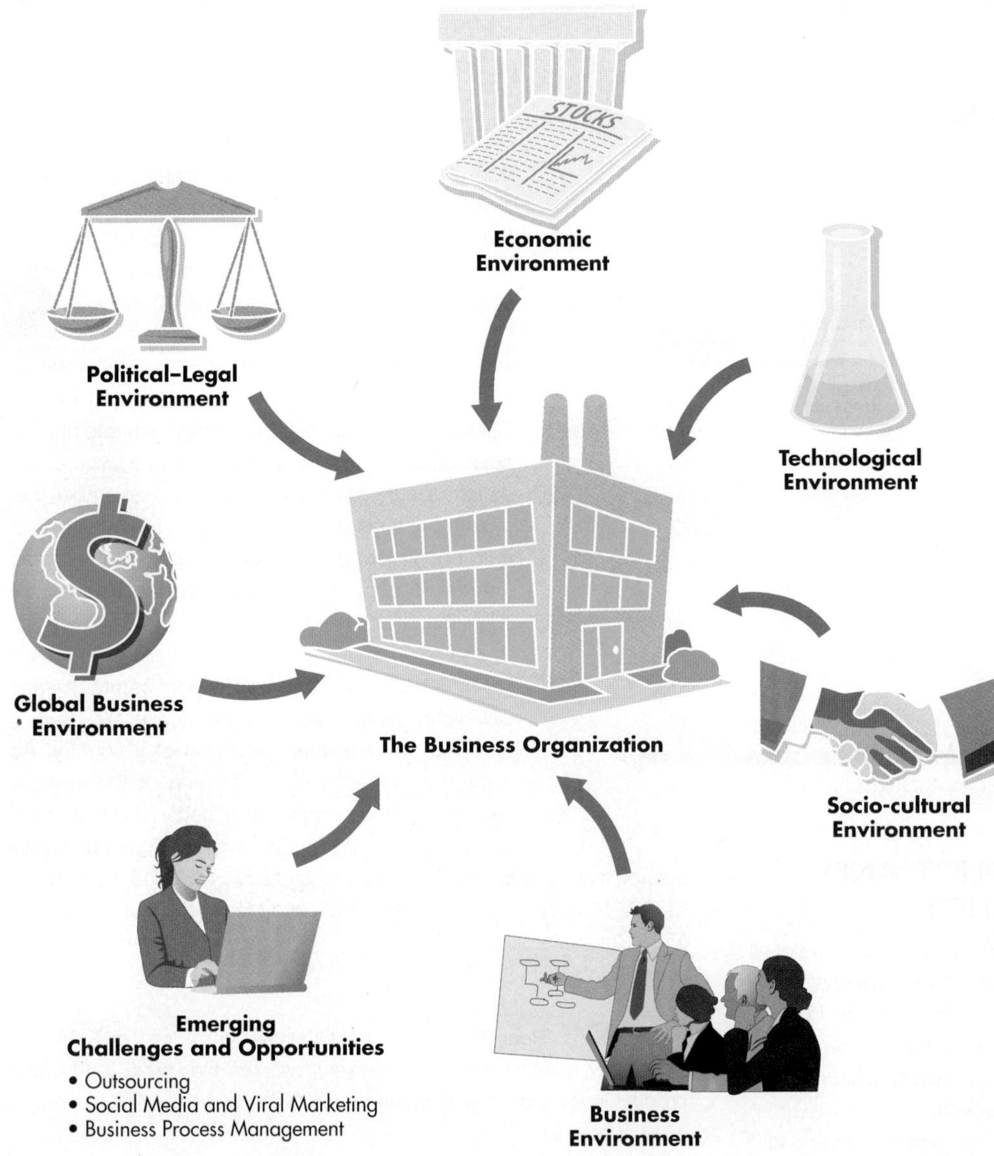

<<< FIGURE 2.1 Dimensions of the external environment

AGGREGATE OUTPUT AND THE STANDARD OF LIVING

How do we know whether or not an economic system is growing? The main measure of growth is **aggregate output**: the total quantity of goods and services produced by an economic system during a given period.[5] To put it simply, an increase in aggregate output is economic growth.[6] When output grows more quickly than the population, two things usually follow: output per capita (the quantity of goods and services per person) goes up and the system provides relatively more of the goods and services that people want.[7] And when these two things occur, people living in an economic system benefit from a higher **standard of living**—the total quantity and quality of goods and services that they can purchase with the currency used in their economic system.

THE BUSINESS CYCLE

The growth (and contraction) pattern of short-term ups and downs in an economy is called the **business cycle**. It has four recognizable phases: peak, recession, trough, and recovery (see Figure 2.2). A recession is usually defined as two consecutive quarters when the economy shrinks, but it is probably more helpful to say that a recession starts just after the peak of the business cycle is reached and ends when the trough is reached.[8] A depression occurs when the trough of the business cycle extends two or more years. Periods of expansion and contraction can vary from several months to several years. During the latter half of the 1990s, the Canadian economy was continuously expanding, leading some people to believe that the business cycle was a thing of the past. That belief was shattered twice in the last 15 years: in 2000, when the high-tech bubble burst, and in 2008, when a major financial crisis and worldwide recession occurred. Many economists correctly predicted that the most recent recession would be long, and some even compared it to the Great Depression of the 1930s.

sectors. Restaurants and grocery stores have increased prices or reduced package sizes to compete and survive. For example, Loblaws raised the price of its President's Choice Granola cereal from $4.99 to $5.79, while simultaneously shrinking the package from 800 grams to 750 grams.[3] Many companies that cater to low-cost interests of consumers, such as Dollarama and Costco, have thrived in the tough economic times as consumers have searched for cheaper prices. Dollarama, which has 761 stores across Canada, saw sales and profit increase by 14 and 23 percent respectively in 2012 from the previous year.[4]

Economic Growth

At one time, about half of the Canadian population was involved in producing the food that we eat. Today, less than 2.5 percent of the population works in agriculture because agricultural efficiency has improved so much that far fewer people are needed to produce the food we need. We can therefore say that agricultural production has grown because the total output of the agricultural sector has increased. We can apply the same idea to a nation's economic system, but the computations are much more complex, as we shall see.

AGGREGATE OUTPUT Total quantity of goods and services produced by an economic system during a given period.

STANDARD OF LIVING Total quantity and quality of goods and services that a country's citizens can purchase with the currency used in their economic system.

BUSINESS CYCLE Pattern of short-term ups and downs (expansions and contractions) in an economy.

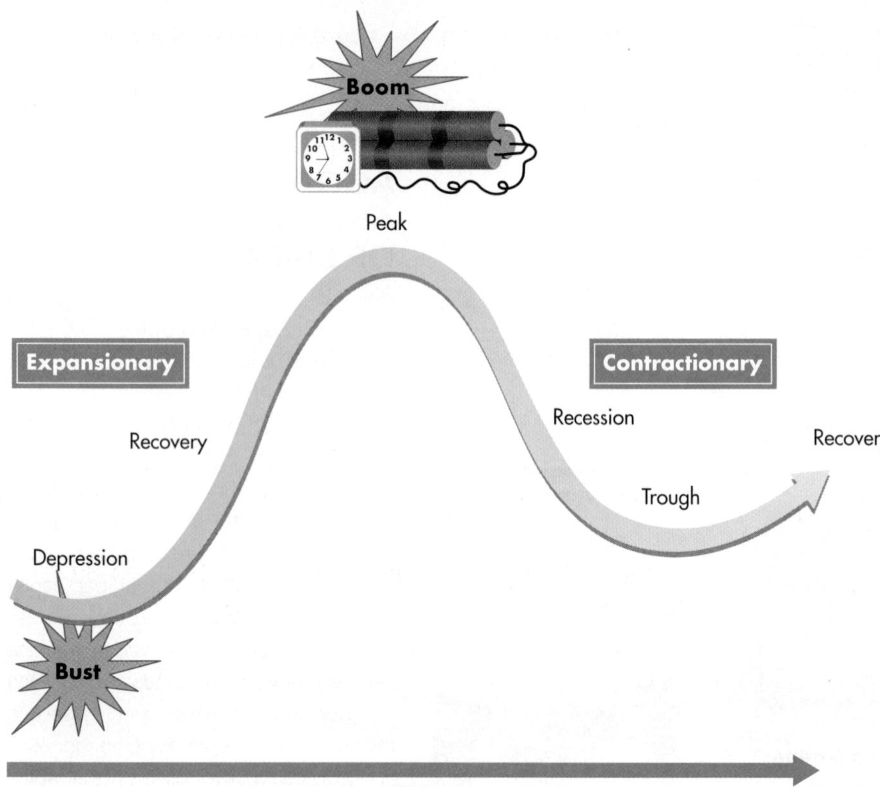

<<< **FIGURE 2.2** The business cycle

GROSS DOMESTIC PRODUCT AND GROSS NATIONAL PRODUCT

The term **gross domestic product (GDP)** refers to the total value of all goods and services produced within a given period by a national economy through domestic factors of production. Canada's GDP in 2012 was $1.7 trillion.[9] Global GDP was approximately $69 trillion; the top five countries were the United States, China, Japan, Germany, and France.[10] If GDP rises, a nation experiences economic growth.

GDP measures all business activity within a nation's borders and it has widely replaced **gross national product (GNP)**, which refers to the total value of all goods and services produced by a national economy within a given period regardless of where the factors of production are located. For example, Bombardier is a Canadian company, but all of the manufacturing that occurs in its foreign plants (Kansas, Mexico, Ireland, and, more recently, Morocco) is included in Canadian GNP—but not in GDP—because its output is not produced in Canada. Conversely, those figures are included in the GDP of those nations (US, Mexico, Ireland, and Morocco respectively) but not their GNP—because they are produced inside their borders by a Canadian company.[11]

Today, GDP is the key measure of economic growth because it tracks an economy's performance over time. However, some argue that such measures are flawed. A commission created by former French president Nicolas Sarkozy and chaired by famous economist Joseph Stiglitz declared that our obsession with GDP helped contribute to the strength of the most recent recession. According to the findings, if a bit more attention had been paid to other indicators, like rising debt, governments may have reacted more cautiously. An article in *The Economist* magazine even referred to GDP as "grossly deceptive product."[12] An organization called Redefining Progress has proposed a more realistic measure to assess economic activity—the Genuine Progress Indicator (GPI). GPI treats activities that harm the environment or our quality of life as costs and gives them negative values.

For example, activities required to clean the mess from the BP Gulf of Mexico oil drilling disaster were included in measurements of economic growth. But the oil spill was not a good thing. The GPI measure shows that while GDP has been increasing for many years, GPI has been falling for over 30 years.[13]

Real Growth Rates GDP is the preferred method of calculating national income and output. The real growth rate of GDP—the growth rate of GDP adjusted for inflation and changes in the value of the country's currency—is what counts. Remember that growth depends on output increasing at a faster rate than population. If the growth rate of GDP exceeds the rate of population growth, then our standard of living should be improving.

GDP per Capita **GDP per capita** means GDP per person. We get this figure by dividing total GDP by the total population of a country. As a measure of economic well-being of the average person, GDP per capita is a better measure than GDP. Luxembourg has the highest GDP per capita (approximately US$114 508), followed by Norway (US$98 102), Qatar (US$92 501), Switzerland (US$83 382), and Macao SAR China (US$65 550). Canada's per capita GDP (US$50 345) is higher than that of the United States (US$48 111).[14]

Real GDP **Real GDP** means that GDP has been adjusted. To understand why adjustments are necessary, assume that pizza is the only product in an economy. Assume that in 2013, a pizza cost $10 and, in 2014, it cost $11.

In both years, exactly 1000 pizzas were produced. In 2013, the GDP was $10 000 ($10 * 1000); in 2014, the GDP was $11 000 ($11 * 1000). Has the economy grown? No. Since 1000 pizzas were produced in both years, aggregate output remained the same. If GDP is not adjusted for 2014, it is called **nominal GDP**, that is, GDP measured in current dollars.[15]

Purchasing Power Parity In our example, current prices would be 2014 prices. On the other hand, we calculate real GDP when

GROSS DOMESTIC PRODUCT (GDP) Total value of all goods and services produced within a given period by a national economy through domestic factors of production.

GROSS NATIONAL PRODUCT (GNP) Total value of all goods and services produced by a national economy within a given period regardless of where the factors of production are located.

GDP PER CAPITA Gross domestic product per person.

REAL GDP GDP calculated to account for changes in currency values and price changes.

NOMINAL GDP GDP measured in current dollars or with all components valued at current prices.

we account for changes in currency values and price changes. When we make this adjustment, we account for both GDP and **purchasing power parity**—the principle that exchange rates are set so that the prices of similar products in different countries are about the same. Purchasing power parity gives us a much better idea of what people can actually buy. In other words, it gives us a better sense of standards of living across the globe.

PRODUCTIVITY

A major factor in the growth of an economic system is **productivity**, which is a measure of economic growth that compares how much a system produces with the resources needed to produce it. Let's say, for instance, that it takes one Canadian worker and 50 Canadian dollars to make 10 pairs of leather boots in an eight-hour workday. Let's also say that it takes 1.2 Spanish workers and the equivalent of $60 (in Euros, the official currency used in Spain) to make 10 pairs of equivalent leather boots in the same eight-hour workday. We can say, then, that the Canadian boot manufacturing industry is more productive than the Spanish boot manufacturing industry.

The two factors of production in this simple case are labour and capital. According to the Organisation for Economic Co-operation and Development (OECD) rankings, Canada stood in twenty-fourth place with a productivity ratio of 76.8 percent compared to the United States. Luxembourg and Norway were the most productive nations at 137.8 and 129.7 percent respectively. Ireland (112.6) was also classified above the benchmark U.S. statistics.[16] If more products are being produced with fewer factors of production, what happens to the prices of these products? They go down. As a consumer, therefore, you would need less of your currency to purchase the same quantity of these products. Thus, your standard of living—at least with regard to these products—has improved. If your entire economic system increases its productivity, then your overall standard of living improves.

PURCHASING POWER PARITY Principle that exchange rates are set so that the prices of similar products in different countries are about the same.

PRODUCTIVITY Measure of economic growth that compares how much a system produces with the resources needed to produce it.

BALANCE OF TRADE The total of a country's exports (sales to other countries) minus its imports (purchases from other countries).

NATIONAL DEBT The total amount of money that a country owes its creditors.

BUDGET DEFICITS The result of the government spending more in one year than it takes in during that year.

In fact, the standard of living improves only through increases in productivity.[17]

THE BALANCE OF TRADE AND THE NATIONAL DEBT

There are several factors that can help or hinder the growth of an economic system, but here we focus on just two of them: balance of trade and the national debt.

Balance of Trade

The **balance of trade** is the economic value of all the products that a country exports minus the economic value of its imported products. Canada traditionally has had a positive balance of trade. It is usually a creditor nation rather than a debtor nation. For example, Canada received $43 to $47 billion more from exports than it spent on imports annually from 2006 to 2008, but that long trend was reversed in 2009 when Canada had a trade deficit of $4.8 billion, followed by a deficit of $8.9 billion in 2010. In 2011, a surplus figure was once again registered, albeit at a very modest $911 million.[18] The United States usually has a negative balance of trade; it spends more on imports than it receives for exports. It is therefore a consistent debtor nation. A trade deficit negatively affects economic growth because the money that flows out of a country can't be used to invest in productive enterprises, either at home or overseas.

National Debt

A country's **national debt** is the amount of money that the government owes its creditors. Like a business, the government takes in revenues (e.g., taxes) and has expenses (e.g., military spending, social programs). For many years, the government of Canada incurred annual **budget deficits**, that is, it spent more money each year than it took in. These accumulated annual deficits created a huge national debt (estimated above $600 billion at the beginning of 2013). This figure amounts to approximately $17 200 per citizen.[19]

<<< The balance of trade looks at the all products including popular imports like the Nintendo Wii. Of course, Nintendo is a very popular Japanese game console manufacturer that makes products in Japan and China.

Chiaki Tsukumo/AP Images

From Confederation (1867) to 1981, the total accumulated debt was only $85.7 billion, but in the period 1981 to 1994, annual deficits were in the $20- to $40-billion range. Fortunately, from 1997 to 2008, Canada was the only highly industrialized country in the world that had annual budget surpluses. That all changed in 2009 when the government announced a deficit of $46.9 billion and followed that with deficits of $36.2 billion and $32.3 billion. Budget deficits are projected until at least 2015 or 2016.[20] Big increases in annual deficits have become the norm in the United States and were made worse because of the multibillion-dollar bailouts that were given to companies in the financial and auto sectors. In spite of this, the United States is still able to borrow large amounts of money from countries like China because the United States is seen as a strong economy and a safe haven in troubled economic times.[21]

How does the national debt affect economic growth? When the government of Canada sells bonds to individuals and organizations (both at home and overseas), this affects economic growth because the Canadian government competes with every other potential borrower—individuals, households, businesses, and other organizations—for the available supply of loanable money. The more money the government borrows, the less money is available for the private borrowing and investment that increases productivity.

Take a look at the following There's an APP for That! feature that outlines three Economics apps.

Economic Stability

A key goal of an economic system is **stability**, a condition in which the amount of money available in an economic system and the quantity of goods and services produced in it are growing at about the same rate. Several factors threaten stability—namely, inflation, deflation, and unemployment.

INFLATION

Inflation is evident when the amount of money injected into an economic system outstrips the increase in actual output. When inflation occurs, people have more money to spend, but there will still be the same quantity of products available for them to buy. As they compete with one another to buy available products, prices go up. Before long, high prices will erase the increase in the amount of money injected into the economy. Purchasing power, therefore, declines.

Inflation varies widely across countries. One dramatic example occurred in Zimbabwe in 2008, when inflation reached an astonishing annual rate above 40 million percent (most countries have rates between 2 and 15 percent). One Zimbabwean dollar from 2005 would have been worth 1 trillion Zimbabwean dollars in 2008. Many workers simply stopped going to their jobs because their pay was not enough to cover their bus fare.[22] The problem was finally solved in 2009 when the government began allowing people to pay their bills using other currencies, like the U.S. dollar or the South African rand.[23] Inflation was projected to be 5.2 percent in 2014 in South Africa (the rand is a more stable measure of value in the region).[24]

Measuring Inflation: The CPI The **consumer price index (CPI)** measures changes in the cost of a "basket" of goods and services that a typical family buys. What is included in the basket has changed over the years. For example, the first CPI in 1913 included items like coal, spirit vinegar, and fruit, while today the index includes bottom-freezer fridges, flat-screen TVs, energy-saving light bulbs, and laser eye surgery.[25] These changes in the CPI reflect changes that have occurred in the pattern of consumer purchases. For example, in 1961, about 53 percent of consumer spending went to necessities like food, housing, and clothing. By the turn of the century, only 40 percent of consumer spending went to necessities.[26] Figure 2.3 shows how inflation has varied over the last 30 years in Canada.

As mentioned earlier, despite the fact that official inflation rates, as measured by the CPI, have remained low, price pressure caused by increased fuel prices is putting great strain on companies in all sectors. Food manufacturers are particularly susceptible. For example, Maple Leaf Foods increased prices in 2012 based on rising costs for inputs such as corn and wheat, which had risen 95 percent and 102 percent, respectively, in the previous 12 months. Increases in food prices were projected at 1.5 to 3.5 percent in 2013 with meat prices rising by as much as 6.5 percent. Inflationary forces are clear, but many consumers are countering the effect by trading down to lower cost alternatives to reduce their grocery bills.[28]

DEFLATION

Deflation (falling prices) is evident when the amount of money injected into an economic system lags behind increases in actual output. Prices may fall because industrial productivity is increasing and cost savings are being passed on to consumers (this is good), or because consumers have high levels of debt and are therefore unwilling to buy very much (this is bad).

UNEMPLOYMENT

At the end of 2012, there were 8 million men and 7.1 million women (over age 25) working in Canada's labour force.[29] But there were many additional people who wanted a job but could not get one.

THERE'S AN APP FOR THAT!

1. **National Debt** >>> **Platforms:** *Apple*
   Source: Caramba App Development
   Key Features: Provides insight into the national debts of more than 180 countries.
2. **World in Figures** >>> **Platforms:** *Android*
   Source: Erik Meier
   Key Features: Facts and Figures for 193 sovereign states (GDP, HDI, Inflation, population, etc.).
3. **Gross Domestic Product (GDP)** >>> **Platforms:** *Apple, Android*
   Source: Samuel Bryant
   Key Features: GDP referenced by year and country.

APP DISCOVERY EXERCISE

Since APP availability changes, conduct your own search for "Top 3" Economic Statistics APPS and identify the key features.

STABILITY Condition in an economic system in which the amount of money available and the quantity of goods and services produced are growing at about the same rate.

INFLATION Occurrence of widespread price increases throughout an economic system.

CONSUMER PRICE INDEX (CPI) Measure of the prices of typical products purchased by consumers living in urban areas.

DEFLATION A period of generally falling prices.

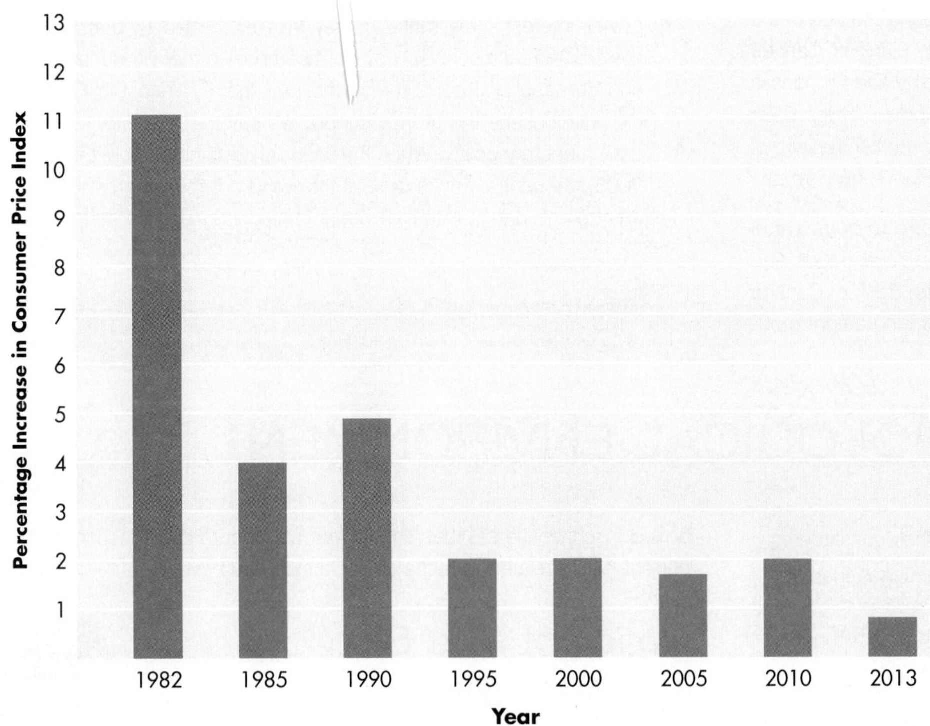

<<< FIGURE 2.3 Price increases in Canada[27]
During the past 15 years, the rate of price increases in Canada has been low and quite stable.

Unemployment is the level of joblessness among people actively seeking work. There are various types of unemployment: frictional unemployment (people are out of work temporarily while looking for a new job), seasonal unemployment (people are out of work because of the seasonal nature of their jobs), cyclical unemployment (people are out of work because of a downturn in the business cycle), and structural unemployment (people are unemployed because they lack the skills needed to perform available jobs). Unemployment rates have varied greatly over the years, as Figure 2.4 shows, with the rates for men generally being higher than the rates for women. At the beginning of 2013, the Canadian unemployment rate stood at 7.3 percent, which was a four-year low at the time.[30]

When unemployment is low, there is a shortage of labour available for businesses. As businesses compete with one another for the available supply of labour, they raise the wages they are willing to pay. Then, because higher labour costs eat into profit margins, businesses raise the prices of their products. If prices get too high, consumers will respond by buying less. Businesses will then reduce their workforces because they don't need to produce as much. But this causes unemployment to go up and the cycle starts all over again.

Managing the Canadian Economy

The federal government manages the Canadian economic system through two sets of policies: fiscal and monetary. **Fiscal policies** involve the collection and spending of government revenues. For example, when the growth rate of the economy is decreasing, tax cuts will normally stimulate renewed

UNEMPLOYMENT The level of joblessness among people actively seeking work in an economic system.

FISCAL POLICIES Policies whereby governments collect and spend revenues.

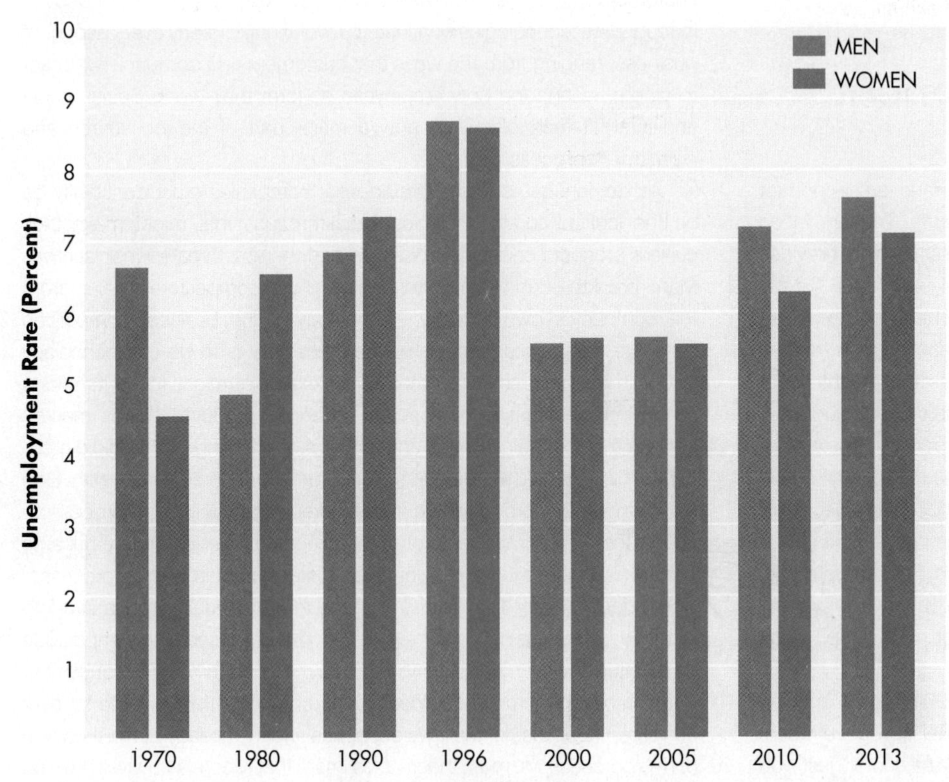

<<< FIGURE 2.4 Historical unemployment rate
From 1970 to 1996, there was a steady upward trend in unemployment rates, but the rate began to decline in the late 1990s. The recession, which began in 2008, caused a clear increase in unemployment, as seen in the chart.

economic growth. **Monetary policies** focus on controlling the size of the nation's money supply. Working primarily through the Bank of Canada (see Chapter 14), the government can influence the ability and willingness of banks throughout the country to lend money. The power of the Bank of Canada to make changes in the supply of money is the centrepiece of the Canadian government's monetary policy. The principle is fairly simple:

- Higher interest rates make money more expensive to borrow and thereby reduce spending by companies that produce goods and services and consumers who buy them. When the Bank of Canada restricts the money supply, we say that it is practising a tight monetary policy.
- Lower interest rates make money less expensive to borrow and thereby increase spending by both companies that produce goods and services and consumers who buy them. When the Bank of Canada loosens the money supply, we say that it is practising an easy monetary policy. When the financial crisis hit back in the fall of 2008, the central banks around the world cut their interest rates in an attempt to stimulate their countries' economies.

MONETARY POLICIES Policies whereby the government controls the size of the nation's money supply.

LO-3 THE TECHNOLOGICAL ENVIRONMENT

TECHNOLOGY All the ways firms create value for their constituents.

RESEARCH AND DEVELOPMENT (R&D) Those activities that are necessary to provide new products, services, and processes.

BASIC (OR PURE) R&D Improving knowledge in an area without a primary focus on whether any discoveries that might occur are immediately marketable.

APPLIED R&D Focusing specifically on how a technological innovation can be put to use in the making of a product or service that can be sold in the marketplace.

As applied to the environment of business, **technology** generally includes all the ways firms create value for their constituents. Technology includes human knowledge, work methods, physical equipment, electronics and telecommunications, and various processing systems that are used to perform business activities. Although technology is applied within organizations, the forms and availability of that technology come from the general environment. Boeing, for example, uses computer-assisted manufacturing and design techniques developed by external vendors to simulate the four miles of hydraulic tubing that run through its new 777 aircraft.

Research and Development (R&D)

Technological improvements and innovation in general are important contributors to the economic development of a country. The innovation process includes **research and development (R&D)**, which provides new ideas for products, services, and processes (see Chapter 13; the importance of R&D in the marketing of products). There are two types of R&D. **Basic (or pure) R&D** involves improving knowledge in an area without a primary focus on whether any discoveries that might occur are immediately marketable. For example, chemists in a laboratory might examine how certain chemical compounds behave. The knowledge gained from this activity might or might not result in a marketable product. **Applied R&D**, on the other hand, means focusing specifically on how a technological innovation can be put to use in the making of a product or service that can be sold in the marketplace. For example, H.J. Heinz developed a tomato that is sweeter than the variety it previously used to make its ketchup. This reduced the need for corn syrup, which had been rapidly increasing in price.[31]

R&D spending in Canada totalled $29.9 billion in 2011. The Canadian private sector accounts for about 52 percent of R&D, the government 10 percent, and universities 38 percent.[32] In the private sector, just 100 businesses account for over half of all R&D money that is spent.[33] The boxed insert entitled "What Should We Do about R&D" describes the current issues related to research in Canada and beyond.

Product and Service Technologies

Product and service technologies are employed for creating products—both physical goods and services—for customers. Although many people associate technology with manufacturing, it is also a significant factor in the service sector. Just as an automobile follows a predetermined pathway along an assembly line, a hamburger at McDonald's is cooked, assembled, and wrapped as it moves along a predefined path. The rapid advancement of the internet into all areas of business is also a reflection of the technological environment. For example, Starbucks Canada now offers a mobile payment program that permits consumers to use their phones as an electronic wallet through the use of an app and a QR code to pay for their "latte grande." According to a senior executive, today's customers may forget their wallet, but they never forget their phones.[34] Indeed, new technologies continue to revolutionize nearly every aspect of business, ranging from the ways that customers and companies interact to where, when, and how employees perform their work. Social media and internet technology are now a major part of the job search and recruitment process.

As demonstrated in the Netflix case, companies must constantly be on the lookout for technological breakthroughs that might make their current products or services obsolete and thereby threaten their survival. Many breakthroughs do not come from direct competitors or even from the company's own industry. Technology is the basis of competition for some companies, especially when their goal is to be the technology leader in their industry. A company, for example, might focus its efforts on having the most technologically advanced products on the market. Intel exemplifies the challenge and the risks of adopting a strategic dependence on technological leadership. Before co-founding Intel with Bob Noyce in 1968, Gordon Moore made a prediction about microprocessors (the processing components of microcomputers) that eventually became known as Moore's Law—the number of transistors in a microprocessor would double every 18 months. In effect, this rate would entail a two-fold increase in processing power every 18 months—a seemingly impossible pace. Intel, however, adopted Moore's Law as a performance requirement for each new generation of processor and has kept up this pace for over 45 years.[35] Because of the laws of physics and the already diminished size of microprocessors, most theorists estimate that Moore's Law will likely be impossible to keep up with sometime between 2015 and 2020.[36]

MANAGING IN TURBULENT TIMES

What Should We Do about R&D?

Canada has a well-educated workforce and competitive corporate tax policies, yet it lags far behind other industrialized countries when it comes to spending on research and development (R&D). Canadian spending on R&D is in the bottom third of the OECD countries, and our productivity growth rate is less than half the OECD average.

In October 2011, the Jenkins report on Canadian R&D was released. The panel—chaired by Tom Jenkins, an entrepreneur and the CEO of the software company Open Text Corp.—examined the structure of tax incentive programs meant to encourage R&D, the granting councils who dole out the money, and the initiatives that are in place to encourage innovation. The panel's most general finding was that the federal government spends a great deal of money each year (approximately $5 billion) trying to get businesses to boost spending on R&D, yet there is has been little change in R&D spending by Canadian companies, and insufficient innovation. Jenkins himself expressed dismay at how little effort has been expended figuring out how inputs (R&D expenditures) are linked to outcomes (commercial products and processes).

The current Scientific Research and Experimental Development program (SR&ED) came in for criticism in a *Globe and Mail* investigation which found many dubious claims, a scatter-gun approach to funding (too many small grants), and the diversion of tax credits to high-priced consultants. A report from the Mowat Centre for Policy Innovation at the University of Toronto urged the government to reduce R&D tax breaks and instead use the money for targeted research grants (a system that is used by innovation leaders like Germany and Sweden).

The situation at Xerox Corp. illustrates the concerns. The company, which has the leading materials science lab in Canada, has developed new inks, toners, and photo receptors, and has generated more than 1500 U.S. patents. That's the good news. But Sophie Vandebroek, who runs the company's global network of research labs, says that Xerox's expertise is an underused asset in Canada, and that Xerox spends about the same amount of money on R&D in Canada as it did 10 years ago. She thinks that Canada's tax credit system for encouraging R&D is not effective.

The Jenkins report contained recommendations to make Canadian companies more globally competitive, including:

- A bigger role for business in how the government allocates its innovations budget
- The formation of an Industrial Research and Innovation Council (IRIC) that would oversee and evaluate the work of the 60 different programs that are currently run by 17 different departments
- More focused distribution of funds to high-performing organizations (turning the current R&D democracy into an R&D meritocracy)
- Overhauling the SR&ED program and put the freed-up funds into other programs, most notably direct grants to businesses and "late-stage" venture capital funding
- Reduce the emphasis on tax breaks and increase the emphasis on direct grants

CRITICAL THINKING QUESTIONS

1. Why do you think Canada lags behind other industrialized countries in R&D?
2. Do you think increased government involvement in R&D will improve Canada's position? Explain your reasoning.

The great R&D spending and efficiency has allowed Intel to remain a leader in microprocessor development.

Ryan McVay/Photodisc/Getty Images

Because of the rapid pace of new developments, keeping a leadership position based on technology is increasingly difficult. **Technology transfer** refers to the process of getting a new technology out of the lab and into the marketplace where it can generate profits for the company. Efficient technology transfer means an increased likelihood of business success, as discussed above. A related challenge is meeting the constant demand to decrease cycle time—the time from beginning to end that it takes a firm to accomplish some recurring activity or function. Since businesses are more competitive if they can decrease cycle times, many companies now focus on decreasing cycle times in areas such as developing products, making deliveries, and collecting credit payments.

TECHNOLOGY TRANSFER The process of getting a new technology out of the lab and into the marketplace.

LO-4 THE POLITICAL–LEGAL ENVIRONMENT

POLITICAL–LEGAL ENVIRONMENT Conditions reflecting the relationship between business and government, usually in the form of government regulation.

The **political–legal environment** reflects the relationship between business and government, including government regulation of business. The legal system defines what an organization can and can't do. Although Canada is a free market economy, there is still significant regulation of business activity, as we saw in Chapter 1. At times, government policy can be tremendously advantageous to businesses. The Yukon government has not raised taxes (royalties) on the extraction of gold since 1906. So the 2.5 percent export royalty is still based on a price per ounce of gold of $15 which translates to a royalty of just 37.5 cents an ounce at a time when gold is selling above $1600 an ounce. This is an extreme example of business-friendly practices.[37] On the other hand, Shoppers Drug Mart has been very vocal about its opposition to Ontario government regulations that have cut the price of generic drug payments to as low as 20 percent of the original brand name product's cost, down from 50 percent. This regulation is saving the province $55 million in costs, but has hurt profits for pharmacies.[38]

Society's general view of business (pro or anti) is also important. During periods of anti-business sentiment, companies may find their competitive activities restricted. Political stability is also an important consideration, especially for multinational firms. No business wants to set up shop in another country unless trade relationships with that country are relatively well defined and stable. Thus, Canadian firms are more likely to do business in England than in Haiti. In recent years, mining companies have been concerned about rumours that members of the South African ruling government were considering nationalization (government takeover of resources, forcing private companies to sell at a price deemed fair by the government) of up to 60 percent of the country's mining sector. This was a dangerous prospect for Vancouver-based Great Basin Gold Ltd., which was developing a $230 million gold mining operation at the time.[39] In another case, when Suncor reinvested in Libya after the fall of Muammar Ghadhafi, the political turmoil there put a $1.4 billion project in jeopardy for a time.[40]

Relations between sovereign governments can also affect business activity. Former CEO of Toronto-based Sherritt International, Ian Delaney, struck a mining deal with Fidel Castro a couple of decades ago which helped Sherritt become one of the largest foreign investors in Cuba. This decision also led to Mr. Delaney being blacklisted from the U.S., however, because of the American embargo of Cuba.[41] On a smaller scale, similar issues also pertain to assessments of local and provincial governments. A new mayor or provincial leader can affect many organizations, especially small firms that do business in a single location and are susceptible to zoning restrictions, property and school taxes, and the like.

LO-5 THE SOCIO-CULTURAL ENVIRONMENT

SOCIO-CULTURAL ENVIRONMENT Conditions including the customs, values, attitudes, and demographic characteristics of the society in which an organization functions.

The **socio-cultural environment** includes the customs, values, attitudes, and demographic characteristics of the society in which a company operates. The socio-cultural environment influences the customer preferences for goods and services, as well as the standards of business conduct that are seen as acceptable.

Customer Preferences and Tastes

Customer preferences and tastes vary both across and within national boundaries. In some countries, consumers are willing and able to pay premium prices for designer clothes with labels such as Armani. But the same clothes have virtually no market in other countries. While differences in tastes across national borders are sometimes clear and obvious, it is important to avoid stereotypical assumptions. Would you be surprised to hear that Canadian lingerie retailers like La Senza and La Vie en Rose have a significant presence in the Middle East? In 2012, La Senza had 96 stores and La Vie en Rose had opened 40 retail outlets in the region (most of them located in Saudi Arabia). Behind the conservative, strict, exterior dress code, there was a significant market for lingerie.[42]

Product usage also varies between nations. In China, bicycles are primarily seen as a mode of transportation, but in Canada, they are marketed primarily for recreational purposes. Consumer preferences can also vary widely within the same country. Customs and product preferences in Quebec, for example, differ from those in other parts of Canada. In the United States, pre-packaged chilli is more popular in the southwest than in the northeast. McDonald's is a good example of a company that is affected by socio-cultural factors. In response to concerns about nutrition and health, McDonald's added salads to its menus and experiments with other low-fat foods.

Consumer preferences and tastes also change over time. Preferences for colour, style, taste, and so forth, change from season to season. In some years, brightly coloured clothes sell best, while in other years, people want more subdued colours. Some of these changes are driven by consumers, and some are driven by companies trying to convince consumers to adopt new styles. These and many other related issues regarding businesses and their customers are explored more fully in Part 4 of this book, which deals with the marketing of goods and services. Read the Entrepreneurship and New Ventures Box entitled "Coalition Music: Entrepreneurial Spirit in the Entertainment Industry," to see how this organization functions in the ever-changing music industry.

La Senza has made inroads in the Middle East. Despite strict rules about dress code, there is a thriving business for undergarments in places like Saudi Arabia.

Matthew Mcvay/Corbis

Ethical Compliance and Responsible Business Behaviour

An especially critical element of the socio-cultural environment is the practice of ethical conduct and social responsibility. We cover these areas in detail in Chapter 3, but they are sufficiently important that we

ENTREPRENEURSHIP AND NEW VENTURES

Coalition Music: Entrepreneurial Spirit in the Entertainment Industry

Entrepreneurs identify opportunities, access resources, improve on, or build something from scratch. Their creations must provide value that other people can appreciate and support through purchases of goods or services. When you think of that entrepreneurial spirit, you might imagine an old traditional manufacturer or retailer or a new high-tech start-up. However, that entrepreneurial spirit can be found in all types of organizations. The people behind Coalition Music are a prime example.

Eric Lawrence and Rob Lanni founded Coalition Music back in 1990. Today, this organization represents some of the biggest names in Canadian music, such as Simple Plan, Our Lady Peace, and Finger Eleven. For all their hard work, Coalition Music was awarded the honour of Company of the Year at the 2012 Canadian Music and Broadcast Industry Awards. This was a nice acknowledgement, but, in this business, long-term success comes down to a few important statistics to prove your worth. Coalition has plenty to be proud of:

- Over 30 commercial albums released
- Over 12 million artist albums sold worldwide
- Loyal and successful clients (partner relationships)
  - Our Lady Peace (19 years)
  - Finger Eleven (15 years)
  - Simple Plan (10 years)

Success in the music business is not just about numbers, but clearly these statistics point to Eric's and Rob's ability to identify opportunities and manage talent. Dealing with artists requires the skill set to handle egos, provide valuable input, and to manage expectations. After spending over two decades building a wealth of industry knowledge, the two entrepreneurs took their passion to a new level.

Artist Entrepreneur Program

While Coalition Music is a distinct business, they represent music artists who have their own brands, unique identities, fan bases, promotional efforts, etc. In other words, they are in the business of helping each artist manage his or her own distinct business identity. It's the artists' music and their ability to connect with their fans (sell music, tickets, and merchandise) that determines their survival. The second you visit the website and read about the company, this core principle is highlighted—Coalition develops "artist–entrepreneurs" and helps them build long-standing careers in both the arena and studio.

So in 2012, Rob and Eric took this idea and created the *Artist Entrepreneur Program*. It allows the firm to leverage their core knowledge and teach diverse music industry topics like production, songwriting, music law, tour logistics, social media networking, marketing and publicity, etc.

Coalition Music recently moved into a new, refurbished facility in Toronto, complete with great rehearsal spaces and a new recording studio (featuring a vintage Neve console) and a classroom. The location has been visited by Drake and MuchMusic.

Simple Plan is one of the great successful acts represented by Coalition Music.

AFP/Getty Images

Do you think you have what it takes to be an artist-entrepreneur? If the answer is yes, you might want to look into this program. If the answer is no (because you lack the raw talent to be a musician) perhaps you might want to reconsider. According to Eric Lawrence, "some of our students have come in dreaming of being a music artist but have left wanting to become entertainment lawyers." Who knows, maybe there is a career for you in the music industry.

CRITICAL THINKING QUESTIONS

1. Describe some of the greatest challenges for Coalition music in their core music business.
2. What do you think of the *Artist Entrepreneur Program*? What are the benefits for the students? What are the secondary benefits (other than potential enrolment) for Coalition Music?

describe a couple of points briefly here: the reporting of a company's financial position and a company's social responsibility toward citizens.

Keeping up with today's increasingly fast-paced business activities is putting a strain on the accounting profession's traditional methods for auditing, financial reporting, and time-honoured standards for professional ethics. The stakeholders of business firms—employees, stockholders, consumers, labour unions, creditors, and the government—are entitled to a fair accounting so they can make enlightened personal and business decisions, but they often get a blurred picture of a firm's competitive health. Nortel went from being the pride and joy of Canada to a historical warning, and a good portion of the downfall could be traced to misleading accounting statements in the final years.

Walmart has a reputation for low prices, but the company has had a very rocky relationship with its employees. For example, Walmart recently agreed to pay US$86 million to settle a lawsuit from 232 000 employees in California. In 2011, when the company bought out a South African retailer named Massmart, the company agreed to respect the union contracts to close the deal. However, the South African union did not stop there—they also publicly urged Walmart to end its adversarial approach with employees in the U.S.[43] In Canada, Walmart has also had a very spotty history, and a court ruling in 2012 found the company guilty of unfair labour practices in its attempt to block a union drive in Weyburn, Saskatchewan.[44]

A few years ago, British Petroleum (BP) was in the news for all the wrong reasons and faced the consequences of the massive Gulf of Mexico oil spill. For months, oil spewed into the Gulf, devastating coastlines, endangering wildlife, and battering the local fishing and tourism businesses. This failure had consequences and the various stakeholders were lining up to make BP pay. Within a few days, a Facebook page promoting a BP boycott had 360 000 supporters. Advocacy groups like Public Citizen held rallies against BP. The U.S. government was planning a legal response to make BP pay for its mistake in the court system. The future of BP was at stake (something that had been unimaginable before the crisis). In the face of all of this pressure, BP created a US$20 billion trust and escrow account to pay for legitimate claims.[45] In 2012, a U.S. district judge awarded a $4 billion fine to settle criminal penalties, but this was just one step in the financial resolution process.[46]

THE BUSINESS ENVIRONMENT

Business today is faster paced, more complex, and more demanding than ever before. As businesses aggressively try to differentiate themselves, there has been a trend toward higher-quality products, planned obsolescence, and product life cycles measured in weeks or months rather than years. This, in turn, has created customer expectations for instant gratification. Final consumers and business customers want high-quality goods and services—often customized—for lower prices and with immediate delivery. Sales offices, service providers, and production facilities are shifting geographically as new markets and resources emerge in other countries. Employees want flexible working hours and opportunities to work at home. Shareholders' expectations also add pressure for productivity increases, growth in market share, and larger profits. At the same time, however, a more vocal public demands more honesty, fair competition, and respect for the environment.

A C-Suite survey found that the three most important issues facing Canadian businesses are (1) the value of the Canadian dollar, (2) a skilled labour shortage, and (3) the environment. These three issues are all important elements of the business environment.[47]

The Industry Environment

Each business firm operates in a specific industry, and each industry has different characteristics. The intensity of the competition in an industry has a big influence on how a company operates. To be effective, managers must understand the competitive situation, and then develop a strategy to exploit opportunities in the industry.

One of the most popular tools to analyze competitive situations in an industry is Michael Porter's five forces model.[48] The model (see Figure 2.5) helps managers analyze five important sources of competitive pressure and then decide what their competitive strategy should be. We briefly discuss each of the elements of the model in the following paragraphs.

RIVALRY AMONG EXISTING COMPETITORS

The amount of rivalry among companies varies across industries. Rivalry can be seen in activities like intense price competition, elaborate advertising campaigns, and an increased emphasis on customer service. For many years, Tim Hortons has dominated the Canadian coffee industry with its extensive coverage of the market and strong brand equity. More recently, however, we have seen some stronger competitive efforts from the likes of Starbucks and McDonald's. In particular, McDonald's has made some aggressive moves (like free coffee for a week, adding fireplaces and Wi-Fi to McCafé locations, etc.) to gain market share. At the beginning of 2013, there were clear signs that the efforts were paying off; McDonald's share of the Canadian coffee market had more than doubled to 10 percent from less than 5 percent four years earlier. Tim Hortons, famous for its double-double, was taking notice.[49]

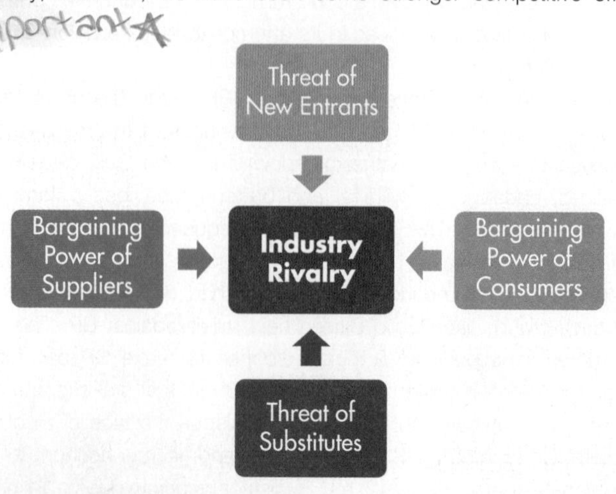

FIGURE 2.5 Michael Porter's five forces model

THREAT OF POTENTIAL ENTRANTS

When new competitors enter an industry, they may cause big changes. If it is easy for new competitors to enter a market, competition will likely be intense and the industry will not be very attractive. Some industries (for example, automobile manufacturing) are very capital intensive and are therefore difficult to enter, but others (for example, home cleaning or lawn care services) are relatively easy to enter.

The entry of Target into the Canadian retail landscape is a great threat for low cost retailers and is also a major opportunity for real estate income trust players like Primaris Retail REIT and RioCan. Target is converting 135 of the 220 former Zellers stores and making major renovations in exchange for favourable leases. It also held options for another 85 locations and sold many options to other retailers or back to the landlords; the scramble to get those prime locations was intense. Walmart secured the rights to 39 of the remaining 85 locations. Other retailers like Canadian Tire were looking at additional sites. The reallocation of 220 locations shook up the industry because one of the greatest barriers (access to prime real estate) was temporarily weakened by the demise of Zellers. Other U.S. chains looking to further expand into Canada, like Marshalls, had a potential opening as well.[50]

SUPPLIERS

The amount of bargaining power suppliers have in relation to buyers helps determine how competitive an industry is. When there are only a few suppliers in an industry, they tend to have great bargaining power. The power of suppliers is influenced by the number of substitute products available (i.e., products that perform the same or similar functions). When there are few substitute products, suppliers obviously have more power.

The threat of Target's entry has materialized and the fall of Zellers is causing a shakeup in the industry as other retailers see the opportunity to enter the market or expand since prime real estate in major malls was temporarily available.

Courtesy of AT&T Archives and History Center

BUYERS

When there are only a few buyers and many suppliers, the buyers have a great deal of bargaining power. Retail powerhouse Walmart, for example, is often cited as a buyer that puts tremendous pressure on its suppliers to reduce their prices. Walmart can do this because it buys so much from these suppliers. In another example, when Canadian Tire purchased Forzani (owner of SportChek and Hockey Experts stores) for $771 million in 2011, it was not necessarily good news for hockey equipment maker Bauer Performance Sports Ltd. When two of your biggest customers merge, it alters the power relationship somewhat. Bauer CEO Scott Davis indicated that this merger may lead to price pressure on his company.[51]

SUBSTITUTES

If there are many substitute products available, the industry is more competitive. For example, various synthetic fibres can be used as substitutes for cotton. The internet has changed the way people pay bills. Because of online banking, people send a lot less mail than they did in the past and thus spend less on stamps as well. Even the federal government recently announced that it would stop issuing pension cheques by mail by 2016. This is bad news for Canada Post as the threat from substitutes is expected to reduce mail volume by another 50 percent in the next decade.[52]

LO-6 EMERGING CHALLENGES AND OPPORTUNITIES IN THE BUSINESS ENVIRONMENT

The most successful firms are dealing with challenges and opportunities in today's business environment by focusing on their **core competencies**—the skills and resources with which they compete best and create the most value for owners. They outsource non-core business processes and pay suppliers and distributors to perform them, thereby increasing their reliance on suppliers. These new business models call for unprecedented coordination—not only among internal activities, but also among customers, suppliers, and strategic partners—and they often involve globally dispersed processes and supply chains.

In this section, we discuss some of the most popular steps that companies have taken to respond to challenges and opportunities in the business environment. These include outsourcing, social media and viral marketing, and business process management.

Outsourcing

Outsourcing is the strategy of paying suppliers and distributors to perform certain business processes or to provide needed materials or services. For example, the cafeteria in a museum may be important to employees and customers, but the museum's primary focus is on exhibits that will interest the general public, not on food-service operations. That's why museums usually outsource cafeteria operations to food-service management companies. The result is more attention to museum exhibits and better food service for customers. Firms today outsource numerous activities, including payroll, employee training, and research and development. When Levon Afeyan, CEO of Montreal-based Seatply Products Inc., searched for a solution to fight low-cost providers from China while simultaneously fending off local competitors providing premium products, he turned to an outsourcing partner in Malaysia. His seat component company now manufacturers about half of its product in Malaysia; it also buys over 80 percent of its partner's output. This partnership has permitted his business to fight the competition under the new, increasingly competitive environment.[53]

Social Media and Viral Marketing

Social media sites, such as Facebook, are now an important part of everyday life for consumers (especially the youth market). Companies are addressing this new reality by providing content and creating various links to connect with consumers. Most organizations are being careful about their online presence because they don't want it to be seen as an imposition, but rather a natural extension to their real-world relationship with clients. As we discuss throughout this book in the E-Business and Social Media Solutions boxes, some companies are making strong inroads as this new model evolves and companies learn to deal with an empowered consumer base. However, the communications are not all good. Read the E-Business and Social Media Solutions box called "Social Media Can Be Just as Dangerous as Hacker Attacks" for more information.

Viral marketing predates the social media craze and first gained prominence through basic email transfer; it describes word of mouth that spreads information like a virus from customer to customer and relies on the internet to replace face-to-face communications. Messages about new cars, sports events, and numerous other goods and services travel on the internet among potential customers, who pass the information on.

Using various formats—games, contests, and instant messaging—marketers encourage potential customers to try out products and tell other people about them.[54] This approach has even more potential today with the likes of Twitter providing even quicker means to move messages.

Viral marketing works because people increasingly rely on the internet for information that they used to get from other media such as radio and newspapers, and because the customer becomes a participant in the process of spreading the word by forwarding information to other internet users.

Business Process Management

A **process** is any activity that adds value to some input, transforming it into an output for a customer (whether external or internal).[55] For example, human resource departments perform interviewing and hiring

CORE COMPETENCIES Skills and resources with which an organization competes best and creates the most value for owners.

OUTSOURCING Strategy of paying suppliers and distributors to perform certain business processes or to provide needed materials or services.

VIRAL MARKETING Strategy of using the internet and word-of-mouth marketing to spread product information.

PROCESS Any activity that adds value to some input, transforming it into an output for a customer (whether external or internal).

E-BUSINESS AND SOCIAL MEDIA SOLUTIONS

Social Media Can Be Just as Dangerous as Hacker Attacks

Computer hackers pose a threat because of their attacks on computer networks, but threats can also be delivered with simple words rather than malicious codes. Managers want their company to have a good reputation in the eyes of consumers, so they keep an eye on the results of "corporate reputation" surveys like "The Most Respected Corporations in Canada," published by KPMG/Ipsos-Reid. Where companies place in these rankings is increasingly influenced by Facebook, Twitter, and YouTube. These social media sources have created a dilemma for managers. On the one hand, if they happen to generate positive "buzz," it will likely enhance the company's reputation. On the other hand, social media can rapidly disseminate negative information that can harm a company's reputation. (Note: Just as social media are facilitated by new technologies, so also is the tracking of company reputations. For example, Radian6 is a New Brunswick–based company that develops software to help companies track what is being said about them online. The company has 2200 clients, including well-known ones like Pepsi and Microsoft.)

Dave Jones, the vice-president for digital communications at Hill & Knowlton, says it can be difficult for a company to know how to respond to repeated bashing from, say, an environmentalist on a blog. Should the company respond to the charges or just ignore them? Consider what happened to Tim Hortons, which is trying to make inroads in the U.S. market. As part of its strategy, it agreed to be one of the sponsors of a family-oriented event in the United States run by a group called The National Organization for Marriage (NOM). When it was discovered that the event was part of NOM's opposition to the legalization of gay marriage, the story developed into an online controversy. Within a few days, Tim Hortons withdrew its support, and bloggers took credit for squelching the sponsorship. But, of course, another segment of the population was unhappy that Tim Hortons withdrew its support for the event. You can't win, it seems.

In another case, a lawsuit was filed against Taco Bell by an unhappy customer who claimed that there was more filler than beef in the company's tacos. When news of this lawsuit began spreading rapidly on the internet, the company decided it had to respond forcefully. It developed Facebook postings and a YouTube video that pointed out that the taco mixture is 88 percent beef, not the 35 percent claimed in the lawsuit.

Taco Bell also took out a full-page newspaper ad that had the aggressive headline Thank You for Suing Us. Although it is too soon to tell what effect the lawsuit will have on the company, Taco Bell says that the response to its advertisements so far has been positive on both Facebook and Twitter.

One thing is clear—the social media arena is a new battlefield and victory or defeat in this domain is based on preparation and a clearly developed strategy of monitoring and appropriate response.

CRITICAL THINKING QUESTION

1. Contrast the responses of Tim Hortons and Taco Bell to the negative online publicity they received. Which response do you think was more effective? Defend your answer.

processes, payroll departments perform the employee-payment process, the purchasing department performs the process of ordering materials, accounting performs the financial reporting process, and marketing performs the process of taking orders from customers.

Business process management means moving away from organizing around departments and moving toward organizing around process-oriented team structures that cut across old departmental boundaries. Often, companies begin by asking, "What must we do well to stay in business and win new orders?" Next, they identify the major processes that must be performed well to achieve these goals. Then they organize resources and skills around those essential processes. By organizing according to processes rather than functional departments, decision making is faster and more customer-oriented, materials and operations are coordinated, and products get to customers more rapidly.[56]

BUSINESS PROCESS MANAGEMENT Approach by which firms move away from department-oriented organization and toward process-oriented team structures that cut across old departmental boundaries.

LO-7 REDRAWING CORPORATE BOUNDARIES

Successful companies are responding to challenges in the external environment by redrawing traditional organizational boundaries and by joining together with other companies to develop new goods and services. Several trends have become evident in recent years: acquisitions and mergers, divestitures and spinoffs, employee-owned corporations, strategic alliances, and subsidiary/parent corporations.

Mergers and Acquisitions

In an **acquisition**, one firm simply buys another firm. For example, Kraft Foods Inc. bought British candy giant Cadbury for US$19 billion.[57] The transaction is similar to buying a car that becomes your property. In contrast, a **merger** is a consolidation of two firms, and the arrangement is more collaborative. In the third quarter of 2012, there were 599 mergers and acquisitions in Canada, with a total value of $58.6 billion; this figure was higher than in the same period in the previous quarter (251 deals worth $45.5 billion).[58]

ACQUISITION The purchase of a company by another, larger firm, which absorbs the smaller company into its operations.

MERGER The union of two companies to form a single new business.

When the companies are in the same industry, as when Molson Inc. merged with Adolph Coors Co., it is called a **horizontal merger**. When one of the companies in the merger is a supplier or customer to the other, it is called a **vertical merger**. When the companies are in unrelated businesses, it is called a **conglomerate merger**.

A merger or acquisition can take place in one of several ways. In a **friendly takeover**, the acquired company welcomes the acquisition, perhaps because it needs cash or sees other benefits in joining the acquiring firm. But in a **hostile takeover**, the acquiring company buys enough of the other company's stock to take control even though the other company is opposed to the takeover.

Montreal-based Couche-Tard has plenty of experience in the merger and takeover game. In the past two decades it has acquired Mac's, Dairy Mart, Circle K, and Winks, to name a few, and is one of the biggest convenience store operators in North America with over 5800 stores. In 2010, it made a US$1.9 billion hostile takeover bid for Iowa-based Casey's after attempting to come to a friendly agreement for the 1500-store chain.[59] Both of those efforts failed. However, in 2012, Couche-Tard's friendly bid for Statoil Fuel and Retail was successful and the $2.8 billion deal gave the company a broad retail network of 2300 stores across Scandinavia, Poland, the Baltic nations, and Russia.[60]

A **poison pill** is a defence tactic that management adopts to make a firm less attractive to an actual or potential hostile suitor in a takeover attempt. The objective is to make the "pill" so distasteful that a potential acquirer will not want to swallow it. Couche-Tard's bid for Casey's was unsuccessful because of a poison pill. Air Canada recently announced plans to institute a poison pill provision which would give all Class A and Class B shareholders the right to purchase stocks, at a discounted price, the moment any group or person announces the intention to buy more than 20 percent of the outstanding shares.[61]

Divestitures and Spinoffs

A **divestiture** occurs when a company decides to sell part of its existing business operations to another corporation. In 2012, when Pfizer Inc. decided to divest its infant-nutrition and animal-health units, competitors jumped at the chance. Nestle and Groupe Danone both showed interest in the strong infant-nutrition assets and Nestle eventually won the auction with a US$11.85 billion bid.[62]

In other cases, a company might set up one or more corporate units as new, independent businesses because a business unit might be more valuable as a separate company. This is known as a **spinoff**. For example, PepsiCo spun off Pizza Hut, KFC, and Taco Bell into a new, separate corporation known as Yum! Brands Inc.

Employee-Owned Corporations

Corporations are sometimes owned by the employees who work for them. The current pattern is for this ownership to take the form of **employee stock ownership plans** or ESOPs. A corporation might decide to set up an ESOP to increase employee motivation or to fight a hostile takeover attempt. The company first secures a loan, which it then uses to buy shares of its stock on the open market. Some of the future profits made by the corporation are used to pay off the loan. The stock, meanwhile, is controlled by a bank or other trustee. Employees gradually gain ownership of the stock, usually on the basis of seniority. But even though they might not have physical possession of the stock for a while, they control its voting rights immediately.

A survey of 471 Canadian and U.S. companies, conducted by Western Compensation & Benefits Consultants of Vancouver, found that three-quarters of the companies that have adopted ESOPs have experienced improvement in both sales and profits. Charlie Spiring, the CEO of Wellington West Holdings Inc., says that one of the fundamental principles of his business is employee ownership. People really have to be entrepreneurs to work well in the company.[63]

Strategic Alliances

A **strategic alliance**, or joint venture, involves two or more enterprises cooperating in the research, development, manufacture, or marketing of a product. For example, Rogers and Walmart have teamed up to launch a new 100-page magazine called *Walmart Live Better.* The circulation will be approximately 1 million copies per issue (six editions per year) distributed inside Walmart stores.[64] Companies form strategic alliances for two main reasons: (1) to help spread the risk of a project, and (2) to get something of value (like technological or industry expertise) from their strategic partner.

Subsidiary and Parent Corporations

A **subsidiary corporation** is one that is owned by another corporation. The corporation that owns the subsidiary is called the **parent corporation**. For example, the Hudson's Bay Company (HBC) is the parent corporation of Home Outfitters.

HORIZONTAL MERGER A merger of two firms that have previously been direct competitors in the same industry.

VERTICAL MERGER A merger of two firms that have previously had a buyer–seller relationship.

CONGLOMERATE MERGER A merger of two firms in completely unrelated businesses.

FRIENDLY TAKEOVER An acquisition in which the management of the acquired company welcomes the firm's buyout by another company.

HOSTILE TAKEOVER An acquisition in which the management of the acquired company fights the firm's buyout by another company.

POISON PILL A defence that management adopts to make a firm less attractive to an actual or potential hostile suitor in a takeover attempt.

DIVESTITURE Occurs when a company sells part of its existing business operations to another company.

SPINOFF Strategy of setting up one or more corporate units as new, independent corporations.

EMPLOYEE STOCK OWNERSHIP PLANS An arrangement whereby a corporation buys its own stock with loaned funds and holds it in trust for its employees. Employees "earn" the stock based on some condition such as seniority. Employees control the stock's voting rights immediately, even though they may not take physical possession of the stock until specified conditions are met.

STRATEGIC ALLIANCE An enterprise in which two or more persons or companies temporarily join forces to undertake a particular project.

SUBSIDIARY CORPORATION One that is owned by another corporation.

PARENT CORPORATION A corporation that owns a subsidiary.

MyBizLab

Visit the MyBizLab website. This online homework and tutorial system puts you in control of your own learning with study and practice tools directly correlated to this chapter's content.

SUMMARY OF LEARNING OBJECTIVES

LO-1 EXPLAIN THE CONCEPTS OF ORGANIZATIONAL BOUNDARIES AND MULTIPLE ORGANIZATIONAL ENVIRONMENTS.

All businesses operate within a larger *external environment* consisting of everything outside an organization's boundaries that might affect it. An *organizational boundary* is that which separates the organization from its environment. Organizations have multiple environments: economic conditions, technology, political–legal considerations, social issues, the global environment, issues of ethical and social responsibility, the business environment itself, and numerous other emerging challenges and opportunities.

LO-2 EXPLAIN THE IMPORTANCE OF THE ECONOMIC ENVIRONMENT TO BUSINESS AND IDENTIFY THE FACTORS USED TO EVALUATE THE PERFORMANCE OF AN ECONOMIC SYSTEM.

The *economic environment* is the economic system in which business firms operate. The key goals of the Canadian system are economic growth, economic stability, and full employment. *Gross domestic product* (GDP) is the total value of all goods and services produced within a given period by a national economy domestically. The government manages the economy through *fiscal and monetary policies*.

LO-3 DESCRIBE THE TECHNOLOGICAL ENVIRONMENT AND ITS ROLE IN BUSINESS.

Technology refers to all the ways firms create value for their constituents, including human knowledge, work methods, physical equipment, electronics and telecommunications, and various processing systems. The innovation process includes *research and development (R&D)*, which provides new ideas for products, services, and processes. There are two general categories of business-related technologies: *product and service technologies* and *business process technologies*.

LO-4 DESCRIBE THE POLITICAL–LEGAL ENVIRONMENT AND ITS ROLE IN BUSINESS.

The *political–legal environment* reflects the relationship between business and government. The legal system defines what an organization can and can't do. Various government agencies regulate important areas such as advertising practices, safety and health considerations, and acceptable standards of business conduct. Pro- or anti-business sentiment in government can further influence business activity.

LO-5 DESCRIBE THE SOCIO-CULTURAL ENVIRONMENT AND ITS ROLE IN BUSINESS.

The *socio-cultural environment* includes the customs, values, and demographic characteristics of society. Socio-cultural processes determine the goods and services as well as the standards of business conduct that a society values and accepts. The shape of the market, the political influence, and the attitudes of its workforce are only a few of the many ways in which culture can affect an organization.

LO-6 IDENTIFY EMERGING CHALLENGES AND OPPORTUNITIES IN THE BUSINESS ENVIRONMENT.

Successful companies are focusing on their core competencies. The innovative ways in which companies respond to emerging challenges and opportunities include *outsourcing, social media and viral marketing,* and *business process management*.

LO-7 UNDERSTAND RECENT TRENDS IN THE REDRAWING OF CORPORATE BOUNDARIES.

An *acquisition* occurs when one firm buys another. A *merger* occurs when two firms combine to create a new company. A *divestiture* occurs when a corporation sells a part of its existing business operations or sets it up as a new and independent corporation. When a firm sells part of itself to raise capital, the strategy is known as a *spin-off.* The *ESOP* plan allows employees to own a significant share of the corporation through trusts established on their behalf. In a *strategic alliance*, two or more organizations collaborate on a project for mutual gain.

QUESTIONS AND EXERCISES

QUESTIONS FOR ANALYSIS

See >>> for Assisted-Graded Writing Assignment in MyBizLab

1. Why is it important for managers to understand the environment in which their businesses operate?
2. It has been argued that inflation is both good and bad. Explain. Are government efforts to control inflation well-advised? Explain.
3. What are the benefits and risks of outsourcing? What, if anything, should be done about the problem of Canadian companies outsourcing jobs to foreign countries? Defend your answer.
4. >>> Explain how current economic indicators such as inflation and unemployment affect you personally. Explain how they affect managers.
5. At first glance, it might seem as though the goals of economic growth and stability are inconsistent with one another. How can this apparent inconsistency be reconciled?
6. >>> What is the current climate in Canada regarding the regulation of business? How might it affect you if you were a manager today?

APPLICATION EXERCISES

7. Select two businesses you are familiar with. Identify the major elements of their external environments that are most likely to affect them in important and meaningful ways.
8. Assume that you are the owner of an internet pharmacy that sells prescription drugs to U.S. citizens. Analyze the factors in the external environment (economic, technological, political–legal, and socio-cultural) that might facilitate your company's activities. Analyze the factors in the external environment that might threaten your company's activities.
9. >>> Select a technology product, such as the Samsung Galaxy smartphone or Amazon's Kindle e-reader, and research how the various environments of business (economic, technological, socio-cultural, global, political–legal, and general business) are currently impacting the sales possibilities of the product or service.
10. Interview two business owners or managers. Ask them to answer the following questions: (a) What business functions, if any, do they outsource? (b) Are they focusing more attention on business process management now than in the past? (c) How have internet applications and the growth of social media changed the way they conduct business?

TEAM EXERCISES

BUILDING YOUR BUSINESS SKILLS

FEELING THE HEAT FROM BAD RESULTS: PRAYING FOR GOOD WEATHER

PURPOSE OF THE ASSIGNMENT

To help students identify the important role played by uncontrollable natural events on the bottom line.

THE SITUATION

Rona Inc. is a Canadian home improvement giant with over $6 billion in annual sales coming from over 830 corporate, franchise, and affiliate stores. It is the largest Canadian retailer of hardware, home renovation, and gardening products and has a roster of over 30 000 employees. Despite its impressive growth, good strategic decisions in the past decade, and locations across the nation, Rona's results are still largely susceptible to natural weather patterns. For example, in the first quarter of a recent year, the retailer lost 23 cents per share based on a 12.6 percent decline in same-store sales from the previous year. The reason, according to CEO Robert Dutton, was that "spring failed to materialize." The extra-long winter that year meant that customers did not rush out to buy things like home gardening supplies, which traditionally pad the bottom line during this sales period. Labour costs remained high while staff had fewer customers to serve. The incentive to discount to attract sales was strong, but company officials stated that they would avoid such tactics. However, the extra build-up of inventory has a direct holding cost; additionally, analysts were worried that the company would likely need to discount (and drastically slash profit margins) to rid itself of the extra stock once the shortened season arrived.[65]

Weather patterns can play an important role in the short-term success or failure of many businesses and clearly Rona was affected by this uncontrollable factor in this case.

ASSIGNMENT

Divide up into groups of four or five students. Each group should begin by doing the following:

Step 1 Identify three ***big companies*** that might be ***positively*** affected by warmer-than-usual weather during a particular season.

Step 2 Identify three ***big companies*** that might be ***negatively*** affected by warmer-than-usual weather patterns during a particular season. If it is appropriate, a company can appear on both lists.

Step 3 Now respond to the following items:

1. For each company that you identify, describe the specific effects on each business.
2. Describe the most logical organizational response to these effects for each company.
3. What kinds of plans, if any, should each organization develop in the event of similar future events?

ALTERNATIVE ASSIGNMENT

Conduct the same exercise on ***small businesses*** and ***entrepreneurs*** and highlight some of the unique challenges that they face. Then proceed with Steps 1–3 above.

QUESTIONS FOR DISCUSSION

1. How could Rona better prepare for and handle negative weather patterns?
2. Are unfavourable natural weather patterns more dangerous for major retailers like Rona or for small businesses? Provide at least one argument on each side before making a choice.
3. Is it possible for a manager to spend too much time trying to anticipate future events? Why or why not?

EXERCISING YOUR ETHICS

PRESCRIBING A DOSE OF COMPETITIVE MEDICINE

THE SITUATION

You are a businessperson in a small town, where you run one of two local pharmacies. The population and economic base are fairly stable. Each pharmacy controls about 50 percent of the market. Each is reasonably profitable, generating solid if unspectacular revenues.

THE DILEMMA

You have just been approached by the owner of the other pharmacy. He has indicated an interest either in buying your pharmacy or in selling his to you. He argues that neither company can substantially increase profits and complains that if one pharmacy raises its prices, customers will simply go to the other one. He tells you outright that if you sell to him, he plans to raise prices by 10 percent.

He believes that the local market will have to accept the increase for two reasons: (1) The town is too small to attract national competitors, such as Shoppers Drug Mart, and (2) local customers can't go elsewhere to shop because the nearest town with a pharmacy is 50 kilometers away.

TEAM ACTIVITY

Form groups of four and assign two members to represent the company that is making the proposition and two members to represent the company that was approached. Answer the questions for discussion found below and then role-play a discussion between the two company owners. Are there alternative solutions? Do they cross ethical lines?

QUESTIONS FOR DISCUSSION

1. What are the roles of supply and demand in this scenario?
2. What are the underlying ethical issues?
3. What would you do if you were actually faced with this situation?

BUSINESS CASE

AIR CANADA'S CHALLENGING ENVIRONMENT

The name Air Canada does not always conjure up warm images for Canadian travellers. But it is the fifteenth-largest airline in the world and it wins international awards. In 2012, it was named the "best international airline in North America" by independent research firm Skytrax (which surveyed over 18.8 million worldwide travellers from 200 airlines). This was the third straight year the airline earned that distinction. It is also the only North American airline to earn the coveted Four-Star ranking, which is an industry benchmark for quality. There have been many ups and downs for Air Canada, but the company continues to control the majority of the domestic market, with WestJet as its main competitor. Back in 2004, Air Canada used bankruptcy protection to deal with major financial problems. It may be tempting to blame that dark period on general turmoil in the travel industry, following the 9/11 terrorist attacks, but placing all the blame on that significant event would be overly simplistic. The airline business is always extremely complicated; it's a difficult business environment that is shaped by relationships with many stakeholders.

Fotosearch/SuperStock

Airlines must efficiently plan their capacity. They don't buy a fleet of planes overnight; airlines make projections and try to maximize the use of planes and other resources. Some of this planning is done two to five or even seven years into the future and this sort of lengthy timeline is complicated. Air Canada must contend with competitor actions at home (e.g., WestJet, Porter), and on international routes (e.g., Air France, British Airways, JAL); it must deal with government regulations (e.g., tax laws, flight restrictions, and international agreements), economic conditions (e.g., recessions, fuel/food prices), and natural weather conditions (e.g., snowstorms and even volcanic ash). Let's take a closer look at these challenges.

In recent years, a major spike in fuel costs hurt air travel and caused ticket prices to skyrocket at times. The global recession decreased tourist and business travel. In fact, back in 2009, the global airline business saw its steepest decline in air traffic since the Second World War. According to the International Air Transport Association (IATA), the global industry lost $10 billion that year. Although IATA predicted industry profits of US$8.4 billion in 2013, it was clear that the industry was experiencing constant pressures. Air Canada worked hard to get its finances under control by creating new agreements with suppliers and major credit providers. However, Air Canada still lost about 20 cents per share in 2012.

At home, Air Canada competes with WestJet and a host of smaller players. The rivalry has pushed it to launch its lower-priced Tango fares (and, more recently, the Rouge brand) to compete in the low-frill, budget travel segment. In addition, the company created a regional partner called Jazz mainly for short-haul flights. In order to effectively compete on the global stage, Air Canada has forged alliances to cut costs. It is a founding member of the leading airline network, Star Alliance. The 27-member airlines of the Star Alliance permit passengers on partner airlines to connect with over 1329 airports in 194 countries. The airlines code-share flights (e.g., booking Air Canada seats on a Lufthansa flight) and share airline lounges in airports around the world.

Governments are strongly linked to airline success or failure. Here are some key facts to consider. The federal government recently negotiated an agreement between Canada and the EU that created new opportunities by reducing restrictions for Air Canada and EU airlines. As a result, Air Canada launched new direct services to five popular European gateway cities: Geneva, Barcelona, Brussels, Copenhagen, and Athens. Of course, the relationship with the government is not all rosy. Air Canada has stated that the government is making it impossible for the airline to be profitable with higher security charges, airport improvement fees, and federal and provincial fuel excise taxes. For example, the federal government collects over $300 million in rent from airports each year. This makes it much more expensive to land a plane in Canada than in the U.S. Air Canada pays $3400 to land an Airbus 320 in Canada's largest airports but less than half that amount ($1650) in the U.S. Total federal tax collected in Halifax alone amounted to $3.2 million in rent charges in one year and is expected to top $5 million by 2014. Since the airline is based in Canada, it has a tax cost disadvantage.

Weather can play a tricky role in airline operations. If you travel on a regular basis, you are very familiar with airline delays. Snowstorms, severe thunder showers, icy weather, and high winds can disrupt travel and cause delays. This creates frustrated passengers and forces airline employees and travel agents to scramble. In 2010, a new issue hit the headlines when a volcano in Iceland halted all air travel to and from Europe for five long days, cancelling over 100 000 flights. The name of the volcano is Eyjafjallajokull (pronounced ay-yah-FYAH-lah-yer-kuhl), and customers were heard muttering similar sounds as they tried to get home. It cost the airline industry huge sums of money through no fault of its own. Air Canada lost about $4 million per day; Air Transat lost approximately $750 000 per day; Air France-KLM lost an estimated $35 million per day.

As you can see, airlines must create efficient strategies and plan for the unexpected. But there are so many elements far outside their control that impact success or failure. In addition to the issues mentioned above, there are massive security challenges, flu pandemics, and political conflicts (e.g., civil war) that can erupt anywhere in the world. This is why it is so hard to find an airline that is profitable on a consistent basis. This is truly a challenging industry.

QUESTIONS FOR DISCUSSION

1. Identify the various environmental factors that influence Air Canada. Which of these are most important? Explain.
2. How does the multi-year planning timeframe regarding the purchasing of aircraft impact management decisions?
3. How do unpredictable events impact Air Canada? Give examples.
4. What can Air Canada do to reduce the negative impact of environmental factors that complicate its activities?
5. How do government regulations of the commercial airline business affect Air Canada?

CHAPTER 03

Conducting Business Ethically *and* Responsibly

LO

AFTER READING THIS CHAPTER, YOU SHOULD BE ABLE TO:

LO-1 Explain how individuals develop their personal *codes of ethics* and why ethics are important in the workplace.

LO-2 Distinguish *ethics* from *social responsibility* and identify *organizational stakeholders*.

LO-3 Show how the concept of social responsibility applies both to environmental issues and to a firm's relationships with customers, employees, and investors.

LO-4 Identify four general *approaches to social responsibility* and describe the four steps a firm must take to implement a *social responsibility program*.

LO-5 Explain how issues of social responsibility and ethics affect small businesses.

Chocolate: Paying the Price

Do you know where the chocolate in your favourite candy bar comes from? It might surprise you to know that over 40 percent of the world's chocolate comes from small farms scattered throughout the West African nation of Côte d'Ivoire. Chocolate comes from small beans that grow on cocoa trees. It takes about 400 beans to make a pound of chocolate. To harvest the beans, labourers chop bean pods from the trees, slice them open, scoop out the beans, spread them on mats, and cover them to ferment. Once the beans are fermented, they are dried, packed in heavy bags, and carried to waiting trucks. At that point, they have entered the supply chain that will take them to Canada, the U.S., or Europe, where they will be turned into all sorts of chocolate products, including Snickers candy bars and Dreyer's Double Fudge Brownie ice cream.

Reports issued by the United Nations Children's Fund (UNICEF) say that much of the labour involved in Côte d'Ivoire chocolate production is performed by children, mostly boys ranging in age from 12 to 16. These child labourers—perhaps as many as 15 000 of them—work 12 hours a day, 7 days a week. They are often beaten to maintain productivity quotas, and they sleep on bare wooden planks in cramped rooms. Most of them were tricked or sold into forced labour, many by destitute parents who couldn't afford to feed them. Efforts to alleviate the problem have met with little success.

Enslaving children became business as usual in the Côte d'Ivoire cocoa industry because the country is heavily dependent on world market prices for cocoa (one-third of the country's economy is based on cocoa exports). Since cocoa prices fluctuate significantly on global markets, profitability in the cocoa industry depends on prices over which farmers have no control. To improve their chances of making a profit, producers look for ways to cut costs, and the use of slave labour is one way to do that.

This sorry situation led to the development of the "fair trade" idea, which tries to ensure that export-dependent farmers in developing countries like Côte d'Ivoire receive fair prices for their crops. Several fair-trade programs are sponsored by Fairtrade Labelling Organizations

age fotostock/SuperStock

International (FLO), a global nonprofit network of fair-trade groups that are headquartered in Germany. FLO works with co-operatives representing cocoa producers in Africa and Latin America to establish standards for the producers' products and operations and for socially relevant policies, such as enforcing anti–child labour laws and providing education and health-care services. In return, FLO guarantees producers a "Fairtrade Minimum Price" for their products. In 2011, for example, FLO guaranteed farmers a price of $1750 per tonne. If the market price falls below that level, FLO covers the difference. If the market exceeds $1750 per tonne, FLO pays producers a premium of $150 per tonne.

The money to do this comes from the importers, manufacturers, and distributors who buy and sell cocoa from FLO-certified producers. These companies are, in turn, monitored by a network of FLO-owned organizations call TransFair, which ensures that FLO criteria are met and that FLO-certified producers receive the fair prices guaranteed by FLO. Products that meet the appropriate FLO-TransFair criteria bear labels attesting that they are "Fair-Trade Certified."

Importers, manufacturers, and distributors have an incentive to not only adopt FLO–TransFair standards, but also to incur the costs of subsidizing overseas producers because they get the right to promote their chocolate products as both fair trade and organic. These categories typically command premium retail prices. When consumers know that they are supporting programs to empower farmers in developing countries, sellers and resellers can charge higher prices, often two to three times higher. A 3.5 ounce candy bar labelled "organic fair trade" may sell for $3.49, compared to about $1.50 for one that's not.

Some critics of fair trade agree in principle with those who advocate its use, but contend that consumers don't need to pay higher prices for fair-trade products. They point out that, according to TransFair's own data, cocoa farmers get only 3 cents of the $3.49 that a socially conscious consumer pays for a Fair Trade–certified candy bar. Consumer researcher Lawrence Solomon says that producers receive very little, and most of the premium price goes to middlemen. Other critics say that sellers of fair-trade products are taking advantage of consumers who are socially conscious, but not price conscious. They point out that if sellers priced that $3.49 candy bar for $2.49 instead, farmers would still get three cents per bar. The price is inflated to $3.49 only because there is a small segment of the market that is willing to pay that price.

HOW WILL THIS HELP ME?

There is a growing dilemma in the business world today: the economic imperatives (real or imagined) facing managers versus pressures to function as good citizens. By understanding the material in this chapter, you will be better able to assess ethical and social responsibility issues that you will face as an *employee* and as a *boss* or *business owner.* It will also help you understand the ethical and social responsibility actions of businesses you deal with as a *consumer* and as an *investor.*

QUESTIONS FOR DISCUSSION

1. Do you think fair trade is a good solution to child labour and related problems? Explain.
2. Are you willing to pay more for fair-trade products? Why or why not?
3. What other options can you identify that might help deal with child labour and other problems in the global cocoa market?

ETHICS IN THE WORKPLACE

The situation described in the opening case clearly demonstrates the controversy that often arises when dealing with the issue of ethics in business. **Ethics** are beliefs about what is right and wrong or good and bad.

ETHICS Individual standards or moral values regarding what is right and wrong or good and bad.

An individual's personal values and morals—and the social context in which they occur—determine whether a particular behaviour is perceived as ethical or unethical. In other words, **ethical behaviour** is behaviour that conforms to individual beliefs and social norms about what is right and good. **Unethical behaviour** is behaviour that individual beliefs and social norms define as wrong and bad. **Business ethics** is a term often used to refer to ethical or unethical behaviours by a manager or employee of a business.

ETHICAL BEHAVIOUR Behaviour that conforms to individual beliefs and social norms about what is right and good.

UNETHICAL BEHAVIOUR Behaviour that individual beliefs and social norms define as wrong and bad.

BUSINESS ETHICS Ethical or unethical behaviours by a manager or employee of an organization.

LO-1 Individual Ethics

Because ethics are based on both individual beliefs and social concepts, they vary from person to person, from situation to situation, and from culture to culture. But there are some commonalities. For example, most societies view stealing as wrong. But what if you happen to see someone drop a $20 bill in a store? Most people would probably say that it would be ethical to return it to the owner, but some might think it is OK to keep it. There will be even less agreement if you find $20 and don't know who dropped it. Should you turn it in to the lost-and-found department? Or, since the rightful owner isn't likely to claim it, can you just keep it?

It is important to make the distinction between *unethical* and *illegal* behaviour. A given behaviour may be ethical and legal (e.g., providing high-quality products to consumers), ethical and illegal (e.g., breaking the law in a totalitarian regime in order to carry out humanitarian efforts), unethical and legal (e.g., paying low wages to workers at a company facility in a foreign country), or unethical and illegal (e.g., "cooking the books" to make a company's financial situation look better than it really is). Some of these distinctions are controversial. For example, consider the case of Netsweeper, a Canadian company that sells web-filtering products that block out pornography and computer viruses. That sounds good, but what if these products are used by a repressive government to block out information it doesn't want its citizens to see (e.g., information on human rights)? While it is perfectly legal for Netsweeper to sell the software, critics argue that the sales are unethical because the company knows that its products can be misused.[1]

Making ethical judgments is also complicated by the fact that practices that are legal in one country may not be legal in another. For example, selling Nazi memorabilia online is legal in the U.S., but not in Germany. In some cultures, ethically ambiguous practices are hallmarks of business activity. Brazilians, for example, apply the philosophy of *jeitinho*—meaning "to find a way"—by using personal connections, bending the rules, or making a "contribution."[2] Suppose you needed to get an official document. You might start out determined to take all the proper bureaucratic steps to get it. However, when you find yourself in a complex maze of rules and regulations and think you'll never get your document, you may resort to *jeitinho* to get the job done.

>> Ethical scandals involving business leaders have made headlines in recent years. Bernie Madoff cost hundreds of major investment clients their entire life savings by running a Ponzi scheme.

Toshifumi Kitamura/AFP/Getty Images

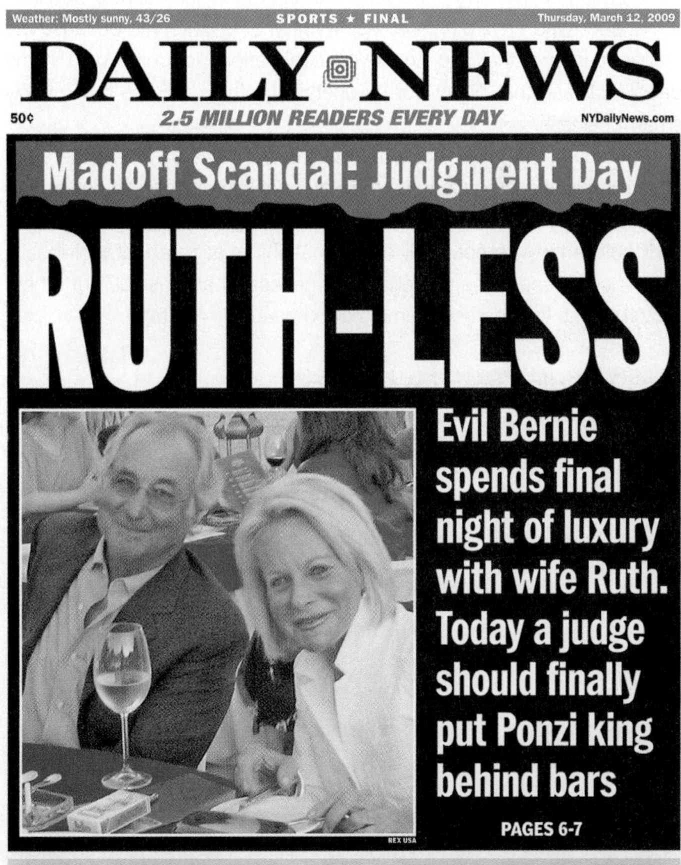
Weather: Mostly sunny, 43/26 | SPORTS ★ FINAL | Thursday, March 12, 2009

DAILY NEWS

50¢ | 2.5 MILLION READERS EVERY DAY | NYDailyNews.com

Madoff Scandal: Judgment Day

RUTH-LESS

Evil Bernie spends final night of luxury with wife Ruth. Today a judge should finally put Ponzi king behind bars

PAGES 6-7

HEY RIHANNA, DON'T BLAME ME!

CHRIS BROWN'S MANAGER DENIES AFFAIR RUMOR – PAGE 5

INDIVIDUAL VALUES AND CODES

The ethical views of individuals in a business—managers, employees, agents, and other legal representatives—are determined by a combination of factors. We start to form ethical standards as children in response to our perceptions of the behaviour of parents and other adults. When we enter school, peers and the entertainment media also shape our lives and contribute to our ethical beliefs and our behaviour. We also develop values and morals that influence our behaviour. If you put financial gain at the top of your priority list, you may develop a code of ethics that supports the pursuit of material comfort. But if you place a high priority on family and friends, you'll probably adopt different standards.

Because ethics are both personally and culturally defined, differences of opinion can arise as to what is ethical or unethical. For example, people who would never think of stealing a candy bar from a grocery store may think it is perfectly legitimate to take home pens and pads of paper from their office. Many otherwise law-abiding citizens have no qualms about using radar detectors to avoid speeding tickets. In each situation, people will use different standards of ethics and will argue that their actions are ethical. These difficulties have led some observers to conclude that individuals can rationalize almost any behaviour as ethical.

Managerial Ethics

Managerial ethics are the standards of behaviour that guide individual managers in their work.[3] Although ethics can affect managerial work in any number of ways, it's helpful to classify behaviour in terms of three broad categories.

MANAGERIAL ETHICS Standards of behaviour that guide individual managers in their work.

CONFLICT OF INTEREST Occurs when an activity benefits the employee at the expense of the employer.

BEHAVIOUR TOWARD EMPLOYEES

There are important ethical questions with regard to issues like hiring and firing, wages and working conditions, and privacy. In Canada, ethical and legal guidelines state that hiring and firing decisions should be based solely on the ability to perform a job. A manager who discriminates against any ethnic minority in hiring therefore exhibits both unethical and illegal behaviour. But what about the manager who hires a friend or relative when someone else might be more qualified? Such decisions may not be illegal, but in Canada they may be seen as objectionable on ethical grounds (but not necessarily in some other countries).

Wages and working conditions are also areas for debate. Consider a manager who pays a worker less than what is deserved because the manager knows that the employee can't afford to quit. While some people will see that behaviour as unethical, others will see it as simply smart business.

Protecting the privacy of employees is another area where there are ethical implications. In Canada, the Personal Information Protection and Electronic Documents Act (PIPEDA) requires organizations to obtain consent before they collect, use, or disclose information about individuals. Many people see these guidelines are necessary and useful, but others view them as yet another example of bureaucratic red tape.

BEHAVIOUR TOWARD THE ORGANIZATION

Ethical issues also arise with respect to employee behaviour toward employers. A **conflict of interest** occurs when an activity benefits an employee at the expense of the employer. For example, suppose the shoe buyer for a large department store chain accepts a free vacation from a shoe manufacturer. If the manufacturer then asks the buyer to increase the size of an order, the buyer may feel an obligation to do so. The buyer might also conclude that more large orders will result in another vacation next year. Most companies have policies that forbid buyers from accepting gifts from suppliers. Businesses in highly competitive industries—software or fashion apparel, for example—have safeguards against designers selling company secrets to competitors. Relatively common problems in the general area of honesty include behaviour such as stealing supplies, padding expense accounts, and using a business phone to make personal long-distance calls. Most employees are honest, but organizations must be vigilant.

BEHAVIOUR TOWARD OTHER ECONOMIC AGENTS

Ethical disputes often arise in the relationship between a company and its customers, competitors, stockholders, suppliers, dealers, and unions. In 2012, for example, Caterpillar Inc. demanded that union workers at its London, Ontario, factory take a 50 percent wage cut in order to help the company's operations become more cost-effective. When the union refused, the company closed the plant and moved the production to the U.S. Some people feel that it is unethical for a company to give employees an ultimatum like Caterpillar did because it seems outrageous and is an attempt to make an offer to employees that the company knows they will not accept. Others would disagree and say the company has to do what it thinks is economically necessary. Businesses in the pharmaceuticals industry are often criticized because of the high prices of drugs. The companies argue that high prices are needed to cover the cost of developing new drugs, but critics argue that the companies are engaging in *price gouging* (charging unreasonably high prices).[4]

After a WestJet executive accessed Air Canada's confidential reservations database, WestJet admitted its actions were unethical and paid Air Canada $5 million.[5] Most people would probably see the WestJet incident as a fairly clear case of unethical behaviour. But what if a manager is given confidential information by an unhappy former employee

Stockbyte/Thinkstock

Kim Steele/Digital Vision/Thinkstock

The intense competition between Air Canada and WestJet motivated a WestJet executive to access Air Canada's confidential reservations database in the hope of gaining a competitive edge for WestJet.

of a competitor who wants to get revenge on his former employer? Is it acceptable in that case for the manager to use the information? Some people would say it's still unethical, but others might argue that since the manager didn't go looking for the information, it's acceptable to use it.[6]

Difficulties may also arise because business practices vary globally. In some countries, bribes are a normal part of doing business, but in Canada (and increasingly in other countries as well), bribes are seen as clearly unethical and illegal. In 2011, Calgary-based Niko Resources was fined $9.5 million for bribing a Bangladeshi government official.[7] In 2012, the president of SNC-Lavalin Group's Candu Energy was charged with bribing a Bangladeshi government official, and several SNC officials have been fired as a result of allegations of corruption, both in Canada and elsewhere.[8] In 2012, Walmart appointed a global officer to oversee compliance with U.S. bribery laws after allegations surfaced that employees may have paid bribes in several countries, including Brazil, Mexico, China, and India.[9] In spite of Canada's condemnation of bribery, the Organisation for Economic Co-operation and Development (OECD) has expressed concerns about loopholes in Canada's bribery laws and the lack of enforcement of bribery penalties.[10] (See Chapter 5 for more information about the issue of bribery.)

Assessing Ethical Behaviour

We can determine whether a particular action or decision is ethical or unethical by using a three-step model to systematically apply ethical judgments to situations that may arise during the course of business activities.[11]

1. Gather the relevant factual information.
2. Determine the most appropriate moral values.
3. Make an ethical judgment based on the rightness or wrongness of the proposed activity or policy.

Let's see how this process might work for a common dilemma faced by managers: expense account claims. Companies routinely cover work-related expenses of employees when they are travelling on company business and/or entertaining clients for business purposes. Common examples of such expenses include hotel bills, meals, rental cars, and so forth. Employees are expected to claim only those expenses that are work-related. Suppose we have the following factual information (Step 1): A manager takes a client to dinner while travelling on business and spends $100; submitting a receipt for that dinner and expecting to be reimbursed for $100 is clearly appropriate. Suppose, however, that the manager also has a $100 dinner the next night in that same city with a good friend for purely social purposes. Submitting that receipt for full reimbursement would be seen by most managers as unethical (but some might try to rationalize that it is acceptable because they are underpaid and this is a way to increase their pay).

Given this information, we need to determine the most appropriate moral values (Step 2). There are four commonly used ethical norms we can use to make this determination:

Utility: Does a particular act optimize what is best for those who are affected by it?

Rights: Does it respect the rights of the individuals involved?

Justice: Is it consistent with what we regard to be fair?

Caring: Is it consistent with people's responsibilities to each other?

Now, let's return to the case of the expense account and make an ethical judgment (Step 3). The *utility* norm would acknowledge that the manager benefits from padding an expense account, but co-workers and owners do not. Likewise, inflating an expense account does not respect the *rights* of others. It is also *unfair* and compromises the manager's *responsibilities* to others. This particular act, then, appears to be clearly unethical. But now suppose that the manager happens to lose the receipt for the legitimate dinner but does not lose the receipt for the social dinner. Would it be ethical to submit the illegitimate receipt because the manager is only doing so to be reimbursed for what he or she is entitled to? Or, is submitting the other receipt unethical under any circumstances? Changes in the factual information about the case may make ethical issues more or less clear-cut.

Technological innovations have created all sorts of new ethical dilemmas: cloning, satellite reconnaissance, email snooping, and bioengineered foods, to name just a few. For every innovation that promises convenience or safety, there seems to be a related ethical issue. The internet and email, for example, are convenient and efficient, but they present business people with a variety of ethics-related problems. For example, a manager in one company sent false emails to his workers, pretending to be a recruiter from a competing firm. Any employees who responded to the emails were skipped for promotion. Electronic communication also makes it possible to run swindles with greater efficiency than ever before. A Ponzi scheme, for example, promises investors large returns on their money, but the money taken in by those running the scheme is not typically invested. Instead, money contributed by later investors is used to pay off early investors. In 2010, investment adviser Earl Jones pleaded guilty to running a Ponzi scheme that defrauded investors of over $50 million. He was sentenced to 11 years in prison.[12]

Encouraging Ethical Behaviour in Organizations

To promote ethical behaviour, managers must understand *why* unethical behaviour occurs in the first place. Three general factors have been identified as important in causing individuals to behave in unethical ways: pressure (the employee has some problem that cannot be solved through legitimate means), opportunity (the employee uses his or her position in the organization to secretly solve the problem), and rationalization (the employee sees himself or herself as a basically an ethical person who was caught up in an unfortunate situation).[13] To reduce the chance of unethical behaviour, organizations should *demonstrate top management commitment to ethical standards, adopt written codes of ethics*, and *provide ethics training to employees*.

DEMONSTRATE TOP MANAGEMENT COMMITMENT TO VALUES AND HIGH ETHICAL STANDARDS

It is crucial that top management demonstrate a serious a public commitment to high ethical standards. For example, Mountain Equipment Co-op is publicly committed to the concept of *ethical sourcing*, which means monitoring factories that produce its products to make sure that those factories are providing good working conditions for their employees, Without this ethical "tone at the top," lower-level employees are not likely to take ethics very seriously.

Figure 3.1 illustrates the essential role that corporate ethics and values should play in corporate policy. It shows that business strategies and practices can change frequently and business objectives may change occasionally, but an organization's core principles and values should remain the same. For example, Google's core principle is "Don't Be Evil." Google adapts its strategies and practices to meet the challenges posed by the rapidly changing technology industry, but Google must do so in a way that does not violate its core principle.

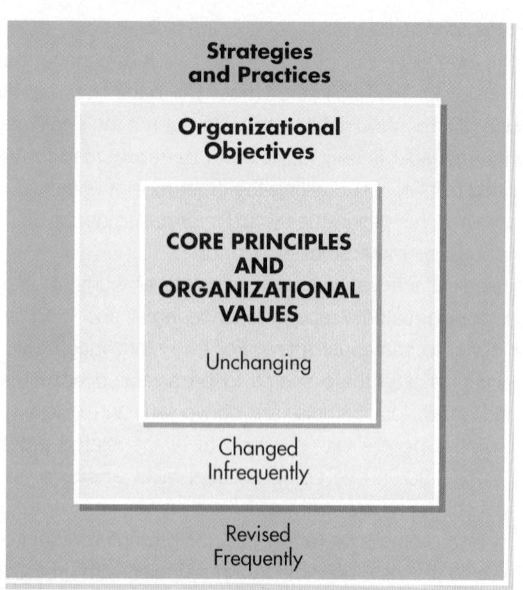

FIGURE 3.1 Core principles and organizational values

Source: Baron, David P. *Business and Its Environment*, 4th edition, © 2003. Reprinted by permission of Pearson Education, Inc., Upper Saddle River, NJ.

ADOPT WRITTEN CODES OF ETHICS

A written code of ethics formally acknowledges that a company intends to do business in an ethical manner. Codes of ethics increase public confidence in a company, improve internal operations, and help managers respond on those occasions when there are problems with illegal or unethical employee behaviour. About two-thirds of Canada's largest corporations have codes of ethics (90 percent of large U.S. firms do). More and more regulatory and professional associations in Canada are recommending that corporations adopt codes of ethics. The Canada Deposit Insurance Corp., for example, requires that all deposit-taking institutions have a code of conduct that is periodically reviewed and ratified by the board of directors. The Canadian Competition Bureau, the Canadian Institute of Chartered Accountants, and the Ontario Human Rights Commission are all pushing for the adoption of codes of ethics by corporations.[14] Many Canadian and U.S. firms are also adding a position called "ethics director" or "ethics officer."

If codes of ethics are to be effective, there must be a control system and consistent enforcement when unethical behaviour occurs. Employees will then know that the company is serious about its pursuit of high ethical standards. This is exactly what did *not* happen in the infamous Enron case. Enron had a code of ethics, but managers did not follow it. On one occasion, Enron's board of directors voted to set aside the code in order to complete a deal that would have violated it. After the deal was completed, they then voted to reinstate the code.

PROVIDE ETHICS TRAINING

Can business ethics be "taught," either in the workplace or in schools? Business schools are important players in the debate about ethics as they sensitize students to academic integrity issues like plagiarism and cheating and how these unethical activities harm students and the educational system. But most analysts agree that companies must take the lead in educating employees about ethics. Imperial Oil, for example, conducts workshops that help employees put Imperial's ethics statement into actual practice. More and more firms are doing ethics training where managers are reminded of the importance of ethical decision making, and are updated on the most current laws and regulations that are relevant for their firm. Mary Gentile, a management consultant, says that employees know the difference between right and wrong, but they occasionally behave in an unethical fashion because they don't know how to resist pressure from peers and bosses to behave unethically.[15] She provides suggestions to help individuals resist such pressure and to act out their ethical values. Some ethics training programs take a more dramatic approach; ethics seminars are taught by former executives who have spent time in prison for their own ethical misdeeds.[16]

Dealing with ethical issues is not a simple matter, and many companies struggle with ethical dilemmas. This is particularly true for those that operate internationally. On several occasions, dangerous working conditions have been discovered in factories in developing countries that produce goods for Western retailers. In 2013, over 1100 workers were killed when a garment factory in Bangladesh collapsed. Soon after the disaster, the Worker Rights Consortium circulated a photo of a Joe Fresh label in the debris.[17] In 2011, allegations were made that some products sold by Victoria's Secret contained cotton that had been produced using child labour.[18]

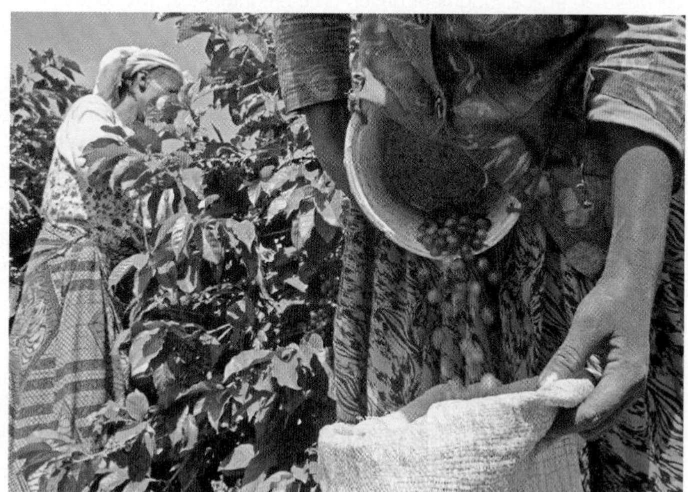

Starbucks helps local farmers gain access to credit, works to develop and maintain sustainability of the coffee crop, and is building farmer support centres in Costa Rica, Ethiopia, and Rwanda to provide local farmers with agricultural and technical education support.

Comstock Images/Thinkstock

LO-2 SOCIAL RESPONSIBILITY

Corporate social responsibility (CSR) refers to the way in which a business tries to balance its commitments to **organizational stakeholders**—those groups, individuals, and organizations that are directly affected by the practices of an organization and that therefore have a stake in its performance.[19] Most companies that strive to be socially responsible concentrate on five stakeholder groups discussed below. They may also select other

CORPORATE SOCIAL RESPONSIBILITY The idea that a business should balance its commitments to individuals and groups that are directly affected by the organization's activities.

ORGANIZATIONAL STAKEHOLDERS Groups, individuals, and organizations that are directly affected by the practices of an organization and that therefore have a stake in its performance.

stakeholders that are particularly important to their particular organization and try to address their needs and expectations as well. As companies place increasing emphasis on their social responsibility to stakeholders, there has been a move to go beyond traditional *financial* measures of return on investment. A new measure—called the Social Return on Investment (SROI)—has been developed which helps companies understand, manage, and communicate the *social* value of their activities for stakeholders.[20]

While everyone seems to accept the idea that attention must be paid to organizational stakeholders, there is debate about which ones should be given the most attention. One view, called *managerial capitalism*, is that a company's only responsibility is to make as much money as possible for its *shareholders*, as long as the company doesn't break any laws. This view has been strongly challenged by an opposing view that says that companies must be responsible to a variety of stakeholders, including *customers*, *employees*, *investors*, *suppliers*, and the *local communities* in which they do business. Opponents of CSR claim that it is being imposed on businesses by a coalition of environmentalists, while supporters of CSR claim that companies have become interested in CSR because that is what consumers prefer.[21]

Mountain Equipment Co-op (MEC) is an example of an organization with a strong sense of social responsibility. The company does not try to maximize shareholder wealth, but rather seeks a balance between financial and social/environmental goals. To demonstrate its concern for social responsibility, MEC provides a safe and healthy workplace for employees, audits suppliers who produce the products it sells, minimizes the negative impact of manufacturing and packaging on the environment, ensures that waste is disposed of in an environmentally responsible manner, treats workers with dignity, pays workers fairly, and emphasizes energy efficiency, pollution control, and recycling potential in MEC buildings.[22]

Another example of CSR in action is the **fair trade** movement, which was motivated by concerns that workers in developing countries who produce commodities like coffee were not receiving fair payment for their products. Companies in developed countries who are concerned about this problem work with non-profit organizations like the Fairtrade Foundation and the Rainforest Alliance. Those non-profit organizations certify that farming co-operatives are paying workers fairly and not damaging the environment. More than 5000 companies—including Kraft Foods, Avon, and Starbucks—sell products with a Fairtrade or Rainforest Alliance logo on them.[23]

When defining their sense of social responsibility, most firms consider four areas: the *environment*, *customers*, *employees*, and *investors*.

LO-3 Responsibility Toward the Environment

Controlling **pollution**—the injection of harmful substances into the environment—is a significant challenge for contemporary business. Air, water, and land pollution are the focus of most anti-pollution efforts by business and governments. The boxed insert entitled "Some Frustrations in the Green Movement" describes some difficulties that are evident as companies and consumers try to behave in a more environmentally friendly way.

FAIR TRADE A movement motivated by concerns that workers in developing countries who produce commodities like coffee were not receiving fair payment for their products.

POLLUTION The introduction of harmful substances into the environment.

THE GREENING OF BUSINESS

Some Frustrations in the Green Movement

Consumers interested in buying products that are environmentally friendly face two key problems. The first is that companies often make misleading claims about the green characteristics of their products. A study of 5296 products by Terrachoice, an environmental marketing company, found that there was at least one misleading green claim on 95.6 percent of the products they studied. The study also found that 100 percent of toy manufacturers and 99.2 percent of baby-product makers were guilty of "greenwashing" (misleading consumers about the environmental benefits of a product). Having a product certified by a recognized, independent third party reduced the incidence of greenwashing, but fake certifications are readily available on the internet. TerraChoice identified several green "sins," including (1) making an environmentally friendly claim but providing no proof, (2) making vague claims (e.g., saying that a product is "all-natural"), (3) making a green claim for a product that is inherently harmful (e.g., cigarettes), and (4) emphasizing a product's positive attributes on a relatively unimportant environmental issue and downplaying a product's negative characteristics on a far more important environmental issue. However, some progress is being made; more and more products have accurate green claims.

The second problem facing consumers is that green products can be very expensive. Governments subsidize the development of electric and hybrid automobiles, but cars like Chevy's hybrid rechargeable Volt (named Car of the Year by *Motor Trend*), Nissan's all-electric Leaf, and Ford's all-electric Focus are expensive enough that many people cannot afford them. A hybrid car like the Prius, for example, costs about 30 percent more than an equivalent gasoline-powered car, and battery-powered cars are 50 to 100 percent higher. Even with fuel savings, it would take more than 10 years for your purchase of an electric or hybrid car to break even with a car like the Ford Fiesta. Gasoline-powered automobiles also outperform electric and hybrid cars on dimensions that are important to consumers (cost, driving range, and power). Consulting firm J.D. Power produced a report entitled "Drive Green 2020: More Hope Than Reality" which noted that hybrid or battery vehicles constituted only 2.2 percent of global vehicle sales in 2010, and that even with healthy growth during the next few years, they will represent just over 7 percent of all vehicles sold by 2020. It's also not clear that electric-powered cars will actually mean less air pollution because providing the electricity to recharge all those electric cars will increase demand on electrical generating plants, and they typically burn fossil fuels to generate electricity. More troubling is a comprehensive life cycle analysis that showed that the manufacturing process for an electric car produces 30 000 pounds of carbon dioxide emissions (the same process for an internal combustion–powered car produces 14 000 pounds).

CRITICAL THINKING QUESTIONS

1. Why are misleading green claims made for so many products?
2. What are the pros and cons of having government actively involved in subsidizing the development of green products?

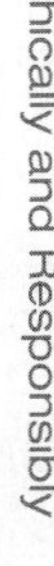

<<< Air pollution is a major problem in some large cities in China because power plants have not installed proper pollution controls. Prior to the 2008 Olympics, the Chinese government forced many factories around Beijing to temporarily cease operations in order to reduce air pollution during the Olympic games.

Keith Brofsky/Photodisc/Getty Images

AIR POLLUTION

Air pollution results when a combination of factors lowers air quality. Large amounts of chemicals such as the carbon monoxide emitted by automobiles contribute to air pollution. So do smoke and other chemicals emitted by manufacturing plants. The rapid industrialization of developing countries has led to increased concerns about air pollution. In China, for example, 100 coal-fired power plants are being built each year, and each plant uses 1.4 million tons of coal and throws off 3.7 million tons of carbon dioxide. Only 5 percent of the coal-fired power plants in China are equipped with pollution-control equipment.[24] Many industrial companies were forcibly shut down by the Chinese government in advance of the 2008 Olympics in an attempt to improve air quality.

The Kyoto Summit in 1997 was an early attempt by various governments to reach an agreement on ways to reduce the threat of pollution. Australia is the world's largest greenhouse gas emitter per capita, contributing 7.3 percent of the world's total. The United States (at 6.5 percent) and Canada (at 6.4 percent) are close behind. Canada is the only one of the three leading emitters that signed the 1997 Protocol, but, in 2006, the Conservative government said Canada would not be able to meet its targets for reducing pollution, and that it would continue with the Protocol only if the targets were renegotiated.[25] The 2009 meetings in Copenhagen on this issue ended without an agreement.

The United Nations has promoted a "cap and trade" system, in which companies in industrialized countries can buy carbon credits, which essentially give them the right to pollute the atmosphere with carbon dioxide. The money collected is then used to help fund clean-air projects in developing countries that would not otherwise be affordable.[26] In 2013, the province of Quebec and the state of California introduced compulsory cap-and-trade rules in an attempt to reduce greenhouse gas emissions. Quebec has set a goal to reduce emissions to 25 percent below 1990 levels.[27] But critics of cap and trade say that the scheme is an open invitation to fraudsters. Suppose, for example, that an Indonesian forest operator sells a carbon permit to a German manufacturing firm that is releasing too much CO_2 into the atmosphere. That one transaction is fine, but what if the Indonesian firm sells the same carbon permit to manufacturers in other countries? That will make it appear like a lot more carbon dioxide has been reduced than is actually the case. Multibillion-dollar fraud has already occurred in the European Union's carbon trading market, and Europol's Criminal Finances and Technology section estimates that up to 90 percent of all carbon market volume in certain EU nations is fraudulent.[28]

Figure 3.2 shows world atmospheric carbon dioxide levels for the period between 1750 and 2000, and it offers three possible scenarios for future levels under different sets of conditions. Energy supplies are measured in exajoules—roughly the annual energy consumption of a large metropolitan area like New York or London. Under the lowest, or best-case, scenario, by 2100 the population would only grow to 6.4 billion people, economic growth would be no more than 1.2 to 2.0 percent a year, and energy supplies would require only 8000 exajoules of conventional oil. However, under the highest, or worst-case, scenario, the population would increase to 11.3 billion people, annual economic growth would be between 3.0 and 3.5 percent, and energy supplies would require as much as 18 400 exajoules of conventional oil.

There is currently a debate about whether **global warming**—an increase in the earth's average temperature—is the result of increased air pollution. The majority of scientists agree that global warming is a fact, but some have argued that warming is simply part of the earth's natural climate cycles. Whatever the answer, the reality is that global warming will benefit some people and hurt others. In normally icy Greenland, for example, the warming climate has resulted in a longer growing season for grain and vegetables, and farmers are planning to start raising cattle because of the increased forage available in the summertime. But the same process warming Greenland is melting the earth's glaciers, and the water released may eventually raise sea levels to the point that many coastal cities around the world will be flooded.[29]

In difficult economic times, like those of the past few years, the general public is less willing to make personal sacrifices in order to battle climate change. A poll of 12 000 people in 11 countries showed that less than half of the respondents were willing to make lifestyle changes to reduce carbon emissions, and only 20 percent said they would be willing to spend extra money to fight climate change.[30]

AIR POLLUTION Pollution that occurs when a combination of factors lowers air quality.

GLOBAL WARMING An increase in the earth's average temperature.

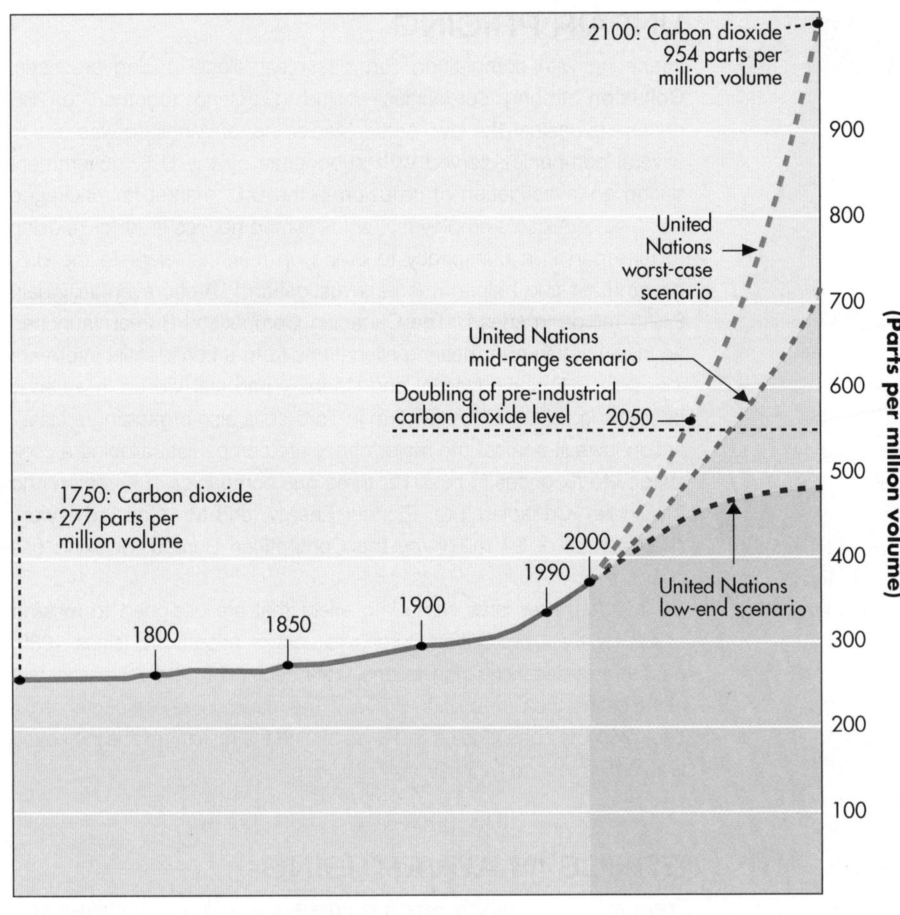

<<< **FIGURE 3.2** CO_2 emissions, past and future

Canadian businesses are now routinely reducing various forms of pollution. However, the road to environmental purity is not easy. Under the Canadian and Ontario Environmental Protection Acts, pollution liability for a business firm can run as high as $2 million per day. To avoid such fines, companies must prove that they showed diligence in avoiding an environmental disaster such as an oil or gasoline spill.[34] The Environmental Choice program, sponsored by the federal government, licenses products that meet environmental standards set by the Canadian Standards Association. Firms whose products meet these standards can put the logo—three doves intertwined to form a maple leaf—on their products.[35]

An interesting problem that highlights some of the complexities in both waste disposal and recycling involves wooden pallets—those splintery wooden platforms used to store and transport consumer goods. Pallets are very recyclable, but since the cost of new ones is so low, many companies just toss used ones aside and buy new ones. Ironically, some environmentalists argue that abandoned pallets actually serve a useful purpose because in urban areas, they often become refuge for animals such as raccoons and abandoned pets.[36]

WATER POLLUTION

For many years, businesses and municipalities dumped their waste into rivers, streams, and lakes with little regard for the effects. Thanks to new stricter legislation and increased awareness on the part of businesses, water quality is improving in many areas. But water pollution is still a concern, and several high-profile oil spills—like the BP disaster in the Gulf of Mexico in 2010—have occurred. Pollution of the oceans—by both cargo and passenger ships—is a continuing problem.

LAND POLLUTION

Toxic wastes are dangerous chemical and/or radioactive by-products of various manufacturing processes that are harmful to humans and animals. In 2010, oil sands giant Syncrude was found guilty of causing the death of 1600 ducks that landed in a tailing pond they had mistaken for a small lake. The company faced fines of up to $800 000 under the federal Migratory Birds Act and the Alberta Environmental Protection and Enhancement Act.[31]

Changes in forestry practices, limits on certain types of mining, and new forms of solid waste disposal are all attempts to address the issue of toxic waste. An entire industry—**recycling**—has developed as part of increased consciousness about land pollution. MET Fine Printers in Vancouver, which used to spend $3000 each month on waste disposal, reduced that to just $300 after introducing a recycling program.[32] Plant and animal waste can be recycled to produce energy; this is referred to as **biomass**. Waste materials like sawdust, manure, and sludge are increasingly being turned into useful products. Ensyn Corp., for example, converts sawdust into liquid fuel by blasting wood waste with a sand-like substance that is heated. What's left is bio-oil.[33]

Canadian firms that do business abroad are increasingly being confronted with environmental issues. In many cases, there is opposition to a project by local residents because they fear that some sort of pollution will result. For example, Calgary-based TVI Pacific Inc.'s planned open-pit mine and cyanide processing plant in the Philippines led to violent clashes between the company and the Subanon people. In Peru, indigenous groups threatened violence if Talisman Energy continued drilling for oil on their land.[37] Multinational firms have also been publicly criticized. For example, Nestlé has received negative publicity on YouTube, Facebook, and Twitter claiming that the company is contributing to destruction of Indonesia's rainforest because it purchases palm oil from an Indonesian company that has cleared the rainforest to make way for a palm oil plantation.[38]

Responsibility Toward Customers

There are three key areas that are currently in the news regarding the social responsibility of business toward customers: *consumer rights*, *unfair pricing*, and *ethics in advertising*.

TOXIC WASTE Pollution resulting from the emission of chemical and/or radioactive by-products of various manufacturing processes into the air, water, or land.

RECYCLING The reconversion of waste materials into useful products.

BIOMASS Plant and animal waste used to produce energy.

THERE'S AN APP FOR THAT!

1. **ecoFootprint** >>> **Platforms:** *Apple, Android*
   Source: Max Gontar
   Key Features: Measures your ecological footprint, based on statistics provided by the World Wildlife Fund.
2. **Green Tips** >>> **Platforms:** *Android*
   Source: Mobilendo
   Key Features: Tips from the European Environment Agency related to water, transport, waste, etc.
3. **Find Green** >>> **Platforms:** *Apple, Android, BlackBerry*
   Source: GenGreen LLC
   Key Features: Helps you find green businesses and resources to help you live a sustainable lifestyle on a local level.

APP DISCOVERY EXERCISE

Since APP availability changes, conduct your own search for "Top 3" Socially Responsible and Green Business APPS and identify the key features.

CONSUMER RIGHTS

Consumerism is a movement dedicated to protecting the rights of consumers in their dealings with businesses. Consumers have the following rights:

1. *The right to safe products.* The right to safe products is not always honoured. In 2008, 20 people died after eating listeria-contaminated meat made by Maple Leaf Foods. Sales dropped by nearly 50 percent once this became public.[39] The government of China has become concerned that negative publicity about faulty toys and contaminated pet food and toothpaste has damaged the "Made in China" label. In a surprising development, Mattel Inc. apologized to China for claiming that a recall of 18 million playsets with dangerous magnets was necessitated by poor quality control at one of its Chinese suppliers. Mattel eventually admitted that its own product design was flawed.[40]
2. *The right to be informed about all relevant aspects of a product.* Food products must list their ingredients, clothing must be labelled with information about its proper care, and banks must tell you exactly how much interest you are paying on a loan.
3. *The right to be heard.* Procter & Gamble puts a toll-free number on many of its products that consumers can call if they have questions or complaints. Many other retailers offer money-back guarantees if consumers are not happy with their purchase.
4. *The right to choose what they buy.* Central to this right is free and open competition among companies. In times past, companies divided up a market so that firms did not have to truly compete against each other. Such practices are illegal today and any attempts by business to block competition can result in fines or other penalties.
5. *The right to be educated about purchases.* All prescription drugs now come with detailed information regarding dosage, possible side effects, and potential interactions with other medications.
6. *The right to courteous service.* This right is hard to legislate, but as consumers become increasingly knowledgeable, they are more willing to complain about bad service. Consumer hotlines can also be used to voice service-related issues.

UNFAIR PRICING

Interfering with competition can also mean illegal pricing practices. **Collusion** among companies—including getting together to "fix" prices—is against the law. Arctic Glacier Inc. of Winnipeg was one of several companies served with subpoenas by the U.S. government during an investigation of collusion in the U.S. market for packaged ice. One of Arctic's employees, who claimed he was fired for refusing to take part in a conspiracy to divide up markets, went to the U.S. government and helped it in its investigation.[41] Arctic eventually paid \$12.5 million in fines.[42] The Canadian Competition Bureau launched an investigation after hearing allegations from a confidential informant that Mars, Hershey, Nestle, and Cadbury had teamed up in a candy price-fixing scheme.[43] A law firm in Toronto is also organizing a class-action lawsuit against the major chocolate companies, alleging a conspiracy to fix prices.[44] In 2012, three gas companies in Kingston and Brockville—Canadian Tire, Pioneer Energy, and Mr. Gas Ltd.—were fined a total of \$2 million by the Competition Bureau for fixing gas prices.[45]

In 2010, new laws came into effect that are designed to make it easier for the Competition Bureau to convict price-fixers (since 1980, only three price-fixing convictions were secured in the 23 cases that came before the Competition Bureau). The maximum prison sentence for price fixing has been tripled to 14 years, and the maximum fine increased from \$10 million to \$25 million.[46]

ETHICS IN ADVERTISING

There are several ethical issues in advertising, including truth-in-advertising claims, the advertising of counterfeit brands, the use of stealth advertising, and advertising that is morally objectionable.

Truth in Advertising Truth in advertising has long been regulated in Canada, but an increased emphasis on this issue is now becoming more noticeable on the international scene. For example, Chinese government officials investigated Procter & Gamble's claim that its Pantene shampoo made hair "10 times stronger." This came shortly after Procter & Gamble was ordered to pay a \$24 000 fine after one consumer complained that SK-II skin cream was not the "miracle water" it claimed to be and that it did not make her skin "look 12 years younger in 28 days."[47]

Advertising of Counterfeit Brands Counterfeit goods are a problem in many different product lines, including perfume, luggage, pharmaceuticals, designer clothing, shoes, cigarettes, watches, sports memorabilia, golf clubs, and fine wines, to name just a few. In 2011, for example, fake jerseys of the re-born Winnipeg Jets hockey team were seized by the RCMP.[48] Canada Goose, a manufacturer of extreme weather outerware, is battling counterfeiters who copy their best-selling products.[49] Because cancer drugs are so expensive, fake versions have started to appear in various countries.[50]

CONSUMERISM A social movement that seeks to protect and expand the rights of consumers in their dealings with businesses.

COLLUSION An illegal agreement among companies in an industry to "fix" prices for their products.

<<< Of all roadway accidents, 25 percent are distraction-related, and the biggest distractions for motorists are handheld gadgets: smartphones, pagers, and the like. In fulfilling its responsibility to consumers, some companies are conducting tests that yield important data about roadway accidents. Ford Motor Co., for example, has a Virtual Test Track Experiment simulator that determines how often drivers get distracted. Under normal circumstances, an adult driver will miss about 3 percent of the simulated "events" (like an ice patch or a deer on the road) that show up in the virtual road trip. If they're on the cell phone, they miss about 14 percent. But teenagers miss a scary 54 percent of the events.

Keith Dannemiller/ZUMAPRESS/Newscom

Counterfeiting has moved beyond the manufacturing of individual products. In China and in New York City, fake Apple stores have popped up, complete with sales assistants wearing blue T-shirts with the Apple logo and signs advertising the latest Apple products.[51] In the Chinese city of Kunming, an Ikea knockoff store called 11 Furniture duplicates Ikea's well-known blue-and-yellow look and has essentially pirated the entire Ikea brand experience.[52]

Counterfeiting is harmful to the companies that have spent a lot of time and money developing brand name goods for sale. While it may seem that consumers benefit because they get low prices for goods that look like the real thing, in fact consumers often pay far too much for counterfeit goods because those goods have very low quality. As well, some counterfeit goods are downright dangerous to use. While a fake handbag simply costs money, fake pharmaceuticals, electrical products, and motorcycles can kill the people who use them.[53]

Stealth (Undercover) Advertising A variation of viral marketing (see Chapter 2), **stealth advertising** involves companies paying individuals to extol the virtues of their products to other individuals who are not aware that they are listening to a paid spokesperson for the company. For example, Student Workforce hires individuals who are 18 to 30 years old to market products to other people in the same age bracket.[54] One advertising agency hired models to pose as tourists. These models asked real tourists to take their picture with a new Sony Ericsson camera cell phone. The models then talked up the advantages of the new product to the unsuspecting real tourists. The ethics of this are questionable when the paid individuals do not reveal that they are being paid by a company, so the recipient of the advertising is not aware that it is advertising. Commercial Alert, a U.S.-based consumer protection group, wants a government investigation of these undercover marketing tactics.[55]

Morally Objectionable Advertising A final ethical issue concerns advertising that consumers consider morally objectionable. Benetton, for example, aired a series of commercials featuring inmates on death row. The ads, dubbed "We, on Death Row," prompted such an outcry that Sears dropped the Benetton USA clothing line.[56] Other ads receiving criticism include Victoria's Secret models in skimpy underwear and campaigns by tobacco and alcohol companies that allegedly target young people. The portrayal of women in some video games is objectionable, and some new products are coming on the market to rectify this situation (see the boxed insert entitled "Silicon Sisters").

Responsibility Toward Employees

In Chapter 8, we describe the human resource management activities essential to a smoothly functioning business. These same activities—recruiting, hiring, training, promoting, and compensating—are also the basis for socially responsible behaviour toward employees. Socially responsible companies hire and promote new workers without regard to race, sex, or other irrelevant factors, provide a safe and non-bullying workplace, do not tolerate abusive managers or managers who sexually harasses subordinates, promote a work–life balance among employees, emphasize employee mental health, and pay a living wage.

Progressive companies go well beyond legal requirements, hiring and training the so-called hard-core unemployed (people with little education and training and a history of unemployment) and those who have disabilities. Bank of Montreal, for example, sponsors a community college skills upgrading course for individuals with hearing impairments. Royal Bank provides managers with discrimination awareness training. Rogers Communications provides individuals with mobility restrictions with telephone and customer-service job opportunities.[57]

STEALTH (UNDERCOVER) ADVERTISING Companies paying individuals to extol the virtues of their products without disclosing that they are paid to do so.

ENTREPRENEURSHIP AND NEW VENTURES

Silicon Sisters: Gaming with a Social Twist

Videos games—which often portray young women in a negative light—have been largely created by young men with the young male consumer in mind. More often than not, these games play to low-level base emotions. According to the Entertainment Software Association of Canada, approximately 59 percent of Canadians play video games and about 39 percent of those people are women. Meeting the specific needs of female gamers is a huge market opportunity that has so far been largely ignored. Silicon Sisters Interactive was created by two women to address this opportunity and to change the face of gaming. Think of it as gaming with a social consciousness: gaming by women, for the female market, with images girls can aspire to, and women can relate to. So put away the guns and explosives—let's talk about a new model for a largely ignored market segment.

The two women behind Silicon Sisters Interactive have first-hand knowledge and experience in all aspects of the gaming industry. Brenda Bailey Gershkovitch is the CEO and focuses on the business side of the company. She earned her stripes as the former COO of Deep Fried Entertainment while working on games like MLB Superstars, Shadow Play, and Fantasy All Stars. She also is on the board of the directors of the Game Developers Conference of Canada. Kristen Forbes is the COO, and she is responsible for production. Kristen gained experience as an Executive Producer at Radical Entertainment where she worked on games like Crash of the Titans, Scarface, Incredible Hulk, and Simpsons Hit and Run.

The shift from gaming consoles to new social gaming platforms (i.e., Facebook) has created an opportunity to connect and create scenarios for collaboration and group interaction. The gaming world is no longer stuck in a dark basement. The success of games like FarmVille (especially among older women) and social forums like Club Penguin (designed for kids up to 12 years old) have led the way. With this in mind, the women behind Silicon Sisters have created games like School 26 and Everlove.

School 26 is a unique casual game designed for girls aged 12 to 16. It follows Kate, a student whose family moves often, making it hard for her to maintain friendships. As she enrolls in her 26th new school, she makes a deal with her parents; if Kate makes good friends here, the family will stay put. Now the player must help Kate use intuition, empathy, and strategy to build friendships and navigate the moral dilemmas (peer pressure, romance, etc.) of high school.

Everlove is a social gaming product aimed at women aged 35 to 50. It is a blend between romance novels and gaming served on a smartphone or tablet.

Will Silicon Sisters Interactive become the next big gaming company? It might or it might not, but this company is changing the face of gaming by thinking about the needs of a large market segment that has been mostly ignored. That is a really good start.

CRITICAL THINKING QUESTIONS

1. What do you think of the potential for gaming products aimed at female consumers?
2. What themes or topics would you recommend for this underserved market?

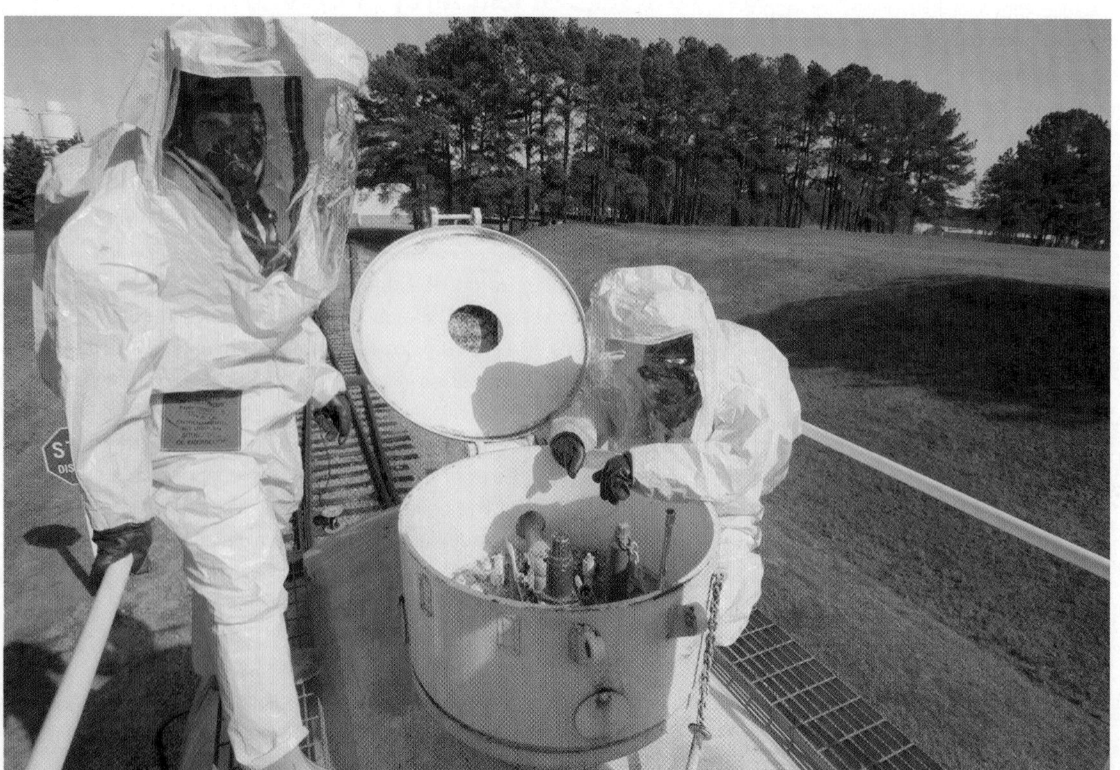

<<< The safety of workers is an important consideration for all organizations. The required use of protective clothing when dealing with toxic substances is just one example of precautions that companies can take to protect workers while they are on the job.

baur/Shutterstock

Businesses also have a responsibility to respect the privacy of their employees, though there is some controversy about exactly how much control companies should have in areas like drug testing and computer monitoring. When the Canadian National Railway instituted drug testing for train, brake, and yard employees, 12 percent failed. Trucking companies have found that nearly one-third of truckers who had an accident were on drugs.[58] It seems likely that safety will be compromised when employees in transportation companies use drugs, but there is controversy about what kind of testing is appropriate.

Differences of opinion are also evident with regard to the computer monitoring of employees while they are at work. New software programs allow bosses to see things like employees' Facebook comments and their opinions about pubs on Foursquare. Social Sentry, a tracking system developed by Social Logix, records employee social media activity from work or home. The program looks for workers who leak sensitive company information or who bad-mouth the company.[59] Workers shouldn't damage the reputation of the company they work for, but there is no consensus on what constitutes going "too far."

WHISTLE-BLOWERS

Respecting employees as people also means respecting their behaviour as ethically responsible individuals. Employees who discover that their company has been engaging in practices that are illegal, unethical, and/or socially irresponsible should be able to report the problem to higher-level management and be confident that managers will stop the questionable practices. If no one in the organization will take action, the employee might decide to inform a regulatory agency or the media. At this point, the person becomes a **whistle-blower**—an employee who discovers and tries to put an end to a company's unethical, illegal, and/or socially irresponsible actions by publicizing them.

John Kopchinski, a sales representative at pharmaceutical giant Pfizer, blew the whistle after he learned that Pfizer was promoting certain drugs for unapproved uses. He received $5.1 million from the U.S. government for his whistle-blowing efforts.[60] In Canada, WestJet employee Melvin Crothers discovered that a fellow WestJet employee was somehow accessing a restricted Air Canada website in order to obtain data about Air Canada's "load factor" (the proportion of seats filled) on certain flights. It turned out that the employee had formerly worked for Air Canada, but his access to confidential Air Canada data had inadvertently not been cancelled. After discovering this, Crothers had a conversation with a former WestJet president who was heading up an Air Canada discount airline, which led to Air Canada filing a lawsuit against WestJet. Crothers resigned from WestJet four days later.[61]

Whistle-blowers are often demoted or fired when they take their accusations public. Even if they retain their jobs, they may still be treated as outsiders and suffer resentment or hostility from co-workers. One recent study found that about half of all whistle-blowers eventually get fired, and about half of those who get fired subsequently lose their homes and/or families.[62]

Federal legislation to protect whistle-blowers was introduced in Canada in 2003. In 2009, the Investment Industry Regulatory Organization of Canada (IIROC) opened a whistle-blower hotline as a result of an increased incidence of securities fraud such as Ponzi schemes in both Canada and the U.S. Calls regarding market fraud are forwarded to four of the top people at the IIROC so that swift action can be taken.[63] The boxed insert entitled "Should Whistle-Blowers Be Paid?" analyzes an interesting issue in whistle-blowing.

WHISTLE-BLOWER An individual who calls attention to an unethical, illegal, and/or socially irresponsible practice on the part of a business or other organization.

MANAGING IN TURBULENT TIMES

Should Whistle-Blowers Be Paid?

In Canada, whistle-blower programs, like the one established in 2009 by the Investment Industry Regulatory Organization of Canada, have not paid whistle-blowers for reporting illegal acts. Rather, attention has focused on protecting whistle-blowers from retaliation by the companies they claim have behaved illegally. This contrasts with the situation in the U.S., where whistle-blowers are paid a bounty between 10 and 30 percent when more than $1 million is recovered from corporate wrongdoers.

In 2011, the Ontario Securities Commission announced that it might implement a whistle-blower program that would be more like the U.S. model. But this raises an important question—are there unanticipated negative consequences that might arise as a result of paying whistle-blowers? There are two opposing views on this question (naturally!).

Supporters argue that paying whistle-blowers is a good idea because whistle-blowers face a great deal of hostility and harassment from their companies when they report managerial misconduct. For example, whistle-blowers are often charged with breaching confidentiality, and they then must pay legal fees as they defend themselves. Companies also try to publicly discredit the whistle-blower, and this likely reduces the person's future job prospects. The practice of "speaking truth to power" is risky for whistle-blowers, so they should be compensated for doing so. Beyond these arguments is the practical fact that the government can recover large sums of money from companies that behave badly. The U.S. government, for example, has recovered more than $28 billion in the last 25 years from companies that made false claims for payments from government contracts.

Opponents argue that if whistle-blowers are paid, they will have an incentive to bypass existing compliance programs and go straight for the money. Undermining existing procedures is probably not a good thing. They also argue that whistle-blowers may make questionable charges as they put their own financial interests ahead of the interests of the company they work for. There may also be a "rush to judgment" about a situation, especially if a new whistle-blower law requires that quick action be taken to resolve a problem. For example, at French carmaker Renault, three high-ranking executives were fired in 2011 after an anonymous tip that they had stashed bribe money in a Swiss bank. The three executives were eventually exonerated, but they were subjected to considerable stress and the company experienced a public humiliation.

CRITICAL THINKING QUESTIONS

1. In your own words, state the pros and cons of paying whistle-blowers for the information they provide.
2. On balance, do you think it is a good idea to pay whistle-blowers? Defend your answer.

Responsibility Toward Investors

It may sound odd to say that managers can be irresponsible toward investors, since the investors are the owners of the company, but managers behave irresponsibly when they pay themselves outlandish salaries and bonuses or spend large amounts of company money for their own personal comfort. If managers do not use the firm's financial resources in a responsible way, the ultimate losers are the owners, since they do not receive the earnings, dividends, or capital appreciation due to them. Financial mismanagement can take many forms, including *improper financial management, misrepresentation of finances*, *cheque kiting*, and *insider trading*.

IMPROPER FINANCIAL MANAGEMENT

Improper financial management can take many forms, including executives making bad financial decisions, paying executives outlandish salaries and bonuses, or sending them on extravagant "retreats" to exotic resorts. For example, managers at American International Group became involved in very-high-risk insurance that caused the company to be on the hook for billions of dollars. The U.S. government ended up giving hundreds of billions of dollars to the company to keep it afloat. In many of these situations, creditors don't have much leverage and shareholders have few viable options. Trying to force a management changeover is not only difficult, but it can also drive down the price of the company's stock, and this is a penalty shareholders are usually unwilling to assign themselves.

MISREPRESENTATION OF FINANCES

Occasionally, managers are guilty of misrepresenting a company's financial condition. In Canada, one of the most highly publicized cases involved Garth Drabinsky and Myron Gottlieb, the top managers at Livent Inc. In 2006, Ken Lay, the CEO of Enron, was convicted of conspiracy and securities fraud, but he died before he was sentenced. In 2007, Conrad Black, CEO of Hollinger International, was convicted of fraud and obstruction of justice and was sentenced to six and a half years in prison. In December 2008, Bernie Madoff pleaded guilty to swindling investors in a $50 billion fraud. He is likely to spend the rest of his life in prison.[64] In 2012, R. Allen Stanford was found guilty of wasting investor money on yachts, failing businesses, and cricket tournaments. He was sentenced to 110 years in prison.[65]

CHEQUE KITING

Cheque kiting involves writing a cheque from one account, depositing it in a second account, and then immediately spending money from the second account while the money from the first account is still in transit. A cheque from the second account can also be used to replenish the money in the first account, and the process starts all over again. This practice obviously benefits the person doing the cheque kiting, but it is irresponsible because it involves using other people's money without paying for it. In 2012, the Bank of Montreal sued several U.S. and Canadian businesspeople, alleging that they ran a cheque kiting scheme that cost BMO $20 million.[66]

INSIDER TRADING

Insider trading occurs when someone uses confidential information to gain from the purchase or sale of stock. In 2011, for example, the Alberta securities regulator charged several executives at Grand Cache Coal Corp. with insider trading for selling company stock before the company disclosed negative news about its sales.[67] Also in 2011, Raj Rajaratnam, the co-founder of Galleon Group, was sentenced to 11 years in prison for insider trading.[68]

CHEQUE KITING The illegal practice of writing cheques against money that has not yet arrived at the bank on which the cheque has been written, relying on that money arriving before the cheque clears.

INSIDER TRADING The use of confidential information to gain from the purchase or sale of stock.

IMPLEMENTING SOCIAL RESPONSIBILITY PROGRAMS

Thus far, we have discussed corporate social responsibility (CSR) as if there is agreement on how companies should behave in most situations. In fact, differences of opinion exist as to the appropriateness of CSR as a business goal. Some people oppose any business activity that cuts into investor profits, while others argue that CSR must take precedence over profits.

Even people who share a common attitude toward CSR by business may have different reasons for their beliefs, and this influences their view about how social responsibility should be implemented. Some people fear that if businesses become too active in social concerns, they will gain too much control over how those concerns are addressed. They point to the influence many businesses have been able to exert on the government agencies that are supposed to regulate their industries. Other critics of business-sponsored social programs argue that companies lack the expertise needed. They believe that technical experts, not businesses, should decide how best to clean up a polluted river, for example.

Supporters of CSR believe that corporations are citizens just like individuals and therefore should help improve our lives. Others point to the vast resources controlled by businesses and note that, since businesses often create many of the problems social programs are designed to alleviate, they should use their resources to help. Still others argue that CSR is wise because it pays off for the firm in terms of good public relations.

The late Max Clarkson, formerly a top-level business executive and director of the Centre for Corporate Social Performance and Ethics at the University of Toronto, designed and applied a CSR rating system for companies. He found that companies that had the highest marks on ethics and CSR also had the highest financial performance.[69]

LO-4 Approaches to Social Responsibility

Given these differences of opinion, it is little wonder that corporations have adopted a variety of approaches to social responsibility. As Figure 3.3 illustrates, the four stances that an organization can take concerning its obligations to society fall along a continuum ranging from the lowest to the highest degree of socially responsible practices. Keep in mind that organizations do not always fit neatly into one category or another. The Ronald McDonald House program has been widely applauded, for example, but McDonald's has also come under fire for allegedly misleading consumers about the nutritional value of its food products. The Exercising Your Ethics exercise at the end of the chapter gives you an opportunity to think about the pros and cons of the various stances toward CSR.

OBSTRUCTIONIST STANCE

Businesses that take an **obstructionist stance** to social responsibility do as little as possible to solve social or environmental problems. When they cross the ethical or legal line that separates acceptable from unacceptable practices, their typical response is to deny or cover up their actions. Firms that adopt this position have little regard for ethical conduct and will generally go to great lengths to hide wrongdoing.

DEFENSIVE STANCE

An organization adopting a **defensive stance** will do everything that is required of it legally, but nothing more. Such a firm, for example, would install pollution-control equipment dictated by law, but would not install higher-quality equipment even though it might further limit pollution. Managers who take a defensive stance insist that their job is to generate profits. Tobacco companies in Canada and the U.S. generally take this position in their marketing efforts since they are legally required to include warnings to smokers on their products and to limit advertising to prescribed media. They follow these rules to the letter of the law, but use more aggressive marketing methods in countries that have no such rules.

ACCOMMODATIVE STANCE

A firm that adopts an **accommodative stance** meets its legal and ethical requirements, but will also go further in certain cases. Such firms may agree to participate in social programs, but solicitors must convince them that these programs are worthy of funding. Many organizations respond to requests for donations to community hockey teams, Girl Guides, youth soccer programs, and so forth. The point, however, is that someone has to knock on the door and ask; accommodative organizations do not necessarily or proactively seek avenues for contributing.

PROACTIVE STANCE

Firms that adopt the **proactive stance** take to heart the arguments in favour of CSR. They view themselves as good citizens of society and they proactively seek opportunities to contribute. The most common—and direct—way to implement this stance is by setting up a foundation to provide direct financial support for various social programs.

Corporate Charitable Donations Donating money to different causes is one way that business firms try to show that they are socially responsible. Every four months, for example, Whole Foods (Toronto) donates 5 percent of one day's sales to a designated non-profit organization.[70] At CIBC, the Miracle Day program has raised a total of $64 million for children's charities in Canada.[71] A survey of 93 large Canadian companies found that 97 percent made a charitable contribution of some sort and that the median value of their contributions was $340 000.[72] More than 80 percent of the companies said that they made contributions because it was a good thing to do, irrespective of any financial benefits they might achieve from giving.[73] Unfortunately, the difficult economic circumstances of the last few years have caused a decline in corporate donations. For example, corporate donations to the Daily Bread Food Bank in Toronto were down 40 percent in 2011. According to Statistics Canada, corporate

OBSTRUCTIONIST STANCE A company that does as little as possible to solve social or environmental problems.

DEFENSIVE STANCE An organization that does only what is legally required and nothing more.

ACCOMMODATIVE STANCE A company that meets all of its legal and ethical requirements and, in some cases, even goes beyond what is required.

PROACTIVE STANCE An organization that actively seeks opportunities to be socially responsible.

Obstructionist Stance | Defensive Stance | Accommodative Stance | Proactive Stance

LOWEST LEVEL OF SOCIAL RESPONSIBILITY — HIGHEST LEVEL OF SOCIAL RESPONSIBILITY

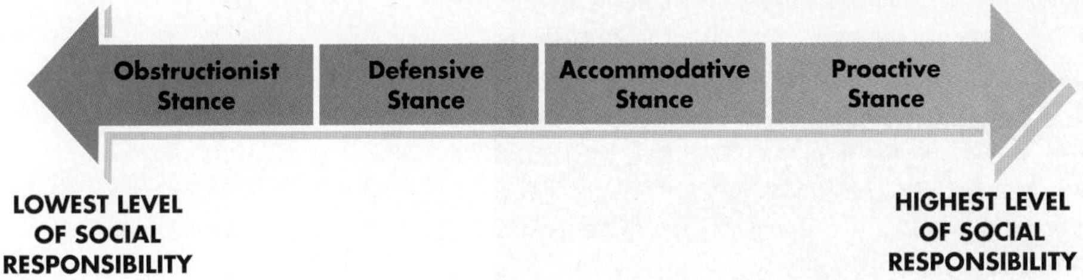

<<< FIGURE 3.3 Spectrum of approaches to social responsibility

donations to charities declined from $2.45 billion in 2008 to $2.26 billion in 2010.[74]

Some companies go beyond simply giving money or products. For example, Unilever Canada gives employees four afternoons a year for community activities.[75] Mars Canada sets aside one day each year for employees to volunteer. In 2013, Tim Hortons' Children's Foundation started construction on a camp for underprivileged children at Sylvia Lake in Manitoba. The Foundation also has a Youth Leadership Program that is currently offered at two sites in Ontario.[76] At Telus Corp.'s annual "day of service" in 2008, employees helped out at a soup kitchen.[77]

SUSTAINABLE DEVELOPMENT Activities that meet current needs, but will not put future generations at a disadvantage when they try to meet their needs.

SOCIAL AUDIT A systematic analysis of how a firm is using funds earmarked for social-responsibility goals and how effective these expenditures have been.

TRIPLE BOTTOM LINE REPORTING Measuring the social, environmental, and economic performance of a company.

Managing Social Responsibility Programs

There are four steps that are required in order for an organization to become truly socially responsible. First, top management must state strong support for CSR and make it a factor in strategic planning. Without the support of top management, no program can succeed.

Second, a committee of top managers needs to develop a plan detailing the level of support that will be provided. Some companies set aside a percentage of profits for social programs. Levi Strauss, for example, has a policy of giving 2.4 percent of its pre-tax earnings to worthy causes. Managers also need to set specific priorities (for example, should the firm focus on training the hard-core unemployed or supporting the arts?).

Third, a specific executive needs to be given the authority to act as director of the firm's social agenda. This individual must monitor the program and ensure that its implementation is consistent with the policy statement and the strategic plan.

Finally, the organization needs to conduct occasional social audits, which are systematic analyses of how a firm is using funds earmarked for its social-responsibility goals.[78] An important related element in a social responsibility program is the idea of **sustainable development**, which means pursuing activities that meet current needs, but which will not put future generations at a disadvantage when they attempt to meet their needs. When making sustainable development decisions, it is important that managers simultaneously consider economic, social, and environmental variables. Research at the London and Harvard Business Schools shows that companies that adopt mandatory sustainability reporting requirements see positive effects on corporate performance.[79] The organization called Student Energy was formed by a student at the University of Calgary in 2008. Its purpose is to educate and inspire the next generation of environmental professionals to move the world to a sustainable energy future.[80]

Canadian businesses publish sustainability reports that explain how the company is performing on issues such as the environment, employee relations, workplace diversity, and business ethics. A study by Ottawa-based Stratos Inc. found that 60 percent of the 100 largest Canadian companies now report at least some sustainability performance information.[81] For example, Artopex Inc., a furniture manufacturer in Quebec, has an active sustainability program.[82] Baxter Corp., a medical products company, publishes an annual Global Sustainability Report measuring the company's progress on nine sustainable priorities, including reductions in its carbon footprint.[83] **Social audits** and sustainability reports together constitute triple bottom line reporting—measuring the social, environmental, and economic performance of a company. Vancouver City Savings Credit Union (Vancity) uses **triple bottom line reporting**.[84]

The Global 100 list of the most sustainable corporations in the world is based on factors like energy productivity (the ratio of sales to energy consumption) and water productivity (sales to water usage). In the 2012 ranking, Novo Nordisk (Denmark) was first, Natura Cosmeticos (Brazil) second, and Statoil (Norway) third. Six Canadian companies made the Top 100, including Suncor (#48), Enbridge (#71), and Encana Corp.

<<< Ronald McDonald House helps the families of children who are in hospital care. It is supported by McDonald's and is an excellent example of socially responsible behaviour by a business.

Walter Zerla/Blend Images/Corbis

(#76).[85] Each year, the Corporate Knights organization publishes its Best 50 Corporate Citizens in Canada list. The rankings are based on an assessment of factors such as pension fund quality, board diversity, tax dollar generation, and Aboriginal relations. The top three companies in 2011 were The Co-operators Group Ltd., Mountain Equipment Co-op, and Domtar Corporation.[86]

LO-5 SOCIAL RESPONSIBILITY AND THE SMALL BUSINESS

In the most general sense, small businesses face many of the same ethical and social responsibility issues as large businesses. But small business owners face many specific ethical dilemmas that have an immediate (and perhaps profound) effect on their business. For example, as the owner of a small garden supply store, how would you respond to a building inspector's suggestion that a cash payment would "expedite" your application for a building permit? As the manager of a nightclub, would you call the police, refuse service, or sell liquor to a customer whose ID card looked forged? Or, as the owner of a small medical laboratory, would you call the board of health to make sure that it has licensed the company you want to contract with to dispose of the lab's medical waste? As the owner of a small manufacturing firm, are you justified in overcharging by 5 percent a customer whose purchasing agent is lax? As the owner of a small computer services company, should you pad your income statement a bit to increase the chance that you will get a much-needed bank loan?

Other dilemmas present themselves to small business owners in the form of social responsibility issues. For example, can a small business afford to pursue CSR objectives? Should it sponsor hockey teams, make donations to the United Way, and buy light bulbs from the Lion's Club? Should it join the chamber of commerce and support the Better Business Bureau because it is the responsible thing to do or just because it is good business? Most of these decisions have financial implications, and the owners of many small firms feel that they do not have any financial flexibility.

MyBizLab Visit the MyBizLab website. This online homework and tutorial system puts you in control of your own learning with study and practice tools directly correlated to this chapter's content.

SUMMARY OF LEARNING OBJECTIVES

LO-1 EXPLAIN HOW INDIVIDUALS DEVELOP THEIR PERSONAL *CODES OF ETHICS* AND WHY ETHICS ARE IMPORTANT IN THE WORKPLACE.

Individual *codes of ethics* are derived from social standards of right and wrong. Ethical behaviour is behaviour that conforms to generally accepted social norms concerning beneficial and harmful actions. Because ethics affect the behaviour of individuals on behalf of the companies that employ them, many firms are adopting formal statements of ethics. Unethical behaviour can result in loss of business, fines, and even imprisonment.

LO-2 DISTINGUISH *ETHICS* FROM *SOCIAL RESPONSIBILITY* AND IDENTIFY *ORGANIZATIONAL STAKEHOLDERS.*

Ethics are individual beliefs about what is right and wrong, while *social responsibility* refers to the way a firm attempts to balance its commitments to organizational stakeholders. Stakeholders are individuals, groups, and organizations that are directly affected by the practices of an organization and that, therefore, have a stake in its performance. The stakeholders that businesses usually pay the most attention to are *investors, employees, customers*, and *local communities*. Businesses formerly paid almost exclusive attention to investors, but public pressure and government regulations have forced businesses to consider other stakeholders as well.

LO-3 SHOW HOW THE CONCEPT OF SOCIAL RESPONSIBILITY APPLIES BOTH TO ENVIRONMENTAL ISSUES AND TO A FIRM'S RELATIONSHIPS WITH CUSTOMERS, EMPLOYEES, AND INVESTORS.

Social responsibility toward the environment requires firms to minimize pollution of air, water, and land. Social responsibility toward customers requires firms to provide products of acceptable quality, to price products fairly, and to respect consumers' rights. Social responsibility toward employees requires firms to respect workers both as resources and as people who are more productive when their needs are met. Social responsibility toward investors requires firms to manage their resources and to represent their financial status honestly.

LO-4 **IDENTIFY FOUR GENERAL *APPROACHES TO SOCIAL RESPONSIBILITY* AND DESCRIBE THE FOUR STEPS A FIRM MUST TAKE TO IMPLEMENT A *SOCIAL RESPONSIBILITY PROGRAM*.**

An *obstructionist* stance on social responsibility is taken by a firm that does as little as possible to address social or environmental problems and that may deny or attempt to cover up problems that may occur. The *defensive* stance emphasizes compliance with legal minimum requirements. Companies adopting the *accommodative* stance go beyond minimum activities, if asked. The *proactive* stance commits a company to actively seeking to contribute to social projects. Implementing a social responsibility program entails four steps: (1) drafting a policy statement with the support of top management, (2) developing a detailed plan, (3) appointing a director to implement the plan, and (4) conducting social audits to monitor results.

LO-5 **EXPLAIN HOW ISSUES OF SOCIAL RESPONSIBILITY AND ETHICS AFFECT SMALL BUSINESSES.**

Managers and employees of small businesses face many of the same ethical questions as their counterparts at larger firms; they also face the same issues of social responsibility and the same need to decide on an approach to social responsibility. The differences are primarily differences of scale.

QUESTIONS AND EXERCISES

QUESTIONS FOR ANALYSIS

See >>> for Assisted-Graded Writing Assignment in MyBizLab

1. >>> In what ways do you think your personal code of ethics might clash with the practices of some companies? How might you resolve these differences?
2. What kind of company wrong doing would most likely prompt you to be a whistle-blower? What kind of wrong doing would be least likely? Explain the difference.
3. In your opinion, which area of social responsibility is most important to you? Why? Are there areas other than those noted in the chapter that you consider important as well? Describe these areas, and indicate why they are important.
4. Identify some specific social responsibility issues that might be faced by small business managers and employees in each of the following areas: environment, customers, employees, and investors.
5. Choose a product or service and explain the social responsibility concerns that are likely to be evident in terms of the environment, customers, employees, and investors.
6. Analyze the forces that are at work from both a company's perspective and a whistle-blower's perspective. Given these forces, what characteristics would a law to protect whistle-blowers have to have to be effective?

APPLICATION EXERCISES

7. Write a one-paragraph description of an ethical dilemma you faced recently (including the outcome). Analyze the situation using the ideas presented in the chapter. Make particular reference to the ethical norms of utility, rights, justice, and caring in terms of how they impacted the situation. What would each of these suggest about the correct decision? Is this analysis consistent with the outcome that actually occurred? Why or why not?
8. Go to the website of the Center for Ethics and Business at Loyola Marymount University and click on "Toolbox." Then click on "Quiz: What's Your Ethical Style?" Take the ethics quiz and analyze what your score implies about how you are likely to react when you are faced with an ethical dilemma.
9. >>> Develop a list of the major stakeholders of your college or university. What priority does the school assign to these stakeholders? Do you agree or disagree with this priority? Explain your reasoning.
10. Interview the owner of a local small business. Ask the owner to (a) describe the kinds of socially responsible activities the company is currently involved in, and (b) identify the factors that facilitate and inhibit socially responsible behaviour in small businesses.

BUILDING YOUR BUSINESS SKILLS

TO LIE OR NOT TO LIE: THAT IS THE QUESTION

METHOD

Step 1 Working with four other students, discuss ways in which you would respond to the following ethical dilemmas. When there is a difference of opinion among group members, try to determine the specific factors that influence different responses.

GOAL

To encourage students to apply general concepts of business ethics to specific situations.

BACKGROUND

Workplace lying, it seems, has become business as usual. According to one survey, one-quarter of working adults said that they had been asked to do something illegal or unethical on the job. Four in ten did what they were told. Another survey of more than 2000 secretaries showed that many employees face ethical dilemmas in their day-to-day work.

- Would you lie about your supervisor's whereabouts to someone on the phone?
- Would you lie about who was responsible for a business decision that cost your company thousands of dollars to protect your own or your supervisor's job?
- Would you inflate sales and revenue data on official company accounting statements to increase stock value?
- Would you say that you witnessed a signature when you did not if you were acting in the role of a notary?
- Would you keep silent if you knew that the official minutes of a corporate meeting had been changed?
- Would you destroy or remove information that could hurt your company if it fell into the wrong hands?

Step 2 Research the commitment to business ethics at Johnson & Johnson (www.jnj.com) and Texas Instruments (www.ti.com/corp/docs/csr/corpgov/ethics/) by clicking on their respective websites. As a group, discuss ways in which these statements are likely to affect the specific behaviours mentioned in Step 1.

Step 3 Working with group members, draft a corporate code of ethics that would discourage the specific behaviours mentioned in Step 1. Limit your code to a single typewritten page, but make it sufficiently broad to cover different ethical dilemmas.

FOLLOW-UP QUESTIONS

1. What personal, social, and cultural factors do you think contribute to lying in the workplace?
2. Do you agree or disagree with the following statement? "The term *business ethics* is an oxymoron." Support your answer with examples from your own work experience or that of a family member.
3. If you were your company's director of human resources, how would you make your code of ethics a "living document"?
4. If you were faced with any of the ethical dilemmas described in Step 1, how would you handle them? How far would you go to maintain your personal ethical standards?

EXERCISING YOUR ETHICS

ASSESSING THE ETHICS OF TRADEOFFS

THE SITUATION

Managers must often make choices among options that are presented by environmental circumstances. This exercise will help you better appreciate the nature and complexity of the kinds of tradeoffs that often result.

THE DILEMMA

You are the CEO of a medium-sized, unionized manufacturing corporation located in a town of about 15 000 people. The nearest major city is about 200 kilometres away. With about 500 workers, you are one of the five largest employers in town. A regional recession has caused two of the other largest employers to close down (one went out of business and the other relocated to another area). A new foreign competitor has set up shop in the area, but local unemployment has still risen sharply. All in all, the regional economic climate and the new competitor are hurting your business. Your sales have dropped 20 percent this year, and you forecast another drop next year before things begin to turn around.

You face two unpleasant choices:

Choice 1: You can tell your employees that you need them to take cuts in pay and benefits. You know that because of the local unemployment rate, you can easily replace anyone who refuses. Unfortunately, you may need your employees to take another cut next year if your forecasts hold true. At the same time, you do have reason to believe that when the economy rebounds (in about two years, according to your forecasts), you can begin restoring pay cuts. Here are the advantages of this choice—you can probably (1) preserve all 500 jobs, (2) maintain your own income, (3) restore pay cuts in the future, and (4) keep the business open indefinitely. The disadvantages are that pay cuts will (1) pose economic hardships for your employees and (2) create hard feelings and undercut morale.

Choice 2: You can maintain the status quo as far as your employees are concerned, but in that case, you'll be facing two problems—(1) you'll have to cut your own salary, and, while you can certainly afford to live on less income, doing so would be a blow to your personal finances and (2) if economic conditions get worse and/or last longer than forecast, you may have to close down altogether. The firm has a cash surplus, but because you'll have to dip into these funds to maintain stable wages, they'll soon run out. The advantages of this option are that you can (1) avoid economic hardship for your workers and (2) maintain good employee relations. The downside is that you will reduce your own standard of living and may eventually cost everyone his or her job.

TEAM ACTIVITY

Assemble a group of four students and assign each group member to one of the following roles:

- CEO of the company
- Vice-president of production
- A stockholder
- An employee who is a member of the union

ACTION STEPS

1. Before hearing any of your group's comments on this situation, and, from the perspective of your assigned role, decide which of the two options you think is the best choice. Write down the reasons for your position.
2. Before hearing any of your group's comments on this situation, and, from the perspective of your assigned role, decide what the underlying ethical issues are in this situation. Write down the issues.
3. Gather the group together and reveal, in turn, each member's comments on the best choice of the two options. Next, reveal the ethical issues listed by each member.
4. Appoint someone to record the main points of agreement and disagreement within the group. How do you explain the results? What accounts for any disagreement?
5. From an ethical standpoint, what does your group conclude is the most appropriate action that should be taken by the company? (You may find the concepts of utility, rights, justice, and caring helpful in making your decision.)

BUSINESS CASE

THE PROBLEM OF CONSUMER SKEPTICISM

In recent years, a consensus seems to be developing that it is important to care for the environment. This "green movement" has motivated many companies to publicize what they are doing to be more eco-friendly. Coca-Cola, for example, pushed its new green image at the 2010 Winter Olympics with its "environmental call to action." Market research suggested that Coke had a lot of work to do to polish up its green image, particularly among consumers in the 13 to 29 age group. Critics have accused Coke of wasting water (it takes 250 litres of water to make one litre of Coca-Cola) and creating a lot of waste for landfills (75 percent of plastic bottles that contain Coca-Cola products end up in landfills). Coke therefore developed a new, eco-friendly container (called the PlantBottle) that is made partly from sugar cane and molasses. The new bottle produces 30 percent fewer emissions because less oil is used in making it.

KHEM SOVANNARA/AFP/Getty Images/Newscom

You might think that any attempt by a company to be more eco-friendly would be viewed positively by those who are concerned about protecting the environment. But that isn't necessarily the case. Skeptics say that the new Coke bottle really doesn't accomplish much because it is still mostly plastic. They note that even though plastic bottles are recyclable, most consumers just throw them out, so simply giving consumers access to plastic bottles is a bad idea.

The criticism that Coca-Cola is getting is not unusual. The fact is that almost any proposed green idea can become caught up in controversy that inhibits the progress of green practices. For example, consider the idea of green roofs, i.e., planting vegetation on the roofs of buildings (see photo). Some companies have had green roofs for years (for example, the green roof on the Manulife Centre parkade in Toronto has been there for 25 years, and the trees are now three storeys high), but the idea is just now starting to really catch on. Toronto's city council passed a bylaw which mandates green roofs on new commercial buildings and high-rise residential buildings. Starting in 2010, such buildings had to have at least part of their roof space devoted to green plantings. It is estimated that a green roof of 350 square metres with 75 percent of its area in greenery would reduce the "heat-island effect" by 26 percent and reduce rainwater runoff by 38 percent. This sounds promising, but critics argue that the new bylaw may actually inhibit the progress of the green movement because it will increase building development costs and limit the options developers can choose from when they are trying to make buildings more environmentally friendly.

The bylaw is seen as one more problem that developers must solve before they can build. And during those periods when the economy is in a fragile state, that is a problem. The recession of 2008 to 2009, for example, caused many businesses to put eco-friendly plans on hold. For example, Horizon Air, a U.S.-based airline, had planned to replace its regional jets with new Q400 turboprops made by Bombardier. The new planes burn 30 percent less fuel and therefore produce fewer emissions. But the economic slowdown forced the company to put those plans on hold. Another example: Clear Skies Solar cancelled plans to build a one-megawatt solar plant because it couldn't get enough financial backing. The plans were cancelled even though government grants are available for the development of solar power.

Consumer attitudes about eco-friendly behaviour can also limit the success of green products. A survey by the Boston Consulting Group in Toronto showed that one-third of Canadians say they often purchase environmentally friendly products, but 78 percent are unwilling to pay the higher price that is often evident for green products. Another online survey of 1000 Canadians showed that people are willing to do certain small things (for example, buying environmentally friendly light bulbs), but they are skeptical about adopting bigger measures. A third study, conducted by Procter & Gamble (P & G), showed that consumers are reluctant to spend more money just because a product is eco-friendly.

Only 10 percent of consumers who were surveyed said they would pay a higher price (or accept a performance decrease) for a product that would benefit the environment. What's worse, 75 percent said they would not accept *any* tradeoff. So, P & G is now focusing on developing sustainable innovation products that are more eco-friendly than earlier products, but which cost about the same price and have the same quality.

Another survey of 10 000 people from Canada and nine other countries analyzed the willingness of consumers to pay a premium for things like improved water quality, renewable (green) energy, and organic food. Here are some illustrative results:

- For improved water quality: on average, respondents were willing to pay a 7.5 percent premium on the median amount of their water bill.
- For renewable energy: 50 percent of respondents said they weren't willing to pay *any* premium, 48 percent were willing (on average) to pay a 5 percent premium; 2 percent were willing to pay a 30 percent premium.
- For organic food: 30 percent said they weren't willing to pay *any* premium; one-third said they would pay a premium between 1 and 5 percent; 2 percent were willing to pay a 50 percent premium.

The level of acceptance of green products has also been influenced by individuals who argue that the green movement has gone too far, and that too many consumers are suffering from eco obsessive-compulsive disorder (consumers being compulsively obsessed with being green in terms of the products they buy). Skeptics argue, for example, that the green movement negatively affects economic growth and increases unemployment. One study in Spain showed that every "green" job that was created destroyed 2.2 jobs elsewhere in the economy. The study concluded that government spending on renewable energy was only half as effective at creating new jobs as an equivalent amount of spending by the private sector.

Consumers may also be reluctant to spend money on eco-friendly products because they are confused by the green claims that are being made by various companies. The Boston Consulting Group study mentioned above also found that consumers are confused about the green options that are available because there is such a wide array of eco-labels on products. Ecolabelling.org is a Vancouver-based company that has identified 274 eco-labels, 23 of them originating in Canada. There are labels touting compostable products, fair trade products, energy efficient products, forest stewardship products, lake-friendly products, and organic products. These eco-labels are supposed to help consumers sift through environmental claims, but what do these labels actually mean? How can shoppers know which products are really eco-friendly and which ones are simply hype? The only thing that seems reasonably certain is that consumers are willing to pay a price premium in the short run if it leads to obvious long-term gains (for example, an energy-efficient refrigerator costs more than a regular one, but it saves money in the long run via lower electric bills).

There are people who are trying to help consumers sort through the maze of conflicting claims. Dara O'Rourke is a university professor who has developed a website called GoodGuide that allows consumers to identify the ingredients found in the products they buy. The website reports on both the environmental impact of products as well as their health effects. Website visitors enter a product name and get a score. The higher the score, the safer and more environmentally friendly the product is. O'Rourke's goal is to help consumers get past the green claims of companies, and get to the actual facts. The goal is to really change the system. Instead of having companies telling consumers what to believe about their products, the idea is to have consumers tell companies what is important to them in the products they buy.

Consumers may also become confused as they try to balance contradictory objectives about products. This problem can be clearly seen in automobile products. On the one hand, we need to sharply reduce carbon emissions by discouraging the use of gas-guzzling cars. This goal could be achieved by raising fuel-efficiency standards. But a study by the Boston Consulting Group concluded that fuel-saving improvements that reduce emissions by 40 percent would also raise the price of the average car by $2000. On the other hand, the governments of both the U.S. and Canada are giving billions of dollars to Chrysler and General Motors in an attempt to save jobs at two companies that have historically produced gas-guzzling cars. These billions of dollars would move us toward the goal of reduced carbon emissions if Chrysler and General Motors could start producing green cars at a price consumers could afford, but industry experts say they can't (at least not in the near term). GM's all-electric car, the Volt, is too expensive to be purchased by a lot of consumers, and GM's financial problems mean that it cannot risk the kind of money it formerly would have on a new product. It is also true that when gas prices are relatively low, consumers don't seem overly interested in green cars. Profit margins are small on green cars, and that is yet another limiting factor.

To cope with all this complexity, consumers need a good measure of ecological intelligence to help them make the distinction between style and substance in ecological claims. One proposal is for consumers to use something called Life Cycle Analysis, which calculates the carbon footprint of various activities (for example, a round-trip flight from Vancouver to Hong Kong, or a bouquet of flowers flown to Toronto from Kenya). But there is no guarantee that providing such detailed information would cause consumers to change their purchasing patterns. Organic foods and so-called "fair trade" products have been around for years, yet most people ignore them.

QUESTIONS FOR DISCUSSION

1. Summarize in your own words the major factors that can inhibit the progress toward greener practices on the part of businesses and consumers.
2. Electric cars create far less pollution than cars powered by the internal combustion engine. In spite of their environmentally friendly nature, it may be quite a few years before there are a lot of electric cars on the road. Why might this be so?
3. Consider the following statement: *It is not worthwhile to provide consumers with detailed information about the content of products or the carbon footprint of various activities because most consumers simply won't use the information. Consumers are struggling to get along financially from day to day, and they don't have the time or inclination to use such information.* Do you agree or disagree with the statement? Explain your reasoning.

CHAPTER SUPPLEMENT 02

Business Law

Law means the set of rules and standards that a society agrees upon to govern the behaviour of its citizens. Both the British and the French influenced the development of law in Canada. In 1867, the British North America (BNA) Act created the nation of Canada. The BNA Act was "patriated" to Canada in 1982 and is now known as the Constitution Act. This act divides legislative powers in Canada between the federal and provincial governments.

LAW The set of rules and standards that a society agrees upon to govern the behaviour of its citizens.

COMMON LAW The unwritten law of England, derived from precedent and legal judgments.

STATUTORY LAW Written law developed by city councils, provincial legislatures, and parliament.

ADMINISTRATIVE LAW The rules and regulations that government agencies and commissions develop based on their interpretations of statutory laws.

BUSINESS LAW Laws that specifically affect how business firms are managed.

CONTRACT An agreement between two parties to act in a specified way or to perform certain acts.

EXPRESS CONTRACT Clearly specifies the terms of an agreement.

IMPLIED CONTRACT Specifies the necessary behaviours of the parties to the contract.

SOURCES OF LAW

The law in Canada has evolved and changed in response to our norms and values. Our laws have arisen from three sources: (1) customs and judicial precedents (the source of common law), (2) the actions of provincial and federal legislatures (the source of statutory law), and (3) rulings by administrative bodies (the source of administrative law).

Common law is the unwritten law of England, derived from ancient precedents and judges' previous legal opinions. Common law is based on the principle of equity, the provision to every person of a just and fair remedy. Canadian legal customs and traditions derive from British common law. All provinces except Quebec, which uses the French Civil Code, have laws based on British common law, and court decisions are often based on precedents from common law. That is, decisions made in earlier cases that involved the same legal point will guide the court.

Statutory law is written law developed by city councils, provincial legislatures, and parliament. Most law in Canada today is statutory law.

Administrative law is the rules and regulations that government agencies and commissions develop based on their interpretations of statutory laws. For example, Consumer and Corporate Affairs Canada develops regulations on false advertising using federal legislation.

THE COURT SYSTEM

In Canada, the judiciary branch of government has the responsibility of settling disputes among organizations or individuals by applying existing laws. Both provincial and federal courts exist to hear both criminal and civil cases. The Supreme Court of Canada is the highest court in Canada. It decides whether to hear appeals from lower courts.

BUSINESS LAW

Business firms, like all other organizations, are affected by the laws of the country. **Business law** refers to laws that specifically affect how business firms are managed. Some laws affect all businesses, regardless of size, industry, or location. For example, the Income Tax Act requires businesses to pay income tax. Other laws may have a greater impact on one industry than on others. For example, pollution regulations are of much greater concern to Vale, a mining corporation, than they are to Carlson Wagonlit Travel.

Business managers should have at least a basic understanding of the following nine important concepts in business law:

1. contracts
2. agency
3. bailment
4. property
5. warranty
6. trademarks, patents, and copyrights
7. torts
8. negotiable instruments
9. bankruptcy

CONTRACTS

Agreements about transactions are common in a business's day-to-day activity. A **contract** is an agreement between two parties to act in a specified way or to perform certain acts. A contract might, for example, apply to a customer buying a product from a retail establishment or to two manufacturers agreeing to buy products or services from each other. A contract may be either **express** or **implied**. An express contract clearly specifies (either orally or in writing) the terms of an agreement. By contrast, an implied contract depends on the two parties' behaviours. For example, if you hire a fishing guide to help you catch fish, you have an implied contract that obligates you to pay the fishing guide for the service you receive.

A valid contract includes several elements:

- an agreement—all parties must consciously agree to the contract.
- consideration—the parties must exchange something of value (e.g., time, products, services, money, and so on).
- competence—all parties to the contract must be legally able to enter into an agreement. Individuals who are below a certain age or who are legally insane, for example, cannot enter into legal agreements.
- legal purpose—what the parties agree to do for or with each other must be legal. An agreement between two manufacturers to fix prices is not legal.

The courts will enforce a contract if it meets the criteria described above. Most parties honour their contracts, but, occasionally, one party does not do what it was supposed to do. **Breach of contract** occurs when one party to an agreement fails, without legal reason, to live up to the agreement's provisions. The party that has not breached the contract has three alternatives under the law in Canada: (1) discharge, (2) sue for damages, or (3) require specific performance.

An example will demonstrate these three alternatives. Suppose that Barrington Farms Inc. agrees to deliver 100 dozen long-stemmed roses to the Blue Violet Flower Shop the week before Mother's Day. One week before the agreed-upon date, Barrington informs Blue Violet that it cannot make the delivery until after Mother's Day. Under the law, the owner of Blue Violet can choose among any of the following actions.

1. *Discharge* Blue Violet can also ignore its obligations in the contract. That is, it can contract with another supplier.
2. *Sue for Damages* Blue Violet can legally demand payment for losses caused by Barrington's failure to deliver the promised goods on time. Losses might include any increased price Blue Violet would have to pay for the roses or court costs incurred in the damage suit.
3. *Require Specific Performance* If monetary damages are not sufficient to reimburse Blue Violet, the court can force Barrington to live up to its original contract.

AGENCY

In many business situations, one person acts as an agent for another person. Well-known examples include actors and athletes represented by agents who negotiate contracts for them. An **agency–principal relationship** is established when one party (the agent) is authorized to act on behalf of another party (the principal).

The agent is under the control of the principal and must act on behalf of the principal and in the principal's best interests. The principal remains liable for the acts of the agent as long as the agent is acting within the scope of authority granted by the principal. A salesperson for IBM, for example, is an agent for IBM, the principal.

BAILMENT

Many business transactions are not covered by the agency–principal relationship. For example, suppose that you take your car to a mechanic to have it repaired. Because the repair shop has temporary possession of something you own, it is responsible for your car. This is a bailor–bailee relationship. In a **bailor–bailee relationship**, the bailor (e.g., the car owner) gives possession of his or her property to the bailee (e.g., the repair shop) but retains ownership of the item. A business firm that stores inventory in a public warehouse is in a bailor–bailee relationship. The business firm is the bailor and the warehouse is the bailee. The warehouse is responsible for storing the goods safely and making them available to the manufacturer upon request.

THE LAW OF PROPERTY

Property includes anything of tangible or intangible value that the owner has the right to possess and use. **Real property** is land and any permanent buildings attached to that land. **Personal property** is tangible or intangible assets other than real property. Personal property includes cars, clothing, furniture, money in bank accounts, stock certificates, and copyrights.

TRANSFERRING PROPERTY

From time to time, businesses and individuals need to transfer property to another person or business. A **deed** is a document that shows ownership of real property. It allows the transfer of title of real property.

A **lease** grants the use of an asset for a specified period of time in return for payment. The business or individual granting the lease is the lessor and the tenant is the lessee. For example, a business (the lessee) may rent space in a mall for one year from a real estate development firm (the lessor).

A **title** shows legal possession of personal property. It allows the transfer of title of personal property. When you buy a snowmobile, for example, the former owner signs the title over to you.

WARRANTY

When you buy a product or service, you want some assurance that it will perform satisfactorily and meet your needs. A **warranty** is a promise that the product or service will perform as the seller has promised it will.

There are two kinds of warranties—express and implied. An **express warranty** is a specific claim that the manufacturer makes about a product. For example, a warranty that a screwdriver blade is made of case-hardened steel is an express warranty. An **implied warranty** suggests that a product will perform as the manufacturer claims it will. Suppose that you buy an outboard motor for your boat and the engine burns out in one week. Because the manufacturer implies by selling the motor that it will work for a reasonable period of time, you can return it and get your money back.

Because opinions vary on what is a "reasonable" time, most manufacturers now give limited-time warranties on their products. For example, they will guarantee their products against defects in materials or manufacture for six months or one year.

TRADEMARKS, PATENTS, AND COPYRIGHTS

Because developing brand names is very expensive, companies do not want others using their brand name and confusing consumers. Many companies therefore apply to the Canadian government and receive a **trademark**, which is the exclusive legal right to use a brand name. Trademarks are granted for 15 years and may be renewed for further periods of 15 years, but only if the company continues to protect its

BREACH OF CONTRACT When one party to an agreement fails, without legal reason, to live up to the agreement's provisions.

AGENCY–PRINCIPAL RELATIONSHIP Established when one party (the agent) is authorized to act on behalf of another party (the principal).

BAILOR–BAILEE RELATIONSHIP In a bailor–bailee relationship, the bailor (the property owner) gives possession of his or her property to the bailee (a custodian) but retains ownership of the item.

PROPERTY Anything of tangible or intangible value that the owner has the right to possess and use.

REAL PROPERTY Land and any permanent buildings attached to that land.

PERSONAL PROPERTY Tangible or intangible assets other than real property.

DEED A document that shows ownership of real property.

LEASE Grants the use of an asset for a specified period of time in return for payment.

TITLE Shows legal possession of personal property.

WARRANTY A promise that the product or service will perform as the seller has promised it will.

EXPRESS WARRANTY A specific claim that the manufacturer makes about a product.

IMPLIED WARRANTY A suggestion that a product will perform as the manufacturer claims it will.

TRADEMARK The exclusive legal right to use a brand name.

brand name. In 2008, a European court ruled that the construction toys made by LEGO could no longer be protected by trademark law. Montreal-based Mega Brands Inc., which makes a competitive product called Mega-Bloks, had challenged LEGO's trademark.[87]

Just what can be trademarked is not always clear. If the company allows the name to lapse into common usage, the courts may take away protection. Common usage occurs when the company fails to use the ® (registered) symbol for its brand. It also occurs if the company fails to correct those who do not acknowledge the brand as a trademark. Windsurfer, a popular brand of sailboards, lost its trademark, and the name can now be used by any sailboard company. The same thing has happened to other names that were formerly brand names—trampoline, yo-yo, thermos, snowmobile, kleenex, and aspirin. But companies like Xerox, Coca-Cola, Jell-O, and Scotch tape have successfully defended their brand names.

A **patent** protects an invention or idea for a period of 20 years. The cost is $1600 to $2500 and it takes 18 months to three years to secure a patent from the Canadian Intellectual Property Office.[88] Patents can be very valuable. In 2006, BlackBerry agreed to pay $612.5 million to NTP Inc., a U.S. firm that claimed BlackBerry was infringing on some patents that NTP held.[89] In 2010, BlackBerry was found not guilty by a judge in the U.K. for a claim by Motorola.[90] In yet another patent dispute, Pfizer Inc. reached an agreement in 2008 with an Indian generic drug maker that kept a cheaper version of the cholesterol-lowering drug Lipitor out of the U.S. market until 2011. Sales revenues of Lipitor are about US$13 billion annually, so this was a very important deal for Pfizer.[91]

Copyrights give exclusive ownership rights to the creators of books, articles, designs, illustrations, photos, films, and music. Computer programs and even semiconductor chips are also protected. Copyrights extend to creators for their entire lives and to their estates for 50 years thereafter. Copyrights apply to the tangible expressions of an idea, not to the idea itself. For example, the idea of cloning dinosaurs from fossil DNA cannot be copyrighted, but Michael Crichton, the author of *Jurassic Park*, could copyright his novel because it is the tangible result of the basic idea.

There is much debate about how copyrights apply to material that appears on the internet. In 2005, the U.S.-based Authors Guild and several publishers sued Google, claiming that its book-scanning project was infringing on their copyrights. In 2008, Google agreed to pay US$125 million to settle the lawsuits. Google can now make available millions of books online.[92] The issue of file sharing is making copyright a big issue these days. New laws and new interpretations of old ones will redefine the role of copyright over the next few years.

TORTS

A **tort** is a wrongful civil act that one party inflicts on another and that results in injury to the person, to the person's property, or to the person's good name. An **intentional tort** is a wrongful act intentionally committed. If a security guard in a department store suspects someone of shoplifting and uses excessive force to prevent him or her from leaving the store, the guard might be guilty of an intentional tort. Other examples are libel, embezzlement, and patent infringement.

Negligence is a wrongful act that inadvertently causes injury to another person. For example, if a maintenance crew in a store mops the floors without placing warning signs in the area, a customer who slips and falls might bring a negligence suit against the store.

In recent years, the most publicized area of negligence has been product liability. **Product liability** means that businesses are liable for injuries caused to product users because of negligence in design or manufacturing. **Strict product liability** means that a business is liable for injuries caused by their products even if there is no evidence of negligence in the design or manufacture of the product.

NEGOTIABLE INSTRUMENTS

Negotiable instruments can be transferred among individuals and business firms. Cheques, bank drafts, and certificates of deposit are examples of negotiable instruments. The Bills of Exchange Act specifies that a negotiable instrument must:

- be written
- be signed by the person who puts it into circulation (the maker or drawer)
- contain an unconditional promise to pay a certain amount of money
- be payable on demand
- be payable to a specific person (or to the bearer of the instrument)

Negotiable instruments are transferred from one party to another through an endorsement. An **endorsement** means signing your name to a negotiable instrument—this makes it transferable to another person or organization. If you sign only your name on the back of a cheque, you are making a blank endorsement. If you state that the instrument is being transferred to a specific person, you are making a special endorsement. A qualified endorsement limits your liability if the instrument is not backed up by sufficient funds. For example, if you get a cheque from a friend and want to use it to buy a new stereo, you can write "without recourse" above your name. If your friend's cheque bounces, you have no liability. A restrictive endorsement limits the negotiability of the instrument. For example, if you write "for deposit only" on the back of a cheque and it is later stolen, no one else can cash it.

BANKRUPTCY

At one time, individuals who could not pay their debts were jailed. Today, however, both organizations and individuals can seek relief by filing for **bankruptcy**, which is the court-granted permission to not pay some or all of their debts.

PATENT Protects an invention or idea for a period of 20 years.

COPYRIGHT Exclusive ownership rights granted to creators for the tangible expression of an idea.

TORT A wrongful civil act that one party inflicts on another and that results in injury to the person, to the person's property, or to the person's good name.

INTENTIONAL TORT A wrongful act intentionally committed.

NEGLIGENCE A wrongful act that inadvertently causes injury to another person.

PRODUCT LIABILITY The liability of businesses for injuries caused to product users because of negligence in design or manufacturing.

STRICT PRODUCT LIABILITY The liability of businesses for injuries caused by their products even if there is no evidence of negligence in the design or manufacture of the product.

NEGOTIABLE INSTRUMENTS Types of commercial paper that can be transferred among individuals and business firms.

ENDORSEMENT Signing your name to a negotiable instrument, making it transferable to another person or organization.

BANKRUPTCY The court-granted permission for organizations or individuals to not pay some or all of their debts.

Thousands of individuals and businesses file for bankruptcy each year. They do so for various reasons, including cash-flow problems, reduced demand for their products, or some other problem that makes it difficult or impossible for them to resolve their financial problems. In recent years, large businesses like Eaton's, Olympia & York, and Enron have sought the protection of bankruptcy laws. Three main factors account for the increase in bankruptcy filings:

1. The increased availability of credit
2. The "fresh-start" provisions in current bankruptcy laws
3. The growing acceptance of bankruptcy as a financial tactic

In Canada, jurisdiction over bankruptcy is provided by the Bankruptcy and Insolvency Act. An **insolvent person (or company)** is defined as one who cannot pay current obligations to creditors as they come due, or whose debts exceed their assets. A **bankrupt person (or company)** is one who has either made a voluntary application to start bankruptcy proceedings (voluntary bankruptcy) or has been forced by creditors into bankruptcy (involuntary bankruptcy) by a process referred to as a receiving order. A person who is insolvent may or may not be bankrupt, and a person who is bankrupt may or may not be insolvent, as there are other bases for bankruptcy under the Act. Another procedure under the Act is referred to as a proposal, which can delay or avoid liquidation by providing the debtor with time to reorganize affairs and/or propose a payment schedule to creditors.

Business bankruptcy under the Act may be resolved or avoided by one of three methods:

1. Under a liquidation plan, the business ceases to exist. Its assets are sold and the proceeds are used to pay creditors.
2. Under a repayment plan, the bankrupt company works out a new payment schedule to meet its obligations. The time frame is usually extended, and payments are collected and distributed by a court-appointed trustee.
3. Reorganization is the most complex form of business bankruptcy. The company must explain the sources of its financial difficulties and propose a new plan for remaining in business. Reorganization may include a new slate of managers and a new financial strategy. A judge may also reduce the firm's debts to ensure its survival. Although creditors naturally dislike debt reduction, they may agree to the proposal, since getting, say, 50 percent of what you are owed is better than getting nothing at all.

THE INTERNATIONAL FRAMEWORK OF BUSINESS LAW

Laws vary from country to country, and many businesses today have international markets, suppliers, and competitors. Managers in such businesses need a basic understanding of the international framework of business law that affects the ways in which they can do business. Issues such as pollution across borders are matters of **international law**—the very general set of co-operative agreements and guidelines established by countries to govern the actions of individuals, businesses, and nations themselves.

International law has several sources. One source is custom and tradition. Among countries that have been trading with one another for centuries, many customs and traditions governing exchanges have gradually evolved into practice. Although some trading practices still follow ancient unwritten agreements, there has been a clear trend in recent years to approach international trade within a formal legal framework. Key features of that framework include a variety of formal trade agreements (see Chapter 5).

Organizations such as the WTO and EU also provide legal frameworks within which participating nations agree to abide.

INSOLVENT PERSON (OR COMPANY) One who cannot pay current obligations to creditors as they come due, or whose debts exceed their assets.

BANKRUPT PERSON (OR COMPANY) One who has either made a voluntary application to start bankruptcy proceedings (voluntary bankruptcy) or has been forced by creditors into bankruptcy (involuntary bankruptcy) by a process referred to as a receiving order.

INTERNATIONAL LAW The very general set of co-operative agreements and guidelines established by countries to govern the actions of individuals, businesses, and nations themselves.

CHAPTER 04

Entrepreneurship, Small Business, and New Venture Creation

LO

AFTER READING THIS CHAPTER, YOU SHOULD BE ABLE TO:

LO-1 Explain the meaning and interrelationship of the terms *small business*, *new venture creation*, and *entrepreneurship*.

LO-2 Describe the role of *small and new businesses* in the Canadian economy.

LO-3 Explain the entrepreneurial process and describe its three key elements.

LO-4 Describe three alternative strategies for becoming a business *owner—starting from scratch, buying an existing business,* and *buying a franchise*.

LO-5 Describe four forms of *legal organization* for a business and discuss the advantages and disadvantages of each.

LO-6 Identify four key *reasons for success* in small businesses and four key *reasons for failure.*

Internet Entrepreneurs: Moving Products Beyond the Rack

© n8n photo/Alamy

Can you name the fastest-growing online retailer in North America? Would you be surprised to find out it is a Canadian company? According to a recent Top 500 list created by *Internet Retailer* magazine, the company to watch is Montreal-based "flash sale" retailer Beyond the Rack. The company was established in 2009 by two ambitious entrepreneurs named Yona Shtern and Robert Gold, along with two full-time employees. By 2013, Beyond the Rack had 400 full-time employees, working in offices in Montreal and New York, while serving over 9 million members from across North America. Beyond the Rack has a working relationship with over 3000 consumer brands and has revenues expected to exceed US$200 million in 2013. Like most successful teams, the two entrepreneurs have complementary skills. Mr. Shtern is the CEO, who spends time taking care of the marketing and merchandising and actively seeks financing, while Mr. Gold is in charge of day-to-day operations.

Business Model

The model was inspired by two highly successful European sites, Gilt and Vente Privee. Beyond the Rack obtains the rights to sell authentic designer brands at major discounted prices (up to 80 percent off retail) exclusively to its members. It is a private shopping club that hosts limited-time, limited-quantity online events. Every day, members can expect up to 15 new events, usually starting at 11 a.m. Eastern Time and lasting 48 hours. Once the event is over, the merchandise is no longer available. The whole model is built on speed. Beyond the Rack does not use a traditional retail approach—it does not buy large quantities of stock, ship it to its warehouse, and hope to sell it. At the prices they are offering, this approach would be unfeasible. Instead, they acquire the rights to sell a specific quantity of discounted products. Once the event is over and the members have committed to purchasing the units, Beyond the Rack orders the physical quantities and then ships them to members around North America. In other words, products do not come to the premises unless member orders are placed. Beyond the Rack has created an efficient win-win-win scenario: (1) customers get designer products at great prices; (2) the designer brands have an efficient way to dispose of excess end-of-season items (from a branding point of view this approach is favourable—it's better to sell to this private club than to have expensive brands sit in cluttered racks in stores like Winners, for example); and (3) Beyond the Rack earns an attractive margin as the facilitator. It's quick, it's efficient, and it's online.

HOW WILL THIS HELP ME?

By understanding the material discussed in this chapter, you'll be better prepared to (1) understand the challenges and opportunities provided in new venture startups, (2) assess the risks and benefits of working in a new business, and (3) evaluate the investment potential inherent in a new business.

Financing

Successful entrepreneurs need more than a good idea; they also require the willingness to take a risk and the energy to work hard, as well as access to financing. If you are opening a small mom-and-pop store, you may need to dip in to your savings or take out a loan to buy equipment and build a storefront. However, when your goals are set high, like becoming the premier online shopping club in North America, you need to be creative and you must convince individuals and organizations to provide major financing to support growth. This is exactly what Yona Shtern and his team have done. Beyond the Rack received US$12 million financing from BDC Venture Capital Inc., a government organization, and Highland Capital Partners LLC, a respected retail investor that has worked with many major organizations including lululemon athletica, MapQuest, and LivePerson. Beyond the Rack raised an additional $4.5 million from Oleg Tscheltzoff and Oliver Jung (two European internet entrepreneurs), Montreal StartUp (a venture fund), and David Chamandy (an "angel investor"). A further round of financing for US$36.6 million was led by Panorama Capital, with additional investments coming from Export Development Canada, Tandem Expansion Fund, Rho Canada, and Inovia Capital. In late 2012, Wellington Financial LP, a privately held specialty finance firm, provided an additional $10 million venture debt financing. According to Beyond the Rack CFO Michael Krebs, "Outside institutional funding is a key element to continued exponential growth." That is how Beyond the Rack generated a membership base of 9 million in four short years.

Growth and Expansion

In 2011, Beyond the Rack acquired selected assets of New York–based BeautyStory.com. This move added to the solid base of members (a key figure for BTR's growth and bargaining power) and strengthened the already successful beauty division. This was yet another important milestone in its brief history. However, as companies grow and structures are put in place, the entrepreneurial spirit of an organization runs the risk of being smothered by bureaucracy. Its trademark creativity, flexibility, and passion will be necessary for Beyond the Rack to sustain its spirit and continue to grow in the dynamic online world. The team at Beyond the Rack is doing everything it can to ensure that employees do not forget the core mission and entrepreneurial spirit of the organization. For example, each month all employees, regardless of their official position, spend some time completing orders in the fulfillment centre. The core message of this approach: "You may be a marketer or an accountant but without these orders and the ultimate satisfaction of the end consumer, there is no business. Never forget who we are."

The Future

Over the next few years, Beyond the Rack will surely experience new challenges and will need to secure additional financing to reach its objectives. Success inevitably brings more competition. For example, Amazon recently launched MyHabit.com to compete with companies like Gilt and Beyond the Rack. What does the future hold for Beyond the Rack? That is unclear. However, the brief history of the firm is a glorious one and the company seems ready for the next challenge. For these internet entrepreneurs, the future, as is the case for more traditional companies, will be based on their ability to satisfy the needs of their brand suppliers and consumers alike, while turning a profit.

QUESTIONS FOR DISCUSSION

1. Entrepreneurs are vital for the success of a free-market economy. Highlight the entrepreneurial process and describe some of the key entrepreneurial characteristics as they relate to this case.
2. Describe some of the major challenges that the entrepreneurs behind Beyond the Rack face.
3. What does this case reveal about the importance of financing a successful growth-oriented start-up business?

SMALL BUSINESS, NEW VENTURE CREATION, AND ENTREPRENEURSHIP

In this chapter we examine old companies with an enduring entrepreneurial spirit (Parasuco), we look at exciting growth-oriented newcomers (Beyond the Rack), and we examine major family organizations that have stood the test of time and a host of small organizations with dreams and aspirations. Each of these examples gives us a glimpse of an important element of the Canadian business landscape. We begin by examining the lifeblood of an economy: small business, entrepreneurship, and new ventures.

One positive result of the most recent recession was a new wave of entrepreneurial efforts. Self-employed Canadians account for 16 percent of the workforce.[1] Every day, approximately 380 businesses are started in Canada.[2] New firms create the most jobs, are noted for their entrepreneurship, and are typically small.[3] But does this mean that most small businesses are entrepreneurial? Not necessarily.

The terms *small business*, *new venture*, and *entrepreneurship* are closely linked terms, but each idea is distinct. In the following paragraphs we will explain these terms to help you understand these topics and how they are interrelated.

LO-1 Small Business

Defining a "small" business can be a bit tricky. Various measures might be used, including the number of people the business employs, the company's sales revenue, the size of the investment required, or the type of ownership structure the business has. Some of the difficulties in defining a small business can be understood by considering the way the Canadian government collects and reports information on small businesses.

Industry Canada is the main federal government agency responsible for small business. In reporting Canadian small-business statistics, the government relies on two distinct sources of information, both provided by Statistics Canada: the *Business Register* (which tracks businesses) and the *Labour Force Survey* (which tracks individuals). To be included in the Register, a business must have at least one paid employee, have annual sales revenues of $30 000 or more, or be incorporated (we describe incorporation later in the chapter). A goods-producing business in the *Register* is considered small if it has fewer than 100 employees, while a service-producing business is considered small if it has fewer than 50 employees. The *Labour Force Survey* uses information from individuals to make estimates of employment and unemployment levels. Individuals are classified as self-employed if they are working owners of a business that is either incorporated or unincorporated, if they work for themselves but do not have a business (some musicians, for example, would fall into this category), or if they work without pay in a family business.[4] In its publication *Key Small Business Statistics* (www.strategis.gc.ca/sbstatistics), Industry Canada reports that there are 2.2 million "business establishments" in Canada and about 2.6 million people who are "self-employed."[5] There is no way of identifying how much overlap there is in these two categories, but we do know that an unincorporated business operated by a self-employed person (with no employees) would not be counted among the 2.2 million businesses in the *Register*. This is an important point because the majority of businesses in Canada have no employees (just the owner), nor are they incorporated.

A study by the Panel Study of Entrepreneurial Dynamics (PSED), conducted by members of the Entrepreneurship Research Consortium (ERC), tracked a sample of Canadian **nascent entrepreneurs**—people who were trying to start a business—over four years. Only 15 percent of those who reported establishing a business had incorporated their firm.[6]

For our purposes, we define a **small business** as an owner-managed business with less than 100 employees. We do so because it enables us to make better use of existing information, and because you are now aware of how definitions can affect our understanding of small businesses. Industry Canada estimates the percentage of small

NASCENT ENTREPRENEURS People who are trying to start a business from scratch.

SMALL BUSINESS An independently owned and managed business that does not dominate its market.

NEW VENTURE A recently formed commercial organization that provides goods and/or services for sale.

ENTREPRENEURSHIP The process of identifying an opportunity in the marketplace and accessing the resources needed to capitalize on it.

ENTREPRENEUR A business person who accepts both the risks and the opportunities involved in creating and operating a new business venture.

business's contribution to Canada's GDP over the past decade at 30 percent annually.[7]

Each year, the Queen's Centre for Business Venturing develops a ranking of the top 50 small- and medium-sized employers to work for in conjunction with Aon Hewitt and *Profit* Magazine. The top 10 firms in the 2013 study are shown in Table 4.1. Each of these companies exhibited superiority in employee recognition, managing performance, career opportunities, and organizational reputation.[8]

The New Venture/Firm

Various criteria can also be used to determine when a new firm comes into existence. Three of the most common are when it was formed, whether it was incorporated, and if it sold goods and/or services.[9] A business is considered to be new if it has become operational within the previous 12 months, if it adopts any of the main organizational forms (proprietorship, partnership, corporation, or co-operative), and if it sells goods or services. Thus, we define a **new venture** as a recently formed commercial organization that provides goods and/or services for sale.

Entrepreneurship

Entrepreneurship is the process of identifying an opportunity in the marketplace and accessing the resources needed to capitalize on it.[11] People start new businesses because they want to control their own destiny and prefer to take a chance rather than looking for a secure job.

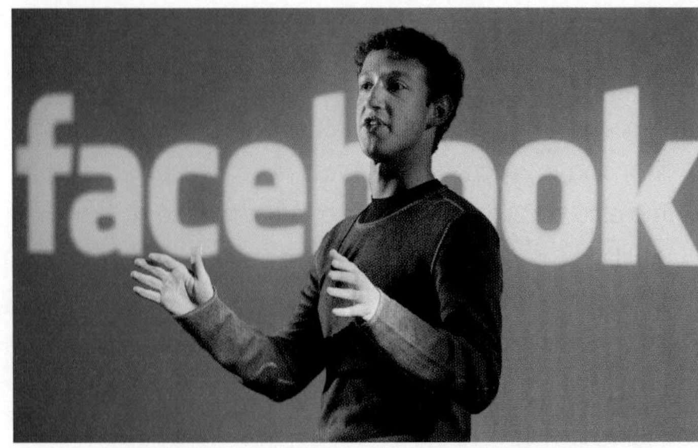

^^ Mark Zuckerberg is the new-age entrepreneur who created Facebook, the wildly successful social networking site.

tacar/Shutterstock

Entrepreneurs are people who recognize and seize these opportunities. For example, Mark Zuckerberg created Facebook, and, in 2013, it had over 1 billion active users. He is one of the richest people in the world under the age of 30. Zuckerberg worked long hours, and he is constantly tailoring the website to suit its expanding audience.[12]

In another example, Rahumathulla Marikkar transformed disappointment into a new business venture when he lost his job as Head of Technology and Environment of Interface Inc., the world's largest modular carpet manufacturer. At a time when manufacturing jobs were disappearing in large volumes, Mr. Marikkar decided to use his knowledge and experience to create Belletile, a Canadian manufacturer. His company is successfully fighting the threat from offshore manufacturing by focusing on high-end niche products that low-cost producers in Asia are unable to produce.[13]

Each year, the Heritage Foundation publishes an index of economic freedom, which assesses the extent to which entrepreneurs have freedom to pursue new business opportunities. In 2013, the top three countries were Hong Kong, Singapore, and Australia, with freedom scores

>>> **TABLE 4.1** Top Small and Medium-Sized Employers in Canada, 2013[10]

	Company	Industry	Location
1.	D.L.G.L. Ltd.	Human Resources Software	Blainville, Quebec
2.	Arrow Professional Services Ltd.	Staffing and Human Resources Services	Toronto, Ontario
3.	Habanero Consulting Group	Information-Technology Consulting	Vancouver, British Columbia
4.	DevFacto Technologies Inc.	Information-Technology Consulting	Edmonton, Alberta
5.	Protegra Inc.	Business-Performance Consulting and Software Development	Winnipeg, Manitoba
6.	iGate Global Solutions Ltd.	Consulting, Information-Technology and Business Process Outsourcing Services	Toronto, Ontario
7.	Cybertech Automation Inc. and i-Gen Solutions Inc.	Engineering and Industrial Information-Technology Services	Edmonton, Alberta
8.	OACIQ	Real Estate	Brossard, Quebec
9.	ISL Engineering and Land Services Ltd.	Engineering Consulting	Edmonton, Alberta
10.	Intelex Technologies Inc.	Software for Environment, Health, Safety and Quality	Toronto, Ontario

INTRAPRENEURS People who create something new within an existing large firm or organization.

of 89.3, 88.0, and 82.6 respectively. Canada ranked sixth with a score of 79.6 and North Korea ranked last with a score of 1.5. Canada now ranks higher than the U.S., partly due to the U.S. government's stimulus spending, which the foundation believes will hurt the U.S. economy's long-term prospects.[14]

Small businesses often provide an environment to use personal attributes—such as creativity—that have come to be associated with entrepreneurs.[15] Because starting a business involves dealing with a great deal of uncertainty, ambiguity, and unpredictability, every new venture founder needs to exercise some of the personal attributes that entrepreneurs are noted for. But do not assume that only small-business owners exhibit entrepreneurial characteristics.[16] Many successful managers in large organizations in both the public and private sectors also exhibit similar characteristics. Entrepreneurship therefore occurs in a wide range of contexts—not just in small or new commercial firms, but also in old firms, in large firms, in firms that grow slowly, in firms that grow rapidly, in non-profit organizations, and in the public sector.[17]

People who exhibit entrepreneurial characteristics and create something new within an existing firm or organization are called **intrapreneurs**. One large firm renowned for encouraging intrapreneurship is Procter & Gamble. It has earned this reputation by having divisions that focus on creating new products for specific markets.[18] The Swiffer product line is one example. Once the basic Swiffer mop was launched successfully, a whole range of products was added, such as the Swiffer WetJet and Swiffer Dusters. A key difference between intrapreneurs and entrepreneurs is that intrapreneurs typically don't have to concern themselves with getting the resources needed to bring the new product to market, since big companies tend to have the necessary resources already available.

As we explore the entrepreneurial process later in the chapter, we will do so within a new-venture context. We begin by outlining the role of small and new businesses in the Canadian economy.

LO-2 THE ROLE OF SMALL AND NEW BUSINESSES IN THE CANADIAN ECONOMY

As we will see in this section, small and new businesses play a key role in the Canadian economy. However, the recognition of this role has really only been acknowledged in the last two decades. Previously, large businesses were the focus of attention in terms of economic impact within industrialized nations.

Small Businesses

It may surprise you to learn that 98.1 percent of all businesses in Canada are small (they have fewer than 100 employees), and more than half of them have fewer than 5 employees. Medium-sized businesses (100–499 employees) comprise 1.7 percent of employer businesses, and large businesses (those with 500 or more employees) represent just 0.2 percent.[19] This pattern is consistent across all provinces. While one large business has many more employees than one small business, as a group, small businesses provide more jobs than large businesses. Small businesses also lead the way when it comes to innovation and new technology and they account for 30 percent of Canadian GDP.

Ontario and Quebec together account for the largest proportion of business establishments in Canada (about 58 percent), followed by the western provinces (37 percent) and the Atlantic provinces (5 percent). Northwest Territories, Yukon, and Nunavut represent just 0.3 percent of Canada's businesses.[20]

While the previous figures profile the number of businesses in Canada by size, we now look at how many people work in small- versus medium- and large-sized businesses. According to Statistics Canada, there were 11 248 400 **private-sector** (companies and organizations not owned or controlled by government) employees in 2013.[21]

PRIVATE-SECTOR The part of the economy that is made up of companies and organizations that are not owned or controlled by the government.

The distribution of employment by size of firm varies considerably across industries. Small businesses account for over two-thirds of employment in five industries: non-institutional health care (88 percent), forestry (77 percent), other services (75 percent), the construction industry (73 percent), and accommodation and food (66 percent).[22]

New Ventures

New firms are not only the main source of job creation, but they are also responsible for the vast majority of new products and services. From 2001 to 2011, small businesses created 43 percent of all the jobs in Canada.[23] Taking into account the businesses that closed during the same time period, there were approximately 9000 companies added each year.[24]

Women are playing a more prominent role than ever before in starting new ventures (see Figure 4.1). More and more women are starting and successfully operating their own small businesses, and women now account for half of all new businesses that are formed. But on a negative note, women lead only 12 percent of the small- and medium-sized businesses that export goods and services.[25]

Female entrepreneurs are honoured each year at the Canadian Woman Entrepreneur Awards. Previous winners included Emily (Shi Yu) Zhang (Vancouver-based Willowest-Hospitality Furnishings), Cora Tsouflidou (Montreal-based Cora Franchise Group), Cathy Buckingham (Barrie, Ontario-based TNR Industrial Doors), and Yvonne Tollens (Okotoks, Alberta-based Computer Aid Professional Services).[26]

Women who run businesses from their homes are sometimes called "mompreneurs."[27] The Mompreneur Networking Group organizes seminars and publishes *Mompreneur*, a free magazine that helps women who want to start a business.

Many young entrepreneurs are also involved in creating new ventures in Canada. Consider the following examples:

- Zane Kelsall was the grand prize winner of the BDC Young Entrepreneurs Award in 2012 for his Two If by Sea Café concept in Halifax, Nova Scotia. The $100 000 grand prize has helped this

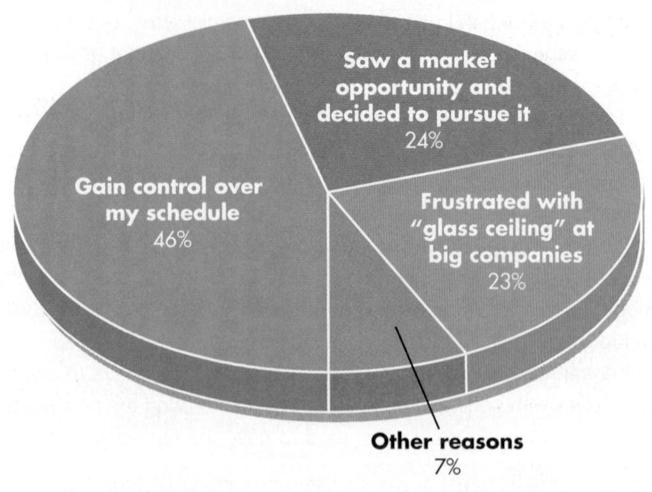

FIGURE 4.1 Reasons women give for starting their own businesses

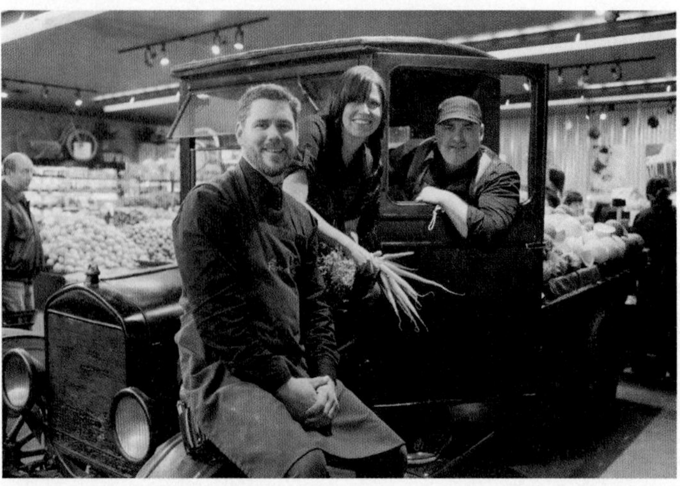

The Root Cellar Village Green Grocer is capitalizing on the movement for fresh local produce and healthier lifestyles.

PETER PARKS/AFP/Getty Images

entrepreneur get a great head start and build a brand name through the exposure and new contacts with marketing specialists at the BDC.

- Rachel Mielke, from Regina, Saskatchewan, transformed her Hillberg & Burk designer jewellery brand from a high-school hobby into a successful business. She makes her hand-made jewellery out of sterling silver, semi-precious stones, and Swarovski crystals. Her designs have ended up in the Academy Award gift bags and her company was featured on *Dragon's Den*.[28]
- Daisy and Adam Orser were previous winners of the award for their Victoria, B.C.–based company called The Root Cellar Village Green Grocer. They are capitalizing on the movement for fresh local produce and healthier lifestyles. The company already employs 50 people and the future looks bright.[29]

LO-3 THE ENTREPRENEURIAL PROCESS

The entrepreneurial process is like a journey (see Figure 4.2). It is influenced by the social, economic, political, and technological factors in the broader environment, but we will focus our attention on understanding the three key elements in the entrepreneurial process—the entrepreneur, the opportunity, and resources—and how they interact. As these key elements interact, they may be mismatched or well matched. For example,

FIGURE 4.2 The entrepreneurial process in a new venture context

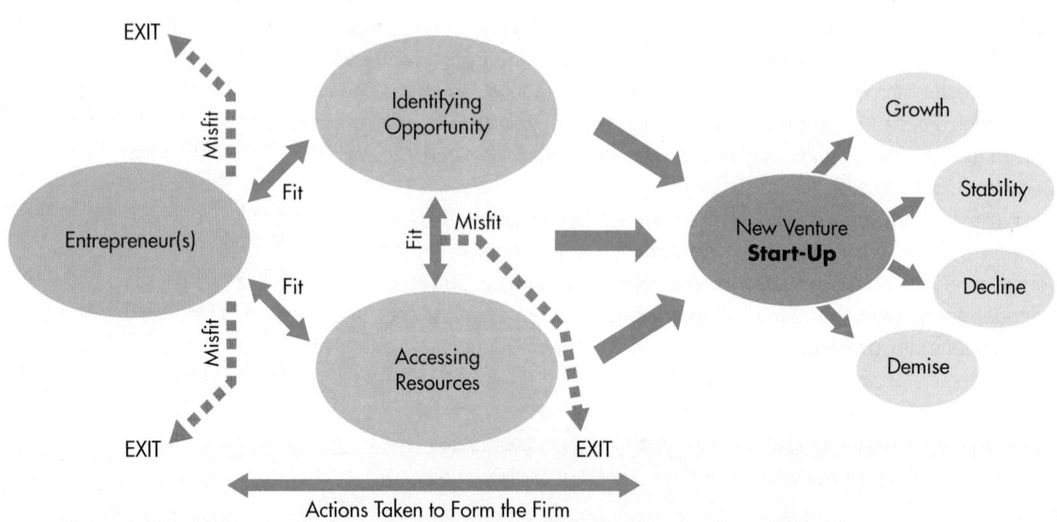

if an entrepreneur identifies an opportunity for a new health service but does not have the relevant background and skills to deliver the service, the business may never get off the ground. However, if all the elements are well matched, the new business will likely become operational at some point.

Since the entrepreneur is at the heart of the entrepreneurial process, considerable attention has been paid to identifying the personal characteristics of entrepreneurs. Research shows that these characteristics are wide-ranging. Some are behavioural (e.g., taking initiative), others are personality traits (e.g., independence), and still others are skills (e.g., problem-solving).[30] Some people think that entrepreneurs are rare, but entrepreneurial characteristics have been found to be widely distributed in the population.[31] We also know that personal characteristics often have less impact on a person's action than the situation a person is in.[32] What is really important is not who the person is but what the person does.[33] Entrepreneurs must (1) identify an opportunity and (2) access resources.

Identifying Opportunities

Identifying opportunities involves generating ideas for new (or improved) products, processes, or services, screening those ideas, and developing the best ones.

IDEA GENERATION

Typically, generating ideas involves abandoning traditional assumptions about how things work and how they ought to be, and seeing what others do not. If the prospective new (or improved) product, process, or service can be profitably produced and is attractive relative to other potential venture ideas, it might present an opportunity. For example, Kevin Systrom developed an app to allow people to virtually check-in at locations visited and broadcast that to a person's social network. The idea eventually changed and evolved into a photo-sharing service, and Kevin's ability to pivot and evolve led to the creation of Instagram, which he sold to Facebook for $1 billion.[34] For another interesting example of success in this modern age, take another look at the E-Business and Social Media Solutions Box entitled *Who Wants To Be a Teen Millionaire*?

Where do ideas come from? Most new ventures do not emerge from a deliberate search for viable business ideas. Rather, the majority originate from events relating to work or everyday life.[35] In fact, work experience is the most common source of ideas, accounting for 45 to 85 percent of those generated. This happens because as employees of a company, prospective entrepreneurs are familiar with the product or service, the customers, the suppliers, and the competitors. They are also aware of marketplace needs, can relate those needs to personal capabilities, and can determine whether they are capable of producing products or services that can fill the void.

E-BUSINESS AND SOCIAL MEDIA SOLUTIONS

Who Wants To Be a Teen Millionaire?

At just 17 years of age, Nick D'Aloisio was living the modern-day entrepreneurial dream. He had identified an opportunity in the mobile app world and turned it into a multi-million dollar payday from Yahoo. The acquisition of Nick's company fit a deliberate strategy at Yahoo. In the past couple of years, Yahoo had purchased a series of small companies in emerging business categories. According to CEO Marissa Meyer, the transactions were helping Yahoo attract more engineers with expertise in creating services for the valuable smartphone and tablet platforms.

Mr. D'Aloisio appeared to have been bitten by the entrepreneurial bug quite early in his life. He started his company at just 15 years of age, creating several apps, with Summly as his biggest hit (before his 18th birthday, anyway). The app uses complex algorithms to compile and simplify news articles for easy viewing on a smartphone. In other words, it is an easy way to get news on the go. From the publishers' perspective, it can drive traffic to content for a new generation of people who are on the go and don't necessarily have traditional subscriptions. Before Yahoo approached Nick, Summly had already been downloaded more than 750 000 times. Clearly, Summly had gained acceptance in a very crowded competitive environment. Just like a small retailer or a manufacturer of goods, the consumer is the one who decides if your offer is worthwhile. In this case, they vote with downloads, not necessarily dollars. But Yahoo identified potential for a long-term revenue-generating model from this app. According to Adam Cahan, a senior vice-president at Yahoo, after the purchase, Summly was taken down while Nick D'Aloisio and a small team integrated the features into existing Yahoo products.

In a clear sign of the times and his age, Nick talked about what a great honour it is to work for a classic internet company. You see, Nick is younger than Yahoo. He may be young, but he clearly sees himself as more than a one-trick wonder. He planned to invest his money wisely, but also talked about an interest in becoming an angel investor at some point. Nick had already earned more than just programming experience. A year before the Yahoo payday, he convinced some big-time investors to support his company; Nick had raised $1.5 million in funding from Zynga's CEO Mark Pincus and a Hong Kong–based businessman. Entrepreneurs must identify opportunities and seize them. Clearly, Nick D'Aloisio had proven he could do just that.

Nick was also quick to point out that his parents were a strong driving force behind his success by encouraging his entrepreneurial passion and supporting his dreams. However, as he approached the important age of 18, he had commitments to Yahoo, but he also had some long-term decisions to make. Should he become an intrapreneur (working within the confines of Yahoo or another company) or should he take advantage of this experience to eventually continue on his path as an independent internet entrepreneur? Only time will tell. But at 17, when most people his age are looking for internships, Nick D'Aloisio had earned some very interesting options.

CRITICAL THINKING QUESTION

1. If you were in Nick's shoes what would you do? Would you be satisfied working with a great internet organization like Yahoo in the long term or would you eventually take the money and go off on your own? Do you consider yourself an entrepreneur at heart?

Stanley Ma (right) is the king of the food court. This entrepreneur owns and operates over 1900 restaurants across the nation.

Photo by Steve Russell/Toronto Star via Getty Images

We have discussed a few technology-based, e-business success stories, but the industry selected is irrelevant. Pure entrepreneurs share a passion and commitment to their businesses. For example, you probably don't know who Stanley Ma is, but chances are you eat at one of his 1900 restaurants across the nation. He is the king of the food court and beyond, operating under 20 brands such as Mr. Sub, Thai Express, Country Style, Jugo Juice, KimChi, Tiki-Ming, Cultures, and Vieux Duluth. His company, MTY, actually owns seven of those 20 brands.[36]

Other frequent sources of new venture ideas include a personal interest/hobby (16 percent) or a chance happening (11 percent).[37] A chance happening refers to a situation in which a venture idea comes about unexpectedly. For example, while on vacation in another country you might try a new snack food that you feel would be in demand if introduced to the Canadian market.

SCREENING

Entrepreneurs often generate many ideas, and screening them is a key part of the entrepreneurial process. The faster you can weed out the "dead-end" venture ideas, the more time and effort you can devote to the ones that remain. The more of the following characteristics that an idea has, the greater the opportunity it presents.

The Idea Creates or Adds Value for the Customer

A product or service that creates or adds value for the customer is one that solves a significant problem or meets a significant need in new or different ways. Consider Polar Mobile, a Toronto-based developer of mobile applications that has made great strides since launching a few years ago. Polar provides a software platform called MediaEverywhere™ that makes it easy for media companies to launch apps for all types of smartphones and tablet devices. The company must be doing something right because major companies are finding value in this relatively new company. In 2013, just six years since it was established, Polar had over 400 customers in 12 countries and powered over 1200 mobile apps with its platform. Its clients include Nokia, BlackBerry, Microsoft, and Dubai-based Emitec Mobile. It seems like Polar has clearly shown the capacity to add value based on this impressive list of partners.[38]

The Idea Provides a Competitive Advantage That Can Be Sustained A competitive advantage exists when potential customers see the product or service as better than that of competitors. Toronto-based Sentinelle Medical is counting on a clear advantage. Cameron Piron spent 10 years developing a better cancer detection technology and another two years getting General Electric to use it in its MRI machines. He recently received the Ontario Government Innovation Award.[39] Sustaining a competitive advantage involves maintaining it in the face of competitors' actions or changes in the industry. All other things being equal, the longer markets are in a state of flux, the greater the likelihood of being able to sustain a competitive advantage. The inability to develop a competitive advantage is a common fatal flaw in many new ventures.[40]

The Idea Is Marketable and Financially Viable While it is important to determine whether there are enough customers who are willing to buy the product or service, it is also important to determine whether sales will lead to profits.[41] Estimating the market demand requires an initial understanding of who the customers are, what their needs are, and how the product or service will satisfy their needs better than competitors' products will. Customers define the competition in terms of who can satisfy their needs best. However, success also requires a thorough understanding of the key competitors who can provide similar products, services, or benefits to the target customer. For example, despite some home-grown success, Vancouver-based ProSnack Natural Foods, a provider of energy bars with organic ingredients, is having difficulty accessing large retailers like MEC that would take them to the next level of sales. The problem is that the market is oversaturated, with more than 50 brands of energy bars lining the shelves of MEC; unfortunately, ProSnack is not one of them.[42]

After learning about the competition and customers, the entrepreneur must prepare a **sales forecast**, which is an estimate of how much of a product or service will be purchased by the prospective customers for a specific period of time—typically one year. Total sales revenue is estimated by multiplying the units expected to be sold by the selling price. The sales forecast forms the foundation for determining the financial viability of the venture and the resources needed to start it.

Determining financial viability involves preparing financial forecasts, two- to three-year projections of a venture's future financial position and performance. They typically consist of an estimate of start-up costs, a cash budget, an income statement, and a balance sheet (see Chapter 11 for more details about these financial documents). These projections serve as the basis for decisions regarding whether to proceed with the venture, and, if so, the amount and type of financing to be used in financing the new business.

The Idea Has Low Exit Costs The final consideration is the venture's exit costs. Exit costs are low if a venture can be shut down without a significant loss of time, money, or reputation.[43] If a venture is not expected to make a profit for a number of years, its exit costs are high, since the project cannot be reasonably abandoned in the short term. For example, Toronto-based zero-emission car manufacturer Zenn Motors has very-long-term projections. On the other hand, if the venture is expected to make a profit quickly, its exit costs will be lower, making the idea more attractive.

SALES FORECAST An estimate of how much of a product or service will be purchased by prospective customers over a specific period.

FRANCHISE An arrangement that gives franchisees (buyers) the right to sell the product of the franchiser (the seller).

BUSINESS PLAN Document in which the entrepreneur summarizes her or his business strategy for the proposed new venture and how that strategy will be implemented.

DEVELOPING THE OPPORTUNITY

As the "dead-end" venture ideas are weeded out, a clear notion of the business concept and an entry strategy for pursuing it must be developed. The business concept often changes from the original plan. Some new ventures develop entirely new markets, products, and sources of competitive advantage once the needs of the marketplace and the economies of the business are understood. So, while a vision of what is to be achieved is important, it is equally important to incorporate new information and to be on the lookout for unanticipated opportunities. For example, if customers are not placing orders, it is important to find out why and make adjustments.

New ventures use one or more of three main entry strategies: they introduce a totally new product or service, they introduce a product or service that will compete directly with existing competitive offerings but adds a new twist (customization of the standard product), or they franchise.[44] A **franchise** is an arrangement in which a buyer (franchisee) purchases the right to sell the product or service of the seller (franchiser). We discuss franchising in more detail later in the chapter.

When capital requirements are high, such as when a manufacturing operation is being proposed, there is a need for considerable research and planning. Similarly, if product development or operations are fairly complex, research and analysis will be needed to ensure that the costs associated with effectively coordinating tasks will be minimized. In these circumstances, or when the aim is to attract potential investors, a comprehensive written business plan is required. A **business plan** is a document that describes the entrepreneur's proposed business venture, explains why it is an opportunity, and outlines its marketing plan, its operational and financial details, and its managers' skills and abilities.[45] The contents of a business plan are shown in Table 4.2.

If market conditions are changing rapidly, the benefits gained from extensive research and planning diminish quickly. By the time the entrepreneur is ready, new competitors may have entered the market, prices may have changed, a location may no longer be available, and so on. Similarly, if the product is highly innovative, market research is of less value, since the development of entirely new products involves creating needs and wants rather than simply responding to existing needs.

Contrary to what many people think, planning does not have to be completed before action is taken. For example, if an electrical contracting business is being proposed in an area where there is a shortage of

TABLE 4.2 A Business Plan

A well-written business plan is formally structured, easy to read, and avoids confusion. Organizing the information into sections makes it more manageable. The amount of detail and the order of presentation may vary from one venture to another and according to the intended audience (if the plan is intended for potential investors it will require more detail than if it is intended for internal use by the entrepreneur). An outline for a standard business plan is provided below.

I.	**Cover Page:** Name of venture and owners, date prepared, contact person, his/her address, telephone and fax numbers, email address, Facebook link, and the name of the organization the plan is being presented to. The easier it is for the reader to contact the entrepreneur, the more likely the contact will occur.
II.	**Executive Summary:** A one- to three-page overview of the total business plan. Written after the other sections are completed, it highlights their significant points and aims to create enough excitement to motivate the reader to continue.
III.	**Table of Contents:** This element lists major sections with page numbers for both the body and the appendices of the plan.
IV.	**Company Description:** Identifies the type of company: manufacturing, retail, etc. It also describes the proposed form of organization: sole proprietorship, partnership, corporation, or co-operative. A typical organization of this section is as follows: name and location, company objectives, nature and primary product or service of the business, current status (start-up, buyout, or expansion) and history, if applicable, and legal form of organization.
V.	**Product or Service Description:** Describes the product or service and indicates what is unique about it. This section explains the value that is added for customers—why people will buy the product or service, features of the product or service providing a competitive advantage, legal protection (patents, copyrights, trademarks, if relevant), and dangers of technical or style obsolescence.
VI.	**Marketing:** This section has two key parts, the market analysis and the marketing plan. The market analysis convinces the reader that the entrepreneur understands the market for the product or service and can deal effectively with the competition to achieve sales projections. The marketing plan explains the strategy for achieving sales projections.
VII.	**Operating Plan:** Explains the type of manufacturing or operating system to be used. Describes the facilities, labour, raw materials, and processing requirements.
VIII.	**Management:** Identifies the key players—the management team, active investors, and directors—and cites the experience and competence they possess. This section includes a description of the management team, outside investors and directors and their qualifications, outside resource people, and plans for recruiting and training employees.
IX.	**Financial Plan:** Specifies financial needs and expected financing sources. Presents projected financial statements, including cash budget, balance sheet, and income statement.
X.	**Supporting Details/Appendix:** Provides supplementary materials to the plan such as résumés and other supporting data.

BOOTSTRAPPING Doing more with less.

COLLATERAL Assets that a borrower uses to secure a loan or other credit, and that are subject to seizure by the lender if the loan isn't repaid according to the specified repayment terms.

tradespeople, it would be important to seek out qualified employees prior to conducting other analyses that are needed to complete the business plan. Such early action also helps to build relationships that can be drawn on later. Obviously, some ventures do not lend themselves to early action, particularly those that are capital intensive. Since most entrepreneurs have limited resources, it is important to concentrate on the issues that can be dealt with, and that will help determine whether to proceed and how to proceed.[46]

Accessing Resources

Typically, entrepreneurs acquire the various resources needed to make the venture a reality by **bootstrapping**, which means "doing more with less." Usually the term refers to financing techniques whereby entrepreneurs make do with less and use other people's resources wherever they can. However, bootstrapping can also refer to the acquisition of other types of resources, such as people, space, equipment, or materials that are loaned or provided free by customers or suppliers.

FINANCIAL RESOURCES

There are two main types of financing—debt and equity (see Chapter 15). Since a business is at its riskiest point during the start-up phase, equity is usually more appropriate and accessible than debt. However, most new venture founders prefer debt because they are reluctant to give up any control to outsiders. To obtain debt financing, the entrepreneur must have an adequate equity investment in the business—typically 20 percent of the business's value—and collateral (or security).

Collateral refers to items (assets) owned by the business (such as a building and equipment) or by the individual (such as a house or car) that the borrower uses to secure a loan or other credit. These items can be seized by the lender if the loan isn't repaid according to the specified terms. To lenders, equity investment demonstrates the commitment of the entrepreneur, as individuals tend to be more committed to a venture if they have a substantial portion of what they own invested in it.

The most common sources of equity financing include:

1. *Personal savings.* New venture founders draw heavily on their own finances to start their businesses. Most save as much as they can in preparation for start-up.
2. *Love money.* This type of financing includes investments from friends, relatives, and business associates. It is called "love money" because it is often given more on the basis of the relationship than on the merit of the business concept.
3. *Private investors.* One popular source of equity is informal capital from private investors called *angels*. Usually, these investors are financially well-off individuals; many are successful entrepreneurs. For example, Gerry Pond provided financial support to Chris Newton in developing Radian6 and Q1 Labs. After a couple of years, the spectacular sale of these two firms accounted for over a billion dollars and created 50 millionaires in New Brunswick. For his contribution Mr. Pond was named Canadian Angel Investor of the Year in 2012. New Brunswick seems to be a hotbed of angel investing because this award was then granted to Dan Martell, a fellow New Brunswick resident, in 2013 for his financial support of 18 start-ups.[47]

ENTREPRENEURSHIP AND NEW VENTURES

Building a Business, Planning a Better Meal

Want to eat better at home, while saving time and money, too? Many people are doing exactly that, using Erika Vitiene's newly launched online meal-planning venture, *GroceryDash*. Vitiene has used her personal shopping experience, together with carefully developed meal-planning steps, to design the *grocerydash.com* website where subscribers get help for their at-home dinner planning.

Ms. Vitiene's motivation is to save overburdened moms the time and money ordinarily spent on planning meals—deciding on menus, exploring grocery aisles to compare prices, and staying within budget—and meal preparation. Every family's meal planner, eventually, feels the challenge of finding new and different dishes, instead of serving "the same old thing, week after week." Although new meal ideas provide greater variety, they also require more time searching for and using different recipes and buying new ingredients at the right price.

While the website doesn't use formal terms such as "methods improvement" and "process flowchart," its contents nevertheless reflect Erika's natural understanding of the steps for improving the "meal planning" process. It identifies the meal planner (the user who will gain better meal planning) and the planner's objectives (good meals at lower cost and time savings), and provides information resources such as ready-made menus, lists of ingredients, and local stores currently offering the ingredients at reduced prices. Menus for seven dinners are displayed weekly, along with their recipes, lists of ingredients, and an aisle-by-aisle shopping list, all arranged around the seasonal price specials at grocery stores. The menus are based on the food pyramid for better nutrition, and recipes minimize the use of processed ingredients. Subscribers can download additional free resources—printable grocery lists, a freezer guide showing how long food will keep (and a list of foods that do not freeze well), and a pantry checklist for an up-to-date inventory of foods on hand at home.

Erika used her system a long time, and proved its effectiveness to herself—saving 25 to 50 percent on her grocery bill—before presenting it online. Although originally intended for moms, and with a subscription price at $4.95 per month, *grocerydash.com* can also become a valued resource to singles, students, and others whose busy schedules and tight budgets can benefit from nutritious ready-planned meals at lower cost, instead of just fast foods. However, in order to succeed in the long-term, she must continue to find ways to generate traffic and ultimately profits.

CRITICAL THINKING QUESTION

1. Do you believe that Erika has created a site with a sustainable business model? What factors will determine her success? What suggestions do you have?

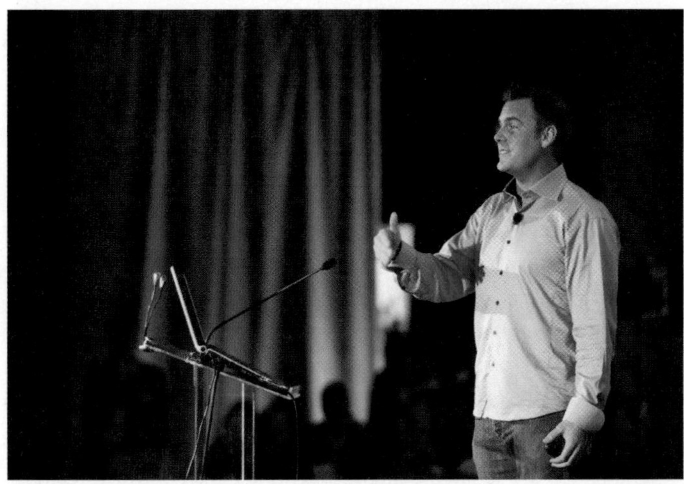

New Brunswick appears to be a hotbed of angel investing as Dan Martell won the award in 2013 for his support of 18 start-ups one year after Gerry Pond won the same award.

© STANCA SANDA/Alamy

4. *Venture capitalists.* Investments by venture capitalists come from professionally managed pools of investor money (venture capital). Since the risk of receiving little or no return on investment is high, only deals that present an attractive, high-growth business opportunity with a return between 35 and 50 percent are considered. Very few new ventures meet this criterion. Venture capital investment in Canada dropped to $1.5 billion in 2012—the levels of VC financing have been reduced in recent years—so angels are becoming more important in providing start-up money to entrepreneurs.[48] The Canadian government recently reduced red-tape hurdles for foreign venture capital firms to invest in Canada. This is good news for firms looking at the venture capital route.[49]

The most common sources of debt financing include:

1. *Financial institutions.* While commercial banks are the main providers of debt financing for established small businesses, it is usually hard for a new business to get a loan. Banks are risk averse and new businesses are considered very risky. Typically, entrepreneurs have more luck obtaining financing for a new venture with a personal loan (as opposed to a business loan). The most common way to obtain a personal loan is to mortgage a house or borrow against the cash value of a life insurance policy. In addition to commercial banks, other sources of debt financing include trust companies, co-operatives, finance companies, equipment companies, credit unions, and government agencies.
2. *Suppliers.* Another source of financing is suppliers who provide goods (i.e., inventory) or services to the entrepreneur with an agreement to bill them later. This is referred to as trade credit. Trade credit can be helpful in getting started, because inventory can be acquired without paying cash, freeing up money to pay other start-up costs. This type of financing is short term; 30 days is the usual payback period. The amount of trade credit available to a new firm depends on the type of business and the supplier's confidence in the firm. Frequently, though, a new business has trouble getting trade credit since its capacity to repay has not been demonstrated.

Besides these conventional sources of financing, the possibilities for bootstrap financing are endless. For example, an entrepreneur might require an advance payment from customers. Equipment can be leased rather than purchased (which reduces the risk of obsolete equipment). Office furniture can be rented, premises can be shared, and manufacturing can be subcontracted, thereby avoiding the expense of procuring material, equipment, and facilities. All of these activities free up cash that can then be used for other purposes. The need for cost reduction services is clear; Regus PLC, a temporary rental space company, based out of Dallas, has opened 30 office centres in Canada in the last decade. It has locations in Calgary, Montreal, Toronto, and Vancouver and is opening new locations in Fort McMurray, Halifax, Barrie, and London.[50]

OTHER RESOURCES

Businesses have other resources to help them with financing, legal, marketing, or operational advice or support. The federal and provincial governments have a wide range of financial assistance programs for small businesses. Among the various forms of assistance are low-interest loans, loan guarantees, interest-free loans, and wage subsidies. We examine three sources of information and assistance below: Business Development Bank of Canada, business incubators, and the internet.

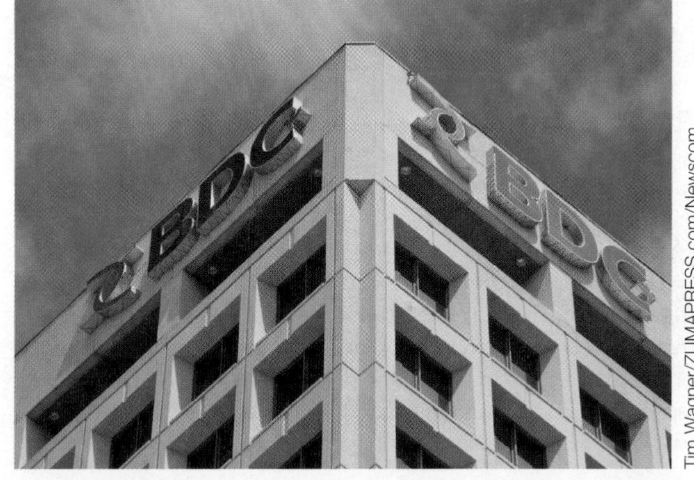

Tim Wagner/ZUMAPRESS.com/Newscom

THERE'S AN APP FOR THAT!

1. **Boss Yourself** >>> **Platforms:** *Apple, Android*
   Source: The Province of British Columbia
   Key Features: Explores the skills you need to start your own business and become a successful and savvy boss.
2. **BDC** >>> **Platforms:** *Apple*
   Source: TechSolComm
   Key Features: The Business Development Bank of Canada's app designed for entrepreneurs.
3. **Equity Terms** >>> **Platforms:** *Apple, BlackBerry*
   Source: Winjit
   Key Features: A practical guide to Venture Capital and Private Equity industry terms.

APP DISCOVERY EXERCISE

Since APP availability changes, conduct your own search for "Top 3" Entrepreneurship, New Venture, and Small Business APPS and identify the key features.

INCUBATORS Facilities that support small businesses during their early growth phase by providing basic services, office space, legal advice, and more.

Business Development Bank of Canada The Business Development Bank of Canada (BDC) has a mandate to help develop Canadian businesses, with a particular focus on small- and medium-sized companies. It provides financing, venture capital, and consulting strategies. The BDC provides services to over 29 000 businesses from coast to coast and serves them through over 100 branch offices. The BDC is a financial institution wholly owned by the Government of Canada. Information can be found at www.bdc.ca or by calling 1-877-BDC-Banx.[51]

Incubators Business **incubators** provide new businesses (newborns) with support to help nurture them into a successful future. The type of support varies, but some key forms of assistance include consulting services, legal advice, accounting services, business contacts, clerical services, and office space. According to the Canadian Association of Business Incubation (CABI), business survival rates are greatly improved by getting involved with an incubator. Survival rates after five years stand at about 80 percent, which is far above the average rates for businesses that don't use incubators. You can learn more by visiting www.cabi.ca. Take a look at Table 4.3 for examples of incubators across the country.

The Internet There are countless resources available online that can help budding entrepreneurs gather research information, write a business plan, and access government grants. The banks all have major sites dedicated to small-business and entrepreneurship resources. For example, Royal Bank of Canada (RBC) has a great site that provides checklists, business plan formats and samples, and advice on selecting business structures and more (www.rbcroyalbank.com/sme/index.html). There are also government sites such as the Canada Business Services for Entrepreneurs dedicated to providing information and advice on every aspect of starting a business, including accessing government grants (www.canadabusiness.ca/eng/).

Building the Right Team

A business may be owned by one person, but entrepreneurship is not a solo process. There are various stakeholders who can provide resources to the venture. When ownership is shared, decisions must be made regarding how much each stakeholder will own, at what cost, and under what conditions. The form of legal organization chosen affects whether ownership can be shared and whether resources can be accessed.

Deciding whether to share ownership by forming a venture team involves consideration of two main issues:

- *the size and scope of the venture*—How many people does the venture require? Can people be hired to fill the key roles as they are required?
- *personal competencies*—What are the talents, know-how, skills, track record, contacts, and resources that the entrepreneur brings to the venture? How do they match with what the venture needs to succeed?

The nature of the team depends upon the match between the lead entrepreneur and the opportunity and how quickly and aggressively he or she plans to proceed. Most teams tend to be formed in one of two ways: (1) one person has an idea (or wants to start a business), and then several associates join the team in the first few years of operation, or (2) an entire team is formed at the outset based on such factors as a shared idea, a friendship, or an experience.

As we saw in the opening case featuring Beyond the Rack, the ideal team consists of people with complementary skills covering the key areas of business (i.e., marketing, finance, production). Small founding teams tend to work better than big ones. It is quite common for the initial team to consist of just two people—a craftsperson and a salesperson.

If the entrepreneur does not intend to establish a high-growth venture, going solo may be a realistic option. Some new venture founders bring on additional team members only as the business can afford them. Most successful solo businesses are simple ventures (e.g., retail stores or service providers).[53] The odds for survival, growth, profitability, and attracting capital are increased by a team approach.[54]

Assessing the "Fit" Between Elements in the Entrepreneurial Process

Assessing the "fit" between the various elements in the entrepreneurial process is an ongoing task, since the shape of the opportunity and, consequently, the resources and people needed to capitalize on it, typi-

>>> TABLE **4.3** Business Incubators across Canada[52]

Name	Location
Entrepreneurship@UBC	Vancouver, British Columbia
NRC National Institute for Nanotechnology	Edmonton, Alberta
Genesys Venture Inc.	Winnipeg, Manitoba
NRC Institute for Marine Biology–IPF	Halifax, Nova Scotia
Genesis Centre	St. John's, Newfoundland
NRC Institute for Information Technology	Fredericton, New Brunswick
Centre for Social Innovation	Toronto, Ontario
Springboard West Innovations	Regina, Saskatchewan
J.-Armand Bombardier Incubator	Montreal, Quebec
LaunchPad Incubator Facility in the Atlantic Technology Centre	Charlottetown, Prince Edward Island

cally change as the opportunity is developed. It is the entrepreneur who stands to gain the most by attending to these "fits" and any changes they may require, although other stakeholders, such as investors, will be considering them as well.

THE ENTREPRENEUR–OPPORTUNITY FIT

The entrepreneur needs to decide whether the opportunity is something he or she can do and wants to do. A realistic self-assessment is important. Prospective ventures that are of limited personal interest and require skills and abilities that do not fit the entrepreneur should be quickly eliminated. No matter how good the product or service concept is, as the opportunity changes shape it may demand skills a single entrepreneur lacks. This may prompt a decision to acquire the needed skills either by forming a team or by getting further training.

THE OPPORTUNITY–RESOURCES FIT

Assessing the opportunity–resources fit involves determining whether the resources needed to capitalize on the opportunity can be acquired. When challenges or risks arise, the aim is to determine whether they can be resolved and to deal with them quickly. For example, if the venture requires a greater financial investment than originally anticipated, this does not necessarily mean that the venture should be abandoned. Other options, such as taking on partners or leasing rather than building a facility, may be viable. Of course, some ventures may not be viable regardless of the alternatives considered.

THE ENTREPRENEUR–RESOURCES FIT

Once the resource requirements of the venture have been determined, the entrepreneur needs to assess whether he or she has the capacity to meet those requirements. For example, an entrepreneur with a strong reputation for software development will have an easier time attracting employees for a venture specializing in software than someone with no track record. If that same entrepreneur is well connected with people in the industry, he or she will be more likely to gain commitments from customers, and in turn, investors.

START-UP AND BEYOND

Entrepreneurs must make the right start-up decisions, but they must also pay attention to how the business will be run once it is started. In this section, we examine three important topics that are relevant to these issues. First, we describe the three main ways that entrepreneurs start up a small business. Next, we look at the four main organizing options that are available to entrepreneurs. We conclude the chapter with a look at the reasons for success and failure in small business.

Starting Up a Small Business

Most entrepreneurs start up a small business in one of three ways: they start from scratch, they buy an existing business, or they buy a franchise. We have already examined the "starting from scratch" alternative in detail in the preceding section, so we turn now to the latter two alternatives.

LO-4 BUYING AN EXISTING BUSINESS

About one-third of all new businesses started in the past decade were bought from someone else. Many experts recommend buying an existing business because it increases the chances of success; it has already proven its ability to attract customers and has established relationships with lenders, suppliers, and other stakeholders. The track record also gives potential buyers a clearer picture of what to expect than any estimate of a new business's prospects.

But an entrepreneur who buys someone else's business may not be able to avoid certain problems. For example, there may be uncertainty about the exact financial shape the business is in, the business may have a poor reputation, the location may be poor, or it may be difficult to determine an appropriate purchase price.

Taking Over a Family Business Taking over a family business poses both opportunities and challenges. On the positive side, a family business can provide otherwise unobtainable financial and management resources—it often has a valuable reputation that can result in important community and business relationships, employee loyalty is often high, and an interested, unified family management and shareholders group may emerge. On the other hand, there may be disagreements over which family members assume control. Choosing an appropriate successor is a key issue for continuity, but it is also a key source of conflict. In addition, if a parent sells his or her interest in the business, the price to be paid may be an issue. Expectations can also be problematic, as some family members may feel that they have a right to a job, promotion, and an impressive title based on birth rights.[55] Handling disagreements among family members about the future of the business can be a challenge. How do you fire a loved one if things are not working out?[56]

BUYING A FRANCHISE

If you drive around any Canadian town or city, you will notice retail outlets with names like McDonald's, Re/Max, Canadian Tire, Chez Cora, and Tim Hortons. These diverse businesses all have one thing in common—they are all franchises, operating under licences issued by parent companies to entrepreneurs who own and manage them. Depending on how it is defined, franchising now accounts for 40 percent of retail sales in Canada. There are approximately 78 000 franchise establishments in Canada that employ over 1 million people and account for over 10 percent of Canadian GDP.[57]

Franchising continues to increase in importance for large and small ambitious companies. For example, Doug Bourgoyne, founder of FrogBox, an eco-friendly moving box rental company, has used this approach to expand. The company was featured on *Dragon's Den* and won the support of Jim Treliving (of Boston Pizza fame) and Brett Wilson (of Canoe Financial). From this exposure, Mr. Bourgoyne received 1500 applications for franchises in Canada.[58]

A **franchising agreement** outlines the duties and responsibilities of each party. It stipulates the amount and type of payment that franchisees must make to the franchiser. These franchise agreements have become

FRANCHISING AGREEMENT Stipulates the duties and responsibilities of the franchisee and the franchiser.

^^ Franchising is very popular in Canada. It offers individuals who want to run their own business an opportunity to establish themselves quickly in a local market.

lightpoet/Shutterstock

increasingly complicated, often 60 or even 100 pages long. Tim Hortons avoids this trend with a streamlined contract of about 26 pages.[59] Franchisees usually make an initial payment for the right to operate an outlet. They also make royalty payments to the franchiser ranging from 2 to 30 percent of the franchisee's annual revenues or profits. The franchisee may also pay an advertising fee to the franchiser. Franchise fees vary widely, from $23 500 for a Mad Science franchise, to over $1 million for a Burger King franchise, to hundreds of millions for a professional sports franchise.

The Advantages of Franchising Both franchisers and franchisees benefit from the franchising way of doing business (see Table 4.4).

The Disadvantages of Franchising There are always two sides to any story. Table 4.4 clearly outlines the obvious advantages. However, many experienced people will tell you that buying a franchise is like buying a job. The agreements are long because franchisers want to protect their image and recipes, and they want franchisees to follow their rules. If they don't, they may be sued. If you have a great new breakfast menu idea for your store and have creative promotional ideas, then franchising may not be for you. If things go well it can be rewarding, but it is important to do your homework because there are many disappointed franchise owners out there.

You should carefully read the agreement and ensure that your territory is protected and that you have the right of first refusal on new potential stores within a certain distance (e.g., 10–15 kilometres or exclusivity of your particular town). Some franchisees have been shocked to see their franchiser place a new franchisee a few blocks away or even across the street. Franchisees can benefit from support and advertising, but that does not come for free. For example, a Harvey's franchisee pays a 5 percent royalty fee and a 4 percent advertising fee (based on gross sales), and these fees are payable each week in addition to regular operating costs and rent.[60] There are plenty of franchisees who belong to popular chains that are barely surviving and are wondering whatever happened to that promised success.

In response to these issues, the provincial governments of Manitoba, Alberta, Ontario, New Brunswick, and Prince Edward Island have created laws to protect franchisees through Franchise Disclosure documents (FDD) that provides clear details of the agreement and helps protect franchisees in these jurisdictions.[61]

Is Franchising for You? Do you think you would be happy being a franchisee? The answer depends on a number of factors, including your willingness to work hard, your ability to find a good franchise to buy, and the financial resources you possess. If you are thinking seriously of going into franchising, you should consider several areas of costs that you will incur:

- the franchise sales price
- expenses that will be incurred before the business opens

>>> TABLE 4.4 The Benefits of Franchising

For the Franchiser	For the Franchisee
• The franchiser can attain rapid growth for the chain by signing up many franchisees in many different locations.	• Franchisees own a small business that has access to big business management skills.
• Franchisees share in the cost of advertising.	• The franchisee does not have to build up a business from scratch.
• The franchiser benefits from the investment money provided by franchisees.	• Franchisee failure rates are lower than when starting one's own business.
• Advertising money is spent more efficiently.	• A well-advertised brand name comes with the franchise and the franchisee's outlet is instantly recognizable.
• Franchisees are motivated to work hard for themselves, which creates profit for the franchiser.	• The franchiser may send the franchisee to a training program run by the franchiser (e.g., the Canadian Institute of Hamburgerology run by McDonald's).
• The franchiser is freed from all details of a local operation, which are handled by the franchisee.	• The franchiser may visit the franchisee and provide expert advice on how to run the business.
• Economies in buying allow franchisees to get lower prices for the raw materials they must purchase.	
• Financial assistance is provided by the franchiser in the form of loans; the franchiser may also help the franchisee obtain loans from local sources.	
• Franchisees are their own bosses and get to keep most of the profit they make.	

- training expenses
- operational expenses for the first six months
- personal financial needs for the first six months
- emergency needs

LO-5 Forms of Business Ownership

Whether they intend to run small farms, large factories, or online e-tailers, entrepreneurs must decide which form of legal ownership best suits their goals: sole proprietorship, partnership, corporation, or co-operative.

THE SOLE PROPRIETORSHIP

The **sole proprietorship** is a business owned and operated by one person. Legally, if you set up a business as a sole proprietorship, your business is considered to be an extension of yourself (and not a separate legal entity). Though usually small, a sole proprietorship may be as large as a steel mill or as small as a lemonade stand. While the majority of businesses in Canada are sole proprietorships, they account for only a small proportion of total business revenues.

Advantages of a Sole Proprietorship Freedom may be the most important benefit of a sole proprietorship. Sole proprietors answer to no one but themselves, since they don't share ownership. A sole proprietorship is also easy to form. If you operate the business under your own name, with no additions, you don't even need to register your business name to start operating as a sole proprietor—you can go into business simply by putting a sign on the door. The simplicity of legal set-up procedures makes this form appealing to self-starters and independent spirits, as do the low start-up costs.

Another attractive feature is the tax benefits. Most businesses suffer losses in their early stages. Since the business and the proprietor are legally one and the same, these losses can be deducted from income the proprietor earns from personal sources other than the business.

Disadvantages of a Sole Proprietorship A major drawback is **unlimited liability**, which means that a sole proprietor is personally liable (responsible) for all debts incurred by the business. If the business fails to generate enough cash, bills must be paid out of the owner's pocket. Another disadvantage is lack of continuity; a sole proprietorship legally dissolves when the owner dies. Finally, a sole proprietorship depends on the resources of one person whose managerial and financial limitations may constrain the business. Sole proprietors often find it hard to borrow money to start up or expand. Many bankers fear that they won't be able to recover loans if the owner becomes disabled.

THE PARTNERSHIP

A **partnership** is established when two or more individuals (partners) agree to combine their financial, managerial, and technical abilities for the purpose of operating a business for profit. This form of ownership is often used by professionals such as accountants, lawyers, and engineers. Partnerships are often an extension of a business that began as a sole proprietorship. The original owner may want to expand, or the business may have grown too big for a single person to handle.

There are two basic types of partners in a partnership. **General partners** are actively involved in managing the firm and have unlimited liability. **Limited partners** don't participate actively in the business, and their liability is limited to the amount they invested in the partnership. A **general partnership** is the most common type and is similar to the sole proprietorship in that all the (general) partners are jointly liable for the obligations of the business. The other type, the **limited partnership,** consists of at least one general partner (who has unlimited liability) and one or more limited partners. The limited partners cannot participate in the day-to-day management of the business or they risk the loss of their limited liability status.

Advantages of a Partnership The most striking advantage of a general partnership is the ability to grow by adding talent and money. Partnerships also have an easier time borrowing funds than sole proprietorships. Banks and other lending institutions prefer to make loans to enterprises that are not dependent on a single individual. Partnerships can also invite new partners to join by investing money.

Like a sole proprietorship, a partnership is simple to organize, with few legal requirements. Even so, all partnerships must begin with an agreement of some kind. It may be written, oral, or even unspoken. Wise partners, however, insist on a written agreement to avoid trouble later. This agreement should answer such questions as:

- Who invested what sums of money in the partnership?
- Who will receive what share of the partnership's profits?
- Who does what and who reports to whom?
- How may the partnership be dissolved?
- How will leftover assets be distributed among the partners?
- How would surviving partners be protected from claims by surviving heirs if a partner dies?
- How will disagreements be resolved?

The partnership agreement is strictly a private document. No laws require partners to file an agreement with any government agency. Nor are partnerships regarded as legal entities. In the eyes of the law, a partnership is nothing more than two or more people working together. The partnership's lack of legal standing means that the partners are taxed as individuals.

SOLE PROPRIETORSHIP Business owned and usually operated by one person who is responsible for all of its debts.

UNLIMITED LIABILITY A person who invests in a business is liable for all debts incurred by the business; personal possessions can be taken to pay debts.

PARTNERSHIP A business with two or more owners who share in the operation of the firm and in financial responsibility for the firm's debts.

GENERAL PARTNER A partner who is actively involved in managing the firm and has unlimited liability.

LIMITED PARTNER A partner who generally does not participate actively in the business, and whose liability is limited to the amount invested in the partnership.

GENERAL PARTNERSHIP A type of partnership in which all partners are jointly liable for the obligations of the business.

LIMITED PARTNERSHIP A type of partnership with at least one general partner (who has unlimited liability) and one or more limited partners. The limited partners cannot participate in the day-to-day management of the business or they risk the loss of their limited liability status.

Disadvantages of a Partnership Unlimited liability is also the biggest disadvantage of a general partnership. By law, each partner may be held personally liable for all debts of the partnership. And if any partner incurs a debt, even if the other partners know nothing about it, they are all liable if the offending partner cannot pay up. Another problem with partnerships is the lack of continuity. When one partner dies or pulls out, a partnership dissolves legally, even if the other partners agree to continue the business.

A related drawback is the difficulty of transferring ownership. No partner may sell out without the other partners' consent. Thus, the life of a partnership may depend on the ability of retiring partners to find someone compatible with the other partners to buy them out. Finally, a partnership provides little or no guidance in resolving conflicts between the partners. For example, suppose one partner wants to expand the business rapidly and the other wants it to grow slowly. If under the partnership agreement the two are equal, it may be difficult for them to decide what to do.

THE CORPORATION

When you think of corporations you probably think of giant businesses such as Air Canada, Walmart, or BlackBerry. The very word "corporation" suggests bigness and power. Yet the tiny corner retailer has as much right to incorporate as a giant oil refiner. Both of them have the same basic characteristics that all corporations share—legal status as a separate entity, property rights and obligations, and an indefinite lifespan. (See Table 4.5 for a list of the top 10 corporations in Canada.)

A corporation has been defined as "an artificial being, invisible, intangible, and existing only in contemplation of the law." As such, corporations may sue and be sued; buy, hold, and sell property; make products and sell them to consumers; and commit crimes and be tried and punished for them. Simply defined, a **corporation** is a business that is a separate legal entity, that is liable for its own debts, and whose owners' liability is limited to their investment.

Shareholders—investors who buy shares of ownership in the form of stock—are the real owners of a corporation. (The different kinds of stockholders are described in Chapter 15.) Profits may be distributed to stockholders in the form of dividends, although corporations are not required to pay dividends. Instead, they often reinvest any profits in the business. Common stockholders have the last claim to any assets if the company folds. Dividends on **common stock** are paid on a per share basis (if a dividend is declared). Thus, a shareholder with 10 shares receives 10 times the dividend paid a shareholder with one share. When investors cannot attend a shareholders' meeting, they can grant voting authority to someone who will attend. This procedure, called voting by proxy, is the way almost all individual investors vote.

TABLE 4.5 Top 10 Corporations in Canada, 2012[63]

Company	Sales Revenues (in billions of $)
1. Manulife Financial Corp.	50.9
2. Manufacturers Life Insurance	49.8
3. Suncor Energy	39.8
4. Royal Bank of Canada	35.8
5. Power Corp. of Canada	32.9
6. Power Financial	32.4
7. George Weston Ltd.	32.4
8. Loblaw Companies	31.4
9. Imperial Oil	30.7
10. Great-West Lifeco	30.01

CORPORATION A business considered by law to be a legal entity separate from its owners with many of the legal rights and privileges of a person; a form of business organization in which the liability of the owners is limited to their investment in the firm.

SHAREHOLDERS Investors who buy shares of ownership in the form of stock.

COMMON STOCK Shares whose owners usually have last claim on the corporation's assets (after creditors and owners of preferred stock) but who have voting rights in the firm.

BOARD OF DIRECTORS A group of individuals elected by a firm's shareholders and charged with overseeing, and taking legal responsibility for, the firm's actions.

INSIDE DIRECTORS Members of a corporation's board of directors who are also full-time employees of the corporation.

OUTSIDE DIRECTORS Members of a corporation's board of directors who are not also employees of the corporation on a day-to-day basis.

CHIEF EXECUTIVE OFFICER (CEO) The highest-ranking executive in a company or organization.

PUBLIC CORPORATION A business whose stock is widely held and available for sale to the general public.

PRIVATE CORPORATION A business whose stock is held by a small group of individuals and is not usually available for sale to the general public.

The **board of directors** is the governing body of a corporation. Its main responsibility is to ensure that the corporation is run in the best interests of the shareholders. The directors choose the president and other officers of the business and delegate the power to run the day-to-day activities of the business to those officers. The directors set policy on paying dividends, on financing major spending, and on executive salaries and benefits. Large corporations tend to have large boards with as many as 20 or 30 directors, whereas smaller corporations tend to have no more than five directors. Usually, these are people with personal or professional ties to the corporation, such as family members, lawyers, and accountants. Each year, the *Globe and Mail* analyzes the governance practices of Canadian companies in four areas: board composition, compensation, shareholder rights, and disclosure. The top-ranked companies in 2012 were Sun Life Financial Inc., Bank of Nova Scotia., and Potash Corp. of Saskatchewan Inc.[62]

Inside directors are employees of the company and have primary responsibility for the corporation. They are top managers, such as the president and executive vice-presidents. **Outside directors** are not employees of the corporation. Attorneys, accountants, university officials, and executives from other firms are commonly used as outside directors.

Corporate officers are the top managers hired by the board to run the corporation on a day-to-day basis. The **chief executive officer (CEO)** is responsible for the firm's overall performance. Other corporate officers typically include the president, who is responsible for internal management, and various vice-presidents, who oversee functional areas such as marketing or operations.

Types of Corporations A **public corporation** is one whose shares of stock are widely held and available for sale to the general public. Anyone who has the funds to pay for them can buy shares of companies such as Petro-Canada, Bombardier, or Air Canada. The stock of a **private corporation**, on the other hand, is held by only a few people and is not generally available for sale. The controlling group may

INITIAL PUBLIC OFFERING (IPO) Selling shares of stock in a company for the first time to a general investing public.

PRIVATE EQUITY FIRMS Companies that buy publicly traded companies and then make them private.

INCOME TRUST A structure allowing companies to avoid paying corporate income tax if they distribute all or most of their earnings to investors.

be a family, employees, or the management group. Pattison and Cirque du Soleil are two well-known Canadian private corporations.

Most new corporations start out as private corporations, because few investors will buy an unknown stock. As the corporation grows and develops a record of success, it may issue shares to the public to raise additional money. This is called an **initial public offering (IPO)**. IPOs are not very attractive to investors during stock market declines, but they become more popular when stock markets recover. There were 52 IPOs in Canada in 2012, raising $1.8 billion in new equity.[64] A public corporation can also "go private," which is the reverse of going public. **Private equity firms** buy publicly traded companies and then take them private. They often make major changes to company operations in order to increase its value.

About a decade ago, many corporations converted to an **income trust** structure, which allowed them to avoid paying corporate income tax if they distributed all or most of their earnings to investors. For example, Bell Canada Enterprises could have avoided an $800 million tax bill in one year by becoming an income trust. The federal government estimated that it was going to lose billions of dollars of tax revenue because so many corporations were becoming income trusts. In a surprise move in 2006, the Canadian government announced that it would begin taxing income trusts more like corporations by 2011. This announcement caused a significant decline in the market value of income trusts and put an end to the rush to convert.[65] In early 2013, there appeared to be renewed interest in income trusts. The reason? Income trusts distribute much of their cash flow to investors each month. Time will tell if this was a minor upswing or the rebirth of interest in this form of business.[66]

Formation of the Corporation

The two most widely used methods of forming a corporation are federal incorporation under the Canada Business Corporations Act and provincial incorporation under any of the provincial corporations acts. The former is used if the company is going to operate in more than one province; the latter is used if the founders intend to carry on business in only one province. Except for banks and certain insurance and loan companies, any company can be federally incorporated under the Canada Business Corporations Act. To do so, articles of incorporation must be drawn up. These articles include such information as the name of the corporation, the type and number of shares to be issued, the number of directors the corporation will have, and the location of the company's operations. The specific procedures and information required for provincial incorporation vary from province to province.

All corporations must attach the word "Limited" (Ltd./Ltée), "Incorporated" (Inc.), or "Corporation" (Corp.) to the company name to indicate clearly to customers and suppliers that the owners have limited liability for corporate debts. The same sorts of rules apply in other countries. British firms, for example, use PLC for "public limited company" and German companies use AG for "Aktiengesellschaft" (corporation).

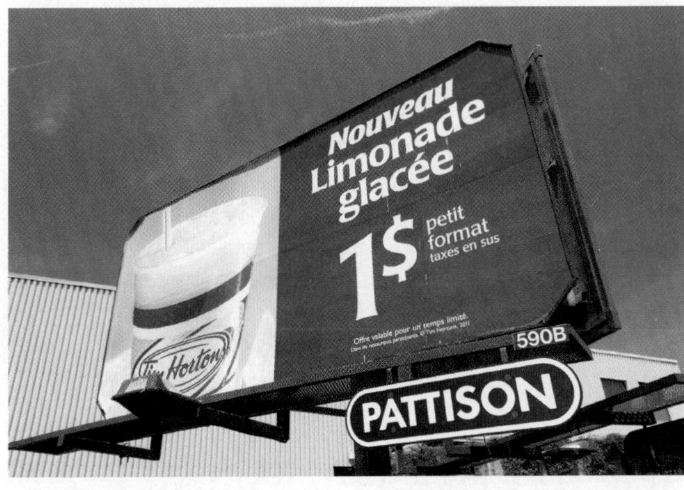

If you are from B.C., you know the Pattison name well but the reach goes across the country and beyond. The company built by this 84-year-old pure entrepreneur has created an empire that employs over 35 000 employees and earned over $7.5 billion in 2012.

© Megapress / Alamy

Advantages of Incorporation

The biggest advantage of the corporate structure is **limited liability**, which means that the liability of investors is limited to their personal investment in the corporation. In the event of failure, the courts may seize a corporation's assets and sell them to pay debts, but the courts cannot touch the investors' personal possessions. If, for example, you invest $25 000 in a corporation that goes bankrupt, you may lose your $25 000, but no more. In other words, $25 000 is the extent of your liability.

Another advantage of a corporation is continuity. Because it has a legal life independent of its founders and owners, a corporation can, in theory, continue forever. Shares of stock may be sold or passed on to heirs, and most corporations also benefit from the continuity provided by professional management. Finally, corporations have advantages in raising money. By selling **stock**, they expand the number of investors and available funds. The term "stock" refers to a share of ownership in a corporation. Continuity and legal status tend to make lenders more willing to grant loans to corporations.

Disadvantages of Incorporation

One of the disadvantages for a new firm in forming a corporation is the cost (approximately $2500). In addition, corporations also need legal help in meeting government regulations because they are far more heavily regulated than proprietorships or general partnerships. Some people say that **double taxation** is another problem with the corporate form of ownership. By this they mean that a corporation must pay income taxes on its profits, and then shareholders must also pay personal income taxes on the **dividends** they receive from the corporation. The dividend a corporation pays is the amount of money, normally a portion of the profits, that is distributed to the shareholders. Since dividends paid by the corporation are paid with after-tax dollars, this amounts to double taxation. Others point out that shareholders get a dividend tax credit, which largely offsets double taxation.

LIMITED LIABILITY Investor liability is limited to their personal investments in the corporation; courts cannot touch the personal assets of investors in the event that the corporation goes bankrupt.

STOCK A share of ownership in a corporation.

DOUBLE TAXATION A corporation must pay income taxes on its profits, and then shareholders must also pay personal income taxes on the dividends they receive from the corporation.

DIVIDENDS The amount of money, normally a portion of the profits, that is distributed to the shareholders.

>>> **TABLE 4.6** A Comparison of Four Forms of Business Ownership

Characteristic	Sole Proprietorship	Partnership	Corporation	Co-operative
Protection against liability for bad debts	low	low	high	high
Ease of formation	high	high	medium	medium
Permanence	low	low	high	high
Ease of ownership transfer	low	low	high	high
Ease of raising money	low	medium	high	high
Freedom from regulation	high	high	low	medium
Tax advantages	high	high	low	high

CO-OPERATIVE An organization that is formed to benefit its owners in the form of reduced prices and/or the distribution of surpluses at year-end.

THE CO-OPERATIVE

A **co-operative** is an incorporated form of business that is organized, owned, and democratically controlled by the people who use its products and services, and whose earnings are distributed on the basis of use of the co-operative rather than level of investment. As such, it is formed to benefit its owners in the form of reduced prices and/or the distribution of surpluses at year-end. The process works like this: Suppose some farmers believe they can get cheaper fertilizer prices if they form their own company and purchase in large volumes. They might then form a co-operative, which can be either federally or provincially chartered. Prices are generally lower to buyers and, at the end of the fiscal year, any surpluses are distributed to members on the basis of how much they purchased. If Farmer Jones bought 5 percent of all co-op sales, he would receive 5 percent of the surplus.

The co-operative's start-up capital usually comes from shares purchased by the co-operative's members. Sometimes all it takes to qualify for membership in a co-operative is the purchase of one share with a fixed (and often nominal) value. Federal co-operatives, however, can raise capital by issuing investment shares to members or non-members. Co-operatives, like investor-owned corporations, have directors and appointed officers.

Types of Co-operatives There are hundreds of different co-operatives, but they generally function in one of six main areas of business:

- *Consumer co-operatives*—These organizations sell goods to both members and the general public (e.g., Mountain Equipment Co-op).
- *Financial co-operatives*—These organizations operate much like banks, accepting deposits from members, giving loans, and providing chequing services (e.g., Vancouver City Savings Credit Union).
- *Insurance co-operatives*—These organizations provide many types of insurance coverage, such as life, fire, and liability (e.g., Co-operative Hail Insurance Company of Manitoba).
- *Marketing co-operatives*—These organizations sell the produce of their farm members and purchase inputs for the production process (e.g., seed and fertilizer). Some, like Federated Co-operatives, also purchase and market finished products.
- *Service co-operatives*—These organizations provide members with services, such as recreation.
- *Housing co-operatives*—These organizations provide housing for members, who purchase a share in the co-operative, which holds the title to the housing complex.

In terms of numbers, co-operatives are the least important form of ownership. However, they are of significance to society and to their members and may provide services that are not readily available or that cost more than the members would otherwise be willing to pay. Table 4.6 compares the various forms of business ownership using different characteristics.

Advantages of a Co-operative Co-operatives have many of the same advantages as investor-owned corporations, such as limited liability of owners and continuity. A key benefit of a co-operative relates to its structure. Each member has only one vote in the affairs of the co-operative, regardless of how many shares he or she owns. This system prevents voting and financial control of the business by a few wealthy individuals. This is particularly attractive to the less-wealthy members of the co-operative.

Unlike corporations, which are not allowed a tax deduction on dividend payments made to shareholders, co-operatives are allowed to deduct patronage refunds to members out of before-tax income. Thus, income may be taxed only at the individual member level rather than at both the co-operative and member level.[67]

Disadvantages of a Co-operative One of the main disadvantages of co-operatives relates to attracting equity investment. Since the benefits from being a member of a co-operative arise through the level of use of the co-operative rather than the level of equity invested, members do not have an incentive to invest in equity capital of the co-operative. Another drawback is that democratic voting arrangements and dividends based purely on patronage discourage some entrepreneurs from forming or joining a co-operative.

LO-6 SUCCESS AND FAILURE IN SMALL BUSINESS

Of every 100 small businesses that begin operation, 85 will still be operating after one year, 70 after three years, and 51 after five years.[68] A study conducted by CIBC World Markets found that small businesses with above-average revenue growth were run by owners who had more education, used professional advisers, adopted the corporate form of ownership, did outsourcing work for other companies, had a high level of internet connectivity, and used the internet to sell outside Canada.[69]

Reasons for Success

Beyond the specific findings like the CIBC study, four general factors typically are cited to explain the success of small-business owners:

1. *Hard work, drive, and dedication.* Small-business owners must be committed to succeeding and be willing to put in the time and effort to make it happen. Long hours and few vacations generally characterize the first few years of new business ownership.
2. *Market demand for the product or service.* Careful analysis of market conditions can help small-business people assess the probable reception of their products. If the area around a college has only one pizza parlour, a new pizzeria is more likely to succeed than if there are already 10 in operation.
3. *Managerial competence.* Successful small-business people have a solid understanding of how to manage a business. They may acquire competence through training (taking courses), experience, or by using the expertise of others. Few, however, succeed alone or straight out of school. Most spend time in successful companies or partner with others to bring expertise to a new business.
4. *Luck.* Luck also plays a role in the success of some firms. For example, after one entrepreneur started an environmental clean-up firm, he struggled to keep his business afloat. Then the government committed a large sum of money for toxic waste clean-up. He was able to get several large contracts, and his business is now thriving.

Reasons for Failure

Small businesses fail for many specific reasons (see Table 4.7). Entrepreneurs may have no control over some of these factors (e.g., weather, accidents), but they can influence most items on the list. Although no set pattern has been established, four general factors contribute to failure:

1. *Managerial incompetence or inexperience.* Some entrepreneurs overestimate their own managerial skills, or believe that hard work alone ensures success. If managers don't know how to make basic business decisions or don't understand basic management principles, they aren't likely to succeed.
2. *Neglect.* Some entrepreneurs try to launch ventures in their spare time, and others devote only limited time to new businesses. But starting a small business demands an overwhelming time commitment.
3. *Weak control systems.* Effective control systems keep a business on track and alert managers to potential trouble. If the control systems don't signal potential problems, the business may be in serious trouble before obvious difficulties are spotted.
4. *Insufficient capital.* Some entrepreneurs are overly optimistic about how soon they'll start earning profits. In most cases, it takes months or even years. Amazon.com didn't earn a profit for 10 years, but obviously still required capital to pay employees and cover expenses. Experts say you need enough capital to operate six months to a year without earning a profit.[70]

On a positive note, business failures were lower than expected in the most recent recession. According to Laurie Campbell, director of the credit counselling organization Credit Canada, this was due to the fact that the recession hit the U.S. first before having an impact in Canada. Many businesses took necessary precautions to cut expenses before it hit.[71]

>>> **TABLE 4.7** Causes of Small-Business Failure

Poor management skills	Personal reasons
• poor delegation and organizational ability	• loss of interest in business
• lack of depth in management team	• accident, illness
• entrepreneurial incompetence, such as a poor understanding of finances and business markets	• death
• lack of experience	• family problems
Inadequate marketing capabilities	**Disasters**
• difficulty in marketing product	• fire
• market too small, non-existent, or declining	• weather
• too much competition	• strikes
• problems with distribution systems	**Other**
Inadequate financial capabilities	• mishandling of large project
• weak skills in accounting and finance	• excessive standard of living
• lack of budgetary control	• lack of time to devote to business
• inadequate costing systems	• difficulties with associates or partners
• incorrect valuation of assets	• government policies change
• unable to obtain financial backing	• fraud by entrepreneur or others
Inadequate production capabilities	
• poorly designed production systems	
• old and inefficient production facilities and equipment	
• inadequate control over quality	
• problems with inventory control	

MyBizLab

Visit the MyBizLab website. This online homework and tutorial system puts you in control of your own learning with study and practice tools directly correlated to this chapter's content.

SUMMARY OF LEARNING OBJECTIVES

LO-1 EXPLAIN THE MEANING AND INTERRELATIONSHIP OF THE TERMS *SMALL BUSINESS, NEW VENTURE CREATION,* AND *ENTREPRENEURSHIP.*

A *small business* has less than 100 employees. A new firm is one that has become operational within the previous 12 months, has adopted any of four main organizational forms—sole proprietorship, partnership, corporation, or co-operative—and sells goods or services. *Entrepreneurship* is the process of identifying an opportunity in the marketplace and accessing the resources needed to capitalize on it. In relation to small and/or new businesses, entrepreneurship is the process by which a small business or a new business is created.

LO-2 DESCRIBE THE ROLE OF *SMALL AND NEW BUSINESSES* IN THE CANADIAN ECONOMY.

While 98 percent of employer businesses in Canada are small (less than 100 employees), about half of the total private-sector labour force work for *small businesses*. The distribution of employment by size of firm varies across industries. The small-business sector's capacity for entrepreneurship and innovation accounts for much of the job creation; this sector contributes to the economy, with start-ups accounting for most of the growth. Women are playing a major role in the growth of small businesses.

LO-3 EXPLAIN THE *ENTREPRENEURIAL PROCESS* AND DESCRIBE ITS THREE KEY ELEMENTS.

The *entrepreneurial process* occurs within a social, political, and economic context and consists of three key elements: the entrepreneur, the opportunity, and resources. Entrepreneurs typically access the various resources needed by bootstrapping—doing more with less. These resources are both financial and non-financial. Two types of financing—debt and equity—can be accessed from a range of sources.

LO-4 DESCRIBE THREE ALTERNATIVE STRATEGIES FOR BECOMING A BUSINESS OWNER—*STARTING FROM SCRATCH, BUYING AN EXISTING BUSINESS,* AND *BUYING A FRANCHISE.*

It is necessary to work through the entrepreneurial process in order to *start a business from scratch*. Whether start-up efforts will result in a new business often depends upon how well matched the entrepreneur's skills and abilities are with the opportunity and the resources required, as well as how well matched the opportunity and resources are. Generally, when someone *buys an existing business*, the odds of success are better because it has existing customers, established relationships (e.g., lenders, suppliers), and an existing track record. Potential buyers have a clearer picture of what to expect. However, the business may have a poor reputation or poor location, and it may be difficult to determine an appropriate purchase price. A special case of buying an existing business involves family businesses, which pose both opportunities and challenges. In *buying a franchise*, the buyer (franchisee) purchases the right to sell the product or service of the seller (franchiser) according to the terms of the franchising agreement. In return, the franchiser provides assistance with the business's start-up as well as with ongoing operations once the business opens its doors.

LO-5 DESCRIBE FOUR FORMS OF *LEGAL ORGANIZATION* FOR A BUSINESS AND DISCUSS THE ADVANTAGES AND DISADVANTAGES OF EACH.

Sole proprietorships are owned and operated by one person, are easy to set up, have low start-up costs, and enjoy tax benefits, and their owners enjoy freedom. However, sole proprietorships have unlimited liability, a lack of continuity, and limited resources.

Under a general partnership, all partners have unlimited liability. Partnerships may lack continuity, and transferring ownership may be difficult. On the positive side, partnerships can grow by adding new talent and money, partners are taxed as individuals, and banks prefer to make loans to enterprises that are not dependent on one individual. All partnerships should have a partnership agreement.

Corporations are separate legal entities; they have property rights and obligations, and they have indefinite life spans. They may sue and be sued; buy, hold, and sell property; make and sell products; and commit crimes and be tried and punished for them. The biggest advantage of incorporation is limited liability. Other advantages include continuity, professional management, and improved ability to raise money by selling stock. Disadvantages of the corporation include high start-up costs, complexity, and double taxation. The vast majority of corporations are privately held. In forming a corporation, a business will incorporate federally if it is going to operate in more than one province and provincially if it is going to operate in only one province.

A co-operative is an organization that is formed to benefit its owners in the form of reduced prices and/or the distribution of surpluses at year-end. On the positive side, co-operatives are democratically controlled, enjoy limited liability and continuity, and are not subject to double taxation. The main disadvantages include difficulty in raising equity. Co-operatives usually function in one of six areas of business: consumer co-operatives, financial co-operatives, insurance co-operatives, marketing co-operatives, service co-operatives, or housing co-operatives.

LO-6 IDENTIFY FOUR KEY *REASONS FOR SUCCESS* IN SMALL BUSINESSES AND FOUR KEY *REASONS FOR FAILURE.*

Four basic factors explain most small-business success: (1) hard work, drive, and dedication; (2) market demand for the products or services being provided; (3) managerial competence; and (4) luck. Four factors contribute to small-business failure: (1) managerial incompetence or inexperience; (2) neglect; (3) weak control systems; and (4) insufficient capital.

QUESTIONS AND EXERCISES

QUESTIONS FOR ANALYSIS

1. Why are new ventures the main source of job creation and new product/service ideas?
2. If you were going to open a new business, what type of business would it be? Why?
3. Would you prefer to buy an existing business or start from scratch? Why?
4. Under what circumstances might it be wise for an entrepreneur to reject venture capital? Under what circumstances might it be advisable to take more venture capital than he or she actually needs?
5. Why might a private corporation choose to remain private? Why might it choose to "go public"?
6. Consider a new product or service that has recently become available for purchase by consumers. To what extent did this product or service possess the "screening" characteristics that are described in the chapter (adding value, providing competitive advantage, etc.)?

APPLICATION EXERCISES

7. There are thousands of mobile applications on the various mobile platforms (you probably use some of them on a weekly or daily basis). Identify an idea for a new application that can serve a consumer need that is currently unmet or can be improved upon.
8. Interview the owner/manager of a sole proprietorship or a general partnership. What characteristics of that business form led the owner to choose it? Does he or she ever plan on changing the form of the business?
9. Identify two or three of the fastest-growing businesses in Canada during the last year. What role has entrepreneurship played in the growth of these firms?
10. Interview the owners of several small businesses in your local area. Ask them what they have done to make their businesses more environmentally friendly. If they have not done anything, ask them what has prevented them from taking the initiative to be more environmentally friendly.

TEAM EXERCISES

BUILDING YOUR BUSINESS SKILLS

BUILDING AN INTERNET STRATEGY

GOAL

To encourage students to define opportunities and problems for small companies doing business on the internet.

SITUATION

Suppose you and two partners own a gift basket store, specializing in special-occasion baskets for individual and corporate clients. Your business is doing well in your community, but you believe there may be opportunity for growth through a virtual storefront on the internet.

METHOD

Step 1 Join with two other students and assume the role of business partners. Start by researching internet businesses. Look at books and articles at the library and search the following websites for help:

- Canada Business Service Centres: www.canadabusiness.ca/eng/
- Small Business Administration (United States): www.sba.gov
- Apple Small Business Home Page: www.apple.com/business/

These sites may lead you to other sites, so keep an open mind.

Step 2 Based on your research, determine the importance of the following small-business issues:

- An analysis of changing company finances as a result of internet applications
- An analysis of your new competitive marketplace (the world) and how it affects your current marketing approach, which focuses on your local community
- Identification of sources of management advice as the expansion proceeds
- The role of technology consultants in launching and maintaining the website
- Customer service policies in your virtual environment

FOLLOW-UP QUESTIONS

1. Do you think your business would be successful on the internet? Why or why not?
2. Based on your analysis, how will extended internet applications affect your current business practices? What specific changes are you likely to make?
3. Do you think that operating a virtual storefront will be harder or easier than doing business in your local community? Explain your answer.

EXERCISING YOUR ETHICS

BREAKING UP IS HARD TO DO

THE SITUATION

Connie and Mark began a 25-year friendship after finishing college and discovering their mutual interest in owning a business. Established as a general partnership, their home-furnishings centre is a successful business that has been sustained for 20 years by a share-and-share-alike relationship. Start-up cash, daily responsibilities, and profits have all been shared equally. The partners both work four days each week except when busy seasons require both of them to be in the store. Shared goals and compatible personalities have led to a solid give-and-take relationship that helps them overcome business problems while maintaining a happy interpersonal relationship.

The division of work is a natural match and successful combination because of the partners' different but complementary interests. Mark buys the merchandise and maintains up-to-date contacts with suppliers; he also handles personnel matters (hiring and training employees). Connie manages the inventory, buys shipping supplies, keeps the books, and manages the finances. Mark does more selling, with Connie helping out only during busy seasons. Both partners share in decisions about advertising and promotions. Mark has taken a particular interest in learning the latest social media tools and has begun to implement these strategies successfully.

THE DILEMMA

Things began changing two years ago, when Connie became less interested in the business and got more involved in other activities. Whereas Mark's enthusiasm remained high, Connie's time was increasingly consumed by travel, recreation, and community-service activities. At first, she reduced her work commitment from four to three days a week. Then she indicated that she wanted to cut back further, to just two days. "In that case," Mark replied, "we'll have to make some changes."

Mark insisted that profit sharing be adjusted to reflect his larger role in running the business from the original 50-50. This was not addressed immediately; however, he also proposed that Connie's monthly salary be cut in half (from $4000 to $2000). Connie agreed. He recommended that the $2000 savings be shifted to his salary because of his increased workload, but this time Connie disagreed, arguing that Mark's current $4000 salary already compensated him for his contributions. She proposed to split the difference, with Mark getting a $1000 increase and the other $1000 going into the firm's cash account. Mark said no and insisted on a full $2000 raise. To avoid a complete falling out, Connie finally gave in, even though she thought it unfair for Mark's salary to jump from $4000 per month to $6000. At that point, she made a promise to herself: "To even things out, I'll find a way to get $2000 worth of inventory for personal use each month and I won't give in on any future profit-sharing adjustments."

TEAM ACTIVITY

Assemble a group of four students and divide the four into two pairs and answer the questions from one of the following perspectives:

- Mark's perspective
- Connie's perspective

(continued)

QUESTIONS TO ADDRESS

1. Identify the ethical issues, if any, regarding Mark's and Connie's respective positions on Mark's proposed $2000 salary increase.
2. What kind of salary and profit adjustments do you think would be fair in this situation? Explain why.
3. There is another way for Mark and Connie to solve their differences—because the terms of participation have changed, it might make sense to dissolve the existing partnership. What do you recommend in this regard?

BUSINESS CASE

PARASUCO JEANS: THE STORY OF A BORN ENTREPRENEUR

In 2013, Salvatore Parasuco's company celebrated its 38th year of operation, so his successful denim business is definitely not a new venture, but it is a great tale of entrepreneurship. Words like "drive," "determination," "self-starter," and "vision" are commonly used to describe entrepreneurs. All of these terms fit the founder of Parasuco Jeans to a T. The story begins with a budding entrepreneur whose ambition is announced at a very young age when he begins selling jeans out of his high-school locker in Montreal. As legend has it, he managed to convince his principal to let him sell the jeans by telling him he needed to make money to help support his family and avoid going down the wrong path. Today, Parasuco Jeans are sold in locations around the world with distribution in Canada, the United States, Europe, and Asia. The company has a particularly good presence in Italy, Hong Kong, Russia, Japan, and Korea. Celebrities such as Justin Bieber, Jessica Alba, Kate Hudson, Carly Rae Jepsen, and many more have been photographed wearing a pair of Parasuco's trendy jeans. Yet despite the success and the longevity of the brand, it does not have as much visibility across Canada as the owner thinks it deserves. He openly wonders why we Canadians (and the local media in particular) aren't as patriotic toward our homegrown brands as Americans are.

Leon Switzer/ZUMAPRESS/Newscom

Salvatore is a Canadian whose family came here from Italy when he was just a young boy. From his humble beginnings, he learned the value of a dollar and credits his father for teaching him the art of negotiation at an early age. The rise of Parasuco Jeans is not a modern-day instant success story with a major internet IPO launch. It is a story about blood, sweat, and some tears. Before getting into the denim design business, Salvatore opened a clothing store, where he learned a lot about the business that would become his life's work. Mr. Parasuco launched Santana Jeans in 1975 and changed the name to Parasuco due to legal issues in 1988. From the early days, it was clear that innovation and design would be at the foundation of the company. Parasuco was the first to launch pre-washed jeans in Canada. The company was also the first brand to introduce stretch denim to the market, a product feature that is central to the company image to this day. In a recent interview, the owner talked about how customers tend to instinctively start to stretch and pull his famous jeans. Success in business requires good vision to compete. This is even more complicated in this industry because staying ahead of the fashion trends is no easy task. The guiding mission of the company is based on eight pillars of strength: (1) respect, (2) people, (3) passion, (4) promotion of innovation, (5) performance, (6) pride, (7) pursuit of excellence, and (8) professionalism. Based on a track record that spans over 35 years, it is obvious that this company has done something right in meeting customer needs. But there are significant existing domestic and emerging international competitors and even other major brands based in Montreal, such as Buffalo by David Bitton (which has its own niche).

Parasuco Jeans is a brand known for its provocative ads. It has shocked and pushed boundaries for years with sexy billboards, magazine spreads, and bus shelter ads. In order to gain more attention, the company placed 25 ads in giant ice blocks around the city of Toronto to coincide with Fashion Week, with a tag line to match: "Styles so hot they will melt the ice." Like most fashion companies, Parasuco uses Twitter and Facebook to build buzz and spread the word. There is also a great deal of content on YouTube, which is a testament to the brand's cult-like following.

Even the most successful businesses have their share of disappointments and failures, but true entrepreneurs know how to overcome them, reduce their losses, and capitalize on the best available opportunity. Back in 2010, when Parasuco decided to close his flagship New York store, he quickly found a tenant (drugstore chain Duane Reade) that agreed to pay $1 million in rent per year, to Parasuco, who had bought the retail condominium four years earlier for about $9 million. At around the same time, he announced intentions to build a high-end boutique hotel in Toronto. In 2012, however, Parasuco sold the site to MOD Developments, who plan to build a 60-story condo unit there.

Salvatore Parasuco is now over 60 years old, but age doesn't seem to be slowing him down one bit. He is still visibly promoting his brand and searching for new opportunities. What do you expect? Salvatore Parasuco has the DNA of a pure entrepreneur.

QUESTIONS FOR DISCUSSION

1. What characteristics did Salvatore Parasuco possess that made him successful as an entrepreneur?
2. The visibility of Parasuco jeans is higher in other countries than in Canada. Why might this be so?
3. How did Salvatore Parasuco's background facilitate his success?

LO

AFTER READING THIS CHAPTER, YOU SHOULD BE ABLE TO:

LO-1 Describe the growing complexity in the *global business environment* and identify the *major world marketplaces.*

LO-2 Identify the evolving role of *emerging markets* and highlight the importance of the *BRICS nations.*

LO-3 Explain how different forms of *competitive advantage, import–export balances, exchange rates,* and *foreign competition* determine how countries and businesses respond to the international environment.

LO-4 Discuss the factors involved in conducting business internationally and in selecting the appropriate levels of *international involvement* and *organizational structure.*

LO-5 Describe some of the ways in which *social, cultural, economic, legal, and political differences* act as barriers to international trade.

LO-6 Explain how *free trade agreements* assist world trade.

Scotiabank: Canadian Bank or Global Player?

If you take a cruise to the Caribbean, you may be surprised to see some familiar Canadian banks at the major ports and as a visible presence in various towns. Scotiabank is a leader in the industry with over 200 branches in the Caribbean, including locations in Aruba, Jamaica, and Barbados. This is, however, just a small glimpse of the international reach of this company. Scotiabank was founded in 1832 in Halifax, Nova Scotia, and now has over 2800 branches in 55 countries. It employs over 82 000 people while providing a wide range of services to more than 19 million customers (13.5 million in international markets). While competitors like TD and BMO have set their sights on expanding in the more familiar U.S. market, Scotiabank took a more speculative expansion approach. It continues to build a strong presence in Central America, Mexico, Latin America, and Asia. As you will see, Scotiabank has various models around the world, designed to respect local laws and adapt to local challenges. For instance, in Mexico, the approach is direct and aggressive; Scotiabank has invested through a holding company called Grupo Financiero Scotiabank Inverlat, S.A. de C.V., which owns two subsidiaries. Scotiabank Inverlat is Mexico's seventh-largest bank with 558 full-service commercial branches and 1172 ATMs. The second is Scotiabank Inverlat Casa de Bolsa, an investment bank, which specializes in equity trading, investment advice, and corporate financing through 45 branches in major Mexican cities. Satisfying customers from different regions of the world requires knowledge of distinct local cultures and economic systems and respect for the unique needs of each market. Managing a portfolio as wide and complicated as Scotiabank's can be extremely challenging, but the company is clearly devoted to its global mission.

Scotiabank has been conducting international business for well over 100 years and earns a great deal of its profits from these operations. The company profile proudly

The Global Context *of* Business

CHAPTER 05

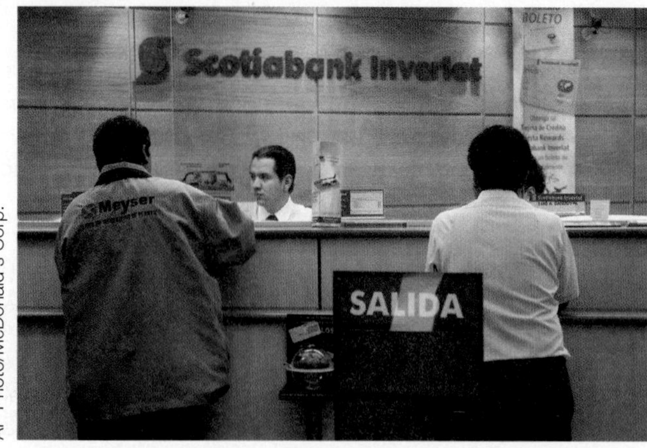

AP Photo/McDonald's Corp.

states that it is the most international of the big Canadian banks. This claim seems to be widely supported because when Prime Minister Stephen Harper was looking for someone to lead a group of chief executives in a forum designed to increase international trade between Canada and Brazil, he turned to Scotiabank CEO Rick Waugh. Waugh agreed to co-chair the forum with the Brazilian CEO of Vale SA, Murilio Ferreira. Why was he chosen? Experience. Scotiabank has been conducting business in Brazil for over 30 years. While some companies look at Brazil and see tough barriers and unwelcome tariffs, Scotiabank sees an established client base, a long-standing relationship, and tremendous potential. Brazil is the world's seventh-largest economy and one of the powerful emerging BRICS nations (the others are Russia, India, China, and South Africa). Scotiabank already earns over $2 billion in trade financing from its Brazilian unit. With the Brazilian middle class predicted to grow by 40 to 45 million people over the next 20 years, Scotiabank is in a good position to benefit in a major way from their early investment in this nation.

Many investments in international markets are designed for long-term gains while sacrificing profits in the short term. However, international banking is nothing new at Scotiabank, and this division is a profit driver for the firm today. Of course, having a presence in markets around the world also means that the bank has increased exposure to risks from around the world. This is particularly dangerous in unstable economic times.

Scotiabank has no intention of slowing down. In recent years, the expansion plan has included 22 acquisitions in Central and South America, with a particular emphasis on Colombia, Peru, and Chile. In fact, Scotiabank has set a target to capture 10 percent of the Chilean market. It recently bought Banco Sud Americano and its 142 full-service branches in that country. In 2012, Scotiabank acquired a majority stake in Banco Colpatria in a $1 billion deal in Colombia. However, such acquisitions are getting more difficult to complete. As a pioneer, Scotiabank was able to make major purchases at very reasonable acquisition prices; however, today more international banks are investing in this region and the prices are getting higher. Nobody ever said it was easy.

There are tremendous prospects in Asia. Scotiabank has operations in key Asian markets including Japan, Korea, and India. Perhaps the greatest opportunities today, and probably for the next 100 years, are in China. In 2011, Scotiabank was clearly trying to deepen its roots in this nation by acquiring a 19.99 percent stake in the Bank of Guangzhou for $719 million. This bank has a network of 84 branches in China's third-largest city. Why 19.99 percent? Doing business internationally often means navigating local rules and regulations. Foreign companies are not allowed to own more than 19.99 percent in any Chinese bank. This latest move follows a purchase of 14.8 percent of the Xi'an City Commercial Bank for $162 million two years earlier. All of the world's major banks are paying attention to this market for obvious reasons; however, for Scotiabank, this latest move will be their last for a while because under current Chinese laws foreign banks are only allowed to have a stake in a maximum of two Chinese banks. To make matters worse, the Bank of Guangzhou deal had still not been officially approved at the beginning of 2013, and Scotiabank executives were getting increasingly frustrated. This is just another example of an obstacle when conducting business abroad.

International growth must always be weighed against the specific challenges in each market (economic,

HOW WILL THIS HELP ME?

Whether you see yourself living abroad, working for a big company, or starting your own business, the global economy will affect you in some way. Exchange rates for different currencies and global markets for buying and selling affect everyone, regardless of their role or perspective. The material in this chapter will help you to (1) understand how global forces impact you as a customer, (2) understand how globalization affects you as an employee, and (3) assess how global opportunities and challenges can affect you as a business owner and as an investor.

legal, political, etc.). Regardless of the latest conditions, Scotiabank has shown its commitment to working with foreign companies, complying with foreign government rules in the quest to grow, and continuing to transform from Canada's leading international bank into Scotiabank-Global bank.

QUESTIONS FOR DISCUSSION

1. In this chapter, you will read about the different ways a company can enter foreign markets. List and describe the effectiveness of various approaches used by Scotiabank across the globe.
2. Describe the key obstacles faced by banks when they try to do business in a foreign nation.
3. Free trade agreements are simplifying trade across the globe, but clearly there are some major challenges for Scotiabank in growing their footprint. Do you believe that the banking industry needs to have more open regulations to allow companies like Scotiabank to expand further across the globe?

THE CONTEMPORARY GLOBAL ECONOMY

GLOBALIZATION Process by which the world economy is becoming a single interdependent system.

IMPORT Product made or grown abroad but sold domestically.

EXPORT Product made or grown domestically but shipped and sold abroad.

The total volume of world trade today is immense—around $15 trillion each year.[1] The world economy is increasingly transforming into a single, interdependent system in a process called **globalization**. Even so, we often take for granted the diversity of goods and services available as a result of international trade. Your tablet, smartphone, clothing, and even the roast lamb on your dinner table may all be **imports**—that is, products made or grown abroad, but sold in Canada. At the same time, the success of many Canadian firms depends on **exports**—products made or grown domestically and shipped abroad.

Trade between nations can be traced back at least as far as 2000 BCE, when North African tribes took dates and clothing to Assyria and Babylonia in the Middle East and traded them for olive oil and spices. International business is nothing new. But international trade has become increasingly central to the fortunes of most nations of the world, as well as businesses. In the past, many nations followed strict policies to protect domestic companies, while today most countries are aggressively encouraging international trade. They are opening their borders to foreign businesses, offering incentives for their own domestic businesses to expand internationally, and making it easier for foreign firms to partner with local firms through various alliances. Today, it is not simply a question of Western nations pushing trade abroad. China is making major inroads and increasing its economic and political influence in Africa with major deals with Nigeria, South Africa, Ethiopia, and Zambia. China is now the largest trading partner in the region with trade totalling more than $114 billion, just ahead of the U.S.[2] It also took the title from Germany as the world's top merchandise exporter a few years ago.[3]

Several forces have combined to spark and sustain globalization. For one thing, governments and businesses have simply become more aware of the benefits of globalization to their countries and stockholders. For another, new technologies have made travel, communication, and commerce easier, faster, and cheaper. The cost of overseas phone calls and seaborne shipping costs per tonne have both declined sharply over the last several decades. Likewise, transatlantic travel takes only a few hours by air. The internet has torn down barriers for large and small companies. Finally, there are competitive pressures; sometimes a firm simply must enter foreign markets just to keep up with its competitors.

Globalization has critics who claim that businesses exploit workers in less-developed countries and avoid domestic environmental and tax regulations. They also charge that globalization leads to the loss of cultural heritage and benefits the rich more than the poor. As a result, many international gatherings of global economic leaders (such as the G8 and G20) have been marked by protests. But despite fears, globalization is part of our evolving existence. A *Globe and Mail* article listed five

Some globalization protestors, like this man, fear that multinational companies will wipe out small domestic businesses like family farms.

© Photo Japan/Alamy

PER-CAPITA INCOME The average income per person of a country.

key trends based on a report from McKinsey: (1) the economic centre of gravity will shift away from North America/Europe/Japan to Asia and Latin America, (2) the productivity imperative (improved productivity is essential to compete in the highly competitive marketplace), (3) the global grid (increasing complex global networks of people and capital), (4) environmental sustainability will take on even more importance, and (5) there will be increased controls on businesses and markets as governments try to cope with the financial crisis.[4]

LO-1 The Major World Marketplaces

The World Bank, an agency of the United Nations, uses **per-capita income**—average income per person—to make distinctions among countries. Its current classification method consists of four categories of countries:[5]

1. *High-income countries:* annual per-capita income greater than US $12 476. They include Canada, the United States, most countries in Europe, Australia, Japan, South Korea, Israel, Kuwait, the United Arab Emirates, and Oman.
2. *Upper-middle-income countries:* annual per-capita income between US $4036 and US $12 475. This group includes China, Colombia, Lebanon, Turkey, Argentina, and South Africa.
3. *Low-middle-income countries:* annual per-capita income between US $1026 and US $4035. This group includes Albania, Armenia, Guatemala, and Vietnam.
4. *Low-income countries* (often called *developing countries*): annual per-capita income of US $1025 or less. Bangladesh, Ethiopia, Haiti, and Afghanistan are among the countries in this group. Due to low literacy rates, weak infrastructures, unstable governments, and related problems, these countries are less attractive for international business.

GEOGRAPHIC CLUSTERS

The world economy is evolving quickly with emerging markets playing an ever-increasing role. However, it still revolves greatly around three major marketplaces: North America, Europe, and Asia. These clusters include relatively more of the upper-middle-income and high-income nations, but relatively few low-income and low-middle-income countries. For instance, because Africa consists primarily of low-income and low-middle-income countries, it is not generally seen as a major marketplace. The three key geographic regions are home to most of the world's largest economies, biggest corporations, influential financial markets, and highest-income consumers.

North America The United States dominates the North American business region. It is the single largest marketplace and has been the most stable economy in the world for decades, but the U.S has major problems due to many issues (e.g., a huge increase in the nation's debt load). Canada also plays a major role in the global economy. Moreover, the United States and Canada are each other's largest trading partners. Many U.S. firms, such as General Motors and Procter & Gamble, have maintained successful Canadian operations for decades, and many Canadian firms, such as BlackBerry and Scotiabank, are also major international competitors.

Mexico has become a major manufacturing centre, especially along the U.S. border, where cheap labour and low transportation costs have encouraged many firms from the United States and other countries to build factories. The auto industry has been very active, with Daimler, General Motors, Volkswagen, Nissan, and Ford all running large assembly plants, and major suppliers have also built facilities in the region. But Mexico's role as a low-cost manufacturing hub has been decreased as companies shift production to China instead.[6]

Europe Europe was traditionally divided into two regions—Western and Eastern. Western Europe, dominated by Germany, the United Kingdom, France, Spain, and Italy, has long been a mature but fragmented marketplace. But the transformation of this region, via the European Union (EU) (discussed later in this chapter), into an integrated economic system has further increased its importance. Major international firms such as Unilever, Renault, Royal Dutch Shell, Michelin, Siemens, and Nestlé, are headquartered in Western Europe. Eastern Europe, once primarily communist, has also gained importance, both as a marketplace and as a producer. Multinational corporations such as Nestlé and General Motors have set up operations in Poland. Ford, General Motors, and Volkswagen built new factories in Hungary. However, governmental instability has slowed development in Bulgaria, Albania, Romania, and other nations.

In recent years, the traditional view of Europe has been severely altered by the European Union, the common currency, and a clear divide between Northern Europe (led by Germany and, to a lesser extent, France) and Southern Europe (including Spain, Italy, Greece, and Portugal). The new dynamics will be discussed in detail below.

Pacific Asia Pacific Asia consists of Japan, China, Thailand, Malaysia, Singapore, Indonesia, South Korea, Taiwan, the Philippines, Vietnam, and Australia (which is technically not in Asia, but is included because of proximity). Fuelled by strong entries in the automobile, electronics, and banking industries, the economies of these countries have grown rapidly in the past three decades.

As the trends indicate, Asia Pacific is a growing force in the world economy and a major source of competition for North American companies. The Japanese dominate the region led by firms like Toyota, Toshiba, and Nippon Steel. However, South Korea (Samsung and Hyundai), Taiwan (Chinese Petroleum and manufacturing for foreign firms), and Hong Kong (a major financial centre) are also successful players in the global economy. China, the world's most densely populated country, has emerged as an important market and now boasts the world's second-largest economy behind that of the United States, after recently passing Japan.[7] In all three key regions, technology is playing an increasingly important role in the future.

BRICS A term used to describe five important and powerful emerging markets in the business world: Brazil, Russia, India, China, and South Africa.

LO-2 New Power Of Emerging Markets: Brics And Beyond

BRIC is a term that describes four increasingly important nations in global trade: Brazil, Russia, India, and China. The BRIC concept was first used by Goldman Sachs in 2001; since that time, BRIC investment funds have become an important group for money managers and international analysts. These four nations have begun to act like a unit, holding unofficial summits and discussing common strategies.

The status of these four nations has risen in international trade for different reasons. Brazil is strong in commodities and agriculture, Russia is a powerful energy supplier, and China is a major hub of manufacturing activity. India has become a leading service provider at various levels ranging from basic customer service call centres to engineering solutions providers. The growth and quick market development of the consumer market in these nations is also providing great sales opportunities for foreign companies that manufacture cars and high-end clothing brands, etc.[8]

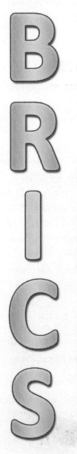

The old international trading patterns and activities are changing. In the past, Western companies used less-developed markets to acquire natural resources supplies and to carry out simple assembly tasks. But the BRIC nations now demonstrate relationships that are much more complex. A clear signal of this shift was evident a few years ago when Indian car maker Tata acquired Jaguar and Land Rover from Ford. This was not quite business in the traditional sense.[9]

While China, India, and Russia have had most of the attention, it is Brazil that is now at the front of the pack in terms of optimism and opportunity, based on positive domestic demand and high levels of investment. According to Transparency International, Brazil is the least corrupt of the BRIC nations, and its rich natural resources and momentum from World Cup 2014 should help propel it for years to come.[10] For example, Brookfield Asset Management is positioned to reap rewards by building major shopping centres to meet the demand of the 30 to 40 million people that have joined the ranks of the Brazilian middle class in the past decade. It is estimated that another 40 to 45 million Brazilians will achieve middle-class status over the next 20 years.[11]

In 2011, the initial group of four extended an invitation to South Africa and transformed into **BRICS.** The move was surprising to many analysts because there seemed to better candidates for admission. However, it was clear that the informal group was developing into an important political club with its own goals. South Africa is rich in minerals resources, something that these emerging markets need to sustain growth. In addition, the new member serves as a gateway to the African continent with over 1 billion potential consumers.[12]

In an even stronger sign of the changing times, a formal BRICS meeting was held in Durban, South Africa, to negotiate a $100 billion reserve fund to protect their currencies and a $50 billion seed-capital plan (to promote new businesses). In addition, they negotiated details for the creation of a development bank to compete with the World Bank. Emerging economies are clearly not relying on "old-world" economies and the BRICS nations clearly have their own independent agenda.[13]

While the BRICS nations have received a lot of publicity, there are tremendous opportunities in other emerging nations, including Thailand, Indonesia, South Korea, and Ukraine, to name just a few. According to the Global Institute of Research, the opportunity in emerging markets amounts to annual projected consumption of $30 trillion by 2025.[14] A new world order is evolving, and "old" economic powers like the U.S., Japan, Germany, and even Canada are going to need to adapt.

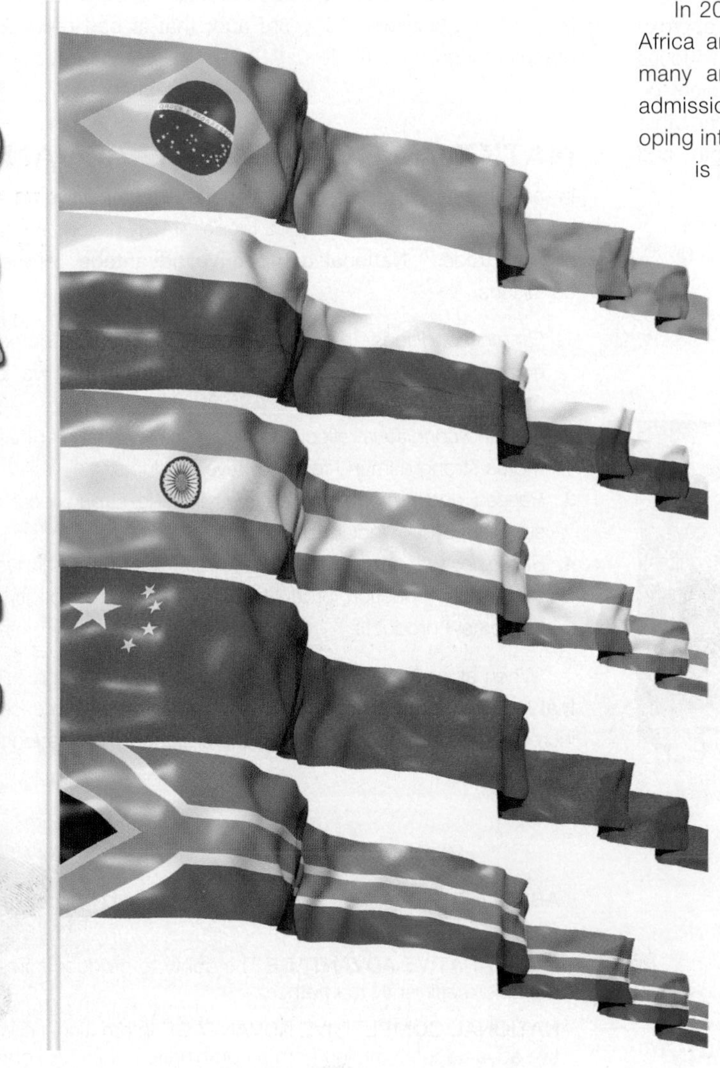

<<< The BRICS nations are a force to be respected in the modern global economy.

© epa european pressphoto agency b.v./Alamy

LO-3 Forms of Competitive Advantage

No country can produce all the goods and services that its people need. Thus, countries export products that they can make more efficiently or cheaper than other countries. The proceeds are then used to import products that they cannot produce effectively. However, this general principle does not fully explain why nations export and import. Such decisions depend on the kind of advantages a particular country may enjoy regarding its abilities to create and/or sell various products and resources.[15] Traditionally, economists have focused on absolute and comparative advantage to explain international trade. But because this approach focuses narrowly on such factors as natural resources and labour costs, the more contemporary view of national competitive advantage has emerged.

ABSOLUTE ADVANTAGE

An **absolute advantage** exists when a country can produce something more efficiently than any other country. In other words, a country can produce a larger output of goods or services using the same or fewer input resources. This concept was first proposed by economist Adam Smith in 1776. Saudi oil, Brazilian coffee beans, and Canadian timber approximate absolute advantage. The theory is simple; countries should focus on producing goods and services that they have an absolute advantage in and buy products that they do not produce more efficiently than other nations.[16] Canada exports timber because of its natural strengths and imports bananas because the climate here does not permit farmers to grow bananas efficiently. If trade was limited to two countries, you could negotiate which nation should produce which items for the greater good. However, the global economy is a complex network and most decisions are not that simple. In addition, true absolute advantages are very rare; the vast majority are actually relative.

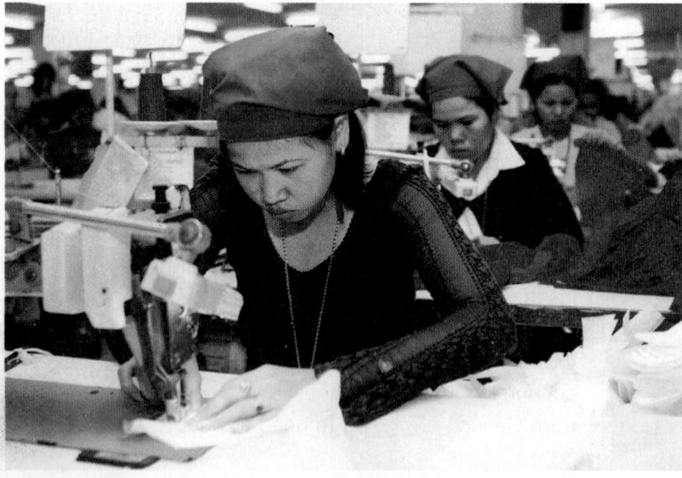

Chinese textile workers are learning what North American textile workers learned years ago. Manufacturers are increasingly moving textile manufacturing to lower-cost locations like Cambodia, where workers (like the ones seen in this photo) earn on average $76 for a 60-hour week as opposed to $280–$460 in China.

Bob Frid/Icon SMI 109/Bob Frid/Icon SMI/Newscom

COMPARATIVE ADVANTAGE

A country has a **comparative advantage** in goods that it can produce more efficiently or better than other goods. For example, if businesses in a given country can make computers more efficiently than they can make automobiles, that nation's firms have a comparative advantage in computer manufacturing. Canada has a comparative advantage in farming (because of fertile land and a temperate climate), while South Korea has a comparative advantage in electronics manufacturing (because of efficient operations and cheap labour). As a result, Canadian firms export grain to South Korea and import electronic equipment from South Korea. All countries have a comparative advantage in some products, but no country has a comparative advantage in all products. Developed countries tend to have a comparative advantage in making high-tech products, while developing countries tend to have a comparative advantage in making products that require lots of low-cost labour. For example, in the past two decades, most of the textile manufacturing jobs in Canada (and elsewhere) have moved to China. But the race to the bottom (in terms of labor costs) now sees countries like Cambodia, Bangladesh, and Vietnam taking manufacturing jobs away from China. Why? In Cambodia, textile workers are paid $76 for a 60-hour week, while in China the wages range from $280 to $460. In other words, Cambodia is just like China was 20 years ago; that is bad news for Chinese manufacturing.[17]

NATIONAL COMPETITIVE ADVANTAGE

In more recent years, the theory of national competitive advantage has become a more widely accepted model of why nations engage in international trade.[18] **National competitive advantage** derives from four conditions:

1. *Factor conditions* (natural resources, human resources, capital, entrepreneurs) are the factors of production that we identified in Chapter 1.
2. *Demand conditions* reflect a large domestic consumer base that promotes strong demand for innovative products.
3. *Related* and *supporting industries* include strong local or regional suppliers and/or industrial customers.
4. *Strategies, structures*, and *rivalries* refer to firms and industries that stress cost reduction, product quality, higher productivity, and innovative new products.

When all of these conditions exist in an industry, the companies in that industry are motivated to be very innovative and to excel. This also increases the likelihood that they will engage in international business.

ABSOLUTE ADVANTAGE The ability to produce something more efficiently than any other country.

COMPARATIVE ADVANTAGE The ability to produce some products more efficiently than others.

NATIONAL COMPETITIVE ADVANTAGE International competitive advantage stemming from a combination of factor conditions; demand conditions; related and supporting industries; and firm strategies, structures, and rivalries.

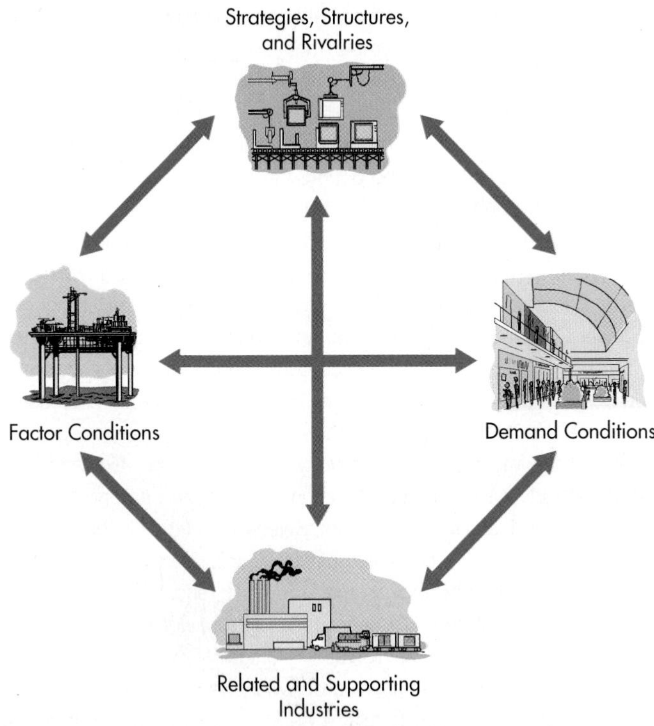

FIGURE 5.1 Attributes of national competitive advantage

Japan, for instance, has strong domestic demand for automobiles. Its automobile producers have well-developed supplier networks, and Japanese firms have competed intensely with each other for decades. This set of circumstances explains why Japanese automobile companies such as Toyota, Honda, Nissan, and Mazda are generally successful in foreign markets.

International competitiveness refers to the ability of a country to generate more wealth than its competitors in world markets. Each year, the World Economic Forum publishes a global competitiveness ranking. The ranking is based on both hard economic data and on a poll of business leaders. In the 2012 to 2013 report, the top three countries on the list were Switzerland, Singapore, and Finland. Canada ranked 14th. Canada's high taxes, regulated industries, relatively large bureaucracy, and overly conservative capital market structure were listed as reasons for a lower rating. The U.S. declined for the fourth straight year and was ranked seventh.[19]

INTERNATIONAL COMPETITIVENESS Competitive marketing of domestic products against foreign products.

BALANCE OF TRADE The economic value of all the products that a country exports minus the economic value of all the products it imports.

SURPLUS Situation in which a country exports more than it imports, creating a favourable balance of trade.

DEFICIT Situation in which a country's imports exceed its exports, creating a negative balance of trade.

BALANCE OF PAYMENTS Flow of all money into or out of a country.

EXCHANGE RATE Rate at which the currency of one nation can be exchanged for the currency of another nation.

TABLE 5.1 Canadian Exports to and Imports from Selected Countries, 2012[21]

Country	Exports (billions)	Imports from (in billions of $)
United States	$338.4	$296.4
European Union	40.9	44.6
Japan	10.8	10.7
All others	53.8	86.7

The Balance of Trade

A country's **balance of trade** is the difference in value between its total exports and its total imports. A country that exports more than it imports has a favourable balance of trade, or a **surplus**. A country that imports more than it exports has an unfavourable balance of trade, or a **deficit**. Canada has enjoyed a favourable balance of merchandise trade for many years, but in 2012, the country had a trade deficit of $11.9 billion. The United States is by far Canada's largest trading partner, and our overall trade balance has been generally favourable only because Canada exports more to the United States than it imports from it. But this is changing, partly due to the higher Canadian dollar. For years, economists had warned against Canada's dependence on the United States. Canada's nearly $47 billion surplus in 2008 turned into a deficit in large part because of a major decline in exports to the U.S. In addition, we also export slightly more than we import from Japan; however, we import more from the countries of the European Union than we export to them (see Table 5.1).[20]

The Balance of Payments

Even if a country has a favourable balance of trade, it can still have an unfavourable balance of payments. A country's **balance of payments** is the difference between money flowing into the country and money flowing out as a result of trade and other transactions. An unfavourable balance means more money is flowing out than in. For Canada to have a favourable balance of payments for a given year, the total of our exports, foreign-tourist spending in this country, foreign investments here, and earnings from overseas investments must be greater than the total of our imports, Canadian-tourist spending overseas, our foreign aid grants, our military spending abroad, the investments made by Canadian firms abroad, and the earnings of foreigners from their investments in this country. Canada has had an unfavourable balance of payments for the last two decades; in 2011, it amounted to $110 billion.[22]

Exchange Rates

An **exchange rate** is the rate at which the currency of one nation can be exchanged for another.[23] For example, if the exchange rate between Canadian dollars and British pounds is 1 to 1.55, this means that it costs $1.55 in Canadian dollars to "buy" one British pound. Alternatively, it would cost only 0.65 of a British pound to "buy" one Canadian dollar. This exchange rate means that 0.65 of a British pound and one Canadian dollar should have exactly the same purchasing power.

THERE'S AN APP FOR THAT!

1. **XE Currency APP** >>> **Platforms:** *Apple, Android, BlackBerry*
   Source: XE.COM Inc.
   Key Features: Allows you to access live rates for every currency in the world.
2. **ExportWise** >>> **Platforms:** *Apple*
   Source: Purple Forge
   Key Features: Allows the user to access *ExportWise* articles, Export Development Canada's (EDC) official magazine.
3. **International Business Etiquette** >>> **Platforms:** *Apple, Android, BlackBerry*
   Source: Kwintessential Ltd.
   Key Features: Guide to understanding other cultures, languages, etiquette, and taboos.

APP DISCOVERY EXERCISE

Since APP availability changes, conduct your own search for "Top 3" Global Business APPS and identify the key features.

The value of one country's currency relative to another varies with market conditions. For example, when many English citizens want to spend pounds to buy Canadian dollars (or goods), the value of the dollar relative to the pound increases, or becomes "stronger," and demand for the Canadian dollar is high. It is also "strong" when there is high demand for goods manufactured in Canada. Thus, the value of the Canadian dollar rises with the demand for Canadian goods. Exchange rates typically fluctuate by very small amounts on a daily basis. More significant variations usually occur over greater spans of time.

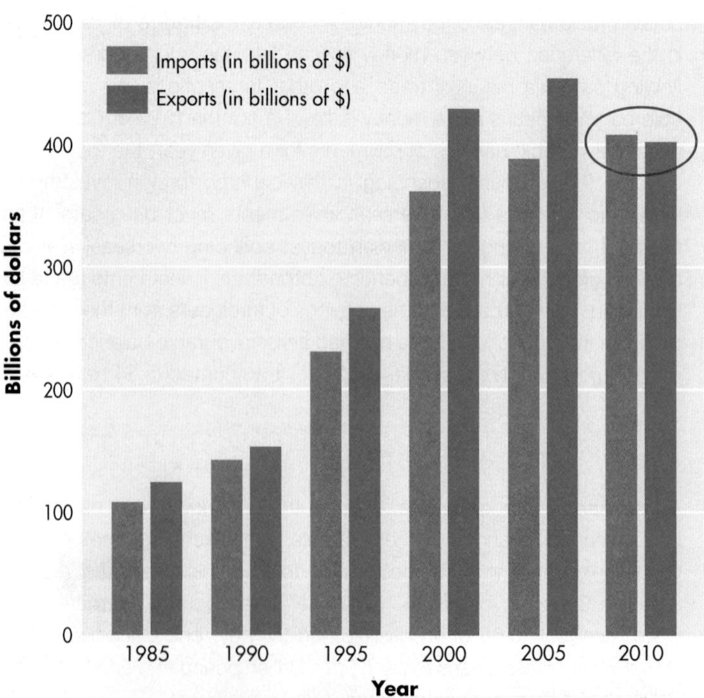

FIGURE 5.2 Canadian imports and exports of merchandise

Fluctuation in exchange rates can have an important impact on the balance of trade. Suppose, for example, that you wanted to buy some British tea for 10 British pounds per box. At an exchange rate of 1.55 Canadian dollars to the British pound, a box will cost you $15.50 (10 pounds * 1.55 = 15.50). But what if the pound gets stronger? At an exchange rate of, say, 2.1 Canadian dollars to the pound, the same box of tea would cost you $21.00 (10 pounds * 2.1 = $21.00). However, if the Canadian dollar gets stronger in relation to the British pound, the prices of all Canadian-made products would rise in the United Kingdom and the prices of all British-made products would fall in Canada. As a result, the British would buy fewer Canadian-made products, and Canadians would spend more on British-made products. The result could conceivably be a Canadian trade deficit with the United Kingdom. This is why the recent increase in the value of the Canadian dollar has Canadian exporters very concerned.

One of the most significant developments in foreign exchange has been the introduction of the **euro**—a common currency among 17 members of the European Union (Denmark, Sweden, and the United Kingdom do not participate). The euro was officially introduced back in 2002. It quickly became as important as the U.S. dollar and the Japanese yen in international commerce. The euro rose in value against the U.S. and Canadian dollars and stood as high as $1.73 against the Canadian dollar in 2008; however, there was a sharp drop when the European crisis began in 2010 and it has dropped to as low as $1.25. It was valued at around $1.40 in early 2013. The primary reason for this drop is the economic instability which has even raised some concerns about the long-term survival of the currency. (See the Managing in Turbulent Times boxed feature entitled "The Neverending European Debt Crisis: The Divided Truth").

EXCHANGE RATES AND COMPETITION

Companies that conduct international operations must watch exchange-rate fluctuations closely because these changes affect overseas demand for their products and can be a major factor in international competition. In general, when the value of a country's domestic currency rises—becomes "stronger"—companies based there find it harder to export products to foreign markets and easier for foreign companies to enter local markets. It also makes it more cost-efficient for domestic companies to move production operations to lower-cost sites in foreign countries. When the value of a country's currency declines—becomes "weaker"—just the opposite patterns occur. Thus, as the value of a country's currency falls, its balance of trade should improve because domestic companies should experience a boost in exports. There should also be a corresponding decrease in the incentives for foreign companies to ship products into the domestic market.

These dollar fluctuations have also had a huge impact on businesses. Canadian companies are finding it harder to compete internationally, since they can no longer rely on a cheap dollar to make their products more affordable across the border and abroad. But after the initial shock, companies are learning to cope. According to the chairman and CEO of Clearwater Seafoods Income Fund, "The way you deal with the stronger Canadian dollar is to increase the efficiency of your operations."[24] Other companies, like Nova Scotia–based High Liner Foods, which buys most of its raw fish on the world markets in U.S. dollars, has seen a net benefit from a stronger Canadian dollar.[25]

EURO A common currency shared among most of the members of the European Union.

MANAGING IN TURBULENT TIMES

The Neverending European Debt Crisis: The Divided Truth

Individuals and businesses must make sure that the debt they carry does not exceed their capacity to do so. The same thing is true for sovereign nations. Well, sort of. Consider the problems that Greece has recently experienced as concerns arose about the country's ability to pay back investors who had purchased its government bonds. During 2010 and 2011, many meetings were held that focused on solving the problem, but no clear resolution emerged. Eventually, it became apparent that some investors were going to take a "haircut" (i.e., lose part of their investment), but there was a disagreement about whether it would be public creditors like the eurozone governments and the European Central Bank (ECB), or private creditors like banks, hedge funds, and asset managers. The ECB resisted taking a haircut because that might cause people to think that the ECB would be less willing in the future to buy the bonds of other countries that were in financial trouble.

The European Central Bank (ECB) agreed to provide Greece a bailout, but said that austerity measures needed to be introduced (like cutting wages and increasing taxes). Citizens then rioted in the streets, protesting high unemployment levels, low economic growth, and business bankruptcies. The austerity measures created a deep recession in Greece, driving unemployment well above 20 percent (53 percent among youth). In 2012, an agreement was reached that gave Greece the money it needed, but imposed losses of up to 75 percent on investors. The ECB took no losses.

In 2013, a new crisis erupted when Cyprus sought a bailout. The European Union initially offered it on the condition that Cyprus impose a tax on bank deposits in order to raise part of the money needed for the bailout. This caused outrage in Cyprus, and the government refused to accept the terms. Eventually an agreement was reached that imposed heavy losses on wealthier investors at the Cyprus Popular Bank. But there was concern that this deal would not be sufficient to solve the country's financial problems, and that further bailouts might be needed later. The European Union also provided bailout money for banks in Spain, but only after stipulating that investors would have to face losses. For example, when Bankia SA was nationalized, shareholders lost nearly all their investment, and bondholders lost 30 percent of their investment.

A great clash of ideologies is evident as attempts are made to solve the problems in Greece, Spain, and Cyprus. One school of thought says that European governments should introduce big stimulus programs to increase economic growth. An opposing school of thought—which is particularly strong in Germany—is that austerity measures are necessary to reduce government debt, and countries with strong economies shouldn't have to bail out countries that do not control their government spending. Clearly this division between the northern and southern European countries is growing. The so-called European crisis has inflicted very different consequences on the partners. Under the current EU system, Spain has taken the position as the Western nation with the highest unemployment rate in the world (closely followed by Greece). Unable to devalue their currency, they search for answers and are told to take their medicine even as they fail to see concrete results. Meanwhile, Germany has simultaneously experienced its lowest unemployment rate in 20 to 30 years (numbers matched in 1981 and 1991), despite the fact that some of its best customers (other European nations) were suffering. A big reason for this obvious contradiction was the fact that a weak euro (due to the crisis) meant that German products were now cheaper for Americans, Canadians, the Japanese, etc., because of the weak exchange rate created by the culprits of the crisis.

One thing is becoming clear: if the euro is to survive in the long term, major structural issues will need to be truly addressed; the band-aid solutions will need to be put aside along with the finger-pointing. Time will tell if the Europeans are serious about a lasting solution.

CRITICAL THINKING QUESTIONS

1. Why is progress toward solutions to financial problems so slow in the European Union? Is this truly a union or a marriage of short-term convenience likely to end up in a messy divorce?
2. What would happen to individual Canadian consumers or Canadian corporations who consistently spent more money than they earned?

LO-4 INTERNATIONAL BUSINESS MANAGEMENT

Wherever a firm is located, its success depends largely on how well it is managed. International business is challenging because the basic management responsibilities—planning, organizing, leading, and controlling—are much more difficult to carry out when a business operates in several markets scattered around the globe. (We discuss the functions of management in Chapter 6.)

Managing means making decisions. In this section, we examine the three most basic decisions managers must make when faced with the prospect of a global market. The first decision is whether to "go international" at all. Often that decision is made because a company feels it has to shift its production to a low-cost foreign country in order to remain competitive. Once that decision has been made, managers must decide on the company's level of international involvement and on the organizational structure that will best meet its global needs.

Going International

The world economy is slowly transforming into one large global village. As Figure 5.3 shows, several factors enter into the decision to go international. One overriding factor is the business climate in other nations. Even experienced firms have encountered cultural, legal, and economic roadblocks, as we shall see later in this chapter. In considering international

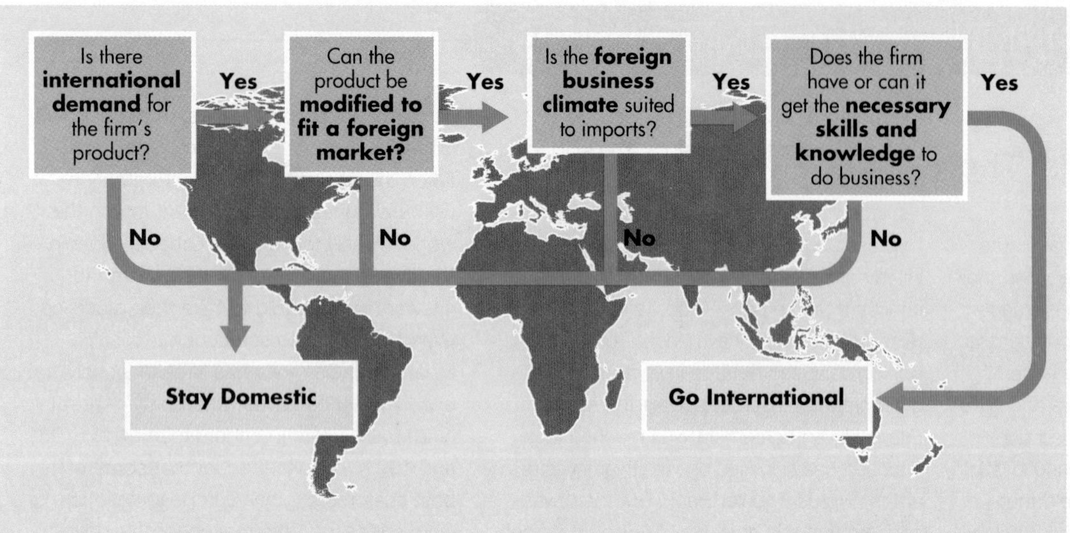
Is there international demand for the firm's product?
Yes
Can the product be modified to fit a foreign market?
Yes
Is the foreign business climate suited to imports?
Yes
Does the firm have or can it get the necessary skills and knowledge to do business?
Yes
No
No
No
No
Stay Domestic
Go International

<<< FIGURE 5.3 Going international

expansion, a company should also consider at least two other questions: Is there a demand for its products abroad? If so, must those products be adapted for international consumption?

GAUGING INTERNATIONAL DEMAND

Products that are seen as vital in one country may be useless in another. Snowmobiles are popular for transportation and recreation in Canada and the northern United States, but there would be no demand at all for this product in Central America. Although this is an extreme example, the point is quite basic to the decision to go international. Specifically, foreign demand for a company's product may be greater than, the same as, or weaker than domestic demand. Even when there is demand, advertising may still need to be adjusted. For instance, in Canada, bicycles and small motorcycles are mainly used for recreation, but in many parts of Asia they are seen as transportation. Market research and/or the prior market entry of competitors may indicate whether there is an international demand for a firm's products.

Some products—like smartphones, Hollywood movies, and video games—are popular all over the world. Movies like *Avatar* and *Twilight* earn significant revenues in North America, but generate even more revenues overseas.

ADAPTING TO CUSTOMER NEEDS

If there is international demand for its product, a firm must still figure out whether or not to adapt the product. If they decide to make changes, they must figure out how to adapt that product to meet the special demands and expectations of foreign customers. For example, New Brunswick–based McCain Foods Limited has worked hard to build market share in South Africa. It even developed single-sized portions of frozen vegetables to serve customers that do not have proper refrigeration.[26] KFC's dishes in China come with a side order of rice and hot soy milk.[27] They must be doing something right because, at last count, KFC had had over 3700 outlets in China (McDonald's had about 1400).[28] Likewise, McDonald's restaurants sell beer in Germany and meatless sandwiches in India to accommodate local tastes and preferences. BlackBerry smartphones may originate in Waterloo, Ontario, but the company has sold over 1.2 million smartphones in Indonesia; in Jakarta, a BlackBerry is an important symbol of success. To succeed in this market, BlackBerry created prepaid scratch cards. This enables consumers to pay a set amount for data and email service each week or month.[29] The boxed insert entitled "Connection That Matters: My World, My Choice!" describes one organization's experience in going international.

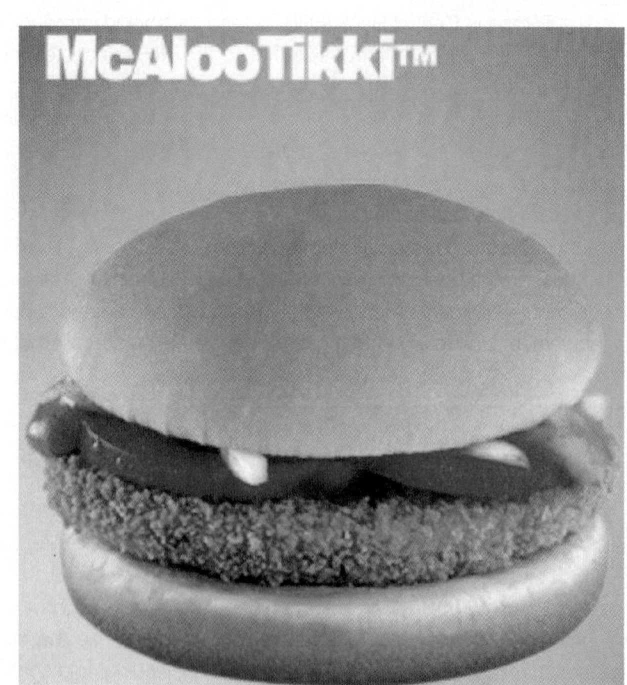
McAlooTikki™

The McAloo Tikki burger is sold in India and in countries with large Indian populations. To meet local needs and religious practices, this is a meatless sandwich made primarily with potato and local spices.

© Chris Howes/Wild Places Photography/Alamy

ENTREPRENEURSHIP AND NEW VENTURES

Connection That Matters: My World, My Choice!

From Bangalore, India, to Calgary, Alberta, there is no doubt that there are cultural and demographic differences that impact the choices made in both areas and all regions in between. The same thread, however, binds all of these choices; whether you are a child in Pakistan or an adult in Germany, making *responsible* choices, according to the founders of My World, My Choice! (MWMC), can make all the difference in the world.

MWMC is an educational program whose mission is to engage students from elementary and secondary schools, and from different regions of the world, to make sustainable choices, while empowering them to become leaders within their own community. These choices are made on a daily basis, from packing bottle-free lunches and composting, to building community gardens. Lianne Foti, director and co-founder of MWMC, says, "We want to show students that the choices they make have a lasting impact on our world. Understanding that the environmental, economic, and social well-being of our planet is tied together through the choices our community makes every day is the first step." This ideology essentially developed into the motivating factor behind creating a program that would become part of the curriculum within school systems and make a diverse impact on the minds of younger generations, the adults of tomorrow.

MWMC began as many entrepreneurial projects do, with co-founders Lianne Foti and Kurt Archer sharing a vision to help make a difference in the choices that impact our world and our future. The adventure began in 2008 in Bangalore, India, where the program reached several hundred students. Its success inspired the pair to take the educational program home to Canada, where their vision shaped into a reality of hundreds of students from Calgary, Alberta, to Guelph, Ontario, inspired to make sustainable choices and a difference in their local communities. This inspirational education program has also reached other regions across the globe in Lahore, Pakistan, and in Kenya, not only as a successful in-class educational tool, but also in developing leadership skills outside the classroom. As a result of their ability to train young and aspiring mentors to volunteer and conduct the simulations, MWMC also has a hand in the development and growth of invaluable leadership skills amongst young professionals. Their sensitivity to cultural differences and their focus on providing a simple and universal goal has contributed to the program's global success.

According to Lianne Foti, "We have seen many insightful ideas result from these projects, and we will continue to challenge students to become the forward-thinking leaders of their generation." Such inspiration from the leaders of MWMC speaks to the impact entrepreneurship can have on curriculum development and education on all sides of the globe.

CRITICAL THINKING QUESTIONS

1. The decision to "go international" requires a high degree of analysis and examination of factors, both internal and external to the business. Assess MWMC's form of competitive advantage and level of involvement in international education.
2. What are some potential barriers to this initiative?

Levels of Involvement in International Business

After a firm decides to go international, it must decide on the level of its international involvement. Several options are available. At the most basic level, it may act as an exporter or importer, organize as an international firm, or operate as a multinational firm. Most of the world's largest industrial firms are multinationals.

EXPORTERS AND IMPORTERS

An **exporter** is a firm that makes products in one country and then distributes and sells them in others. An **importer** buys products in foreign markets and then imports them for resale in its home country. These approaches represent the lowest level of involvement in international operations and are excellent ways to learn the fine points of global business. Exporters and importers tend to conduct most of their business in their home nations. It is not just large companies that are exporting; small firms also export products and services.

Canada ranks first among the G8 countries in the proportion of its production that is exported (almost 40 percent).[30] Large and small Canadian firms export products and services. For example, McCain Foods is a formidable presence in Europe, where it holds a 75 percent share of the market for "oven fries" in Germany; Sabian Cymbals sells 90 percent of its products in 80 different countries; Electrovert Ltd. does 95 percent of its business outside Canada.

INTERNATIONAL FIRMS

As firms gain experience and success as exporters and importers, they may move to the next level. An **international firm** conducts a significant portion of its business abroad. Hershey, for example, sells its products in 90 foreign countries, and it buys ingredients for its chocolates from several foreign suppliers. But it manufactures the vast majority of its products in the United States (there is one plant in Mexico). In fact, most of that manufacturing occurs in Pennsylvania.[31] So an international firm may be large and influential in the global economy, but remain basically a domestic firm with international operations. Its central concern is its own domestic market.

MULTINATIONAL FIRMS

Most **multinational firms** do not think of themselves as having domestic and international divisions. Instead, planning and decision making

EXPORTER Firm that distributes and sells products to one or more foreign countries.

IMPORTER Firm that buys products in foreign markets and then imports them for resale in its home country.

INTERNATIONAL FIRM Firm that conducts a significant portion of its business in foreign countries.

MULTINATIONAL FIRM Firm that designs, produces, and markets products in many nations.

are geared toward global markets.[32] The locations of headquarters are almost irrelevant. Royal Dutch Shell, Nestlé, IBM, and Ford are well-known multinationals.

The economic importance of multinational firms should not be underestimated. Consider the economic impact of the 500 largest multinational corporations; they employ millions of people, buy supplies, parts, equipment, and materials from thousands of other firms; and pay billions of dollars in taxes. Moreover, their activities and products affect the lives of hundreds of millions of consumers, competitors, and investors (sometimes not in a very positive way). Organized protests against the activities of multinational corporations have become quite common. In 2012, Royal Dutch Shell ranked first with $484 billion in sales and 90 000 employees.[33]

International Organizational Structures

Different levels of involvement in international business require different kinds of organizational structure. For example, a structure that would help coordinate an exporter's activities would be inadequate for the activities of a multinational firm. In this section, we briefly consider the international organizational strategies, including independent agents, licensing arrangements, branch offices, strategic alliances, and foreign direct investment.

INDEPENDENT AGENTS

An **independent agent** is a foreign individual or organization that agrees to represent an exporter's interests in foreign markets. Independent agents often act as sales representatives—they sell the exporter's products, collect payment, and ensure that customers are satisfied. Independent agents often represent several firms at once and usually do not specialize in a particular product or market. Levi Strauss uses agents to market clothing products in many small countries in Africa, Asia, and South America.

LICENSING ARRANGEMENTS

Canadian companies seeking more involvement in international business may choose **licensing arrangements**. Firms give individuals or companies in a foreign country the exclusive right to manufacture or market their products in that area. In return, the exporter typically receives a fee plus ongoing payments called **royalties**.[34] Royalties are usually calculated as a percentage of the licence holder's sales. For example, Can-Eng Manufacturing, Canada's largest supplier of industrial furnaces, exports its furnaces under licensing arrangements to Japan, Brazil, Germany, Korea, Taiwan, and Mexico. Franchising is a special form of licensing that is also very popular.[35] McDonald's and Pizza Hut franchise around the world. Similarly, Accor SA, a French hotel chain, franchises its Ibis, Sofitel, and Novotel hotels.

BRANCH OFFICES

Instead of developing relationships with foreign companies or independent agents, a firm may simply send some of its own managers to overseas branch offices. A company has more direct control over branch managers than agents or licence holders. **Branch offices** also provide a more visible public presence in foreign countries. Potential customers tend to feel more secure when a business has branch offices in their country.

When a business operates branches, plants, or subsidiaries in several countries, it may assign one plant or subsidiary the responsibility for researching, developing, manufacturing, and marketing one product or line of products. This is known as **world product mandating**.

STRATEGIC ALLIANCES

The concept of a strategic alliance was introduced in Chapter 2. In international business, it means that a company finds a partner in a foreign country where it would like to conduct business. Each party agrees to invest resources and capital in a new business or else to cooperate in some way for mutual benefit. This new business—the alliance—is then owned by the partners, which divide its profits.

The number of strategic alliances among major companies has increased significantly over the last decade and is likely to grow further. In many countries, including Mexico, India, and China, laws make alliances virtually the only way to do business within their borders.[36] Whirlpool, the world's largest manufacturer of home appliances, has partnered with Hisene Kelon Electrical Holdings Co. in China to manufacture appliances locally. In addition, the company has signed a preferential distribution agreement with Suning Appliance Co., which owns 1700 retail stores in 300 Chinese cities.[37] This approach eases the way into new markets; alliances also give firms greater control over their foreign activities than independent agents and licensing arrangements. (All partners in an alliance retain some say in its decisions.) Perhaps most important, alliances allow firms to benefit from the knowledge and expertise of their foreign partners. In India, Walmart partnered with Bharti Enterprises to build 10 to 15 large cash-and-carry stores. Walmart wanted to capture a share of the booming retail market without angering the local mom-and-pop merchants and middlemen that dominate the industry.[38]

There are clear advantages of forming strategic alliances, but there are many obstacles as well. Groupon, the successful online coupon company, faced major problems after it formed a joint venture with GaoPeng in China. After some early promise, many offices were shut down in 2011 and approximately 400 former employees and their lawyers took legal action. Part of the problem was that the joint venture had to deal with strong competitors, including one that had already acquired the right to use the groupon.cn domain name.[39]

FOREIGN DIRECT INVESTMENT

The term **foreign direct investment (FDI)** means buying or establishing tangible assets (e.g., a manufacturing plant) in another country.[40]

INDEPENDENT AGENT Foreign individual or organization that agrees to represent an exporter's interests.

LICENSING ARRANGEMENT Arrangement in which firms choose foreign individuals or organizations to manufacture or market their products in another country.

ROYALTIES Fees that an exporter receives for allowing a company in a foreign country to manufacture or market the exporter's products.

BRANCH OFFICE A location that an exporting firm establishes in a foreign country to sell its products more effectively.

WORLD PRODUCT MANDATING The assignment by a multinational of a product responsibility to a particular branch.

FOREIGN DIRECT INVESTMENT (FDI) Buying or establishing tangible assets in another country.

For example, in 2013, Bombardier built a manufacturing facility in Casablanca, Morocco.[41] The Bank of Montreal recently purchased Milwaukee-based Marshall and Ilsley bank branches (374 in all) and nearly doubled its presence in the U.S.[42] However, despite such moves, a debate has been going on for years about how FDI by foreign firms in Canada affects Canadians. Recently, foreign buyouts of major Canadian firms like Inco, Four Seasons Hotels, and Alcan have caused some Canadian business leaders to express concern. The most general fear is that foreign buyouts of Canadian firms will damage the economy because the head offices will move to foreign countries and major decisions will be made there, not in Canada.

Investment Canada has a mandate to help attract foreign investment to the nation and, in the past three decades, foreign direct investment in Canada has been growing steadily; it now averages over $600 billion annually. More than half of that amount is flowing from the U.S.; however, nearly half of FDI flowing from Canadian firms goes to the United States as well.[43]

TABLE 5.2 Top 10 Foreign-Controlled Companies in Canada, 2012[44]

Rank	Company	Annual Revenues (in billions of $)
1.	Imperial Oil	30.7
2.	Husky Energy	24.7
3.	Walmart Canada	22.3
4.	Costco Wholesale Canada	13.3
5.	Novelis Inc.	10.4
6.	Ultramar Ltd	10.1
7.	Ford Motor Co. of Canada	9.5
8.	Direct Energy Marketing Ltd.	9.4
9.	IBM Canada	9.1
10.	Honda Canada	8.1

LO-5 BARRIERS TO INTERNATIONAL TRADE

Whether a business is selling to just a few foreign markets or is a true multinational, a number of differences between countries will affect its international operations. How a firm responds to and manages social, economic, and political issues will go a long way toward determining its success.

Social and Cultural Differences

Any firm involved in international business needs to understand something about the society and culture in the countries it plans to operate in. Unless a firm understands these cultural differences—either itself or by acquiring a partner that does—it will probably not be successful in its international activities. A French lingerie company called Jours Apres Lunes recently got into trouble for a new line of products aimed at children aged four to twelve years old. The line, along with an ad campaign that featured young girls posing in a manner beyond their years, received little attention in France, but was widely criticized as inappropriate and creepy outside of Europe.[45]

Some differences are relatively obvious. Language barriers can cause inappropriate naming of products. In addition, the physical stature of people in different countries can make a difference. For example, the Japanese are slimmer and shorter on average than Canadians, an important consideration for firms that intend to sell clothes in these markets. Differences in the average age of the local population can also impact product development and marketing. Countries with growing populations tend to have a high percentage of young people. Thus, electronics and fashionable clothing would likely do well. Countries with stable or declining populations tend to have more old people. Generic pharmaceuticals might be more successful in such markets.

In addition to such obvious differences, a wide range of subtle value differences can have an important impact. For example, many Europeans shop daily. To Canadians, used to weekly trips to the supermarket, the European pattern may seem like a waste of time. But for Europeans, shopping is not just "buying food." It is also meeting friends, exchanging political views, gossiping, and socializing.

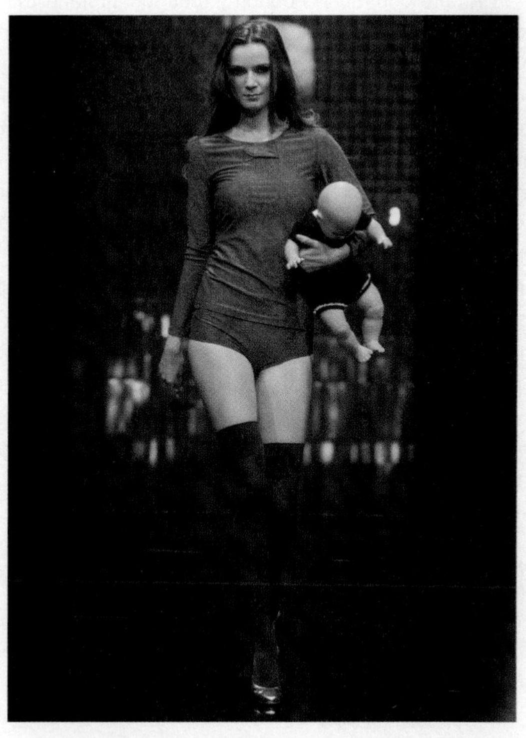

Jours Apres Lunes upset many people with a series of controversial ads depicting children in images that appear beyond their age.

© B Christopher/Alamy

What implications does this kind of shopping have for firms selling in European markets? First, those who go shopping each day do not need the large refrigerators and freezers common in North America. Second, the large supermarkets one sees in Canada are not an appropriate retail outlet in Europe. Finally, the kinds of food Europeans buy differ from those Canadians buy. In Canada, prepared and frozen foods are important, but Europeans often prefer to buy fresh ingredients to do their own food preparation. These differences are gradually disappearing, however, so firms need to be on the lookout for future opportunities as they emerge.

Even more subtle behavioural differences that can influence business activity exist. For example, crossing your legs in a business meeting in Saudi Arabia is inappropriate, because showing the sole of your foot is viewed as an insult to the other people in the room. In Portugal, it is considered rude to discuss business during dinner, and, in Taiwan, tapping your fingers on the table is a sign of appreciation for a meal. In China, don't give a businessman a green hat and don't wrap a gift in white or black (a green hat on a Chinese man is said to indicate that his wife is unfaithful, and black and white are associated with death). Deals can be lost based on cultural misunderstandings. Knowledge of local dos and don'ts is important in international business activity. Do your homework.[46]

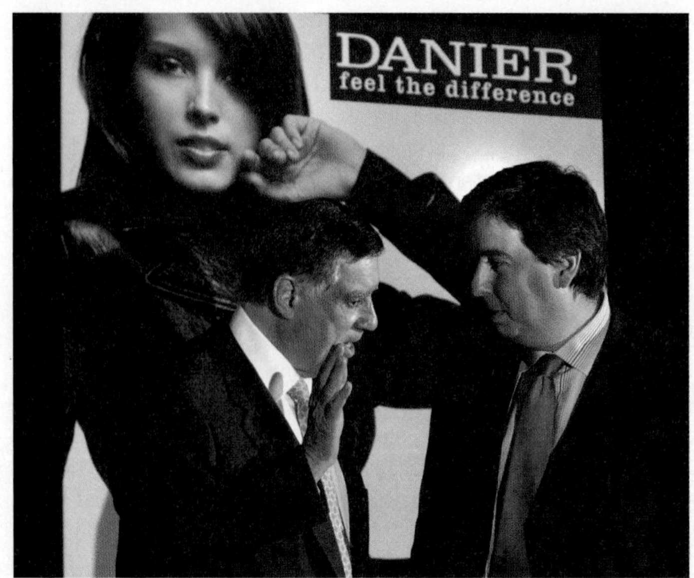

New tougher tariffs imposed on goods imported from 72 countries translate directly into an estimated additional cost of $1.2 million for Danier Leather (or about $10 to $20 per leather jacket).

AP Photo/Canadian Press, Tom Hanson

Economic Differences

Although cultural differences are often subtle, economic differences can be fairly pronounced. In dealing with economies like those of France and Sweden, firms must be aware of the extent of government involvement. For example, the French government is heavily involved in all aspects of airplane design and manufacturing. Similarly, a foreign firm doing business in a pure command economy must understand the unfamiliar relationship of government to business. Another very important consideration is the level of economic development and the financial infrastructure in a country. What percentage of retail transactions are completed by credit card? Is financing readily available? Is it a cash economy? And so on.

Navigating the economic differences and identifying the global opportunities is a major challenge for today's corporations. Growth is quite often fuelled by nations across the globe. For instance, luxury goods manufacturers can see major benefits as economies grow and a taste for global brands increases. Swiss watch-maker Patek Philippe experienced growth of 19 percent in 2012 and averaged 20 percent in the two previous years, due largely to growing demand in China, where Swiss watches are often given to government officials. However, in the first three months of 2013, an economic slowdown in China brought an unexpected 26 percent decline in sales.[47]

Legal and Political Differences

Legal and political differences are often closely linked to the structure of the economic systems in different countries. These issues include tariffs and quotas, local-content laws, and business-practice laws.

QUOTAS, TARIFFS, AND SUBSIDIES

Even free-market economies often use some form of quota and/or tariff that affects the prices and quantities of foreign-made products in those nations. A **quota** restricts the total number of certain products that can be imported into a country. It indirectly raises the prices of those imports by reducing their supply. The ultimate form of quota is an **embargo**, a government order forbidding exportation and/or importation of a particular product—or even all the products—of a particular country.

A **tariff** is a tax charged on imported products. Tariffs directly affect the prices of products, effectively raising the price of imports to consumers. Tariffs raise money for the government and somewhat discourage the sale of imported products. Governments from around the world impose quotas and tariffs. For example, Italy imposes high tariffs on imported electronic goods. In 2013, the Canadian government announced a reduction in tariffs on sporting goods and baby clothes, which could lead to potential annual savings of $76 million for consumers. However, at the same time, the government announced higher tariffs on goods imported from 72 countries which could lead to a $330 million increase in costs for Canadian shoppers. For example, the new rules will cost Danier Leather an estimated $1.2 million a year (or about $10–$20 per jacket). You can bet this extra cost will be passed along to the consumer.[48]

A **subsidy** is a government payment given to a domestic business to help it compete with foreign firms. Bombardier has received subsidies from both federal and provincial governments. These funds and low-interest loans have helped the company compete and develop its major projects. Bombardier and its main rival, Brazil-based Embraer, have accused each other of receiving excessive unfair government support, which has led to disputes at the WTO.

QUOTA A restriction by one nation on the total number of products of a certain type that can be imported from another nation.

EMBARGO A government order forbidding exportation and/or importation of a particular product.

TARIFF A tax levied on imported products.

SUBSIDY A government payment to help domestic business compete with foreign firms.

When the government of a country pays subsidies to one of its domestic companies or industries, this can have a negative effect on producers in other countries. For example, the WTO ruled that the U.S. government's subsidies to its cotton growers broke trade rules, depressed world cotton prices, and hurt Brazilian cotton producers.[49] These subsidies also hurt small cotton farmers in Africa because they caused highly productive U.S. farmers to produce a lot of cotton, which drove down the price African farmers received.[50] Canada's supply management system, which restricts imports and guarantees markets for producers of chickens, turkeys, eggs, and milk, could also come under fire since the WTO views the system as an unfair subsidy to producers.[51] More information about the WTO is available at the end of the chapter.

Subsidies are designed to support domestic companies; however, in this free-trade era, governments are increasingly generous with foreign firms that can help develop local industries and provide local jobs. A few years ago Warner Bros. opened up a new studio to develop high-end video games in Montreal. Local talent, reputation, and knowledge were key factors, but government funding helped close the deal. The Quebec government provided $7.5 million to get the studio off the ground.

© UrbanZone/Alamy

Protectionism—the practice of protecting domestic business at the expense of free market competition—has advocates and critics. Supporters argue that tariffs and quotas protect domestic firms and jobs. In particular, they protect new industries until they are able to compete internationally. Some claim they are necessary because other nations have such measures. Still others justify protectionism in the name of national security and argue that advanced technology should not be sold to potential enemies.

But opponents of protectionism are equally vocal. They note that protectionism reduces competition and drives up prices. Protectionism is also a cause of friction between nations. They maintain that while jobs in some industries would be lost if protectionism ceased, jobs in other industries would expand if all countries abolished tariffs and quotas.

At times, protectionism takes on almost comic proportions. Many of you may enjoy Cheetos Cheesy snacks, but you probably never realized that the brand has been in trouble with the law. A few years back, the company (Frito-Lay) incorrectly labelled several shipments of Cheetos from the U.S. into Canada as cardboard boxes. When the company realized the error they immediately informed the authorities. Since neither cardboard boxes nor Cheetos snacks are subject to tariffs, they figured that this would not be a problem. They were wrong. The Canadian Border Services put a retroactive 11 percent tariff on all the shipments going back three years. For five additional years, the agency refused to listen. In 2013, a tribunal ruled that this was an excessive example of protectionism; Frito-Lay was taken on an "administrative ride" for an innocent clerical mistake.[52]

LOCAL-CONTENT LAWS

A country can affect how a foreign firm does business there by enacting **local-content laws** that require products sold in a particular country be at least partly made in that country. These laws typically mean that firms seeking to do business there must either invest directly or have a local joint-venture partner. In this way, some of the profits in a foreign country are shared with the people who live there.

Many countries have local-content laws. In a fairly extreme case, Venezuela forbids the import of any product if a similar product is made there. A few years ago, Venezuela's president said he would cancel all mining licences and stop issuing new ones to foreign companies. This move was designed to protect the many small, local miners. Oil and gas licences held by foreign companies had already been cancelled. These actions make foreign companies more reluctant to invest in Venezuela.[53] In a recent case in Canada, Public Mobile challenged a government ruling which cleared Globalive's Wind Mobile and declared it a Canadian company in compliance with telecommunications rules. This industry is still highly regulated and Public Mobile is fighting the ruling concerning a direct competitor, because it was heavily financed by Orascom Telecom, a Cairo-based corporation.[54]

Local-content laws may even exist within a country and when they do, they act just like trade barriers. In Canada, for example, a low bid on a bridge in British Columbia was rejected because the company that made the bid was from Alberta. The job was given to a B.C. company. A window manufacturer from New Brunswick lost a contract in Nova Scotia despite having made the lowest bid, and the job went to a company in Nova Scotia. The Agreement on Internal Trade (AIT) requires all 10 Canadian provinces to remove barriers to agricultural trade. However, internal conflicts are still common. According to Perrin Beatty, former president of the Canadian Chamber of Commerce, interprovincial trade barriers are putting Canadian companies at a huge disadvantage. This has to change if Canadian companies are to survive and thrive in a global marketplace.[55]

PROTECTIONISM Protecting domestic business at the expense of free market competition.

LOCAL-CONTENT LAWS Laws requiring that products sold in a particular country be at least partly made in that country.

BUSINESS-PRACTICE LAWS

Many businesses entering new markets encounter problems in meeting strict regulations and bureaucratic barriers. Such practices are affected by the **business-practice laws** that host countries set in their jurisdictions. They can be frustratingly effective. Walmart left Germany and South Korea because the company did not effectively adapt to local tastes or rules and was unable to achieve economies of scale.[56] In Germany, for example, Walmart had to stop refunding price differences on items sold for less by other stores because the practice is illegal in Germany. In another case, Google agreed to pay $500 million to settle a case with the U.S. government over advertising revenue earned from Canadian online pharmacies. The government accused Google of enabling the illegal importation of drugs.[57]

Paying bribes to government officials to get business is another problem area. In 2013, SNC-Lavalin executives Ben Aissa and Stefane Roy were accused of paying $160 million to Saadi Gadhafi and other Libyan officials (under the old regime) to secure over $2 billion worth of contracts in Libya (to build an airport, a prison, and a water filtration plant) over a 10-year span.[58] The Canadian Corruption of Foreign Public Officials Act prohibits bribery of foreign officials, but as more Canadian companies do business abroad, they find themselves competing against companies that are happy to pay bribes to get business. In an attempt to create fairer competition among multinational companies, ministers from the Organisation for Economic Co-operation and Development (OECD) agreed in 1997 to criminalize bribery of foreign public officials.[59]

Transparency International (TI) publishes a "Corruption Perceptions Index," which ranks countries based on the amount of corruption that is perceived to exist, based on ratings by business people, academics, and risk analysts. The index showed that the least corrupt countries are Denmark, Finland, and New Zealand, while the most corrupt countries are North Korea, Afghanistan, and Somalia. Canada ranked ninth and the United States was 19th on the list.[60]

Cartels and Dumping A **cartel** is an association of producers whose purpose is to control the supply and price of a commodity. The most famous cartel is the Organization of the Petroleum Exporting Countries (OPEC). It has given oil-producing countries great power in the last 40 years. At various times, other cartels have been evident in diamonds, shipping, and coffee. While nothing much can be done when governments form a cartel like OPEC, private-sector businesses can be prosecuted for doing so. Canada is involved in a potash cartel with Belarus and Russia (these three nations account for almost 80 percent of production); the price has quadrupled in just a few years.[61]

Many countries forbid **dumping**—selling a product abroad for less than the comparable price charged in the home country. Antidumping legislation typically defines dumping as occurring if products are being sold at prices less than fair value, or if the result unfairly harms domestic industry. Recently, the U.S. imposed duties of 10.36 to 15.78 percent on steel pipes produced in China. China denounced the U.S. protectionist approach.[62] However, the U.S. is not alone in its concerns; India has accused China of dumping products on the Indian market that it can't sell elsewhere.[63]

BUSINESS-PRACTICE LAW Law or regulation governing business practices in given countries.

CARTEL Any association of producers whose purpose is to control supply of and prices for a given product.

DUMPING Selling a product for less abroad than in the producing nation.

LO-6 OVERCOMING BARRIERS TO TRADE

Despite the barriers to trade described so far, international trade is flourishing. This is because both organizations and free-trade treaties exist to promote trade. The most significant of these are the General Agreement on Tariffs and Trade (GATT), the World Trade Organization (WTO), the European Union (EU), and the North American Free Trade Agreement (NAFTA).

General Agreement on Tariffs and Trade (GATT)

Governments typically view exports as good (because they create jobs in the country) and imports as bad (because they cause job losses in the country). Because of this, governments may be tempted to build trade barriers to discourage imports. But if every country does this, international trade is damaged. To avoid this problem, the **General Agreement on Tariffs and Trade (GATT)** was signed after the Second World War. Its purpose was to reduce or eliminate trade barriers, such as tariffs and quotas. It did so by encouraging nations to protect domestic industries within agreed-upon limits and to engage in multilateral negotiations. While 92 countries signed GATT, not all complied with its rules. The United States was one of the worst offenders. A revision of GATT went into effect in 1994, but many issues remained unresolved—for example, the opening of foreign markets to most financial services.

World Trade Organization

On January 1, 1995, the **World Trade Organization (WTO)** came into existence as the successor to GATT. The 159 member countries are required to open markets to international trade, and the WTO is empowered to pursue three goals:

1. Promote trade by encouraging members to adopt fair trade practices.
2. Reduce trade barriers by promoting multilateral negotiations.
3. Establish fair procedures for resolving disputes among members.

The WTO is overseeing reductions in import duties on thousands of products that are traded between countries. Canada, the United States, and the European Union are founding members of the WTO.[64] Unlike GATT, the WTO's decisions are binding, and many people feared that it would make sweeping decisions and boss countries around. These

GENERAL AGREEMENT ON TARIFFS AND TRADE (GATT) International trade agreement to encourage the multilateral reduction or elimination of trade barriers.

WORLD TRADE ORGANIZATION (WTO) Organization through which member nations negotiate trading agreements and resolve disputes about trade policies and practices.

fears were overstated.[65] The WTO has served its role as a ruling body but appeals can often drag on for years. For example, Boeing recently won a ruling against Airbus because it received US$4.1 billion in loans from European governments while developing its A380 jets. Despite the ruling, there appears to be even more money being given to Airbus for development of the new A350. It has been over five years since the case was first presented and it could be years before Boeing sees any rewards from the ruling.[66]

A recent wave of new free trade agreements (e.g., Canada-Europe Agreement & the Trans Pacific Partnership, with its 21 members) have senior trade officials openly questioning the long-term relevance of the WTO if the members don't make adjustments. Many of the new agreements have more modern, faster rules. For example, the new trading agreements include better coordination of standards and regulations (which sometimes act as obstacles to trade).[67] In this day and age, the WTO structure must adapt to the needs of its various constituents.

The European Union

Originally called the Common Market, the **European Union (EU)** initially included only the principal Western European nations like Italy, Germany, France, and the United Kingdom. But by 2013, 27 countries belonged to the EU (see Figure 5.4). Other countries are in the process of applying for membership, including Croatia and Turkey. The EU has eliminated most quotas and set uniform tariff levels on products imported and exported within its group. The EU is the largest free marketplace in the world and produces nearly one-quarter of total global wealth.[68]

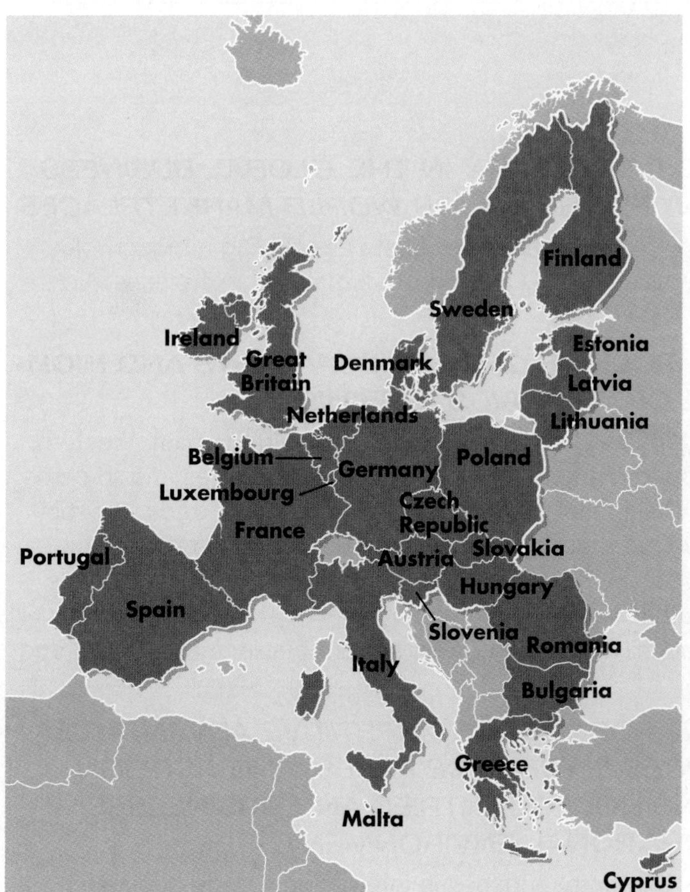

FIGURE 5.4 The nations of the European Union

Source: Based on, Nations of the European Union, Source: Europe, at http://europa.eu/abc/maps/index_en.htm, accessed October 22, 2011.

EUROPEAN UNION (EU) Agreement among major Western European nations to eliminate or make uniform most trade barriers affecting group members.

NORTH AMERICAN FREE TRADE AGREEMENT (NAFTA) Agreement to gradually eliminate tariffs and other trade barriers among the United States, Canada, and Mexico.

The North American Free Trade Agreement

On January 1, 1994, the **North American Free Trade Agreement (NAFTA)** took effect. The objective of NAFTA was to create a free trade area for Canada, the United States, and Mexico. It eliminates trade barriers, promotes fair competition, and increases investment opportunities.

Surveys conducted before the deal had a majority of Canadians opposed to NAFTA. They feared that jobs would be lost to other countries or that Canada's sovereignty would be threatened, and that Canada would be flooded with products manufactured in Mexico, where wages are much lower. Supporters of NAFTA argued that the agreement would open up U.S. markets for Canadian products and create more employment, would create more employment possibilities for women, and would not threaten Canada's sovereignty.

What has actually happened since NAFTA took effect? A group of economists at the Canadian Economics Association concluded that free trade has not been as good for Canada as predicted by its supporters, nor as bad for Canada as predicted by its detractors.[69] Several specific effects are noticeable:

- NAFTA has created a much more active North American market.
- Direct foreign investment has increased in Canada.
- U.S. imports from (and exports to) Mexico have increased.
- Canada has become an exporting powerhouse.
- Trade between the United States and Canada rose sharply, and Canada enjoys a large trade surplus with the United States.

In the last few years, there is evidence that the benefits of NAFTA are slowly being eroded by ever-increasing delays at border crossings because of security concerns. However, on the positive side, there is now an extensive Canadian presence in Mexico in everything from mining, to auto parts, to banking. For example, as we saw in the opening case, Scotiabank, the most international Canadian bank, has made great inroads in Mexico with over 2 million Mexican clients.[70] There is also a renewed effort to increase direct trade between Mexico and Canada. Mexico recently eliminated nearly 14 000 rules and regulations to improve trade competitiveness. At the time, trade minister Bruno Ferrari called on Canada to increase its relationship with Mexico and help ensure that the $20 billion in trade between the nations continues to increase over the next decade.[71]

Other Free Trade Agreements

On January 1, 1995, a free trade agreement known as Mercosur went into effect between Argentina, Brazil, Uruguay, and Paraguay. Venezuela became the fifth member in 2012. Within the first decade of its existence, tariffs had been eliminated on 80 percent of the goods traded between the original members. Brazil has proposed enlarging Mercosur into a South American Free Trade Area (SAFTA), which might eventually negotiate with NAFTA to form an Americas Free Trade Area (AFTA).

Around the world, groups of nations are banding together to form regional trade associations for their own benefit. Some examples include

- the ASEAN Free Trade Area (see Figure 5.5)
- the Asia-Pacific Economic Cooperation (many nations of the Pacific Rim, as well as the United States, Canada, and Mexico)
- the Economic Community of Central African States (many nations in equatorial Africa)
- the Gulf Cooperation Council (Bahrain, Kuwait, Oman, Qatar, Saudi Arabia, and United Arab Emirates)

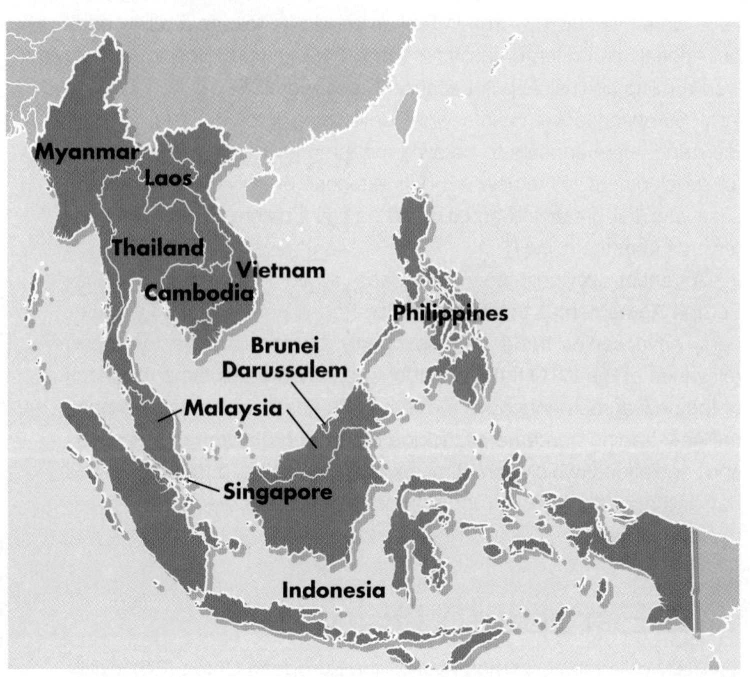

>>> **FIGURE 5.5** The nations of the Association of Southeast Asian Nations (ASEAN)

Source: Based on Association of Southeast Asian Nations, at http://www.aseansec.org/

MyBizLab Visit the MyBizLab website. This online homework and tutorial system puts you in control of your own learning with study and practice tools directly correlated to this chapter's content.

SUMMARY OF LEARNING OBJECTIVES

LO-1 DESCRIBE THE GROWING COMPLEXITY IN THE *GLOBAL BUSINESS ENVIRONMENT* AND IDENTIFY THE *MAJOR WORLD MARKETPLACES.*

The world economy is changing and emerging markets are playing a bigger role. However, world trade still revolves greatly around three major marketplaces: North America, Europe, and Asia.

LO-2 IDENTIFY THE EVOLVING ROLE OF *EMERGING MARKETS* AND HIGHLIGHT THE IMPORTANCE OF THE *BRICS NATIONS.*

Old international trading patterns and activities are changing. In the past, Western companies used less-developed markets to acquire natural resources and to carry out simple assembly tasks. While this is still evident in international trade, the relationships have become much more complex and many former have-nots are now exploiting relationships for their own gain. There are great opportunities in places like Thailand, Indonesia, South Korea, and Ukraine. However, the BRICS nations are getting most of the attention. BRICS stands for Brazil, Russia, India, China, and South Africa.

LO-3 EXPLAIN HOW DIFFERENT FORMS OF *COMPETITIVE ADVANTAGE, IMPORT-EXPORT BALANCES, EXCHANGE RATES,* AND *FOREIGN COMPETITION* DETERMINE HOW COUNTRIES AND BUSINESSES RESPOND TO THE INTERNATIONAL ENVIRONMENT.

With an absolute advantage, a country engages in international trade because it can produce a good or service more efficiently than any other nation. Countries usually trade because they enjoy comparative advantages; they can produce some items more efficiently than they can produce other items. A country that exports more than it imports has a favourable balance of trade, while a country that imports more than it exports has an unfavourable balance of trade. If the exchange rate decreases, our exports become less expensive for other countries, so they will buy more of what we produce. The reverse happens if the value of the Canadian dollar increases. Changes in the exchange rate, therefore, have a strong impact on our international competitiveness.

LO-4 DISCUSS THE FACTORS INVOLVED IN CONDUCTING BUSINESS INTERNATIONALLY AND IN SELECTING THE APPROPRIATE LEVELS OF *INTERNATIONAL INVOLVEMENT* AND *INTERNATIONAL ORGANIZATIONAL STRUCTURE*.

In deciding whether to do business internationally, a firm must determine whether a market for its product exists abroad and whether the firm has the skills and knowledge to manage such a business. Firms must also assess the business climates in other nations and the preferred level of international involvement: (1) exporter or importer, (2) international firm, or (3) multinational firm. The choice will influence the organizational structure of its international operations, specifically, its use of independent agents, licensing arrangements, branch offices, strategic alliances, and direct investment.

LO-5 DESCRIBE SOME OF THE WAYS IN WHICH *SOCIAL, CULTURAL, ECONOMIC, LEGAL, AND POLITICAL DIFFERENCES* ACT AS BARRIERS TO INTERNATIONAL TRADE.

Social and cultural differences that can serve as barriers to trade include language, social values, and traditional buying patterns. Differences in economic systems may force businesses to establish close relationships with foreign governments before they are permitted to do business abroad. Quotas, tariffs, subsidies, and local-content laws offer protection to local industries. Differences in business-practice laws can make standard business practices in one nation illegal in another.

LO-6 EXPLAIN HOW *FREE TRADE AGREEMENTS* ASSIST WORLD TRADE.

Several trade agreements have attempted to eliminate restrictions on free trade internationally. The World Trade Organization (WTO) has 159 members with the mandate to help open up markets to international trade. The European Union (EU) has eliminated virtually all trade barriers among the 27 member nations. The North American Free Trade Agreement (NAFTA) eliminates many of the barriers to free trade among the United States, Canada, and Mexico.

QUESTIONS AND EXERCISES

QUESTIONS FOR ANALYSIS

1. Explain how the economic system of a country affects foreign firms interested in doing business there.
2. Assume that you are the manager of a small firm seeking to enter the international arena. What information would you need about the market that you're thinking of entering?
3. Do you think that a firm operating internationally is better advised to adopt a single standard of ethical conduct or to adapt to local conditions? Under what conditions might each approach be preferable?
4. Explain how it is possible for a country to have a positive balance of trade and a negative balance of payments.
5. Is NAFTA good or bad for Canada? Give supporting reasons for your answer.
6. The EU includes most of the Western European countries, but some (such as Switzerland) have chosen not to join. Why might that be? What are the implications for countries that do not join?

APPLICATION EXERCISES

7. Interview the manager of a local firm that does at least some business internationally. Identify reasons why the company decided to "go international," as well as the level of the firm's involvement and the organizational structure it uses for its international operations.
8. Select a familiar product. Using library references, learn something about the culture of India and identify the problems that might arise in trying to market this product to India's citizens.

(continued)

9. What attributes of your province or region (cultural, geographical, economic, etc.) would be of interest to a foreign firm thinking about locating there? Visit provincial government sites and find resources that are available for businesses to help them invest in your province. Identify a company that has recently invested in your province. What reasons did it give for its decision?

10. Visit the website of a major global company such as Coca-Cola and enter some of its international sites. Make sure to choose countries from different parts of the world. What are some of the differences that you see in the websites? Identify some of the similar themes and report your findings.

TEAM EXERCISES

BUILDING YOUR BUSINESS SKILLS

FINDING YOUR PLACE

GOAL

To encourage students to apply global business strategies to a small-business situation.

SITUATION

Some people might say that Yolanda Lang is a bit too confident. Others might say that she needs confidence—and more—to succeed in the business she's chosen. But one thing is certain: Lang is determined to grow INDE, her handbag design company, into a global enterprise. At only 28 years of age, she has time on her side—if she makes the right business moves now.

These days, Lang spends most of her time in Milan, Italy. Backed by $50 000 of her parents' personal savings, she is trying to compete with Gucci, Fendi, and other high-end handbag makers. Her target market is women willing to spend $400 on a purse. Ironically, Lang was forced to set up shop in Italy because of the snobbishness of these customers, who buy high-end bags only if they're European-made. "Strangely enough," she muses, "I need to be in Europe to sell in North America."

To succeed, she must first find ways to keep production costs down—a tough task for a woman in a male-dominated business culture. Her fluent Italian is an advantage, but she's often forced to turn down inappropriate dinner invitations. She also has to figure out how to get her 22-bag collection into stores worldwide. Retailers are showing her bags in Italy and Japan, but she's had little luck in the United States. "I intend to be a global company," says Lang. The question is how to succeed first as a small business.

METHOD

Step 1 Join together with three or four other students to discuss the steps that Lang has taken so far to break into the U.S. retail market. These steps include:

- buying a mailing list of 5000 shoppers from high-end department store Neiman Marcus and selling directly to these customers; and
- linking with a manufacturer's representative to sell her line in major U.S. cities while she concentrates on Europe.

Step 2 Based on what you learned in this chapter, suggest other strategies that might help Lang grow her business. Working with group members, consider whether the following options would help or hurt Lang's business. Explain why a strategy is likely to work or likely to fail.

- Lang could relocate to the United States and sell abroad through an independent agent.
- Lang could relocate to the United States and set up a branch office in Italy.
- Lang could find a partner in Italy and form a strategic alliance that would allow her to build her business on both continents.

Step 3 Working alone, create a written marketing plan for INDE. What steps would you recommend that Lang take to reach her goal of becoming a global company? Compare your written response with those of other group members.

FOLLOW-UP QUESTIONS

1. What are the most promising steps that Lang can take to grow her business? What are the least promising?
2. Lang thinks that her trouble breaking into the U.S. retail market stems from the fact that her company is unknown. How would this circumstance affect the strategies suggested in Steps 1 and 2?
3. When Lang deals with Italian manufacturers, she is a young, attractive woman in a man's world. Often, she must convince men that her purpose is business and nothing else. How should Lang handle personal invitations that get in the way of business? How can she say no while still maintaining business relationships? Why is it often difficult for women to do business in male-dominated cultures?
4. The American consulate has given Lang little business help because her products are made in Italy. Do you think the consulate's treatment of an American business person is fair or unfair? Explain your answer.
5. Do you think Lang's relocation to Italy will pay off? Why or why not?
6. With Lang's goals of creating a global company, can INDE continue to be a one-person operation?

EXERCISING YOUR ETHICS

PAYING ATTENTION TO FOREIGN PRACTICES

THE SITUATION

Assume that you're an up-and-coming manager in a regional Canadian distribution company. Firms in your industry are just beginning to enter foreign markets, and you've been assigned to head up your company's new operations in a Latin American country. Because at least two of your competitors are also trying to enter this same market, your boss wants you to move as quickly as possible. You also sense that your success in this assignment will likely determine your future with the company.

You have just completed meetings with local government officials, and you're pessimistic about your ability to get things moving quickly. You've learned, for example, that it will take 10 months to get a building permit for a needed facility. Moreover, once the building is up, it will take another six months to get utilities. Finally, the phone company says that it may take up to six additional months to get high-speed internet access.

THE DILEMMA

Various officials have indicated that time frames could be considerably shortened if you were willing to pay special "fees." You realize that these "fees" are bribes, and you're well aware that the practice of paying such "fees" is both unethical and illegal in Canada. In this foreign country, however, it's not illegal and not even considered unethical. Moreover, if you don't pay and one of your competitors does, you'll be at a major competitive disadvantage. In any case, your boss isn't likely to understand the long lead times necessary to get the operation running. Fortunately, you have access to a source of funds that you could spend without the knowledge of anyone in the home office.

TEAM ACTIVITY

Assemble a group of four students and divide the four into two pairs and answer the questions from one of the following perspectives:

- Your perspective as an employee who is being tasked with the authority to complete the job.
- The perspective of the boss (assume that despite your assumptions this manager is actually well aware of the business practices in this country).

QUESTIONS TO ADDRESS

1. What are the key ethical issues in this situation?
2. What do you think most managers would do in this situation?
3. What would you do?

BUSINESS CASE

TIM HORTONS' SLOW U.S. EXPANSION AND THE NEW PUSH TOWARDS THE MIDDLE EAST

When you think of Tim Hortons, what images come to mind? Students typically use the following words: hockey, Timbits, maple, Canada, doughnuts, coffee, Sidney Crosby, inexpensive. Tim Hortons is very successful in Canada, and its doughnuts have become the Canadian equivalent of American apple pie or the Big Mac. The company has worked hard to create a warm, homegrown image in the minds of the Canadian consumer. Its low-cost/high-volume approach, its tremendous channel domination, and its unapologetic links to Canadian symbols are all sources of competitive advantage for Tim Hortons in Canada. According to its website, Tim Hortons is the fourth-largest quick-service restaurant chain in North America. It is the largest in Canada with over 3400 stores. To put this figure into perspective, McDonald's has approximately 1400 stores in Canada. But can Tim Hortons successfully export its business model to the U.S. and beyond?

Chris Mueller/Redux

THE U.S. EXPANSION CHALLENGE

The first U.S. Tim Hortons opened in Buffalo, New York, in 1984, and, in 2013, there were 804 stores in 12 northern U.S. states. Recently, the company announced plans for more U.S. expansion, and it now seems ready for a more concentrated push into the U.S. But what approach should be used? Should the same standardized approach that has worked in Canada be used or will the model have to be adapted for the U.S. market?

For obvious reasons, Tim Hortons has not focused on hockey and Canadian symbols to sell its doughnuts and coffee in the U.S. It might try to replace hockey with baseball, but Dunkin' Donuts already has strong grassroots links to that sport. It could wrap itself in the U.S. flag, but that would leave it open to charges of being fake, and that approach might also confuse or upset Canadians who visit the U.S. Another problem—Tim Hortons cannot rely on a large marketing channel advantage in the United States. In Canada, there is one Tim Hortons for every 10 000 consumers, but this is not the case across the border. In the U.S., there are thousands of local coffee shops in addition to major players like Dunkin' Donuts, Starbucks, and even McDonald's (especially with its recent McCafé push). In the U.S., these companies have the sort of market penetration that Tim Hortons enjoys in Canada.

So, what can be done? Until now, Tim Hortons' central message in the United States has focused on value and freshness. This was not a very original idea, but at least it was an honest approach. Unfortunately, this hasn't differentiated Tim Hortons from its competitors. Something else is needed. But what? The company is now pursuing several strategies, including the acquisition of prime locations, co-branding, and going upscale.

ACQUIRING PRIME LOCATIONS

A few years ago, Tim Hortons opened its first outlets in New York City after reaching an agreement with a former Dunkin' Donuts franchisee who owned 12 prime locations in Manhattan and Brooklyn. This gave Tim Hortons a great opportunity to develop its brand and gain exposure in this key market because prime locations are difficult to find, especially in New York City. The fact that people were already accustomed to going to these particular locations for their coffee fix should also help. As a result of this deal, Tim Hortons has some much-needed exposure, including a location in Madison Square Garden.

CO-BRANDING

A few years ago, Tim Hortons and Kahala Corporation, owner of the Cold Stone Creamery—an ice cream parlour franchise—announced a co-branding agreement that would see the development of up to 100 combined stores in the U.S. At the same time, approximately 60 outlets across Canada were converted to test this new co-branded format. This should help Tim Hortons to get noticed and to improve its competitive position in the U.S. market.

GOING UPSCALE

Back in 2010, Tim Hortons announced that it was planning to create upscale café/bake shops with a different menu that would include pastries baked onsite. These new stores were scheduled to open in existing markets such as New York and Michigan. The announcement raised several new questions. Could a high-end Tim Hortons work? How would the company manage the traditional stores alongside the new outlets? Would there be a sub-brand created or would it eventually transform all U.S. locations? This strategy should help relieve some of the stress of the rising food costs that have recently been squeezing low-cost food providers like Tim Hortons. But can the company manage the brand and not confuse consumers? Should it even try?

BREAKING NEW GROUND

Tim Hortons is taking a concept that has worked in Canada and is trying to make it work in a foreign market. In order to succeed, Tim Hortons must develop a clear strategy that U.S. consumers can identify with. That approach is what made the company successful in Canada. Succeeding in new markets is not easy and the American expansion is still a work in progress. However, despite the challenges in a similar market down south, Tim Hortons made a bold announcement recently when it decided to open a location in the United Arab Emirates and announced intentions to open 120 new outlets in the Gulf region (Kuwait, Bahrain, Saudi Arabia, and Oman were identified). In 2013, the company had already opened 24 locations in the region. Clearly, this would present a whole new set of challenges, but it was also an indication that Tim Hortons was serious about expansion. With the Canadian market already developed, growth will need to come from outside the borders. Only time will tell if the concept will work, but one thing is certain—they probably won't be selling many Timbits by using images of Sydney Crosby in Dubai.

QUESTIONS FOR DISCUSSION

1. Can the same business model that has been so successful in Canada work in the U.S.?
2. Tim Hortons has focused on hockey and Canadian symbols in Canada. What might replace hockey as an emphasis in the U.S. market? How can Tim Hortons compete with the myriad of small local coffee shops in the U.S.?
3. Tim Hortons' strategy is to acquire prime locations, engage in co-branding, and go upscale in an attempt to penetrate the U.S. market. What are the advantages and disadvantages of this strategy?
4. In what ways will expanding in places like Dubai be easier than expanding in the United States? In what ways will it be harder? (Hint: Will the Canadian image play well in Dubai? Is it marketable?)
5. Do you believe that Tim Hortons will be successful if it follows through with a full expansion into the Gulf region? Explain. Should Tim Hortons use a standardized or adapted approach in this region?

THE CONTEMPORARY BUSINESS ENVIRONMENT

GOAL OF THE EXERCISE

In Chapter 4, we discussed how the starting point for virtually every new business is a business plan. Business plans describe the business strategy for any new business and demonstrate how that strategy will be implemented. One benefit of a business plan is that in preparing it, would-be entrepreneurs must develop their idea on paper and firm up their thinking about how to launch their business before investing time and money in it. In this exercise, you'll get started on creating your own business plan.

EXERCISE BACKGROUND: PART 1 OF THE BUSINESS PLAN

The starting point for any business plan is coming up with a "great idea." This might be a business that you've already considered setting up. If you don't have ideas for a business already, look around. What are some businesses that you come into contact with on a regular basis? Restaurants, childcare services, and specialty stores are a few examples you might consider. You may also wish to create a business that is connected with a talent or interest you have, such as crafts, cooking, or car repair. It's important that you create a company from scratch rather than use a company that already exists. You'll learn more if you use your own ideas.

Once you have your business idea, your next step is to create an "identity" for your business. This includes determining a name for your business and an idea of what your business will do. It also includes identifying the type of ownership your business will take, a topic we discussed in Chapter 4. The first part of the plan also briefly looks at who your ideal customers are, as well as how your business will stand out from the crowd. Part 1 of the plan also looks at how the business will interact with the community and demonstrate social responsibility, topics we discussed in Chapter 3. Finally, almost all business plans today include a perspective on the impact of global business, which we discussed in Chapter 5.

YOUR ASSIGNMENT

MyBizLab

STEP 1

To complete this assignment, you first need to download the Business Plan Student Template file from this book's MyBizLab. This is a Microsoft Word file you can use to complete your business plan. For this assignment, you will fill in Part 1 of the plan.

STEP 2

Once you have the Business Plan Student Template file, you can begin to answer the following questions in Part 1: The Contemporary Business World.

1. What is the name of your business?

   Hint: *When you think of the name of your business, make sure that it captures the spirit of the business you're creating.*

2. What will your business do?

   Hint: *Imagine that you are explaining your idea to a family member or a friend. Keep your description to 30 words or fewer.*

3. What form of business ownership (sole proprietorship, partnership, or corporation) will your business take? Why did you choose this form?

   Hint: *For more information on types of business ownership, refer to the discussion in Chapter 4.*

4. Briefly describe your ideal customer. What are they like in terms of age, income level, and so on?

   Hint: *You don't have to give too much detail in this part of the plan; you'll provide more details about customers and marketing in later parts of the plan.*

5. Why will customers choose to buy from your business instead of your competition?

   Hint: *In this section, describe what will be unique about your business. For example, is the product special, or will you offer the product at a lower price?*

6. All businesses have to deal with ethical issues. One way to address these issues is to create a code of ethics. List three core principles your business will follow.

   Hint: *To help you consider the ethical issues that your business might face, refer to the discussion in Chapter 3.*

7. A business shows social responsibility by respecting all of its stakeholders. What steps will you take to create a socially responsible business?

   Hint: *Refer to the discussion of social responsibility in Chapter 3. What steps can you take to be a "good citizen" in the community? Also consider how you may need to be socially responsible toward your customers and, if applicable, investors, employees, and suppliers.*

8. Will you sell your product in another country? If so, what countries and why? What challenges will you face?

   Hint: *To help you consider issues of global business, refer to this chapter. Consider how you will expand internationally (e.g., independent agent, licensing). Do you expect global competition for your product? What advantages will foreign competitors have?*

Note: Once you have answered the questions, save your Word document. You'll be answering additional questions in later chapters.

CBC VIDEO CASE 1-1

POSILIGHT

THE COMPANY

Energy efficiency and cost-saving solutions are increasingly important in today's society. It is not often that both are able to come together in one product and be successful. But Posilight, a lighting product for grocery and variety stores, provides both cost-saving and energy-efficient solutions for retailers' refrigerators and freezer cases, and can save up to

65 percent on energy costs. Posilight is able to fit in existing refrigerator cases, and this creates additional savings because replacement display cases are not necessary. President and founder Robert Simoneau developed the Posilight idea after he decided to enter the $1.5-billion lighting industry.

Posilight differs from other light solutions in that it is an LED bulb that creates rays from the front of the glass door of a freezer to the back of the merchandise. An even amount of light is cast, with no light bands or shadows. This so-called "positional lighting" is based on the same concept as that of a spotlight on stage, where focused light is provided to attract the audience's attention. "If the light is not on the merchandise you want people to see, then it's useless and you're consuming energy for nothing," says Simoneau.

THE PITCH

In his appearance on *Dragon's Den*, Simoneau asked for $75 000 in return for giving the dragons 10 percent ownership of his company (valued at $750 000). This investment would help Simoneau get his product into more test stores, and give him some of the dragons' expertise in marketing.

THE DRAGONS' POINT OF VIEW

Initially, the dragons seemed interested in Simoneau's proposal. One asked about how many sales he had thus far, but interest waned when Simoneau said that he hasn't seen much sales interest after showing the product in two test stores. "It is hard to impress financial investors unless you improve sales," said Arlene Dickinson. Simoneau expressed a desire to increase the company's sales revenue and then sell the patent to a manufacturer. The dragons did not agree with this idea. "It is easier to go to a manufacturing company and say, 'Buy the license to make this product,' so why not get the money from them? It is just easier," said one dragon. Based on this concern, one dragon declined the investment opportunity, saying, "There is a gap in the logic for me. I don't see the business. I'm out."

When Kevin O'Leary asked fellow dragon Jim whether or not he thought there was something to this idea, Jim said he thought there was: "We go through $75 000 worth of bulbs every year; there is money to be made here for sure."

THE OUTCOME

After a request to get participation from the dragons, and with an interest in taking advantage of Arlene Dickinson's marketing expertise, Simoneau once again began stirring up the dragons' interest. He was eventually able to convince four of the dragons to invest in his product idea after they concluded that it would be a unique product and might be a huge success in the market. The final investment deal included $75 000, with Simoneau paying an initial 11.5 percent royalty fee for every dollar of sales revenue he generated; the fee would then drop (permanently) to 5 percent after the $75 000 had been recovered. Simoneau was able to leave still owning 99 percent of the company. The dragons own just 1 percent, but will be able to say that they are partners when Posilight becomes a huge success and they will collect a handsome royalty for their efforts.

QUESTIONS FOR DISCUSSION

1. What is quality? What quality attributes does Posilight possess?
2. The dragons thought that it was a better idea to license the product than to sell the patent to a manufacturer. Why do you think they took that position?
3. Why did the dragons conclude that Posilight had good market potential?

Source: Video Resource: "Posilight," *Dragon's Den,* Season 4, episode 16 (February 3, 2010). www.Posilight.com.

CBC VIDEO CASE 1-2

MAKING MONEY BY GOING GREEN?

As concern for the environment increases, more and more Canadian businesses are going green (and trying to make a profit by doing so). Here are three examples.

MARITIME GEOTHERMAL LTD.

Glen Kaye, of Maritime Geothermal Ltd., says that Canadians are starting to become interested in geothermal heat, which is a clean alternative to fossil fuels. Linda Naccarato, a Burlington, Ontario, homeowner, is drilling for this heat in her yard. With it, she can heat her home, swimming pool, and driveway (to melt snow in the winter). This "energy from the ground" produces only one-quarter of the greenhouse gas emissions produced by fossil fuels. The initial installation cost of the system is pretty high, but the system pays for itself within 5 to 7 years. After that, the homeowner gets cheap heat. Electricity is needed to run the heat pump, but the cost of that is only one-quarter of the cost of a traditional furnace burning fossil fuels. Customers using geothermal heat have the added advantage of not having to worry about changes in the price of fossil fuels.

Geothermal heating works because (1) heat travels from something warm to something colder, and (2) a great deal of heat is retained in the ground as a result of the radioactive decay of minerals and solar energy falling on the planet. There are two main ways to capture geothermal heat. The most efficient method is used in areas where very hot ground-water is available (usually where tectonic plates come together). This water is pumped directly into radiators to heat homes and offices. This type of heat has been used for many years in Iceland. Thermal water is also used in Boise, Idaho, and Squamish, B.C. Hot water can also be used to run turbines to generate electricity.

The second method involves getting heat from the ground. This is possible because the temperature of the ground three metres below the surface has a fairly stable temperature of about 10 degrees Celsius. Here's how it works: holes are drilled in the ground and small-diameter pipes filled with a mix of water and ethanol are installed in the holes. In the winter, the liquid is colder than the soil, so it absorbs heat from the ground. A heat pump brings the heat to the surface, and fans blow it around. The pipes are connected to a heat exchanger in the home, so no furnace is needed. Once the liquid cools off, it is then pumped back into the ground and the process starts all over again. In summer, when above-ground temperatures exceed 10 degrees, the system is reversed (i.e., the heat pump moves heat from the home or office into the ground where the liquid in the pipes is cooled by the earth and then transported back into the building to cool it).

Worldwide, less than 1 percent of the world's total energy needs are provided by geothermal heat. In Canada, about 1 percent of Canadian homes are heated this way.

THE ZENN ELECTRIC CAR

The eco-friendly Zenn electric car (*Z*ero *E*missions, *N*o *N*oise) was designed for use in low-speed urban areas (less than 50 km/h), but the company had trouble getting the car certified as roadworthy. The car was made in St. Jérôme, Quebec, and sold in the U.S. and other foreign countries, but Transport Canada was reluctant to certify the vehicle on safety grounds. Specifically, the concern was that low-speed vehicles (LSVs) are not required to meet the same safety standards as other cars, so safety is compromised when these cars share the road with faster, heavier vehicles. Frustration with the federal government led Zenn to cease production in 2010. Another company (Dynasty Electric Car Co.) also gave up and stopped producing its electric car.

MINAS BASIS PULP & POWER

Nova Scotia–based Minas Basis Pulp & Power paper mill doesn't use any trees; instead, it uses 100 percent recycled cardboard. Like other mills, it uses hydro power, but it recaptures heat and reuses it, not once but several times. Therefore, less fuel is used, which means fewer emissions. The mill also recycles all of the water it uses. As a result of these conservation measures, 1.5 million trees are spared and 270 000 tonnes of greenhouse gases are not emitted, and enough electricity to power 38 000 homes is saved each year. The company is also looking at generating energy by harnessing the power of the tides. The nearby Bay of Fundy has the world's highest tides, and clean, renewable energy can be generated by placing turbines underwater to extract energy from tidal movements.

Minas wants to become the greenest paper mill in North America. If it succeeds, it will be doing its part to help save the planet and become a profitable company in the process. Minas hopes it can charge a premium price for its paper because buyers will want to buy products from a green paper mill.

QUESTIONS FOR DISCUSSION

1. What kind of challenges and opportunities are evident when a company decides to go green?
2. What is social responsibility? To what extent does "going green" qualify as socially responsible behaviour by a company? Explain your reasoning.
3. Consider the following statement: *Geothermal heating is environmentally friendly and also provides cheap power, so in the next few years Canadians are going to rapidly adopt this method of heating their homes.* Do you agree or disagree with the statement? Explain your reasoning.

Sources: *CBC News in Review*, "Making Money by Going Green," May 2008; www.en.wikipedia.org/wiki/Geothermal_heating.

PART 2 THE BUSINESS OF MANAGING

J. B. Handelsman/Cartoonbank.com

LO

AFTER READING THIS CHAPTER, YOU SHOULD BE ABLE TO:

LO-1 Describe the four activities that constitute the *management process.*

LO-2 Identify *types of managers* by level and area.

LO-3 Describe the five basic *management skills.*

LO-4 Explain the importance of *goal setting* and *strategic management* in organizational success.

LO-5 Discuss *contingency planning* and *crisis management* in today's business world.

LO-6 Explain the idea of *corporate culture* and why it is important.

A Crisis for the 787 Dreamliner

On January 7, 2013, the lithium-ion batteries in a brand-new Boeing 787 Dreamliner owned by Japan Airlines caught fire while the plane was parked at Boston's Logan Airport. Then, on January 16, an All Nippon Airways Dreamliner made an emergency landing after pilots noticed a burning smell. Passengers exited the plane on emergency slides. As a result of these two incidents, the U.S. Federal Aviation Administration (FAA) grounded all 787s until the cause of the problem could be identified and fixed (the first time since 1979 that the FAA had taken such an action). The grounding order meant that the eight airlines that had purchased the plane had to cancel hundreds of flights, and that reduced their revenues. It also meant that Boeing couldn't deliver dozens of already-built Dreamliners until the FAA ban was lifted. The problem is one of Boeing's biggest crises in years and could cost the company a lot of money, including penalty payments to buyers who do not receive their planes on time.

Jim McNerney—the CEO of Boeing—immediately took action to deal with the crisis. He sent handwritten apologies to the leaders of the two Japanese airlines, and persuaded General Motors and General Electric to lend their electrical experts to help find the cause of the problem. He also met with officials at the FAA to brief them on what Boeing was doing to deal with the crisis. McNerney's strategy was to work behind the scenes to deal with the crisis rather than to get involved in a lot of public relations activity with the media. In a meeting with Boeing's Chief Technology Officer, McNerney pointed out in strong terms that the problem wasn't simply about electrochemistry in a battery, but about safety and the confidence of the general public in Boeing's plane. But McNerney took flak for not being more

© pizuttipics/Fotolia

Managing *the* Business Enterprise

CHAPTER 06

forthcoming with investors and the public about the nature of the problem.

At a press conference on January 30, McNerney talked about fourth-quarter financial results and told investors and financial analysts that the company was planning to increase 787 production from five to ten planes a month. He said he couldn't answer questions about the battery problems because the company was in the middle of an investigation. Investors were nervous because they didn't know how much the problem would cost to fix.

On February 22, FAA officials met with Boeing managers and reviewed a proposal to get the Dreamliner flying again, but the FAA representatives said they wouldn't let the plane back in service until they were convinced that the safety risks with the lithium-ion batteries had been addressed. Both Japanese and U.S. investigators agreed that the batteries had caught fire after short circuits caused thermal reactions among the battery cells which then produced temperatures that were high enough to melt metal. But they disagreed over what caused the short circuits. Japanese investigators from GS Yuasa Corp. (the company that makes the batteries) felt that a power surge that originated outside the battery was the cause of the problem. They therefore suggested that a voltage regulator be installed to prevent electrical current from flowing to the batteries if a problem developed. By contrast, Boeing's investigators proposed stronger and better separated battery cells, as well as a fireproof container for the batteries. One of the reasons for this disagreement is that investigators didn't have much experience with the use of lithium-ion batteries on commercial jetliners. But the disagreement meant that Boeing was facing the possibility that the root cause of the problem might be very difficult to identify.

HOW WILL THIS HELP ME?

From the perspective of a *manager*, after reading this chapter you will have a clearer understanding of how to effectively carry out various management responsibilities. From the perspective of a *consumer* or *investor*, you'll be better able to assess and appreciate the quality of management in various companies.

On March 12, the FAA gave initial approval to Boeing's proposed fix-ups to the batteries. This meant that flight tests could begin to see if the problem had really been solved. But test flights are a lengthy process, and it appeared that commercial flights might not be able to resume until May 2013.

The negative publicity about the problems with the 787 created a public relations challenge for Boeing, because it had to convince passengers that the airplane was really safe to fly. Boeing responded to the crisis with various initiatives. For example, when curious web users Googled search terms such as "Dreamliner fire," the first item they saw was a sponsored link that directed them to a page where they could read details of Boeing's changes to the plane's batteries. Boeing also downplayed the severity of the battery fires by noting that there had been thousands of instances over the years where batteries in airplanes malfunctioned. A top executive at Boeing also said that he would be on the first 787 flight after the FAA lifted its grounding order.

The crisis also grounded the pilots who fly the Dreamliner. They passed the time by practising on flight simulators and giving lectures to school-children. One Air India 787 pilot made a rap video for YouTube lamenting his lack of flight time.

On April 25, 2013, the FAA approved the changes to the battery system that Boeing proposed, and the Dreamliner was cleared for flights carrying passengers once again.

QUESTIONS FOR DISCUSSION

1. How well do you think Boeing CEO Jim McNerney handled the Dreamliner crisis? Explain.
2. Use the steps in the rational decision-making process that are presented in this chapter to describe the progression of events that occurred in the 787 Dreamliner crisis.

WHO ARE MANAGERS?

<<< As top managers, (a) Marjorie Scardino (former CEO of Pearson PLC), (b) Colin Rovinescu, president and CEO of Air Canada, and (c) James Sinegal (co-founder and CEO of Costco) are important resources for their companies. They set the strategic direction for their companies and provide leadership to other managers. They are also accountable to shareholders, employees, customers, and other key constituents for the performance and effectiveness of their businesses.

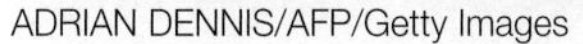

ADRIAN DENNIS/AFP/Getty Images Images Distribution/Newscom AP Photo/Paul Sakuma

MANAGERS The people who plan, organize, lead, and control the operations of an organization.

Managers are the people who plan, organize, lead, and control the operations of an organization. All businesses depend on effective management. Regardless of the type of organization they work in, managers perform many of the same basic functions, are responsible for many of the same tasks, and have many of the same responsibilities. Although our focus is on managers in business settings, management is important for all kinds of organizations, including charities, religious organizations, community organizations, educational institutions, and government agencies. The prime minister of Canada, the president of the University of Toronto, the executive director of the United Way, the dean of your business school, and the chief administrator of your local hospital are all managers. Regardless of the nature and size of an organization, managers are among its most important resources.

LO-1 THE MANAGEMENT PROCESS

Management is the process of planning, organizing, leading, and controlling an enterprise's financial, physical, human, and information resources to achieve the organization's goals. There are two important overall points to keep in mind when thinking about the management process. First, the planning, organizing, leading, and controlling aspects of a manager's job are interrelated. This means that a manager is likely to be engaged in all these activities during the course of any given business day.

Second, there is a difference between management effectiveness and management efficiency. **Efficiency** means achieving the greatest level of output with a given amount of input. **Effectiveness**, on the other hand, means achieving organizational goals that have been set. Thus, efficiency means doing things right, while effectiveness means doing the right things. A manager who focuses on being effective will likely also be efficient, but a manager who focuses on being efficient may or may not be effective.

MANAGEMENT The process of planning, organizing, leading, and controlling a business's financial, physical, human, and information resources in order to achieve its goals.

EFFICIENCY Achieving the greatest level of output with a given amount of input.

EFFECTIVENESS Achieving organizational goals.

PLANNING That portion of a manager's job concerned with determining what the business needs to do and the best way to achieve it.

Planning

Planning is the process of determining the firm's goals and developing a strategy for achieving those goals. The planning process involves five steps:

- In Step 1, goals are established for the organization. A commercial airline, for example, may set a goal to fill 90 percent of the seats on each flight.
- In Step 2, managers identify whether a gap exists between the company's desired and actual position. For example, the airline may analyze load data and find that only 73 percent of the seats on the average flight are filled.
- In Step 3, managers develop plans to achieve the desired objectives. For example, the airline may reduce fares on heavily travelled routes in order to increase the percentage of the seats that are filled.
- In Step 4, the plans that have been decided upon are implemented. For example, the fare from Toronto to Montreal may be reduced by 10 percent.
- In Step 5, the effectiveness of the plan is assessed. The airline would measure the percentage of seats that were filled after the change was implemented to determine whether the goal was reached.

McDonald's experience in Canada over the past decade demonstrates the importance of the planning process. Until 2002, McDonald's was the largest fast-food chain in Canada. But then it was overtaken by Tim Hortons. In response to this development, McDonald's set a goal to reinvent itself and begin to grow again (Step 1). The gap between where McDonald's was and where it wanted to be (Step 2) was obvious, so McDonald's top managers developed a strategic plan (called "Plan to Win") in order to achieve the new objective (Step 3). This involved developing many new menu items (like the Angus Burger, new salads, and snack wraps), renovating restaurants to look more like contemporary cafés or bistros (with polished stone tabletops and fireplaces), letting franchisees target local tastes with their menus (like the McLobster sandwich in the Maritimes), and staying open longer (60 percent of McDonald's restaurants are now open 24 hours a day). These plans were implemented beginning in 2003 and 2004 (Step 4). The effectiveness of the plan has now been assessed (Step 5). Sales were $2.9 billion in 2008 (a record) and $3 billion in 2009 (another record).[1] These sales levels were achieved in spite of the recession of 2008 to 2009. In 2011, McDonald's announced that it planned to spend $1 billion on further interior and exterior renovations to its restaurants.[2]

A HIERARCHY OF PLANS

Plans can be made on three general levels, with each level reflecting plans for which managers at that level are responsible. These levels constitute a hierarchy because implementing plans is practical only when there is a logical flow from one level to the next. **Strategic plans** reflect decisions about resource allocations, company priorities, and the steps needed to meet strategic goals, and are usually set by top management. In 2010, Maple Leaf Foods developed a five-year strategic plan which was designed to increase its earnings by more than 75 percent by 2015.[3] When organizations like Bell Canada make strategic plans, they must take into account certain technological developments that affect their business (see the boxed insert entitled "Should You Say Goodbye to Traditional Land Lines?")

By contrast, **tactical plans** are shorter-range plans concerned with implementing specific aspects of the company's strategic plan. They typically involve upper and middle management. Coca-Cola's decision to increase sales in Europe by building European bottling facilities is an example of tactical planning. **Operational plans**, developed by middle and lower-level managers, set short-term targets for daily, weekly, or monthly performance. McDonald's, for example, establishes operational plans when it explains precisely how Big Macs are to be cooked, warmed, and served.

STRATEGIC PLANS Plans that reflect decisions about resource allocations, company priorities, and steps needed to meet strategic goals.

Organizing

Organizing involves mobilizing the resources that are required to complete a particular task (this topic is examined in detail in Chapter 7). The

TACTICAL PLANS Generally, short-range plans concerned with implementing specific aspects of a company's strategic plans.

OPERATIONAL PLANS Plans setting short-term targets for daily, weekly, or monthly performance.

ORGANIZING That portion of a manager's job concerned with mobilizing the necessary resources to complete a particular task.

E-BUSINESS AND SOCIAL MEDIA SOLUTIONS

Should You Say Goodbye to Traditional Land Lines?

Older Canadians remember the days when telephone operators and telephone cords were an integral part of everyday conversations. Today, consumers use words like VoIP and Skype, and they use tools like smartphones and tablets. In the past two decades, there has been a steady decline of land-line usage and an increase in wireless communication. And pay phones, which were once a powerful revenue source for phone companies, were available in numerous locations, such as local restaurants, malls, and street-corner stand-alone phone booths. But it's getting tougher and tougher to spot these relics of the past. Your home land-line phone may be next.

Part of the transition is due to the introduction and tremendous growth of VoIP (which stands for Voice-over-Internet Protocol). When you think of VoIP, you may think of pure play companies like Vonage or even a firm like Magic Jack, but it also includes computer-based options like Skype and Google Voice. The big name cable companies like Rogers are also in on the action, but they tend to charge much higher prices than pure VoIP organizations. It is projected that by 2015 this category will account for over 68 percent of the market. This number should be reached and quickly surpassed partly because of some new regulations. A recent ruling gives consumers the ability to transfer their regular phone numbers to new VoIP service accounts if they decide to leave their current provider. In early 2013, NetTalk jumped on the opportunity and was actively encouraging consumers to transfer their service and save money.

There is another trend that threatens traditional phone companies. According to Convergence Consulting Group Ltd., one in five Canadians (an estimated 21.6 percent in 2013) are cancelling their home phone line altogether. This is up from about 14 percent two years earlier. This is happening because:

- Mobile plans are getting cheaper as new competition drives down prices.
- Competition has led to more favourable unlimited plans.
- Younger consumers who grew up with mobile phones are feeling no need to sign up to a land-line service when they leave their parents' home.

The net result is that wireless is seen as the only way to go for a large number of Canadians. You can't really blame companies like Bell for wishing things would stay the same (land lines and mobiles for everyone), but they have already started to respond to the mobile market. As the communications industry continues to change, all the players will need to adapt or risk becoming as irrelevant as the lonely phone booth.

CRITICAL THINKING QUESTIONS

1. Do you have a traditional home line? A VoIP line? Are you one of the growing number of people that are part of the wireless-only generation?
2. What can traditional phone and wireless providers do to keep your business or regain your loyalty? Think of solutions beyond just pricing.

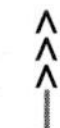

LEADING That portion of a manager's job concerned with guiding and motivating employees to meet the firm's objectives.

CONTROLLING That portion of a manager's job concerned with monitoring the firm's performance and, if necessary, acting to bring it in line with the firm's goals.

importance and complexity of the organizing function can be seen by considering the restructuring that has taken place at Hewlett-Packard in recent years. HP had long prided itself on being a corporate confederation of individual businesses. Each business made its own decisions quickly and efficiently, and the competition kept each unit on its toes. This structure served the firm well for many years. But as time passed, HP somehow lost its competitive edge. The decision was then made to centralize company activities and develop an integrated, organization-wide internet strategy. A reorganized HP then bounced back, at least for a few years.[4] But when HP began again to experience profitability problems in its PC division in 2005, then-CEO Carly Fiorina decided to combine the PC and printing divisions in order to increase hardware sales to customers. When Fiorina left HP shortly thereafter, her successor (Mark Hurd) undid her changes. When Hurd left the firm a few years later, the new CEO, Meg Whitman, once again combined the two divisions.[5]

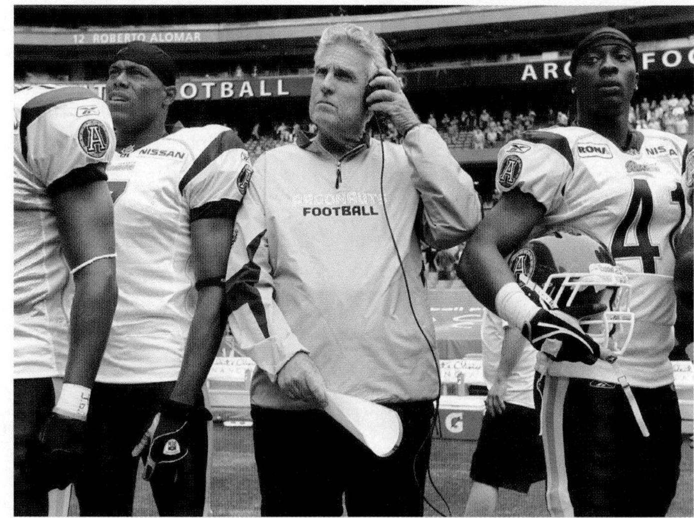

Managers are needed in all kinds of business firms, including professional sports teams. A head coach is a first-line manager who is responsible for the day-to-day success of the team.

AP Photo/The Canadian Press, Darren Calabrese

Leading

Leading (or directing) involves the interactions between managers and their subordinates as they both work to meet the firm's objectives. Legendary leaders like Sam Walton (Walmart), Clive Beddoe (WestJet), and Steve Jobs (Apple) were able to unite their employees in a clear and targeted manner, and motivate them to work in the best interests of the company. While managers have the power to give orders and demand results, leading goes beyond merely giving orders. Leaders must also have the ability to motivate their employees to set challenging goals and to work hard to achieve them. This means that employees will respect their leaders, trust them, and believe that by working together, both the company and its employees will benefit. We discuss leadership in more detail in Chapter 10.

Controlling

Controlling is the process of monitoring a firm's performance to make sure that it is meeting its goals. Managers at WestJet and Air Canada, for example, focus relentlessly on numerous indicators of performance that they can measure and adjust. Everything, from on-time arrivals to baggage-handling errors to the number of empty seats on an airplane to surveys of employee and customer satisfaction, are regularly and routinely monitored. If on-time arrivals start to slip, managers focus on the problem and get it fixed. No single element of the firm's performance can slip too far before it is noticed and fixed.

Figure 6.1 illustrates the control process, which begins when management establishes standards (often for financial performance). If, for example, a company sets a goal of increasing its sales by 20 percent over the next five years, an appropriate standard to assess progress toward the 20 percent goal might be an increase of about 4 percent a year. Managers then measure actual performance each year against standards. If the two amounts agree, the organization continues along its present course. If they vary significantly, however, one or the other needs adjustment. If sales have increased 3.9 percent by the end of the first year, things are probably fine. But if sales have dropped 1 percent, some revision in plans is needed.

Consider how controlling applies to the courses that you are now taking. The instructor first indicates the knowledge areas where you must show competence and the level of competence you must show. Next, the instructor measures your performance, usually through assignments and exams. The instructor then determines whether your performance meets the standard. If your performance is satisfactory (or unsatisfactory), you receive feedback in the form of a passing (or failing) grade in the course.

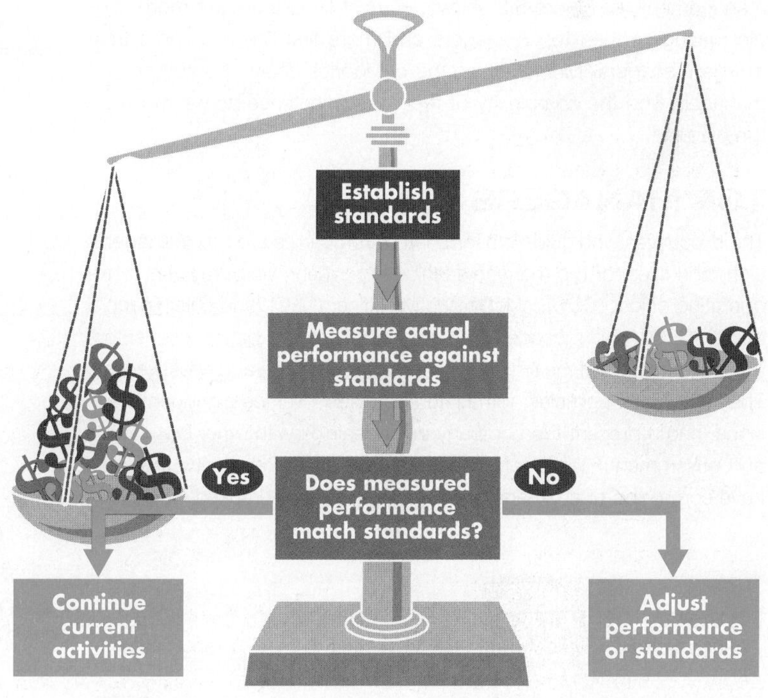

FIGURE 6.1 The control process

Control can also show where performance is better (or worse) than expected and can serve as a basis for providing rewards or reducing costs. For example, when the distributor of the surprise hit movie *The March of the Penguins* saw how popular the movie was becoming, the firm was able to increase advertising and distribution, making the niche movie into a major commercial success. In contrast, when the sales of the Chevrolet Super Sport Roadster (a classic, late-1940s pickup-style vehicle with a two-seat roadster design) were much lower than expected, production of the vehicle was suspended.

Management Roles vs. Management Functions

Describing managers' jobs by referring to functions like planning, organizing, leading, and controlling gives us a good *general* picture of what managers do, but it may not give a clear idea of the *specific* activities that managers are involved in. The answer to the question "What do managers actually do?" is that they play a variety of roles in organizations. The work of Henry Mintzberg of McGill University illustrates the roles approach to management. In a now-classic work, Mintzberg conducted a detailed study of the work of five chief executive officers and found that (1) they worked at an unrelenting pace, (2) their activities were characterized by brevity, variety, and fragmentation, (3) they preferred "live" action and emphasized work activities that were current, specific, and well defined, and (4) they were attracted to verbal media.[6]

Mintzberg believes that a manager's job can be described as 10 roles (in three general categories) that must be performed. The manager's formal authority and status give rise to three *interpersonal roles*: (1) figurehead (duties of a ceremonial nature, such as attending a subordinate's wedding), (2) leader (being responsible for the work of the unit), and (3) liaison (making contact outside the vertical chain of command). These interpersonal roles give rise to three *informational roles*: (1) monitor (scanning the environment for relevant information), (2) disseminator (passing information to subordinates), and (3) spokesperson (sending information to people outside the unit).

The interpersonal and informational roles allow the manager to carry out four *decision-making roles*: (1) entrepreneur (improving the performance of the unit), (2) disturbance handler (responding to high-pressure disturbances, such as a strike at a supplier), (3) resource allocator (deciding who will get what in the unit), and (4) negotiator (working out agreements on a wide variety of issues, such as the amount of authority an individual will be given).

LO-2 TYPES OF MANAGERS

Although all managers plan, organize, lead, and control, not all managers have the same degree of responsibility for each activity. Moreover, managers differ in the specific application of these activities. Thus, we can differentiate between managers based on their level of responsibility and their area of responsibility.

Levels of Management

The three basic levels of management are top, middle, and first-line management. As Figure 6.2 shows, in most firms there are more middle managers than top managers and more first-line managers than middle managers. Moreover, as the categories imply, the authority of managers and the complexity of their duties increase as we move up the pyramid.

TOP MANAGERS

The executives who guide the fortunes of companies are **top managers**. Common titles for top managers include president, vice-president, chief operating officer (COO), chief executive officer (CEO), and chief financial officer (CFO). Top managers are responsible to the board of directors and shareholders of the firm for its overall performance and effectiveness. They set general policies, formulate strategies, oversee significant decisions, and represent the company in its dealings with other businesses and government.[7] While top managers have a lot of authority, they also have something of an image problem. A 2012 study ranked CEOs very low on the "trust" dimension, and this means that some of Canada's most successful people have low credibility.[8]

MIDDLE MANAGERS

Although below the ranks of the top executives, **middle managers** still occupy positions of considerable autonomy and importance. Titles such as plant manager, operations manager, and division manager are typical

TOP MANAGERS Those managers responsible for a firm's overall performance and effectiveness and for developing long-range plans for the company.

MIDDLE MANAGERS Those managers responsible for implementing the decisions made by top managers.

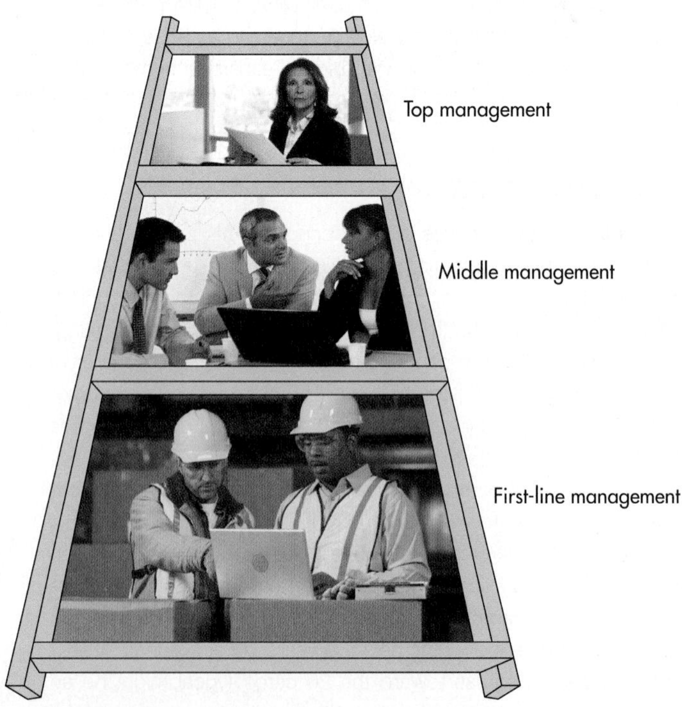

FIGURE 6.2 Organizations have three basic levels of management

(Top to Bottom) © Trains and Planes/Alamy; © Photos 12/Alamy; Scott Houston/Polaris/Newscom

FIRST-LINE MANAGERS Those managers responsible for supervising the work of employees.

HUMAN RESOURCE MANAGERS Those managers responsible for hiring, training, evaluating, and compensating employees.

of middle-management positions. The producer of a Lion's Gate film, like *Precious,* is a middle manager. In general, middle managers are responsible for implementing the strategies, policies, and decisions made by top managers. For example, if top management decides to bring out a new product in 12 months or to cut costs by 5 percent, middle management will have to decide to increase the pace of new product development or to reduce the plant's workforce.

FIRST-LINE MANAGERS

First-line managers spend most of their time working with and supervising the employees who report to them. Common titles include supervisor, office manager, and group leader. A transit supervisor who monitors bus schedules, passenger safety, and the behaviour of bus drivers is a first-line supervisor. So is the flight-services manager for a specific Air Canada flight. Table 6.1 summarizes the duties of the three basic levels of management.

Areas of Management

Within any large company, the top, middle, and first-line managers work in a variety of areas, including human resources, operations, information, marketing, and finance.

HUMAN RESOURCE MANAGERS

Human resource managers can be found in most companies; they hire employees, train them, evaluate their performance, decide how they should be compensated, and deal with labour unions (if the workforce is unionized). Large firms may have several human resource departments, each dealing with specialized activities. Imperial Oil, for example, has separate departments to deal with recruiting and hiring, wage and salary levels, and labour relations. Smaller firms may have a single department, while very small organizations may have a single person responsible for all human resource activities. Chapters 8 and 9 address human resource management issues.

OPERATIONS MANAGERS

Operations managers are responsible for a company's system for creating goods and services. This includes production control, inventory control, and quality control, among other duties. Manufacturing companies like Steelcase, Bristol Aerospace, and Sony need operations managers at many levels. Such firms typically have a vice-president for operations (top), plant managers (middle), and supervisors (first-line). In recent years, sound operations management practices have also become increasingly important to service-producing organizations like hospitals, the government, and colleges and universities. Operations management is the subject of Chapter 10.

INFORMATION MANAGERS

Dramatic increases in both the amount of information available to managers and the ability to manage it have led to the emergence of **information managers**. These managers are responsible for designing and implementing various systems to gather, process, and disseminate information. Federal Express, for example, has a chief information officer. Middle managers engaged in information management help design information systems for divisions or plants. Computer systems managers within smaller businesses or operations are first-line managers. Information management is discussed in the Chapter 11 Supplement.

MARKETING MANAGERS

Marketing includes the development, pricing, promotion, and distribution of products and services. **Marketing managers** are responsible for getting these products and services to buyers. Marketing is especially

OPERATIONS MANAGERS Managers responsible for controlling production, inventory, and quality of a firm's products.

INFORMATION MANAGERS Managers responsible for the design and implementation of systems to gather, process, and disseminate information.

MARKETING MANAGERS Managers responsible for developing, pricing, promoting, and distributing goods and services to buyers.

>>> **TABLE 6.1** The Three Levels of Management

Level	Examples	Responsibilities
Top managers	President, vice president, treasurer, chief executive officer (CEO), chief financial officer (CFO)	• Responsible for the overall performance and effectiveness of the firm • Set general policies, formulate strategies, and approve all significant decisions • Represent the company in dealings with other firms and with government bodies
Middle managers	Plant manager, operations manager, division manager, regional sales manager	• Responsible for implementing the strategies of and working toward the goals set by top managers
First-line managers	Supervisor, office manager, project manager, group leader, sales manager	• Responsible for supervising the work of employees who report to them • Ensure employees understand and are properly trained in company policies and procedures

important for firms producing consumer products, such as Procter & Gamble, Coca-Cola, and Sun Ice. These firms may have large numbers of marketing managers at various levels. For example, a large firm will probably have a vice-president for marketing (top manager), regional marketing managers (middle managers), and several district sales managers (first-line managers). We examine marketing in Chapters 12–13.

FINANCIAL MANAGERS

Management of a firm's finances is extremely important to its survival. Nearly every company has **financial managers** to plan and oversee its financial resources. Levels of financial management may include a vice-president for finance (top), division controller (middle), and accounting supervisor (first-line). For large financial institutions, effective financial

FINANCIAL MANAGERS Managers responsible for planning and overseeing the financial resources of a firm.

management is the company's reason for being. Chapters 14 and 15 describe financial management in detail.

OTHER MANAGERS

Some firms have more specialized managers. Chemical companies like CIL have research and development managers, for example, whereas companies like Petro-Canada and Apple have public relations managers. The range of possibilities is almost endless, and the areas of management are limited only by the needs and imagination of the company.

LO-3 BASIC MANAGEMENT SKILLS

TECHNICAL SKILLS Skills associated with performing specialized tasks within a firm.

The degree of success that people achieve in management positions is determined by the skills and abilities they possess. Effective managers must have several skills, including technical, human relations, conceptual, time management, and decision-making skills.

Technical Skills

Technical skills allow managers to perform specialized tasks. A secretary's ability to type, an animator's ability to draw a cartoon, and an accountant's ability to audit a company's records are all technical skills. People develop their technical skills through education and experience. The secretary, for example, probably took an office systems technology course and has had many hours of practice both on and off the job. The animator may have had training in an art school and probably learned a great deal from experienced animators on the job. The accountant earned a university degree and a professional certification.

As Figure 6.3 shows, technical skills are especially important for first-line managers. Most first-line managers spend considerable time helping employees solve work-related problems, monitoring their performance, and training them in more efficient work procedures. Such managers need a basic understanding of the jobs they supervise. As a manager moves up the corporate ladder, however, technical skills become less and less important. Top managers, for example, often need only a general familiarity with the mechanics of basic tasks performed within the company. A top manager at Disney, for example, probably can't draw Mickey Mouse or build a ride for Disney World.

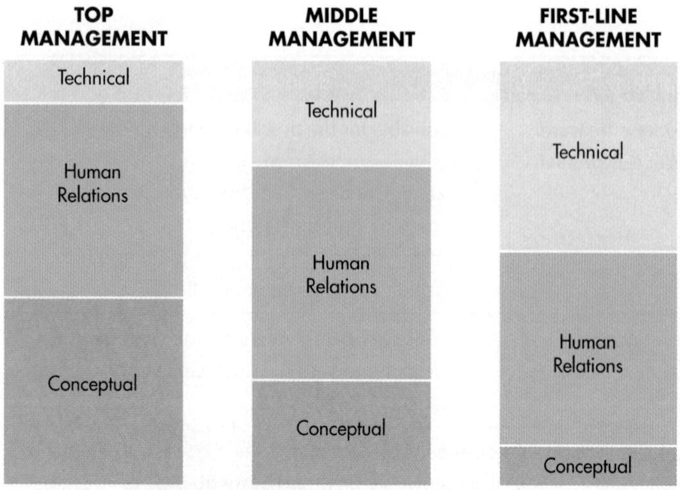

FIGURE 6.3 Different levels in an organization require different combinations of managerial skills

Human Relations Skills

Human relations skills help managers lead, motivate, communicate with, and get along with their subordinates. Managers with poor human relations skills will likely have conflicts with subordinates, cause valuable employees to quit or transfer, and contribute to poor morale. Figure 6.3 shows that human relations skills are important at all levels of management. This is true because all managers in the hierarchy act as "bridges" between their bosses, their subordinates, and other managers at the same level in the hierarchy. A study by DDI Canada found that the top reason for managerial failure was poor people skills,[9] and a study by Google found that technical expertise ranked last among a list of eight "Habits of Highly Effective Google Managers." At the top of the list were even-tempered bosses who made time for one-on-one meetings, and who helped subordinates work through problems.[10]

To improve their insights into employee needs and company operations, some managers work alongside lower-level employees on a temporary basis. For example, the CEO of ING DIRECT sits beside call centre agents and personally answers caller inquiries.[11] When the CEO of 7-Eleven (Joseph De Pinto) worked undercover at a 7-Eleven outlet, he discovered how hard the people worked and why the location was selling so much coffee. Larry O'Donnell, the CEO of Waste Management, did jobs like sorting trash, picking up paper at a landfill, and cleaning portable toilets. The experience taught him the pressure for production that employees had to cope with, and he introduced changes based on what he had learned on the job.[12]

HUMAN RELATIONS SKILLS Skills in understanding and getting along with people.

CONCEPTUAL SKILLS Abilities to think in the abstract, diagnose and analyze various situations, and see beyond the present situation.

TIME MANAGEMENT SKILLS Skills associated with the productive use of time.

DECISION-MAKING SKILLS Skills in defining problems and selecting the best courses of action.

Conceptual Skills

Conceptual skills refer to a person's ability to think in the abstract, to diagnose and analyze various situations, and to see beyond the present situation. Conceptual skills help managers recognize new market opportunities and threats. For example, in e-commerce businesses, conceptual skills help managers foresee how a particular business application will be affected by, or can be translated to, the internet. Figure 6.3 shows that top managers depend most on conceptual skills, and first-line managers least, but some conceptual skills are needed in almost any management job.

Time Management Skills

Time management skills refer to the productive use that managers make of their time. Effective time management is particularly important for highly paid top managers. For example, in 2010 Aaron Regent, CEO of Barrick Resources, was paid a total of $24 217 040.[13] Assuming that he worked 50 hours a week and took two weeks' vacation, Regent earned about $9686 per hour, or about $161 per minute. Any time that Regent wastes represents a large cost to Barrick and its stockholders.

To manage time effectively, managers must address four leading causes of wasted time:

- *Paperwork*. Some managers spend too much time deciding what to do with letters and reports. Most documents of this sort are routine and can be handled quickly. Managers must learn to recognize those documents that require more attention.
- *The telephone*. Experts estimate that managers are interrupted by the telephone every five minutes. To manage time more effectively, they suggest having a secretary screen all calls and setting aside a certain block of time each day to return the important ones.
- *Meetings*. Many managers spend as much as four hours per day in meetings. To help keep this time productive, the person handling the meeting should specify a clear agenda, start on time, keep everyone focused on the agenda, and end on time.
- *Email*. With the introduction of devices like the BlackBerry, managers are relying more heavily on email and other forms of electronic communication. But many email messages are not important, and some are downright trivial. As the number of electronic messages grows, the potential time wasted also increases.

Decision-Making Skills

Decision-making skills help managers define problems and select the best course of action. It is a critical management skill because decision making affects all the functions of management. The Alternative Board (TAB) is devoted to improving management decision making and has 1000 peer groups around North America. These peer groups—attended by managers looking for solutions to problems they are experiencing—provide a forum for discussions among managers who have had similar problems.[14]

THE RATIONAL DECISION-MAKING PROCESS

Table 6.2 shows the steps in the rational decision-making process. The key elements of each step are described below.

>>> TABLE **6.2** Steps in the Rational Decision-Making Process

	Step	Detail	Example
1.	Recognizing and defining the decision situation	Some stimulus indicates that a decision must be made. The stimulus may be positive or negative.	The plant manager sees that employee turnover has increased by 5 percent.
2.	Identifying alternatives	Both obvious and creative alternatives are desired. In general, the more important the decision, the more alternatives should be generated.	The plant manager can increase wages, increase benefits, or change hiring standards.
3.	Evaluating alternatives	Each alternative is evaluated to determine its feasibility, its satisfactoriness, and its consequences.	Increasing benefits may not be feasible. Increasing wages and changing hiring standards may satisfy all conditions.
4.	Selecting the best alternative	Consider all situational factors and choose the alternative that best fits the manager's situation.	Changing hiring standards will take an extended period of time to cut turnover, so increase wages.
5.	Implementing the chosen alternative	The chosen alternative is implemented into the organizational system.	The plant manager may need permission from corporate headquarters. The human resource department establishes a new wage structure.
6.	Following up and evaluating the results	At some time in the future, the manager should ascertain the extent to which the alternative chosen in step 4 and implemented in step 5 has worked.	The plant manager notes that six months later, turnover dropped to its previous level.

Recognizing and Defining the Decision Situation The first step in rational decision making is recognizing that a decision is necessary. There must be some stimulus or spark to initiate this process. For example, when equipment malfunctions, managers must decide whether to repair it or to replace it. The stimulus for a decision may be either a problem or an opportunity. A manager facing cost overruns on a project is faced with a problem decision, while a manager who is trying to decide how to invest surplus funds is faced with an opportunity decision.

Understanding precisely what the problem or opportunity is comes from careful analysis and thoughtful consideration of the situation. Consider the international air travel industry. Because of the growth of international travel related to business, education, and tourism, global carriers like Singapore Airlines, KLM, JAL, British Airways, and American Airlines need to increase their capacity for international travel. Because most major international airports are already operating at or near capacity, adding a significant number of new flights to existing schedules is not feasible. As a result, the most logical alternative is to increase capacity on existing flights. Thus, Boeing and Airbus, the world's only manufacturers of large commercial aircraft, recognized an important opportunity and defined their decision situation as how best to respond to the need for increased global travel capacity.[15]

After a long decision-making process, Airbus decided to design its own new jumbo jet. Boeing, meanwhile, went through a similar decision-making process, but concluded that the risks were too great to gamble on such an enormous project. Instead, the company decided to modify its existing 747 design and develop a new fuel-efficient aircraft called the 787.

© Hero Images Inc./Alamy

Identifying Alternatives Once the need for a decision has been recognized and defined, the second step is to identify possible alternative courses of effective action. In general, the more important the decision, the more attention is directed to developing alternatives. If the decision involves a multimillion-dollar relocation, a great deal of time and expertise should be devoted to identifying alternatives, but if the decision involves choosing a name for the company softball team, many fewer resources should be devoted to the task (although there may be a lot of arguing about what the name should be!).

Managers must accept that factors such as legal restrictions, moral and ethical norms, and available technology can limit their alternatives. For example, after assessing the question of how to increase international airline capacity, Boeing and Airbus identified three alternatives: They could independently develop new large planes, they could collaborate in a joint venture to create a single new large plane, or they could modify their largest existing planes to increase their capacity.

Evaluating Alternatives Once alternatives have been identified, they must be thoroughly evaluated to increase the chance that the alternative finally chosen will be successful. During its analysis of alternatives, Airbus concluded that it would be at a disadvantage if it tried to simply enlarge its existing planes, because the competitive Boeing 747 is already the largest aircraft being made and could readily be expanded. Boeing, meanwhile, was seriously concerned about the risk inherent in building a new and even larger plane, even if it shared the risk with Airbus as a joint venture.

Selecting the Best Alternative Choosing the best available alternative is a key activity in decision making. Even though many situations do not lend themselves to objective mathematical analysis, managers and leaders can often develop subjective estimates for choosing an alternative. Decision makers should also remember that finding multiple acceptable alternatives may be possible, so selecting just one alternative and rejecting all the others might not be necessary. For example, Airbus proposed a joint venture with Boeing, but Boeing decided that its best course of action was to modify its existing 747 to increase its capacity. Airbus then decided to proceed on its own to develop and manufacture a new jumbo jet called the A380. Meanwhile, Boeing decided that, in addition to modifying its 747, it would also develop a new plane (the 787).

Implementing the Chosen Alternative After an alternative has been selected, managers must implement it. In the case of an acquisition, for example, managers must decide how to integrate the activities of the new business into the firm's existing organizational framework. One of the key considerations during implementation is employee resistance to change. The reasons for such resistance include insecurity, inconvenience, and fear of the unknown. Managers must also recognize that even when all alternatives have been evaluated as precisely as possible and the consequences of each alternative have been weighed, unanticipated consequences are still likely. For example, both Boeing and Airbus have experienced unexpected delays in bringing their new planes to market.

Following Up and Evaluating the Results The final step in the decision-making process requires managers to evaluate the effectiveness of their decision—that is, they should make sure that the chosen alternative has served its original purpose. If an implemented alternative appears not to be working, they can respond in several ways. One possibility is to adopt an alternative that had previously been discarded. Or they might recognize that the situation was not correctly defined to begin with and start the process all over again. In the Boeing–Airbus case, both companies have gotten some feedback about whether or not they made a good decision. For example, increasing fuel prices mean that the 787 was the best decision because it is so fuel efficient.

BEHAVIOURAL ASPECTS OF DECISION MAKING

Most managers try to be logical when they make decisions. But even when they try, they may not succeed. When Starbucks opened its first coffee shops in New York, it relied on scientific marketing research, taste tests, and rational deliberation in making a decision to emphasize drip over espresso coffee. However, that decision proved wrong when it became clear that New Yorkers strongly preferred the same espresso-style coffees that were Starbucks' mainstays in the west.

Hence, the firm had to reconfigure its stores hastily to meet customer preferences.

To complicate matters, non-logical and emotional factors often influence managerial decision making. These factors include *organizational politics, intuition, escalation of commitment*, and *risk propensity*.

Organizational Politics The term **organizational politics** refers to the actions that people take as they try to get what they want. These actions may or may not be beneficial to the organization, but they do influence decision making, particularly if the person taking the action is a powerful manager. A study of 293 Canadian office workers found that 71 percent believed that office politics was at least somewhat necessary in order to get ahead in their organization.[16]

Intuition Managers sometimes decide to do something because it "feels right" or they have a "hunch." **Intuition** is usually based on years of experience and practice in making decisions in similar situations. Such an inner sense may actually help managers make an occasional decision without going through a rational sequence of steps. For example, the New York Yankees once contacted three major sneaker manufacturers—Nike, Reebok, and Adidas—and informed them that they were interested in signing a sponsorship deal. While Nike and Reebok were carefully and rationally assessing the possibilities, managers at Adidas quickly responded to the idea and ended up hammering out a contract while the competitors were still analyzing details.[17] These occasional successes can be very dramatic, but they should not cause managers to rely too heavily on intuition.

Escalation of Commitment When a manager makes a decision and then remains committed to its implementation in spite of clear evidence that it was a bad decision, **escalation of commitment** has occurred.[18] A good example of this is Expo '86, the world's fair that was held in British Columbia. When the project was first conceived, the deficit was projected at about $56 million. Over the next few years, the projected deficit kept rising until it was over $300 million. In spite of that, the project went forward. Managers can avoid overcommitment by setting specific goals ahead of time that deal with how much time and money they are willing to spend on a given project. These goals make it harder for managers to interpret unfavourable news in a positive light.

Risk Propensity **Risk Propensity** refers to how much a manager is willing to gamble when making decisions. Managers who are very cautious when making decisions are more likely to avoid mistakes, and they are unlikely to make decisions that lead to big losses (or big gains). Other managers are extremely aggressive in making decisions and are willing to take risks.[19] They rely heavily on intuition, reach decisions quickly, and often risk big money on their decisions. These managers are more likely than their conservative counterparts to achieve big successes, but they are also more likely to incur greater losses.[20] The organization's culture is a prime ingredient in fostering different levels of risk propensity.

ORGANIZATIONAL POLITICS The actions that people take as they try to get what they want.

INTUITION An innate belief about something, often without conscious consideration.

ESCALATION OF COMMITMENT Condition in which a decision maker becomes so committed to a course of action that he or she stays with it even when there is evidence that the decision was wrong.

RISK PROPENSITY Extent to which a decision maker is willing to gamble when making a decision.

LO-4 STRATEGIC MANAGEMENT: SETTING GOALS AND FORMULATING STRATEGY

Strategic management is the process of effectively aligning the organization with its external environment. The starting point in strategic management is setting goals that a business wants to achieve. Every business needs goals. Remember, however, that deciding what it intends to do is only the first step for an organization. Managers must also make decisions about what actions will and will not achieve company goals. Decisions cannot be made on a problem-by-problem basis or merely to meet needs as they arise. In most companies, a broad program underlies those decisions. That program is called a **strategy**—the broad set of organizational plans for implementing the decisions made for achieving organizational goals.

Setting Business Goals

Goals are performance targets, the means by which organizations and their managers measure success or failure at every level. Goals indicate *what* results are desired, while plans indicate *how* these goals are to be achieved. Managers must understand the purposes of goal setting and the kinds of goals that need to be set.

STRATEGIC MANAGEMENT The process of helping an organization maintain an effective alignment with its environment.

STRATEGY The broad set of organizational plans for implementing the decisions made for achieving organizational goals.

THE PURPOSES OF GOAL SETTING

There are four main purposes in organizational goal setting:

1. *Goal setting provides direction, guidance, and motivation for all managers.* Toyota set a goal to sell 200 000 vehicles in Canada in 2012. That was a 25 percent increase over actual sales in 2011.[21] WestJet's goal is to challenge Air Canada for the top spot in domestic air travel by 2016.[22]
2. *Goal setting helps firms allocate resources.* Areas that are expected to grow will get first priority. Thus, 3M allocates more resources to new projects with large sales potential than it allocates to mature products with low growth potential.
3. *Goal setting helps to define corporate culture.* General Electric's goal is to have each of its divisions be #1 or #2 in its industry. The result is a competitive, often stressful, environment and a culture that rewards success and has little tolerance for failure.
4. *Goal setting helps managers assess performance.* At Port Metro Vancouver, the goal for container "dwell time"—the time containers

VISION (OR PURPOSE) A statement indicating why an organization exists and what kind of organization it wants to be.

MISSION STATEMENT An organization's statement of how it will achieve its purpose in the environment in which it conducts its business.

sit on the dock—is three days (the North American standard). In January 2010, the dwell time was 3.7 days, but by November 2011, it had been reduced to 2.5 days. Setting specific goals like this helps managers assess their performance.[23]

Goal setting is effective for individuals as well as organizations. When students set goals, they achieve higher grades, lower their chance for dropping out of school, and experience greater well-being as adults. Unfortunately, less than half of the students aged 10 to 18 are aggressively pursuing goals.[24]

KINDS OF GOALS

Goals differ from company to company, depending on the firm's vision and mission. Every organization has a **vision (or purpose)** that indicates why it exists and what kind of organization it wants to be. For example, businesses seek profit, universities discover and transmit new knowledge, and government agencies provide services to the public. Most organizations also have a **mission statement**—a statement of how they will achieve their purpose. DaimlerChrysler's mission statement emphasizes "delighted customers," while Atco Ltd.'s mission is to provide products and services to the energy and resource industries and to invest in energy-related assets in North America. Mission statements often include some statement about the company's core values and its commitment to ethical behaviour.

Two business firms can have the same vision—for example, to sell watches at a profit—yet have very different missions. Timex sells low-cost, reliable watches in outlets ranging from department stores to corner drugstores. Rolex, on the other hand, sells high-quality, high-priced fashion watches through selected jewellery stores. Regardless of a company's purpose and mission, it must set long-term, intermediate, and short-term goals.

- **Long-term goals** relate to extended periods of time—typically five years or more into the future. American Express, for example, might set a long-term goal of doubling the number of participating merchants during the next 10 years.
- **Intermediate goals** are set for a period of one to five years into the future. When Kazuo Hirai became CEO of Sony in 2012, he was determined to improve the performance of the consumer electronics company. He therefore set a sales target of US$105 billion for the division that makes medical equipment and electric car batteries. The goal is to be achieved in two years. He also set a goal to triple revenue in the mobile phone division.[25]
- Like intermediate goals, **short-term goals**—which are set for one year or less—are developed for several different areas. Increasing sales by 2 percent this year, cutting costs by 1 percent next quarter, and reducing turnover by 4 percent over the next six months are all short-term goals.

Whatever the time frame of the goals that are set, research shows that managers who set **SMART goals** (goals that are Specific, Measurable, Achievable, Relevant, and Time-framed) have higher performance than managers who don't. The boxed insert entitled "Extending the Logic of Goal Setting" describes the importance of setting goals that take the environment into account.

Formulating Strategy

After a firm has set its goals, it must develop a strategy for achieving them. In contrast to planning, strategy is wider in scope and is a broad program that describes how a business intends to meet its goals, how it will respond to new challenges, and how it will meet new needs. For example, Brookfield Asset Management's strategy is to buy high-quality assets at less than replacement cost.[26] **Strategy formulation** involves three basic steps: (1) setting strategic goals, (2) analyzing the organization and its environment, and (3) matching the organization and its environment (see Figure 6.4).

LONG-TERM GOALS Goals set for extended periods of time, typically five years or more into the future.

INTERMEDIATE GOALS Goals set for a period of one to five years.

SHORT-TERM GOALS Goals set for the very near future, typically less than one year.

SMART GOALS Goals that are Specific, Measurable, Achievable, Relevant, and Time-framed.

STRATEGY FORMULATION Creation of a broad program for defining and meeting an organization's goals.

>>> **FIGURE 6.4** Strategy formulation

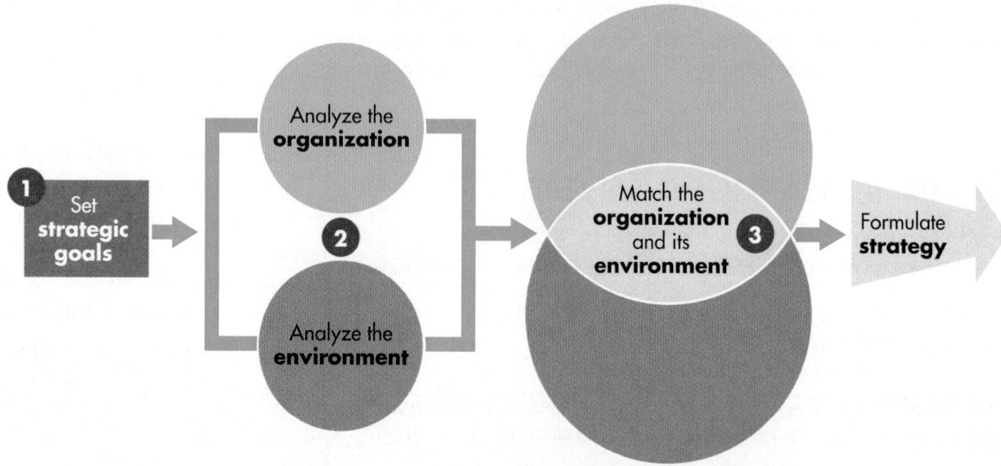

THE GREENING OF BUSINESS

Extending the Logic of Goal Setting

The logic of goal setting is being extended to make businesses greener. Green goals may be developed by managers, or they may be imposed on companies by external groups. Consider the following:

- Scotiabank set a goal to be in the top 10 percent of the companies listed on the Dow Jones Sustainability World Index.
- Employees on different floors of the Air Miles building in Toronto compete to see who can reduce energy usage the most in a specific month.
- Ford Motor Co. has set a goal of tripling its production of electric vehicles and hybrids by 2013.
- Co-operators Life Insurance Co. has set a goal to reduce emissions from business travel and climate control by 50 percent by 2014.
- Dillon Consulting Ltd. (Toronto) has a goal to invest 1 percent of revenue into social, environmental, and community initiatives.
- DuPont Canada has a goal to double investment in research and development programs with quantifiable environmental benefits.

For some organizations, their entire mission is being green. For example, the mission of B.C.–based Greener Footprints (a non-profit organization) is to reduce the use of plastic bags in Canada. For other organizations, the setting of green goals is closely tied to the success of their business. For example, the CEO of Honda, Takeo Fukui, recognized that Toyota's popular Prius hybrid automobile outsold Honda's hybrid car by a wide margin during the last decade, so he set a goal to make Honda the greenest company in the automobile industry. Honda has set a goal to sell 500 000 hybrid automobiles each year (Toyota's goal is 1 million). In 2008, Honda introduced its Clarity FCX, which was powered by a hydrogen fuel cell that generates no pollution at all. Honda also launched a new gas-electric hybrid in 2009 and plans to launch several other hybrids by 2015.

Rona Inc., the home renovation chain, has set a goal of doing business only with suppliers who address environmental sustainability and do not contribute to deforestation. The goal for 2009 was to have all the plywood panels Rona sells made only from lumber that comes from forests that have been certified as sustainable. By 2010, the same goal applied to spruce, pine, and fir. By 2012, Rona's goal was to have 25 percent of its total wood sales come from forests that are certified by the Forest Stewardship Council.

CRITICAL THINKING QUESTIONS

1. What are the advantages of setting green goals? Are there disadvantages? Explain.
2. What difficulties might Rona encounter as it tries to reach the goal of having 25 percent of its total wood sales come from forests that are certified by the Forest Stewardship Council?

SETTING STRATEGIC GOALS

Strategic goals are long-term goals derived directly from the firm's mission statement. General Electric, for example, is pursuing four strategic goals to ensure continued success for the company: an emphasis on quality control, an emphasis on selling services and not just products, concentrating on niche acquisitions, and global expansion.

ANALYZING THE ORGANIZATION AND ITS ENVIRONMENT

After strategic goals have been set, managers assess both their organization and its environment using a **SWOT analysis**. This involves identifying organizational Strengths and Weaknesses, and identifying environmental Opportunities and Threats. Strengths and weaknesses are factors internal to the firm, and are assessed using **organizational analysis**. Strengths might include surplus cash, a dedicated workforce, an ample supply of managerial talent, technical expertise, or weak competitors. For example, Pepsi's strength in beverage distribution through its network of soft-drink distributors was successfully extended to distribution of its Aquafina brand of bottled water. Weaknesses might include a cash shortage, aging factories, and a poor public image. Garden.com's reliance on the internet-based e-tailing model became its downfall when the dot-com bubble burst.

Opportunities and threats are factors external to the firm and are assessed using **environmental analysis**. Opportunities include things like market demand for new products, favourable government legislation, or shortages of raw materials that the company is good at producing.

STRATEGIC GOALS Long-term goals derived directly from the firm's mission statement.

SWOT ANALYSIS Identification and analysis of organizational strengths and weaknesses and environmental opportunities and threats as part of strategy formulation.

ORGANIZATIONAL ANALYSIS The process of analyzing a firm's strengths and weaknesses.

ENVIRONMENTAL ANALYSIS The process of scanning the environment for threats and opportunities.

THERE'S AN APP FOR THAT!

1. SWOT Chart >>> **Platforms:** *Apple, Android, BlackBerry*
   Source: K. Kaleeswaran
   Key Features: Strategic planning method used to evaluate the Strengths, Weaknesses, Opportunities, and Threats.
2. Goal Tracker: SmartGoals >>> **Platforms:** *Android*
   Source: MSurf Lab.
   Key Features: A tool to help you set SMART (specific, measurable, achievable, relevant, and time-framed) goals.
3. Strategy + Business Magazine >>> **Platforms:** *Apple, Android*
   Source: Booz and Company
   Key Features: In-depth feature stories, leader interviews, and strategic commentaries.

APP DISCOVERY EXERCISE

Since APP availability changes, conduct your own search for "Top 3" Management APPS and identify the key features.

For example, when Pepsi managers recognized a market opportunity for bottled water, they moved quickly to launch their Aquafina brand and to position it for rapid growth. Threats include new products developed by competitors, unfavourable government regulations, and changes in consumer tastes. For example, in 2010, the Province of Ontario proposed new legislation that sharply reduced the revenue that pharmacies would receive for dispensing prescription drugs. Some external threats are unpredictable, like the volcanic eruption in Iceland in 2010 that halted air travel in Europe for a week. Commercial airlines lost hundreds of millions of dollars of revenue, while alternative service providers like trains saw demand for their services soar.

MATCHING THE ORGANIZATION AND ITS ENVIRONMENT

The final step in strategy formulation is matching environmental threats and opportunities with corporate strengths and weaknesses. Matching companies with their environments lays the foundation for successfully planning and conducting business. Over the long term, this process may also determine whether a firm typically takes risks or behaves more conservatively. Just because two companies are in the same industry does not mean that they will use the same strategies. The Toronto-Dominion Bank, for example, aggressively expanded into the U.S. retail banking industry by acquiring U.S. banks, but the Royal Bank of Canada has been much less aggressive in this area.[27]

Levels of Strategy

There are three levels of strategy in a business firm (see Figure 6.5). A **corporate-level strategy** identifies the various businesses that a company will be in and how these businesses will relate to each other. A **business-level (competitive) strategy** identifies the ways a business will compete in its chosen line of products or services. **Functional strategies** identify the basic courses of action that each department in the firm will pursue so that it contributes to the attainment of the business's overall goals.

CORPORATE-LEVEL STRATEGY Identifies the various businesses that a company will be in, and how these businesses will relate to each other.

BUSINESS-LEVEL (COMPETITIVE) STRATEGY Identifies the ways a business will compete in its chosen line of products or services.

FUNCTIONAL STRATEGIES Identify the basic courses of action that each department in the firm will pursue so that it contributes to the attainment of the business's overall goals.

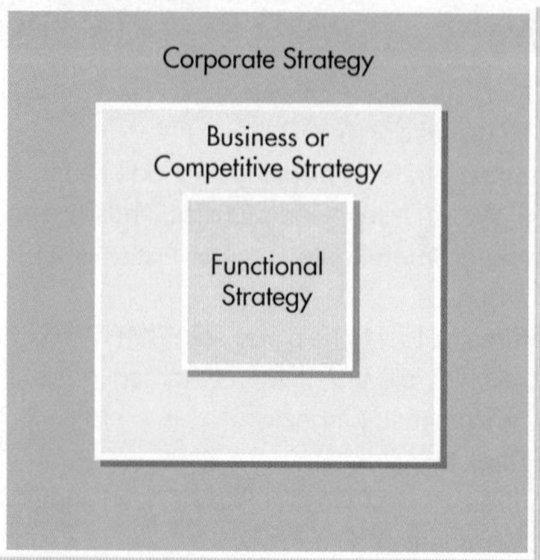

FIGURE 6.5 Hierarchy of strategy

Source: Based on Thomas L. Wheelen and J. David Hunger, *Strategic Management and Business Policy*, 8th edition. (Upper Saddle River, NJ: Prentice Hall, 2002), 14.

CONCENTRATION STRATEGY Involves focusing the company on one product or product line.

MARKET PENETRATION Boosting sales of present products by more aggressive selling in the firm's current markets.

GEOGRAPHIC EXPANSION Expanding operations in new geographic areas or countries.

CORPORATE-LEVEL STRATEGIES

There are several different corporate-level strategies that a company might pursue, including concentration, growth, integration, diversification, and investment reduction.

Concentration A **concentration strategy** involves focusing the company on one product or product line that it knows very well. Organizations that have successfully pursued a concentration strategy include McDonald's and Canadian National Railway.

Growth Companies have several growth strategies available to them, including **market penetration** (boosting sales of present products by more aggressive selling in the firm's current markets), **geographic expansion** (expanding operations in new geographic areas),

Target used a horizontal integration strategy when it entered the Canadian market. It purchased over 200 Zellers stores and then remade them in the Target style.

© Jonathan Larsen/Diadem Images/Alamy

PRODUCT DEVELOPMENT Developing improved products for current markets.

HORIZONTAL INTEGRATION Acquiring control of competitors in the same or similar markets with the same or similar products.

VERTICAL INTEGRATION Owning or controlling the inputs to the firm's processes and/or the channels through which the products or services are distributed.

DIVERSIFICATION Expanding into related or unrelated products or market segments.

INVESTMENT REDUCTION Reducing the company's investment in one or more of its lines of business.

and **product development** (developing improved products for current markets). These three strategies focus on internal activities that will result in growth.

Integration There are two basic integration strategies. **Horizontal integration** means acquiring control of competitors in the same or similar markets with the same or similar products. For example, Hudson's Bay owns Home Outfitters (Deco Decouverte in Quebec), and U.S.-based Target acquired many Zellers stores as it prepared to enter the Canadian market. **Vertical integration** means owning or controlling the inputs to the firm's processes and/or the channels through which the products or services are distributed. Oil companies like Shell not only drill and produce their own oil, but also sell it through company-controlled outlets across Canada. These two strategies focus on external activities that will result in growth.

Diversification **Diversification** helps the firm avoid the problem of having all of its eggs in one basket by spreading risk among several products or markets. *Related diversification* means adding new, but related, products or services to an existing business. For example, Maple Leaf Gardens Ltd., which already owned the Toronto Maple Leafs, acquired the Toronto Raptors basketball team. *Conglomerate diversification* means diversifying into products or markets that are not related to the firm's present businesses. Eastman Kodak was the leader for many years in the film-based photography business, but it fell on hard times when digital cameras were introduced (Kodak invented the digital camera in the 1970s, but somehow never capitalized on the idea). Kodak then adopted a diversification strategy in an attempt to survive (and tried to reinvent itself as a printing and graphics company), but it fell into bankruptcy anyway.[28]

Investment Reduction **Investment reduction** means reducing the company's investment in one or more of its lines of business. One investment-reduction strategy is *retrenchment*, which means the reduction of activity or operations. For example, Federal Industries was formerly a conglomerate with interests in trucking, railways, metals, and other product lines, but it has now retrenched and focuses on a more limited set of products and customers. *Divestment* involves selling or liquidating one or more of a firm's businesses. For example, BCE sold its Yellow Pages and White Pages for $4 billion.

The boxed insert entitled "Will This Strategy Fly?" describes corporate-level strategic thinking at Bombardier.

MANAGING IN TURBULENT TIMES

Will This Strategy Fly?

Montreal-based Bombardier is a world leader in the production of commercial jets, business jets, and trains. Bombardier's fortunes are often influenced by political decisions made by governments, so developing corporate strategy is difficult. For example, Bombardier and Brazil-based Embraer have repeatedly charged each other with violating World Trade Organization rules about receiving government subsidies from their home governments.

Bombardier's corporate strategy involves aggressively pursuing customers in two distinct markets: business jets and commercial jets. In the *business jet* market, Bombardier's current product offering is the Global Express XRS high-end jet. But in order to compete with U.S. rival Gulfstream Aerospace, Bombardier is planning to spend more than $1 billion to develop two new, ultra-luxurious, long-range business jets that are derivatives of the Global Express. The Global 7000, which is slated for delivery in 2016, will be 20 percent wider than Gulfstream's G650 (but the G650 will come on the market in 2012). The Global 8000 is designed to compete on distance and will fly slightly faster than the G650. In the *commercial jet* market, Bombardier is developing the CSeries jet, which is designed to compete in the 100- to 150-seat segment of the market. The new jet will have advanced avionics, new wings made of composite materials, and a fuselage made of a lithium-aluminum alloy. There are actually two planes in the series: the CS100 (which seats 100 to 124 people) and the CS300 (which seats 120 to 145 people). With its new entries, Bombardier feels that it can successfully compete against planes made by Airbus and Boeing, the two giants in the industry. But developing a new product is risky because of the complexity of the product, the long time frame needed for its development, and the high cost of each unit (for example, the new CSeries jets will sell for about $65 million each).

At the 2011 Paris Air Show, executives of both Boeing and Airbus conceded that aircraft manufacturers in Canada, Russia, Brazil, and China are going be competitive with Boeing and Airbus. AirInsight, an aviation consultancy company, released a report showing that the CSeries aircraft will have advantages over both the Airbus A319neo and the Boeing 737. But Boeing and Airbus could also respond to the CSeries threat by lowering prices on their planes. Since they are much larger companies, Bombardier could probably not meet their prices.

If Bombardier's strategy succeeds, it will mean huge sales revenues and profits for the company, but Bombardier also has to worry about other competition, which will come from China's C919 aircraft, which is being developed by Commercial Aircraft Corp. of China (also known as Comac). Ryanair, Europe's biggest discount carrier, is working together with Comac, so that could make it difficult for Bombardier to sell any planes to Ryanair. New planes are also being developed by Embraer (Brazil) and Sukhoi (Russia).

CRITICAL THINKING QUESTIONS

1. What are the various levels of strategy that exist in a business firm?
2. What corporate-level strategy is Bombardier pursuing? Explain your reasoning.

COST LEADERSHIP Becoming the low-cost leader in an industry.

DIFFERENTIATION STRATEGY A firm seeks to be unique in its industry along some dimension that is valued by buyers.

FOCUS STRATEGY Selecting a market segment and serving the customers in that market niche better than competitors.

BUSINESS-LEVEL (COMPETITIVE) STRATEGIES

Whatever corporate-level strategy a firm decides on, it must also have a competitive strategy. A competitive strategy is a plan to establish a profitable and sustainable competitive position.[29] Michael Porter identifies three competitive strategies. **Cost leadership** means becoming the low-cost leader in an industry. Walmart is the best-known industry cost leader. Montreal-based Gildan Activewear is dedicated to achieving the lowest possible costs in producing its T-shirts. The company has captured 29 percent of the U.S. imprinted T-shirt market with this strategy.[30]

A firm using a **differentiation strategy** tries to be unique in its industry along some dimension that is valued by buyers. For example, Caterpillar emphasizes durability, Volvo stresses safety, Apple stresses user-friendly products, and Mercedes-Benz emphasizes quality. A **focus strategy** means selecting a market segment and serving the customers in that market niche better than competitors. Before it was acquired by Nexfor, Fraser Inc. focused on producing high-quality, durable, lightweight paper that is used in bibles.

FUNCTIONAL STRATEGIES

Each business's choice of a competitive strategy (cost leadership, differentiation, or focus) is translated into supporting functional strategies for each of its departments to pursue. A functional strategy is the basic course of action that each department follows so that the business accomplishes its overall goals. To implement its cost-leadership strategy, for example, Walmart's distribution department pursued a functional strategy of satellite-based warehousing that ultimately drove distribution costs down below those of its competitors.

LO-5 CONTINGENCY PLANNING AND CRISIS MANAGEMENT

Business environments are often difficult to predict because unexpected events may occur. Two common methods of dealing with the unforeseen are *contingency planning* and *crisis management*.

Contingency Planning

Contingency planning means identifying in advance changes that might occur that would affect a business and developing a plan to respond to such changes. For example, airlines know that snowstorms at, say, Toronto's Pearson International Airport are likely, so they develop contingency plans for coping with that eventuality. These plans typically involve rescheduling flights into neighbouring airports and providing passengers with ground transportation into Toronto. Assessing the costs and benefits of these and other options ahead of time helps managers cope with problems when they arise.

Commercial airlines have contingency plans to deal with problems like major snowstorms. These contingency plans involve making sure that planes are not stranded at airports that are experiencing snow delays.

EDHAR/Shutterstock

Crisis Management

Crisis management means dealing with an emergency that demands an immediate response. Crisis management plans outline who will be in charge in different kinds of circumstances, how the organization will respond, and the plans that exist for assembling and deploying crisis-management teams.

Business crises are more common than you might think. For example, as we saw in the opening case, Boeing faced a crisis when batteries in the 787 Dreamliner caught fire. BP also faced a crisis when an explosion at a drilling rig in the Gulf of Mexico resulted in the death of 11 workers and caused a huge oil spill. Toyota faced a crisis when consumers claimed that some models of its cars were accelerating out of control. Carnival Corp. faced a crisis when one of its cruise ships lost power and stranded 4000 passengers at sea for four days with no working toilets. Maple Leaf Foods was confronted with a crisis when listeria (tainted meat) was discovered at one of its processing plants. Maple Leaf quickly recalled 686 000 kilograms of meat (an action that cost the company $19 million). CEO Michael McCain publicly apologized at news conferences and in television commercials and assured consumers that the company would solve the problem.[31] A few months later, a survey revealed that 78 percent of respondents had recently purchased a Maple Leaf product (that was up from only 20 percent right after the crisis occurred).[32]

CONTINGENCY PLANNING Identifying aspects of a business or its environment that might require changes in strategy.

CRISIS MANAGEMENT An organization's methods for dealing with emergencies.

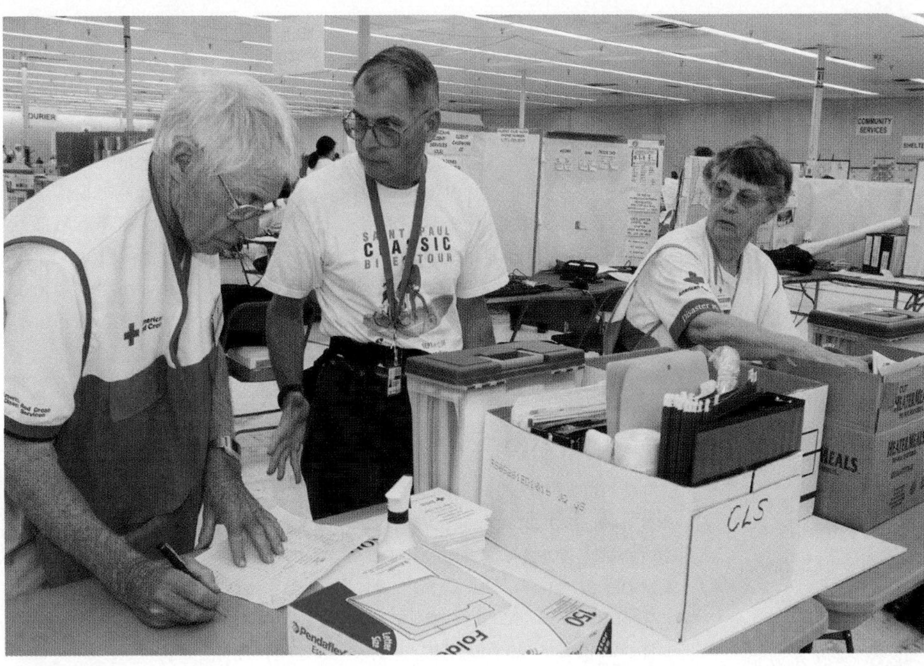

<<< Crisis management involves an organization's methods for dealing with emergencies. Here, Red Cross volunteers organize and file paperwork submitted by Hurricane Katrina victims.

© Jim West/Alamy

LO-6 MANAGEMENT AND THE CORPORATE CULTURE

Just as every individual has a unique personality, every company has a unique identity. This is its **corporate culture**—the shared experiences, stories, beliefs, and norms that characterize it. Here are some examples:

- At ING DIRECT, the culture encourages employees to challenge the status quo, both within the company and the banking industry.[33]
- The culture of the Toronto Blue Jays organization is designed to make employees feel like they are part of a family. To facilitate the culture, employees have "snacks with the president" so they can talk about how the organization is operating.
- Google creates a culture of "yes" in order to encourage innovation. Employees focus on what is right with a new idea rather than what is wrong with it.[34]
- Magna International, a large Canadian producer of auto parts, is a firm with a strong culture. Its founder, Frank Stronach, is well known for his views about employees, working conditions, daycare centres, unions, the free enterprise system, and profit distribution.[35]
- Four Seasons Hotels and Resorts has a different, but equally strong, culture. Managers are judged by deeds, not words, and act as role models; employees take their cues from the managers.[36]

Companies that focus largely on one type of product (for example, Starbucks Coffee Company) may have a fairly homogeneous culture throughout the organization. But companies with many different divisions and many different types of customers (for example, the Royal Bank of Canada) are likely to have several different subcultures because the various divisions pursue different goals and because different types of people are found in the different divisions.

CORPORATE CULTURE The shared experiences, stories, beliefs, and norms that characterize a firm.

^^^ The founder or CEO of a business plays a major role in shaping the company's culture. For example, the late Steve Jobs, co-founder and former CEO of Apple, helped establish an informal and laid-back culture at the company, which featured casual business attire and an open-door policy. That culture helps Apple continue to attract and retain talented people.

© Mart of Images/Alamy

A strong corporate culture guides everyone to work toward the same goals and helps newcomers learn accepted behaviours. In a strong culture where financial success is the key issue, newcomers quickly learn that they are expected to work long, hard hours and that the "winner" is the one who brings in the most revenue. But if quality of life is more fundamental to the culture, newcomers learn that it's acceptable to balance work and non-work activities. Cameron Herold—a Vancouver entrepreneur who has had a string of successes in franchising, including College Pro Painters, Boyd Autobody, and 1-800-GOT-JUNK—says that a cult-like culture is crucial for attracting great employees. He says what's needed is a culture that is "more than a business and slightly less than a religion."[37]

Each year, Waterstone Human Capital conducts in-depth interviews with senior managers at many different Canadian companies and asks them which corporate cultures they admire most. The 2011 winners included Agrium Inc., CIBC, Coast Capital Savings Credit Union, and ING DIRECT Canada.[38] Although many companies do not systematically monitor their corporate cultures, Starbucks is one company that does. Once every 18 months, employees fill out a Partner View Survey containing questions that are designed to help the company determine whether it is making progress toward one of its key values—providing a work environment where people treat one another with respect and dignity. The survey is voluntary, but about 90 percent of employees fill it out (on company time). One reason the participation rate is so high is that the company actually pays attention to what employees say in the survey. For example, when one survey showed that employees were not clear about career progression possibilities in the company, Starbucks held career fairs in several Canadian cities, where company managers spoke with employees about management opportunities at Starbucks.[39]

Communicating the Culture and Managing Change

Managers must carefully consider the kind of culture they want for their organization, then work to nourish that culture by communicating with everyone who works there. Walmart, for example, assigns veteran managers to lead employees in new territories. Starbucks Coffee surveys employees every 18 months regarding several aspects of its culture. Royal Bank of Canada and Four Seasons Hotels and Resorts also survey their employees to determine how well they are progressing toward their corporate culture goals.[40]

COMMUNICATING THE CULTURE

To use a company's culture to full advantage, its managers must accomplish several tasks, all of which hinge on effective communication. First, managers themselves must have a clear understanding of the culture. Second, they must transmit the culture to others in the organization. Communication is a key aim in training and orienting newcomers. A clear and meaningful statement of the organization's mission is also a valuable communication tool. Finally, managers can maintain the culture by rewarding and promoting those who understand it and work toward maintaining it.

MANAGING CHANGE

Organizations must sometimes change their cultures. Ontario Hydro, for example, had an "engineering" culture for many years. That meant that everything was planned and analyzed down to the last detail before any action was taken. But Ontario Hydro's culture has changed to a more consumer-oriented, risk-taking culture as it tries to cope with large debt and changes in its markets.

Changing an organization's culture can be difficult, so just because someone recognizes the need for cultural change does not mean that it will actually be implemented. For example, when several RCMP officers alleged that there were problems with senior management, lawyer David Brown was appointed by the government to look into the matter. His report concluded that the Commissioner had exercised absolute power, that no one questioned his management style, and that there was a "tone" at the top of the organization that resulted in little respect for employees. The report also said that whistle-blowers within the RCMP were punished when they pointed out that there were problems. The report concluded that the culture and management structure at the RCMP were "horribly broken."[41] These developments are discouraging because just a few years earlier the RCMP had completed a "visioning" process that resulted in a new mission statement, a new set of core values, and a commitment to the communities where it worked. At that time, it was reported that the culture of the RCMP was quite different than it had been in the days when military tradition dominated the organization, but subsequent events suggested that the culture had not actually changed much.

MyBizLab Visit the MyBizLab website. This online homework and tutorial system puts you in control of your own learning with study and practice tools directly correlated to this chapter's content.

SUMMARY OF LEARNING OBJECTIVES

LO-1 DESCRIBE THE FOUR ACTIVITIES THAT CONSTITUTE THE *MANAGEMENT PROCESS.*

Management is the process of planning, organizing, leading, and controlling an organization's financial, physical, human, and information resources to achieve the organization's goals. *Planning* means determining what the company needs to do and how best to get it done. *Organizing* means determining how best to arrange a business's resources and the necessary jobs into an overall structure.

Leading means guiding and motivating employees to meet the firm's objectives. *Controlling* means monitoring the firm's performance to ensure that it is meeting its goals.

LO-2 IDENTIFY *TYPES OF MANAGERS* BY LEVEL AND AREA.

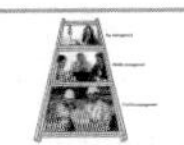

Managers can be differentiated in two ways: by level and by area. By level, *top managers* set policies, formulate strategies, and approve decisions. *Middle managers* implement policies, strategies, and decisions. *First-line managers* usually work with and supervise employees. By area, managers focus on *marketing, finance, operations, human resource*, and *information*. Managers at all levels may be found in every area of a company.

LO-3 DESCRIBE THE FIVE BASIC *MANAGEMENT SKILLS*.

Most managers agree that five basic management skills are necessary for success. *Technical skills* are needed to perform specialized tasks ranging from typing to auditing. *Human relations skills* are needed to understand and get along with other people. *Conceptual skills* allow managers to think in the abstract, to diagnose and analyze various situations, and to see beyond present circumstances. *Decision-making skills* allow managers to define problems and to select the best course of action. *Time management skills* refer to managers' ability to make productive use of the time available to them.

LO-4 EXPLAIN THE IMPORTANCE OF *GOAL SETTING* AND *STRATEGIC MANAGEMENT* IN ORGANIZATIONAL SUCCESS.

Goals—the performance targets of an organization—can be *long term, intermediate,* and *short term*. They provide direction for managers, they help managers decide how to allocate limited resources, they define the corporate culture, and they help managers assess performance. *Strategic management* involves three major activities: setting strategic goals, analyzing the organization and its environment, and matching the organization and its environment. The strategies that are decided upon are then translated into *strategic*, *tactical*, and *operational* plans.

LO-5 DISCUSS *CONTINGENCY PLANNING* AND *CRISIS MANAGEMENT* IN TODAY'S BUSINESS WORLD.

To deal with crises or major environmental changes, companies develop contingency plans and plans for crisis management. *Contingency planning* tries to identify in advance the important aspects of a business or its markets that might change and how the company will respond if such changes actually occur. *Crisis management* means developing methods and actions for dealing with an emergency that requires an immediate response. To prepare for such emergencies, organizations develop crisis plans.

LO-6 EXPLAIN THE IDEA OF *CORPORATE CULTURE* AND WHY IT IS IMPORTANT.

Corporate culture is the shared experiences, stories, beliefs, and norms that characterize an organization. A strong, well-defined culture can help a business reach its goals and can influence management styles. Culture is determined by several factors, including top management, the organization's history, stories and legends, and behavioural norms. If carefully communicated and flexible enough to accommodate change, corporate culture can be managed for the betterment of the organization.

QUESTIONS AND EXERCISES

QUESTIONS FOR ANALYSIS

See >>> for Assisted-Graded Writing Assignment in MyBizLab

1. How are the four *functions* of management related to the five *skills* of management? Use examples to clarify your answer.
2. What is the relationship between Mintzberg's *roles* of management and the more traditional *functions* of management? Use examples to clarify your answer.
3. Identify the managers by level and area at your college or university.
4. Can you identify any organizations where the technical skills of top managers are more important than human relations or conceptual skills? Can you identify organizations where conceptual skills are not important?
5. >>> What differences might you expect to find in the corporate cultures of a 100-year-old manufacturing firm based in Winnipeg and a five-year-old e-commerce firm based in Ottawa?
6. Consider the various corporate-level strategies discussed in the text (concentration, growth, integration, diversification, investment, reduction). What is the relationship between these various strategies? Are they mutually exclusive? Are they complementary? Explain.

APPLICATION EXERCISES

7. Interview a manager at any level of a local company. Identify the manager's job according to level and area. Explain what planning, organizing, directing, and controlling mean in terms of the manager's job. Give examples. Also indicate which management skills are most important for the manager's job.
8. Review the example of the decisions made by Airbus and Boeing regarding new large aircraft. Then research the most current information on the status of the two planes. Which company seems to have made the better decision?
9. Interview an administrator at your college or university. Ask the administrator to give his or her views on the school's strengths and weaknesses and on the threats and opportunities the school is facing. Then use this information to write up a SWOT analysis for the school.
10. Select any organization of which you are a member (your company, your family, your place of worship, or a club). Explain the relevance of the management functions of planning, organizing, directing, and controlling for that organization.

TEAM EXERCISES

BUILDING YOUR BUSINESS SKILLS

SPEAKING WITH POWER

GOAL

To encourage students to appreciate effective speaking as a critical human relations skill.

BACKGROUND

A manager's ability to understand and get along with supervisors, peers, and subordinates is a critical human relations skill. At the heart of this skill, says Harvard University professor of education Sarah McGinty, is the ability to speak with power and control. McGinty defines "powerful speech" in terms of the following characteristics:

- The ability to speak at length and in complete sentences
- The ability to set a conversational agenda
- The ability to deter interruption
- The ability to argue openly and to express strong opinions about ideas, not people
- The ability to make statements that offer solutions rather than pose questions
- The ability to express humour

Taken together, says McGinty, "all this creates a sense of confidence in listeners."

METHOD

Step 1 Working alone, compare your own personal speaking style with McGinty's description of powerful speech by taping yourself as you speak during a meeting with classmates or during a phone conversation.

(Tape both sides of the conversation only if the person to whom you are speaking gives permission.) Listen for the following problems:

- Unfinished sentences
- An absence of solutions
- Too many disclaimers ("I'm not sure I have enough information to say this, but . . .")
- The habit of seeking support from others instead of making definitive statements of personal conviction (saying, "As Emily stated in her report, I recommend consolidating the medical and fitness functions," instead of, "I recommend consolidating the medical and fitness functions.")
- Language fillers (saying, "you know," "like," and "um" when you are unsure of your facts or uneasy about expressing your opinion)

Step 2 Join with three or four other classmates to evaluate each other's speaking styles.

- Have a 10-minute group discussion on the importance of human relations skills in business.
- Listen to other group members, and take notes on the "power" content of what you hear.
- Offer constructive criticism by focusing on what speakers say rather than on personal characteristics (say, "Bob, you sympathized with Paul's position, but I still don't know what you think," instead of, "Bob, you sounded like a weakling.").

FOLLOW-UP QUESTIONS

1. How do you think the power content of speech affects a manager's ability to communicate? Evaluate some of the ways in which effects may differ among supervisors, peers, and subordinates.
2. How do you evaluate yourself and group members in terms of powerful and powerless speech? List the strengths and weaknesses of the group.
3. Do you agree or disagree with McGinty that business success depends on gaining insight into your own language habits? Explain your answer.
4. In our age of computers and email, why do you think personal presentation continues to be important in management?
5. McGinty believes that power language differs from company to company and that it is linked to the corporate culture. Do you agree, or do you believe that people express themselves in similar ways no matter where they are?

EXERCISING YOUR ETHICS

CLEAN UP NOW OR CLEAN UP LATER?

THE SITUATION

The top management team of a medium-sized manufacturing company is on a strategic planning "retreat" where it is formulating ideas and plans for spurring new growth in the company. As one part of this activity, the team, working with the assistance of a consultant, has conducted a SWOT analysis. During this activity, an interesting and complex situation has been identified. Next year, the federal government will be issuing new—and much more stringent—pollution standards for the company's industry. The management team sees this as a potential threat in that the company will have to buy new equipment and change some of its manufacturing methods in order to comply with the new standards.

THE DILEMMA

One member of the team, James Smith, has posed an interesting option—not complying. His logic can be summarized as follows:

1. The firm has already developed its capital budgets for the next two years. Any additional capital expenditures will cause major problems with the company's cash flow and budget allocations.
2. The company has a large uncommitted capital budget entry available in three years; those funds could be used to upgrade pollution control systems at that time.
3. Because the company has a spotless environmental record so far, James Smith argues that if the company does not buy the equipment for three years, the most likely outcomes will be (a) a warning in year 1; (b) a small fine in year 2; and (c) a substantial fine in year 3. However, the total amounts of the years 2 and 3 fines will be much lower than the cost of redoing the company budgets and complying with the new law next year.

TEAM ACTIVITY

Assemble a group of four students and assign each group member to one of the following roles:

- Management team member
- Lower-level employee at the company
- Company customer
- Company investor

ACTION STEPS

1. Before hearing any of your group's comments on this situation and from the perspective of your assigned role, decide whether James Smith's suggestion regarding ignoring pollution standards is a good one. Write down the reasons for your position.
2. Before hearing any of your group's comments on this situation and from the perspective of your assigned role, determine what the underlying ethical issues are in this situation.
3. Gather your group together and reveal, in turn, each member's comments on James Smith's suggestion. Next, reveal the ethical issues listed by each member.
4. Appoint someone to record main points of agreement and disagreement within the group. How do you explain the results? What accounts for any disagreement?
5. From an ethical standpoint, what does your group conclude is the most appropriate action that should be taken by the company in this situation?
6. Develop a group response to the following question: What are the respective roles of profits, obligations to customers, and obligations to the community for the firm in this situation?

BUSINESS CASE

THE OVERTIME PAY CONTROVERSY

Under the terms of the Canada Labour Code, individuals in supervisory roles are not entitled to overtime pay for work beyond 40 hours per week. But this provision is now being challenged. It all started in 2003, when Sharon Michalowski, a manager at Nygard International Ltd., filed a complaint with the Manitoba Labour Board arguing that she should have been paid overtime for the extra hours that she was required to work. Nygard took the position that since Michalowski was a manager, that she was required to work whatever hours were necessary to do the job. But the Board ruled in Michalowski's favour and awarded her $10 000 in overtime pay. Nygard appealed the case to the Supreme Court of Canada, but lost. Soon after, the province of Manitoba fell into line with other provinces and passed legislation that exempted managers from overtime pay rules in its labour laws. But that didn't end the debate.

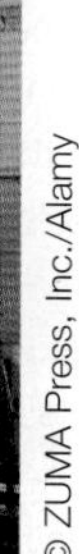
© ZUMA Press, Inc./Alamy

In 2010, a $250 million overtime class action lawsuit was launched by 1500 first-line supervisors at Canadian National Railway who oversee the movement of trains and the maintenance of track. The supervisors said they had to work 50 hours a week on average, and sometimes as much as 90 hours per week. The lawsuit was certified (approved to go to trial) by the Ontario Superior Court. An important issue in this case was whether a person who is designated as a "supervisor" can claim overtime, that is, the case hinges on whether first-line supervisors at CN are properly classified as "managers" and whether they actually have managerial duties. In June 2012, the Ontario Court of Appeals denied certification of the CN case and concluded that it wouldn't work as a class action because it depended on the definition of "manager" and "employee," and that would have to be determined on a case-by-case basis. The Appeals Court decision means that individual first-line supervisors at CN will have to decide whether to pursue an appeal or not.

It is not just groups of employees who are filing lawsuits. Massimo Sanago, the executive chef at the Glendale Golf and Country Club in Hamilton, had the responsibility of managing kitchen operations. But because of staff shortages, he spent over half his time cooking. He also had to work long hours to finish all his other work. Glendale gave him a $5000 bonus in recognition of his efforts, but he felt that was insufficient, so he filed a claim for overtime pay with the Ministry of Labour. Glendale disputed the claim, arguing that Sanago's job was managerial and that he, therefore, did not qualify for overtime pay. The company said that his core job was managerial in nature, and that he performed cooking duties only on an emergency basis. But the Ontario Labour Relations Board ruled that the company had to pay him overtime.

Cases like those above should not be confused with overtime class action lawsuits that have been filed by *non-management* workers. In 2008, for example, a $360 million class-action lawsuit was filed against CIBC World Markets Inc. by salaried stock analysts, financial advisors, and investment bankers who claimed they had not been compensated for overtime work they had done. Early in 2012, a judge quashed the lawsuit, saying that some employees who are classified as "analysts" are actually managers and do not qualify for overtime. A similar class action overtime lawsuit was filed by bank tellers at the CIBC. The Ontario Divisional Court ruled that CIBC's overtime policy didn't violate the law, but it also ruled that there were not enough common issues among the 31 000 tellers at CIBC to warrant a class-action lawsuit. But in June 2012, the Ontario Court of Appeal overturned the earlier rulings and decided that the case could go forward.

In 2010, non-management workers at the Bank of Nova Scotia also filed a class action lawsuit claiming that they were not paid for overtime that they had worked. The bank appealed a judge's ruling that the case could go to trial, but in 2011, the Ontario Divisional Court rejected the bank's appeal and concluded that there was evidence of systemic wrongs in Scotiabank's overtime policy. In June 2012, the Ontario Court of Appeal agreed with the Divisional Court and certified the class action suit. Note that such certification does not mean that the judge agrees with the plaintiff; rather, it simply means that the plaintiffs can be included in a single case for a single trial. The two banks may now appeal the ruling to the Supreme Court of Canada.

The threat of lawsuits has influenced other companies to take action. For example, KMPG was sued by employees who claimed that the company forced them to work as much as 90 hours a week in order to complete their work. While the lawsuit was still before the courts, KPMG agreed to fix the problem, and it may have to spend up to $10 million to do so.

Class action suits against employers are partly the result of the way labour laws are written. For example, unless a person's occupation is specifically excluded by legislation, that person is entitled to overtime pay for each hour they work beyond the provincial maximum (in Ontario, that is 44 hours per week). In Ontario, occupations such as lawyers, accountants, dentists, veterinarians, farmers, salespeople, gardeners, janitors, taxi drivers, and IT professionals are excluded. Critics of the legislation argue that the first five occupations make some sense because they require independent work, but it makes little sense to exclude the latter four occupations.

QUESTIONS FOR DISCUSSION

1. Identify the positive and negative implications of not paying *managers* for overtime. Do the same for *non-management* workers.
2. Consider the following statement: *Managers should not expect to be paid overtime. They are highly paid, and they should focus on getting the job done, rather than on how many hours it takes to complete the job. People who don't have a "get-the-job-done" attitude shouldn't be managers*. Do you agree or disagree with the statement? Defend your answer.

Organizing *the* Business Enterprise

CHAPTER 07

LO

AFTER READING THIS CHAPTER, YOU SHOULD BE ABLE TO:

LO-1 Discuss the elements that influence a firm's *organizational structure.*

LO-2 Explain how *specialization* and *departmentalization* are the building blocks of organizational structure.

LO-3 Distinguish between *responsibility* and *authority* and explain the differences in decision making in *centralized* and *decentralized organizations.*

LO-4 Explain the differences between *functional, divisional, project*, and *international organization structures*, and describe the most popular forms of organizational design.

LO-5 Understand how the *informal organization* is different from the formal organization.

What Happened To the "Occupy Wall Street" Movement?

Do you remember the "Occupy Wall Street" movement that received so much publicity in 2011? The movement started at Vancouver-based Adbusters, an organization that publishes a magazine that is critical of excessive consumer consumption. Inspired by the so-called "Arab Spring" in the Middle East earlier in 2011, the staff at Adbusters got together for a brainstorming session and came up with the image of a ballerina balanced on top of Wall Street's iconic charging bull sculpture. A simple Twitter hashtag was chosen: #OccupyWallStreet. Thousands of people became excited about the idea and before long a big protest demonstration was planned for New York City. By mid-October, protests were also taking place in major Canadian and European cities. Protest groups set up camps in many places, including city parks, the Vancouver Art Gallery, Zuccotti Park in New York City, and the Toronto Stock Exchange. Protestors met together in large and small groups, played drums, and sang together. Unions and community groups also joined the movement, and a website called "Occupy Together" was started. The movement appeared leaderless, and stood for open, participatory, non-hierarchical decision making, with everyone entitled to provide input and push their own ideas. As one protestor said, "No one is a leader because everyone is a leader."

The Occupy Wall Street movement struck a responsive chord in both Canadians and Americans who were frustrated with a political/economic system they saw as favouring corporations and rich individuals. The movement had many goals, the most general one being an end to economic inequality. The central message was "we are the 99%," but that message was combined with a dizzying array of other demands: raise taxes on corporations, offer free college education, stop climate change, stop unfair treatment of Muslims, stop home foreclosures, reduce high unemployment, and nationalize the banks.

© Andre Jenny/Alamy

HOW WILL THIS HELP ME?

Companies frequently introduce changes to improve their organizational structures. By understanding the material in this chapter, as an *employee*, you'll understand your "place" in the organization that employs you. As a *boss* or *owner*, you'll be better equipped to decide on the optimal structure for your own organization.

While the situation seemed rather chaotic, there actually was *some* structure in the movement. For example, daily meetings (called assemblies) were held, which planned the occupation, decided where marches would be held, developed communication with the media, and organized the supplies that had been donated. Anyone could participate in the assemblies, and minutes of assemblies were posted online. Since a New York bylaw prevented use of bullhorns without a permit, protestors adopted "the people's microphone" system where someone shouted a message a few words at a time to the crowd, then people who heard that message repeated it for others who were further away.

But opposition to the camps soon developed. City officials, for example, became frustrated by the movement's occupation of public spaces. As police moved protestors out of public parks, and as winter approached, the movement started to fizzle out. A few camps were still occupied in January 2012, and a few others reappeared in May 2012, but the movement had lost a great deal of momentum.

Why did the Occupy Wall Street movement decline? Observers said that the movement did not succeed because (1) it was not as egalitarian as generally assumed (the camps exhibited a hierarchy, and a few people dominated everyone else), (2) it had no central message and no clear goal, (3) assemblies were very inefficient and time-consuming, (4) the movement lacked an endgame (under what conditions would protestors end their protest?), (5) the movement's culture was one of entitlement (the protests were dominated by the younger generation, who expected to be handed the wealth of their parents), (6) it cost money (city officials wanted the encampments dismantled because costs were being incurred to control the protestors), and (7) internal dissension developed as the tent camps became havens for the disenfranchised members of society.

The anti-hierarchical nature of the Occupy Wall Street movement was supposed to help it succeed. Kalle Lasn, one of the founders of Adbusters, said that critics didn't understand that the Occupy movement was a new-style revolution. It was not vertical, and it didn't have (or want) a designated leader. Instead, it was horizontal because it grew out of the culture of the internet. When asked about the future of the movement, Lasn said that it would adopt a different strategy for 2012, one which involved "surprise attacks" in diverse settings like university economics departments and banks, rather than continuous occupations of city parks.

As interest in the Occupy Wall Street movement declined, attention turned to a website called leadnow.ca, which some thought would become the focal point for a leaderless organization. The website was used to organize "vote mobs" on university and community college campuses, and in just a few months, it attracted 60 000 members. Its goal is to have half a million members before the next federal election in Canada.

QUESTIONS FOR DISCUSSION

1. What are the key features of organizational structure? Which ones are evident in the Occupy Wall Street movement? Which ones are absent?
2. Consider the following statement: *In order to be effective, every organization needs a hierarchical structure with bosses and subordinates. Without such a structure, there is no one in charge, no one knows how much authority they have, and people can't be held accountable for their work.* Do you agree or disagree with the statement? Explain your reasoning.

WHAT IS ORGANIZATIONAL STRUCTURE?

ORGANIZATIONAL STRUCTURE The specification of the jobs to be done within a business and how those jobs relate to one another.

Organizational structure is the specification of the jobs to be done within a business and how those jobs relate to one another. To understand what organizational structure is all about, consider an analogy—a business is like an automobile. All automobiles have an engine, four wheels, fenders and other structural components, an interior compartment for passengers, and various operating systems including those for fuel, brakes, and climate control. Each component has a distinct purpose, but must also work in harmony with all the others. Automobiles made by competing firms all have the same basic components, although the way they look and fit together may vary. Similarly, all businesses have common structural and operating components, each of which has a specific purpose. Each component must fulfill its own purpose while simultaneously fitting in with the others. And, just like automobiles made by different companies, how these components look and fit together varies from company to company.

Every institution—be it a for-profit business like Frantic Films, a not-for-profit organization like the University of Saskatchewan, or a government agency like the Competition Bureau—must develop an appropriate structure for its own unique situation. What works for Air Canada is not likely to work for the Canada Revenue Agency. Likewise, the structure of the Red Cross will not likely work for the University of Toronto.

LO-1 Determinants of Organizational Structure

How is an organization's structure determined? Does it happen by chance or is there some strategy that managers use to create structure? Or is it a combination of the two? Ideally, managers should assess a variety of factors as they plan for and then create a structure that will make their organization effective. But with the busyness that is evident in most organizations, structure may often develop without much planning.

What factors influence structure? The organization's purpose, mission, and strategy are obviously important. A dynamic and rapidly growing enterprise, for example, needs a structure that contributes to flexibility and growth, while a stable organization with only modest growth will function best with a different structure. Size, technology, and changes in environmental circumstances also affect structure. A large manufacturing firm operating in a strongly competitive environment requires a different structure than a local barbershop or video store.

Whatever structure an organization adopts, it is rarely fixed for long. Indeed, most organizations change their structures almost continually. Since it was first incorporated in 1903, for example, Ford Motor Co. has undergone literally dozens of major structural changes, hundreds of moderate changes, and thousands of minor changes. In just the last 15 years, Ford has initiated several major structural changes which were designed to eliminate corporate bureaucracy, speed up decision making, and improve communication and working relationships among people at different levels of the organization.

The Chain of Command

Most businesses prepare **organization charts** that illustrate the company's structure and show employees where they fit into the firm's operations. Figure 7.1 shows the organization chart for a hypothetical company. Each box represents a job within the company. The solid lines that connect the boxes define the **chain of command**, or the reporting relationships within the company. Thus, each plant manager reports directly to the vice-president of production who, in turn, reports to the president. When the chain of command is not clear, many different kinds of problems can result. An actual organization chart would, of course, be far more complex and include individuals at many more levels. Large firms cannot easily draw an organization chart with everyone on it. The chart might also show some unusual features. For example, until recently, the organization chart of BlackBerry showed two CEOs and two chairmen of the board. But in 2011, investor pressure caused the company to change the structure so that just one person did each job.[1]

ORGANIZATION CHART A physical depiction of the company's structure showing employee titles and their relationship to one another.

CHAIN OF COMMAND Reporting relationships within a business; the flow of decision-making power in a firm.

THE BUILDING BLOCKS OF ORGANIZATIONAL STRUCTURE

The most fundamental building blocks of organizational structure are *specialization* (determining who will do what) and *departmentalization* (determining how people performing certain tasks can most appropriately be grouped together).

LO-2 Specialization

Job specialization is the process of identifying the specific jobs that need to be done and designating the people who will perform them. In a sense, all businesses have only one major "job"—making a profit by selling products and services to consumers. But this big job must be broken into smaller components which are then assigned to individuals. Consider the manufacturing of men's shirts. Because several steps are required to produce a shirt, each job is broken down into its component

JOB SPECIALIZATION The process of identifying the specific jobs that need to be done and designating the people who will perform them.

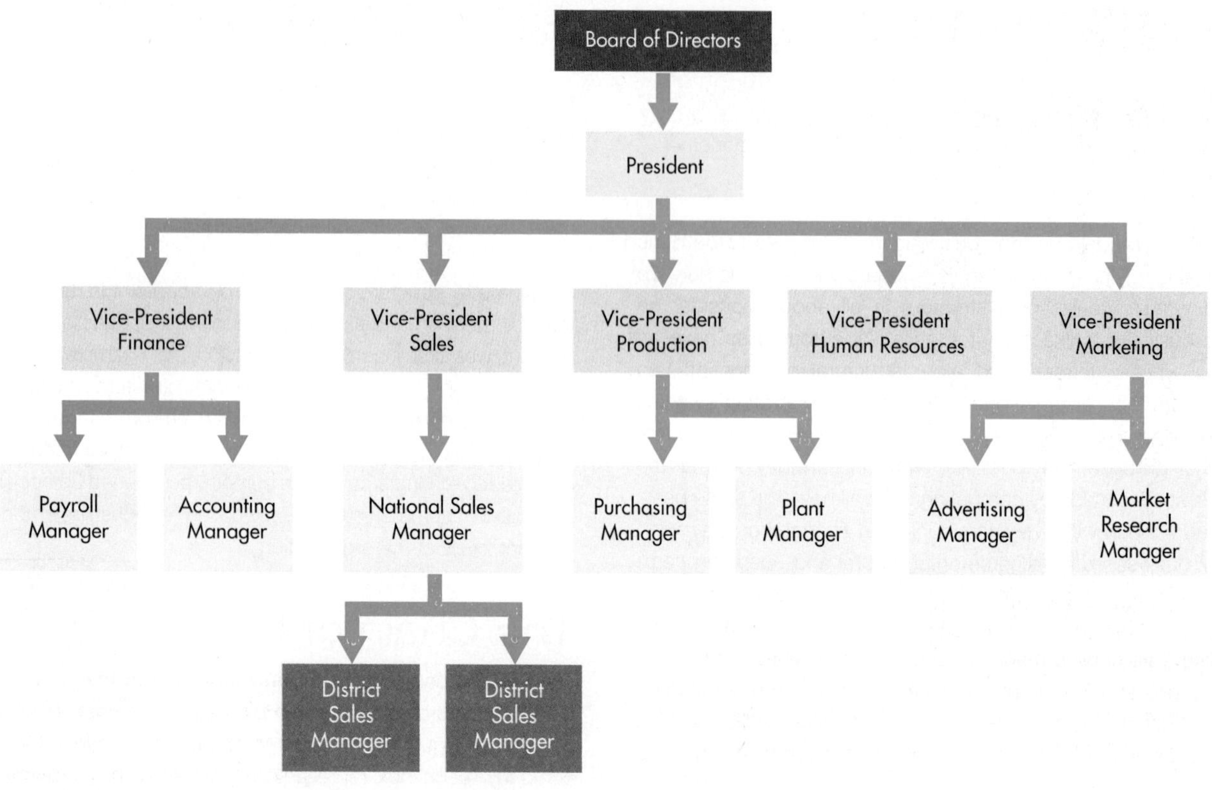

FIGURE 7.1 An organization chart

An organization chart shows key positions in the organization and interrelationships among them. An actual organization chart would, of course, be far more complex and include individuals at many more levels. Indeed, because of their size, larger firms cannot easily draw a diagram with everyone on it.

parts—that is, into a set of tasks to be completed by a series of individuals or machines. One person, for example, cuts material for the shirt body, another cuts material for the sleeves, and a third cuts material for the collar. Components are then shipped to a sewing room, where a fourth person assembles the shirt. In the final stage, a fifth person sews on the buttons.[2]

SPECIALIZATION AND GROWTH

In a very small organization, the owner may perform every job. As the firm grows, however, so does the need to specialize jobs so that others can perform them. When Mrs. Fields Cookies began, Debbi Fields did everything herself: bought the equipment, negotiated the lease, baked the cookies, operated the store, and kept the records. As the business grew, however, she found that her job was becoming too much for one person. She first hired a bookkeeper to handle her financial records, then an in-store manager and a cookie baker. Her second store required another set of employees—another manager, another baker, and some salespeople. While Fields focused her attention on other expansion opportunities, she turned promotions over to a professional advertising director. Thus, the job that she once did all by herself was increasingly broken down into components and assigned to different individuals.

Job specialization is a natural part of organizational growth. It is neither a new idea nor limited to factory work. It carries with it certain advantages—individual jobs can be performed more efficiently, the jobs are easier to learn, and it is easier to replace people who leave the organization. But if job specialization is carried too far and jobs become too narrowly defined, people get bored, become less satisfied with their jobs, and lose sight of how their contributions fit into the overall organization.

Departmentalization

Departmentalization is the process of grouping specialized jobs into logical units. Departmentalization improves control and coordination because managers can see more easily how various units are performing. Departmentalization allows the firm to treat a department as a **profit centre**—a separate unit responsible for its own costs and profits. Thus, by assessing profits from sales in a particular area—for example, men's clothing—Sears can decide whether to expand or curtail promotions in that area. Departmentalization may occur along *functional*, *customer*, *product*, *geographic*, or *process* lines (or some combination of these).

FUNCTIONAL DEPARTMENTALIZATION

Functional departmentalization means organizing departments according to the function they perform—marketing, finance, production,

DEPARTMENTALIZATION The process of grouping jobs into logical units.

PROFIT CENTRE A separate company unit responsible for its own costs and profits.

FUNCTIONAL DEPARTMENTALIZATION Departmentalization according to functions or activities.

CP PHOTO/Andrew Vaughan

wavebreakmedia/Shutterstock

When Walt Disney was just starting out, he did most of the work on his animated features all by himself. But today's features, like Disney's hit movie *Cars II,* require the work of hundreds of people.

human resources, etc. Each of these departments may be further subdivided; for example, the marketing department might be divided geographically or into separate staff for market research and advertising.

CUSTOMER DEPARTMENTALIZATION

Customer departmentalization involves setting up departments or divisions that focus on meeting the needs of specific customers. Some retail stores actually derive their generic name—department stores—from the manner in which they are structured. Stores like HMV are divided into departments—a classical music department, an R&B department, a pop department, and so on. Each department targets a specific customer category (people who want different genres of music). Customer departmentalization makes shopping easier by providing identifiable store segments. Thus, a customer shopping for Shania Twain's latest CD can bypass World Music and head straight for Country. Stores can also group products in locations designated for deliveries, special sales, and other service-oriented purposes. In general, the store is more efficient and customers get better service—in part because salespeople tend to specialize and gain expertise in their departments.[3]

PRODUCT DEPARTMENTALIZATION

Product departmentalization means dividing an organization according to the specific products or services that are being created. 3M Corp.,

CUSTOMER DEPARTMENTALIZATION Departmentalization according to the types of customers likely to buy a given product.

PRODUCT DEPARTMENTALIZATION Departmentalization according to the products being created or sold.

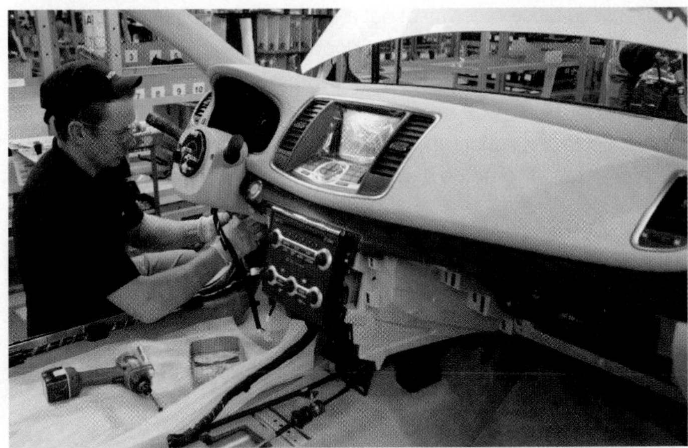

Nissan has developed an assembly process that is so efficient that it can turn out a vehicle in 10 fewer hours than Ford can. The key is the organization of the workstations. At this station, workers install just about everything that the driver touches inside the truck cab. Other stations take care of the whole vehicle frame, the entire electrical system, or completed doors.

PRNewsFoto/Commerce Bank

Many department stores are departmentalized by product. Concentrating different products in different areas of the store makes shopping easier for customers.

Photo by Scott Gries/Getty Images

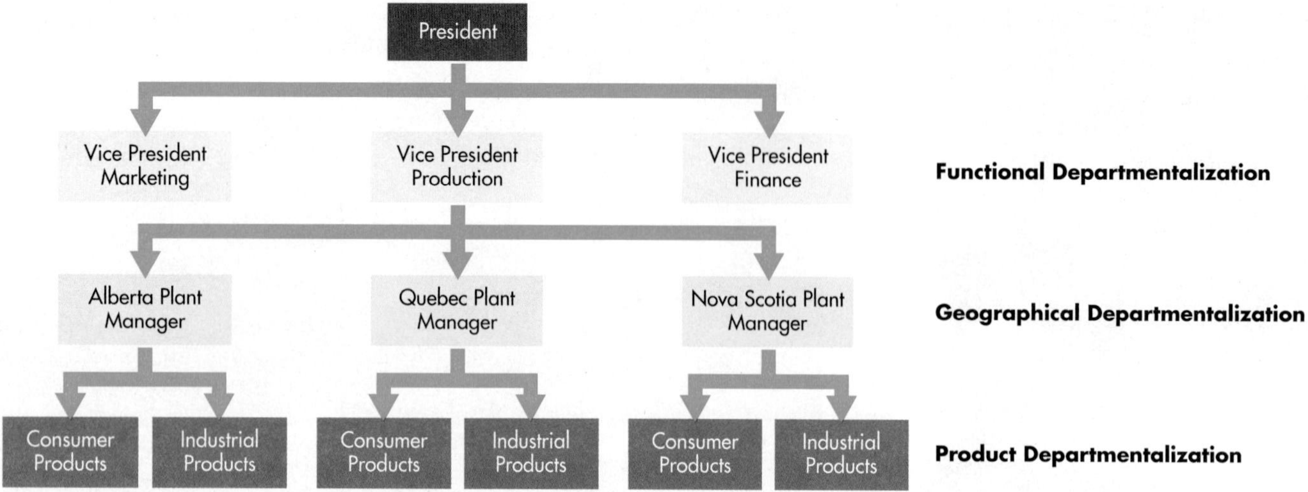

FIGURE 7.2 Multiple forms of departmentalization
Most organizations use multiple bases of departmentalization. This organization, for example, is using functional, geographic, and product departmentalization.

which makes both consumer and industrial products, operates different divisions for Post-it brand tape flags, Scotch-Brite scrub sponges, and the Sarns 9000 perfusion system for open-heart surgery. In 2011, home improvement giant Lowe's reorganized its merchandising operations into two product divisions: (1) building and outdoor products, and (2) kitchen, bath, and home décor products.[4]

PROCESS DEPARTMENTALIZATION

Process departmentalization means dividing the company according to the production process used. Vlasic, a pickle maker, has separate departments that transform cucumbers into fresh-packed pickles, relishes, or pickles cured in brine.

GEOGRAPHIC DEPARTMENTALIZATION

Geographic departmentalization means creating departments based on the area of the country—or even the world—they serve. In 2011, Lowe's also created three divisions: north, south, and west.[5] In 2009, Nike introduced a new structure that was organized around six geographic regions: North America, Western Europe, Eastern/Central Europe, Greater China, Japan, and emerging markets.[6]

Choosing Between Product and Geographic Departmentalization It may be difficult for managers to decide whether to use geographical or product departmentalization. Geographic departmentalization ensures quick, responsive reaction to the needs of the company's customers in specific geographic areas, but it may also lead to duplicate production and other facilities and compartmentalization of knowledge in those same geographic areas. Many years ago, when relatively limited communications made it difficult to take the pulse of consumer needs or monitor operations abroad, it made sense to let local managers in foreign countries run their regional or country businesses as more or less autonomous companies. However, in today's global economy, competition is so intense that firms can't afford to miss an opportunity to quickly transfer product improvements from one region to another. So, some firms are switching from geographic to product departmentalization. For example, PepsiCo was formerly organized around geographic areas (North America and International). When Indra Nooyi became CEO, she reorganized the company into three divisions: Americas Foods, Americas Beverages, and International. The new structure—which is actually a combination of product and geographic departmentalization—better reflects PepsiCo's focus on snack foods (which account for nearly half its total revenue).

Because different forms of departmentalization offer different advantages, larger companies tend to adopt different types of departmentalization at various levels of the corporation. For example, the company illustrated in Figure 7.2 uses functional departmentalization at the top level, geographic departmentalization at the mid-level, and product departmentalization at the lowest level.

PROCESS DEPARTMENTALIZATION Departmentalization according to the production process used to create a good or service.

GEOGRAPHIC DEPARTMENTALIZATION Departmentalization according to the area of the country or world supplied.

ESTABLISHING THE DECISION-MAKING HIERARCHY

A major question that must be asked about any organization is this: Who makes which decisions? This leads to a consideration of the decision-making hierarchy, which generally results from a three-step process:

1. *Assigning tasks*: determining who can make decisions and specifying how they should be made.
2. *Performing tasks*: implementing decisions that have been made.
3. *Distributing authority*: determining whether the organization is to be centralized or decentralized.

LO-3 Assigning Tasks

Authority is the power to make the decisions necessary to complete a task. **Responsibility** is the duty to perform an assigned task. These ideas may seem simple, but two distinct problems may arise when they are applied in practice. First, authority and responsibility may not be balanced. For example, suppose a buyer for a department store has an unexpected opportunity to make a large purchase at an extremely good price, but does not have the authority to make the purchase without confirmation from above. The company's policies on authority and responsibility are inconsistent because the buyer is responsible for purchasing the clothes that will be sold in the store, but lacks the authority to make the needed purchases. Second, when things go wrong, there is often debate about who is responsible. In the *News of the World* phone-hacking scandal, Rupert Murdoch said he wasn't responsible for the phone hacking that some of his reporters engaged in. But observers say that top managers *were* responsible because they put pressure on reporters to get "scoops" so the paper's circulation would increase, and this drove the reporters to take extreme measures to get stories.[7]

Performing Tasks

Delegation means assigning a task to a subordinate. Once authority has been delegated, **accountability** falls to the subordinate, who must then complete the task. When Winnipeg-based Frantic Films first began operations, the principal shareholders made all the decisions. But the CEO, Jamie Brown, thought that it was important to delegate more authority to lower-level workers so they would gain experience in making decisions that affected the company. So, he gave lower-level managers the authority to spend up to $5000 without having to get the approval of top management. This change was also made because the top managers were spending too much time dealing with requests for small amounts of money.[8]

FEAR OF DELEGATING

Some managers have trouble delegating tasks because (a) they assume that subordinates can never do anything as well as the manager can, (b) they fear that their subordinates will "show them up" in front of others by doing a superb job, or (c) they want to control everything. Managers who fail to delegate don't have time to do long-range planning, and they may be uninformed about important industry trends and competitive products because they are too involved in day-to-day operations. Jeffrey Kindler, the former CEO of Pfizer Inc., quit after he lost the support of other executives who were frustrated with his focus on detail and his micromanaging style.[9]

There are remedies for these problems. First, managers should recognize that they cannot do everything themselves. Second, if subordinates cannot do a job, they should be trained so that they can assume more responsibility. Third, managers should recognize that if a subordinate performs well, that reflects favourably on the manager. Fourth, managers should surround themselves with a team of strong subordinates, and then delegate sufficient authority to those subordinates so they can get the job done. Barry Salzberg, the global CEO for Deloitte Touche Tohmatsu Ltd., says that senior management exists to help their staff become more successful, not the other way around.[10]

Managers should keep the following points in mind when they are delegating authority:

- decide on the nature of the work to be done
- match the job with the skills of subordinates
- make sure the person chosen understands the objectives he or she is supposed to achieve
- make sure subordinates have the time and training necessary to do the task

Distributing Authority

In a **centralized organization**, top management retains the right to make most decisions that need to be made. Most lower-level decisions must be approved by upper management before they can be implemented.[11] McDonald's, for example, uses centralization as a way to standardize its operations. All restaurants must follow precise steps in buying products and making and packaging burgers and other menu items. Most advertising is handled at the corporate level, and any local advertising must be approved by a regional manager. Restaurants even have to follow prescribed schedules for facilities' maintenance and upgrades like floor polishing and parking-lot cleaning.[12]

In a **decentralized organization**, more decision-making authority is delegated to managers at lower levels in the hierarchy. The purpose of decentralization is to make a company more responsive to its environment by giving lower-level managers more autonomy. At FedEx, for example, the commitment to decentralization promotes innovation. Managers are encouraged and rewarded for questioning, challenging, and developing new ideas, which are always given serious consideration. Developments have included teaming up with Motorola and Microsoft to create a proprietary pocket-size PC, sending package information to cell phones, and creating software products for small business logistics.[13]

There are advantages and disadvantages of decentralization, and they can clearly be seen in the long history of General Motors. In the 1920s, GM's legendary president, Alfred Sloan, introduced a decentralized structure that gave each car division considerable autonomy to produce cars that would attract whatever market segment the division was pursuing. It worked so well that GM became the largest automobile manufacturer in the world by the middle of the twentieth century. But all this autonomy resulted in widely differing car designs that were very expensive to produce. As decades passed, costs soared and competition from cost-conscious Japanese automakers became ferocious. GM's sales and overall profitability plummeted. In response, GM then took away much of the autonomy from managers in various international divisions and instituted a requirement that its worldwide units work much more closely together to design cars that could be sold (with modest

AUTHORITY The power to make the decisions necessary to complete a task.

RESPONSIBILITY The duty to perform an assigned task.

DELEGATION Assignment of a task, a responsibility, or authority by a manager to a subordinate.

ACCOUNTABILITY Liability of subordinates for accomplishing tasks assigned by managers.

CENTRALIZED ORGANIZATION Top managers retain most decision-making rights for themselves.

DECENTRALIZED ORGANIZATION Lower- and middle-level managers are allowed to make significant decisions.

variations) worldwide. A "Global Council" in Detroit made key decisions about how much would be spent on new car development. When GM engineers at its Daewoo joint venture with South Korea wanted to develop a sport utility vehicle especially suited for the South Korean market, the request was denied.[14] But even these actions were not sufficient to stem GM's decline, and, in 2008, the company was bailed out by the U.S. and Canadian governments and entered bankruptcy protection as it tried to recover. By 2011, the company's performance had once again improved.

SPAN OF CONTROL

The **span of control** refers to how many people are supervised by an individual manager. The span of control may be wide (many subordinates reporting to a boss) or narrow (few subordinates reporting to a boss). Factors influencing the span of control include employees' abilities, the supervisor's managerial skills, the nature of the tasks being performed, and the extent to which tasks are interrelated. For example, when many employees perform the same simple task or a group of interrelated assembly-line tasks, a wide span of control is possible. Because all the jobs are routine, one supervisor may well control an entire assembly line with 40 or more workers. Since tasks are interrelated—if one workstation stops, they all stop—having one supervisor ensures that all stations receive equal attention. In contrast, when jobs are not routine, or when they are unrelated, a narrower span of control is preferable.

Downsizing—the planned reduction in the scope of an organization's activity—affects the span of control. When downsizing involves cutting large numbers of managers, entire layers of management are eliminated. When this happens, the remaining managers often end up with larger spans of control. Because spans of control are wider, corporate structures are flatter after downsizing.

SPAN OF CONTROL The number of people managed by one manager.

DOWNSIZING The planned reduction in the scope of an organization's activity.

LINE AUTHORITY An organizational structure in which authority flows in a direct chain of command from the top of the company to the bottom.

LINE DEPARTMENT A department directly linked to the production and sale of a specific product.

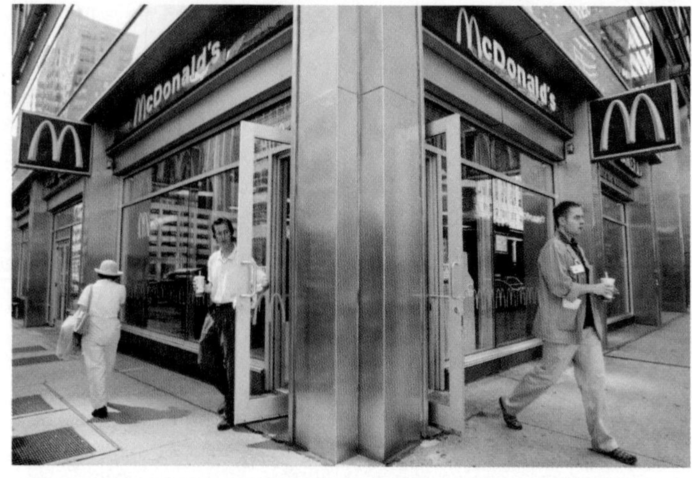

^^^ McDonald's emphasis on centralization ensures standardization in its product offerings. Customers will have a consistent dining experience whenever and wherever they eat at a McDonald's restaurant.

© Pictorial Press Ltd/Alamy

Three Forms of Authority

As individuals are delegated responsibility and authority, a complex web of interactions develops. These interactions may take one of three forms of authority: line, staff, or committee and team. All three forms of authority may be found in a single company, especially if it is a large one.

LINE AUTHORITY

Line authority is authority that flows up and down the chain of command (refer back to Figure 7.1). Most companies rely on **line departments**, those that are directly linked to the production and sale of specific products. For example, Clark, an equipment manufacturer, has a division that produces forklifts and small earth movers (see Figure 7.3). In this division, line departments include purchasing, materials handling, fabrication, painting, and assembly (all of which are directly linked to production), along with sales and distribution (both of which are directly linked to sales).

Each line department is essential in achieving the goals the company has set. Line employees are the "doers" and producers in a company. If any line department fails to complete its task, the company cannot sell and deliver finished goods. Thus, significant authority is usually delegated to line departments.

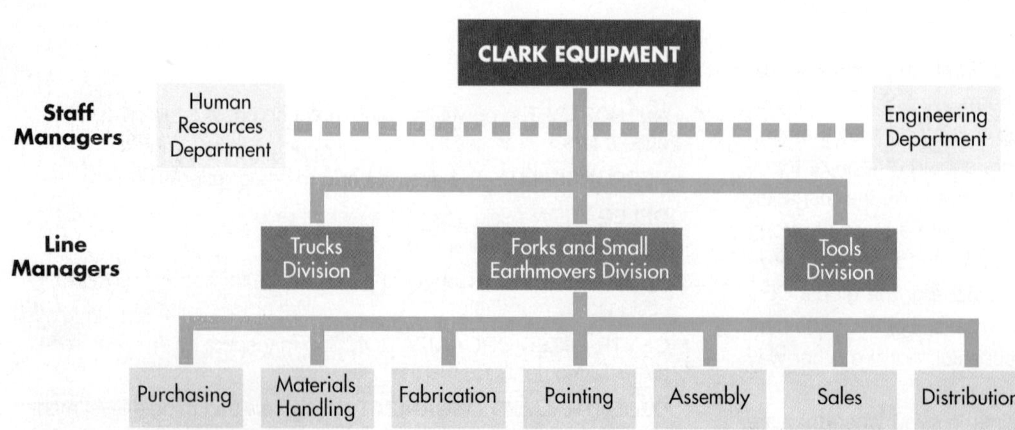

<<< **FIGURE 7.3** Line and staff organization

STAFF AUTHORITY

Companies often employ individuals with technical expertise in areas like law, accounting, marketing research, and human resources. These experts may be given **staff authority**; that is, they help line departments in making decisions, but they do not have the authority to make the final decision. For example, if the fabrication department at Clark has an employee with a drinking problem, the line manager of the department might consult a human resource staff expert for advice on how to handle the situation. The staff expert might suggest that the worker stay on the job, but enter a counselling program. But if the line manager decides that the job is too dangerous to be handled by a person whose judgment is impaired by alcohol, the line manager's decision will most likely prevail.

Typically, line authority is represented on organization charts by solid lines, while staff authority is shown by dotted lines. Line managers are directly involved in producing the firm's products or services, while staff members generally provide services to management. But remember, the goals of the organization influence the distinction between line and staff authority. At Aluminum Company of Canada, for example, the director of personnel has staff authority because the personnel department supports the primary function of the company (the production and marketing of aluminum). But at Office Overload, the director of personnel is a line manager because the primary goal of that firm is to provide personnel to other firms.

COMMITTEE AND TEAM AUTHORITY

More and more organizations have started to use **committee and team authority**—authority granted to committees or work teams that play central roles in the firm's daily operations. A committee, for example, may consist of top managers from several major areas of the company. If the work of the committee is especially important, and if the committee will be working together for an extended time, the organization may even grant it special authority as a decision-making body that goes beyond the individual authority possessed by each of its members.

Firms are also increasingly using work teams at the operating level. These teams are made up of workers (not managers) and are empowered to plan, organize, and perform their work with a minimum of supervision. Organizations usually find it beneficial to grant special authority to work teams so that they will function more effectively.[15] More information about teams is presented in Chapter 9.

STAFF AUTHORITY Authority that is based on expertise and that usually involves advising line managers.

COMMITTEE AND TEAM AUTHORITY Authority granted to committees or work teams involved in a firm's daily operations.

LO-4 BASIC ORGANIZATIONAL STRUCTURES

A glance at the organization charts of many organizations reveals what appears to be an almost infinite variety of structures. However, closer examination shows that most of them fit into one of four basic categories: functional, divisional, project, or international.

The Functional Structure

In the **functional structure**, the various units in the organization are formed based on the key functions that must be carried out to reach organizational goals. The functional structure—an example of which was shown in Figure 7.1—makes use of departmentalization by function. The advantages and disadvantages of the functional structure are summarized in Table 7.1. To overcome one of the disadvantages of the functional structure—poor interdepartmental communication—some companies have established *customer innovation centres* which have expertise on product development, brand management, and sales. At these centres, key customers provide feedback on product performance and brainstorm new ideas for products that will better satisfy customers.[16]

FUNCTIONAL STRUCTURE Various units are included in a group based on functions that need to be performed for the organization to reach its goals.

TABLE 7.1 Advantages and Disadvantages of a Functional Structure

Advantages	Disadvantages
1. It focuses attention on the key activities that must be performed.	1. Conflicts may arise among the functional areas.
2. Expertise develops within each function.	2. No single function is responsible for overall organizational performance.
3. Employees have clearly defined career paths.	3. Employees in each functional area have a narrow view of the organization.
4. The structure is simple and easy to understand.	4. Decision making is slowed because functional areas must get approval from top management for a variety of decisions.
5. It eliminates duplication of activities.	5. Coordinating highly specialized functions may be difficult.

The Divisional Structure

The **divisional structure** divides the organization into several divisions, each of which operates as a semi-autonomous unit and profit centre. Divisions in organizations can be based on products, customers, or geography. For example, Winnipeg-based Frantic Films has three product divisions: live action (which produces programs like *Pioneer Quest* and *'Til Debt Do Us Part*), TV commercials (which produces television commercials for national and international clients), and software (which creates new, stand-alone software to enhance certain visual effects).[17] Bell Canada created three customer-based divisions: consumers, small- and medium-sized businesses, and large corporations. This structure replaced the former divisional structure that was geographically based.[18] Sometimes a company reorganizes divisions in order to be more effective. In 2012, Yahoo Inc. established three divisions—consumers, regions, and technology—in order to focus its activities and to increase growth prospects.[19]

Whatever basis is used, divisional performance can be assessed because each division operates almost as a separate company. Divisionalized companies can buy, sell, create, and disband divisions without disrupting the rest of their operations. Different divisions can sponsor separate advertising campaigns and foster different corporate identities. They can also share certain corporate-level resources (such as market research data). But sometimes unhealthy competition develops between divisions, or the efforts of one division may be duplicated by those of another. At PepsiCo, for example, each of the company's three major beverage brands—Pepsi, Gatorade, and Tropicana—formerly operated as independent divisions. But this independence became a problem because the three brands were competing for the same resources and there was very little coordination and sharing of information between the divisions. Now, all three brands are in one division so that a unified approach to brand management is achieved. The advantages and disadvantages of the divisional structure are summarized in Table 7.2.

Project Organization

A typical organization is characterized by unchanging vertical authority relationships because the organization produces a product or service in a repetitive and predictable way. Procter & Gamble, for example, produces millions of tubes of Crest toothpaste each year using standardized production methods. The company has done this for years and intends to do so indefinitely. But some organizations find themselves faced with new product opportunities, or with projects that have a definite starting and ending point. These organizations often use a project structure to deal with the uncertainty encountered in new situations.

Business firms are increasingly using work teams and allowing groups of employees to plan and organize their own work with a minimum of supervision. This contributes to employee empowerment.

MONICA M. DAVEY/EPA/Newscom

Project organization involves forming a team of specialists from different functional areas of the organization to work on a specific project.[20] A project structure may be temporary or permanent; if it is temporary, the project team disbands once the project is completed and team members return to their regular functional area or are assigned to a new project.

Project organization is used extensively by Canadian firms in the construction of hydroelectric generating stations like those developed by Hydro-Québec on the La Grande River and by Manitoba Hydro on the Nelson River. Once the generating station is complete, it becomes part of the traditional structure of the utility. Project organization is also used at Genstar Shipyards Ltd. in Vancouver. Each ship that is built is treated as a project and supervised by a project manager, who is responsible for ensuring that the ship is completed on time and within budget.[21] Project organization has also proven useful for coordinating the many elements needed to extract oil from the tar sands.

DIVISIONAL STRUCTURE Divides the organization into divisions, each of which operates as a semi-autonomous unit.

PROJECT ORGANIZATION An organization that uses teams of specialists to complete specific projects.

TABLE 7.2 Advantages and Disadvantages of a Divisional Structure

Advantages	Disadvantages
1. It accommodates change and expansion.	1. Activities may be duplicated across divisions.
2. It increases accountability.	2. A lack of communication among divisions may occur.
3. It develops expertise in the various divisions.	3. Adding diverse divisions may blur the focus of the organization.
4. It encourages training for top management.	4. Company politics may affect the allocation of resources.

The project organization structure is very useful for construction projects like this hydroelectric generating station on the La Grande River in Quebec. The construction of installations like this has a specific beginning and ending point. Once completed, the generating station becomes part of the traditional organization structure of the provincial utility.

© Cultura RM/Alamy

A **matrix organization** is a variation of the project structure in which the project manager and the regular line managers share authority. When a project is concluded, the matrix is disbanded. Ford, for example, uses a matrix organization to design new car models. A design team composed of people from engineering, marketing, operations, and finance is created to design the new car. After the team's work is completed, team members move back to their permanent functional jobs.

Martha Stewart Living Omnimedia, Inc. has created a permanent matrix organization for its lifestyle business. The company is organized broadly into media and merchandising groups, each of which has specific products and product groups. Layered on top of this structure are teams of lifestyle experts organized into groups such as cooking, crafts, weddings, and so forth (see Figure 7.4). Although each group targets specific customer needs, they all work across all product groups. A wedding expert, for example, might contribute to an article on wedding planning for a Martha Stewart magazine, develop a story idea for a Martha Stewart cable television program, and supply content for a Martha Stewart website. This same individual might also help select fabrics suitable for wedding gowns that are to be retailed.[22]

MATRIX ORGANIZATION A project structure in which the project manager and the regular line managers share authority until the project is concluded.

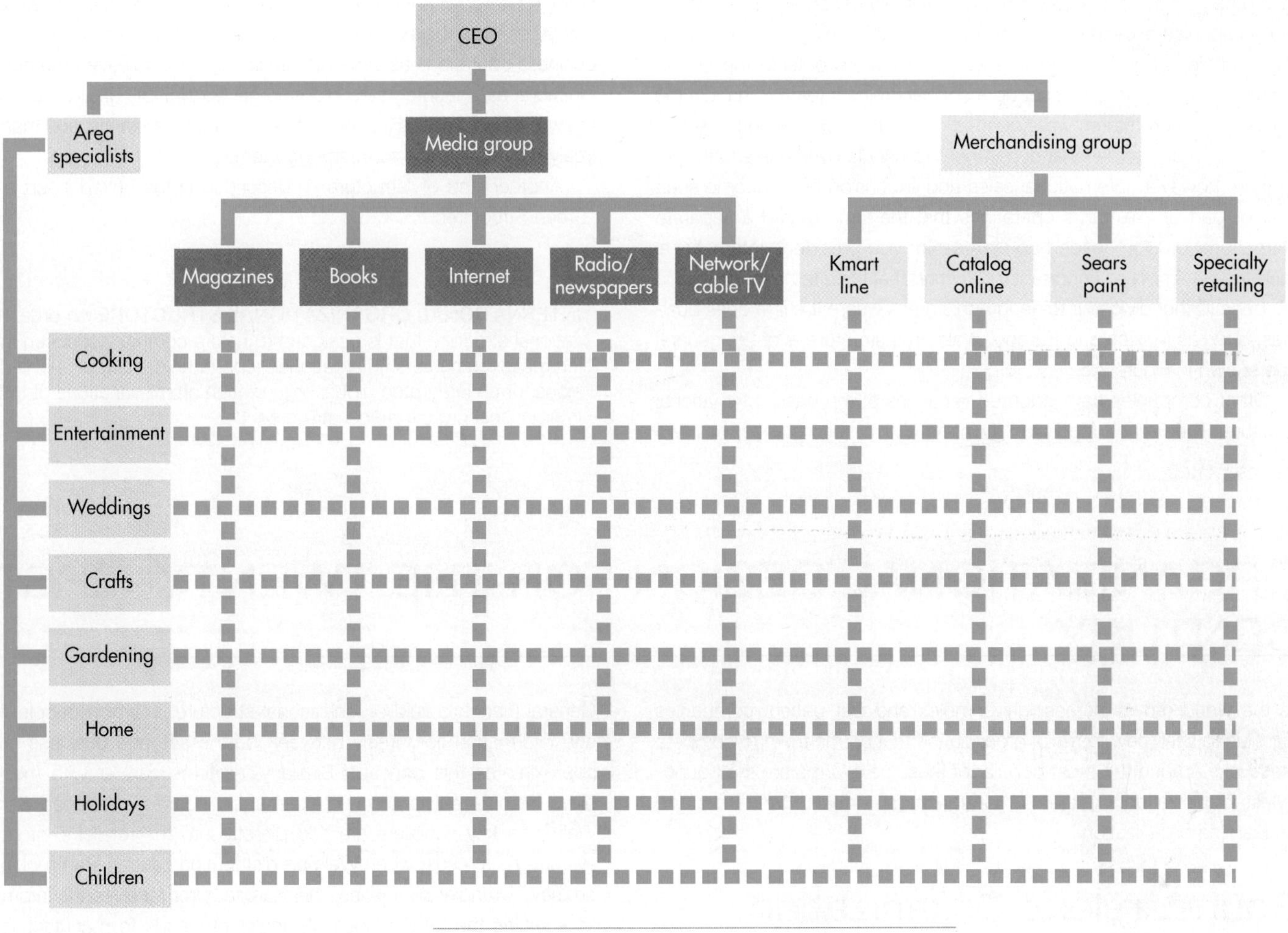

CEO

Area specialists

Media group

Merchandising group

Magazines
Books
Internet
Radio/ newspapers
Network/ cable TV
Kmart line
Catalog online
Sears paint
Specialty retailing

Cooking
Entertainment
Weddings
Crafts
Gardening
Home
Holidays
Children

FIGURE 7.4 Matrix organization of Martha Stewart

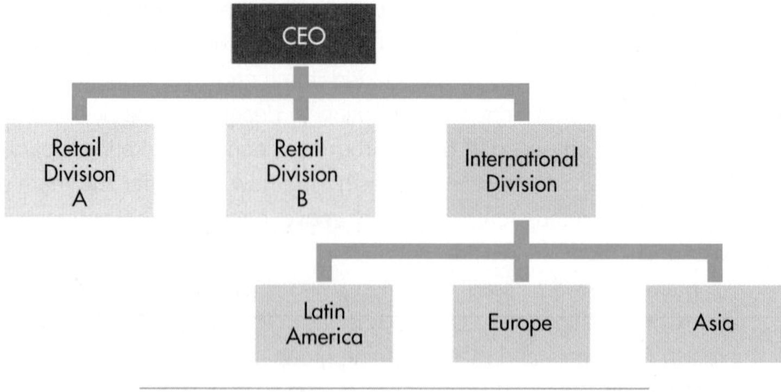

FIGURE 7.5 International division structure

All the signs at this 8000-square-metre store in Numazu identify it as a Seiyu outlet run by Japan's fifth-largest supermarket chain. However, Walmart owns 38 percent of Seiyu, and this giant store is part of Walmart's effort to enter the world's second-largest retail market.

yuri arcurs/Fotolia

The matrix structure is not always effective. In 2009, Carol Bartz—the new CEO at Yahoo!—announced a restructuring that was designed to make managers more accountable and to speed up decision making. The new structure essentially did away with the matrix structure and workers no longer report to multiple bosses.[23]

International Organization Structures

There are several types of **international organizational structures** that have emerged as competition on a global scale becomes more intense and companies experiment with the ways in which they might respond. For example, when Walmart opened its first store outside the United States in the early 1990s, it set up a special projects team to handle the logistics. As more stores were opened during the next decade, the firm created a small international department to handle overseas expansion. By then, however, international sales and expansion had become such a major part of Walmart's operations that the firm created a separate international division headed up by a senior vice-president. International operations are now so important to Walmart that the international division has been further divided into geographic areas where the firm does business, such as Mexico and Europe. Walmart's structure is of the general type shown in Figure 7.5.

Other companies have adopted variations of the basic international structure. The French food giant Danone Group, for instance, has two major product groups: dairy products (Danone yogurt) and bottled water (Evian). Danone's structure does not differentiate internationally, but rather integrates global operations within each product group.[24]

Some companies adopt a truly global structure in which they acquire resources (including capital), produce goods and services, engage in research and development, and sell products in whatever local market is appropriate, without any consideration of national boundaries. Until a few years ago, for example, General Electric (GE) kept its international business operations as separate divisions. Now, however, the company functions as one integrated global organization. GE businesses around the world connect and interact with each other constantly, and managers freely move back and forth among them.[25]

Another kind of "structure" is described in the boxed insert entitled "Green Structures."

INTERNATIONAL ORGANIZATIONAL STRUCTURE An organizational structure that is designed to help a company succeed in international markets. International departments, international divisions, or an integrated global organization are all variations of the international organizational structure.

ORGANIZATIONAL DESIGN FOR THE TWENTY-FIRST CENTURY

As the world grows increasingly complex and fast paced, companies continue to seek new forms of organization that permit them to compete effectively. Among the most popular of these new forms are the boundaryless organization, the team organization, the virtual organization, and the learning organization.

Boundaryless Organization

The boundaryless organization is one in which traditional boundaries and structures are minimized or eliminated altogether. For example, General Electric's fluid organizational structure, in which people, ideas, and information flow freely between businesses and business groups, approximates this concept. Similarly, as firms partner with their suppliers in more efficient ways, external boundaries disappear. Some of Walmart's key suppliers are tied directly into the retailer's information system. As a result, when Walmart distribution centres start running low on, say, Wrangler blue jeans, the manufacturer receives the information as soon as the retailer does. Wrangler proceeds to manufacture new inventory and restock the distribution centre without Walmart having to place a new order.

THE GREENING OF BUSINESS

Green Structures

The term "organizational structure" is commonly used to explain *theoretical* concepts like departmentalization, authority, responsibility, and the hierarchical patterns within organizations. But organizations also need *physical* structures like office buildings and factories to do their work, and managers in both the public and private sector are beginning to realize that their physical structures present significant opportunities to be eco-friendly. Sustainable buildings make sense because they reduce energy costs, attract more tenants, improve a company's image, and are a hedge against future changes in municipal building regulations. Consider these examples:

- Winnipeg's new airport (which opened in October 2011) may be the most energy-efficient building of its size in the world. It is designed to achieve Leadership in Energy and Environmental Design (LEED) certification.
- On the 20th floor of the LEED-certified offices of Ontario Realty Corp. (ORC), the emphasis is on natural light (and smart motion-sensor lights), with heating and cooling provided by clean energy systems.
- In the Fremont Village Shopping Centre in Port Coquitlam, B.C., the roofs of Walmart and Canadian Tire are covered with thousands of plants which provide insulation (reducing energy costs) and also reduce storm water runoff and the "heat-island" effect.
- Esri Canada's green-roof building in the Toronto suburb of Don Mills contains 53 types of trees, shrubs, and flowers; employees benefit from having access to the natural world while at work; the green roof is one of about 135 that exist in the Toronto area.
- In October 2011, the Toronto-Dominion Bank opened a renovated branch in London, Ontario, that will produce as much energy as it uses.
- In 2012, construction began on the GreenLife Business Centre in Milton, Ontario. The building will produce more energy than it consumes with its huge solar panel array.

Some architects think that over the next decade it may be possible to have buildings that require no energy at all from public utilities. Gerrit de Boer, president of Toronto-based Idomo Furniture Company, says that his firm will be "off the grid" in less than 10 years as a result of the geothermal heating system and the photovoltaic solar array being installed in the company's 200 000-square-foot building.

The physical advantages of green structures are only part of the story. Employees may feel more pride in their company when working in a green building, and they may also be more engaged in their work because the surroundings are so pleasant. A survey showed that ORC employees had a 96 percent satisfaction rate with their new offices (compared to 43 percent in their old offices).

CRITICAL THINKING QUESTIONS

1. What are the advantages of "green" buildings? Are there any disadvantages? Explain.
2. Consider the following statement: *It is very expensive to build eco-friendly buildings, so expenditures like these should generally not be made. Rather, companies should focus on upgrading their production facilities so they can make higher-quality, lower-priced products for consumers and more profits for their shareholders.* Do you agree or disagree with the statement? Explain your reasoning.

Team Organization

Team organization relies almost exclusively on project-type teams, with little or no underlying functional hierarchy. People "float" from project to project as dictated by their skills and the demands of those projects. At Cypress Semiconductor, units or groups that become large are simply split into smaller units. Not surprisingly, the organization is composed entirely of small units. This strategy allows each unit to change direction, explore new ideas, and try new methods without having to deal with a rigid bureaucratic superstructure. Although few large organizations have actually reached this level of adaptability, Apple and Xerox are among those moving toward it.

Virtual Organization

Closely related to the team organization is the virtual organization. A virtual organization has little or no formal structure. Typically, it has only a handful of permanent employees, a very small staff, and a modest administrative facility. As the needs of the organization change, its managers bring in temporary workers, lease facilities, and outsource basic support services to meet the demands of each unique situation. As the situation changes, the temporary workforce changes in parallel, with some people leaving the organization and others entering it. Facilities and subcontracted services also change. In other words, the virtual organization exists only in response to its own needs.

Global Research Consortium (GRC) is a virtual organization. GRC offers research and consulting services to firms doing business in Asia. As clients request various services, GRC's staff of three permanent employees subcontracts the work to an appropriate set of several dozen independent consultants and/or researchers with whom it has relationships. At any given time, therefore, GRC may have several projects underway and 20 or 30 people working in various capacities. As the projects change, so does the composition of the organization. Figure 7.6 illustrates the basic structure of a virtual organization.

Learning Organization

A learning organization facilitates the lifelong learning and personal development of all of its employees while continually transforming itself to respond to changing demands and needs. The most frequent goals are improved quality, continuous improvement, and performance measurement. The idea is that the most consistent and logical strategy for achieving continuous improvement is to constantly upgrade employee talent, skill, and knowledge. For example, if each employee

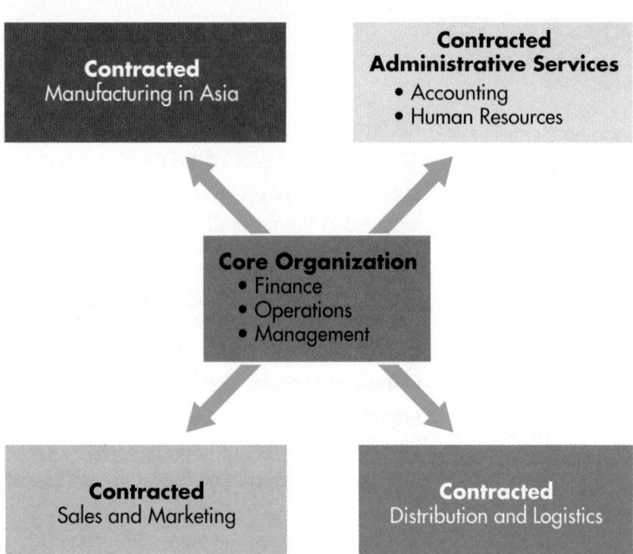

in an organization learns one new thing each day and can translate that knowledge into work-related practice, continuous improvement will logically follow.

In recent years, many different organizations have implemented this approach on various levels. Shell, for example, purchased an executive conference centre called the Shell Learning Center. The facility boasts state-of-the-art classrooms and instructional technology, lodging facilities, a restaurant, and recreational amenities such as a golf course, swimming pool, and tennis courts. Line managers at the firm rotate through the centre and serve as teaching faculty. All Shell employees routinely attend training programs, seminars, and related activities, gathering the latest information they need to contribute more effectively to the firm.

<<< **FIGURE 7.6** The virtual organization

LO-5 THE INFORMAL ORGANIZATION

The formal organization of a business is the part that can be seen and represented on the organization chart. The structure of a company, however, is not limited to the organization chart and the formal assignment of authority. Frequently, the **informal organization**—the everyday social interactions among employees that transcend formal jobs and job interrelationships—effectively alters a company's formal structure. Indeed, the informal organization is sometimes more powerful than the formal structure. The power of the informal organization was evident in the highly publicized rescue of the Chilean miners in 2010. In the underground cavern where they were trapped, there were no top managers, so much of what the miners did was informal (dividing up chores, singing, providing mutual support, etc.) These activities kept the miners' hopes alive until they were rescued.[26] The team ethics exercise at the end of this chapter presents an interesting situation that illustrates the informal organization.

Is the informal organization good or bad? On the positive side, the informal organization can help employees feel that they "belong," and it gives them an outlet for "letting off steam" in a safe environment. It also provides information that employees are interested in hearing. On the negative side, the informal organization can reinforce office politics that put the interests of individuals ahead of those of the company. Likewise, a great deal of harm can be caused by distorted or inaccurate information communicated without management input or review. For example, if the informal organization is generating false information about impending layoffs, valuable employees may act quickly (and unnecessarily) to seek other employment. Two important elements of the informal organization are informal groups and the organizational grapevine.

INFORMAL ORGANIZATION A network of personal interactions and relationships among employees unrelated to the firm's formal authority structure.

GRAPEVINE An informal communications network that carries gossip and other information throughout an organization.

Informal Groups

Informal groups are simply groups of people who decide to interact among themselves even though they may not be required to do so by the formal organization. They may be made up of people who work together in a formal sense or who simply get together for lunch, during breaks, or after work. They may talk about business, the boss, or non-work-related topics such as families, movies, or sports. For example, at the New York Metropolitan Opera, musicians and singers play poker during the intermissions. Most pots are in the $30 to $40 range. The late Luciano Pavarotti, the famed tenor, once played (he lost).[27]

The Organizational Grapevine

The **grapevine** is the informal communication network that runs through the entire organization.[28] The grapevine is found in all organizations, and it

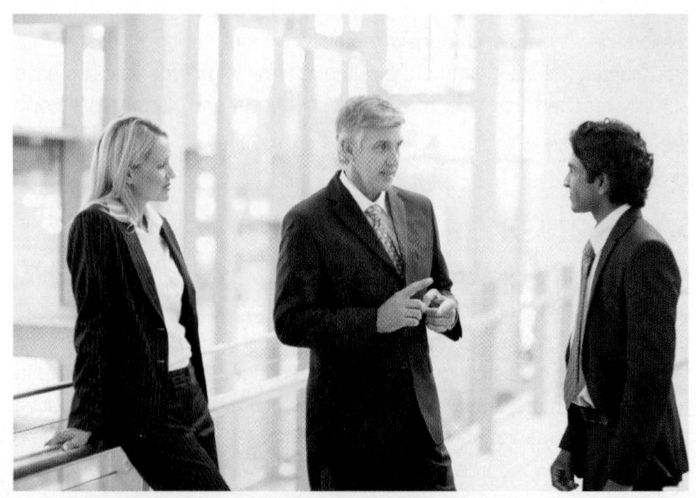

>>> The grapevine is a powerful communications network in most organizations. These workers may be talking about any number of things—an upcoming deadline on an important project, tonight's hockey game, the stock market, rumours about an impending takeover, gossip about who's getting promoted, or the weather.

© S K D/Alamy

E-BUSINESS AND SOCIAL MEDIA SOLUTIONS

Virtual Water Coolers: Encouraging Employee Engagement

Beyond an organization's official communication channels lies a complex web of interpersonal relationships. Employees may receive formal instructions at meetings from supervisors and senior management, but they discuss the details informally during social interactions. Managers group people together and create formal teams, but employees really bond with each other in those informal moments of discussion standing by the water cooler. So what happens to these bonds when many employees work from home as telecommuters? How can organizations make sure that employees (both telecommuters and regulars) are connected and communicate effectively?

Susan Cranston, a senior business advisor at Manulife, says the traditional approach of using memos and meetings is not enough, and Twitter, YouTube, Facebook, and internal social media tools have become the digital water cooler. They permit employees to gather key facts, increase information sharing, transfer knowledge, and ultimately promote creativity and innovation. Organizations can promote better communication by officially adopting social media.

At Telus, this issue was of the highest importance because the company had over 1200 telecommuters in 2013 and had set an aggressive objective of having 70 percent of their workforce work from home by 2015. To improve teamwork and build social bonds among this growing community, Telus decided to bring social media into the process. According to company officials, it starts with basic tools like instant messenger that enable quick communications, but it goes well beyond that. Their "Fireside Chats" give employees an informal vehicle to build networks and get to know each other better. The company also plans to improve and create more seamless integration of popular social media like wikis, blogs, and Facebook-like tools.

Once a company acknowledges the need to build a modern communications platform, they then must decide how to build it. Virtual spaces must be clearly identified so it is easy for employees in different locations (and times zones) to interact. Top management must show their support not only in words, but also in actions. Some basic rules are necessary, but the environment needs to be open and people need to feel comfortable posting. Finally, the tools must be easily accessible on employees' screens when they log on to the network.

Like the traditional water cooler, there is a lot of information that is productive and helps build bonds, but there is a significant part which is meant to be private. Employees will definitely use their own private social media tools to communicate the latter to colleagues, but companies that formally encourage effective social communications can reap the rewards of increased efficiency.

CRITICAL THINKING QUESTIONS

1. What do you think of the Telus approach? Is it a positive attempt to engage employees or do you see it as an artificial distraction?
2. The "water cooler" approach can be beneficial, but it is also a potential source for unfounded gossip which could have a negative effect on the organization. Debate the pros and cons of the virtual water cooler concept.

does not always follow the same patterns as formal channels of authority and communication. Formerly, when people gathered around the water cooler or on the golf course to exchange gossip and pass on information, they had names and faces. But with the internet (a worldwide grapevine), you may not know who you are talking to, or how reliable the person providing the information is.[29] The boxed insert entitled "Virtual Water Coolers" explains how social media can facilitate effective communication.

Because the grapevine typically passes information orally, messages may become distorted in the process. In addition to miscommunication and attempts by some people to manipulate it for their own ends, the grapevine may carry rumours with absolutely no basis in fact. Such rumours are most common when there is a complete lack of information. Human nature abhors a vacuum and the grapevine may fill the vacuum with something, even if that something is just rumours. Baseless rumours can be very hard to kill, however.

Attempts to eliminate the grapevine are fruitless, so managers shouldn't waste their time trying to do so. Rather, they should maintain open channels of communication and respond vigorously to inaccurate information because this will minimize the damage the grapevine can cause. In fact, the grapevine can actually be an asset. By getting to know the key people who are part of the grapevine, the manager can partially control the information received and use the grapevine to determine employee reactions to new ideas (e.g., a change in human resource policies or benefit packages). Wise managers will tune in to the grapevine's message because it is often a corporate early-warning system. Ignoring this valuable source of information can cause managers to be the last to know that they are about to get a new boss, or that they have a potentially fatal image problem.

THERE'S AN APP FOR THAT!

1. **Project Management** >>> **Platforms:** *Android, BlackBerry*
   Source: WagMobKey
   Features: Provides short project management chapters, flashcards, and quizzes for self-assessment.
2. **Let's Get Organized** >>> **Platforms:** *Android*
   Source: KoolAppz
   Key Features: Provides tips for individuals to be more organized at home and in the workplace.
3. **Work Teams** >>> **Platforms:** *Apple*
   Source: Samzol Saleh
   Key Features: Helps you map out an organization's people in a flexible organizational diagram.

APP DISCOVERY EXERCISE

Since APP availability changes, conduct your own search for "Top 3" Business Organization APPS and identify the key features.

MyBizLab

Visit the MyBizLab website. This online homework and tutorial system puts you in control of your own learning with study and practice tools directly correlated to this chapter's content.

SUMMARY OF LEARNING OBJECTIVES

LO-1 DISCUSS THE ELEMENTS THAT INFLUENCE A FIRM'S *ORGANIZATIONAL STRUCTURE*.

Every business needs structure to operate. *Organizational structure* varies according to a firm's mission, purpose, and strategy. Size, technology, and changes in environmental circumstances also influence structure. In general, while all organizations have the same basic elements, each develops the structure that contributes to the most efficient operations.

LO-2 EXPLAIN HOW *SPECIALIZATION* AND *DEPARTMENTALIZATION* ARE THE BUILDING BLOCKS OF ORGANIZATIONAL STRUCTURE.

As a firm grows, it usually has a greater need for people to perform specialized tasks (specialization). It also has a greater need to group types of work into logical units (departmentalization). Common forms of departmentalization are *customer, product, process, geographic*, and *functional*. Large businesses often use more than one form of departmentalization.

LO-3 DISTINGUISH BETWEEN *RESPONSIBILITY* AND *AUTHORITY* AND EXPLAIN THE DIFFERENCES IN DECISION MAKING IN *CENTRALIZED* AND *DECENTRALIZED ORGANIZATIONS*.

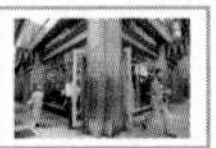

Responsibility is the duty to perform a task, while *authority* is the power to make the decisions necessary to complete tasks. *Delegation* begins when a manager assigns a task to a subordinate; *accountability* means that the subordinate must complete the task. *Span of control* refers to the number of people who work for a manager. The more people supervised by a manager, the wider his or her span of control. Wide spans are usually desirable when employees perform simple or unrelated tasks. When jobs are diversified or prone to change, a narrower span is generally preferable.

In a *centralized organization*, only a few individuals in top management have real decision-making authority. In a *decentralized organization*, much authority is delegated to lower-level management. Where both *line* and *line-and-staff authority* exist in an organization, *line departments* generally have authority to make decisions while *staff departments* have a responsibility to advise. *Committee and team authority* empowers committees or work teams to make decisions about various aspects of operations.

LO-4 EXPLAIN THE DIFFERENCES BETWEEN *FUNCTIONAL, DIVISIONAL, PROJECT*, AND *INTERNATIONAL ORGANIZATION STRUCTURES*, AND DESCRIBE THE MOST POPULAR FORMS OF ORGANIZATIONAL DESIGN.

In a *functional organization*, authority is usually distributed among such basic functions as marketing and finance. In a *divisional organization*, the various divisions operate in a relatively autonomous fashion. In *project organization*, a company creates project teams to address specific problems or to complete specific projects. A company that has divisions in many countries may require an additional level of *international organization* to coordinate those operations. Four of the most popular forms of organizational design are *boundaryless organizations* (traditional boundaries and structures are minimized or eliminated), *team organizations* (relying on project-type teams, with little or no functional hierarchy), *virtual organizations* (which have little formal structure and only a handful of permanent employees, a small staff, and a modest administrative facility), and *learning organizations* (which facilitate employees' lifelong learning and personal development while transforming the organization to meet changing demands and needs).

LO-5 UNDERSTAND HOW THE *INFORMAL ORGANIZATION* IS DIFFERENT FROM THE FORMAL ORGANIZATION.

The *informal organization* consists of the everyday social interactions among employees that transcend formal jobs and job interrelationships. The informal organization exists within the formal structure of every organization and cannot be suppressed. Effective managers work with the informal organization and try to harness it for the good of the formal organization.

QUESTIONS AND EXERCISES

QUESTIONS FOR ANALYSIS

See >>> for **Assisted-Graded Writing Assignment** in **MyBizLab**

1. Explain the significance of organizational size as it relates to organizational structure. Describe the changes that are likely to occur as an organization grows.
2. Why do some managers have difficulties in delegating authority? Why do you think this problem might be more pronounced in small businesses?
3. What might the organization structure of a small printing firm look like? Describe changes that might be necessary as the business grows.
4. >>> Compare and contrast the matrix and divisional approaches to organizational structure. How would you feel personally about working in a matrix organization in which you were assigned simultaneously to multiple units or groups *and* had multiple bosses?
5. If a company has a formal organization structure, why should managers pay attention to the informal organization?
6. The argument has been made that, compared to the functional organization structure, the divisional structure does a better job of training managers for top-level positions. Do you agree or disagree with this argument? Explain your reasoning.

APPLICATION EXERCISES

7. Draw up an organization chart for your college or university.
8. Think about the organization where you currently work (or one where you previously worked). Which of the four basic structural types was it most consistent with (functional, divisional, project, international)? What was the basis of departmentalization in the organization? Why was that particular basis used?
9. Interview the manager of a local service business (for example, a fast-food restaurant). What types of tasks does this manager typically delegate? Is the appropriate authority also delegated in each case? What problems occur when authority is not delegated appropriately?
10. Review the discussion of intrapreneurs in Chapter 4. Then identify a person who has succeeded as an intrapreneur. In what ways did the structure of the intrapreneur's company help this individual succeed? In what ways did the structure pose problems?

TEAM EXERCISES

BUILDING YOUR BUSINESS SKILLS

GETTING WITH THE PROGRAM

GOAL

To encourage students to understand the relationship between organization structure and a company's ability to attract and keep valued employees.

SITUATION

You are the founder of a small but growing high-tech company that develops new computer software. With your current workload and new contracts in the pipeline, your business is thriving, except for one problem—you cannot find computer programmers for product development. Worse yet, current staff members are being lured away by other high-tech firms. After suffering a particularly discouraging personnel raid in which competitors captured three of your most valued employees, you schedule a meeting with your director of human resources to plan organizational changes designed to encourage worker loyalty. You already pay top dollar, but the continuing exodus tells you that programmers are looking for something more.

METHOD

Working with three or four classmates, identify some ways in which specific organizational changes might improve the working environment and encourage employee loyalty. As you analyze the following factors, ask yourself the obvious question, *If I were a programmer, what organizational changes would encourage me to stay?*

- Level of job specialization. With many programmers describing their jobs as tedious because of the focus on detail in a narrow work area, what changes, if any, would you make in job specialization? Right now, for instance, few of your programmers have any say in product design.
- Decision-making hierarchy. What decision-making authority would encourage people to stay? Is expanding employee authority likely to work better in a centralized or decentralized organization?
- Team authority. Can team empowerment make a difference? Taking the point of view of the worker, describe the ideal team.
- Intrapreneuring. What can your company do to encourage and reward innovation?

FOLLOW-UP QUESTIONS

1. With the average computer programmer earning nearly $70 000, and with all competitive firms paying top dollar, why might organizational issues be critical in determining employee loyalty?
2. If you were a programmer, what organizational factors would make a difference to you? Why?
3. As the company founder, how willing would you be to make major organizational changes in light of the shortage of qualified programmers?

EXERCISING YOUR ETHICS

TO POACH, OR NOT TO POACH

THE SITUATION

The Hails Corporation, a manufacturing plant, has recently moved toward an all-team-based organization structure. That is, all workers are divided into teams. Each team has the autonomy to divide up the work assigned to it among its individual members. In addition, each team handles its own scheduling for members to take vacations and other time off. The teams also handle the interviews and hiring of new team members when the need arises. Team A has just lost one of its members, who moved to another city to be closer to his ailing parents.

THE DILEMMA

Since moving to the team structure, every time a team has needed new members, it has advertised in the local newspaper and hired someone from outside the company. However, Team A is considering a different approach to fill its opening. Specifically, a key member of another team (Team B) has made it known that she would like to join Team A. She likes the team members, sees the team's work as being enjoyable, and is somewhat bored with her team's current assignment.

The concern is that if Team A chooses this individual to join the team, several problems may occur. For one thing, her current team will clearly be angry with the members of Team A. Further, "poaching" new team members from other teams inside the plant is likely to become a common occurrence. On the other hand, though, it seems reasonable that she should have the same opportunity to join Team A as an outsider would. Team A needs to decide how to proceed.

TEAM ACTIVITY

Assemble a group of four students and assign each group member to one of the following roles:

- Member of Team A
- Member of Team B
- Manager of both teams
- Hails investor

ACTION STEPS

1. Before hearing any of your group's comments on this situation and, from the perspective of your assigned role, decide whether you think that the member of Team B should be allowed to join Team A. Write down the reasons for your position.
2. Before hearing any of your group's comments on this situation and from the perspective of your assigned role, determine the underlying ethical issues, if any, in this situation. Write down the issues.
3. Gather your group together and reveal, in turn, each member's comments on the situation. Next, reveal the ethical issues listed by each member.
4. Appoint someone to record main points of agreement and disagreement within the group. How do you explain the results? What accounts for any disagreement?
5. From an ethical standpoint, what does your group conclude is the most appropriate action that should be taken by Hails in this situation? Should Team B's member be allowed to join Team A?
6. Develop a group response to the following questions: *Assuming Team A asks the Team B member to join its team, how might it go about minimizing repercussions? Assuming Team A does not ask the Team B member to join its team, how might it go about minimizing repercussions?*

BUSINESS CASE

KODAK'S TROUBLING MOMENT

If you ask anyone who was born before 1990 what comes to mind when they hear the word "Kodak," they will likely respond by saying "Kodak moment" (referring to a famous Kodak advertising campaign from yesteryear). When Eastman Kodak filed for bankruptcy in January 2012, it joined the list of companies whose brands had once dominated their markets, but who had failed to adapt to changing conditions. What happened to Kodak? Here's the story.

Canadian Press via AP Images

In 1885, George Eastman invented roll film. Within three years, the first Kodak camera was produced. The company prospered by making it easy for consumers to take pictures (prior to that time, the process was very cumbersome). In 1900, the now-legendary Brownie camera was marketed, and, in 1935, the first colour film—called Kodachrome—was made available to consumers. By the mid-1970s, Kodak controlled 90 percent of the market for photographic film. At that same time, however, Fujifilm began to aggressively compete with Kodak and gradually took away some of Kodak's market share. But the most significant development was the invention of the digital camera by an engineer at Kodak in 1975. The company developed a variety of digital cameras over the next few years, but top managers apparently had difficulty envisioning a world without film. In spite of Kodak's less-than-aggressive digital strategy, it was actually No. 1 in digital camera sales in the U.S. in 2005. But things went downhill fast after that because Kodak was unable to compete with lower-priced digital cameras offered by Asian competitors, and because Kodak failed to anticipate that many photos would eventually be taken on smartphones rather than with cameras. By 2010, Kodak was in seventh place behind companies like Nikon, Canon, and Sony.

Kodak responded to its declining fortunes by cutting costs through outsourcing many of its production activities and by drastically cutting its workforce. In the 1980s, the company employed 145 000 people worldwide, but, by 2012, that number had dropped to just 17 000. The company stopped selling film cameras (in 2004), Kodachrome film (in 2009), and digital cameras, pocket video cameras, and digital picture frames (in 2012). It also restructured from three business units (commercial film, consumer film, and printing) into just two business units (commercial and consumer printing). The new structure is expected to reduce costs and increase productivity. Kodak's new strategy is to focus on commercial and consumer inkjet printing, workflow software, and packaging. In printing, Kodak currently ranks fifth worldwide, with a 2.6 percent market share.

All these difficulties led to a drastic decline in the price of Kodak stock. During 2011, for example, the stock price declined 88 percent, and by early 2012, it was selling for just 36 cents a share. The share price improved somewhat when it was announced that the board of directors had appointed Laura Quatela, the company's general counsel, as a co-president to serve with Philip Faraci. They will both report to the CEO, Antonio Perez.

Kodak has a lot of patents that it may be able to sell for billions of dollars, just like Nortel Networks did a few years ago. In an attempt to generate much-needed cash, Kodak also filed lawsuits against Apple, BlackBerry, and HTC, claiming that those companies violated patents that Kodak held on processes like sending photos from mobile devices and previewing images with an electronic camera.

Some observers think that there was nothing Kodak could have done to avoid its bankruptcy. But consider Fujifilm, which used to be a small company that played catch-up with Kodak for many years. When digital photography burst upon the scene, Fujifilm diversified into other areas. That restructuring meant cutting billions from its photographic businesses and spending large amounts of money getting into new businesses like cosmetics and electronics. Fujifilm is now a very profitable company.

Kodak's bankruptcy filing marks an astonishing fall from prominence for a company that had dominated the photography business for well over 100 years. The company hopes to emerge from bankruptcy as a smaller company that has very little involvement in photography. But it remains to be seen whether it can effectively compete with its new product lines.

QUESTIONS FOR DISCUSSION

1. What are the key differences between the functional and divisional organizational structures? Which type is Kodak using? Explain.
2. What corporate-level strategy did Kodak pursue in the twentieth century? What are the advantages and disadvantages of such a strategy? What corporate-level strategy is Kodak pursuing in the twenty-first century? (Review the discussion on corporate-level strategy in Chapter 6 before answering this question.)
3. It is ironic that Kodak invented the digital camera, yet was unable to capitalize on that invention. Why do you think Kodak was unable to compete in the digital camera market?
4. At the time you read this case, how is the newly structured Kodak performing?

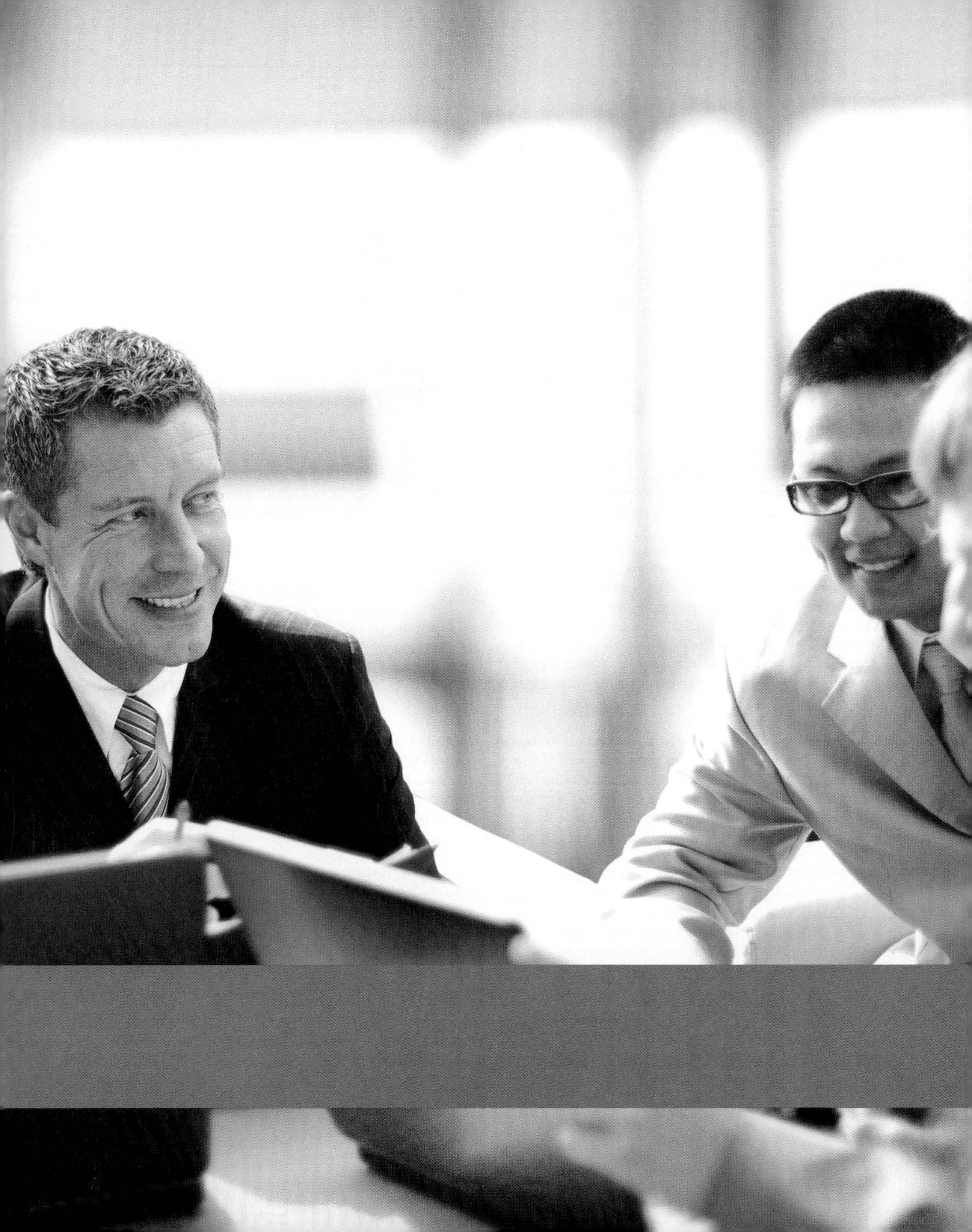

LO

AFTER READING THIS CHAPTER, YOU WILL BE ABLE TO:

- LO-1 Define *human resource management*, discuss its strategic significance, and explain how managers plan for human resources.
- LO-2 Identify the issues involved in staffing a company, including *internal* and *external recruiting* and *selection*.
- LO-3 Discuss different ways in which organizations go about developing the capabilities of employees and managers.
- LO-4 Discuss the importance of *wages and salaries, incentives*, and *benefit programs* in attracting and keeping skilled workers.
- LO-5 Describe some of the key legal issues involved in hiring, compensating, and managing workers in today's workplace.
- LO-6 Discuss *workforce diversity*, the *management of knowledge workers*, and the use of *contingent* and *temporary workers* as important changes in the contemporary workplace.
- LO-7 Trace the evolution of, and discuss trends in, *unionism* in Canada.
- LO-8 Describe the *major laws governing unionism*.
- LO-9 Identify the steps in the *collective bargaining process*.

Hard Hits in Professional Sports

When people think of labour–management disputes, they often think of modestly paid production workers going on strike at a factory in an attempt to improve their wages and benefits. But labour disputes also occur in situations where workers are highly paid. The most obvious example of this is professional sports. The average working person can only dream of getting paid as much as a professional athlete, yet *all* professional athletes in the four major professional sports in North America—hockey, baseball, football, and basketball—belong to unions. This is interesting, especially given that only 16 percent of private-sector workers in Canada and only 8 percent in the U.S. belong to unions.

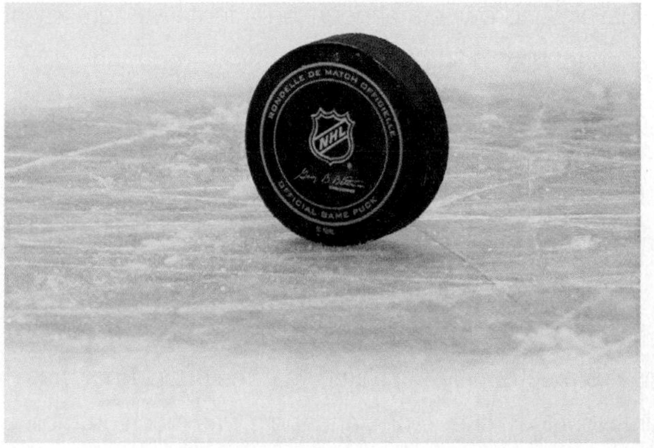

© Jim West/Alamy

Labour–management disputes are common in professional sports. Consider the National Hockey League (NHL). During much of 2012, players and team owners were trying

Managing Human Resources *and* Labour Relations

CHAPTER 08

to fashion a new collective bargaining agreement. The most contentious issue was how to split up the $3.3 billion in annual revenue the NHL receives. In the previous collective agreement, team owners received 43 percent and players got 57 percent. Team owners started negotiations by proposing to reverse those percentages. Not surprisingly, the players rejected that idea. As tensions increased and negotiations stalled, owners decided to lock out the players. During the four-month lockout, mediators were called in to try to move the disputing parties closer to an agreement, but progress was very slow. As the end of 2012 approached, it was clear that if an agreement was not reached very soon, the entire season would be lost (that is what happened in 2004 to 2005 when the two sides couldn't reach an agreement). Finally, the players and owners announced a tentative agreement on January 6, 2013. The agreement covered many different issues, with the key one being a 50–50 revenue split. Because the dispute lasted so long, there was only time for each team to play about 50 games during the January to April 2013 period.

HOW WILL THIS HELP ME?

Effectively managing human resources is critical to the success of organizations. A firm that handles this activity well has a better chance for success than a firm that simply goes through the motions. After reading the material in this chapter, you'll be better able to understand—from the perspective of a *manager*—the importance of properly managing human resources in a department or business you own or supervise. You'll also understand—from the perspective of an *employee*—why your employer has adopted certain approaches to dealing with issues like hiring, training, compensation, and benefits.

The lockout meant millions of dollars of lost revenues for owners and millions of dollars of lost salaries for players. Fans were extremely frustrated that they could not watch their favourite hockey team, and there was much grumbling about how the dispute between "millionaire players and billionaire owners" was hurting loyal fans. A study by Level 5 Strategy Group estimated that the NHL lost approximately $300 million in brand value as a result of the lockout. The dispute didn't affect just team owners and players. One study showed that game-day spending at restaurants close to arenas in Vancouver, Toronto, Montreal, Calgary, and Winnipeg decreased by 11 percent during the lockout. Revenues at drinking establishments fell by 35 percent. When the lockout ended, credit-card receipts jumped 34 percent at bars in Winnipeg and 22 percent in Vancouver. In spite of all the frustration experienced by fans, hockey remains the most popular professional sport in Canada (56 percent of respondents in a poll named hockey as their favourite sport).

Labour disputes have also been evident in the other major professional sports in North America. In baseball, the Major League Baseball Players Association (MLBPA) went on strike from August 1994 to April 1995 after failing to negotiate a new collective agreement with team owners. As a result, postseason play, including the World Series, was cancelled. Many businesses that counted on baseball—including broadcasters, advertisers, retailers, and restaurants—suffered economic losses when games were not played. In basketball, the 2011 season began two months late due to a labour dispute, and a full schedule was not played. The players were also locked out in 1998 to 1999, and that season was shortened by 50 games. There were also shorter lockouts in 1995 and 1996.

In football, a strike/lockout threat loomed in 2011. The main area of dispute was how to divide up the $9.4 billion in annual revenue that the league takes in (sound familiar?). In March 2011, the players decertified their union and then filed an antitrust suit against the NFL. The suit asked for an injunction to prevent the owners from locking out the players. The NFL then filed a complaint with the National Labor Relations Board claiming that the union was not bargaining in good faith, and that the decertification was an attempt by the union to avoid its bargaining responsibilities. Soon after, the NFL locked out the players, and the two sides dug in to prepare for a lengthy battle. In May 2011, a federal appeals court ruled that the lockout would remain in force because it did not grow out of a labour dispute (since the players were no longer represented by a union). The players were not impressed with that logic. During this period, multiple days of court-ordered mediation also took place as owners and players continued to negotiate in an attempt to reach a new agreement. The first positive news came in July 2011, when rumours began circulating that the players might give tentative approval to the most recent proposal made by the

NFL owners. The players' group executive committee and team reps met for 10 hours one day to carefully look over the proposal. The NFL owners group also met to see if all owners were in agreement with the proposed terms. A few days later, both team owners and players voted in favour of the proposal. The new 10-year agreement gave owners 53 percent of league revenues and players 47 percent (the old agreement had a 50–50 split).

QUESTIONS FOR DISCUSSION

1. What labour relations concepts discussed in this chapter are evident in the description above?
2. Why would professional athletes be willing to go on strike to win salary increases when they already have multimillion dollar contracts?
3. Consider the following statement: *The owners of professional sports teams and the athletes that play for those teams earn far too much money. Fans should boycott sports contests until team owners reduce ticket prices (and the salaries that players are paid).* Do you agree or disagree with the statement? Explain your reasoning.

LO-1 THE FOUNDATIONS OF HUMAN RESOURCE MANAGEMENT

Human resource management (HRM) is the set of organizational activities directed at attracting, developing, and maintaining an effective workforce. Human resource management takes place within a complex and ever-changing environmental context and is increasingly being recognized for its strategic importance.[1]

The Strategic Importance of HRM

Human resources are critical for effective organizational functioning. HRM (or personnel) was once relegated to second-class status in many organizations, but its importance has grown dramatically in the last two decades, stemming from increased legal complexities, the recognition that human resources are a valuable means for improving productivity, and an awareness of the costs associated with poor human resource management.

Managers now realize that the effectiveness of their HR function has a substantial impact on a firm's bottom-line performance. Poor human resource planning can result in spurts of hiring followed by layoffs—a process that is costly in terms of unemployment compensation payments, training expenses, and morale. Haphazard compensation systems do not attract, keep, and motivate good employees, and outmoded recruitment practices can expose the firm to expensive and embarrassing legal action. Consequently, the chief human resource executive of most large businesses is a vice-president directly accountable to the CEO, and many firms are developing strategic HR plans that are integrated with other strategic planning activities.

HUMAN RESOURCE MANAGEMENT (HRM) Set of organizational activities directed at attracting, developing, and maintaining an effective workforce.

JOB ANALYSIS A detailed study of the specific duties in a particular job and the human qualities required for that job.

JOB DESCRIPTION The objectives, responsibilities, and key tasks of a job; the conditions under which it will be done; its relationship to other positions; and the skills needed to perform it.

JOB SPECIFICATION The specific skills, education, and experience needed to perform a job.

Human Resource Planning

Planning is the starting point in attracting qualified human resources. Human resource (HR) planning involves job analysis, forecasting the demand for and supply of labour, and matching supply and demand.

JOB ANALYSIS

Job analysis is a systematic analysis of jobs within an organization. A job analysis is made up of two parts:

1. The **job description** lists the duties of a job, its working conditions, and the tools, materials, and equipment used to perform it.
2. The **job specification** lists the skills, abilities, and other credentials needed to do the job.

Job analysis information is used in many HR activities. For instance, knowing about job content and job requirements is necessary to develop appropriate selection methods and job-relevant performance appraisal systems and to set equitable compensation rates.

FORECASTING HR DEMAND AND SUPPLY

After managers fully understand the jobs to be performed within an organization, they can start planning for the organization's future HR needs. The manager starts by assessing trends in past HR usage, future organizational plans, and general economic trends. A good sales forecast is often the foundation, especially for smaller organizations. Historical ratios can then be used to predict demand for types of employees, such as operating employees and sales representatives. Large organizations use much more complicated models to predict HR needs.

REPLACEMENT CHART An HR technique that lists each important managerial position, who occupies it, how long he or she will probably stay in it before moving on, and who (by name) is now qualified or soon will be qualified to move into it.

EMPLOYEE INFORMATION SYSTEMS (SKILLS INVENTORIES) Computerized systems that contain information on each employee's education, skills, work experience, and career aspirations.

Forecasting the supply of labour involves two tasks:

- Forecasting internal supply—the number and type of employees who will be in the firm at some future date
- Forecasting external supply—the number and type of people who will be available for hiring from the labour market at large

The simplest approach in forecasting *internal* supply simply adjusts present staffing levels for anticipated turnover and promotions. Large organizations often use extremely sophisticated models to keep track of the present and future distributions of professionals and managers. This allows the company to spot areas where there will eventually be too many qualified professionals competing for too few promotions or, conversely, too few good people available to fill important positions.

Replacement Charts At higher levels of the organization, managers plan for specific people and positions. The technique most commonly used is the **replacement chart**, which lists each important managerial position, who occupies it, how long he or she will probably stay in it before moving on, and who is now qualified or soon will be qualified to move into it. This technique allows ample time to plan developmental experiences for people identified as potential successors to critical managerial jobs. WestJet had a smooth transition of power when Sean Durfy took over as CEO from Clive Beddoe. In 2010, when Mr. Durfy had to leave abruptly for personal reasons, after just 18 months on the job, Gregg Saretsky took over. He was regarded as the logical successor, having been hired nine months earlier as vice-president of WestJet Vacations, but nobody expected him to get the CEO opportunity so quickly.[2]

Skills Inventories To facilitate planning and to identify people for transfer or promotion, some organizations also have **employee information systems**, or **skills inventories**. These systems are usually computerized and contain information on each employee's education, skills, work experience, and career aspirations. Such a system can quickly locate every employee in the company who is qualified to fill a position requiring, say, a degree in chemical engineering, three years of experience in an oil refinery, and fluency in French.

Forecasting the *external* supply of labour is more difficult. For example, how does a manager predict how many electrical engineers will be seeking work in Ontario or British Columbia three years from now? To get an idea of the future availability of labour, planners must rely on information from outside sources, including population and demographic statistics and figures supplied by colleges and universities on the number of students in major fields. Some people argue that these statistics suggest that Canada is soon likely to face a severe labour shortage because so many baby boomers are reaching retirement age.[3] A 2012 report from the Canadian Chamber of Commerce predicted shortages in a variety of industries, including construction, nursing, and trucking.[4] But others disagree, noting that people now have healthier lifestyles and are therefore more able and willing to work past the typical retirement age.[5]

MATCHING HR SUPPLY AND DEMAND

After comparing future demand and internal supply, managers can make plans to navigate predicted shortfalls or overstaffing. If a shortfall is predicted, new employees can be hired, present employees can be retrained and transferred into understaffed areas, individuals approaching retirement can be persuaded to stay on, or labour-saving or productivity-enhancing systems can be installed.

If the organization needs to hire, the external labour-supply forecast helps managers plan how to recruit according to whether the type of person needed is readily available or scarce in the labour market. The use of temporary workers also helps managers by giving them extra flexibility in staffing. If overstaffing is expected to be a problem, the main options are transferring the extra employees, not replacing individuals who quit, encouraging early retirement, and laying people off.

LO-2 RECRUITING HUMAN RESOURCES

Once managers have decided what positions they need to fill, they must find and hire individuals who meet the job requirements. Staffing a business with qualified individuals is one of the most complex and important aspects of good human resource management. A study by the Canadian Federation of Independent Business found that the top three characteristics employers are looking for are a good work ethic, reliability, and willingness to stay on the job.[6]

Recruiting is the process of attracting qualified people to apply for available jobs. **Internal recruiting** means considering present employees as candidates for openings. Promotion from within can help build morale and keep high-quality employees from leaving. In unionized firms, the procedures for notifying employees of internal job-change opportunities are usually spelled out in the union contract. For higher-level positions, a skills inventory system may be used to identify internal candidates, or managers may be asked to recommend individuals who should be considered.

RECRUITING The phase in the staffing of a company in which the firm seeks to develop a pool of interested, qualified applicants for a position.

INTERNAL RECRUITING Considering present employees as candidates for job openings.

EXTERNAL RECRUITING Attracting people outside the organization to apply for jobs.

External recruiting means attracting people outside the organization to apply for jobs. External recruiting methods include advertising, campus interviews, employment agencies or executive search firms, union hiring halls, referrals by present employees, and hiring "walk-ins" (people who show up without being solicited). Private employment agencies can be a good source of clerical and technical employees, and executive search firms specialize in locating top-management talent. Newspaper and job-search website ads are often used because they reach a wide audience and thus allow minorities "equal opportunity" to learn about and apply for job openings.

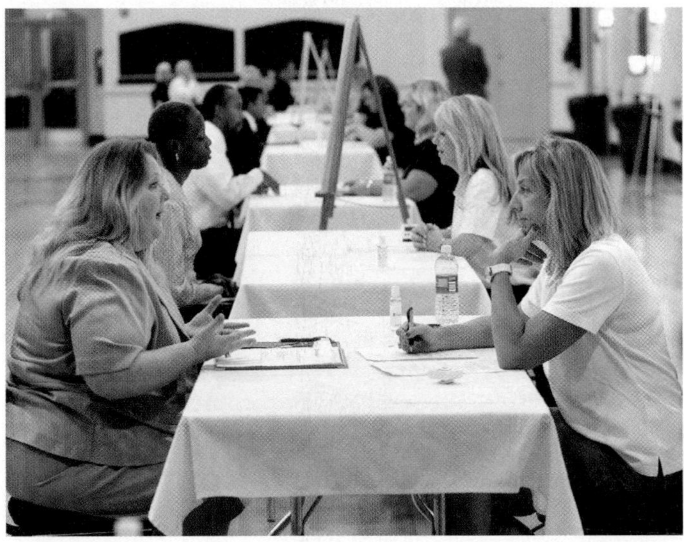

At job fairs, students and recruiters talk face-to-face about jobs that are available and the characteristics and training that applicants must have to secure a job.

AFP/Getty Images/Newscom

THERE'S AN APP FOR THAT!

1. **Search Jobs Beyond.com** >>> **Platforms:** *Apple, BlackBerry*
   Source: Beyond.com
   Key Features: Users can locate thousands of jobs across more than 25 industries by area and keyword.
2. **Canadian Job Force.com** >>> **Platforms:** *Apple, BlackBerry*
   Source: Beyond.com
   Key Features: Enables users to search for jobs in over 25 industries in the Canadian job market.
3. **HR at Your Fingertips** >>> **Platforms:** *Apple, Android*
   Source: HR Sentry
   Key Features: Contains a glossary of HR terms + tips for entrepreneurs to create an employee handbook.

APP DISCOVERY EXERCISE

Since APP availability changes, conduct your own search for "Top 3" Human Resources APPS and identify the key features.

At a job fair, candidates browse through the positions available and talk face-to-face with recruiters. Job fairs are cheaper than posting jobs with an employment agency. In 2011, more than 10 000 people signed up for a *virtual job fair* that was run by Monster.ca. Unlike campus job fairs, individuals from all career stages were involved. Participants clicked on the virtual booths of employers they were interested in. Employers interviewed candidates via video.[7]

Internships are short-term paid or unpaid positions where students focus on a specific project. Hari Pemasani, who came to Canada from India, completed a pharmacy program at the University of Toronto and then had an internship with Loblaw Cos. Ltd. He was then hired for a full-time position and soon became the pharmacy manager for the store where he worked.[8] The Canadian Undergraduate Survey Consortium found that 55 percent of graduating students had completed an internship.[9]

The boxed insert entitled "Green Careers" illustrates the increasing importance of environmental considerations in recruiting.

The biggest change in recent years has been the advent of online recruiting. Companies post positions on websites like Monster.com, Workopolis.com, or LinkedIn, and interested applicants respond. Internet recruiting gives employers and those seeking employment a fast, easy, and inexpensive way of interacting. But there are drawbacks. Employers receive huge numbers of applications, and many are from unqualified people. Starbucks, for example, received 7.6 million applications during 2011. To cope with this situation, many companies now use resume-filtering software which searches out key words on applications. If the key words aren't there, the applicant is not contacted.[10] IGN Entertainment, a gaming and media company, doesn't even ask for a resume. Instead, candidates respond to challenges on IGN's website which are designed to gauge applicants' thought processes.[11]

Selecting Human Resources

Once the recruiting process has attracted a pool of applicants, the next step is to select someone to hire. The intent of the selection process is to gather information from applicants that will predict their job success and then to hire the candidates likely to be most successful. The process of determining the predictive value of information is called **validation**.

To reduce the element of uncertainty, managers use a variety of selection techniques, the most common of which are shown in Figure 8.1. Each organization develops its own mix of selection techniques and may use them in almost any order.

APPLICATION FORMS

The first step in selection is asking the candidate to fill out an application form. An application form is an efficient method of gathering information about the applicant's previous work history, educational background, and other job-related demographic data. It should not contain questions about areas unrelated to the job, such as gender, religion, or national origin. Application-form data are generally used informally to decide whether a candidate merits further evaluation, and interviewers use application forms to familiarize themselves with candidates before interviewing them.

TESTS

Employers sometimes ask candidates to take tests during the selection process. Tests of ability, skill, aptitude, or knowledge relevant to a particular job are usually the best predictors of job success, although tests of general intelligence or personality are occasionally useful as well. At Astral Media, job candidates are required to take a series of tests that measure verbal and numerical skills, as well as psychological traits.[12] Some companies administer tests to determine how well applicants score on the "big five" personality dimensions discussed in Chapter 9. These scores are used to help make hiring decisions. In addition to being validated, tests should be administered and scored consistently. All candidates should be given the same directions, allowed the same amount of time, and offered the same testing environment, including temperature, lighting, and distractions.

INTERNSHIPS Short-term paid or unpaid positions where students focus on a specific project.

VALIDATION The process of determining the predictive value of information.

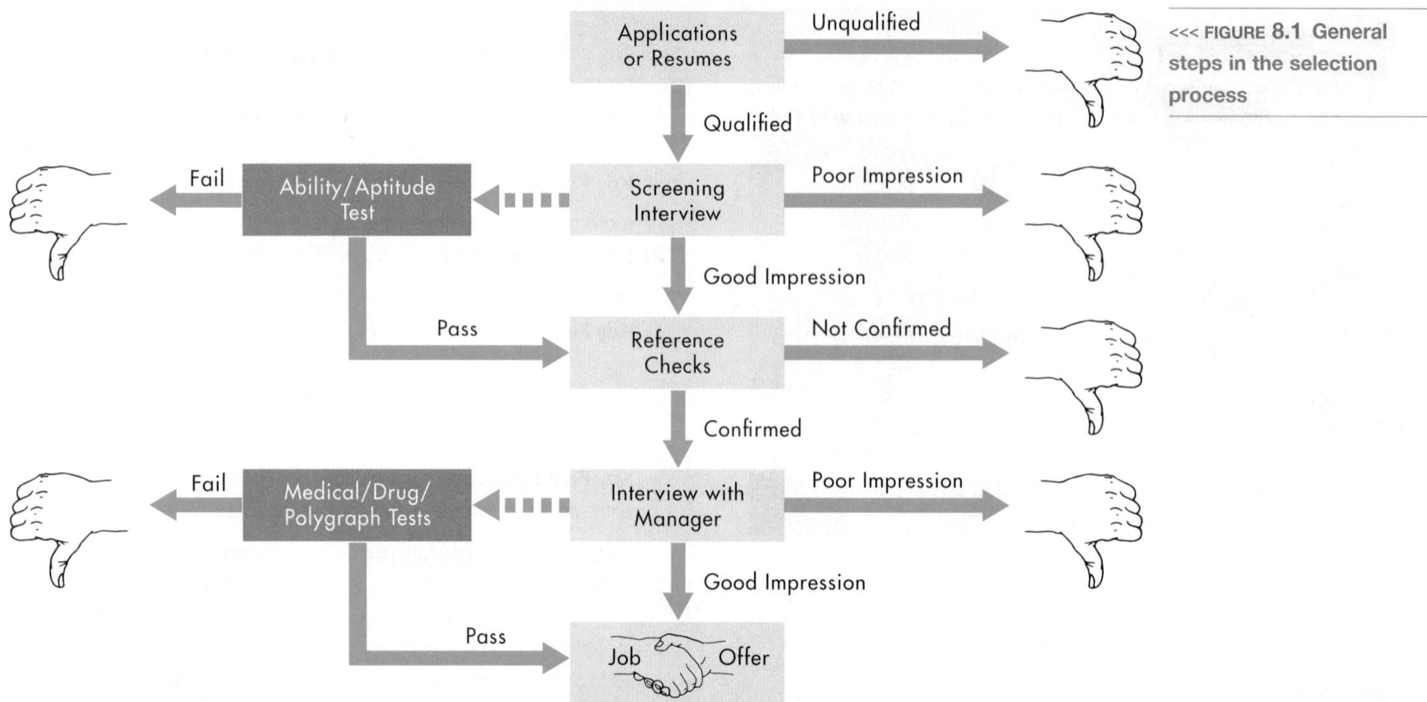

<<< **FIGURE 8.1** General steps in the selection process

An **assessment centre** is a series of exercises in which candidates perform realistic management tasks under the watchful eye of expert appraisers. During this time, potential managers take selection tests, engage in management simulations, make individual presentations, and

ASSESSMENT CENTRE A series of exercises in which management candidates perform realistic management tasks while being observed by appraisers.

THE GREENING OF BUSINESS

Green Careers

In recent years, Canadians have become more concerned about the environment, and many people say they want to work for companies that share their concerns. After Chad Hunt graduated from university, he took a job with Husky Injection Molding because of the company's emphasis on protecting the environment. Sara Wong said it was the zero waste program at Hudson's Bay Co. (HBC) that caught her attention when she was job-hunting. When Kali Taylor was a student at the University of Calgary, she started an environmentally focused group called Student Energy. The purpose of the group is to educate and inspire students to become environmental professionals and to facilitate the transition to a sustainable energy future. In 2013, students from more than 50 countries attended the group's International Student Energy Summit in Norway.

A Green Careers Summit in Calgary—hosted by ECO Canada—helped Grade 11 and 12 students to explore possible career paths with several business leaders who worked in various environmental fields. Environmental careers are available in virtually every sector of the economy. Over half a million Canadians are now employed in environmentally related jobs (e.g., consultants who assess homes to see how energy efficient they are). Many of these jobs didn't even exist a generation ago. According to the Environmental Careers Organization of Canada, the top five green careers are environmental engineer, environmental technologist, conservation biologist, geographic information system analyst, and environmental communications officer.

In a survey conducted by Monster.ca, 78 percent of respondents said they would quit their current job if they could get one at a company that had an environmentally friendly focus. In a second survey, 81 percent of the respondents said that their current employer was not environmentally friendly. Only 18 percent said the employer was "extremely green." An environmentally friendly workplace is important to both current and prospective employees. Aon Hewitt's annual "Green 30" list is based on employee perceptions of their companies' environmental efforts. A recent list included Lush Fresh Handmade Cosmetics, ISL Engineering and Land Services, and Nexen. In these and other companies, employees are often the ones that push for green initiatives. For example, David Huang saved his company (BLJC) $400 000 by suggesting a variety of energy-saving actions. At VanCity Credit Union, Maureen Cureton encouraged other employees to buy from green and socially conscious retailers. That evolved into the Beehive, a searchable database that lists sustainable retailers.

CRITICAL THINKING QUESTIONS

1. What are the advantages of working for an environmentally friendly company? Are there any disadvantages?
2. Consider the following statement: *All the publicity about graduates looking for jobs at environmentally friendly companies is exaggerated. Many graduates are merely claiming they want to work for an environmentally friendly company, even though most of them really don't care that much about the environment.* Do you agree or disagree with the statement? Explain your reasoning.

conduct group discussions. Assessors check to see how each participant reacts to stress or to criticism by colleagues. A relatively new type of test is **video assessment**, which involves showing potential hires videos of realistic work situations and asking them to choose a course of action to deal with the situation.

INTERVIEWS

The interview is a popular selection device, but it is sometimes a poor predictor of job success because biases inherent in the way people perceive and judge others on first meeting affect subsequent evaluations. Many companies are placing more emphasis on testing and less emphasis on interviewing because job candidates are becoming clever at giving all the "right" answers during interviews.[13] Interview validity can be improved by training interviewers to be aware of potential biases, and by writing out questions in advance and asking all interviewees the same set of questions.

Interviewers can also increase interview validity by asking "curveball" questions—that is, questions that job applicants would never expect to be asked—to see how well they think on their feet. Questions such as "How would you move Mount Fuji?" or "How would you sell me a glass of water?" are curveball questions.[14]

Another approach to improving interview validity is **behaviour-based interviewing**. Instead of asking a traditional interview question like "Do you often take the initiative?" behaviour-based interviewing asks, "Tell me about a situation where you became aware of a problem. What did you do?" This approach puts a spotlight on behaviour rather than on what a person says. It can be used to test for technical skills (e.g., accounting, welding, or computer programming), management skills (e.g., organizing, motivating others, or communicating), and individual skills (e.g., dependability, discipline, or the ability to work on a team). For more information on behaviour-based interviewing, see the Business Case at the end of this chapter.

VIDEO ASSESSMENT Involves showing potential hires videos of realistic work situations and asking them to choose a course of action to deal with the situation.

BEHAVIOUR-BASED INTERVIEWING An approach to improving interview validity by asking questions that focuses the interview much more on behaviour than on what a person says.

OTHER TECHNIQUES

Organizations also use other selection techniques that vary with the circumstances. A manufacturer afraid of injuries to workers on the job might require new employees to have a physical examination. This gives the company some information about whether the applicants are physically fit to do the work and what (if any) pre-existing injuries they might have.

Drug tests are coming under fire. According to the Canadian Human Rights Commission policy, pre-employment drug testing and random drug testing are not permitted. However, recent legal decisions make this anything but a black-and-white issue. Rulings related to the Greater Toronto Airport Authority (GTAA) and Goodyear Canada are open to other interpretations. The decisions upheld the rights of these organizations to use drug and alcohol testing for safety-sensitive positions and as a post-treatment check for employees with a history of drug abuse. However, it was also deemed unreasonable to deny selection because of a pre-employment positive drug test. This is an area of law that will continue to evolve and be debated.[15]

Reference checks with previous employers are also used but may be of limited value because individuals are likely to provide the names of only those references who will give them positive recommendations. It is also getting harder to get good reference information because many HR people are worried about legal rulings south of the border as high as $1.4 million. But many legal experts say that the fear is unwarranted; the law protects them in giving honest, even if negative, information.[16]

LO-3 DEVELOPING HUMAN RESOURCES

After a company has hired new employees, it must acquaint them with the firm and their new jobs. This process begins with a formal orientation to welcome the employee and provide information about the company history, structure, culture, benefits programs, and much more. Managers also take steps to train employees and develop necessary job skills. In addition, every firm has some system for performance appraisal and feedback.

New Employee Orientation

A new employee's first 30 days on the job have a big influence on whether the person will stay with the company.[17] An Ipsos Reid survey of over 1000 workers revealed that 50 percent of them felt that they didn't always fit in well at work.[18] Thus, orientation of new workers is a very important activity. **Orientation** is the process of introducing new employees to the company's policies and programs, the co-workers and supervisors they will interact with, and the nature of their job. Orientation allows new employees to feel like part of a team and to become effective contributors to the organization more rapidly. It also plays a key role in job satisfaction, performance, and retention. Overall, orientation eases the transition from outsider to insider. Poor orientation, on the other hand, can result in disenchantment, dissatisfaction, anxiety, and turnover. The dating website PlentyofFish uses its matchmaking techniques to find appropriate employees. Just as a friend would recommend a potential partner, employees are encouraged to refer people they may know that would be a great fit to the company as well.[19]

Training and Development

On-the-job training occurs while employees are in the actual work situation. Much on-the-job training is informal, as when one employee shows another how to operate the photocopy machine. Training may also be formal, as when a trainer shows employees how to operate a new software program. In **job rotation**, employees learn a wide array of tasks and acquire more abilities as they are moved from one job to another.

ORIENTATION The process of introducing new employees to the company's policies and programs, the co-workers and supervisors they will interact with, and the nature of their job.

ON-THE-JOB TRAINING Development programs in which employees gain new skills while performing them at work.

JOB ROTATION A technique in which an employee is rotated or transferred from one job to another.

Off-the-job training is performed at a location away from the work site. For example, **vestibule training** involves employees performing work under conditions closely simulating the actual work environment. Montreal-based CAE is famous for building flight simulators that enable airline pilots to learn how to fly a new jet without ever leaving the ground. CAE also develops mock-up operating rooms where medical students can learn in a simulated environment.[20]

Management development programs try to enhance conceptual, analytical, and problem-solving skills. Most large companies run formal in-house management development programs or send managers to programs on university campuses. In the Build for the Future program at TD Bank, top managers meet once a month to plan leadership training and coaching of subordinates.[21] But in many companies, training for managers is not so systematic. In one survey of over 1000 managers, 57 percent said they had to learn how to manage by trial and error, and 89 percent said they had not been groomed to be a leader.[22]

Some management development takes place informally, often through processes such as networking and mentoring. **Networking** refers to informal interactions among managers for the purpose of discussing mutual problems, solutions, and opportunities. Networking takes place in a variety of settings, both inside and outside the office. **Mentoring** means having a more experienced manager sponsor and teach a less experienced manager. Men still occupy the majority of top management positions, and they are important in mentoring women who aspire to top management jobs.[23] For both men and women, *reverse mentoring* is becoming common—younger, more tech-savvy employees mentor senior staff members on everything from viral marketing to blogging to the use of Facebook and YouTube.[24]

OFF-THE-JOB TRAINING Development programs in which employees learn new skills at a location away from the normal work site.

VESTIBULE TRAINING A work simulation in which the job is performed under conditions closely simulating the actual work environment.

MANAGEMENT DEVELOPMENT PROGRAMS Development programs in which managers' conceptual, analytical, and problem-solving skills are enhanced.

NETWORKING Informal interactions among managers, both inside and outside the office, for the purpose of discussing mutual problems, solutions, and opportunities.

MENTORING Having a more experienced manager sponsor and teach a less experienced manager.

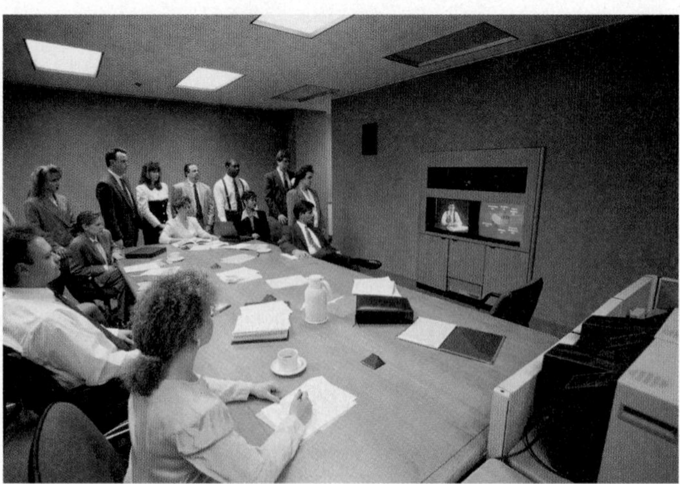

Video conferencing has become an important part of the training function. Travel costs are reduced, and interactions between the trainer and the trainees are facilitated.

© music Alan King/Alamy

Team Building and Group-Based Training

Since more and more organizations are using teams as a basis for doing their jobs, it should not be surprising that many of the same companies are developing training programs specifically designed to facilitate co-operation among team members. For example, Eagle's Flight is an innovative leader in the development and delivery of practical training programs for the global business community. Their offering of training programs includes team and training experiences, as well as leadership development and learning.[25]

Evaluating Employee Performance

Performance appraisals are designed to show how well workers are doing their jobs. Typically, the appraisal process involves a written assessment issued on a regular basis. As a rule, however, the written evaluation is only one part of a multi-step process. The appraisal process begins when a manager defines performance standards for an employee. The manager then observes the employee's performance. If the standards are clear, the manager should have little difficulty comparing expectations with performance. The process is completed when the manager and employee meet to discuss the appraisal.

It is best to rely on several information sources when conducting appraisals. A system called **360-degree feedback** gathers information from supervisors, subordinates, and co-workers. The most accurate information comes from individuals who have known the person being appraised for one to three years. Eight or ten individuals should take part in the evaluation.[26] The use of social media in appraisal is increasing. When Facebook decided that traditional appraisals were not suited to its employees, it turned to Toronto-based Rypple, a company that specializes in software tools to provide real-time feedback using a Facebook-style interface. Managers can "like" tasks, ask for feedback, and monitor employee progress toward goals.[27]

PROVIDING PERFORMANCE FEEDBACK

Many managers are not effective when providing performance feedback, partly because they don't understand how to do it properly and partly because they don't enjoy it. As a result, managers may have a tendency to avoid giving negative feedback because they know that an employee who receives it may be angry, hurt, discouraged, or argumentative. But

PERFORMANCE APPRAISALS A formal program for evaluating how well an employee is performing the job; helps managers to determine how effective they are in recruiting and selecting employees.

360-DEGREE FEEDBACK Gathering information from a manager's subordinates, peers, and superiors when assessing the manager's performance.

if employees are not told about their shortcomings, they will have no concrete reason to try to improve and will receive no guidance as to how to improve. Because of the problems with performance appraisal, some companies have abandoned them. Australian-based Atlassian Inc., for example, replaced annual appraisals with weekly one-on-one meetings between managers and workers. Discussions focus on goals and performance.[28]

SIMPLE RANKING METHOD A method of performance appraisal that requires a manager to rank-order from top to bottom or from best to worst each member of a particular workgroup or department.

GRAPHIC RATING SCALE A statement or question about some aspect of an individual's job performance for which the rater must select the response that fits best.

CRITICAL INCIDENT METHOD A technique of performance appraisal in which raters recall examples of especially good or poor performance by an employee and then describe what the employee did (or did not do) that led to success or failure.

METHODS FOR APPRAISING PERFORMANCE

The **simple ranking method** requires a manager to rank-order from top to bottom or from best to worst each member of a particular workgroup or department. The individual ranked first is the top performer; the individual ranked second is the second-best performer, and so forth. Another ranking method, the forced distribution method, involves grouping employees into predefined frequencies of performance ratings. Those frequencies are determined in advance and are imposed on the rater. A decision might be made, for instance, that 10 percent of the employees in a workgroup will be categorized as outstanding, 20 percent as very good, 40 percent as average, 20 percent as below average, and the remaining 10 percent as poor. The forced distribution method is familiar to students because it is the principle used by professors who grade on a so-called "bell curve" or "normal curve."

One of the most popular and widely used methods is the **graphic rating scale**, which consists simply of a statement or question about some aspect of an individual's job performance. Figure 8.2 shows a sample graphic rating scale.

The **critical incident method** focuses attention on an example of especially good or poor performance on the part of the employee. Raters then describe what the employee did (or did not do) that led to success or failure. This technique not only provides information for feedback but also defines performance in fairly clear behavioural terms.

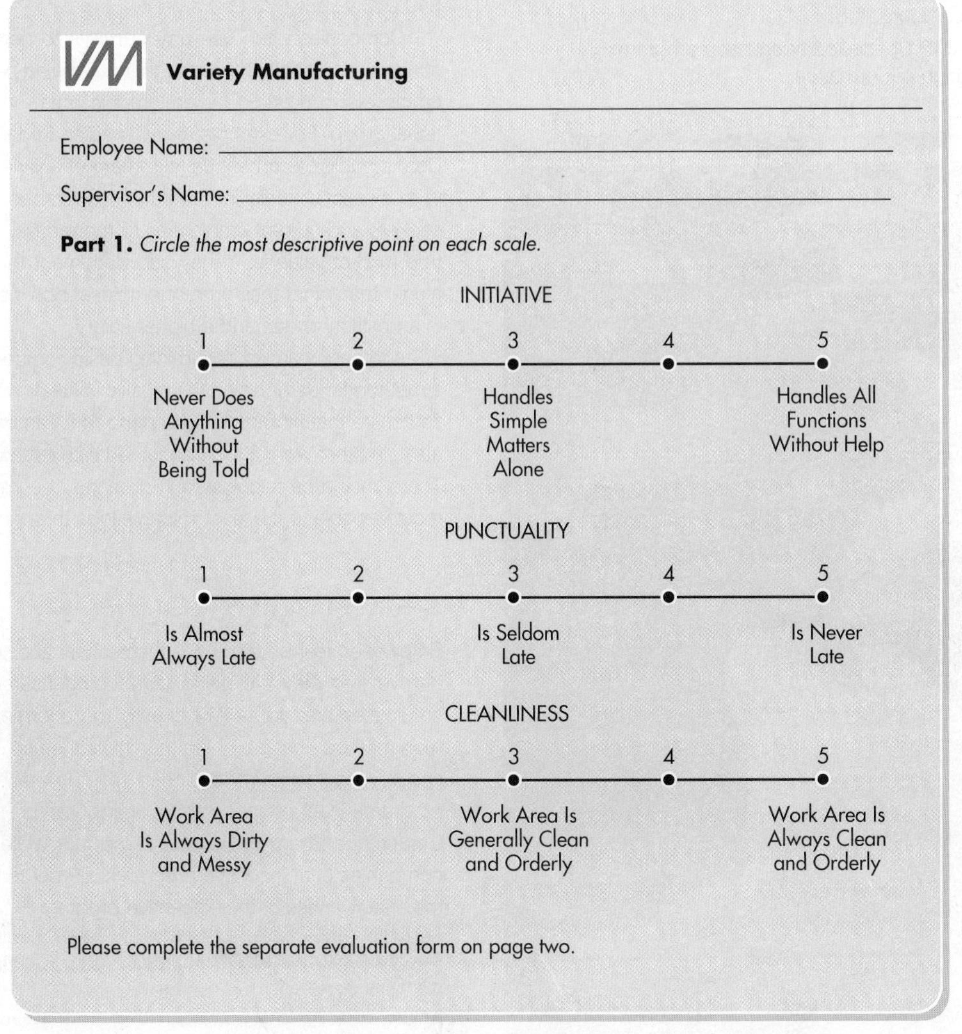
VM **Variety Manufacturing**

Employee Name: ______________________

Supervisor's Name: ______________________

Part 1. *Circle the most descriptive point on each scale.*

INITIATIVE

1	2	3	4	5
Never Does Anything Without Being Told		Handles Simple Matters Alone		Handles All Functions Without Help

PUNCTUALITY

1	2	3	4	5
Is Almost Always Late		Is Seldom Late		Is Never Late

CLEANLINESS

1	2	3	4	5
Work Area Is Always Dirty and Messy		Work Area Is Generally Clean and Orderly		Work Area Is Always Clean and Orderly

Please complete the separate evaluation form on page two.

FIGURE 8.2 Performance rating scale (AKA Graphic rating scale)

LO-4 COMPENSATION AND BENEFITS

Compensation refers to the rewards that organizations provide to individuals in return for their willingness to perform various jobs and tasks within the organization. Compensation includes a number of different elements, such as base salary, incentives, bonuses, benefits, and other rewards. The compensation received by CEOs can be extremely large, especially when bonuses are included. The top 100 Canadian CEOs were paid an average of $8.4 million in 2010.[29] By comparison, the average Canadian worker earned $44 366.[30] Frank Stronach of Magna International earned $61.8 million in 2011.[31] Critics have frequently questioned the wisdom of giving executives such large amounts of money, but most attempts to rein in executive salaries have failed. In 2009, there was a huge outcry in the United States about bonuses paid to executives of AIG, a company that was in deep financial trouble and had been bailed out by taxpayers. Shareholders at CIBC and the Royal Bank of Canada passed motions demanding that the companies give them a voice in executive compensation through non-binding shareholder votes.[32] In Sweden, Norway, and the Netherlands, shareholders have a binding vote on executive pay packages. Whether binding or non-binding, investor feedback may help boards of directors rein in executive compensation that is perceived as too high.[33]

COMPENSATION What a firm offers its employees in return for their labour.

WAGES Dollars paid based on the number of hours worked.

SALARY Dollars paid at regular intervals in return for doing a job, regardless of the amount of time or output involved.

PAY SURVEYS A survey of compensation paid to employees by other employers in a particular geographic area, an industry, or an occupational group.

JOB EVALUATION A method for determining the relative value or worth of a job to the organization so that individuals who perform it can be appropriately compensated.

INCENTIVE PROGRAMS Special compensation programs designed to motivate high performance.

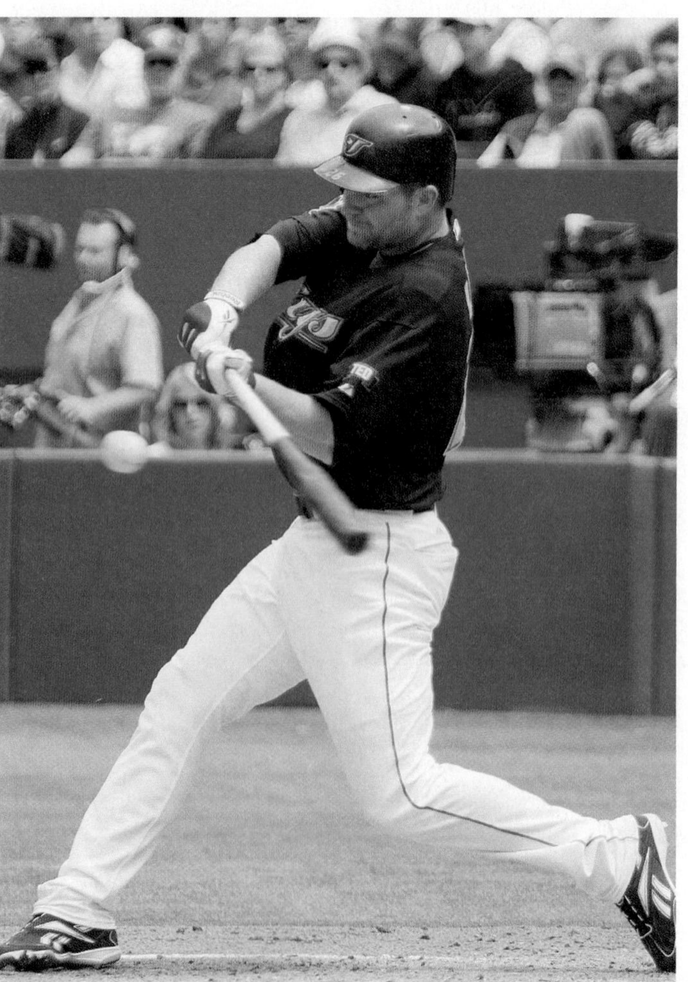

Determining Basic Compensation

Wages generally refer to hourly compensation paid to operating employees. Most of the jobs that are paid on an hourly wage basis are lower-level and/or operating-level jobs. In 2012, the average hourly wage in manufacturing was $19.76, while in retailing it was only $15.73. The manufacturing sector is shrinking, and retailers are now the biggest employers in Canada.[34] Rather than expressing compensation on an hourly basis, the organization may instead describe compensation on an annual or monthly basis. Many college and university graduates, for example, compare job offers on the basis of annual **salary**, such as $40 000 versus $38 000 a year.

Companies often use **pay surveys** to determine pay levels. These surveys show the compensation that is being paid to employees by other employers in a particular geographic area, an industry, or an occupational group. For example, the Canadian Federation of Business School Deans publishes an annual summary of salaries for professors teaching in business schools in Canadian universities. The internet allows job seekers and current employees to more easily get a sense of what their true market value is. If they can document the claim that their value is higher than what their current employer now pays or is offering, they are in a position to demand a higher salary.

Another means of determining basic compensation is **job evaluation**, a method for determining the relative value or worth of a job to the organization, so that individuals who perform it can be compensated appropriately. In other words, it is concerned with establishing internal pay equity. There should be a logical rank-ordering of compensation levels from the most valuable to the least valuable jobs throughout the organization.

Incentive Programs

Employees feel better about themselves and their company when they believe that they are being fairly compensated. But money motivates employees only if it is tied directly to performance, and the most common method of establishing this link is the use of **incentive programs**—special pay programs designed to motivate high performance. These programs can be applied to individuals or teams. A survey by the Conference Board of Canada found that while 80 percent of Canadian companies offer incentive programs, 69 percent of them don't measure the effectiveness of their incentive program.[35]

<<< Individual incentive plans have been a big part of professional sports for many years. Players receive multimillion dollar annual compensation for outstanding individual performance.

Frontpage/Shutterstock

INDIVIDUAL INCENTIVES

Under a **piece-rate incentive plan**, employees receive a certain amount of money for every unit they produce. An assembly-line worker might be paid $1 for every 12 units of a product successfully completed. Sales employees are often paid a **bonus**—a special payment above their salaries—when they sell a certain number or certain dollar amount of goods for the year. Bonuses are also given in non-sales jobs. For example, many baseball players have contract clauses that pay them bonuses for hitting over .300, making the all-star team, or being named Most Valuable Player. Despite public outcries, large bonuses at the "Big Six" Canadian banks continue to rise. For example, in 2010, the Royal Bank of Canada was expected to pay $1.87 billion in bonuses, up from $1.7 billion a year earlier.[36]

With **pay for performance** (or **variable pay**) schemes, managers are rewarded for especially productive output—for producing earnings that significantly exceed the cost of bonuses. Such incentives go to middle managers on the basis of company-wide performance, business-unit performance, personal record, or all three factors. Eligible managers must often forgo merit or entitlement raises (increases for staying on and reporting to work every day), but many firms say that variable pay is a better motivator because the range between generous and mediocre merit raises is usually quite small.

TEAM AND GROUP INCENTIVES

Some incentive programs apply to all the employees in a firm. Under **profit-sharing plans**, profits earned above a certain level are distributed to employees. At the Great Little Box Company in Richmond, B.C., 15 percent of company profits are split evenly among staff. The company also has an "open book" policy of providing financial information to employees so they can relate financial performance of the company to their share of the profits.[37]

Gainsharing plans distribute bonuses to employees when a company's costs are reduced through greater work efficiency. **Pay-for-knowledge plans** encourage workers to learn new skills and to become proficient at different jobs. These workers receive additional pay for each new skill or job they master.

PIECE-RATE INCENTIVE PLAN A compensation system in which an organization pays an employee a certain amount of money for every unit produced.

BONUS Individual performance incentive in the form of a special payment made over and above the employee's salary.

PAY FOR PERFORMANCE (VARIABLE PAY) Individual incentive that rewards a manager for especially productive output.

PROFIT-SHARING PLANS An incentive program in which employees receive a bonus depending on the firm's profits.

GAINSHARING PLANS An incentive program in which employees receive a bonus if the firm's costs are reduced because of greater worker efficiency and/or productivity.

PAY-FOR-KNOWLEDGE PLANS Incentive plan to encourage employees to learn new skills or become proficient at different jobs.

BENEFITS What a firm offers its workers other than wages and salaries in return for their labour.

PROTECTION PLANS A plan that protects employees when their income is threatened or reduced by illness, disability, death, unemployment, or retirement.

EMPLOYMENT INSURANCE A protection plan that provides a basic subsistence payment to employees who are between jobs.

CANADA PENSION PLAN A plan that provides income to retired individuals through employee and employer taxes that are withheld from payroll.

WORKERS' COMPENSATION Mandated insurance that covers individuals who suffer a job-related illness or accident.

Benefits

Benefits are rewards, incentives, and other things of value that an organization gives to employees in addition to wages, salaries, and other forms of direct financial compensation. Because these benefits have tangible value, they represent a meaningful form of compensation even though they are not generally expressed in financial terms. According to a PricewaterhouseCoopers survey, some of the top benefits sought, other than money, were gift cards, extra vacation days, and being fast-tracked for promotion.[38]

MANDATED PROTECTION PLANS

Protection plans assist employees when their income is threatened or reduced by illness, disability, unemployment, or retirement. **Employment insurance** provides a basic subsistence payment to employees who are unemployed but are actively seeking employment. Both employers and employees pay premiums to an employment insurance fund. The 2012 premium rate cannot exceed $1.83 per $100 of insurable earnings.[39] Employment Insurance also covers maternity leave of 55 percent of a new mother's annual earnings (to a maximum of $44 200).[40]

The **Canada Pension Plan** provides income for retired individuals to help them supplement their personal savings, private pensions, part-time work, etc. It is funded through employee and employer taxes that are withheld from payroll.

Workers' compensation is mandated insurance that covers individuals who suffer a job-related illness or accident. Employers bear the cost of workers' compensation insurance. The premium is related to each employer's past experience with job-related accidents and illnesses. For example, a steel company might pay $20 per $100 of wages, while an accounting firm might pay only $0.10 per $100 of wages.

OPTIONAL PROTECTION PLANS

Health insurance is the most important type of coverage, and has expanded in recent years to include vision care, mental health services, dental care, and prescription drugs. Employee prescription drug plan costs are doubling about every five years, and companies are increasingly concerned about their ability to offer this kind of coverage.[41] Pension liabilities are also a problem.

PAID TIME OFF

Paid vacations are usually for periods of one, two, or more weeks. Most organizations vary the amount of paid vacation with an individual's seniority, but some companies are reducing the time required to qualify for paid vacations. At Carlson Wagonlit Travel Canada, employees get four weeks of paid vacation after working at the company for just five years. Formerly, 10 years of service was required.[42]

Another common paid time-off plan is sick leave, which is provided when an individual is sick or otherwise physically unable to perform his or her job. Sometimes an organization will allow an employee to take off a small number of days simply for "personal business." The Catholic Children's Aid Society provides its child protection workers with time off when they need it because they routinely face high-stress situations.[43]

OTHER TYPES OF BENEFITS

In addition to protection plans and paid time off, many organizations offer a number of other benefit programs. **Wellness programs**, for example, concentrate on preventing illness in employees rather than simply paying their expenses when they become sick. **Cafeteria-style benefit plans** allow employees to choose the benefits they really want. The organization typically establishes a budget, indicating how much it is willing to spend, per employee, on benefits. Employees are then presented with a list of possible benefits and the cost of each. They are free to put the benefits together in any combination they wish.

WELLNESS PROGRAMS A program that concentrates on preventing illness in employees rather than simply paying their expenses when they become sick.

CAFETERIA-STYLE BENEFIT PLANS A flexible approach to providing benefits in which employees are allocated a certain sum to cover benefits and can "spend" this allocation on the specific benefits they prefer.

LO-5 THE LEGAL CONTEXT OF HRM

HRM is influenced by federal and provincial law, so managers must be aware of the most important and far-reaching areas of HR regulation. These include *equal employment opportunity*, *comparable worth*, *sexual harassment*, *employee health and safety*, and *retirement*.

Equal Employment Opportunity

The basic goal of all **equal employment opportunity regulations** is to protect people from unfair or inappropriate discrimination in the workplace. Note that differentiating between employees—for example, giving one person a raise and denying the raise to another person—is not illegal. As long as the basis for this distinction is purely job related (e.g., based on performance or qualifications) and is applied objectively and consistently, the action is legal and appropriate. Problems arise when distinctions among people are not job related. In such cases, the resulting discrimination is illegal.

ANTI-DISCRIMINATION LAWS

The key federal anti-discrimination legislation is the **Canadian Human Rights Act** of 1977 (each province has also enacted human rights legislation). The goal of the Act is to ensure that any individual who wishes to obtain a job has an equal opportunity. The Act applies to all federal agencies, federal Crown corporations, any employee of the federal government, and business firms that do business inter-provincially. The Act prohibits a wide variety of practices in recruiting, selecting, promoting, and dismissing personnel. It specifically prohibits discrimination on the basis of age, race and colour, national and ethnic origin, physical handicap, religion, gender, marital status, or prison record (if pardoned). Some exceptions to these blanket prohibitions are permitted. Discrimination cannot be charged if a blind person is refused a position as a bus driver or crane operator. Likewise, a firm cannot be charged with discrimination if it does not hire a deaf person as an audio engineer.

Difficulties in determining whether discrimination has occurred are sometimes dealt with by using the concept of **bona fide occupational requirement**. That is, an employer may choose one person over another based on overriding characteristics of the job in question. If a fitness centre wants to hire only women to supervise its women's locker room and sauna, it can do so without being discriminatory because it established a bona fide occupational requirement.

Enforcement of the Human Rights Act is carried out by the Canadian Human Rights Commission. The commission can either respond to complaints from individuals who believe they have been discriminated against or launch an investigation on its own if it has reason to believe that discrimination has occurred. If a claim of discrimination is substantiated, the offending organization or individual may be ordered to compensate the victim.

The **Employment Equity Act of 1986** addresses the issue of discrimination in employment by designating four groups as employment-disadvantaged—women, visible minorities, Aboriginal people, and people with disabilities. These four groups contain six of every ten individuals in the Canadian workforce, and it is estimated that their underemployment costs the Canadian economy around $50 billion each year.[44] Companies covered by the Employment Equity Act are required to publish statistics on their employment of people in the four designated groups. In 2010, the Royal Bank of Canada received an award from Catalyst recognizing the bank's success in promoting diversity. For example, women at RBC now occupy nearly 40 percent of executive roles in the company, and this figure is growing.[45]

EQUAL EMPLOYMENT OPPORTUNITY REGULATIONS Regulations to protect people from unfair or inappropriate discrimination in the workplace.

CANADIAN HUMAN RIGHTS ACT Ensures that any individual who wishes to obtain a job has an equal opportunity to apply for it.

BONA FIDE OCCUPATIONAL REQUIREMENT When an employer may choose one applicant over another based on overriding characteristics of the job.

EMPLOYMENT EQUITY ACT OF 1986 Federal legislation that designates four groups as employment disadvantaged—women, visible minorities, Aboriginal people, and people with disabilities.

COMPARABLE WORTH A legal concept that aims to pay equal wages for work of equal value.

Comparable Worth

Comparable worth is a legal concept that aims at paying equal wages for jobs that are of comparable value to the employer. This might mean comparing dissimilar jobs, such as those of secretaries and mechanics or nurses and electricians. Proponents of comparable worth say that all the jobs in a company must be evaluated and then rated in terms of basic dimensions such as the level of skill they require. All jobs could then be compared based on a common index. People in different jobs that rate the same on this index would be paid the same. Experts hope that this will help to reduce the gap between men's and women's pay. In a long-standing comparable worth dis-

© Deklofenak/Fotolia

© vectorlib.com/Fotolia

^^ The idea behind comparable worth is to pay equal wages for jobs that are of comparable value to the employer. This may require a comparison of jobs that are quite different.

pute, the Supreme Court of Canada ruled that flight attendants at Air Canada—who have been trying for years to achieve pay equity with male-dominated groups of employees—could compare their pay with the pay of ground crews and pilots because all these employees work for the same company.[46]

Critics of comparable worth object on the grounds that it ignores the supply and demand aspects of labour. They say that legislation forcing a company to pay people more than the open market price for their labour (which may happen in jobs where there is a surplus of workers) is another example of unreasonable government interference in business activities. They also say that implementing comparable worth will cost business firms too much money.

Sexual Harassment

Within the job context, **sexual harassment** refers to requests for sexual favours, unwelcome sexual advances, or verbal or physical conduct of a sexual nature that creates an intimidating or hostile environment for a given employee. The Canadian Human Rights Act takes precedence over any policies that a company might have developed on its own to deal with sexual harassment problems.

Quid pro quo harassment is the most blatant form of sexual harassment. It occurs when the harasser offers to exchange something of value—for example, a promotion—for sexual favours. The creation of a **hostile work environment** is a subtler form of sexual harassment. For example, a group of male employees who continually make off-colour jokes may create a hostile work environment for female employees. Other situations are harder to assess. In 2010, for example, Debrahlee Lorenzana sued Citibank, claiming that she was fired because she dressed too provocatively and was, therefore, a workplace distraction. But some of her co-workers said she was just an attention-seeking gold digger who was simply fired for poor performance.[47] In 2012, she dropped her lawsuit against the company and did not receive any money.[48]

Regardless of the details of a particular case, the same strict rules apply—sexual harassment is illegal, and the organization is responsible for controlling it. If a manager is found guilty of sexual harassment, the company is liable because the manager is an agent of the company.

Employee Safety and Health

Employee health and safety programs help to reduce absenteeism and turnover, raise productivity, and boost morale by making jobs safer and more healthful. In Canada, each province has developed its own workplace health and safety regulations. The Ontario Occupational Health and Safety Act illustrates current legislation in Canada. It requires all employers to ensure that equipment and safety devices are used properly. Employers must also show workers the proper way to operate machinery. At the job site, supervisors are charged with the responsibility of ensuring that workers use equipment properly. The Act also requires workers to behave appropriately on the job. Employees have the right to refuse to work on a job if they believe it is unsafe; a legal procedure exists for resolving any disputes in this area. In most provinces, the Ministry of Labour appoints inspectors to enforce health and safety regulations.

SEXUAL HARASSMENT Requests for sexual favours, unwelcome sexual advances, or verbal or physical conduct of a sexual nature that creates an intimidating or hostile environment for a given employee.

QUID PRO QUO HARASSMENT Form of sexual harassment in which sexual favours are requested in return for job-related benefits.

HOSTILE WORK ENVIRONMENT Form of sexual harassment deriving from off-colour jokes, lewd comments, and so forth.

If the inspector finds a sufficient hazard, he or she has the authority to clear the workplace. Inspectors can usually arrive at a firm unannounced to conduct an inspection.

Some industrial work—logging, construction, fishing, and mining—can put workers at risk of injury in obvious ways. But other types of work—such as typing or lifting—can also cause painful injuries. **Repetitive strain injuries (RSIs)** occur when workers perform the same functions over and over again. These injuries disable more than 200 000 Canadians each year and account for nearly half of all work-related lost-time claims.

REPETITIVE STRAIN INJURY (RSI) An injury that occurs when a worker performs the same functions over and over again.

Retirement

Until the 1990s, Canadian courts generally upheld 65 as the mandatory retirement age, but most Canadian provinces have now abolished mandatory retirement. New rules took effect in December 2012 abolishing mandatory retirement at federally regulated employers like Air Canada.[49] In spite of changes like these, workers are actually retiring earlier than they used to. In the late 1970s, the average retirement age in Canada was 65, but, by 2009, it had dropped to 62.[50] A Statistics Canada study showed that "boomer" couples are unlikely to retire at the same time, with the woman often staying in the workforce longer than her husband.[51] Some managers fear that the abolition of mandatory retirement will allow less productive employees to remain at work after age 65, but research shows that the employees who stay on the job past 65 are usually the most productive ones. But there are two other interesting facts that should not be ignored: workers over age 65 are nearly four times as likely to die from work-related causes as younger workers, and older workers have double the health-care costs of workers in their forties.[52]

Concerns have been expressed that Canadians who will be retiring in the future will not have enough income to meet their expenses. In response, the federal Pooled Registered Pension Plan Act became law in 2012. It allows individuals to contribute to a defined contribution pension plan even if their employer does not offer a pension plan.

LO-6 NEW CHALLENGES IN THE CHANGING WORKPLACE

As we have seen throughout this chapter, HR managers face various challenges in their efforts to keep their organizations staffed with effective workers. To complicate matters, new challenges arise as the economic and social environments of business change. Several of the most important HRM issues facing business today are managing workforce diversity, managing knowledge workers, and managing contingent and temporary workers.

Managing Workforce Diversity

One extremely important set of human resource challenges centres on **workforce diversity**—the range of workers' attitudes, values, beliefs, and behaviours that differ by gender, race, age, ethnicity, physical ability, and other characteristics. The situation for visible minorities is currently one of the most publicized aspects of diversity. Consider these facts:

- By 2015, 20 percent of Saskatchewan's population will be Aboriginal.
- In 2001, approximately 4 million Canadians were visible minorities; by 2017, that number could increase to as much as 8.5 million.
- Visible minorities currently make up more than 40 percent of the population of Vancouver.
- By 2017, visible minorities will form more than 50 percent of the populations of Toronto and Vancouver.
- By 2017, 22 percent of the total Canadian population will be visible minorities.[53]

Many Canadian companies are actively pursuing the management of diversity. At Procter & Gamble Canada, employees come from 40 different countries and speak at least 30 different languages. Diversity is recognized through "affinity groups," such as the Women's Leadership Council, the French Canadian Network, the Asian Professional Network, the Christian Network, and the Jewish Network. The goal of these networks is to help employees feel comfortable about participating in corporate life and to act as a resource for employees who want insights about how to target specific markets.[54]

Western Union hires people who speak the language of their target market (individuals who want to send money back to relatives in their home country) and who know what it feels like to be an immigrant in Canada. This approach has yielded some interesting activities. In one area of Toronto, for example, customers who wanted to transfer money back to their family in the Philippines got a free loaf of Pan de Sal bread from a local Filipino baker.[55]

At the Royal Bank of Canada, the Diversity Leadership Council (DLC)—which is chaired by CEO Gordon Nixon—developed the RBC Diversity Blueprint, a three-year plan to support diversity within the company and in the external marketplace and community it serves.[56]

All of these examples demonstrate that organizations are increasingly recognizing that diversity can be a competitive advantage. By hiring the best people available from every group—rather than hiring from just one or a few groups—a firm can develop a higher-quality workforce. A diverse workforce can bring a wider array of information to bear on problems and can provide insights on marketing products to a wider range of consumers.

Managing Knowledge Workers

Traditionally, employees added value to organizations because of what they did or because of their experience. In the "information age," however, many employees add value because of what they know.[57]

WORKFORCE DIVERSITY The range of workers' attitudes, values, beliefs, and behaviours that differ by gender, race, age, ethnicity, physical ability, and other relevant characteristics.

THE NATURE OF KNOWLEDGE WORK

These employees are usually called **knowledge workers**, and the skill with which they are managed is a major factor in determining which firms will be successful in the future. Knowledge workers, including computer scientists, engineers, and physical scientists, provide special challenges for the HR manager. They tend to work for high-tech firms and are usually experts in some abstract knowledge base. They often prefer to work independently and tend to identify more strongly with their profession than with the organization that pays them—even to the extent of defining performance in terms recognized by other members of their profession.

As the importance of information-driven jobs grows, the need for knowledge workers increases. But these employees require extensive and highly specialized training, and not every organization is willing to make the human capital investments necessary to take advantage of these employees. Even after knowledge workers are on the job, training updates are critical to prevent their skills from becoming obsolete. The failure to update such skills not only results in the loss of competitive advantage, but it also increases the likelihood that knowledge workers will move to another firm that is more committed to updating their knowledge.

KNOWLEDGE WORKER MANAGEMENT AND LABOUR MARKETS

Organizations that need knowledge workers must introduce regular market adjustments (upward) to pay them enough to keep them. This is especially critical in areas in which demand is growing, as even entry-level salaries for these employees are skyrocketing. Once an employee accepts a job with a firm, the employer faces yet another dilemma. Once hired, workers are subject to the company's internal labour market, which is not likely to be growing as quickly as the external market for knowledge workers as a whole. Consequently, the longer knowledge workers remain with a firm, the further behind the market their pay falls—unless it is regularly adjusted upward.

Managing Contingent Workers

A contingent worker is one who works for an organization on something other than a permanent or full-time basis. Categories of contingent workers include part-time workers, independent contractors (freelancers), on-call workers, temporary employees (usually hired through outside "temp" agencies), contract workers, and guest workers (foreigners working in Canada for a limited time).

TRENDS IN CONTINGENT EMPLOYMENT

Contingent employment is on the rise in Canada. Part-time employment in all categories was 7.75 percent higher in 2011 than in 2007.[58] In Canada, there is increasing demand for temporary workers in top management because the economic downturn has created a lot of turnover in this area. These "temps at the top" usually stay for a year or less until a permanent person is found.[59]

KNOWLEDGE WORKERS Workers who are experts in specific fields like computer technology and engineering, and who add value because of what they know, rather than how long they have worked or the job they do.

The number of guest workers in Canada—one category of contingent workers—is increasing. They work in all kinds of industries, including agriculture, manufacturing, and services. Each year there are over 150 000 guest workers in Canada. The number is predicted to rise in the future.[60]

MANAGEMENT OF CONTINGENT WORKERS

The effective management of contingent workers requires consideration of three issues. First, careful planning must be done so the organization brings in contingent workers only when they are actually needed and in the quantity needed to complete necessary tasks. Second, the costs and benefits of using contingent workers must be understood. Many firms bring in contingent workers in order to reduce labour costs, but if contingent workers are less productive than permanent workers, there may be no gain for the organization. Third, contingent workers should be integrated into the mainstream activities of the organization as much as possible. This involves deciding how they will be treated relative to permanent workers. For example, should contingent workers be invited to the company holiday party? Should they have the same access to employee benefits? Managers must develop a strategy for integrating contingent workers according to some sound logic and then follow that strategy consistently over time.[61]

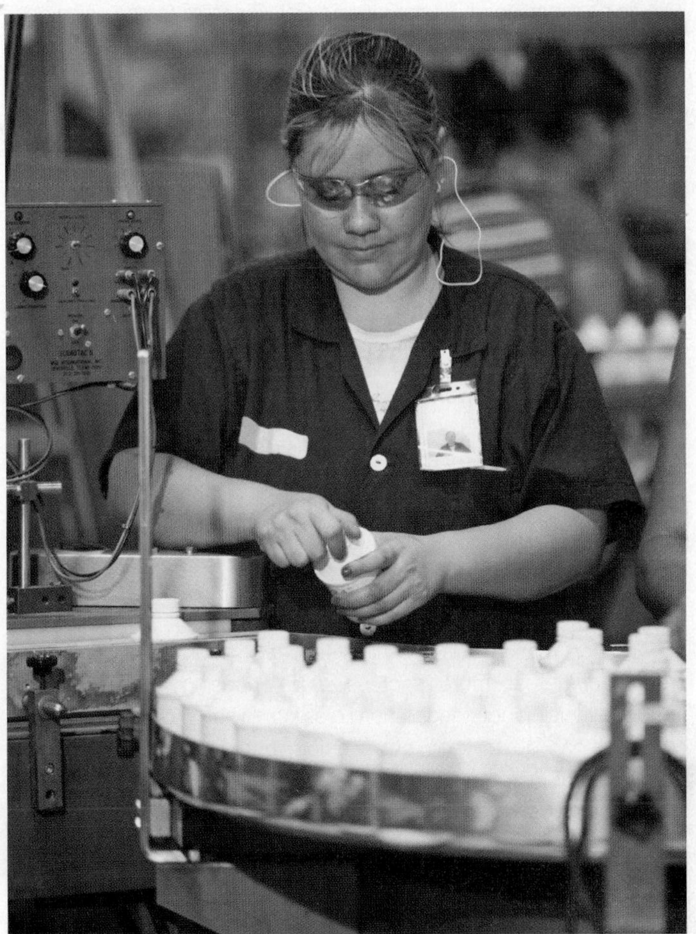

Organizations are increasingly using contingent workers. This allows human resource managers both scheduling flexibility and the opportunity to try out potential permanent employees.

© V. Yakobchuk/Fotolia

LO-7 DEALING WITH ORGANIZED LABOUR

A **labour union** is a group of individuals working together to achieve shared job-related goals, such as higher pay, shorter working hours, greater benefits, or better working conditions.[62] Labour unions grew in popularity in Canada in the nineteenth and early twentieth centuries. At that time, work hours were long, pay was minimal, and working conditions were often unsafe. Workers had no job security and received few benefits. Many companies employed large numbers of children and paid them poverty-level wages. If people complained, they were fired.

Unions forced management to listen to the complaints of all workers rather than to just those few who were brave enough to speak out. Thus, the power of unions comes from collective action. **Collective bargaining** is the process by which union leaders and company management negotiate terms and conditions of employment for those workers represented by unions. We discuss the role of collective bargaining in detail below.

Unionism Today

Although 4.3 million workers belonged to unions in 2011, union membership as a proportion of the non-agricultural workforce (called *union density*) has stagnated, and less than one-third of Canadian workers belong to unions. Union density varies widely across countries. In Canada, union density is about 30 percent; in the U.S., 11 percent; in France, 9 percent; and in Sweden, 82 percent.[63]

The highest rates of unionization are found in Newfoundland and Labrador (37.7 percent) and Quebec (37.5 percent). The lowest rates are found in Alberta (23.0 percent) and New Brunswick (26.4 percent). The public sector is quite heavily unionized (72.7 percent), but the private sector is not (18.1 percent).[64] In some occupations, like teaching and nursing, over 80 percent of workers are unionized. In other occupations, like management and food and beverage services, less than 10 percent of workers belong to unions.[65]

Many years ago, unions routinely won certification votes. But in recent years, they have had less success. One reason is that today's workforce is increasingly diverse. Women and ethnic minorities have weaker traditions of union affiliation than white males (who dominated the blue-collar jobs in the past). The workforce is also increasingly employed in the service sector, which traditionally has been less heavily unionized.

Another reason for declining unionization is that companies have become far more aggressive in opposing unions. Federal and provincial labour legislation restricts what management of a company can do to keep out a union, but companies are free to pursue certain strategies to minimize unionization, such as creating a more employee-friendly work environment. For example, Japanese manufacturers who have set up shop in North America have avoided unionization efforts by the United Auto Workers (UAW) by providing job security, higher wages, and a work environment in which employees are allowed to participate and be actively involved in plant management.

LABOUR UNION A group of individuals who work together to achieve shared job-related goals.

COLLECTIVE BARGAINING The process through which union leaders and management personnel negotiate common terms and conditions of employment for those workers represented by the union.

TRENDS IN UNION–MANAGEMENT RELATIONS

The problems that have been experienced by unions have caused some significant changes in union–management relations. Not so long ago, most union–management bargaining was very adversarial, with unions making demands for dramatic improvements in wages, benefits, and job security. But with organizational downsizing and a decade of low inflation in Canada, many unions today find themselves able to achieve only modest improvements in wages and benefits. A common goal of union strategy is, therefore, to preserve what has already been won. For example, unions are well aware that companies have an incentive to relocate jobs to lower-wage foreign countries, so unions have to work hard to keep jobs in Canada and thus maintain job security for members.

Today, unions must cooperate with employers if both companies and unions are to survive and prosper. The goal is to create win-win partnerships in which managers and workers share the same goals: profitability, growth, and effectiveness, with equitable rewards for everyone. Even in those sectors of the economy where unions remain quite strong—most notably in the automobile and steel industries—unions have changed their tactics. In the automobile industry, Buzz Hargrove, former president of the Canadian Auto Workers, has urged members of the union bargaining team to come up with new ideas for improving quality and productivity so that Canadian factories will be more attractive for new investment.[66]

The Future of Unions

Unions face some serious challenges. In the *private sector*, companies have become much more aggressive when negotiating with unions. For example, in 2012, Electro-Motive Canada moved production from its London, Ontario, plant to the U.S. when workers wouldn't agree to a 50 percent wage cut.[67] In the *public sector*, the federal and provincial governments are looking for ways to save money because of large budget deficits, so there will be pressure to hold the line on wages and benefits. The boxed insert entitled "Public Sector Unions" describes some interesting developments in public sector unionism.

Unions are facing other challenges as well: the decline of the so-called "smokestack industries" (where union power was formerly very strong), the globalization of business (which has caused the movement of jobs to areas of the world with lower labour costs), and technological change (which often reduces the number of workers that are needed). Unions are responding to these challenges in a variety of ways. For example, in 2012, two of Canada's largest unions—the Canadian Auto Workers and the Communications, Energy and Paperworkers—held merger talks.[68]

MANAGING IN TURBULENT TIMES

Public Sector Unions

In 2011, there was a showdown between public-sector unions and the state of Wisconsin when governor Scott Walker introduced a bill that proposed to end collective bargaining for state workers (except for base wage rates), required unions to hold recertification votes annually, and curtailed the practice of withholding union dues from employee paycheques. Despite noisy protests by state workers, the bill passed. Other U.S. states—Ohio, Michigan, and Indiana—were also considering changes to their labour legislation.

Are these developments relevant for Canadian labour unions? Some observers say "no," because Canadian society has a more favourable view of unions (for example, 71 percent of public-sector workers are unionized in Canada, but only 37 percent are in the U.S.). They note that when the province of B.C. tried to throw out a collective agreement with health-care workers in order to save money, the Supreme Court of Canada ruled that collective bargaining in the public sector is a constitutional right. But other experts say the U.S. developments are relevant and point out that unionization rates in northern U.S. states are similar to those in Ontario, and much lower in the southern states. In other words, the real dividing line is not the Canadian-U.S. border, but the Mason-Dixon line (the line often viewed as separating the "northern" and "southern" cultures in the U.S.). Even some union officials are concerned. For example, Mark Ferguson, president of a Toronto branch of the Canadian Union of Public Employees, says that the public hates unions. And Ken Georgetti, president of the Canadian Labour Congress, says that unions are increasingly seen as "out for themselves" and no longer have the respect of the general public in Canada.

Critics of unions say that taxpayers are increasingly unhappy with what they perceive to be the "rich" compensation and benefits that are available to public-sector workers. For example, federal workers usually have a defined benefit pension that, after 35 years, pays 70 percent of the worker's highest five-year earning average. By contrast, in the private sector, two-thirds of workers don't even have a pension. Pressure is already being put on Canadian public sector unions. In Toronto, there is a move to privatize garbage collection to reduce costs and to avoid problems like the 39-day strike of garbage collectors a few years ago. Also, the provincial premier is trying to push through legislation that takes away the right to strike from Toronto transit workers. Attempts are being made in Saskatchewan to "rebalance" the ratio between unionized and non-unionized government workers, and Quebec wants to reduce pension payments to public-sector retirees.

CRITICAL THINKING QUESTIONS

1. Will the pressures that are being put on public-sector unions in the U.S. also develop in Canada? Support your conclusion.
2. Consider the following statement: *The rich benefits that members of public-sector unions receive must be reduced. It is not fair that public sector workers are given pensions that are so much better than private-sector workers.* Do you agree or disagree with the statement? Defend your answer.

LO-8 THE LEGAL ENVIRONMENT FOR UNIONS IN CANADA

CONSTITUTION ACT Divided authority over labour regulations between the federal and provincial governments.

Political and legal barriers to collective bargaining existed until well into the twentieth century (see Table 8.1). Courts held that some unions were conspirators in restraint of trade. Employers viewed their employees' efforts to unionize as attempts to deprive the employers of their private property. The employment contract, employers contended, was between the individual worker and the employer—not between the employer and employees as a group. The balance of bargaining power was very much in favour of the employer.

The employer–employee relationship became much less direct as firms grew in size. Managers were themselves employees, and hired managers dealt with other employees. Communication among owners, managers, and workers became more formalized. Big business had more power than workers. Because of mounting public concern, laws were passed to place workers on a more even footing with employers.

The **Constitution Act** (originally the BNA Act), passed in 1867, has also affected labour legislation. This Act allocated certain activities to the

TABLE 8.1 Key Canadian Labour Legislation

Date	Legislation	Accomplishments/Goals
1900	Conciliation Act	• designed to help settle labour disputes through voluntary conciliation • first step in creating more favourable labour conditions
1907	Industrial Disputes Investigation Act	• compulsory investigation of labour disputes by a government-appointed board before any strike action (found to violate a provision of the British North America [BNA] Act)
1943	Privy Council Order 1003	• recognized the right of employees to bargain collectively • prohibited unfair management labour practices • established a labour board to certify bargaining authority • prohibited strikes and lockouts (except in collective bargaining agreements [CBAs])

federal government (e.g., labour legislation for companies operating interprovincially) and others to individual provinces (labour relations regulations in general). Thus, labour legislation comes from both the federal and provincial governments, but is basically a provincial matter. That is why certain groups of similar employees might be allowed to go on strike in one province but not in another.

Federal Legislation—The Canada Labour Code

The **Canada Labour Code** is a comprehensive piece of legislation that applies to the labour practices of firms operating under the legislative authority of parliament. In 2005, a sweeping review of the Canada Labour Code was announced by the federal Minister of Labour. One of the issues that the review will focus on is whether managers and supervisors should also be protected by labour code restrictions on the number of hours they work each week, and whether they should receive overtime pay. The issue came to the forefront after the Manitoba Labour Board ruled that Sharon Michalowski, a manager at Nygard International, was entitled to overtime pay, even though she was a manager and had signed a contract stipulating that she would work whatever hours were required to earn her annual salary of $42 000.[69] Managers are still not covered by the provisions of the Canada Labour Code.

The Canada Labour Code has four main sections: fair employment practices; standard hours, wages, vacations, and holidays; safety of employees; and Canada industrial relations regulations.

FAIR EMPLOYMENT PRACTICES

This section prohibits an employer from either refusing employment on the basis of a person's race or religion or using an employment agency that discriminates against people on the basis of their race or religion. These prohibitions apply to trade unions as well, but not to non-profit, charitable, and philanthropic organizations. Any individual who believes a violation has occurred may make a complaint in writing to Labour Canada. The allegation will then be investigated and, if necessary, an Industrial Inquiry Commission will be appointed to make a recommendation in the case. Since 1982, fair employment practices have been covered by the Canadian Human Rights Act; they are also covered by the Canadian Charter of Rights and Freedoms.

STANDARD HOURS, WAGES, VACATIONS, AND HOLIDAYS

This section deals with a wide variety of mechanical issues such as standard hours of work (8-hour day and 40-hour week), maximum hours of work per week (48), overtime pay (at least one and a half times the regular pay), minimum wages, equal wages for men and women doing the same jobs, vacations, general holidays, and parental leave. The specific provisions are changed frequently to take into account changes in the economic and social structure of Canada, but their basic goal is to ensure consistent treatment of employees in these areas.

SAFETY OF EMPLOYEES

This section requires that every person running a federal work project do so in a way that will not endanger the health or safety of any employee. It also requires that safety procedures and techniques be implemented to reduce the risk of employment injury. This section requires employees to exercise care to ensure their own safety; however, even if it can be shown that the employee did not exercise proper care, compensation must still be paid. This section also makes provisions for a safety officer whose duty is to assure that the provisions of the code are fulfilled. The safety officer has the right to enter any federal project "at any reasonable time."

CANADA INDUSTRIAL RELATIONS REGULATIONS

The final major section of the Canada Labour Code deals with all matters related to collective bargaining.

Provincial Labour Legislation

Each province has enacted legislation to deal with the personnel practices covered in the Canada Labour Code. These laws vary across provinces and are frequently revised; however, their basic approach and substance is the same as in the Canada Labour Code. Certain provinces may exceed the minimum code requirements on some issues (e.g., minimum wage).

Union Organizing Strategy

A union might try to organize workers when some workers in a firm are members and the union wants to represent other workers, or when it is attempting to outdo a rival union, or when it wants to increase the number of workers who belong to the union. The Canadian Auto Workers (CAW) union, for example, is trying to offset the loss of thousands of jobs in the automobile industry. In 2013, the CAW launched a drive to unionize 7000 workers at two Toyota assembly plants in Ontario.[70] The United Food and Commercial Workers (UFCW) union has also been active as it tries to organize workers in several companies, including Holt Renfrew & Co., Walmart, and Loblaw Cos. Ltd. In 2012, the UFCW tried to become the sole bargaining agent for workers at Holt Renfrew & Co., but workers voted against joining the union.[71]

Management often becomes aware of a union organizing effort through gossip on the company grapevine. When management discovers that an organizing drive is underway, it may try to counteract it. However, management must know what it can legally do to discourage the union. Each province has somewhat different rules for certifying unions as representatives of employees. For example, suppose that a union is trying to organize employees of a Manitoba company. If the union can show that at least 50 percent of the employees are members of the union, it can apply to the Manitoba Labour Board (MLB) for certification as the sole bargaining agent for the employees. During the process, there may be an issue regarding the right of different types of workers to join or not join the union. For example, supervisors may or may not be included in a bargaining unit along with non-management workers. The **bargaining unit** includes those individuals deemed appropriate by the province, and the MLB has final authority in determining the appropriateness of the bargaining unit. Once the MLB has determined that the unit is appropriate, it may order a **certification vote**. If a majority of those voting are in favour of the union, it is certified as the sole bargaining agent for the unit.

CANADA LABOUR CODE Legislation that applies to the labour practices of firms operating under the legislative authority of parliament.

BARGAINING UNIT Individuals grouped together for purposes of collective bargaining.

CERTIFICATION VOTE A vote supervised by a government representative to determine whether a union will be certified as the sole bargaining agent for the unit.

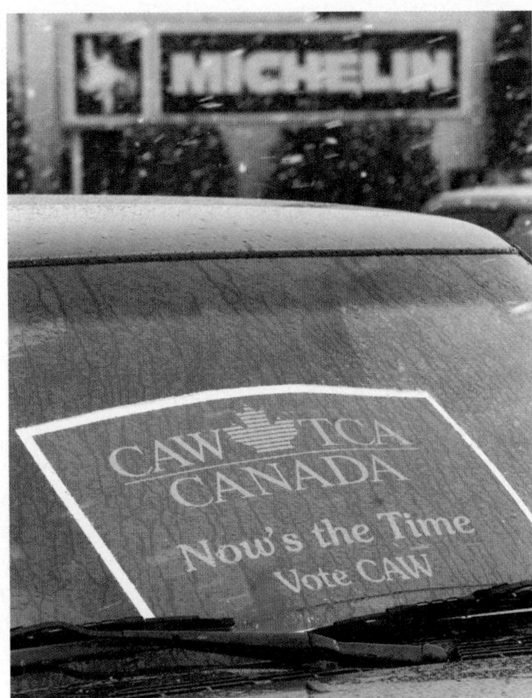

<<< The outcome of this certification vote will determine whether these workers at Michelin will be represented by the CAW.

AP Photo/Mary Altaffer

The same law that grants employees the right to unionize also allows them to cease being represented by a union. **Decertification** is the process by which employees legally terminate their union's right to represent them. This happened during a labour dispute over job security and safety that arose at Goldcorp Inc.'s mine near Red Lake, Ontario, which led to a strike involving 100 workers. The strike was settled when workers agreed to decertify their union in return for severance pay that was four times the rate mandated by Ontario law.[72]

Union Security

The greatest union security exists in the **closed shop**, where an employer can hire only union members. For example, a plumbing or electrical contractor who hires workers through a union hiring hall can hire only union members. In a **union shop**, an employer may hire non-union workers even if the employer's current employees are unionized. But newly hired workers must join the union within a stipulated period of time (usually 30 days). In an **agency shop**, all employees for whom the union bargains must pay union dues, but they need not join the union. In an **open shop**, an employer may hire union and/or non-union labour. Employees need not join a union or pay dues to a union.

DECERTIFICATION The process by which employees legally terminate their union's right to represent them.

CLOSED SHOP An employer can hire only union members.

UNION SHOP An employer can hire non-unionized workers, but they must join the union within a certain period.

AGENCY SHOP All employees for whom the union bargains must pay dues, but they are not required to join the union.

OPEN SHOP An employer may hire union or non-union workers.

LO-9 COLLECTIVE BARGAINING

People often associate collective bargaining with the specific act of signing a contract between a union and a company or industry. In fact, collective bargaining is an ongoing process involving both the drafting and administration of the terms of a labour contract.

Reaching Agreement on the Contract's Terms

The collective bargaining process begins when the union is recognized as the exclusive negotiator for its members. The bargaining cycle begins when union leaders meet with management representatives to begin working on a new contract. By law, both parties must negotiate "in good faith." When each side has presented its demands, sessions focus on identifying the bargaining zone. This process is shown in Figure 8.3. For example, although an employer may initially offer no pay raise, it may expect that it may eventually have to grant a raise of up to 6 percent. Likewise, the union may initially demand a 10 percent pay raise while expecting to accept a raise as low as 4 percent. The bargaining zone, then, is a raise between 4 and 6 percent. Obviously, compromise is needed on both sides if agreement is to be reached. The new tentative agreement is then submitted for a ratification vote by union membership.

Contract Issues

Most of the issues in the labour contract arise from demands that unions make on behalf of their members. Issues that are typically most important to union negotiators include *compensation*, *benefits*, and *job security*. Certain management rights issues are also negotiated in most bargaining agreements.

COMPENSATION

The most common issue is compensation. Unions want their employees to earn higher wages immediately, so they try to convince management to

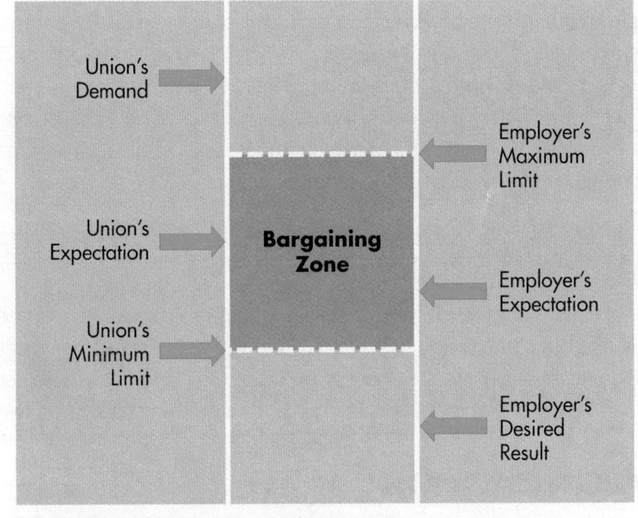

FIGURE 8.3 The bargaining zone

raise wages for all or some employees. Of equal concern to unions is future compensation that is to be paid during subsequent years of the contract. One common tool for securing wage increases is a **cost-of-living adjustment (COLA)**. Most COLA clauses tie future raises to the Consumer Price Index (CPI), a government statistic that reflects changes in consumer purchasing power. A **wage reopener clause**—which allows wage rates to be renegotiated at preset times during the life of the contract—is sometimes included in labour contracts where a union is uncomfortable with a long-term contract based solely on COLA wage increases.

BENEFITS

Benefits that are commonly addressed during negotiations include insurance, retirement benefits, paid holidays, working conditions, and the cost of supplementary health care (prescription drugs, eye care, dental care, etc.). The health-care issue is becoming increasingly contentious during negotiations because the cost of health care is rapidly increasing.

JOB SECURITY

In some cases, a contract may dictate that if the workforce is reduced, seniority will be used to determine which employees keep their jobs. Unions are also increasingly setting their sights on preserving jobs for workers in Canada in the face of business efforts to outsource production in some sectors to countries where labour costs are cheaper. For example, Gildan Activewear outsources much of its production to low-wage countries in the Caribbean.

OTHER UNION ISSUES

Other possible issues might include such specific details as working hours, overtime policies, rest periods, differential pay plans for shift employees, the use of temporary workers, grievance procedures, and allowable union activities (dues collection, union bulletin boards, etc.). In addition, some contracts are beginning to include formal mechanisms for greater worker input into management decisions.

MANAGEMENT RIGHTS

Management wants as much control as possible over hiring policies, work assignments, and so forth. Unions, meanwhile, often try to limit management rights by specifying hiring, assignment, and other policies. At one Chrysler plant the contract stipulates that three workers are needed to change fuses in robots: a machinist to open the robot, an electrician to change the fuse, and a supervisor to oversee the process. Such contracts often bar workers in one job category from performing work that falls within the domain of another. Unions try to secure jobs by defining as many different categories as possible (the Chrysler plant has over 100). Of course, management resists this practice, which limits flexibility and makes it difficult to reassign workers.

When Bargaining Fails

An impasse occurs when, after a series of bargaining sessions, management and labour are unable to agree on a first-time contract or a contract to replace an agreement that is about to expire. Both union and management may try various tactics to support their demands until the impasse is resolved.

UNION TACTICS

A **strike** occurs when employees temporarily walk off the job and refuse to work. In 2011, postal workers went on strike until they were forced back to work by government legislation. At Montreal-based Tembec Holdings, workers were on strike for three months before management and union negotiators were able to fashion a new collective agreement.[73] During a strike, unions may picket or launch a boycott. **Picketing** involves having workers march at the entrance to the company with signs explaining their reasons for striking. **Sympathy strikes** (also called **secondary strikes**) occur when one union strikes in sympathy with a strike initiated by another union. **Wildcat strikes**—those that are not authorized by the union or that occur during the life of a contract—deprive strikers of their status as employees and thus of the protection of labour laws. Air Canada ground crews engaged in a wildcat strike in 2012 which caused hundreds of flights to be delayed or cancelled.[74]

A **boycott** occurs when union members agree not to buy the products of the firm that employs them. Workers may also urge other consumers to shun their firm's products. In a **work slowdown**, workers perform their jobs at a much slower pace than normal. A variation is the "sickout," during which large numbers of workers call in sick. Sometimes a union is not permitted to strike. In 2011, for example, Air Canada flight attendants were not allowed to go on strike after the Labour Minister referred the dispute to the Labour Board.[75]

MANAGEMENT TACTICS

Management can also respond forcefully to an impasse. A **lockout** occurs when employers physically deny employees access to the workplace. Management might lock workers out if they fear that workers will damage expensive equipment. In 2012 in Quebec, Rio Tinto Alcan Inc. locked out 780 workers for six months when the union voted to go on strike.[76] As an alternative to a lockout, firms can hire temporary or permanent replacements (**strikebreakers**) for the absent employees. However, the use of replacement workers is illegal in Quebec and British Columbia.

Companies can also lessen the impact of unions by contracting out—to non-union contractors—a lot of assembly work they used to do themselves. This results in fewer union workers within the company.

COST-OF-LIVING ADJUSTMENT (COLA) A contract clause specifying that wages will increase automatically with the rate of inflation.

WAGE REOPENER CLAUSE A contract clause that allows wage rates to be renegotiated at preset times during the life of the contract.

STRIKE A tactic of labour unions in which members temporarily walk off the job and refuse to work, in order to win concessions from management.

PICKETING A tactic of labour unions in which members march at the entrance to the company with signs explaining their reasons for striking.

SYMPATHY STRIKE (OR SECONDARY STRIKE) When one union strikes in sympathy with a strike initiated by another union.

WILDCAT STRIKE A strike that is not authorized by the union or that occurs during the life of a contract.

BOYCOTT Union members agree not to buy the product of the firm that employs them.

WORK SLOWDOWN Workers perform their jobs at a much slower pace than normal.

LOCKOUT A tactic of management in which the firm physically denies employees access to the workplace to pressure workers to agree to the company's latest contract offer.

STRIKEBREAKER An individual hired by a firm to replace a worker on strike; a tactic of management in disputes with labour unions.

Companies can also join **employers' associations**—groups of companies that get together to plan strategies and exchange information about how to manage their relations with unions. The British Columbia Maritime Employers Association—which includes 67 companies that employ longshoremen in Vancouver and other seaports in B.C.—is an example of an employers' association. In extreme cases, management may simply close down a plant if an agreement cannot be reached with the union. For example, Maple Leaf Foods closed its Edmonton hog processing plant when the workers went on strike there. That cost 850 workers their jobs.

Conciliation, Mediation, and Arbitration

Rather than using their weapons on one another, labour and management can agree to call in a third party to help resolve a dispute. In **conciliation**, a neutral third party (the conciliator) helps the two sides clarify the issues that are separating them. The conciliator cannot impose a settlement on the disputing parties. In 2012, the Canadian Press asked the federal government to appoint a conciliator to help with negotiations with the Canadian Media Guild, whose contract expired at the end of 2011.[77]

In **mediation**, a neutral third party (the mediator) goes beyond conciliation and advises the disputing parties about specific steps they might take to reach a settlement. The mediator, however, cannot impose a settlement either. In 2012, when the Air Canada Pilots Association received support from its members for a strike, a mediator was appointed to assist in the negotiations between Air Canada and the union in the hope of reaching a negotiated settlement without a strike occurring.[78]

In **voluntary arbitration**, a neutral third party (the arbitrator) imposes a settlement on the disputing parties that have agreed to submit the dispute to outside judgment. In 2011, for example, a pension dispute between Air Canada and the Canadian Auto Workers was sent to an arbitrator for resolution. The arbitrator ruled in favour of the union's proposal for a hybrid pension plan that included elements of both defined benefit and defined contribution pension plans.[79] In some cases, arbitration is legally required to settle bargaining disputes. This **compulsory arbitration** is used to settle disputes between government and public employees such as firefighters and police officers.

EMPLOYERS' ASSOCIATIONS A group of companies that get together to plan strategies and exchange information about how to manage their relations with unions.

CONCILIATION A neutral third party helps the two sides clarify the issues that are separating them.

MEDIATION A method of settling a contract dispute in which a neutral third party is asked to hear arguments from both the union and management and offer a suggested resolution.

VOLUNTARY ARBITRATION A method of settling a contract dispute in which the union and management ask a neutral third party to hear their arguments and issue a binding resolution.

COMPULSORY ARBITRATION A method of settling a contract dispute in which the union and management are forced to explain their positions to a neutral third party, which issues a binding resolution.

MyBizLab

Visit the MyBizLab website. This online homework and tutorial system puts you in control of your own learning with study and practice tools directly correlated to this chapter's content.

SUMMARY OF LEARNING OBJECTIVES

LO-1 DEFINE *HUMAN RESOURCE MANAGEMENT*, DISCUSS ITS STRATEGIC SIGNIFICANCE, AND EXPLAIN HOW MANAGERS PLAN FOR HUMAN RESOURCES.

Human resource management, or *HRM*, is the set of organizational activities directed at attracting, developing, and maintaining an effective workforce. HRM plays a key strategic role in organizational performance. Planning for human resource needs entails several steps: (1) conducting a job analysis, (2) forecasting demand and supply, and (3) matching HR supply and demand.

LO-2 IDENTIFY THE ISSUES INVOLVED IN STAFFING A COMPANY, INCLUDING *INTERNAL* AND *EXTERNAL RECRUITING* AND *SELECTION*.

Recruiting is the process of attracting qualified people to apply for open jobs. *Internal recruiting* involves considering present employees for new jobs. It builds morale and rewards the best employees. *External recruiting* means attracting people from outside the organization. Key *selection techniques* include application forms, tests, and interviews. The techniques must be valid predictors of expected performance.

LO-3 DISCUSS DIFFERENT WAYS IN WHICH ORGANIZATIONS GO ABOUT DEVELOPING THE CAPABILITIES OF EMPLOYEES AND MANAGERS.

Nearly all employees undergo some initial *orientation* process. Many employees are also given the opportunity to acquire new skills through various *work-based* and/or *instructional-based programs*.

LO-4 DISCUSS THE IMPORTANCE OF *WAGES AND SALARIES*, *INCENTIVES*, AND *BENEFIT PROGRAMS* IN ATTRACTING AND KEEPING SKILLED WORKERS.

Wages and salaries, *incentives*, and *benefit packages* may all be parts of a company's *compensation program*. By providing competitive compensation levels, a business can attract and keep qualified personnel. *Incentive programs* can also motivate people to work more productively. *Indirect compensation* also plays a major role in effective and well-designed compensation systems.

LO-5 DESCRIBE SOME OF THE KEY LEGAL ISSUES INVOLVED IN HIRING, COMPENSATING, AND MANAGING WORKERS IN TODAY'S WORKPLACE.

Managers must obey a variety of federal and provincial laws in the areas of *equal opportunity* and *equal pay*, *sexual harassment*, and *comparable worth*. Firms are also required to provide employees with safe working environments, as per the guidelines of provincial occupational health and safety acts.

LO-6 DISCUSS *WORKFORCE DIVERSITY*, THE *MANAGEMENT OF KNOWLEDGE WORKERS*, AND THE USE OF *CONTINGENT* AND *TEMPORARY WORKERS* AS IMPORTANT CHANGES IN THE CONTEMPORARY WORKPLACE.

Workforce diversity refers to the range of workers' attitudes, values, beliefs, and behaviours that differ by gender, race, ethnicity, age, and physical ability. Many firms now see diversity as a source of competitive advantage and work actively to achieve diversity in their ranks. Additional challenges exist in *managing knowledge workers* (rapidly increasing salaries and high turnover). *Contingent workers* are hired to supplement an organization's permanent workforce. The use of contingent workers gives managers flexibility; also, these workers are usually not covered by employers' benefit programs—two reasons why their numbers are growing.

LO-7 TRACE THE EVOLUTION OF, AND DISCUSS TRENDS IN, *UNIONISM* IN CANADA.

The first unions were formed in the early nineteenth century in the Maritime provinces. Labour organizations sprang up and faded away during the nineteenth century and unions began to develop in the twentieth century. Since the mid-1970s, labour unions in Canada have had difficulty attracting new members. Membership as a percentage of total workforce has declined. Increasingly, unions recognize that they have lost significant power and that it is in everyone's best interests to work with management instead of against it.

LO-8 DESCRIBE THE *MAJOR LAWS GOVERNING UNIONISM*.

Privy Council Order 1003 gave unions the right to bargain collectively in Canada. *The Constitution Act of 1867* allows the federal government to pass labour legislation (e.g., the *Canada Labour Code*) for companies that operate inter-provincially, and allowed the provincial governments to pass legislation (e.g., the Ontario Labour Relations Act) for companies that operate in only one province.

LO-9 IDENTIFY THE STEPS IN THE *COLLECTIVE BARGAINING PROCESS*.

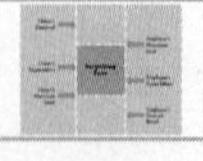

Once certified, the union engages in collective bargaining with the organization. The initial step is reaching agreement on a *labour contract*. Contract demands usually involve wages, job security, or management rights. Both labour and management have several tactics that can be used against the other if negotiations break down. Unions may attempt a *strike*, a *boycott*, or a *work slowdown*. Companies may hire *strikebreakers* or *lockout* workers. Sometimes *mediation* or *arbitration* may be used to settle disputes.

QUESTIONS AND EXERCISES

QUESTIONS FOR ANALYSIS

1. Why is the formal training of workers so important to most employers? Why don't employers simply let people learn about their jobs as they perform them?
2. Why is a good employee–job match important? Who benefits more, the organization or the employee? Explain your reasoning.
3. How is it possible for unemployment to be high while at the same time companies are complaining that they are having trouble hiring people?
4. Obtain a copy of an employment application. What are its strengths and weaknesses in terms of helping a company to decide whether to hire the applicant?

See >>> for Assisted-Graded Writing Assignment in MyBizLab

5. Why do you think the unionization rate in the public sector is so much higher than in the private sector? Do you think this will change in the foreseeable future? Explain your reasoning.
6. Consider the following statement: *In a union shop, newly hired employees must join the union within 30 days of starting work. Forcing workers to join a union in order to keep their job is unreasonable and violates their freedom of choice. Workers should be allowed to decide whether they want to join a union or not. Union shops should therefore not be allowed.* Do you agree or disagree with this statement? Explain your reasoning.

APPLICATION EXERCISES

7. Interview a human resource manager at a local company. Select a position for which the firm is currently recruiting applicants and identify the steps in the selection process. Do the steps match those shown in Figure 8.1? Why or why not?
8. >>> Survey 10 of your acquaintances and determine (a) how important benefits are to them as opposed to salary, (b) the benefits that are the least and most important in attracting and keeping workers, (c) the extent to which their opinions about benefits vs. salary will influence their choice of an employer after graduation.
9. Select a job currently held by you or a close friend. Draw up a job description and job specification for this position.
10. Interview the managers at two local companies, one unionized and one non-unionized. Compare the wage and salary levels, benefits, and working conditions at the two firms. Do you find any differences? If so, what are they?

TEAM EXERCISES

BUILDING YOUR BUSINESS SKILLS

GETTING ONLINE FOR A JOB

THE PURPOSE OF THE ASSIGNMENT

To introduce students to career-search resources available on the internet.

THE SITUATION

If companies are on one side of the external staffing process, people looking for work are on the other. Companies need qualified candidates to fill job openings and candidates need jobs that are right for them. The challenge, of course, is to make successful matches. Increasingly, this match-making is being conducted on the internet. Companies are posting jobs in cyberspace, and job seekers are posting résumés in response. The number of job postings has grown dramatically in recent years. On a typical Sunday, you might find as many as 50 000 postings on the Monster Board, a leading job site. With so many companies looking for qualified candidates online, it makes good business sense to learn how to use the system.

ASSIGNMENT

Using internet career resources means locating job databases and preparing and posting a résumé. (You will therefore need access to the internet to complete this exercise.)

Step 1 Team up with three classmates to investigate and analyze specific job databases. In each case, write a short report describing the database (which you and other group members may use during an actual job search). Summarize the site and its features as well as its advantages, disadvantages, and costs. Start with the following sites and add others you may find on your own:

Monster Canada, www.monster.ca
Careerbuilder, www.careerbuilder.ca
College Grad Job Hunter, www.collegegrad.com

Step 2 Investigate the job opportunities listed on the home pages of various companies. Consider trying the following companies:

Air Canada, www.aircanada.com
Dofasco, www.dofasco.ca
Royal Bank, www.rbcroyalbank.com
IBM, www.ibm.com/ca
Walmart, www.walmartstores.com
McDonald's, www.mcdonalds.com
Bombardier, www.bombardier.com

Write a summary of the specific career-related information you find on each site.

Step 3 Working with group members, research strategies for composing effective cyber résumés. The following websites provide some helpful information on formats and personal and job-related information that should be included in your résumé. They also offer hints on the art of creating a scannable résumé:

Workopolis, www.workopolis.com

Career Magazine, www.careermag.com

Two books by Joyce Lain Kennedy, *Electronic Job Search Revolution* and *Electronic Résumé Revolution*, also contain valuable information.

Step 4 Working as a group, create an effective electronic résumé for a fictitious college or university graduate looking for a first job. Pay attention to format, language, style, and the effective communication of background and goals.

Step 5 Working as a group, learn how to post your résumé online. (Do not submit the résumé you created for this exercise, which is, after all, fictitious.) The databases provided will guide you in this process.

QUESTIONS FOR DISCUSSION

1. Why is it necessary to learn how to conduct an electronic job search? Do you think it will be more or less necessary in the years ahead?
2. Why do you think more computer-related jobs than non-technical jobs are posted online? Do you think this situation will change?
3. Why is it a waste of time to stylize your résumé with different fonts, point sizes, and centred headings?
4. What is the advantage of emailing your résumé directly to a company rather than applying for the same job through an online databank?

EXERCISING YOUR ETHICS

HANDLING THE LAYOFFS

THE SITUATION

The CEO of a moderate-sized company is developing a plan for laying off employees. He wants each manager to rank his or her employees according to the order in which they should be laid off, from first to last.

THE DILEMMA

One manager has just asked for help. He is new to his position and has little experience to draw from. The members of the manager's team are as follows:

- Tony Jones: white male, 10 years with the company, average performer, reportedly drinks a lot after work
- Amanda Wiggens: white female, very ambitious, three years with the company, above-average performer, puts in extra time at work; is known to be abrasive when dealing with others
- George Sinclair: Aboriginal, 20 years with the company, average performer, was previously laid off but called back when business picked up
- Dorothy Henderson: white female, 25 years with the company, below-average performer, has filed five sexual harassment complaints in the last 10 years
- Wanda Jackson: black female, eight years with the company, outstanding performer, is rumoured to be looking for another job
- Jerry Loudder: white male, single parent, five years with the company, average performer
- Martha Strawser: white female, six years with company, excellent performer but spotty attendance, is putting husband through university

TEAM ACTIVITY

Assemble a group of four students. Your group has agreed to provide the manager with a suggested rank ordering of the manager's employees.

ACTION STEPS

1. Working together, prepare this list, ranking the manager's employees according to the order in which they should be laid off, from first to last. Identify any disagreements that occurred along the way, and indicate how they were resolved.
2. As a group, discuss the underlying ethical issues in this situation and write them down.
3. As a group, brainstorm any legal issues involved in this situation and write them down.
4. Do the ethical and legal implications of your choices always align?
5. Do the ethical and performance implications of your choices always align?

BUSINESS CASE

BEHAVIOUR-BASED INTERVIEWING

Interviewing job candidates is a long-standing practice in companies, but it is clear that interviewing often does not yield critical information that recruiters need to make good hiring decisions. One of the key problems is the types of questions that are asked in interviews. Often they take the form of "What are your strengths and weaknesses?" or "What kind of communication skills do you have?" Candidates who are good talkers (but maybe not such good performers) can do well in interviews, but not perform well on the job. Dissatisfaction with traditional interview questions has led to the development of behaviour-based interviewing, which emphasizes action-oriented questions that require interviewees to describe what they have actually done when confronted with certain situations.

Behaviour-based interviewing assumes that a person's past behaviour is a good predictor of their future behaviour. It therefore assesses the *behaviours* of individuals as they have dealt with difficult and/or important job situations in the past, and then assumes that these behaviours are a good indicator of how the person will react to similar job situations in the future. As noted in the chapter, this approach can be used to

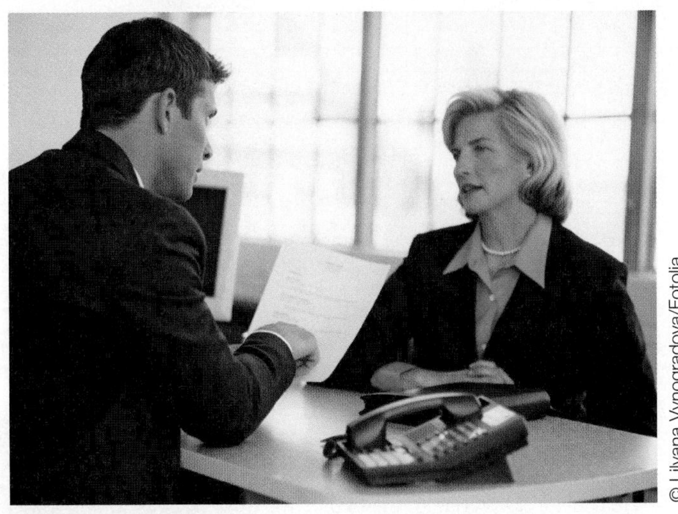
© Lilyana Vynogradova/Fotolia

test for technical skills, management skills, and individual characteristics. Typical questions that interviewers ask in behaviour-based interviewing are as follows:

- Think of a time when you had to deal with a customer who you thought was being unreasonable. How did you deal with that person?
- Tell me about the most unpopular decision you have ever made. What did you do when you found out that your decision was unpopular?
- Think of a time when you had to cope with a major change in your job. What did you do?
- Think of a time when you had to work with a person who was not "pulling their weight." What did you do?
- Tell me about a time when you worked effectively under pressure.
- Think of a time when you had to achieve consensus on a work team but encountered unexpected resistance. What did you do to facilitate the reaching of consensus?

Inexperienced candidates may not be able to adequately answer these questions because they haven't yet dealt with these situations in their career. Further behaviour-based questions—such as "Think about a time when you were in over your head on a job and tell me what you did to resolve that problem"—can be asked to determine whether the person is creative and has good problem-solving abilities. But an experienced person who cannot answer these questions is another story entirely; in those cases, the interviewer is likely to make a "no hire" decision.

Behaviour-based interviewing requires the interviewer to first identify the characteristics, skills, and behaviours that are important in the job that needs to be filled. This can be done by carefully observing current employees who excel in their jobs, and then identifying the key behaviours that are necessary for effectiveness. The interviewer then constructs open-ended questions which will determine if the interviewee possesses those characteristics, skills, and behaviours. The overall goal is to find out what it would be like working with the candidate on a daily basis.

Behaviour-based interviewing is becoming more common because companies are facing increasingly competitive environments. Since these competitive environments often lead to downsizing, it is important to determine which individuals are capable of high performance. There is also more emphasis on working in teams and that means increased importance for interpersonal skills. These changing work situations have motivated companies to be much more focused in their hiring because they want workers who are more skilled and motivated than previously.

The increasing use of behaviour-based interviewing means that you are likely to be exposed to it at some point in your job search. What should you do to prepare for a behaviour-based interview? The main thing is to think about the job you are interviewing for and the skills that will be required to do it. Try to tell an interesting story (from a previous paid or volunteer position) that succinctly describes a situation you faced, the actions you took, and the outcome that resulted from your actions. If the outcome was good, the interviewer will likely be favourably impressed with your logical thinking and actions. If the outcome wasn't so good, you can indicate what you learned from the experience and how that experience will benefit your new employer.

Be sure to outline the specifics of the situation, how you dealt with it, what happened as a result of your decision, and what you learned from it. It is important to be able to communicate things about *you*. The best way to answer the interviewer's questions is to use the *SAB* acronym: describe the situation (S), the actions you took that made a difference (A), and how the situation benefited from your actions (B).

Also, reviewing the job posting and job description before your interview will help you develop a list of skills that are required for the job; you can then match them to your own when speaking with the interviewer.

QUESTIONS FOR DISCUSSION

1. There seem to be many advantages to behaviour-based interviewing. Are there disadvantages as well? Explain.
2. Why is behaviour-based interviewing becoming so common?
3. Consider the following statement: *Behaviour-based interviewing sounds like a good idea because it forces interviewees to describe their actual behaviour. Realistically, however, it probably won't work as well as expected because people who are good* talkers *will always be able to present themselves well, even if they are not very good performers.* Do you agree or disagree with the statement? Explain your reasoning.

Motivating, Satisfying, *and* Leading Employees

CHAPTER 09

LO

AFTER READING THIS CHAPTER, YOU SHOULD BE ABLE TO:

LO-1 Identify and discuss the basic *forms of behaviour* that employees exhibit in organizations.

LO-2 Describe the nature and importance of *individual differences* among employees.

LO-3 Explain the meaning and importance of *psychological contracts* and the person–job fit in the workplace.

LO-4 Identify and summarize the most important models of *employee motivation*.

LO-5 Describe the *strategies* used by organizations to improve job satisfaction and employee motivation.

LO-6 Define *leadership* and distinguish it from *management*.

LO-7 Summarize the *approaches to leadership* that developed during the twentieth century.

LO-8 Describe the most recent ideas about effective leadership.

Happiness and Satisfaction in the Workplace

A 2011 survey of 30 000 workers from 17 countries (including 2000 Canadians) was conducted by Mercer, a global consulting firm. Their *What's Working* survey showed that 36 percent of Canadian respondents were so unhappy with their jobs that they were considering quitting (26 percent held this view in the 2006 survey). The deterioration in happiness was influenced by the poor economic climate of the last few years, which had led to wage freezes, smaller merit increases, and fewer promotion opportunities. Employees in the 16 to 24 and 25 to 34 age brackets were the most likely to be thinking about leaving their jobs. Compared to workers who were not considering leaving their job, those that were considering leaving were consistently less satisfied, felt less fairly treated by their employer, were less proud to work for their organization, got less of a feeling of accomplishment from their work, and were less likely to recommend their organization to others as a good place to work.

Hurst Photo/Shutterstock

Several of the concerns in the *What's Working* survey flow from employee concerns about money. But what role does money play in happiness? A study in the *Proceedings* of the National Academy of Sciences reported that beyond an annual income of about $75 000, more money does not increase happiness. Lack of money does make people unhappy, but having a lot of money does not guarantee happiness. Students who set a goal of making a lot of money (for example, those majoring in business, engineering, and economics) generally achieved their goal. People who didn't care as much about money were more likely to be in liberal arts and the social sciences. Other research shows that achieving a feeling of happiness may not be as important as having a sense of purpose in life. People with a sense of purpose are more likely to remain cognitively intact as they age and even live longer than people who simply focus on being happy.

HOW WILL THIS HELP ME?

The connections that employees have with their jobs can go a long way toward determining how happy they are with their work. Some people love their jobs, while others hate theirs. Most people, however, fall somewhere in between. After studying the information in this chapter, you'll be better able to understand (1) your own feelings toward your work from the perspective of an *employee*, (2) the feelings of others toward their work from the perspective of a *manager* or an *owner*, (3) how you can more effectively function as a *leader*, and (4) how your manager or boss strives to motivate you through his or her own leadership.

Happiness with money is not the only consideration in employee satisfaction. Another survey—this one of 3000 Canadians—revealed some interesting things about what people valued in their work lives. The views of four age groups were examined:

- "Matures" (born before 1947)
- "Baby Boomers" (born between 1947 and 1966)
- "GenXers" (born between 1967 and 1979)
- "Millennials," also called "Generation Y" (born in 1980 or later)

Individuals in these four groups value similar things, but their priorities differ. For example, GenXers put the highest value on achieving a balance between work and home life, while Baby Boomers value continuing to grow and using their skills. Surprisingly, Matures value advancement more than either Baby Boomers or GenXers. Other findings: Millennials change jobs three times as much as Baby Boomers formerly did, apparently moving around looking for jobs that will satisfy their needs. Millennials also have very high expectations and assume that their pay will increase rather rapidly within five years (likely a naïve hope). Matures place less emphasis on fun at work than Baby Boomers, who in turn place less emphasis on fun than GenXers.

GenXers are most disappointed with how their careers have unfolded. They report the lowest levels of satisfaction of all four groups, the lowest levels of met expectations, and the greatest levels of conflict between work and family life. Part of the problem seems to be that GenXers are caught between Millennials and Baby Boomers, who are generally seen as more influential in society. One important implication of the findings is this—as the Baby Boomers retire in the next few years, the GenXers are going to become important to the success of the companies they work for. But if GenXers are unhappy with their work and career situation, this could cause problems.

How can managers address the problems that are evident in the above surveys? The easy answer is to give employees what they want. *But what do employees want?* Managers often *assume* they know the answer to this question, but consider the results of a survey by the Canadian Payroll Association, which analyzed the frequency with which 39 specific benefits were provided by *companies* to their employees. The top five items were term life insurance, car allowances, tuition fees, disability-related employment benefits, and professional membership dues. But a survey of *worker* opinions found that they rated flexible working hours, casual dress, unlimited internet access, opportunities to telecommute, and nap time as the most desirable. There are obviously major differences in these two lists, so managers are having some difficulty assessing what employees want.

Managers can improve this unfortunate situation by gaining a greater understanding of employee needs. They can do this by asking the following questions:

- What do employees expect from their role? Employee satisfaction increases when their role provides adequate challenge and fits well with their personal purpose.
- What motivates employees? Answering this question yields information about employee needs, which are important in job satisfaction.

- What kind of work environment do employees want? If employees want a meritocracy, they are not going to be happy if everyone receives equal rewards. If they want a lot of autonomy, they are not going to be happy with a rigidly structured job. In other words, the work environment must be structured to emphasize the things that employees value.
- What career development help do employees want? Employees want to improve their skills and learning, and they want to feel that management is investing in their careers.

Beyond these specific issues, managers should also ask a very general question: "Under what circumstances will employees feel happy and be willing to work enthusiastically for the company?" The answer to this question may be evident in yet another survey, this one based on responses by 8000 Canadians. The survey found that the three most important things (for employees of *all* ages) were (1) to be treated with respect, (2) to be dealt with fairly, and (3) to feel a sense of "connection" with the organization they work for. Managers can have a very positive influence on all of these things.

QUESTIONS FOR DISCUSSION

1. Why do you think the different groups (Matures, Baby Boomers, Gen Xers, and Millennials) have different satisfaction levels?
2. Consider the following statement: *Surveys of employee values and satisfaction levels are very useful to managers because they help managers be more effective in motivating their employees*. Do you agree or disagree with the statement? Explain your reasoning.

LO-1 FORMS OF EMPLOYEE BEHAVIOUR

EMPLOYEE BEHAVIOUR The pattern of actions by the members of an organization that directly or indirectly influences the organization's effectiveness.

PERFORMANCE BEHAVIOURS The total set of work-related behaviours that the organization expects employees to display.

ORGANIZATIONAL CITIZENSHIP Positive behaviours that do not directly contribute to the bottom line.

COUNTERPRODUCTIVE BEHAVIOURS Behaviours that detract from organizational performance.

ABSENTEEISM When an employee does not show up for work.

TURNOVER Annual percentage of an organization's workforce that leaves and must be replaced.

Employee behaviour is the pattern of actions by the members of an organization that directly or indirectly influences the organization's effectiveness. **Performance behaviours** are those that are directly involved in performing a job. An assembly-line worker who sits by a moving conveyor and attaches parts to a product as it passes by has relatively simple performance behaviours, but a research-and-development scientist who works in a lab trying to find new scientific breakthroughs that have commercial potential has much more complex performance behaviours.

Other behaviours—called **organizational citizenship**—provide positive benefits to the organization in more indirect ways. An employee who does satisfactory work in terms of quantity and quality, but refuses to work overtime, won't help newcomers learn the ropes, and is generally unwilling to make any contribution beyond the strict performance requirements of the job is not a good organizational citizen. In contrast, an employee with a satisfactory level of performance who works late when the boss asks and takes time to help newcomers learn their way around is a good organizational citizen.

Counterproductive behaviours are those that detract from organizational performance. **Absenteeism** occurs when an employee does not show up for work. When an employee is absent, legitimately or not, that person's work does not get done and a substitute must be hired to do it, or others in the organization must pick up the slack. Tardiness is also a counterproductive behaviour. A survey conducted by CareerBuilder.com revealed that 19 percent of workers admitted being late for work at least once a week.[1]

Turnover occurs when people quit their jobs. It results from a number of factors, including the nature of the job, the nature of supervision, a poor person–job fit, the external labour market, and family influences.

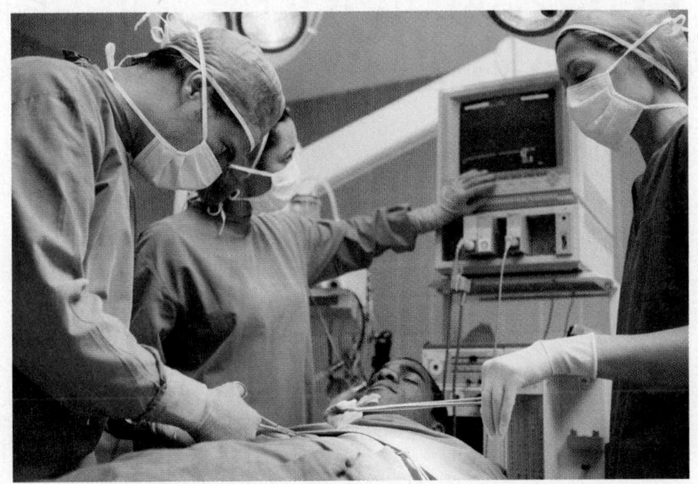

For some jobs, performance behaviours can be narrowly defined and easily measured. For many other jobs, such as those held by scientists or doctors, performance behaviours are less objective, more diverse, and more difficult to assess.

Ethical Funds Company Image

E-BUSINESS AND SOCIAL MEDIA SOLUTIONS

Tweet, Post: You're Fired

Today we are dealing with an unprecedented generational gap. Historically, there has always been some tension as the next generation enters the workplace, but the gap between Generation Y (Millennials) and Baby Boomers and Generation Xers (who had previously learned to work together) has been heightened by a technology gap. Employee-manager relationships can be complicated at times, but when you add the additional element of social media tools like Facebook and Twitter you have a new outlet for potential misunderstandings and incidents. While the dangers are particularly clear for younger workers who have embraced this technology, this is a cautionary note for all workers looking for a new and powerful outlet to complain.

Let's take a look at a few examples.

- Canadian broadcaster Damian Goddard was fired for a tweet containing a negative comment about same-sex marriage that he sent on his private Twitter account on his own time. He filed a human rights complaint claiming that the firing was unjust on the grounds that the action went against freedom of religion and freedom of speech. However, in 2013, the Human Rights Commission dismissed his case.
- Two employees at a car dealership in B.C. were fired after they posted extremely negative comments about their employer and their managers. The two workers complained about the legitimacy of the decision, but the British Columbia Labour Relations Board supported the dismissal.
- An employee at Chrysler, who was hired as a social media consultant, was fired after he used the F-word in one of his official company tweets when describing how people drive in the Motor City.

Employer interests seem to be well protected in such cases in Canada. Up to this point the labour tribunals have supported the management position and indicated that such acts violate the legal "duty of loyalty." However, this is a quickly evolving frontier in employee relations which is complicated by union–management contracts, outdated legislation, and ground-breaking new rulings.

So, pay attention to what you write in your social media posts, because your employer may already be doing so.

CRITICAL THINKING QUESTIONS

1. Do you believe that employers should have the right to terminate an employee based on tweets and Facebook posts?
2. Consider the following statement: *Canadian legislation is hurting the right to freedom of speech of its citizens with these types of rulings*. Do you agree with the statement? Defend your answer.

One survey of 660 workers showed that 84 percent who worked for a "kind" manager planned to stay with their company a long time, while only 47 percent of those who worked for a "bully" said they planned to stay.[2]

Other forms of counterproductive behaviour are also costly. Theft and sabotage, for example, result in direct financial costs for an organization. Sexual and racial harassment also cost an organization, both directly (through financial liability if the organization responds inappropriately) and indirectly (by lowering morale, producing fear, and driving off valuable employees). Workplace aggression and violence are also counterproductive. While some forms of behaviour are obviously counterproductive, there can be debate about others (see the boxed insert entitled "Tweet, Post: You're Fired").

LO-2 INDIVIDUAL DIFFERENCES AMONG EMPLOYEES

INDIVIDUAL DIFFERENCES Personal attributes that vary from one person to another.

PERSONALITY The relatively stable set of psychological attributes that distinguish one person from another.

Individual differences are physical, psychological, and emotional attributes that vary from one person to another. The individual differences that characterize a specific person make that person unique. Personality and attitudes are two main categories of individual differences.

Personality

Personality is the relatively stable set of psychological attributes that distinguish one person from another. In recent years, researchers have identified five fundamental traits that are especially relevant to organizations. These "big five" personality traits (shown in Figure 9.1) can be summarized as follows:

- *Agreeableness* is a person's ability to get along with others. A person with a high level of agreeableness is gentle, cooperative, forgiving, understanding, and good-natured in their dealings with others. A person with a low level of agreeableness is often irritable, short-tempered, uncooperative, and generally antagonistic toward other people. Highly agreeable people are better at developing good working relationships with co-workers, whereas less agreeable people are not likely to have particularly good working relationships.
- *Conscientiousness* refers to the number of things a person tries to accomplish. Highly conscientious people tend to focus on relatively few tasks at one time; as a result, they are likely to be organized, systematic, careful, thorough, responsible, and self-disciplined. Less conscientious people tend to pursue a wider array of tasks; as a result, they are often more disorganized and irresponsible, as well as less thorough and self-disciplined. Highly conscientious people tend to be relatively higher performers in a variety of different jobs.
- *Emotionality* refers to the degree to which people tend to be positive or negative in their outlook and behaviours toward others. People

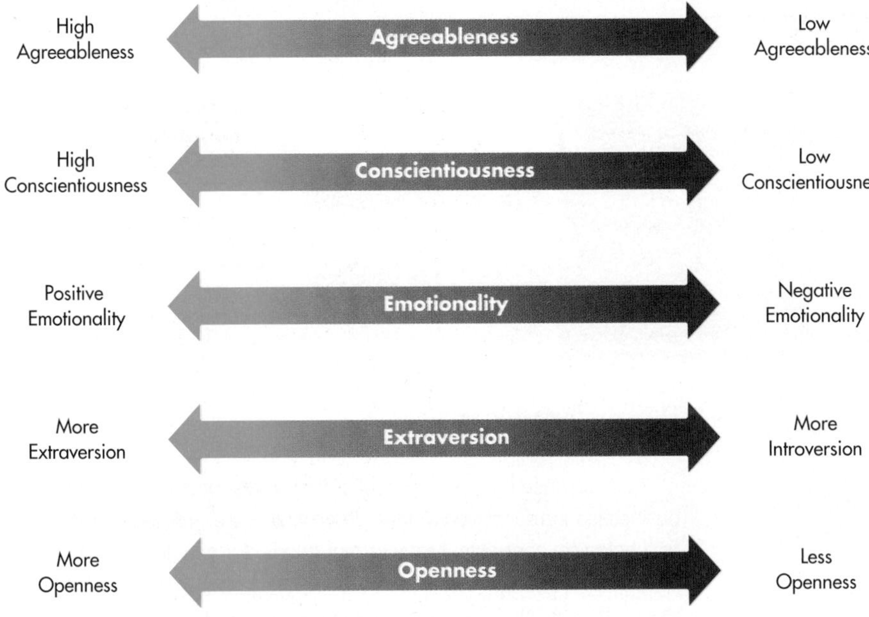

<<< FIGURE 9.1 The "big five" personality traits

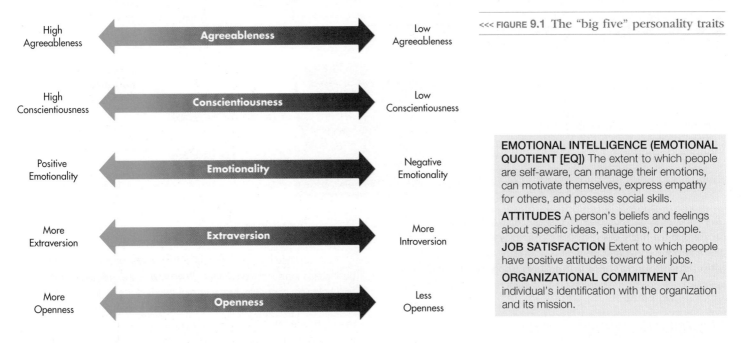

EMOTIONAL INTELLIGENCE (EMOTIONAL QUOTIENT [EQ]) The extent to which people are self-aware, can manage their emotions, can motivate themselves, express empathy for others, and possess social skills.

ATTITUDES A person's beliefs and feelings about specific ideas, situations, or people.

JOB SATISFACTION Extent to which people have positive attitudes toward their jobs.

ORGANIZATIONAL COMMITMENT An individual's identification with the organization and its mission.

with positive emotionality are relatively poised, calm, resilient, and secure; people with negative emotionality are more excitable, insecure, reactive, and subject to mood swings. People with positive emotionality are better able to handle job stress, pressure, and tension. Their stability might also cause them to be seen as more reliable than their less stable counterparts.

- *Extraversion* refers to a person's comfort level with relationships. Extroverts are sociable, talkative, assertive, and open to establishing new relationships, while introverts are much less sociable, talkative, and assertive, and more reluctant to begin new relationships. Extroverts tend to be higher overall job performers than introverts and are more likely to be attracted to jobs based on personal relationships, such as sales and marketing positions.
- *Openness* reflects how open or rigid a person is in terms of his or her beliefs. People with high levels of openness are curious and willing to listen to new ideas and to change their own ideas, beliefs, and attitudes in response to new information. People with low levels of openness tend to be less receptive to new ideas and less willing to change their minds. People with more openness are often better performers due to their flexibility and the likelihood that they will be better accepted by others in the organization.

EMOTIONAL INTELLIGENCE

Emotional intelligence, or **emotional quotient (EQ)**, refers to the extent to which people possess social skills, are self-aware, can manage their emotions, can motivate themselves, and can express empathy for others.[3] Research suggests that people with high EQs may perform better than others, especially in jobs that require a high degree of interpersonal interaction and that involve influencing or directing the work of others. EQ appears to be something that isn't biologically based, but that can be developed.[4] A survey of 2660 managers conducted by CareerBuilder.com found that 34 percent of hiring managers put a high priority on emotional intelligence when making hiring decisions. Seventy-one percent of the respondents placed a higher priority on emotional intelligence than on mental intelligence when making hiring decisions.[5]

Attitudes

People's attitudes also affect their behaviour in organizations. **Attitudes** reflect our beliefs and feelings about specific ideas, situations, or other people. People in organizations have attitudes about many different things: their salary, their promotion possibilities, their boss, their employee benefits, and so on. Especially important attitudes are job satisfaction and organizational commitment.

- **Job satisfaction** reflects the extent to which people have positive attitudes toward their jobs. (A related concept—morale—refers to the overall attitude people have toward their workplace.) A Workopolis survey of 577 Canadians showed that 53 percent loved their jobs, 16 percent kept their job simply because it helped pay the bills, and 14 percent felt that their current job had the potential to lead to something better.[6] A survey of workers in 23 countries found that workers in Norway, Denmark, and Canada were the most satisfied with their current employer.[7] Satisfied employees tend to be absent less often, to be good organizational citizens, and to stay with the organization. Dissatisfied employees may be absent more often, may experience stress that disrupts co-workers, and may be continually looking for another job. Contrary to what a lot of managers believe, however, high levels of job satisfaction do not automatically lead to high levels of productivity.
- **Organizational commitment** (also called job commitment) reflects an individual's identification with the organization and its mission. Highly committed employees see themselves as true members of the firm, overlook minor sources of dissatisfaction, and see themselves remaining members of the organization. Less committed employees are more likely to see themselves as outsiders, to express more dissatisfaction about the work situation, and to not see themselves as long-term members of the organization. One way to increase employee commitment is to give employees a voice. BBVA, Spain's second-largest bank, accomplishes this by including employees in the performance evaluation process. Not only is the employee's own self-evaluation considered, but co-workers also answer questions about each employee's performance. Infosys Technologies in Bangalore, India, started a Voice of Youth program, which gives top-performing young employees a seat on its management council.[8]

LO-3 MATCHING PEOPLE AND JOBS

PSYCHOLOGICAL CONTRACT The set of expectations held by an employee concerning what he or she will contribute to an organization (contributions) and what the organization will provide the employee (inducements) in return.

PERSON–JOB FIT The extent to which a person's contributions and the organization's inducements match one another.

Contributions from the Individual
- effort
- ability
- loyalty
- skills
- time
- competency

Inducements from the Organization
- pay
- benefits
- job security
- status
- promotion opportunities
- career opportunities

FIGURE 9.2 The psychological contract

Given the array of individual differences that exist across people and the many different forms of employee behaviour that can occur in organizations, it is important to have a good match between people and the jobs they are performing. Two key methods for facilitating this match are psychological contracts and the person–job fit.

Psychological Contracts

A **psychological contract** is the set of expectations held by an employee concerning what he or she will contribute to an organization (referred to as contributions) and what the organization will provide to the employee (referred to as inducements). If either party perceives an inequity in the contract, that party may seek a change. The employee, for example, might ask for a pay raise, a promotion, or a bigger office, or might put forth less effort or look for a better job elsewhere. The organization can also initiate change by training workers to improve their skills, transferring them to new jobs, or terminating them. Unlike a business contract, a psychological contract is not written on paper, nor are all of its terms explicitly negotiated. Figure 9.2 illustrates the essential features of a psychological contract.

The downsizing and cutbacks that have occurred in Canadian businesses in recent years have complicated the process of managing psychological contracts. Many organizations, for example, used to offer at least some assurance of job security as a fundamental inducement to employees. Now, however, because job security is lower, alternative inducements (like improved benefits, more flexible working hours, bonuses, etc.) may be needed.

The Person–Job Fit

The **person–job fit** refers to the extent to which a person's contributions and the organization's inducements match one another. Each employee has a specific set of needs that he or she wants fulfilled, and a set of job-related behaviours and abilities to contribute. If the organization can take perfect advantage of those behaviours and abilities and exactly fulfill those needs, it will have achieved a perfect person–job fit. A good person–job fit can result in higher performance and more positive attitudes, whereas a poor person–job fit can have just the opposite effect.

MOTIVATION IN THE WORKPLACE

Motivation means the set of forces that causes people to behave in certain ways. While one worker may be motivated to work hard to produce as much as possible, another may be motivated to do just enough to get by. As we saw in the opening case, effective managers recognize that different employees have different needs and are motivated by different things. One company that stopped handing out T-shirts with the company logo on them found that professional workers didn't much care, but immigrant workers in entry-level jobs were unhappy because the T-shirts had symbolic value for them (the T-shirts apparently made them feel like they belonged in Canada).[9] This example, and thousands more, show that managers must think very carefully about how to motivate employees.

Over the last century, many theories have been proposed to explain the complex issue of motivation. In this section, we will focus on three major approaches that reflect a chronology of thinking in the area of motivation: classical theory/scientific management, early behavioural theory, and contemporary motivational theories.

Classical Theory

In the **classical theory of motivation**, it is assumed that workers are motivated solely by money. In his book, *The Principles of Scientific Management* (1911), industrial engineer Frederick Taylor proposed a way for both companies and workers to benefit from this view of life in the workplace.[10] If workers are motivated by money, Taylor reasoned, then paying them more would prompt them to produce more. Meanwhile, the firm that analyzed jobs and found better ways to perform them would be able to produce goods more cheaply, make higher profits, and thus pay—and motivate—workers better than its competitors.

Taylor's approach is known as **scientific management**, and his ideas captured the imagination of many managers in the early twentieth century. Soon, plants across Canada and the United States were hiring experts to perform **time-and-motion studies**, which were the first

MOTIVATION The set of forces that causes people to behave in certain ways.

CLASSICAL THEORY OF MOTIVATION A theory of motivation that presumes that workers are motivated almost solely by money.

SCIENTIFIC MANAGEMENT Analyzing jobs and finding better, more efficient ways to perform them.

TIME-AND-MOTION STUDIES The use of industrial-engineering techniques to study every aspect of a specific job to determine how to perform it most efficiently.

The Hawthorne studies were an important step in developing an appreciation for the human factor at work. These women worked under different lighting conditions as researchers monitored their productivity. The researchers were amazed to find that productivity increased regardless of whether lighting levels increased or decreased.

© Monkey Business/Fotolia

"scientific" attempts to break jobs down into easily repeated components and to devise more efficient tools and machines for performing them. [11] The results were impressive. For example, studies of workers loading iron on rail cars showed that productivity tripled when scientific management principles were used.

Early Behavioural Theory

In 1925, a group of Harvard researchers began a study at the Hawthorne Works of the Western Electric Company. Their intent was to examine the relationship between changes in the physical environment and worker output, with an eye to increasing productivity. The results of the experiment at first confused, then amazed, the scientists. Increasing lighting levels improved productivity, but so did lowering lighting levels. And, against all expectations, raising the pay of workers failed to increase their productivity. Gradually, they pieced together the puzzle—the explanation for the contradictory findings lay in workers' response to the attention being paid to them. In essence, the researchers determined that almost any action on the part of management that made workers believe they were receiving special attention caused worker productivity to rise. This result, known as the **Hawthorne effect**, convinced many managers that paying attention to employees is indeed good for business.

Following the Hawthorne studies, managers and researchers alike focused more attention on how good *human relations*—the interactions between employers and employees and their attitudes toward one another—helped in motivating employees. Researchers eventually developed several now-classic motivation theories, including the *human resources model*, the *hierarchy of needs model*, and *two-factor theory*.

LO-4 THE HUMAN RESOURCES MODEL: THEORIES X AND Y

Behavioural scientist Douglas McGregor concluded that managers had different beliefs about how best to use the human resources at a firm's disposal. He classified these beliefs into sets of assumptions that he labelled "Theory X" and "Theory Y."[12] Managers who subscribe to **Theory X** tend to believe that people are naturally lazy and uncooperative and must therefore be either punished or rewarded to be made productive. Managers who subscribe to **Theory Y** tend to believe that people are naturally energetic, growth-oriented, self-motivated, and interested in being productive.

McGregor generally favoured Theory Y beliefs and argued that Theory Y managers are more likely to have satisfied, motivated employees. Of course, Theory X and Y distinctions are somewhat simplistic and offer little concrete basis for action. Their value lies primarily in their ability to highlight and analyze the behaviour of managers as a result of their attitudes toward employees.

MASLOW'S HIERARCHY OF HUMAN NEEDS MODEL

Psychologist Abraham Maslow's **hierarchy of human needs model** proposed that people have a number of different needs that they attempt to satisfy in their work.[13] He classified these needs into five basic types and suggested that they are arranged in a hierarchy of importance, where lower-level needs must be met before a person will try to satisfy those on a higher level (see Figure 9.3).

- *Physiological needs* are those concerned with survival; they include food, water, shelter, and sleep. Businesses address these needs by providing both comfortable working environments and salaries sufficient to buy food and shelter.
- *Security needs* include the needs for stability and protection from the unknown. Many employers thus offer pension plans and job security.
- *Social needs* include the needs for friendship and companionship. Making friends at work can help to satisfy social needs, as can the feeling that you "belong" in a company.
- *Esteem needs* include the needs for status, recognition, and self-respect. Job titles and large offices are among the things that businesses can provide to address these needs.
- *Self-actualization needs* are needs for self-fulfillment. They include the needs to grow and develop one's capabilities and to achieve new and meaningful goals. Challenging job assignments can help satisfy these needs.

According to Maslow, once needs at one level have been satisfied, they cease to motivate behaviour. For example, if you feel secure in your job, a new pension plan will probably be less important to you than the chance to make new friends and join an informal

HAWTHORNE EFFECT The tendency for workers' productivity to increase when they feel they are receiving special attention from management.

THEORY X A management approach based on the belief that people must be forced to be productive because they are naturally lazy, irresponsible, and uncooperative.

THEORY Y A management approach based on the belief that people want to be productive because they are naturally energetic, responsible, and cooperative.

HIERARCHY OF HUMAN NEEDS MODEL Theory of motivation describing five levels of human needs and arguing that basic needs must be fulfilled before people work to satisfy higher-level needs.

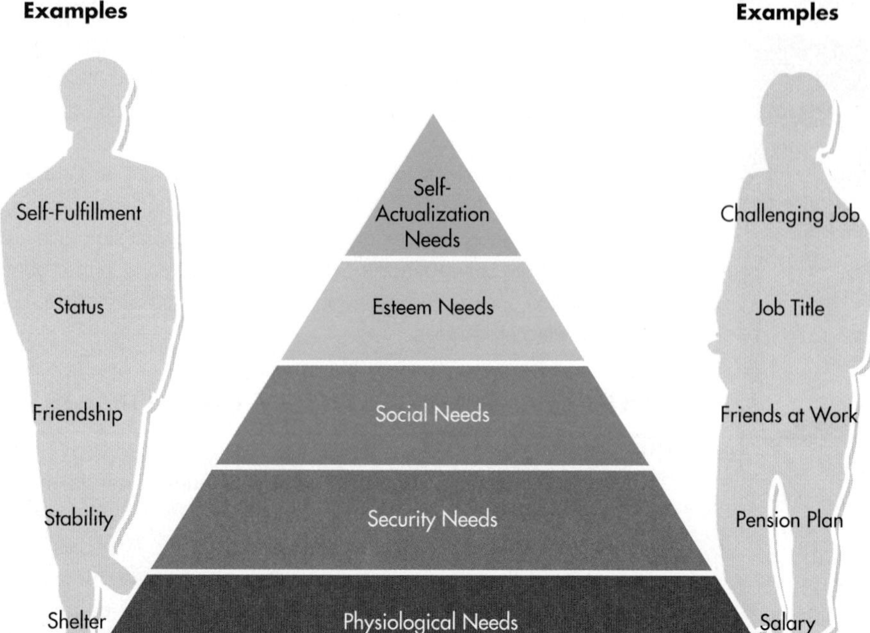

<<< **FIGURE 9.3** Maslow's hierarchy of human needs

Source: A. H. Maslow, *Motivation and Personality*, 2nd edition. (Upper Saddle River, NJ: Prentice Hall, 1970). Reprinted with permission of Pearson Education, Inc.

TWO-FACTOR THEORY A theory of human relations developed by Frederick Herzberg that identifies factors that must be present for employees to be satisfied with their jobs and factors that, if increased, lead employees to work harder.

network among your co-workers. If, however, a lower-level need suddenly becomes unfulfilled, most people immediately refocus on that lower level. For example, if you are trying to meet your esteem needs by working as a divisional manager at a major company and you learn that your division and your job may be eliminated, you might very well find the promise of job security at a new firm very motivating. The boxed insert entitled "Moving People to Move Movies" describes how one company focuses on employee needs.

TWO-FACTOR (MOTIVATOR–HYGIENE) THEORY

After studying a group of accountants and engineers, psychologist Frederick Herzberg proposed the **two-factor theory**, which says that job satisfaction and dissatisfaction depend on two separate factors: *hygiene factors* (such as working conditions,

ENTREPRENEURSHIP AND NEW VENTURES

Moving People to Move Movies

Selling movies to consumers is a dynamic and challenging industry today. In order to cope with the complex and rapidly evolving nature of the industry, Netflix CEO and founder Reed Hastings recruited a team of top performers in fields as diverse as marketing, content management, and website operations. But then he had to find a way to motivate these stars to fulfill their potential. Netflix does use monetary rewards as a motivator ("We're unafraid to pay high," says Hastings), but the company achieves its greatest results by focusing on employee needs.

One important set of needs that Netflix fulfills is the desire to work with friends, to be part of a team, and to "belong." The atmosphere is casual and collaborative, but, as Michelle Conlin of *BusinessWeek* puts it, "Netflix is no frat party with beer bashes and foosball tables." The Netflix values statement says, "The benefit of a high-performance culture is that you work with consistently outstanding colleagues, which is exhilarating. We're a high-performance team, not a family. A strong family is together forever, no matter what. A strong company, on the other hand, is more like a professional sports team, which is built to win."

Netflix works to fulfill employees' needs for esteem by being an employer that is well liked. The job pages of the company's website say, "It is satisfying to work at a company that people love. We're ranked number one in customer satisfaction across the entire Internet, narrowly besting such great companies as Apple and Amazon."

Another need is employees' passion to achieve. The "best in class" personnel at this firm of just 400 workers are attracted by the opportunity to have a significant impact on a successful and ever-changing company. Before founding Netflix, Hastings started Pure Software. At first, the start-up was an exciting place to work, but it became more humdrum and bureaucratic as it grew. When Pure was sold to IBM, Hastings vowed to never repeat that mistake. The Netflix values statement summarizes Hastings's viewpoint as follows: "Rules inhibit creativity and entrepreneurship, leading to a lack of innovation. Our solution to increased complexity is to increase talent density. Great people make great judgment calls, despite ambiguity. We believe in freedom and responsibility, not rules."

The Netflix motivation scheme is not for everyone. "At most companies, average performers get an average raise," says Hastings. "At Netflix, they get a generous severance package." Netflix is getting maximum performance from its workers in order to gain a competitive advantage over its key competitors.

CRITICAL THINKING QUESTIONS

1. Why do you think the Netflix motivation scheme is not for everyone?
2. Consider the following statement: *Trying to motivate employees by focusing on their needs is not a good idea because it is hard to find out just what employee needs are, and, even if you find out, that doesn't tell you specifically what you should do to satisfy those needs.* Do you agree or disagree with the statement? Defend your answer.

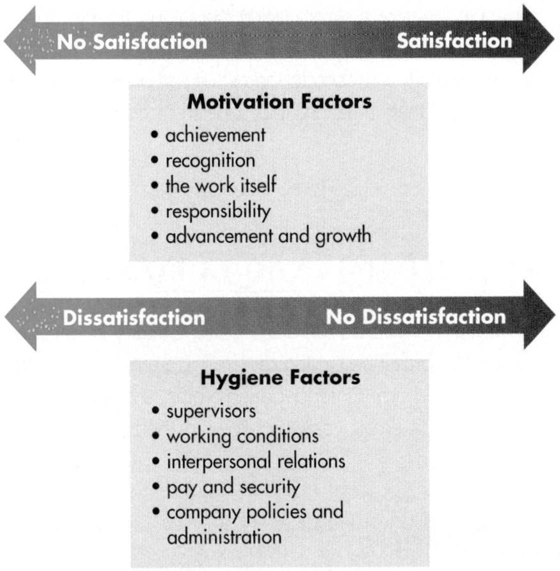

No Satisfaction — Satisfaction

Motivation Factors

- achievement
- recognition
- the work itself
- responsibility
- advancement and growth

Dissatisfaction — No Dissatisfaction

Hygiene Factors

- supervisors
- working conditions
- interpersonal relations
- pay and security
- company policies and administration

FIGURE 9.4 Two-factor theory of human motivation

quality of supervision, interpersonal relations, pay, and job security) and *motivating factors* (such as recognition, responsibility, advancement, and achievement).[14] Motivation factors cause movement along a continuum from no satisfaction to satisfaction. For example, if workers receive no recognition for successful work, they may not be satisfied, but neither will they be dissatisfied. If recognition is provided, they will likely become more satisfied. Hygiene factors cause movement along a different continuum, one from no dissatisfaction to dissatisfaction. For example, workers will be dissatisfied if they feel that working conditions are poor, but if working conditions are improved, workers will not become satisfied; rather, they will no longer be dissatisfied. Overall, motivation factors are directly related to the work that employees actually perform, while hygiene factors refer to the environment in which they perform it (see Figure 9.4). This theory suggests that managers must first ensure that hygiene factors are acceptable (to avoid worker dissatisfaction) and then offer motivating factors (to improve satisfaction and motivation).

Contemporary Motivation Theory

In recent years, other, more complex models of employee behaviour and motivation have been developed. Two of the more interesting and useful ones are *expectancy theory* and *equity theory*.

EXPECTANCY THEORY

Expectancy theory suggests that people are motivated to work toward rewards they want and which they believe they have a reasonable chance—or expectancy—of obtaining.[15] A reward that seems out of reach, for example, is not likely to be motivating even if it is intrinsically positive (see Figure 9.5). Suppose that an assistant department manager learns that a division manager has retired and that the firm is looking for a replacement. Even though she wants the job, the assistant manager does not apply for it because she doubts that she would be selected. Then she learns that the firm is looking for a production manager on a later shift. She thinks that she could get this job but does not apply for that one either, because she does not want to change shifts. But when she learns of an opening one level higher—full department manager—in her own division, she applies for this job because she both wants it and thinks that she has a good chance of getting it.

Expectancy theory helps to explain why some people do not work as hard as they can when their salaries are based purely on seniority. Because they are paid the same whether they work very hard or just hard enough to get by, there is no financial incentive for them to work harder. Similarly, if hard work will result in one or more undesirable outcomes—say, a transfer to another location or a promotion to a job that requires unwanted travel—employees may not be motivated to work hard.

EQUITY THEORY

Equity theory focuses on social comparisons—people evaluating their treatment by the organization relative to the treatment of others. This approach says that people begin by analyzing what they contribute to their jobs (time, effort, education, experience, and so forth) relative to what they get in return (salary, benefits, recognition, security). The result is a ratio of contribution to return. Employees compare their own ratios to those of "comparison others" (employees who are similar in terms of experience and training). Depending on their assessments, they experience feelings of equity or inequity.[16]

For example, suppose a new college graduate gets a starting job at a large manufacturing firm. His starting salary is $38 000 per year, he

EXPECTANCY THEORY The theory that people are motivated to work toward rewards that they want and that they believe they have a reasonable chance of obtaining.

EQUITY THEORY The theory that people compare (1) what they contribute to their job with what they get in return, and (2) their input/output ratio with that of other employees.

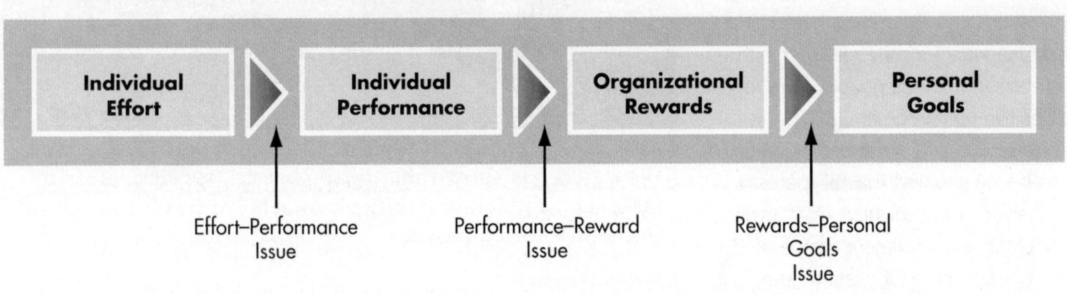

FIGURE 9.5 Expectancy theory model

gets a compact company car, and he shares an office with another new employee. If he later learns that another new employee has received the same salary, car, and office arrangement, he will feel equitably treated. But if he finds out that another newcomer received $40 000, a full-size company car, and a private office, he may feel that he has been inequitably treated.

When people feel that they are being inequitably treated, they may do various things to restore fairness. For example, they may ask for a raise, reduce their work effort, work shorter hours, or complain to their boss. They may also rationalize their situation, find a different comparison person, or simply quit.

LO-5 STRATEGIES FOR ENHANCING MOTIVATION

REINFORCEMENT Controlling and modifying employee behaviour through the use of systematic rewards and punishments for specific behaviours.

GOAL-SETTING THEORY The theory that people perform better when they set specific, quantified, time-framed goals.

MANAGEMENT BY OBJECTIVES (MBO) A system of collaborative goal setting that extends from the top of an organization to its bottom.

Understanding what motivates workers and provides job satisfaction is only part of the manager's job. The other part is to apply that knowledge. Experts have suggested—and many companies have instituted—a wide range of programs designed to make jobs more interesting and rewarding and the work environment more pleasant. Six of the most common strategies are reinforcement/behaviour modification, goal setting, participative management and empowerment, team management, job enrichment and redesign, and modified work schedules.

Reinforcement/Behaviour Modification

Reinforcement is a two-step process. The first step is to define the specific behaviours that managers want their employees to exhibit (working hard, being courteous to customers, stressing quality, etc.), and the specific behaviours they want to eliminate (wasting time, being rude to customers, ignoring quality, etc.). The second step is to "shape" employee behaviour by using reinforcement.

Reinforcement means applying (or withholding) positive (or negative) consequences in order to motivate employees to exhibit behaviour the manager wants. A manager has four basic reinforcement options: (1) *positive reinforcement* (apply positive consequences when employees exhibit desired behaviours), (2) *punishment* (apply negative consequences when employees exhibit undesirable behaviours), (3) *omission* (withhold positive consequences when employees exhibit undesirable behaviours), and (4) *negative reinforcement* (withhold negative consequences when employees exhibit desired behaviours).

Managers generally prefer positive reinforcement because it contributes to good employer–employee relationships. Managers generally dislike punishing employees, partly because workers may respond with anger, resentment, hostility, or even retaliation. Most people think of monetary rewards when they think of positive reinforcement, but one of the simplest, but uncommon, ways for managers to motivate workers is to praise them. A *Globe and Mail* web poll showed that 27 percent of the 2331 respondents had *never* received a compliment from their boss. Another 10 percent had not received a compliment in the last year, and 18 percent had not received a compliment in the last month.[17] Other non-monetary rewards are also useful. Calgary-based Pacesetter Directional and Performance Drilling rewards top employees with time off from work, and Markham, Ontario–based Nobis, a manufacturer of hats and apparel, rewards employees by allowing them to name hats after family and friends.[18]

Goal-Setting Theory

Goal-setting theory focuses on setting goals that will motivate employees. Research has shown that SMART goals (Specific, Measurable, Achievable, Relevant, and Time-framed) are most likely to result in increased employee performance. It is also true that on occasion, goal setting may lead to bad behaviour on the part of managers. For example, if managers are told they will receive a bonus if they achieve a certain level of sales revenue, they may focus all their attention on generating sales revenue, and not pay any attention to profits. At Enron, managers received large bonuses for achieving revenue goals even though the company was failing.[19]

One of the most popular methods for setting performance goals is called **management by objectives (MBO)**, which involves managers and subordinates in setting goals and evaluating progress. The motivational impact is perhaps the biggest advantage of MBO. When employees meet with managers to set goals, they learn more about company-wide objectives, feel that they are an important part of a team, and see how they can improve company-wide performance by achieving their own goals.

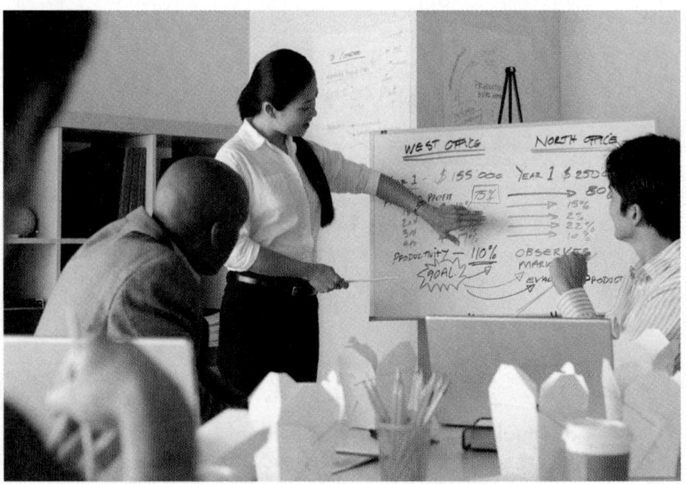

Research has shown that goals that are specific, measurable, and moderately difficult to achieve result in high performance for employees.

Ben Nelms/Landov LLC

Investors Group Financial Services has used MBO for many years to motivate its sales force in selling financial services. The MBO process begins when the vice-president of sales develops general goals for the entire sales force. Sales reps review their financial accomplishments and think through their personal and financial goals for the coming year. They then meet with their division managers and reach a consensus about the specific goals the sales reps will pursue during the next year. Each division manager then forwards the proposed objectives for his or her division to the appropriate regional manager. This process continues all the way up to the vice-president of sales, who gives final approval to the overall sales objectives of the company for the coming year.[20]

Participative Management and Empowerment

Participative management and empowerment involves tapping into workers' knowledge about the job, encouraging them to be self-motivated and to make suggestions for improvements, and giving them more authority and responsibility so that they feel they are a real part of the company's success. In 2009, Texas-based WorldBlu published a list of the 100 most democratic workplaces in the world. Seven Canadian companies made the list, including 1-800-GOT-JUNK?, I Love Rewards, and TakingITGlobal.[21] Some companies try to operate without the usual hierarchy and give workers a large amount of discretion. For example, at Morning Star Company—the world's largest tomato processor—workers write up a mission statement which describes how they will contribute to the overall goals of the company. Employees are expected to propose the hiring of new people if they are overloaded or if they see a need that should be met. Each employee also develops a "Colleague Letter of Understanding" with other employees who are affected by the person's work. At the end of the year, employees receive feedback on their performance from colleagues with whom they have a Letter of Understanding. Pay is determined by a committee that is elected. All business units are ranked (based on performance), and those that rank poorly have to explain what happened. One employee said that "nobody is your boss, everyone is."[22]

There are many other examples of empowerment in Canadian and international businesses:

- At WestJet, front-line staff have the right to issue travel credits to customers they feel have not been treated properly. WestJet thinks that the goodwill generated by the practice will increase repeat business.[23]
- At Toronto's Delta Chelsea Hotel, employees noticed that in the summer months there were fewer business guests and more vacationers' children in the hotel. As a result of employee suggestions, the hotel installed a waterslide, appointed a "kids' concierge," and set up a game room for teens to better serve this market segment.[24]
- At ING DIRECT Canada, a webpage has been set up that allows employees to submit ideas for peers to vote on. An innovation team then evaluates the ideas.[25]
- AES Corporation is a large energy company where multifunctional teams manage themselves without the assistance of any legal, human resources, or other functional department, or any written policies or procedures. No one person is in charge of the teams. As a result of this structure (some call it "empowerment gone mad"), employees exhibit flexibility and continuous learning.[26]

To enhance employee productivity, some companies are now using **wikis**—websites that allow employees to add content on issues that are of interest to the business. This is part of a move to "mass collaboration" that is going on in businesses.[27] Another technique to encourage participative management is the **quality circle**, a group of employees who meet regularly to consider solutions for problems in their work area. At Great-West Life Assurance Company, for example, quality circles are made up of volunteers who meet once a week (on company time) to consider ways to do higher quality, more effective work.

Empowerment is not desired by all employees. Some will be frustrated by responsibilities they are not equipped to handle, and others will be dissatisfied if they see the invitation to participate as more symbolic than real. A good approach is to invite participation if employees want to have input and if participation will have real value for an organization.

Team Management

Companies have traditionally given individual employees the responsibility to complete certain tasks, but in recent years, an emphasis on teams has become increasingly common. These teams take a variety of forms. **Problem-solving teams** focus on developing solutions to specific problems. They are based on the idea that the best solutions to problems are likely to come from the employees who actually do the work. For example, at the Bowmanville, Ontario, plant of St. Mary's Cement Inc., members of various departments joined a problem-solving team whose goal was to find ways to reduce the company's energy bills. After analyzing the situation, the committee developed a list of energy-saving initiatives and created plans to implement them. Over a recent three-year period, the initiatives saved the company $800 000.[28]

The problem-solving idea is developed even further in **self-managed teams**, which set their own goals, select their own team members, evaluate their own performance, and generally manage themselves. At Johnsonville Foods, self-managing teams recruit, hire, evaluate, and terminate low performers on their own.[29]

Project teams (also called **venture teams**) work on specific projects like developing new processes, new products, or new businesses. The classic example of a project team is the one that developed IBM's first personal computer many years ago. **Transnational teams**, composed

PARTICIPATIVE MANAGEMENT AND EMPOWERMENT Method of increasing job satisfaction by giving employees a voice in the management of their jobs and the company.

WIKIS Websites that allow employees to add content on issues that are of use to the business.

QUALITY CIRCLE A technique for maximizing quality of production. Employees are grouped into small teams that define, analyze, and solve quality and other process-related problems within their area.

PROBLEM-SOLVING TEAMS Teams that focus on developing solutions to specific problems a company is facing.

SELF-MANAGED TEAMS Teams that set their own goals, select their own team members, evaluate their own performance, and generally manage themselves.

PROJECT TEAMS (VENTURE TEAMS) Teams that work on specific projects, such as developing new processes, new products, or new businesses.

TRANSNATIONAL TEAMS Teams composed of members working in different countries.

of members from many different countries, have also become common. For example, Fuji-Xerox sent 15 engineers from Tokyo to New York to work with U.S. engineers as they developed a "world copier," a product that became a big success.[30] **Virtual teams** are groups of geographically dispersed co-workers that are assembled to accomplish a specific task, using a combination of telecommunications and information technologies. These teams are becoming increasingly popular because of globalization.

Teams provide monetary benefits for companies that use them, but they can also provide non-monetary benefits such as increasing motivation and job satisfaction levels for employees, enhancing company-wide communication, and making members feel like they are an integral part of the organization.[31] But, as with participative management, managers must remember that teams are not for everyone, nor are they effective in every situation.[32] At Levi Strauss, for example, individual workers who performed repetitive tasks like sewing zippers into jeans were paid according to the number of jobs they completed each day. In an attempt to boost productivity, company management reorganized everyone into teams of 10 to 35 workers and assigned tasks to the entire team. Each team member's pay was determined by the team's level of productivity. But faster workers became resentful of slower workers because they reduced the group's total output. Slower workers, meanwhile, resented the pressure put on them by faster-working co-workers. As a result, motivation, satisfaction, and morale all dropped, and Levi Strauss eventually abandoned the teamwork plan altogether.[33]

Teams work best when successful task completion requires input from several people, when there is interdependence between tasks (as in team sports), and when working together can accomplish tasks that an individual could not do alone (as in a hospital surgical team).[34]

Job Enrichment and Redesign

While MBO programs and participative management can work in a variety of settings, job enrichment and job redesign programs can increase satisfaction only if a job lacks motivating factors to begin with.[35] **Job enrichment** means adding one or more motivating factors to a job. In a now-classic study, a group of eight typists worked in isolated cubicles taking calls from field sales representatives and then typing up service orders. They had no client contact, so if they had a question about the order, they had to call the sales representative. They also received little performance feedback. Interviews with these workers suggested that they were bored with their jobs and did not feel valued. As part of a job enrichment program, each typist was paired with a small group of designated sales representatives and became a part of their team. Typists were also given permission to call clients directly if they had questions about the order. Finally, a new feedback system was installed to give the typists more information about their performance. As a result, their performance improved and absenteeism decreased markedly.[36]

^ This pit crew must work as a team in order to minimize the time the race car is in the pit. Coordination among team members is crucial, since even a few wasted seconds can make the difference between victory or defeat in the race.

© ITAR-TASS Photo Agency/Alamy

VIRTUAL TEAMS Teams of geographically dispersed individuals who use telecommunications and information technologies to accomplish specific tasks.

JOB ENRICHMENT A method of increasing employees' job satisfaction by extending or adding motivating factors such as responsibility or growth.

JOB REDESIGN A method of increasing employees' job satisfaction by improving the person–job fit through combining tasks, creating natural work groups, and/or establishing client relationships.

Job enrichment is accomplished by **job redesign**, which involves combining tasks to increase job variety, forming natural work groups, and establishing client relationships. By redesigning work to achieve a more satisfactory person–job fit, job redesign motivates individuals who have a high need for growth or achievement.[37]

COMBINING TASKS

This involves enlarging jobs and increasing their variety to make employees feel that their work is more meaningful. In turn, workers are more motivated. For example, the job done by a computer programmer who maintains computer systems might be redesigned to include some system design and development work. The programmer is then able to use additional skills and is involved in the overall system package.

FORMING NATURAL WORKGROUPS

People who do different jobs on the same project are good candidates for natural workgroups. These groups help employees get an overview of their jobs and see their importance in the total structure. They also help managers, and the firm in general, because the people working on a project are usually the most knowledgeable about it and are thus able to solve problems related to it. Consider a group where each employee does a small part of the job of assembling iPhones. One worker may see his job as working on the internal components, while another worker may see her job as working on the external components. The jobs could be redesigned to allow the group to decide who does what and in what order. The workers can exchange jobs and plan their work schedules. Now they all see themselves as part of a team that assembles iPhones.

ESTABLISHING CLIENT RELATIONSHIPS

A third way of redesigning a job is to establish client relationships, that is, to let employees interact with customers. This approach increases the variety of a job. It also gives workers greater feelings of control over their jobs and more feedback about their performance. Instead of responding to instructions from marketing managers on how to develop new products, software writers at Lotus are encouraged to work directly with customers. Similarly, software writers at Microsoft watch test users work with programs and discuss problems with them directly rather than receive feedback from third-party researchers.

Modified Work Schedules

Several types of modified work schedules have been developed to increase job satisfaction, including *flextime,* the *compressed workweek, telecommuting,* and *workshare programs*.

FLEXTIME

Flextime allows people to pick their working hours. Figure 9.6 illustrates how a flextime system might be arranged and how different people might use it. The office is open from 6 a.m. until 7 p.m. Core time is 9 a.m. until 11 a.m. and 1 p.m. until 3 p.m. Joe, being an early riser, comes in at 6 a.m., takes an hour lunch between 11 a.m. and noon, and finishes his day by 3 p.m. Sue, on the other hand, prefers a later day. She comes in at 9 a.m., takes a long lunch from 11 a.m. to 1 p.m., and then works until 7 p.m. Pat works a more traditional day from 8 a.m. until 5 p.m.

One survey found that 88 percent of Canadian businesses offer some form of flexible work arrangements (but many businesses offer them to only the most senior employees).[38] Since many employees work more than 40 hours per week, more and more companies are offering flexible working schedules to help them cope.[39] Flextime options are provided at organizations like Next Level Games Inc. (Vancouver), the National Energy Board (Calgary), and the Office of the Auditor General (Ottawa).[40] Alexandra Jacobs, a single mother who works for the Royal Bank of Canada, works three days a week from home. Jacobs manages a staff of five, and each of those people also has a flexible work schedule.[41]

COMPRESSED WORKWEEKS

In the **compressed workweek**, employees work fewer days per week but more hours on the days they do work. The most popular compressed workweek is four days, 10 hours per day, which is used in many companies and municipalities. Companies providing a compressed workweek option include Chubb Insurance Company of Canada (Toronto), Next Level Games Inc. (Vancouver), and Cameco Corp. (Saskatoon).[42] The Catholic Children's Aid Society of Toronto has introduced the compressed workweek to help staff cope with long, unpredictable hours.[43]

^^^ Telecommuting has become increasingly common in organizations, but it may not work for every organization. In 2013, for example, Marissa Mayer (the CEO of Yahoo! Inc.) announced that telecommuting would no longer be allowed at Yahoo. She said that the strategy was not the right one for Yahoo "at this time."

© Cary Ulrich Photography/Alamy

TELECOMMUTING

A third variation in work design is **telecommuting**, which allows people to do some or all of their work away from their office. The availability of networked computers, fax machines, smartphones, tablets, email, and overnight delivery services makes it possible for many

FLEXTIME A method of increasing employees' job satisfaction by allowing them some choice in the hours they work.

COMPRESSED WORKWEEK Employees work fewer days per week, but more hours on the days they do work.

TELECOMMUTING Allowing employees to do all or some of their work away from the office.

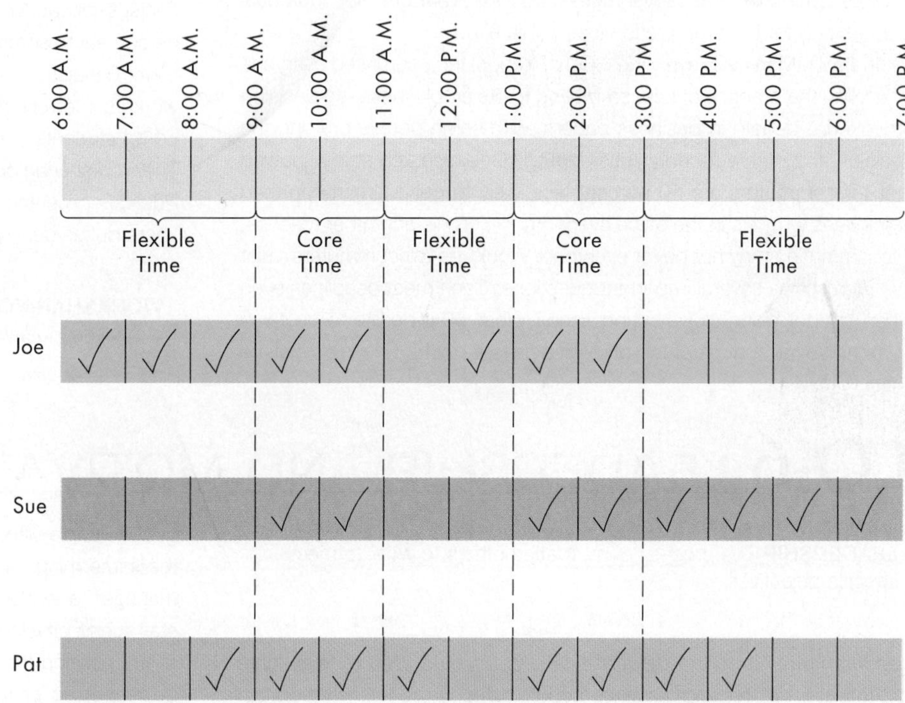

>>> **FIGURE 9.6 Flextime schedules**
Flextime schedules include core time, when everyone must be at work, and flexible time, during which employees can set their own working hours.

TABLE 9.1 Advantages and Disadvantages of Telecommuting

ADVANTAGES OF TELECOMMUTING	DISADVANTAGES OF TELECOMMUTING
For Employees	**For Employees**
• health benefits (lower stress levels) • lower costs (reduced car expenses) • better use of time (no commuting long distances) • better use of time (no interruptions)	• feeling "out of the loop" (not being knowledgeable about important business issues or interesting personal gossip) • having difficulty separating personal and professional life (work intrudes at home) • feeling ill-suited for telework (lack of discipline and feeling lonesome) • finding it difficult to work closely with colleagues when necessary • fear of career derailment
For the Organization	**For the Organization**
• increases productivity (two-thirds of employers surveyed said that employee productivity went up) • cost savings (fewer offices and office supplies are needed; lower vehicle expenses) • lower electric bills (fewer lights and computers are turned on in offices) • access to qualified staff (who otherwise wouldn't be available because they don't live in the area or don't want to drive so far to work) • lower travel expenses (teleconferencing, email, networking systems take the place of travel) • lower employee turnover	• requires a change in management thinking (forces managers to adopt an attitude of trust regarding employees) • many managers still think if they can't see employees, they aren't working (may threaten the control of bosses who are used to having employees in sight) • bosses have to spend more time with subordinates on the phone or other media (they may prefer face-to-face communication) • bosses don't know when employees are actually working • telecommuting may not work well for companies where customers are frequently in the office • telecommuting may not work well if colleagues frequently need intense face-to-face collaboration to complete rush jobs on time

independent professionals to work at home or while travelling. About one-third of the world's labour force now works wherever they are, not just in the office.[44] Many Canadian organizations offer telecommuting as an option. At BC Biomedical Laboratories, 15 percent of the administrative staff work from home, and at LoyaltyOne, 50 percent of call centre representatives don't commute.[45] At Cisco Systems, 90 percent of internal meetings are conducted using virtual meeting software. While 500 people work out of the downtown Toronto office, there are only 200 desks there.[46] In some business functions like customer service and telemarketing, most employees are telecommuters.[47]

Telecommuting has advantages and disadvantages for individual workers and for the organization (see Table 9.1).

In 2013, Marissa Mayer, the CEO of Yahoo! Inc., surprised everyone by ending the practice of telecommuting for its employees. The decision provoked a debate in business papers, with some people praising the decision and others roundly criticizing it.[48] One research study showed that telecommuters are 50 percent less likely to get a promotion than employees who are in the office every day.[49] For this and other reasons, telecommuting may not be for everyone. Would-be telecommuters must ask themselves several important questions: Can I meet deadlines even when I'm not being closely supervised? What will it be like to be away from the social context of the office five days a week? Can I renegotiate family rules so my spouse doesn't come home expecting to see dinner on the table just because I've been home all day?

WORKSHARE PROGRAMS

A fourth type of modified work schedule, **worksharing** (also called **job sharing**), benefits both employees and the employer. This approach allows two (or more) people to share one full-time job. For example, two people might share a position advising the human resources department. One person works Mondays through Wednesdays, and the other works Wednesdays through Fridays. Or, five people might share one reservationist's job at Air Canada, with each working one day a week. Each person earns some money, remains in the job market, and enjoys some travel benefits. Worksharing programs can also help ease experienced workers into retirement while training their replacements, and they allow co-op students to combine academic learning with practical experience. The worksharing option is used in organizations as diverse as the Ontario Public Service and the National Hockey League, where two goalies often share duties during the high-stress playoffs.[50]

WORKSHARING (JOB SHARING) A method of increasing employee job satisfaction by allowing two people to share one job.

LO-6 LEADERSHIP AND MOTIVATION

LEADERSHIP The process of motivating others to work to meet specific objectives.

Leadership refers to the processes and behaviours used by managers to motivate, inspire, and influence subordinates to work toward certain goals. People often assume that "leadership" and "management" mean the same thing, but there are important differences. A person can be a manager, a leader, or both.[51] Consider a hospital setting. The chief of staff (chief physician) of a large hospital is clearly a manager by virtue of the position the person occupies. But this individual may or may not be respected or trusted by others and may have to rely solely on the

TABLE 9.2 Kotter's Distinctions between Management and Leadership

Activity	Management	Leadership
Creating an Agenda	Planning and budgeting. Establishing detailed steps and timetables for achieving needed results; allocating the resources necessary to make those needed results happen.	Establishing direction. Developing a vision of the future, often the distant future, and strategies for producing the changes needed to achieve that vision.
Developing a Human Network for Achieving the Agenda	Organizing and staffing. Establishing some structure for accomplishing plan requirements, staffing that structure with individuals, delegating responsibility and authority for carrying out the plan, providing policies and procedures to help guide people, and creating methods or systems to monitor implementation.	Aligning people. Communicating the direction by words and deeds to all those whose cooperation may be needed to influence the creation of teams and coalitions that understand the vision and strategies and accept their validity.
Executing Plans	Controlling and problem solving. Monitoring results vs. plan in some detail, identifying deviations, and then planning and organizing to solve these problems.	Motivating and inspiring. Energizing people to overcome major political, bureaucratic, and resource barriers to change, by satisfying very basic, but often unfulfilled, human needs.
Outcomes	Produces a degree of predictability and order and has the potential to consistently produce major results expected by various shareholders (e.g., for customers, always being on time; for stockholders, being on budget).	Produces change, often to a dramatic degree, and has the potential to produce extremely useful change (e.g., new products that customers want, new approaches to labour relations that help make a firm more competitive).

authority vested in the position to get people to do things. Thus, being a manager does not ensure that a person is also a leader. In contrast, an emergency-room nurse with no formal authority may be quite effective at taking charge of a chaotic situation and directing others in how to deal with specific patient problems. Others in the emergency room may respond because they trust the nurse's judgment and have confidence in the nurse's decision-making skills. In this case, the emergency-room nurse is a leader, but not a manager. Finally, the head of pediatrics, supervising a staff of 20 other doctors, nurses, and attendants, may also enjoy the staff's complete respect, confidence, and trust. They readily take the head's advice, follow directives without question, and often go far beyond what is necessary to help carry out the unit's mission. In this case, the head of pediatrics is both a manager and a leader. The key distinctions between leadership and management are summarized in Table 9.2.[52]

Organizations need both management and leadership if they are to be effective. Leadership is necessary to create and direct change and to help the organization get through tough times, and management is necessary to achieve coordination and systematic results and to handle administrative activities during times of stability and predictability.[53] Management—in conjunction with leadership—can help achieve planned orderly change. Leadership—in conjunction with management—can keep the organization properly aligned with its environment. Both managers and leaders play a major role in establishing the moral climate of the organization and in determining the role of ethics in its culture.[54]

LO-7 Approaches to Leadership

Political, religious, and business leaders have influenced the course of human events throughout history, but careful scientific study of leadership began only about a century ago. In the following paragraphs, we briefly summarize the development of this research.

THE TRAIT APPROACH

The **trait approach**—which was emphasized by researchers in the first two decades of the twentieth century—was based on the idea that leaders had unique traits that distinguished them from non-leaders. Many traits were thought to be important, including intelligence, dominance, self-confidence, energy, height, and knowledge about the job. As time passed, the list became so long that it lost any practical value. The trait approach was all but abandoned by the middle of the twentieth century, but in recent years it has resurfaced. Some researchers now argue that certain traits (for example, intelligence, drive, motivation, honesty, integrity, and self-confidence) provide the potential for effective leadership, but only if the person is really motivated to be a leader. The implication is that people without these traits are not likely to be successful leaders even if they try.[55] Recall that the emotional intelligence idea that was discussed earlier in this chapter identified five somewhat different traits of successful leaders.[56]

THE BEHAVIOURAL APPROACH

Because the trait approach was a poor predictor of leadership success, attention shifted from managers' traits to their behaviours. The goal of the **behavioural approach** was to determine how the behaviours of effective leaders differed from the behaviours of less effective leaders. This research led to the identification of two basic forms of leader behaviour: **task-oriented** (the manager focuses on how tasks should be performed in order to achieve important goals) and **employee-oriented** (the manager focuses on the satisfaction, motivation, and well-being of employees). Task-oriented managers tend to have higher performing subordinates, while employee-oriented managers tend to have more satisfied subordinates.

TRAIT APPROACH A leadership approach focused on identifying the essential traits that distinguished leaders.

BEHAVIOURAL APPROACH A leadership approach focused on determining what behaviours are employed by leaders.

TASK-ORIENTED LEADER BEHAVIOUR Leader behaviour focusing on how tasks should be performed in order to meet certain goals and to achieve certain performance standards.

EMPLOYEE-ORIENTED LEADER BEHAVIOUR Leader behaviour focusing on satisfaction, motivation, and well-being of employees.

AUTOCRATIC STYLE A form of leader behaviour in which the manager issues orders and expects them to be obeyed without question.

DEMOCRATIC STYLE A form of leader behaviour in which the manager requests input from subordinates before making decisions, but the manager retains the decision-making power.

FREE-REIN STYLE A form of leader behaviour in which the manager serves as an adviser to subordinates who are given a lot of discretion when making decisions.

SITUATIONAL (CONTINGENCY) APPROACH TO LEADERSHIP Leadership approach that assumes that appropriate leader behaviour varies from one situation to another.

Researchers have also identified three main leadership styles: the **autocratic style** (the manager issues orders and expects them to be obeyed without question), the **democratic style** (the manager requests input from subordinates before making decisions, but retains final decision-making power), and the **free-rein style** (the manager serves as an adviser to subordinates who are given a lot of discretion when making decisions). Most leaders tend to regularly use one style, and may, in fact, find it difficult to change from one style to another. But some leaders do manage to change their style. For example, Andrall (Andy) Pearson was an abrasive, numbers-oriented, hard-to-please manager when he was president and COO of PepsiCo. But as director of Yum Brands, he softened and transformed and truly cared about employees.[57]

THE SITUATIONAL APPROACH TO LEADERSHIP

As time passed, researchers began to realize that different combinations of leader behaviour might be effective in different situations. For instance, if workers are satisfied but not very motivated to work hard, a leader should most likely focus on task-focused behaviours in order to improve productivity. If worker productivity is high, but workers are stressed out about their jobs and have low levels of job satisfaction, the leader should most likely concentrate on employee-focused behaviours so as to improve their job satisfaction. This line of thinking led to the development of the **situational (or contingency) approach to leadership**.

The contingency approach was first proposed as a continuum of leadership behaviour. At one extreme, the leader makes decisions alone; at the other extreme, the leader has employees make decisions with only minimal guidance from the leader. Each point on the continuum is influenced by characteristics of the leader (including the manager's value system, confidence in subordinates, personal inclinations, and feelings of security), characteristics of the subordinates (including the subordinates' need for independence, readiness to assume responsibility, tolerance for ambiguity, interest in the problem, understanding of goals, knowledge, experience, and expectations), and the characteristics of the situation (including the type of organization, group effectiveness, the problem itself, and time pressures). Thus, many variables beyond the leader's behaviour were considered. Later models proposed additional factors (in the leader, in the subordinates, and in the environment) that influenced subordinate satisfaction and productivity.

THERE'S AN APP FOR THAT!

1. **Deloitte Leadership Academy** >>> **Platforms:** *Apple, Android, BlackBerry*
   Source: Deloitte Touche Tohmatsu
   Key Features: Leadership lessons from the world's best business schools and most inspiring leaders.
2. **Leadership Qualities** >>> **Platforms:** *Android, BlackBerry*
   Source: Bigo
   Key Features: Learn 12 winning Leadership Qualities of a competent and influential leader.
3. **Leadership Quotes** >>> **Platforms:** *Android, BlackBerry*
   Source: Juniper Islet
   Key Features: Excellent quotes about being a leader and leadership!

APP DISCOVERY EXERCISE

Since APP availability changes, conduct your own search for "Top 3" Motivational and Leadership APPS and identify the key features.

LO-8 RECENT TRENDS IN LEADERSHIP

During the late twentieth and early twenty-first centuries, many new ideas about leadership have been developed. We conclude this chapter with a brief discussion of several of these ideas.

TRANSFORMATIONAL LEADERSHIP

Transformational leadership is the set of abilities that allows a leader to recognize the need for change, to create a vision to guide that change, and to execute the change effectively. In contrast, **transactional leadership** involves routine, regimented activities that are necessary during periods of stability.

Many leaders may find it difficult to exercise both types of leadership. For example, when Michael Eisner took over the Walt Disney organization in the early 1990s, the company was stagnant and was heading into decline. Relying on transformational skills, Eisner turned things around in dramatic fashion. Among many other things, he quickly expanded the company's theme parks, built new hotels, improved Disney's movie business, created a successful Disney cruise line, launched several other major initiatives, and changed the company into a global media powerhouse. But when the firm began to plateau and needed some time to let the changes all settle in, Eisner was unsuccessful at changing his own approach from transformational leadership to transactional leadership and was pressured into retiring.

CHARISMATIC LEADERSHIP

Charismatic leadership is a type of influence based on the leader's personal charisma. Figure 9.7 portrays the three key elements of charismatic leadership that most experts acknowledge today.[58]

Charismatic leaders have a high level of self-confidence and a strong need to influence others. They also communicate high expectations about follower performance and express confidence in their followers. A highly charismatic supervisor will generally be more successful in

TRANSFORMATIONAL LEADERSHIP The set of abilities that allows a leader to recognize the need for change, to create a vision to guide that change, and to execute the change effectively.

TRANSACTIONAL LEADERSHIP Comparable to management, it involves routine, regimented activities.

CHARISMATIC LEADERSHIP Type of influence based on the leader's personal charisma.

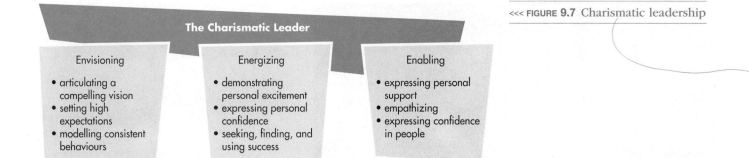

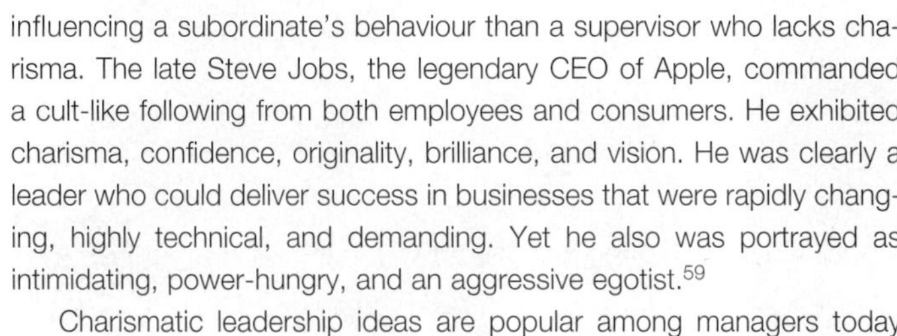

The Charismatic Leader
Envisioning
• articulating a compelling vision
• setting high expectations
• modelling consistent behaviours
Energizing
• demonstrating personal excitement
• expressing personal confidence
• seeking, finding, and using success
Enabling
• expressing personal support
• empathizing
• expressing confidence in people

<<< FIGURE 9.7 Charismatic leadership

influencing a subordinate's behaviour than a supervisor who lacks charisma. The late Steve Jobs, the legendary CEO of Apple, commanded a cult-like following from both employees and consumers. He exhibited charisma, confidence, originality, brilliance, and vision. He was clearly a leader who could deliver success in businesses that were rapidly changing, highly technical, and demanding. Yet he also was portrayed as intimidating, power-hungry, and an aggressive egotist.[59]

Charismatic leadership ideas are popular among managers today and are the subject of numerous books and articles.[60] One concern is that some charismatic leaders will inspire such blind faith in their followers that the followers may engage in inappropriate, unethical, or even illegal behaviours simply because the leader instructs them to do so. This tendency likely played a role in the collapse of both Enron and Arthur Andersen, as people followed orders from their charismatic bosses to hide information, shred documents, and mislead investigators. The film *Enron: The Smartest Guys in the Room* documents this problem.

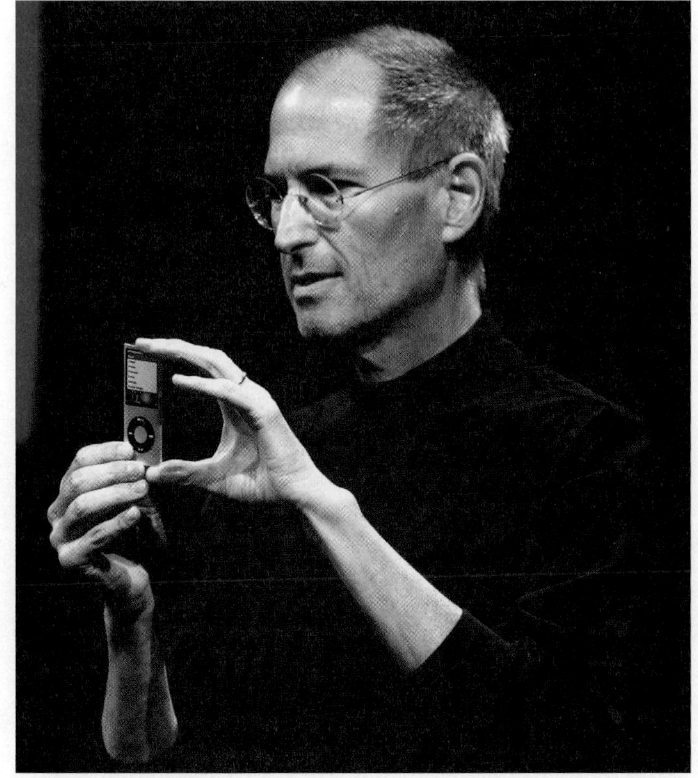

^^ The late Steve Jobs, former CEO of Apple, was a prime example of a charismatic leader.

Harry Sieplinga/HMS Images

LEADERS AS COACHES

Many organizations are now attempting to become less hierarchical—that is, to eliminate the old-fashioned command-and-control mentality often inherent in bureaucratic organizations—and to motivate and empower individuals to work independently. This changes the role of leaders. Whereas leaders were once expected to control situations, direct work, supervise people, closely monitor performance, make decisions, and structure activities, many leaders today are being asked to become coaches instead of overseers.[61]

Consider the parallel with an athletic team. The coach selects the players for the team and decides on the general direction to take (such as emphasizing offence versus defence). The coach also helps develop player talent and teaches team members how to execute specific plays. But at game time, it's up to the players to execute plays and get the job done. While the coach may get some of the credit for the victory, he or she didn't actually score any of the points.

For business leaders, a coaching perspective calls for the leader to help select team members and other new employees, to provide overall direction, to help train and develop the team and the skills of its members, and to help the team get the information and other resources it needs. The leader may also have to help resolve conflict among team members and mediate other disputes that arise. And coaches from different teams need to link the activities and functions of their respective teams. But beyond these activities, the leader is expected to keep a low profile and let the group get its work done without overly close supervision.

GENDER AND LEADERSHIP

Another factor that is altering the face of leadership is the growing number of women advancing to the highest levels in organizations. Given that most leadership theories and research studies have focused on male leaders, developing a better understanding of how women lead is clearly an important next step. For example, do women and men lead differently? Some early observers, for instance, predicted that (consistent with prevailing stereotypes) female leaders would be relatively warm, supportive, and nurturing as compared to their male counterparts. But, in reality, research suggests that female leaders are not necessarily more nurturing or supportive than male leaders. Likewise, male leaders are not systematically more harsh, controlling, or task focused than female leaders. Women do seem to have a tendency to be more democratic when making decisions, whereas men have a tendency to be somewhat more autocratic.[62]

CROSS-CULTURAL LEADERSHIP

Culture is a broad concept that encompasses both international differences and diversity-based differences within one culture. For instance, when a Japanese firm sends an executive to head up the firm's operation in Canada, that person will need to be sensitive to the cultural differences

AP Photo/Peter Lennihan

© Adrian Weinbrecht/Alamy

Elyse Allan (President and CEO of GE Canada) reads a report in her Mississauga office (left). Bonnie Brooks (President and CEO of The Bay and Lord & Taylor) speaks during an interview prior to the presentation of the Ivanka Trump Ready-to-Wear Collection at the Lord & Taylor flagship store in New York (right).

that exist between the two countries and consider changing his or her leadership style accordingly. Japan is generally characterized by collectivism (group before individual), whereas Canada is based more on individualism (individual before group). The Japanese executive, then, will find it necessary to recognize the importance of individual contributions and rewards and the differences in individual and group roles that exist in Japanese and Canadian businesses.

Cross-cultural factors also play a growing role in organizations as their workforces become more diverse. Most leadership research, for instance, has analyzed white male leaders because those individuals dominated leadership positions in North America. But as Asians, Blacks, Aboriginals, and Hispanics achieve leadership positions, it will be necessary to reassess how applicable current models of leadership are when applied to an increasingly diverse pool of leaders.

Canadian versus American Management Styles The management styles of Canadian managers might look a lot like that of Americans, but there are several notable differences. In general, Canadian managers are more subtle and subdued than American managers, more committed to their companies, less willing to mindlessly follow the latest management fad, and more open to different cultures because of the multicultural nature of Canada.[63] The Global Leadership and Organizational Behavior Effectiveness study found that Canadian managers are very oriented toward fairness, are less likely to protect their own interests above those of their teams, and put more emphasis on long-term goals rather than short-term gratification.[64] All of these characteristics are advantageous for Canadian companies that increasingly compete in global markets.

During the past decade, many Canadian-born managers have achieved significant success in companies that operate internationally. These include Bob Kelly (CEO of the Bank of New York Mellon Corp.), Henry McKinnell (former CEO of Pfizer), Steven McArthur (president of Expedia), Patricia Arnold (vice-president of Credit Suisse First Boston), Clara Furse (former CEO of the London Stock Exchange), Simon Cooper (CEO of Ritz-Carlton Hotel), and Dominic Barton (chairman of McKinsey & Company's Asia Region).[65]

STRATEGIC LEADERSHIP

Strategic leadership—which focuses on leadership in top management—is a leader's ability to understand the complexities of both the organization and its environment in order to lead change toward enhanced competitiveness. The late Steve Jobs, former CEO of Apple, was an effective strategic leader. For example, he recognized the potential growth of MP3 players and the fact that those devices used technology that was similar to that found in computers. He therefore directed the development of the Apple iPod, the iPhone, and iTunes, which have become enormously successful and profitable products.

ETHICAL LEADERSHIP

In the wake of corporate scandals at firms like AIG, Enron, and WorldCom, faith in business leaders has been shaken. Business leaders are now being called on to maintain high ethical standards for their own conduct, to unfailingly exhibit ethical behaviour, and to hold others in their organizations to the same standards—in short, to practice **ethical leadership**. Those responsible for hiring new leaders are looking more closely at the backgrounds of candidates. The emerging pressure for stronger corporate governance models is likely to further increase the

STRATEGIC LEADERSHIP Leader's ability to understand the complexities of both the organization and its environment and to lead change in the organization so as to enhance its competitiveness.

ETHICAL LEADERSHIP Leader behaviours that reflect high ethical standards.

VIRTUAL LEADERSHIP Leadership in settings where leaders and followers interact electronically rather than in face-to-face settings.

commitment to select for leadership positions only those individuals with high ethical standards and to hold them more accountable for both their actions and the consequences of those actions.

VIRTUAL LEADERSHIP

Virtual leadership involves carrying out leadership activities when the leader does not have regular personal contact with followers. This contrasts with earlier times, when leaders and their employees worked together in the same physical location and engaged in personal (i.e., face-to-face) interactions on a regular basis. The challenges of virtual leadership have confronted Alexey Saltykov, the CEO of InsureEye Inc., a company that helps consumers understand their insurance costs. Alexey is located in Toronto, but he has two employees in Russia, one in Montreal, and a business adviser in Australia. The company uses Skype and web-based collaboration software, but neither approach works as well as Alexey would like. He wants more in-person communication with all the people in one room.[66]

Under virtual leadership, communication between leaders and their subordinates still occurs, but it may be largely by videoconferencing, telephone, and email. In these situations, leaders have to work harder at creating and maintaining relationships with their employees. Nonverbal communication is not possible with email, for example, so managers have to make a special effort to convey appreciation, reinforcement, and constructive feedback to subordinates.

MyBizLab

Visit the MyBizLab website. This online homework and tutorial system puts you in control of your own learning with study and practice tools directly correlated to this chapter's content.

SUMMARY OF LEARNING OBJECTIVES

LO-1 IDENTIFY AND DISCUSS THE BASIC *FORMS OF BEHAVIOUR* THAT EMPLOYEES EXHIBIT IN ORGANIZATIONS.

Employee behaviour is the pattern of actions by the members of an organization that directly or indirectly influences the organization's effectiveness. *Performance behaviours* are the total set of work-related behaviours that the organization expects employees to display. *Organizational citizenship* refers to the behaviour of individuals who make a positive overall contribution to the organization. *Counterproductive behaviours* are those that detract from, rather than contribute to, organizational performance.

LO-2 DESCRIBE THE NATURE AND IMPORTANCE OF *INDIVIDUAL DIFFERENCES* AMONG EMPLOYEES.

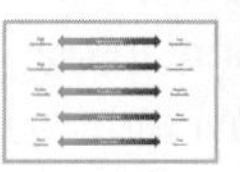

Individual differences are personal attributes that vary from one person to another. *Personality* is the relatively stable set of psychological attributes that distinguish one person from another. The *"big five" personality traits* are agreeableness, conscientiousness, emotionality, extraversion, and openness. *Emotional intelligence*, or emotional quotient (EQ), refers to the extent to which people are self-aware, can manage their emotions, can motivate themselves, express empathy for others, and possess social skills. *Attitudes* reflect our beliefs and feelings about specific ideas, situations, or other people. Especially important attitudes are *job satisfaction and organizational commitment.*

LO-3 EXPLAIN THE MEANING AND IMPORTANCE OF *PSYCHOLOGICAL CONTRACTS* AND THE PERSON–JOB FIT IN THE WORKPLACE.

A *psychological contract* is the overall set of expectations held by employees and the organization regarding what employees will contribute to the organization and what the organization will provide in return. A good *person–job fit* is achieved when the employee's contributions match the inducements the organization offers. Having a good match between people and their jobs can help enhance performance, job satisfaction, and motivation.

LO-4 IDENTIFY AND SUMMARIZE THE MOST IMPORTANT MODELS OF *EMPLOYEE MOTIVATION*.

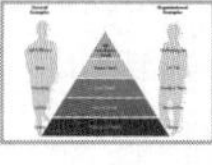

Motivation is the set of forces that cause people to behave in certain ways. Early approaches to motivation were first based on the assumption that people work only for money, and then on the assumption that social needs are the primary way to motivate people. The *hierarchy of human needs* model holds that people at work try to satisfy one or more of five different needs. The *two-factor theory* argues that job satisfaction is influenced by motivation factors such as recognition for a job well done, while job dissatisfaction depends on hygiene factors such as working conditions. *Expectancy theory* suggests that people are motivated to work toward rewards that they desire and have a reasonable expectancy of obtaining. *Equity theory* focuses on social comparisons—people evaluating their treatment by the organization relative to the treatment of others.

LO-5 DESCRIBE THE *STRATEGIES* USED BY ORGANIZATIONS TO IMPROVE JOB SATISFACTION AND EMPLOYEE MOTIVATION.

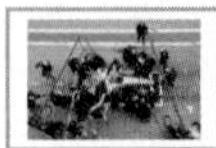

Reinforcement involves applying (or withholding) positive (or negative) consequences in an attempt to motivate employees to exhibit behaviour the manager wants. *Goal setting* involves setting SMART goals that will motivate workers to high performance. *Participative management and empowerment* involves tapping into workers' knowledge about the job, encouraging them to be self-motivated, and giving them more authority and responsibility so that they feel they are a real part of the company's success. *Team management* means forming teams of employees and empowering the team to make decisions on issues like production scheduling, work procedures, work schedules, and the hiring of new employees. *Job enrichment* means adding motivating factors to job activities. *Modified work schedules*—such as *work sharing* (job sharing), *flextime*, and *telecommuting*—increase employee satisfaction by providing increased flexibility for workers.

LO-6 DEFINE *LEADERSHIP* AND DISTINGUISH IT FROM *MANAGEMENT*.

Leadership refers to the processes and behaviours used by a person in order to motivate, inspire, and influence the behaviours of others. Leadership and management are not the same thing. Leadership involves such things as developing a vision, communicating that vision, and directing change. *Management*, meanwhile, focuses more on outlining procedures, monitoring results, and working toward outcomes.

LO-7 SUMMARIZE THE *APPROACHES TO LEADERSHIP* THAT DEVELOPED DURING THE TWENTIETH CENTURY.

The *trait approach* to leadership focused on identifying the traits of successful leaders. Recent research has focused on traits such as emotional intelligence, drive, honesty and integrity, self-confidence, and charisma. The *behavioural approach* identified two common leader behaviours: *task-focused* and *employee-focused* behaviours. Three leadership styles—*autocratic, democratic*, and *free-rein*—were also identified. The *situational approach* to leadership assumes that factors in the leader, factors in the followers, and factors in the situation determine which leadership behaviour is most effective.

LO-8 DESCRIBE THE MOST RECENT IDEAS ABOUT EFFECTIVE LEADERSHIP.

Transformational leadership (as distinguished from *transactional leadership*) focuses on the set of abilities that allows a leader to recognize the need for change, to create a vision to guide that change, and to execute the change effectively. *Charismatic leadership* is influence based on the leader's personal charisma. Leaders are often expected to play the role of *coach*, which involves selecting team members; providing direction, training, and developing; and allowing the group to function autonomously. Research on *gender and leadership* is re-examining assumptions about how men and women lead. *Cross-cultural leadership* is becoming increasingly important as companies become more diverse in a globalized economic system. *Strategic leadership* is the leader's ability to lead change in the organization so as to enhance its competitiveness. *Ethical leadership* requires that leaders maintain high ethical standards for their own conduct, and to hold others in their organizations to the same standards. *Virtual leadership* is becoming important as more leaders and their followers work in physically separate places.

QUESTIONS AND EXERCISES

QUESTIONS FOR ANALYSIS

1. Describe the psychological contract you currently have or have had in the past with an employer. If you have never worked, describe the psychological contract that you have with the instructor in this class.
2. Explain how each of the "big five" personality traits influence leadership effectiveness.
3. How is the job enrichment/job redesign approach to motivation different from the modified work schedules (flextime, compressed workweek) approach to motivation? Are there similarities between the two approaches? Explain.
4. How can participative management programs enhance employee satisfaction and motivation? Why do some employees not want to get involved in participative management?
5. What is the relationship between performance behaviours and organizational citizenship behaviours? Which are more important to an organization?
6. Describe the type of circumstance in which it would be appropriate to apply each of the theories of motivation discussed in this chapter. Which theory would be easiest to use? Which one would be hardest? Why?

APPLICATION EXERCISES

7. Identify two Canadian and two U.S. managers who you think would also qualify as great leaders. Explain your choices.
8. Ask a manager what traits he or she thinks are necessary for success. How does the manager's list compare with the "big five" list in this chapter? How many differences are there? Why would these differences exist?
9. Interview the human resource manager of a local company and ask what strategies the company uses to enhance employee job satisfaction.
10. Interview a manager and ask whether he or she believes that leadership can be taught. What are the implications of the manager's answer?

TEAM EXERCISES

BUILDING YOUR BUSINESS SKILLS

LEARNING TO LEAD

GOAL

To encourage you to understand your own strengths and weaknesses as they relate to critical leadership skills.

BACKGROUND INFORMATION

Most large businesses devote considerable resources to identifying those managers with the most leadership potential, and then providing training and development opportunities for those managers to enhance and refine their leadership skills. One company, for instance, has identified the following traits, characteristics, and skills, as important in leadership:

- Personal integrity
- Decision-making skills
- Interpersonal skills
- Communication skills
- Strategic thinking skills
- Global awareness skills
- Financial management skills

METHOD

Step 1 Working with three other students (as assigned by your instructor), develop and describe indicators and measures a business could use to *assess* each of the traits, characteristics, and skills listed above in managers, so the company could select those managers with the strongest potential for leadership. In other words, describe how you would go about selecting managers for special leadership training and development.

Step 2 Work with your group to develop or describe the techniques and methods that would *enhance* the traits, characteristics, and skills listed above. In other words, after you have identified the managers with the strongest potential for growth as leaders in Step 1, in Step 2 describe how you would go about teaching and developing those individuals so as to enhance their leadership potential and capacity.

FOLLOW-UP QUESTIONS

1. Comment on the traits, characteristics, and skills in the above list. Do you agree or disagree that these would differentiate between those who are both managers and leaders versus those who are simply managers? Are there others items that should be added to the list?
2. How easy do you think it would be to select managers for leadership and development in a company?
3. Do you believe that leadership can be taught? What are the assumptions underlying your answer?
4. If you personally were selected for a leadership development program, what would you expect to encounter during the training and development? How do you think you might be different after the training and development were completed?

EXERCISING YOUR ETHICS

TAKING ONE FOR THE TEAM

THE SITUATION

You are a skilled technician who has worked for a major electronics firm for the past 10 years. You love your job—it is interesting, stimulating, and enjoyable, and you are well paid for what you do. The plant where you work is one of five manufacturing centres your firm operates in a major metropolitan area. The firm is currently developing a new prototype for one of its next-generation products. To ensure that all perspectives are reflected, the company has identified a set of technicians from each plant who will work together as a team for the next two months.

THE DILEMMA

You have just met with your new teammates and are quite confused about what you might do next. As it turns out, the technicians from two of the manufacturing centres have heard rumours that your company is planning to close at least three of the centres and move production to a lower-cost factory in another country. These individuals are very upset. Moreover, they have made it clear that they (1) do not intend to put forth much extra effort on this project, and (2) are all looking for new jobs. You and the other technicians, though, have heard none of these rumours. Moreover, these individuals seem as excited as you about their jobs.

TEAM ACTIVITY

First, working alone, write a brief summary of how you would handle this situation. For instance, would you seek more information or just go about your work? Would you start looking for another job, would you try to form a sub-group just with those technicians who share your views, or would you try to work with everyone?

Second, form a small group with some of your classmates. Share with each other the various ideas you each identified. Then, formulate a group description of what you think most people in your situation would do. Finally, share your description with the rest of the class.

BUSINESS CASE

GETTING EMPLOYEES INVOLVED

In a 2011 Psychometrics Canada poll of 368 Canadian HR managers, 69 percent of respondents said that low employee engagement was a problem in their organization, and 82 percent felt that company management should be doing more to increase employee engagement. The HR managers didn't think that employee motivation was low; rather, they felt that managers were not creating the working conditions that would make employees feel engaged. The respondents also expressed the opinion that managers should give employees more recognition and praise (58 percent), listen more to employee opinions (71 percent), and provide employees with more learning and development opportunities (57 percent).

Another 2011 survey—this one involving 30 000 workers in 17 different countries—also found reason for concern about employee engagement. The survey was conducted by the global consulting firm Mercer; they defined employee engagement as a situation where employees have a vested interest in a company's success and are motivated to perform at levels that exceed stated job requirements. The survey found that one-third of workers are seriously considering leaving their current employer, and that there has been a decline in employee engagement since 2005 when a similar survey was conducted. Specifically, declines were evident in (1) the sense of commitment employees felt to their organization, (2) the pride they had in their organization, (3) employee willingness to go beyond stated job requirements, and (4) the feeling of accomplishment that employees got from their job.

A lack of employee engagement is a serious problem because employees are a great source of ideas for improving company operations. Consider these examples:

- At Algoma Steel, a shop-floor employee came up with a more efficient process for producing heat-treated steel plates that resulted in $90 million in additional revenue for the company.
- At ISL Engineering and Land Services, a senior urban designer was interested in making the company "greener," but he didn't want to force the idea on employees from the top down. Rather, he wanted them to help develop ideas. So, 25 employees who were known to be particularly keen about sustainability were named "green champions." They were encouraged to spend up to 10 percent of their time each day working on environmental issues. Project manager Jason Kopman, one of the champions, is analyzing energy-efficient upgrades for the ISL building.
- When Razor Suleman, CEO of I Love Rewards, noticed employee morale and motivation issues in his company, he decided to directly involve 10 to 12 current employees in interviewing prospective new employees. The process means that employees essentially "sell" the company to applicants, and by having staff members directly involved in hiring, it helps ensure that new hires will be a "fit" with the company culture. Employee involvement also extends to participation in objective setting, reinforced by an employee stock ownership program. Employees are also privy to the company's financial statements and can query management on any budget line expense.

Brad Hams, an organizational-change expert, says that employee engagement is typically low because business owners and employees have different perspectives. Owners are concerned about things like profit, cash flow, and cost control, while employees are concerned about things like pay, benefits, and job security. Employee engagement can be increased by giving employees the right incentives (so that they benefit when company performance improves), providing the right education for employees (so that they understand how the business works), and adopting the right performance measures (to help employees accurately monitor their performance).

Another way to increase employee engagement is to use social media. When social media first came on the scene, businesses saw it as a tool for marketing the company's products and services to external groups like customers. But now, managers are realizing that social media can be helpful in connecting workers with each other. A survey by the International Association of Business Communicators found that 70 percent of companies use social media for internal communications (up from 45 percent the previous year).

About 75 percent of Canadian workers now use social networking sites while on the job. A poll conducted by Robert Half Technology of Canada asked information officers at 270 companies about their company's policy on the use of social media at work. Forty-four percent of the companies allowed employees to use social media sites such as Twitter, Facebook, and LinkedIn for business purposes (up from only 22 percent a year earlier). About one-third of the companies still prohibit the use of social media in the office (down from 58 percent a year earlier).

Many companies are taking very specific actions to capitalize on the employee engagement characteristics of social media. At Toronto-Dominion Bank, the company's internal website has been made into a social media platform that includes blogs, chat forums, surveys, and a feature that allows employees to leave comments on blog pages, news items, and memos. Wendy Arnott, the vice-president of social media and digital communications, says that social media is a great way to increase employee engagement.

Alec Soth/Magnum Photos, Inc. (US)

Sun Life Financial Inc. also uses social media—blogs, online communities, and wikis—to get ideas from employees, and the company has pilot-tested a social media feature that allows employees to respond to the ideas of colleagues. Bill McCollam, the vice-president of digital strategy, said the company got a lot of good ideas as a result of the pilot test. Sun's social media site also allows each employee to develop a personal profile, and this helps managers find people with certain skills that are needed for specific projects. Managers have also noticed that the more casual nature of social media encourages timid employees to speak up and become engaged, whereas they often wouldn't do so in formal meetings.

The push in recent years to make management greener is another area that offers many specific opportunities to increase employee engagement. Jeremy Osborn is the founder of Good Energy, a company that helps other companies get their employees engaged in thinking about sustainability. He says that innovation has to come up from employees, and that increasing employee engagement contributes positively to increased social responsibility.

While employees often come up with good ideas for improvement in work processes and methods, getting them to actually share such improvements with management can be tricky, particularly when employees do not trust management. There are several reasons why workers do not share ideas for improvement. First, some workers fear that such sharing will allow others to take credit for their hard-earned knowledge, or that sharing their knowledge will weaken their position in the company. For example, a long-time employee at a small Canadian manufacturing plant taught a younger replacement worker how to run a complicated machine. Shortly thereafter, the older worker became ill and was off work for several weeks. When he returned, he found that the younger worker had essentially taken over his job. The older worker had this to say: "To pass on your experience or your knowledge to others, or to pass on to your fellow workers your secrets, how you assemble it faster, better, or more efficiently for the company, be careful; tomorrow you might have lost your job."

Second, there is a lot of "informal learning" that goes on in companies, but it is not generally recognized or rewarded in Canadian workplaces. The executive director of the Winnipeg-based Centre for Education and Work observes that if informal learning is not rewarded, we should not be surprised if employees do not share with management the efficient short-cuts they have discovered that allow them to work faster.

Third, employees fear that if they share their knowledge, management will use that knowledge to increase output. That's OK in the abstract, but if increased output leads management to conclude that they can get by with fewer workers, then layoffs will occur and employees will conclude that sharing ideas helps the company and hurts workers. Many workers have developed extra-fast ways of doing their work, but are reluctant to share those ideas with management. Since managers are always under pressure to improve productivity, the refusal of these workers to share information is frustrating.

Fourth, employees may be afraid of how they will be viewed by the boss if they suggest changes. One study of 400 employees in four different industries found that "social concerns" prevented employees from suggesting changes (they feared that bosses and co-workers would be unhappy with suggested changes to the status quo). One way to overcome this problem is to have each employee's job description include a statement to the effect that everyone in the company is responsible for suggesting improvements in the way work is done.

Fifth, employees may be intimidated by the power differences that exist between them and their managers. It is easy to say that managers should listen to employees, but that may not result in much useful information because employees are hesitant to speak their mind. A better strategy is for managers to ask employees what they need to do their jobs better. This strategy moves the focus away from the power difference between the employee and the manager, and instead puts the focus on improving the way work is done.

Sixth, workers don't share their knowledge because they have become convinced that management doesn't think they have anything to contribute. At one manufacturing plant, a new plant manager was trying to resolve some production problems that had developed under his predecessor. He asked for worker participation so that he could understand what was wrong in the plant and how things might be improved. Workers were surprised they were being asked for their ideas, because previous management had not solicited worker input. But in this case the workers agreed to help, and the story eventually had a happy ending.

QUESTIONS FOR DISCUSSION

1. Consider the following statement: *The use of social media by employees is harmful to productivity because employees are distracted from their work and spend too much time on personal matters instead.* Do you agree or disagree with the statement? Support your position.
2. Why do some workers refuse to share their job knowledge with either their co-workers or with management? What can management do to encourage workers to share their job knowledge?
3. Many managers feel that since companies provide jobs for people, the company has every right to expect that employees will do things like sharing their job knowledge with their co-workers because this will make the company more successful and allow it to continue to provide jobs. Do you agree or disagree with this viewpoint? Explain your reasoning.

PART 2(A): THE BUSINESS OF MANAGING

GOAL OF THE EXERCISE

In Part 1 of the business plan project, you formulated a basic identity for your business. Part 2(a) asks you to think about the goals of your business, some internal and external factors affecting the business, and the organizational structure of the business.

EXERCISE BACKGROUND: PART 2(A) OF THE BUSINESS PLAN

As you learned in Chapter 6, every business sets goals. In this part of the plan, you'll define some of the goals for your business. Part 2(a) also asks you to perform a basic SWOT analysis for your business. As you'll recall from Chapter 6, a SWOT analysis looks at the business's strengths, weaknesses, opportunities, and threats. The strengths and weaknesses are internal factors—things that the business can control. The opportunities and threats are generally external factors that affect the business:

Socio-cultural forces—Will changes in population or culture help your business or hurt it?

Economic forces—Will changes in the economy help your business or hurt it?

Technological forces—Will changes in technology help your business or hurt it?

Competitive forces—Does your business face much competition or very little?

Political–legal forces—Will changes in laws help your business or hurt it?

Each of these forces will affect different businesses in different ways, and some of these may not apply to your business at all.

Part 2(a) of the business plan also asks you to determine how the business is to be run. One thing you'll need to do is create an organizational chart to get you thinking about the different tasks needed for a successful business. You'll also examine various factors relating to operating your business.

YOUR ASSIGNMENT

STEP 1

Open the saved Business Plan file you began working on in Part 1. You will continue to work from this file.

STEP 2

For the purposes of this assignment, you will answer the questions in Part 2(a): The Business of Managing:

1. Provide a brief mission statement for your business.

   Hint: *Refer to the discussion of mission statements in Chapter 6. Be sure to include the name of your business, how you will stand out from your competition, and why a customer will buy from you.*

2. Consider the goals for your business. What are three of your business goals for the first year? What are two intermediate- to long-term goals?

   Hint: *Refer to the discussion of goal setting in Chapter 6. Be as specific and realistic as possible with the goals you set. For example, if you plan on selling a service, how many customers do you want by the end of the first year, and how much do you want each customer to spend?*

3. Perform a basic SWOT analysis for your business, listing its main strengths, weaknesses, opportunities, and threats.

   Hint: *We explained previously which factors you should consider in your basic SWOT analysis. Look around at your world, talk to classmates, or talk to your instructor for other ideas in performing your SWOT analysis.*

4. Who will manage the business?

   Hint: *Refer to the discussion of managers in Chapter 6. Think about how many levels of management as well as what kinds of managers your business needs.*

5. Show how the "team" fits together by creating a simple organizational chart for your business. Your chart should indicate who will work for each manager, as well as each person's job title.

   Hint: *As you create your organizational chart, consider the different tasks involved in the business. To whom will each person report? Refer to the discussion of organizational structure in Chapter 7 for information to get you started.*

   Note: Once you have answered the questions, save your Word document. You'll be answering additional questions in later chapters.

PART 2(B): THE BUSINESS OF MANAGING

GOAL OF THE EXERCISE

At this point, your business has an identity and you've described the factors that will affect your business and how you will operate it. Part 2(b) of the business plan project asks you to think about your employees, the jobs they will be performing, and the ways in which you can lead and motivate them.

EXERCISE BACKGROUND: PART 2(B) OF THE BUSINESS PLAN

To complete this part of the plan, you need to refer to the organizational chart that you created in Part 2(a). In this part of the business plan exercise, you'll take the different job titles you created in the organizational chart and give thought to the skills that employees will need to bring to the job before they begin. You'll also consider training you'll need to provide after they are hired, as well as how you'll compensate your employees. Part 2(b) of the business plan also asks you to consider how you'll lead your employees and keep them happy and motivated.

YOUR ASSIGNMENT

STEP 1

Open the Business Plan file you have been working on.

STEP 2

For the purposes of this assignment, you will answer the questions in Part 2(b): The Business of Managing:

1. What do you see as the "corporate culture" of your business? What types of employee behaviours, such as organizational citizenship, will you expect?

   Hint: *Will your business demand a casual environment or a more professional environment? Refer to the discussion on employee behaviour in this chapter for information on organizational citizenship and other employee behaviours.*

2. What is your philosophy on leadership? How will you manage your employees on a day-to-day basis?

   Hint: *Refer to the discussion on leadership in this chapter to help you formulate your thoughts.*

3. Looking back at your organizational chart in Part 2(a), briefly create a job description for each team member.

   Hint: *As you learned in Chapter 8, a job description lists the duties and responsibilities of a job; its working conditions; and the tools, materials, equipment, and information used to perform it. Imagine your business on a typical day. Who is working, and what are each person's responsibilities?*

4. Next, create a job specification for each job, listing the skills and other credentials and qualifications needed to perform the job effectively.

   Hint: *As you write your job specifications, consider what you would write if you were making an ad for the position. What would the new employee need to bring to the job in order to qualify for the position?*

5. What sort of training, if any, will your employees need once they are hired? How will you provide this training?

   Hint: *Refer to the discussion of training in Chapter 8. Will you offer your employees on-the-job training? Off-the-job training? Vestibule training?*

6. A major factor in retaining skilled workers is a company's compensation system—the total package of rewards that it offers employees in return for their labour. Part of this compensation system includes wages/salaries. What wages or salaries will you offer for each job? Why did you decide on that pay rate?

   Hint: *Refer to Chapter 8 for more information on forms of compensation.*

7. As you learned in Chapter 8, incentive programs are special programs designed to motivate high performance. What incentives will you use to motivate your workforce?

   Hint: *Be creative and look beyond a simple answer, such as giving pay increases. Ask yourself, who are my employees and what is important to them? Refer to Chapter 8 for more information on the types of incentives you may want to consider.*

Note: Once you have answered the questions, save your Word document. You'll be answering additional questions in later chapters.

CBC VIDEO CASE 2-1

CBC

NAIL SALONS

Sushi restaurants and coffee shops are just two of the symbols of the diversity that is evident in Canada. Another feature of Canadian society is immigrant groups who tend to cluster in certain occupations—Italians in construction, Koreans in convenience stores, and Filipinos in child care, for example. But no immigrant group has transformed its industry like the Vietnamese immigrants who own and operate nail salons. The salons are everywhere now, and they cater to women who want to pamper themselves by having their nails done. In past years, nail salons were of interest mostly to wealthy women, or to women who wanted their nails done for a special occasion like a wedding. Now, however, the cost of a nail job is low enough ($7–$15) that most women can afford it. These salons are like social clubs because there are so many repeat customers who get to know each other.

The growth of nail salons in Canada and the U.S. has been driven by global immigration from Asia and by help from a Hollywood actress. When the Vietnam War ended in 1975, one million Vietnamese fled the country to escape the reunification of Vietnam under communist rule. About 100 000 of these refugees came to Canada. Tippi Hedren, an American actress who achieved some fame as a result of her appearance in Alfred Hitchcock's movie *The Birds*, heard about the plight of the Vietnamese boat people and wanted to help Vietnamese women find jobs. The women admired her manicured fingernails, so she brought in a manicurist to teach them how to do their own nails. The women became interested in this activity and, being entrepreneurial, started opening up their own nail salons in the U.S. Over the next few years, the movement gradually spread across the U.S. from west to east, and eventually to Canada.

One of the original boat people was 11 when his family escaped. He spent two years in a refugee camp in Cambodia, then came to Canada and opened a Vietnamese restaurant in Vancouver. His wife eventually took a manicurist course and then she and her sister opened a nail salon. Some other relatives also work in the salon. The man sold his restaurant and now works in the salon as well. The tight-knit nature of families has helped the Vietnamese gain success; they want to be their own bosses and do things their way.

Like all businesses, nail salons must deal with both challenges and opportunities. First, early in the history of the nail salon business, there was some concern that Vietnamese women were being exploited because they worked long hours for low wages. But now these women can often make $1000 per week or more. Second, the pioneering wave of boat people has long since dried up, and people from other countries are now entering the industry. For example, one woman from Kazakhstan went from working in a bakery to working in a Vietnamese nail salon.

Third, the reputation of Vietnamese nail salons has been tarnished a bit in recent years because of reports of a lack of sanitation, inadequate sterilization of equipment, and the use of certain harmful chemicals. Most nail salons also do pedicures, and the water used in pedicure chairs poses a potential problem. It must be regularly filtered or the customer's feet are sitting in water that may be contaminated with fungus or warts. New pedicure chairs solve this problem by having water come out the top and drain out the bottom, but these chairs are expensive. Overall, what is needed is a nationwide system of licensing to reassure customers.

On the positive side, however, new products such as elaborate nail designs provide immense revenue potential for nail salons.

All things considered, the domination of the nail salon business by Vietnamese immigrants should serve as an inspiration for other entrepreneurs. These immigrants created a new industry and have managed to prosper with no government subsidies. And the nail industry has boomed even during the tough economic times of the last few years.

QUESTIONS FOR DISCUSSION

1. What does the term "workforce diversity" mean? What are the advantages of a diverse work force? How diverse is the nail salon business?
2. What is meant by the term "motivation"? To what extent are motivational factors different for immigrants than for individuals who were born in Canada? To what extent are they similar?
3. Consider the following statement: *The concentration of certain immigrant groups in certain industries is not a good thing because these immigrants become isolated from the broader Canadian society. As a result, their loyalty to Canada is not very high.* Do you agree or disagree with the statement? Explain your reasoning.

Source: *The National*, "Hands-Down Success," May 5, 2011.

CBC VIDEO CASE 2-2

CBC

CLASH OF THE CO-WORKERS

Venture conducted a survey to determine workers' perceptions of the main causes of conflict in the workplace. Respondents were presented with a list of 10 common worker complaints and asked to list their top three. The top three vote-getters were: (1) people who talk too loudly on the phone, (2) office gossip, and (3) co-workers who waste your time. *Venture* further examined the impact of office gossip, and also looked at the issues of co-workers who don't pull their weight, and clashes between older and younger workers.

OFFICE GOSSIP

Office gossip can poison a workplace. A tanning salon owner who had worked hard to build her company encountered big problems when employees starting spreading rumours about each other. After one salon manager disciplined a worker, other workers began spreading rumours that the salon manager was incompetent. When the owner became aware of the large amount of gossip that was evident at the company, she called all employees into the head office and asked them to sign a contract that prohibited gossip—for example, talking about a co-worker when that co-worker isn't present. A year after introducing the contract idea, the salon owner is getting calls from other companies asking about the policy.

Bob Summerhurst, an HR specialist, says that gossip occurs when bosses play favourites or when they don't communicate properly. Any information void will be filled with gossip, and that gossip is often negative. His solution is not a ban on gossip, but rather regular meetings of managers and employees.

CO-WORKERS WHO DON'T PULL THEIR WEIGHT

Jerry Steinberg, a Vancouver teacher, says that workers with children are often treated as "special" and he thinks it's not fair. He says an extra burden is being borne by people like him when they are asked to work a few extra hours a week to cover for parents who are tending to their children. The problem is worst during the holiday season because people with no children are asked to work holidays so that workers with children can spend time with their kids.

Steinberg is speaking up about his concerns. He has started a website called "No Kidding" where child-free members can vent their frustrations about the unfair treatment they are receiving at their place of work. But Steinberg says it is hard to stand up for yourself because you don't want to rock the boat or be a whiner. He recognizes that it sounds heartless to be unsympathetic to parents' wishes to spend time with their children. But he also observes that these people made a choice to have children, and they shouldn't expect to have an advantage because they made that choice. He is also unhappy about the extra benefits that parents get. He has a simple solution for that problem: give each employee a certain dollar amount that they can spend on whatever benefits they want.

THE GENERATION GAP

Young people in their 20s have generally grown up in an environment where their Baby Boomer parents gave them lots of things. Now those young people are entering the work force, and they want more things: benefits, money, authority, and free time. And they want them right now.

Consider John and Ryan, who are recent college grads. They are part of a generation that is a problem for business. They feel that they work very hard, but they don't necessarily want to do what their predecessors did (like wearing a suit and tie to work, or working from 9 to 5). Mike Farrell, who researches attitudes of young people, notes that most young people are plugged in and well informed, and these are qualities that employers crave. Theresa Williams, who hires workers for the *Halifax Chronicle-Herald*, recognizes that young people today are different from their predecessors. For example, they don't seem grateful to be offered a job like people in her generation were. She tries to overcome the difficulties in recruiting young people by emphasizing the good working conditions at the *Chronicle-Herald*.

The way students look for jobs is also changing. The job fair approach is still used, but some companies find it doesn't attract the kind of employees they want. One company therefore came up with a gimmick: they posted a job competition on the internet, with the prize being a job for a year, a free apartment, and a trip home for the holidays. The two winners—John and Ryan—moved to Halifax. A year later, they moved out of their free apartment, but stayed on with the company. Now they are helping to design this year's job competition, and they're on board with "the old guys."

QUESTIONS FOR DISCUSSION

1. What are the various forms of employee behaviour that can be observed in organizations, and what is the impact of the various forms on organizations? Identify the forms of employee behaviour evident in each of the three situations described above, and how they affected the organization in which they occurred.
2. What is the difference between "management" and "leadership"? What is the relevance of management and leadership in each of the situations described above?
3. What is the difference between the formal organization and the informal organization? How is the distinction relevant for each of the three situations described above?
4. Consider the following statement with respect to the first incident described above (office gossip): *The grapevine carries a lot of inaccurate information that prevents employees from doing their jobs well. To overcome this problem, managers should provide accurate information through formal communication channels, and that will negate the need for the grapevine.* Do you agree or disagree with the statement? Explain your reasoning.

Source: CBC's *Venture*, "Clash of the Co-Workers," March 26, 2006.

PART 3 MANAGING OPERATIONS AND INFORMATION

Blend Images - Dave and Les Jacobs/Getty Images

AFTER READING THIS CHAPTER, YOU WILL BE ABLE TO:

- LO-1 Explain the meaning of the term *production* (or *operations*) and describe the four kinds of *utility* it provides.
- LO-2 Identify the characteristics that distinguish *service operations* from *goods production* and explain the main differences in the *service focus*.
- LO-3 Describe two types of *operations processes*.
- LO-4 Describe the factors involved in *operations planning* and *operations control*.
- LO-5 Explain the connection between *productivity* and *quality*.
- LO-6 Understand the concept of *total quality management* and describe nine tools that companies can use to achieve it.
- LO-7 Explain how a *supply-chain strategy* differs from traditional strategies for coordinating operations among businesses.

What's Happening to Manufacturing in Canada?

During the past decade, there have been some interesting trends in the manufacturing sector in Canada. Between 1981 and 2010, factory *output* increased 59 percent, but factory *employment* fell 16 percent. During the last decade, 500 000 manufacturing jobs vanished, and, in 2011, factory employment in Canada dropped to its lowest level on record. Manufacturing now accounts for just 10 percent of the jobs in Canada (down from 16 percent in 2000). From 1976 to 1990, manufacturing was the biggest sector in the Canadian economy, but now it is third.

The difficulties in manufacturing are most obvious in the automobile manufacturing industry. In the 1990s, the auto industry had an annual trade surplus of $20 billion, which has now fallen to an annual deficit of $12 billion. In 2000, 198 000 people worked in the auto industry, but, by the end of 2011, that number was down to 131 000. Canada now produces two million cars, compared to three million in 2000. Many-auto parts plants have also disappeared (it is estimated that one well-paying job at an auto plant supports another 7.5 jobs elsewhere). Ontario is now the world's highest-cost place to make automobiles. Both General Motors Canada and Chrysler Canada have received bailout money from the federal government, but many problems remain. During the last few years, GM has closed manufacturing plants in Toronto, Windsor, and St. Therese, Quebec. In 2011, GM announced that it would close its Oshawa plant in June 2013. After that closure, GM will have just 8000 workers in Canada (down from 40 000 in the early 1990s).

Three key factors explain the decline of the manufacturing sector in Canada (not just automobile manufacturing). First, the application of new technology and automation

Operations Management, Productivity, *and* Quality

CHAPTER 10

has allowed companies to increase output while employing fewer workers. For example, Maple Leaf Foods announced in 2012 that it would close five old and inefficient food processing factories that could not compete with companies in the U.S. The old plants will be replaced with one new highly efficient factory in Hamilton that will produce more than the five old plants combined. About 1500 jobs, however, will be lost in the process. One reason for this change is the need for the company to improve its financial performance. In 2010, Maple Leaf earned nearly $50 million in pre-tax profits, but that represented only 1 cent on each dollar of sales.

© auremar/Fotolia

Second, the Canadian dollar has increased sharply against the U.S. dollar during the past decade, rising from $0.62 in 2001 to parity in 2012. This has increased the cost of Canadian-made products in foreign markets and has led to declining export sales.

Third, in addition to intense foreign competition, other countries aggressively try to attract manufacturing plants. Some U.S. states, for example, have given companies millions of dollars in incentives to encourage them to open manufacturing facilities in their jurisdiction. Volkswagen recently received more than $500 million from the state of Tennessee, and Mexico has convinced both Honda and Nissan to build new plants there. Representatives of foreign organizations also come to Canada to tout the benefits of their location. For example, Greg Wathen, CEO of the Economic Development Coalition of Southwest Indiana, came to Canada to encourage Canadian auto parts makers to set up shop in the state of Indiana.

HOW WILL THIS HELP ME?

You will benefit in three ways by reading and understanding methods that managers use for managing production operations and improving quality: (1) as an *employee*, you'll get a clearer picture of why everyone in a business should be concerned about productivity and quality, and how your job depends on the goods and services your company provides; (2) as a *manager,* you'll understand that, if companies want to remain competitive, they must continually analyze their production methods so they can efficiently produce high-quality products and services; and (3) as a *consumer*, you'll gain an appreciation of the significant efforts that companies expend in order to efficiently produce high-quality goods and services for consumers.

All of these developments sound pretty ominous, but keep in mind that the decline of manufacturing as a share of GDP is not something that has suddenly started recently; rather, the trend has been evident since the end of World War II. During the war, the manufacturing-to-GDP ratio was nearly 30 percent, but, by the 1960s, it had declined to 23 percent and then to just 14 percent in the most recent decade. Over the past 60 years, most developed economies have also experienced declines in manufacturing as a share of GDP, so Canada has lots of company. For example, in the U.S., manufacturing as a share of GDP has dropped from 24 percent in 1970 to just 13 percent at present.

There is some good news. There have actually been increases in some manufacturing activity, particularly in the energy industry. Consider the Nisku industrial complex south of Edmonton, the second-biggest energy park in North America (the biggest one is in Houston, Texas). Pipes are the building blocks of refineries, petrochemical plants, and oil-sand extraction sites, and they are fitted together at Nisku into the necessary configurations. Manufacturing here is not mass production; rather, it is engineered-to-order modules made one at a time. The oil-sands boom has drastically increased the number of jobs available for welders, pipefitters, and electricians. In Edmonton, manufacturing jobs are up 50 percent since the recession ended.

There are some success stories in the automobile business as well. Magna International's Newmarket, Ontario, factory, which makes door latches for automobiles, has become a world-class manufacturing plant. It defies the claim that low-cost countries will automatically kill manufacturing in advanced industrial countries. The Newmarket plant is so efficient that it ships door latches to auto makers in China.

QUESTIONS FOR DISCUSSION

1. Explain, in your own words, the developments during the last few decades that have created problems for Canadian manufacturing.
2. Should the Canadian government intervene more aggressively in the automobile industry to maintain employment? Explain your reasoning.
3. Consider the following statement: *The Alberta oil-sands development has had a negative effect on manufacturing in Canada because the emphasis on oil has driven up the value of the Canadian dollar and made Canadian manufacturers less competitive in export markets.* Do you agree or disagree with the statement? Defend your reasoning.

LO-1 WHAT DOES "PRODUCTION" MEAN TODAY?

SERVICE OPERATIONS Production activities that yield tangible and intangible service products.

GOODS PRODUCTION Production activities that yield tangible products.

Everywhere you go, you encounter businesses that provide goods and services to their customers. You wake up in the morning, for example, to the sound of your favourite radio station. You stop at the corner store for a newspaper on your way to the bus stop, where you catch the bus to work or school. Your instructors, the bus driver, the clerk at the 7-Eleven, and the morning radio announcer are all examples of people who work in **service operations**. They provide you with tangible and intangible service products, such as entertainment, transportation, education, and food preparation. Firms that make tangible products—radios, newspapers, buses, textbooks—are engaged in **goods production**.

Because the term *production* has historically been associated with manufacturing, it has been replaced in recent years by *operations*, a term that reflects both services and goods production. All businesses are service operations to some extent, and many of the things that we need or want—from health care to fast food—are produced by service operations. As a rule, service-sector managers focus less on equipment and technology than on the human element in operations because success or failure may depend on the quality of provider–customer contact.

Changes in Production Operations

Over the last 300 years, there have been several industrial revolutions. The first occurred in Britain in the 1800s, and the second in the U.S. in the early 1900s. Now, a third industrial revolution is underway, which is based on new technologies, software, robots, and miniaturization.[1] For example, 3-D printing produces goods like car parts and dresses using successive layers of plastic ink, and Ford Motor Company is using this process to design and test new engineering ideas.[2] The technology means that new product prototypes can be developed within a day or two of the development of a new design, rather than the three- to four-month time frame required with traditional methods. Other new technologies allow machines to run more cleanly, quickly, and safely, and to operate on a global scale. In a modern factory with online manufacturing, machines can log on to the internet, adjust their own settings, and make minor decisions without human help. They can communicate with other machines in the company (via an intranet) and with other companies' machines (via the internet). So-called "smart" equipment stores performance data that becomes available on desktops around the world, where designers can click on machine data, simulate machine action, and evaluate performance, before the machines themselves ever swing into action. With the internet, producers of both services and goods are integrating their production activities with those of far-off suppliers and customers.

CREATING VALUE THROUGH PRODUCTION

Products (both goods and services) provide customers with **utility** (want satisfaction). By making a product available at a time when consumers want it, production creates **time utility**, as when a company turns out ornaments in time for Christmas. By making a product available in a place convenient for consumers, production creates **place utility**, as when a local department store creates a "Trim-a-Tree" section. By making a product that consumers can take pleasure in owning, production creates **ownership (possession) utility**, as when you take a box of ornaments home and decorate your tree. By turning raw materials into finished

UTILITY The power of a product to satisfy a human want; something of value.

TIME UTILITY Quality of a product that satisfies a human want because of the time at which it is made available.

PLACE UTILITY Quality of a product that satisfies a human want because of where it is made available.

OWNERSHIP (POSSESSION) UTILITY Quality of a product that satisfies a human want during its consumption or use.

<<< The decorations for a Christmas tree clearly illustrate the importance of time, place, ownership, and form utility to consumers.

© David R. Frazier Photolibrary, Inc./Alamy

FORM UTILITY Quality of a product that satisfies a human want because of its form; requires raw materials to be transformed into a finished product.

OPERATIONS (OR PRODUCTION) MANAGEMENT A set of methods and technologies used in the production of a good or a service.

PRODUCTION MANAGERS Managers responsible for ensuring that operations processes create value and provide benefits.

goods, production creates **form utility**, as when an ornament maker combines glass, plastic, and other materials to create tree decorations.

Operations (or **production**) **management** is the systematic direction and control of the processes that transform resources into finished goods and services. As Figure 10.1 shows, **production managers** must bring raw materials, equipment, and labour together under a production plan that effectively uses all the resources available in the production facility. As the demand for a product increases, managers must schedule and control work to produce the amount required. Meanwhile, they must control costs, quality levels, inventory, and plant and equipment. The impact of production activity on the environment must also be considered. The boxed insert entitled "Producing Green Energy" describes the dilemma that exists in the production of energy.

LO-2 Differences between Service and Manufacturing Operations

Both service and manufacturing operations transform raw materials into finished products. In service operations, however, the raw materials, or inputs, are not things like glass or steel. Rather, they are people who have either unsatisfied needs or possessions needing care or alteration. The output of service operations is not physical products, but people with needs met and possessions serviced. Service operations are more complicated than goods production in four ways: (1) interacting with consumers, (2) the intangible and unstorable nature of some services, (3) the customer's presence in the process, and (4) service quality considerations.

INTERACTING WITH CONSUMERS

Manufacturing operations emphasize outcomes in terms of physical goods—for example, a new jacket. But the outcomes of most service

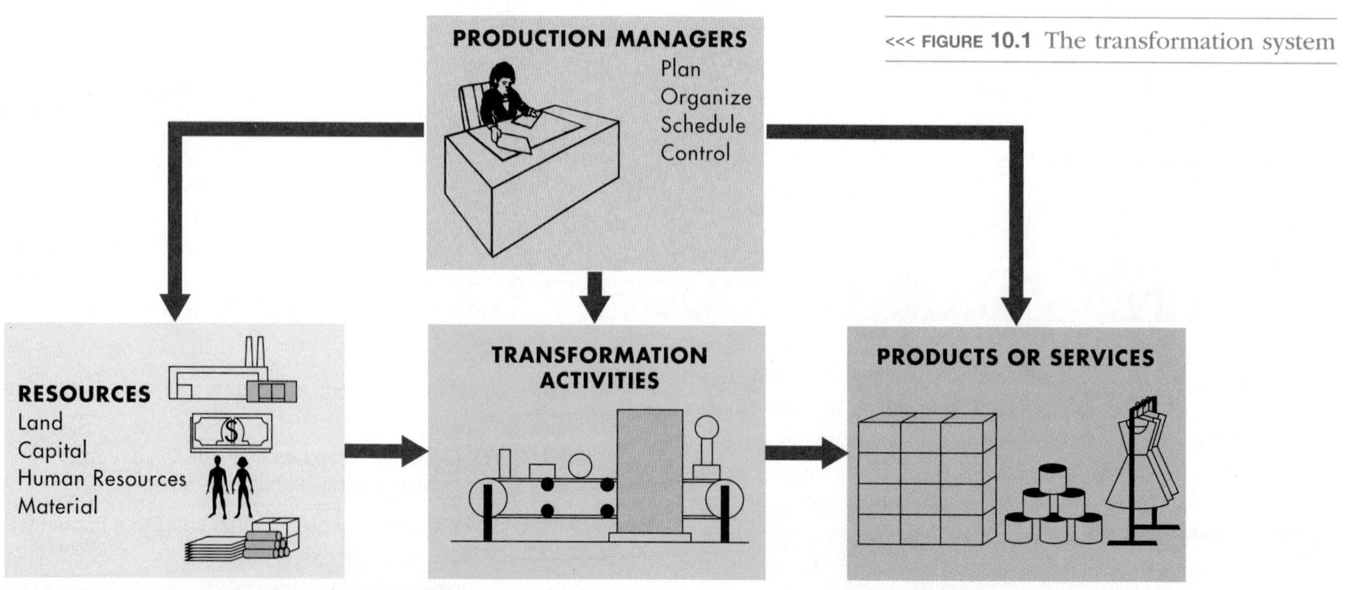

<<< FIGURE 10.1 The transformation system

THE GREENING OF BUSINESS

Producing Green Energy

When people think about the production of goods, they usually think of products like automobiles, home appliances, computers, toothpaste, and so forth. But the production of *energy* is also a crucial activity in our society, and, in recent years, there has been a big push to produce "greener" forms of energy, like wind and solar. But it is also becoming clear that making green decisions about energy is very complicated, because each type of energy (oil, coal, gas, nuclear, hydroelectric, wind, solar, and biofuels) has both advantages and disadvantages.

The dilemma is very clear—the most abundant and cheapest sources of energy (coal, oil, and natural gas) create significant environmental pollution when they are burned, while the least available and most expensive sources of energy (wind, solar, and nuclear) create very little pollution. The fact that consumers want to pay the lowest price possible for energy likely means that there will continue to be a reliance on coal, oil, and natural gas for most of our energy needs.

There are several other factors that complicate decisions about the production of energy. First, some scientists are now questioning whether carbon dioxide is really the driver of global warming. If their views become dominant, that will reduce the push for "greener" energy sources, like wind and solar. Second, critics have noted that without large government subsidies, wind and solar power are not competitive with coal and oil, and, as a result, wind and solar will not constitute a significant proportion of total energy for many years. Third, technological advances in the extraction of traditional fossil fuels have increased the supply of those fuels, which, in turn, lowers their price and makes them more attractive than wind and solar power.

Biofuels—the production of energy from sources like corn (used to make ethanol) and palm oil (used to make biodiesel)—looked promising at one time, but several unanticipated problems have arisen with this idea. For example, the increased demand for corn to make ethanol has driven up corn prices and increased the costs for all businesses that use corn. That, in turn, resulted in higher prices paid by consumers. Poor people were hurt the most, because they spend a larger proportion of their total income on food.

It seems that every way we turn there are problems.

CRITICAL THINKING QUESTIONS

1. Consult the sources listed for this boxed insert (found at the end of the book), and then develop a list of the advantages and disadvantages of each type of energy. Based on the list, which source of energy do you think is best? What problems did you encounter as you tried to make your decision about which form is best?
2. Consider the following statement: *It is unwise to continue spending large amounts of money to develop wind and solar power because these sources are too unreliable and too expensive. Instead, more emphasis should be placed on developing technologies to make traditional fossil fuels less polluting.* Do you agree or disagree with the statement? Defend your reasoning.

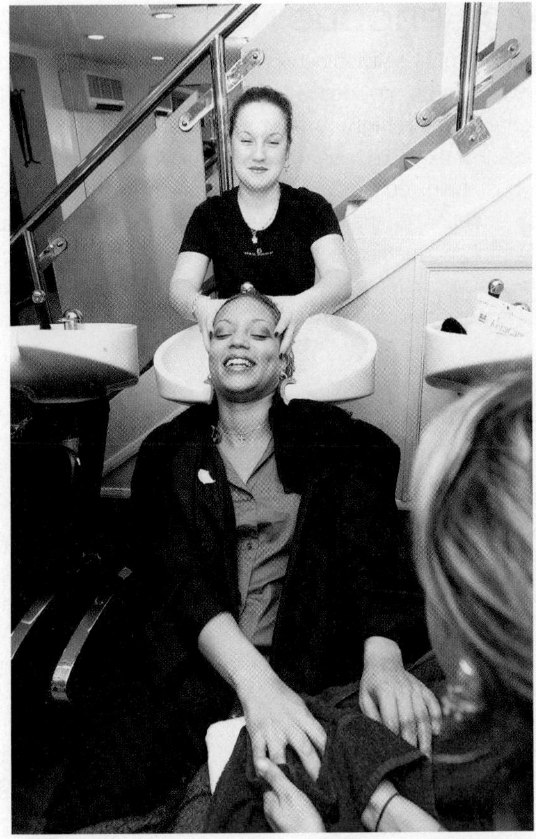

<<< The hair styling and manicure services being provided to this customer are classified as "high-contact," because the customer must be part of the operations process. The services also illustrate the three key features of service operations: *intangibility* (customer pleasure or satisfaction with the service), *customization* (the service each person gets is customized for them), and *unstorability* (the service cannot be produced ahead of time).

Gary Douglas/iStockphoto

operations are really combinations of goods and services—both making a pizza and serving (or delivering) it. Service workers need human relations skills. For example, gas company employees may need to calm frightened customers who have reported gas leaks. Thus, their job includes more than just repairing pipes. In contrast, factory workers who install gas pipes in manufactured homes have no contact with customers and don't need such skills.

SERVICES CAN BE INTANGIBLE AND UNSTORABLE

Often, services can't be touched, tasted, smelled, or seen. An important satisfier for customers, therefore, is the intangible value they receive in the form of pleasure, gratification, or a feeling of safety. For example, when you hire an attorney, you purchase not only the intangible quality of legal expertise, but also the equally intangible reassurance that help is at hand. Many services—such as trash collection, transportation, child care, and house cleaning—can't be produced ahead of time and then stored for high-demand periods. If a service isn't used when available, it is usually wasted. Services, then, are typically unstorable. Airline companies try to cope with unstorability by scheduling more aircraft maintenance during the slower winter months, when consumer demand for seats is lower.[3]

THE CUSTOMER'S PRESENCE IN THE OPERATIONS PROCESS

The customer is often present in the operations process. To get a haircut, for example, most of us have to go to the barbershop or hair salon. As they participate in the operations process, consumers can affect it. As a customer, you expect the salon to be conveniently located (place utility), to be open for business at convenient times (time utility), to provide safe and comfortable facilities, and to offer quality grooming (form utility) at reasonable prices (value for money spent). Accordingly, the manager sets hours of operation, available services, and an appropriate number of employees to meet customer requirements. But what happens if a customer, scheduled to receive a haircut, also asks for additional services, such as highlights or a shave, when he or she arrives? In this case, the service provider must balance customer satisfaction with a tight schedule. High customer contact has the potential to significantly affect the process.

The growth of e-commerce has introduced a "virtual presence," as opposed to a physical presence, of the customer. Consumers interact electronically and in real time with sellers, collecting information about product features, delivery availability, and after-sales service. Many companies have invited "the virtual customer" into their service systems by building customer-communications relationships. For example, the online travel agency Expedia.ca responds to your personalized profile with a welcome email, presents you with a tailor-made webpage the next time you sign in, offers chat rooms in which you can compare notes with other customers, and notifies you of upcoming special travel opportunities.

SERVICE QUALITY CONSIDERATIONS

Consumers use different measures to judge services and goods because services include intangibles, not just physical objects. Service managers know that quality of *work* and quality of *service* are not necessarily the same thing. Your car, for example, may have been flawlessly repaired (quality of work), but you'll probably be unhappy with the service if you're forced to pick it up a day later than promised (quality of service).

LO-3 Operations Processes

An **operations process** is a set of methods and technologies used in the production of a good or a service. At the most fundamental level, operations processes for the production of physical products are either *make-to-order* (producing custom-designed products for special order) or *make-to-stock* (producing standard items in large quantities for consumers in general).

GOODS-PRODUCING PROCESSES

Operations processes in manufacturing firms can be classified based on the kind of transformation technology that is used or whether the operations process combines resources or breaks them into component parts.

Types of Transformation Technologies Manufacturers use the following types of transformation technologies to turn raw materials into finished goods:

- In *chemical* processes, raw materials are chemically altered. Such techniques are common in the aluminum, steel, fertilizer, petroleum, and paint industries.
- *Fabrication* processes mechanically alter the basic shape or form of a product. Fabrication occurs in the metal forming, woodworking, and textile industries.
- *Assembly* processes put together various components. These techniques are common in the electronics, appliance, and automotive industries.
- In *transport* processes, goods acquire place utility by being moved from one location to another. For example, bicycles are routinely moved from manufacturing plants to consumers by truck and through warehouses and discount stores.
- *Clerical* processes transform information. Combining data on employee absences and machine breakdowns into a productivity report is a clerical process. So is compiling inventory reports at a retail outlet.

Analytic versus Synthetic Processes An **analytic process** breaks down basic resources into their component parts. For example, Rio Tinto Alcan manufactures aluminum by extracting it from an ore called bauxite. The reverse approach, a **synthetic process**, combines a number of raw materials to produce a finished product such as fertilizer or paint.

SERVICE-PRODUCING PROCESSES

One useful way of classifying services is to determine whether or not a given service can be provided without the customer being part of the production system. In **high-contact systems**, the customer is part of the process. For example, when you purchase transportation, you must board a bus, train, or airplane. Transportation managers, therefore, must pay attention to the cleanliness of the trains, buses, and airplanes. Dental and medical services, hair salons, and guided tours are also high-contact systems. By contrast, in **low-contact systems**, the customer is not physically present. The cheque-processing centre at

OPERATIONS PROCESS A set of methods and technologies used in the production of a good or a service.

ANALYTIC PROCESS Any production process in which resources are broken down into their component parts.

SYNTHETIC PROCESS Any production process in which resources are combined.

HIGH-CONTACT SYSTEM A system in which the service cannot be provided without the customer being physically in the system (e.g., transit systems).

LOW-CONTACT SYSTEM A system in which the service can be provided without the customer being physically in the system (e.g., lawn-care services).

Hydro Quebec

Yuri Arcurs/Shutterstock

© Dmitry/Fotolia

dapd/AP PHOTO

Mile Atanasov/Shutterstock

<<< The various types of transformation technologies used by businesses provide an impressive array of products and services to consumers. The basic technologies shown here are *chemical* (top left), *fabrication* (top centre), *assembly* (top right), *transport* (bottom left), and *clerical* (bottom right).

a bank is a low-contact system because customers are not in contact with the bank while the service is being performed. Gas and electric utilities, auto repair shops, and lawn-care services are also low-contact systems.

Business Strategy as the Driver of Operations

Production is a flexible activity that can be moulded into many shapes to give quite different capabilities for different purposes. The kind of production that is best for a particular company should be decided from above by the firm's business strategy.[4] In the following paragraphs, we present examples of four firms—two in goods production and two in services—that have different business strategies and, therefore, different operations capabilities. As shown in Table 10.1, each company has identified a business strategy that it can use to attract customers in its industry. Toyota chose quality as their strategy for competing in selling cars. No Frills Grocery (owned by Loblaw Companies) emphasizes discount prices. The flexibility strategy at 3M prioritizes new product development in an ever-changing line of products for home and office, and FedEx captures the overnight delivery market with delivery dependability. Firms design their operations to support the company's business strategy.

Since the four firms have different business strategies, we should expect to see differences in their operations. The top-priority **operations capability (production capability)**—the activity or process

OPERATIONS CAPABILITY (PRODUCTION CAPABILITY) The activity or process that production must do especially well and with high proficiency.

>>> **TABLE 10.1** Business Strategies That Win Customers for Four Companies

Company	Strategy for Attracting Customers	What the Company Does to Implement Its Strategy
Toyota	Quality	Cars perform reliably, have an appealing fit and finish, and consistently meet or exceed customer expectations at a competitive price
No Frills	Low price	Foods and everyday items offered at prices significantly lower than conventional food chains
3M	Flexibility	Innovation, with more than 55 000 products in a constantly changing line of convenience items for home and office
FedEx	Dependability	Every delivery is fast and on time, as promised

TABLE 10.2 Operations Capabilities and Characteristics for Four Companies

Operations Capability	Key Operations Characteristics
Quality (Toyota)	• High-quality standards for materials suppliers • Just-in-time materials flow for lean manufacturing • Specialized, automated equipment for consistent product buildup • Operations personnel expert on continuous improvement of product, work methods, and materials
Low Cost (No Frills)	• Avoids excess overhead and costly inventory (no floral departments, sushi bars, or banks that drive up costs) • Originally provided a limited assortment of "No Name" products and only the most basic customer service (more recently, stores have expanded both products and customer services) • Customers are required to pack their own groceries and provide their own bags • Low labour costs are achieved by minimum staffing • Labour and shelving costs are reduced by selling merchandise out of custom shipping cartons (in recent years, more conventional product displays have been introduced)
Flexibility (3M)	• Maintains some excess (expensive) production capacity available for fast start-up on new products • Adaptable equipment/facilities for production changeovers from old to new products • Hires operations personnel who thrive on change • Many medium- to small-sized facilities in diverse locations to enhance creativity
Dependability (FedEx)	• Customer automation: uses electronic and online tools with customers to shorten shipping time • Wireless information system for package scanning by courier, updating of package movement, and package tracking by customer • Maintains a company air force, global weather forecasting centre, and ground transportation for pickup and delivery, with backup vehicles for emergencies • Each of 30 automated regional distribution hubs processes up to 45 000 packages per hour for next-day deliveries

that production must do especially well, with high proficiency—is listed for each firm in Table 10.2, along with key operations characteristics for implementing that capability. Each company's operations capability matches up with its business strategy, so that the firm's activities—from top to bottom—are focused in a particular direction. For example, Toyota's top priority is quality, so its operations—inputs, transformation activities, and outputs—are devoted first and foremost to quality. All production processes, equipment, and training are designed to build better cars. The entire culture supports a quality emphasis among employees, suppliers, and dealerships. As described in the Business Case at the end of the chapter, Toyota had a significant setback with respect to quality in 2010, but those problems motivated its managers to redouble their efforts to produce high-quality cars.

LO-4 OPERATIONS PLANNING

FORECASTS Estimates of future demand for both new and existing products.

CAPACITY The amount of a good that a firm can produce under normal working conditions.

Managers from many departments contribute to the firm's decisions about operations management. As Figure 10.2 shows, however, no matter how many decision makers are involved, the process can be described as a series of logical steps. The business plan and forecasts developed by top managers guide operations planning. The business plan outlines goals and objectives, including the specific goods and services that the firm will offer. Managers also develop long-range production plans through **forecasts** of future demand for both new and existing products. Covering a period of two to five years, the production plan specifies the number of plants or service facilities and the amount of labour, equipment, transportation, and storage that will be needed to meet demand. It also specifies how resources will be obtained. There are five main categories of operations planning: *capacity, location, layout, quality*, and *methods planning*.

Capacity Planning

The amount of a product that a company can produce under normal working conditions is its **capacity**. A firm's capacity depends on how many people it employs and the number and size of its facilities.

CAPACITY PLANNING FOR PRODUCING GOODS

Capacity planning means ensuring that a firm's capacity just slightly exceeds the normal demand for its product. If capacity is too small to meet demand, the company must turn away customers, and it will lose profit opportunities. If capacity is too large, the firm wastes money by having too many machines and too many employees.

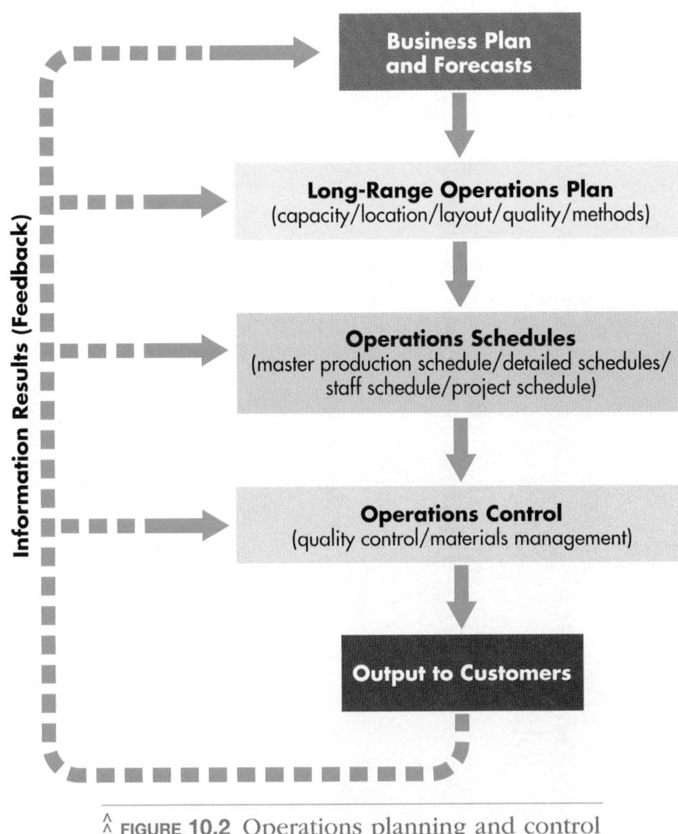

FIGURE 10.2 Operations planning and control

CAPACITY PLANNING FOR PRODUCING SERVICES

In low-contact systems, capacity should be set at the level of average demand. Orders that arrive faster than expected can be set aside in a "to be done" file and processed later, during a slower period. In high-contact systems, managers must plan capacity to meet peak demand. A supermarket, for instance, has far more cash registers than it needs on an average day. But on a Saturday morning or during the three days before Christmas, all registers will be running at full speed. By introducing self-service check-in machines and manned "bag drop" stations, Alaska Airlines doubled its capacity, halved its staffing needs, and cut costs, all while speeding travellers through the check-in process.[5]

Location Planning

Because the location of a factory, office, or store affects its production costs and flexibility, sound location planning is crucial. Companies that locate in high-cost areas will find themselves at a cost disadvantage relative to their competitors.

LOCATION PLANNING FOR PRODUCING GOODS

In goods-producing operations, location decisions are influenced by proximity to raw materials and markets, availability of labour, energy and transportation costs, local regulations and taxes, and community living conditions.

LOCATION PLANNING FOR PRODUCING SERVICES

Low-contact services can be located near resource supplies, labour, or transportation outlets. For example, the typical Walmart distribution centre is located near the hundreds of Walmart stores it supplies, not near the companies that supply the distribution centre. Distribution managers regard Walmart stores as their customers. By contrast, high-contact services must locate near the customers who are a part of the system. Accordingly, fast-food restaurants such as Taco Bell, McDonald's, and Burger King have begun moving into non-traditional locations with high traffic—dormitories, hospital cafeterias, museums, and shopping malls.

Layout Planning

Once a site has been selected, managers must decide on plant layout. Layout of machinery, equipment, and supplies determines whether a company can respond quickly and efficiently to customer requests for more and different products, or whether it will find itself unable to match competitors' production speed or convenience of service.

LAYOUT PLANNING FOR PRODUCING GOODS

In facilities that produce physical goods, layout must be planned for three types of space: (1) the actual workstations and equipment for transforming raw materials into finished products, (2) storage and maintenance areas, and (3) support facilities like offices, restrooms, parking lots, and cafeterias. Goods may be produced using *process*, *cellular*, or *product* layouts.

Process Layouts In a **process layout**, equipment and people are grouped according to function—this layout is well suited to job shops specializing in custom work. In a woodworking shop, for example, machines cut the wood in one area, sanding occurs in another area, and jobs that need painting are taken to a dust-free area where all the painting equipment is located. The job shop produces many one-of-a-kind products, and each product requires different kinds of work (see Figure 10.3a). While Product X may need only three production steps prior to packaging, Product Y needs four. Machine shops, custom bakeries, and dry cleaning shops often feature process layouts.

Cellular Layouts The **cellular layout** is used when a group of similar products follows a fixed flow path. A clothing manufacturer, for example, may establish a cell that is dedicated to making a family of pockets—for example, pockets for shirts, coats, blouses, trousers, and slacks. Within the cell, various types of equipment (e.g., for cutting, trimming, and sewing) are arranged close together in the appropriate sequence. Figure 10.3b shows two production cells, one each for Products X and Y, while all other smaller-volume products are produced elsewhere in the plant.

Product Layouts In a **product layout**, equipment and people are set up to produce one type of product in a fixed sequence of steps (see Figure 10.3c). Product layouts are efficient for producing large

PROCESS LAYOUT A way of organizing production activities such that equipment and people are grouped together according to their function.

CELLULAR LAYOUT Used to produce goods when families of products can follow similar flow paths.

PRODUCT LAYOUT A way of organizing production activities such that equipment and people are set up to produce only one type of good.

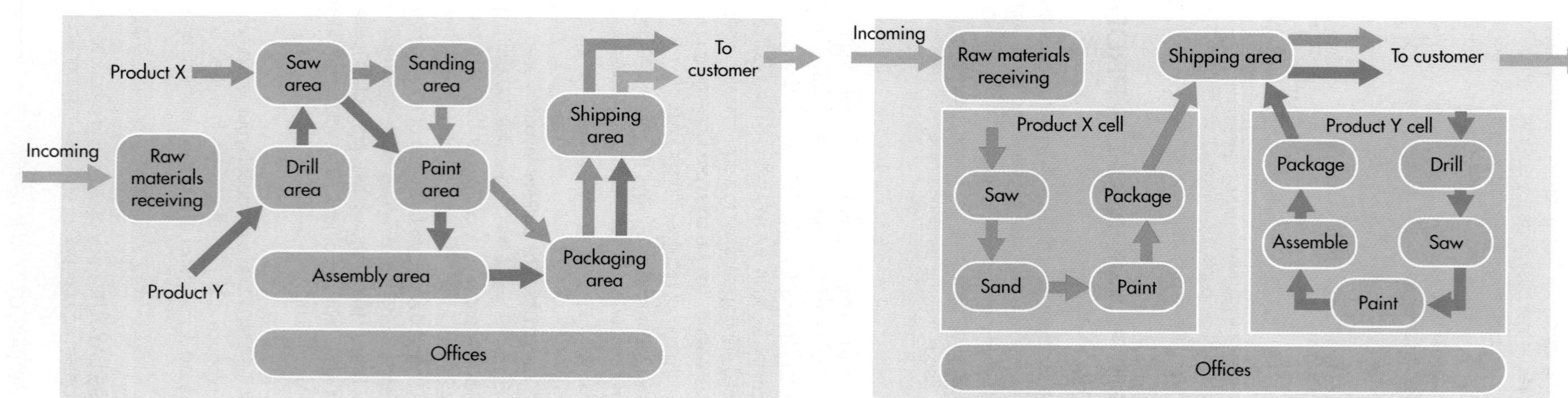

(a) Process Layout for Wood Shop

Arrows indicate unique path of workflow for each product.
Orange = Product X; Blue = Product Y

(b) Cellular Layout for Wood Shop

Arrows indicate unique path of workflow for each product.
Orange = Product X; Blue = Product Y

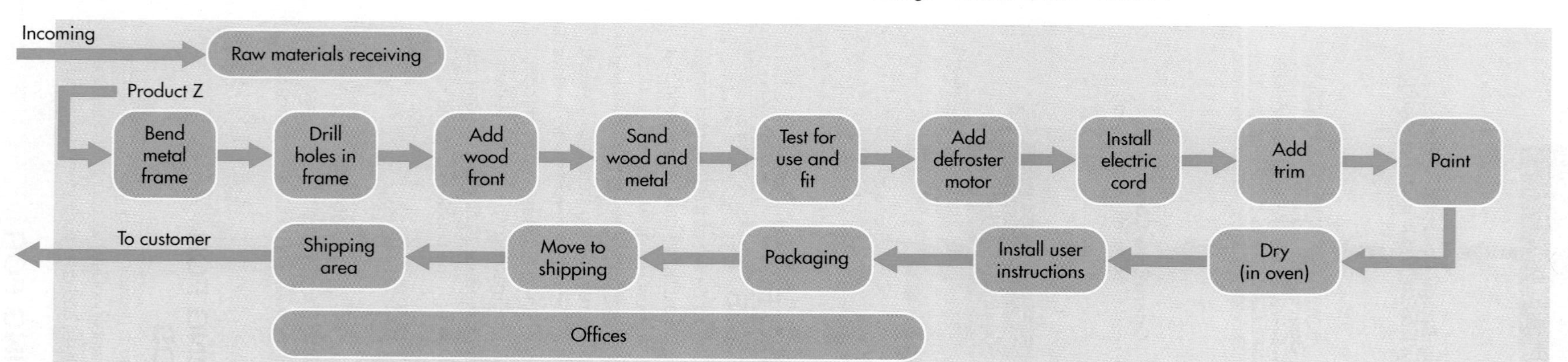

(c) Product Layout—Assembly Line

Arrows indicate the fixed path of workflow for all units of Product Z

FIGURE 10.3 Layouts for producing goods

volumes of product quickly and often use **assembly lines**. Automobile, food processing, and television-assembly plants use product layouts. In an attempt to improve productivity even more, many companies have introduced **lean manufacturing**, which emphasizes the elimination of all forms of waste, including overproduction, excess inventory, and wasted motions. Louis Vuitton, the maker of luxury handbags, has adopted lean manufacturing in order to quickly respond to changes in customer preferences.[6]

Many assembly lines use *industrial robots*—computer-controlled machines, like spot welders, that perform repetitive operations quickly and accurately. Robots are also used in other situations; at Amazon.com, robots are used to locate items in customers' orders and to move products around the warehouse.[7] In agriculture, robots are used to pick fruit and to milk cows,[8] and hospitals use "service robots" to carry trays of medication or loads of laundry.[9]

Other Developments in Layout Flexibility With a **flexible manufacturing system (FMS)**, a single factory can produce a wide variety of products. Automobile manufacturers, for example, now build several models of cars using the same basic "platform" (the underbody of the car). Nissan, Toyota, and Honda make the majority of their cars using FMS, and North American carmakers are now rapidly adopting the strategy.[10] The Oakville, Ontario, Ford plant was the first flexible assembly plant in Canada.[11]

Some companies have experimented with so-called **soft manufacturing**—reducing huge FMS operations to smaller, more manageable groups of machines. Automation is less likely to fail when relegated to jobs it does best, while human workers perform the assembly-line jobs that require dexterity and decision making. Both are supported by networks of computers programmed to assist in all sorts of tasks.

The latest development is the **movable factory**. Because FMS is so expensive, some developing countries with lots of labour, but little capital, are buying up equipment from industrialized countries that is still relatively modern and then using it to produce new and untested products in their own country. For example, a used press from the Buffalo-Niagara region, capable of shaping steel with its 14 000 tonnes of pressure per square inch, is used to manufacture the internal workings of new Chinese nuclear power plants.[12]

LAYOUT PLANNING FOR SERVICES

In a low-contact system, like the mail-processing facility at UPS or FedEx, the system looks very much like a product layout in a factory. Machines and people are arranged in the order in which they are used in the mass processing of mail. In contrast, FedEx Kinko's Office and Print Centers use process layouts for diverse custom jobs. Specific functions such as photocopying, computing, binding, photography, and laminating are each performed in specialized areas of the store.

With the "Kiva MFS" system, operators stand still while products come to them. Pallets, cases, and orders are stored on inventory pods that are picked up and moved by mobile robotic drive units (the small orange device under the shelves in the centre of the picture).

© Ian Dagnall/Alamy

High-contact service systems are arranged to meet customer needs and expectations. For example, a cafeteria focuses both layout and services on the groups that constitute its primary market—families and elderly people. As shown in Figure 10.4, families enter to find an array of highchairs and rolling baby beds that make it convenient to wheel children through the line. Meanwhile, servers are willing to carry trays for elderly people and for those pushing strollers.

ASSEMBLY LINE A type of product layout in which a partially finished product moves through a plant on a conveyor belt or other equipment.

LEAN MANUFACTURING A system designed for smooth production flows that avoid inefficiencies, eliminate unnecessary inventories, and continuously improve production processes.

FLEXIBLE MANUFACTURING SYSTEM (FMS) A production system that allows a single factory to produce small batches of different goods on the same production line.

SOFT MANUFACTURING Emphasizes computer software and computer networks instead of production machines.

MOVABLE FACTORY Purchasing relatively modern production equipment and transporting it to another location to create a new manufacturing plant, typically in a developing country.

>>> **FIGURE 10.4** Layout of a typical Piccadilly cafeteria

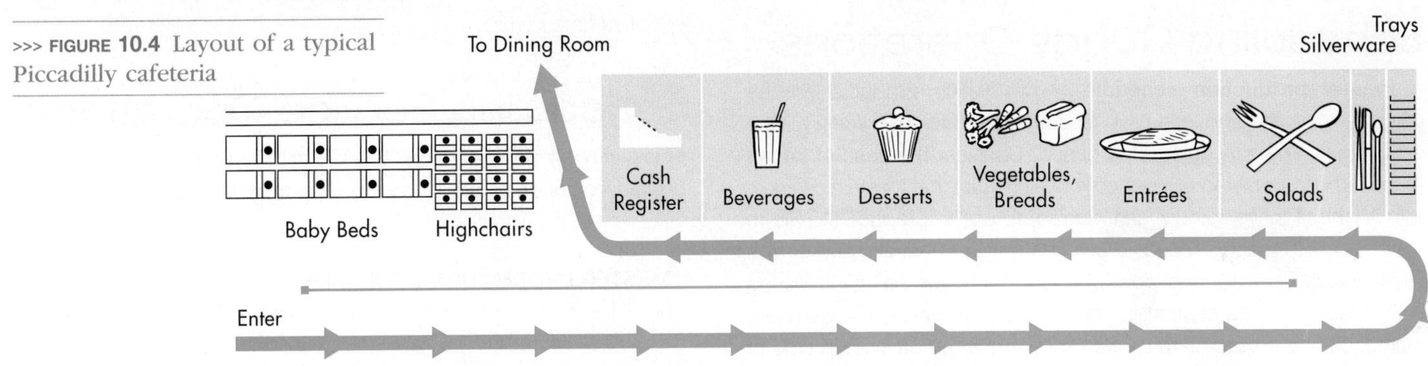

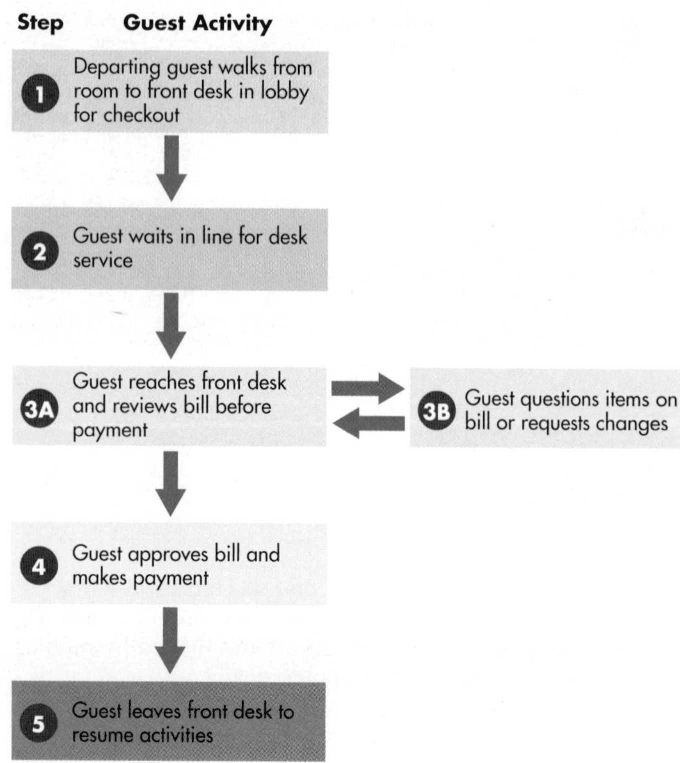

Step
Guest Activity
1 Departing guest walks from room to front desk in lobby for checkout
2 Guest waits in line for desk service
3A Guest reaches front desk and reviews bill before payment
3B Guest questions items on bill or requests changes
4 Guest approves bill and makes payment
5 Guest leaves front desk to resume activities

<<< FIGURE 10.5 Flow chart of a traditional guest checkout

Quality Planning

In planning production systems and facilities, managers must keep in mind the firm's quality goals.[13] Thus, any complete production plan includes systems for ensuring that goods are produced to meet the firm's quality standards. The issues of productivity and quality are discussed in more detail later in this chapter.

Methods Planning

In designing production systems, managers must clearly identify all production steps and the specific methods for performing them. They can then work to reduce waste, inefficiency, and poor performance by examining procedures on a step-by-step basis, an approach sometimes called methods improvement.

METHODS IMPROVEMENTS IN GOODS

Improvement of production for goods begins when a manager documents the current method using a diagram called the process flow chart. The chart identifies the sequence of production activities, movements of materials, and work performed at each stage, as the product flows through production. The flow can then be analyzed to identify wasteful activities, sources of delay in production flows, and other inefficiencies.

METHODS IMPROVEMENTS IN SERVICES

Similar procedures are useful in designing and evaluating low-contact service systems. At a bank, for example, the cash-management unit collects accounts receivable for corporate clients; the sooner cheques are collected and deposited, the sooner the client begins collecting interest. In high-contact services, the demands of systems analysis are somewhat different. Here, the steps in the process must be analyzed to see where improvements can be made. Consider the traditional checkout method at hotels. The process flow chart in Figure 10.5 shows five stages of customer activities. A more efficient checkout method eliminates steps 1, 2, 3A, and 5. Customers now scan their bills on the TV in their rooms before departure. If the bill is correct, no further checkout is required, and the hotel submits the charges against the credit card the customer showed at check-in.

OPERATIONS SCHEDULING

Once plans identify the necessary resources and how to use those resources to reach a firm's quantity and quality goals, managers must develop timetables for acquiring the resources. This aspect of operations is called scheduling.

Scheduling Goods Operations

A **master production schedule** shows which products will be produced, when production will occur, and what resources will be used during the scheduled time period. Consider the case of Logan Aluminum Inc., which produces coils of aluminum that its main customers, Atlantic Richfield and Alcan Aluminum, use to produce aluminum cans. Logan's master schedule extends out to 60 weeks and shows which types of coils, and how many of each, will be made during each week. This information is not complete, however. For example, manufacturing personnel must also know on which days each type of coil will be run. Machine start-up and stop times must be assigned, and employees must be given scheduled work assignments. Short-term detailed schedules answer questions like these on a daily or weekly basis. These schedules use incoming orders and weekly sales forecasts to determine what size and variety of coils to make within a specified time period.

Scheduling Service Operations

In low-contact services, work scheduling may be based either on the desired completion date or on the time of order arrival. For example,

MASTER PRODUCTION SCHEDULE Schedule showing which products will be produced, when production will take place, and what resources will be used.

>>> **FIGURE 10.6** A Gantt chart

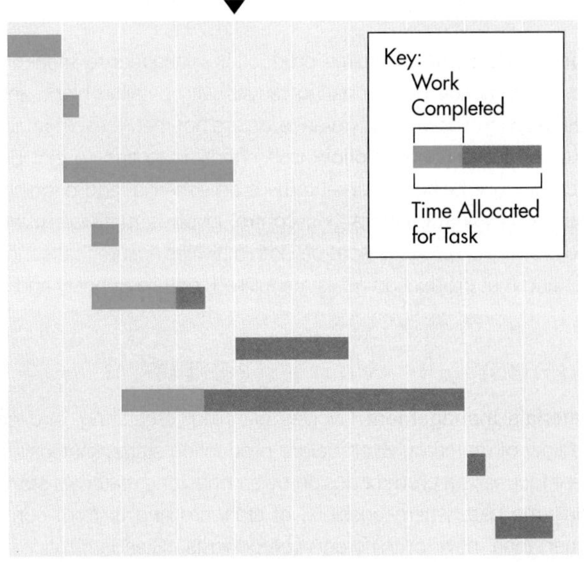

several cars may be scheduled for repairs at a local garage. Thus, if your car is not scheduled for work until 3:30 p.m., it may sit idle for several hours, even if it was the first to be dropped off. In such businesses, reservation and appointment systems can help to smooth demand.

In high-contact services, the customer is part of the system and must be accommodated. Thus, precise scheduling of services may not be possible in high-contact systems. For example, if a hospital emergency room is overloaded, patients cannot be asked to make an appointment and come back later.

Tools for Scheduling

Special projects, such as plant renovations or relocations, often require close coordination and precise timing. In these cases, special tools, such as Gantt and PERT charts, facilitate scheduling.

GANTT CHARTS

A **Gantt chart** diagrams steps to be performed and specifies the time required to complete each step. The manager lists all activities needed to complete the work, estimates the time required for each step, and checks the progress of the project against the chart. If it is ahead of schedule, some workers may be shifted to another project. If it is behind schedule, workers may be added or completion delayed.[14]

GANTT CHART Scheduling tool that diagrams steps to be performed and specifies the time required to complete each step.

PERT CHART Production schedule specifying the sequence and critical path for performing the steps in a project.

Figure 10.6 shows a Gantt chart for the renovation of a college classroom. It shows progress to date and schedules for the remaining work. The current date is 5/11. Note that workers are about one-half week behind in removing old floor tiles and reworking tables and chairs.

PERT CHARTS

The Program Evaluation and Review Technique (PERT) is useful for customized projects in which numerous activities must be coordinated. Like Gantt charts, **PERT charts** break down large projects into steps and specify the time required to perform each one. Unlike Gantt charts, however, PERT charts not only show the necessary sequence of activities, but also identify the critical path for meeting project goals.[15] Figure 10.7 shows a PERT chart for the classroom renovation that we reviewed above. The critical path consists of activities A, B, D, G, H, and I. It is critical because any delay in completing any activity will cause workers to miss the completion deadline (nine and one-half weeks after start-up). No activity along the critical path can be started until all preceding activities are done. Chairs and tables can't be returned to the classroom (H) until after they've been reworked (G) and after new tiles are installed (F). The chart also identifies activities that will cause delays unless special action is taken at the right time. By reassigning workers and equipment, managers can speed up potentially late activities and keep on schedule.

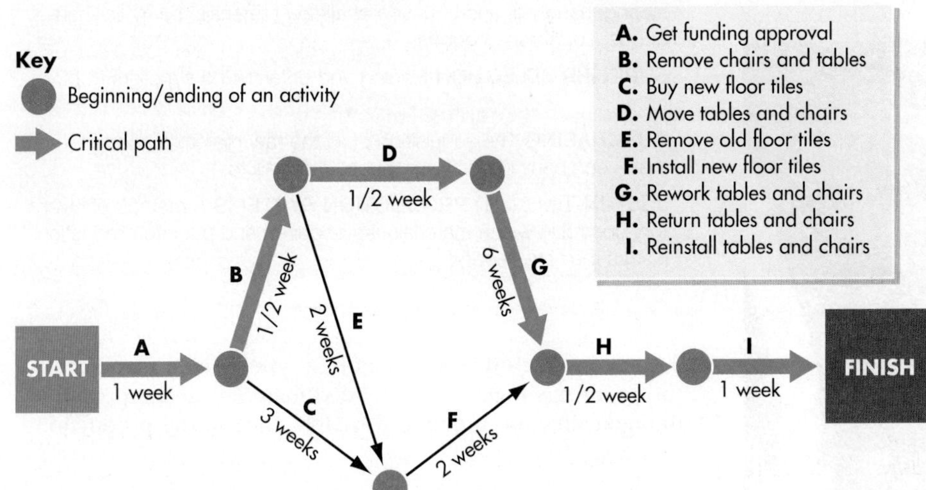

<<< **FIGURE 10.7** A PERT chart

LO-5 OPERATIONS CONTROL

Operations control requires production managers to monitor production performance by comparing results with detailed plans and schedules. If schedules or quality standards are not met, these managers must take corrective action. **Follow-up**—checking to ensure that production decisions are being implemented—is an essential and ongoing facet of operations control. Operations control involves *materials management* and *production process control*. Both activities ensure that schedules are met and that production goals are fulfilled, both in quantity and in quality.

Materials Management

Materials management involves planning, organizing, and controlling the flow of materials. Even before production starts, materials management focuses on product design by emphasizing materials **standardization**—the use, where possible, of standard and uniform components, rather than new or different components. Standardization simplifies paperwork, reduces storage requirements, eliminates unnecessary material flows, and saves money, by reducing the number of different parts that are needed. The five major areas of materials management are as follows:

- **Transportation**—includes the means of transporting resources to the company and finished goods to buyers.
- **Warehousing**—storage of both incoming materials for production and finished goods for physical distribution to customers.
- **Inventory control**—includes the receiving, storing, handling, and counting of all raw materials, partly finished goods, and finished goods. It ensures that enough material inventories are available to meet production schedules.
- **Supplier selection**—finding and choosing suppliers of services and materials to buy from. It includes evaluating potential suppliers, negotiating terms of service, and maintaining positive buyer–seller relations.
- **Purchasing**—acquisition of all the raw materials and services that a company needs to produce its products; most large firms have purchasing departments to buy proper materials in the amounts needed.

<<< Just-in-time (JIT) production, a type of lean manufacturing, brings together all needed materials at the precise moment they are required for each stage in the production process.

© Blend Images/Alamy

Production Process Control

Companies use various tools for process control, including *worker training*, *just-in-time production systems*, *material requirements planning*, and *quality control*.

WORKER TRAINING

When providing services, employees are both producers and salespeople. Thus, human relations skills are vital for anyone who has contact with the public. Service employees with poor attitudes reduce sales, but the right attitude is a powerful sales tool. Disney World has a team of sweepers constantly at work picking up bits of trash as soon as they fall to the ground. When visitors have questions about directions or time, they often ask one of the sweepers. Because their responses affect visitors' overall impressions of Disney World, sweepers are trained to respond in appropriate ways. Their work is evaluated and rewarded based on strict performance appraisal standards.[16]

JUST-IN-TIME PRODUCTION SYSTEMS

To minimize manufacturing inventory costs, many companies use **just-in-time (JIT) production systems**. JIT brings together all the needed materials and parts at the precise moment they are required for each production stage, and not before. JIT reduces inventory of goods

OPERATIONS CONTROL Managers monitor production performance by comparing results with plans and schedules.

FOLLOW-UP Checking to ensure that production decisions are being implemented.

MATERIALS MANAGEMENT Planning, organizing, and controlling the flow of materials from purchase through distribution of finished goods.

STANDARDIZATION Using standard and uniform components in the production process.

TRANSPORTATION The means of transporting resources to the company and finished goods to buyers.

WAREHOUSING The storage of both incoming materials for production and finished goods for physical distribution to customers.

INVENTORY CONTROL In materials management, receiving, storing, handling, and counting of all raw materials, partly finished goods, and finished goods.

SUPPLIER SELECTION Finding and determining suppliers to buy from.

PURCHASING The acquisition of all the raw materials and services that a company needs to produce its products.

JUST-IN-TIME (JIT) PRODUCTION SYSTEMS A method of inventory control in which materials are acquired and put into production just as they are needed.

in process to practically nothing and saves money by replacing stop-and-go production with smooth movement. Sobeys, for example, has invested in more efficient inventory management that has allowed it to reduce the size of storage rooms by 10 percent, because products now move more quickly to the shelves.[17]

MATERIAL REQUIREMENTS PLANNING

Material requirements planning (MRP) uses a **bill of materials** that is basically a "recipe" for the finished product. It specifies the necessary raw materials, the order in which they should be combined, and the quantity of each ingredient needed to make one "batch" of the product (say, 2000 finished telephones). The recipe is fed into a computer that controls inventory and schedules each stage of production. The result is fewer early arrivals, less frequent stock shortages, and lower storage costs.

Manufacturing resource planning, or **MRP II,** is an advanced version of MRP that ties together all parts of the organization into the company's production activities. For example, MRP inventory and production schedules are translated into cost requirements for the financial management department and personnel requirements for the human resources department. Information on capacity availability for new customer orders goes to the marketing department.

QUALITY CONTROL

Quality control refers to the management of the production process so as to manufacture goods or supply services that meet specific quality standards. McDonald's, for example, is a pioneer in quality control in the restaurant industry. The company oversees everything from the farming of potatoes for French fries to the packing of meat for Big Macs. Quality-assurance staffers even check standards for ketchup sweetness and French-fry length. We discuss quality control in more detail in the following section.

MATERIAL REQUIREMENTS PLANNING (MRP) A method of inventory control in which a computerized bill of materials is used to estimate production needs, so that resources are acquired and put into production only as needed.

BILL OF MATERIALS Production-control tool that specifies the necessary ingredients of a product, the order in which they should be combined, and how many of each are needed to make one batch.

MANUFACTURING RESOURCE PLANNING (MRP II) An advanced version of MRP that ties together all parts of the organization into the company's production activities.

QUALITY CONTROL The management of the production process so as to manufacture goods or supply services that meet specific quality standards.

THE PRODUCTIVITY–QUALITY CONNECTION

Productivity measures how much is produced relative to the resources used to produce it. By using resources more efficiently, the quantity of output will be greater for a given amount of input. But unless the resulting goods and services are of satisfactory quality, consumers will not want them. **Quality**, then, means fitness for use—offering features that consumers want.

Meeting the Productivity Challenge

A nation's productivity determines how large a piece of the global economic-resource pie it gets. A country whose productivity fails to increase as rapidly as that of other countries will see its people's standard of living fall relative to the rest of the world.

MEASURING PRODUCTIVITY

How do we know how productive a country is? Most countries use **labour productivity** to measure their level of productivity:

labour productivity of a country = gross domestic product/total number of workers

The focus on labour, rather than on other resources such as capital or energy, is popular because most countries keep records on employment and hours worked.

PRODUCTIVITY AMONG GLOBAL COMPETITORS

A 2011 study by the Organisation for Economic Co-operation and Development (OECD) reported on productivity levels in selected

QUALITY A product's fitness for use in terms of offering the features that consumers want.

LABOUR PRODUCTIVITY Partial productivity ratio calculated by dividing gross domestic product by total number of workers.

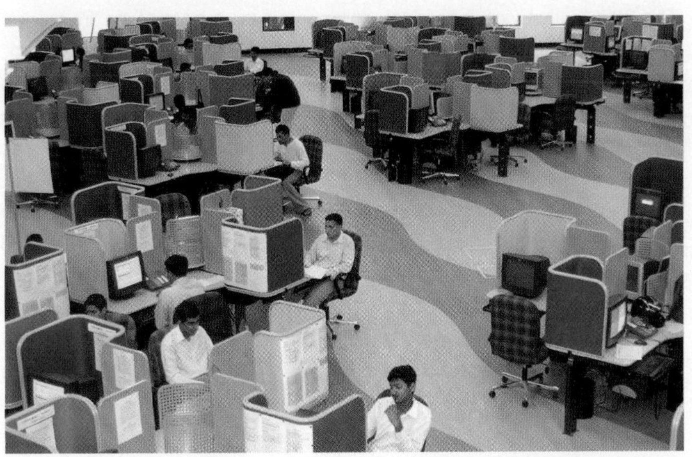

<<< Workers at this call centre in Bangalore, India, field calls from the customers of multinational firms headquartered in North America and Europe. Many jobs like these are outsourced to service suppliers in India because workers there receive lower wages than their North American counterparts. This translates into higher productivity, because costs are lower for a given level of output.

© Blend Images/Fotolia

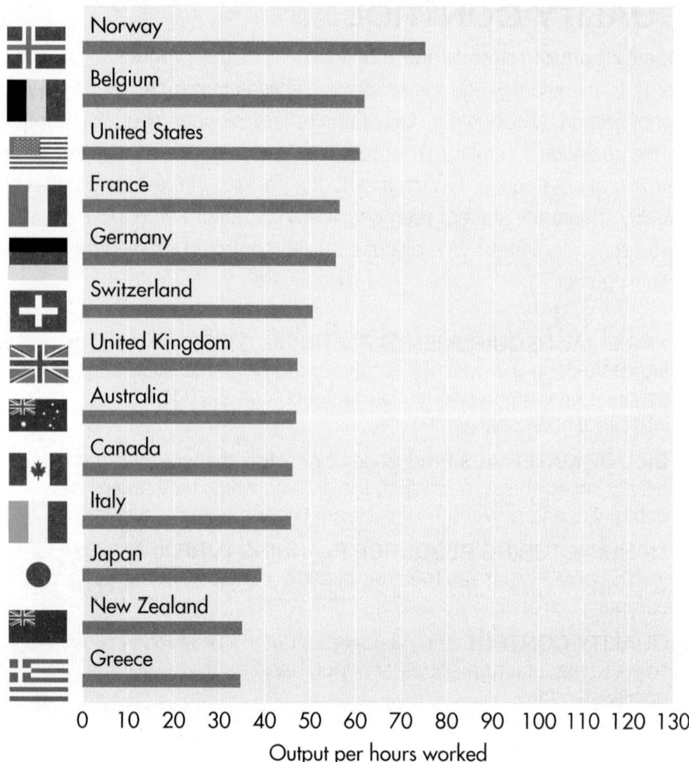

<<< **FIGURE 10.8** International productivity comparisons (selected countries, 2011)

Source: Organisation for Economic Co-operation and Development (OECD)

countries (see Figure 10.8). Output per hour worked was the highest in Norway (74.9) and lowest in Mexico (20.4, not shown). Canadian productivity (46.6) usually lags behind that of the U.S. (60.9), but, in 2011, Canadian productivity growth outpaced the U.S. for the first time since 2006.[18]

Why are there such productivity differences from nation to nation? The answer lies in many factors: technologies, human skills, economic policies, natural resources, and even traditions. In Japan, for example, the food-production industry is fragmented and highly protected, and, compared with Canadian and U.S. food production, it is extremely inefficient (the average U.S. worker produces 3.5 times as much food as a Japanese worker).[19]

According to Michael Porter, a Harvard University expert on international competitiveness, Canada's international competitiveness is a concern because we have been living off our rich diet of natural resources. Porter criticizes Canadian business, government, and labour for failing to abandon outdated ways of thinking regarding productivity and innovation.[20] Other critics say that Canada is stuck in a "productivity trap," meaning that Canadians are collectively working harder and using up more natural resources, but the benefits and outputs we receive aren't proportional. The productivity trap is reducing Canada's ability to compete in international markets.[21]

DOMESTIC PRODUCTIVITY

A country that improves its ability to make something out of its existing resources can increase the wealth of all its inhabitants. Conversely, a decline in productivity shrinks a nation's total wealth. Additional wealth from higher productivity can be shared among workers (as higher wages), investors (as higher profits), and customers (as stable or declining prices).

MANUFACTURING VERSUS SERVICE PRODUCTIVITY

Manufacturing productivity is higher than service productivity. It is important to improve service productivity because the service sector is an important and growing part of the Canadian economy. From 1998 to 2008, for example, the service sector grew by 40.5 percent, compared to only 18.5 percent for the goods-producing sector. More than 75 percent of employed Canadians work in the service sector.[22] For many years, it was believed that the service sector suffered from "Baumol's Disease," named after economist William Baumol. He argued that since the service sector focused more on hands-on activity that machines couldn't replace, it would be more difficult to increase productivity in services. But the Opera Company of Brooklyn is challenging that notion. It now puts on the opera *The Marriage of Figaro* with only 12 musicians and a technician who oversees a computer program that plays all the other parts. The orchestra's productivity has increased sharply because it does not have to pay for the usual complement of musicians.[23]

INDUSTRY PRODUCTIVITY

Productivity varies across different industries (for example, manufacturing is more productive than services). Productivity within a given industry also varies across countries (for example, Canadian agriculture is more productive than agriculture in many other nations, because we use more sophisticated technology and possess superior natural resources). The productivity of many industries has increased over time. In the steel industry, for example, about 10 hours of labour were required to produce a tonne of steel in the 1980s, but now only about four hours of labour are needed. In forestry, Canfor Corporation developed a strategic-planning tool called Genus to manage its forestry operations. It is used to determine how the company should adjust its logging plans to reflect market demand.[24]

COMPANY PRODUCTIVITY

The productivity of individual companies is important to investors, workers, and managers. High productivity gives a company a competitive edge because its costs are lower. As a result, it can offer its product at a lower price (and gain more customers), or it can make a greater profit on each item sold. Some companies have found that they can increase their productivity by monitoring employee interactions. At Cubist Pharmaceutical, for example, sales and marketing employees wore badges that collected data on their conversational patterns and their movements. The company discovered that more face-to-face interactions among employees were associated with higher levels of productivity. It, therefore, remodeled its cafeteria and provided better food, so that employees would be more likely to have lunch together.[25]

MEETING THE QUALITY CHALLENGE

In the decades after the World War II, American business consultant W. Edwards Deming tried to persuade U.S. firms that they needed to improve the quality of their products. Like many a prophet, he was not honoured in his homeland. But his arguments won over the Japanese. Through years of meticulous hard work, Japan's manufacturers have changed "Made in Japan" from a synonym for cheap, shoddy merchandise into a hallmark of reliability. Eventually, North American businesses came to understand that Deming was right.

Quality advocates such as Joseph Juran and Kaoru Ishikawa introduced methods and tools for improving quality. Ishikawa, for example, developed "fishbone diagrams" (also known as "cause-and-effect diagrams" or "Ishikawa diagrams") that help employees figure out the causes of quality problems in their work areas. The diagram in Figure 10.9, for instance, was developed to help an airport manager find out why the facility had so many delayed departures. Focusing on five major categories of possible causes, the manager then noted several potential causes of the problem in each. It turns out that there weren't enough tow trucks to handle baggage transfers.[26]

THERE'S AN APP FOR THAT!

1. **Quality Management** >>> **Platforms:** *Apple, Android, BlackBerry*
   Source: WagMob
   Key Features: On-the-go learning tool for quality management issues.
2. **Gantt Charts** >>> **Platforms:** *Apple*
   Source: YBOOM International
   Key Features: Allows the user to track the progress of a project.
3. **Pert Estimator** >>> **Platforms:** *Apple, Android*
   Source: Burriss Consulting Group LLC
   Key Features: This tool takes best, worst, and most-likely estimates along with the hourly cost to provide an accurate estimate for a given task.

APP DISCOVERY EXERCISE

Since APP availability changes, conduct your own search for "Top 3" Operations Management APPS and identify the key features.

LO-6 Managing for Quality

Total quality management (TQM) includes all of the activities necessary for getting high-quality goods and services into the marketplace. TQM emphasizes that no defects are tolerable, and that employees are responsible for maintaining quality standards. For example, at Toyota's Cambridge, Ontario, plant, workers can push a button or pull a rope to stop the production line when something is not up to standard.[27]

A customer focus is the starting point for TQM. It includes using methods for determining what customers want and then making sure that all the company's activities and people are focused on fulfilling those needs. Total participation is critical; if all employees are not working toward improved quality, the firm is wasting potential contributions from its human resources and is missing a chance to become a stronger competitor in the marketplace. TQM in today's competitive markets demands continuous improvement of products, after-sales service, and all of the

TOTAL QUALITY MANAGEMENT (TQM) A concept that emphasizes that no defects are tolerable and that all employees are responsible for maintaining quality standards.

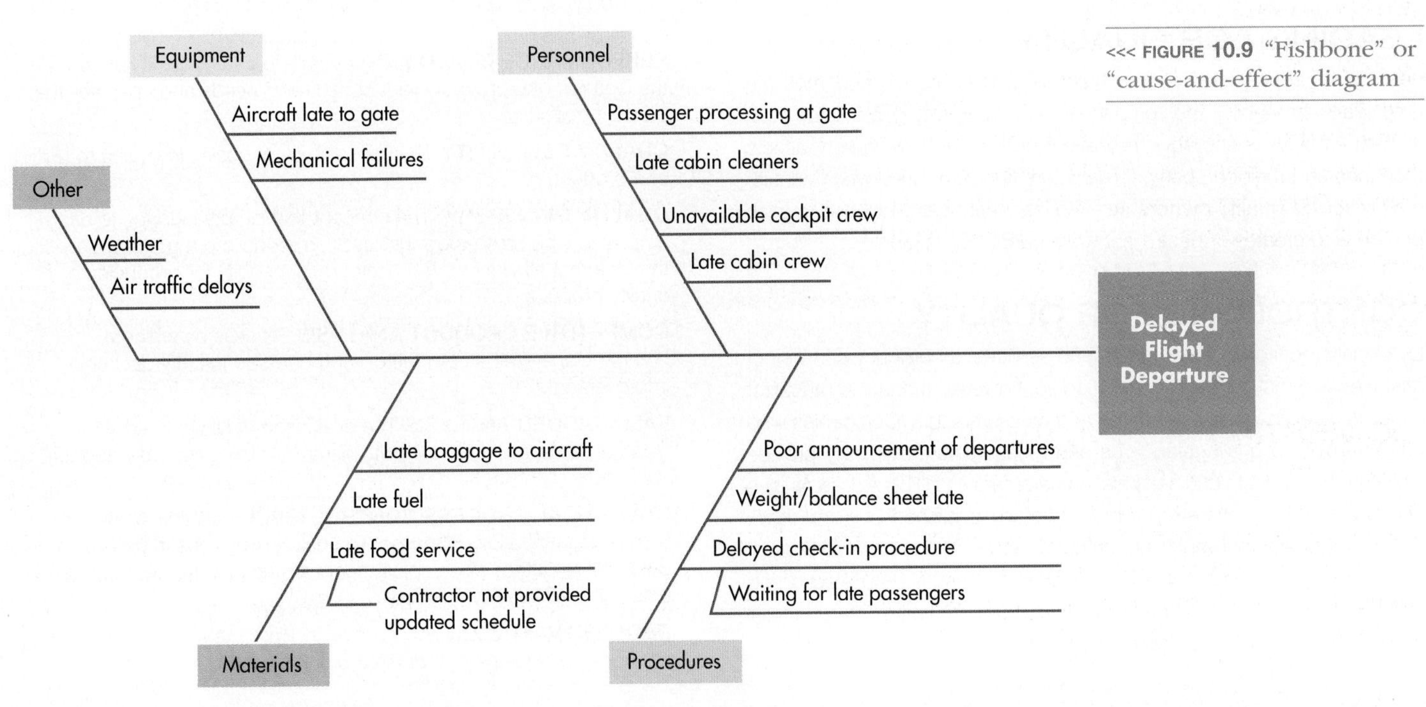

<<< FIGURE 10.9 "Fishbone" or "cause-and-effect" diagram

company's internal processes, such as accounting, delivery, billing, and information flow.

Consider the example of Standard Aero in Winnipeg, which is in the business of aircraft overhaul. When the company instituted TQM, the process began with the formation of a "change council" consisting of the CEO and five senior managers. Next, a nine-person task force was formed that consisted of employees who had done the full range of jobs on one of Standard's major overhaul contracts. The task force's first job was to find out what the customer wanted. It did this by designing a questionnaire and visiting customer plants around the world to gather information. It also worked within Standard Aero to determine exactly how the company did its aircraft overhaul work. After weeks of analysis, the task force was able to reduce the time required for overhaul work significantly. The number of times a certain gearbox was handled as it moved through the repair process, for example, was reduced by 84 percent.[28]

PLANNING FOR QUALITY

Planning for quality should begin before products are designed or redesigned. **Performance quality** refers to the features of a product and how well it performs. For example, Maytag gets a price premium because its washers and dryers offer a high level of performance quality. Customers perceive Maytag products as having more advanced features and being more durable than other brands.

Quality reliability refers to the consistency or repeatability of performance. At Courtyard by Marriott hotels, for example, consistency is achieved by maintaining the same features at all of Marriott's nearly 700 locations (high-speed internet access, meeting space, access to an exercise room and swimming pool, and 24-hour access to food).

ORGANIZING FOR QUALITY

Having a separate "quality control" department is no longer enough. Everyone, from the chair of the board to the part-time clerk, must work to assure quality. At Germany's Messerschmitt-Boelkow-Blohm aerospace company, for example, all employees are responsible for inspecting their own work. The goal is to minimize problems by making the product correctly from the beginning.

LEADING FOR QUALITY

Leading for quality means that managers must inspire and motivate employees throughout the company to achieve quality goals. They need to help employees see how they affect quality and how quality affects their jobs and their company. If managers succeed, employees will ultimately accept **quality ownership**—the idea that quality belongs to each person who creates or destroys it while performing a job.

CONTROLLING FOR QUALITY

By closely monitoring its products and services, a company can detect mistakes and make corrections. To do so, however, managers must first establish specific quality standards and measurements. Companies who pay attention to quality standards and measurements typically provide high-quality products and services to customers. In 2012, Alaska Airlines and Delta Air Lines were top rated in a study published by *The Middle Seat*, a company that ranks air carriers on key quality measures like on-time arrivals, cancelled flights, and mishandled bags. Both Alaska and Delta had ranked poorly in previous years, but both had instituted major operational overhauls that focused on improving quality.[29]

Tools for Quality Assurance

There are many tools that can be used to achieve the desired level of quality: *competitive product analysis, value-added analysis, statistical process control, quality/cost studies, quality improvement teams, benchmarking, getting closer to the customer, ISO 9000:2000 and ISO 14000, re-engineering*, and *adding value through supply chains*.

COMPETITIVE PRODUCT ANALYSIS

Ideas for improving both the product and the production process may come from **competitive product analysis**. For example, Toshiba will take apart a Xerox photocopier and test each component to see how it compares with Toshiba's competing product. It can then decide which Toshiba product features are satisfactory, which product features need to be upgraded, and whether Toshiba's production processes need improvement.

VALUE-ADDED ANALYSIS

Value-added analysis means evaluating all work activities, material flows, and paperwork to determine the value that they add for customers. Value-added analysis often reveals wasteful or unnecessary activities that can be eliminated without harming customer service. For example, when Hewlett-Packard reduced its customer contracts from 20 pages to as few as 2, computer sales rose by more than 18 percent.

STATISTICAL PROCESS CONTROL

Companies can improve uniformity in their outputs by understanding the sources of variation. **Statistical process control (SPC)** methods—especially process variation studies and control charts—allow managers to analyze variations in production data.

Process Variation While some amount of **process variation** is acceptable, too much can result in poor quality and excessive operating costs. Consider the box-filling operation for Honey Nuggets cereal. Each automated machine fills two 400-gram boxes per second. Even under

PERFORMANCE QUALITY The overall degree of quality; how well the features of a product meet consumers' needs and how well the product performs.

QUALITY RELIABILITY The consistency of quality from unit to unit of a product.

QUALITY OWNERSHIP The concept that quality belongs to each employee who creates or destroys it in producing a good or service; the idea that all workers must take responsibility for producing a quality product.

COMPETITIVE PRODUCT ANALYSIS Process by which a company analyzes a competitor's products to identify desirable improvements.

VALUE-ADDED ANALYSIS The evaluation of all work activities, material flows, and paperwork to determine the value they add for customers.

STATISTICAL PROCESS CONTROL (SPC) Statistical analysis techniques that allow managers to analyze variations in production data and to detect when adjustments are needed to create products with high-quality reliability.

PROCESS VARIATION Any change in employees, materials, work methods, or equipment that affects output quality.

proper conditions, slight variations in cereal weight from box to box are normal. Equipment and tools wear out, the cereal may be overly moist, and machinists make occasional adjustments. But how much variation is occurring? How much is acceptable?

Information about variation in a process can be obtained from a process capability study. Boxes are taken from the filling machines and weighed. The results are plotted, as in Figure 10.10, and compared with the upper and lower specification limits (quality limits) for weight. These limits define good and bad quality for box filling. Boxes with more than 410 grams are a wasteful "giveaway." Underfilling has a cost because it is unlawful.

In Figure 10.10, we see that none of Machine A's output violates the quality limits, and it is fully capable of meeting the company's quality standards. But Machines B and C have problems and cannot reliably meet Honey Nuggets' quality standards. The company must take special—and costly—actions to sort the good from the bad boxes before releasing the cereal for shipment.

Control Charts Knowing that a process is capable of meeting quality standards is not enough. Managers must still monitor the process to prevent its going astray during production. To detect the beginning of bad conditions, managers can check production periodically and plot the results on a **control chart**. For example, several times a day, a machine operator at Honey Nuggets might weigh several boxes of cereal together to ascertain the average weight.

QUALITY/COST STUDIES FOR QUALITY IMPROVEMENT

Quality/cost studies identify a firm's current costs and also reveal areas with the largest cost-saving potential.[30] For example, Honey Nuggets must determine its costs for **internal failures**. These are expenses—including the costs of overfilling boxes and the costs of sorting out bad boxes—incurred during production and before bad product leaves the plant. **External failures** occur when bad boxes get out of the factory and reach the customer. The costs of correcting them—refunds to customers, transportation costs to return bad boxes to the factory, possible lawsuits, factory recalls—are also tabulated in a quality/cost study.

QUALITY IMPROVEMENT TEAMS

Quality improvement (QI) teams are groups of employees from various work areas who meet regularly to define, analyze, and solve common production problems. Their goal is to improve both their own work methods and the products they make.[31] Many QI teams organize their own work, select leaders, and address problems in the workplace. Motorola, for example, sponsors company-wide team competitions to emphasize the value of the team approach, to recognize outstanding team performance, and to reaffirm the team's role in the company's continuous-improvement culture. Teams get higher marks for dealing with projects closely tied to Motorola's key initiatives.[32]

CONTROL CHART A statistical process control method in which results of test sampling of a product are plotted on a diagram that reveals when the process is beginning to depart from normal operating conditions.

QUALITY/COST STUDIES A method of improving product quality by assessing a firm's current quality-related costs and identifying areas with the greatest cost-saving potential.

INTERNAL FAILURES Expenses incurred during production and before bad product leaves the plant.

EXTERNAL FAILURES Allowing defective products to leave the factory and get into consumers' hands.

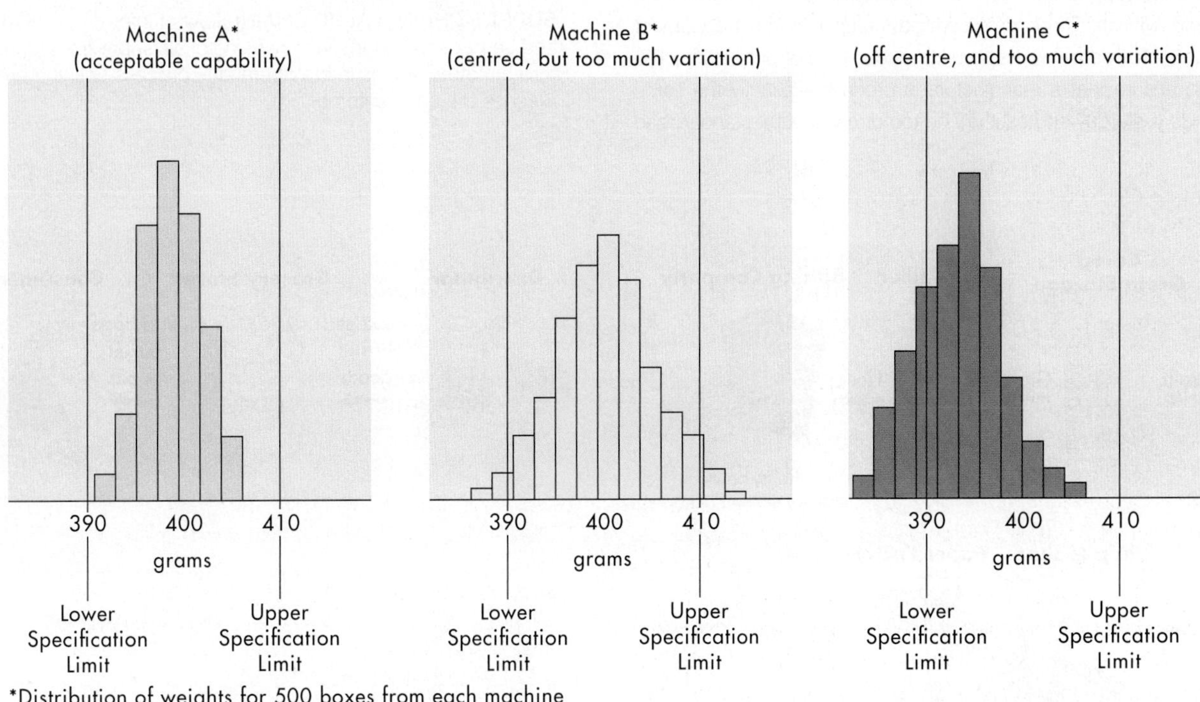

FIGURE 10.10 Process variation in box filling for Honey Nuggets cereal

BENCHMARKING

With **benchmarking**, a company compares its current performance against its own past performance (internal benchmarking), or against the performance of its competitors (external benchmarking). As an example of the former, the percentage of customer phone calls last month requiring more than two minutes of response time may be compared to the required response time the month before that. As an example of the latter, Toronto Hospital gathered performance data on 26 indicators from various Canadian hospitals so it could determine how well it was performing compared to other organizations in the health-care industry.[33]

GETTING CLOSER TO THE CUSTOMER

Successful businesses take steps to know what their customers want in the products or services they buy. For example, the Coast Capital Savings Credit Union branch in Surrey, B.C., simplified the banking experience of its customers and developed an innovative new service called "You're the Boss Mortgage" which was named the Mortgage of the Year by canadianmortgagetrends.com.[34]

ISO 9000:2000

DuPont had a problem—a moulding press used to make plastic connectors for computers had a 30-percent defect rate. Efforts to solve the problem went nowhere until, as part of a plant-wide quality program, press operators were asked to submit detailed written reports describing how they did their jobs. After comparing notes, operators realized that they were incorrectly measuring the temperature of the moulding press; as a result, temperature adjustments were often wrong. With the mystery solved, the defect rate dropped to 8 percent.

The quality program that led to this solution is called **ISO 9000**—a certification program attesting to the fact that a factory, a laboratory, or an office has met the rigorous quality management requirements set by the International Organization for Standardization. ISO 9000 (pronounced ICE-o nine thousand) originated in Europe as an attempt to standardize materials received from suppliers in high-tech industries such as electronics, chemicals, and aviation. To become certified, companies must document the procedures followed by workers during every stage of production. The purpose is to ensure that a manufacturer's product is exactly the same today as it was yesterday and as it will be tomorrow. Ideally, standardized processes would ensure that goods are produced at the same level of quality, even if all employees were replaced by a new set of workers.

BUSINESS PROCESS RE-ENGINEERING

Business process re-engineering is the fundamental rethinking and radical redesign of business processes to achieve dramatic improvements as measured by cost, quality, service, and speed.[35] It requires rethinking of each of the steps in a process, starting from scratch. For example, when Caterpillar Financial Services changed to an online system for customers, it reengineered the whole payments and financing process by improving equipment, retraining employees, and connecting customers to its databases.[36]

LO-7 ADDING VALUE THROUGH SUPPLY CHAINS

Companies usually belong to a network of firms that must coordinate their activities. As each firm performs its transformation processes, it relies on others in the network. A **supply chain** (or **value chain**) for any product is the flow of information, materials, and services that starts with raw-materials suppliers and continues adding value through other stages in the network of firms until the product reaches the end customer.[37]

Figure 10.11 shows the supply-chain activities involved in supplying baked goods to consumers. Each stage adds value for the final customer, and each stage depends on the others for success in getting fresh-baked goods to consumers.

BENCHMARKING Comparing the quality of the firm's output with the quality of the output of the industry's leaders.

ISO 9000 Certification program attesting to the fact that a factory, a laboratory, or an office has met the rigorous quality management requirements set by the International Organization for Standardization.

BUSINESS PROCESS RE-ENGINEERING Redesigning of business processes to improve performance, quality, and productivity.

SUPPLY CHAIN (VALUE CHAIN) Flow of information, materials, and services that starts with raw-materials suppliers and continues through other stages in the operations process until the product reaches the end customer.

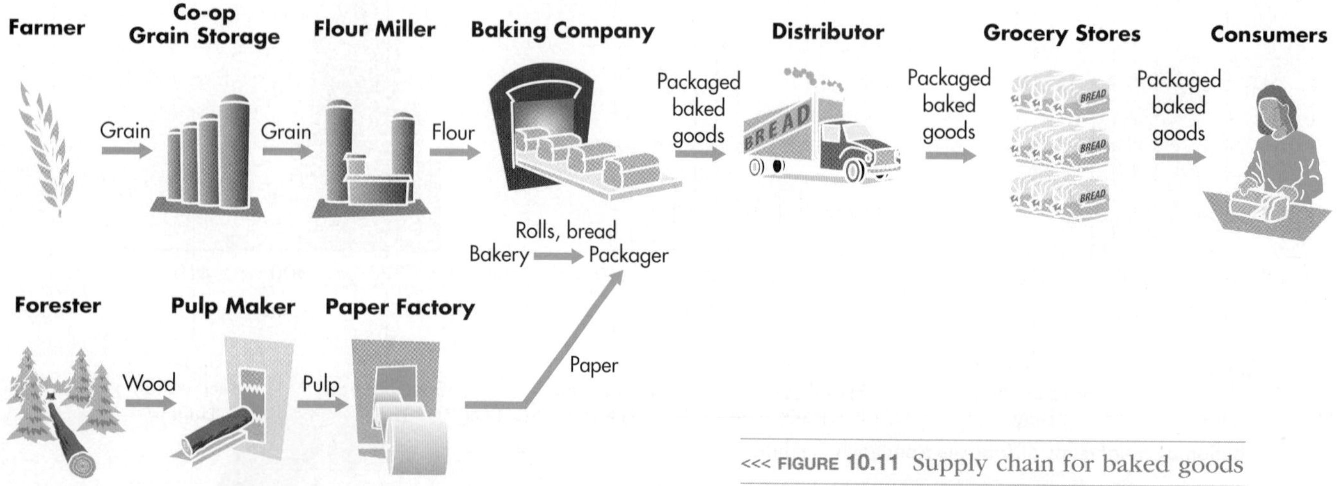

<<< **FIGURE 10.11** Supply chain for baked goods

Supply-chain management (SCM) tries to improve the overall flow through a system composed of companies working together. The smooth flow of accurate information along the chain reduces unwanted inventories, avoids delays, and cuts supply times. Materials move faster to other businesses and, ultimately, consumers, and the efficiency of SCM means faster deliveries and lower costs than customers could get if each member acted only according to its own operations requirements. Because customers ultimately get better value, SCM gains competitive advantage for each supply-chain member.[38] A traditionally managed bakery, for example, would focus simply on getting production inputs from flour millers and paper suppliers and supplying baked goods to distributors. Unfortunately, this approach limits the chain's performance and doesn't allow for possible improvements when activities are more carefully coordinated. Supply-chain management can improve performance and, as a result, provide higher quality at lower prices.

Supply-chain management is also important for services. As mentioned in Chapter 6, Port Metro Vancouver developed a supply-chain strategy that reduced container "dwell time"—the time containers sit on the dock—from 3.7 days to 2.5 days, after managers determined that the port had to become more competitive with American ports. This reduction in dwell time also improved the port's relationships with operators like Canadian National Railway and Canadian Pacific Railway Ltd.[39] Supply chains are also becoming increasingly global. For example, an architect from Malaysia might sketch out a new office tower for the city of London, an architect from the Philippines might do the detailed renderings, and an engineer from China might assess the structural soundness of the building.[40] Occasionally, problems arise in global supply chains, as the boxed insert "Supply-Chain Disruption" demonstrates.

SUPPLY-CHAIN MANAGEMENT (SCM) Principle of looking at the chain as a whole to improve the overall flow through the system.

MANAGING IN TURBULENT TIMES

Supply-Chain Disruptions

The devastating earthquake and tsunami that struck northeastern Japan in 2011 killed thousands of people and destroyed entire communities. The disaster also disrupted the production of automobiles, automobile parts, and electronic components like flash memory and dynamic random-access memory for computing devices and smartphones. The earthquake damaged a Sony factory which produces HDCAM-SR tapes used by movie and television producers. Since Sony is the only supplier in the world of that product, the sharply reduced supply caused prices to suddenly triple for the tapes.

When a supply-chain shock occurs at one of its suppliers, a manufacturer may have to scramble to find another supplier. For example, Advanced Semiconductor Engineering Inc., a Taiwan-based chip-packaging company, had to look for new suppliers in China and South Korea after its Japanese supplier was unable to deliver supplies of plastic moulding compounds used to wrap semiconductors.

Just-in-time inventory systems (JIT) were negatively impacted by the Japanese earthquake. Manufacturing plants in various countries around the world had to be shut down for a period of time due to parts shortages. Ford Motor closed its manufacturing plants in South Africa, China, and Taiwan, and Toyota and Honda shut down production at Canadian assembly plants during the months of April and May 2011. In November 2011, Toyota and Honda had to again shut down assembly lines in Canada because of parts shortages caused by flooding in Thailand, and Intel also warned of shortages of hard disks because of the flooding. Companies continue to use JIT, but many of them are starting to hold larger stocks of inventory in case of supply disruptions.

Supply-chain disruptions seem to be occurring with greater frequency. Political unrest in the Middle East and China's restrictions on the export of rare earth metals are just two illustrations of how supply chains can be disrupted. But companies are reacting very quickly to disruptions. Just after the Japanese earthquake, for example, there was concern that supply-chain disruptions would cause worldwide shutdowns of manufacturing plants. But that didn't happen because companies had diversified their sources of supply for critical inputs to their production processes. So, if a disruption occurs at one supplier, the company already has an alternative in place. Another (somewhat surprising) reason is that Japan is simply not a key foreign supplier for many companies. In a survey of supply-chain managers, it was discovered that only 2 percent of respondents said that Japan was their top foreign supplier.

CRITICAL THINKING QUESTIONS

1. What can companies do to lessen the impact of supply-chain disruptions?
2. Consider the following statement: *Companies should reconsider their use of just-in-time inventory systems because if a supply disruption occurs, the manufacturing process will almost immediately have to be shut down because the company carries virtually no inventory.* Do you agree or disagree with the statement? Explain your reasoning.

MyBizLab

Visit the MyBizLab website. This online homework and tutorial system puts you in control of your own learning with study and practice tools directly correlated to this chapter's content.

SUMMARY OF

LEARNING OBJECTIVES

LO-1 EXPLAIN THE MEANING OF THE TERM *PRODUCTION* (OR *OPERATIONS*) AND DESCRIBE THE FOUR KINDS OF *UTILITY* IT PROVIDES.

Production (or *operations*) refers to the processes and activities for transforming resources into finished services and goods for customers. Production creates *time utility* (products are available when customers want them), *place utility* (products are available where they are convenient for customers), *ownership utility* (customers benefit from possessing and using the product), and *form utility* (products are in a form that is useful to the customer).

LO-2 IDENTIFY THE CHARACTERISTICS THAT DISTINGUISH *SERVICE OPERATIONS* FROM *GOODS PRODUCTION* AND EXPLAIN THE MAIN DIFFERENCES IN THE *SERVICE FOCUS*.

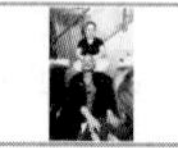

In service production, raw materials are not things but rather people, so services are performed, while goods are produced. Also, services are largely *intangible,* more likely than physical goods to be *customized* to meet the purchaser's needs, and more *unstorable* than most products. Because services are intangible, for instance, providers work to ensure that customers receive value in the form of pleasure, satisfaction, or a feeling of safety. Service providers also focus on the *customer-service link*, often acknowledging the customer as part of the operations process.

LO-3 DESCRIBE TWO TYPES OF *OPERATIONS PROCESSES*.

In manufacturing, *analytic processes* break down resources into component parts and *synthetic processes* combine raw materials to produce a finished product. Services use either *high-contact processes* (the customer is in the system while the service is being performed) or *low-contact processes* (the customer is not in the system while the service is being performed).

LO-4 DESCRIBE THE FACTORS INVOLVED IN *OPERATIONS PLANNING* AND *OPERATIONS CONTROL*.

Operations planning involves *forecasting* (determining future demand for products), *capacity planning* (calculating how much of a product can be produced), *location planning* (analyzing proposed facility sites), *layout planning* (designing a facility to enhance production efficiency), *quality planning* (ensuring that products meet a firm's quality standards), and *methods planning* (identifying specific production steps and methods for performing them). *Operations control* requires production managers to monitor production performance (by comparing results with detailed plans and schedules) and then to take corrective action as needed. *Materials management* involves the planning, organizing, and controlling of the flow of materials. There are several tools for helping managers control operations processes, including *worker training programs*, *just-in-time (JIT) production systems*, *material requirements planning (MRP)*, and *quality control*.

LO-5 EXPLAIN THE CONNECTION BETWEEN *PRODUCTIVITY* AND *QUALITY*.

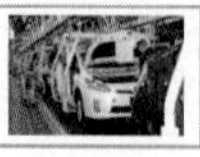

Productivity is a measure of economic performance; it compares how much is produced with the resources used to produce it. *Quality* is a product's fitness for use. However, an emphasis solely on productivity or solely on quality is not enough. Profitable competition in today's business world demands high levels of both productivity and quality.

LO-6 UNDERSTAND THE CONCEPT OF *TOTAL QUALITY MANAGEMENT* AND DESCRIBE NINE TOOLS THAT COMPANIES CAN USE TO ACHIEVE IT.

Total quality management (TQM) includes all the activities that are necessary for getting high-quality goods and services into the marketplace. Tools that are available to managers include *value-added analysis*, *statistical process control methods*, *quality/cost studies*, *quality improvement teams*, *benchmarking*, *getting closer to the customer*, *ISO 9000:2000*, *re-engineering*, and *supply-chain management*.

LO-7 EXPLAIN HOW A *SUPPLY-CHAIN STRATEGY* DIFFERS FROM TRADITIONAL STRATEGIES FOR COORDINATING OPERATIONS AMONG BUSINESSES.

The *supply-chain strategy* is based on the idea that members of the supply chain can gain competitive advantage by working together as a coordinated system of units. Sharing information allows companies to reduce inventories, improve quality, and speed the delivery of products to consumers.

QUESTIONS AND EXERCISES

QUESTIONS FOR ANALYSIS

See >>> for Assisted-Graded Writing Assignment in MyBizLab

1. >>> What are the resources needed and the finished "products" that are produced in the following services: real-estate firm, child-care facility, bank, city water and electric department, and hotel?
2. Explain how the functions of management (planning, organizing, leading, and controlling) relate to one another in the pursuit of quality.
3. >>> Pick three products (not services) that you regularly use. Do some research to determine which of the basic production processes are used to produce these products (chemical, fabrication, assembly, transport, or clerical processes). To what extent are multiple processes used in the production of the product?
4. Pick three services (not physical goods) that you regularly use. Explain what customization, unstorability, and intangibility mean for each of the services. How do these factors influence the way the service is delivered to customers?
5. Develop a service-flow analysis for some service that you use frequently, such as buying lunch at a cafeteria, having your hair cut, or riding a bus. Identify areas of potential quality or productivity failures in the process.
6. Historically, high productivity in the service sector has been difficult to achieve. Why was this so? What might be changing in this area that will cause service productivity to increase during the next decade?

APPLICATION EXERCISES

7. Develop a list of internal customers and internal suppliers for the organization where you work. Identify areas of potential quality improvement in these internal customer–supplier relationships.
8. Choose a consumer item and trace its supply chain. Can you see areas where improvements might be made?
9. Interview a production manager in a local firm and determine which of the tools for total quality management the company is using. Also determine why the company has chosen not to use some other tools.
10. Think of an everyday activity—either personal or professional—that you would like to do more efficiently. Describe how you would use methods planning to achieve increased efficiency in that activity. Draw a process flow chart that shows the stages in the activity you chose, and then explain how you would use it.

TEAM EXERCISES

BUILDING YOUR BUSINESS SKILLS

THE IMPACT OF EFFICIENCY

PURPOSE OF THE ASSIGNMENT

To encourage students to think critically about the idea of productivity and its effects on people and organizations.

THE SITUATION

In 1865 (yes, 1865), William Jevons published a book entitled *The Coal Question*. In it, he argued that increased efficiency in the use of coal in iron-making would not lead to less consumption of coal (as most people would think), but to more consumption of coal. He gave an example to support this seemingly counterintuitive argument: if some technological improvement allowed more iron to be made with less coal than previously, the iron company's profits would increase and new investment dollars would flow into the company. The company's reduced costs would allow it to reduce the price of its products. That price reduction, in turn, would cause increased demand from customers. Over time, as more and more companies efficiently produced more and more iron, the total consumption of coal needed to make all that iron would be greater than it was before the increase in efficiency occurred. The most general point that Jevons made was that increased economy in the use of fuel would actually lead to increased consumption of that fuel. This is because increasing energy efficiency really means increasing the productivity of energy. And when you increase the productivity of something, its price goes down.

In 2011, David Owen wrote a book entitled *The Conundrum* (New York: Riverhead Books) which contains many examples of how Jevons' basic idea works in modern society. He notes, for example, that improving roads (i.e., making them more efficient) does not reduce traffic congestion, but makes it worse over time. Why? Because better roads attract more drivers, and this increases congestion. All of these extra cars also produce a large amount of air pollution. If governments want to reduce air pollution by attracting more people to public transit, they must increase the cost of driving. That can be accomplished by providing poor (i.e., congested) roads for drivers, who will then get so fed up with driving that they will be motivated to use public transit.

ASSIGNMENT

Step 1 Get together with three other students. Assign one or two of the chapters in Owen's recent book to each group member (the chapters are very short). Chapters 1, 2, 6, 12, 13, 19, 20, and 21 are particularly recommended.

Step 2 Gather the group together for a discussion of the idea that increased efficiency actually results in increased use, rather than decreased use. Use the "Follow-up Questions" below as a starting point.

Step 3 Write a brief report summarizing your group's conclusions.

FOLLOW-UP QUESTIONS

1. Is Jevons' idea sound? Defend your answer.
2. Briefly describe several areas where Jevons' ideas apply. Are there areas where his ideas do not apply?
3. Assume for a moment that you agree with the argument that increased efficiency means more consumption rather than less. If you wanted to decrease consumption, give a specific example of the actions you would take. Also note whether you think the actions are politically feasible.

EXERCISING YOUR ETHICS

CALCULATING THE COST OF CONSCIENCE

THE SITUATION

Product quality and cost affect every firm's reputation and profitability, as well as the satisfaction of customers. This exercise will expose you to some ethical considerations that pertain to certain cost and service decisions that must be made by operations managers.

THE DILEMMA

As director of quality for a major appliance manufacturer, Ruth was reporting to the executive committee on the results of a program for correcting problems with a newly redesigned compressor that the company had recently begun putting in its refrigerators. Following several customer complaints, the quality lab had determined that some of the new compressor units ran more loudly than expected. One corrective option was to simply wait until customers complained and responding to each complaint if and when it occurred. Ruth, however, decided that this approach was inconsistent with the company's policy of being the high-quality leader in the industry. Insisting on a proactive, "pro-quality" approach, Ruth initiated a program for contacting all customers who had purchased refrigerators containing the new compressor.

Unfortunately, her "quality-and-customers-first" policy was expensive. Service representatives across Canada had to phone every customer, make appointments for home visits, and replace original compressors with a newer model. Because replacement time was only 30 minutes, customers were hardly inconvenienced, and food stayed refrigerated without interruption. Customer response to the replacement program was overwhelmingly favourable.

Near the end of Ruth's report, an executive vice-president was overheard to comment, "Ruth's program has cost this company $400 million in service expenses." Two weeks later, Ruth was fired.

TEAM ACTIVITY

Assemble a group of four students and assign each group member to one of the following roles:

- Ruth
- Ruth's boss
- A customer
- A company investor

ACTION STEPS

1. Before hearing any of your group's comments on this situation and from the perspective of your assigned role, take a moment to consider whether Ruth's firing is consistent with the company's desire for industry leadership in quality. Write down the reasons for your position.
2. Before hearing any of your group's comments on this situation and from the perspective of your assigned role, consider what underlying ethical issues, if any, exist in this situation. Write down the issues.
3. Gather your group together and reveal, in turn, each member's comments on Ruth's firing. Next, reveal the ethical issues listed by each member.
4. Appoint someone to record the main points of agreement and disagreement within the group. How do you explain the results? What accounts for any disagreement?
5. From an ethical standpoint, what does your group conclude is the most appropriate action that should have been taken by the company in this situation?
6. Develop a group response to the following question: What are the respective roles of profits, obligations to customers, and employee considerations for the firm in this situation?

BUSINESS CASE

KEEPING THE QUALITY HIGH AT TOYOTA

J.D. Power & Associates is a marketing information services company that produces two annual rankings of automobile quality and reliability. The Initial Quality Study assesses consumer satisfaction with new-vehicle quality during the first 90 days of ownership, while the Vehicle Dependability Study assesses consumer satisfaction after three years of vehicle ownership. Both studies are based on feedback from thousands of car owners. In both studies, the measure is problems per 100 vehicles (PP 100).

In the 2012 Initial Quality Study (IQS), the top three vehicles were the Toyota Lexus ES350 (73 PP100), Jaguar (75 PP100), and Porsche (75 PP100). The initial quality average was 102 PP100, down from 105 PP100 in 2011 (the lower the number, the higher the quality). Of the 34 *brands* that were ranked, 26 showed improved quality over 2011. Of the 185 *models* that were ranked, 65 percent improved their quality over 2011. Toyota automobile models exhibited very high quality, ranking in the top three in multiple categories, including "sub-compact car" (Toyota Yaris and Toyota Sedan), "compact car" (Toyota Corolla and Prius Hatchback), "large car" (Toyota Avalon), "compact MPV" (Toyota Prius v Wagon), "premium car" (Lexus ES350), "mid-size van" (Toyota Sienna), "compact crossover SUV" (Toyota RAV4 SUV and FJ Cruiser SUV), and "mid-size pickup" (Toyota Tacoma truck).

Zuma Press/Newscom

In the 2013 Vehicle Dependability Study (VDS), the top three vehicles were the Toyota Lexus (57 PP100), Porsche (112 PP100), and Lincoln (112 PP100). The overall dependability average was 126 PP100, down from 132 PP100 in 2012 (again, the lower the number, the higher the dependability). Toyota automobile models exhibited very high dependability, ranking in the top three in multiple categories, including "compact car" (Toyota Prius), "large car" (Toyota Avalon), "premium car" (Lexus ES350), "mid-size premium crossover SUV" (Lexus RX), "compact crossover" (Toyota FJ Cruiser), "mid-size crossover" (Toyota Venza), and "minivans" (Toyota Sienna).

Over the years, Toyota has received lots of positive publicity about "The Toyota Way," which emphasizes efficient production methods, continuous improvement, and high quality products. Toyota's production system was so impressive that executives from other automobile companies regularly toured Toyota's manufacturing plants in an attempt to discover Toyota's secret. One of the most highly publicized achievements for Toyota came in 2009, when it overtook General Motors as the largest car manufacturer in the world.

But Toyota ran into significant problems in 2009 when it reported the first operating loss in its history. Then Toyota announced that it was recalling more than five million of its cars because accelerator pedals were getting jammed in the driver's side car mat and causing the car to surge forward uncontrollably. In 2010, Toyota announced another recall—this one involving 2.3 million vehicles (270 000 in Canada)—that also had to do with jamming accelerators. These recalls created great concern among Toyota owners, who were suddenly scared to drive their cars. Toyota worked frantically with its supplier, CTS Corp., to figure out a way to fix the problem. The solution was to insert a steel reinforcement bar in the accelerator pedal assembly which reduced the tension that was causing the pedal to stick. CTS began producing the redesigned pedal in just a few days. Toyota admitted that the accelerator had a design flaw and that CTS was not at fault (CTS also produces accelerator pedals for Honda and Nissan and no problems were found in those cars). In 2012, Toyota agreed to pay $1.1 billion to settle a class-action suit brought by consumers who cars had experienced unintended acceleration.

The recall was a public relations nightmare for Toyota because the company had always had a good reputation for producing high-quality automobiles. In the J.D. Power 2009 Initial Quality Study, Toyota had 10 cars rated as the best in 18 different vehicle categories, and many consumers in Canada and the U.S. did, in fact, have the perception that Toyota produced higher-quality cars than those produced by Ford, Chrysler, and GM. But the recalls changed those perceptions, at least temporarily. In May 2010, a *Consumer Reports* survey found that Toyota lost the top spot in terms of customer loyalty (it was passed by both Ford and Honda). And in the 2010 Initial Quality Survey, Chrysler, Ford, and GM had fewer design-related problems and defects than their foreign competitors. That was the first time in nearly 50 years that domestic car makers had beaten foreign rivals in quality. Toyota also lost its top spot as the biggest company in the automobile business.

A Canadian class-action lawsuit against Toyota and CTS Corp. claimed that Toyota knew (or should have known) that there were also design defects in Toyota's electronic throttle control system. Toyota also faced a lawsuit in the U.S. because of 19 deaths caused by jammed accelerators. The law firm bringing the suit claimed that Toyota knew about the defect, but didn't do anything about it. These claims eventually led the U.S. government to ask the National Highway Traffic Safety Administration (NHTSA) to examine the possibility that there were faults in the electronic throttle system. The NHTSA then called on the Engineering and Safety Center of NASA to study Toyota vehicles. While the engineers did find a few cases where Lexus floor mats that had been installed in Toyotas caused the throttle to remain open, they could find no evidence of any electronic cause of unintended acceleration. This led many people to conclude that drivers were hitting the accelerator rather than the brake.

In the aftermath of the crisis, Toyota implemented several new quality- and safety-related changes to its operations, including the appointment of a high-level manager to oversee safety issues, and a global computer database that tracks vehicle repairs and customer complaints. The latest J.D. Power quality and reliability ratings seem to indicate that Toyota has weathered the crisis. In 2012, Toyota was once again the largest carmaker in the world. But Toyota also announced in November 2012 that it was recalling 2.7 million vehicles because of problems with their steering and water pump systems. The quest for quality goes on.

QUESTIONS FOR DISCUSSION

1. What is total quality management? How is it relevant for automobiles?
2. What is the difference between internal and external benchmarking? Do the J.D. Power Initial Quality and Vehicle Dependability studies facilitate benchmarking? Explain.
3. Consider the following statement: *Consumer opinions about which cars have the best quality or dependability are unreliable because people have preferences for a certain car before they buy it. They are therefore unlikely to give an objective opinion about the car's quality or dependability.* Do you agree or disagree with the statement? Defend your reasoning.

LO

AFTER READING THIS CHAPTER, YOU SHOULD BE ABLE TO:

LO-1 Explain the *role of accountants*, distinguish between the three types of traditional *professional accounting designations* in Canada, and outline the unification process towards the *Canadian Chartered Professional Accounting (CPA) designation.*

LO-2 Explain how the *accounting equation* is used.

LO-3 Describe three basic *financial statements* and show how they reflect the activity and financial condition of a business.

LO-4 Explain the key *standards* and *principles* for *reporting financial statements.*

LO-5 Explain how computing *financial ratios* can help in analyzing the financial strengths of a business.

LO-6 Discuss the role of *ethics in accounting.*

Stolen Maple Syrup: Accounting for Missing Inventory

You might think accountants spend all of their time sitting in comfortable offices, but that picture fails to consider many important functions. For example, auditing inventory levels is a vital business task conducted by accountants. The goal of this exercise is to ensure that the numbers on paper match the real numbers. This process requires different (often complicated) methods depending on the industry. Some young accountants are surprised to find themselves boarding tiny airplanes to remote northern regions where they will manually measure mineral reserves. To complete these tasks, accountants must roll up their sleeves or even

Bloomberg via Getty Images

© Web Pix/Alamy

Understanding Accounting

CHAPTER 11

climb onto stockpiles (e.g., coal, dolomite, etc.) in order to estimate reserves.

When Michel Gauvreau was assigned the task of auditing the Global Strategic Maple Syrup Reserve, he probably expected it to be just another job. There were 16 000 barrels listed in the storage facility, and as he entered the complex and saw row after row (of barrels), he had no reason for concern. As he manoeuvered through the warehouse, however, Michel quickly realized that this task was anything but routine; his audit would lead to the discovery of a major theft and organized fraud. First, Michel found a series of empty barrels. As he continued the audit, he found more empty barrels, and then realized that many of the "full" containers did not contain maple syrup at all. They were filled with water instead. At $32 per gallon, each missing barrel represented $1800 of missing maple syrup inventory. What Mr. Gauvreau had discovered was no error; it was an unbelievable, systematic theft of approximately $20 million worth of maple syrup. Enough to put a tablespoon on 183 million pancakes!

HOW WILL THIS HELP ME?

By understanding the material presented in this chapter, you will benefit in three ways: (1) if you're an *entrepreneur* thinking about starting your own business, you'll discover your obligations for reporting your firm's financial status, (2) as an *employee or manager,* you'll better understand how your company's operations influence its financial performance, and (3) as an *investor,* you'll learn how to interpret financial statements so that you can evaluate a company's financial condition and its prospects for the future.

So, what exactly is the Global Strategic Maple Syrup Reserve? Quebec produces about 70 percent of the world's maple syrup supply. A few years ago, this federation was created to help manage the supply. Overproduction leads to lower prices, and this can be countered by keeping a strategic reserve stockpile in good years. These reserves help to balance supply and meet demand in bad years (years with poor production). Ultimately, this creates more stable (usually inflated) prices, so that producers have a steadier income stream. However, like all managed supply systems, it requires cooperation from all local producers. The federation has had many legal run-ins with rogue producers. But this case was something much more eye-opening and devious. The storage facility did not have a sophisticated security system. However, since it would take about 100 truckloads to move this amount of maple syrup, it appeared that the theft was an inside job. This scenario became more likely when it was revealed that the thieves had taken the time to transfer some of the contents from the original barrels with bar codes (to identify their origins) into seemingly untraceable containers.

Now that Michel had done his job, the theft was a police matter. Was there any hope of recovering the stolen inventory? Isn't maple syrup untraceable? Well, you might think that this was a perfect crime. But, taking the inventory is just phase one; selling it is another challenge. How do you unload this much product discreetly? Selling such a huge quantity of maple syrup within Canada would raise suspicions, but if the thieves tried to cross the border with their syrup, they would leave a major paper trail behind. So, although phase one went off without a hitch (until the accountants uncovered it), phase two was another matter.

Officers from various agencies (the RCMP, Canada Border Services Agency, U.S. Immigration, and the QPP) interviewed over 300 people in Quebec, New Brunswick, Ontario, and the northeastern United States. They reviewed export documents and statistics, and conducted forensic analysis of syrup kettles, forklifts, and scales. They eventually traced two-thirds of the stolen goods before the arrests and accusations were made public.

- Twenty-three people were arrested.
- Companies and individuals in three provinces were implicated.
- Twelve tanker trucks worth of stolen maple syrup were found at a Vermont candy producer's factory.

Regardless of your beliefs about the appropriateness of an organized supply system, it is clear that Michel Gauvreau helped to protect all the legal stakeholders. He alerted everyone that the numbers on the paper did not match the numbers in the warehouse, thus ensuring the integrity of this system, flawed as it may be. In late 2013, it was announced that this story was being used to create a Hollywood film starring Jason Segel.

QUESTIONS FOR DISCUSSION

1. How does the case of the maple syrup robbery demonstrate the important role of accountants?
2. Conduct some research and find articles discussing this case. What are the latest findings? What have investigators revealed by looking at the accounting paper trail?

WHAT IS ACCOUNTING?

ACCOUNTING A comprehensive system for collecting, analyzing, and communicating financial information.

BOOKKEEPING Recording accounting transactions.

ACCOUNTING INFORMATION SYSTEM (AIS) An organized procedure for identifying, measuring, recording, and retaining financial information so that it can be used in accounting statements and management reports.

Accounting is a comprehensive information system for collecting, analyzing, and communicating financial information. It measures business performance and translates the findings into information for management decisions. Accountants prepare performance reports for owners, the public, and regulatory agencies. To perform these functions, accountants keep records of transactions such as taxes paid, income received, and expenses incurred, and they analyze the effects of these transactions on particular business activities. By sorting, analyzing, and recording thousands of transactions, accountants can determine how well a business is being managed and how financially strong it is. **Bookkeeping** is just one phase of accounting—the recording of accounting transactions.

Because businesses engage in many thousands of transactions, ensuring that financial information is consistent and dependable is mandatory. This is the job of the **accounting information system (AIS)**: an organized procedure for identifying, measuring, recording, and retaining financial information so that it can be used in accounting statements and management reports. The system includes all of the people, reports, computers, procedures, and resources for compiling financial transactions.[1] The boxed insert entitled "Greener Accounting Practices" describes several ways that accountants are becoming more environmentally responsible.

Users of accounting information are numerous:

- Business managers use accounting information to set goals, develop plans, set budgets, and evaluate future prospects.
- Employees and unions use accounting information to get paid and to plan for and receive benefits such as health care, insurance, vacation time, and retirement pay.
- Investors and creditors use accounting information to estimate returns to stockholders, determine a company's growth prospects, and determine whether it is a good credit risk before investing or lending.
- Tax authorities use accounting information to plan for tax inflows, determine the tax liabilities of individuals and businesses, and ensure that correct amounts are paid on time.
- Government regulatory agencies rely on accounting information to fulfill their duties. Provincial securities regulators, for example, require firms to file financial disclosures so that potential investors have valid information about a company's financial status.

If a company does not produce accurate accounting information, all of these groups may be hurt. As we saw in the opening case, inventory counts at the Global Strategic Maple Syrup Reserve were inaccurate. Standard accounting procedures identified the inconsistency, thus

THE GREENING OF BUSINESS

Greener Accounting Practices

In accounting, there is at least one important activity that impacts the environment: the use of paper for all those financial statements. But the electronic revolution has provided accountants with the opportunities to reduce paper waste; respond quickly to clients; reduce the costs associated with storing, tracking, and accessing documents; and work virtually anywhere in the world via the internet. Traditional accounting firms spend a lot of valuable time handling paperwork, such as invoices. A paperless system eliminates the need to store paper invoices by storing their digital images and retrieving the images as needed. Firms now have easier access to more data, facilitating analyses that can save thousands of dollars.

There are real incentives for companies to embrace environmentally friendly business practices like saving paper. But careful thought has to be given to how this will be done because of the well-known tendency of human beings to resist change. To resolve any resistance based on *technical* concerns, management must ensure that the IT infrastructure is working properly and that there is an adequate storage and security system. To deal with resistance based on *emotional* concerns, management needs to provide incentives to motivate people to change. Digital files, for example, reduce the need to travel in order to share documents with clients and other associates. This also enables companies to reduce their dependency on a traditional work environment because more employees can choose to work flexible hours and have a more balanced work and family life. Another incentive is the increased efficiency that will be evident with the use of electronic technology. Increased efficiency means that a given amount of work can be done with fewer people than were previously needed, and this will increase competitiveness.

It is anticipated that accounting firms will increasingly train their clients to perform more of the initial data entry to allow for the electronic exchange of information. Firms will no longer be limited by geographic boundaries. They can also bill for higher-level accounting tasks and be much more selective about their clients. These new methods will help eliminate the bottom 10 to 20 percent of unproductive clients and allow more time to cultivate the profitable files.

CRITICAL THINKING QUESTIONS

1. There are clearly benefits for firms that embrace green accounting practices, but are there also benefits to clients? If so, describe them.
2. Why might there be reluctance on the part of accounting firms or their clients to embrace green initiatives like paperless systems?

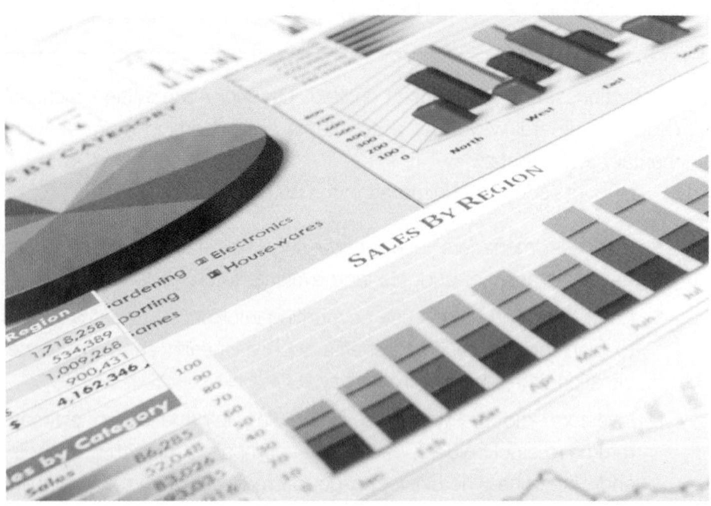

<<< A financial report is an integral component of the financial accounting system.

INDRANIL MUKHERJEE/AFP/GETTY IMAGES/Newscom

revealing the theft. The discovery had important implications for maple syrup producers, government agencies, and customers who ultimately may have purchased stolen products unknowingly. A few years ago, General Motors warned its investors that it did not yet have an effective accounting control system in place, and that it could not guarantee the reliability of its financial statements.[2] The Sarbanes-Oxley Act (passed in the U.S. in 2002) required senior managers in companies to certify that their company had an effective internal control system in place. In Canada, this idea was partially adopted two years later through National Instrument 52-109. Critics of this type of legislation argue that it has been very expensive to implement and has not achieved the goal of more reliable accounting information.[3]

LO-1 WHO ARE ACCOUNTANTS AND WHAT DO THEY DO?

CONTROLLER The individual who manages all the firm's accounting activities.

FINANCIAL ACCOUNTING SYSTEM The process whereby interested groups are kept informed about the financial condition of a firm.

MANAGERIAL (OR MANAGEMENT) ACCOUNTING Internal procedures that alert managers to problems and aid them in planning and decision making.

CHARTERED PROFESSIONAL ACCOUNTANT (CPA) The banner (designation) which is being used to unify the accounting profession in Canada.

CHARTERED ACCOUNTANT (CA) An individual who has met certain experience and education requirements and has passed a licensing examination; acts as an outside accountant for other firms.

At the head of the accounting system is the **controller**, who manages all of the firm's accounting activities. As chief accounting officer, the controller ensures that the accounting system provides the reports and statements needed for planning, controlling, and decision-making activities. This broad range of activities requires different types of expertise among accounting specialists. We begin our discussion by distinguishing between the two main fields of accounting: financial and managerial. Then, we discuss the different functions and activities of the three professional accounting groups in Canada.

Financial and Managerial Accounting

As we have just seen, it is important to distinguish between users of accounting information who are outside a company and users who are inside the company. This same distinction allows us to categorize accounting systems as either *financial* or *managerial*.

FINANCIAL ACCOUNTING

A firm's **financial accounting system** is concerned with external users of information such as consumer groups, unions, stockholders, and government agencies. Companies prepare and publish income statements and balance sheets at regular intervals, as well as other financial reports that are useful for stockholders and the general public. All of these documents focus on the activities of the company as a whole, rather than on individual departments or divisions.

MANAGERIAL ACCOUNTING

In contrast, **managerial (or management) accounting** serves internal users. Managers at all levels need information to make decisions for their departments, to monitor current projects, and to plan for future activities. Other employees also need accounting information. Engineers, for instance, want to know the costs for materials and production so they can make product operation improvements. To set performance goals, salespeople need data on past sales by geographic region. Purchasing agents use information on material costs to negotiate terms with suppliers.

Professional Accountants

Three professional accounting organizations have developed in Canada to certify accounting expertise. The three designations are Chartered Accountants (CA), Certified Management Accountants (CMA), and Certified General Accountants (CGA). Below, we discuss each of the designations and their traditional strengths and roles; however, there is a process well underway toward unifying these organizations and certifications under the **Chartered Professional Accountant (CPA)** banner. We will examine the implications of this process in detail at the end of this section.

CHARTERED ACCOUNTANTS

The Canadian Institute of Chartered Accountants (CICA) grants the **chartered accountant (CA)** designation. To achieve this designation, a person must earn a university degree, then complete an educational program and pass a national exam. About half of all CAs work in CA firms that offer accounting services to the public; the other half work in government or industry. CA firms typically provide audit, tax, and management

TABLE 11.1 Top 10 Accounting Firms in Canada, 2013[5]

	Company	Annual Revenues (millions of dollars)
1	Deloitte LLP	1881
2	PricewaterhouseCoopers LLP	1202
3	KPMG LLP	1162
4	Ernst & Young LLP	911
5	Grant Thornton Canada	545
6	BDO Canada LLP	446
7	MNP LLP	430
8	Collins Barrow National Cooperative Inc.	156
9	Richter LLP	80
10	Mallette	56

services. CAs focus on external financial reporting, that is, certifying for various interested parties (stockholders, lenders, the Canada Revenue Agency, etc.) that the financial records of a company accurately reflect the true financial condition of the firm. In 2013, there were about 83 000 CAs in Canada.[4]

CERTIFIED GENERAL ACCOUNTANTS

The Certified General Accountants Association of Canada grants the **certified general accountant (CGA)** designation. To become a CGA, a person must complete an education program and pass a national exam; to be eligible, a person must have an accounting job with a company. CGAs can audit corporate financial statements in most provinces. Most CGAs work in private companies, but there are a few CGA firms. Some CGAs also work in CA firms. CGAs also focus on external financial reporting and emphasize the use of the computer as a management accounting tool. In 2013, there were about 75 000 CGAs in Canada, the Caribbean, and China.[6]

Take a look at the following feature called "There's an APP for That!" as it outlines three accounting apps.

CERTIFIED MANAGEMENT ACCOUNTANTS

The Society of Management Accountants of Canada grants the **certified management accountant (CMA)** designation. To achieve the designation, a person must have a university degree, pass a two-part national entrance examination, and complete a strategic leadership program while gaining practical experience in a management accounting environment. CMAs work in organizations of all sizes and focus on applying best management practices in all of the operations of a business. CMAs bring

CERTIFIED GENERAL ACCOUNTANT (CGA) An individual who has completed an education program and passed a national exam; works in private industry or a CGA firm.

CERTIFIED MANAGEMENT ACCOUNTANT (CMA) An individual who has completed a university degree, passed a national examination, and completed a strategic leadership program; works in industry and focuses on internal management accounting.

THERE'S AN APP FOR THAT!

1. Need an Accountant App >>> **Platforms:** *Apple, Android*
   Source: Certified General Accountant Association (CGA-Canada).
   Key Features: Searchable directory of CGAs in Canada (dial automatically through the APP, provides directions).
2. QuickBooks App >>> **Platforms:** *Apple, Android*
   Source: Intuit
   Key Features: Allows you to manage customers, invoices, sales receipts, estimates, and small business finances.
3. Kashoo Accounting App >>> **Platforms:** *Apple*
   Source: Kashoo (Vancouver)
   Key Features: Permits small business owners to keep track of receipts, invoices, and bank balances on the go.

APP DISCOVERY EXERCISE

Since APP availability changes, conduct your own search for "Top 3" Accounting APPS and identify the key features.

a strong market focus to strategic management and resource deployment, synthesizing and analyzing financial and non-financial information to help organizations maintain a competitive advantage. CMAs emphasize the role of accountants in the planning and overall strategy of the firm in which they work. In 2013, there were about 40 000 CMAs in Canada, with an additional 10 000 students in the program.[7]

THE UNIFICATION PROCESS: FROM CA, CGA, CMA TO CPA

Over the years, there have been many discussions about a possible merger between the three Canadian designations. In January 2012, however, after months of consultations, "the Canadian Institute of Chartered Accountants (CICA), the Society of Management Accountants of Canada (CMA Canada), and Certified General Accountants of Canada (CGA-Canada) issued A Framework for Uniting the Canadian Accounting Profession under a new Canadian Chartered Professional Accountant (CPA) designation."[8] However, because the accounting profession is regulated provincially, the implementation and ultimate approval is taking place at different rates. In New Brunswick, a unifications proposal was put forward in March of 2013. This process was completed a year earlier in Newfoundland and Labrador. In Quebec, the unification agreement was completed in May 2012. In other jurisdictions, the process has moved a bit slower. By March 2013, the CA and CMA provincial members had approved the proposal in British Columbia, Manitoba, Saskatchewan, Nova Scotia, Prince Edward Island, Northwest Territories, and Yukon. In Alberta, the CGA and CMA designations had approved the proposal. In Ontario, the process has been approved by the CA (ICAO), and CMA Ontario has indicated they are working toward this recommendation as well.

Once fully approved in these jurisdictions, the members will use combined designations for a period of 10 years: CPA, CA; CPA, CMA; CPA, CGA. After 10 years, a member can simply refer to themselves as a CPA. New rules for earning this designation are also being established. More information on the unification process can be found at www.CPACanada.ca.

Accounting Services

CAs and CGAs usually perform several accounting services for their clients. The most common of these are auditing, tax services, and management services.

AUDITING

In an **audit**, accountants examine a company's AIS to ensure that it adheres to **generally accepted accounting principles (GAAP)**—a body of theory and procedure developed and monitored by the CICA. An audit involves examination of receipts such as shipping documents, cancelled cheques, payroll records, and cash receipts records. In some cases, an auditor may physically check inventories, equipment, or other assets, even if it means descending 200 metres into an underground mine. The opening case about stolen maple syrup provides some concrete evidence as to why accountants must be thorough in their evaluations of assets. At the end of an audit, the auditor will certify whether the client's financial reports comply with GAAP.

International Accounting Standards In a globalized economy, users of financial information want assurances that accounting procedures are comparable from country to country. So, the International Accounting Standards Board (IASB) has developed International Financial Reporting Standards (IFRS), a sort of "global GAAP," which is now being used by more than 100 countries.[9] Canadian companies adopted the IFRS on January 1, 2011, but it required a lot of work to determine how to present accounting information in a way that satisfies the new standards.[10] IASB financial statements require an income statement, balance sheet, and statement of cash flows, which are similar to those that have historically been developed by Canadian accountants, but a variety of formats are used since a uniform format has not been developed. Some accounting experts argue that IFRS gives managers too much leeway to report the figures they want, which means less protection for investors.[11] The U.S. has resisted the adoption of IFRS, but the standard has been adopted by three-quarters of the powerful G20 nations.[12]

The new IASB standards may have a noticeable impact on the way Canadian companies report some financial results. For example, suppose a company has a customer loyalty plan that gives customers points for purchases they make, and then these points can be redeemed for free products. If a customer makes $1000 in purchases and earns points that can be redeemed for $25 worth of merchandise, the company may have historically counted the $1000 as sales revenue and then also counted the $25 as sales revenue when the points were redeemed. But under the new IFRS, companies cannot add the $25 to the original $1000. The new rules will reduce the apparent same-stores sales growth numbers for these companies.[13]

Detecting Fraud In recent years, there has been much publicity about the failure of auditors to detect fraud. Therefore, when audits are being conducted, **forensic accountants** may be used to track down hidden funds in business firms. Because of the increase in white-collar crime, forensic accounting is one of the fastest-growing areas in the field. Forensic accountants must be good detectives. They look behind the corporate walls instead of accepting financial records at face value. In combining investigative skills with accounting, auditing, and the instincts of a bloodhound, they assist in the investigation of business and financial issues that may have application to a court of law. Forensic accountants may be called upon by law enforcement agencies, insurance companies, law firms, and business firms. They may conduct criminal investigations of internet scams and misuse of government funds. Forensic accountants also assist business firms in tracing and recovering lost assets from employee business fraud or theft.

Fraud examiners interview high-level executives, pursue tips from employees or outsiders, and search through emails, looking for suspicious words and phrases. The CA designation in investigative and forensic accounting (CA IFA) provides in-depth knowledge and experience in investigative and forensic accounting. You can get more information on the topic at the website for the Association of Forensic Examiners at http://ACFE.org.

AUDIT An accountant's examination of a company's financial records to determine if it used proper procedures to prepare its financial reports.

GENERALLY ACCEPTED ACCOUNTING PRINCIPLES (GAAP) Standard rules and methods used by accountants in preparing financial reports.

FORENSIC ACCOUNTANT Accountants who track down hidden funds in business firms.

MANAGEMENT CONSULTING SERVICES Specialized accounting services to help managers resolve a variety of problems in finance, production scheduling, and other areas.

TAX SERVICES

Tax services include helping clients not only with preparing their tax returns, but also in their tax planning. Tax laws are complex, and an accountant's advice can help a business structure (or restructure) its operations and investments and save millions of dollars in taxes. To serve their clients best, of course, accountants must stay abreast of changes in tax laws—no simple matter.

MANAGEMENT CONSULTING SERVICES

Management consulting services range from personal financial planning to planning corporate mergers. Other services include plant layout and design, marketing studies, production scheduling, computer feasibility studies, and design and implementation of accounting systems. Some CA firms even assist in executive recruitment. Small wonder that the staffs of CA firms include engineers, architects, mathematicians, and even psychologists.

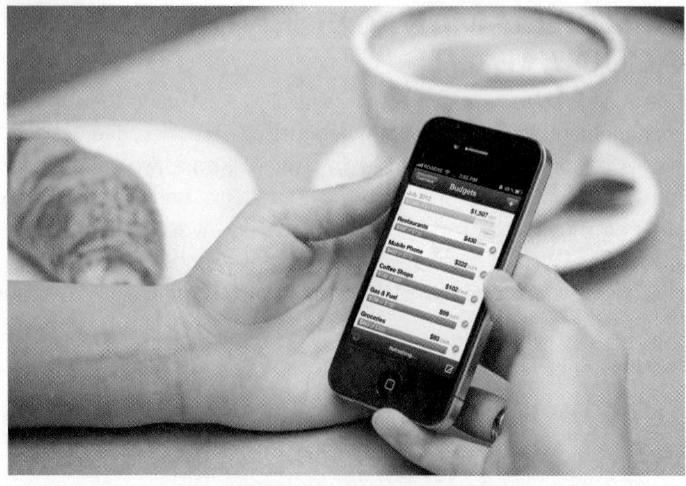

Thanks to smartphones, financial information is now much more accessible wherever you might be located at the time.

Getty Images

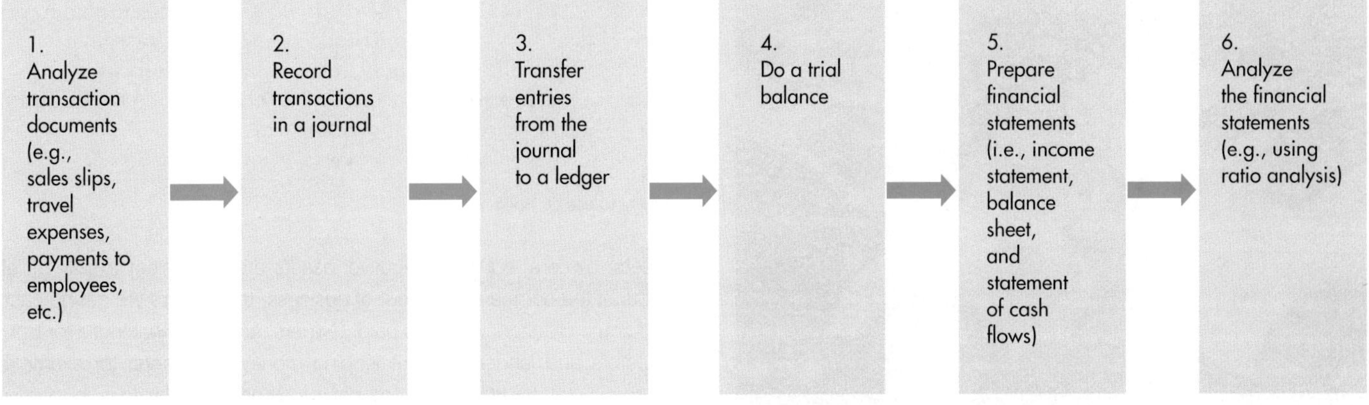

FIGURE 11.1 The accounting cycle

Private Accountants

Private accountants are salaried employees who deal with a company's day-to-day accounting needs. Large businesses employ specialized accountants in such areas as budgets, financial planning, internal auditing, payroll, and taxation. In a small firm, a single individual may handle all accounting tasks. The work of private accountants varies, depending on the nature of the specific business and the activities needed to make that business a success. An internal auditor at Petro-Canada, for example, might fly to the Hibernia site to confirm the accuracy of oil-flow meters on the offshore drilling platform. But a supervisor responsible for $200 million in monthly accounts payable to vendors and employees may travel no further than the executive suite.

PRIVATE ACCOUNTANT An accountant hired as a salaried employee to deal with a company's day-to-day accounting needs.

THE ACCOUNTING CYCLE

Private accountants use a six-step process to develop and analyze a company's financial reports (see Figure 11.1). The first step is to analyze data that are generated as a result of the company's regular business operations (sales revenue, income tax payments, interest income, inventory purchases, etc.). These transactions are entered in a journal (which lists them in chronological order) and then in a ledger (which shows the increases and decreases in the various asset, liability, and equity accounts). Then, the ledger amounts for each account are listed in a trial balance (which assesses the accuracy of the figures). Financial statements (balance sheet, income statement, and statement of cash flows) are then prepared using GAAP. The last step in the process involves analyzing the financial statements (for example, by using ratio analysis). Many years ago, these steps were done laboriously by hand, but now computers are used to help private accountants efficiently work through the six steps.

LO-2 THE ACCOUNTING EQUATION

All accountants, whether public or private, rely on record keeping. Underlying all record-keeping procedures is the most basic tool of accounting: the **accounting equation**. At various points in the year, accountants use the following equation to balance the data pertaining to financial transactions:

Assets = Liabilities + Owners' equity

After each transaction (e.g., payments to suppliers, sales to customers, wages to employees), the accounting equation must be in balance. To understand the importance of this equation, we must understand the terms *assets*, *liabilities*, and *owners' equity*.[14]

Assets and Liabilities

An **asset** is any economic resource that is expected to benefit a firm or an individual who owns it. Assets include land, buildings, equipment, inventory, and payments due to the company (accounts receivable). A **liability** is a debt that the firm owes to an outside party.

Owners' Equity

You may have heard of the equity that a homeowner has in a house—that is, the amount of money that could be made by selling the house and paying off the mortgage. Similarly, **owners' equity** is the amount of

ACCOUNTING EQUATION Assets = Liabilities + Owners' equity; the formula used by accountants to balance data for the firm's financial transactions at various points in the year.

ASSET Anything of economic value owned by a firm or individual.

LIABILITY Any debt owed by a firm or individual to others.

OWNERS' EQUITY Any positive difference between a firm's assets and its liabilities; what would remain for a firm's owners if the company were liquidated, all its assets were sold, and all its debts were paid.

<<< The inventory at this car dealership is part of the company's assets. The cars constitute an economic resource because the firm will benefit financially as it sells them. After they are sold and at the end of the company's accounting period, the dealership will convert the cost of the cars as expenses and show them as costs of goods sold.

AP Photo/Jae C. Hong

money that owners would receive if they sold all of a company's assets and paid all of its liabilities. We can rewrite the accounting equation to highlight this definition:

Assets − Liabilities = Owners' equity

If a company's assets exceed its liabilities, owners' equity is positive; if the company goes out of business, the owners will receive some cash (a gain) after selling assets and paying off liabilities. If liabilities outweigh assets, owners' equity is negative; assets are insufficient to pay off all debts. If the company goes out of business, the owners will get no cash and some creditors won't be paid. Owners' equity is meaningful for both investors and lenders. Before lending money to owners, for example, lenders want to know the amount of owners' equity in a business. Owners' equity consists of two sources of capital:

1. The amount that the owners originally invested.
2. Profits earned by and reinvested in the company.

When a company operates profitably, its assets increase faster than its liabilities. Owners' equity, therefore, will increase if profits are retained in the business instead of paid out as dividends to stockholders. Owners' equity also increases if owners invest more of their own money to increase assets. However, owners' equity can shrink if the company operates at a loss or if owners withdraw assets.

LO-3 FINANCIAL STATEMENTS

If a business purchases inventory with cash, then cash decreases and inventory increases. Similarly, if the business purchases supplies on credit, then supplies increase and so do accounts payable. Since every transaction affects two accounts, **double-entry accounting systems** are used to record the dual effects of financial transactions. These transactions are reflected in three important **financial statements**: balance sheets, income statements, and statements of cash flows.[15]

Balance Sheets

Balance sheets supply detailed information about the accounting equation factors: assets, liabilities, and owners' equity. Figure 11.2 shows the balance sheet for Perfect Posters.

ASSETS

As we have seen, an asset is any economic resource that a company owns and from which it can expect to derive some future benefit. Most companies have three types of assets: current, fixed, and intangible.

Current Assets **Current assets** include cash, money in the bank, and assets that can be converted into cash within a year. They are normally listed in order of **liquidity**, that is, the ease with which they can be converted into cash. Business debts, for example, can usually be satisfied only through payments of cash. A company that needs cash, but does not have it—in other words, a company that is not liquid—may be forced to sell assets at sacrifice prices or even go out of business.

By definition, cash is completely liquid. Marketable securities (e.g., stocks or bonds of other companies, government securities, and money market certificates) are slightly less liquid, but can be sold quickly if necessary. Three other non-liquid assets are **accounts receivable** (amounts due from customers who have purchased goods on credit), **merchandise inventory** (merchandise that has been acquired for sale to customers and is still on hand), and **prepaid expenses** (supplies on hand and rent paid for the period to come). Figure 11.2 shows that Perfect Posters' current assets as of December 31, 2013, totalled $57 210.

DOUBLE-ENTRY ACCOUNTING SYSTEM A bookkeeping system, developed in the fifteenth century and still in use, that requires every transaction to be entered in two ways—how it affects assets and how it affects liabilities and owners' equity—so that the accounting equation is always in balance.

FINANCIAL STATEMENTS Any of several types of broad reports regarding a company's financial status; most often used in reference to balance sheets, income statements, and/or statements of cash flows.

BALANCE SHEET A type of financial statement that summarizes a firm's financial position on a particular date in terms of its assets, liabilities, and owners' equity.

CURRENT ASSETS Cash and other assets that can be converted into cash within a year.

LIQUIDITY The ease and speed with which an asset can be converted to cash; cash is said to be perfectly liquid.

ACCOUNTS RECEIVABLE Amounts due to the firm from customers who have purchased goods or services on credit; a form of current asset.

MERCHANDISE INVENTORY The cost of merchandise that has been acquired for sale to customers but is still on hand.

PREPAID EXPENSES Includes supplies on hand and rent paid for the period to come.

Perfect Posters, Inc.
555 Riverview, Toronto, Ontario

Perfect Posters, Inc.
Balance Sheet
As of December 31, 2013

Assets			
Current Assets:			
Cash		$7,050	
Marketable securities. . . .		2,300	
Accounts receivable.	$26,210		
Less: Allowance of doubtful accounts.	(650)	25,560	
Merchandise inventory.		21,250	
Prepaid expenses		1,050	
Total current assets			**$57,210**
Fixed Assets:			
Land		18,000	
Building	65,000		
Less: Accumulated depreciation	(22,500)	42,500	
Equipment	72,195		
Less: Accumulated depreciation	(24,815)	47,380	
Total fixed assets. . .			**107,880**
Intangible Assets:			
Patents	7,100		
Trademarks	900		
Total intangible assets			**8,000**
Total assets			**$173,090**

Liabilities and Owners' Equity			
Current liabilities:			
Accounts payable.	$16,315		
Wages payable.	3,700		
Taxes payable.	1,920		
Total current liabilities			**$21,935**
Long-term liabilities:			
Notes payable, 8% due 2014	10,000		
Bonds payable, 9% due 2016	30,000		
Total long-term liabilities			**40,000**
Total liabilities			**$61,935**
Owners' Equity			
Common stock, $5 par		40,000	
Additional paid-in capital		15,000	
Retained earnings		56,155	
Total owners' equity			**111,155**
Total liabilities and owners' equity . . .			**$173,090**

FIGURE 11.2 Perfect Posters' balance sheet
This balance sheet shows clearly that the firm's total assets equal its total liabilities and owners' equity.

Fixed Assets **Fixed assets** (e.g., land, buildings, and equipment) have long-term use or value. As buildings and equipment wear out or become obsolete, their value depreciates. Various methods can be used to calculate depreciation, but, in its simplest sense, **depreciation** means determining an asset's useful life in years, dividing its worth by that many years, and then subtracting the resulting amount each year. The asset's remaining value therefore decreases each year. In Figure 11.2, Perfect Posters shows fixed assets of $107 880 after depreciation.

Intangible Assets Although their worth is hard to set, intangible assets have monetary value. **Intangible assets** usually include the cost of obtaining rights or privileges such as patents, trademarks, copyrights, and franchise fees. **Goodwill** is the amount paid for an existing business beyond the value of its other assets. Perfect Posters has no goodwill assets, but it does own trademarks and patents for specialized storage equipment. These intangible assets are worth $8000. Larger companies have intangible assets that are worth much more.

LIABILITIES

Current liabilities are debts that must be paid within one year. These include **accounts payable** (unpaid bills to suppliers for materials, as well as wages and taxes that must be paid in the coming year). Perfect Posters has current liabilities of $21 935.

Long-term liabilities are debts that are not due for at least one year. These normally represent borrowed funds on which the company must pay interest. Perfect Posters' long-term liabilities are $40 000.

FIXED ASSETS Assets that have long-term use or value to the firm, such as land, buildings, and machinery.

DEPRECIATION Distributing the cost of a major asset over the years in which it produces revenues; calculated each year by subtracting the asset's original value divided by the number of years in its productive life.

INTANGIBLE ASSETS Non-physical assets, such as patents, trademarks, copyrights, and franchise fees, that have economic value, but whose precise value is difficult to calculate.

GOODWILL The amount paid for an existing business beyond the value of its other assets.

CURRENT LIABILITIES Any debts owed by the firm that must be paid within one year.

ACCOUNTS PAYABLE Amounts due from the firm to its suppliers for goods and/or services purchased on credit; a form of current liability.

LONG-TERM LIABILITIES Any debts owed by the firm that are not due for at least one year.

OWNERS' EQUITY

The final section of the balance sheet in Figure 11.2 shows owners' equity broken down into *common stock, paid-in capital*, and *retained earnings*. When Perfect Posters was formed, the declared legal value of its common stock was $5 per share. By law, this $40 000 ($5 multiplied by 8000 shares) cannot be distributed as dividends. **Paid-in capital** is additional money invested in the firm by its owners. Perfect Posters has $15 000 in paid-in capital.

Retained earnings are net profits minus dividend payments to shareholders. Retained earnings accumulate when profits, which could have been distributed to shareholders, are kept instead for use by the company. At the close of 2013, Perfect Posters had retained earnings of $56 155.

LO-4 Income Statements

The **income statement** is sometimes called a profit-and-loss statement, because its description of revenues and expenses results in a figure showing the firm's annual profit or loss. In other words,

Revenues – Expenses = Profit (or loss)

Popularly known as "the bottom line," profit or loss is probably the most important figure in any business enterprise. The boxed insert entitled "How Will Twitter Turn Tweets into Treasure?" contains information about profit uncertainties in new start-ups.

Figure 11.3 shows the 2013 income statement for Perfect Posters, whose bottom line that year was $12 585. The income statement is divided into three major categories: revenues, cost of goods sold, and operating expenses.

REVENUES

When a law firm receives $250 for preparing a will or when a supermarket collects $65 from a customer buying groceries, both are receiving **revenues**—the funds that flow into a business from the sale of goods or services. In 2013, Perfect Posters reported revenues of $256 425 from the sale of art prints and other posters.

PAID-IN CAPITAL Any additional money invested in the firm by the owners.

RETAINED EARNINGS A company's net profits less any dividend payments to shareholders.

INCOME STATEMENT (PROFIT-AND-LOSS STATEMENT) A type of financial statement that describes a firm's revenues and expenses and indicates whether the firm has earned a profit or suffered a loss during a given period.

REVENUES Any monies received by a firm as a result of selling a good or service or from other sources such as interest, rent, and licensing fees.

ENTREPRENEURSHIP AND NEW VENTURES

How Will Twitter Turn Tweets into Treasure?

Widely accepted accounting measurements provide useful information about established firms, but are a bit foggier with start-ups. Consider the continuing questions from the investment community about Twitter's ambiguous financial status. With several firms interested in buying Twitter, how can they know its market value (estimated at $10 billion in 2013) without solid financial data? The real numbers are confidential and closely guarded by Twitter. As to its profitability, Twitter reports, "we spend more money than we make." Since Twitter was launched in 2006, its total losses have not been reported publicly. When (and how) will losses blossom into profitability? As stated by co-founder and former CEO Evan Williams, "We will make money, and I can't say exactly how because … we can't predict how the business we're in will work." And until they know *how*, they don't know *when* profits will occur. Twitter's balance sheet is another source of ambiguity. The accounting equation requires a fixed relationship among three items: Assets = Liabilities + Owners' equity. Twitter insiders have a clear accounting of its outstanding liabilities, and paid-in capital (a part of shareholders' equity) is known, too. It includes the co-founders' personal investments plus a series of venture capital infusions, bringing the suspected total to over $800 million.

But there are difficulties valuing Twitter's assets. For example, Twitter acquired the assets of a company called *Values of n* to get needed technology and intellectual property into its operations. Exactly how Twitter will use them is unknown, so how should they be valued? Twitter's greatest asset is a massive loyal customer base with a phenomenal growth rate—200 million active users who account for 400 million daily tweets—and its enormous advertising potential. Celebrities, media, politicians, and organizations such as Warner Bros Pictures and Toyota, are using Twitter for sales and marketing promotions. Should this advertising potential be recognized as an intangible asset? At what value? While the company's market, customer base, and products are rapidly emerging, how should its many assets—tangible and intangible—be valued?

On what basis can those evaluations be justified? Clearly, these issues at Twitter are less well settled than at more established firms. In order to become a public corporation Twitter had to answer these questions (in late 2013) and reveal numbers to the general public.

CRITICAL THINKING QUESTION

1. Consider the following statement: *Accounting information is meaningful and useful for well-established companies and is particularly helpful for individuals and organizations when making investment decisions. But accounting information is not very helpful in making investment decisions for newly established companies.* Do you agree or disagree with the statement? Defend your answer.

Perfect Posters, Inc.
555 Riverview, Toronto, Ontario

Perfect Posters, Inc.
Income Statement
Year ended December 31, 2013

Revenues (gross sales)			**$256,425**
Costs of goods sold:			
Merchandise inventory, January 1, 2013	$22,380		
Merchandise purchases during year	103,635		
Goods available for sale		$126,015	
Less: Merchandise inventory, December 31, 2013		21,250	
Cost of goods sold			**104,765**
Gross profit			**151,660**
Operating expenses:			
Selling and repackaging expenses:			
Salaries and wages	49,750		
Advertising	6,380		
Depreciation—warehouse and repackaging equipment	3,350		
Total selling and repackaging expenses		59,480	
Administrative expenses:			
Salaries and wages	55,100		
Supplies	4,150		
Utilities	3,800		
Depreciation—office equipment	3,420		
Interest expense	2,900		
Miscellaneous expenses	1,835		
Total administration expenses		71,205	
Total operating expenses			**130,685**
Operating income (income before taxes)			20,975
Income taxes			8,390
Net income			**$12,585**

FIGURE 11.3 Perfect Posters' Income Statement
The final entry on the income statement, the bottom line, reports the firm's profit or loss.

Revenue Recognition and Matching

Revenue recognition is the formal recording and reporting of revenues in the financial statements. Although any firm earns revenues continuously as it makes sales, earnings are not reported until the earnings cycle is completed. Revenues are recorded for the accounting period in which sales are completed and collectible (or collected).

REVENUE RECOGNITION The formal recording and reporting of revenues in the financial statements.

MATCHING PRINCIPLE Expenses should be matched with revenues to determine net income for an accounting period.

COST OF GOODS SOLD Any expenses directly involved in producing or selling a good or service during a given time period.

GROSS PROFIT (GROSS MARGIN) A firm's revenues (gross sales) less its cost of goods sold.

OPERATING EXPENSES Costs incurred by a firm other than those included in cost of goods sold.

OPERATING INCOME Compares the gross profit from business operations against operating expenses.

NET INCOME (NET PROFIT OR NET EARNINGS) A firm's gross profit less its operating expenses and income taxes.

The **matching principle** states that expenses will be matched with revenues to determine net income for an accounting period.[16] This principle is important because it permits the user of the statement to see how much net gain resulted from the assets that had to be given up to generate revenues during the period covered in the statement.

COST OF GOODS SOLD

In Perfect Posters' income statement, the **cost of goods sold** category shows the costs of obtaining materials to make the products sold during the year. Perfect Posters began 2013 with posters valued at $22 380. Over the year, it spent $103 635 to purchase posters. During 2013, then, the company had $126 015 worth of merchandise available to sell. By the end of the year, it had sold all but $21 250 of those posters, which remained as merchandise inventory. The cost of obtaining the goods sold by the firm was thus $104 765.

Gross Profit (or Gross Margin)

To calculate **gross profit** (or **gross margin**), subtract the cost of goods sold from revenues. Perfect Posters' gross profit in 2013 was $151 660 ($256 425 minus $104 765). Expressed as a percentage of sales, gross profit is 59.1 percent ($151 660 divided by $256 425).

Gross profit percentages vary widely across industries. In retailing, Home Depot reports 34 percent; in manufacturing, Harley-Davidson reports 36 percent; and in pharmaceuticals, Pfizer Inc. reports 80 percent. For companies with low gross margins, product costs are a big expense. If a company has a high gross margin, it probably has low cost-of-goods-sold, but high selling and administrative expenses.

OPERATING EXPENSES

In addition to costs directly related to acquiring goods, every company has general expenses ranging from erasers to the president's salary. Like cost of goods sold, **operating expenses** are resources that must flow out of a company for it to earn revenues. As you can see in Figure 11.3, Perfect Posters had operating expenses of $130 685 in 2013. This figure consists of $59 480 in selling and repackaging expenses and $71 205 in administrative expenses.

Selling expenses result from activities related to selling the firm's goods or services. These may include salaries for the sales force, delivery costs, and advertising expenses. General and administrative expenses, such as management salaries, insurance expenses, and maintenance costs, are expenses related to the general management of the company.

Operating Income and Net Income

Sometimes managers calculate **operating income**, which compares the gross profit from business operations against operating expenses. This calculation for Perfect Posters ($151 660 minus $130 685) reveals an operating income, or income before taxes, of $20 975. Subtracting income taxes from operating income ($20 975 minus $8390) reveals **net income** (also called net profit or net earnings). In 2013, Perfect Posters' net income was $12 585.

Statements of Cash Flows

In order to survive, a business must earn a profit (that is, its sales revenues must exceed its expenses), but it must also make sure it has cash available when it needs it (for example, to pay employees). Cash flow

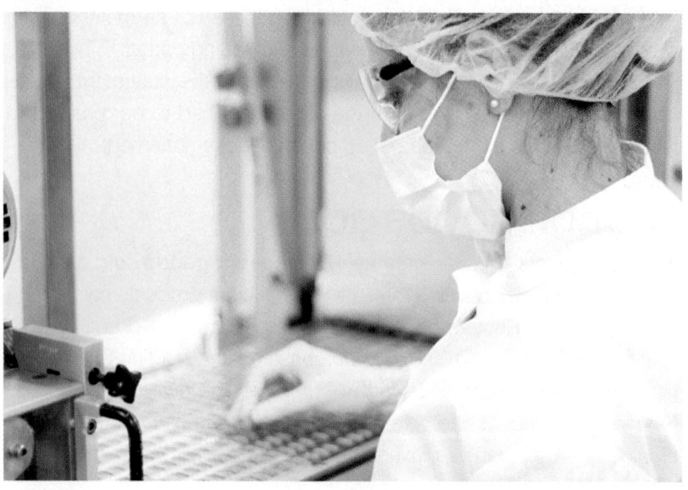

At the end of its accounting period, this pharmaceuticals company will subtract the cost of making the goods that it sells from the revenues it receives from sales. The difference will be its gross profit (or gross margin).

AP Photo/Jae C. Hong

STATEMENT OF CASH FLOWS A financial statement that describes a firm's generation and use of cash during a given period.

BUDGET A detailed financial plan for estimated receipts and expenditures for a period of time in the future, usually one year.

management requires the development of a **statement of cash flows**, which describes a company's yearly cash receipts and cash payments. It shows the effects on cash of three important business activities:

- *Cash flows from operations.* This part of the statement is concerned with the firm's main operating activities: the cash transactions involved in buying and selling goods and services. It reveals how much of the year's profits result from the firm's main line of business (e.g., Ferrari's sales of automobiles), rather than from secondary activities (e.g., licensing fees that a clothing firm paid to Ferrari to use their logo).
- *Cash flows from investing.* This section reports net cash used in or provided by investing. It includes cash receipts and payments from buying and selling stocks, bonds, property, equipment, and other productive assets.
- *Cash flows from financing.* The final section reports net cash from all financing activities. It includes cash inflows from borrowing or issuing stock, as well as outflows for payment of dividends and repayment of borrowed money.

The overall change in cash from these three sources provides information to lenders and investors. When creditors and stockholders know how firms obtained and used their funds during the course of a year, it is easier for them to interpret the year-to-year changes in the firm's balance sheet and income statement.

The Budget: An Internal Financial Statement

In addition to financial statements, managers need other types of accounting information to aid in internal planning, controlling, and decision making. Probably the most crucial internal financial statement is the budget. A **budget** is a detailed statement of estimated receipts and expenditures for a period of time in the future. Although that period is usually one year, some companies also prepare budgets for three- or five-year periods, especially when considering major capital expenditures.

Budgets are also useful for keeping track of weekly or monthly performance. For example, Procter & Gamble evaluates all of its business units monthly, by comparing actual financial results with monthly budgeted amounts. Discrepancies in "actual versus budget" totals signal potential problems and initiate action to get financial performance back on track.

LO-5 ANALYZING FINANCIAL STATEMENTS

SOLVENCY RATIOS Ratios that estimate the financial risk that is evident in a company.

SHORT-TERM SOLVENCY RATIO Financial ratio for measuring a company's ability to pay immediate debts.

CURRENT RATIO Financial ratio for measuring a company's ability to pay current debts out of current assets.

Financial statements present a great deal of information, but what does it all mean? How, for example, can statements help investors decide what stock to buy or help managers decide whether to extend credit? Statements provide data, which in turn can be used to compute solvency, profitability, and activity ratios that are useful in analyzing the financial health of a company compared to other companies and to check a firm's progress by comparing its current and past statements.

Solvency Ratios

What are the chances that a borrower will be able to repay a loan and the interest due? This question is first and foremost in the minds of bank lending officers, managers of pension funds and other investors, suppliers, and the borrowing company's own financial managers. **Solvency ratios** measure the firm's ability to meet its debt obligations.

SHORT-TERM SOLVENCY RATIOS

Short-term solvency ratios measure a company's liquidity and its ability to pay immediate debts. The most commonly used ratio is the **current ratio**, which reflects a firm's ability to generate cash to meet obligations through the normal, orderly process of selling inventories and collecting revenues from customers. It is calculated by dividing current assets by current liabilities. The higher a firm's current ratio, the lower the risk it represents to investors. For many years, the guideline was a current ratio of 2:1 or higher—which meant that current assets were at least double current liabilities. More recently, many firms that are financially strong operate with current ratios of less than 2:1.

How does Perfect Posters measure up? Look again at the balance sheet in Figure 11.2. Judging from its current assets and current

DEBT A company's total liabilities.

DEBT-TO-EQUITY RATIOS A form of debt ratio calculated as total liabilities divided by owners' equity.

LEVERAGE Using borrowed funds to make purchases, thus increasing the user's purchasing power, potential rate of return, and risk of loss.

PROFITABILITY RATIOS Measures of a firm's overall financial performance in terms of its likely profits; used by investors to assess their probable returns.

RETURN ON EQUITY A form of profitability ratio calculated as net income divided by total owners' equity.

RETURN ON SALES Ratio calculated by dividing net income by sales revenue.

EARNINGS PER SHARE A form of profitability ratio calculated as net income divided by the number of common shares outstanding.

ACTIVITY RATIOS Measures of how efficiently a firm uses its resources; used by investors to assess their probable returns.

INVENTORY TURNOVER RATIO An activity ratio that measures the average number of times inventory is sold and restocked during the year.

liabilities at the end of 2013, we see that the company looks like a good credit risk:

$$\frac{\text{Current assets}}{\text{Current liabilities}} = \frac{\$57\ 210}{\$21\ 935} = 2.61$$

LONG-TERM SOLVENCY

A firm that can't meet its long-term debt obligations is in danger of collapse or takeover—a risk that makes creditors and investors quite cautious. To evaluate a company's risk of running into this problem, creditors turn to the balance sheet to see the extent to which a firm is financed through borrowed money. Long-term solvency is calculated by dividing **debt**—total liabilities—by owners' equity. The lower a firm's debt, the lower the risk to investors and creditors. Companies with **debt-to-equity ratios** above 1.0 may be relying too much on debt. In the case of Perfect Posters, we can see from the balance sheet in Figure 11.2 that the debt-to-equity ratio calculates as follows:

$$\frac{\text{Debt}}{\text{Owners' equity}} = \frac{\$61\ 935}{\$111\ 155} = \$0.56$$

Sometimes, high debt can not only be acceptable, but also desirable. Borrowing funds gives a firm **leverage**—the ability to make otherwise unaffordable investments. In leveraged buyouts, firms have sometimes taken on huge debt in order to get the money to buy out other companies. If owning the purchased company generates profits above the cost of borrowing the purchase price, leveraging makes sense. Unfortunately, many buyouts have caused problems because profits fell short of expected levels or because rising interest rates increased payments on the buyer's debt.

Profitability Ratios

Although it is important to know that a company is solvent, safety or risk alone is not an adequate basis for investment decisions. Investors also want some measure of the returns they can expect. Return on equity, return on sales, and earnings per share are three commonly used **profitability ratios** (sometimes these are called shareholder return ratios or performance ratios).

RETURN ON EQUITY

Owners are interested in the net income earned by a business for each dollar invested. **Return on equity** measures this performance by dividing net income (recorded on the income statement, Figure 11.3) by total owners' equity (recorded on the balance sheet, Figure 11.2). For Perfect Posters, the return-on-equity ratio in 2013 is:

$$\frac{\text{Net income}}{\text{Total owners' equity}} = \frac{\$12\ 585}{\$111\ 155} = 11.3\%$$

Is this ratio good or bad? There is no set answer. If Perfect Posters' ratio for 2013 is higher than in previous years, owners and investors should be encouraged. But if 11.3 percent is lower than the ratios of other companies in the same industry, they should be concerned.

RETURN ON SALES

Companies want to generate as much profit as they can from each dollar of sales revenue they receive. The **return on sales** ratio is calculated by dividing net income by sales revenue (see Figure 11.3). For Perfect Posters, the return on sales ratio for 2013 is:

$$\frac{\text{Net income}}{\text{Sales revenue}} = \frac{\$12\ 585}{\$256\ 425} = 4.9\%$$

Is this figure good or bad? Once again, there is no set answer. If Perfect Posters' ratio for 2013 is higher than in previous years, owners and investors should be encouraged, but if 4.9 percent is lower than the ratios of other companies in the same industry, they will likely be concerned.

EARNINGS PER SHARE

Earnings per share—calculated by dividing net income by the number of shares of common stock outstanding—influences the size of the dividend a company can pay to its shareholders. Investors use this ratio to decide whether to buy or sell a company's stock. As the ratio gets higher, the stock value increases because investors know that the firm can better afford to pay dividends. The market value of a stock will typically decline if the latest financial statements report a decline in earnings per share. For Perfect Posters, we can use the net income total from the income statement in Figure 11.3 to calculate earnings per share as follows:

$$\frac{\text{Net income}}{\text{Number of common shares outstanding}} = \frac{\$12\ 585}{\$8000} = \$1.57 \text{ per share}$$

Activity Ratios

Activity ratios measure how efficient a company is in using the resources that it has. Potential investors want to know which company gets more "mileage" from its resources. For example, suppose that two firms use the same amount of resources or assets. If Firm A generates greater profits or sales, it is more efficient and, thus, has a better activity ratio.

One of the most important activity ratios is the **inventory turnover ratio**, which calculates the average number of times that inventory is sold and restocked during the year.[17] Once a company knows its average inventory (calculated by adding end-of-year inventory to beginning-of-year inventory and dividing by 2), it can calculate the inventory turnover ratio, which is expressed as the cost of goods sold divided by average inventory:

$$\frac{\text{Cost of goods sold}}{\text{Average inventory}} = \frac{\text{Cost of goods sold}}{(\text{Beginning inventory} + \text{Ending inventory}) \div 2}$$

<<< The inventory turnover ratio measures the average number of times that a store sells and restocks its inventory in one year. The higher the ratio, the more products get sold and the more revenue comes in. In almost all retail stores, products with the highest ratios get the shelf space that generates the most customer traffic and sales.

AP Photo/file

To calculate Perfect Posters' inventory turnover ratio for 2013, we take the merchandise inventory figures for the income statement in Figure 11.3. The ratio can be expressed as follows:

$$\frac{\$104\ 765}{(\$22\ 380 + \$21\ 250) \div 2} = 4.8$$

In other words, new merchandise replaces old merchandise every 76 days (365 days divided by 4.8). The 4.8 ratio is below the industry average of 7.0 for comparable wholesaling operations, indicating that the business is somewhat inefficient.

LO-6 BRINGING ETHICS INTO THE ACCOUNTING EQUATION

The ultimate purpose of strong ethical standards in accounting is to maintain public confidence in business institutions, financial markets, and the products and services of the accounting profession. Without ethics, all accounting tools and methods would be meaningless because their usefulness depends, ultimately, on their honest application.

Why Accounting Ethics?

In recent years, we have seen many corporations demonstrate poor judgment and experience ethical lapses. In some cases, this has led to a minor problem; in others (as we will see in the closing case on Nortel), it has helped lead to the demise of a company. Ethics remains an area where one person who is willing to "do the right thing" can make a difference—and people do, every day. With the unification process for accounting designations moving forward, a new Canadian Chartered Professional Accounting Code of Ethics is being developed that will borrow from the best practices of the three current designations. In Table 11.2, you can see the existing CPA code of ethics in the U.S.

A code of ethics is a good start; it clearly outlines good practices and points out improper behaviour. Ultimately, the actions of conscientious

TABLE 11.2 Highlights from the CPA Code of Ethics[18]

The new Canadian CPA designation will likely outline a similar code to the one found south of the border for American Certified Public Accountants.
Responsibilities as a Professional
To exercise their duties with a high level of morality and in a manner that is sensitive to bringing credit to their profession.
Serving the Public Interest
Demonstrate commitment to the profession by respecting and maintaining the public trust and serving the public honorably.
Maintaining Integrity
Perform all professional activities with highest regards for integrity, including sincerity and honesty, so as to promote the public's confidence in the profession.
Being Objective and Independent
Avoid conflicts of interest, and the appearance of conflicts of interest, in performing their professional responsibilities. They should be independent from clients when certifying to the public that the client's statements are true and genuine.
Maintaining Technical and Ethical Standards
Exercise "due care," through professional improvement, abiding by ethical standards, updating personal competence through continuing accounting education, and improving the quality of services.
Professional Conduct in Providing Services
The CPA in public practice should abide by the meaning and intent of the Code of Professional Conduct when deciding on the kinds of services and the range of actions to be supplied for clients.

accountants will maintain and improve the level of faith investors have in accounting reports. As discussed earlier in the chapter, legislation to improve clarity and increase accountability, the Sarbanes-Oxley Act in the U.S. and the National Instrument 52-109 in Canada, has been developed to ensure public confidence.

MyBizLab Visit the MyBizLab website. This online homework and tutorial system puts you in control of your own learning with study and practice tools directly correlated to this chapter's content.

SUMMARY OF LEARNING OBJECTIVES

LO-1 EXPLAIN THE *ROLE OF ACCOUNTANTS,* DISTINGUISH BETWEEN THE THREE TYPES OF TRADITIONAL *PROFESSIONAL ACCOUNTING DESIGNATIONS* IN CANADA, AND OUTLINE THE UNIFICATION PROCESS TOWARDS THE *CANADIAN CHARTERED PROFESSIONAL ACCOUNTING (CPA) DESIGNATION.*

By collecting, analyzing, and communicating financial information, accountants provide business managers and investors with an accurate picture of a firm's financial health. Traditionally, Chartered Accountants (CAs) and Certified General Accountants (CGAs) provide accounting expertise for client organizations that must report their financial condition to external stakeholders. Certified Management Accountants (CMAs) provide accounting expertise for the firms that employ them. However, in January 2012, a framework for uniting the Canadian accounting profession under a new Canadian Chartered Professional Accountant (CPA) designation was developed. Since the accounting profession is regulated provincially, the implementation and ultimate approval is taking place at different rates across the country.

LO-2 EXPLAIN HOW THE *ACCOUNTING EQUATION* IS USED.

Accountants use the following equation to balance the data pertaining to financial transactions:

Assets – Liabilities = Owners' Equity

After each financial transaction (e.g., payments to suppliers, sales to customers, wages to employees), the accounting equation must be in balance. If it isn't, then an accounting error has occurred. The equation also provides an indication of the firm's financial health. If assets exceed liabilities, owners' equity is positive; if the firm goes out of business, owners will receive some cash (a gain) after selling assets and paying off liabilities. If liabilities outweigh assets, owners' equity is negative and assets aren't enough to pay off debts. If the company goes under, owners will get no cash and some creditors won't be paid, thus losing their remaining investments in the company.

LO-3 DESCRIBE THREE BASIC *FINANCIAL STATEMENTS* AND SHOW HOW THEY REFLECT THE ACTIVITY AND FINANCIAL CONDITION OF A BUSINESS.

The balance sheet summarizes a company's assets, liabilities, and owners' equity at a given point in time. The income statement details revenues and expenses for a given period of time and identifies any profit or loss. The statement of cash flows reports cash receipts and payment from operating, investing, and financial activities.

LO-4 EXPLAIN THE KEY *STANDARDS* AND *PRINCIPLES* FOR *REPORTING FINANCIAL STATEMENTS.*

Accountants follow standard reporting practices and principles when they prepare financial statements. Otherwise, users wouldn't be able to compare information from different companies, and they might misunderstand—or be led to misread—a company's true financial status. Revenue recognition is the formal recording and reporting of revenues in financial statements. The earnings cycle is complete when the sale has been made, the product is delivered, and the sale price has been collected or is collectible. This practice assures interested parties that the statement gives a fair comparison of what was gained for the resources that were given up. The matching principle states that expenses will be matched with revenues to determine net income for an accounting period. This permits the user of the statement to see how much net gain resulted from the assets that had to be given up to generate revenues during the period covered in the statement.

LO-5 EXPLAIN HOW COMPUTING *FINANCIAL RATIOS* CAN HELP IN ANALYZING THE FINANCIAL STRENGTHS OF A BUSINESS.

Drawing upon data from financial statements, ratios can help creditors, investors, and managers assess a firm's finances. The *current, short-term solvency (liquidity)*, and *debt-to-owners' equity ratios* all measure solvency, a firm's ability to pay its debt in both the short and long terms. Return on sales, return on equity, and earnings per share are all ratios that measure profitability. The inventory turnover ratio shows how efficiently a firm is using its funds.

LO-6 DISCUSS THE ROLE OF *ETHICS IN ACCOUNTING.*

The purpose of ethics in accounting is to maintain public confidence in business institutions, financial markets, and the products and services of the accounting profession. Without ethics, all of accounting's tools and methods would be meaningless, because their usefulness depends, ultimately, on truthfulness in their application. Accordingly, professional accounting associations enforce codes of professional conduct that include ethics-related areas, such as the accountant's responsibilities, the public interest, integrity, etc. The associations include ethics as an area of study to meet requirements for certification. The codes prohibit, among other things, misrepresentation and fraud in financial statements. While the accounting profession generally relies on self-compliance to professional codes, accounting associations maintain ethical conduct committees to receive allegations, hold hearings, reach settlements, and impose penalties for misconduct.

QUESTIONS AND EXERCISES

QUESTIONS FOR ANALYSIS

See >>> for **Assisted-Graded Writing Assignment** in **MyBizLab**

1. Balance sheets and income statements are supposed to be objective assessments of the financial condition of a company. But the accounting scandals of the last few years show that certain pressures may be put on accountants as they audit a company's financial statements. Describe these pressures. To what extent do these pressures make the audit more subjective?
2. >>> If you were planning to invest in a company, which of the three types of financial statements would you want most to see? Why?
3. A business hires a professional accountant to assess the financial condition of the company. Why would the business also employ a private accountant?
4. How does the double-entry system reduce the chances of mistakes or fraud in accounting?
5. How do financial ratios help managers to monitor their own efficiency and effectiveness?
6. Explain the difference between financial and managerial accounting. In your answer, describe the different audiences for the two types of accounting and the various individuals involved in the process.

APPLICATION EXERCISES

7. Suppose that Inflatables Inc., makers of air mattresses for swimming pools, has the following transactions in one week:
   - sold three deluxe mattresses to Al Wett (paid cash $50, remaining $25 on credit) on 7/16
   - received cheque from Ima Flotein as payment for mattresses bought on credit ($120) on 7/13
   - received new shipment of 200 mattresses from Airheads Mfg. (total cost $3000, paid 50 percent cash on delivery) on 7/17

   Construct a journal for Inflatables Inc.
8. Flynn Plastics Company reports the following data in its September 30, 2013 financial statements:
   - Gross sales $225 000
   - Current assets $50 000
   - Long-term assets $130 000
   - Current liabilities $33 000
   - Long-term liabilities $52 000
   - Net income $11 250

   a. Compute the owners' equity.
   b. Compute the current ratio.
   c. Compute the debt-to-equity ratio.
   d. Compute the return on sales.
   e. Compute the return on owners' equity.
9. Interview an accountant at a local manufacturing firm. Trace the process by which budgets are developed in that company. How does the firm use budgets? How does budgeting help its managers plan business activities? How does budgeting help them control business activities? Give examples.
10. >>> Interview the manager of a local business and ask about the role of ethics in the company's accounting practices. How important is ethics in accounting? What measures does the firm take to ensure that its internal reporting is ethical? What steps does the company take to maintain ethical relationships in its dealing with external accounting firms?

TEAM EXERCISES

BUILDING YOUR BUSINESS SKILLS

PUTTING THE BUZZ IN BILLING

GOAL

To encourage students to think about the advantages and disadvantages of using an electronic system for handling accounts receivable and accounts payable.

METHOD

Step 1 As the CFO of a utility company, you are analyzing the feasibility of switching from a paper-based system to an electronic one. You decide to discuss the ramifications of the choice with three associates (choose three classmates to take on these roles). Your discussion requires that you research existing electronic payment systems. Specifically, using online and library research, you must find out as much as you can about the electronic bill-paying systems being developed by companies like VISA International, Intuit, IBM, and the Checkfree Corporation.

Step 2 After you have researched this information, brainstorm the advantages and disadvantages of switching to an electronic system.

FOLLOW-UP QUESTIONS

1. What cost savings are inherent in the electronic system for both your company and its customers? In your answer, consider such costs as handling, postage, and paper.
2. What consequences would your decision to adopt an electronic system have on others with whom you do business, including manufacturers of cheque-sorting equipment, Canada Post, and banks?
3. Switching to an electronic system would mean a large capital expense for new computers and software. How could analyzing the company's income statement help you justify this expense?
4. How are consumers likely to respond to paying bills electronically? Are you likely to get a different response from individuals than you get from business customers?

EXERCISING YOUR ETHICS

CONFIDENTIALLY YOURS

THE SITUATION

Accountants are often entrusted with private, sensitive information that should be used confidentially. In this exercise, you are encouraged to think about ethical considerations that might arise when an accountant's career choices come up against a professional obligation to maintain confidentiality.

THE DILEMMA

Assume that you're the head accountant in Turbatron, a large electronics firm that makes components for other manufacturing firms. Your responsibilities include preparing Turbatron's financial statements, which are then audited for financial reporting to shareholders. In addition, you regularly prepare confidential budgets for internal use by managers responsible for planning departmental activities, including future investments in new assets. You've also worked with auditors and CA consultants that assess financial problems and suggest solutions.

Now let's suppose that you're approached by another company, Electrolast, one of the electronics industry's most successful firms and offered a higher-level position. If you accept, your new job will include developing Electrolast's financial plans and serving on the strategic-planning committee. Thus, you'd be involved not only in developing strategy, but also in evaluating the competition, perhaps even using your knowledge of Turbatron's competitive strengths and weaknesses.

Your contractual commitments with Turbatron do not bar you from employment with other electronics firms.

TEAM ACTIVITY

Assemble a group of four to five students and assign each group member to one of the following roles:

- Head accountant (leaving Turbatron)
- General manager of Turbatron
- Shareholder of Turbatron
- Customer of Turbatron
- General manager of Electrolast (if your group has five members)

ACTION STEPS

1. Before hearing any of your group's comments on this situation and from the perspective of your assigned role, decide if there are any ethical issues confronting the head accountant in this situation. If so, write them down.
2. Return to your group and reveal ethical issues identified by each member. Were the issues the same among all roles or did differences in roles result in different issues?
3. Among the ethical issues that were identified, decide, as a group, which one is most important for the head accountant. Which is most important for Turbatron?
4. What does your group finally recommend be done to resolve the most important ethical issue(s)?
5. What steps do you think Turbatron might take in advance of such a situation to avoid any difficulties it now faces?

BUSINESS CASE

UNTANGLING AN ACCOUNTING MESS AT BANKRUPT NORTEL

In 2012, the trial of three former top executives of Nortel Networks finally began. They were charged by the RCMP with criminal fraud and with allegedly manipulating the company's accounting system in order to inflate profits during a difficult time in Nortel's history. In other words, the executives were charged with "cooking the books." The three defendants acknowledged that there were accounting mistakes, but rejected the claim that they had engaged in fraudulent behaviour.

© Ian Dagnall/Alamy

In 1895, Northern Electric and Manufacturing Co. was established to manufacture Bell telephones. That company eventually became Nortel Networks. By the late twentieth century, Nortel had become the "crown jewel" in Canada's high-tech sector, dominating global markets for digital telephone-switching and fibre-optic transmission systems. By 2000, Nortel employed 95 000 people, had a market value of $440 billion, and shares of stock were priced as high as $124 per share. But over the next few years, the company experienced significant problems, and, by 2009 (when the company was delisted from the Toronto Exchange), its shares were selling for just 18 cents each.

What happened? Richard Powers, a professor at the Rotman School of Management at the University of Toronto, says, "Nortel rode the tech boom and became complacent." But complacency wasn't Nortel's only problem. When the tech bubble burst in 2000, Nortel could not maintain its growth trajectory. Its share price plummeted from $124 per share in August 2000 to just $7.56 in September 2001, and there were nearly 50 000 fewer employees in the company than there had been in 2000. The CEO, John Roth, left the company (and received $86 million after cashing in his stock options). He was replaced by Frank Dunn, who took various steps to turn Nortel around. After incurring massive losses in 2001 and 2002, the company reported a profit of $54 million in 2003, and Dunn was seen as having rescued the company. In 2003, Nortel reported its third consecutive quarterly profit, and these profits triggered a total of $43.6 million in bonuses for senior managers.

But dark clouds appeared on the horizon after Nortel's auditor, Deloitte & Touche, expressed concerns that the profits were not what they seemed, and that some accounting adjustments had been made that turned losses into profits. The crisis deepened when Nortel said it was going to restate about $900 million of liabilities that were on its balance sheet because it had overestimated what these liabilities would be. Nortel's audit committee then set about finding out how Nortel could have overstated liabilities by $900 million. The group concluded that there were significant accounting irregularities and a "tone at the top" that encouraged the manipulation of accounting rules in order to reach profit targets.

In 2004, Frank Dunn (CEO), Douglas Beatty (Chief Financial Officer), and Michael Gollogly (Controller) were fired after a report by a U.S. law firm concluded that the three had used financial practices that did not comply with U.S. rules. The report also noted that top managers had created an "aggressive accounting culture" in order to exploit the bonus system to their advantage. The three managers filed a wrongful dismissal lawsuit against Nortel in 2006, alleging defamation and mental stress.

Between 2003 and 2007, the release of Nortel's audited financial statements was delayed on four separate occasions as the company tried to determine its actual financial position. These delays created much uncertainty and anxiety among shareholders, and they finally ran out of patience. In 2009, Nortel filed for bankruptcy protection. Richard

Powers says, "I don't think the accounting scandal destroyed the company, but it certainly contributed to it by becoming a huge distraction."

In 2013, the three executives were acquitted of the charges. According to the judge, Nortel had a long history (over 20 years) of excessive reserves that could be used to meet earnings targets. In other words, the aggressive system was established long before these particular executives took charge of the mess. In addition, he indicated that the burden of proof had not been met. This did not mean that their actions were ethical or sound in business terms. It just meant that the legal system did not find enough clear evidence for a conviction. The executives had not walked away totally untouched; they faced this threat of litigation for over a decade, but when you consider the thousands of workers negatively impacted and the billions of dollars lost by investors and employees, it was a small price to pay.

This does not mark the end of the legal process for the defunct Nortel. In early 2013, Nortel reached an agreement to pay $67 million to a group of U.S. retirees that were suing the company. The sale of Nortel assets (after the bankruptcy) raised billions of dollars and there are still many legal claims to be dealt with.

QUESTIONS FOR DISCUSSION

1. How is it possible for there to be so much uncertainty about whether or not a company made a profit in a given year? Isn't profit simply computed by subtracting expenses from revenues?
2. It is alleged that the top executives at Nortel who were put on trial manipulated the accounting system in order to make the company look profitable. Did the top managers have an incentive to manipulate the accounting system?
3. What do you think of the outcome of the trial of the three top executives? Conduct some further research about the case. What evidence needed to be shown to prove that the accounting system had been manipulated?

CHAPTER SUPPLEMENT 03

Using Technology to Manage Information in the Internet and Social Media Era

INFORMATION TECHNOLOGY (IT) The various devices for creating, storing, exchanging, and using information in diverse modes, including visual images, voice, multimedia, and business data.

E-COMMERCE Buying and selling processes that make use of electronic technology.

INTERNET MARKETING The promotional efforts of companies to sell their products and services to consumers over the internet.

Throughout the text, we examine how the internet and the emergence of social media have improved communications, revolutionized distribution, augmented human resources practices, revolutionized industries (and threatened others), developed new marketing communication channels, and changed the most basic business systems. In this supplement, we will begin by providing additional information about the internet and social media. We will also examine the evolving role of technology in managing information.

INTERNET USAGE

Before we look into the specific impact of the internet on business, let's examine some of the key Canadian internet statistics. In terms of speed, Hong Kong has the fastest internet connections in the world; Canada ranks thirteenth.[1] However, Canada is ranked ninth among G20 countries in terms of internet contribution to GDP. It is expected to rank twelfth by 2016, with Saudi Arabia, Australia, and Mexico climbing ahead. There are 25.5 million Canadian internet users, and the average time spent online is 41.3 hours per month, which ranks second in the world behind only the United States.[2] In addition, 94 percent of Canadians that live in households with incomes above $85 000 are connected (only 56 percent for households with incomes below $30 000 per year).[3] These figures will continue to increase for the next few years. The federal government has also set its sights on increasing and improving the connectivity in rural settings; it invested in 52 projects worth over $225 million in 2010. At that time, it cost approximately $89 per month for 5Mbps (megabits per second) connections in most rural areas. But consumers could get 10Mbps for about $47 a month in most cities, or get 50 Mbps (a 10-times faster connection) for about the same fee as rural customers paid for only 5Mbps. The improved infrastructure will help increase rural access, build further opportunities for companies wishing to sell to rural Canadian clients, and also provide more incentive and opportunity for small businesses to operate in rural settings.[4]

THE IMPACT OF INFORMATION TECHNOLOGY (IT)

No matter where we go, we can't escape the impact of **information technology (IT)**—the various devices for creating, storing, exchanging, and using information in diverse modes, including visual images, voice, multimedia, and business data. We see ads all the time for the latest smartphones, laptops, iPads and other tablets, and software products, and most of us connect daily to the internet (many of you never disconnect). Email and BlackBerry (BBM) messaging have become staples in business, and even such traditionally "low-tech" businesses as hair salons and garbage collection companies are becoming dependent on the internet, computers, and networks. As consumers, we interact with databases every time we withdraw money from an ATM, order food at McDonald's, use an Apple or Android application to order food or movie tickets, or check on the status of a package at UPS or FedEx.

IT has had an immense effect on businesses—in fact, the growth of IT has changed the very structure of business organizations. Its adoption has altered workforces in many companies, contributed to greater flexibility in dealing with customers, and changed the way that employees interact with each other. E-commerce has created new market relationships around the globe. We begin by looking at how businesses are using IT to bolster productivity, improve operations and processes, create new opportunities, and communicate and work in ways not possible before.

THE IMPACT OF THE INTERNET ON MARKETING

E-commerce refers to buying and selling processes that make use of electronic technology, while **internet marketing** refers to the promotional efforts of companies to sell their products and services to consumers over the internet.[5]

While internet marketing has some obvious advantages for both buyers (access to information, convenience, etc.) and sellers (reach, direct distribution, etc.), it also has weaknesses, including profitability problems (many internet marketers are still unprofitable and the failure rates are high), information overload (consumers may not know what to do with all the information available to them), and somewhat limited markets (consumers who use the web are typically more highly educated). In addition to these weaknesses, internet marketers must also cope with consumer concerns about two security-related issues.

Consumers also object to spyware software, which monitors websites they visit and observes their shopping habits. This software is often implanted on their personal computers as they wander through the web. It then generates advertisements that are targeted to that particular consumer.

<<< In 2013, Barack Obama was still an avid BlackBerry user. Despite calls for him to join the iPhone crowd, he resisted. That is the type of loyalty that BlackBerry is counting on in launching its Q10, Z10, Q30, and Z30 phones for core users like the president. This picture is indicative of the times we live in. Think of how often you see classmates and work colleagues walking down a hall, smartphone in hand.

© ZUMA Press, Inc./Alamy

CREATING PORTABLE OFFICES: PROVIDING REMOTE ACCESS TO INSTANT INFORMATION

The packing list for Barry Martin's upcoming fishing trip reflects his new outlook on how he gets his work done. It reads, in part, as follows: (1) fly rod, (2) dry-pack food, (3) tent, and (4) BlackBerry. Ten years ago, a much longer list would have included a cellphone, road and area maps, phone directory, appointments calendar, office files, and client project folders, all of which are now replaced by just one item—his BlackBerry—a device that allows him to take the office with him wherever he goes. Even in the Canadian wilderness, Martin can place phone calls and read new email and BBM messages. Along with internet browsing, his BlackBerry also allows access to desktop tools—such as an organizer and an address book—for managing work and staying in touch with customers, suppliers, and employees from any location. The mobile messaging capabilities of devices like the BlackBerry offer businesses powerful tools that save time and travel expenses.[6] In recent years, we have seen Apple and Android devices eat into BlackBerry's market share and even in their core market: business people. As we described in Chapter 4's E-Business and Social Media Solutions box "Who Wants To Be a Teen Millionaire?" the range of current applications is immense and increasing to meet the needs of business and consumers. We have also included a new feature in the text called "There's an App for That!" to encourage you to use your smartphone or tablet to access resources related to all the functions of business.

ENABLING BETTER SERVICE BY COORDINATING REMOTE DELIVERIES

With access to the internet, company activities may be geographically scattered, but remain coordinated through a networked system that provides better service for customers. Many businesses, for example, coordinate activities from one centralized location, but their deliveries flow from several remote locations, often at lower cost. When you order furniture from an internet storefront—a chair, a sofa, a table, and two lamps—the chair may come from a warehouse in Toronto, the lamps from a manufacturer in China, and the sofa and table from a supplier in North Carolina. Beginning with the customer's order, activities are coordinated through the company's network, as if the whole order were being processed at one place. This avoids the expensive in-between step of first shipping all the items to a central location.

In 2012, approximately 20 percent of holiday gifts were bought online and, with improved shipping and easy deliveries, Canadian retailers must also be aware that many U.S. retailers like Macy's, Neiman Marcus, and Nordstrom have made it much easier for Canadians to shop online and bypass their traditional local retailers.[7]

CREATING LEANER, MORE EFFICIENT ORGANIZATIONS

Networks and technology are also leading to leaner companies with fewer employees and simpler structures. Because networks enable firms to maintain information linkages between employees and customers, more work and customer satisfaction can be accomplished with fewer people. Bank customers can access 24-hour information systems and monitor their accounts without employee assistance. Instructions that once were given to assembly workers by supervisors are now delivered to workstations electronically. Truck drivers delivering freight used to return to the trucking terminal to receive instructions from supervisors on reloading for the next delivery, but now instructions arrive on electronic screens in the trucks, so drivers know in advance what will be happening next.

ENABLING INCREASED COLLABORATION

Collaboration among internal units and with outside firms is greater when firms use collaboration software and other IT communications devices (which we discuss below). Companies are learning that complex problems can be solved better through IT-supported collaboration, either with formal teams or spontaneous interaction among people and departments. The design of new products was once largely an engineering responsibility. Now it is a shared activity using information from people in marketing, finance, production, engineering, and purchasing, who, collectively, determine the best design. For example, the design of Boeing's 787 Dreamliner aircraft is the result of collaboration, not just among engineers, but also from passengers (who wanted electronic outlets to recharge personal electronic devices), cabin crews (who wanted more bathrooms and wider aisles), and air-traffic controllers (who wanted larger, safer airbrakes).

ENABLING GLOBAL EXCHANGE

The global reach of IT is enabling business collaboration on a scale that was unheard of just a few years ago. Consider Lockheed Martin's contract for designing the Joint Strike Fighter and supplying thousands of the planes in different versions for Canada, the United States, Britain, Italy, Denmark, and Norway. Lockheed can't do the job alone. Over the project's 20-year life, more than 1500 companies will supply everything from radar systems to engines to bolts. Web collaboration on a massive scale is essential for coordinating design, testing, and construction, while avoiding delays, holding down costs, and maintaining quality.[8]

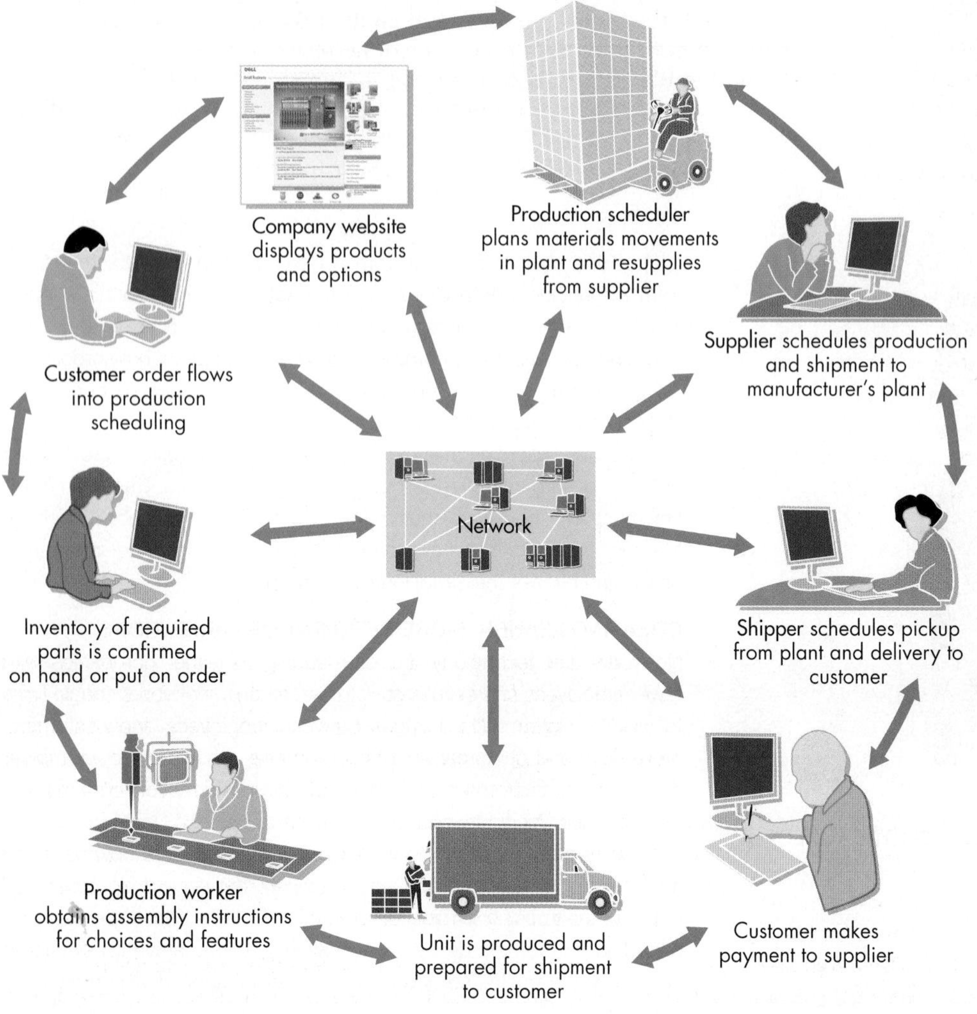
Company website displays products and options
Production scheduler plans materials movements in plant and resupplies from supplier
Supplier schedules production and shipment to manufacturer's plant
Customer order flows into production scheduling
Network
Inventory of required parts is confirmed on hand or put on order
Shipper schedules pickup from plant and delivery to customer
Production worker obtains assembly instructions for choices and features
Unit is produced and prepared for shipment to customer
Customer makes payment to supplier

<<< **FIGURE IT.1** Networking for mass customization

IMPROVING MANAGEMENT PROCESSES

IT has also changed the nature of the management process. At one time, upper-level managers didn't concern themselves with all of the detailed information filtering upward from the workplace, because it was expensive to gather, slow in coming, and quickly became out of date. Rather, workplace management was delegated to middle and first-line managers.

With databases, specialized software, and networks, however, instantaneous information is accessible and useful to all levels of management. For example, consider *enterprise resource planning* (ERP), a system for organizing and managing a firm's activities across product lines, departments, and geographic locations. An ERP stores real-time information on work status and upcoming transactions and notifies employees when action is required if certain schedules are to be met. It coordinates internal operations with activities of outside suppliers and notifies customers of upcoming deliveries and billings. Consequently, more managers use it routinely for planning and controlling operations. A manager at Hershey Foods might use ERP to check on the current status of any customer order for Hershey Kisses, inspect productivity statistics for each workstation, and analyze the delivery performance on any shipment. Managers can better coordinate company-wide performance because they can identify departments that are working well together and those that are lagging behind schedule and creating bottlenecks.

PROVIDING FLEXIBILITY FOR CUSTOMIZATION

IT has also created new manufacturing capabilities that enable businesses to offer customers greater variety and faster delivery cycles. Whether it's a personal computer from Dell, one of Samsung's smartphones, or Vaughn goalie pads, today's design-it-yourself world has become possible through fast, flexible manufacturing using IT networks. At Timbuk2's website, for example, you can "build your own" custom messenger bag at different price levels with choices of size, fabric, colour combinations, accessories, liner material, strap, and even left- or right-hand access.[9] The principle is called **mass customization**—although companies produce in large volumes, each unit features the unique options the customer prefers. As shown in Figure IT.1, flexible production and speedy delivery depend on an integrated network of information to coordinate all the activities among customers, manufacturers, suppliers, and shippers.

32
VAUGHN
VAUGHN
LA
VAUGHN
WARRIOR

^^ Vaughn goalie pads are used by some of the top goaltenders in the NHL, like Tukka Rask of the Boston Bruins and Jonathan Quick of the LA Kings. You can purchase the gear off the rack, but Vaughn offers a mass customization series that permits you to make adjustments to your gear to suit your needs (for colour, size, etc.).

Keith Dannemiller/Newscom

MASS CUSTOMIZATION Although companies produce in large volumes, each unit features the unique options the customer prefers.

PROVIDING NEW BUSINESS OPPORTUNITIES

Not only is IT improving existing businesses, but it is also creating entirely new businesses. For big businesses, this means developing new products, offering new services, and reaching new clients. Only a few years ago, Google was a fledgling search engine. In 2013, the company had nearly $48 billion in cash and short-term investments and it was no longer simply a search engine company; Google had email (Gmail) and other productivity software (Google Docs, etc.), the Android cellphone platform, and YouTube.[10]

The IT landscape has also presented small business owners with new e-business opportunities. To assist start-up businesses, eBay's services network is a ready-made online business model, not just an auction market. Services range from credit financing to protection from fraud and misrepresentation, information security, international currency exchanges, and post-sales management. These features enable users to complete sales transactions, deliver merchandise, and get new merchandise for future resale, all from the comfort of their own homes.

Technology continues to provide new and improved business models. For example, Instinet Inc. was a pioneer in electronic trading. It recently launched a service called Meet the Street, which matches companies with potential investors. This service competes directly with investment companies like the Royal Bank of Canada (RBC) and Goldman Sachs that are known for creating "road shows" (days packed with meetings with potential investors). The service enables business owners to book their own meetings, make travel arrangements, suggest dining spots, and use GPS technology to organize meetings efficiently to save time.[11]

IMPROVING THE WORLD AND OUR LIVES

Can advancements in IT really make the world a better place? Hospitals and medical equipment companies certainly think so. For example, when treating combat injuries, surgeons at Walter Reed National Military Medical Center in the U.S. rely on high-tech graphics displays that are converted into three-dimensional physical models for pre-surgical planning. These 3-D mock-ups of shoulders, femurs, and facial bones give doctors the opportunity to see and feel the anatomy as it will be seen in the operating room, before they even use their scalpels.[12] Meanwhile, vitamin-sized cameras that patients swallow are providing doctors with computer images of the insides of the human body, helping them make better diagnoses for ailments such as ulcers and cancer.[13]

THE IMPACT OF THE INTERNET ON YOUR POCKET BOOK

Many people complain that the cost of internet service is yet another expense in their lives that did not exist in the past. However, these complaints fail to recognize the cost-saving benefits. A recent study conducted by the Internet Innovation Alliance (IIA) indicates that the average person saves approximately $9000 per year because of the internet (compared to those who are not connected). See Table IT.1.[14]

SOCIAL NETWORKING: PROVIDING A SERVICE

The many forms of social media—blogs and networks such as LinkedIn, Twitter, and Facebook—are no longer just playthings for gossips and hobbyists. Today, job seekers routinely turn to online networking—tapping leads from friends, colleagues, and acquaintances—for contacts with companies that may be hiring. Peers and recruiters are networking using social media sites, company website tools, professional associations and trade groups, technical schools, and alumni organizations. Some social sites provide occupation-specific career coaching and job tips. For example, scientists are connecting with Epernicus, top managers use Meet the Boss, and graduate students are connecting with Graduate Junction.[15]

TABLE IT.1 Source of Internet Savings

Typical Sources of Savings From Internet Connections	Result
1. Online Comparison Shopping	• Better-negotiated deals based on online research (savings of hundreds or even thousands of dollars) • Savings on fuel (less running around)
2. Paying Bills Online	• Savings on fuel • No stamps, envelopes, etc.
3. Accessing Cheaper Inventory (Deals)	• Easy access to online aggregator sites (discount retailers, coupons, etc.)

IT BUILDING BLOCKS: BUSINESS RESOURCES

Businesses today have a wide variety of IT resources at their disposal. In addition to the internet and email, these include communications technologies, networks, hardware devices, and software, as shown at technology media sites such as TechWeb.com.

The amount of traffic on the internet has increased dramatically over the years, and certain individuals, such as scientists, have found that it is often slow going when they try to transmit or manipulate large databases. So **Internet2** has been created, which is faster than the regular internet. Internet2 is generally available only to universities, corporations, and government agencies that have applications that put heavy demands on the internet (for example, videoconferencing).

The internet has spawned a number of other business communications technologies, including intranets, extranets, electronic conferencing, and VSAT satellite communications.

Intranets Many companies have extended internet technology by maintaining internal websites linked throughout the firm. These private networks, or **intranets**, are accessible only to employees and may contain confidential information on benefits programs, a learning library, production management tools, or product design resources. For firms such as Ford Motor Company, whose intranet is accessible to 200 000 people daily, sharing information on engineering, distribution, and marketing has reduced the lead time for getting new models into production and has shortened customer delivery times.[16]

Extranets **Extranets** allow outsiders limited access to a firm's internal information network. The most common application allows buyers to enter a system to see which products are available for sale and delivery, thus providing convenient product availability information. Industrial suppliers are often linked into customers' information networks so that they can see planned production schedules and prepare supplies for customers' upcoming operations.

Electronic Conferencing **Electronic conferencing** allows groups of people to communicate simultaneously from various locations via email,

INTERNET2 Faster than regular internet, Internet2 is generally available only to universities, corporations, and government agencies that have applications with heavy demands.

INTRANET An organization's private network of internally linked websites accessible only to employees.

EXTRANET A system that allows outsiders limited access to a firm's internal information network.

ELECTRONIC CONFERENCING IT that allows groups of people to communicate simultaneously from various locations via email, phone, or video.

VSAT SATELLITE COMMUNICATIONS A network of geographically dispersed transmitter-receivers (transceivers) that send signals to and receive signals from a satellite, exchanging voice, video, and data transmissions.

COMPUTER NETWORK A group of two or more computers linked together by some form of cabling or by wireless technology to share data or resources, such as a printer.

CLIENT-SERVER NETWORK A common business network in which clients make requests for information or resources and servers provide the services.

WIDE AREA NETWORKS (WANS) Computers that are linked over long distances through telephone lines, microwave signals, or satellite communications.

LOCAL AREA NETWORKS (LANS) Computers that are linked in a small area, such as all of a firm's computers within a single building.

VIRTUAL PRIVATE NETWORKS (VPNS) Connecting two or more LANs through a public network, like the internet, to save money for a firm.

WIRELESS WIDE AREA NETWORKS (WWAN) A network that uses airborne electronic signals instead of wires to link computers and electronic devices over long distances.

WI-FI Short for wireless fidelity; a wireless local area network.

WIRELESS LOCAL AREA NETWORK (WIRELESS LAN OR WLAN) A local area network with wireless access points.

HARDWARE The physical components of a computer network, such as keyboards, monitors, system units, and printers.

SOFTWARE Programs that tell the computer's hardware what resources to use and how.

phone, or video, thereby eliminating travel time and saving money. One form, called data conferencing, allows people in remote locations to work simultaneously on one document. Videoconferencing allows participants to see one another on video screens while the conference is in progress. For example, Lockheed Martin's Joint Strike Fighter project, discussed earlier, uses internet collaboration systems with both voice and video capabilities. Although separated by oceans, partners can communicate as if they were in the same room while redesigning components and creating production schedules. Electronic conferencing is attractive to many businesses because it eliminates travel and saves money.

VSAT Satellite Communications Another internet technology businesses use to communicate is **VSAT satellite communications**. VSAT (short for very small aperture terminal) systems have a transmitter-receiver (transceiver) that sits outdoors with a direct line of sight to a satellite. The hub—a ground-station computer at the company's headquarters—sends signals to and receives signals from the satellite, exchanging voice, video, and data transmissions. An advantage of VSAT is privacy. A company that operates its own VSAT system has total control over communications among its facilities, no matter their location, without dependence on other companies. A firm might use VSAT to exchange sales and inventory information, advertising messages, and visual presentations between headquarters and store managers at remote sites.

NETWORKS: SYSTEM ARCHITECTURE

A **computer network** is a group of two or more computers linked together, either hardwired or wirelessly, to share data or resources (e.g., a printer). The most common type of network used in businesses is a **client-server network**. In client-server networks, clients are usually the laptop or desktop computers through which users make requests for information or resources. Servers are the computers that provide the services shared by users. In big organizations, servers are usually assigned a specific task. For example, in a local university or college network, an application server stores the word-processing, spreadsheet, and other programs used by all computers connected to the network. A print server controls the printers, stores printing requests from client computers, and routes jobs as the printers become available. An email server handles all incoming and outgoing email. With a client-server system, users can share resources and internet connections—and avoid costly duplication.

Networks can be classified according to geographic scope and means of connection (either wired or wireless).

Wide Area Networks (WANs) Computers that are linked over long distances—province-wide or even nationwide—through telephone lines, microwave signals, or satellite communications make up what are called **wide area networks (WANs)**. Firms can lease lines from communications vendors or maintain private WANs. Walmart, for example, depends heavily on a private satellite network that links thousands of U.S. and international retail stores to its Bentonville, Arkansas, headquarters.

Local Area Networks (LANs) In **local area networks (LANs)**, computers are linked in a smaller area, such as an office or a building. For example, a LAN unites hundreds of operators who enter call-in orders at TV's Home Shopping Network facility. The arrangement requires only one computer system with one database and one software system. **Virtual private networks (VPNs)** connect two or more LANs through a public network like the internet. This saves companies money because they don't have to pay for private lines, but it is important that strong security measures are in place, so that unauthorized persons can't gain access.

Wireless Networks Wireless networks use airborne electronic signals to link network computers and devices. Like wired networks, wireless networks can reach across long distances or exist within a single building or small area. For example, the BlackBerry system shown in Figure IT.2 consists of devices that send and receive transmissions on the **wireless wide area networks (WWANs)** of more than 100 service providers—such as Rogers (Canada), T-Mobile (United Kingdom and United States), and Vodafone (Italy)—in countries throughout the world. The wireless format that the system relies on to control wireless messaging is supplied by BlackBerry and is installed on the user-company's computer.[17] A firewall provides privacy protection. We'll discuss firewalls in more detail later in this supplement.

Wi-Fi Hotspots are locations such as coffee shops, hotels, and airports that provide wireless internet connections for people on the go. Each hotspot, or **Wi-Fi** (short for wireless fidelity) access point, uses its own small network, called a **wireless local area network (wireless LAN or WLAN)**. Although wireless service is free at some hotspots, others charge a fee—a daily or hourly rate—for the convenience of Wi-Fi service. For example, in an attempt to find new revenue sources, airlines are scrambling to provide Wi-Fi services to passengers (for a fee) on their planes through ground-based or satellite connections. WestJet is working with a U.S.-based air-to-ground service provider named Gogo LLC to establish its service.[18]

HARDWARE AND SOFTWARE

Any computer network or system needs **hardware**—the physical components, such as keyboards, monitors, system units, and printers. In addition to laptops, desktop computers, tablets, and smartphones are also used in businesses. For example, Walmart employees roam store aisles using handheld devices to identify, count, and order items, track deliveries, and update backup stock at distribution centres to keep store shelves replenished with merchandise.

The other essential component in any computer system is **software**—programs that tell the computer how to function. Software

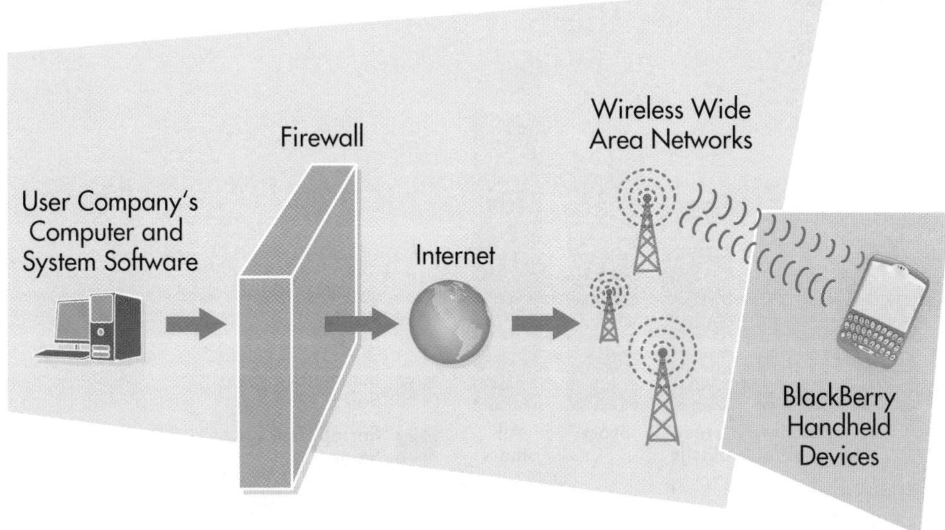

<<< **Figure IT.2** BlackBerry wireless internet architecture

includes system software, such as the latest version of Microsoft Windows, which tells the computer's hardware how to interact with the software. It also includes application software, which meets the needs of specific users (e.g., Adobe Photoshop). Some application programs are used to address common, long-standing needs such as database management and inventory control, whereas others have been developed for a variety of specialized tasks ranging from mapping the underground structure of oil fields to analyzing the anatomical structure of the human body.

Computer graphics convert numeric and character data into pictorial information like charts and graphs. They allow managers to see relationships more easily and generate clearer and more persuasive reports and presentations. As Figure IT.3 shows, both types of graphics can convey different kinds of information—in this case, the types of materials that should be ordered by a picture framing shop like Artists' Frame Service.

Groupware—software that connects group members for email distribution, electronic meetings, message storing, appointments and schedules, and group writing—allows people to collaborate from their own desktop PCs, even if they're remotely located. It is especially useful when people work together regularly and rely heavily on information sharing. Groupware systems include IBM Domino, Microsoft Exchange Server, and Novell GroupWise.

INFORMATION SYSTEMS: HARNESSING THE COMPETITIVE POWER OF INFORMATION TECHNOLOGY

Business today relies on information management in ways that no one could foresee even a decade ago. Managers now treat IT as a basic organizational resource for conducting daily business. At major firms, every activity—designing services, ensuring product delivery and cash flow, evaluating personnel—is linked to information systems. An **information system (IS)** uses IT resources and enables managers to take **data**—raw facts and figures that by themselves may not have much meaning—and turn that data into **information**—the meaningful, useful interpretation of data. Information systems also enable managers to collect, process, and transmit that information for use in decision making.

One of the most widely publicized examples of the strategic use of information systems is Walmart. Their IS drives down costs and increases efficiency because the same methods and systems are applied for all 5000-plus stores in Europe, Asia, and North America. Data on

^^^ After conquering the consumer market (taking sales away from other major players including Apple), Samsung is pushing its smartphone platform and trying to carve out a bigger share of the business market (taking market share from BlackBerry) by emphasizing SAFE, the extra security and manageability layer for Samsung Android phones like the Galaxy.

Islemount Images/Alamy

COMPUTER GRAPHICS Programs that convert numeric and character data into pictorial information like charts and graphs.

GROUPWARE Software that connects group members for email distribution, electronic meetings, message storing, appointments and schedules, and group writing.

INFORMATION SYSTEM (IS) A system that uses IT resources to convert data into information and to collect, process, and transmit that information for use in decision making.

DATA Raw facts and figures that by themselves may not have much meaning.

INFORMATION The meaningful, useful interpretation of data.

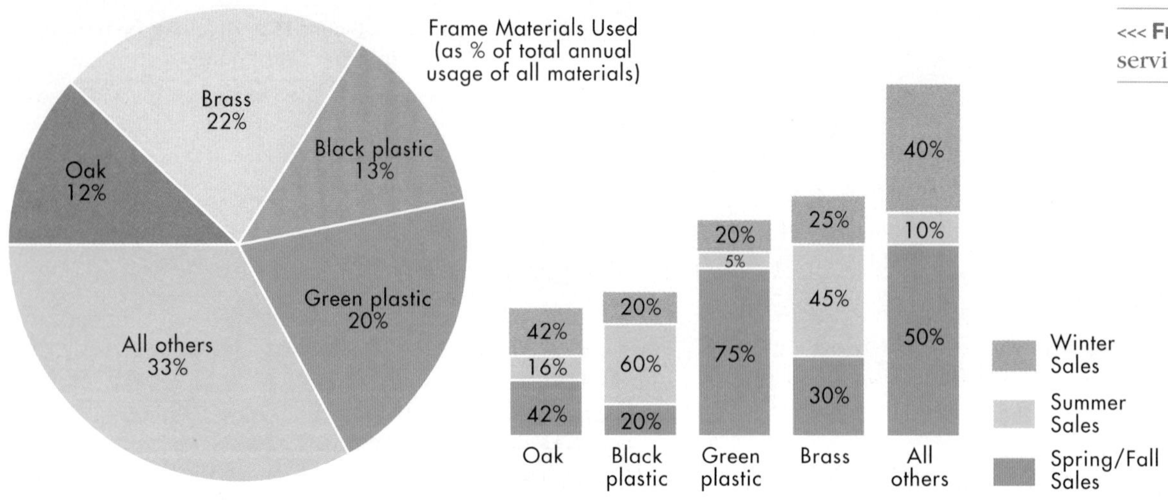

<<< **FIGURE IT.3** Artists' frame service

the billions of sales transactions—time, date, place—flows to company headquarters in Bentonville, Arkansas. Keeping track of nearly 700 million stock-keeping units (SKUs) weekly, the information system enforces uniform reordering and delivery procedures—on packaging, timing, and quantities—for more than 30 000 suppliers. It also regulates the flow of more than five billion cases through its distribution centres and deliveries by nearly 8000 Walmart truck drivers to its stores. Beyond the firm's daily operations, information systems are also crucial in planning. Managers routinely use the IS to decide on products and markets for the next 5 to 10 years. The company's vast database enables marketing managers to analyze demographics, and it is also used for financial planning, materials handling, and electronic funds transfers with suppliers and customers.

Like most businesses, Walmart regards its information as an asset that is planned, developed, and protected. Therefore, it's not surprising that businesses have *information systems managers* who operate the systems used for gathering, organizing, and distributing information, just as they have production, marketing, and finance managers. These managers use many of the IT resources we discussed earlier to sift through this information and apply it to their jobs. The effective use of information is so critical that many companies have appointed **chief information officers** who are responsible for managing all aspects of information resources and information processes.

There are so many new challenges and opportunities for IT managers. For example, **cloud computing** is a major buzz word in IT circles and it has different meanings to different people. In essence, it refers to internet-based development and use of computer technology. Individuals have been using this approach for years with email and photo sharing (think Google and Flickr). Organizations are now taking a closer look at the prospects of shared data centres through internet technology. At the conceptual level, cloud computing means placing some infrastructure online and having someone else run it rather than doing it in-house.

CHIEF INFORMATION OFFICERS Managers who are responsible for managing all aspects of information resources and information processes.

CLOUD COMPUTING Internet-based development and use of computer technology; at the conceptual level, it means placing some infrastructure online and having someone else run it rather than doing it in-house.

DATA WAREHOUSING The collection, storage, and retrieval of data in electronic files.

Some of the major advantages promised by this approach include lower costs, quicker set-up, easy scalability, easier software integration, reduced financial risk, decreased downtime, potential services for small business (that otherwise could not afford them), automatic updates that don't disrupt or endanger other systems, and empowered users.[19]

While many of you routinely use such services (e.g., iCloud), the question still remains if major companies will adopt this approach in large numbers. According to a Telus survey of IT managers, 71 percent of large Canadian companies want nothing to do with cloud computing. Most companies (85 percent) said they were concerned with security issues, particularly with public clouds.[20] However, other firms are embracing the approach in its various forms and receiving the benefits. For example, Cadillac Fairview, the Toronto-based commercial real-estate company, switched its email service to Gmail and reduced its costs to $50 per person from $210 per person with their previous provider. In addition, Cadillac Fairview gets an impressive amount of storage for the service. Cadillac Fairview is also looking at adopting Salesforce.com, which is a customer relationship management provider that would allow the company to eliminate in-house servers for their customer relationship needs.[21]

LEVERAGING INFORMATION RESOURCES: DATA WAREHOUSING, BIG DATA, AND DATA MINING

Almost everything you do leaves a trail of information about you. Your preferences in movie rentals, television viewing, internet sites, and groceries; the destinations of your phone calls, your credit-card charges, your financial status; and personal information about age, gender, marital status, and even your health are just a few of the items about each of us that are stored in scattered databases. The behaviour patterns of millions of users can be traced by analyzing files of information gathered over time from their internet usage and in-store purchases.

Data Warehousing The collection, storage, and retrieval of such data in electronic files is called **data warehousing**. In recent years, many data warehouses have been locating or re-locating existing facilities to Canada partly because of the cold climate. Data warehouses generate a lot of heat and the natural environment in a northern climate helps cool facilities. But the natural cooling effect of our winters is only part of the story; cheaper, clean energy sources are another important consideration. According to Mike O'Neil, president of IT Market Dynamics, "It is far cheaper and easier to set up a data center next to a hydro dam." Along with Canada, Finland and Sweden are also popular destinations.[22]

Big Data and Data Mining Companies are increasingly faced with larger and larger sets of data collected about their consumers. Every

Many data warehouses are setting up in or relocating to cold-weather countries like Canada, Finland, and Sweden to take advantage of the natural cooling provided by the weather (during winter) and because of inexpensive electricity.

Enigma/Alamy

single day we create 2.5 quintillion bits of data. If it sounds like a big number, it is! According to IBM, 90 percent of the data in the world has been created in the last two years alone. This data originates from purchase transaction records, sensors, digital pictures and video posts on social media sites, as well as smartphone GPS signals, to name a few.[23] This surge in information is forcing IT specialists to change their perspective and adapt. *Big data* can be defined as "high-volume, high-velocity and high-variety information assets that demand cost-effective, innovative forms of information processing for enhanced insight and decision making."[24] In other words, we have more data than ever before and our processes are now quicker than ever. The real test for businesses is to create systems to extract this information in a fast, cost-effective manner. Some firms are actively using this information in real time, while other firms have information resources that remain untapped.

According to market researcher IDC, in Canada alone businesses are expected to produce over 90 trillion gigabytes by 2020. But Canadian businesses lag in the use of big data. The arrival of Target, a heavy user of big data, into the Canadian retail space may force other retailers to accelerate their adoption of current applications. Internet retailers like Shop.ca have been early adopters. According to Trevor Newell, president of Shop.ca, sales of a projector increased by 800 percent after the company sent automated targeted emails to members and promoted the product on social media sites.[25]

Trying to access the gold mine of information in company databases is nothing new. In order to make sense of the mountains of information, companies have used **data mining**—the application of electronic technologies for searching, sifting, and reorganizing pools of data to uncover useful information for years. Data mining helps managers plan for new products, set prices, and identify trends and shopping patterns. By analyzing what consumers actually do, businesses can determine what subsequent purchases they are likely to make and then send them tailor-made ads. For example, a grocery chain can collect data on customer shopping habits to find ways to gain greater customer loyalty. It can accumulate information from its shopper cards, analyze the data to uncover shopping patterns, and send money-saving coupons to regular customers for the specific products they usually buy.

Philosophically, "big data" is replacing "data mining" from a perspective of searching for that golden nugget of information after the fact (data mining) to a quick moving, interactive, systematic flow of real-time (or near-time) information (big data approach).[26]

DATA MINING The application of electronic technologies for searching, sifting, and reorganizing pools of data to uncover useful information.

TRANSACTION PROCESSING SYSTEM (TPS) Applications of information processing for basic day-to-day business transactions.

Information Linkages with Suppliers The top priority for Walmart's IS—improving in-stock reliability—requires integration of Walmart's and suppliers' activities with store sales. That's why Procter & Gamble, Johnson & Johnson, and other suppliers connect into Walmart's information system to observe up-to-the-minute sales data on individual items, by store. They can use the system's computer-based tools—spreadsheets, sales forecasting, and weather information—to forecast sales demand and plan delivery schedules. Coordinated planning avoids excessive inventories, speeds up deliveries, and holds down costs throughout the supply chain, while keeping shelves stocked for retail customers.

TYPES OF INFORMATION SYSTEMS

Since employees have a variety of responsibilities and decision-making needs, a firm's information system may actually be a set of several information systems that share data, while serving different levels of the organization, different departments, or different operations. One popular information system is called the **transaction processing system (TPS)**, which processes information for many different, day-to-day business transactions like customer order-taking by online retailers, approval of claims at insurance companies, receiving and confirming reservations by airlines, and payroll processing.

Because they work on different kinds of problems, managers and their subordinates need access to the specialized information systems that satisfy their different information needs. In addition to different types of users, each business function—marketing, human resources, accounting, production, finance—has its own information needs, as do groups working on major projects. Each user group and department, therefore, may need a special IS. Two important groups are knowledge workers and managers.

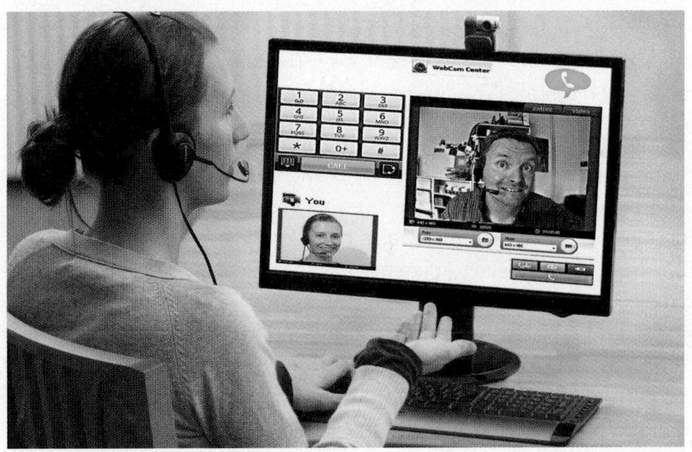

Quick communication within an organization is more important than ever. New tools are available to managers to help deal with the flood of data and exchanges of information. Companies are always looking for cost-effective ways to manage the sharing of knowledge.

TONY KARUMBA/Getty Images, Inc.

KNOWLEDGE INFORMATION SYSTEMS Information system that supports knowledge workers by providing resources to create, store, use, and transmit new knowledge for useful applications.

COMPUTER-AIDED DESIGN (CAD) IS with software that helps knowledge workers design products by simulating them and displaying them in three-dimensional graphics.

MANAGEMENT INFORMATION SYSTEM (MIS) Computer system that supports managers by providing information—reports, schedules, plans, and budgets—that can be used for making decisions.

DECISION SUPPORT SYSTEM (DSS) Interactive system that creates virtual business models for a particular kind of decision and tests them with different data to see how they respond.

ARTIFICIAL INTELLIGENCE (AI) The development of computer systems to imitate human thought and behaviour.

EXPERT SYSTEM A form of AI designed to imitate the thought processes of human experts in a particular field.

HACKER Cyber-criminal who gains unauthorized access to a computer or network, either to steal information, money, trade secrets, or property, or to tamper with data.

Information Systems for Knowledge Workers As we discussed in Chapter 8, knowledge workers are employees for whom information and knowledge are the raw materials of their work, such as engineers, scientists, and IT specialists who rely on IT to design new products or create new processes. These workers require **knowledge information systems**, which provide resources to create, store, use, and transmit new knowledge for useful applications—for instance, databases to organize and retrieve information, and computational power for data analysis.

Specialized support systems have also increased the productivity of knowledge workers. **Computer-aided design (CAD)** helps knowledge workers design products ranging from cellphones to jewellery to auto parts, by simulating them and displaying them in 3-D graphics. The older method—making handcrafted prototypes from wood, plastic, or clay—is replaced with faster, cheaper prototyping—the CAD system electronically transfers instructions to a computer-controlled machine that builds the prototypes.

Information Systems for Managers Each manager's information activities and IS needs vary according to his or her functional area (accounting, marketing, etc.) and management level. The following are some popular information systems used by managers for different purposes.

Management Information Systems **Management information systems (MISs)** support managers by providing reports, schedules, plans, and budgets that can then be used for making decisions, both short- and long-term. For example, at a publishing company, managers rely on detailed information—current customer orders, staffing schedules, employee attendance, production schedules, equipment status, and materials availability—for moment-to-moment decisions during the day. They require similar information to plan mid-range activities such as personnel training, materials movements, and cash flows. They also need to anticipate the status of the jobs and projects assigned to their departments. Many MISs—cash flow, sales, production scheduling, and shipping—are indispensable for helping managers complete these tasks.

For longer-range decisions involving business strategy, managers need information to analyze trends in the publishing industry and overall company performance. They need both external and internal information, current and future, to compare current performance data to data from previous years and to analyze consumer trends and economic forecasts.

Decision Support Systems Managers who face a particular kind of decision repeatedly can get assistance from **decision support systems (DSSs)**—interactive systems that create virtual business models and test them with different data to see how they respond. When faced with decisions on plant capacity, managers can use a capacity DSS. The manager inputs data on anticipated sales, working capital, and customer-delivery requirements. The data flows into the DSS processor, which then simulates the plant's performance under the proposed data conditions. After experimenting with various data conditions, the DSS makes recommendations on the best levels of plant capacity for each future time period.

Artificial Intelligence **Artificial intelligence (AI)** refers to the development of computer systems to imitate human behaviour—in other words, systems that perform physical tasks, use thought processes, and learn. In developing AI systems, business specialists, modellers, and information-technology experts try to design computer-based systems capable of reasoning, so that computers, instead of people, can perform certain activities. For example, a credit-evaluation system may decide which loan applicants are creditworthy and which are too risky, and it may then compose acceptance and rejection letters accordingly. Some AI systems possess sensory capabilities, such as lasers that "see," "hear," and "feel."

The **expert system** is designed to imitate the thought processes of human experts in a particular field.[27] Expert systems incorporate the rules that an expert applies to specific types of problems, such as the judgments a physician makes when diagnosing illnesses. In effect, expert systems supply everyday users with "instant expertise."

IT RISKS AND THREATS

As with other technologies throughout history, IT has attracted abusers that are intent on doing mischief, with severity ranging from a small annoyance to outright destruction. Eager IT users everywhere are finding that even social networking and cell phones have a "dark side"—privacy invasion. Facebook postings of personal information about users can be intercepted and misused by intruders. Beacon, a now defunct part of Facebook's advertising system, caused a public uproar when it published peoples' online purchases in their Facebook newsfeeds. Maintaining privacy is a problem with cell-phone advancements. Bluetooth connections allow savvy intruders to read a victim's text messages, listen in on live conversations, and even view users' photos.[28] Smartphone sales are likely to surpass regular cell-phone sales by 2015, so this presents an increased challenge, since more personal information is usually contained on these multipurpose devices.[29]

Businesses, too, are troubled with IT's dark side. Hackers break into computers, stealing personal information and company secrets, and launching attacks on other computers. Meanwhile, the ease of information sharing on the internet has proven costly for companies that are having increasing difficulty protecting their intellectual property, and viruses that crash computers have cost companies millions. In this section, we'll look at these and other IT risks.

HACKERS

Breaking and entering no longer refers only to physical intrusion. Today, it applies to IT intrusions as well. **Hackers** are cybercriminals who gain unauthorized access to a computer or network, either to steal information, money, trade secrets, or property, or to tamper with data. Another common hacker activity is to launch denial of service (DoS) attacks. DoS attacks flood networks or websites with bogus requests for information and resources, thereby shutting the networks or websites down and preventing legitimate users from accessing them.

At Acxiom, computer systems track consumer data provided by nearly every credit-card issuer, bank, and insurance company in North America. The company is currently improving its computer-security models, but many people who worry about the potential for abuse point out that Acxiom itself has been successfully "hacked" more than once in the past couple of years.

CP Picture Archive/Andrew Vaughan

Accessing unsecured wireless networks is a profitable industry for cybercriminals. Once inside, hackers can commit identity theft and steal credit-card numbers, among other things. When police officers try to track down these criminals, they're long gone, leaving the network host exposed to criminal prosecution.

IDENTITY THEFT

Once inside a computer network, hackers are able to commit **identity theft**, the unauthorized stealing of personal information (such as social insurance numbers and addresses) to get loans, credit cards, or other monetary benefits by impersonating the victim. Clever crooks get information on unsuspecting victims by digging in trash, stealing mail, or using phishing or pharming schemes to lure internet users to bogus websites. For instance, a cybercriminal might send TD Bank online customers an email notifying them of a billing problem with their accounts. When the customers click on the link, they are transferred to a spoofed (falsified) webpage, modelled after TD Bank's site. The customers then submit the requested information—credit-card number, social insurance number, and PIN—into the hands of the thief. Today, consumers are more aware of these scams, but they are still effective. Major organizations like the Canadian Bankers Association and the Competition Bureau are working with organizations to identify patterns and inform consumers.[30]

In Canada, the federal government has created new privacy legislation in the Personal Information Protection and Electronic Documents Act (PIPEDA). It was designed to promote e-commerce, while protecting personal information. The Act outlines the rules for managing personal information in the private sector.[31]

INTELLECTUAL PROPERTY THEFT

Nearly every company faces the dilemma of protecting product plans, new inventions, industrial processes, and other **intellectual property**—something produced by the intellect or mind that has commercial value. Its ownership and the right to its use may be protected by patent, copyright, trademark, and other means. Intellectual property theft is evident when, for example, individuals illegally download unpaid-for movies, music, and other resources from file-swapping networks. But the activities are not limited to illegal entertainment downloads. For example, according to the U.S. Intelligence Agency, Chinese cyber-spies steal about $40 to $50 billion worth of intellectual property each year.[32]

COMPUTER VIRUSES, WORMS, AND TROJAN HORSES

Another IT risk facing businesses is rogue programmers who disrupt IT operations by contaminating and destroying software, hardware, or data files. Viruses, worms, and Trojan horses are three kinds of malicious programs that, once installed, can shut down any computer system. A computer *virus* exists in a file that attaches itself to a program and migrates from computer to computer as a shared program or as an email attachment. It does not infect the system unless the user opens the contaminated file, and users typically are unaware they are spreading the virus by file sharing. It can, for example, quickly copy itself over and over again, using up all available memory and effectively shutting down the computer.

Worms are a particular kind of virus that travel from computer to computer within networked computer systems, without the need for any software to be opened to spread the contaminated file. In a matter of days, the notorious Blaster worm infected some 400 000 computer networks, destroying files and even allowing outsiders to take over computers remotely. The worm replicates itself rapidly, sending out thousands of copies to other computers in the network. Travelling through internet connections and email address books in the network's computers, it absorbs system memory and shuts down network servers, web servers, and individual computers.

Unlike viruses, a *Trojan horse* does not replicate itself. Instead, it most often comes into the computer, at your request, masquerading as a harmless, legitimate software product or data file. Once installed, the damage begins. For instance, it may simply redesign desktop icons or, more maliciously, delete files and destroy information.

SPYWARE

As if forced intrusion isn't bad enough, internet users unwittingly invite spies masquerading as friendly files available as a giveaway or shared among individual users on their PCs. This so-called **spyware** is downloaded by users that are lured by "free" software. Once installed, it crawls around to monitor the host's computer activities, gathering email addresses, credit-card numbers, passwords, and other inside information that it transmits back to someone outside the host system. Spyware authors assemble incoming stolen information to create their own "intellectual property" that they then sell to other parties to use for marketing and advertising purposes or for identity theft.[33]

Spam **Spam**—junk email sent to a mailing list or a newsgroup (an online discussion group)—is a greater nuisance than postal junk mail because the internet is open to the public, email costs are negligible,

IDENTITY THEFT Stealing of personal information (such as social insurance number and address) to get loans, credit cards, or other monetary benefits by impersonating the victim.

INTELLECTUAL PROPERTY A product of the mind that has commercial value.

SPYWARE Program unknowingly downloaded by users that monitors their computer activities, gathering email addresses, credit-card numbers, and other information that it transmits to someone outside the host system.

SPAM Junk email sent to a mailing list or a newsgroup.

FIREWALL Security system with special software or hardware devices designed to keep computers safe from hackers.

ANTI-VIRUS SOFTWARE Product that protects systems by searching incoming emails and data files for "signatures" of known viruses and virus-like characteristics.

ENCRYPTION SYSTEM Software that assigns an email message to a unique code number (digital fingerprint) for each computer, so only that computer, not others, can open and read the message.

and massive mailing lists are accessible through file sharing or by theft. Spam operators send unwanted messages. In addition to wasting users' time, spam also consumes a network's bandwidth, thereby reducing the amount of data that can be transmitted in a fixed amount of time for useful purposes.

IT PROTECTION MEASURES

Security measures against intrusion and viruses are a constant challenge. Businesses guard themselves against intrusion, identity theft, and viruses by using firewalls, special software, and encryption.

FIREWALLS

Firewalls are security systems with special software or hardware devices designed to keep computers safe from hackers. A firewall is located where two networks—for example, the internet and a company's internal network—meet. It contains two components for filtering each incoming data:

1. The company's *security policy*—access rules that identify every type of message that the company doesn't want to pass through the firewall.
2. A *router*—a table of available routes or paths, a "traffic switch" that determines which routes or paths on the network to send each message to after it is tested against the security policy.

Only those messages that meet the conditions of the user's security policy are routed through the firewall and permitted to flow between the two networks. Messages that fail the access test are blocked and cannot flow between the two networks.

PREVENTING IDENTITY THEFT

Internet privacy experts say that a completely new identity verification system is needed to stop the rising tide of internet identity theft. One possibility is an "infocard," which would act like a credit card and would allow websites to verify a customer's identity without keeping personal information on the customer. While foolproof prevention is impossible, steps can be taken to reduce the chance that you will be victimized. A visit to the Identity Theft Resource Center (www.idtheftcenter.org) is a valuable first step to get information on everything from scam alerts to victim issues—including assistance on lost and stolen wallets—to media resources, current laws, and prevention of identity theft in the workplace.

PREVENTING VIRUSES: ANTI-VIRUS SOFTWARE

Many viruses take advantage of weaknesses in operating systems in order to spread. Network administrators must make sure that the computers on their systems are using the most up-to-date operating system that includes the latest security protection. Combating viruses, worms, and Trojan horses has become a major industry for systems designers and software developers. Installation of **anti-virus software** products protects systems by searching incoming email and data files for "signatures" of known viruses and virus-like characteristics. Contaminated files are discarded or placed in quarantine for safekeeping.

PROTECTING ELECTRONIC COMMUNICATIONS: ENCRYPTION SOFTWARE

Unprotected email can be intercepted, diverted to unintended computers, and opened, revealing contents to intruders. Protective software is available to guard against those intrusions, adding a layer of security by encoding emails so that only intended recipients can open them. An **encryption system** works by scrambling an email message so that it looks like garbled nonsense to anyone who doesn't possess the key.

AVOIDING SPAM AND SPYWARE

To help their employees avoid privacy invasion and to improve productivity, businesses often install anti-spyware and spam-filtering software on their systems. Dozens of anti-spyware products provide protection—software such as Webroot's Spy Sweeper and Microsoft Windows Defender—but they must be continually updated to keep pace with new spyware techniques. While it cannot be prevented entirely, spam is reduced by many internet service providers (ISPs) that ban the spamming of ISP subscribers.

MANAGING OPERATIONS AND INFORMATION

GOAL OF THE EXERCISE

This part of the business plan project asks you to think about your business in terms of both accounting concepts and information technology (IT) needs and costs. See Chapter Supplement 03 for material on IT.

MANAGING OPERATIONS AND INFORMATION

An increasingly important part of a business plan is a consideration of how IT—computers, the internet, social media, software, and so on—influences businesses. This part of the business plan asks you to assess how you will use technology to improve your business. Will you, for example, use a database to keep track of your customers? How will you protect your business from hackers and other IT security risks?

This part of the business plan also asks you to consider the costs of doing business, such as salaries, rent, and utilities. You'll also be asked to complete the following financial statements:

- Balance Sheet. The balance sheet is a foundation for financial reporting. This report identifies the valued items of the business (its assets) as well as the debts that it owes (its liabilities). This information gives the owner and potential investors a snapshot into the health of the business.
- Income Statement (or Profit-and-Loss Statement). This is the focus of the financial plan. This document will show you what it takes to be profitable and successful as a business owner for your first year.

YOUR ASSIGNMENT

MyBizLab

STEP 1

Open the saved Business Plan file you have been working on.

STEP 2

For the purposes of this assignment, you will answer the following questions in Managing Operations and Information:

1. What kinds of IT resources will your business require?

   Hint: Think about the employees in your business and what they will need in order to do their jobs. What computer hardware and software will they need? Will your business need a network and an internet connection? What type of network? Refer to Chapter Supplement 03 for a discussion of IT resources you may want to consider.

2. How will you use IT to keep track of your customers and potential customers?

   Hint: Many businesses—even small businesses—use databases to keep track of their customers. Will your business require a database? What about other information systems? Refer to Chapter Supplement 03 for more information on these topics.

3. What are the costs of doing business? Equipment, supplies, salaries, rent, utilities, and insurance are just some of these expenses. Estimate what it will cost to do business for one year.

   Hint: The Business Plan Student Template provides a table for you to insert the costs associated with doing business. Note that these are just estimates—just try your best to include accurate costs for the expenses you think will be a part of doing business.

4. How much will you charge for your product? How many products do you believe you can sell in one year (or how many customers do you think your business can attract)? Multiply the price that you will charge by the number of products that you hope to sell or the amount you hope each customer will spend. This will give you an estimate of your revenues for one year.

   Hint: You will use the amounts you calculate in the costs and revenues questions in this part of the plan in the accounting statements in the next part, so be as realistic as you can.

5. Create a balance sheet and an income statement (profit-and-loss statement) for your business.

   Hint: You have two options for creating these reports. The first option is to use the Microsoft Word versions that are found within the Business Plan Student Template itself. The second option is to use the specific Microsoft Excel templates created for each statement, which can be found on this book's MyBizLab. These Excel files are handy to use because they already have the worksheet calculations preset—all you have to do is plug in the numbers and the calculations will be performed automatically for you. If you make adjustments to the different values in the Excel worksheets, you'll automatically see how changes to expenses, for example, can improve the bottom line.

6. Create a floor plan of the business. What does it look like when you walk through the door?

   Hint: When sketching your floor plan, consider where equipment, supplies, and furniture will be located.

7. Explain what types of raw materials and supplies you will need to run your business. How will you produce your good or service? What equipment do you need? What hours will you operate?

   Hint: Refer to the discussion of operations in Chapter 10 for information to get you started.

8. What steps will you take to ensure that the quality of the product or service stays at a high level? Who will be responsible for maintaining quality standards?

   Hint: Refer to the discussion of quality improvement and total quality management in Chapter 10 for information to get you started.

Note: Once you have answered the questions, save your Word document. You'll be answering additional questions in later chapters.

CBC VIDEO CASE 3-1

TICKLE YOUR TUMMY NUT-FREE COOKIE COMPANY

THE COMPANY

Tickle Your Tummy Nut-Free Cookie Company is an Aurora, Ontario–based company that sells all-natural, nut-free cookies made with whole ingredients. The company was established in 2003 by Jennifer Montoni, a single, stay-at-home mom with three children. Tickle Your Tummy has recently expanded its product offerings to include cupcakes, cakes, brownies, and oatmeal bars, all with a quality guarantee.

Montoni first saw the potential and market need for a nut-free cookie when one of her daughters was discovered to be allergic to peanuts and tree nuts. Montoni then decided to create baked goods that tasted great and were safe to eat. With a limited amount of simple, quality, whole ingredients to work with, she made her first shortbread cookies with elaborate and fun designs and saw $20 000 worth of cookie sales in her first year of business. Now, her cookies are available for online purchasing and are also sold in specialty food stores across North America for $5.00/package. Sales revenue for Tickle Your Tummy Nut-Free Cookie Company was $800 000 in 2009 and the company has seen 50 to 100 percent growth per year.

The company's success is due mainly to Montoni's dedication to quality during the production of her cookies. Each step in the production process adheres to the highest-quality standards of freshness. From using whole ingredients, to cutting, decorating, and packaging cookies individually, production and quality are always at the heart of it all with nut-free safety in mind. Personalized baked goods can also be ordered from the company and this contributes to the company's quality image.

THE PITCH

Montoni's desire to take her business to the next level led her to be a candidate on *Dragon's Den*, where she pitched her nut-free cookie business to the dragons. She asked for $300 000 in return for giving the dragons 30 percent of her company.

Montoni was hopeful that the investment would help her automate the company's current handmade cookie process, and thereby enable the company to continue its rapid growth and keep up with consumer demand. She also wanted to be able to pursue her goal to inspire others and become an allergy educator for parents through various marketing initiatives.

THE DRAGONS' POINT OF VIEW

Dragon Kevin O'Leary was skeptical of Montoni's claim that her company should be valued at $900 000. He said, "The cookie business is a low-growth business. You're making $70 000, worth $400 000, and you value your business at $900 000, and you are not worth that much." O'Leary argued that the business was worth only about $450 000, and he wondered whether Montoni would still be motivated if he (O'Leary) invested $300 000 and therefore owned 66 percent of the business. Montoni stood her ground, saying that "there is a lot of speculation on how to value a business in the real world; you don't have the formula and neither do I, and my valuation is based on the fact that my company has seen growth from 50 to 100 percent per year."

The other dragons were impressed with the amount of cookies that were being sold each year and thought that Montoni was a great sales rep. In particular, Arlene Dickinson was impressed by the allergy educator idea as well as Montoni's credibility and knowledge.

THE OUTCOME

Once O'Leary finished debating her valuation of the business, the other dragons thought about their potential interest in the offer. One said, "You're generating $250 000 a year; if you took a smaller salary, your company would be larger in terms of the valuation that Mr. O'Leary is so worried about. I can take 50 percent of the business for $300 000."

Three of the dragons, including Arlene Dickinson, eventually decided to invest $100 000 each. They felt that Montoni had made a great presentation and had an inspiring story to tell. Robert Herjavec said, "I just don't know why she would sell that much of her business for $300 000 when she built it out of her basement." Dickinson responded by saying, "I know why: she's been on her own with three kids running a business and she is smart enough that she knows she needs people to help her along now, to help her with the next level, and she gets it."

Despite one dragon's reluctance because of the low growth rate in the cookie industry, Montoni was finally able to make a deal with three of the dragons. They are now partners, having invested $300 000 in total for a 50 percent ownership share in her company (remember that Montoni was originally offering just 30 percent ownership for $300 000).

The big lesson here is ownership and control. An entrepreneur must know when to relinquish control in order to be able to expand and grow the business.

QUESTIONS FOR DISCUSSION

1. What is quality? What factors define quality for Montoni's products?
2. What lessons about valuing a business can you take away from this video?
3. What do you think of the market potential for this product? Do you think Tickle Your Tummy Nut-Free Cookie Company has a future? Explain your answer.

CBC VIDEO CASE 3-2

TREE PLANTERS

At Touchwood Lake, Alberta, 36 rookie tree planters (as well as a group of veteran planters) meet Cal Dyck, who has contracts to plant seven million white and black spruce seedlings in Alberta and Saskatchewan. The trees won't be ready to harvest for 90 years. The tree planting industry was born in the 1970s when the idea of sustainable forestry caught on. Originally, convicts were used, but then the forestry companies found out that hippies were cheaper.

During a two-day orientation session, Cal gives the students a lot of information about tree planting. He knows most of them want to make a lot of money in a short period of time, and he tells them they can do that if they are highly motivated and committed to working hard (planters can burn up to 7000 calories per day). Students are paid between 10 and 25 cents per tree, depending on the terrain. For a $30 per day charge, Cal will feed the workers and move them around to various planting sites. He also provides hot showers.

Among the rookies at the orientation are three friends: Misha (who is studying journalism at Concordia University in Montreal), Megan (a student at the Emily Carr Institute in Vancouver), and Lianne (also a student at the Emily Carr Institute). They will soon learn about the frailty of the human body in the business of tree planting (blisters, tendonitis, twisted ankles, and so on). The orientation also includes all-important demonstrations about how to properly plant a seedling. Spacing the seedlings, planting them at the right depth, choosing the right type of soil, and having the seedlings at the right temperature are all important considerations. The rookies train as a group, but then they're on their own and can work at their own pace. Their work is constantly checked for quality. If planting is not done right, it must be redone.

The rookies plant for just four hours during their first day on the job. While rookies are learning how to plant, they may plant fewer than 100 trees a day, but an experienced veteran can plant 3000 trees in a day. These high-volume planters—called "pounders" because of their intense work ethic—can earn $15 000 during the summer season. They set high production goals for themselves and that motivates them to work hard.

For the rookies, the first week is already starting to blur. They eat, sleep, and plant. The work cycle is four days on and one day off. Within just a few weeks, some rookies are already starting to wonder why they are in the bush, especially on days when the rain is pouring down and they are soaked through. At Kananaskis, Alberta, work slows down because the terrain is rough and steep. It's only halfway through the season, but some planters already have bad cases of tendonitis from the repeated motions of jamming their shovel into the ground as they plant seedlings. Already 8 of the 36 rookies have quit.

Lianne has made $2500 so far, and she is one of the top rookie planters. By season's end, Lianne will have planted over 98 000 trees. Megan (Lianne's school buddy) is starting to waver. She is fighting a sinus infection and is not even making minimum wage. Misha has decided to quit. A friend of hers is getting married back east and she will not return after the wedding. A week later, Megan quits as well.

At Candle Lake, Saskatchewan, the planting crews are behind schedule as the season nears its end. They still have 1.2 million trees to plant, and the ranks of rookie planters are thinning fast. Only 14 of 36 rookies are still on the job. Smaller work crews mean more work for those who are left, and the opportunity to make more money. After more than three months in the bush, each rookie who is still on the job has planted thousands of trees. Lianne has learned to stop calculating her daily earnings. Brad, a veteran planter, says that he admires the rookies who have pulled through. He says that it's amazing that people can be brought into the bush from the city to do this kind of work.

QUESTIONS FOR DISCUSSION

1. Explain what the terms *productivity* and *quality* mean. How are they related in the actual practice of tree planting?
2. Consider the following statement: *The productivity and quality of rookie tree planters is very low, and the turnover rate is very high. Tree-planting companies should therefore hire only experienced tree planters*. Do you agree or disagree with the statement? Defend your answer.
3. Why do you think tree planters are paid on a piece-rate basis? What are the advantages and disadvantages of paying tree planters this way? (Review the relevant material in Chapter 8 before answering this question.)
4. Explain the various forms of employee behaviour. How does each one of these forms of behaviour impact the productivity and quality of tree planters? (Review the relevant material in Chapter 9 before answering this question.)

PART 4 PRINCIPLES OF MARKETING

Tyler Olson/Shutterstock

AFTER READING THIS CHAPTER, YOU SHOULD BE ABLE TO:

- LO-1 Explain the concept of *marketing* and identify the five forces that constitute the *external marketing environment*.
- LO-2 Explain the purpose of a *marketing plan* and identify the four components of the *marketing mix*.
- LO-3 Explain *market segmentation* and how it is used in *target marketing* and *positioning*.
- LO-4 Explain the purpose and value of *marketing research*.
- LO-5 Describe the key factors that influence the *consumer buying process*.
- LO-6 Discuss the three categories of *organizational markets*.
- LO-7 Explain the definition of a product as a *value package* and classify *goods and services*.
- LO-8 Describe the key considerations in the *new product development process*, and explain the importance of *branding and packaging*.

New Product Development Strategies & the Power of Brand Equity

© ZUMA Press, Inc./Alamy

What's in a brand name? Why do people choose one product over another? When you choose between two items, how much of your decision is based on the brand's reputation and how much is based on the actual features? If you had to choose between two cars with identical features, how would the brand make the difference?

As you will see below, you don't need to imagine this scenario. In order to reduce new product development costs,

Understanding Marketing Principles *and* Developing Products

CHAPTER 12

companies are using many techniques, including outsourcing and even partnerships with competing brands. This is especially true in the automobile sector, where development is long and costs are high. Recently, Toyota (which owns the Scion brand) and Subaru teamed up their engineering capabilities to create one new sports car and sell it under two different brand names: the Subaru BRZ and the Scion FRS.

HOW WILL THIS HELP ME?

Adjusting its *marketing strategy* is an example of how a company can apply marketing basics to appeal to the forces of the *external marketing environment*. This chapter examines the *marketing plan*, components of the *marketing mix*, as well as the role of *targeting, market segmentation*, and *positioning*. It also explores the fundamentals of *market research* and the key factors that influence the *consumer and organizational buying processes*. The chapter concludes with a look at how new products are developed and how they are defined by *branding* and *packaging*. By grasping the marketing methods and ideas in this chapter, you will not only be better prepared as a marketing professional, but also as an informed consumer.

Outsourcing

Outsourcing is a popular cost- and time-reduction technique in the auto sector; it involves farming out some or all of the development and manufacturing process to external companies. Magna International (headquartered in Aurora, Ontario) is a company that many manufacturers turn to for solutions. Magna was founded in 1957, but today has 288 manufacturing and 88 product development facilities in 26 countries. Here are just a few examples of Magna's product content solutions in the car industry:

- Dodge Caravan—door panels and transmission components
- Mercedes Benz M-Class—body structure stamping and assembly
- Lincoln MKZ—engine, underbody stamping, and assembly
- BMW X3—full vehicle assembly, original engineering design

Direct Partnerships

Some companies have created joint ventures and built common manufacturing plants with competitors to assemble their vehicles (e.g., Toyota and Peugeot Citroen in the Czech Republic). In order to truly leverage strengths, some companies even make the ultimate commitment and merge (Renault-Nissan have had a positive union, while Daimler-Chrysler split up after a turbulent marriage). This latest "project" partnership between Subaru and Toyota (Scion) enables these companies to share their expertise to build a better car. Scion is strong in design, geared for the Generation Y drivers, and Subaru is famous for its advanced technology and the symmetrical all-wheel drive system.

Brand Equity

Why do people pay premium prices for a Louis Vuitton purse or a Mercedes car? The material is top quality, but we all know that the cost to manufacture does not fully justify the extra price. People are willing to pay extra for a brand logo, for the positive association, for the status granted, and for the image. In the case of Toyota and Subaru, the two cars are the same, so which one would you buy if you had the choice—the Subaru or the Scion? Most consumers will never know the truth about these cars, but you do. Your answer will be based on the brand you value more. There is no other rational basis for comparison in this case. However, if you did not know the truth, your perception of each brand might blur your opinions. One thing is clear: Both companies believed that they could produce a better product at a lower base cost by teaming up. In the end, the market will decide their fates.

QUESTIONS FOR DISCUSSION

1. What lessons about product development does this case demonstrate?
2. Why might it be advantageous for competitors to cooperate in the development of new products? Provide additional product examples.
3. Why would consumers be willing to pay a higher price for a product that is essentially identical to one with a lower price?

LO-1 WHAT IS MARKETING?

What comes to mind when you think of marketing? Most people think of marketing as advertisements for detergents, social networking, and soft drinks. Marketing, however, covers a much wider range of activities. **Marketing** can be defined as "an organizational function and a set of processes for creating, communicating, and delivering value to customers and for managing customer relationships in ways that benefit the organization and its stakeholders."[1]

A company that employs the **marketing concept** is coordinated to achieve one goal—to serve its present and potential customers at a profit. This concept means that a firm must get to know what customers really want and closely follow evolving tastes. The various departments of the firm—marketing, production, finance, and human resources—must operate as a well-coordinated system that is unified in the pursuit of customer satisfaction.

Delivering Value

What attracts buyers to one product instead of another? Although our desires for the many goods and services available to us may be unlimited, financial resources force most of us to be selective. Accordingly, customers buy products that offer the best value when it comes to meeting their needs and wants.

VALUE AND BENEFITS

The **value** of a product compares its benefits with its costs. Benefits include not only the functions of the product, but also the emotional satisfaction associated with owning, experiencing, or possessing it. But every product has costs, including sales price, the expenditure of the buyer's time, and even the emotional costs of making a purchase decision. A satisfied customer perceives the benefits derived from the purchase to be greater than its costs. Thus, the simple but important ratio for value is derived as follows:

$$\text{Value} = \text{Benefits}/\text{Costs}$$

The marketing strategies of leading firms focus on increasing value for customers. Marketing resources are deployed to add benefits and decrease costs of products to provide greater value. To satisfy customers, a company may, for example, do any of the following:

- Develop an entirely new product that performs better (provides greater performance benefits) than existing products.
- Keep a store open longer hours during a busy season (adding the benefit of greater shopping convenience).
- Offer price reductions (the benefit of lower costs).
- Offer information that explains how a product can be used in new ways (the benefit of new uses at no added cost).

VALUE AND UTILITY

To understand how marketing creates value for customers, we need to know the kind of benefits that buyers get from a firm's goods or services. As we discussed in Chapter 10, those benefits provide customers with **utility**—the ability of a product to satisfy a human want or need. Marketing strives to provide four kinds of utility in the following ways:

- *Form utility.* Marketing has a voice in designing products with features that customers want.
- *Time utility.* Marketing creates a time utility by providing products when customers will want them.
- *Place utility.* Marketing creates a place utility by providing products where customers will want them.
- *Possession utility.* Marketing creates a possession utility by transferring product ownership to customers by setting selling prices, setting terms for customer credit payments, if needed, and providing ownership documents.

Because they determine product features, and the timing, place, and terms of sale that provide utility and add value for customers, marketers must understand customers' wants and needs. Their methods for creating utility are described in this and the following chapter.

Goods, Services, and Ideas

The marketing of tangible goods is obvious in everyday life. It applies to two types of customers: those who buy consumer goods and those who buy industrial goods. Think of the products that you bought the last time you went to the mall or the grocery store or on the internet. In a department store, an employee asks if you'd like to try a new brand of cologne. A pharmaceutical company proclaims the virtues of its new cold medicine. Your local auto dealer offers an economy car at an economy price. These products are all **consumer goods**: tangible goods that you may buy for personal use. Firms that sell goods to consumers for personal consumption are engaged in consumer marketing, also known as B2C (business-to-consumer) marketing.

Marketing also applies to **industrial goods**: physical items used by companies to produce other products. Surgical instruments and bulldozers are industrial goods, as are many components and raw materials such as integrated circuits, steel, and plastic. Firms that sell goods to other companies are involved in industrial marketing, also known as B2B (business-to-business) marketing.

But marketing techniques are also applied to **services**—products with intangible (non-physical) features, such as professional advice, timely information for decisions, or arrangements for a vacation. Service marketing—the application of marketing for services—continues to be a major growth area in Canada. Insurance companies, airlines, public

MARKETING An organizational function and a set of processes for creating, communicating, and delivering value to customers, and for managing customer relationships in ways that benefit the organization and its stakeholders.

MARKETING CONCEPT The idea that the whole firm is directed toward serving present and potential customers at a profit.

VALUE A relative comparison of a product's benefits versus its costs.

UTILITY The ability of a product to satisfy a human want or need.

CONSUMER GOODS Physical products purchased by consumers for personal use.

INDUSTRIAL GOODS Physical products purchased by companies to produce other products.

SERVICES Products with non-physical features, such as information, expertise, or an activity that can be purchased.

>>> Fairmont Hotels actively use CRM techniques to satisfy customers in over 60 luxury properties across the globe, including the scenic Fairmont Banff Springs Hotel.

Stuart Forster/Alamy

RELATIONSHIP MARKETING A marketing strategy that emphasizes building lasting relationships with customers and suppliers.

CUSTOMER RELATIONSHIP MANAGEMENT (CRM) Organized methods that a firm uses to build better information connections with clients, so that stronger company–client relationships are developed.

accountants, and health clinics all engage in service marketing, both to individuals (consumer markets) and to other companies (industrial markets).

Finally, marketers also promote ideas. Ads in theatres, for example, warn us against copyright infringement and piracy. Other marketing campaigns may stress the advantages of avoiding fast foods, avoiding texting while driving, or quitting smoking—or they may promote a political party or candidate.

Relationship Marketing and Customer Relationship Management

Although marketing often focuses on single transactions for products, services, or ideas, marketers also take a longer-term perspective. Thus, **relationship marketing** emphasizes building lasting relationships with customers and suppliers. Stronger relationships—including stronger economic and social ties—can result in greater long-term satisfaction, customer loyalty, and customer retention.[2] Starbucks's Card Rewards attracts return customers with free coffee refills and other extras.

CUSTOMER RELATIONSHIP MANAGEMENT

Like many other marketing areas, the ways that marketers go about building relationships with customers have changed dramatically. **Customer relationship management (CRM)** is an organized method that an enterprise uses to build better information connections with clients, so that stronger enterprise–client relationships are developed. The power of internet communications, coupled with the ability to gather and assemble information on customer preferences, allows marketers to better predict what clients will want and buy. Compiling and storage of customers' data, known as data warehousing, provides the raw materials from which marketers can gather information that allows them to find new clients. It also identifies their best customers who can then be informed about upcoming new products and supplied with special information such as post-purchase service reminders. Data mining automates the massive analysis of data by using computers to sort and search for previously undiscovered clues about what customers look at, react to, and how they might be influenced. The hoped-for result is a clearer picture of how marketing, knowing a client's preferences, can more effectively use its resources to better satisfy those particular needs, thereby building closer, stronger relationships with customers.[3]

Toronto-based Fairmont Resort Hotels, for example, first used data mining to rebuild its customer-relations package by finding out what kinds of vacations their customers prefer, and then placing ads where they were more likely to reach those customers. When data mining revealed the worldwide destinations of Fairmont customers, it helped determine Fairmont's decision to buy their customers' number-one preference—the Savoy in London.[4] More recently, Fairmont's enhanced CRM is attracting new guests, along with heightening relationships and loyalty among existing clients, through web-based promotions and incentives. Using profiles of guest information, Fairmont identifies target traveller segments and supplies travellers with personalized price discounts and special hotel services.[5] For a more detailed discussion on data warehousing and data mining refer to the Supplement 3: Using Technology to Manage Information in the Internet and Social Media Era.

The Marketing Environment

Marketing strategies are not determined unilaterally by any business—rather, they are strongly influenced by powerful outside forces. As you see in Figure 12.1, every marketing program must recognize the factors in a company's external environment, that is, everything outside an organization's boundaries that might affect it. In this section, we will discuss how these external forces affect the marketing environment in particular.

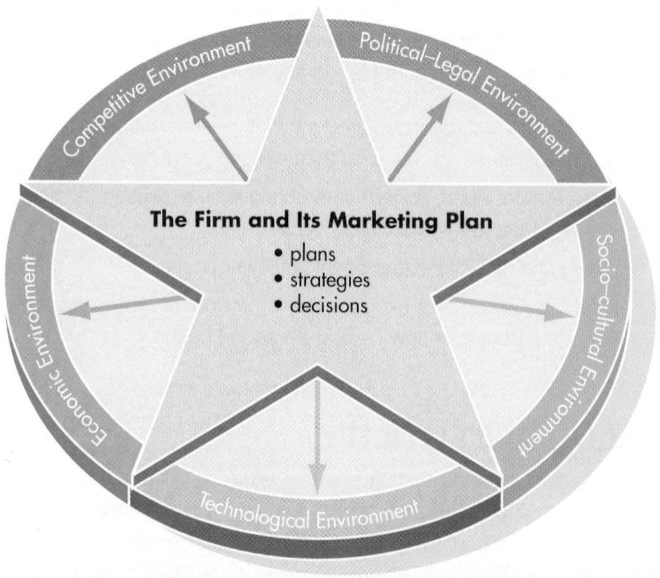

FIGURE 12.1 The external marketing environment

POLITICAL–LEGAL ENVIRONMENT

Political activities, both global and domestic, have a major influence on marketing. For example, environmental legislation has determined the destinies of entire industries. The political push for alternative energy sources is creating new markets and products for emerging companies, such as India's Suzlon Energy Limited (large wind turbines), wind-powered electric generators from Germany's Nordex AG, and wind farms and power plants created by Spain's Gamesa Corporation. Marketing managers try to maintain favourable political and legal environments in several ways. To gain public support for products and activities, marketers use ad campaigns to raise public awareness of important issues, and companies contribute to political candidates.

SOCIO-CULTURAL ENVIRONMENT

Changing social values force companies to develop and promote new products. Just a few years ago, organic foods were available only in specialty food stores like Whole Foods. Today, in response to a growing demand for healthy foods, Target's Archer Farms product line brings affordable organic food to a much larger audience. In addition, Whole Foods and other grocers like it are expanding. In 2013, Whole Foods had 345 stores in Canada, the U.S., and the U.K., but it had plans to reach 1000 stores in short order. With same-store sales increases averaging between 7 to 10 percent in recent years, it is clear that consumers are becoming more willing to pay higher prices for better quality food.[6] For another interesting look at environmentally friendly products and practices, read the Greening of Business box entitled "Green Products and Services."

TECHNOLOGICAL ENVIRONMENT

New technologies create new goods and services. New products make existing products obsolete, and many products change our values and lifestyles. In turn, lifestyle changes often stimulate new products not directly related to the new technologies themselves. For example, smartphones facilitate business communication just as prepackaged meals provide convenience for busy household cooks. Both kinds of products also free up time for recreation and leisure.

ECONOMIC ENVIRONMENT

Because they determine spending patterns by consumers, businesses, and governments, economic conditions influence marketing plans for product offerings, pricing, and promotional strategies. Marketers are concerned with such economic variables as inflation, interest rates, and recession. Thus, they monitor the general business cycle to anticipate trends in consumer and business spending.

The interconnected global economy has become an increasingly important concern for marketers worldwide—for example, in 2008, rising oil prices broke records on an almost daily basis. Fed up with gas prices, drivers drove less, decreasing the demand and prices for gasoline. As the global economy continued to sour, the Canadian government demanded its automakers reduce production costs and auto prices to qualify for the government's bailout fund. Meanwhile, the continuing U.S. housing crisis left many former homeowners down south stuck with debt they could not afford to repay. As a result, money-strapped consumers shifted to used cars (instead of new) and to downsized, more modest housing. This product shift by consumers affected all areas of marketing—target markets, pricing, promotion, and distribution—for cars, fuel, and housing.[7]

COMPETITIVE ENVIRONMENT

In a competitive environment, marketers must convince buyers that they should purchase one company's products rather than those of some other seller. Because both consumers and commercial buyers have limited resources, every dollar spent on one product is no longer available for other purchases. Each marketing program, therefore, seeks to make its product the most attractive. Expressed in business terms, a failed program loses the buyer's dollar forever (or at least until it is time for the next purchase decision).

To promote products effectively, marketers must first understand which of three types of competition they face:

- **Substitute products** may not look alike or they may seem very different from one another, but they can fulfill the same need. For example, your cholesterol level may be controlled with either of two competing products: a physical fitness program or a drug regimen. The fitness program and the drugs compete as substitute products.
- **Brand competition** occurs between similar products and is based on buyers' perceptions of the benefits of products offered by particular companies. For internet searches do you turn to the Google or Bing search engine? Brand competition is based on users' perceptions of the benefits offered by each product.
- **International competition** matches the products of domestic marketers against those of foreign competitors. The intensity of international competition has been heightened by the formation of alliances, such as the European Union and NAFTA.

Having identified the kind of competition, marketers can then develop a strategy for attracting more customers.

Marketing strategies are strongly influenced by powerful outside forces. For example, new technologies create new products, such as the cell-phone "gas station" shown here. These recharging stations enable customers to recharge their mobile devices just as they would refuel their cars. The screens at the stations also provide marketers with a new way to display ads to waiting customers.

© Michael Kemp/Alamy

SUBSTITUTE PRODUCT A competing product (which may be dissimilar in nature) that can fulfil the same need.

BRAND COMPETITION Competitive marketing that appeals to consumer perceptions of benefits of products offered by particular companies.

INTERNATIONAL COMPETITION Competitive marketing of domestic products against foreign products.

THE GREENING OF BUSINESS

Green Products and Services

During the last few years, more and more companies are responding to consumers' concerns about the environment by developing and marketing products and services that are environmentally friendly. Consider the following examples:

- Quebec-based Cascades Inc. developed a new technology that makes it possible to use recycled paper to produce toilet paper that is as soft as toilet paper produced from new wood. Previously, toilet paper made from recycled paper had a rougher texture than toilet paper made from newly cut trees because the recycling process damages the wood fibres. Cascades' new product—called Enviro—is designed to compete with products like Charmin and Cottonelle Ultra.
- Ford Motor Co. has set a goal to make one-quarter of the vehicles it produces either electric or hybrid by 2013. The company is not just tinkering around the edges, but is investing $135 million to redesign its core models.
- PepsiCo introduced a new bottle in 2012 that is fully recyclable. It is made from switchgrass, corn husks, and pine bark—by-products left over from the company's food business (e.g., orange and potato peels) may also be used in the future. The new technology creates a molecular structure from these waste materials that is very similar to the petroleum-based plastic bottles that currently dominate the market. Coca-Cola—which introduced a plastic bottle in 2009 that was 30 percent plant-based—will also introduce a new bottle that is completely plant-based within a couple of years.
- Bridgestone, Goodyear, Michelin, and Pirelli have developed new tires that reduce fuel consumption (and, therefore, exhaust emissions).
- Con-way Inc., a large trucking firm, has been involved in discovering new ways to increase the fuel efficiency of trucks and, thereby, reduce greenhouse gas emissions. The company joined with truck and engine manufacturers, transport firms, and scientists to develop regulations that are expected to save companies $50 billion in fuel costs, reduce oil consumption by 530 million barrels, and reduce greenhouse gas emissions by 270 million tonnes.
- Canadian National Railways knows that many of its customers are very conscious of their carbon footprint, so CN has made sustainability an integral part of its business. The company estimates that it can now move one tonne of freight 197 miles using only one litre of diesel fuel.

The emphasis on products and services that are environmentally friendly is welcomed by consumers who are concerned about the environment. But environmentally friendly products can be expensive. For example, electric cars like the Chevrolet Volt and Nissan Leaf produce less air pollution than cars powered by the traditional internal combustion engine, but many consumers cannot afford these new products (the sticker price for the Volt is $41 545 and for the Leaf $38 395). Even consumers who can afford these cars may not be willing to pay the price premium.

CRITICAL THINKING QUESTION

1. What other environmentally friendly products and services are you aware of from your own personal experience?

LO-2 STRATEGY: THE MARKETING MIX

MARKETING MANAGER A manager who plans and implements the marketing activities that result in the transfer of products from producer to consumer.

MARKETING PLAN A detailed strategy for focusing marketing efforts on consumers' needs and wants.

MARKETING MIX A combination of product, pricing, promotion, and place (distribution) strategies used to market products.

A company's **marketing managers** are responsible for planning and implementing all the activities that result in the transfer of goods or services to its customers. These activities lead to the **marketing plan**—a detailed strategy for focusing marketing efforts on customers' needs and wants. Therefore, marketing strategy begins when a company identifies a customer need and develops a product to meet it. In planning and implementing strategies, marketing managers develop the four basic components (often called the "Four Ps") of the **marketing mix**: product, pricing, place, and promotion.

You can learn more about many of the key terms and concepts in this chapter by examining and downloading the contents from the box entitled "There's An App for That!"

THERE'S AN APP FOR THAT!

1. **Marketing 101** >>> **Platforms:** *Apple, BlackBerry*
   Source: WAGMob
   Key Features: Offers online tutorials to help you learn marketing concepts.
2. **Brand Finance App** >>> **Platforms:** *Apple, Android*
   Source: MagazineCloner.com Ltd.
   Key Features: Highlights practical issues in brand strategy & brand building.
3. **Marketing Checklist** >>> **Platforms:** *BlackBerry*
   Source: GENOA net works
   Key Features: Helps guide the user to create a marketing plan step-by-step.

APP DISCOVERY EXERCISE

Since APP availability changes, conduct your own search for "Top 3" Marketing APPS and identify the key features.

PRODUCT Good, service, or idea that is marketed to fill consumers' needs and wants.

PRODUCT DIFFERENTIATION Creation of a product feature or product image that differs enough from existing products to attract customers.

PRICING The process of determining the best price at which to sell a product.

PLACE (DISTRIBUTION) The part of the marketing mix concerned with getting products from producers to consumers.

PROMOTION The aspect of the marketing mix concerned with the most effective techniques for communicating information about products.

Product

Marketing begins with a **product**—a good, a service, or an idea designed to fill a customer's need or want. Conceiving and developing new products is a constant challenge for marketers, who must always consider the factor of change—changing technology, changing wants and needs of customers, and changing economic conditions. Meeting these changing conditions often means changing existing products—such as Starbucks's introduction of its new line of instant coffee—to keep pace with emerging markets and competitors.

PRODUCT DIFFERENTIATION

Producers often promote particular features of products in order to distinguish them in the marketplace. **Product differentiation** is the creation of a feature or image that makes a product differ enough from existing products to attract customers. As you will see in detail in the closing case, Lululemon has a clear identity based on a yoga-inspired theme and has carved out a strong presence in the athletic clothing market. We cover the development process and the branding of products in detail in the final section of the chapter.

Pricing

Pricing a product—selecting the best price at which to sell it—requires consideration of several variables. For example, car manufacturers are always looking for ways to satisfy consumers and increase sales. Despite a powerful brand, when BMW Canada sets prices for its 3 Series line of cars, it needs to consider the competition. For example, in one recent year, the Acura TL was offering $3000 rebates and the Audi A4 was available at 2.9 percent financing.[8] Determining the best price at which to sell a product is a difficult balancing act. From a manufacturer's point of view, prices must support the organization's operating, administrative, research, and marketing costs. On the other hand, prices cannot be so high that consumers turn to competing products. Successful pricing means finding a profitable middle ground between these two requirements.

Both low- and high-price strategies can be effective, depending on the situation. For example, Canadian Tire maintained healthy sales in patio furniture and barbecues during the most recent recession by stocking additional lower-priced items and scaling back their stock of more expensive items.[9] At the same time, de Grisogono was launching The Meccanico watch in style, by winning the Prix du Public at a prestigious competition in Geneva. The company proclaims that The Meccanico is the world's most complicated watch and it retails for about $200 000 or roughly as much as a Ferrari.[10] Low prices will generally lead to a larger volume of sales. High prices will usually limit the size of the market, but will increase a firm's profits per unit. In some cases, however, high prices may actually attract customers by implying that the product is especially good or rare. We will discuss pricing in more detail in Chapter 13.

Place (Distribution)

In the marketing mix, **place** refers to **distribution**. Placing a product in the proper outlet—for example, a retail store—requires decisions about several activities, all of which are concerned with getting the product from the producer to the consumer. Decisions about warehousing and inventory control are distribution decisions, as are decisions about transportation options.

Firms must also make decisions about the channels through which they distribute products. Many manufacturers, for example, sell goods to other companies that, in turn, distribute them to retailers. Others sell directly to major retailers, such as Target and The Bay. Still others sell directly to final consumers. We explain distribution decisions further in Chapter 13.

Promotion

The most visible component of the marketing mix is, no doubt, **promotion**, which refers to techniques for communicating information about products. The most important promotional tools include advertising, personal selling, sales promotions, publicity/public relations, and direct or interactive marketing. Promotion decisions are discussed further in Chapter 13.

American Eagle Outfitters (AEO) is a chain of more than 900 stores specializing in clothes, accessories, and personal-care products designed to appeal to a demographic consisting of girls and guys ages 15 to 25. In 2006, the brand expanded its line with Aerie, a chain of stand-alone stores in the U.S. and Canada, and an online store, that sell girls' intimates, workout wear, and Aerie's Dormwear—a collection of leggings, hoodies, and fashionable sweats appropriate for lounging in the dorm or wearing to a morning class.

Helene Rogers/AGE Fotostock America Inc.

Blending It All Together: Integrated Strategy

An **integrated marketing strategy** ensures that the Four Ps blend together, so that they are compatible with one another and with the company's non-marketing activities as well. As an example, Toyota has become the world's largest automaker. Its nearly 30-year auto superiority, despite massive product recalls from 2009 to 2011, stems from a coherent marketing mix that is tightly integrated with its production strategy. Offering a relatively small number of different models, Toyota targets auto customers that want high quality, excellent performance reliability, and moderate prices (good value for the price). With a smaller number of different models than American automakers, fewer components and parts are needed, purchasing costs are lower, and less factory space is required for inventory and assembly in Toyota's lean production system. Lean production's assembly simplicity yields higher quality, the factory's cost savings lead to lower product prices, and speedy production allows shorter delivery times through Toyota's distribution system. Taken together, this integrated strategy is completed when Toyota's advertising communicates its message of industry-high customer satisfaction.[11]

INTEGRATED MARKETING STRATEGY A strategy that blends together the Four Ps of marketing to ensure their compatibility with one another and with the company's non-marketing activities as well.

LO-3 TARGET MARKETING AND MARKET SEGMENTATION

Marketers have long known that products cannot be all things to all people. The emergence of the marketing concept and the recognition of customers' needs and wants has led marketers to think in terms of **target markets**—groups of people or organizations with similar wants and needs, who can be expected to show interest in the same products.

Target marketing requires **market segmentation**—dividing a market into categories of customer types or "segments." Once they have identified segments, companies may adopt a variety of strategies. Some firms market products to more than one segment. General Motors, for example, once offered automobiles with various features at almost every price point. GM's past strategy was to provide an automobile for nearly every segment of the market. The financial crisis, however, forced GM's changeover to fewer target markets and associated brands by closing Saturn, phasing out Pontiac, and selling or shutting down Hummer and Saab.

In contrast, some businesses offer a narrower range of products, such as Ferrari's high-priced sports cars, aiming at a narrow segment. Note that segmentation is a strategy for analyzing consumers, not products. Once a target segment is identified, the marketing of products for that segment begins. The process of fixing, adapting, and communicating the nature of the product itself is called **product positioning**. In the Canadian coffee-house landscape, two companies stand out with very different value propositions and positioning approaches. Tim Hortons emphasizes a standardized product and provides fast service to people in a hurry, while Starbucks provides more customized products in more leisurely surroundings.

Identifying Market Segments

By definition, members of a market segment must share some common traits that affect their purchasing decisions. In identifying consumer segments, researchers look at several different influences on consumer behaviour. Following are five of the most important variables.

GEOGRAPHIC SEGMENTATION

Many buying decisions are affected by the places people call home. **Geographic variables** are the geographical units, from countries to neighbourhoods, that may be important in a segmentation strategy. For example, the heavy rainfall in British Columbia prompts its inhabitants to purchase more umbrellas than people living in Arizona's desert climate. Urban dwellers have less demand for pickup trucks than their rural counterparts. Sailboats sell better along both coasts than they do in the prairie provinces. These patterns affect marketing decisions about what products to offer, at what price to sell them, how to promote them, and how to distribute them. Consider the marketing of down parkas in rural Saskatchewan. Demand will be high, price competition may be limited, local newspaper advertising may be very effective, and the best location may be one easily reached from several small towns.

DEMOGRAPHIC SEGMENTATION

Demographic variables describe populations by identifying characteristics such as age, income, gender, ethnic background, marital status, race, religion, and social class as detailed in Table 12.1. Note that these are objective criteria that cannot be altered. Marketers must work with or around them.

Depending on the marketer's purpose, a segment can be a single classification (e.g., age 20 to 34) or a combination of categories (e.g., age 20 to 34, married with children, earning $25 000 to $34 999). Foreign competitors are gaining market share in auto sales by appealing to young buyers (under 30) with limited incomes (under $30 000). While companies such as Hyundai and Kia are winning entry-level customers with high quality and generous warranties, Volkswagen targets under-35 buyers with its entertainment-styled VW Jetta.[12] Hot Topic is a California-based chain that specializes in clothes, accessories, and jewellery designed to appeal to the youth market, whereas the Bank of Montreal is paying particular attention to the large baby-boomer population (born between 1947 and 1966), which represents approximately 40 percent of the

TARGET MARKET A group of people who have similar wants and needs and can be expected to show interest in the same products.

MARKET SEGMENTATION The process of dividing a market into categories of customer types or "segments."

PRODUCT POSITIONING The process of fixing, adapting, and communicating the nature of a product.

GEOGRAPHIC VARIABLES Geographic units that may be considered in developing a segmentation strategy.

DEMOGRAPHIC VARIABLES Characteristics of populations that may be considered in developing a segmentation strategy.

>>> TABLE 12.1 Demographic Variables

Age	Under 5; 5–11; 12–19; 20–34; 35–49; 50–64; 65+
Education	Grade school or less; some high school; graduated high school; some college or university; college diploma or university degree; advanced degree
Family Life Cycle	Young single; young married without children; young married with children; older married with children under 18; older married without children under 18; older single; other
Family Size	1, 2–3, 4–5, 6+
Income	Under $15 000; $15 000–$24 999; $25 000–$34 999; $35 000–$44 999; $45 000 and over
Nationality	Including but not limited to African, Asian, British, Eastern European, French, German, Irish, Italian, Latin American, Middle Eastern, and Scandinavian
Race	Including but not limited to Inuit, Asian, black, and white
Religion	Including but not limited to Buddhist, Catholic, Hindu, Jewish, Muslim, and Protestant
Sex	Male, female
Language	Including but not limited to English, French, Inuktitut, Italian, Ukrainian, and German

working population. Specialized services and products are being developed to serve the growing retirement needs of this group.[13] For more information take a look at the Managing in Turbulent Times box entitled "Marketing to the Boomers."

Canada's great ethnic diversity requires companies to pay close attention to ethnicity as a segmentation variable. Visible minorities in Canada control $76 billion in annual buying power, and to be effective in *multicultural marketing*, companies must understand the underlying values that ethnic minority customers hold.[14] These consumers can be precisely targeted using one of the 358 media outlets geared toward 93 ethnic groups in Canada. Ethnic TV stations include the Fairchild Network (Cantonese and Mandarin) and ATN (South Asian). There are 44 language groups represented in 240 publications ranging from Punjabi to Italian. There are 66 languages represented on 70 radio stations across the country, including CHIN in Toronto, CFMB in Montreal, and CJVB in Vancouver.[15]

In another sign of the growing consumer power and potential of the multi-billion dollar ethnic marketing segment, Metro purchased a 55 percent stake in Adonis, a Montreal-based ethnic grocery store for an

MANAGING IN TURBULENT TIMES

Marketing to the Boomers

One of the important demographic variables that marketers must take into account is changes in the age distribution of the population of Canada, particularly the increasing proportion of older people. In 2011, for example, there were four million people in Canada aged 65 or over, an increase of 11.5 percent since 2001. The proportion of seniors in Canada is projected to double in the next 25 years as a result of increased life expectancy (currently 82.5 years for women and 77.7 years for men).

These numbers represent both problems and opportunities. The *opportunities* include more sales of prescription drugs (because older people take more medications), more demand for financial services (because older people want advice on how to invest their pension earnings), and more demand for leisure activities like cruising (because older people have the time and money to travel). But companies have found that boomers aren't receptive to marketing that treats them as "old."

Opportunities also exist in terms of housing, where boomers have been the driving force for many years. When they were young, boomers demanded the traditional single-family residences, but, when they retire, they are more likely to demand a condominium (because they don't want the hassle of home maintenance) or assisted-living facilities (because of declining health). A study conducted by the Conference Board of Canada predicts that, by 2030, about 80 percent of new housing demand will come from seniors shopping for condominiums or seniors' residences. Since there will be less demand for traditional homes, the price of those is likely to stagnate or decline.

But there are also *problems* with an aging population. A key one is the impact that an aging population will have on the stock market. When large numbers of baby boomers retire between 2015 and 2025, it will mean less investment in equity markets, and this could well mean relatively poor stock market performance. Here's the reason: most people save the most money during middle age, but after that they save very little. These so-called "prime savers" increase demand for equity investments and, therefore, drive up the price of stocks (other things being equal). The problem is that the ratio of prime savers to other consumers (seniors and younger adults) peaked in 2010. When the ratio peaked in Japan in the early 1990s, it started a two-decade long stagnation of the Japanese economy and the Japanese stock market. The same thing may happen in Canada. Boomers will likely "de-risk" their portfolios by selling stocks and buying bonds as they get older. Some analysts predict that there won't be any significant growth in the stock market until after 2025.

Things might not turn out so badly if Canadians retire later than expected (and thus have more money to invest), or if investors from developing countries (with larger proportions of younger people in their populations) make investments in Canada through sovereign wealth funds.

CRITICAL THINKING QUESTION

1. Develop a list of products and services for which demand will increase in the next two decades. Then develop a list of products and services for which demand will decrease. Defend your conclusions.

undisclosed sum. This deal was designed to acquire a piece of a very successful chain, but also to gain expertise and access to supplier networks in order to increase the profile of ethnic foods in Metro's regular grocery stores. In 2013, Metro opened its first Adonis outlet outside Quebec and plans for expansion were underway. Two years earlier, Loblaws Inc. purchased T&T Supermarket Inc., Canada's largest Asian food retailer, for $225 million.[16] Clearly both retailers see ethnic food as a top priority.

GEO-DEMOGRAPHIC SEGMENTATION

Geo-demographic variables are a combination of geographic and demographic traits, and they are becoming the most common segmentation tool. An example would be Young Urban Professionals—well-educated, 25- to 34-year-olds with high-paying professional jobs living in the "downtown" core of major cities. This type of segmentation is more effective because the greater number of variables defines the market more precisely.

PSYCHOGRAPHIC SEGMENTATION

Members of a market can also be segmented according to **psychographic variables** such as lifestyles, opinions, interests, and attitudes. Psychographics are particularly important to marketers because, unlike demographics and geographics, they can sometimes be changed by marketing efforts. For example, Polish companies have overcome consumer resistance by promoting the safety and desirability of using credit cards rather than depending solely on cash.[17] Many companies have succeeded in changing some consumers' opinions by running ads highlighting products that they have improved directly in response to consumer desires. For example, Las Vegas began courting the gay community a few years ago as part of a broader effort to target a range of minority audiences. According to research from Community Marketing Inc., gay and lesbian travel accounts for $55 billion of the overall U.S. travel market, and is one of the most lucrative segments of the travel markets.[18]

BEHAVIOURAL SEGMENTATION

Behavioural segmentation refers to dividing a market into groups based on consumer knowledge, use, or response to a product.[19] **Behavioural variables** include *benefits sought* (e.g., Head and Shoulders shampoo addresses dandruff control), *user status* (i.e., ex-users, current users, non-users etc.), *usage rate* (i.e., heavy users vs. light users), *loyalty status* (i.e., highly brand loyal vs. brand promiscuous), and *occasion for use* (e.g., time of day, special occasion, etc.).

Market Segmentation: A Caution

Segmentation must be done carefully. A group of people may share an age category, income level, or some other segmentation variable, but their spending habits may be quite different. Look at your friends in school. You may all be approximately the same age, but you have different needs and wants. Some of you may wear cashmere sweaters, while others wear sweatshirts. The same holds true for income. University professors and truck drivers earn about the same level of income; however, their spending patterns, tastes, and wants are generally quite different. That is why it is important to look at multiple variables.

In Canada, the two dominant cultures—English and French—have historically shown significant differences in consumer attitudes and behaviour. Researchers have found that compared with English Canadians, French Canadians are more involved with home and family, attend the ballet more often, travel less, eat more chocolate, and are less interested in convenience food. But this does not necessarily mean that companies must have different product offerings in Quebec. The adoption process for new products varies from one individual to another, according to socio-economic and demographic characteristics.

GEO-DEMOGRAPHIC VARIABLES A combination of geographic and demographic traits used in developing a segmentation strategy.

PSYCHOGRAPHIC VARIABLES Consumer characteristics, such as lifestyles, opinions, interests, and attitudes, that may be considered in developing a segmentation strategy.

BEHAVIOURAL VARIABLES Behavioural considerations, such as benefits sought, loyalty status, usage rate, user status, and occasion for use, that may be used in developing a segmentation strategy.

LO-4 MARKET RESEARCH

MARKET RESEARCH The systematic study of what buyers need and how best to meet those needs.

SECONDARY DATA Information already available to market researchers as a result of previous research by the firm or other agencies.

Market research, the study of what buyers need and how best to meet those needs, can address any element in the marketing mix. Business firms spend millions of dollars each year trying to figure out their customers' habits and preferences. Market research can greatly improve the accuracy and effectiveness of market segmentation.[20] For example, comic books have historically not been of much interest to girls, but DC Comics and Marvel Entertainment are convinced they can change that after observing the success of upstart companies like Tokyopop and Viz Media, which produce translated Japanese comics called manga. These companies have succeeded in attracting female readers by having "girl-friendly" content and by distributing their products in both comic book shops and mainstream bookstores.[21]

The Research Process

Market research can occur at almost any point in a product's existence, but it is most frequently used when a new or altered product is being considered. There are five steps in performing market research:[22]

1. *Study the current situation.* What is the need and what is currently being done to meet it?
2. *Select a research method.* In choosing a method, marketers must bear in mind the effectiveness and costs of different methods.
3. *Collect data.* **Secondary data** refers to information already available as a result of previous research by the firm or other organizations. For example, Statistics Canada publishes a great deal of useful data for business firms. Using secondary data can save time, effort, and money. But in some cases, secondary data are unavailable or inadequate,

so **primary data**—new research by the firm or its agents—must be obtained. When the Metro grocery chain wanted to increase sales among a key target group—the yoga set (i.e., health-conscious women)—it added three metres of space for yogurt in its coolers, while reducing space for products like margarine. The resulting data showed no loss in margarine sales, but significant growth in yogurt sales.[23]

4. *Analyze the data.* Data is not useful until it has been organized into clear information.
5. *Prepare a report.* This report normally includes a summary of the study's methodology and findings, various alternative solutions (where appropriate), and recommendations for an appropriate course of action.

Research Methods

The four basic types of methods used by market researchers are *observation, survey, focus groups*, and *experimentation.*

OBSERVATION

Probably the oldest form of market research is simple **observation**. It is also a popular research method because it is relatively low in cost, often drawing on data that must be collected for some other reason, such as reordering. In earlier times, when a store owner noticed that customers were buying red children's wagons, not green ones, the owner reordered more red wagons, the manufacturer's records showed high sales of red wagons, and the marketing department concluded that customers wanted red wagons. But observation is now much more sophisticated. For example, Retail guru Paco Underhill collects approximately 50 000 hours of video every year for customers like Walmart, Best Buy, and Gap.[24] Using video equipment to observe consumer behaviour is called *video mining*. It is being adopted by many retailers in North America, who

PRIMARY DATA Information developed through new research by the firm or its agents.

OBSERVATION A market research technique involving viewing or otherwise monitoring consumer buying patterns.

E-BUSINESS AND SOCIAL MEDIA SOLUTIONS

Retailers Are Tracking Your Every Move

Understanding what consumers want and providing it when they want it has always been good business practice for retailers. In small towns, general stores carried a variety of goods and the owner's ability to understand individual customer needs went a long way in meeting satisfaction. Today, retailers may not have a personal relationship with you, but they have a wealth of information to help them understand who you are and what you buy. In addition, they can track your location, monitor your actions in high definition, and see how much time you spend in certain departments. Retailers are only beginning to scratch the surface of what is possible with modern technology, but you might be surprised to find out just how far they have already come. Here are a few examples:

- Retailers and malls have set up Wi-Fi networks to satisfy customer needs, but that same technology permits them to keep track of customers. Boingo Wireless Inc. is testing a system that tracks traffic patterns in malls. Nearbuy Systems is pushing a system that is supposed to enable retailers to cross-reference the websites shoppers visit on their phones with their location in the outlet.
- Mac's and Couche-Tard outlets will take this technology even further in an attempt to turn your smartphone into a mini-billboard. Using a technology from iSign Media Solutions Inc., Couche-Tard will strategically send ads to anyone within a 300-foot radius of one of their stores. The messages will request your permission, but the reminder of the location proximity is automatic and potentially quite effective.
- Many retailers are tapping into their video surveillance to track customer behaviour and analyze buying patterns. Alexander Fernandes founded Vancouver-based QImaging for medical and industrial use, but has found a great market in shopping-mall and retail-store surveillance. Most of the pre-existing camera equipment was dated and provided poor, grainy images. So, Fernandes and his team developed High Definition Stream Management which makes it less expensive and easier to store and send images. His customers include shopping malls, arenas, banks, and many other outlets.
- The most fundamental way to track consumers is through actual sales data. Charles Brown, president of The Source, noticed that shoppers were buying more headphones. Armed with this information, he started stocking more upscale lines (e.g., Beats by Dr. Dre) and sales in this category increased by 40 percent. Many chains, like The Source, supplement this data by analyzing real-time chatter on social media sites and examining online consumer product reviews and commentary.
- In another example, Target uses its REDcard loyalty program to track purchase habits. Its system is sophisticated enough to tell if a young female consumer is pregnant based on previous purchases and can therefore target promotions (such as a sale on baby cribs) to those individuals.

All of this brings up questions of privacy, but the companies pushing the intrusive cellphone technology point out that you could always turn off your phone or the tracking capability. But, of course, most consumers are oblivious to all that is going on around them. Even if they were aware, would they really care? Retailers will argue that they are just trying to understand your needs to meet demands efficiently. Is this any different than the digital greeter named Anna that says hello to shoppers as they enter The Bay's flagship store in Toronto? What do you think? Is this all bordering on creepy behaviour or is it just the way things are today?

QUESTIONS FOR DISCUSSION

1. Which of the techniques that were described above do you find the most effective? Which do you find least effective?
2. Do you believe that retailers are crossing ethical lines with some of this new technology?

use hidden cameras to determine the percentage of shoppers who buy and the percentage who only browse. Some consumer organizations are raising privacy concerns about this practice, since shoppers are unaware that they are being taped.[25]

For an interesting modern look at the subject, take a close look at the E-Business and Social Media box entitled "Retailers Are Tracking Your Every Move."

SURVEY

Sometimes observation of current events is not enough and marketers need to conduct a **survey** to find out what consumers want. The heart of any survey is a questionnaire that contains carefully constructed questions designed to give the company honest answers about specific research issues. Surveys can be expensive to carry out and may vary widely in their accuracy. Because no firm can afford to survey everyone, marketers must carefully select a representative group of respondents. In the past, surveys have been mailed to individuals for their completion, but online surveys are now extremely popular. When Sara Lee Corp. acquired Kiwi shoe polish, it surveyed 3500 people in eight countries about their shoe-care needs. It learned that people do not care as much about the shine on their shoes as they do about how fresh and comfortable they are on the inside. The firm has since unveiled several new products based on this research under the Kiwi name and is doing quite well.[26]

FOCUS GROUPS

Many firms also use **focus groups**, where 6 to 15 people are brought together to talk about a product or service. A moderator leads the group's discussion, and employees from the sponsoring company may observe the proceedings from behind a one-way mirror. The comments of people in the focus group are taped, and researchers go through the data looking for common themes. The people in the focus group are not usually told which company is sponsoring the research. When Procter & Gamble was developing a new air freshener, it asked people in focus groups to describe their "desired scent experience." They discovered that people get used to a scent after about half an hour and no longer notice it. P&G used this information to develop Febreze Scentstories, which gives off one of five scents every 30 minutes.[27]

Consumers don't necessarily tell the truth when participating in focus groups or when filling out surveys. They may say one thing and think something else. This has led marketers to look at other ways of gathering information. For example, Sensory Logic Inc. studies facial expressions and eye movements to determine what consumers really think of a product.[28]

EXPERIMENTATION

Experimentation compares the responses of the same or similar individuals under different circumstances. For example, a firm that is trying to decide whether to include walnuts in a new candy bar probably would not learn much by asking people what they thought of the idea. But if it made some bars with nuts and some without and then asked people to try both, the responses could be very helpful.[29]

SURVEY A market research technique based on questioning a representative sample of consumers about purchasing attitudes and practices.

FOCUS GROUP A market research technique involving a small group of people brought together and allowed to discuss selected issues in depth.

EXPERIMENTATION A market research technique in which the reactions of similar people are compared under different circumstances.

LO-5 UNDERSTANDING CONSUMER BEHAVIOUR

Market research in its many forms can help marketing managers understand how common traits of a market segment affect consumers' purchasing decisions. It helps with fundamental questions: Why do people buy a certain product? What desire are they fulfilling with the product? Is there a psychological or sociological explanation for why they purchase one product and not another? These questions and many others are addressed in the study of **consumer behaviour**—the study of the decision process by which people buy and consume products.

Influences on Consumer Behaviour

To understand consumer behaviour, marketers draw heavily on such fields as psychology and sociology. The result is a focus on four major influences on consumer behaviour: psychological, personal, social, and cultural. By identifying which influences are most active in certain circumstances, marketers try to explain consumer choices and predict future buying behaviour.

- *Psychological influences* include an individual's motivations, perceptions, ability to learn, and attitudes.
- *Personal influences* include lifestyle, personality, and economic status.
- *Social influences* include family, opinion leaders (people whose opinions are sought by others), and such reference groups such as friends, co-workers, and professional associates.
- *Cultural influences* include culture (the way of living that distinguishes one large group from another), subculture (smaller groups with shared values), and social class (the cultural ranking of groups according to such criteria as background, occupation, and income).

Although these factors can have a strong impact on a consumer's choices, their effect on actual purchases is sometimes weak or negligible. Some consumers, for example, exhibit high **brand loyalty**—they

CONSUMER BEHAVIOUR The study of the decision process by which people buy and consume products.

BRAND LOYALTY A pattern of regular consumer purchasing based on satisfaction with a product's performance.

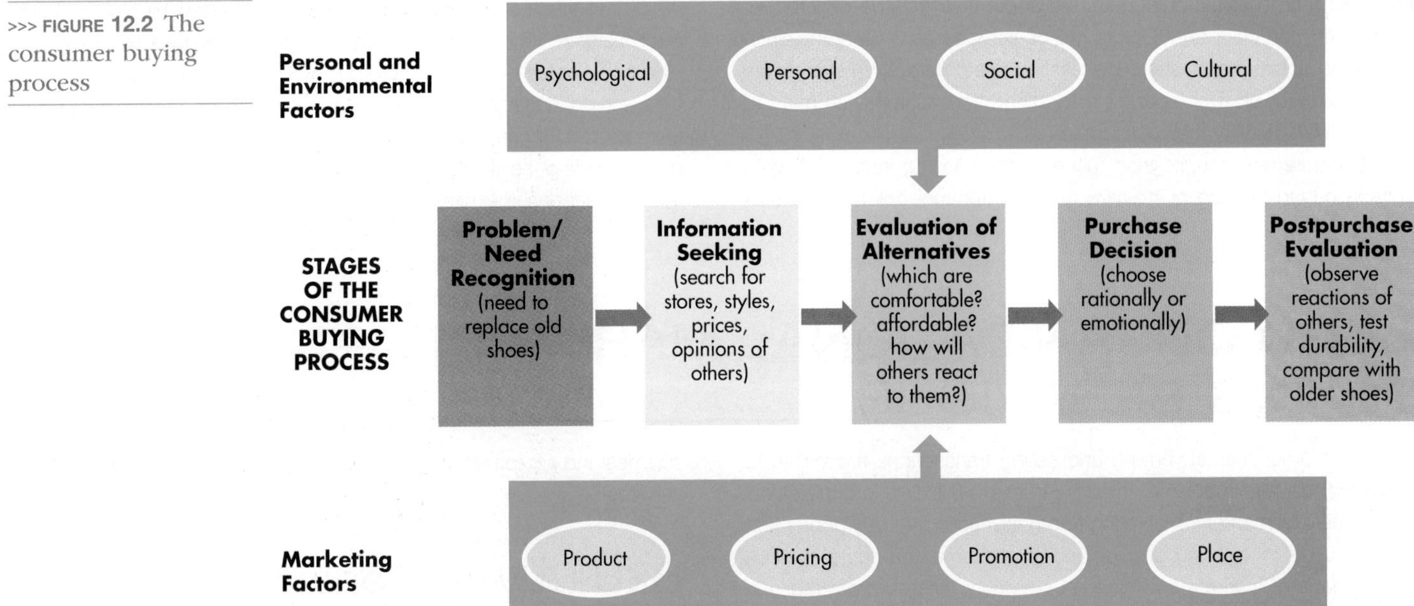

>>> FIGURE 12.2 The consumer buying process

regularly purchase products, such as Pepsi, because they are satisfied with their performance. Such people are less subject to influence and will stick with preferred brands.[30] (We will examine the effects of branding in more detail at the end of this chapter.) On the other hand, the clothes you wear, the social network you choose, and the way you decorate your room, often reflect social and psychological influences on your consumer behaviour.

The Consumer Buying Process

Students of consumer behaviour have constructed various models to help show how consumers decide to buy products. Figure 12.2 presents one such model. At the core of this and similar models is an awareness of the many influences that lead to consumption. Ultimately, marketers use this information to develop marketing plans.

PROBLEM/NEED RECOGNITION

This process begins when the consumer recognizes a problem or need. Need recognition also occurs when you have a chance to change your buying habits. After an exercise workout, you recognize that you are thirsty and in need of a refreshment. When you obtain your first job after graduation, your new income may let you buy things that were once too expensive for you. You may find that you need professional clothing, apartment furnishings, and a car. RBC and Scotiabank cater to such shifts in needs when they market credit cards to graduates.

INFORMATION SEEKING

Having recognized a need, consumers often seek information. The search is not always extensive. When you are thirsty you may simply look for the nearest vending machine; however, before making major purchases, most people seek information from personal sources, public sources, and experience. When buying a new car you may take months to gather information from various sources (online, from friends, mechanics, etc.) before you even consider a purchase.

EVALUATION OF ALTERNATIVES

If someone is in the market for skis, they probably have some idea of who makes skis and how they differ. By analyzing product attributes (price, prestige, quality) of the consideration set (the group of brands they will consider buying), consumers compare products before deciding which one best meets their needs.

PURCHASE DECISION

Ultimately, consumers make purchase decisions. "Buy" decisions are based on rational motives, emotional motives, or both. **Rational motives** involve the logical evaluation of product attributes: cost, quality, and usefulness. **Emotional motives** involve non-objective factors and include sociability, imitation of others, and aesthetics. For example, you might buy the same brand of jeans as your friends to feel accepted in a certain group, not because your friends happen to have the good sense to prefer durable, comfortable, low-priced jeans (usually it is the opposite scenario).

POST-PURCHASE EVALUATION

Marketing does not stop with the sale of a product. What happens after the sale is important. Marketers want consumers to be happy after buying products so that they are more likely to buy them again. Because consumers do not want to go through a complex decision process for every purchase, they often repurchase products they have used and liked.

Not all consumers are satisfied with their purchases. Dissatisfied consumers may complain, file a lawsuit, or publicly criticize the product and the company. They are unlikely to purchase the product again, and they are much more likely to speak about their negative experience with

RATIONAL MOTIVES Reasons for purchasing a product that are based on a logical evaluation of product attributes.

EMOTIONAL MOTIVES Reasons for purchasing a product that are based on non-objective factors.

a product than satisfied customers are about their positive experience. People can complain about products or services at www.complaints.com or on social media sites. Dissatisfied customers can have a very negative impact on a company's marketing effort. Companies need to be proactive to satisfy their consumers.

After a recent tough year full of embarrassing recalls, Toyota Canada began offering customers free maintenance for two years or 48 000 kilometres. This approach is commonly used by high-end auto manufacturers. This response could be effective for three reasons: (1) it allows Toyota to identify unsatisfied customers and fix their problems before they spread negative word of mouth, (2) it is relatively inexpensive—in essence, four oil changes, and (3) it ensures that customers will get into the habit of visiting the dealership, a behaviour that can be very lucrative after the two-year period expires.[31]

LO-6 ORGANIZATIONAL MARKETING AND BUYING BEHAVIOUR

In the consumer market, buying and selling transactions are visible to the public. Equally important, though far less visible, are organizational (or commercial) markets. Marketing to organizations that buy goods and services used in creating and delivering consumer products involves various kinds of markets and buying behaviours different from those in consumer markets.

Business Marketing

Business marketing involves organizational or commercial markets that fall into three B2B categories: industrial, reseller, and government/institutional markets. Taken together, B2B markets account for more than two times the sales amount of the consumer market.[32]

INDUSTRIAL MARKET

The **industrial market** includes businesses that buy goods to be converted into other products or that are used up during production. It includes farmers, manufacturers, and some retailers. For example, clock-making company Seth Thomas buys electronics, metal components, and glass from other companies to make clocks for the consumer market. The company also buys office supplies, tools, and factory equipment—items never seen by clock buyers—that are used during production.

RESELLER MARKET

Before products reach consumers, they pass through a **reseller market** consisting of intermediaries, including wholesalers and retailers that buy and resell finished goods. For example, as a leading distributor of parts and accessories for the pleasure boat market, Coast Distribution System buys lights, steering wheels, and propellers and resells them to marinas and boat-repair shops.

GOVERNMENT AND INSTITUTIONAL MARKET

Federal, provincial, and municipal governments are very important, not only for the laws they create and maintain, but for their economic spending power. The Canadian federal government, for example, spent an estimated $282 billion in 2013. A new website enables Canadians to track this spending at www.tbs-sct.gc.ca/ems-sgd/edb-bdd/index-eng.html.[33] The **institutional market** consists of non-governmental organizations, such as churches, museums, and charities, that also use supplies and equipment as well as legal, accounting, and transportation services.

B2B Buying Behaviour

In some respects, organizational buying behaviour bears little resemblance to consumer buying practices. Differences include the buyers' purchasing skills and an emphasis on buyer–seller relationships.

DIFFERENCES IN BUYERS

Unlike most consumers, organizational buyers purchase in large quantities and are professional, specialized, and well informed.

- Industrial buyers buy in bulk or large quantities. Because of this fact, and with so much money at stake, the following are also characteristics of organizational buyers.
- As professionals, B2B buyers are trained in methods for negotiating purchase terms. Once buyer–seller agreements have been reached, they also arrange formal contracts.
- As a rule, industrial buyers are company specialists in a line of items and are often experts about the products they buy.

DIFFERENCES IN THE BUYER–SELLER RELATIONSHIP

Consumer–seller relationships are often impersonal, short-lived, one-time interactions. In contrast, B2B situations often involve frequent and long-term buyer–seller relationships. The development of a long-term relationship provides each party with access to the technical strengths of the other, as well as the security of knowing what future business to expect. Thus, a buyer and a supplier may form a design team to create products to benefit both parties. Accordingly, industrial sellers emphasize personal selling by trained representatives who understand the needs of each customer.

INDUSTRIAL MARKET An organizational market consisting of firms that buy goods that are either converted into products or used during production.

RESELLER MARKET An organizational market consisting of intermediaries that buy and resell finished goods.

INSTITUTIONAL MARKET An organizational market consisting of such non-governmental buyers of goods and services as hospitals, churches, museums, and charitable organizations.

LO-7 WHAT IS A PRODUCT?

In developing the marketing mix for any product, whether goods or services, marketers must consider what customers really want when they purchase products. Only then can these marketers plan strategies effectively.

The Value Package

Whether it is a physical good, a service, or some combination of the two, customers get value from the various benefits, features, and even intangible rewards associated with a product. **Product features** are the qualities, tangible and intangible, that a company builds into its products. However, as we discussed earlier, to attract buyers, features must also provide benefits.

For example, Gibson Guitars sells more than just the sum of the features for its legendary Les Paul guitars (mahogany headstock and neck, nickel and silver frets, rosewood fingerboard, solid mahogany back and body, and a maple top); it also sells a powerful package that is linked to the very history of rock and roll. Some of the greatest legends of music have used this guitar, including Jimmy Page of Led Zeppelin. Consumers ultimately purchase based on the benefits that are provided by those features. In the case of Gibson's Les Paul guitars, it is not simply the maple top or the fact that the Gibson carefully glues the necks of the guitars onto the main bodies (a more expensive, time-consuming process compared to simply bolting them on, as most other makers do). It is also the results and ultimate benefits that guitar enthusiasts seek; Gibson believes this approach leads to a warmer tone and a more resonant sound. According to Jimmy Vivino, the bandleader of the *Conan* show, "The mahogany-necked Gibson creates a lingering sound, with more 'fur' around the notes. That's the sound I want."[34]

Today's customer regards a product as a bundle of attributes—benefits and features—that, taken together, marketers call the **value package**. Increasingly, buyers expect to receive products with greater value—with more benefits and features at reasonable costs—so firms must compete on the basis of enhanced value packages.

Gibson's Les Paul Guitars have been used by some of the most famous guitarists in rock 'n' roll history. Jimmy Page of Led Zeppelin and Slash from Guns N' Roses are two of the most iconic music figures that have enhanced the legend of this guitar.

MAURITZ ANTIN/EPA/Newscom

PRODUCT FEATURES Tangible and intangible qualities that a company builds into its products.

VALUE PACKAGE A product marketed as a bundle of value-adding attributes, including reasonable cost.

CONVENIENCE GOOD/CONVENIENCE SERVICE An inexpensive good or service purchased and consumed rapidly and regularly.

SHOPPING GOOD/SHOPPING SERVICE A moderately expensive, infrequently purchased good or service.

SPECIALTY GOOD/SPECIALTY SERVICE An expensive, rarely purchased good or service.

PRODUCTION ITEM An industrial product purchased and used directly in the production process that creates other goods or services.

EXPENSE ITEM An industrial product purchased and consumed within a year by firms producing other products.

CAPITAL ITEM An expensive, long-lasting, infrequently purchased industrial product, such as a building, or an industrial service, such as a long-term agreement for data warehousing services.

Classifying Goods and Services

We can classify products according to expected buyers, who fall into two groups: buyers of consumer products and buyers of organizational products. As we saw earlier in this chapter, the consumer and industrial buying processes differ significantly. Similarly, marketing products to consumers is vastly different from marketing products to companies and other organizations.

CLASSIFYING CONSUMER PRODUCTS

Consumer products are commonly divided into three categories that reflect buyer behaviour: **convenience goods and services**, **shopping goods and services**, and **specialty goods and services**. These are outlined in Table 12.2.

CLASSIFYING ORGANIZATIONAL PRODUCTS

Depending on how much they cost and how they will be used, organizational products can be divided into three categories: **production items**, **expense items**, and **capital items**. These are explained in Table 12.3.

>>> TABLE 12.2 Categories of Consumer Products

Category	Description	Examples
Convenience Goods and Services	• Consumed rapidly and regularly • Inexpensive • Purchased often and with little input of time and effort	• Milk • Newspaper • Fast food
Shopping Goods and Services	• Purchased less often • More expensive • Consumers may shop around and compare products based on style, performance, colour, price, and other criteria.	• Television set • Tires • Car insurance
Specialty Goods and Services	• Purchased infrequently • Expensive • Consumer decides on a precise product and will not accept substitutions and spends a good deal of time choosing the "perfect" item.	• Jewellery • Wedding gown • Catering

>>> TABLE 12.3 Categories of Organizational Products

Category	Description	Examples
Production Items	• Goods or services used directly in the production process	• Loads of tea processed into tea bags • Information processing for real-time production
Expense Items	• Goods or services that are consumed within a year by firms producing other goods or supplying other services	• Oil and electricity for machines • Building maintenance • Legal services
Capital Items	• Permanent (expensive and long-lasting) goods and services • Life expectancy of more than a year • Purchased infrequently so transactions often involve decisions by high-level managers	• Buildings (offices, factories) • Fixed equipment (water towers, baking ovens) • Accessory equipment (computers, airplanes)

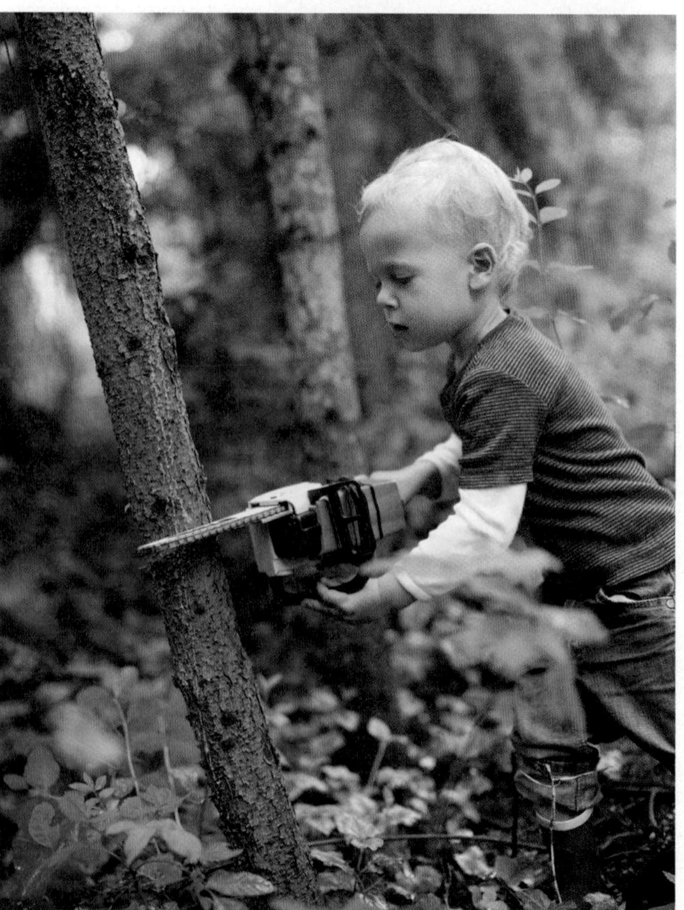

The Product Mix

The group of products that a company makes available for sale, whether consumer, industrial, or both, is its **product mix**. Black & Decker, for example, makes toasters, vacuum cleaners, electric drills, and a variety of other appliances, tools and, more recently (based on the popular Bob the Builder wave), children's toys. 3M makes everything from Post-it Notes to laser optics.

PRODUCT LINES

Many companies begin with a single product. Over time, they find that the initial product fails to suit every customer shopping for the product type. To meet market demand, they introduce similar products—such as flavoured coffees and various roasts—designed to reach more customers. Starbucks stores, for example, expanded their line of coffees by adding various Italian-style espresso beverages, including mochas, cappuccinos, lattes (hot and iced), and flavoured blended cremes. A group of products that are closely related because they function in a

PRODUCT MIX A group of products that a firm makes available for sale.

<<< Black & Decker has a wide range of product categories, but one fairly recent addition has proven to be quite successful. The company now sells branded toy replicas to kids so they can catch the do-it-yourself bug from a young age.

© RGtimeline/Fotolia

similar manner (e.g., flavoured coffees) or are sold to the same customer group (e.g., stop-in coffee drinkers) who will use them in similar ways is a **product line**.

Companies may extend their horizons and identify opportunities outside existing product lines. The result—multiple (or diversified) product lines—is evident at Starbucks. Beyond just serving beverages to customers at coffee bars, Starbucks has lines of home-brewing equipment, supermarket products, music products, and industry services. Multiple product lines allow a company to grow rapidly and can help offset the consequences of slow sales in any one product line.

PRODUCT LINE A group of products that are closely related because they function in a similar manner or are sold to the same customer group who will use them in similar ways.

LO-8 DEVELOPING NEW PRODUCTS AND BRANDING

To expand or diversify product lines—in fact, just to survive—firms must develop and introduce streams of new products. Faced with competition and shifting customer preferences, no firm can count on a single successful product to carry it forever.

The New Product Development Process

For many years, the growing demand for improved health care has stimulated the development of new dietary supplements, heart medicines, and other pharmaceuticals. However, companies that develop and sell these products face a big problem—it costs well over $100 million, sometimes over $1 billion, and can take as long as eight to ten years to get a new product through the official approval process.

Testing, both for government approval and for marketing, can be the most time-consuming stage of development. For example, Merck & Co. is developing an experimental heart drug—called anacetrapib—to raise levels of good cholesterol, thereby reducing the risk of heart attack. Years of laboratory work were followed by a lengthy test study using 1600 patients, and the results of that study must undergo further analysis. Thereafter, a major 30 000-patient study, beginning in 2011, must be completed before the drug may be deemed ready for approval and use sometime after 2015.[35] If successful, Merck could cash in on the growth of the cholesterol-lowering drug market, but it requires an immense amount of time, patience, money, and risk of failure.

Product development is a long and expensive process, and, like Merck & Co., many firms have research and development (R&D) departments for exploring new product possibilities. Why do they devote so many resources to exploring product possibilities, rejecting many seemingly good ideas along the way? First, high mortality rates for new ideas mean that only a few new products reach the market. Second, for many companies, speed to market with a product is as important as care in developing it.

Product Mortality Rates

It is estimated that it takes 50 new product ideas to generate one product that finally reaches the market. Even then, only a few of these survivors become successful products. Many seemingly great ideas have failed as products. Creating a successful new product has become increasingly difficult—even for the most experienced marketers. Why? The number of new products hitting the market each year has increased dramatically; more than 180 000 new household, grocery, and drugstore items are introduced annually. At any given time, however, the average North American supermarket carries a total of only 45 000 different items. Because of lack of space and customer demand, about nine out of ten new products will fail. Those with the best chances are innovative and deliver unique benefits. The single greatest factor in product failure is the lack of significant difference (i.e., the new product is a "me-too" product). Take a look at Figure 12.3 for some recent and some classic examples of spectacular product failures.

SPEED TO MARKET

The more rapidly a product moves from the laboratory to the marketplace, the more likely it is to survive. By introducing new products ahead of competitors, companies establish market leadership. They become popular in the market before being challenged by newer competitors. How important is **speed to market** (or time compression)—that is, a firm's success in responding rapidly to customer demand or market changes? One study reports that a product that is only three months late to market (three months behind the leader) loses 12 percent of its lifetime profit potential. At six months, it will lose 33 percent.

The Seven-Step Development Process

To increase their chances of developing successful new products or services, many firms use a basic seven-step process. Steps 2, 3, 4, 6, and 7 are the same for both products and services, but there are some differences in Steps 1 and 5.

1. *Product ideas.* Product development begins with a search for ideas for new products. Product ideas can come from consumers, the sales force, research and development, or engineering. Procter & Gamble invented hundreds of products including many category firsts: household detergent, fluoride toothpaste (Crest), stackable chips (Pringles), and a time-saving cleaning system (Swiffer). A record of over 130 years of successful innovation is no coincidence. The company has over 1000 PhDs among 8000 employees located in 26 research facilities around the world.[36]
2. *Screening.* This stage is an attempt to eliminate all product ideas that do not mesh with the firm's abilities, expertise, or objectives. Representatives from marketing, engineering, and production must have input at this stage.

SPEED TO MARKET A strategy of introducing new products to respond quickly to customer or market changes.

FIGURE 12.3 Recent and classic product failures

Famous Product and Brand Failures	Reasons for Failure
Qwikster	Is this the biggest product failure since New Coke? When Netflix announced that it was splitting its online streaming and DVD mail service, consumers were outraged. The DVD-by-mail service was going to be called Qwikster, but the outrage over the loss of convenience and increased prices led to the loss of about 800 000 customers. Netflix ultimately reversed the decision and killed the Qwikster brand.
Pepsi Blue	Despite a good marketing campaign linked to hip-hop artists, the X-games, and the March Madness Basketball tournament, Pepsi Blue was a failure. The ultimate test for any product is consumer response; Pepsi's Blue cola did not taste or look right and consumers rejected it.
Toshiba's HD DVD	Consider the battle between Toshiba (HD DVD) and Sony (Blu-ray) for global dominance in the format of high-definition DVDs. Both companies invested millions of dollars, and experts predicted that there would be a long fight between the two companies. But in less than two years, Toshiba gave up and stopped producing its product. Why? Because Sony was successful in convincing movie studios like Warner to release movies only in Blu-ray. Major retail outlets like Walmart and Netflix also announced they would only sell Blu-ray. [4]
New Coke	This example dates back over 30 years but teaches a big lesson in marketing research. At the time, Coke reformulated its century-old flagship brand to deal with the threat of Pepsi. The new beverage tested well in research labs but consumers did not realize that Coke was going to replace its original formula. The new formula was launched, the public was outraged, and the company quickly came back with Coca-Cola Classic.
XFL	Vince McMahon (the founder of WWE wrestling) founded the XFL to compete indirectly with the NFL. There were great gimmicks and exciting camera angles but consumers were not fooled. The league quickly folded because the ultimate product was inferior.

(Top to Bottom) © Terese Loeb Kreuzer/Alamy; Masterfile Corporation; Courtesy of Jaguar Cars Limited; © Islemount Images/Alamy; Kurhan/Fotolia

3. *Concept testing.* Once ideas have been initially reviewed, companies use market research to solicit consumers' input. Firms can identify benefits that the product must provide, as well as an appropriate price level for the product.
4. *Business analysis.* This involves developing a comparison of costs and benefits for the proposed product. Preliminary sales projections are compared with cost projections from finance and production to determine whether the product can meet minimum profitability goals.
5. *Prototype development.* Using input from the concept-testing phase, engineering and/or research and development produce a preliminary version of the product. Prototypes can be extremely expensive, often requiring extensive hand crafting, tooling, and development of components, but this phase can help identify potential production problems.
6. *Product testing and test marketing.* The company begins limited production of the item. If the product meets performance requirements, it is made available for sale in limited areas (test markets). This stage is very costly, since promotional campaigns and distribution channels must be established. Test marketing gives a company its first information on how consumers will respond to a product under real market conditions.
7. *Commercialization.* If test-marketing results are positive, the company will begin full-scale production and marketing of the product. Gradual commercialization, with the firm moving the product into more and more areas over time, reduces stress on the firm's initial production capabilities, but delays in commercialization may give competitors a chance to bring out their own version.

Product Life Cycle

When a product reaches the market, it enters the **product life cycle (PLC)**, a series of stages through which it passes during its commercial life. Depending on the product's ability to attract and keep customers, its PLC may be a matter of months, years, or decades. Strong, mature products (such as Clorox bleach and H&R Block tax preparation) have had long, productive lives.

PRODUCT LIFE CYCLE (PLC) A series of stages in a product's commercial life.

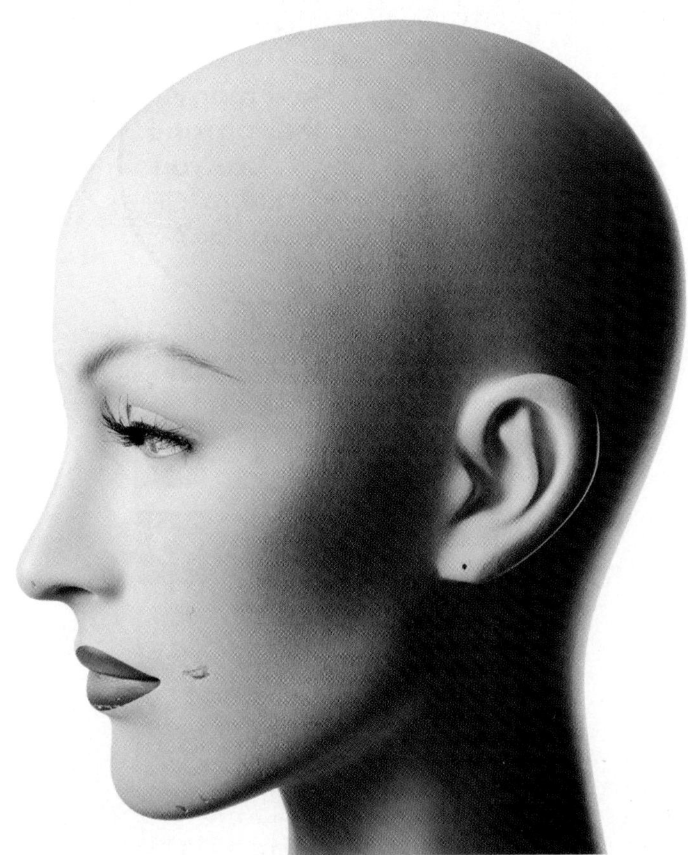

<<< Designers used to create products, such as this head for a human-like toy, by sculpting models out of clay. Now they use "rapid prototyping," a technology that allows several employees to work simultaneously on 3D digital/visual "models" that can be emailed to clients for instant review. It now takes days, or just hours, instead of weeks to make an initial sculpture.

iStockphoto/Thinkstock

STAGES IN THE PLC

The life cycle for both goods and services is a natural process in which products are born, grow in stature, mature, and finally decline and die. Look at the two graphics in Figure 12.4. In Figure 12.4(a), the four phases of the PLC are applied to several products with which you are familiar:

1. *Introduction.* This stage begins when the product reaches the marketplace. Marketers focus on making potential customers aware of the product and its benefits. Because of extensive promotional and development costs, profits are non-existent. But the use of modern media tools like Twitter and YouTube is providing cost-efficient alternatives for companies to generate attention and buzz.
2. *Growth.* If the new product attracts and satisfies enough consumers, sales begin to climb rapidly. During this stage, the product begins to show a profit. Other firms in the industry move speedily to introduce their own versions. Heavy promotion is often required to build brand preference over the competition.
3. *Maturity.* Sales growth starts to slow. Although the product earns its highest profit level early in this stage, increased competition eventually forces price-cutting, increasing advertising and promotional expenditures, and lower profits. Toward the end of the stage, sales start to fall.
4. *Decline.* Sales and profits continue to fall, as new products in the introduction stage take away sales. Firms end or reduce promotional support (ads and salespeople), but may let the product linger to provide some profits.

Figure 12.4(b) plots the relationship of the PLC to a product's typical profits or losses. Although the early stages of the PLC often show financial losses, increased sales for successful products recover earlier losses and continue to generate profits until the decline stage. For many products, profitable life spans are short—thus, the importance placed by so many firms on the constant replenishment of product lines.

EXTENDING PRODUCT LIFE: AN ALTERNATIVE TO NEW PRODUCTS

Companies try to keep products in the maturity stage as long as they can. Sales of TV sets, for example, have been revitalized by such feature

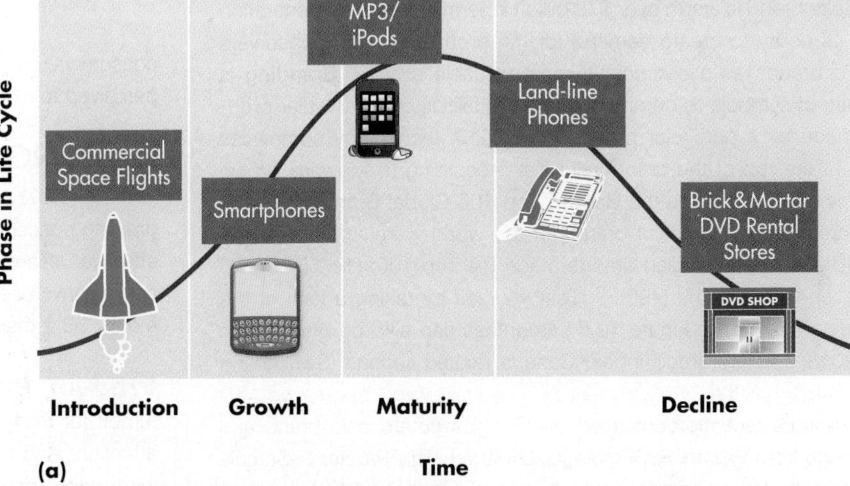

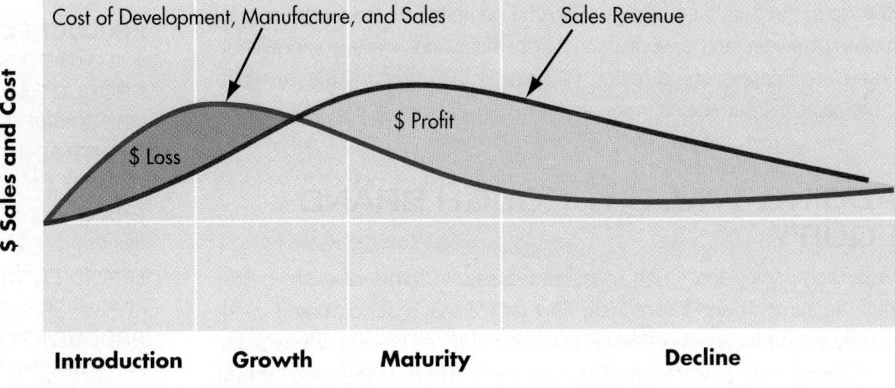

>>> FIGURE 12.4 Products in the life cycle: (a) Phases and (b) Profit (or loss)

changes as colour, portability, miniaturization, stereo capability, high definition, and 3D. Companies can extend product life through a number of creative means. Foreign markets offer three possibilities for lengthening product life cycles:

1. In **product extension**, an existing product is marketed globally; Coca-Cola is a prime example of international product extensions.
2. With **product adaptation**, the product is modified for greater appeal in different countries. In Germany, a McDonald's meal includes beer; in Japan, Ford puts the steering wheel on the right side. After Kraft Foods changed the shape of the traditional round Oreo Cookie to be long and thin (and coated the cookie in chocolate), it became the bestselling cookie in China. The new shape is also sold in Canada.[37]
3. **Reintroduction** means reviving, for new markets, products that are becoming obsolete in older ones. NCR has reintroduced manually operated cash registers in Latin America.

Identifying Products

Marketers must also identify products so that consumers recognize them. Two important tools for this task are branding and packaging.

BRANDING PRODUCTS

Coca-Cola is the best-known brand in the world. Some Coke executives claim that if all the company's other assets were obliterated, they could go to the bank and borrow $100 billion on the strength of the brand name alone. Indeed, Interbrand, the brand-ranking firm, says the Coke brand is worth over $70 billion in terms of revenue generation from its ability to create demand for the product. Industry observers regard brands as a company's most valuable asset.[38] **Branding** is the use of symbols to communicate the qualities of a particular product made by a particular producer. In 2013, technology companies were at the top of the brand value list. According to Millward Brown Optimor, which creates the BrandZ Top 100 Global Brands Ranking, the three most successful brands in the world were Apple, Google, and IBM. Three Canadian brands made the Top 100: RBC (#39), TD (#46), and Scotiabank (#96).[39] (Test yourself by taking a look at the branding exercise in Figure 12.5.) Countries can also be branded. In the 2013 Country Brand Index, Canada ranked second (Switzerland was first).[40]

Kellogg's recently purchased the Pringles potato chip brand and its assets from Procter & Gamble for US$2.7 billion. Procter & Gamble is turning its focus to household goods and beauty and personal care products; Pringles was the last remaining asset in its food business. For Kellogg's, the purchase helps solidify the company as the fourth-largest maker of sweet and savoury snacks in the world. Having a powerful brand like Pringles on its roster will help as the company tries to gain more sales in international markets.[41]

ADDING VALUE THROUGH BRAND EQUITY

Many companies that once measured assets in terms of cash, buildings, equipment, and inventories, now realize that a strong brand is an equally important asset. Widely known and admired brands are valuable because of their power to attract customers. Those with higher **brand equity** generate greater brand awareness and loyalty on the part of consumers, have larger market shares than competing brands, and are perceived to have greater quality.

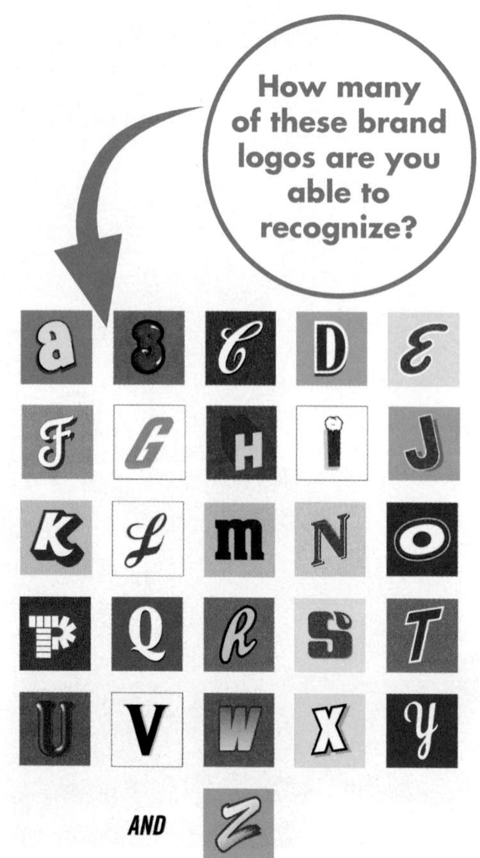

How many of these brand logos are you able to recognize?
AND

FIGURE 12.5 Branding exercise: Name that logo

GAINING BRAND AWARENESS

The expensive, sometimes fierce, struggle for brand recognition is a growing concern in most industries. Today, marketers are finding more effective, less expensive ways to gain brand awareness. Recent successes have been found with several methods, including product placements, buzz marketing, and viral marketing and social networking.

Product Placements Television commercials can be a real turnoff for many viewers, but entertainment programming gets our full attention. And that's when marketers are turning up the promotional juice with **product placement**—a promotional tactic for brand

PRODUCT EXTENSION The process of marketing an existing, unmodified product globally.

PRODUCT ADAPTATION The process of modifying a product to have greater appeal in foreign markets.

REINTRODUCTION The process of reviving, for new markets, products that are obsolete in older ones.

BRANDING A process of using symbols to communicate the qualities of a product made by a particular producer.

BRAND EQUITY The added value a brand name provides to a product beyond its basic functional benefits.

PRODUCT PLACEMENT A promotional tactic for brand exposure in which characters in television, film, music, magazines, or video games use a real product with its brand visible to viewers.

<<< Canada Goose has benefited from various product placements in movies and magazines. Kate Upton wore a Canada Goose jacket on the cover of the 2013 *Sports Illustrated* Swimsuit Edition.

Chen Chao/Dorling Kindersley Limited

exposure in which characters in television, film, music, magazines, or video games use a real product with a brand visible to viewers. In 2013, Canada Goose was thrilled to be front and centre in the *Sports Illustrated* Swimsuit edition as model Kate Upton posed in one of their jackets for a shoot in Antarctica.[42]

Product placements are effective because the message is delivered in an attractive setting that holds the customer's interest. When used in successful films and TV shows, the brand's association with famous performers is an implied celebrity endorsement. The idea is to legitimize the brand in the mind of the customer. In all, nearly $5 billion is spent annually on product placements, especially in television, and major marketers are putting more into product placements instead of television advertisements. Television placements are widespread, including Hyundai in *Leverage* and *Burn Notice*, and are especially effective as digital video recorders (DVRs) become more popular. Viewers can use their DVRs to skip commercials in recorded shows, but product placements are unavoidable.

Buzz Marketing One method for increasing brand awareness is **buzz marketing**, which relies on word-of-mouth to spread "buzz" about a particular product or idea. Buzz marketing agencies provide volunteer participants with new products to try and ask them to share the buzz with their friends, family, co-workers, and others in their social network. Here's the key—most companies running word-of-mouth campaigns require full disclosure, which means the participants should let people know they are participating in a campaign. This is essential so that those on the receiving end of the "buzz" don't feel tricked or taken advantage of.

Viral Marketing and Social Networking **Viral marketing** is buzz that relies on social networking on the internet to spread information like a "virus" from person to person. Messages about new cars, sports events, and numerous other goods and services flow via networks among potential customers who pass the information on to others. Using various social network formats—games, contests, chat rooms, blogs, and bulletin boards—marketers encourage potential customers to try out products and tell other people about them. Marketers—including such giants as eBay—are increasingly using **corporate blogs** for public relations, branding, and otherwise spreading messages that stimulate chat about products to target markets.[43] Most major consumer companies now have their own Facebook page.

How effective can it be? Viral marketing can lead to consumer awareness faster and with wider reach than traditional media messages—and at a lower cost. It works for two reasons. First, people rely on the internet for information that they used to get from newspapers, magazines, and television. Equally important, however, is the interactive element: The customer becomes a participant in the process of spreading the word by forwarding information to other internet users.

Types of Brand Names

National brands are those that are produced and distributed by the manufacturer across an entire country (e.g., Chips Ahoy). When a company with a well-known brand sells another company the right to place that brand on its products, these are called **licensed brands**. Harley-Davidson's famous logo—emblazoned on boots, eyewear, gloves, purses, lighters, and watches—brings the motorcycle maker more than $210 million annually. Along with brands such as Coors and Ferrari, licensing for character-based brands like Spider-Man is equally lucrative.

Private brands carry the retailer's own brand name, even though they are manufactured by another firm. Sears has two well-known private brands—Craftsman tools and Kenmore appliances. Loblaw Companies Ltd. created a line of upscale products under the private brand President's Choice (PC). If you want Loblaws' famous PC Decadent

BUZZ MARKETING Marketing that relies on word-of-mouth to spread "buzz" about a particular product or idea.

VIRAL MARKETING Buzz that relies on social networking on the internet to spread information like a "virus" from person to person.

CORPORATE BLOG Blogs run by major corporations for public relations, branding, and otherwise spreading messages that stimulate chat about products to target markets.

NATIONAL BRANDS Products distributed by and carrying a name associated with the manufacturer.

LICENSED BRANDS Selling the limited rights, to another company, to use a brand name on a product.

PRIVATE BRANDS Products promoted by and carrying a name associated with the retailer or wholesaler, not the manufacturer.

<<< Loblaws' PC Decadent Chocolate Chip Cookies have built a reputation that all private-label brands strive for. Consumers that love these cookies must go to Loblaws, or one of their subsidiaries, to buy them.

Library of Congress (Photoduplication)

chocolate chip cookies, you need to visit a Loblaws outlet or one of its subsidiaries. Shoppers Drug Mart has tried to copy the success of President's Choice with its private label brands: Life for a wide range of products and Quo for cosmetics.[44] In fact, Shoppers Drug Mart has set a goal to increase its private-label shelf space to 25 percent of overall product offerings. These brands are often 25 percent cheaper for consumers and yet the profit margins tend to be 15 percent higher for the company. This is a clear win-win scenario.[45] Private brands account for 19 percent of the overall market and $10.9 billion in the grocery market.[46]

Generic brands are also gaining more shelf space; they are the products that you see in grocery stores that simply state a category name like "bacon" or "peanut butter." If you've been to Costco recently, you may have picked up its very popular generic chocolate chip cookies. Major retailers are carrying fewer national brands and more of their own private brands as well as these less-expensive, no-frills generic brands.

Global Branding Issues

How do you take a successful domestic brand and launch it internationally? For many companies with Canadian origins, it seems as though an infusion of cash or support from larger American or European companies is step number one. Brands like MAC, Club Monaco, and La Senza have all established a strong presence abroad after building a name as domestic Canadian brands. In these three cases, the road to stronger global presence began with takeovers by Estée Lauder, Ralph Lauren, and Limited Brands for the respective companies. As you read in Chapter 5, Tim Hortons is having a hard time selecting the right brand image as it expands further into the United States. The large, spread-out Canadian market landscape, combined with the relatively small population, makes it more difficult to gain the monetary resources to expand without support. However, there are success stories like Montreal-based Aldo group, which has stores in over 60 countries.[47]

Firms that sell products internationally also face another branding strategy issue. They must consider how product names will translate in various languages. Chevrolet learned this lesson decades ago when it entered the Latin American market with the Nova. This name was not well received simply because "no va" translates into "it does not go."[48] More recently, the Buick Lacrosse has been catching attention in Quebec for the wrong reasons: In French slang, *lacrosse* is a term for pleasuring yourself. What's even more surprising is that GM was aware of this unfortunate naming issue and originally released the car back in 2005 as the Buick Allure. But in an effort to cut down marketing costs, it ignored the potential embarrassment and decided to eventually launch the Lacrosse.[49]

Packaging Products

Except for products like fresh fruits and vegetables and structural steel, almost all products need some form of **packaging** so they can be transported to the market. Packaging also serves several other functions—it is an in-store advertisement that makes the product attractive; it clearly displays the brand; it identifies product features and benefits; and it reduces the risk of damage, breakage, or spoilage. The package is the marketer's last chance to say "buy me" to the consumer. Maison Orphee, a Quebec City–based maker of oils, mustards, sea salts, and vinegars, took the advice of consultants and redesigned their packaging with slimmer bottles and a high-end label design. The result was a 70 percent increase in sales without a dime spent on traditional advertising.[50] Packaging counts!

Companies are also paying close attention to consumer concerns about packaging. Beyond concerns about product tampering, packaging must be tight enough to withstand shipping, but not so tight that it frustrates consumers when they try to open the package. Nestlé—which spends more than $6 billion annually on packaging—spent nine months coming up with a new, easier-to-open lid and an easier-to-grip container for its Country Creamery ice cream. In general, companies have found that packaging costs can be as high as 15 percent of the total cost to make a product, and features like zip-lock tops can add 20 percent to the price that is charged.[51]

Labelling Products

Every product has a **label** on its package. Like packaging, labelling can help market the product. First, it identifies the product or the brand, such as the name "Campbell" on a can of soup or "Chiquita" on a banana. Labels also promote products by getting consumers' attention. Attractive colours and graphics provide visual cues to products that otherwise might be overlooked on the shelf. Finally, the label describes the product by providing information about nutritional content, directions for use, proper disposal, and safety.

GENERIC BRANDS No-frills products sold under the general category name rather than a specific company name.

PACKAGING Physical container in which a product is sold, advertised, or protected.

LABEL That part of a product's packaging that identifies the product's name and contents and sometimes its benefits.

The federal government regulates the information on package labels. The **Consumer Packaging and Labelling Act** has two main purposes: first, to provide a comprehensive set of rules for packaging and labelling of consumer products, and second to ensure that manufacturers provide full and factual information on labels. All pre-packaged products must state in French and English the quantity enclosed in metric units, as well as the name and description of the product.

Sellers are very sensitive to what is on the label of the products they sell. However, consumers can also be very sensitive and loyal to the visual presentation of a brand. A few years ago, Tropicana learned that consumers were fond of the company's classic logo with the orange and straw as the centrepiece. When the company tried to replace it with a new design, consumers responded with emails, letters, and complaints. PepsiCo, which owns Tropicana, immediately reversed the decision.[52]

CONSUMER PACKAGING AND LABELLING ACT A federal law that provides comprehensive rules for the packaging and labelling of consumer products.

MyBizLab — Visit the MyBizLab website. This online homework and tutorial system puts you in control of your own learning with study and practice tools directly correlated to this chapter's content.

SUMMARY OF LEARNING OBJECTIVES

LO-1 EXPLAIN THE CONCEPT OF *MARKETING* AND IDENTIFY THE FIVE FORCES THAT CONSTITUTE THE *EXTERNAL MARKETING ENVIRONMENT*.

Marketing is responsible for creating, communicating, and delivering value and satisfaction to customers at a profit. Marketing manages customer relationships to benefit the organization and its stakeholders. After identifying customers' needs and wants, it develops plans to satisfy them by creating products, and establishing their prices, methods for distributing them, and ways of promoting them to potential customers. Marketing is successful if satisfied buyers perceive that the benefits derived from each purchase outweigh its costs, and if the firm, in exchange for providing the products, meets its organizational goals. Five outside factors comprise a company's external environment and influence its marketing programs: (1) political and legal actions, (2) socio-cultural factors, (3) technological changes, (4) economics, and (5) competition.

LO-2 EXPLAIN THE PURPOSE OF A *MARKETING PLAN* AND IDENTIFY THE FOUR COMPONENTS OF THE *MARKETING MIX*.

The marketing plan is a detailed strategy for focusing marketing efforts on meeting consumer needs and wants. The plan defines the organization's marketing goals, and identifies all the activities for reaching those goals that will result in the successful transfer of goods and services to its customers. In planning and implementing strategies, marketing managers focus on the four elements (Four Ps) of the marketing mix: (1) products for consumers, (2) pricing of products, (3) place (distribution) of products to consumers, and (4) promotion of products.

LO-3 EXPLAIN *MARKET SEGMENTATION* AND HOW IT IS USED IN *TARGET MARKETING* AND *POSITIONING*.

Marketers think in terms of target markets—groups of people or organizations with similar wants and needs and who can be expected to show interest in the same products. Target marketing requires market segmentation—dividing a market into categories of customer types or "segments." Members of a market segment must share some common traits that influence purchasing decisions. Once they identify segments, companies adopt a variety of strategies for attracting customers in one or more of the chosen target segments. The following are five variables used for segmentation: (1) Geographic variables are the geographical units that may be considered in developing a segmentation strategy. (2) Demographic variables describe populations by identifying such traits as age, income, gender, ethnic background, and marital status. (3) Geo-demographic variables combine demographic variables with geographic variables, such as an age category coupled with urban areas. (4) Psychographic variables include lifestyles, interests, and attitudes. (5) Behavioural variables include benefit sought, user status, usage rate, loyalty status, and occasion for use.

LO-4 EXPLAIN THE PURPOSE AND VALUE OF *MARKETING RESEARCH.*

Market research is the study of what buyers need and the best ways to meet those needs. This process involves (1) studying the current situation, (2) selecting a research method, (3) collecting and analyzing data, and (4) preparing the report. The four most common research methods are observation, surveys, focus groups, and experimentation.

LO-5 DESCRIBE THE KEY FACTORS THAT INFLUENCE THE *CONSUMER BUYING PROCESS.*

One consumer behaviour model considers five influences that lead to consumption: (1) Problem/need recognition: The buying process begins when the consumer recognizes a problem or need. (2) Information seeking: Having recognized a need, consumers seek information. The information search leads to a consideration set—a group of products they will consider buying. (3) Evaluation of alternatives: By analyzing product attributes (price, prestige, quality) of the consideration set, consumers compare products to decide which product best meets their needs. (4) Purchase decision: "Buy" decisions are based on rational motives, emotional motives, or both. (5) Post-purchase evaluations: Consumers continue to form opinions after their purchase. Marketers want consumers to be happy after the consumption of products so that they are more likely to buy them again.

LO-6 DISCUSS THE THREE CATEGORIES OF *ORGANIZATIONAL MARKETS.*

(1) The industrial market consists of businesses that buy goods to be converted into other products or that are used during production. This market includes farmers, manufacturers, and some retailers. (2) Before products reach consumers, they pass through a reseller market consisting of intermediaries—wholesalers and retailers—that buy finished goods and resell them. (3) The government and institutional market includes federal, state, and local governments, and non-governmental buyers—hospitals, churches, and charities—that purchase goods and services needed for serving their clients. Taken together, these organizational markets do more than two times the business annually than the consumer markets.

LO-7 EXPLAIN THE DEFINITION OF A PRODUCT AS A *VALUE PACKAGE* AND CLASSIFY *GOODS AND SERVICES.*

Customers buy products to receive value that satisfies a want or a need. Thus, a successful product is a value package—a bundle of attributes that, taken together, provides the right features and offers the right benefits that satisfy customers' wants and needs. Features are the qualities, tangible and intangible, that are included with the product. To be satisfying, features must provide benefits that allow customers to achieve the end results they want. The value package has services and features that add value by providing benefits that increase the customer's satisfaction.

Products (both goods and services) can be classified according to expected buyers as either consumer products or organizational products. Convenience products are inexpensive consumer goods and services that are consumed rapidly and regularly. Shopping products are more expensive and are purchased less often than convenience products. Specialty products are extremely important and expensive goods and services. Organizational products are classified as either production items, expense items, or capital items. Production items are goods and services used directly in the production process. Expense items are goods or services consumed within a year to produce other products. Capital items are expensive and long-lasting goods and services that have expected lives of several years.

LO-8 DESCRIBE THE KEY CONSIDERATIONS IN THE *NEW PRODUCT DEVELOPMENT PROCESS,* AND EXPLAIN THE IMPORTANCE OF *BRANDING AND PACKAGING.*

To expand or diversify product lines, new products must be developed and introduced. Many firms have research and development (R&D) departments for continuously exploring new product possibilities, because high mortality rates for new ideas result in only a few new products reaching the market. Even then, only a few of these survivors become successful products. Speed to market—how fast a firm responds with new products or market changes—determines a product's profitability and success. A continuous product development process is necessary because every product has a product life cycle—a series of stages through which it passes during its commercial life. The development of new products, then, is the source for renewal of the firm's product offerings in the marketplace.

Branding and packaging identify products so that consumers recognize them. Branding is the use of names and symbols, like Coca-Cola or McDonald's golden arches, to communicate the qualities of a particular product made by a particular producer. The goal in developing a brand is to distinguish a product from others so that consumers develop a preference for that particular brand name. Most products need some form of packaging—a physical container in which it is sold, advertised, or protected. A package makes the product attractive, displays the brand name, and identifies features and benefits. It also reduces the risk of damage, breakage, or spoilage, and it lessens the likelihood of theft.

QUESTIONS AND EXERCISES

QUESTIONS FOR ANALYSIS

See >>> for **Assisted-Graded Writing Assignment** in **MyBizLab**

1. What does *brand equity* mean and how do companies like Apple take advantage of their strong brand equity?
2. Select a good or service that you have purchased recently. Try to retrace the relevant steps in the buyer decision process as you experienced it. Which steps were most important to you?
3. What are the various classifications of consumer and industrial products? Give an example of a good and a service for each category other than those discussed in the text.
4. How is the concept of the value package useful in marketing to consumers and industrial customers?
5. Why has the in-store use of hidden cameras become so popular? Is this "video mining" ethical? If not, how could it be made more acceptable?
6. Consider a service product, such as transportation, entertainment, or health care. What are some ways that more customer value might be added to this product? Why would your improvements add value for the buyer?

APPLICATION EXERCISES

7. Identify a company with a product that interests you. Consider ways the company could use customer relationship management (CRM) to strengthen relationships with its target market. Specifically, explain your recommendations on how the company can use each of the four basic components of the marketing mix in its CRM efforts.
8. >>> Select a product made by a foreign company and sold in Canada. What is the product's target market? What is the basis on which the target market is segmented? Do you think that this basis is appropriate? How might another approach, if any, be beneficial? Why?
9. Choose a product that could benefit from word-of-mouth buzz marketing. Then create a marketing campaign kit for participants to spread the word about this product.
10. Interview the manager of a local manufacturing firm. Identify the company's different products according to their positions in the product life cycle.

TEAM EXERCISES

BUILDING YOUR BUSINESS SKILLS

DEALING WITH VARIABLES

GOAL

To encourage students to analyze the ways in which various market segmentation variables affect business success.

SITUATION

You and four partners are thinking of purchasing a heating and air conditioning (H/AC) dealership that specializes in residential applications priced between $2000 and $40 000. You are now in the process of deciding where that dealership should be. You are considering four locations: Miami, Florida; Toronto, Ontario; Vancouver, British Columbia; and Dallas, Texas.

METHOD

Step 1 Working with four classmates (your partnership group), conduct library research to learn how H/AC makers market their residential products. Check for articles in the *Globe and Mail*, *Canadian Business*, the *Wall Street Journal*, and other business publications.

Step 2 Continue your research. This time, focus on the specific marketing variables that define each prospective location. Check Statistics Canada data at your library and on the internet and contact local chambers of commerce (by phone and via the internet) to learn about the following factors for each location:

- Geography
- Demography (especially age, income, gender, family status, and social class)
- Psychographic variables (lifestyles, interests, and attitudes)

Step 3 Meet with group members to analyze which location holds the greatest promise as a dealership site. Base your decision on your analysis of market segment variables and their effect on H/AC sales.

FOLLOW-UP QUESTIONS

1. Which location did you choose? Describe the market segmentation factors that influenced your decision.
2. Identify the two variables you believe will have the greatest impact on the dealership's success. Why are these factors so important?
3. Which factors were least important in your decision? Why?
4. When equipment manufacturers advertise residential H/AC products, they often show them in different climate situations (in winter, summer, or high-humidity conditions). Which market segments are these ads targeting? Describe these segments in terms of demographic and psychographic characteristics.

EXERCISING YOUR ETHICS

DRIVING A LEGITIMATE BARGAIN

THE SITUATION

A firm's marketing methods are sometimes at odds with the consumer's buying process. This exercise illustrates how ethical issues can become entwined with personal selling activities, product pricing, and customer relations.

THE DILEMMA

In buying his first new car, Matt visited showrooms and websites for every make of SUV truck. After weeks of reading and test-driving, he settled on a well-known Japanese-made vehicle with a manufacturer's suggested retail price of $37 500 for the 2013 model. The price included accessories and options that Matt considered essential. Because he planned to own the car for at least five years, he was willing to wait for just the right package rather than accept a lesser-equipped car already on the lot. Negotiations with Gary, the sales representative, continued for two weeks. Finally, a sales contract was signed for $33 600, with delivery due no more than two or three months later, if the vehicle had to be special-ordered from the factory, and earlier if Gary found the exact car when he searched other dealers around the country. On April 30, to close the deal, Matt had to write a check for $1000.

Matt received a call on June 14 from Angela, Gary's sales manager. "We cannot get your car before October," she reported, "so it will have to be a 2014 model. You will have to pay the 2014 price." Matt replied that the agreement called for a stated price and delivery deadline for 2013, pointing out that money had exchanged hands for the contract. When asked what the 2014 price would be, Angela responded that it had not yet been announced. Angrily, Matt replied that he would be foolish to agree now on some unknown future price. Moreover, he didn't like the way the dealership was treating him. He told Angela to send him back everything he had signed; the deal was off.

TEAM ACTIVITY

Assemble a group of four students and assign each group member to one of the following roles:

- The salesperson
- The manager of the dealership
- Matt (the customer)
- A representative from the Automobile Protection Agency (consumer rights group)

ACTION STEPS

1. Before hearing any of your group's comments on this situation and from the perspective of your assigned role, what do you recommend to resolve this situation? Provide a detailed explanation of your position.
2. Gather your group together and reveal, in turn, each member's recommendation.
3. Appoint someone to record main points of agreement and disagreement within the group. How do you explain the results? What accounts for any disagreement?
4. Given the factors involved in the consumer buying process, how would you characterize the particular ethical issues in this situation?
5. From an ethical standpoint, what are the obligations of the sales representative and the manager regarding the pricing of the product in this situation?
6. If you were responsible for maintaining good customer relations at the dealership, how would you handle this matter?

BUSINESS CASE

LULULEMON: PROVEN MODEL, NEW TARGETS, AND EMERGING THREATS

Lululemon is a Canadian retail success story built on a clear vision and well-defined products aimed at a specific target market (the yoga set). In 2013, revenues were quite healthy, estimated between $1.616 and $1.64 billion. However, there was a change coming. Lululemon's success was being copied and their price undercut by companies like Gap (with its new Athleta brand). At the same time, lululemon was looking at a major international expansion, while simultaneously considering a fairly radical move: actively targeting men with a female-dominated brand. Before we look at the present day issues facing lululemon, let's take a look at the reasons behind the lululemon success story.

Jochen Tack/Alamy

HOW THE MODEL WAS BUILT

Chip Wilson founded lululemon after taking a rejuvenating yoga class in 1998. After two decades in the ski, snowboard, and skate business, he made an abrupt change and built this yoga-inspired athletic gear retailer. The first outlet opened in Vancouver's Kitsilano area in 2000. By 2013, lululemon had 211 stores in Canada, the United States, Australia, Germany, the Netherlands, New Zealand, Singapore, the U.K., and China. Lululemon had transformed people's buying behaviour while creating a lifestyle community; the strength of the brand was based on its mission to provide quality, design, innovation, and unique positioning.

Lululemon strives to be more than just a retailer. According to the company, the intent is to elevate the world from mediocrity to greatness. Strong words for a clothing retailer. Its mission is to create components for people to live longer, healthier, and more fun lives. To further distinguish itself, lululemon developed a mantra, a manifesto, ambassadors, and a community hub to get the message out. Their values are a major stretch (no pun intended) from the tainted corporate image that defines so many firms these days.

From day one, Chip Wilson set out to provide superior products for his target consumer. It was clear to Chip that traditional sweatpants were totally unfit for yoga, and an opportunity was identified. But he needed to educate consumers and offer better alternatives than the pure cotton clothing most people were wearing in yoga studios. His previous experience in developing technical athletic fabrics led to the creation of a design studio that moonlighted as a yoga studio in the evenings. Experts were consulted, yoga instructors were given clothing and enlisted as product testers, and the efforts paid off. Lululemon created a fabric called "luon," which is moisture wicking and preshrunk, has improved stretching ability, and maintains its shape. Today, lululemon makes products from Luxtreme, Coolmax, Silverscent, and Beechlu (to name a few); these fabrics are lighter weight and antibacterial.

Lululemon offers important services to supplement its goods and build its community. Every outlet offers weekly complimentary yoga classes. In addition, they offer running clinics, boot camps, and Pilates courses. Lululemon still consults yogis and elite athletes; a continuous improvement approach is the foundation of its product development cycle. Even the brand name was developed in this manner. Before the original launch, it surveyed 100 individuals to select the name and logo from a list of 20 options. Clearly, lululemon is a firm by the people, for the people.

In terms of place or distribution, over 211 retail outlets are being supplemented by showrooms, non-permanent, leased spaces that aim to test new market locations and create buzz. In 2009, the successful launch of lululemon's e-commerce site was another major step in improving distribution. At the same time, the expansion of its wholesale business, to more yoga studios and gyms, helped create stronger ties and increased selling avenues. Lululemon was also investing in its supply chain to ensure that popular products were kept in stock.

Lululemon uses virtually no traditional advertising, with the exception of strategically placed ads in highly targeted magazines like *Yoga Journal*. According to the CEO, a single email notification to clients about a new product can generate more than $6000 of sales. It has an ambassador program designed for loyal devotees who embody the lifestyle. You can go to the website and read about or get in touch with hundreds of ambassadors. In addition, there are approximately 60 "elite" ambassadors like Olympians Clara Hughes, Jennifer Heil, and Thomas Grandi. There are plenty of other ways to communicate with a yogi or fellow devotees; the website creates synergy with all modern communication tools, including basic blogging and the ever-popular social media sites Twitter, Facebook, and Flickr.

High-end quality is usually accompanied by high-end prices. Lululemon's products are expensive and the company is unapologetic; the focus is on value, not price. Having a strategy is one thing, but sticking to it is something else. Many organizations overreact to current market circumstances and forget who they are. In the face of the most recent recession and price pressure from competitors, lululemon stood firm. Prices were kept high.

COPYCAT THREATS, DEFECTS, AND NEW TARGET MARKETS

Great success leads to copycats. Gap Inc. bought Athleta, a small online retailer, and is using this brand to stalk lululemon by strategically opening locations near existing lululemon locations and undercutting them on price. Gap Inc. plans to have 50 Athleta outlets open across North America by the end of 2013. Nike is also said to be very interested in capturing some of this yoga-inspired success. Clearly these companies are capable of knocking off the product, but can they match the lulu community? Early signs suggest that they will try to copy the whole model. For example, the Athleta site talks about how to stay "Chi" and the company offers "Zen Webinars."

In the middle of defending itself against the copycats, lululemon was in the headlines for all the wrong reasons. A brand that charges premium prices for products must deliver premium quality. So in 2013, it was a scandal when the company announced a recall of 17 percent of its "luon" pants. Apparently, there was an error in manufacturing for a large batch of pants that made them too sheer (see-through). This was quite the embarrassment considering their pants are the company's core product. Lululemon estimated short-term losses at $57–67 million, but the damage to its reputation as a premium product producer was much greater.

With all of these challenges and with investors demanding a continuation of the growth model, lululemon has set yet another ambitious goal: to target and capture a greater share of the male market (by focusing on the CrossFit training craze). The goal is to go from 8 percent of sales to men to 20 percent within a few years. But the question remains, will men be attracted (in large numbers) to a brand that has defined itself largely with a female identity? What will the core customer think of this new lulu message?

Lululemon embodies and displays the confidence that it tries to instill in its members. It will be interesting to see how it addresses these new threats and implement new strategies and tactics over the next decade.

QUESTIONS FOR DISCUSSION

1. What is the relative emphasis placed on each of the 4 Ps of marketing at lululemon?
2. What is the basis for the market segmentation used at lululemon?
3. What factors in the marketing environment have the most impact on lululemon?
4. Do you believe that lululemon's push to lure more male consumers is wise, or do you believe the company should focus on its traditional image?

CHAPTER 13

Pricing, Promoting, *and* Distributing Products

AFTER READING THIS CHAPTER, YOU SHOULD BE ABLE TO:

LO-1 Identify the various *pricing objectives* that govern pricing decisions, and describe the *price-setting tools* used in making these decisions

LO-2 Discuss *pricing strategies* that can be used for different competitive situations and identify the *pricing tactics* that can be used for setting prices.

LO-3 Identify the important *objectives of promotion* and discuss the considerations in selecting a *promotional mix*.

LO-4 Define the *role of advertising* and describe the key *advertising media*.

LO-5 Outline the tasks involved in *personal selling*, describe the various types of *sales promotions*, and distinguish between *publicity* and *public relations*.

LO-6 Explain the *distribution mix* and identify the different *channels of distribution*.

LO-7 Describe the role of *intermediaries*. Explain the functions of *wholesalers* and identify the types of *retailers* and *e-intermediaries*.

LO-8 Describe the *physical distribution process*.

Promoting a Successful Yogurt Craze

In recent years, there have been many product introductions in the yogurt aisles, with each one promising a unique benefit or ingredient to capture market share. However, in this competitive industry it is hard to make a real dent. With food costs rising and consumers watching their wallets, there has been a noticeable trend—prices have increased or, alternatively, package sizes have been reduced and prices have been maintained (which essentially means that prices have been increased in a more creative manner). It seems like every year the packages get smaller and smaller and smaller. If you had collected large yogurt containers to see what you could buy for approximately $3.99 in each of the past 10 years, you would likely have the yogurt equivalent of the classic wooden Russian Matryoshka dolls—in other words, you could probably fit the successive new containers into the old containers based on the year manufactured.

Old Product, New Market

In the fight for yogurt supremacy, something interesting has been occurring and it is not exactly a new product that is leading the way (unless you believe that products that have been around for centuries are new). What's old is now new in Canadian yogurt aisles, and leading the revolution is the Greek yogurt category. According to Nielsen, Greek yogurt accounted for about 6 percent of the Canadian market, by volume, at the beginning of 2013. This represents significant traction. For example, in its first year, the President's

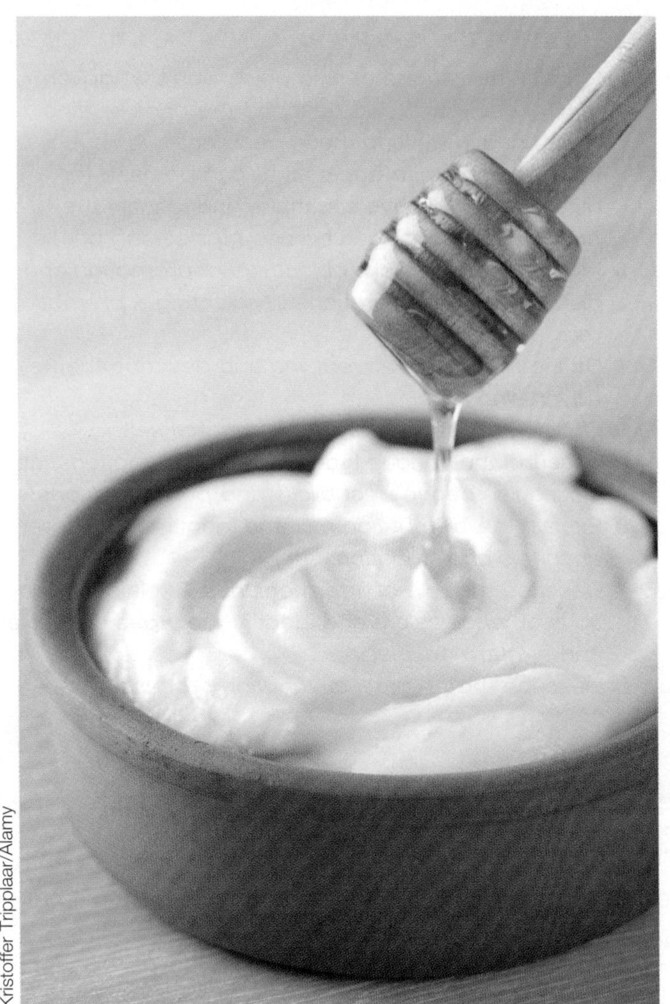
Kristoffer Tripplaar/Alamy

Choice Greek brand has become the number-one-selling yogurt at Loblaws. To truly appreciate the potential for growth, we need to look south of the border, where the Greek yogurt craze started two years earlier than in Canada and achieved a 13 percent market share in just three years (it took energy drinks twice as long to get an equivalent share of the beverage market). According to Consumer Edge Research, Greek yogurt could actually capture as much as half of the U.S. market, which is expected to be worth $9 billion by 2015 (Euromonitor). These numbers are all impressive, and what is even more spectacular is that this product is usually sold in smaller packages for significantly higher prices than regular yogurt. With all of this potential, it seems like everyone is trying to take advantage of the trend. Even Ben & Jerry's has created a frozen Greek yogurt.

Product Fundamentals

The success of this sub-category is based on some very solid fundamentals. The product fits in with the increased trend toward healthy living and eating habits. People are willing to pay more for good, healthy products, and, in this case, the creamier taste is not created by artificial flavours or unhealthy ingredients. Rather, Greek yogurt is unique because it is strained using a cheesecloth filter to remove the liquid. That is why it is thicker and has a different texture that consumers seem to appreciate.

Creative Marketing, Building Buzz

Like any great launch, the marketing has been a key ingredient to the product's success. In Canada, the President's Choice brand was supported by a significant marketing campaign. Liberté brand launched with an emphasis on health and conducted sampling events and taste tests in gyms and other health-related venues. Down south, Chobani is the market leader ahead of Fage (an authentic imported Greek brand). Chobani spread the word using a roving truck it called the "Chomobile," which travelled around promoting the health benefits of its yogurt and supplying product samples.

These grassroots approaches built the initial buzz, but it is clear that the stakes are rising along with the popularity. Danone (the French multinational) recently invested in a mass marketing campaign and spent $3.5 million on a Super

HOW WILL THIS HELP ME?

To become the number-one brand or retailer in any market takes a solid understanding of how best to set prices, reach market-share objectives, promote and distribute products to customers, and, ultimately, achieve profits. This chapter also examines the different types of intermediaries with an emphasis on wholesalers and retailers. We also highlight how the online marketplace has changed the nature of how companies do business. By understanding this chapter's methods for pricing, distributing, and promoting products, you'll be more prepared to evaluate a company's marketing programs, distribution methods, and competitive potential.

As we saw in Chapter 12, product development managers decide which products a company will offer to its customers. In this chapter, we'll look at three of the four Ps of the marketing mix. We'll start by looking at the concept of pricing and the tools used in making pricing decisions. Then we'll look at promotion and discuss the considerations in selecting a promotional mix. We will also highlight the tasks involved in personal selling, sales promotions, publicity, and public relations. Finally, we'll discuss place—the distribution mix and the different channels and methods of distribution.

Bowl advertisement featuring John Stamos for its Oikos Greek yogurt brand. This was a clear signal that this niche was quickly transforming into a major segment. Who will win the battle of the Greek yogurt brands? Time will tell, but, after centuries in existence, this "new" segment in the North American market appears to be here to stay.

QUESTIONS FOR DISCUSSION

1. What are the primary features and benefits that help explain the successful commercialization of this yogurt category in the North American market?
2. In the case, we identified both private brands and national brands. Categorize each of the brands mentioned, and explain the difference between national and private brands (as discussed in Chapter 12).
3. If you were involved in launching a new brand of Greek yogurt for a major food manufacturer, what strategy would you employ?
4. If you were in charge of creating a new campaign for the President's Choice Greek yogurt brand, what elements of the promotion mix would you employ? How would you use social media tools to get the message out?

LO-1 DETERMINING PRICES

After product, the second major component of the marketing mix is **pricing**—determining what the customer pays and the seller receives in exchange for a product. Setting prices involves understanding how they contribute to achieving the firm's sales objectives.

Pricing to Meet Business Objectives

eBay, the popular internet auction site, has a straightforward pricing structure that's a consumer favourite: Let buyers make offers until a price is finally settled. While eBay sellers hope for a high price, they sometimes are willing to give up some profit in return for a quick sale. Unfortunately, the eBay pricing model, one-on-one price setting, isn't feasible for all companies with lots of customers and products. **Pricing objectives** are the goals that sellers hope to achieve in pricing products for sale. Some companies have profit-maximizing pricing objectives, while others have market-share pricing objectives. Pricing decisions are also influenced by the need to compete in the marketplace, by social and ethical concerns, and even by corporate image.

PROFIT-MAXIMIZING OBJECTIVES

The seller's pricing decision is critical for determining the firm's revenue, which is calculated using the following formula:

Revenue = Selling price × Units sold

Companies that set prices to maximize profits want to set the selling price to sell the number of units that will generate the highest possible total profits. If a company sets prices too low, it will probably sell many units, but may miss out on additional profits on each unit (and may even lose money on each exchange). If a company sets prices too high, it will make a large profit on each item, but will sell fewer units. Again, the firm loses money, and it may also be left with excess inventory.

In calculating profits, managers weigh sales revenues against costs for materials and labour, as well as capital resources (plant and equipment) and marketing costs (such as maintaining a large sales staff). To use these resources efficiently, many firms set prices to cover costs and achieve a targeted level of return for owners.

MARKET-SHARE (MARKET PENETRATION) OBJECTIVES

In the long run, a business must make a profit to survive. Because they are willing to accept minimal profits, even losses, to get buyers to try products, companies may initially set low prices for new products to establish **market share** (or **market penetration**)—a company's percentage of the total industry sales for a specific product type. In some cases, companies set strategic objectives based on events and on declining share. For example, a couple of years ago Toyota cut prices in an attempt to regain lost market share after millions of its cars were recalled due to reports of uncontrollable acceleration.[1]

Price-Setting Tools

Whether a company's central objective is maximizing profits or market share, managers like to measure the potential impact of price before finalizing what they will charge for their product. Two tools used for this purpose are cost-oriented pricing and breakeven analysis. Although each can be used alone, both are often used because they provide different kinds of information for determining prices that will allow the company to reach its objectives.

COST-ORIENTED PRICING

Cost-oriented pricing considers a firm's desire to make a profit and its need to cover production costs.

Selling price = Seller's costs + Profit

PRICING Process of determining what a company will receive in exchange for its products.

PRICING OBJECTIVES The goals that sellers hope to achieve in pricing products for sale.

MARKET SHARE (OR MARKET PENETRATION) A company's percentage of the total industry sales for a specific product type.

COST-ORIENTED PRICING Pricing that considers the firm's desire to make a profit and its need to cover production costs.

For example, a manager at HMV would price DVDs by calculating the cost of making them available to shoppers. Thus, price would include the costs of store rent, employee wages, utilities, product displays, insurance, and the DVD manufacturer's price.

If the manufacturer's price is $8 per DVD and the store sells DVDs for $8, the store won't make any profit. Nor will it make a profit if it sells DVDs for $8.50 each—or even $10 or $11. To be profitable, the company must charge enough to cover product and other costs. Together, these factors determine the **markup**—the amount added to an item's purchase cost to sell it at a profit. In this case, a reasonable markup of $7 over the purchase cost means a $15 selling price. The following equation calculates the markup percentage and determines what percent of every dollar of revenue is gross profit:

$$\text{Markup percentage} = \frac{\text{Markup}}{\text{Sales price}}$$

For our DVD retailer, the markup percentage is 46.7:

$$\text{Markup percentage} = \frac{\$7}{\$15} = 46.7\%$$

Out of every $1.00 taken in, $0.467 will be gross profit. Out of gross profit, the store must still pay rent, utilities, insurance, and all other costs.

For experienced price setters, an even simpler method uses a standard cost-of-goods percentage to determine the markup amount. Many retailers, for example, use 100 percent of cost-of-goods as the standard markup. If the manufacturer's price is $8 per DVD, the markup (100 percent) is also $8, so the selling price is $16.

BREAKEVEN ANALYSIS: COST-VOLUME-PROFIT RELATIONSHIPS

Using cost-oriented pricing, a firm will cover **variable costs**—costs that change with the number of units of a product produced and sold, such as raw materials, sales commissions, and shipping. Firms also need to pay **fixed costs**—costs, such as rent, insurance, and utilities, that must be paid *regardless of the number of units produced and sold.*

Costs, selling price, and the number of units sold determine how many units a company must sell before all costs, both variable and fixed, are covered, and it begins to make a profit. **Breakeven analyses** assess costs versus revenues for various sales volumes and show, at any particular selling price, the amount of loss or profit for each possible volume of sales.

Assume you are the manager of a store that only sells DVDs. How would you determine how many DVDs you needed to sell to break even? We know that the variable cost of buying each DVD from the manufacturer is $8. This means that the store's annual variable costs depend on how many DVDs are sold—the number of DVDs sold times the $8 cost for each DVD. Say that *fixed costs* for keeping the store open for one year are $100 000 (no matter how many DVDs are sold). At a selling price of $15 each, how many DVDs must be sold so *that total revenues exactly cover both fixed and variable costs*? The answer is the **breakeven point**, which is 14 286 DVDs:

$$\text{Breakeven point (in units)} = \frac{\text{Total Fixed Cost}}{\text{Price} - \text{Variable Cost}}$$

$$= \frac{\$100\,000}{\$15 - \$8} = 14\,286 \text{ DVDs}$$

Look at Figure 13.1. If the store sells fewer than 14 286 DVDs, it loses money for the year. If sales go over 14 286, profits grow by $7 for each additional DVD. If the store sells exactly 14 286 DVDs, it will cover all its costs, but earn zero profit.

Zero profitability at the breakeven point can also be seen by using the profit equation:

$$\text{Profit} = \begin{matrix}\text{Total}\\\text{Revenue}\end{matrix} - \left(\begin{matrix}\text{Total}\\\text{Fixed}\\\text{Cost}\end{matrix} + \begin{matrix}\text{Total}\\\text{Variable}\\\text{Cost}\end{matrix}\right)$$

$$= (14\,286 \text{ DVDs} \times \$15) - (\$100\,000 \text{ Fixed Cost}$$

$$+ [14\,286 \text{ DVDs} \times \$8 \text{ Variable Cost}])$$

$$\$0 = (\$214\,290) - (\$100\,000 + \$114\,288)$$

(rounded to the nearest whole DVD)

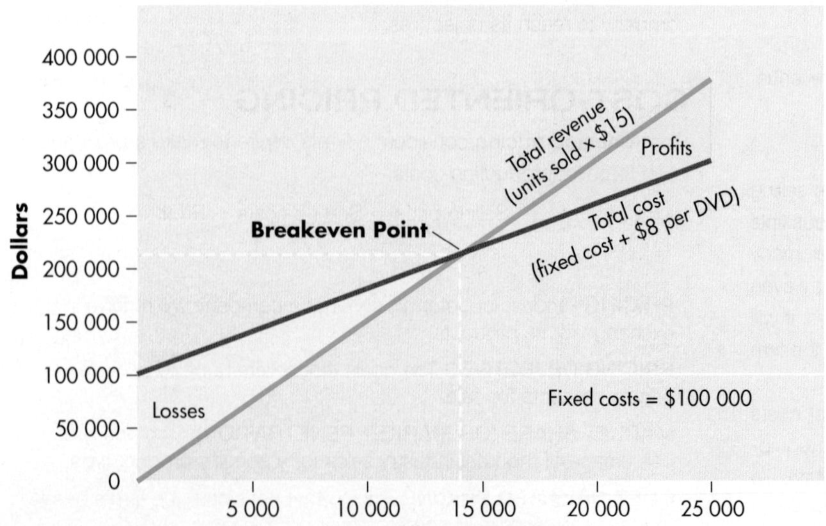

<<< **FIGURE 13.1** Breakeven analysis

MARKUP Amount added to an item's purchase cost to sell it at a profit.

VARIABLE COST Cost that changes with the quantity of a product produced and sold.

FIXED COST Cost that is incurred regardless of the quantity of a product produced and sold.

BREAKEVEN ANALYSIS For a particular selling price, assessment of the seller's costs versus revenues at various sales volumes.

BREAKEVEN POINT The sales volume at which the seller's total revenue from sales equals total costs (variable and fixed) with neither profit nor loss.

LO-2 PRICING STRATEGIES AND TACTICS

The pricing tools discussed in the previous section help managers set prices on specific goods. They do not, however, help them decide on pricing philosophies for diverse competitive situations. In this section, we discuss pricing strategy (pricing as a planning activity) and some basic pricing tactics (ways in which managers implement a firm's pricing strategies).

Pricing Strategies

Pricing is an extremely important element in the marketing mix, as well as a flexible marketing tool—it is certainly easier to change prices than to change products or distribution channels. This section will look at how pricing strategies can result in widely differing prices for very similar products.

PRICING EXISTING PRODUCTS

A firm has three options for pricing existing products:

1. Pricing *above* prevailing market prices for similar products to take advantage of the common assumption that higher price means higher quality
2. Pricing *below* market prices while offering a product of comparable quality to higher-priced competitors
3. Pricing *at* or near market prices

Godiva chocolates and Patek Phillipe watches price high by promoting prestige and quality images. In contrast, both Budget and Dollar car-rental companies promote themselves as low-priced alternatives to Hertz and Avis. Pricing below prevailing market price works if a firm offers a product of acceptable quality while keeping costs below those of higher-priced competitors.

PRICING NEW PRODUCTS

When introducing new products, companies must often choose between very high prices or very low prices. **Price skimming**—setting an initial high price to cover development and introduction costs and generate a large profit on each item sold—works only if marketers can convince customers that a new product is truly different from existing products and there is no foreseeable major competition on the horizon. Apple's iPod is a good example. With no strong competitors entering the market for several years, Apple was able to maintain a high retail price with little discounting, even at Walmart. In contrast, **penetration pricing**—setting an initial low price to establish a new product in the market—seeks to create customer interest and stimulate trial purchases. This is the best strategy when introducing a product which has or expects to have competitors very quickly.

Godiva chocolates are definitely not the cheapest on the market; the company chooses to provide quality for a premium price.

Elena Elisseeva/Shutterstock

Startup firms often use one-price, fixed pricing for launching new products. Carbonite, Inc., started its online backup service with "one-flat-low price," no matter how much space you needed to back up your PC files.[2] To date, the company has backed up more than 80 billion files, using a $54.95-per-year one-price strategy. The initial policy of Apple's iTunes was to use one low price per song, $0.99, to attract and build a customer base in the first five years. After achieving sales from over 75 million customers, a three-tier pricing was adopted to reflect differences in value among songs. Older or obscure tunes of lesser value are priced at $0.69, while current hot songs are priced at $1.29, and still others sell for $0.99.

FIXED VERSUS DYNAMIC PRICING FOR ONLINE BUSINESS

The digital marketplace has introduced a highly variable pricing system as an alternative to conventional fixed pricing for both consumer and business-to-business (B2B) products. At present, fixed pricing is still the most common option for cybershoppers. E-commerce giant Amazon.com has maintained this practice as its pricing strategy for its millions of retail items. In contrast, dynamic pricing, like eBay's auction bidding, uses flexibility between buyers and sellers in setting a price and uses the web to instantly notify millions of buyers of product availability and price changes.

Another kind of dynamic pricing—the reverse auction—allows sellers to alter prices privately on an individual basis. At Priceline.com, for example, consumers set a price (below the published fixed price) they are willing to pay for airfare (or a rental car or a hotel room); then an airline can complete the sale by accepting the bid price. For B2B purchases, MediaBids.com uses reverse advertising auctions to sell ad space. A company will notify MediaBids that it is going to spend $1000 for advertising. Publications then use their ad space as currency to place bids for the advertising dollars. The company can then accept the bid that offers the most ad exposure in the best publication.[3]

Pricing Tactics

Regardless of its pricing strategy, a company may adopt one or more pricing tactics. Companies selling multiple items in a product category

PRICE SKIMMING Setting an initially high price to cover new product costs and generate a profit.

PENETRATION PRICING Setting an initially low price to establish a new product in the market.

^^ Dynamic pricing, with online bidding screens on the wall, is a mainstream feature of this salesroom for the British Car Auctions (BCA) site in Brighouse, West Yorkshire, U.K.

Mike Cassese/Landov LLC

THERE'S AN APP FOR THAT!

1. **Ad Age Latest News** >>> **Platforms:** *Apple, Android, BlackBerry*
   Source: Polar Mobile
   Key Features: Recent news from Ad Age, the leading global source of marketing and intelligence.
2. **Marketing Hoopla** >>> **Platforms:** *Apple, Android, BlackBerry*
   Source: 3H Communications
   Key Features: Regular posts on marketing, branding, advertising, social media, and design trends.
3. **Gross Margin** >>> **Platforms:** *Apple, Android*
   Source: Golden Delicious Apps
   Key Features: Helps you calculate your gross margin in percent and dollars terms.

APP DISCOVERY EXERCISE

Since APP availability changes, conduct your own search for "Top 3" Marketing APPS and identify the key features.

often use **price lining**—offering all items in certain categories at a limited number of prices. A clothing retailer, for example, might predetermine $199, $299, $399, and $499 as the price points for men's suits, so all men's suits would be set at one of these four prices. This allows the store to have a suit for all of the different customer segments it hopes to attract. Grocery stores utilize this strategy as well; for example, in canned goods they will carry a national brand, a store brand, and a generic brand at different price points.

Psychological pricing takes advantage of the fact that customers are not completely rational when making buying decisions. One type, **odd-even pricing**, is based on the theory that customers prefer prices that are not stated in even dollar amounts. Thus, customers regard prices of $1000, $100, $50, and $10 as significantly higher than $999.95, $99.95, $49.95, and $9.95, respectively. Finally, sellers must often resort to price reductions—**discounts**—to stimulate sales.

Before moving to the next section, take a look at the boxed feature called "There's an App for That!" It highlights pricing, promotion, and general marketing apps.

PRICE LINING Setting a limited number of prices for certain categories of products.

PSYCHOLOGICAL PRICING A pricing tactic that takes advantage of the fact that consumers do not always respond rationally to stated prices.

ODD-EVEN PRICING A psychological pricing tactic based on the premise that customers prefer prices not stated in even dollar amounts.

DISCOUNT A price reduction offered as an incentive to purchase.

LO-3 PROMOTING PRODUCTS AND SERVICES

Promotion refers to techniques for communicating information about products and is part of the communication mix—the total message any company sends to customers about its product. Promotional techniques, especially advertising, must communicate the uses, features, and benefits of products, and marketers use an array of tools for this purpose.

The ultimate objective of promotion is to increase sales. However, marketers also use promotion to increase consumer awareness of their products, to make consumers more knowledgeable about product features, and to persuade consumers to prefer their brand over others. Today's value-conscious customers gain benefits when the specific elements in the promotional mix are varied so as to communicate value-added benefits. Burger King shifted its promotional mix by cutting back on advertising and using those funds for customer discounts. Receiving the same food at a lower price is "value added" for Burger King's customers. Many companies, like Hallmark Cards, experience seasonal sales patterns. By increasing their promotional activities in slow periods, they can achieve a more stable sales volume throughout the year. As a result, they can keep their production and distribution systems running evenly. Tim Hortons achieves the same goal with its annual Roll up the Rim contest.

Promotional Strategies

Once a firm's promotional objectives are clear, it must develop a promotional strategy to achieve these objectives. Promotional strategies may be of the push or pull variety. A company with a **push strategy** will "push" its product to wholesalers and retailers, who then persuade customers

PROMOTION Aspect of the marketing mix concerned with the most effective techniques for communicating information about and selling a product.

PUSH STRATEGY A promotional strategy in which a company aggressively pushes its product through wholesalers and retailers, which persuade customers to buy it.

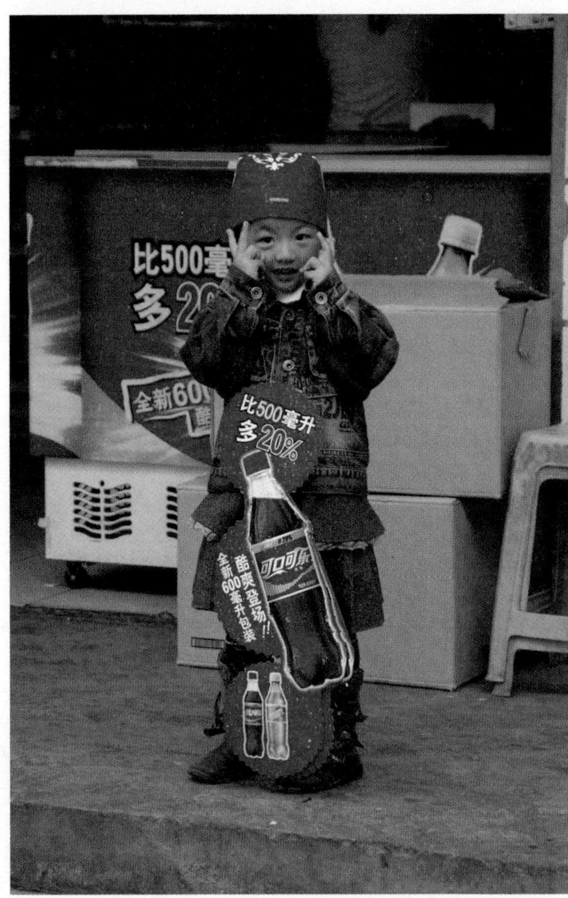

<<< Coca-Cola must design unique ads for each of its brands and it must also ensure that the message fits the nation or region targeted. Before creating an international ad like this Chinese advertisement, it is crucial to research what disparities, such as meaning of words, traditions, and taboos, exist between different societies.

© Jim Blaylock/The Augusta Chronicle/ZUMAPRESS.com

to buy it. In contrast, a company with a **pull strategy** appeals directly to customers, who demand the product from retailers, who in turn demand the product from wholesalers, who in turn demand the product from the manufacturer. Advertising "pulls," while personal selling "pushes."

Makers of industrial products often use a push strategy, while makers of consumer products often use a pull strategy. Many large firms use a combination of the two. For example, Coca-Cola uses advertising to create consumer demand (pull) for its various beverages—Coke, Fruitopia, Dasani, and Powerade. It also pushes wholesalers and retailers to stock these products. In total, the company has over 3500 products worldwide.[4]

PULL STRATEGY A promotional strategy in which a company appeals directly to customers, who demand the product from retailers, which demand the product from wholesalers.

PROMOTIONAL MIX That portion of marketing concerned with choosing the best combination of advertising, personal selling, sales promotions, and publicity to sell a product.

The Promotional Mix

Four of marketing's most powerful promotional tools are advertising, personal selling, sales promotions, and publicity and public relations. The best combination of these tools—the best **promotional mix**—depends on many factors. The most important is the target audience.

THE TARGET AUDIENCE: PROMOTION AND THE CONSUMER DECISION PROCESS

In establishing a promotional mix, marketers match promotional tools with the five stages in the buyer decision process:

1. When consumers first recognize the need to make a purchase, marketers use advertising and publicity, which can reach many people quickly, to make sure buyers are *aware of their products*.
2. As consumers search for information about available products, advertising and personal selling are important methods *to educate them*.
3. Personal selling can become vital as consumers compare competing products. Sales representatives can *demonstrate product quality, features, benefits,* and *performance* in comparison with competitors' products.
4. When buyers are ready to purchase products, sales promotion can give consumers *an incentive to buy*. Personal selling can help by bringing products to convenient purchase locations.
5. After making purchases, consumers evaluate products and note (and remember) their strengths and deficiencies. At this stage, advertising and personal selling can *remind customers that they made wise purchases.*

Figure 13.2 summarizes the effective promotional tools for each stage in the consumer buying process.

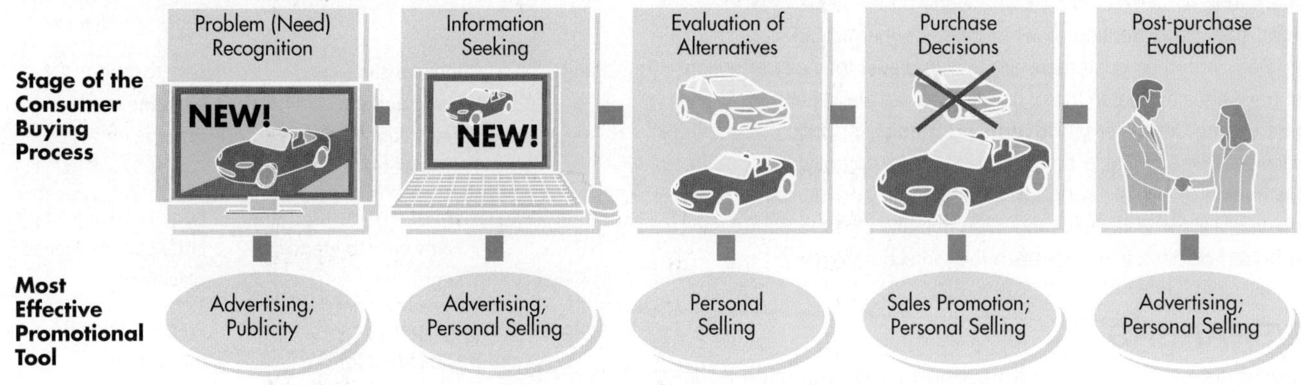

FIGURE 13.2 The consumer buying process and the promotional mix

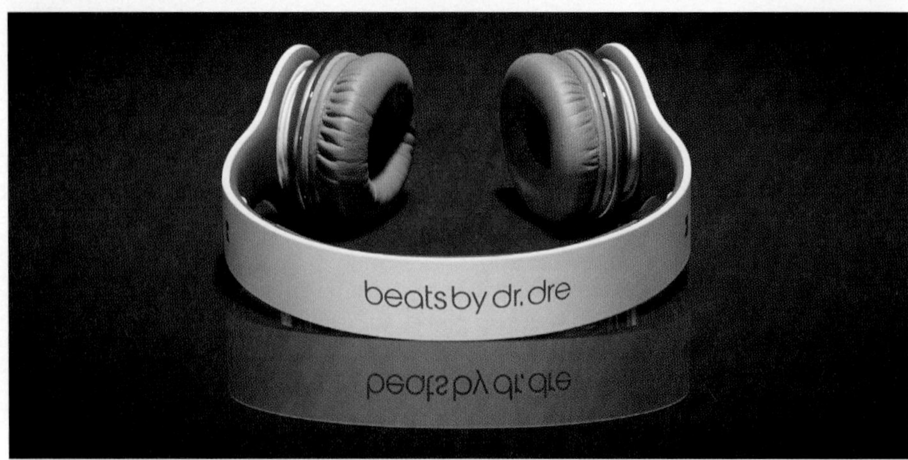

<<< The Beats by Dr. Dre have been built though a non-traditional approach; the message and reputation has spread through online buzz, YouTube videos, and more traditional techniques like cinema ads. As we will discuss below, this modern approach is revolutionizing the whole business of promotion.

Kathy deWitt/Alamy

LO-4 ADVERTISING PROMOTIONS AND MEDIA

ADVERTISING Paid, non-personal communication by which an identified sponsor informs an audience about a product.

ADVERTISING MEDIA The specific communication device—television, radio, internet, newspapers, direct mail, magazines, billboards—used to carry a firm's advertising message to potential customers.

Advertising is paid, non-personal communication by which an identified sponsor informs an audience about a product. You can probably remember many jingles and slogans from your early childhood. If a friend tells you that he or she has dandruff, you may instinctively tell them to use Head and Shoulders shampoo. Companies have been planting messages in your mind for years. Like it or not, we are all a little bit brainwashed. Consumers remember brand names more easily if the company has a catchy advertising slogan. Buckley's Cough Mixture is well known in Canada. You remember the slogan, don't you? "It tastes awful, and it works." Advertising can convince customers to try a company's product or service, but it has limits. It is the customers' experience with the product or service that determines whether they will make repeat purchases.

Advertising Media

Consumers tend to ignore the bulk of advertising messages that bombard them; they pay attention to what interests them. Marketers must find out, then, who their customers are, which media they pay attention to, what messages appeal to them, and how to get their attention. Thus, marketers use several different **advertising media**—specific communication devices for carrying a seller's message to potential customers. The combination of media through which a company advertises is called its media mix. Table 13.1 shows the strengths and weaknesses of various media and below we analyze each form in some detail.

NEWSPAPERS

Newspapers are still a widely used traditional advertising medium; in 2011, Canadian advertisers spent $1.97 billion on this medium. This figure was down 6 percent from the previous year and is down over 20 percent from the corresponding figures 10 years earlier.[5] Newspapers offer excellent coverage, since each local market has at least one daily newspaper, and many people read the paper every day. This medium offers flexible, rapid coverage, since ads can change from day to day.

TABLE 13.1 Total Media Usage, Strengths, and Weaknesses

Advertising Medium	Strengths	Weaknesses
Television	Program demographics allow for customized ads Large audience	Most expensive
Direct mail	Targeted audience Personal messages Predictable results	Easily discarded Environmentally irresponsible
Internet	Targeted audience Measurable success	Nuisance to consumers Easy to ignore
Newspapers	Broad coverage Ads can be changed daily	Quickly discarded Broad readership limits ability to target specific audience
Radio	Inexpensive Large audience Fairly easy to identify segments	Easy to ignore Message quickly disappears
Magazines	Often reread and shared Fairly easy to identify segments	Require advanced planning Little control over ad placement
Outdoor	Inexpensive Difficult to ignore Repeat exposure	Presents limited information Little control over audience

Newspapers also offer believable coverage, since ads are presented next to news. In addition, a larger percentage of individuals with higher education and income level tend to read newspapers on a daily basis. For example, newspapers attract a 47 percent readership from individual households with an income of $75 000 or above, as opposed to only a 5 percent readership of individual households under $20 000.[6]

However, the focus in the newspaper business is definitely changing. Postmedia Network Canada has the largest roster of papers in the nation; this company officially adopted a "digital first" strategy and saw an 8.6 percent increase in sales within the first quarter. Some papers are even trying unorthodox tricks to catch viewer attention. For example, the *Los Angeles Times* had a full front-page ad a couple of years ago.[7] This could not have been imagined decades ago, but newspapers are looking for revenues and new ways to get noticed and survive in a digital age.

Clearly traditional media is transforming and suffering in the process. The Entrepreneurship and New Ventures box called "A 'Helping Hand' for Professional Inspiration: wowOwow!" provides information about a site that was created based on an opportunity presented by this decline in traditional media.

TELEVISION

Television allows advertisers to combine sight, sound, and motion, thus appealing to almost all of the viewer's senses. Information on viewer demographics for a particular program allows advertisers to promote to their target audiences. National advertising is done on television, because it reaches more people than any other medium. One disadvantage of television is that there are too many commercials, which causes viewers to confuse products. In addition, viewers who record programs on DVRs (digital video recorders) often fast-forward through the ads appearing on the TV shows they have recorded. This is a growing concern, since 29 percent of Canadians owned DVRs in 2013.[8] The brevity of TV ads also makes television a poor medium to educate viewers about complex products.

Spending on television advertising in Canada totalled $3.55 billion in 2011, up nearly 5 percent.[9] Television is the most expensive advertising medium. In 2013, a 30-second commercial on U.S. television during the NFL Super Bowl cost over $4 million, and some experts are predicting that the amount could climb to $10 million within a few years.[10] A national 30-second spot in Canada during the Super Bowl costs approximately $130 000.[11] A comparable 30-second Grey Cup spot costs about $65 000.[12]

As discussed in Chapter 12, product placement, which involves using brand-name products as part of the actual storyline of TV shows, is gaining popularity. Shows like *Survivor* and *American Idol* are noticeably full of placements. *American Idol* contestants are interviewed in the Coca-Cola room and the judges drink from prominently placed Coca-Cola glasses. The contestants film a music video featuring a Ford product each week, which is presented as part of the show. Finally, the audience is invited to vote using AT&T. In all, there were over 4100 plugs in one recent season of *American Idol*.[13] In the early days of TV, live commercials featured actors or characters like Howdy Doody selling the merits of products. Decades later, in an attempt to break through the clutter, it appears as if this old technique has been revived and updated.

ENTREPRENEURSHIP AND NEW VENTURES

A "Helping Hand" for Professional Inspiration: wowOwow!

The five founders of a new social networking service back in 2008 had no idea that wowOwow.com would reinvigorate the talents of midlife professionals into new, more promising careers during the economic downturn. After just two years, its inspiring content led to the website's selection as one of Forbes.com's "Top 100 Websites for Women." The site's business concept is simple: (a) Women over 40 enjoy social networking, but with different interests than the younger crowd. (b) The fame and sophistication of its founders' personal lives, interests, and experiences is an attraction for the target audience. Plus, a contributing cast, including Whoopi Goldberg, Candice Bergen, and Lily Tomlin, provides added punch. (c) The $1 million start-up investment is shared equally among its media-savvy founders—all of whom are pace-setting veteran businesswomen: Lesley Stahl (broadcast journalist), Mary Wells (advertising executive), Joni Evans (publishing executive), Peggy Noonan (political commentator), and Liz Smith (gossip columnist). (d) Branding—the distinctive wowOwow.com (for Women on the Web)—signifies the site's mature audience and its goal of sharing professional and personal experiences to encourage one another and to make the world better. (e) The price is right for social networkers: Sign-up is free. Revenues from advertisers will be firmed up later, after wowOwow demonstrates that it can attract a massive audience—grow the audience, and advertisers will come. (f) Publicity gives wowOwow's message a powerful boost, including interviews on National Public Radio, prominent articles in the *New York Times*, and television features on NBC's *Today Show*.

The surprising career-change twist came with wowOwow.com's Executive Intern Program. It's not for newcomer youth interns but, rather, for experienced businesswomen with marketable skills, who, in the business downturn, especially in media industries, need new skills leading to another job. With more and more newspapers and magazines moving online, newer print-web skills are required, while traditional print media personnel are being displaced. That was the situation for the first intern (unpaid), who, at age 55, started listening, watching, and learning by doing and asking for help from much younger, tech-savvy web writers at WOW's offices. She learned new skills in writing URLs, tags, headlines, subheads, and links in story development for wowOwow.com content. Positive buzz created by the internship program confirms that wowOwow's social network endorses the site's goal of sharing professional and personal experiences to encourage others and to make the world better.

CRITICAL THINKING QUESTION

1. Part of the incentive for the creation of this site was the transformation in the news and media business; the founders took a negative situation and identified an opportunity to create a community for women. What do you think of the long-term potential of this site?

DIRECT MAIL

Direct mail involves flyers or other types of printed advertisements that are mailed directly to consumers' homes or places of business. Direct mail allows the company to select its audience and personalize its message. The goal is to generate an immediate response and to have the customer contact a firm directly. Although many people discard "junk mail," targeted recipients with stronger-than-average interest are more likely to buy. Although direct mail involves the largest advance costs of any advertising technique, it does appear to have the highest cost-effectiveness. Advertisers spent $1.243 billion on direct-mail promotion in 2011.[14] Targeted emails are a more modern and cost effective way to serve this purpose.

RADIO

According to BBM research, more than 90 percent of Canadians aged 12 years and over listen to the radio more than 19 hours a week.[15] Radio ads are fairly inexpensive and, since most radio is programmed locally, this medium gives advertisers a high degree of customer selectivity. For example, radio stations are already segmented into listening categories such as classic rock, country and western, jazz, talk, news, and religious programming. Radio only permits an audio presentation and ads are over quickly. As well, people tend to use the radio as "background" while they are doing other things, so they may pay little attention to advertisements. Spending on radio advertisements totalled $1.575 billion in Canada in 2011.[16] Subscriber-based satellite radio poses a significant long-term threat to the traditional radio model.

MAGAZINES

The many different magazines on the market provide a high level of consumer selectivity. The person who reads *Popular Photography* is more likely to be interested in the latest specialized lenses from Canon than a *Gourmet* magazine subscriber. Magazine advertising allows for excellent reproduction of photographs and artwork that not only grab buyers' attention, but also may convince them of the product's value. Magazines also provide advertisers with plenty of space for detailed product information. Magazines have a long life and tend to be passed from person to person, thus doubling and tripling the number of exposures. The Canadian magazine with the largest readership is *Reader's Digest* with 557 701 subscribers; unfortunately, the magazine saw a 10 percent decrease in subscribers in 2012. *Chatelaine* had the second-highest number of subscribers at 536 447, and *Canadian Living* was third with 508 479 subscribers.[17] Spending on magazine advertisements totalled $593 million in Canada in 2011.[18]

OUTDOOR ADVERTISING

Outdoor advertising—billboards, signs, and advertisements on buses, taxis, and subways—is relatively inexpensive, faces little competition for customers' attention, and is subject to high repeat exposure. Like many other areas of advertising, outdoor advertising has gone high-tech. For example, Titan Worldwide has developed an LED display that shows commercials on New York City buses. The display contains GPS technology, so it can target audiences based on the time of day and the postal code where the bus is located. The technology will also be introduced to Canada and Ireland.[19] A Montreal-based company called iGotcha Media has built a network of LCD screens for malls and golf courses.[20] Many billboards now feature animation and changing images, and today's billboard messages are cheaper because they can be digitally printed in colour in large quantities. On the downside, outdoor ads can present only limited information, and sellers have little control over who sees their advertisements. Outdoor advertising in Canada totalled $485 million in 2011.[21]

WORD-OF-MOUTH ADVERTISING

Word-of-mouth advertising occurs when consumers talk to each other about products they are using. According to the Word of Mouth Marketing Association, there are several varieties of word-of-mouth advertising. These include buzz marketing (using high-profile news to get consumers talking about a product), viral marketing (consumers passing product information around on the internet), product seeding (providing free product samples to influential consumers), and cause marketing (involving consumers who feel strongly about a cause such as reducing poverty).[22]

Consumers form very strong opinions about products as a result of conversations with friends and acquaintances, so when consumers start talking about a new product or idea, the information can build momentum and spread like wildfire. This "spreading the word" can happen without any expenditure of money by the company selling the product in question. But companies do spend money developing formal word-of-mouth advertising campaigns, because they recognize how powerful those campaigns are. For example, Toronto-based Hook Communications launched its Voice Over Internet Protocol (VOIP) service with an incentive to spread the word. Customers were asked to provide the emails of friends and then Hook sent friendly messages on their behalf. If two people joined the service, the referrer received a year of free service and $100 in loyalty rewards.[23]

THE INTERNET AND THE POWER OF CONSUMER ENGAGEMENT

Online ad sales were valued at $2.6 billion in Canada in 2011, a net increase of 16 percent since the previous year. The growth in this area has been tremendous and the power of this medium is unquestionable, encompassing various powerful forms including search, display,

The value of YouTube as an advertising destination is unquestionable, with masses of people visiting the site daily for entertainment purposes. Google (which owns YouTube) is determined to cash in on the traffic.

NY Daily News via Getty Images

classifieds, and email.[24] A survey conducted by the Solutions Research Group indicated that Canadians are truly hooked on YouTube. They asked respondents: when was the last time you visited YouTube? The results demonstrate the power of this site: 57 percent within 24 hours, 25 percent within the last week, 9 percent within the last month, with only 8 percent more than a month, and 12 percent answering never.[25]

To understand the transformational power of this medium, consider the strategic fortress of TV advertising—the Super Bowl. Even this sacred advertising event has changed. Instead of tightly guarding secret campaigns for the big day, companies are now creating teaser campaigns on YouTube and Facebook to build interest weeks before the big day and encouraging consumers to participate in events. In addition, the immense audience is being directed from TV to the internet during the game. For example, Budweiser Canada used the Super Bowl to drive people to its Facebook page in order to enter a live contest that concluded at the end of the game.[26] In another example, the media check-in service Get Glue worked with Pepsi to help the company maximize its expensive half-time show sponsorship (starring Beyonce). The result was that 95 747 virtual stickers were unlocked (and could be posted by the participants) reaching an estimated 36 million people (who saw those messages).[27] For a detailed example, take a look at the e-Business and Social Media Solutions Box entitled "The 'Gamification' of Promotions."

Internet advertising offers advantages for both buyers and sellers. For buyers, advantages include convenience, privacy, selection, easily accessible information, and control. For sellers, advantages include reach, direct distribution, reduced expenses, relationship building (with customers on interactive websites), flexibility, and feedback (sellers can measure the success of messages by counting how many people see each ad and track the number of click-throughs to their own websites).[28] More and more companies are also asking the consumer to get involved with the brand and actually influence marketing decisions. You can include Starbucks (name a flavour), Crayola (new colours), and Frito Lay (flavour ideas and ad themes) in the growing crowd.[29]

Online marketing can be very profitable for companies, but what happens when consumers turn against them? With so many individuals participating in social networking sites, like Facebook, and keeping personal blogs, it's increasingly common for a single unhappy customer to wage war against a company for selling faulty products or providing poor service. Individuals may post negative reviews of prod-

E-BUSINESS AND SOCIAL MEDIA SOLUTIONS

The "Gamification" of Promotions

For many years, the predominant approach used by marketers was to tell customers about the benefits of using their company's products and hope that consumers would respond favourably to the promotional message. Of course, there have always been some exceptions to this approach. For example, the rock band The Grateful Dead was an early user of what we now call "social media," because it encouraged fans to tape the band's concerts. This reduced record sales, but the band developed a huge fan following because people who taped the concerts passed the tapes around to their friends. The band, therefore, made a lot of money from live concerts.

In recent years, the use of social media in marketing has become widespread and sophisticated, partly because of advances in technology. The term "social media" refers to many different activities, including (but not limited to) social networking (e.g., Facebook, Twitter, Orkut), blogs (e.g., Xanga, WordPress, LiveJournal), wikis (e.g., PBworks, Wetpaint), microblogging (e.g., Foursquare, Facebook places), video (e.g., YouTube), social bookmarking (e.g., Google Reader, CiteULike), and online games (e.g., Farmville).

Companies are actively using social media to promote products. Consider a few examples:

- Farmville recently incorporated Cascadian Farm, an organic food company, into the game (players can virtually plant Cascadian's blueberries). One million players got involved in the first three days of the promotion.
- In another Farmville promotion, players who purchased certain drinks at 7-Eleven received codes which could be redeemed for virtual products in the Farmville game.
- Rapper Jay-Z's autobiography was promoted by having fans log on to a dedicated page on Bing. Fans could win an autographed copy of a page of the book if they correctly decoded clues online or via a smartphone.

Traditional loyalty programs (where customers get rewards for being a frequent user) are a common marketing tactic that has also entered the realm of social media. For example, Foursquare is a smartphone app that allows users to earn free products or receive price discounts at retail stores they frequently visit. Users "check in" at a retail location (e.g., Starbucks) and let their friends know where they are. If the user is the most frequent visitor at a retail outlet, they get the title of "mayor" of that outlet and also get free or reduced-price products. Such new techniques may even threaten traditional loyalty programs because: (a) people get a kick out of playing online games, and (b) the high-tech version may be cheaper for companies because some games provide only virtual rewards to customers. The popularity of so-called "gamification" is behind the explosive growth of companies like Groupon as well. There is even a Gamification Summit held to show marketers how to use gaming effectively.

Finally, social media has influenced the way marketers assess the success of promotional efforts. Brand engagement is now an important metric to evaluate social media marketing efforts.

QUESTIONS FOR DISCUSSION

1. What is promotion? What are the five specific areas within the general area of promotion? Where do social media fit within the overall area of promotion?
2. Consider the following statement: *Social media are rapidly going to become more important than traditional media in promoting the products and services of companies.* Do you agree with this statement? Defend your answer.

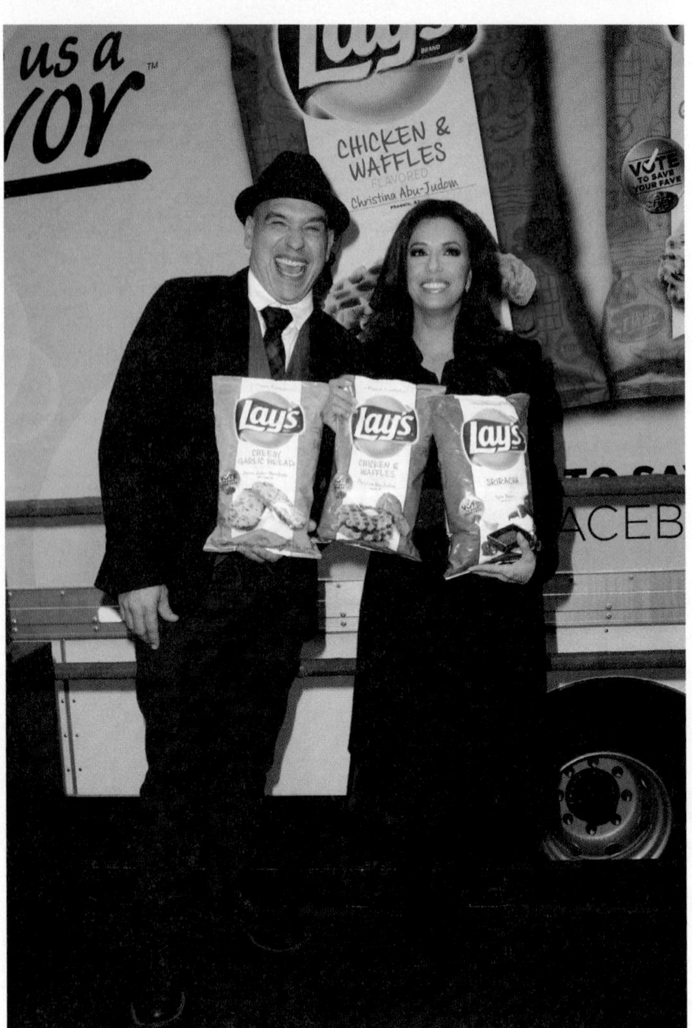

<<< More and more companies are engaging their customers to name flavours, create ads, and otherwise perform marketing functions.

Handout/MCT/Newscom

ucts on blogs, upload angry videos outlining complaints on YouTube, or join public discussion forums where they can voice their opinion. While companies benefit from the viral spread of good news, they must also be on guard against an online backlash that can damage their reputation.[30]

MOBILE AND OTHER ADVERTISING MEDIA

Mobile phone ads are growing in importance for obvious reasons. There are 25.9 million Canadian wireless phone subscribers. In addition, with more of these users moving to smartphones, the range of ad possibilities is improving.[31] The importance of the smartphone market should not be underestimated; it is one of the reasons Facebook paid over US$1 billion to acquire the photo-based service Instagram.[32] According to E-Marketer, by 2016, worldwide mobile ad spending is expected to reach US$23.6 billion.[33]

A combination of many additional media—including catalogues, sidewalk handouts, Yellow Pages, skywriting, special events, and door-to-door communications—make up the remaining advertisements to which Canadians are exposed. The combination of media that a company chooses for advertising is called its media mix. Although different industries use different mixes, most depend on multiple media to advertise their products and services. Advergaming is also a major venue for advertising. There were approximately 170 million console and computer gamers in North America in 2013.[34]

LO-5 PERSONAL SELLING, SALES PROMOTIONS, PUBLIC RELATIONS AND PUBLICITY

In this section, we outline the tasks involved in personal selling, describe the various types of sales promotions, and distinguish between publicity and public relations.

Personal Selling

Virtually everyone has done some selling. Perhaps you had a lemonade stand or sold candy for the drama club. Or you may have gone on a job interview, selling your abilities and services as an employee to the interviewer's company. **Personal selling**—the oldest form of selling—provides the personal link between seller and buyer. It adds to a firm's credibility because it gives buyers a contact person who will answer their questions. Because it involves personal interaction, personal selling requires a level of trust between the buyer and the seller. When a buyer feels cheated by the seller, that trust has been broken and a negative attitude toward salespeople in general can develop.

Personal selling is the most expensive form of promotion per contact, because presentations are generally made to one or two individuals at a time. Personal-selling expenses include salespeople's compensation and their overhead (travel, food, and lodging). The average cost of an industrial sales call has been estimated at $300 to $500.[35] Costs have prompted many companies to turn to telemarketing, using telephone solicitations to conduct the personal-selling process. Telemarketing is useful in handling any stage of this process and in arranging appointments for salespeople. It cuts the cost of personal sales visits to industrial customers, who require about four visits to complete a sale. Such savings are stimulating the growth of telemarketing, which provides 150 000 jobs in Canada and generates $25 billion in annual sales. Telemarketing returns $6.25 for every dollar spent.[36] However, because many consumers are annoyed by telemarketing pitches, a do-not-call registry was set up in Canada in 2008, and six million people quickly registered. Heavy fines can be levied on companies that ignore the new rules.[37]

PERSONAL SELLING Promotional tool in which a salesperson communicates one to one with potential customers.

Sales Promotions

Sales promotions are short-term promotional activities designed to stimulate consumer buying or cooperation from distributors, sales agents, or other members of the trade. They are important because they increase the likelihood that buyers will try products. They also enhance product recognition and can increase purchase size and amount. For example, soap is often bound into packages of four with the promotion, "Buy three and get one free."

To be successful, sales promotions must be convenient and accessible when the decision to purchase occurs. If Harley-Davidson has a one-week motorcycle promotion and you have no local dealer, the promotion is neither convenient nor accessible to you, and you will not buy. But if Herbal Essences offers a 20 percent–off coupon that you can save for use later, the promotion is convenient and accessible. Like anything else, too much of a good thing can be destructive. The Bay has been criticized for holding too many scratch-and-save "Bay Days." The goal of such programs is to generate immediate sales, as people are given an incentive to buy now or buy before the end of the weekend. But in the case of The Bay, many customers have been conditioned to expect these sales. The end result is that some customers delay purchases, waiting for the next sale. This is clearly not the goal of a sales promotion program.

TYPES OF SALES PROMOTIONS

Most consumers have taken part in a variety of sales promotions, such as free samples (giveaways), which let customers try products without risk, and **coupon** promotions, which use certificates entitling buyers to discounts in order to encourage customers to try new products, lure them away from competitors, or induce them to buy more of a product. **Premiums** are free or reduced-price items, such as pencils, coffee mugs, and six-month low-interest credit cards, given to consumers in return for buying a specified product. Contests can boost sales by rewarding high-producing distributors and sales representatives with vacation trips to Hawaii or Paris. For example, during one promotion, Molson Canadian included a free T-shirt with certain packages of its beer.[38]

To grab customers' attention in stores, companies use **point-of-purchase (or sale) displays** at the ends of aisles or near checkout counters to ease finding products and to eliminate competitors from consideration. In addition to physical goods, POS pedestals also provide services, namely information for consumers. Bank lobbies and physicians' waiting rooms, for example, can have computer-interactive kiosks inviting clients to learn more about bank products and educational information about available treatments on consumer-friendly touch-screen displays. For B2B promotions, industries sponsor **trade shows** where companies rent booths to display and demonstrate products to customers who have a special interest or who are ready to buy.

Publicity and Public Relations

Much to the delight of marketing managers with tight budgets, **publicity** is free. Moreover, because it is presented in a news format, consumers see publicity as objective and believable. However, marketers may have little control over bad publicity, and that can have a very negative impact. For example, a YouTube video showing what appeared to be a Guinness beer commercial portrayed several people in a suggestive sexual arrangement with the title "Share One with a Friend." Guinness was quick to distance itself from the fake advertisement, saying that was not how it wanted its product portrayed.

SALES PROMOTIONS Short-term promotional activities designed to stimulate consumer buying or cooperation from distributors and other members of the trade.

COUPON A method of sales promotion featuring a certificate that entitles the bearer to stated savings off a product's regular price.

PREMIUM A method of sales promotion in which some item is offered free or at a bargain price to customers in return for buying a specified product.

POINT-OF-PURCHASE (OR SALE) A method of sales promotion in which a product display is located in a retail store in order to encourage consumers to buy the product.

TRADE SHOW A method of sales promotion in which members of a particular industry gather for displays and product demonstrations designed to sell products to customers.

PUBLICITY Information about a company, a product, or an event transmitted by the general mass media (with no direct cost to the company).

>>> Ciroc Vodka is a strong beneficiary of PR and publicity; this is the reason why Diageo, the world's largest producer of alcohol products, teamed up with Sean "Diddy" Combs, the entertainment artist and entrepreneur, and made him a brand ambassador. He does not miss a chance to promote this brand.

PRNewsFoto/Nintendo/Associated Press

In contrast, **public relations** is a term that describes company-influenced publicity. It attempts to create goodwill between the company and its customers through public-service announcements that enhance the company's image. For example, a bank may announce that senior citizens' groups can have free use of a meeting room for their social activities. As well, company executives may make appearances as guest speakers representing their companies at professional meetings and civic events. They also may serve as leaders in civic activities, like the United Way campaign and university fundraising.

In 2012, in a surprising but interesting move, McDonald's talked honestly about their food to any customer willing to ask questions in an online campaign called "Our Food, Your Questions." In recent years, the company has made an effort to improve quality and offer healthier choices, but clearly they opened themselves up to some difficult answers. For example, they confirmed that a strawberry milkshake has 1100 calories! Not all the questions led to unfavourable responses though, and McDonald's clearly felt that this dialogue was already occurring in cyberspace, especially since the film *Super Size Me* was released a few years ago. Why not address the point directly and also dismiss some myths as well?[39]

PUBLIC RELATIONS Company-influenced information directed at building goodwill with the public or dealing with unfavourable events.

LO-6 THE DISTRIBUTION MIX

In addition to a good product mix and effective pricing and promotion, the success of any product also depends on its **distribution mix**—the combination of distribution channels by which a firm gets products to end users. In this section, we look at intermediaries and different kinds of distribution channels. Then, we discuss some benefits consumers reap from services provided by intermediaries.

Intermediaries and Distribution Channels

Once called middlemen, **intermediaries** help to distribute goods, either by moving them or by providing information that stimulates their movement from sellers to customers. **Wholesalers** are intermediaries who sell products to other businesses for resale to final consumers. **Retailers** sell products directly to consumers.

DISTRIBUTION OF GOODS AND SERVICES

A **distribution channel** is the path a product follows from producer to end user. Figure 13.3 shows how four popular distribution channels can be identified according to the channel members involved in getting products to buyers.

Channel 1: Direct Distribution In a **direct channel**, the product travels from the producer to the consumer or organizational buyer without intermediaries. Dell built its name using this channel approach. Most business goods, especially those bought in large quantities, are sold directly by the manufacturer to the industrial buyer.

Channel 2: Retail Distribution In Channel 2, producers distribute consumer products through retailers. Goodyear, for example, maintains its own system of retail outlets. Levi's has its own outlets, but also produces jeans for other retailers. Large outlets, such as Walmart, buy merchandise directly from producers. Many industrial buyers, such as businesses buying office supplies at Staples (Bureau en Gros), rely on this channel.

DISTRIBUTION MIX The combination of distribution channels by which a firm gets its products to end users.

INTERMEDIARY An individual or firm that helps to distribute a product.

WHOLESALER An intermediary who sells products to other businesses for resale to final consumers.

RETAILER An intermediary who sells products directly to consumers.

DISTRIBUTION CHANNEL The network of interdependent companies through which a product passes from producer to end user.

DIRECT CHANNEL A distribution channel in which a product travels from producer to consumer without intermediaries.

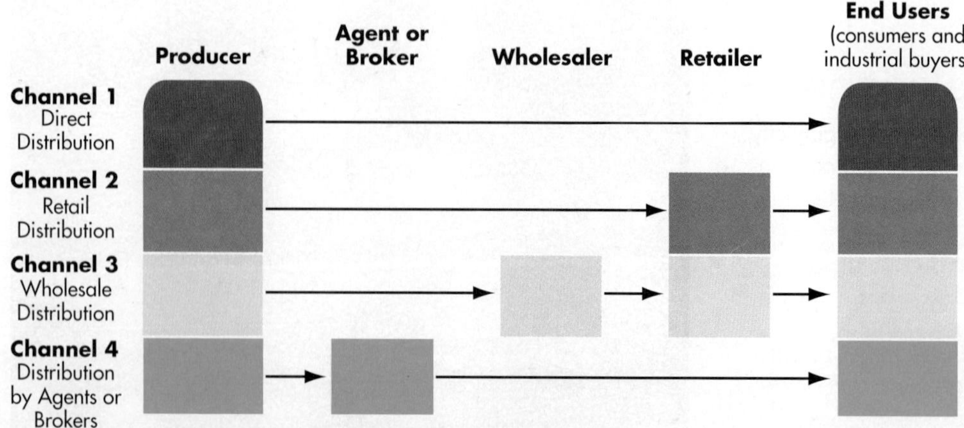

<<< FIGURE 13.3 Channels of distribution

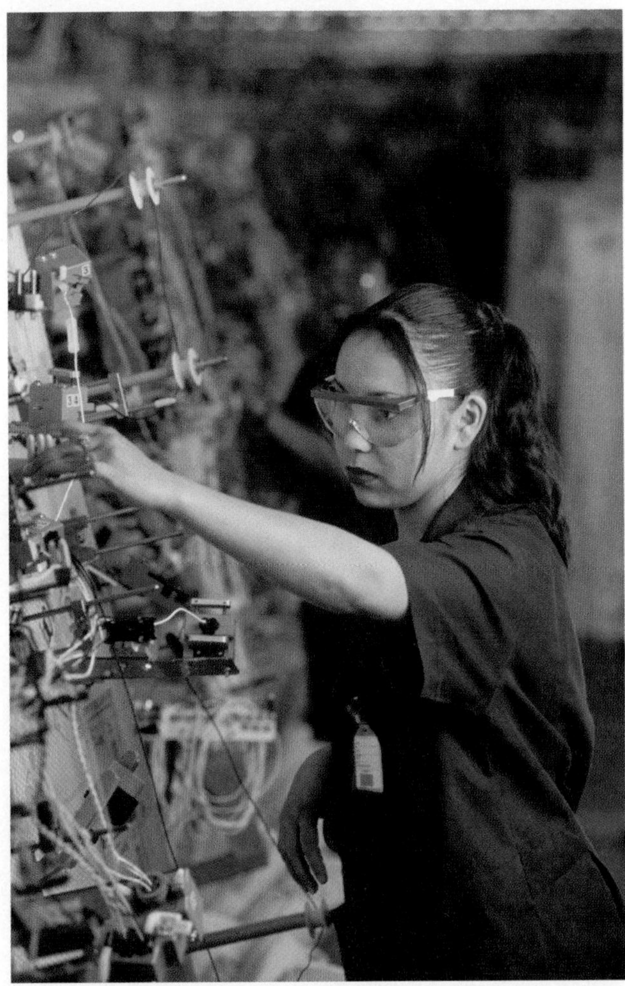

<<< At this plant of an electrical components supplier, this employee assembles electrical systems according to a process that meets the requirements for their industrial customers. The finished assemblies are shipped from the plant to customers' facilities, illustrating a direct (producer to customer) channel of distribution.

Keith Dannemiller/Newscom

Channel 3: Wholesale Distribution Once the most widely used method of non-direct distribution, Channel 2 requires a large and costly amount of floor space for storing and displaying merchandise. Wholesalers relieve the space problem by storing merchandise and restocking store displays frequently. With approximately 90 percent of its space used to display merchandise and only 10 percent left for storage and office facilities, the combination convenience store/gas station's use of wholesalers is an example of Channel 3.

Channel 4: Distribution by Agents or Brokers Sales agents or brokers represent producers and receive commissions on the goods they sell to consumers or industrial users. **Sales agents**, including many travel agents, generally deal in the related product lines of a few producers, such as tour companies, to meet the needs of many customers. Vancouver-based Uniglobe Travel International, a travel agency representing airlines, car-rental companies, hotels, and tour companies, books flight reservations and arranges complete recreational travel services for consumers. The firm also services companies whose employees need lodging and transportation for business travel. In contrast to agents, **brokers**, in industries such as real estate and stock exchanges, match numerous sellers and buyers as needed to sell properties, often without knowing in advance who they will be.

THE PROS AND CONS OF NON-DIRECT DISTRIBUTION

One problem with non-direct distribution is higher prices. The more members there are in the channel—the more intermediaries making a profit by charging a markup or commission—the higher the final price. Intermediaries, however, can provide added value by providing time-saving information and making the right quantities of products available where and when consumers need them. Figure 13.4 illustrates the problem of making chili without the benefit of a common intermediary—the supermarket. As a consumer, you would obviously spend a lot more time, money, and energy if you tried to gather all the ingredients from separate producers. In short, intermediaries exist because they provide necessary services that get products efficiently from producers to users.

SALES AGENT An independent intermediary who generally deals in the related product lines of a few producers and forms long-term relationships to represent those producers and meet the needs of many customers.

BROKER An independent intermediary who matches numerous sellers and buyers as needed, often without knowing in advance who they will be.

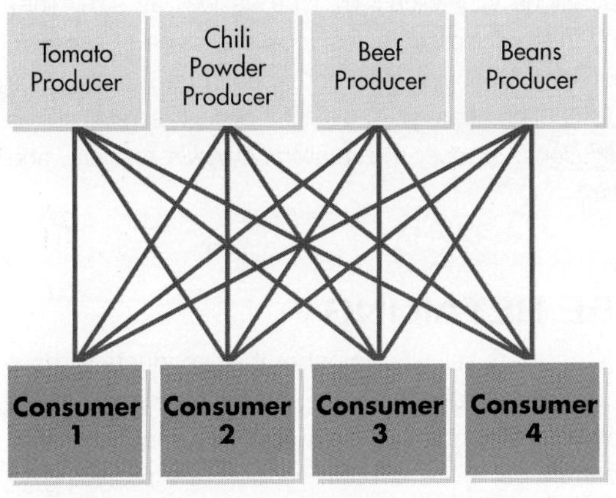

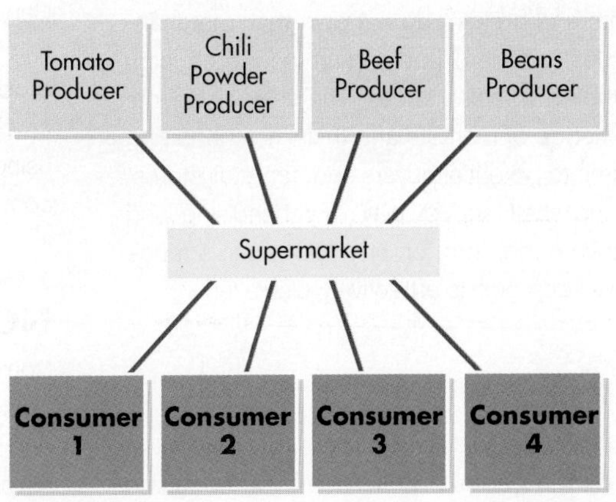

<<< FIGURE 13.4 The value-adding intermediary

Distribution Strategies

The choice of a distribution strategy determines the amount of market exposure the product gets and the cost of that exposure. **Intensive distribution** occurs when a product is distributed through as many channels and channel members as possible. Doritos chips flood the market through many different outlets. Intensive distribution is normally used for low-cost consumer goods, such as candy and magazines. In contrast, **exclusive distribution** occurs when a manufacturer grants the exclusive right to distribute or sell a product to one wholesaler or retailer in a given geographic area. For example, Jaguar automobiles are sold by only a single dealer servicing a large metropolitan area. **Selective distribution** falls between intensive and exclusive distribution. A company that uses this strategy selects only wholesalers and retailers who will give special attention to the product in terms of sales efforts, display position, etc. This method is usually embraced by companies like Black & Decker, whose product lines do not require intense market exposure to increase sales.

Channel Conflict and Channel Leadership

Channel conflict occurs when members of the distribution channel disagree over the roles they should play or the rewards they should receive. John Deere, for example, would no doubt object if its dealers began distributing Russian and Japanese tractors. Channel conflict may also arise if one member has more power than the others or is viewed as receiving preferential treatment. Such conflicts defeat the purpose of the system by disrupting the flow of goods to their destinations. Usually, one channel member—the **channel captain**—is the most powerful in determining the roles and rewards of other members. The channel captain might be a manufacturer, or it might be a large retailer like Walmart that generates large sales volumes.

Vertical marketing systems (VMSs) are designed to overcome the problems of channel conflict. In a VMS, separate businesses join to form a unified distribution channel, with one member coordinating the activities of the whole channel. In a corporate VMS, all stages in the channel are under single ownership. The Limited, for example, owns both the production facilities that manufacture its apparel and the retail stores that sell it. In a contractual VMS, channel members sign contracts agreeing to specific duties and rewards. The Independent Grocers Alliance (IGA), for example, consists of independent retail grocers joined with a wholesaler who contractually leads—but does not own—the VMS. Most franchises are contractual VMSs.

INTENSIVE DISTRIBUTION A distribution strategy in which a product is distributed in nearly every possible outlet, using many channels and channel members.

EXCLUSIVE DISTRIBUTION A distribution strategy in which a product's distribution is limited to only one wholesaler or retailer in a given geographic area.

SELECTIVE DISTRIBUTION A distribution strategy that falls between intensive and exclusive distribution, calling for the use of a limited number of outlets for a product.

CHANNEL CONFLICT Conflict arising when the members of a distribution channel disagree over the roles they should play or the rewards they should receive.

CHANNEL CAPTAIN The channel member that is the most powerful in determining the roles and rewards of organizations involved in a given channel of distribution.

VERTICAL MARKETING SYSTEM (VMS) A system in which there is a high degree of coordination among all the units in the distribution channel so that a product moves efficiently from manufacturer to consumer.

LO-7 THE ROLE OF INTERMEDIARIES

Wholesaling

The roles differ among the various intermediaries in distribution channels. As noted earlier, most wholesalers are independent operations that buy products from manufacturers and sell them to various consumers or other businesses. They usually provide storage, delivery, and additional value-adding services, including credit, marketing advice, and merchandising services, such as marking prices and setting up displays. Merchant wholesalers take title to merchandise; that is, they buy and own the goods they resell to other businesses.

Unlike wholesalers, agents and brokers do not own their merchandise. Rather, they serve as sales and merchandising arms for producers or sellers who do not have their own sales forces. The value of agents and brokers lies in their knowledge of markets and their merchandising expertise. They show sale items to potential buyers and, for retail stores, they provide such services as shelf and display merchandising and advertising layout. They remove open, torn, or dirty packages; arrange products neatly; and generally keep goods attractively displayed.

Retailing

You may not have had much contact with wholesalers, but, like most Canadians, you buy nearly all the goods and services you consume from retailers. Most retailers are small operations, often consisting of just the owners and part-time help. Retailers also include huge operations, such as Walmart, the world's largest corporate employer, as well as other global players like Carrefour in France and Daiei in Japan.

TYPES OF BRICK-AND-MORTAR RETAIL OUTLETS

Canadian retail operations vary widely by type as well as size. They can be classified by their pricing strategies, location, range of services, or range of product lines. Choosing the right types of retail outlets is a crucial aspect of distribution strategy. Table 13.2 describes retail stores using three classifications: *product-line retailers*, *bargain retailers*, and *convenience stores*.

NON-STORE RETAILING

Some of the largest retailers sell all or most of their products without brick-and-mortar stores. Certain types of products—snack foods and candy—sell well from card- and coin-operated machines. For all products, global annual sales through vending are projected to

TABLE 13.2 Types of Retailers

Product Line Retailers	Description	Examples
Department Stores	Organized into specialized departments (e.g., shoes, furniture, women's petite sizes, etc.), they are usually large, handle a wide range of goods, and provide a variety of services.	**The Bay, Sears**
Supermarkets	Organized and divided into departments of related products (e.g., food products, household products, etc.), they stress low prices, self-service, and wide selection.	**Loblaws, Sobeys, Safeway**
Specialty Stores	They serve specific market segments with full product lines and knowledgeable sales personnel in narrow product fields.	**Aldo Shoes, Sunglass Hut**
Category Killers	A very large form of specialty store which focuses on particular categories on a giant scale and often dominates retail sales in the category.	**Toys "R" Us, Staples (Bureau en Gros)**
Bargain Retailers	**Description**	**Examples**
Discount Stores	They provide a wide variety of merchandise with minimal service at low prices.	**Walmart**
Factory Outlets	Large discount stores that usually sell last season's merchandise, discontinued items, and factory seconds at a low price.	**Nike Outlet Store**
Wholesale Clubs	They offer large discounts on a wide range of brand-name merchandise to customers who pay annual membership.	**Costco**
Convenience Stores	**Description**	**Examples**
Convenience Stores	Characterized by easily accessible locations, extended store hours, and speedy service; in recent years, more than 2300 convenience stores closed across Canada, partly because contraband cigarettes eliminated about $2.5 billion in sales.[40]	**Couche-Tard, Mac's**

DIRECT-RESPONSE RETAILING A form of non-store retailing in which firms directly interact with customers to inform them of products and to receive sales orders.

E-INTERMEDIARY An internet distribution channel member that assists in delivering products to customers or that collects information about various sellers to be presented to consumers.

SHOPPING AGENT (E-AGENT) An e-intermediary (middleman) in the internet distribution channel that assists users in finding products and prices, but does not take possession of products.

reach nearly $200 billion by 2015. But this is still a very small percentage (1 to 2 percent) of total retail sales.[41] Non-store retailing also includes **direct-response retailing**, in which firms contact customers directly to inform them about products and to receive sales orders. Take a look at Table 13.3 for a description of certain forms of direct-response retailing.

E-INTERMEDIARIES

The ability of e-commerce to bring together millions of widely dispersed consumers and businesses has changed the types and roles of intermediaries. **E-intermediaries** are internet-based channel members who perform one or both of two functions: (1) They collect information about sellers and present it to consumers, or (2) they help deliver internet products to buyers. We will examine two types of e-intermediaries: shopping agents and e-retailers.

Online Shopping Agents **Shopping agents (e-agents)**, like PriceSCAN.com, help internet shoppers by gathering and sorting information. Although they don't take possession of products, they know which websites and stores to visit, give accurate comparison prices, identify product features, and help customers complete transactions by presenting information in a usable format.

TABLE 13.3 Non-Store & Direct-Response Retailing

Direct-Response	Description
Mail Order Catalogue Marketing	A form of non-store retailing in which customers place orders for merchandise in catalogues and receive orders by mail.
Telemarketing	Uses telephone calls to sell directly to consumers. Telemarketing also includes inbound toll-free calls, which most catalogue and other retail stores make available.
Direct Selling	The oldest form of retailing, selling door-to-door or through home-selling parties. Avon Products, the world's largest direct seller, has 6 million door-to-door sales representatives in more than 100 countries.[42]
Video/TV	A form of retailing that lets viewers shop at home from special channels on their TVs. For example, QVC displays and demonstrates products on TV, as well as on Facebook, YouTube, and Twitter, and allows viewers to phone in or email orders.

Electronic Retailing Over 85 percent of the world's online population—over one billion consumers—have made purchases on the internet. iTunes has outsold brick-and-mortar music retailers, and Amazon.com is the world's largest online retailer, with annual sales of $24 billion.[43] **Electronic retailing (online retailing)** allows sellers to inform, sell to, and distribute to consumers via the web. In addition to large companies, millions of small businesses around the globe have their own websites. Online spending in Canada is expected to top $30.9 billion in 2015.[44]

More than 30 000 Canadians are "small retailers" who make a significant portion of their annual income by selling goods and services on sites like eBay and Kijiji. But they often do not pay income or sales tax on their sales, so both the Canada Revenue Agency and the federal government are losing millions of dollars in tax revenues each year. The Federal Court of Appeal has ordered eBay to provide information on people who sell more than $1000 per month on its site.[45]

Interactive Retailing Today, both retail and B2B customers interact with multimedia sites using voice, graphics, animation, film clips, and access to live-human advice. As an example of **interactive retailing**, LivePerson.com is a leading provider of real-time sales and customer service that allows customers to enter a live chat room with a service operator who can answer their specific product questions.

ELECTRONIC RETAILING (ONLINE RETAILING) Non-store retailing in which information about the seller's products and services is connected to consumers' computers, allowing consumers to receive the information and purchase the products in the home.

INTERACTIVE RETAILING Non-store retailing that uses a website to provide real-time sales and customer service.

LO-8 PHYSICAL DISTRIBUTION

PHYSICAL DISTRIBUTION Activities needed to move a product efficiently from manufacturer to consumer.

WAREHOUSING A physical distribution operation concerned with the storage of goods.

Physical distribution refers to the activities needed to move products from manufacturer to customer and includes warehousing and transportation operations. Its purpose is to make goods available when and where customers want them, keep costs low, and provide services to satisfy customers. Because of its importance for customer satisfaction, some firms have adopted distribution as their core marketing strategy of choice.

For example, Maersk Line and Aqualife AS have partnered to create a transport system to ship seafood from Canada's east coast aquaculture companies to customers in Europe. Specialized tanks on board the ships oxygenate water without having to use pumps. The new system will help to open new markets for aquaculture products grown in Canada.[46] In another example, Coca-Cola Co. decided to take over Coca-Cola Enterprises (CCE)—which focused on bottling and distribution—because Coca-Cola Co. thought it could better manage its various brands and cut distribution costs.[47]

Warehousing Operations

Warehousing—the physical distribution operation concerned with the storage of goods—is a major part of distribution management. In selecting a strategy, managers must keep in mind both the different characteristics and costs of warehousing operations. Warehouses may be owned by a single manufacturer, wholesaler, or retailer, which deals in mass quantities and needs regular storage (such as The Brick). Other warehouses are independently owned and rent space to companies as required (e.g., during peak periods).

NON-PHYSICAL STORAGE

The digital age brings with it massive quantities of data that need to be safely stored, preserved, organized, and accessible to users. Many companies rely on remote off-site digital storage services as a safety net to protect their valuable data resources. Home users, too, use daily online backup services, such as Carbonite Backup, to protect against losing data when their computers crash. In the event of any physical catastrophe—floods, fires, earthquakes—at the client's facility, data can be restored online from the backup system.[48]

Transportation Operations

Physically moving a product creates the highest cost many companies face. In addition to transportation methods, firms must also consider the nature of the product, the distance it must travel, the speed with which it must be received, and customer wants and needs.

TRANSPORTATION MODES

Differences in cost among the major transportation modes—trucks, railroads, planes, digital transmission, water carriers, and pipelines—are usually most directly related to delivery speed. See Table 13.4 for more details about transportation modes.

For more information about pipelines, take a look at the Greening of Business box entitled "The Keystone XL Pipeline." It discusses a major project that has been in the news quite a bit lately.

FedEx has over 140 000 employees worldwide and operates a fleet of 654 airplanes that help the company deliver speedy service to clients around the world.

Enigma/Alamy

TABLE 13.4 Pros and Cons of the Various Modes of Transporting Goods

Mode of Transport	Pros and Cons
Trucks	+ Flexibility, fast service, and dependability − Increased truck traffic is raising safety concerns
Planes	+ Fastest traditional method (potential for lower-inventory costs; reduces the need to store items that might spoil) − Most expensive approach
Digital Transmission	+ Newest, fastest, and least expensive method − Restricted to certain products (e.g., music, movies, software, etc.)
Water Carriers	+ Least expensive traditional mode − Slowest method
Railroads	+ Economically transport high-volume, heavy, bulky items (e.g., cars, steel) − Delivery routes are limited by fixed railway lines
Pipelines	+ Good for specialized products (liquids and gases); economical and reliable − Slow, lack of flexibility

Distribution through Supply Chains as a Marketing Strategy

Instead of just offering advantages in product features, quality, price, and promotion, many firms have turned to supply chains that depend on distribution as a cornerstone of business strategy. This approach means assessing, improving, and integrating the entire stream of activities—upstream suppliers, wholesaling, warehousing, transportation, delivery, and follow-up services—involved in getting products to customers.

Walmart built its distribution system utilizing the best practices of both Just-in-Time and supply chains (as discussed in Chapter 7), instead of the industry practice of relying on outside freight companies and wholesalers. When you buy a product (like Tide) at Walmart, the checkout scanner reads the barcode on the box and Walmart's inventory system is updated instantly, showing that a replacement is needed on the shelf. Once the supply of Tide dwindles to its automatic triggering number, Walmart's distribution centre receives a digital signal notifying that this store needs more Tide and, at the same time, the system also notifies the manufacturer (in this case, Procter & Gamble) that this location needs a replenishment supply—a predetermined number of boxes of Tide. Walmart's data mining system determines the reorder number for every product based on sales (daily, weekly, and even by time of the year). Because of Walmart's constant rapid restocking from upstream sources, its store shelves are re-supplied without having to keep large inventories in its warehouses and retail stores, thus reducing inventory costs and providing lower prices.

THE GREENING OF BUSINESS

The Keystone XL Pipeline

Oil is Canada's largest export, and it has a significant positive effect on our favourable balance of trade and on our national wealth. The U.S. imports more oil from Canada than from any other country, and, to facilitate the exporting of even more oil, TransCanada wants to build the Keystone XL pipeline to carry oil from Alberta to Houston, Texas (where many oil refineries are located).

After studying the proposal, the U.S. State Department concluded that the pipeline would not be an environmental threat, but environmental groups in both Canada and the U.S. disagreed. Their concerns about pipeline safety intensified after several recent incidents of pipelines leaking. For example, an Enbridge pipeline ruptured during July 2010 and spilled 3.8 million litres of oil into the Kalamazoo River in Michigan, and an Exxon Mobil pipeline later spilled 95 000 litres of oil into the Yellowstone River in Montana. Environmental groups also claimed that U.S. State Department officials advised TransCanada Corp. how to build public support for the Keystone pipeline, even though the State Department was, at that time, in the process of deciding whether to approve the project.

Canadian activists—led by Greenpeace Canada, the Council of Canadians, and the Indigenous Environmental Network—organized a protest in Ottawa in September 2011 to raise awareness of the problem and stop approval for the pipeline. On November 7, 2011, thousands of protestors demonstrated outside the U.S. White House. Their goal was to convince President Barack Obama to deny approval for the Keystone pipeline. After that, the pipeline was put on hold. Cynics claimed that Obama was fearful that if he ignored the protestors, many people who voted for him in 2008 would not vote for him in 2012.

In April 2012, in a further attempt to get the pipeline approved, TransCanada submitted a revised proposal that avoided an environmentally sensitive area in Nebraska. If the Keystone pipeline fails to get approval, one alternative is for Canada to export more oil to the Far East, where demand is expected to be high. Enbridge, for example, is planning a Northern Gateway pipeline that would move oil across northern B.C. to Kitimat. But that pipeline idea has run into resistance from Canadian aboriginal groups who claim it will be an environmental hazard. When opposition like this develops and there are many different groups with different agendas, the approval process can be very drawn out and the outcome is not certain. For example, the Mackenzie Valley pipeline, which had been under discussion for 40 years, was finally cancelled in 2011.

CRITICAL THINKING QUESTIONS

1. What is "the external environment of business"? How does it impact companies like TransCanada Corp. and Enbridge? (Review the material in Chapter 2 before answering this question.)
2. Do you think the Keystone XL pipeline should be approved? Defend your answer.

Walmart's JIT system has allowed it to achieve a short (as low as two-day) turnaround from manufacturer to the store shelf, thus providing cost control and product availability. It maintains lower levels of inventory, meets customer demand, and keeps the lowest prices in the retail industry.

These close partnership relationships also have other benefits when competitors try to enter their territory. For example, as Target began to open stores across Canada in 2013, it complained of difficulty in finding vendors for certain products in Canada. For smaller vendors that receive 80 to 90 percent of their business from companies like Walmart and HBC, there may have been capacity issues, but there also may have been direct verbal or implied pressure to stay loyal and avoid the new player on the block.[49]

MyBizLab Visit the MyBizLab website. This online homework and tutorial system puts you in control of your own learning with study and practice tools directly correlated to this chapter's content.

SUMMARY OF LEARNING OBJECTIVES

LO-1 IDENTIFY THE VARIOUS *PRICING OBJECTIVES* THAT GOVERN PRICING DECISIONS, AND DESCRIBE THE *PRICE-SETTING TOOLS* USED IN MAKING THESE DECISIONS.

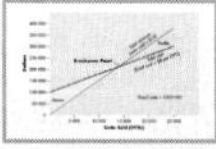

Two major pricing objectives are (1) pricing to maximize profits—set the price to sell the number of units that will generate the highest possible total profits, and (2) market-share objectives—pricing is used for establishing market share. The seller is willing to accept minimal profits, even losses, to get buyers to try products. Two basic tools are used: (1) Cost-oriented pricing begins by determining total costs for making products available to shoppers, then a figure for profit is added in to arrive at a selling price, and (2) breakeven analysis assesses total costs versus revenues for various sales volumes. It shows, at each possible sales volume, the amount of loss or profit for any chosen sales price. It also shows the breakeven point, the number of sales units for total revenue to equal total costs.

LO-2 DISCUSS *PRICING STRATEGIES* THAT CAN BE USED FOR DIFFERENT COMPETITIVE SITUATIONS AND IDENTIFY THE *PRICING TACTICS* THAT CAN BE USED FOR SETTING PRICES.

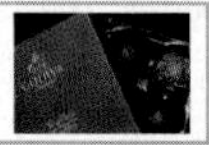

Pricing for existing products can be set above, at, or below market prices for similar products. High pricing is often interpreted as meaning higher quality and prestige, while low pricing may attract greater sales volume. Strategies for new products include price skimming, setting an initially high price to cover costs and generate a profit, and penetration pricing, setting a low price to establish a new product in the market. Strategies for e-businesses include dynamic versus fixed pricing. Dynamic pricing establishes individual prices by real-time interaction between the seller and each customer on the Internet. Fixed pricing is the traditional one-price-for-all arrangement.

Three tactics are often used for setting prices: (1) With price lining, any product category (such as ladies' shoes) will be set at three or four price levels, and all shoes will be priced at one of those levels. (2) Psychological pricing acknowledges that customers are not completely rational when making buying decisions, as with odd-even pricing where customers regard prices such as $10 as being significantly higher than $9.95. (3) Discount pricing uses price reductions to stimulate sales.

LO-3 IDENTIFY THE IMPORTANT *OBJECTIVES OF PROMOTION* AND DISCUSS THE CONSIDERATIONS IN SELECTING A *PROMOTIONAL MIX*.

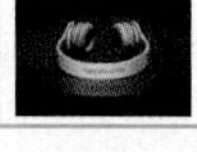

Although the ultimate goal of any promotion is to increase sales, other goals include communicating information, positioning a product, adding value, and controlling sales volume. In deciding on the appropriate promotional mix, the best combination of promotional tools (e.g., advertising, personal selling, sales promotions, direct marketing, public relations), marketers must consider the good or service being offered, characteristics of the target audience, the buyer's decision process, and the promotional mix budget.

LO-4 DEFINE THE *ROLE OF ADVERTISING* AND DESCRIBE THE KEY *ADVERTISING MEDIA*.

Advertising is paid, non-personal communication, by which an identified sponsor informs an audience about a product. Marketers use several different advertising media—specific communication devices for carrying a seller's message to potential customers—each with its specific advantages and drawbacks. The most common media—television, newspapers, direct mail, radio, magazines, outdoor advertising, internet, mobile—differ in their cost and their ability to segment target markets.

LO-5 OUTLINE THE TASKS INVOLVED IN *PERSONAL SELLING,* DESCRIBE THE VARIOUS TYPES OF *SALES PROMOTIONS,* AND DISTINGUISH BETWEEN *PUBLICITY* AND *PUBLIC RELATIONS*.

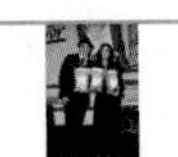

Personal selling is a promotional tool in which a salesperson communicates one to one with potential customers; it provides the personal link between seller and buyer. Sales promotions include point-of-purchase (or sale) displays to attract consumer attention, help them find products in stores and offices, and provide product information. Other sales promotions give purchasing incentives, such as samples (customers can try products without having to buy them), coupons (a certificate for price reduction), and premiums (free or reduced-price rewards for buying products). At trade shows, B2B sellers rent booths to display products to industrial customers. Contests intend to stimulate sales, with prizes to high-producing intermediaries and consumers who use the seller's products.

Publicity is information about a company, a product, or an event transmitted by the general mass media to attract public attention. Control of the message's content is determined by outside writers and reporters. In contrast to publicity, public relations is company-influenced information that seeks to either build good relations with the public or to deal with unfavourable events.

LO-6 EXPLAIN THE MEANING OF *DISTRIBUTION MIX* AND IDENTIFY THE DIFFERENT *CHANNELS OF DISTRIBUTION*.

The combination of distribution channels for getting products to end users—consumers and industrial buyers—is the distribution mix. Intermediaries help to distribute a producer's goods by moving them from sellers to customers; wholesalers sell products to other businesses, which resell them to final users. Retailers, sales agents, and brokers sell products directly to end users. In the simplest of the four distribution channels, the producer sells directly to users. Channel 2 includes a retailer, Channel 3 involves both a retailer and a wholesaler, and Channel 4 includes an agent or broker.

LO-7 DESCRIBE THE ROLE OF *INTERMEDIARIES.* EXPLAIN THE FUNCTION OF *WHOLESALERS* AND IDENTIFY THE DIFFERENT TYPES OF *RETAILERS* AND *E-INTERMEDIARIES*.

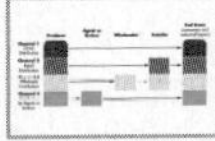

The roles differ among the various intermediaries in distribution channels. Wholesalers provide a variety of services, including delivery, credit arrangements, and product information. In buying and reselling an assortment of products, wholesalers provide storage, marketing advice, and assist customers by marking prices and setting up displays. Retail stores range from broad product-line department stores and supermarkets, to small specialty stores for specific market segments seeking narrow product lines. Non-store retailing includes direct-response retailing, mail order (or catalogue marketing), telemarketing, and direct selling.

E-intermediaries are internet-based channel members who perform one or both of two functions: (1) They collect information about sellers and present it to consumers, and (2) they help deliver internet products to buyers. Two prominent types of e-intermediaries are shopping agents and electronic retailers: (1) Shopping agents (e-agents) help online consumers by gathering and sorting information (such as comparison prices and product features) for making purchases. They add value for sellers by listing sellers' web addresses for consumers. (2) Electronic retailers interact online with customers and add value by informing, selling to, and distributing products to them.

LO-8 DESCRIBE THE *PHYSICAL DISTRIBUTION PROCESS.*

Physical distribution activities include providing customer services, warehousing, and transportation of products. Warehouses provide storage for products, whereas transportation operations physically move products from suppliers to customers. Trucks, railroads, planes, water carriers (boats and barges), digital transmission, and pipelines are the major transportation modes used in the distribution process.

QUESTIONS AND EXERCISES

QUESTIONS FOR ANALYSIS

See >>> for **Assisted-Graded Writing Assignment** in **MyBizLab**

1. Discuss the goal of price skimming and penetration pricing.
2. How do cost-oriented pricing and breakeven analysis help managers measure the potential impact of prices? What general factors motivate marketing managers to price their products at, above, or below prevailing market prices?
3. From the manufacturer's point of view, what are the advantages and disadvantages of using intermediaries to distribute products? How about from the end-user's point of view?
4. Explain how e-intermediaries differ from traditional agents or brokers.
5. Select four advertising media and compare the advantages and disadvantages of each.
6. Give three examples (other than those provided in the chapter) of products that use intensive distribution. Do the same for products that use exclusive distribution and selective distribution. What are the characteristics of the products in each category? For which category was it easiest to find examples? Why?

APPLICATION EXERCISES

7. >>> Select a product and analyze pricing objectives for it. What information would you want if you were to adopt a profit-maximizing objective or a market-share objective?
8. Consider the various kinds of non-store retailing. Give examples of two products that typify the kinds of products sold through each form of non-store retailing. Are different products best suited to each form of non-store retailing? Explain.
9. Identify a company that is a member in a supply chain. Explain how its presence in the chain affects the company's marketing decisions for pricing, promoting, and distributing its products.
10. Choose two advertising campaigns that have recently been conducted by business firms in your area. Choose one that you think is effective and one that you think is ineffective. What differences in the campaigns make one better than the other? Why would a business use a push strategy rather than a pull strategy?

TEAM EXERCISES

BUILDING YOUR BUSINESS SKILLS

GREETING CARD START-UP DECISIONS

GOAL

To encourage you to analyze the potential usefulness of two promotional methods—personal selling and direct mail—for a start-up greeting card company.

BACKGROUND INFORMATION

You are the marketing adviser for a local start-up company that makes and sells specialty greeting cards in a city of 400 000. Last year's sales totaled 14 000 cards, including personalized holiday cards, birthday cards, and special-events cards for individuals. Although revenues increased last year, you see a way of further boosting sales by expanding into card shops, grocery stores, and gift shops. You see two alternatives for entering these outlets:

1. Use direct mail to reach more individual customers for specialty cards.
2. Use personal selling to gain display space in retail stores.

Your challenge is to convince the owner of the start-up company which alternative is the more financially sound decision.

METHOD

Step 1 Get together with four or five classmates to research the two kinds of product segments: personalized cards and retail-store cards. Find out which of the two kinds of marketing promotions will be more effective for each of the two segments. What will be the reaction to each method by customers, retailers, and card-company owners?

Step 2 Draft a proposal to the company owner. Leaving budget and production details to other staffers, list as many reasons as possible for adopting direct mail. Then, list as many reasons as possible for adopting personal selling. Defend each reason. Consider the following reasons in your argument:

- *Competitive environment.* Analyze the impact of other card suppliers that offer personalized cards and cards for sale in retail stores.
- *Expectations of target markets.* Who buys personalized cards and who buys ready-made cards from retail stores?
- *Overall cost of the promotional effort.* Which method, direct mail or personal selling, will be more costly?
- *Marketing effectiveness.* Which promotional method will result in greater consumer response?

FOLLOW-UP QUESTIONS

1. Why do you think some buyers want personalized cards? Why do some consumers want ready-made cards from retail stores?
2. Consider today's easy access to online sources of cards and to software for designing and making cards on home PCs. How does the availability of these resources affect your recommendation?
3. What was your most convincing argument for using direct mail? For using personal selling?
4. Can a start-up company compete in retail stores against industry giants, such as Hallmark?

EXERCISING YOUR ETHICS

THE CHAIN OF RESPONSIBILITY

THE SITUATION

Because several stages are involved when distribution chains move products from supply sources to end consumers, the process offers ample opportunity for ethical issues to arise. This exercise encourages you to examine some of the ethical issues that can emerge during transactions among suppliers and customers.

THE DILEMMA

A customer bought an expensive wedding gift at a local store and asked that it be shipped to the bride in another province. Several weeks after the wedding, the customer contacted the bride, who had not confirmed the arrival of the gift. It hadn't arrived. Charging that the merchandise had not been delivered, the customer requested a refund from the retailer. The store manager uncovered the following facts:

- All shipments from the store are handled by a well-known national delivery firm.
- The delivery firm verified that the package had been delivered to the designated address two days after the sale.
- Normally, the delivery firm does not obtain recipient signatures; deliveries are made to the address of record, regardless of the name on the package.

The gift giver argued that even though the package had been delivered to the right address, it had not been delivered to the named recipient. It turns out that, unbeknownst to the gift giver, the bride had moved. It stood to reason, then, that the gift was in the hands of the new occupant at the bride's former address. The manager informed the gift giver that the store had fulfilled its obligation. The cause of the problem, she explained, was the incorrect address given by the customer. She refused to refund the customer's money and suggested that the customer might want to recover the gift by contacting the stranger who received it at the bride's old address.

TEAM ACTIVITY

Assemble a group of four students and assign each group member to one of the following roles:

- Customer (the person who had originally purchased the gift)
- Employee (of the store where the gift was purchased)
- Bride (the person who was supposed to receive the gift)
- Customer service manager (of the delivery company)

QUESTIONS FOR DISCUSSION

1. Before hearing any of your group's comments and from the perspective of your assigned role, decide whether there are any ethical issues in this situation. If so, write them down.
2. Before hearing any of your group's comments and from the perspective of your assigned role, decide how this dispute should be resolved.
3. Together with your group, share the ethical issues that were identified. What responsibilities does each party—the customer, the store, and the delivery company—have in this situation?
4. What does your group recommend be done to resolve this dispute? What are the advantages and disadvantages of your recommendations?

BUSINESS CASE

TRANSFORMING THE REAL ESTATE DISTRIBUTION MODEL

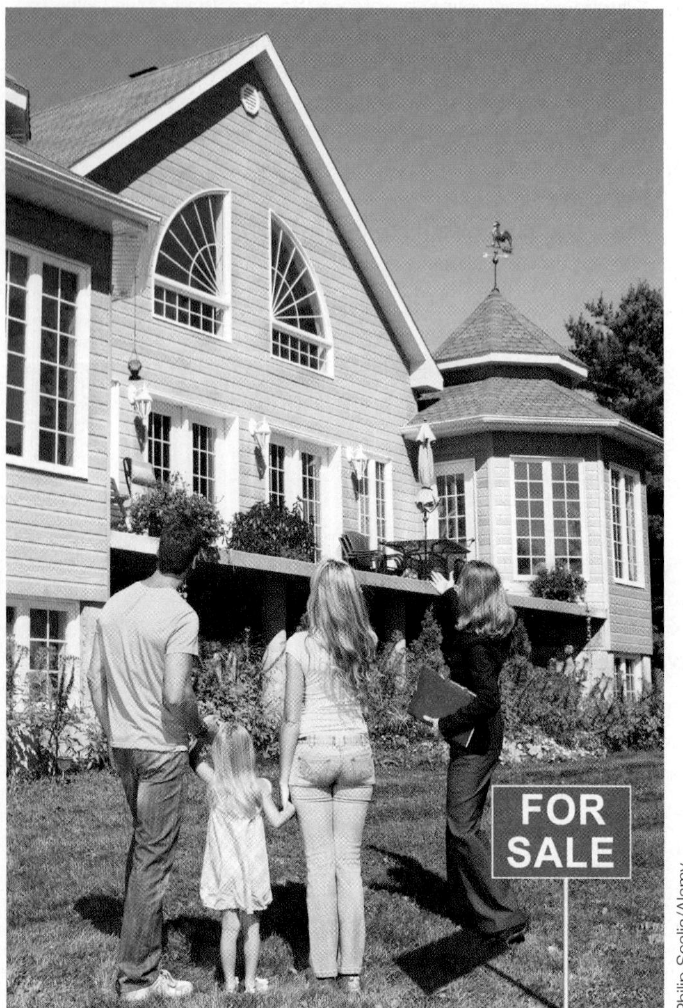

Philip Scalia/Alamy

Intermediaries, like real estate agents, bring buyers and sellers together. For many years, the Canadian Real Estate Association (CREA) allowed only "full service" real estate agents access to its Multiple Listing Service (MLS), the database that lists most of the houses for sale in Canada. Since 90 percent of all homes are sold through MLS, this meant that people who were selling their home really had no alternative but to pay for the "full service" that an agent would give them, even if they didn't want all the services. These services did not come cheap. For example, a real estate agent would typically receive a $20 000 commission when selling a $400 000 house for a client (half of that amount would be shared with the buyer's agent).

Buyers and sellers have long felt that these commissions were way too high. In recent years, e-brokers have emerged who charge a flat rate for selling a house, and their rate is far below what traditional real-estate agents charge (as little as $100). This has created competition for traditional real estate agents, and it is not surprising that they view e-brokers with alarm (even though e-brokers were not allowed access to the MLS). E-brokers began appearing on the scene in the mid-1990s. For example, Nicolas Bouchard founded Duproprio.com, which focused on private sales without an agent. At first, the site attracted mostly people who knew each other or had seen someone's *For Sale* sign on their lawn. Bouchard's company developed slowly over the years, but he says it now has 1.25 million visitors each month (although this is still a lot smaller than the 12 million visits on the MLS).

Beyond the competition from e-brokers, another problem developed for CREA in 2010, when the Canadian Competition Bureau filed a complaint with the Competition Tribunal, alleging that CREA was engaging in anti-competitive restrictions that were designed to maintain high fees for traditional real estate brokers by denying e-brokers access to the MLS, and by not allowing CREA agents to provide less than full service. The outcome of the Competition Bureau's investigation of CREA was the signing of a consent agreement that allows people who are selling their home to buy whatever level of service they want from their real estate agent (anything from a cheap, flat-rate MLS listing, all the way up to "full service"). The agreement essentially prohibits CREA members from discriminating against e-brokers who simply want to post homes for sale on the MLS. Sellers who buy a flat-rate listing are now guaranteed that their house will appear on the MLS listing. The seller must offer a finder's fee to any real estate agent who brings them a buyer for their house, but no minimum payment is required. Sellers who are willing to do most of the work of negotiating the sale of their house will, therefore, pay far less to an agent than they used to. Agents are required by the agreement to show their clients any listing that the client is interested in, including those that are posted by low-fee brokers.

After the consent agreement, the Competition Bureau said that it was satisfied that its anti-competitive concerns had been dealt with, but critics then began charging that the system was still rigged because CREA was trying to keep agents from doing business across provincial boundaries. After the consent agreement, e-brokers thought that they would be able to deal with clients across Canada. But real estate boards in several provinces interpreted provincial legislation in such a way as to prohibit real estate agents from other provinces from competing in their province. For example, Joe William, an Ottawa-based real estate agent who charged just $100 for putting a listing on the MLS, got multiple requests from people outside Ontario, but he was fined by the province of Quebec, which claimed he was violating provincial law. He dropped his listings in Quebec, but appealed the decision. William also got an email from the Manitoba Securities Commission saying that before he could do real estate transactions in Manitoba, he had to have a Manitoba license. He says he can't understand why he needs a license simply to post real estate listings online.

So, the situation is still not clear. The question is this: Are flat-fee real estate agents actually trading in real estate or are they simply posting houses for sale online? The answer to this seemingly simple question is important because if agents *are* trading, they must have a license in the province where they are trading. But flat-fee real estate agents say that all they are doing is newspaper or online advertising, and that homeowners are handling the actual sale.

Critics have also complained that real estate agents have a basic conflict of interest because the agent for the buyer typically receives a commission from the seller. So, a buyer's agent could inform a seller that he or she has a buyer for the house, but that the agent wants 2.5 percent of the sales price before the agent will bring the buyer to look at the house. If the seller says no, will the agent still bring the buyer to look at the house? If not, the agent is not looking out for the buyer, but is instead looking out for his or her own interests (i.e., showing the buyer a house where the seller is willing to pay the agent a 2.5 percent commission).

Overall, critics say that the high commissions in the industry attract too many people to the business. One industry executive says the industry is overrun with people who lack experience and knowledge. If commissions decline under the new system, fewer people may seek employment in the industry.

Supporters of CREA responded to these complaints by noting that the consent agreement really didn't change anything because real estate agents have never been able to sell in different provinces. As well, they argue that, since CREA developed the MLS, it shouldn't be forced to share it with competitors. In terms of agent knowledge and experience, they say that should be addressed by licensing and apprenticeship programs for aspiring agents.

In 2011, the Competition Bureau filed another lawsuit, this one against the Toronto Real Estate Board (TREB), arguing that its practices were still preventing brokers from sharing information over the internet. The Competition Bureau acknowledged that real estate agents were allowed to give customers information in person or via fax, but said that TREB's guidelines did not allow customers access to websites that would give them the detailed information they needed to make housing purchase decisions. TREB responded by adopting a new policy that it claimed would give consumers access to information on the Multiple Listing Service. Whether this new policy will resolve the dispute is unclear. What is clear is that the internet has already shaken up several industries (book and music sellers, travel agents, and classified ads), and is now in the process of shaking up the business of selling homes.

In 2013, CREA launched a TV ad campaign demonstrating nightmare scenarios for homeowners that decided to sell their own homes without an agent. They used humor to show errors made by individuals who lacked professional experience. Was this simply an interesting way to demonstrate their value or a sign of desperation for an industry that sees a major transformation on the horizon? Time will tell, but with total agent commissions amounting to $8.26 billion in 2012 (up from $3.96 billion 10 years earlier) the stakes were very high. With the housing boom fizzling and prices stabilizing (and falling in many markets) there was a new threat for CREA. In a rising market, people may be willing to pay commissions of $25 000 when they can sell a property and earn $100 000 to $200 000 in capital gains profit. But what will occur in a prolonged period where prices remain flat or decline and that $25 000 commission is coming straight from the homeowner's equity? This combination of new technology and a downturn in the market may lead to the type of change that CREA has feared for years.

QUESTIONS FOR DISCUSSION

1. Do you think that changes in the way real estate agents are paid will end up saving money for people who buy a home? For people who sell their home?
2. Consider the following statement: *It is unreasonable for the Competition Bureau to force CREA to share its MLS listings with e-brokers because CREA has spent a lot of time and money developing the MLS. Why should CREA have to share information with its competitors when other companies are not forced to?* Do you agree or disagree with this statement? Defend your answer.

MANAGING MARKETING

GOAL OF THE EXERCISE

So far, your business has an identity, you've described the factors that will affect your business, and you've examined your employees, the jobs they'll be performing, and the ways in which you can motivate them. Part 4 of the business plan project asks you to think about marketing's 4 Ps—product, price, place (distribution), and promotion—and how they apply to your business. You'll also examine how you might target your marketing toward a certain group of consumers.

EXERCISE BACKGROUND: PART 4 OF THE BUSINESS PLAN

In Part 1, you briefly described what your business will do. The first step in Part 4 of the plan is to more fully describe the product (good or service) you are planning to sell. Once you have a clear picture of the product, you'll need to describe how this product will stand out in the marketplace—that is, how will it differentiate itself from other products?

In Part 1, you also briefly described who your customers would be. The first step in Part 4 of the plan is to describe your ideal buyer, or target market, in more detail, listing their income level, education level, lifestyle, age, and so forth. This part of the business plan project also asks you to discuss the price of your products, as well as where the buyer can find your product.

Finally, you'll examine how your business will get the attention and interest of the buyer through its promotional mix—advertising, personal selling, sales promotions, and publicity and public relations.

This part of the business plan encourages you to be creative. Have fun! Provide as many details as you possibly can, as this reflects an understanding of your product and your buyer. Marketing is all about finding a need and filling it. Does your product fill a need in the marketplace?

YOUR ASSIGNMENT

MyBizLab

STEP 1

Open the saved Business Plan file you have been working on.

STEP 2

For the purposes of this assignment, you will answer the following questions in Part 4: Managing Marketing:

1. Describe your target market in terms of age, education level, income, and other demographic variables.

   Hint: *Refer to Chapter 12 for more information on the aspects of target marketing and market segmentation that you may want to consider. Be as detailed as possible about who you think your customers will be.*

2. Describe the features and benefits of your product or service.

   Hint: *As you learned in Chapter 12, a product is a bundle of attributes—features and benefits. What features does your product have—what does it look like and what does it do? How will the product benefit the buyer?*

3. How will you make your product stand out in the crowd?

   Hint: *There are many ways to stand out in the crowd, such as having a unique product, outstanding service, or great location. What makes your great idea special? Does it fill an unmet need in the marketplace? How will you differentiate your product to make sure that it succeeds?*

4. What pricing strategy will you choose for your product, and what are the reasons for this strategy?

   Hint: *Refer to Chapter 13 for more information on pricing strategies and tactics. Since your business is new, so is the product. Therefore, you probably want to choose between price skimming and penetration pricing. Which will you choose and why?*

5. Where will customers find your product or service? (That is, what issues of the distribution mix should you consider?)

   Hint: *If your business does not sell its product directly to consumers, what types of retail stores will sell your product? If your product will be sold to another business, which channel of distribution will you use? Refer to Chapter 13 for more information on aspects of distribution you may want to consider.*

6. How will you advertise to your target market? Why have you chosen these forms of advertisement?

   Hint: *Marketers use several different advertising media—specific communication devices for carrying a seller's message to potential customers—each with advantages and drawbacks. Refer to Chapter 13 for a discussion of the types of advertising media you may wish to consider here.*

7. What other methods of promotion will you use and why?

   Hint: *There's more to promotion than simple advertising. Other methods include personal selling, sales promotions, and publicity and public relations. Refer to the discussion of promotion in Chapter 13 for ideas on how to promote your product that go beyond just advertising.*

Note: Once you have answered the questions, save your Word document. You'll be answering additional questions in later chapters.

CBC VIDEOCASE 4-1

BOOMER ADS

The general population is getting older and baby boomers (people born between 1947 and 1966 in Canada) continue to dominate. They have transformed major aspects of society for years. Their large numbers led to the construction of new schools and had an impact on everything from housing trends to vacation needs and pharmaceuticals. Today you may be noticing more individuals with grey hair and wrinkles in advertisements. Marketers are starting to focus on the real needs of the 50-plus age demographic. In addition, there has clearly been a shift to a more open and frank language in ads, with terms like *menopausal skin* being employed. Marketers are creating products aimed specifically at boomers, with a focus not on age but rather on lifestyle. Louis Vuitton's "personal journey" campaign is a perfect example. The luxury brand had once been resistant to using images of older consumers, choosing instead to focus on flashier photos of youthful individuals. Now, however, Louis Vuitton caters to wealthy customers who are more often than not a bit older. The "personal journey" campaign, for example, featured many older celebrities like Sean Connery, Keith Richards, and Catherine Deneuve.

Baby boomers were the original "Pepsi Generation" and, back in the 60s, they defined what it meant to be young. Advertisers believe youth sells and constantly bombard consumers with images of youth. However, with one in three Canadians now belonging to the boomer classification, and coming face to face with the aches and pains of age, marketers are now catering to these needs. For example, *Zoomer* magazine is designed for and geared towards boomers. Instead of images of sweet grandmothers on the cover, however, *Zoomer* paints a more youthful picture using stars like Wayne Gretzky, Margaret Atwood, and Bryan Adams.

Traditionally, it was mainly financial institutions, retirement homes, and pharmaceutical companies that catered to this age group; but today it is not uncommon to see luxury brands and high-end cosmetics companies creating entire campaigns based on the boomers. Demographer David Foot believed that this change was inevitable; however, for a time, as the first baby boomers entered their fifties, marketers were still consumed with images of youth and often ignored this massive generation. Part of the thinking was based on an assumption that boomers were very brand loyal and less likely to switch brands so there was less need to advertise to them. However, research is showing otherwise: a 55-year-old is just as likely to switch brands as a 25-year-old.

One thing is clear: the boomers are a lucrative market. Even as the economy crashed a few years ago, the boomers still had money to spend because most had paid off their mortgages and had savings to tap into. Life expectancy is going up; 50 really is the new 40. Boomers are healthy, they grew up with marketing, and they are willing to spend on themselves and their loved ones. Based on those facts, boomers will be heavily pitched to for many years to come.

QUESTIONS FOR DISCUSSION

1. What do you think of the approach taken by some marketers in using very direct language (such as *menopausal skin*) in their ads?
2. Explain the basic elements of segmentation, targeting, and positioning by using the Louis Vuitton "Personal Journey" campaign as an example.
3. What forms of media would you use to capture the boomer demographic? Avoid stereotypical assumptions and think carefully about social media approaches (that fit) as well as traditional media.
4. List the various influences on consumer behaviour and identify how these influences might have a greater or a less important impact on a baby boomer as opposed to a millennial (Generation Y) consumer.

CBC VIDEOCASE 4-2

CBC

JOE FRESH

At a recent Toronto fashion event, one brand stood out from the crowd. It was different not because of outrageous styling but because of the retailer supporting it. Joe Fresh is the brainchild of Joe Mimran, who is a legend of the Canadian fashion scene. He is the man behind famous brands like Club Monaco and Caban. What is Joe Fresh? Think fashionable merchandise at very low prices offered conveniently at your local Loblaw grocery stores. According to Joe Mimran, the challenge presented by Loblaw was to create fashions that could appeal to various tastes across the country and yet also be stylish at very low prices. Joe could provide the fashion expertise but there was also a need for a brand "that would actually resonate with the consumer." Clearly, Joe Fresh is a nice play on words that both fits consumers' constant insatiable search for new product styles and pays respect to the retail home of the brand. Although this combination is a very unlikely fit for the fashion catwalk, Joe Fresh is already making a major impression on the industry.

You may be wondering why Loblaw would go down this route and make a major stake on the clothing business (which is not part of their core strength). However, if you examine the market it is clear that there is a growing consolidation and sticking to the status quo was dangerous. At the time, Loblaw was struggling after installing a new inventory management system. Competitors like Walmart were hurting Loblaw by selling food items and providing low-cost clothing. Walmart was also planning to add new superstores. Joe Fresh was Loblaw's way of addressing this growing threat. While Walmart has strong clothing sales figures, its retail brand perception is low. If Joe Fresh can meet low price points and add cachet, there is a great opportunity for Loblaw. It is all part of the market evolution. Pharmacies (like Shoppers Drug Mart) are selling groceries, Walmart and Loblaw are now selling pharmaceuticals, and naturally Loblaw is now selling clothes.

Joe Fresh is trying to help capture some of Loblaw's previous glory. Low-cost fashion is a potential hit, especially in troubled economic times. According to the video, Joe Fresh is now the second-largest clothing line (by sales) in Canada. The company does not disclose its statistics but its goal is to reach $1 billion a year in sales. Based on its initial success, Loblaw has asked Joe Mimran to design other household goods to add unique flavour and freshness to those categories. Mr. Mimran knows a thing or two about such an expansion, as his Caban business failed after a similar attempt. But he plans to use this first-hand knowledge and the lessons learned to make Joe Fresh a success across product lines. Time will tell whether this relationship continues to bear fruit or starts to rot in the attempt to expand.

QUESTIONS FOR DISCUSSION

1. How does the Joe Fresh brand of fashion products create value for consumers? What is their value equation?
2. Describe the target market for Joe Fresh fashions across various market segmentation variables.
3. Explain the concept of brand equity and link it to the growth of the Joe Fresh brand. How does the Joe Fresh brand stack up to Walmart's low-cost fashion? How does it stack up to popular fashionable brands like Zara?
4. What do you think of the brand extension of Joe Fresh into other categories such as housewares? Do you think it is a good idea? Why or why not?
5. How can Loblaw use social media to create extra buzz for the Joe Fresh brand? Provide concrete examples and a framework of ideas (slogan, social media campaigns, advergaming, etc.).

PART 5 MANAGING FINANCIAL ISSUES

© microworks - Fotolia.com

Money *and* Banking

CHAPTER 14

LO AFTER READING THIS CHAPTER, YOU SHOULD BE ABLE TO:

- LO-1 Define *money* and identify the different forms it takes in Canada's money supply.
- LO-2 Understand the different kinds of *financial institutions* that make up the *Canadian financial system* and explain the services they offer.
- LO-3 Explain the functions of the *Bank of Canada* and describe the tools it uses to control the money supply.
- LO-4 Explain the role of *alternate banks*, *specialized lending and savings intermediaries*, and *investment dealers* in the Canadian financial system.
- LO-5 Discuss some of the institutions and activities in *international banking and finance*.

Beware of the Credit-Card Trap!

© Sam Spiro/Fotolia

As you walk in the downtown core of any major metropolitan city, what do you see on top of the buildings? You will notice that many of them bear the names of banks and insurance companies. The financial services industry is very healthy; the top five banks in Canada earned combined profits of $28 billion in 2012 alone. Despite some recent missteps, the fundamental math is strong. In 2013, the Canadian banking system was ranked number one in the world for the fifth straight year. The industry is governed by the rules of the Bank Act and supported by internal company policies. In recent years, banks have expanded their services to meet a wider range of consumer investment needs, and service fees have grown and added to the bottom line. Credit cards are another major source of revenues.

How many bank-issued credit cards do you possess? How responsible are you with those credit cards? How much interest do you pay every year? Do you even know the answer to these questions? Look around your lecture hall. Let's say there are 100 people in your class and they are all clients of your local bank. Your classmates deposit money in their accounts (thus, providing funds) and receive a very low interest rate in return (in recent years it has been below the 1 percent range). You use your bank-issued credit card to charge $1000 to pay for your spring break vacation. You don't have the money to pay it back, so you have contractually agreed to pay back interest of 20 percent.

Most people won't think twice about how much interest they pay every year because the credit-card issuers allow individuals to pay back borrowed money slowly with the help of minimum payments. If you only pay the minimum, it will take you years—and hundreds of dollars—to pay off even this minor debt.

Beware of the Minimum Payment

> **HOW WILL THIS HELP ME?**
>
> By understanding the material in this chapter, you will learn what money is, where it comes from, how the supply of money grows, and the kinds of services that are available to you from the financial services industry.

It may seem like you are getting a great deal by being generously allowed to make only the minimum payment of $50 (or 2 to 3 percent of the balance), but, of course, this deal comes with a major price. If you are carrying $10 000 of credit-card debt at 20 percent interest, for example, you are paying about $2000 in interest per year. Could you think of anything else you could do with an extra $2000 (a trip, a nice music system, new furniture)? For many people, the whole credit-card experience is like getting onto a defective treadmill that actually starts off slowly, and then gets progressively quicker before the button gets stuck on high speed. In that situation, you would need to find an effective way to jump off or get someone to pull the plug for you. Unfortunately, many people do not know how to help themselves get out of the credit-card trap.

Some people even delude themselves into thinking that their situation is better than it actually is. They make the minimum payments and may carry a debt load of, say, $10 000 on their credit cards, but in the meantime they have the same amount of money sitting in a bank account. Why would someone collect 1 percent on a $10 000 bank-account balance and simultaneously pay 20 percent interest on a credit-card debt? It's illogical. Under these circumstances, it is costing you $1900 annually (–$2000 cost of credit +$100 interest from the account) to fool yourself.

Some people just never do the math. They can't be bothered or they just don't understand. (You have been warned.) Others are fearful that if they pay off their credit-card bills, they will just load their cards up again. If that is the case for you, then you need to use your scissors to cut up your credit cards. Discipline is required.

If you don't have the money to pay for previous debts, you can use other sources of lower-interest borrowing to pay off the bills.

Here are *some short-term options:*

- A home-equity line of credit (HELOC) can be used to pay down your debt. These days you can get a rate of 4 to 5 percent (total savings: $1500 to $1600 per year on the same $10 000 debt). So why not transfer the credit-card debt to this lower-rate option and use the savings to pay down your debt quicker?
- Credit-card issuers often offer cheque transfers at, say, 0.99 to 3.99 percent for six to nine months. You can transfer the 20 percent debt on your Visa, for example, to your MasterCard, when it is offering a temporary 1.99 percent deal. This sort of offer can save you hundreds of dollars and gives you extra funds to pay off principal. The catch is that, at the end of the six to nine months, you will be charged a high rate again. (Remember, this is only a short-term solution. Don't add to your debt; instead, use the time to pay it off).
- If you must take on debt by credit card, there are some products that charge more reasonable rates. According to the Canadian Bankers Association (CBA), there are over 70 low-interest credit cards on the market. The CBA define low interest as below 12 percent (which is still very high). RBC launched a credit card called the RBC My Project Credit MasterCard. It provides as much as $40 000 with 0 percent interest for six months and interest of 4.99 percent above prime after that.

The real solution: Buy what you can afford and pay cash. Then there is no need for long-term calculations and financially troubling interest payments.

Benefits and the Best Advice

Credit cards are still a great way to make purchases conveniently without carrying large sums of money—if you act responsibly. They provide a 21- to 30-day interest-free loan if you pay on time. In addition, you can earn points that can lead to free travel and free products.

If you are responsible, you can take advantage of the benefits without over-contributing to the construction of another downtown high-rise building. In this chapter, we learn about the definition of money. Credit cards are not money. They can be used as a medium of exchange, but they must be used wisely or they will have a very negative effect on your personal wealth.

QUESTIONS FOR DISCUSSION

1. Identify and explain two of the fundamental warnings about credit cards that are contained in this opening case.
2. Do you believe the typical consumer understands the full extent of the so-called "credit-card trap?" What elements of the credit game are the most difficult to comprehend for most consumers?
3. Do you believe the government should place tighter controls on interest rates and ban credit-card companies from charging rates above 15 percent? Why? Why not?

LO-1 WHAT IS MONEY?

MONEY Any object generally accepted by people as payment for goods and services.

When someone asks you how much money you have, what do you say? Do you count the bills and coins in your pockets? Do you mention the funds in your chequing and savings accounts? What about stocks, or bonds, or your car? Taken together, the value of everything you own is your personal wealth. Not all of it, however, is money.

The Characteristics of Money

Modern money generally takes the form of stamped metal or printed paper issued by governments (e.g., Canadian dollars or euros). The Chinese were using metal money to represent the objects they were exchanging as early as 1100 BCE. However, many different objects (cows, shells, stones, and dolphin teeth) have been used as money in different societies. Theoretically, just about anything *portable*, *divisible*, *durable*, and *stable* can serve as **money**. To appreciate these qualities, imagine using something that lacks these characteristics:

- **Portability.** Try lugging 1000 pounds of cow as a unit of exchange from shop to shop, as was done in ancient agrarian economies. In contrast, modern currency is light and easy to handle.
- **Divisibility.** How would you divide your cow if you wanted to buy a hat, a book, and a radio from three different stores? Is a pound of head worth as much as a pound of leg? Modern currency is easily divisible into smaller parts with fixed values—for example, a dollar for 10 dimes.
- **Durability.** Your cow will lose value every day (and eventually die). Modern currency, however, neither dies nor spoils, and, if it wears out, it can be replaced. The Canadian government recently converted paper bills into polymer plastic bills to increase durability. However, just months after the release, there were questions about the bills' ability to withstand heat when a family claimed that the bills shrivelled and melted after being placed close to a heater.[1]
- **Stability.** If cows were in short supply, you might be able to make quite a deal for yourself. In the middle of a year with an abundant cow supply, however, the market would be flooded with cows, so their value would fall. The value of our paper money also fluctuates, but it is considerably more stable and predictable.

The Functions of Money

Imagine, for a moment, a successful cow rancher who needs a new fence. In a *barter economy*—one in which goods are exchanged directly for one another—he or she would have to find someone who is willing to exchange a fence for a cow (or parts of it). If no fence maker wants a cow, the rancher must find someone else—for example, a wagon maker—who does want a cow. Then, the rancher must hope that the fence maker will trade for a new wagon. In a money economy, the rancher would sell his or her cow, receive money, and exchange the money for goods, like a new fence.

Thus, the barter economy is relatively inefficient. This example demonstrates the three functions of money:

<<< Cattle are not portable, durable, or stable, making them an unsuitable medium of exchange in the modern monetized economy.

© Sam Spiro/Fotolia

1. **It is a medium of exchange.** Like the rancher "trading" money for a new fence, money is used to buy and sell things. Without money, we would be bogged down in a system of barter.
2. **It is a store of value.** Pity the rancher whose cow gets sick on Monday and who wants to buy some clothes on the following Saturday, by which time the cow may have died and lost its value. In the form of currency, however, money can be used for future purchases, since it "stores" value.
3. **It is a unit of account**. Money lets us measure the relative values of goods and services. It acts as a measure of worth because all products can be valued and accounted for in terms of money. For example, the concepts of $1000 worth of clothes or $500 in labour costs have universal meaning.

The Spendable Money Supply: M-1

For money to serve as a medium of exchange, a store of value, or a unit of account, buyers and sellers must agree on its value. The value of money depends in part on its supply (how much money is in circulation). When the money supply is high, the value of money drops. When the money supply is low, the value of money increases.

It is not easy to measure the supply of money, nor is there complete agreement on exactly how it should be measured. The "narrow" definition of the money supply is called **M-1**, which includes only the most liquid forms of money—currency and demand deposits (chequing accounts) in banks. As of September 2012, M-1 totalled $675.2 billion in Canada.[2]

Currency is paper money and coins issued by the Canadian government. It is widely used to pay small bills. Canadian currency—which clearly states, "This note is legal tender"—is money the law requires a creditor to accept in payment of a debt. Counterfeiting of paper currency is now a worldwide problem, partly because new technologies allow counterfeiters to make real-looking bills rather easily. In 2011, there were over 1.5 billion Bank of Canada notes in circulation with over 52 000 counterfeit bills detected.[3] To reduce counterfeiting, the Bank of Canada has issued new high-tech polymer $20, $50, and, $100 bills.[4]

A **cheque** is an order instructing the bank to pay a given sum to a specified person or firm. Cheques enable buyers to make large purchases without having to carry large amounts of cash. Money in chequing accounts, known as **demand deposits**, is counted in M-1 because such funds may be withdrawn at any time without notice.

M-1 Plus the Convertible Money Supply: M-2

M-2 includes everything in M-1 plus items that cannot be spent directly, but that are easily converted to spendable forms: time deposits, money market mutual funds, and savings deposits. M-2 accounts for nearly all the nation's money supply. As this overall supply of money increases, more is available for consumer purchases and business investment. When this supply decreases, less is available for consumer purchases and business investment. As of October 2012, M-2 totalled $1128.7 billion in Canada.[5] M-2 was up about 10 percent in 2012 from the previous year and, despite low inflation at the time, this statistic brought renewed fears of higher inflation ahead.[6]

Unlike demand deposits, **time deposits** require prior notice of withdrawal and cannot be transferred by cheque. The supply of money in time deposits—such as *certificates of deposit (CDs)* and *savings certificates*—are not nearly as popular today in a low-interest rate environment as they were when 10 to 15 percent interest rates were common.

Money market mutual funds are operated by investment companies that bring together pools of assets from many investors. The fund buys a collection of short-term, low-risk financial securities. Ownership of and profits (or losses) from the sale of these securities are shared among the fund's investors.

Credit Cards: Plastic Money?

Although not included in M-1 or M-2, credit—especially through credit cards—has become a major factor in the purchase of consumer goods in Canada. The use of MasterCard, Visa, American Express, and credit cards issued by individual businesses has become so widespread that many people refer to credit cards as "plastic money." Credit cards are actually a money substitute; they serve as a temporary medium of exchange, but are not a store of value. With growing fears of rising debt as an incentive, the Canadian government is planning to adopt a new code of conduct to further regulate credit and debit cards.[7] Canadians hold 74.5 million MasterCard and Visa credit cards. The value of goods and services bought with credit cards in Canada amounts to approximately US$30 billion annually.[8] Worldwide, the total value of goods purchased with Visa cards is above $3 trillion annually.[9] Banks like the Bank of Montreal, the Canadian Imperial Bank of Commerce, the Bank of Nova Scotia, and TD Canada Trust are the biggest issuers of Visa cards in Canada. Each time a card is used, the banks receive an "interchange" fee, a percentage of the purchase value of the transaction. The banks use these fees to offset costs they incur with loyalty and points programs. Despite rising fees, merchants understand the value of plastic to their businesses; there are over 1.25 million merchant outlets that accept Visa and MasterCard in Canada.[10]

Credit-card fraud is a major concern for both consumers and retailers. In 2011, criminals were responsible for over $366 million in fraudulent charges against nearly half a million Canadian customers. To deal with these problems, credit-card companies have developed new chip encryption technology that requires an additional password. However, this does not mean that these new cards are totally safe, only safer. Just like debit cards, there are ways for crooks to bypass the added layer of security (ranging from simple observation

M-1 Only the most liquid forms of money (currency and demand deposits).

CURRENCY Paper money and coins issued by the government.

CHEQUE An order instructing the bank to pay a given sum to a specified person or firm.

DEMAND DEPOSITS Money in chequing accounts; counted as M-1 because such funds may be withdrawn at any time without notice.

M-2 Everything in M-1 plus savings deposits, time deposits, and money market mutual funds.

TIME DEPOSIT A deposit that requires prior notice to make a withdrawal; cannot be transferred to others by cheque.

MONEY MARKET MUTUAL FUNDS Funds operated by investment companies that bring together pools of assets from many investors to buy short-term, low-risk financial securities.

>>> Chip encryption technology was introduced to reduce credit-card fraud.

Image Source/Fotolia

to hidden cameras). In addition, the new chip cards in Canada are also equipped with the traditional magnetic stripes (that can have information skimmed from compromised terminals) because many merchants are still not equipped with the new chip terminals, and the United States is resisting this change. The credit card companies don't want to lose potential transactions, so they are currently supplying cards with both features.[11] Industry sources still claim there has been a reduction of fraud with the new cards.

LO-2 THE CANADIAN FINANCIAL SYSTEM

Many forms of money, especially demand deposits and time deposits, depend on the existence of financial institutions to provide a broad spectrum of services to both individuals and businesses. In this section, we describe the major types of financial institutions, explain how they work, and describe some of the special services they offer. We also explain their role as creators of money and discuss the regulation of the Canadian banking system.

Financial Institutions

There are several types of financial institutions in Canada, but the main function of all of them is to facilitate the flow of money from sectors with surpluses to those with deficits, by attracting funds into chequing and savings accounts. Incoming funds are loaned to individuals and businesses and, perhaps, invested in government securities.

For many years, the financial community in Canada has been divided rather clearly into four distinct legal areas. These "four financial pillars" are (1) chartered banks, (2) alternate banks (e.g., trust companies and credit unions/caisses populaires), (3) life insurance companies and other specialized lending and saving intermediaries (e.g., factors, finance companies, venture capital firms, mutual funds, and pension funds), and (4) investment dealers. We will discuss each of these financial institutions in detail in this chapter, but it is important to understand that many changes have taken place in the financial services industry in the last couple of decades, and the lines between these four pillars have blurred.

Changes Affecting Financial Institutions

The crumbling of the four financial pillars began in 1980 when changes were made to the Bank Act. Since then, many other changes have been made. For example, banks are now permitted to own securities dealers, to establish subsidiaries to sell mutual funds, and to sell commercial paper (see Chapter 15). Trust companies have declined in importance, and many trust companies have been bought by banks or insurance companies. The largest trust company—Canada Trust—merged with the Toronto-Dominion Bank and became TD Canada Trust.

FINANCIAL PILLAR #1—CHARTERED BANKS

A **chartered bank** is a privately owned, profit-seeking financial intermediary that serves individuals, businesses, and non-business organizations. Chartered banks are the largest and most important financial institutions in Canada. In November 2012, Canadian chartered banks had assets totaling $2.35 trillion.[12] Chartered banks offer chequing and savings accounts, make loans, and provide many services to their customers. They are the main source of short-term loans for business firms. As you will see in the Managing in Turbulent Times Box entitled "Canadian Banks: Soundest in the World," there is a lot of praise directed at the Canadian banking system. The *Guardian* referred to Canadian banks as the envy of the world, and the *Economist* referred to them as the primary reason for Canada's economic resilience.[13]

Unlike in the United States, where there are hundreds of banks each with only a few branches, in Canada, there are only a few banks, each with hundreds of branches. The five largest Canadian banks account for about 90 percent of total bank assets. Schedule I banks are those that are Canadian-owned and have no more than 10 percent of voting shares controlled by a single interest. Schedule II banks are those that may be domestically owned, but do not meet the 10 percent limit, or may be foreign-controlled. Several foreign banks have set up Schedule II subsidiaries in Canada. The Bank Act limits foreign-controlled banks to deposits that do not exceed 8 percent of the total domestic assets of all banks in Canada. The largest chartered banks in Canada are shown in Table 14.1, ranked based on revenues.

Services Offered by Banks

The banking business is highly competitive; therefore, banks no longer just accept deposits and make loans. Most banks now offer pension

CHARTERED BANK A privately owned, profit-seeking firm that serves individuals, non-business organizations, and businesses as a financial intermediary.

MANAGING IN TURBULENT TIMES

Canadian Banks: Soundest in the World

In 2012, the World Economic Forum ranked Canadian banks as the soundest in the world. It was the fourth year in a row that Canadian banks achieved the top ranking. The ranking was particularly impressive given the widespread uncertainty about the global economic situation, stock-market volatility, and sovereign debt crisis in Europe. Canada's strong banking system began to receive publicity during the worldwide recession of 2008 to 2009, amidst concern that U.S. banks were in financial trouble. The situation was much different in Canada, where the top five Canadian banks at that time earned $18.9 billion in profits, while the top five U.S. banks lost $37 billion.

Canadian banks are strictly regulated. For example, they must maintain a large financial cushion to absorb potential losses, and their shares must be widely held. The Office of the Superintendent of Financial Institutions (OSFI), Canada's banking regulator, is very conservative and keeps a close watch on the activities of Canadian banks. The OSFI's rules on Canadian banks are stricter than the rules that many foreign countries impose on their banks. At Canada's six largest banks, for example, levels of the most secure capital (known as Tier 1 capital) are almost double the OSFI standard (and more than three times the global standard). There is a bit of irony here, because the conservative nature of the Canadian banking system has been a source of complaints from Canadian consumers in the past. But consumers now appreciate the strength of the Canadian banking system.

Mortgage loans are an important activity for banks, and Canadian banks have been very conservative (until fairly recently—see this chapter's closing case) relative to their U.S. counterparts. This conservatism can be seen in mortgage arrears statistics; less than 1 percent of Canadian mortgage holders have gone more than three months without making a payment. By contrast, the U.S. financial system has received multibillion-dollar bailouts, and President Obama admitted that the Canadian banking system was managed much better than the U.S. system. Canadian banks in the U.S.—Royal Bank's RBC Bank, Bank of Montreal's Harris Bank, and Toronto Dominion's TD Bank—have all noted a surge in deposits as their U.S. rivals struggled with financial problems.

Canadian banks are also better off because they are shielded from a certain amount of foreign competition. Because of that, Canadian banks did not feel compelled to get involved in the kinds of risky mortgages that got U.S. banks into trouble. When Canadian banks did get involved (on a much smaller scale), they showed the risky mortgages on their balance sheets, so the public knew exactly what their financial condition was.

CRITICAL THINKING QUESTION

1. Consider the following statement: *Governments around the world should continuously apply very strict standards for banks, even in good economic times, so that the kinds of financial problems that have developed in Europe and the U.S. will not happen again.* Do you agree or disagree with this statement? Explain your reasoning.

TABLE 14.1 Top 10 Banks in Canada (ranked by revenues)[14]

Company	Sales Revenue (billions of dollars)
1. Royal Bank of Canada	36.0
2. Toronto-Dominion Bank	25.4
3. Bank of Nova Scotia	23.7
4. Bank of Montreal	15.4
5. Canadian Imperial Bank of Commerce	14.9
6. National Bank of Canada	5.3
7. HSBC Bank Canada	3.1 (*Schedule II Bank)
8. Laurentian Bank	1.19
9. Amex Bank of Canada	1.03 (*Schedule II Bank)
10. MBNA Canada Bank	1.02 (*Schedule II Bank)

"And, hey, don't kill yourself trying to pay it back. You know our motto—'What the hell, it's only money.'"

© Mikhail Olykainen/Shutterstock

services, trust services, international services, financial advice, and electronic money transfer.

PENSION SERVICES

Most banks help customers establish savings plans for retirement. Banks serve as financial intermediaries by receiving funds and investing them as directed by customers. They also provide customers with information on investment possibilities.

TRUST SERVICES

Many banks offer trust services—the management of funds left "in the bank's trust." In return for a fee, the trust department will perform such tasks as making your monthly bill payments and managing your investment portfolio. Trust departments also manage the estates of deceased persons.

INTERNATIONAL SERVICES

The three main international services offered by banks are currency exchange, letters of credit, and banker's acceptances. Suppose that a Canadian company wants to buy a product from a French supplier. For a fee, it can use one or more of three services offered by its bank:

1. It can exchange Canadian dollars for euros at a Canadian bank and then pay the French supplier in euros.
2. It can pay its bank to issue a **letter of credit**—a promise by the bank to pay the French firm a certain amount if specified conditions are met.
3. It can pay its bank to draw up a **banker's acceptance**, which promises that the bank will pay some specified amount at a future date.

FINANCIAL ADVICE

Many banks, both large and small, help their customers manage their money. Depending on the customer's situation, the bank may recommend different investment opportunities. The recommended mix might include guaranteed investment certificates, mutual funds, stocks, and bonds. Today, bank advertisements often stress the growing role of banks as financial advisers. CIBC's first quarter profit for its wealth management division was $100 million in 2012, an increase of 50 percent.[15]

Take a look at the following "There's an APP for That!" feature that outlines three banking and financial investment apps.

ELECTRONIC FUNDS TRANSFER

Electronic funds transfer (EFT) provides for payments and collections by transferring financial information electronically. Such systems can help a businessperson close an important business deal by transferring money from Vancouver to Halifax within seconds. In addition to internet and telephone banking, examples include automated banking machines, direct deposits and withdrawals, point-of-sale transfers, smart cards, and mobile digital wallets.

- *Automated Banking Machines (ABMs)* **ABMs** (also called automated teller machines—ATMs) let you bank at almost any time of day or night. There are over 60 000 ABMs in Canada and more than 17 500 are bank-owned.[16] The independent "white label" machines usually charge higher fees. FirstOntario Credit Union recently launched a new version it calls the Personal Assistant Teller (PAT). This system provides a video link with a teller who can talk to the consumer about loans or listen to complaints in addition to offering the traditional ABM transactions.[17] (See Figure 14.1 for more about ABMs/ATMs.)

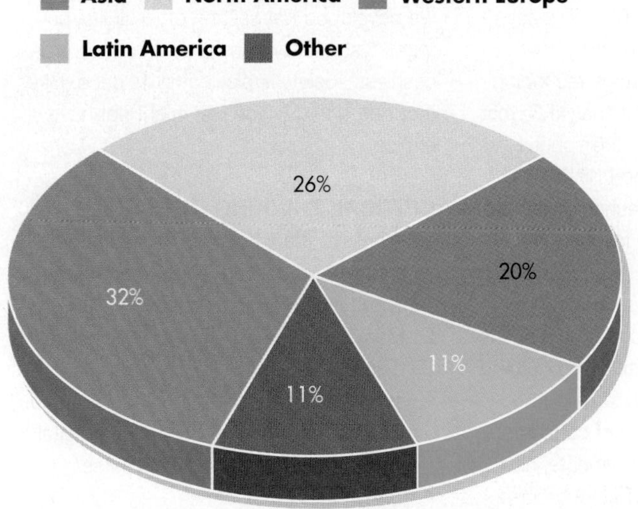

FIGURE 14.1 Global dispersion of ABMs (ATMs)

- *Direct Deposits and Withdrawals* These enable a user to authorize, in advance, specific, regular deposits and withdrawals. You can arrange to have paycheques and social assistance cheques automatically deposited and recurring expenses, such as insurance premiums and utility bills, automatically paid.
- *Point-of-Sale Transfers* These permits consumers to pay for retail purchases with a **debit card**, a type of plastic money that immediately reduces the balance in the user's bank account when used. Approximately 94 percent of Canadians have a debit card and they are accepted in over 450 000 retail establishments across the nation. Over four billion transactions are completed annually using the Interac network.[18]
- *Smart Cards* **Smart cards** (e.g., phone cards) can be programmed with "electronic money" at ATM machines or with special hookups. After using your card to purchase an item, you can then check an electronic display to see how much money is left. European and Asian consumers are the most avid users. In North America, smart cards are most popular in gas pump payments,

THERE'S AN APP FOR THAT!

1. **TD (Canada)** >>> **Platforms:** *Apple, Android, BlackBerry*
   Source: TD Bank Group
   Key Features: Provides quick, easy, secure access to accounts, helpful information, and convenient tools.
2. **Mint.com Personal Finance** >>> **Platforms:** *Apple, Android, BlackBerry*
   Source: mint.com
   Key Features: Allows you to track, budget, and manage your money in one place.
3. **Globe Investor** >>> **Platforms:** *Apple, BlackBerry*
   Source: The Globe and Mail
   Key Features: A guide to help you take control of your investments; Canada's authoritative source of business news and of up-to-the minute market data.

APP DISCOVERY EXERCISE

Since APP availability changes, conduct your own search for "Top 3" Finance APPS and identify the key features.

LETTER OF CREDIT A promise by a bank to pay money to a business firm if certain conditions are met.

BANKER'S ACCEPTANCE A promise that a bank will pay a specified amount of money at a future date.

AUTOMATED BANKING MACHINES (ABMs) Electronic machines that enable bank customers to conduct account related transactions 24 hours a day, 7 days a week.

DEBIT CARD A type of plastic money that immediately upon use reduces the balance in the user's bank account and transfers it to the store's account.

SMART-CARDS A credit-card-sized computer that can be programmed with "electronic money."

followed by prepaid phone service, ATMs, self-operated check-outs, and automated banking services.[19] Analysts predict that in the near future smart cards will function as much more than electronic purses.

- *Mobile (Digital) Wallet* At a recent meeting of the Canadian Bankers Association, the country's largest banks agreed to standards to set the tone for the transition from plastic cards to mobile wallets. Financial institutions and telecommunications companies will embed credit and debit card information in smartphones, allowing you to pay for groceries and shop for clothes using your mobile device.[20] CIBC and Rogers Communications have already signed a deal; the service is launching on BlackBerry devices first and will quickly expand to include other platforms.[21] In a sign of the times, Starbucks recently launched an app that allows customers to pay for their grande latte with their mobile phones.[22] Read the E-Business and Social Media Solutions box entitled "Say Hello to Your Digital Wallet," to learn more about evolving methods of exchange.

Figure 14.2 summarizes the services that chartered banks offer. Banks are chartered by the federal government and are closely regulated when they provide these services.

Bank Loans

Banks are the major source of short-term loans for business. Although banks make long-term loans to some firms, they prefer to specialize in providing short-term funds to finance inventories and accounts receivable. A secured loan is backed by collateral (e.g., accounts receivable). If the borrower cannot repay the loan, the bank sells the collateral. An unsecured loan is backed only by the borrower's promise to repay it. Only the most credit-worthy borrowers can get unsecured loans.

Borrowers pay interest on their loans. Large firms with excellent credit records pay the **prime rate of interest**, which is the lowest rate charged to borrowers. This rate changes often because of changes in the demand and supply of loanable funds, as well as Bank of Canada policies. The so-called "Big Six" Canadian banks (Royal Bank, CIBC, Bank of Montreal, Bank of Nova Scotia, TD Canada Trust, and National Bank of Canada) typically act in concert with respect to the prime rate.

PRIME RATE OF INTEREST The lowest rate charged to borrowers.

E-BUSINESS AND SOCIAL MEDIA SOLUTIONS

Say Hello to Your Digital Wallet

Are you ready to put away your old-fashioned leather wallet (filled with paper and coins) for the future of business transactions? If you are fearful of technology, your answer is clear: No. However, if you are an innovative consumer, looking to get a head start on the future, you are in luck: the digital wallet has arrived in Canada.

Hand-out/TIM HORTONS INC./ Newscom

Simon Whitfield is a famous Canadian athlete who has achieved great victories (most notably, an Olympic gold in triathlon). In November 2012, he also became the first Canadian to use a tap-and-go digital payment app (from Rogers and CIBC) to pay for a retail credit-card purchase with a smartphone within the country. Mr. Whitfield was chosen to demonstrate the first point-of-sale mobile-credit transaction at a Tim Hortons in downtown Toronto. As he pointed his telephone at a scanner to pay for his coffee, he symbolically broke a barrier that may very well revolutionize how Canadians pay for products. This is the wave of the future, and, in places like South Korea and Japan, there is nothing new about it. Consumers can use their smartphones to purchase everything from public-transportation fares to groceries.

The digital wallet will link to your various credit cards, debit cards, and loyalty and reward cards. Imagine a day when you will no longer need to carry 10 to 20 plastic cards. The day is coming soon. So, how does it work? The system uses a technology called Near Field Communications (NFC) that enables the consumer to use their phone to transmit data over very short distances. There are other competing technologies, but the major banks seem to be favouring this system.

Will consumers evolve? A significant percentage of people have already grown accustomed to e-tickets and smartphone boarding passes for airplane flights. According to a ComScore survey, 30 percent of consumers are open to in-store mobile payments, and that number rises to over half among current smartphone users. In addition, 52 percent of those consumers would like to use their digital wallet in stores and online. These mobile payments are just one part of a growing move towards machine-to-machine payments (M2M); connections between devices without the need for human intervention. In 2013, there were approximately 140 million M2M transactions, and that number is expected to reach 50 billion by 2020.

Once upon a time, people used cows and shells to barter for goods. Society moved to precious metals and later to minted coins and paper. In the early days of the internet, we developed Paypal and other digital payment systems, but now the march towards a cashless society is picking up its pace. Like it or not, one day you just might not have a choice.

CRITICAL THINKING QUESTIONS

1. What are the financial implications of the digital wallet for retailers? What are the implications for consumers?
2. Many individuals are fearful of the growing digitization of our world. A cashless digital society is a very scary thought for some. Debate the pros and cons of the digital wallet with one of your classmates.

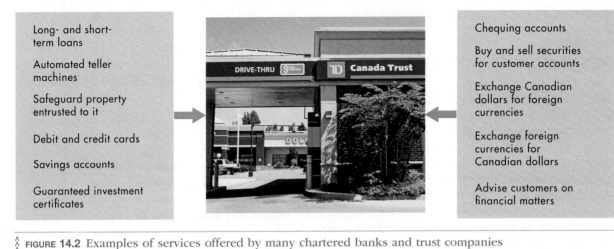

Long- and short-term loans

Automated teller machines

Safeguard property entrusted to it

Debit and credit cards

Savings accounts

Guaranteed investment certificates

Chequing accounts

Buy and sell securities for customer accounts

Exchange Canadian dollars for foreign currencies

Exchange foreign currencies for Canadian dollars

Advise customers on financial matters

FIGURE 14.2 Examples of services offered by many chartered banks and trust companies

Francis Vachon/Alamy

Banks as Creators of Money

Financial institutions provide a special service to the economy—they create money. They don't mint bills and coins, but by taking in deposits and making loans, they expand the money supply. We will first look at how this expansion process works, assuming that banks have a **reserve requirement**, which means they must keep a portion of their chequable deposits in vault cash or as deposits with the Bank of Canada. (The reserve requirement was dropped over two decades ago, and the implications of this change are described later.)

Suppose you saved $100, took it to a bank, and opened a chequing account. Let's assume, for the moment, that there is a reserve requirement, and that it is 10 percent. Your bank must therefore keep $10 of your $100 deposit in reserve, so it has only $90 to lend to other borrowers. Now, suppose a person named Jennifer Leclerc borrows $90 from your bank. She now has $90 added to her chequing account. Assume that she writes a cheque for $90 payable to Canadian Tire. Canadian Tire's bank ends up with a $90 deposit, and that bank is also required to keep $9 in reserve. It therefore has $81 to lend out to someone else. This process of deposit expansion can continue as shown in Figure 14.3, and your original deposit of $100 could result in an increase of $1000 in new deposits for all banks in the system.

But what happens if there is no reserve requirement? At the extreme, it means that banks could (theoretically) create infinite amounts of money, because they wouldn't have to keep any in reserve. But banks will not do this because it is risky. So, in practice, the dropping of the reserve requirement simply means that banks will be able to create more money than they did when there was a reserve requirement.

RESERVE REQUIREMENT The requirement (until 1991) that banks keep a portion of their chequable deposits in vault cash or as deposits with the Bank of Canada.

Deposit	Money Held in Reserve by Bank	Money to Lend	Total Supply
$100.00	$10.00	$90.00	**$190.00**
90.00	9.00	81.00	**271.00**
81.00	8.10	72.90	**343.90**
72.90	7.29	65.61	**409.51**
65.61	6.56	59.05	**468.56**

>>> FIGURE 14.3 How the chartered banking system creates money

Other Changes in Banking

Substantial changes in addition to those already described are taking place in banking, including *deregulation*, changes in *customer demands*, and changes in *international banking*.

DEREGULATION

Deregulation has allowed banks to alter their historical role as intermediaries between depositors and borrowers. Canada's banks have been diversifying to provide more financial products to their clients. Training bankers to be effective in this environment is necessary, and over 100 executives at TD Canada Trust attended a Harvard University course that taught them to think like investment bankers. They have learned the lessons well and have embraced their new role. In fact, the major Canadian banks recently petitioned U.S. regulators to exempt them from the Volker Rule (part of the Dodd Frank Wall Street Reform Consumer Protection Act), which would prevent them from investing in private equity funds and other speculative investments because they are deposit-taking banks.[23]

Deregulation has opened up new revenue streams for Canadian banks but, in an interesting twist, a few years ago the "Big Six" banks actually asked the government to get tougher with mortgage rules (new regulations) to cool off the housing market. They called for a return to tougher rules moving the minimum down-payment from 5 percent to 10 percent and reducing amortization maximum periods from 35 to 30 years.[24] The Canadian government responded to this request in 2011 and then actually reduced the maximum amortization period for insured mortgages to 25 years in 2012.[25]

CHANGES IN CONSUMER DEMANDS

Consumers are no longer content to keep money in a bank when they can get more elsewhere. They are turning to electronic banks like ING Direct and President's Choice Financial (a Loblaw subsidiary) that pay higher interest on savings accounts. Such companies can pay higher rates because they don't incur the costs associated with having branches like traditional banks do.

Traditional banks are responding to this new competition by selling a growing array of services in their branches. For example, the Bank of Montreal recently started providing bereavement services. If a customer's mother dies, BMO offers a service that takes care of everything from the funeral planning to redirecting the deceased person's mail.[26] Banks are finding new ways to attract and serve their clientele in order to remain competitive and attract a new generation that does not have the same loyalties as previous generations.

Banks also want to get much more involved in selling insurance, but, as of 2013, the Bank Act prohibited banks from selling insurance in their branch offices (they are allowed to sell insurance at other locations). Canadian banks are being "creative" in keeping insurance and banking activities separate (but not too separate). In Oakville, Ontario, Royal Bank of Canada consumers who enter the branch will notice the RBC bank on the right and RBC Insurance on the left. The two operations are separated by only a glass wall. Dan Danyluk, the CEO of the Insurance Brokers Association of Canada, says that RBC's strategy is ignoring the intent of the law. He argues that credit-granting institutions like banks should not be allowed to sell insurance in their branches because they may try to tie the buying of, say, car insurance to the approval of the loan to buy the car.[27] The government agrees and it recently sent a message by banning banks from selling unauthorized insurance on their websites.[28]

All of this activity is transforming the profit base of banks. In the past, they made most of their money from the spread between interest rates paid to depositors and the rates charged on loans. Investment banking, on the other hand, is fee-based. Banks are making a larger proportion of their profits from fees, and this is blurring the traditional boundary between banks and securities firms.

BANK OF CANADA Canada's central bank; formed in 1935.

BANK RATE (REDISCOUNT RATE) The rate at which chartered banks can borrow from the Bank of Canada.

CHANGES IN INTERNATIONAL BANKING

Canada's banks are going to experience increased competition because foreign banks are now allowed to do business in Canada. Canadian banks are responding to this threat with a variety of tactics, including attempts to merge with one another. But bank mergers have been blocked by the federal government because it feared the mergers would reduce competition and harm consumers. However, as we saw in Chapter 5 (and, in particular, the opening case on Scotiabank), Canadian banks have grown and strengthened through acquisitions overseas and through improved efficiencies in their home market.

LO-3 The Bank of Canada

The **Bank of Canada**, formed in 1935, is Canada's central bank. It has a crucial role in managing the Canadian economy and in regulating certain aspects of chartered bank operations. The Bank of Canada is managed by a board of governors composed of a governor, a deputy governor, and 12 directors appointed from different regions.

The rate at which chartered banks can borrow from the Bank of Canada is called the **bank rate**, or **rediscount rate**. It serves as the basis for establishing the chartered banks' prime interest rates. In practice, chartered banks seldom have to borrow from the Bank of Canada. However, the bank rate is an important instrument of monetary policy as a determinant of interest rates. In recent years, the Bank of Canada and central banks across the globe have kept rates very low. This extended period of low rates has led citizens to increase their debt load and has fuelled housing price booms, but there are increasing calls for the governor of the Bank of Canada to increase rates and restore some order, even if the U.S. Federal Reserve and others don't follow its lead.[29]

THE MONEY SUPPLY AND THE BANK OF CANADA

The Bank of Canada plays an important role in managing the money supply in Canada (see Figure 14.4). If the Bank of Canada wants to

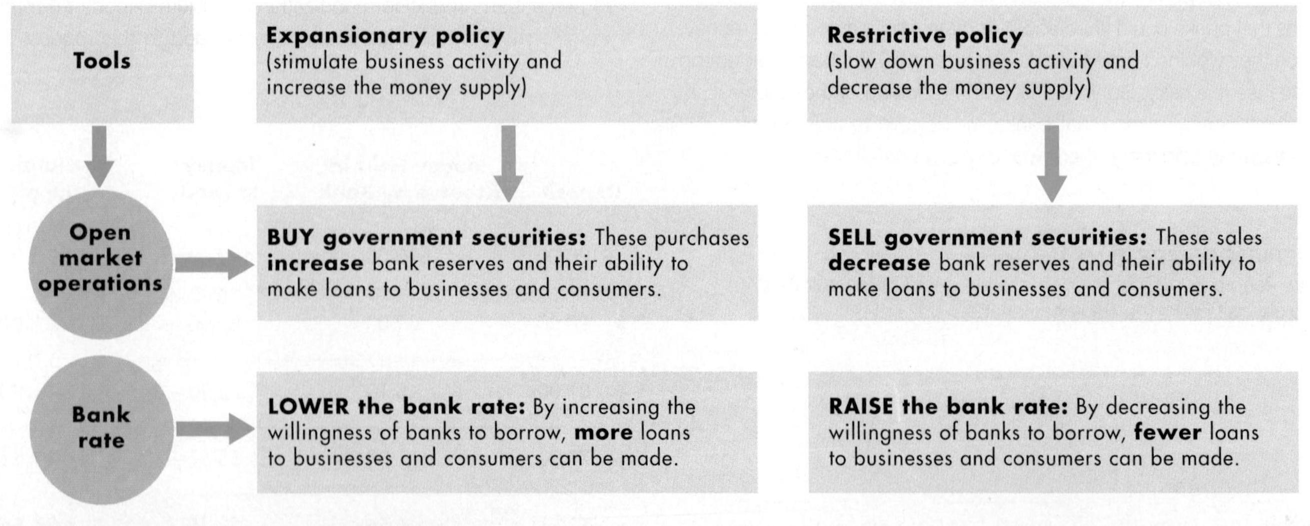

Tools
Expansionary policy
(stimulate business activity and increase the money supply)
Restrictive policy
(slow down business activity and decrease the money supply)
Open market operations
BUY government securities: These purchases increase bank reserves and their ability to make loans to businesses and consumers.
SELL government securities: These sales decrease bank reserves and their ability to make loans to businesses and consumers.
Bank rate
LOWER the bank rate: By increasing the willingness of banks to borrow, more loans to businesses and consumers can be made.
RAISE the bank rate: By decreasing the willingness of banks to borrow, fewer loans to businesses and consumers can be made.

FIGURE 14.4 Bank of Canada monetary policy actions

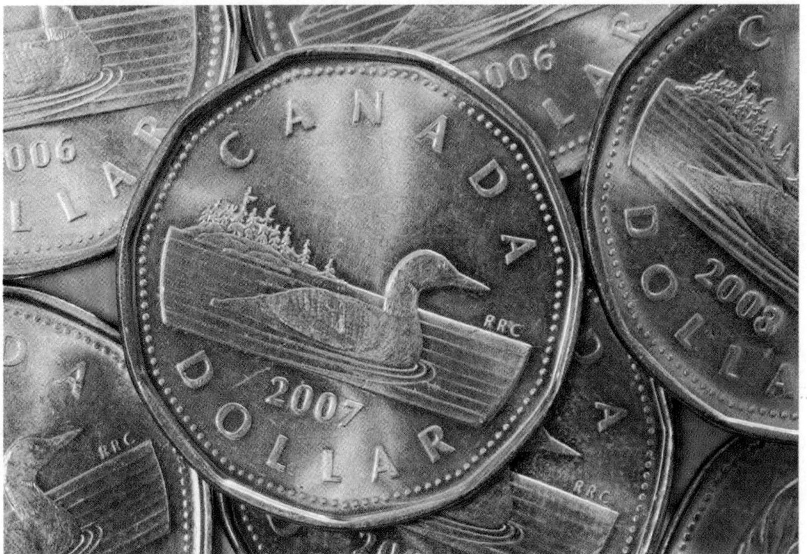

Will the Canadian loonie be seen swimming in Icelandic waters? As Iceland considers a move to the Canadian dollar, one thing is clear: the historically underrated currency has earned respect as a stable force backed by strong government policy

Bloomberg via Getty Images; © maximimages.com/Alamy

increase the money supply, it can buy government securities. The people who sell these bonds then deposit the proceeds in their banks. These deposits increase banks' reserves and their willingness to make loans. The Bank of Canada can also lower the bank rate; this action will cause increased demand for loans from businesses and households because these customers borrow more money when interest rates drop.

If the Bank of Canada wants to decrease the money supply, it can sell government securities. People spend money to buy bonds, and these withdrawals bring down banks' reserves and reduce their willingness to make loans. The Bank of Canada can also raise the bank rate; this action will cause decreased demand for loans from businesses and households because these customers borrow less money when interest rates rise.

In 2012, the federal government and the Bank of Canada were given a strong endorsement of their management of the money supply when it was reported that Iceland was considering adopting the Canadian dollar as its official currency. It is still unclear if Iceland will begin to take serious actions in that direction, but the option is being discussed at high levels and the strong monetary and fiscal policy in recent years has made our currency an attractive stable alternative for Iceland.[30] In another sign of the approval of the Canadian system, Mark Carney, former governor of the Bank of Canada, was hired by the Bank of England and took over the British post during the summer of 2013. According to George Osborne, chancellor of the Bank of England, Mark Carney is "simply the best, most experienced and most qualified person in the world" to handle that country's economic challenges.[31]

LO-4 FINANCIAL PILLAR #2—ALTERNATE BANKS

Trust Companies

A **trust company** safeguards property—funds and estates—entrusted to it. It may also serve as trustee, transfer agent, and registrar for corporations, and provide other services. For example, a corporation selling bonds to investors appoints a trustee, usually a trust company, to protect the bondholders' interests. A trust company can also serve as a transfer agent and registrar for corporations. A transfer agent records changes in ownership of a corporation's shares of stock, and a registrar certifies to the investing public that stock issues are correctly stated and comply with the corporate charter. Other services include preparing and issuing dividend cheques to stockholders and serving as trustee for employee profit-sharing funds. Trust companies also accept deposits and pay interest on them. As noted previously, trust companies have declined in importance during the last couple of decades.

Credit Unions/Caisses Populaires

One in every three Canadians is a member of a credit union (called *caisses populaires* in Quebec), with 5 million members in Quebec and 5.1 million members in the rest of Canada.[32] **Credit unions** and **caisses populaires** are cooperative savings and lending associations formed by a group with common interests. They are important because they lend money to businesses and to consumers who use the money to buy

TRUST COMPANY Safeguards funds and estates entrusted to it; may also serve as trustee, transfer agent, and registrar for corporations.

CREDIT UNIONS (CAISSES POPULAIRES) Cooperative savings and lending association formed by a group with common interests.

>>> **TABLE 14.2** Top 10 Credit Unions/Caisse Populaires in Canada, 2012 (ranked by number of members)[33]

Company	Members
1. Mouvement des Caisses Desjardins	5 581 000
2. Coast Capital Savings Credit Union	495 350
3. Vancouver City Savings Credit Union	486 484
4. Servus Credit Union Ltd.	371 407
5. Meridian Credit Union Ltd.	212 169
6. First West Credit Union	151 304
7. Conexus Credit Union	115 008
8. Assiniboine Credit Union	108 037
9. Alterna Savings	104 466
10. Affinity Credit Union	102 245

durable goods such as cars and furniture from businesses. Members (owners) can add to their savings accounts by authorizing deductions from their paycheques or by making direct deposits. They can borrow short-term, long-term, or mortgage funds from the credit union. Credit unions invest substantial amounts of money in corporate and government securities and sell certificates of deposits to the general public. According to a Moody's Investor Services report, credit unions are gaining popularity because they offer many services available at banks and they tend to pay dividends to their members when they make profits. Table 14.2 identifies the top 10 credit unions in Canada ranked by total members.

FINANCIAL PILLAR #3—SPECIALIZED LENDING AND SAVINGS INTERMEDIARIES

Life Insurance Companies

A **life insurance company** shares risk with its policyholders in return for payment of a premium from those policyholders. It lends some of the money it collects from premiums to borrowers. Life insurance companies are substantial investors in real estate mortgages and in corporate and government bonds. Next to chartered banks, they are the largest financial intermediaries in Canada. The industry as a whole has over $514 billion invested in Canada (10 percent of all provincial and federal bonds, 15 percent of corporate bonds, and 20 percent of mutual fund assets), and employs over 135 000 people.[34]

Factoring Companies

An important source of short-term funds for many firms is factoring companies. A **factoring company** (or **factor**) buys accounts receivable (amounts due from credit customers) from a firm. It pays less than the face value of the accounts, but collects the entire face value of the accounts. The difference, minus the cost of doing business, is the factor's profit. A firm that sells its accounts receivable to a factor shifts the risk of credit loss to the factor. If an account turns out to be uncollectible, the factor suffers the loss. Canada Factoring Company is an example of a domestic factoring company.

Financial Corporations

A **sales finance company** specializes in financing installment purchases made by individuals and firms. When you buy durable goods from a retailer on an installment plan with a sales finance company, the loan is made directly to you. The item itself serves as security for the loan. Sales finance companies enable firms to sell on credit, even though the firms could not afford to finance credit sales on their own. General Motors Acceptance Corporation (GMAC) is a sales finance company that finances installment contracts resulting from sales made by General Motors. Industrial Acceptance Corporation is a large Canadian sales finance company.

A **consumer finance company** makes personal loans to consumers. Often, the borrower pledges no security (collateral) for the loan. For larger loans, collateral may be required. These companies do not make loans to businesses, but they do provide the financing that allows consumers to buy goods and services from businesses. Household Finance Corporation is an example of a consumer finance company.

Venture Capital Firms

A **venture capital firm** provides funds for new or expanding firms that seem to have significant potential. For example, Google started a venture capital fund to support "young companies with awesome potential."[35] Venture capital firms may demand an ownership stake of 50 percent or more before they will buy into a company. Because financing new, untested businesses is risky, venture capital firms also want to earn a higher-than-normal return on their investment. They may insist that they be given at least one seat on the board of directors to observe how their investment is faring. Venture capital firms look for companies with growth potential that could lead to substantial increases in stock value.

Venture capital firms obtain their funds from initial capital subscriptions, from loans from other financial intermediaries, and from retained earnings. The amount of venture capital that is raised varies according to economic conditions. In 2011, venture capital firms raised a total of $1.5 billion in Canada. This figure was up 34 percent from the previous year, but was

LIFE INSURANCE COMPANY A mutual or stock company that shares risk with its policyholders for payment of premiums.

FACTORING COMPANY (OR FACTOR) Buys accounts receivable from a firm for less than their face value and then collects the face value of the receivables.

SALES FINANCE COMPANY Specializes in financing installment purchases made by individuals or firms.

CONSUMER FINANCE COMPANY Makes personal loans to consumers.

VENTURE CAPITAL FIRM Provides funds for new or expanding firms thought to have significant potential.

<<< Many of you are quite familiar with TV programs like *Dragon's Den* and *Shark Tank* that provide a simplified made-for-TV version of the venture capital process.

© kolvenbach/Alamy

well shy of the $2.1 billion raised four years earlier.[36] Canada's venture capital industry has been experiencing serious problems and many Canadian entrepreneurs have turned to U.S.-based venture capital companies for funding.[37]

Pension Funds

A **pension fund** accumulates money that will be paid out to plan subscribers at some time in the future. The money collected is invested in corporate stocks and bonds, government bonds, or mortgages until it is to be paid out. Many private pension funds are being evaluated, and there are great concerns about funding and management in this area. For example, the pension fund at Air Canada was estimated to have a funding deficit of $4.2 billion in 2012.[38]

PENSION FUND Accumulates money that will be paid out to plan subscribers in the future.

FINANCIAL PILLAR #4—INVESTMENT DEALERS

Investment dealers (called stockbrokers or underwriters) are the primary distributors of new stock and bond issues (the underwriting function). They also facilitate secondary trading of stocks and bonds, both on stock exchanges and on over-the-counter stock and bond markets (the brokerage function). These functions are described in more detail in Chapter 15.

OTHER SOURCES OF FUNDS

Government Financial Institutions and Granting Agencies

In Canada, a number of government suppliers of funds are important to business. In general, they supply funds to new and/or growing companies. However, established firms can also use some of them.

The Business Development Bank of Canada (BDC) makes term loans, primarily to smaller firms judged to have growth potential but which are unable to secure funds at reasonable terms from traditional sources. It provides proportionally more equity financing and more management counselling services. A variety of provincial industrial development corporations also provide funds to developing business firms in the hope that they will provide jobs in the province. A number of federal and provincial programs are specifically designed to provide loans to agricultural operators. Most of these, with the exception of farm improvement loans that guarantee bank loans to farmers, are long-term loans for land purchase.

The federal government's Export Development Corporation (EDC) finances and insures export sales for Canadian companies. The Canada Mortgage and Housing Corporation (CMHC) is involved in providing and guaranteeing mortgages. The CMHC is particularly important to the construction industry. Governments are also involved in providing grants to business operations.

International Sources of Funds

The Canadian capital market is just one part of the international capital market. Canadian provinces borrow extensively in foreign markets, such as those in London and New York. Canadian corporations likewise find it attractive to borrow in foreign markets. Foreign sources of funds have been important throughout the economic development of Canada. Although many groups and individuals have expressed concern about foreign ownership of Canadian businesses, projections of Canada's future capital requirements indicate that we will continue to need these funds. Canadian financial institutions will continue to play a large role in making these funds available.

LO-5 INTERNATIONAL BANKING AND FINANCE

Banks and other financial institutions play an important role in the international movement of money and in the value that is placed on the currency of various countries. Each nation tries to influence its currency exchange rates for economic advantage in international trade. The subsequent country-to-country transactions result in an international payments process that moves money between buyers and sellers on different continents.

Citizens of the Republic of Belarus, along with visitors from other countries, rely on information about current exchange rates between the Belarusian ruble (Br) and currencies of other countries. The Belarus Bank is a local provider of currency exchange services.

© Caro/Alamy

Exchange Rates and International Trade

The value of a given currency, such as the Canadian dollar, reflects the overall supply and demand for Canadian dollars both at home and abroad. This value changes with economic conditions worldwide; therefore, firms watch for trends.

A good case in point is the fluctuation in the Canadian dollar relative to the American dollar. As we entered the new millennium, Canadians had grown accustomed to a weak dollar—in the 65 to 70 cent range against the U.S. dollar. A dollar at parity with the American dollar was almost unthinkable. Yet, on November 9, 2007, the dollar reached US$1.09, a level that had not been seen for decades. That movement and strength encouraged Canadians to cross the border and purchase everything from clothing to cars. Over the next few years, the dollar retreated at bit, but a new era was upon Canadians. In October 2013, the Canadian dollar was valued at approximately US $0.96.[39]

These dollar fluctuations have also had a huge impact on businesses. Canadian companies are finding it more difficult to compete internationally since they can no longer rely on a cheap dollar to make their products more affordable across the border and abroad. But after the initial shock, companies are learning to cope. According to chairman and CEO of Clearwater Seafoods Income Fund, "The way you deal with the stronger Canadian dollar is to increase the efficiency of your operations."[40] Other companies, like Nova Scotia–based High Liner Foods, which buys most of its raw fish on the world markets in U.S. dollars, has seen a net benefit. The rise in the Canadian dollar helped that company increase profits by 40 percent in one year.[41]

THE LAW OF ONE PRICE

When a country's currency is overvalued, its exchange rate is higher than warranted by its economic conditions, and its high costs make it less competitive. In contrast, an undervalued currency means low costs and low prices. When a currency becomes overvalued, a nation's economic authorities may devalue the nation's currency. This causes a decrease in the country's exchange value, making it less expensive for other countries to buy the country's products. If a nation's currency is undervalued, the government can revalue the currency, which will make it more expensive for other countries to buy its products.

But how do we know whether a currency is overvalued or undervalued? One method involves a simple concept called the **law of one price**: the principle that identical products should sell for the same price in all countries. In other words, if the different prices of a Rolex watch in different countries were converted into a common currency, the common-denominator price should be the same everywhere.

A simple example that illustrates over- and undervalued currencies is the Big Mac Index, published annually in the *Economist*. The index lists a variety of countries and their Big Mac prices in terms of

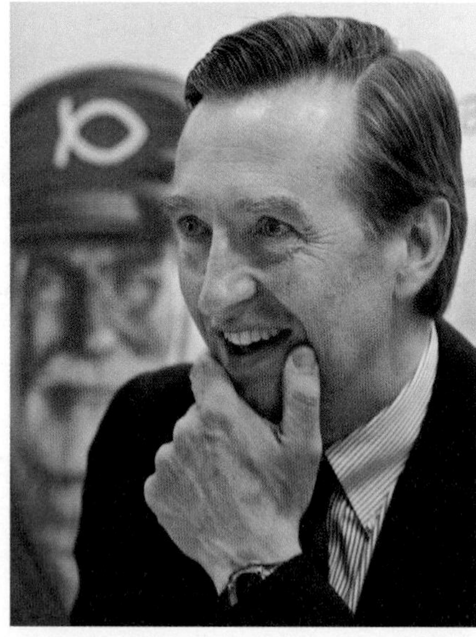

While many Canadian companies find it more difficult to compete or earn high margins because of the increase in the value of the Canadian dollar, High Liner Food has been a beneficiary because it buys most of its fish in U.S. dollars on the world market. The stronger loonie is a big ally in this case.

© Per Andersen/Alamy

LAW OF ONE PRICE The principle that identical products should sell for the same price in all countries.

TABLE 14.3 The Big Mac Index

Country	Price in $US	Country	Price in $US
India	1.50	Canada	5.26
South Africa	1.82	Sweden	6.16
Hong Kong	2.19	Switzerland	6.72
Malaysia	2.30	Venezuela	7.15
US	**4.56**	Norway	7.51

U.S. dollars (see Table 14.3 for examples).[42] In July 2013, a Big Mac cost $4.56 in the United States. If a Big Mac in another country costs more than $4.56, the currency is overvalued; if it costs less than $4.37, the currency is undervalued. In 2013, the most overvalued currencies were Norway ($7.51), Venezuela ($7.15), Switzerland ($6.72), and Sweden ($6.16). Canada ranked sixth at $5.26. The most undervalued currencies were India ($1.50), South Africa ($1.82), and Hong Kong ($2.19). These different values mean that, in theory, you could buy Big Macs in China and sell them in Norway at a profit. If you did that, the demand for burgers would increase in China, driving up the price to match the other countries. In other words, the law of one price would set it.

The International Payments Process

Transactions among buyers and sellers in different countries are simplified through the services provided by their banks. For example, payments from buyers flow through a local bank that converts them from the local currency into the foreign currency of the seller. Likewise, the local bank receives and converts incoming money from the banks of foreign buyers.[43] Let's take a look at an international transaction to highlight the process.

Step 1 A Canadian olive importer withdraws $1000 from its chequing account to buy olives from a Greek exporter. The local Canadian bank converts those dollars into euros at the current exchange rate (0.73809 euros per dollar).

Step 2 The Canadian bank sends the cheque for 738.09 euros (EUR 738.09 = 0.73809 multiplied by 1000) to the exporter in Greece.

Steps 3 and 4 The exporter sends olives to its Canadian customer and deposits the cheque in its local Greek bank. While the exporter now has euros that can be spent in Greece, the importer has olives to sell in Canada. At the same time, a separate transaction is being made between a Canadian machine exporter and a Greek olive oil producer. This time, the importer/exporter roles are reversed between the two countries: the Greek firm needs to import a $1000 olive oil press from Canada.

Steps 5 and 6 EUR 738.09 withdrawn from a local Greek bank account is converted into $1000 Canadian and sent via cheque to the Canadian exporter.

Steps 7 and 8 The olive oil press is sent to the Greek importer, and the importer's cheque is deposited in the Canadian exporter's local bank account.

The International Bank Structure

There is no worldwide banking system that is comparable, in terms of policymaking and regulatory power, to the system of any single industrialized nation. Rather, worldwide banking stability relies on a loose structure of agreements among individual countries or groups of countries. In addition, local standards and laws vary greatly.

THE WORLD BANK AND THE IMF

Two United Nations agencies, the World Bank and the International Monetary Fund, help to finance international trade. Unlike true banks, the **World Bank** actually provides only a very limited scope of services. For instance, it funds national improvements by making loans to build roads, schools, power plants, and hospitals. The resulting improvements eventually enable borrowing countries to increase productive capacity and international trade. The **International Monetary Fund (IMF)** is a group of 188 nations that have combined their resources for the following purposes:

- to promote the stability of exchange rates
- to provide temporary, short-term loans to member countries
- to encourage members to cooperate on international monetary issues
- to encourage development of a system for international payments

In 2011, the IMF had about $396 billion available for loans.[44] With the recent economic turmoil created by the housing and commercial paper crisis in the U.S. and the European debt crisis, economists and governments are openly questioning the efficiency of these international

WORLD BANK A United Nations agency that provides a limited scope of financial services, such as funding national improvements in undeveloped countries.

INTERNATIONAL MONETARY FUND (IMF) United Nations agency consisting of 188 nations that have combined resources to promote stable exchange rates, provide temporary short-term loans, and serve other purposes.

structures. At the beginning of 2013, the IMF itself was openly admitting that miscalculations were made in handling the European debt crisis by preaching austerity at all costs. The IMF's top economists Olivier Blanchard and Daniel Leigh drafted a document which highlighted errors in predicting the impact of austerity (cuts) in the European economies. In particular, they pointed to a very large underestimation of the increase in unemployment and the decline in domestic demand that would result from such policies.[45]

It is now clearly up to the group of 20 major economies (G20), the IMF, and the other major economic bodies to improve the clarity of rules and reexamine and improve the overall international financial structure.[46]

MyBizLab

Visit the MyBizLab website. This online homework and tutorial system puts you in control of your own learning with study and practice tools directly correlated to this chapter's content.

SUMMARY OF LEARNING OBJECTIVES

LO-1 DEFINE *MONEY* AND IDENTIFY THE DIFFERENT FORMS IT TAKES IN CANADA'S MONEY SUPPLY.

Any item that is portable, divisible, durable, and stable satisfies the four basic *characteristics of money*. Money also serves three functions: a *medium of exchange*, a *store of value*, and a *unit of account*. The nation's money supply is often determined by two measures. *M-1* includes liquid (or spendable) forms of money: currency (bills and coins), demand deposits, and other "chequable" deposits. *M-2* includes M-1 plus items that cannot be directly spent but that can be easily converted to spendable forms: time deposits, money market funds, and savings deposits. Credit must also be considered as a factor in the money supply.

LO-2 UNDERSTAND THE DIFFERENT KINDS OF *FINANCIAL INSTITUTIONS* THAT MAKE UP THE *CANADIAN FINANCIAL SYSTEM* AND EXPLAIN THE SERVICES THEY OFFER.

There are four financial pillars in Canada: *chartered banks*, *alternate banks*, *life insurance companies*, and *investment dealers*. Chartered banks are the most important source of short-term funds for business firms. They create money in the form of expanding demand deposits. The four types of institutions offer services like financial advice, brokerage services, electronic funds transfer, pension and trust services, and lending of money. Some of the differences between these institutions are disappearing. The financial services industry continues to evolve in Canada.

LO-3 EXPLAIN THE FUNCTIONS OF THE *BANK OF CANADA* AND DESCRIBE THE TOOLS IT USES TO CONTROL THE MONEY SUPPLY.

The Bank of Canada manages the Canadian economy, controls the *money supply*, and regulates certain aspects of chartered banking operations. If the Bank of Canada wants to increase the money supply, it can buy government securities or lower the *bank rate*. If it wants to decrease the money supply, it can sell government securities or increase the bank rate.

LO-4 EXPLAIN THE ROLE OF *ALTERNATE BANKS, SPECIALIZED LENDING AND SAVINGS INTERMEDIARIES*, AND *INVESTMENT DEALERS* IN THE CANADIAN FINANCIAL SYSTEM.

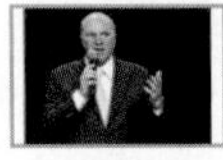

Alternate banks include trust companies and credit unions. *Trust companies* safeguard property that is entrusted to them. *Credit unions* are co-operative savings and lending associations formed by a group with common interests. They lend money to both businesses and consumers. *Specialized lending* and *savings intermediaries* include life insurance companies, (which share risks with their policyholders in return for payment of a premium), *factoring companies* (which buy accounts receivable from businesses at a discount and then collect the face value of the account receivable), *financial corporations* (which specialize in financing installment purchases made by businesses and individuals), *venture capital* firms (which provide funds for new or expanding businesses), and *pension funds* (which accumulate and invest money that will be paid out to plan subscribers at some time in the future).

LO-5 DISCUSS SOME OF THE INSTITUTIONS AND ACTIVITIES IN *INTERNATIONAL BANKING* AND *FINANCE*.

Changes in currency values and exchange rates reflect global supply and demand for various currencies. Policies by central banks on money supplies and interest rates influence the values of currencies on the foreign currency exchange markets. Electronic technologies now permit speedy global financial transactions to support the growing importance of international finance. Country-to-country transactions rely on an *international payments process* that moves money between buyers and sellers in different nations. If trade between two countries is in balance—if money inflows and outflows are equal for both countries—money does not have to flow between the two countries. If inflows and outflows are not in balance, then a flow of money between them is made to cover the difference. The *World Bank* and the *International Monetary Fund* were developed by the United National with the goal of providing stability to encourage international trade.

QUESTIONS AND EXERCISES

QUESTIONS FOR ANALYSIS

1. What specific changes in banking are shifting banks away from their historical role?
2. Do we really need all the different types of financial institutions we have in Canada? Could we make do with just chartered banks? Why or why not?
3. Should credit cards be counted in the money supply? Why or why not? Support your answer by using the definition of money.
4. Should banks be regulated, or should market forces be allowed to determine the money supply? Defend your answer.
5. Customers who deposit their money in online-only chequing and savings accounts can often get higher interest rates than at brick-and-mortar banks. Why do you think that online banks can offer these rates? What might be some drawbacks to online-only banking?
6. What is the logic behind the "law of one price" concept? Give an example using Switzerland and China.

APPLICATION EXERCISES

7. Start with a $1000 deposit and assume a reserve requirement of 15 percent. Now trace the amount of money created by the banking system after five lending cycles.
8. Interview several consumers to determine which banking services and products they use (debit cards, ATMs, smart cards, online brokerage, etc.). If interviewees are using these services, determine the reasons. If they are not, find out why.
9. Interview the manager of a local chartered bank branch. Identify the ways in which the Bank of Canada helps the bank and the ways in which it limits the bank.
10. Consider historical currency exchange rates for the Canadian dollar versus the U.S. dollar and the euro. If you had bought those currencies with Canadian dollars five years ago, what would their Canadian dollar values be today?

TEAM EXERCISES

BUILDING YOUR BUSINESS SKILLS

FOUR ECONOMISTS IN A ROOM

GOAL

To encourage you to understand the economic factors considered by the Bank of Canada in determining current interest rates.

BACKGROUND INFORMATION

One of the Bank of Canada's most important tools in setting monetary policy is the adjustment of the interest rates it charges member banks to borrow money. To determine interest rate policy, the Bank of Canada analyzes current economic conditions. Its findings are published on their website and are contained in a quarterly *Monetary Policy Report*.

METHOD

Step 1 Working with three other students, access the Bank of Canada's website at http://www.bankofcanada.ca/. Access the most recent *Monetary Policy Report* and read it carefully.

Step 2 Working with group members, pick out three key economic highlights. Discuss the ways each factor influences the Bank of Canada's decision to raise, lower, or maintain interest rates, and what the implications are on regular consumers.

Step 3 Find articles published in the *Globe and Mail* or the *National Post* or another major newspaper. Look for articles published immediately following the appearance of the most recent report. Discuss with group members what the articles say about current economic conditions and interest rates.

Step 4 Based on your research and analysis, what factors do you think the Bank of Canada will take into account to control inflation? Working with group members, explain your answer in writing.

Step 5 Working with group members, research what the governor of the Bank of Canada says about interest rates. Do reasons for raising, lowering, or maintaining rates agree with your team's analysis?

FOLLOW-UP QUESTIONS

1. What are the most important factors in the Bank of Canada's interest-rate decisions?
2. Consider the old joke about economists that goes like this: *When there are four economists in a room analyzing current economic conditions, there are at least eight different opinions.* Based on your research and analysis, why do you think economists have such varying opinions?

EXERCISING YOUR ETHICS

TELLING THE ETHICAL FROM THE STRICTLY LEGAL

THE SITUATION

When upgrading services for convenience to customers, chartered banks are concerned about setting prices that cover all costs so that, ultimately, they make a profit. This exercise challenges you to evaluate one banking service—ABM transactions—to determine if there are also ethical issues that should be considered in a bank's pricing decisions.

THE DILEMMA

Assume that a bank has more than 300 ABMs serving the nearly 400 000 chequing and savings accounts of its customers. Customers are not charged a fee for their 30 million ABM transactions each year, so long as they use their bank's ABMs. For issuing cash to non-customers, however, the bank charges a $2 ABM fee. The bank's officers are reexamining their policies on ABM surcharges because of public protests.

In considering its current policies, the bank's vice-president for community relations is concerned about more than mere legalities. She wants to ensure that her company is "being a good citizen and doing the right thing." Any decision on ABM fees will ultimately affect the bank's customers, its image in the community and industry, and its profitability for its owners.

TEAM ACTIVITY

Assemble a group of four students and assign each group member to one of the following roles:

- a bank customer
- the bank's vice-president for community relations
- a bank shareholder
- the bank's CEO

QUESTIONS FOR DISCUSSION

1. Before discussing the situation with your group and from the perspective of your assigned role, do you think there are any ethical issues in this situation? If so, write them down.
2. Before discussing the situation with your group and from the perspective of your assigned role, decide how this dispute should be resolved.
3. For the various ethical issues that were identified, decide as a group which one is the most important for the bank to resolve. Which issue is second in importance?
4. From an ethical standpoint, what does your group recommend be done to resolve the most important ethical issue? To resolve the second-most important ethical issue? What are the advantages and disadvantages of your recommendations?

BUSINESS CASE

CANADIAN BANKS: ON THE EDGE OF A MORTGAGE CRISIS?

In 2013, potential home buyers were facing a difficult question: To buy or not to buy? They had seen home prices soar for years with the help of cheap mortgage rates, but a softening of the market appeared to have arrived. For anyone considering this question in the previous decade, the correct answer was clearly to buy. But could the positive upward trend continue? Some experts were calling for a major correction in housing prices by as much as 20 to 25 percent, while others were predicting a soft landing without too much fuss. We had seen a dramatic rise in home prices across the country: A year earlier, the values were soaring in Vancouver (average price $775 693), Toronto (average price $494 879), and Montreal (average price $402 455). Overall, the average price across Canada stood at $360 396; this figure had more than doubled in a decade. A year later, not much had changed as the average price stood at $355 777. However, there were major signs of weakness in the overheated Vancouver and Toronto condo markets and the alarm bells were ringing across the nation (for those willing to listen). More homeowners who had seen their equity rise sharply were now asking the opposite question: to sell or not to sell? In the previous decade, most people sold and bought bigger homes with their newfound wealth. That strategy is beneficial if prices continue to rise and if you are not too overextended with debt.

If you examined these rising valuations and thought that this large increase could not be sustained because the trend in salaries and inflation was not keeping pace with housing price increases, you had a very sound traditional argument. However, if you acted on this logic and took a conservative approach, you may have missed out on the wealth accumulation trend. The majority have bought into the following train of thought: "The prices will keep rising, and if I wait I will have to pay more. So I might as well buy as much house as I can and get the maximum loan the bank is offering."

© ClassicStock/Alamy

Investors who have been waiting on the sidelines for a market correction have been punished. Of course, the housing market, like other investment vehicles, goes in cycles. At times it can be flat and at others it booms. The long-term trend is up, but not at this pace. A correction will hit the housing market at some point and prices will stabilize for a period. The question really is, what should you do today? In order to answer this, you have to look at the fundamentals, despite their poor performance in predicting the market lately: the regulators, the role of the banks, the lessons from history and the U.S crisis, and, ultimately, your long-term ability to pay. With new warnings being issued daily, it appeared that the pendulum may be about to swing back in favour of the conservative home buyer.

THE ROLE OF THE BANKS

When it comes to mortgages, banks are in the business of making money by lending to people who can pay back their loans and the interest. Canadian banks have traditionally been prudent in providing mortgage loans; however, in recent years, this conservative approach has taken a dangerous turn. The big banks (with the full support of the Bank of Canada) have been severe enablers in the rise of housing prices. Low rates and great terms have made it possible for more people to buy homes and for all potential customers to buy bigger (and/or more expensive) homes than they could rationally afford. After years of low interest rates, it seemed like the housing market could not be given any additional stimulus. Or so it seemed. In 2012, the Bank of Montreal caused new waves with an unbelievably low five-year mortgage rate of 2.99 percent. The competitors quickly followed, although they offered the rate for four years rather than five. These are the types of deals that we expect from used car salespeople, not responsible banks. However, something interesting occurred—within a few weeks, some of the other banks retreated from this overly aggressive stance; the Bank of Nova Scotia was the first to step back. There was also a bizarre plea for help as some bank executives began to ask for tighter regulations.

THE REGULATORS

Part of Jim Flaherty's job as finance minister is to cool down the economy when it is too hot. However, his task is difficult because, on the one hand, we see a major bubble forming in the housing market. The appropriate response to this problem is to raise rates to dampen consumer appetite for debt. On the other hand, rates are so low worldwide that an increase in the Canadian rate would lead to a potentially damaging increase in the Canadian dollar. The U.S. Federal Reserve Chairman had already indicated that he would not increase rates until at least 2014 and that the U.S. rate would remain near zero until that time. So any increase in Canadian rates would mean that the Canadian dollar would likely soar even higher, which could further hurt exports. So what could the finance minister do?

Mr. Flaherty warned Canadians against taking on too much debt—good fatherly advice. In addition, other subtle steps were taken. For example, Ottawa has made some adjustments through the Canadian Mortgage and Housing Corporation (CMHC), which provides mortgage insurance to financial institutions, determining which mortgages are insurable and which are not. For years, mortgages in Canada had a maximum amortization period of 25 years. But in 2006, this policy changed to allow mortgages to be granted for 40 years with very little or no down payment. This meant that people's monthly payments were now much lower (pay back the same mortgage amount over 40 years vs. 25 years) and it also meant that people could take on much more debt. The end result was soaring housing prices and massive accumulated debt for consumers. The average household-debt-to-disposable-income ratio reached 153 percent in Canada. The Americans and the British reached levels of 160 percent before it caught up to them in the form of a major housing market crisis. In response to this concern, Mr. Flaherty lowered the amortization maximum to 35 years and later to 30 years, and more recently back to 25 years. This move was fully supported by key industry players like Ed Clark, CEO of TD Bank.

WHY SHOULD YOU CARE?

Many people think that the housing mortgage crisis in the United States only hurt individuals who could not pay their mortgages. Of course, many of these individuals lost their homes, but some who bought homes they could not afford actually made a lot of money by selling before the crisis hit. Probably the biggest victims of the crisis are the responsible home buyers who were forced to overpay for their homes because of a false market bubble. For example, Jane and Tom paid $550 000 for a house that was actually worth only $300 000. They saved their money, made a down payment of $150 000, and took out a mortgage for $400 000. They have very strong incomes and could afford this major mortgage even though they were very nervous about taking out such a big loan. They never missed their payments.

After the crisis, however, their property's market value dropped to $250 000 but they still owe $375 000 on their mortgage—and, don't forget, they also made a down payment of $150 000. Jane and Tom are victims of a system that was out of control and now they are stuck with a mortgage that does not make sense. The consumers who put a zero down payment on a house they could not afford lived in that home for a few years and walked away from their mortgage. For Jane and Tom, however, the nightmare is just beginning.

FUNDAMENTAL MATH

The sustained low-interest-rate environment has encouraged people to purchase more house than they can probably afford. Some people believe that these low rates will last forever or do not understand what even a small increase can mean. Let's take a look at an example.

John and Mary buy a home for $500 000. They make a down payment of $150 000 and take out a mortgage for $350 000. They lock in their mortgage of $350 000 for five years at a rate of 2.99 percent, with an amortization of 30 years.

Rate 2.99
Period 5 years
Amortization 30 years
Monthly Payment $1470.25

What would that same house cost in monthly payments under traditional terms?

They lock in their mortgage rate for five years at an amortization of 25 years.

Rate 5.99 (historically a very good rate)
Period 5 years
Amortization 25 years (traditional approach)
Monthly Payment $2237.24

The same house costs $767 more per month and that is with a very conservative 5.99 percent figure. Nobody expects to see rates above double digits in the foreseeable future, but reasonable rates should be part of your long-term "what if" planning. If you can afford the home either way, then you are probably okay. If not, maybe you should take some time to think about it before you sign.

CONCLUSION

Time will tell if the market was indeed out of control in early 2013, but, as investors and homeowners, you should know the facts. There are great opportunities in real estate, but do your homework and understand the implications of interest rates and the functions of the banking system.

QUESTIONS FOR DISCUSSION

1. How has the change in government policy with regard to amortization periods and down payments influenced the housing market?
2. Why are bank executives asking the government to increase regulations? Isn't it in the interest of all business executives to have less regulation to enable them to create profits for their shareholders?
3. Visit the TD Canada Trust website and access the Mortgage Calculator tool at www.tdcanadatrust.com. How much is the posted rate for a five-year mortgage? How much will it cost you (monthly payment) to get a mortgage of $250 000 with a 25-year amortization? What is the total cost of your interest payments over the lifetime of the loan?
4. Based on the scenario provided in the case, what should Jane and Tom do in the situation that they are facing? Should they wait for the market to improve and stay in their home? Should they walk away and buy another home? What other factors must they consider?

CHAPTER SUPPLEMENT 04

Managing Your Personal Finances: A Synopsis

The contents below highlight some important personal finance tips and practical hands-on examples. For a more detailed description complete with additional worksheets and analysis of these financial planning tips, visit the online appendix in MyBizLab.

DEVELOPING A PERSONAL FINANCIAL PLAN

Like it or not, dealing with personal finances is a life-long job. As a rule, it involves rational management of your personal finances—controlling them as a way of life and helping them grow. Figure F.1 provides a summary of the key steps in developing a financial plan.

TABLE F.1 Tips for Personal Financial Wealth

1. Develop a Financial Plan
2. Understand the Time Value of Money & Never Forget the Rule of 72!
3. Use Credit Cards Responsibly
4. Invest Wisely in Real Estate
5. Cash Out From (Legal) Tax Avoidance
6. Protect Your Net Worth

THE TIME VALUE OF MONEY AND THE RULE OF 72

The time value of money is perhaps the single most important concept in personal finance. It's especially relevant for setting financial goals and evaluating investments. The concept of *time value* recognizes the basic fact that, while it's invested, money grows by earning interest or yielding some other form of return. Thus, whenever you make everyday purchases, you're giving up interest that you could have earned with the same money if you'd invested it instead. From a financial standpoint, "idle" or uninvested money is a wasted resource.

How long does it take to double an investment? A handy rule of thumb is called the "Rule of 72." You can find the number of years needed to double your money by dividing the annual interest rate (in percent) into 72. If, for example, you reinvest annually at 8 percent, you'll double your money in about 9 years.

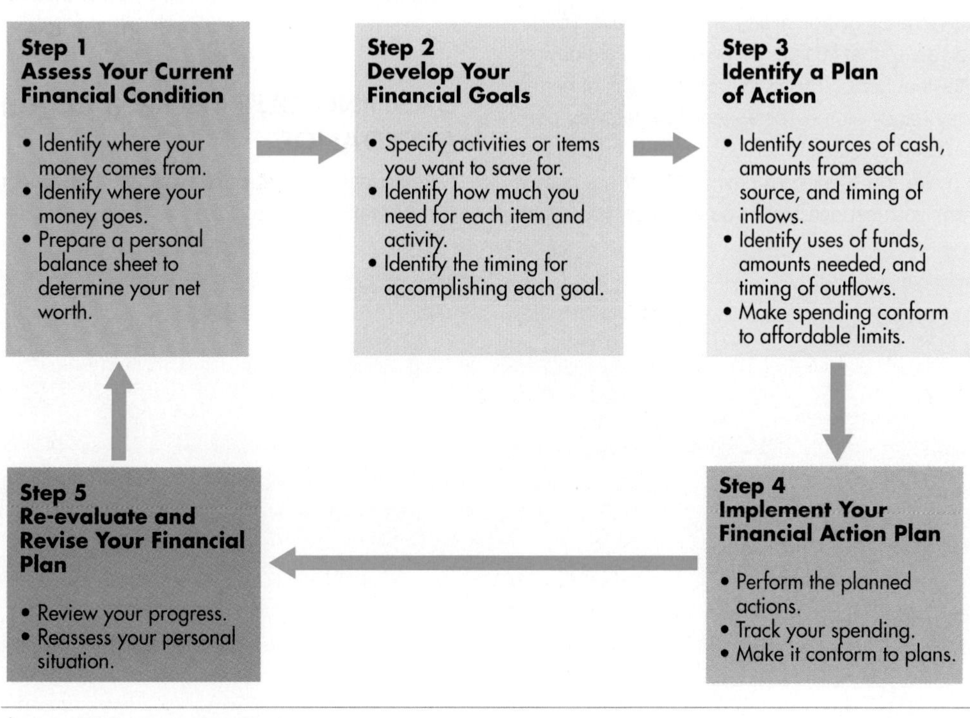

Step 1
Assess Your Current Financial Condition
• Identify where your money comes from.
• Identify where your money goes.
• Prepare a personal balance sheet to determine your net worth.
Step 2
Develop Your Financial Goals
• Specify activities or items you want to save for.
• Identify how much you need for each item and activity.
• Identify the timing for accomplishing each goal.
Step 3
Identify a Plan of Action
• Identify sources of cash, amounts from each source, and timing of inflows.
• Identify uses of funds, amounts needed, and timing of outflows.
• Make spending conform to affordable limits.
Step 4
Implement Your Financial Action Plan
• Perform the planned actions.
• Track your spending.
• Make it conform to plans.
Step 5
Re-evaluate and Revise Your Financial Plan
• Review your progress.
• Reassess your personal situation.

FIGURE F.1 Developing a personal financial plan

>>> TABLE F.2 The Rule of 72 and the Time Value of Money

The Number 72	Interest Rate	Number of years for money to double	How much is a $10 000 investment worth after 30 years?
72	1	72	**$13 800**
72	4	18	$32 430
72	6	12	$57 430
72	8	9	$100 620
72	10	7.2	**$174 490**

Take a look at Table F.1 for a clearer picture of the importance of this simple rule.

How does a $10 000 investment grow under different interest-rate scenarios? These days most banks pay 1 percent interest (if you're lucky). You would have to live another 72 years to see your money double at that rate. Thirty years later that $10 000 initial investment would only be worth $13 800, whereas the same investment would be worth $174 000 if you earned 10 percent. On average, the stock market has earned an average return of 10 percent in the last 75 years. However, if you are risk averse, you could still put the money in something safer (like bonds) and still turn that $10 000 in $32 430 or more. There are more detailed explanations and examples available in the online appendix.

Where you invest your money counts! Never forget the rule of 72 and the time value of money!

USE CREDIT CARDS RESPONSIBLY

Although some credit cards don't charge annual fees, all of them charge interest on unpaid (outstanding) balances. Because credit-card debt is one of the most expensive sources of funds, you need to understand the costs before you start charging. For example, if you have $5000 worth of credit-card debt on a Visa that charges 18 percent, you are paying $960 in interest per year for that debt. You could probably think of better ways to spend that money (fancy clothes or a weekend getaway perhaps). Most people never make that calculation because the credit-card companies allow you to make the "minimum payment" and are happy collecting the interest from you (especially as you increase your debt from $5000 to $10 000 to $20 000 over time). If you only make the minimum payment, that *$5000 credit-card debt (at 18 percent) will take 115 months to pay off.* Guess what, the rule of 72 also applies to your debts. So be smart.

Don't destroy your personal wealth by ignoring the cost of your interest payments. If you are stuck with debt, try to transfer it to lower-cost sources of financing and pay it off as soon as possible!

INVEST CAREFULLY IN REAL ESTATE

Should you rent or buy? The answer to that question involves a variety of considerations, including life stage, family needs, career, financial situation, and preferred lifestyle. If you decide to buy, you have to ask yourself how much house you can afford. To answer that question, you need to ask a number of questions about your personal financial condition and your capacity for borrowing. Buy wisely.

Step 1: Don't spend beyond your means!
Step 2: When signing a mortgage deal, look around and compare; even a 0.25 percent lower interest rate translates into significant savings.

CASHING OUT FROM (LEGAL) TAX AVOIDANCE

Take advantage of all of the various government programs and rules to cut your tax bill. Some of the most important methods for tax relief and/or untaxed accumulation of funds include Registered Retirement Savings Plan (RRSP), Tax-Free Savings Accounts (TSFAs), and Registered Education Savings Plans (RESP).

Lower your tax bill, increase your personal equity.

PROTECT YOUR NET WORTH

With careful attention, thoughtful saving and spending, and skillful financial planning (and a little luck), you can build up your net worth over time. However, every financial plan should consider steps for preserving it. One approach involves the risk–return relationship. Do you prefer to protect your current assets, or are you willing to risk them in return for greater growth? At various life stages, and whenever you reach a designated level of wealth, you should adjust your asset portfolio to conform to your risk and return preferences—conservative, moderate, or aggressive.

Another approach is life insurance. From a personal-finance perspective, the purpose of life insurance is to replace income upon the death of the policyholder. Accordingly, the amount of insurance you need depends on how many other people rely on your income. Insurance, for example, is crucial for the married parent who is a family's sole source of income. On the other hand, a single person with no financial dependents needs little or no insurance and will probably prefer to put money into higher-paying investments.

Buy the right life insurance and the right amount. For an explanation of the difference between term and whole life insurance refer to the online site.

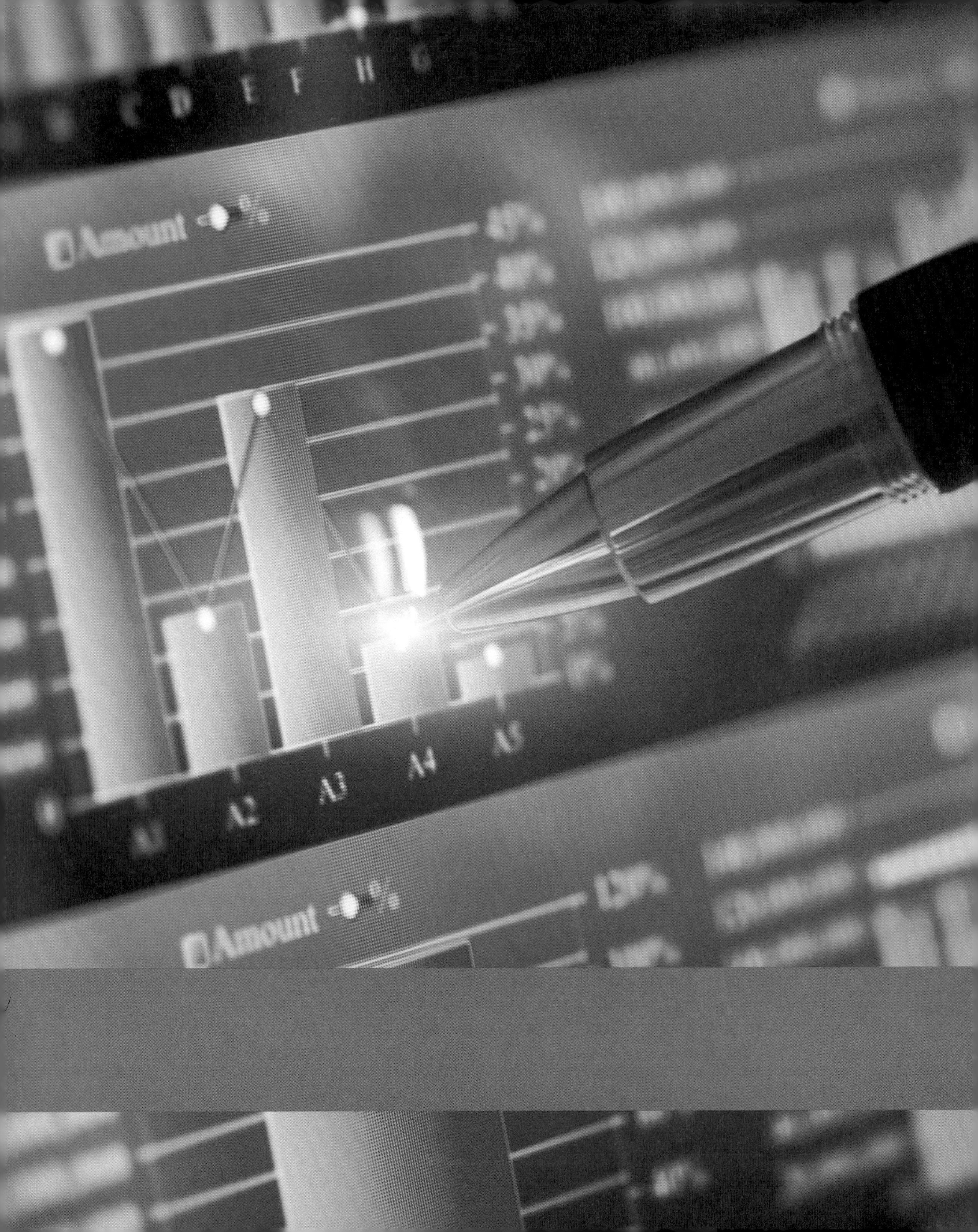
Amount
A1
A2
A3
A4
A5
Amount

Financial Decisions *and* Risk Management

CHAPTER 15

LO

AFTER READING THIS CHAPTER, YOU SHOULD BE ABLE TO:

LO-1 Describe the responsibilities of a *financial manager*.

LO-2 Distinguish between *short-term* (operating) and *long-term* (capital) expenditures.

LO-3 Identify three sources of *short-term financing* for businesses.

LO-4 Identify three sources of *long-term financing* for businesses.

LO-5 Discuss the value of *common stock and preferred stock* to stockholders, and describe the secondary market for each type of security.

LO-6 Explain the process by which securities are bought and sold.

LO-7 Describe the investment opportunities offered by *mutual funds*, *hedge funds*, *commodities*, and *stock options*.

LO-8 Explain how *risk* affects business operations and identify the five steps in the *risk management process*.

Hoarding Cash: Good or Bad Idea?

In 2012, corporations in Europe, Japan, Canada, and the U.S. held large amounts of cash—a total of $7.75 *trillion,* according to the Institute of International Finance. Canadian corporations were sitting on $526 billion in liquid assets, while U.S. corporations had almost $2 trillion. Canadian mining company Teck Resources Ltd., for example, held $4.5 billion as a result of high prices for coal, copper, and other commodities the company mines. The company wanted to maintain a large cash balance because it expected lowered production of certain commodities and lower commodity prices in 2012 because of weaker demand. In Europe, the ratio of investment to GDP is at a 60-year low, even though companies have large amounts of cash and are maintaining so-called "fortress balance sheets." In the U.S., companies with fortress balance sheets include General Electric ($91 billion), Pfizer ($36.4 billion), General Motors ($33 billion), and Coca-Cola ($13.8 billion). Technology companies hold particularly large amounts of cash (Apple—$97 billion, Microsoft—$41 billion, Cisco Systems—$40 billion, Google—$34 billion). While some Canadian companies do hold large amounts of cash, they are not nearly as cash-rich as U.S. companies. For example, the average cash-to-book-value of companies on the S&P 500 is 37.2 percent, but only 14.5 percent for companies on the S&P/TSX.

Hoarding of cash is viewed as a bad thing by many people. Critics say that companies made the financial crisis of 2008 worse because they hoarded cash instead of spending it on job creation. They argue that would have constituted a "second stimulus" beyond the government's stimulus spending. There were many specific critical comments. For example, a *Washington Post* columnist concluded that corporations who sit on large sums of money do not invest in any job-creating enterprises. The *Wall Street Journal* said that it would be good if cash-rich companies stepped up their hiring so that the high unemployment rate would be reduced. David Bianco, the chief equity strategist at Merrill Lynch, criticized chief financial officers of companies for holding too much cash and said that cash hoarding was depressing share prices. He noted that shareholders were unhappy because dividend payout ratios were near historical lows. Some critics went so far as to suggest a 2 percent tax on corporation cash balances. A study of 25 companies that had $10 billion or more cash on hand showed that their stock prices were underperforming compared to the general market, and that they had slow growth rates. Bank of Canada governor Mark Carney offered the view that businesses should either spend their cash or give it back to shareholders in the form of dividends. If shareholders received more dividends, they would boost the economy because they would have more money to spend.

Bloomberg via Getty Images

HOW WILL THIS HELP ME?

The material in this chapter will benefit you in two ways: (1) you will be better able to use your knowledge about finance in your career as both an *employee* and as a *manager*, and (2) you will be a more informed *consumer*, with greater awareness of how businesses use financial instruments to support their activities.

But financial managers have a different perspective on the appropriateness of holding large amounts of cash. Even though several years have passed since the economic downturn hit in 2008, financial managers are still wary. They see many possible problems on the horizon—the possibility of a "double-dip" recession, a slowdown in China's economy, volatility in commodity markets, and low consumer confidence, to name just a few. Financial managers are, therefore, being very conservative in how they manage cash. Cost-cutting and cash hoarding have become key strategies, and financial managers have adopted a wait-and-see attitude before spending large amounts of money on things like hiring more staff.

The view that it is bad for financial managers to hoard cash is also challenged by Alan Reynolds, a senior fellow at the U.S.-based Cato Institute. He says that such a view reveals ignorance about basic financial realities. (He analyzes data from U.S. corporations, but the same principles apply to Canadian companies.) Reynolds makes four key points. First, net worth indicates the health of a corporation, not the form in which assets are held (e.g., cash, accounts receivable, fixed assets, etc.). The net worth of U.S. nonfinancial corporations dropped from $15.9 trillion in 2007 to $12.6 trillion in 2011. The ratio of cash to total assets rose because the value of total assets fell, not because the corporation was hoarding large amounts of cash. Second, liquid assets, like cash, serve as a safety cushion to deal with unexpected business difficulties. To characterize the holding of cash as "hoarding," without also considering the level of short-term debt, is meaningless. U.S. corporations hold nearly $2 trillion in cash, but that is far less than the $3.67 trillion in short-term debt on their books. Third, there is a big difference between the assets a corporation owns (which are shown on the balance sheet) and the money it spends and receives (which is shown on the income statement and statement of cash flows). Companies don't draw down assets (liquid or otherwise) to meet payroll expenses; rather, they add workers when they think that they can increase their after-tax revenues by doing so. Fourth, the idea that investing in liquid assets (e.g., bonds, time deposits, and mutual funds) somehow reduces hiring is simply wrong. Corporations can, and do, make capital expenditures (e.g., in buildings and inventories) at the same time as they are making investments in liquid assets. It's also true that even if cash-rich technology companies like Apple spend some of their cash, it would likely create jobs in foreign countries, not North America.

QUESTIONS FOR DISCUSSION

1. What are three main responsibilities of financial managers? How do these responsibilities influence the amount of cash that companies hold?
2. If companies paid out more money in dividends, do you think that consumers would spend more money and thereby boost the economy? Defend your answer.
3. Which of the two claims—that companies are hoarding cash or companies are not hoarding cash—do you think is most persuasive? Explain.

LO-1 THE ROLE OF THE FINANCIAL MANAGER

Financial managers plan and control the acquisition and dispersal of the company's financial assets. The business activity known as **finance** (or corporate finance) typically involves four responsibilities:

1. determining a firm's long-term investments
2. obtaining funds to pay for those investments
3. conducting the firm's everyday financial activities
4. managing the risks that the firm takes

In recent years, more and more chief financial officers (CFOs) have been appointed as chief executives officers (CEOs). For example, at Pepsico, Indra Nooyi was promoted from CFO to CEO. About 20 percent of CEOs were formerly CFOs.[1] The skill set of CFOs is expanding because they have access to a great deal of information about the internal workings of companies, and because they are responsible for setting budgets and dealing with regulatory agencies.[2]

Objectives of the Financial Manager

A financial manager's overall objective is to increase a firm's value and stockholders' wealth. Financial managers do many specific things to increase a firm's value: collect funds, pay debts, establish trade credit, obtain loans, control cash balances, and plan for future financial needs. Whereas accountants create data to reflect a firm's financial status, financial managers make decisions for improving that status. Financial managers must ensure that a company's revenues exceed its costs—in other words, that it earns a profit. In sole proprietorships and partnerships, profits translate directly into increases in owners' wealth. In corporations, profits translate into an increase in the value of common stock.

FINANCIAL MANAGERS Managers responsible for planning and overseeing the financial resources of a firm.

FINANCE The business function involving decisions about a firm's long-term investments and obtaining the funds to pay for those investments.

CASH-FLOW MANAGEMENT Managing the pattern in which cash flows into the firm in the form of revenues and out of the firm in the form of debt payments.

FINANCIAL CONTROL The process of checking actual performance against plans to ensure that the desired financial status is achieved.

FINANCIAL PLAN A description of how a business will reach some financial position it seeks for the future; includes projections for sources and uses of funds.

Responsibilities of the Financial Manager

The various responsibilities of the financial manager in increasing a firm's wealth fall into three general categories: *cash-flow management*, *financial control*, and *financial planning*.

CASH-FLOW MANAGEMENT

To increase a firm's value, financial managers must ensure that it always has enough funds on hand to purchase the materials and human resources that it needs to produce goods and services. Funds that are not needed immediately must be invested to earn more money. This activity—**cash-flow management**—requires careful planning. If excess cash balances are allowed to sit idle instead of being invested, a firm loses the interest that it could have earned. One study revealed that companies averaging $2 million in annual sales typically hold $40 000 in non-interest-bearing accounts. Larger companies hold even larger sums. By putting idle cash to work, firms gain additional investment income.

FINANCIAL CONTROL

Because things never go exactly as planned, financial managers must be prepared to make adjustments for actual financial changes that occur each day. **Financial control** is the process of checking actual performance against plans to ensure that the desired financial outcome occurs. For example, planned revenues based on forecasts usually turn out to be higher or lower than actual revenues. Why? Simply because sales are unpredictable. Control involves monitoring revenue inflows and making appropriate financial adjustments. Higher-than-expected revenues, for instance, may be deposited in short-term interest-bearing accounts, or they may be used to pay off short-term debt. Otherwise earmarked resources can be saved or put to better use. In contrast, lower-than-expected revenues may necessitate short-term borrowing to meet current debt obligations.

Budgets are important in financial control (see Chapter 11) and provide the "measuring stick" against which performance is evaluated. The cash flows, debts, and assets, not only of the whole company, but of each department, are compared at regular intervals against budgeted amounts. Discrepancies indicate the need for financial adjustments so that resources are used to the best advantage.

FINANCIAL PLANNING

The cornerstone of effective financial management is the development of a **financial plan**, which describes a firm's strategies for reaching some future financial position. In 2012, for example, Canadian Pacific

Financial managers have the responsibility of ensuring that the financial assets of their company are used effectively. This includes investments the company may have in other companies in the form of shares of stock. Regular assessment of how these investments are performing is an important responsibility of financial managers.

Photos.com/Jupiterimages

Railway Ltd. announced that it would make strategic investments totalling $1.2 billion in order to improve its operating ratio (which, in 2011, was the worst among North America's Big Six railways).[3] When constructing a financial plan, several questions must be answered:

- What funds are needed to meet immediate plans?
- When will the firm need more funds?
- Where can the firm get the funds to meet both its short- and long-term needs?

To answer these questions, a financial manager must develop a clear picture of why a firm needs funds. Managers must also assess the relative costs and benefits of potential funding sources. In the following sections, we examine the main reasons why companies generate funds and describe the main sources of business funding, both for the short and long term.

LO-2 WHY BUSINESSES NEED FUNDS

Every company needs money to survive. Failure to make a contractually obligated payment can lead to bankruptcy and the dissolution of the firm. Financial managers must distinguish between short-term (operating) expenditures and long-term (capital) expenditures. The time frame for short-term expenditures is typically less than one year, while for long-term expenditures the time frame is greater than one year.

Short-Term (Operating) Expenditures

A firm incurs short-term expenditures regularly in its everyday business activities. To handle these expenditures, financial managers must pay attention to *accounts payable*, *accounts receivable*, and *inventories*.

ACCOUNTS PAYABLE

In Chapter 11, we defined accounts payable as unpaid bills owed to suppliers plus wages and taxes due within a year. For most companies, this is the largest single category of short-term debt. To plan for funding flows, financial managers want to know in advance the amounts of new accounts payable, as well as when they must be repaid. For information about such obligations and needs—say, the quantity of supplies required by a certain department in an upcoming period—financial managers must rely on other managers. The Team Ethics exercise at the end of the chapter presents an interesting dilemma regarding accounts payable.

ACCOUNTS RECEIVABLE

Accounts receivable refer to funds due from customers who have bought on credit. Because accounts receivable represent an investment in products for which a firm has not yet received payment, they temporarily tie up its funds. Clearly, the seller wants to receive payment as quickly as possible. A sound financial plan requires financial managers to project accurately both how much credit is advanced to buyers and when they will make payments. For example, managers at Kraft Foods must know how many dollars worth of cheddar cheese Safeway supermarkets will order each month; they must also know Safeway's payment schedule.

Credit Policies Predicting payment schedules is a function of **credit policy**—the rules governing a firm's extension of credit to customers. This policy sets standards as to which buyers are eligible for what type of credit. Typically, credit is extended to customers who have the ability to pay and who honour their obligations. Credit is denied to firms with poor payment histories.

Credit policy also sets specific payment terms. For example, credit terms of "2/10, net 30" mean that the selling company offers a 2 percent discount if the customer pays within 10 days. The customer has 30 days to pay the regular price. Under these terms, the buyer would have to pay only $980 on a $1000 invoice on days 1 to 10, but all $1000 on days 11 to 30. The higher the discount, the more incentive buyers have to pay early. Sellers can thus adjust credit terms to influence when customers pay their bills.

INVENTORIES

Between the time a firm buys raw materials and the time it sells finished products, it ties up funds in **inventory**—materials and goods that it will sell within the year. Failure to manage inventory can have grave financial

CREDIT POLICY Rules governing a firm's extension of credit to customers.

INVENTORY Materials and goods currently held by the company that will be sold within the year.

consequences. Too little inventory of any kind can cost a firm sales, while too much inventory means tied-up funds that cannot be used elsewhere. In extreme cases, a company may have to sell excess inventory at low prices simply to raise cash.

The basic supplies a firm buys to use in its production process are its **raw-materials inventory**. Levi Strauss's raw-materials inventory includes huge rolls of denim. **Work-in-process inventory** consists of goods partway through the production process. Cut-out but not-yet-sewn jeans are part of the work-in-process inventory at Levi's. Finally, **finished-goods inventory** are the items that are ready for sale (completed blue jeans ready for shipment to Levi's dealers).

RAW-MATERIALS INVENTORY That portion of a firm's inventory consisting of basic supplies used to manufacture products for sale.

WORK-IN-PROCESS INVENTORY That portion of a firm's inventory consisting of goods partway through the production process.

FINISHED-GOODS INVENTORY That portion of a firm's inventory consisting of completed goods ready for sale.

Long-Term (Capital) Expenditures

Companies need funds to cover long-term expenditures for fixed assets like land, buildings, and machinery. In 2012, for example, Walmart Canada spent $750 million on remodelling, expanding, or relocating 73 different retail outlets.[4] Long-term expenditures are more carefully planned than short-term outlays because they pose special problems. They differ from short-term outlays in the following ways, all of which influence the ways that long-term outlays are funded:

- unlike inventories and other short-term assets, they are not normally sold or converted to cash
- their acquisition requires a very large investment
- they represent a binding commitment of company funds that continues long into the future

LO-3 SOURCES OF SHORT-TERM FUNDS

Firms can call on many sources for the funds they need to finance day-to-day operations and to implement short-term plans. These sources include *trade credit*, *secured short-term loans*, and *unsecured short-term loans*.

Trade Credit

Accounts payable are not merely an expenditure. They are also a source of funds to the company, which has the use of both the product purchased and the price of the product until the time it pays its bill. **Trade credit**, the granting of credit by one firm to another, is effectively a short-term loan. Trade credit can take several forms.

- The most common form, **open-book credit**, is essentially a "gentlemen's agreement." Buyers receive merchandise along with invoices stating credit terms. Sellers ship products on faith that payment will be forthcoming.
- When sellers want more reassurance, they may insist that buyers sign legally binding **promissory notes** before merchandise is shipped. The agreement states when and how much money will be paid to the seller.
- The **trade draft** is attached to the merchandise shipment by the seller and states the promised date and amount of payment due. To take possession of the merchandise, the buyer must sign the draft. Once signed by the buyer, the document becomes a **trade acceptance**. Trade drafts and trade acceptances are useful forms of credit in international transactions.

TRADE CREDIT The granting of credit by a selling firm to a buying firm.

OPEN-BOOK CREDIT Form of trade credit in which sellers ship merchandise on faith that payment will be forthcoming.

PROMISSORY NOTE Form of trade credit in which buyers sign promise-to-pay agreements before merchandise is shipped.

TRADE DRAFT Form of trade credit in which buyers must sign statements of payment terms attached to merchandise by sellers.

TRADE ACCEPTANCE Trade draft that has been signed by the buyer.

SECURED LOANS A short-term loan in which the borrower is required to put up collateral.

COLLATERAL Any asset that a lender has the right to seize if a borrower does not repay a loan.

PLEDGING ACCOUNTS RECEIVABLE Using accounts receivable as collateral for a loan.

Secured Short-Term Loans

For most firms, bank loans are a vital source of short-term funding. Such loans almost always involve a promissory note in which the borrower promises to repay the loan plus interest. In **secured loans**, banks also require the borrower to put up collateral—to give the bank the right to seize certain assets if payments are not made. Inventories, accounts receivable, and other assets (e.g., stocks and bonds) may serve as **collateral** for a secured loan. Secured loans allow borrowers to get funds when they might not qualify for unsecured credit. Moreover, they generally carry lower interest rates than unsecured loans.

INVENTORY AS COLLATERAL

When a loan is made with inventory as a collateral asset, the lender lends the borrower some portion of the stated value of the inventory. Inventory is more attractive as collateral when it can be readily converted into cash. Boxes full of expensive, partially completed lenses for eyeglasses are of little value on the open market, but a thousand crates of canned tomatoes might well be convertible into cash.

ACCOUNTS RECEIVABLE AS COLLATERAL

When accounts receivable are used as collateral, the process is called **pledging accounts receivable**. In the event of non-payment, the lender may seize the receivables (funds owed the borrower by its customers). If these assets are not enough to cover the loan, the borrower must make up the difference. This option is especially important to service companies such as accounting firms and law offices. Because they do not maintain inventories, accounts receivable are their main source of collateral. Typically, lenders that will accept accounts receivable as collateral are financial institutions with credit departments capable of evaluating the quality of the receivables.

Factoring Accounts Receivable A firm can also raise funds by *factoring* (that is, selling) its accounts receivable. The purchaser of the receivables (called a factor) might, for example, buy $50 000 worth of receivables for 80 percent of that sum ($40 000). The factor then tries to collect on the receivables and profits to the extent that the money it eventually collects exceeds the amount it paid for the receivables. Usually the factor ends up with a profit of 2 to 4 percent, depending on the quality of the receivables, the cost of collecting them, and interest rates. Factoring essentially means outsourcing the collection process. About $4 billion worth of goods are factored each year in Canada, but this is far below the $300 billion in the U.S. Toronto-based Liquid Capital Advance Corp., a factoring company, had revenues of almost $2 billion in 2011.[5]

Unsecured Short-Term Loans

With an **unsecured loan**, the borrower does not have to put up collateral. In many cases, however, the bank requires the borrower to maintain a compensating balance—the borrower must keep a portion of the loan amount on deposit with the bank in a non-interest-bearing account.

The terms of an unsecured loan—amount, duration, interest rate, and payment schedule—are negotiated. To receive such a loan, a firm must ordinarily have a good banking relationship with the lender. Once an agreement is made, a promissory note will be executed and the funds transferred to the borrower. There are three common types of unsecured loans: *lines of credit*, *revolving credit agreements*, and *commercial paper*.

LINES OF CREDIT

A standing agreement with a bank to lend a firm a maximum amount of funds on request is called a **line of credit**. With a line of credit, the firm knows the maximum amount it will be allowed to borrow if the bank has sufficient funds. The bank does not guarantee that the funds will be available when requested. For example, suppose that RBC gives Sunshine Tanning Inc. a $100 000 line of credit for the coming year. By signing promissory notes, Sunshine's borrowings can total up to $100 000 at any time. The bank may not always have sufficient funds when Sunshine needs them. But Sunshine benefits from the arrangement by knowing in advance that the bank regards the firm as creditworthy and will lend funds to it on short notice.

REVOLVING CREDIT AGREEMENTS

Revolving credit agreements are similar to bank credit cards for consumers. Under a **revolving credit agreement**, a lender agrees to make some amount of funds available on demand to a firm for continuing short-term loans. The lending institution guarantees that funds will be available when sought by the borrower. In return, the bank charges a commitment fee—a charge for holding open a line of credit for a customer even if the customer does not borrow any funds. The commitment fee is often expressed as a percentage of the loan amount, usually 0.5 to 1 percent of the committed amount. For example, suppose that RBC agrees to lend Sunshine Tanning up to $100 000 under a revolving credit agreement. If Sunshine borrows $80 000, it still has access to $20 000. If it pays off $50 000 of the debt, reducing its debt to $30 000, then $70 000 is available. Sunshine pays interest on the borrowed funds and also pays a fee on the unused funds in the line of credit.

COMMERCIAL PAPER

Commercial paper, which is backed solely by the issuing firm's promise to pay, is an option for only the largest and most creditworthy firms. Here's how it works: Corporations issue commercial paper with a face value. Companies that buy commercial paper pay less than that value. At the end of a specified period (usually 30 to 90 days, but legally up to 270 days), the issuing company buys back the paper—at the face value. The difference between the price the buying company paid and the face value is the buyer's interest earned. For example, if Air Canada needs to borrow $10 million for 90 days, it might issue commercial paper with a face value of $10.2 million. If an insurance company with $10 million in excess cash buys the paper, after 90 days Air Canada would pay $10.2 million to the insurance company. So, the insurance company earns $200 000 for its $10 million investment (an interest rate of approximately 2 percent).

UNSECURED LOAN A short-term loan in which the borrower is not required to put up collateral.

LINE OF CREDIT A standing agreement between a bank and a firm in which the bank specifies the maximum amount it will make available to the borrower for a short-term unsecured loan; the borrower can then draw on those funds, when available.

REVOLVING CREDIT AGREEMENT A guaranteed line of credit for which the firm pays the bank interest on funds borrowed, as well as a fee for extending the line of credit.

COMMERCIAL PAPER A method of short-run fundraising in which a firm sells unsecured notes for less than the face value and then repurchases them at the face value within 270 days; buyers' profits are the difference between the original price paid and the face value.

LO-4 SOURCES OF LONG-TERM FUNDS

Firms need long-term funding to finance expenditures on fixed assets like the buildings and equipment that is necessary for conducting business. They may seek long-term funds through *debt financing*, *equity financing*, or *hybrid financing*.

Debt Financing

Long-term borrowing from outside the company—**debt financing**—is a major component of most firms' long-term financial planning. Debt financing is most appealing to companies that have predictable profits and cash-flow patterns. For example, demand for electric power is quite steady from year to year and predictable from month to month. Thus, provincial hydroelectric utilities rely heavily on debt financing. There are two primary sources of debt financing: *long-term loans* and the sale of *bonds*.

DEBT FINANCING Raising money to meet long-term expenditures by borrowing from outside the company; usually takes the form of long-term loans or the sale of corporate bonds.

LONG-TERM LOANS

Most corporations get their long-term loans from a chartered bank, usually one with which the firm has developed a long-standing relationship. Long-term loans are usually matched with long-term assets. Interest rates for the loan are negotiated between the borrower and lender. Although some bank loans have fixed rates, others have floating rates tied to the prime rate that they charge their most creditworthy customers (see Chapter 14). For example, a company may negotiate a loan at "prime +1 percent." If prime is 3 percent at that particular time, the company will pay 4 percent. Credit companies, insurance companies, and pension funds also grant long-term business loans.

Long-term loans have several advantages. They can be arranged quickly, the duration of the loan is easily matched to the borrower's needs, and if the firm's needs change, the loan usually contain clauses making it possible to change the terms. But long-term loans also have some disadvantages. Large borrowers may have trouble finding lenders to supply enough funds. Long-term borrowers may also have restrictions placed on them as conditions of the loan. They may have to pledge long-term assets as collateral. And they may have to agree not to take on any more debt until the borrowed funds are repaid.

BONDS

A **corporate bond** is a contract—a promise by the issuing company or organization to pay the bondholder a certain amount of money (the principal) on a specified date, plus interest in return for use of the investor's money. The **bond indenture** spells out the terms of the bond, including the interest rate that will be paid, the maturity date of the bond, and which of the firm's assets, if any, are pledged as collateral.

Bonds are the major source of long-term debt financing for most large corporations. Bonds are attractive when companies need large amounts of funds for long periods of time; in many cases, bonds may not be redeemed for 30 years. But bonds involve expensive administrative and selling costs, and they may also require high interest payments if the issuing company has a poor credit rating. If a company fails to make a bond payment, it is in *default*.

Registered bonds register the names of holders with the company, which then mails out cheques to the bondholders. **Bearer (or coupon) bonds** require bondholders to clip coupons from certificates and send them to the issuer to receive payment. Coupons can be redeemed by anyone, regardless of ownership. With **secured bonds**, borrowers can reduce the risk of their bonds by pledging assets to bondholders in the event of default. If the corporation does not pay interest when it is due, the firm's assets can be sold and the proceeds used to pay the bondholders. Unsecured bonds are called **debentures**. No specific property is pledged as security for these bonds. Holders of unsecured bonds generally have claims against property not otherwise pledged in the company's other bonds. Accordingly, debentures have inferior claims on the corporation's assets. Financially strong corporations often use debentures.

With regard to maturity dates, there are three types of bonds: *callable*, *serial*, and *convertible*.

Callable Bonds The issuer of **callable bonds** may call them in and pay them off before the maturity date at a price stipulated in the indenture. Usually the issuer cannot call the bond for a certain period of time after issue, often within the first five years. Issuers usually call in existing bonds when prevailing interest rates are lower than the rate being paid on the bond. The issuer must still pay a *call* price to call in the bond. The call price usually gives a premium to the bondholder. The premium is merely the difference between the face value and call price. For example, a bond that bears a $100 face value might be callable by the firm for $108.67 any time during the first year after issue. The call price (and therefore the premium) decreases annually as the bonds approach maturity.

CORPORATE BOND A promise by the issuing company to pay the holder a certain amount of money on a specified date, with stated interest payments in the interim; a form of long-term debt financing.

BOND INDENTURE Indicates the key terms of a bond, such as the amount, the interest rate, and the maturity date.

REGISTERED BONDS Bonds where the names of holders are registered with the company.

BEARER (OR COUPON) BONDS Bonds that require bondholders to clip coupons from certificates and send them to the issuer to receive interest payments.

SECURED BONDS Bonds issued by borrowers who pledge assets as collateral in the event of non-payment.

DEBENTURES Unsecured bonds.

CALLABLE BONDS Bonds that can be called in and paid off before the maturity date at a price stipulated in the indenture.

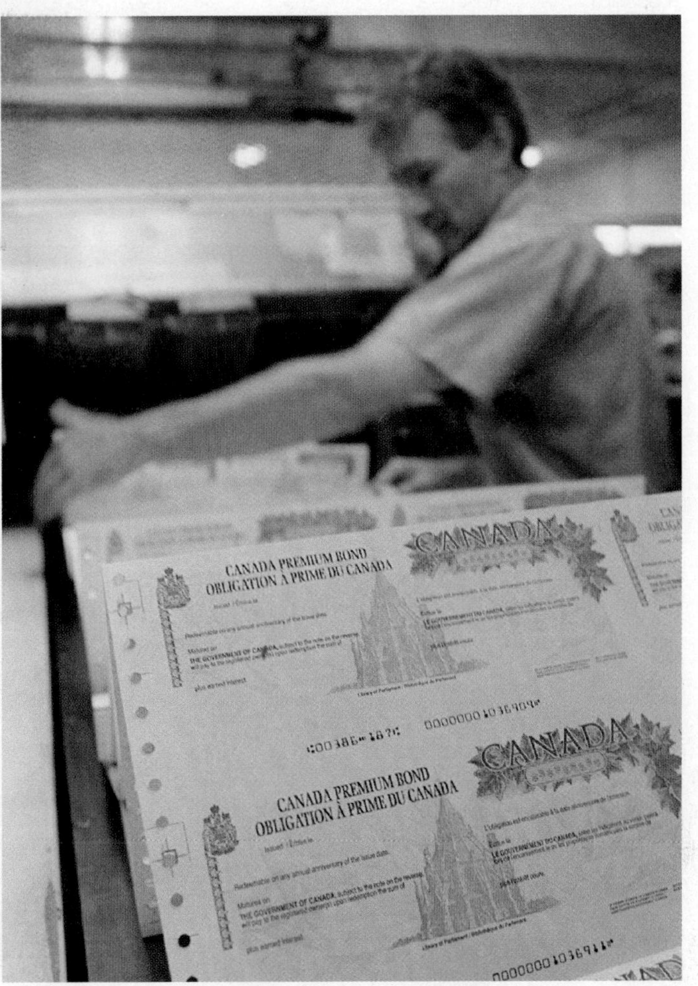

Corporations aren't the only organizations that sell bonds. The government of Canada also sells bonds to finance its activities.

branislavpudar/Shutterstock

Callable bonds are often retired by the use of **sinking-fund provisions**. The issuing company is required to put a certain amount of money into a special bank account annually. At the end of a certain number of years, the money (including interest) will be sufficient to redeem the bonds. Failure to meet the sinking-fund provision places the issue in default. Such bonds are generally regarded as safer investments than many other bonds.

Serial Bonds Some corporations issue serial or convertible bonds. With a **serial bond**, the firm retires portions of the bond issue in a series of different preset dates. For example, a company with a $100-million issue maturing in 20 years may retire $5 million each year.

Convertible Bonds **Convertible bonds** can be converted into the common stock of the issuing company. For example, suppose that Bell Canada Enterprises sold a $100-million issue of 4.5 percent convertible bonds in 2010. The bonds were issued in $1000 denominations, and they mature in 2020. At any time before maturity, each bond of $1000 is convertible into 19.125 shares of the company's common stock. Suppose that between October 2010 and March 2017, the stock price ranged from a low of $28 to a high of $67. In that time, then, 19.125 common shares had a market value ranging from $535 to $1281. The bondholder could have exchanged the $1000 bond in return for stock to be kept or sold at a possible profit (or loss).

Bonds differ from one another in terms of their level of risk. To help bond investors make assessments, several services rate the quality of bonds from different issuers. Table 15.1 shows ratings by Moody's and Standard & Poor's. The rating measures the bond's default risk—the chance that one or more promised payments will be deferred or missed altogether. The financial crisis of 2008 revealed some significant problems with bond rating agencies. The credibility of companies like Moody's and Standard & Poor's declined because they gave overly favourable ratings to certain securities that were actually very risky. People who made investments based on the ratings lost billions of dollars when bonds they thought were safe turned out not to be.[6]

TABLE 15.1 Bond Ratings

	High Grade	Medium Grade (Investment Grade)	Speculative	Poor Grade
Moody's	Aaa Aa	A Baa	Ba B	Caa to C
Standard & Poor's	AAA AA	A BBB	BB B	CCC to D

SINKING-FUND PROVISIONS Money an issuing company puts into a special bank account annually to be used to redeem the issued bonds.

SERIAL BOND A bond that a firm retires in portions on a series of different preset dates.

CONVERTIBLE BONDS Bonds that can be converted into the common stock of the issuing company.

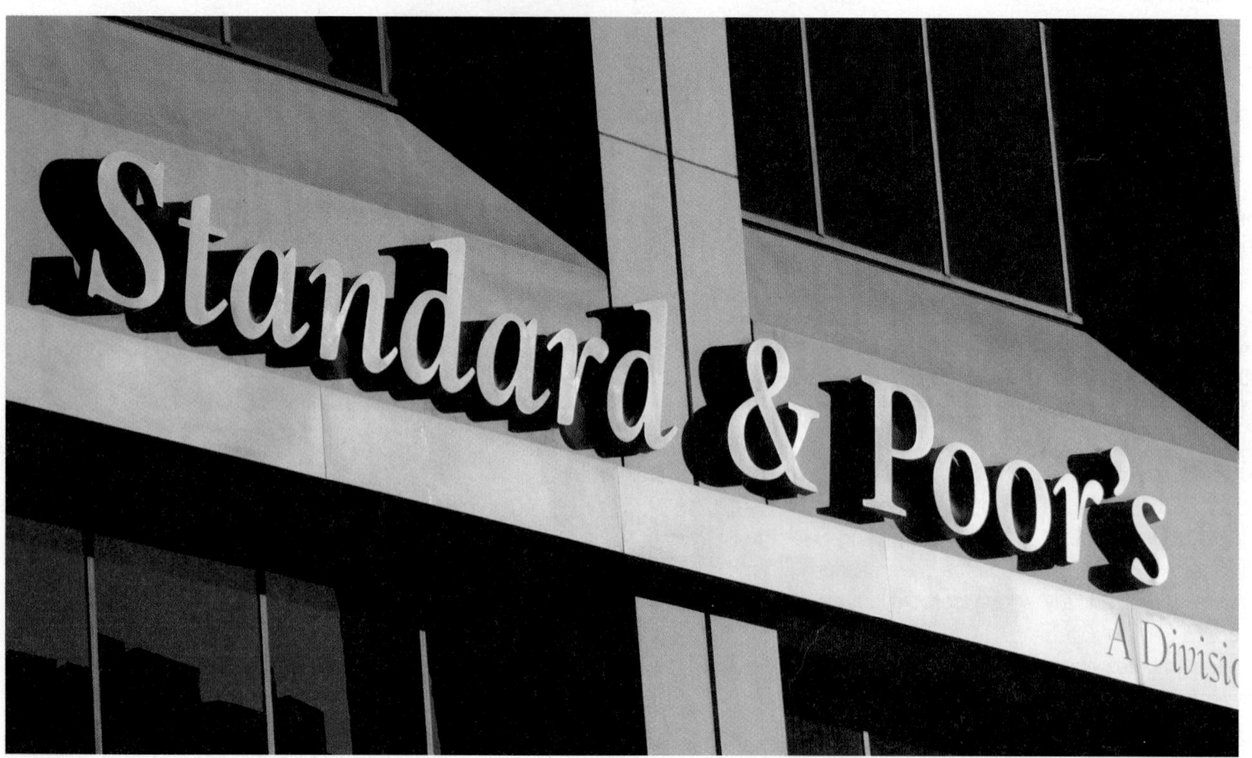

If bond rating agencies like Moody's, Standard & Poor's, or Fitch downgrade a company's ratings to low enough levels, its bonds become junk bonds. When that happens, investors demand higher interest rates to reflect the increased risk of investing in the company.

Genin Nicolas/ABACA/Newscom

LO-5 Equity Financing

Sometimes, looking inside the company for long-term funding is preferable to looking outside. In most cases, **equity financing** takes the form of *issuing stock* or *retaining the firm's earnings*. Both options involve putting the owners' capital to work.

ISSUING COMMON STOCK

By selling shares of common stock, the company obtains the funds it needs to buy land, buildings, and equipment. Individuals and companies buy a firm's stock, hoping that it will increase in value (a capital gain) and/or will provide dividend income. Let's look at an example. Suppose that Sunshine Tanning's founders invested $10 000 in buying the original 500 shares of common stock (at $20 per share) in 2003. If the company used these funds to buy equipment and succeeded financially, by 2012 it may have needed further funds for expansion. A pattern of profitable operations and regularly paid dividends enabled Sunshine to raise $50 000 by selling 500 new shares of stock for $100 per share. This additional paid-in capital would increase the total shareholders' equity to $60 000, as shown in Table 15.2.

Common stock values are expressed in three ways. The face value of a share of stock—its **par value**—is set by the issuing company's board of directors. The **book value** of common stock represents stockholders' equity (the sum of a company's common stock par value, retained earnings, and additional paid-in capital) divided by the number of shares. A stock's real value is its **market value**—the current price of a share in the stock market. For successful companies, the market value is usually greater than its book value. Thus, when market price falls to near book value, some investors buy the stock on the principle that it is underpriced and will increase in value in the future. The price of a share of stock can be influenced by both objective factors (company profits) and by subjective factors, like *rumours* (e.g., claims that a company has made a big gold strike), *investor relations* (publicizing the positive aspects of a company's financial condition to financial analysts and financial institutions), and *stockbroker recommendations* (a recommendation to buy a stock may increase demand and cause its price to increase, while a recommendation to sell may decrease demand and cause the price to fall).

The **market capitalization** of a company's stock is computed by multiplying the number of a company's outstanding shares times the market value of each share. Because stock prices change every day, so do market capitalizations. The Royal Bank topped the Canadian list in 2012 with a market capitalization of approximately $80 billion.[7]

TABLE 15.2 Stockholders' Equity for Sunshine Tanning

Common Stockholders' Equity, 2003	
Initial common stock (500 shares issued @ $20 per share, 2003)	$10 000
Total stockholders' equity	$10 000
Common Stockholders' Equity, 2012	
Initial common stock (500 shares issued @ $20 per share, 2003)	$10 000
Additional paid-in capital (500 shares issued @ $100 per share, 2012)	50 000
Total stockholders' equity	$60 000

In Canada, banks and resource companies dominate the top 10 list of companies with the largest market capitalizations.

The use of equity financing via common stock can be expensive because paying dividends is more expensive than paying bond interest. This is because interest paid to bondholders is tax deductible, but dividends paid to stockholders are not. Even though equity financing is expensive, financial managers cannot rely totally on debt capital because long-term loans and bonds carry fixed interest rates and represent a promise to pay regardless of the profitability of the firm. If the firm defaults on its obligations, it may lose its assets and even go into bankruptcy. In 2012, for example, Yellow Media Inc. was trying to pay off a $1.5 billion debt it had accumulated. To get money to pay bondholders, the company cut off dividends for preferred shareholders, but that caused the value of those shares to drop by up to 55 percent. Common shares dropped in value by 97 percent.[8]

RETAINING THE FIRM'S EARNINGS

Another approach to equity financing is to use retained earnings. These earnings represent profits not paid out in dividends. Using retained earnings means that the firm will not have to borrow money and pay interest on loans or bonds. A firm that has a history of reaping much higher profits by successfully reinvesting retained earnings may be attractive to some investors. But the smaller dividends that can be paid to shareholders as a result of retained earnings may decrease demand for—and thus the price of—the company's stock. Let's revisit our Sunshine Tanning example. If the company had net earnings of $50 000 in 2012, it could pay a $50-per-share dividend on its 1000 shares of common stock. But if it plans to remodel at a cost of $30 000 and retains $30 000 of earnings to finance the project, only $20 000 is left to distribute for stock dividends ($20 per share).

Hybrid Financing: Preferred Stock

Preferred stock is a hybrid because it has some of the features of corporate bonds and some features of common stock. As with bonds, payments on preferred stock are for fixed amounts. Unlike bonds, however, preferred stock never matures. It can be held indefinitely, like common stock. And dividends need not be paid if the company makes no profit. If dividends are paid, preferred stockholders receive them first in preference to dividends on common stock. A major advantage of preferred stock to the issuing corporation is its flexibility. It secures funds for the firm without relinquishing control, since preferred stockholders have no voting rights. It does not require repayment of principal or the payment of dividends in lean times.

EQUITY FINANCING Raising money to meet long-term expenditures by issuing common stock or by retaining earnings.

PAR VALUE The arbitrary value of a stock set by the issuing company's board of directors and stated on stock certificates; used by accountants but of little significance to investors.

BOOK VALUE Value of a common stock expressed as total stockholders' equity divided by the number of shares of stock.

MARKET VALUE The current price of one share of a stock in the secondary securities market; the real value of a stock.

MARKET CAPITALIZATION The dollar value (market value) of stocks listed on a stock exchange.

Preferred stock is usually issued with a stated par value, such as $100. Dividends paid on preferred stock are usually expressed as a percentage of the par value. For example, if a preferred stock with a $100 par value pays a 6 percent dividend, stockholders would receive an annual dividend of $6 on each share.

Some preferred stock is *callable*, meaning that the issuing firm can require the preferred stockholders to surrender their shares in exchange for a cash payment. The amount of this cash payment, known as the call price, is specified in the agreement between the preferred stockholders and the firm.

Choosing between Debt and Equity Financing

Financial planning involves striking a balance between debt and equity financing to meet the firm's long-term need for funds. The mix of debt and equity a firm uses is called its **capital structure**. Financial plans contain targets for the capital structure, but choosing a target is not easy. A wide range of debt-versus-equity mixes is possible.

The most conservative strategy is to use all equity financing and no debt, because a company has no formal obligations for financial payouts. But as we have noted, equity is a very expensive source of capital. The riskiest strategy would be to use all debt financing. While less expensive than equity funding, indebtedness increases the risk that a firm will be unable to meet its obligations and will go bankrupt. Financial managers try to find a mix somewhere between these two extremes that will maximize stockholders' wealth. Figure 15.1 summarizes the factors management takes into account when deciding between debt and equity financing.

THE RISK–RETURN RELATIONSHIP

Every investor has a personal preference for safety versus risk. Investors generally expect only modest returns for secure investments such as government-insured bonds, but expect higher returns for riskier investments. Each type of investment, then, has a **risk–return relationship**. Figure 15.2 shows the general risk–return relationship for various financial instruments. High-grade corporate bonds, for example, rate low in terms of risk, but they also provide low returns. Junk bonds, on the other hand,

CAPITAL STRUCTURE Relative mix of a firm's debt and equity financing.

RISK–RETURN RELATIONSHIP Shows the amount of risk and the likely rate of return on various financial instruments.

Debt financing	Equity financing
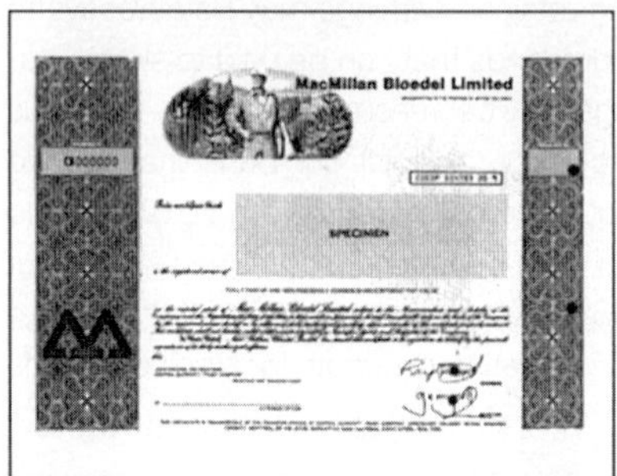	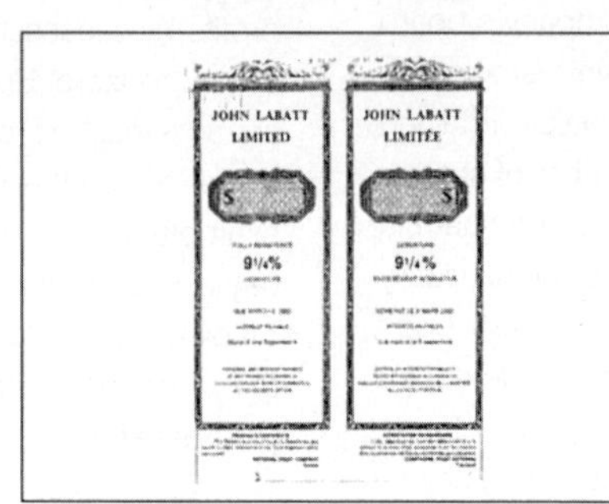
When must it be repaid?	
Fixed deadline	No limit
Will it make claims on income?	
Yes, regular and fixed	Only residual claim
Will it have claims on assets?	
In liquidation, creditors come first	In liquidation, shareholders must wait until creditors are paid and preferred equity precedes common equity
Will it affect management control?	
No	May cause challenge for corporation control
How are taxes affected?	
Bond interest is deductible	Dividends are not deductible
Will it affect management flexibility?	
Yes, many constraints	No, few constraints

<<< FIGURE **15.1** Comparing debt and equity financing

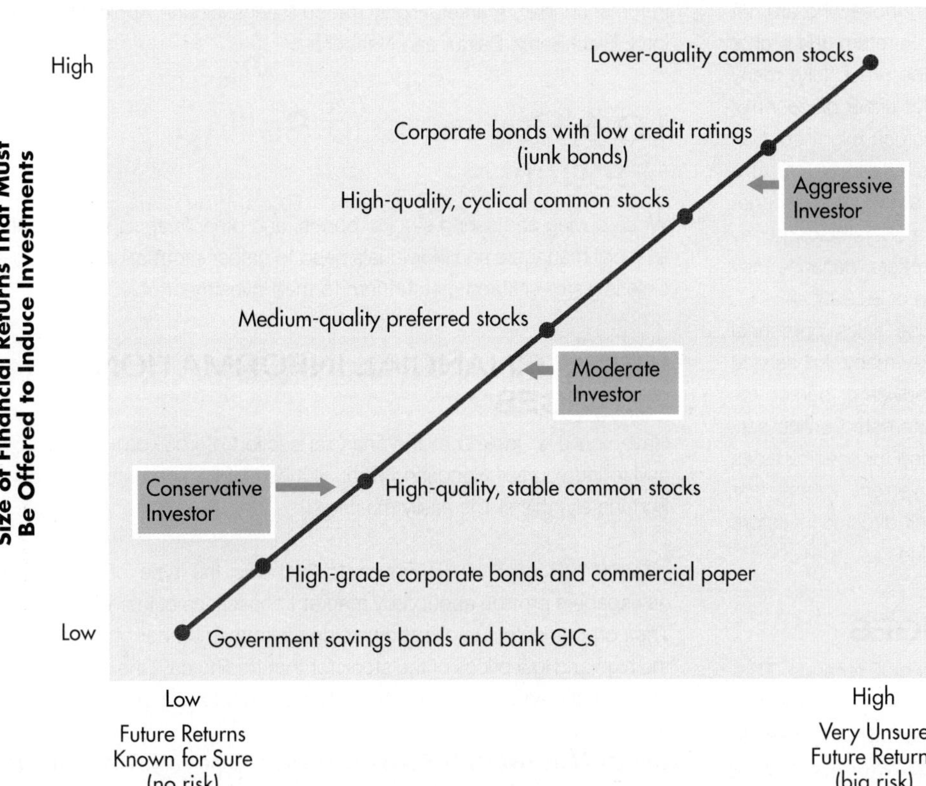

rate high in terms of risk (because the company might default), but they also provide high returns to attract investors.

Risk–return differences are recognized by financial planners, who try to gain access to the greatest funding at the lowest possible cost. By gauging investors' perceptions of their riskiness, a firm's managers can estimate how much it must pay to attract funds to its offerings. Over time, a company can reposition itself on the risk continuum by improving its record on dividends, interest payments, and debt repayment.

<<< **FIGURE 15.2** The risk–return relationship

SECURITIES MARKETS

Stocks and bonds are known as **securities** because they represent a secured (asset-based) claim on the part of investors. Collectively, the market in which stocks and bonds are sold is called the securities market. **Primary securities markets** handle the buying and selling of new shares (initial public offerings or IPOs) of stocks and bonds by firms or governments. When new securities are sold to one buyer or a small group of buyers, these *private placements* allow the businesses that use them to keep their plans confidential. But new securities represent only a small portion of securities traded. The market for existing stocks and bonds—the **secondary securities market**—is handled by organizations like the Toronto Stock Exchange. Companies do not receive any money when shares of stock are bought and sold in the secondary securities market.

Corporate financial managers (and individual investors) need to be knowledgeable about securities markets if they hope to be successful. In this section, we look at the following aspects of securities markets: *investment banking*, *stock exchanges*, *buying and selling securities*, and *financing securities purchases*. We also describe several other investments that investors may purchase.

Investment Banking

Most new stocks and some bonds are sold to the public market. To bring a new security to market, the issuing corporation must obtain approval from a provincial securities commission. It also needs the services of an investment banker. **Investment bankers** serve as financial specialists in issuing new securities. Well-known institutions like RBC Dominion Securities and TD Securities provide the following services:

1. They advise companies on the timing and financial terms for a new issue.
2. By underwriting (buying) the new securities, investment bankers bear some of the risk of issuing a new security.
3. They create the distribution network that moves the new securities through groups of other banks and brokers into the hands of individual investors.

Stock Exchanges

A **stock exchange** is composed of individuals (stockbrokers) and organizations (investment banks) that provide a setting in which shares of stock can be bought and sold. The exchange enforces certain rules to govern its members' trading activities. Most exchanges are non-profit corporations established to serve their members. To become a member, an individual must purchase one of a limited number of "seats" on the exchange. Only members (or their representatives) are allowed to trade on the exchange. In this sense, because all orders to buy or sell must flow through members, they have a legal monopoly. Memberships can be bought and sold like other assets.

SECURITIES Stocks, bonds, and mutual funds representing secured, or asset-based, claims by investors against issuers.

PRIMARY SECURITIES MARKET Market in which new stocks and bonds are bought and sold.

SECONDARY SECURITIES MARKET The sale and purchase of previously issued stocks and bonds.

INVESTMENT BANKERS Financial specialists in issuing new securities.

STOCK EXCHANGE A voluntary organization of individuals formed to provide an institutional setting where members can buy and sell stock for themselves and their clients in accordance with the exchange's rules.

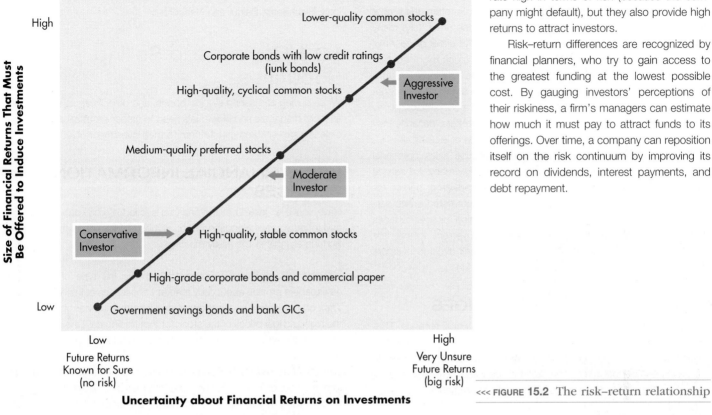

A **stockbroker** receives buy and sell orders from those who are not members of the exchange and executes the orders. In return, the broker earns a commission from the person who placed the order. Like many products, brokerage assistance can be purchased at either *discount* or at *full-service* prices. Buying 200 shares of a $20 stock might cost an investor up to $100 at a full-service broker, but as little as $6.99 at a discount broker. Price differences are evident even among the discount brokers. For example, you could buy 100 shares of a $50 stock and pay just $1 in brokers' commissions if you use Virtual Brokers, because they charge only $0.01 per share with a minimum charge of $0.99.[9]

Discount brokerage services cost less because sales personnel receive fees or salaries, not commissions. Unlike many full-service brokers, discount brokers do not offer investment advice or person-to-person sales consultations. However, they offer automated online services: stock research, industry analysis, and screening for specific types of stocks. Online trading is popular because of convenient access, fast no-nonsense transactions, and the opportunity for self-directed investors to manage their own investments while paying low fees.

CANADIAN STOCK EXCHANGES

The TMX Group owns and operates the Toronto Stock Exchange (TSX) and the TSX Venture Exchange. The TSX is the largest stock exchange in Canada. It is made up of about 110 individual members who hold seats. The securities of most major corporations are listed here. A company must pay a fee before it can list its security on the exchange.

FOREIGN STOCK EXCHANGES

Many foreign countries also have active stock exchanges, and several foreign stock exchanges—most notably those in the United States and United Kingdom—trade far more shares each day than the TSX does. For many people, "the stock market" means the New York Stock Exchange (NYSE). In 1980, the U.S. stock market accounted for more than half the value of the *world* market in traded stocks. Market activities, however, have shifted as the value of shares listed on foreign exchanges continues to grow rapidly. The annual dollar value of trades on exchanges in London, Tokyo, and other cities is now in the trillions. In fact, the London Stock Exchange exceeds even the NYSE in the number of stocks listed.

THE OVER-THE-COUNTER MARKET

The **over-the-counter (OTC)** market is so-called because its original traders were somewhat like retailers—they kept supplies of shares on hand and, as opportunities arose, sold them over the counter to interested buyers. Even today, the OTC market has no trading floor. It consists of many people in different locations who hold an inventory of securities that are not listed on any of the major exchanges. The OTC market consists of independent dealers who own the securities that they buy and sell at their own risk.

NASDAQ

The **National Association of Securities Dealers Automated Quotation (NASDAQ)** is the world's first electronic stock market.[10] The NASDAQ telecommunications system operates the NASDAQ Stock Market by broadcasting trading information on an intranet to over 350 000 terminals worldwide. NASDAQ orders are paired and executed on a computer network. The stocks of nearly 3700 companies are traded by NASDAQ. Many newer firms are listed here when their stocks first become available in the secondary market. Highly traded listings include Apple, Microsoft, Intel, BlackBerry, Baidu, and Netflix.[11]

LO-6 Buying and Selling Securities

When buying and selling stocks, bonds, and other financial instruments, financial managers and individuals need to gather information about possible investments and match them to their investment objectives.

USING FINANCIAL INFORMATION SERVICES

Have you ever looked at the financial section of your daily newspaper and found yourself wondering what all those tables and numbers mean? Fortunately, this skill is easily mastered.

Stock Quotations Figure 15.3 shows the type of information newspapers provide about daily market transactions of individual stocks. The corporation's name is shown along with the number of shares sold, the high and low prices of the stock for that trading day, the closing price of the stock, and the change from the closing price on the previous day.

Bond Quotations Bond prices also change daily. These changes form the coupon rate, which provides information for firms about the cost of borrowing funds. Prices of domestic corporation bonds, Canadian government bonds, and foreign bonds are reported separately. Bond prices are expressed in terms of 100, even though most have a face value of $1000. Thus, a quote of 85 means that the bond's price is 85 percent of its face value, or $850.

A corporate bond selling at 155¼ would cost a buyer $1552.50 ($1000 face value multiplied by 1.5525), plus commission. The interest (coupon) rate on bonds is also quoted as a percentage of par, or face, value. Thus "6½s" pay 6.5 percent of par value per year. Typically, interest is paid semi-annually at half of the stated interest or coupon rate.

The market value (selling price) of a bond at any given time depends on three things: its stated interest rate, the "going rate" of interest in the market, and its redemption or maturity date. A bond with a higher stated interest rate than the going rate on similar quality bonds will probably sell at a premium above its face value—its selling price will be above its redemption price. A bond with a lower stated interest rate than the going rate on similar quality bonds will probably sell at a discount—its selling price will be below its redemption price. How much the premium or discount is depends largely on how far in the future the maturity date is. The maturity date is shown after the interest rate. Figure 15.4 shows the type of information daily newspapers provide.

STOCKBROKER An individual licensed to buy and sell securities for customers in the secondary market; may also provide other financial services.

OVER-THE-COUNTER (OTC) MARKET Organization of securities dealers formed to trade stock outside the formal institutional setting of the organized stock exchanges.

NATIONAL ASSOCIATION OF SECURITIES DEALERS AUTOMATED QUOTATION (NASDAQ) A stock market implemented by NASD that operates by broadcasting trading information on an intranet to more than 350 000 terminals worldwide.

Hand-out/TIM HORTONS INC./Newscom

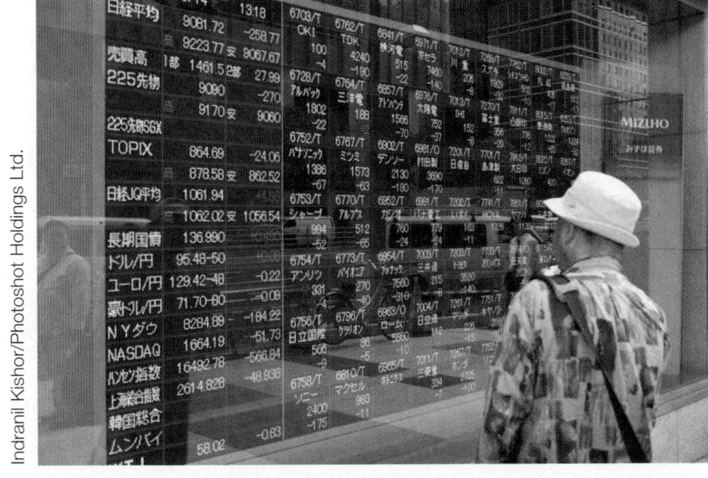
Indranil Kishor/Photoshot Holdings Ltd.

^^^ Stock-market procedures and tools have changed a lot over the years, but the fundamentals remain the same. Investors must do their homework and conduct careful research before shares of stock are purchased.

Company	Volume	High	Low	Close	Change
Bombardier	5875	3.82	3.66	3.67	–0.11
Goldcorp	**6203**	**41.52**	**38.70**	**40.93**	**+3.23**
Royal Bank	3664	50.89	49.84	49.99	–1.56
Magna Intl.	892	41.30	39.14	39.50	–2.25
IAMGold	4615	12.26	11.36	12.15	+1.08
Kinross	3232	8.41	8.94	8.88	+0.59

- *Stock*
  Goldcorp Inc. (Name of Company).
- *Volume*
  6203 (total number of shares traded on this date [in 100s]).
- *High and Low*
  During the trading day, the highest price was $41.52 and the lowest price was $38.70.
- *Close*
  At the close of trading on this date, the last price paid per share was $40.93.
- *Net Change*
  Difference between today's closing price and the previous day's closing price. Price increased by $3.23 per share.

^^^ FIGURE **15.3** How to read a daily stock quotation

Issuer	Coupon	Maturity	Price	Yield
		GOVERNMENT OF CANADA		
Canada	4.20	June 1, 18	117.45	3.57
Canada	3.5	June 1, 20	115.40	3.03
		PROVINCIALS		
Hy Que	6.50	Feb. 15, 35	147.09	4.42
BC	4.7	June 18, 37	124.83	3.76
		CORPORATE		
Telus	**4.95**	**Mar. 3, 17**	**101.92**	**4.86**
Bank of Mon.	5.10	Apr. 21, 21	109.38	4.66

- *Issuer*
  Company name is Telus.
- *Coupon*
  The annual rate of interest at face value is 4.95 percent.
- *Maturity*
  The maturity date is March 3, 2017.
- *Price*
  On this date, $101.92 was the price of the last transaction.
- *Yield*
  The yield is computed by dividing the annual interest paid by the current market price. (Note: Yield to Maturity [YTM] would also take into account duration and capital repayment.)

<<< FIGURE **15.4** How to read a bond quotation

Suppose you bought a $1000 par-value bond in 1995 for $650. Its stated interest rate is 6 percent, and its maturity or redemption date is 2015. You therefore receive $60 per year in interest. Based on your actual investment of $650, your *bond yield* is 9.2 percent. If you hold it to maturity, you get $1000 for a bond that originally cost you only $650. This extra $350 increases your true, or effective, yield.

Market Indexes Although they do not indicate how specific securities are doing, **market indexes** provide a useful summary of trends in specific industries and the stock market as a whole. Such information can be crucial in choosing investments. For example, market indexes reveal bull and bear market trends. **Bull markets** are periods of upward-moving stock prices. The years 1981 to 1989, 1993 to 1999, and 2004 to 2006 were bull markets. Periods of falling stock prices are called **bear markets**. The years 1972 to 1974, 1991 to 1992, 2000 to 2002, and 2008 to 2009 were bear markets.

The most widely cited market index is the **Dow Jones Industrial Average (DJIA)**, which is the sum of market prices for 30 of the largest industrial firms listed on the NYSE. By tradition, the Dow is an indicator of blue-chip (top-quality) stock price movements. Because of the small number of firms it considers, however, it is a limited gauge of the overall stock market. The Dow increased sharply in the 1990s. It reached 11 000 early in 2000 but dropped to less than 6500 in 2009. By mid-2013, it had surged to a record high of over 15 000.

The **S&P/TSX index** is an average computed from 225 large Canadian stocks from various industry groups.[12] The index has also been very volatile during the last few years. It moved sharply upward during the bull market of the 1990s and topped 11 000 in the summer of 2000. It dropped below 8000 by 2009, but increased again to 12 700 by mid-2013.

The **S&P 500** (Standard & Poor's Composite Index) consists of 500 stocks, including 400 industrial firms, 40 utilities, 40 financial institutions, and 20 transportation companies. The index average is weighted according to market capitalization of each stock, so the more highly valued companies exercise a greater influence on the index.

Some stock-market observers regard the **NASDAQ Composite Index** as the most important of all market indexes. Unlike the Dow and the S&P 500, all NASDAQ-listed companies are included in the index. The NASDAQ market has been very volatile. In early 2000, it reached 5000, but by 2001 had dropped to just 1300. In mid-2013 it had risen to 3150.

BUYING AND SELLING STOCKS

Based on your own investigations and/or recommendations from your stockbroker, you can place many types of orders. A **market order** requests the broker buy or sell a certain security at the prevailing market price at the time. A **limit order** authorizes the purchase of a stock only if its price is less than or equal to a given limit. For example, a limit order to buy a stock at $80 per share means that the broker is to buy it if and only if the stock becomes available for a price of $80 or less. Similarly, a stop order instructs the broker to sell a stock if its price falls to a certain level. For example, a **stop order** of $85 on a particular stock means that the broker is to sell it if and only if its price falls to $85 or below.

You can also place orders of different sizes. A **round lot** order requests 100 shares or some multiple thereof. Fractions of a round lot are called odd lots. Trading **odd lots** is usually more expensive than trading round lots, because an intermediary called an odd-lot broker is often involved, which increases brokerage fees.

The business of buying and selling stocks is changing rapidly. Formerly, a person had to have a broker to buy and sell stocks. More and more individuals are now buying and selling stocks on the internet, and traditional brokers are worried that before long customers will avoid using their services.

Financing Securities Purchases

When you place a buy order of any kind, you must tell your broker how you will pay for the purchase. You might maintain a cash account with your broker. Then, as stocks are bought and sold, proceeds are added into the account and commissions and costs of purchases are withdrawn by the broker. You can also buy shares on credit.

MARGIN TRADING

Shares of stock can be purchased on **margin**—putting down only a portion of the stock's price. You borrow the rest from your broker, who, in turn, borrows from the banks at a special rate and secures the loans with stock. Suppose you purchase $100 000 worth of stock in WestJet. Let's also say that you paid $50 000 of your own money and borrowed the other $50 000 from your broker at 10 percent interest. Valued at its market price, your stock serves as your collateral. If shares have risen in value to $115 000 after one year, you can sell them and pay your broker $55 000 ($50 000 principal plus $5000 interest). You will have $60 000 left over. Your original investment of $50 000 will have earned a 20 percent profit of $10 000. If you had paid the entire price out of your own pocket, you would have earned only a 15 percent return.

Although investors often recognize possible profits to be made in margin trading, they sometimes fail to consider that losses can be amplified. If the value of your initial WestJet investment of $100 000 had instead fallen to $85 000 after one year, you would have lost 15 percent if you had paid out of pocket. However, if you had used margin trading, you would have lost $20 000 ($5000 interest payment + $15 000 share decrease) on a $50 000 investment, which amounts to a 40 percent loss.

MARKET INDEX A measure of the market value of stocks; provides a summary of price trends in a specific industry or of the stock market as a whole.

BULL MARKET A period of rising stock prices; a period in which investors act on a belief that stock prices will rise.

BEAR MARKET A period of falling stock prices; a period in which investors act on a belief that stock prices will fall.

DOW JONES INDUSTRIAL AVERAGE (DJIA) Market index based on the prices of 30 of the largest firms listed on NYSE.

S&P/TSX INDEX An average computed from 225 large Canadian stocks from various industry groups.

STANDARD & POOR'S COMPOSITE INDEX (S&P 500) Market index based on the performance of 400 industrial firms, 40 utilities, 40 financial institutions, and 20 transportation companies.

NASDAQ COMPOSITE INDEX Value-weighted market index that includes all NASDAQ-listed companies, both domestic and foreign.

MARKET ORDER An order to a broker to buy or sell a certain security at the current market price.

LIMIT ORDER An order to a broker to buy a certain security only if its price is less than or equal to a given limit.

STOP ORDER An order to a broker to sell a certain security if its price falls to a certain level or below.

ROUND LOT The purchase or sale of stock in units of 100 shares.

ODD LOT The purchase or sale of stock in units of other than 100 shares.

MARGIN The percentage of the total sales price that a buyer must put up to place an order for stock or a futures contract.

<<< When the stock market is volatile, there are often spreads between bid prices (what traders pay for a share of stock) and ask prices (what they charge for it). The difference isn't necessarily large, but if you can make a number of quick hits during the day, you can make money. That strategy appeals to traders at large firms, but also to individual traders working on their own.

THE CANADIAN PRESS/Pawel Dwulit

The rising use of margin credit by investors was a growing concern during the bull market of 2004–2006. Investors focused on the upside benefits but were not sensitive enough to the downside risks. Especially at online brokerages, inexperienced traders were borrowing at an alarming rate, and some were using the borrowed funds for risky and speculative day trading. So-called *day traders* visited websites online to buy and sell a stock in the same day (so-called intraday trades), seeking quick in-and-out fractional gains on large volumes (many shares) of each stock. While some day traders were successful, most ended up as financial losers.

SHORT SALES

In addition to money, brokerages also lend buyers securities. A **short sale** involves borrowing a security from your broker and selling it (one of the few times it is legal to sell what you do not own). At a given time in the future, you must restore an equal number of shares of that issue to the brokerage, along with a fee.

For example, suppose that in June you believe the price of Bombardier stock will soon fall. You order your broker to sell short 1000 shares at the market price of $5 per share. Your broker will make the sale and credit $5000 to your account. If Bombardier's price falls to $3.50 per share in July, you can buy 1000 shares for $3500 and give them to your broker, leaving you with a $1500 profit (before commissions). The risk is that Bombardier's price will not fall but will hold steady or rise, leaving you with a loss. The boxed insert entitled "Short Selling: Herbalife and Sino-Forest" describes two recent cases of short selling that caused a lot of controversy.

SHORT SALE Selling borrowed shares of stock in the expectation that their price will fall before they must be replaced, so that replacement shares can be bought for less than the original shares were sold for.

MANAGING IN TURBULENT TIMES

Short Selling: Herbalife and Sino-Forest

Herbalife Ltd. sells energy drinks, vitamins, and body-care products using a multi-level marketing system. Distributors earn money not only from selling the company's products, but also from recruiting new salespeople. In 2013, William Ackman, the head of Pershing Square Capital Management, "shorted" the stock of Herbalife Ltd., claiming that Herbalife was a pyramid scheme. He did so after reading a report that claimed Herbalife's distributors were buying the company's products so they could earn commissions, not so they could actually sell the products to consumers. Supporters of the company said that was nonsense. In 2012, Herbalife's share price declined about 40 percent when a hedge fund, Greenlight Capital, also shorted the stock.

Another highly publicized case of short selling occurred in Canada in 2011 when a company called Muddy Waters released a report which was critical of the accounting practices of Sino-Forest Corp., a company that owns timber lands in China. The report essentially questioned whether Sino-Forest actually owned the timber assets it claimed, and whether it was actually receiving the revenue it claimed. The report, and a review of Sino-Forest by Moody's Rating Service, had an immediate impact. On June 1, Sino-Forest shares were trading for $18.21 each, but by June 21, they were trading for just $1.29. By that time, Paulson & Co., the biggest shareholder of Sino-Forest, had sold all of the 34.7 million shares that it owned.

The incentives for short sellers are very high if they can demonstrate that there are problems in a company (or if they can convince investors that there *might* be problems). For example, if you had borrowed 1000 shares of Sino-Forest from your broker on June 1, 2011, and sold them, you would have received $18 210 (1000 x $18.21). You could then have purchased 1000 replacement shares on June 21 for just $1290.00 (1000 x $1.29). Your profit would have been $16 920 ($18 210 minus $1290).

On June 8, Richard Kelertas, an analyst at Dundee Capital Markets, vigorously attacked the Muddy Waters report, saying that it was "a pile of crap." He accused Muddy Waters' founder, Carson Block, of promoting his report to hedge funds five weeks before making it public in an attempt to generate interest in short sales of Sino-Forest shares. But the comments by Kelertas had little effect, and the market price of Sino-Forest shares continued to decline. In 2012, Sino-Forest filed for bankruptcy. Shareholders who lost a lot of money when the share price declined are now suing the company.

CRITICAL THINKING QUESTION

1. Consider the following statement: *Short selling should be banned because it creates instability in the price of a company's stock.* Do you agree or disagree with the statement? Defend your reasoning.

LO-7 OTHER INVESTMENTS

Although stocks and bonds are very important, they are not the only marketable securities for businesses. Financial managers are also concerned with investment opportunities in *mutual funds*, *hedge funds*, *commodities*, and *stock options*.

Mutual Funds

Mutual funds pool investments from individuals and other firms to purchase a portfolio of stocks, bonds, and short-term securities. For example, if you invest $1000 in a mutual fund that has a portfolio worth $100 000, you own 1 percent of the portfolio. Mutual funds usually have portfolios worth many millions of dollars. Investors in **no-load funds** are not charged a sales commission when they buy into or sell out of the mutual fund. **Load funds** carry a charge of between 2 and 8 percent of the invested funds. Mutual funds give small investors access to professional financial management. Their managers have up-to-date information about market conditions and the best large-scale investment opportunities.

Mutual funds vary by the investment goals they stress. Some stress safety and invest in treasury bills and other safe issues that offer income (liquidity). Other funds seek higher current income and are willing to sacrifice some safety. Still other mutual funds stress growth. Aggressive-growth mutual funds seek maximum capital appreciation; they sacrifice current income and safety and invest in new companies and other high-risk securities.

Mutual funds that stress socially responsible investing are called **ethical funds**. They will not invest in cigarette manufacturers or companies that make weapons, for example, and instead focus on investing in companies that produce safe and useful products and show concern for their employees, for the environment, and for human rights. While many companies offer such investments, the company Ethical Funds is dedicated to this mission.

An **exchange-traded fund (ETF)** is a bundle of stocks (or bonds) that is in an index that tracks the overall movement of a market. Unlike

MUTUAL FUND Any company that pools the resources of many investors and uses those funds to purchase various types of financial securities, depending on the fund's financial goals.

NO-LOAD FUND A mutual fund in which investors are not charged a sales commission when they buy into or sell out of the fund.

LOAD FUND A mutual fund in which investors are charged a sales commission when they buy into or sell out of the fund.

ETHICAL FUNDS Mutual funds that stress socially responsible investing.

EXCHANGE-TRADED FUND (ETF) A bundle of stocks (or bonds) that is in an index that tracks the overall movement of the market.

E-BUSINESS AND SOCIAL MEDIA SOLUTIONS

The Next Frontier, Mobile Investing

Quick, what are all the different ways you access money, make payments, or invest using electronic means? Online banking, mobile banking, ATMs, credit cards, debit cards, email money transfer, quick swipe passes, QR codes, etc. The list goes on and the methods are quickly multiplying. Now, mobile investing is emerging as an important investment tool in Canada.

Basic mobile banking has been around for a while, but most Canadian institutions have been much slower to build mobile investing apps (trading platforms designed for your smartphone). TD Waterhouse experimented with the possibility a decade ago, but found that the infrastructure and conditions in Canada (number of clients, high cost of data plans, and customer readiness) were not right at the time. Instead, American institutions led the way in this area. Mobile trades, for example, accounted for 5 percent of all transactions at TD Ameritrade Holding Corp in 2011. This figure was double that of the previous year and with the accelerated market penetration of smartphones in the consumer market, it was clear that the growth potential meant that similar services were now more necessary north of the border. In 2012, most of the major Canadian banks and discount brokerages were quickly pushing forward to build effective mobile investing apps. According to an Ipsos Reid poll, about one in five discount brokerage customers are interested in mobile investing and, not surprisingly, the positive results are directly correlated with the age of the investor. Younger consumers are much more likely to use this approach. Another informal *Globe and Mail* poll showed similar results with 22 percent of individuals claiming that they were either currently conducting mobile trading or were open to it.

The convenience of taking care of your investing needs from anywhere, at any time, on a smartphone, is clear; however, there is always that lingering security issue that makes a large portion of the population hesitate with newer financial transaction tools. According to the president of TD Waterhouse, John See, their mobile investing protection is already just as secure as it is for basic online transactions. Beyond the fear of mobile fund theft, this approach still has one very fundamental issue that exists no matter what tools you use: you still need to pick the right stocks to invest in. Before making your first mobile investing trade, make sure to do your homework. In the spirit of the times, you might want to look at some popular investment blogs found on sites such as Canadian Capitalist (canadiancapitalist.com), Money Index (moneyindex.org/Canada), The *Wall Street Journal*'s Deal Journal (wsj.com/deals), or Tech Finance (techfinance.ca). Good luck.

CRITICAL THINKING QUESTIONS

1. Have you ever bought or sold securities using a mobile investing platform? Are you open to this approach? Explain your response.
2. Consider the following statement: *Mobile investing is dangerous. People need to carefully analyze investment data and not make quick on-the-go decisions. This approach may cause inexperienced investors to feel a false sense of security and will lead to more foolish impulse investments.* Do you agree with the statement? Defend your answer.

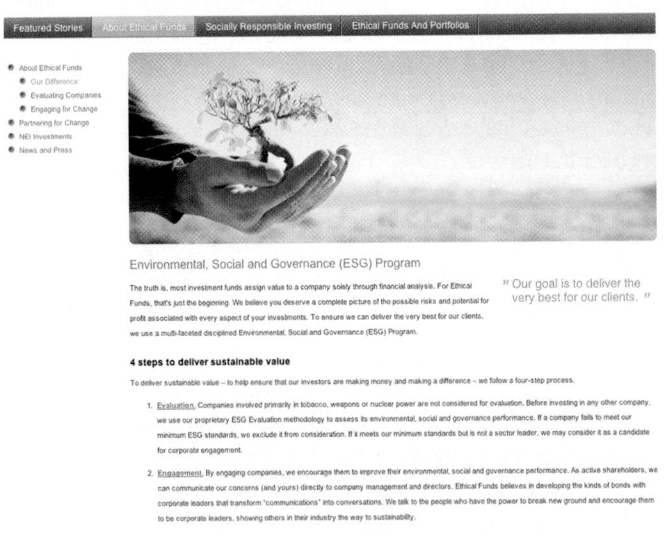

MAKE MONEY. MAKE A DIFFERENCE.
Home | Advisor Site | Investor Trax | Contact us | Français
Search
Search
Featured Stories
About Ethical Funds
Socially Responsible Investing
Ethical Funds And Portfolios
About Ethical Funds
Our Difference
Evaluating Companies
Engaging for Change
Partnering for Change
NEI Investments
News and Press
Environmental, Social and Governance (ESG) Program
The truth is, most investment funds assign value to a company solely through financial analysis. For Ethical Funds, that's just the beginning. We believe you deserve a complete picture of the possible risks and potential for profit associated with every aspect of your investments. To ensure we can deliver the very best for our clients, we use a multi-faceted disciplined Environmental, Social and Governance (ESG) Program.
" Our goal is to deliver the very best for our clients. "
4 steps to deliver sustainable value
To deliver sustainable value -- to help ensure that our investors are making money and making a difference -- we follow a four-step process.
1. Evaluation. Companies involved primarily in tobacco, weapons or nuclear power are not considered for evaluation. Before investing in any other company, we use our proprietary ESG Evaluation methodology to assess its environmental, social and governance performance. If a company fails to meet our minimum ESG standards, we exclude it from consideration. If it meets our minimum standards but is not a sector leader, we may consider it as a candidate for corporate engagement.
2. Engagement. By engaging companies, we encourage them to improve their environmental, social and governance performance. As active shareholders, we can communicate our concerns (and yours) directly to company management and directors. Ethical Funds believes in developing the kinds of bonds with corporate leaders that transform "communications" into conversations. We talk to the people who have the power to break new ground and encourage them to be corporate leaders, showing others in their industry the way to sustainability.

^^^ Ethical Funds, a division of NEI Investments, does not invest in companies involved primarily in the production of tobacco, weapons, or nuclear power.

GLENN BROWN/ERNST & YOUNG/Newscom

mutual funds—which are priced only at the end of each day—you can buy or sell ETFs at any time during the day when the market reaches your target price. Also unlike mutual funds—which incur the costs of active management—ETFs have lower operating expenses because they are bound by rules that specify what stocks will be purchased and when. Once the rule is established, little human action is needed, and this reduces management expenses. Annual fees for mutual funds average 1.4 percent of assets, but for ETFs the rate is as low as 0.09 percent.[13]

Hedge Funds

Hedge funds are private pools of money that try to give investors a positive return regardless of stock-market performance. Hedge funds often engage in risky practices like short selling (essentially betting that a company's stock price will go down) and leveraging (borrowing money against principal). Historically, interest in hedge funds has been limited to wealthy people (called "accredited investors") who are assumed to be very knowledgeable about financial matters and are able to weigh the risks of investing. But recently, hedge funds have begun marketing their products to the average investor with something called "principal-protected notes." They guarantee that investors will get their original investment back at a certain time, but they do not guarantee that any additional returns will be forthcoming. Some hedge funds have been in the news for all the wrong reasons. For example, an Ontario Securities Commission panel ruled that two executives from the now defunct Norshield Asset Management Ltd. knowingly misled their clients and investigators and failed to keep proper books. Losses are estimated at $159 million from 1900 retail investors.[14]

Commodities

Futures contracts—agreements to purchase a specified amount of a commodity at a given price on a set date in the future—are available for commodities ranging from coffee beans and live hogs to propane and platinum, as well as for stocks. Since selling prices reflect traders' beliefs about the future, prices of such contracts are very volatile, and futures trading is very risky.

For example, on January 3, 2012, the price of gold was $1625 per ounce. If futures gold contracts for July 2013 were selling for $1575 per ounce, this price would reflect investors' judgment that gold prices would be slightly lower in July. Now, suppose that you purchased a 100-ounce gold futures contract in January for $157 500 ($1575 x 100). If, in March 2013, the July gold futures sold for $1700, you could sell your contract for $170 000. Your profit after the two months would be $12 500. Of course, if the futures contract had been selling for less than $1575, you would have lost money. Usually, buyers of futures contracts need not put up the full purchase amount. Rather, the buyer posts a smaller amount—the margin—that may be as little as $3000 for contracts of $100 000.

Let us look again at our gold futures example. If you had posted a $4250 margin for your July gold contract, you would have earned a $12 500 profit on that investment of $4250 in only two months. However, you also took a big risk involving two big ifs: If you had held on to your contract until July and if gold had dropped, say to $1525, you would have lost $5000 ($157 500 – $152 500). If you had posted a $4250 margin to buy the contract, you would have lost that entire margin and would owe an additional $750. Between 75 and 90 percent of all small-time investors lose money in the futures market.

Stock Options

A **stock option** is the right to buy or sell a stock. A **call option** gives its owner the right to buy a particular stock at a certain price, with that right lasting until a particular date. A **put option** gives its owner

THERE'S AN APP FOR THAT!

1. CFA Institute >>> **Platforms:** *Apple, Android*
   Source: Willow Tree Apps
   Key Features: Provides summaries and blog posts on the latest developments in finance and investing.
2. Bloomberg >>> **Platforms:** *Apple, Android, BlackBerry*
   Source: Bloomberg Finance LP
   Key Features: Offers news, stock quotes, company descriptions, market leaders/laggers, price charts, & more.
3. Rule of 72 >>> **Platforms:** *Apple*
   Source: Insurance Technologies LLC.
   Key Features: Determines how long it will take for an investment to double given a fixed rate of interest.

APP DISCOVERY EXERCISE

Since APP availability changes, conduct your own search for "Top 3" Finance APPS and identify the key features.

HEDGE FUNDS Private pools of money that try to give investors a positive return regardless of stock-market performance.

FUTURES CONTRACTS Agreement to purchase specified amounts of a commodity (or stock) at a given price on a set future date.

STOCK OPTION The purchased right to buy or sell a stock.

CALL OPTION The purchased right to buy a particular stock at a certain price until a specified date.

PUT OPTION The purchased right to sell a particular stock at a certain price until a specified date.

the right to sell a particular stock at a specified price, with that right lasting until a particular date. These options are traded on several stock exchanges.

If you thought the price of Goldcorp Inc. (G) (which sold for $40 per share in June 2012) was going to go up, you might buy a call option giving you the right to buy 100 shares any time in the next two months at a so-called strike price of $50. If the stock rose to $60 before July, you would exercise your call option. Your profit would be $10 per share ($60-50) less the price you paid to buy the option. However, if the stock price fell instead of rising, you would not exercise your call option because Goldcorp shares would be available on the open market for less than $50 per share. Your stock option would be "under water"; that is, it would be worthless. You would lose whatever you paid for the option. In recent years, there has been much negative publicity about stock options that are given to executives to motivate them to work hard for the company.

SECURITIES REGULATION

Canada, unlike the United States, does not have comprehensive federal securities legislation or a federal regulatory body. Government regulation is primarily provincial and emphasizes self-regulation through the various provincial securities exchanges. A report by a government-appointed committee that studied Canada's system of securities regulation concluded that it is in dire need of reform. The committee noted that Canada is the only country in the industrialized world with a patchwork of provincial regulations, and it recommended a single regulator for Canada. The main complaints the committee noted were lack of meaningful enforcement of securities laws and unnecessary costs and time delays that make Canada's capital markets uncompetitive internationally. As of 2013, changes had still not been made.

Ontario is generally regarded as having the most progressive securities legislation in Canada. The Ontario Securities Act contains disclosure provisions for new and existing issues, prevention of fraud, regulation of the Toronto Stock Exchange, and takeover bids. It also prohibits insider trading. The Toronto Stock Exchange provides an example of self-regulation by the industry. The TSX has regulations concerning listing and delisting of securities, disclosure requirements, and issuing of prospectuses for new securities.

In 1912, the Manitoba government pioneered Canadian laws applying mainly to the sale of new securities. Under these **blue-sky laws**, corporations issuing securities must back them up with something more than the "blue sky." Similar laws were passed in other provinces.

BLUE-SKY LAWS Laws regulating how corporations must back up securities.

ENTREPRENEURSHIP AND NEW VENTURES

Crowdfunding for Entrepreneurs

Crowdfunding means raising money online through the use of social media, usually by getting a small amount of money from a large number of investors. As of 2013, Canadian provincial securities regulations do not allow crowdfunding to be used to raise equity funds from the *average* investor. But crowdfunding can be used to raise equity funds from *accredited* investors (those with a high net worth). For example, the crowdfunding site CircleUp raises funds from accredited investors for companies with sales in the $1 million to $10 million range.

Crowdfunding is legal if the company gives investors a product rather than an equity stake. When Calgary native Eric Migicovsky could not get financial backing from venture capitalists for the high-tech watch he was developing, he turned to crowdfunding site Kickstarter to raise the $100 000 he needed. He ended up getting $10.2 *million* from 69 000 different investors. He did not violate the "no equity funding" rule, because he offered a watch to each investor instead of an equity stake in his company. Crowdfunding is also legal for charitable purposes. For example, the crowdfunding site Pursu.it helps Olympic hopefuls get funds to help them train for the Olympics.

In the United States, the Jumpstart Our Business Startups (JOBS) program allows companies to use crowdfunding to attract equity funds from small investors (up to a limit of $1 million) without requiring companies to provide an audited financial statement. The National Crowdfunding Association of Canada and the Canadian Advanced Technology Alliance both support the idea of having a U.S.-style law here so that investment money does not leave Canada and go south. If crowdfunding is eventually allowed for the average investor, it will be a way for start-up companies (which have trouble generating funds through traditional sources) to get the money they need to develop their products and services. Calgary businessman Jim Richardson is working on a site called crowdcapital.ca. The idea is that companies would go to the website and indicate how much money they want. Investors would also visit the site and decide whether to invest in the product that is being developed.

Proponents of crowdfunding say that it is a way to turn social media enthusiasts into venture capitalists. But critics argue that crowdfunding will lead to fraud because unscrupulous operators will see an opportunity to fleece unsophisticated investors. They point out that if a start-up is really promising, it will attract the attention of venture capital firms. They conclude that most of the companies that would do crowdfunding would be those that are not good investment options.

CRITICAL THINKING QUESTION

1. Consider the following statement: *Crowdfunding should not be allowed because it will allow con artists to fleece unsophisticated investors. The current securities regulations protect potential investors and these regulations should remain in force.* Do you agree or disagree with the statement? Explain your reasoning.

Provincial laws also generally require that stockbrokers be licensed and securities be registered before they can be sold. In each province, issuers of proposed new securities must file a **prospectus** with the provincial securities exchange. The prospectus must be made available to investors who might want to invest. The boxed insert entitled "Crowdfunding for Entrepreneurs" provides information on a somewhat controversial new type of fund-raising that relies on social media.

PROSPECTUS A detailed registration statement about a new stock filed with a provincial securities exchange; it must include any data helpful to a potential buyer.

FINANCIAL MANAGEMENT FOR SMALL BUSINESSES

Most new businesses have inadequate funding. Why are so many start-ups underfunded? Entrepreneurs often underestimate the value of establishing bank credit as a source of funds and use trade credit ineffectively. In addition, they often fail to consider venture capital as a source of funding, and they are notorious for not planning cash-flow needs properly. Many of them are also not aware of government programs that are available for support. For example, programs like the Canada Small Business Funding Program enable entrepreneurs to receive up to $350 000 worth of loans and up to $500 000 for the purchase of real property. Each year, the program provides approximately 10 000 loans for over $1 billion of financing.[15] Of course, companies that do not apply, or are unaware of the program, get $0 even if they are good potential candidates.

Establishing Bank Credit and Trade Credit

Some banks have liberal credit policies and offer financial analysis, cash-flow planning, and knowledgeable advice. Some provide loans to small businesses in bad times and work to keep them going. Obtaining credit, therefore, begins with finding a bank that can—and will—support a small firm's financial needs. Once a line of credit is obtained, the small business can seek more liberal credit policies from other businesses. Sometimes suppliers give customers longer credit periods—say, 45 or 60 days rather than 30 days. Liberal trade credit terms with their suppliers lets firms increase short-term funds and avoid additional borrowing from banks.

Start-up firms without proven financial success usually must present a business plan to demonstrate creditworthiness.[16] As we saw in Chapter 4, a business plan is a document that tells potential lenders why the money is needed, the amount needed, how the money will be used to improve the company, and when it will be paid back.

Venture Capital

Many newer businesses—especially those undergoing rapid growth—cannot get the funds they need through borrowing alone. They may, therefore, turn to venture capital—outside equity funding provided in return for part ownership of the firm (see Chapter 4).

Planning for Cash-Flow Requirements

All businesses should plan for their cash flows, but it is especially important for small businesses to do so. Success or failure may hinge on anticipating times when cash will be short and when excess cash is expected. Figure 15.5 shows possible cash inflows, cash outflows, and net cash position (inflows minus outflows), month by month, for Slippery Fish Bait Supply. In this highly seasonal business, bait stores buy heavily from Slippery during the spring and summer months. Revenues outpace expenses, leaving surplus funds that can be invested. During the fall and winter, expenses exceed revenues. Slippery must borrow funds to keep going until sales revenues pick up again in the spring. Comparing predicted cash inflows from sales with outflows for expenses shows the firm's monthly cash-flow position.

By anticipating shortfalls, a financial manager can seek advance funds and minimize their cost. By anticipating excess cash, a manager can plan to put the funds to work in short-term, interest-earning investments.

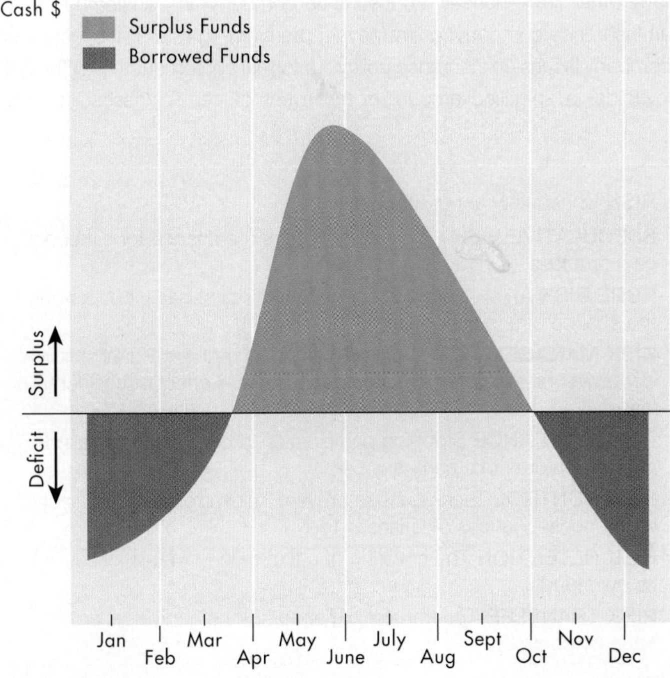

<<< **FIGURE 15.5** Cash flow for Slippery Fish Bait Supply Company

LO-8 RISK MANAGEMENT

Risk—uncertainty about future events—is a factor in every manager's job because nearly every managerial action raises the possibility for either positive or negative outcomes. Risk management is therefore essential.[17] Firms devote considerable resources not only to recognizing potential risks, but also to positioning themselves to make the most advantageous decisions regarding risk.

The financial crisis that erupted in 2008 caused many firms to take a second look at their risk-management practices. For example, the Caisse de dépôt et placement du Québec incurred heavy losses in 2008 as a result of its involvement in currency and stock-related derivatives and the commercial paper crisis.[18] The Bank of Montreal (BMO) also had problems and reported write-downs of $490 million. That was on top of the $850 million charge it incurred as the result of fraud committed by one of its traders. As a result of the losses, BMO did a complete review of its risk-management systems and procedures. Bill Downe, the CEO, admitted that BMO got involved in some business activities that were beyond the company's risk tolerance and strategic plan.[19]

According to a survey of 600 executives conducted by Toronto-based recruitment firm Watson Gardner Brown, the most difficult jobs to staff are in the risk management and compliance areas. Why? Firms are increasing the size of these divisions because of the scandals and the meltdown in some securities in recent years. Institutional investors are demanding more attention to risk oversight before they will trust their funds to such organizations. Finding enough highly qualified people to fill these spots, even with generous salaries, has been a challenge.[20]

Coping with Risk

Businesses constantly face two basic types of risk—**speculative risks**, such as financial investments, which involve the possibility of gain or loss, and **pure risks**, which involve only the possibility of loss or no loss. For example, designing and distributing a new product is a speculative risk. The product may fail or succeed. The chance of a warehouse fire is a pure risk.

For a company to survive and prosper, it must manage both types of risk in a cost-effective manner. We can thus define the process of **risk management** as "conserving the firm's earning power and assets by reducing the threat of losses due to uncontrollable events."[21] The risk-management process usually involves five steps.

STEP 1: IDENTIFY RISKS AND POTENTIAL LOSSES

Managers analyze a firm's risks to identify potential losses. For example, a firm with a fleet of delivery trucks can expect that one of them will eventually be involved in an accident. The accident may cause bodily injury to the driver or others, and may cause physical damage to the truck or other vehicles.

STEP 2: MEASURE THE FREQUENCY AND SEVERITY OF LOSSES AND THEIR IMPACT

To measure the frequency and severity of losses, managers must consider both past history and current activities. How often can the firm expect the loss to occur? What is the likely size of the loss in dollars? For example, our firm with the fleet of delivery trucks may have had two accidents per year in the past. If it adds more trucks to its fleet, it may reasonably expect the number of accidents to increase.

STEP 3: EVALUATE ALTERNATIVES AND CHOOSE TECHNIQUES THAT WILL BEST HANDLE LOSSES

Having identified and measured potential losses, managers are in a better position to decide how to handle them. They generally have four choices: *risk avoidance*, *control*, *retention*, or *transfer*.

Risk Avoidance A firm opts for **risk avoidance** by declining to enter or by ceasing to participate in a risky activity. For example, the firm with the delivery trucks could avoid any risk of physical damage or bodily injury by closing down its delivery service. Similarly, a pharmaceutical maker may withdraw a new drug for fear of liability lawsuits.

Risk Control When avoidance is not practical or desirable, firms can practise **risk control**—say, the use of loss-prevention techniques to minimize the frequency of losses. A delivery service, for instance, can prevent losses by training its drivers in defensive-driving techniques, mapping out safe routes, and conscientiously maintaining its trucks.

Risk Retention When losses cannot be avoided or controlled, firms must cope with the consequences. When such losses are manageable and predictable, they may decide to cover them out of company funds. The firm is thus said to "assume" or "retain" the financial consequences of the loss: hence the practice known as **risk retention**. For example, the firm with the fleet of trucks may find that each vehicle suffers vandalism totalling $300 per year. Depending on its coverage, the company may find it cheaper to pay for repairs out of pocket rather than to submit claims to its insurance company.

Risk Transfer When the potential for large risks cannot be avoided or controlled, managers often opt for **risk transfer**. They transfer the risk to another firm—namely, an insurance company. In transferring risk to an insurance company, a firm pays a premium. In return, the insurance company issues an insurance policy—a formal agreement to pay the policyholder a specified amount in the event of certain losses. In some

RISK Uncertainty about future events.

SPECULATIVE RISK An event that offers the chance for either a gain or a loss.

PURE RISK An event that offers no possibility of gain; it offers only the chance of a loss or no loss.

RISK MANAGEMENT Conserving a firm's (or an individual's) financial power or assets by minimizing the financial effect of accidental losses.

RISK AVOIDANCE Stopping participation in or refusing to participate in ventures that carry any risk.

RISK CONTROL Techniques to prevent, minimize, or reduce losses or the consequences of losses.

RISK RETENTION The covering of a firm's unavoidable losses with its own funds.

RISK TRANSFER The transfer of risk to another individual or firm, often by contract.

cases, the insured party must also pay a deductible—an agreed-upon amount of the loss that the insured must absorb prior to reimbursement. Thus, the truck company may buy insurance to protect itself against theft, physical damage to trucks, and bodily injury to drivers and others involved in an accident.

STEP 4: IMPLEMENT THE RISK-MANAGEMENT PROGRAM

The means of implementing risk-management decisions depend on both the technique chosen and the activity being managed. For example, risk avoidance for certain activities can be implemented by purchasing those activities from outside providers, such as hiring delivery services instead of operating delivery vehicles. Risk control might be implemented by training employees and designing new work methods and equipment for on-the-job safety. For situations in which risk retention is preferred, reserve funds can be set aside out of revenues. When risk transfer is needed, implementation means selecting an insurance company and buying the right policies.

STEP 5: MONITOR RESULTS

Because risk management is an ongoing activity, follow-up is always essential. New types of risks emerge with changes in customers, facilities, employees, and products. Insurance regulations change, and new types of insurance become available. Consequently, managers must continually monitor a company's risks, re-evaluate the methods used for handling them, and revise them as necessary.

MyBizLab	Visit the MyBizLab website. This online homework and tutorial system puts you in control of your own learning with study and practice tools directly correlated to this chapter's content.

SUMMARY OF

LEARNING OBJECTIVES

LO-1 DESCRIBE THE RESPONSIBILITIES OF A *FINANCIAL MANAGER*.

A financial manager's overall objective is to increase a firm's value and stockholders' wealth. They must ensure that earnings exceed costs, so that the firm generates a profit. The responsibilities of the financial manager fall into two general categories: (1) *cash-flow management*, and (2) *financial control*.

LO-2 DISTINGUISH BETWEEN *SHORT-TERM* (OPERATING) AND *LONG-TERM* (CAPITAL) EXPENDITURES.

Short-term (operating) expenditures are incurred in a firm's everyday business activities. To handle these expenditures, managers must pay attention to accounts payable, accounts receivable, and inventories. *Long-term* (capital) expenditures are required to purchase fixed assets.

LO-3 IDENTIFY THREE SOURCES OF *SHORT-TERM FINANCING* FOR BUSINESSES.

Trade credit is really a short-term loan from one firm to another. *Secured short-term loans*, like bank loans, usually involve promissory notes in which the borrower promises to repay the loan plus interest. These loans require collateral, which can be seized if payments are not made as promised. *Unsecured short-term loans* are those where a borrower does not have to put up collateral. The bank may, however, require the borrower to maintain a compensating balance—a portion of the loan amount kept on deposit with the bank.

LO-4 IDENTIFY THREE SOURCES OF *LONG-TERM FINANCING* FOR BUSINESSES.

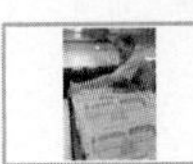

The three sources of long-term financing for businesses are debt financing, equity financing, and hybrid financing. *Debt financing* involves long-term borrowing from outside the company; it is a major component of most firms' long-term financial planning. The most common forms of debt financing are long-term loans and the issuing of bonds. A *bond* is a contract—a promise by the issuing company or organization to pay the bondholder a certain amount of money (the principal) on a specified date, plus interest, in return for use of the investor's money. *Equity financing* takes the form of issuing stock or retaining the firm's earnings. Both options involve putting the owners' capital to work. By selling shares of common stock, the company obtains the funds it needs to buy land, buildings, and equipment. The use of preferred stock is a *hybrid* approach; it has features of both corporate bonds and common stocks.

LO-5 DISCUSS THE VALUE OF *COMMON STOCK* AND *PREFERRED STOCK* TO STOCKHOLDERS, AND DESCRIBE THE SECONDARY MARKET FOR EACH TYPE OF SECURITY.

Common stock gives investors the prospect of capital gains and dividend income. Common stock values are expressed in three ways: *par value* (the value set by the issuing company's board of directors), *market value* (the current price of a share on the stock market), and *book value* (stockholders' equity divided by the number of shares). *Preferred stock* is less risky than common stock because dividends are paid before common shareholders receive any returns. Both common and preferred stock are traded on stock exchanges (and in over-the-counter [OTC] markets).

LO-6 EXPLAIN THE PROCESS BY WHICH SECURITIES ARE BOUGHT AND SOLD.

Investors generally use such financial information services as newspapers and online stock, bond, and OTC quotations. Market indexes such as the Toronto Stock Exchange index, the Dow Jones Industrial Average, the Standard & Poor's Composite Index, and the NASDAQ Composite provide useful summaries of trends. Investors can then place different types of orders. Market orders are orders to buy or sell at current prevailing prices. Investors can issue limit or stop orders that are executed only if prices rise or fall below specified levels. Round lots are purchased in multiples of 100 shares. Odd lots are purchased in fractions of round lots. Securities can be bought on margin or as part of short sales.

LO-7 DESCRIBE THE INVESTMENT OPPORTUNITIES OFFERED BY *MUTUAL FUNDS, HEDGE FUNDS, COMMODITIES,* AND *STOCK OPTIONS*.

Mutual funds offer investors different levels of risk and growth potential. Load funds require investors to pay commissions of 2 to 8 percent; no-load funds do not charge commissions when investors buy in or out. *Hedge funds* are private pools of money that try to give investors a positive return, regardless of stock-market performance. Futures contracts (agreements to buy specified amounts of *commodities*, like coffee, at given prices on preset dates) are traded in the commodities market. Commodities traders often buy on margins, which means that only a percentage of the total sales price is put up to order futures contracts. A *stock option* gives the holder the right to buy or sell a stock at a certain price until a specific date.

LO-8 EXPLAIN HOW *RISK* AFFECTS BUSINESS OPERATIONS AND IDENTIFY THE FIVE STEPS IN THE *RISK MANAGEMENT PROCESS*.

Businesses face both *speculative risks* (where a gain or loss is possible), and *pure risks* (where only a loss or no loss is possible). Risk management means conserving earning power and assets by reducing the threat of losses due to uncontrollable events. The five-step *risk management process* requires managers to (1) identify risks and potential losses, (2) measure the frequency and severity of losses and their impact, (3) evaluate alternatives, (4) implement the risk management program, *and* (5) monitor results.

QUESTIONS AND EXERCISES

QUESTIONS FOR ANALYSIS

See >>> for Assisted-Graded Writing Assignment in MyBizLab

1. >>> In what ways do the two sources of debt financing differ from each other? How do they differ from the two sources of equity financing?
2. Explain how an investor might make money in a commodities trade. Then explain how an investor might lose money in a commodities trade.

3. What is the basic relationship between the amount of risk associated with a project and the likelihood of gains (or losses) on the project? Explain how several financial instruments (GICs, common stocks, preferred stocks, corporate bonds) illustrate this basic relationship.
4. Which of the three measures of common stock value is most important? Why?
5. Why would a business "factor" its accounts receivable?
6. What are the risks and benefits associated with the sources of short-term funds (trade credit, secured loans, and unsecured loans)? How do these risks and benefits compare with those associated with sources of long-term funds (debt and equity)?

APPLICATION EXERCISES

7. >>> Interview the financial manager of a local business. What are the investment goals of the organization? What mix of securities does it use? What advantages and disadvantages do you see in its portfolio?
8. Contact a stock broker for information about setting up a personal account for trading securities. Prepare a report on the broker's requirements for placing buy/sell orders, credit terms, cash account requirements, services available to investors, and commissions/fees schedules.
9. Go to Sedar.com and find the balance sheets of two corporations operating in the same industry. Determine the relative emphasis each company has placed on raising money through debt versus equity. Why might these differences exist?
10. Visit an online stock site such as globeinvestor.com and find the latest prices for the following stocks: Canadian Tire, BlackBerry, and Rona. What are the trends? Has the stock price risen or declined in the past six months?

TEAM EXERCISES

BUILDING YOUR BUSINESS SKILLS

MARKET UPS AND DOWNS

See >>> for Assisted-Graded Writing Assignment in **MyBizLab**

GOAL

To encourage students to understand the forces that affect fluctuations in stock prices.

SITUATION

Investing in stocks requires an understanding of the various factors that affect stock prices. These factors may be intrinsic to the company itself or part of the external environment.

- Internal factors relate to the company itself, such as an announcement of poor or favourable earnings, earnings that are more or less than expected, major layoffs, labour problems, management issues, and mergers.
- External factors relate to world or national events, such as a threatened war in the Persian Gulf, the BP oil spill in the Gulf of Mexico, weather conditions that affect sales, the Bank of Canada's adjustment of interest rates, and employment figures that were higher or lower than expected. By analyzing these factors, you will often learn a lot about why a stock did well or why it did poorly. Being aware of these influences will help you anticipate future stock movements.

METHOD

>>> Step 1 Working alone, choose a common stock that has experienced considerable price fluctuations in the past few years. Here are several examples (but there are many others): IBM, Amazon.com, BlackBerry, and Apple Computer. Find the symbol for the stock and the exchange on which it is traded.

>>> Step 2 Visit the Globe Investor website (or a similar site) and gather information on the particular stock and study its trading pattern. You can also visit your library and find the *Daily Stock Price Record*, a publication that provides a historical picture of daily stock closings. There are separate copies for the various stock exchanges.

>>> Step 3 Find four or five days over a period of several months or even a year when there have been major price fluctuations in the stock. (A two- or three-point price change from one day to the next is considered major.) Then research what happened on that day that might have contributed to the fluctuation. The best place to begin is the *Globe and Mail* or the *Wall Street Journal*.

>>> Step 4 Write a short analysis linking changes in stock price to internal and external factors. As you analyze the data, be aware that it is sometimes difficult to know why a stock price fluctuates.

Step 5 Get together with three other students who studied different stocks. As a group, discuss your findings, looking for fluctuation patterns.

FOLLOW-UP QUESTIONS

1. Do you see any similarities in the movement of the various stocks during the same period? For example, did the stocks move up or down at about the same time? If so, do you think the stocks were affected by the same factors? Explain your thinking.
2. Based on your analysis, did internal or external factors have the greater impact on stock price? Which factors had the longer-lasting effect? Which factors had the shorter effect?
3. Why do you think it is so hard to predict changes in stock price on a day to day basis?

EXERCISING YOUR ETHICS

DOING YOUR DUTY WHEN PAYABLES COME DUE

THE SITUATION

Sarah Keats is the vice-president of finance at Multiverse, a large firm that manufactures consumer products. On December 15, 2010 (two weeks before the end of the fiscal year), she attends an executive committee meeting at which Jack Malvo, the CEO, expresses concern that the firm's year-end cash position will be less favourable than projected.

The firm has exceeded analysts' performance expectations in each of his eight years at the helm, and Malvo is determined that stockholders will never be disappointed as long as he is CEO. The purpose of the meeting is to find solutions to the cash problem and decide on a course of action.

THE DILEMMA

To open the meeting, Malvo announces, "We have just two weeks to reduce expenses or increase revenues. We need a $100 million swing to get us where market analysts predicted we'd be on cash flows for the year. Any suggestions?"

In the discussion that ensues, it is noted that Multiverse owes $150 million to about 80 companies that supply component parts and other operating supplies to Multiverse. The money is due before year-end. Sarah Keats says, "Our cash outflows for the year will be lower if we delay paying suppliers, which will help the bottom line. And, it's like getting a free loan." The procurement director, Julie Levin, expresses the following concern: "Our agreements with suppliers call for faithful payments at designated times, and many of the smaller firms depend on receiving that cash to meet their obligations. Also, we've worked hard for two years at improving relationships with all suppliers, and that effort could go down the drain if we don't meet our financial commitments as promised."

As the meeting draws to a close, Malvo announces, "Keep me posted on any unexpected developments, but if nothing helpful comes up in the next few days, let's go ahead and withhold supplier payments for three weeks."

TEAM ACTIVITY

Assemble a group of four students and assign each group member to one of the following roles:

- Jack Malvo (CEO of Multiverse)
- Sarah Keats (vice-president of finance)
- Julie Levin (procurement director)
- A stockholder of Multiverse

ACTION STEPS

1. Before discussing the situation with your group and from the perspective of your assigned role, decide whether there are any ethical issues here.
2. Before discussing the situation with your group and from the perspective of your assigned role, decide what action you think should be taken. Write down your recommended action.
3. Gather your group together and reveal, in turn, each member's comments and recommendations.
4. Appoint someone to record the main points of agreement and disagreement within the group. How do you explain the results? What accounts for any disagreements?
5. From an ethical standpoint, what does your group recommend?

BUSINESS CASE

GROWING UP SOCIAL: GRADUATING TO AN IPO

What do you get when you mix the investment banking establishment with new-age internet companies? It is not quite a marriage made in heaven, is it? For example, some traditionalists were upset at the sight of young Mark Zuckerberg showing up to important meetings still sporting a "hoody" sweatshirt despite being a wealthy businessman (they felt it was disrespectful). There can be some awkward moments, but the stock market is designed to raise money and support companies that have the potential to earn more of it, regardless of dress attire. In the past few years, a string of social media companies have taken the leap and matured from radical idea seekers to publicly traded companies. The initial public offering (IPO) is a key moment in that growing process when companies launch into the public domain. Let's take a look at some notable recent examples.

FACEBOOK

In May 2012, Facebook was making all the headlines with its highly anticipated IPO. Based on the initial price, the company was valued at US$104 billion, a figure that was 104 times higher than the company's profit levels from the previous year. While the market believed in Facebook's growth potential, there were certain fundamental rules of the IPO game that had experts openly saying that the stock was overpriced. Two weeks after the IPO (when the stock was priced at $38 per share), Facebook shares had lost 25 percent of their value, and by September 2012, their price had dropped to $17.55 per share. The costs of running the business were a major concern to investors. In addition, with relatively low barriers to entry, new threats were emerging that could threaten current and future revenue streams. For example, the $1 billion acquisition of Instagram was a bit of an eye opener, given that Facebook has developed its own version of this app. Officially, the company was purchasing a stronger presence on the smartphone platform, but Facebook paid a big price considering they were not acquiring the technology; they were essentially buying a threat. Instagram had 12 employees, at the time, but over 50 million users (in this business "users are king"). The potential advertising dollars are correlated to the number of eyeballs. But if Instagram could transform into a threat after just two years in operation, what did this mean for the future of Facebook? By January 2013, the price of a share of Facebook had risen to $30, so perhaps investors will actually profit in the long run. But the initial marriage did not include the traditional honeymoon.

GROUPON

Groupon's IPO, six months earlier, was not exactly a mirror image of Facebook, but there were distinct highs and lows as well. The IPO price valuation was set at about $12 billion. The online daily discount site launched its stock at a price of $20 per share and saw the market react favourably. In fact, in the post-wedding honeymoon period, the stock rose over 30 percent in the first two weeks. However, problems for Groupon actually became evident before the IPO ceremony, and there were many legitimate questions which caused the company to restate previous financial statements. At the time, the company had posted net operating losses of $218 million on revenue of $1.1 billion and was trying to manage growth with a sales force of over 10 000 people, but that was proving to be difficult. By early 2013, amid a new round of financial irregularities, Groupon was trading at just $4.43 a share, sharply down from its IPO price of $20 per share. There were also concerns that Groupon's business model (which is focused on daily coupon deals) was fundamentally flawed. A survey of merchants who had used daily deals found that nearly 40 percent of them were not likely to run another Groupon promotion. Their reasons included commission rates that were too high, repeat business that was too low, and the belief that other forms of marketing were more effective than coupons. In February 2013, Groupon's CEO was fired.

LINKEDIN

LinkedIn can be considered the more mature version of Facebook. After all, it was designed with a business slant from day one. So you might expect this IPO to run a bit more smoothly. At the time of its IPO, LinkedIn had 202 million users. While this number paled in comparison to the 900 million users on Facebook, it was LinkedIn's revenue potential that impressed the investment community (companies like Starbucks and Pepsico pay LinkedIn for things like job ads and career pages). LinkedIn had a growing number of "paid subscribers" and the company was increasing revenues in the area of "hiring solutions," which enables employers to post job openings and search for candidates. The lower membership numbers also meant that there was more room for growth ahead. LinkedIn went public in 2011 and, within a day, the stock price had doubled from the original $45 to over $90. A year later, the stock exceeded $100 per share, and, by February 2013, the price was $168. LinkedIn's market value went from $4 billion in 2011 to $18 billion in 2013. By contrast, the market values of Facebook, Zynga, and Groupon were all down 25 to 60 percent from their IPO prices. The early returns from the stock market seem to be a clear signal that LinkedIn is indeed a more mature business venture with solid financial prospects.

PLANNING IPOs

The success or failure of an IPO is based on a lot of factors, including timing. But the long-term fate of any stock is based on fundamental stock-market factors such as revenue, growth, and profitability. Some of the social media players have now graduated, but they must compete in the "real world" of stock evaluations and it can be a brutal world. Other social media firms, such as Twitter, were still building their models before taking the IPO leap. In order to earn the respect of the market, they must show maturity and the ability to generate long term growth and earnings.

Tatyana Zenkovich/Photoshot Holdings Ltd.

QUESTIONS FOR DISCUSSION

1. Why is it so difficult to predict which IPOs will be long-term successes?
2. What factors influence the market price of a share of stock? Which factors were most important for each of the companies mentioned above?
3. What other social media IPOs have taken place beyond those companies mentioned above? How have they performed during their first year of public ownership?

CHAPTER SUPPLEMENT 05

Insurance *as* Risk Management

To deal with some risks, both businesses and individuals may choose to purchase one or more of the products offered by insurance companies. Buyers find insurance appealing for a very basic reason—in return for a relatively small sum of money, they are protected against specific losses, some of which are potentially devastating. With insurance, individuals and businesses share risks by contributing to a fund out of which those who suffer losses are paid. Insurance companies are willing to accept these risks for other companies because they make profits by taking in more in **premiums** than they pay out to cover policyholders' losses. Although many policyholders are paying for protection against the same type of loss, it is unlikely that all of them will suffer such a loss.

INSURABLE VS. UNINSURABLE RISKS

Like every other business, insurance companies must avoid certain risks. Insurers thus divide potential sources of loss into *insurable* and *uninsurable risks*.[22] Obviously, they issue policies only for insurable risks, which must satisfy the four criteria of *predictability*, *casualty*, *unconnectedness*, and *verifiability*.

Predictability The insurer must be able to use statistical tools to forecast the likelihood of a loss. For example, an auto insurer needs information about the number of car accidents in the past year to estimate the expected number of accidents for the following year. With this knowledge, the insurer can translate expected numbers and types of accidents into expected dollar losses. The same forecast also helps insurers determine premiums charged to policyholders.

Casualty A loss must result from an accident, not from an intentional act by the policyholder. For example, an insurer does not have to cover damages if a policyholder deliberately sets fire to a business. To avoid paying in cases of fraud, insurers may refuse to cover losses when they cannot determine whether policyholders' actions contributed to them.

Unconnectedness Potential losses must be random and must occur independently of other losses. No insurer can afford to write insurance when a large percentage of those who are exposed to a particular kind of loss are likely to suffer such a loss. One insurance company, for instance, would not want all the hail coverage in Saskatchewan or all the earthquake coverage in Vancouver. By carefully choosing the risks it will insure, an insurance company can reduce its chances of a large loss.

Verifiability Finally, insured losses must be verifiable as to cause, time, place, and amount. Did an employee develop emphysema because of a chemical to which she was exposed or because she smoked 40 cigarettes per day for 30 years? Did the policyholder pay the renewal premium before the fire destroyed his factory? Were the goods stolen from the company's office or from the president's home? What was the insurable value of the destroyed inventory? When all these points have been verified, payment by the insurer goes more smoothly.

THE INSURANCE PRODUCT

Some insurers offer only one area of coverage—life insurance, for example—while others offer a broad range. In this section, we briefly describe three major categories of business insurance—*liability*, *property*, and *life*.

Liability Insurance Liability means responsibility for damages in case of accidental or deliberate harm to individuals or property. **Liability insurance** covers losses resulting from damage to people or property when the insured party is judged liable. A business is liable for

PREMIUMS Money paid to an insurance company by customers in return for being covered for certain types of losses should they occur.

LIABILITY INSURANCE Covers losses resulting from damage to people or property when the insured party is judged liable.

Losses are reduced or prevented when this security specialist uses electronic surveillance (left), when valuables are stored under lock and key (middle), and when workers are reminded to wear safety gear at this construction site (right).

© Everett Collection Inc/Alamy; Photo by Dick Loek/Toronto Star via Getty Images; © Arco Images GmbH/Alamy any injury to an employee when the injury arises from activities related to occupation. When workers are permanently or temporarily disabled by job-related accidents or disease, employers are required by law to provide **workers' compensation coverage** for medical expenses, loss of wages, and rehabilitation services.

Every year in Canada, well over $1 billion is lost to insurance fraud. The insurance industry estimates that between $10 and $15 of every $100 you pay in premiums goes to cover fraud losses. The Insurance Bureau of Canada (IBC) is an industry association that represents Canadian companies that provide car, home, and business insurance. The IBC protects honest policyholders by monitoring insurance claims and determining which ones are fraudulent. Two areas of particular concern are organized crime rings and fraudulent injury claims. One popular scam is the "staged accident." The swindler purposely (but carefully) runs into, say, a telephone pole, and then everyone in the car claims that they are suffering from whiplash. After the accident is reported, the insurance company contacts the car's occupants and sends them accident benefit packages. Sometimes people who aren't even insured are paid benefits because they use counterfeit "proof of insurance" cards.[23] The IBC also lobbies the government to make legislative changes that will deter insurance fraud. Visit the IBC website at www.ibc.ca.

Property Insurance Firms purchase **property insurance** to cover injuries resulting from physical damage to real estate or personal property. Property losses may result from fire, lightning, wind, hail, explosion, theft, vandalism, or other destructive forces, such as hurricanes. In 2005, insurance companies received claims exceeding $55 billion as a result of several hurricanes that hit the southern United States and flooded New Orleans. That figure was double the previous record (set in 2004). Canadian insurers were expected to pay out about $570 million of the 2005 total.

In some cases, loss to property is minimal in comparison with loss of income. A manufacturer, for example, may have to close down for an extended time while fire damage is being repaired. During that time, the company is not generating any income, but certain expenses—such as taxes, insurance premiums, and salaries for key personnel—may continue. To cover such losses, a firm may buy *business interruption insurance*.

Life Insurance Insurance can also protect a company's human assets. As part of their benefits packages, many businesses purchase **life insurance** for employees. Life insurance companies receive premiums in return for the promise to pay beneficiaries after the death of insured parties. As with other types of insurance, a portion of the premium is used to cover the insurer's own expenses.

Life insurance can, of course, also be purchased by individuals. For many years, Canadian life insurance companies have sold insurance policies to Canadians, but now they are rapidly expanding overseas,

WORKERS' COMPENSATION COVERAGE Compensation for medical expenses, loss of wages, and rehabilitation services for injuries arising from activities related to occupation.

PROPERTY INSURANCE Covers injuries to firms resulting from physical damage to or loss of real estate or personal property.

LIFE INSURANCE Insurance that pays benefits to survivors of a policyholder.

GROUP LIFE INSURANCE Life insurance underwritten for a group as a whole rather than for each individual member.

KEY PERSON INSURANCE Insurance that protects a company against loss of the talents and skills of key employees.

BUSINESS CONTINUATION AGREEMENT An agreement in which owners of a business make plans to buy the ownership interest of a deceased associate from his or her heirs.

Catastrophic losses like those caused by fire are avoided when a business buys property insurance. The cost of the rebuilding will be paid by the insurance company. But interruption of the firm's normal operations will also be harmful, so many businesses buy business interruption insurance as well.

© vario images GmbH & Co.KG/Alamy

particularly in China and India. Sun Life Financial, for example, has formed a joint venture with Aditya Birla Group to sell life insurance and mutual funds in India. As a result of this partnership, Sun Life is the second-largest privately owned life insurance company in India.[24] But in 2011, both Sun Life and Standard Life Assurance decided to stop selling individual life insurance policies in the U.S. because low interest rates and volatile stock markets made it difficult to make a profit selling such policies.[25] In some areas of the world, unstable and dangerous situations have motivated entrepreneurs to sell special kinds of insurance. For example, the al Ameen Insurance Co. pays out $3500 to beneficiaries of people who are killed as a result of insurgent activity in Iraq. The annual premium is about $35.[26]

Most companies buy **group life insurance**, which is underwritten for groups as a whole rather than for each individual member. The insurer's assessment of potential losses and its pricing of premiums are based on the characteristics of the entire group.

SPECIAL FORMS OF BUSINESS INSURANCE

Many forms of insurance are attractive to both businesses and individuals. For example, homeowners are as concerned about insuring property from fire and theft as businesses are. Businesses, however, have some special insurable concerns—the departure or death of key employees or owners.

Key Person Insurance Many businesses choose to protect themselves against loss of the talents and skills of key employees. If a salesperson who brings in $2.5 million of sales revenue dies or takes a new job, the firm will suffer loss. It will also incur recruitment costs to find a replacement and training expenses once a replacement is hired. **Key person insurance** is designed to offset both lost income and additional expenses.[27]

Business Continuation Agreements Who takes control of a business when a partner or an associate dies? Surviving partners are often faced with the possibility of having to accept an inexperienced heir as a management partner. This contingency can be handled in **business continuation agreements**, whereby owners make plans to buy the ownership interest of a deceased associate from his or her heirs. The value of the ownership interest is determined when the agreement is made. Special policies can also provide survivors with the funds needed to make the purchase.

CRAFTING A BUSINESS PLAN | PART 5:

MANAGING FINANCIAL ISSUES

GOAL OF THE EXERCISE

In this final part of the business plan project, you'll consider how you'll finance your business as well as create an executive summary for your plan.

EXERCISE BACKGROUND: PART 5 OF THE BUSINESS PLAN

In a previous part of the business plan, you discussed the costs of doing business, as well as how much revenue you expect to earn in one year. It's now time to think about how to finance the business. To get a great idea off the ground requires money. But how will you get these funds?

You'll then conclude this project by creating an executive summary. The purpose of the executive summary is to give the reader a quick snapshot into your proposed business. Although this exercise comes at the end of the project, once you're done writing it, you'll end up placing the executive summary at the beginning of your completed business plan.

YOUR ASSIGNMENT

STEP 1

Open the saved Business Plan file you have been working on.

STEP 2

For the purposes of this assignment, you will answer the following questions, shown in Part 5: Managing Financial Issues.

1. How much money will you need to get your business started?

   Hint: *Refer to Part 3 of the plan where you analyzed the costs involved in running your business. Approximately how much will you need to get your business started?*

2. How will you finance your business? For example, will you seek a bank loan? Borrow from friends? Sell stocks or bonds initially or as your business grows?

   Hint: *Refer to Chapter 15 for information on securities such as stocks and bonds. Refer also to Chapters 4 and 15 for more information on sources of short-term and long-term funds.*

3. Now, create an executive summary for your business plan. The executive summary should be brief—no more than two pages—and cover the following points:

   - The name of your business
   - Where your business will be located
   - The mission of your business
   - The product or service you are selling
   - Who your ideal customers are
   - How your product or business will stand out in the crowd
   - Who the owners of the business are and what experience they have
   - An overview of the future prospects for your business and industry

   Hint: *At this point, you've already answered all of these questions, so what you need to do here is put the ideas together into a "snapshot" format. The executive summary is really a sales pitch—it's the investor's first impression of your idea. Therefore, as with all parts of the plan, write in a clear and professional way.*

Congratulations on completing the business plan project!

CBC VIDEO CASE 5-1

CREDIT-CARD FRAUD

A new trend is evident in criminal activity: smash-and-grab thieves are stealing hard drives from retail stores. When a big Canadian grocery chain hired an expert to find out why their point-of-sale (POS) terminals were being stolen, they discovered that the thieves wanted the credit and debit card information on the POS. Businesses are supposed to wipe these terminals clean at the end of each business day so that customers' credit- and debit-card numbers are not left on the terminals overnight, but businesses may not do this on a regular basis. The grocery chain's problem is not an isolated occurrence. Starbucks, Boston Pizza, and Husky have all been hit by POS terminal theft.

Thieves use the credit- and debit-card numbers they get from the POS terminals to make counterfeit credit cards. Blank gift cards are run through a reader, and the stolen credit- or debit-card numbers are put on the stripe on the back of the gift card. But crooks don't just buy stuff with the fake credit or debit cards they make: with your credit-card numbers in hand, criminals can go into your bank and use the data there to impersonate you. They can even transfer your line of credit to another bank account that they have opened up in someone else's name. Criminals no longer have to rob banks because POS terminals are "open bank vaults" and they are everywhere.

Twice in one week, thieves stole POS terminals from a Sammy J. Peppers restaurant in Coquitlam, B.C. *Marketplace* brought in a security expert to look into the problem. The restaurant owner said the POS terminals were checked to see that no customer data was kept on them overnight. The computer expert removed the hard drive from the restaurant's POS terminal to see what was stored there. Fortunately, he found that the hard drive had indeed been wiped clean. So, even if thieves stole the POS terminal, they wouldn't get any of the customers' credit- or debit-card numbers. But other retail establishments are not doing such a good job. Husky, for example, admits it is not sure what was on the hard drives that were stolen from it.

There are 630 000 POS terminals in Canada processing thousands of transactions every day. In Abbotsford, B.C., 28 retail businesses were broken into in a short time period. An Abbotsford detective says that one company was targeted 100 times. Retailers have been keeping quiet about this problem, and although credit-card companies make good on customers' losses, we all ultimately pay a price because overall costs go up.

It is not uncommon for consumers to get a notice from their credit-card company saying that their card has been "compromised," but it is hard to pinpoint where the problem occurred. A representative from the Retail Council of Canada admits there is a problem, but says it is hard to keep up with the innovative activities of thieves who are always one step ahead of security measures. The representative says that customers know about the possibility that their credit or debit card could be compromised, but the people that *Marketplace* interviewed seemed oblivious to this fact. Stores should therefore tell consumers about the problem instead of keeping silent, but there is no law in Canada requiring retailers to tell you your card has been stolen. Companies are often confident that nothing is on the POS hard drives that would be helpful to thieves, but in reality there often is. Crown Prosecutor Peter Stabler says that retailers know that important information is on their POS hard drives and so do the crooks.

QUESTIONS FOR DISCUSSION

1. Why aren't POS terminals wiped more often?
2. What actions can retailers take to reduce credit-card fraud?
3. Consider the following statement: *Retail outlets should be required by law to put up signs warning customers that their credit- and debit-card numbers may be stolen.* Do you agree or disagree with the statement? Defend your position.

CBC VIDEO CASE 5-2

CBC

SOAKWASH

THE COMPANY

When Jacqueline Sava walked into the Dragon's Den, she had already amassed over $1 million worth of sales. Soakwash is designed to clean women's delicate items such as bras and lingerie; it is formulated specifically for hand-washable items. The products are sold in yarn shops, quilting shops, lingerie shops, and apparel stores. As an added benefit, customers using Soakwash do not need to rinse out the items (a significant point of differentiation from the competition).

THE PITCH

After presenting the benefits of her product, Jacqueline requested $300 000 for a 25 percent equity stake in her company. She informed the dragons that the funding would help her create a salesforce to garner a stronger presence in the market and hurt her competitors. According to Jacqueline, she needed to hire salespeople to take her company to the next level. Specifically, she pointed to an estimated 6000 upper-end lingerie shops in the United States. Jacqueline explained that she had a proven track record of training retail stores to up-sell the product but asserted that at present she could not reach enough retailers to convince them to carry her products.

THE DRAGONS' POINT OF VIEW

After Jacqueline's pitch, it was clear that there were many questions and more concern than enthusiasm. First, the dragons pointed to a huge well-known competitor, namely Zero fabric wash. Second, when asked about her sales figures, Jacqueline revealed that the $1 million was actually a total that spanned more than two-and-a-half years. It also became clear that her sales were not growing and had remained at $400 000 for each of the last two years. Third, the dragons were very concerned that she had a bank loan of $300 000 in addition to the $200 000 that she had already invested out of her own pocket. When pressed about this issue, Jacqueline replied, "It's a great time to have debt." Kevin O'Leary (always the compassionate one) bluntly told her she was wrong and said, "They are going to call your loan and squeeze your head like a pimple."

THE OUTCOME

When it was time for the dragons to make their decisions, the questions had already mounted and one by one the dragons walked away from the deal with the following comments:

- "You valued your company at more than a million dollars. I can't get near the valuation, I'm out."
- "Your sales are flat-lining. Slug it out one retailer at a time. I don't see the market. I'm out."
- "You came out asking for three times the value of the company. I think the valuation is outrageous. I'm out."
- "When you have sales of 400k and 300k of debt, it's an issue. I'm out."
- "I love you as an entrepreneur, love your product, but for 300k I'd have to own your company! I'm out."

The big lesson: the numbers... the numbers... the numbers. The panel of experts thought the numbers were out of line and that Jacqueline's request was outrageous, and every one of them backed out while giving her some stern advice.

QUESTIONS FOR DISCUSSION

1. What lessons about financing a business can you take away from this video? If Jacqueline were given a second opportunity to make a pitch to the dragons, what advice would you give her?
2. What do you think of the market potential for this product? Do you think Soakwash has a bright future? Explain why or why not.
3. In your opinion, which of the dragons made the most compelling point?

NOTES, SOURCES, AND CREDITS

ENDNOTES

CHAPTER 1

1. "Best Country for Business: Canada," *Globe and Mail*, October 5, 2011, B2.
2. Robert A. Collinge and Ronald M. Ayers, *Economics by Design: Principles and Issues*, 2nd ed. (Upper Saddle River, NJ: Prentice Hall, 2000), 41–42; Michael J. Mandel, "The New Economy," *BusinessWeek*, January 31, 2000, 73–77.
3. Sean Wise, "Social Networks Reshaping Economics," *Winnipeg Free Press*, May 18, 2011, A11.
4. Richard I. Kirkland Jr., "The Death of Socialism," *Fortune*, January 4, 1988, 64–72.
5. Andres Oppenheimer, "Latin America Is Skeptical," *Orlando Sentinel*, February 20, 2006, A19.
6. James Kynge, "Private Firms' Growth in China Striking: Report," *National Post*, May 11, 2000, C14.
7. "Cuba Allows Private Ads in Phone Book," *Globe and Mail*, December 9, 2011, B7.
8. Karl E. Case and Ray C. Fair, *Principles of Economics*, 5th ed. (Upper Saddle River, NJ: Prentice Hall, 1999), 69–74; Robert A. Collinge and Ronald M. Ayers, *Economics by Design: Principles and Issues*, 2nd ed. (Upper Saddle River, NJ: Prentice Hall, 2000), 51–52.
9. Andres Oppenheimer, "While Latin America Nationalizes, India Opens Up," *Orlando Sentinel*, January 22, 2007, A11.
10. Barry Critchley, "Canada Post Should Be Privatized: OECD; Productivity Issue," *National Post*, March 11, 2010, FP2.
11. John Greenwood, "Study Cites Privatization in Productivity Gains," *National Post*, June 26, 2009, FP1.
12. *Bank of Canada Banking and Financial Statistics*, Series G1, Government of Canada Fiscal Position, April 26, 2012, S84.
13. *Financial Post*, June, 2009, 82.
14. "UFC May Have Long Wait to Crack Ontario Market," thestar.com, May 23, 2010, www.thestar.com/printarticle/783892.
15. Andy Hoffman, "Labatt Convicted in Quebec Discount Beer Case," *Globe and Mail*, November 24, 2005, B10.
16. Jim Middlemiss, "Don't Get Caught Offside in Rules Changes; Wrong Advice on Competition Act Could Be Costly," *National Post*, March 23, 2009, FP6. For an analysis of the current situation in the U.S. regarding resale price maintenance, see Joseph Pereira, "Price-Fixing Makes Comeback after Supreme Court Hearing," *Wall Street Journal*, August 18, 2008, A1, A12.
17. Hollie Shaw, "Bogus Ads: If You Mislead the Consumer, Be Ready to Suffer the Financial Fallout," *National Post*, May 22, 2009, FP12.
18. Shirley Won and Jacquie McNish, "Antitrust Watchdog Loses Beer Battle," *Globe and Mail*, March 29, 2007, B1, B6.
19. Steven Chase and Jacquie McNish, "Prentice Probes Watchdog's Court Conduct," *Globe and Mail*, January 30, 2008, B1–B2.
20. John Gray, "Texas Fold 'Em," *Canadian Business*, October 9–22, 2006, 44–46.
21. "Video Gaming: The Next Level," *Venture*, March 20, 2005.
22. "Alberta Film, TV Production Faces Decline," May 19, 2010, CBC News, www.cbc.ca/arts/film/story/2010/05/18/alberta-film-production-decline.html.
23. Jennifer Allen, "New Lobby Rules Mean More Work for Lawyers," *Globe and Mail*, August 13, 2008, B5.
24. Andy Hoffman, "Global Demand for Maple Syrup Keeps Rising. Sweet!," *Globe and Mail*, March 12, 2009, B1.
25. Joel Millman, "Metal Is So Precious that Scrap Thieves Now Tap Beer Kegs," *Wall Street Journal*, March 14, 2006, pp. A1, A15.
26. Paul Heyne, Peter J. Boettke, and David L. Prychitko, *The Economic Way of Thinking*, 10th ed. (Upper Saddle River, NJ: Prentice Hall, 2003), 190, 358–359.
27. Karl E. Case and Ray C. Fair, *Principles of Economics*, 6th ed., updated (Upper Saddle River, NJ: Prentice Hall, 2003), 300–309.
28. *Hoover's Handbook of World Business 2002* (Austin: Hoover's Business Press, 2002), 74–75.
29. Timothy Aeppel, "Show Stopper: How Plastic Popped the Cork Monopoly," *Wall Street Journal*, May 1, 2010, A1.
30. Barrie McKenna, "Snail Mail Corp. Tries to Break Out of its Shell," *Globe and Mail*, January 21, 2011, B1.
31. Vincent Geloso and Youri Chassin, "Postal Monopoly is Becoming a Dead Letter," *National Post*, June 2, 2011, FP11.

CHAPTER 2

1. Bertrand Marotte, "Bauer Aims to Rebound from NHL Lockout with Lacrosse Power Play," *Globe and Mail*, October 8, 2012, B1.
2. See Jay B. Barney and William G. Ouchi, eds., *Organizational Economics* (San Francisco: Jossey-Bass, 1986), for a detailed analysis of linkages between economics and organizations.
3. Marina Strauss, "Grocers Scramble to Offset Higher Food Costs," *Globe and Mail*, May 2, 2011, B4.
4. Matthew Levin, "Dollarama Profit Rises 23% on Higher Sales," *Financial Post*, December 6, 2012.
5. Karl E. Case and Ray C. Fair, *Principles of Economics*, 6th ed., updated (Upper Saddle River, NJ: Prentice Hall, 2003), 432–433.
6. Karl E. Case and Ray C. Fair, *Principles of Economics*, 6th ed., updated (Upper Saddle River, NJ: Prentice Hall, 2003), 15.
7. Karl E. Case and Ray C. Fair, *Principles of Economics*, 6th ed., updated (Upper Saddle River, NJ: Prentice Hall, 2003), 15.
8. Richard Blackwell, "The 'R' Word," *Globe and Mail*, October 16, 2008, B5.
9. Bank of Canada Banking and Financial Statistics, Table H1 (January 2013): S98.
10. World Bank Website, GDP statistics, http://search.worldbank.org/data?qterm=gdp&language=&format= [accessed February 1, 2013].
11. Bertrand Marotte, "Bombardier Setting Up Shop in Morocco," *Globe and Mail*, September 6, 2012.
12. Matthew McLearn, "Our Dangerous Addiction to GDP," *Canadian Business*, October 12, 2009, 23.
13. Green Economics website, www.greeneconomics.ca/gpi, accessed June 9, 2010; Barry Marquardson, "GDP Fails as a Measurement," *Globe and Mail*, July 16, 1998, B2.

14. World Bank Website, GDP statistics, http://search.worldbank.org/data?qterm=gdp%20per%20capita&language=EN [accessed February 1, 2013].

15. Olivier Blanchard, *Macroeconomics*, 3rd ed. (Upper Saddle River, NJ: Prentice Hall, 2003), 24–26.

16. OECD website, http://stats.oecd.org/Index.aspx?DatasetCode=LEVEL [accessed February 1, 2013].

17. Jay Heizer and Barry Render, *Operations Management*, 6th ed. (Upper Saddle River, NJ: Prentice Hall, 2001), 15–16.

18. Statistics Canada website, http://www.statcan.gc.ca/tables-tableaux/sum-som/l01/cst01/gblec02a-eng.htm [accessed February 2, 2013].

19. Canadian Press, "Canada Urged to 'Get Act Together' As National Debt to Hit $600-billion Saturday," *Financial Post*, November 23rd, 2012.

20. CBC News website, Federal Deficit Shrinking Faster than Expected, http://www.cbc.ca/news/business/story/2013/01/25/deficit-november.html [accessed February 2, 2013].

21. Neil Reynolds, "U.S. Debt: Don't Worry, Be Happy (till 2017)," *Globe and Mail*, April 3, 2009, B2.

22. Celia Dugger, "Life in Zimbabwe: Wait for Useless Money, Then Scour for Food," *New York Times*, October 2, 2008, A1, A14.

23. Geoffrey York, "How Zimbabwe Slew the Dragon of Hyperinflation," *Globe and Mail*, March 23, 2009, B1.

24. Mike Cohen & Franz Wild, Bloomberg Website, South Africa Holds Rate as Rand Sparks Inflation Fears. January 24, 2013.

25. Tavia Grant, "A Snapshot of How We Spend," *Globe and Mail*, April 20, 2010, B2; Tavia Grant, "Lard in 1913, Plasma TV Now: CPI Tracks Changes," *Globe and Mail*, April 21, 2005, B1, B15.

26. Bruce Little, "There's Been a Huge Shift in How Consumers Spend," *Globe and Mail*, July 5, 2004, B4.

27. Figure 2.3: Bank of Canada website, CPI Statistics, www.bankofcanada.ca/en/cpi.html [accessed June 10, 2010].

28. Tavia Grant, "Food Prices to Rise in 2013, Report Says," *Globe and Mail*, December 6, 2012, B8; Rita Trichur, "Maple Leaf Takes on Challenge of Food Inflation," *Globe and Mail*, April 29, 2011, B9.

29. *Bank of Canada Banking and Financial Statistics*, Series H5, Labour Force Status of the Population, December 2011, S103.

30. "Canada's Unemployment Rate Drops to a 4 Year Low, CTV News Website, http://www.ctvnews.ca/business/canada-s-unemployment-rate-drops-to-4-year-low-1.1100775 [accessed February 2, 2013].

31. Julie Jargon, "Seeking Sweet Savings," *Wall Street Journal*, October 2, 2007, B1–B2.

32. Statistics Canada. "Spending on Research And Development," http://www.statcan.gc.ca/daily-quotidien/120113/dq120113d-eng.htm [accessed February 2, 2013].

33. Statistics Canada, 2008, Industrial Research and Development: Intentions, Catalogue no. 88-202-X, Table 4, Concentration of Total Intramural Research and Development Expenditures by Companies Size, http://www.statcan.gc.ca/pub/88-202-x/2012000/t050-eng.htm [accessed February 2, 2013].

34. Marina Strauss, "Starbucks Rolls Out Smart Phone Payments," *Globe and Mail*, November 11, 2011, B4.

35. Intel website, Moore's Law, www.intel.com/technology/mooreslaw/ [accessed June 11, 2010].

36. Timothy Taylor, "Welcome to the Machines," *Report on Business*, September 2011, 14.

37. Nathan Vanderklippe, "Yukon's Golden Dilemma," *Globe and Mail*, February 2, 2013, B1.

38. Marina Strauss and Kevin Howlett, "Ontario Cuts Generic Drug Payments Again," *Globe and Mail*, April 24, 2012, B4; Michael Babad, "How Ontario's Drug Reforms Could Hit Shoppers Drug Mart," *Globe and Mail*, April 8, 2010, B1.

39. Geoffrey York, "Nationalization Talks Put Miners on Edge," *Globe and Mail*, February 2, 2010, B3.

40. Carrie Tait, "Suncor Gears Up to Go Back into Libya," *Globe and Mail*, February 2, 2010, B3.

41. Brenda Boum, "No Regrets From the Capitalist Miner Who Built Bridges to Communist Cuba," *Globe and Mail*, November 25, 2011, B1.

42. Angelina Chapin, "Under Cover Economy," *Canadian Business*, September 26, 2011, 50–52.

43. Ira Boudway, "Labour Disputes: The Wal-Mart Way," *Bloomberg BusinessWeek*, 57–60.

44. CBC Website, "Wal-Mart runs afoul of Sask. Labour Laws," http://www.cbc.ca/news/canada/saskatchewan/story/2012/10/23/sk-weyburn-wal-mart-union-121023.html [accessed February 2, 2013].

45. David Ebner, "BP Spill Causes Transatlantic Tensions," *Globe and Mail*, September 27, 2011, B3; Eric Reguly, "Now Come the Lawyers," *Globe and Mail*, June 5, 2010, B1, B4; Peter Coy and Stanley Reed, "Lessons of the Spill," *Bloomberg BusinessWeek*, May 10–16, 2010; BP website, http://www.bp.com/sectiongenericarticle.do?categoryId=9036580&contentId=7067577 [accessed December 28, 2011].

46. CBC News Website, "Judge Approves Record Fine in BP Oil Spill Settlement," http://www.cbc.ca/news/world/story/2013/01/29/business-bp-gulf-spill-settlement.html [accessed February 2, 2013].

47. Richard Blackwell, "The Greening of the Corner Office," *Globe and Mail*, March 26, 2007, B1, B4.

48. Michael Porter, *Competitive Strategy: Techniques for Analyzing Industries and Competitors* (New York: The Free Press, 1980).

49. Jeff Beer, "Fresh Trouble for the Double-Double," *Canadian Business*, February 18, 2013, 11.

50. Hollie Shaw, "Target Unveils Canadian Stores," *Financial Post*, May 26, 2011; Marina Strauss, "Target's Rejected Sites in High Demand by Rivals," *Globe and Mail*, September 24, 2011, B5.

51. "Bauer Expects Price Pressure as Big Customers Merge," *Globe and Mail*, August 19, 2011, B5.

52. Barrie McKenna, "Canada Post in the Red For First Time in 16 Years," *Globe and Mail*, May 2nd, 2012, B1, B8.

53. Diane Peters, "Setting the Bar High for Outsourcing," *Globe and Mail*, November 29, 2011, B15.

54. Judy Strauss and Raymond Frost, *E-Marketing* (Upper Saddle River, NJ: Prentice Hall, 2001), 245–246.

55. Lee J. Krajewski and Larry P. Ritzman, *Operations Management: Strategy and Analysis*, 6th ed. (Upper Saddle River, NJ: Prentice Hall, 2002), 3–4.

56. Lee J. Krajewski and Larry P. Ritzman, *Operations Management: Strategy and Analysis*, 6th ed. (Upper Saddle River, NJ: Prentice Hall, 2002), Chapter 3.

57. Gordon Pitts, "Kraft CEO Still Digesting Cadbury Takeover," *Globe and Mail*, June 7, 2010, B8.

58. David Pett, "Canadian M&A Activity Sputters in Third Quarter," *Financial Post*, October 18, 2012.

59. Andrew Willis, "Couche-Tard Shows No Stomach for Casey's Fight," *Globe and Mail*, June 9, 2010, B16.

60. Couche-Tard Website, http://www.couche-tard.com/corporatif/ [accessed February 2, 2013].

61. Ross Marowits, "Air Canada Adopts Poison Pill," *Globe and Mail*, March 31, 2011, B1.

62. Dana Cimilluca, Jonathan Rockoff, and Anupreeta Das, "Nestle Wins Pfizer's Baby Food Division," *Globe and Mail*, April 24, 2012, B11.

63. "Culture of Fun Benefits Clients, Staff," *National Post*, October 27, 2008, FP12.

64. Susan Krashinsky, "Rogers and Wal-Mart to Launch Magazine," *Globe and Mail*, December 6, 2012, B3.

65. Rona Website, Company Fact Sheet, http://www.rona.ca/corporate [accessed February 2, 2013]; David Milstead, "Rona Forecast Remains Cloudy Despite Sunny Days Ahead," *Globe and Mail*, May 24, 2011, B13.

CHAPTER 3

1. Chris MacDonald, "Sweeping Ethics under the Rug," *Canadian Business*, January 23, 2012, 12.

2. Ronald Ebert and Ricky Griffin, *Business Essentials*, 7th edition (Upper Saddle River, NJ: Prentice Hall, 2009).

3. Thomas Donaldson and Thomas W. Dunfee, "Toward a Unified Conception of Business Ethics: An Integrative Social Contracts Theory," *Academy of Management Review*, Vol. 19, Issue 2 (1994): 252–284.

4. "Drug Companies Face Assault on Prices," *W all Street Journal*, May 11, 2000, B1, B4.

5. John Saunders, "Bitter Air Carrier Dogfight Heads to Court," *Globe and Mail*, July 8, 2004, B3.

6. Andrew Crane, "Spying Doesn't Pay; Intelligence Gathering is Still an Ethical and Legal Minefield," *National Post*, November 11, 2008, FP12.

7. "Niko Penalized $9.5 M for Bangladesh Bribe," *Winnipeg Free Press*, June 25, 2011, B5.

8. G. McArthur, "New Corruption Allegations Hit SNC-Lavalin," *Globe and Mail*, December 19, 2012, B1.

9. "Walmart India Unit suspends CFO, Others; Alleged Bribery," *National Post*, November 24, 2012, FP13; Brad Dorfman, "Wal-Mart Hires Global Anti-Bribery Watchdog; Mexico Stores Scandal," *National Post*, April 25, 2012, FP2.

10. Julian Sher, "OECD Slams Canada's Record on Prosecuting Bribery," *Globe and Mail*, March 28, 2011, B4.

11. Various other models have been proposed. See J. Rest, "Background Theory and Research" in J. Rest and T. Narvaez (eds.), *Moral Development in the Professions: Psychology and Applied Ethics*, 1991, 1–26 (New Jersey: Lawrence Earlbaum Associates Inc.). Also, T. Jones, "Ethical Decision Making by Individuals in Organizations: An Issue-Contingent Model," *Academy of Management Review*, 1991, 16, 366–395. Rest's model, for example, includes four phases: *moral sensitivity* (awareness that a situation contains a moral issue), *moral judgment* (determining which possible solutions can be morally justified), *moral motivation* (the intention to make a moral decision), and *moral action* (the action the individual takes).

12. Bertrand Marotte, "Victims Unmoved by Fraudster's Courtroom Tears," *Globe and Mail*, January 16, 2010, A16.

13. These three factors were included as part of a "fraud triangle" (see Donald R. Cressey, *Other People's Money* (Montclair: Patterson Smith, 1973, p. 30). The factors were originally described in terms of financial fraud carried out by a trusted individual, but the factors can be applied to both financial and non-financial issues.

14. Mark Schwartz, "Heat's on to Get an Effective Code," *Globe and Mail*, November 27, 1997, B2.

15. Mary Gentile, *Giving Voice to Values*. New Haven: Yale University Press, 2010.

16. Jeffrey S. Harrison and R. Edward Freeman, "Stakeholders, Social Responsibility, and Performance: Empirical Evidence and Theoretical Perspectives," *Academy of Management Journal*, 1999, Vol. 42, No. 5, 479-485. See also David P. Baron, *Business and Its Environment*, 5th Ed. (Upper Saddle River, NJ: Prentice Hall, 2006), Chapter 18.

17. "A Wake-Up Call for Canadian Consumers," *Winnipeg Free Press*, April 26, 2013, A15.

18. "Parent Company of Victoria's Secret to Probe Claims of Child Labour," *National Post*, December 16, 2011, FP6.

19. Jeffrey S. Harrison and R. Edward Freeman, "Stakeholders, Social Responsibility, and Performance: Empirical Evidence and Theoretical Perspectives," *Academy of Management Journal* 42, no. 5 (1999): 479–485. See also David P. Baron, *Business and Its Environment*, 3rd ed. (Upper Saddle River, NJ: Prentice Hall, 2000), Chapter 17.

20. See SROI Canada website, http://www.sroi-canada.ca/about/index.html [accessed July 22, 2013]; see also SROI Network International website, http://www.thesroinetwork.org/publications [accessed July 22, 2013].

21. An idea of the conflicting ideas that exist in this debate can be seen in two articles: Peter Foster, "Milton's Loophole," *National Post*, June 22, 2011, FP15, and Eleanor Vaughan, "Just What Milton Would Have Wanted?" *National Post*, June 24, 2011, FP11.

22. Laura Pratt, "Sustainability Reporting," *CGA Magazine*, September-October, 2007, 18-21; also Sharda Prashad, "Good Green Goals," *The Toronto Star*, April 27, 2007, www.thestar.com/printArticle/205855; also Ralph Shaw, "Peak Performance (Mountain Equipment Co-op)," *Alternatives Journal*, 31, No. 1 (2005), 19-20.

23. John Lyons, "Skin-Deep Gains for Amazon Tribe," *Wall Street Journal*, May 5, 2011, A1.

24. Neil Reynolds, "The Dirty Truth of China's Energy," *Globe and Mail*, March 28, 2007, B2.

25. Bill Curry, "Ottawa Wants Kyoto Softened," *Globe and Mail*, May 12, 2006, A1, A7.

26. Jeffrey Ball, "U.N. Effort to Curtail Emissions in Turmoil," *Wall Street Journal*, April 12–13, 2008, A1, A5.

27. K. Dougherty, "Cap and Trade Comes into Force; Quebec, California," *National Post*, January 2, 2013, FP4.

28. Patricia Adams, "The Next Big Scam," *National Post*, January 13, 2010, FP15.

29. Lauren Etter, "For Icy Greenland, Global Warming Has a Bright Side," *Wall Street Journal*, July 18, 2006, A1, A12.

30. "Going Green Losing Its Shine Among World's Citizens: Poll," *Winnipeg Free Press*, November 28, 2008, A20.

31. "Syncrude Guilty in Duck Deaths," *Winnipeg Free Press*, June 26, 2010, A10; also Tim Shufelt, "Trial Goes Far Beyond Ducks; Syncrude Case Affects All Tailings Pond Users," *National Post*, March 19, 2010, FP1.

32. Brian Morton, "Green Practices Are Both Right and Profitable; Helped Get Clients," *National Post*, June 11, 2012, FP8.

33. Egle Procuta, "One Man's Garbage Is Another's Gold," *Globe and Mail*, April 11, 2006, B7.

34. Geoffrey Scotton, "Cleanups Can Hurt, Companies Warned," *Financial Post*, June 25, 1991, 4.

35. Marc Huber, "A Double-Edged Endorsement," *Canadian Business*, January 1990, 69–71.

36. Daniel Machalaba, "As Old Pallets Pile Up, Critics Hammer Them as New Eco-Menace," *Wall Street Journal*, April 1, 1998, A1.

37. Claudia Cattaneo, "Talisman Braces for Jungle Standoff: Threats of Violence," *National Post*, November 14, 2008, FP1.

38. Emily Steel, "Nestlé Takes a Beating on Social Media Sites," *Wall Street Journal*, March 29, 2010, B5.

39. Steve Ladurantaye, "Maple Leaf Battered by Meat Recall Costs," *Globe and Mail*, October 30, 2008, B3.

40. Nicholas Casey, Nicholas Zamiska, and Andy Pasztor, "Mattel Seeks to Placate China with Apology on Toys," *Wall Street Journal*, September 22–23, 2007, A1, A7.

41. John Wilke, "U.S. Probes Ice Makers Collusion Case," *Wall Street Journal*, August 7, 2008, B1, B10.

42. Martin Cash, "Icemaker Facing Heat Over Finances," *Winnipeg Free Press*, July 20, 2011, B5.

43. Paul Waldie, "Chocolate Bar Makers Probe Over Prices," *Globe and Mail*, November 28, 2007, B1, B10.

44. "Chocolate Makers Face Legal Challenges," *Globe and Mail*, February 20, 2008, B9.

45. Christine Dobby, "Three Gas Retailers Fined in Price Fixing," *National Post*, March 22, 2012, FP4.

46. Jacquie McNish and Jeff Gray, "'Quaint' Canada Called No Match for Price-Fixers," *Globe and Mail*, January 27, 2010, B11.

47. Jonathan Cheng, "False Ads: Chinese Consumers Awaken to a Western Problem," *Wall Street Journal*, July 8, 2005, B9.

48. "These Just Won't Fly," *Winnipeg Free Press*, September 1, 2011, B1.

49. "Canada Goose vs. Counterfeiters," *National Post*, July 19, 2011, FP16; also "Down With Counterfeits," *National Post*, November 7, 2011, FP8.

50. Jeanne Whalen and Benoit Faucon, "Counterfeit Cancer Medicines Multiply," *Wall Street Journal*, December 31, 2012, B1.

51. Louise Watt, "Fake Apple Stores Pop Up in China," *Winnipeg Free Press*, July 22, 2011, B11; also "Apple Hits New York's Fake Stores with Lawsuit," *Globe and Mail*, August 6, 2011, B2.

52. Melanie Lee, "Blue, Yellow and Fake; China's Penchant for Fake Products Expands to the Whole Brand Experience," *National Post*, August 2, 2011, FP3.

53. Jeanne Whalen and Benoit Faucon, "Counterfeit Cancer Medicines Multiply," *Wall Street Journal*, December 31, 2012, B1; also Daryl-Lynn Carlson, "The Costly Reality of Fakes," *National Post*, December 5, 2007.

54. Holly Shaw, "Buzzing Influencers," *National Post*, March 13, 2008, FP12.

55. Tim Barker, "Word-of-Mouth Advertising Grows in Influence, Concern," *Orlando Sentinel*, March 17, 2006, A1, A19.

56. Michael McCarthy and Lorrie Grant, "Sears Drops Benetton after Controversial Death Row Ads," *USA Today*, February 18, 2000, 2B.

57. Shona McKay, "Willing and Able," *Report on Business*, October 1991, 58–63.

58. J. Southerst, "In Pursuit of Drugs," *Canadian Transportation*, November 1989, 58–65.

59. Steve Lambert, "Pushing Boundaries: Keeping an Eye on Employees," *Globe and Mail*, August 20, 2011, B15.

60. Joshua Gallu and Dawn Kopecki, "Whistleblower Awarded Record US$5.1 Million; Firm Fined US$2.3 Billion; Former Salesman Was Appalled by Pfizer's Tactics," *National Post*, September 4, 2009, FP3.

61. Brent Jang and Patrick Brethour, "This WestJet Staffer Blew the Whistle on His Employer's Corporate Spying: He's Still Waiting for Someone to Say Thanks," *Globe and Mail*, October 18, 2006, A1, A12.

62. Cora Daniels, "'It's a Living Hell,'" *Fortune*, April 15, 2002, 367–368.

63. Boyd Erman, "Whistleblower Hotline Opens," *Globe and Mail*, May 26, 2009, B5.

64. Grant McCool and John Poirier, "Madoff Mess Manoeuvres," *National Post*, December 18, 2008, FP3.

65. Laurel Brubaker Calkins and Andrew Harris, "Stanford Gets 110 Years for Ponzi Scheme," *National Post*, June 15, 2012, FP12.

66. Jeff Gray, "BMO Lawsuit Targets 'Cheque-Kiting' Scheme," *Globe and Mail*, July 4, 2012, B6.

67. Janet McFarland, "Five Grand Cache Executives Accused of Insider Trading," *Globe and Mail*, December 9, 2011, B5.

68. David Glovin, Patricia Hurtado, and Bob Van Voris, "Galleon Boss Gets 11-Year Term; Rajaratnam Stays Silent in Facing Prison Time," *National Post*, October 14, 2011, FP1.

69. Daniel Stoffman, "Good Behaviour and the Bottom Line," *Canadian Business*, May 1991, 28–32.

70. "Looking Good in Green," *Maclean's*, May 9, 2011, 47.

71. "Giving's a Hit with CIBC Employees; CIBC," *National Post*, February 3, 2012, JV5.

72. Diana McLaren, "Spirit of Philanthropy Is Thriving," *Globe and Mail*, December 10, 2008, B7.

73. "Survey Shows Canadian Businesses Engaged in Meeting Community Need," *Canada NewsWire*, February 7, 2008, 1.

74. Rita Trichur, "Strings Attached; Corporations Want More for Their Money," *Globe and Mail*, October 29, 2011, B1.

75. Diane McLaren, "Doing Their Part—with Goals in Mind," *Globe and Mail*, December 10, 2008, B7.

76. Bruce Owen, "Camp Tim on Its Way," *Winnipeg Free Press*, May 28, 2010, A6.

77. Kira Vermond, "A Great Way to Engage Your Employees," *Globe and Mail*, July 26, 2008, B16.

78. Sandra Waddock and Neil Smith, "Corporate Responsibility Audits: Doing Well by Doing Good," *Sloan Management Review*, Winter 2000: 75–85.

79. Richard Blackwell, "The Double-Edged Sword of Corporate Altruism," *Globe and Mail*, November 10, 2008, B5.

80. Edward Waitzer, "Bottom Lines Benefit When Social Reporting is Embraced," *Globe and Mail*, November 17, 2011, B2.

81. Derek Sankey, "Green Careers Available in Every Sector; Student Energy; Youth Need to Find Sustainable Energy Future," *National Post*, November 7, 2012, FP11.

82. Marjo Johne, "Sustainability Performance a New Essential," *Globe and Mail*, May 19, 2011, B8.

83. "Looking Good in Green," *Maclean's*, May 9, 2011, 47.

84. Alison Arnot, "The Triple Bottom Line," *CGA Magazine* (January–February 2004), 27–32.

85. Richard Blackwell, "Six Canadian Firms on Global Top 100 List," *Globe and Mail*, January 25, 2012, B2.

86. The Corporate Knights website, http://www.corporateknights.com/ [accessed July 22, 2013].

87. "Mega Brands Wins Case over Lego," *Globe and Mail*, November 13, 2008, B3.

88. Canadian Intellectual Patent Office (CIPO) website, www.cipo.ic.gc.ca/eic/site/cipointernet-internetopic.nsf/eng/Home [accessed April 25, 2010]; Canadian Western Diversification Canada website, www.wd.gc.ca/eng/7133.asp [accessed April 25, 2010].

89. Paul Waldie, "How RIM's Big Deal Was Done," *Globe and Mail*, March 6, 2006, B1, B14.

90. *Globe and Mail* website, "Judge Rules for RIM in Patent Dispute," February 3, 2010, www.theglobeandmail.com [accessed April 25, 2010].

91. Avery Johnson, "Pfizer Buys More Time for Lipitor," *Wall Street Journal*, June 19, 2008, B1.

92. "Google to Pay US$125 Million to Settle Copyright Lawsuits Over Book Project," *National Post*, October 29, 2008, FP6.

CHAPTER 4

1. Statistics Canada Website, "Financial Well-being of the Self Employed," http://www.statcan.gc.ca/daily-quotidien/110923/dq110923a-eng.htm [accessed September 26, 2011]; Tavia Grant, "Call It the Entrepreneurial Era," *Globe and Mail*, March 30, 2010, Section B.

2. Statistics Canada, *Business Dynamics in Canada*, Catalogue no. 61–534-XIE (Ottawa: Minister of Industry, 2006).

3. P.D. Reynolds, S.M. Camp, W.D. Bygrave, E. Autio, and M. Hay, *Global Entrepreneurship Monitor: 2001 Executive Report* (Kansas City, MO: Kauffman Center for Entrepreneurial Leadership, 2001); P.D. Reynolds, M. Hay, W.D. Bygrave, S.M. Camp, and E. Autio, *Global Entrepreneurship Monitor: 2000 Executive Report* (Kansas City, MO: Kauffman Center for Entrepreneurial Leadership, 2000).

4. Industry Canada, *Key Small Business Statistics* (Ottawa: Public Works and Government Services Canada, 2006), 24.

5. Industry Canada, *Key Small Business Statistics*, http://www23.statcan.gc.ca/imdb-bmdi/document/1105_D2_T1_V3-eng.pdf, 1 [accessed March 29, 2013].

6. Monica Diochon, Teresa Menzies, and Yvon Gasse, "Exploring the Relationship between Start-Up Activities and New Venture Emergence: A Longitudinal Study of Canadian Nascent Entrepreneurs," *International Journal of Management and Enterprise Development, Vol. 2*, Issue 3/4 (2005): 408–426.

7. Industry Canada, *Key Small Business Statistics*, (July 2012), 23.

8. "Best Small and Medium Sized Employers in Canada," http://business.queensu.ca/centres/qcbv/bsme/bsme50.php [accessed March 30, 2013].

9. Nancy M. Carter, William B. Gartner, and Paul D. Reynolds, "Firm Founding," in W.B. Gartner, K.G. Shaver, N.M. Carter, and P.D. Reynolds, eds., *Handbook of Entrepreneurial Dynamics: The Process of Business Creation* (Thousand Oaks, CA: Sage, 2004), 311–323.

10. Data from Queen's School of Business/Profit Magazine, "Canada's Smartest Employers 2013".

11. William D. Bygrave and C.W. Hofer, "Theorizing about Entrepreneurship," *Entrepreneurship Theory and Practice, Vol. 16*, Issue 2 (Winter 1991): 14; Donald Sexton and Nancy Bowman-Upton, *Entrepreneurship: Creativity and Growth* (New York: Macmillan, 1991), 7.

12. Facebook website, http://www.facebook.com/press/info.php?statistics [accessed September 11, 2011]; Fred Vogelstein, "How Mark Zuckerberg Turned Facebook into the Web's Hottest Platform," *Wired*, September 6, 2007, www.wired.com/techbiz/startups/news/2007/09/ff_facebook?currentPage=3; Ellen McGirt, "Hacker, Dropout, CEO," *Fast Company*, May 2007, www.fastcompany.com/magazine/115/open_features-hacker-dropout-ceo.html.

13. Greg Keenan and Kevin Carmichael, "From the Ashes," *Globe and Mail*, June 11, 2011, B9.

14. Heritage Foundation Index of Economic Freedom website, http://www.heritage.org/index/ranking [accessed March 30, 2013].

15. Angela Dale, "Self-Employment and Entrepreneurship: Notes on Two Problematic Concepts," in Roger Burrows, ed., *Deciphering the Enterprise Culture* (London: Routledge, 1991), 45, 48; Holt 1992, 11.

16. Donald Sexton and Nancy Bowman-Upton, *Entrepreneurship: Creativity and Growth* (New York: Macmillan, 1991), 11; Kao, 1991, 21.

17. Allan A. Gibb, "The Enterprise Culture and Education: Understanding Enterprise Education and Its Links with Small Business, Entrepreneurship and Wider Educational Goals," *International Small Business Journal, Vol. 11*, Issue 3 (1993): 13–34; Donald Sexton and Nancy Bowman-Upton, *Entrepreneurship: Creativity and Growth* (New York: Macmillan, 1991).

18. Terrence Belford, "Intrapreneurs Combine Big-Biz Clout with Entrepreneurial Style," *CanWest News* (March 23, 2005). Retrieved June 25, 2006, from CBCA Current Events database. (Document ID: 1009719591.)

19. Industry Canada, Small Business Research and Policy, *Key Small Business Statistics*, Table 2 (July 2012), http://www.ic.gc.ca/eic/site/061.nsf/vwapj/KSBS-PSRPE_July-Juillet2012_eng.pdf/$FILE/KSBS-PSRPE_July-Juillet2012_eng.pdf [accessed March 30, 2013].

20. Industry Canada, Small Business Research and Policy, *Key Small Business Statistics*, (July 2012), http://www.ic.gc.ca/eic/site/061.nsf/vwapj/KSBS-PSRPE_July-Juillet2012_eng.pdf/$FILE/KSBS-PSRPE_July-Juillet2012_eng.pdf [accessed March 30, 2013], P9.

21. Statistics Canada website, Employment by Class of Worker and Industry, http://www.statcan.gc.ca/daily-quotidien/120706/t120706a002-eng.htm [accessed March 30, 2013].

22. Industry Canada, Small Business Research and Policy, *Key Small Business Statistics* (June 2012), 18.

23. Industry Canada, Small Business Research and Policy, *Key Small Business Statistics* (Ottawa: Public Works and Government Services Canada, July 2012), 3.

24. Industry Canada, *Key Small Business Statistics* (Ottawa: Public Works and Government Services Canada, June 2011), 38.

25. Lauren McKeon, "Tied to Home," *Canadian Business*, April 14, 2008, 33.

26. Women of Influence, Female Entrepreneur Awards, http://www.womenofinfluence.ca/theawards/past-winners/ [accessed March 29, 2013].

27. Roma Luciw, "Stay-at-Home Moms Stay the Business Course," *Globe and Mail*, March 3, 2007, B10.

28. *BDC Newsletter*, Canadian Small Business Week, 2011 Young Entrepreneur Awards, P8.

29. BDC website, Young Entrepreneurs Award, www.bdc.ca [accessed March 30, 2013].

30. Donald F. Kuratko and Richard M. Hodgetts, *Entrepreneurship: Theory, Process, Practice*, 7th ed. (Mason, OH: Thomson South-Western, 2007), 118–125; John A. Hornday, "Research about Living Entrepreneurs," in *Encyclopedia of Entrepreneurship*, Calvin Kent, Donald Sexton, and Karl Vesper, eds. (Englewood Cliffs, NJ: Prentice Hall, 1982), 26–27; Jeffry A. Timmons and Stephen Spinelli, *New Venture Creation: Entrepreneurship for the 21st Century* (Boston: McGraw-Hill Irwin, 2007), 9.

31. J.D. Kyle, R. Blais, R. Blatt, and A.J. Szonyi, "The Culture of the Entrepreneur: Fact or Fiction," *Journal of Small Business and Entrepreneurship*, 1991: 3–14.

32. R.H. Brockhaus and Pam S. Horwitz, "The Psychology of the Entrepreneur," in *The Art and Science of Entrepreneurship*, D.L. Sexton and Raymond W. Smilor, eds. (Cambridge, MA: Ballinger, 1986); William B. Gartner, "What Are We Talking about When We Talk about Entrepreneurship?" *Journal of Business Venturing, Vol. 5*, Issue 1 (1990): 15–29; Allan A. Gibb, "The Enterprise Culture and Education: Understanding Enterprise Education and Its Links with Small Business, Entrepreneurship and Wider Educational Goals," *International Small Business Journal, Vol. 11*, Issue 3 (1993): 13–34; J.C. Mitchell, "Case and Situation Analysis," *Sociological Review, Vol. 31*, Issue 2 (1983): 187–211.

33. Donald Sexton and Nancy Bowman-Upton, *Entrepreneurship: Creativity and Growth* (New York: Macmillan, 1991); Karl H. Vesper, *New Venture Strategies* (Englewood Cliffs, NJ: Prentice Hall, 1990); W.D. Bygrave and C.W. Hofer, "Theorizing about Entrepreneurship," *Entrepreneurship Theory and Practice, Vol. 16*, Issue 2 (Winter 1991): 14.

34. Lizette Chapman, "'Pivoting' Pays Off For Tech Entrepreneurs" *Globe and Mail*, April, 26, 2012, B11.

35. Walter Good, *Building a Dream* (Toronto: McGraw-Hill Ryerson, 1998), 40.

36. Richard Blackwell, "An Empire Served on a Plastic Tray," *Globe and Mail*, October 8, 2011, B3.

37. Wayne A. Long and W. Ed McMullan, *Developing New Ventures* (San Diego: Harcourt Brace Jovanovich, 1990), 374–375.

38. May Jeong, "Fast-Growing Apps Developer Polar Mobile Looks East," *Globe and Mail*, August 24, 2011, B4; Omar El Akkad, "Nokia Picks Polar to Build 300 Mobile Apps," *Globe and Mail*, August 27, 2011, B3.

39. Rasha Mourtada, "Tested to the Limit," *Globe and Mail*, April 14, 2009, B4.

40. Michael E. Porter, "Know Your Place," *Inc., Vol. 13*, Issue 9 (September 1992): 90–93.

41. Howard H. Stevenson, H. Irving Grousbeck, Michael J. Roberts, and Amarnath Bhide, *New Business Ventures and the Entrepreneur* (Boston: Irwin McGraw-Hill, 1999), 19.

42. Matt Braga, "The Fight for Shelf Space" *Globe and Mail*, May 4, 2011, B10.

43. Howard H. Stevenson, H. Irving Grousbeck, Michael J. Roberts, and Amarnath Bhide, *New Business Ventures and the Entrepreneur* (Boston: Irwin McGraw-Hill, 1999), 21.

44. Marc J. Dollinger, *Entrepreneurship: Strategies and Resources* (Upper Saddle River, NJ: Prentice Hall, 1999), 94–101.

45. Thomas W. Zimmerer and Norman M. Scarborough, *Essentials of Entrepreneurship and Small Business Management*, 4th ed. (Upper Saddle River, NJ: Pearson Prentice Hall), 359.

46. Michael E. Porter, "Know Your Place," *Inc., Vol. 13*, Issue 9 (September 1992): 90–93.

47. Gordon Pitts, "Two Deals, $1 Billion and 50 Millionaires," *Globe and Mail*, October, 17, 2011, B1, B6; Quentin Casey, "Moncton CEO Named Top Angel Investor," *Telegraph-Journal*, January, 30, 2013.

48. Canada's Venture Capital and Private Equity website, http://www.cvca.ca/files/Downloads/VC_Data_Deck_2012_Final.pdf [accessed March 30, 2013].

49. Steve Ladurantaye, "New Rules Set Stage for Wave of Foreign Capital," *Globe and Mail*, March 6, 2010, B1.

50. Wallace Immen, "Co-Work Spaces Help Businesses Blossom," *Globe and Mail*, June 18, 2011, B21.

51. Business Development Bank of Canada website, www.bdc.ca [accessed June 24, 2010].

52. Canadian Association of Business Incubation, http://www.cabi.ca/docs/Incubators-in-Canada.pdf [accessed March 30, 2013].

53. Karl H. Vesper, *New Venture Mechanics* (Englewood Cliffs, NJ: Prentice Hall, 1993), 105.

54. Jeffry A. Timmons, *New Venture Creation* (Boston: Irwin McGraw-Hill, 1999), 277.

55. George Anders, Carol Hymowitz, Joann Lublin, and Don Clark, "All in the Family," *Wall Street Journal*, August 1, 2005, B1, B4.

56. Harvey Schacter, "Honey, You're Fired," *Globe and Mail*, October 18, 2010, E5.

57. Canadian Franchise Association, http://www.cfa.ca/Publications_Research/FastFacts.aspx [accessed September 26, 2011].

58. Anita Elash, "Frogbox Needs a Plan to Jump into the US Market," *Globe and Mail*, June 15, 2011, B17.

59. Tony Wilson, "Legal Advice on Starting a Franchise," *Globe and Mail*, March 16, 2010.

60. Harvey's website, http://harveysfranchising.ca/eng/franchising_2.php [accessed June 24, 2010].

61. Tony Wilson, "A Hodge-Podge Mix of Provincial Franchise Laws Cries Out For a Fix," *Globe and Mail*, October 19, 2011, E10.

62. "Rankings for Corporate Governance Practices," *Globe and Mail*, November 25, 2012.

63. "Canada's 100 Biggest Companies by Revenue in 2012," *Globe and Mail*, June 28, 2012.

64. Jennifer Kwan, "Canadian IPO's to Rebound in 2012?" http://ca.finance.yahoo.com/blogs/insight/canadian-ipos-rebound-2013-153055731.html [accessed March 31, 2013].

65. Terry Pedwell, "Income Trusts Face Tough Rules," *Winnipeg Free Press*, November 1, 2006, B7.

66. Marzena Czarnecka, "Income Trusts Are Back," *Canadian Business*, December 8, 2012.

67. "An Overview of Available Business Structures," www.umanitoba.ca/afs/agric_economics/MRAC/structures.html#Cooperatives [accessed July 22, 2013].

68. Industry Canada, Small Business Research and Policy, *Key Small Business Statistics* (Ottawa: Public Works and Government Services Canada, July 2012), p. 3.

69. Kevin Marron, "Want to Succeed? Read This," *Globe and Mail*, October 19, 2005, E1, E5. Several excellent articles on starting and operating a small business are found in Section E, "Report on Small Business" in the *Globe and Mail*, October 19, 2005.

70. See Norman M. Scarborough and Thomas W. Zimmerer, *Effective Small Business Management: An Entrepreneurial Approach*, 7th ed. (Upper Saddle River, NJ: Prentice Hall, 2003).

71. Virginia Galt, "Business Bankruptcies Fall in Canada," *Globe and Mail*, May 13, 2009, B4.

CHAPTER 5

1. World Trade Organization Website, http://www.wto.org/english/news_e/pres11_e/pr628_e.pdf [accessed August 28, 2011], "Trade Growth to Ease in 2011, but Despite 2010 Record Surge, Crisis Hangover Persists, Press."
2. Peter Wonascott, "U.S. Takes Notice of China's Expanding Ties to Africa," *Globe and Mail*, September 2, 2011, B9.
3. John W. Miller and Marcus Walker, "China Passes Germany as Top Exporter," *Globe and Mail*, January 6, 2010, B8.
4. Jiri Maly, "Five Trends That Will Shape the Global Economy," *Globe and Mail*, June 7, 2010, B5.
5. World Bank website [accessed April 14, 2013], http://data.worldbank.org/about/country-classifications/country-and-lending-groups#Low_income; Ricky Griffin and Michael W. Pustay, *International Business: A Managerial Perspective*, 5th ed. (Upper Saddle River, NJ: Prentice Hall, 2007).
6. Thomas Friedman, *The World Is Flat* (New York: Farrar, Straus, and Giroux, 2005).
7. BBC News Website, "China Overtakes Japan as World's Second-Biggest Economy," February 14, 2011, http://www.bbc.co.uk/news/business-12427321 [accessed September 16, 2011].
8. Paul Brent, "A Few BRICS Short of a Load," *Canadian Business*, November 23, 2009, 21; Courtland L. Bovee, John V. Thill and George Dracopoulos, *Business In Action,* 2nd Canadian Edition, (Pearson Education, 2008), Chapter 2; Shirley Won, "BRIC May Cure any Resource Sector Ills," *Globe and Mail*, November 22, 2007, B17; Andrew Mills, "The Face of Brazil's Ascent," *Globe and Mail*, March 12 2010, B11.
9. Tom Krishner, "Indian Car Maker May Land Jaguar, Land Rover," *Globe and Mail*, January 4, 2008, B3.
10. Tavia Grant and Brian Milner, "Why Brazil Stands Out," *Globe and Mail*, June 10, 2010, B1 & B6.
11. Steven Chase, "In Brazil, the Rise of the Mall," *Globe and Mail*, Sept 2, 2011, B1.
12. The *Guardian* website [accessed September 10, 2011], http://www.guardian.co.uk/world/2011/apr/19/south-africa-joins-bric-club.
13. Geoffrey York, "BRICS Nations Bicker Over Bank," *Globe and Mail*, March 28, 2013, B12.
14. Dominic Barton, "A $30-Trillion Opportunity," *Canadian Business*, November 15, 2012, P25.
15. Ricky W. Griffin and Michael W. Pustay, *International Business: A Managerial Perspective*, 2nd ed. (Reading, MA: Addison-Wesley, 1999), Chapter 3; Dominick Salvatore, *International Economics*, 6th ed. (Upper Saddle River, NJ: Prentice Hall, 1998), 27–33; Karl E. Case and Ray C. Fair, *Principles of Economics*, 5th ed. (Upper Saddle River, NJ: Prentice Hall, 1999), 813–817.
16. John J Wild, Kenneth L. Wild, and Jerry C. Han, *International Business: The Challenges of Globalization*, 4th ed. (Upper Saddle River, NJ: Prentice Hall, 2008), 159-160.
17. Dexter Roberts. "Made in Cambodia—For Now," *Bloomberg Businessweek*, January 16–January 22, 2012, 16.
18. This section is based on Michael Porter, *The Competitive Advantage of Nations* (Boston: Harvard Business School Press, 1990), Chapter 3 and 4; Warren J. Keegan, *Global Marketing Management*, 6th ed. (Upper Saddle River, NJ: Prentice Hall, 1999), 312–321; John J. Wild, Kenneth L. Wild, and Jerry C.Y. Han, *International Business: An Integrated Approach* (Upper Saddle River, NJ: Prentice Hall, 2000), 175–178.
19. World Economic Forum website, Global Competitiveness Report [accessed April 14, 2013], http://www.weforum.org/issues/global-competitiveness.
20. Bank of Canada, Banking and Financial Statistics, Series J2, Canadian Balance of Payments, January 2011, S116-S117; Table 5.1 Statistics Canada website, http://www.statcan.gc.ca/tables-tableaux/sum-som/l01/cst01/gblec02a-eng.htm [accessed April 14, 2013].
21. Statistics Canada website [accessed September 11, 2011], http://www40.statcan.gc.ca/l01/cst01/gblec02a-eng.htm.
22. Bank of Canada website, http://www.bankofcanada.ca/wp-content/uploads/2013/03/bfs_mar2013.pdf (March 2013): S-112 [accessed April 14, 2013].
23. Karl E. Case and Ray C. Fair, *Principles of Economics*, 5th ed. (Upper Saddle River, NJ: Prentice Hall, 1999), 818–821.
24. LûAnn LaSalle, "Clearwater Eyes Productivity to Offset High Loonie," *Globe and Mail*, March 24, 2010, B1.
25. Gordon Pitts, "How Captain High Liner Beat the Dollar Odds," *Globe and Mail*, March 16, 2010, B1–B4.
26. Geoffrey York, "McCain Laying Down its Chips on African strategy," *Globe and Mail*, December 22, 2009, B3.
27. Carolyne Wheeler, "Yum Brands' Recipe for Fast-Food Success in China? Adapt to Local Tastes," *Globe and Mail*, May 11, 2011, B5.
28. Dianne Brady, "Yum's Big Game of Chicken," *Bloomberg Businessweek*, March 29, 2012, 63-69.
29. Mark MacKinnon, "RIM's Indonesian Bonanza," *Globe and Mail*, March 25, 2010, B1.
30. Barrie McKenna, Rise as Auto-Parts Power Reflects New Manufacturing Edge," *Wall Street Journal*, August 1, 2006, A1, A6.
31. The Hershey Company website, http://www.thehersheycompany.com/about-hershey.aspx [accessed April 15, 2013].
32. Ray August, *International Business Law: Text, Cases, and Readings*, 3rd ed. (Upper Saddle River, NJ: Prentice Hall, 2000), 192–197.
33. Fortune 500 Website, Global500 Rankings 2012, http://money.cnn.com/magazines/fortune/global500/2012/snapshots/6388.html?iid=splwinners [accessed April 15, 2013].
34. Warren J. Keegan, *Global Marketing Management*, 6th ed. (Upper Saddle River, NJ: Prentice Hall, 1999), 290–292; Ricky W. Griffin and Michael W. Pustay, *International Business: A Managerial Perspective*, 2nd ed. (Reading, MA: Addison-Wesley, 1999), 427–431; John J. Wild, Kenneth L. Wild, and Jerry C.Y. Han, *International Business: An Integrated Approach* (Upper Saddle River, NJ: Prentice Hall, 2000), 454–456.
35. Ricky W. Griffin and Michael W. Pustay, *International Business: A Managerial Perspective*, 2nd ed. (Reading, MA: Addison-Wesley, 1999), 431–433; John J. Wild, Kenneth L. Wild, and Jerry C.Y. Han, *International Business: An Integrated Approach* (Upper Saddle River, NJ: Prentice Hall, 2000), 456–458.
36. Shirley Won, "Small Firms Beating a Path to the Middle Kingdom," *Globe and Mail*, August 31, 2004, B7.
37. James R. Haggerty, "Whirlpool Strikes Deal to Boost Chinese Market Share," *Wall Street Journal*, March 20, 2012, B7.
38. Gaurav Raghuvanshi and Eric Bellman, "Wal-Mart Tiptoes into India's Marketplace," *Globe and Mail*, February 21, 2010, B13.
39. Loretta Chao, "Groupon Shutters Offices as Chinese Venture Stumbles," *Globe and Mail*, August 24, 2011, B11.
40. John J. Wild, Kenneth L. Wild, and Jerry C.Y. Han, *International Business: An Integrated Approach* (Upper Saddle River, NJ:

Prentice Hall, 2000), Chapter 7; Ricky W. Griffin and Michael W. Pustay, *International Business: A Managerial Perspective*, 2nd ed. (Reading, MA: Addison-Wesley, 1999), 436–439.

41. Ross Marowits, "Bombardier Looking to Morocco for Production," *Globe and Mail*, May 7, 2011, B8; Bombardier Website, http://www.bombardier.ca/en/corporate/media-centre/press-releases/details?docID=0901260d8029499b [accessed April 14, 2013].
42. Grant Robertson, "A Once-Cautious Bank Takes a Bold Leap South," *Globe and Mail*, August 20, 2011, B6–B7.
43. Dawn Calleja, "Foreign Investment: Opportunity + Danger," *Globe and Mail*, March 28, 2013, B6.
44. Based on Canada's Biggest Companies by Revenues, Globe and Mail, 2012.
45. Anita Elash, "French Lingerie Firm's Pretty Babies Prompt Calls to Let Girls be Girls, *Globe and Mail*, August 19, 2011, A3.
46. Marcus Gee, "Green Hats and Other Ways to Blow a Deal in China," *Globe and Mail*, August 27, 2007, B1.
47. Elizabeth Holmes, "The Return of the Luxe Life," *Globe and Mail*, May 4, 2011, B17.
48. Marina Strauss, "Retailers Warn of Price Hikes as Ottawa Boosts Tariffs," *Globe and Mail*, March 23, 2013, B1–B5.
49. "WTO Strikes Down U.S. Cotton Subsidy Appeal," *Globe and Mail*, March 4, 2005, B10.
50. Scott Kilman and Roger Thurow, "To Soothe Anger over Subsidies, U.S. Cotton Tries Wooing Africa," *Wall Street Journal*, August 5, 2005, A1, A6.
51. Simon Tuck, "Farmers to WTO: If It Ain't Broke ...," *Globe and Mail*, August 9, 2004, B1–B2.
52. Barrie McKenna, "In a Bureaucratic Box: Cardboard, Cheetos and the Canadian Border," *Globe and Mail*, January 10, 2013, B1–B4.
53. Ronald Ebert and Ricky Griffin, *Business Essentials*, 7th edition (Upper Saddle River, NJ: Prentice Hall, 2009).
54. Iain Marlow, "Public Mobile Wants Top Court to Weigh In on Foreign Ownership," *Globe and Mail*, June 10, 2011, B3.
55. Richard Blackwell, "Free Trade Abroad but Not at Home?" *Globe and Mail*, April 25, 2013, B4.
56. Gary McWilliams, "Wal-Mart Era Wanes amid Big Shifts in Retail," *Wall Street Journal*, October 3, 2007, A1, A17.
57. Brian Womack and Sara Forden, "Google to Pay $500 Million in Settlement Over Online Drug Ads," *Globe and Mail*, August 25, 2011, B1.
58. Christopher Curtis, "SNC-Lavalin Paid $160-Million in Libyan Bribes, RCMP Says," *Montreal Gazette*, March 6, 2013.
59. Nicholas Bray, "OECD Ministers Agree to Ban Bribery as Means for Companies to Win Business," *Wall Street Journal*, May 27, 1997, A2.
60. Transparency International Website, http://www.transparency.org/cpi2012/results [accessed April 14, 2013].
61. Toby Heaps, "Potash Politics," *Corporate Knights*, Winter 2009, 19–23.
62. Canadian Press, "China Decries U.S. Duties on Steel Pipes," *Globe and Mail*, January 1, 2010, B4.
63. Peter Wonacott, "Downturn Heightens China–India Tension on Trade," *Wall Street Journal*, March 20, 2009, A8.
64. Peter Wonacott, "Downturn Heightens China–India Tension on Trade," *Wall Street Journal*, March 20, 2009, A8.
65. "New Global Trade Regulator Starts Operations Tomorrow," *Winnipeg Free Press*, December 31, 1994, A5.
66. Barrie McKenna, "Boeing's WTO Win May Prove a Hollow Victory," *Globe and Mail*, September 5, 2009, B5.
67. Barrie McKenna, "Aspiring WTO Head Warns Organization Risks Irrelevancy," *Globe and Mail*, March 28, 2013, B12.
68. Europa website, http://europa.eu/index_en.htm [accessed March 23, 2010].
69. Bruce Little, "Free-Trade Pact Gets Mixed Reviews," *Globe and Mail*, June 7, 2004, B3.
70. Rachel Pulfer, "NAFTA's Third Amigo," *Canadian Business*, June 15, 2009, 27.
71. Barrie McKenna, "Putting Canada-Mexico Trade in High Gear," *Globe and Mail*, June 16, 2011, B12.

CHAPTER 6

1. Chris Knight, "McDonald's New Recipe for Success; The Golden Arches Has Fought Its Way Back, Not with the Burger, but with Coffee, Snack Wraps, and a Restaurant Facelift," *National Post*, September 5, 2009, FP1.
2. "McDonald's Canada Plans $1B Store Overhaul," *Reuters*, September 7, 2011, www.bnn.ca/News/2011/9/7.
3. "Maple Leaf Rolls Out New Five-Year Plan; Goal Is to Simplify; Part of Strategy is to Cut Product Portfolio by 60%," *National Post*, October 7, 2010, FP6.
4. Peter Burrows, "The Hottest Property in the Valley?" *Business Week*, August 30, 1999, 69–74.
5. Ben Worthen, "CEO Whitman Tells H-Ps Workers 'Everything is on Table' in Overhaul," *Wall Street Journal*, March 22, 2012, B7; "Hewlett Packard Reorganizes under Onslaught from Mobile Devices," *National Post*, March 21, 2012, FP6.
6. Henry Mintzberg, *The Nature of Managerial Work*. New York: Harper and Row, 1973.
7. Alex Taylor III, "How a Top Boss Manages His Day," *Fortune*, June 19, 1989, 95–100.
8. Dan Ovsey, "Will Anyone Repair the C-Suite Brand?" *National Post*, March 13, 2012, FP7.
9. Roma Luciw, "No. 1 Employee Not Always Your No. 1 Manager," *Globe and Mail*, February 17, 2007, B10.
10. Adam Bryant, "Quest to Build a Better Boss; Google Looks at What Makes a Good Manager," *National Post*, March 16, 2011, FP12.
11. "Hands-On from the Top Down; ING Direct," *National Post*, February 3, 2012, JV3.
12. The experiences of these and other bosses are depicted in the CBS television series *Undercover Boss*, which premiered in 2010. CEOs work with entry-level employees (who don't know they are working with the CEO). The program summarizes the lessons the CEOs learned. In 2012, a Canadian edition began on the W network. Another series, the "Big Switcheroo" on CBC, portrays situations where bosses trade jobs with lower-level workers.
13. Jason Buckland, "Canada's 10 Highest Paid CEOs," www.money.ca.msn.com/savings [accessed April 20, 2012].
14. Rick Spence, "As a Leader, Are You a Cop or a Coach? Top Secret Meet Reveals Great Coaches Are Rare," *National Post*, July 21, 2009, FP11.
15. Jerry Useem, "Boeing vs. Boeing," *Fortune*, October 2, 2000, 148–160; "Airbus Prepares to 'Bet the Company' as It Builds a Huge New Jet," *Wall Street Journal*, November 3, 1999, A1, A10.

16. "Office Politics Seen as Key to Advancing," *Globe and Mail*, March 2, 2012, B15.

17. Charles P. Wallace, "Adidas—Back in the Game," *Fortune*, August 18, 1997, 176–182.

18. Barry M. Staw and Jerry Ross, "Good Money after Bad," *Psychology Today*, February 1988, 30–33.

19. Gerry McNamara and Philip Bromiley, "Risk and Return in Organizational Decision Making," *Academy of Management Journal, Vol. 42* (1999), 330–339.

20. Brian O'Reilly, "What It Takes to Start a Startup," *Fortune*, June 7, 1999, 135–140.

21. Greg Keenan, "Toyota Canada's New Head Lays Out Recovery Plan," *Globe and Mail*, January 9, 2012, B1.

22. Brent Jang, "WestJet Sets Sights on Air Canada's Title," *Globe and Mail*, January 2, 2012, B1.

23. Nick Rockel, "Keeping the Containers Moving," *Globe and Mail*, November 15, 2011, B15.

24. Sue Shellenbarger, "Making Kids Work on Goals (And Not Just Soccer)," *Wall Street Journal*, March 9, 2011, D1.

25. "Sony CEO Wields Ax, Sets Turnaround Targets," *BNN*, April 12, 2012.

26. Joanna Pachner, "A Perfect Predator," *Canadian Business*, July 20–August 16, 2010, 51.

27. Sinclair Stewart and Derek DeCloet, "It's Mr. Focus v. Mr. Diversification," *Globe and Mail*, June 3, 2006, B4.

28. Martin Mittelstaedt, "A Conflicting Moment for Kodak," *Globe and Mail*, May 24, 2011, B13.

29. Michael Porter, *Competitive Strategy: Techniques for Analyzing Industries and Competitors* (New York: The Free Press, 1980).

30. Bertrand Marotte, "Gildan Takes T-Shirt Making to the Cutting-Edge of Casual Apparel," *Globe and Mail*, July 3, 2004, B3.

31. Steve Ladurantaye, "Maple Leaf Battered by Meat Recall Costs," *Globe and Mail*, October 30, 2008, B3.

32. Kristine Owram, "Maple Leaf Claims 'Progress' After Recall," *Globe and Mail*, February 25, 2009, B5.

33. "Hands-On from the Top Down; ING DIRECT," *National Post*, February 3, 2012, JV3.

34. Chrystia Freeland, "Americans Struggle to Adjust to New Culture of 'No'," *Globe and Mail*, November 26, 2010, B2.

35. Ric Dolphin, "Magna Force," *Canadian Business*, May, 1988.

36. Isadore Sharp, "Quality for All Seasons," *Canadian Business Review*, Spring, 1990, 21–23.

37. Derek Sankey, "Cult-Like Culture Is Key," *Financial Post*, July 28, 2008, www.nationalpost.com/story-printer.html?id=684225.

38. "Canada's 10 Most Admired Corporate Cultures of 2011 Announced Today," Waterstone Human Capital, www.waterstonehc.com/news-events/news.

39. Calvin Leung, "Culture Club," *Canadian Business*, October 9-22, 2006, 115.

40. "Golden Rule Is Measure of Success: 10 Most Admired Corporate Cultures," *National Post*, December 3, 2008, FP16; Calvin Leung, "Culture Club," *Canadian Business*, October 9–22, 2006, 115, 116, 118, 120.

41. Meagan Fitzpatrick, "RCMP 'Horribly Broken,' Need Fix Quickly: Report," *Winnipeg Free Press*, June 16, 2007, A9.

CHAPTER 7

1. Tim Kiladze and Iain Marlow, "RIM Shakeup Gets Chilly Welcome," *Globe and Mail*, January 24, 2012, B1.

2. John A. Wagner and John R. Hollenbeck, *Management of Organizational Behavior* (Englewood Cliffs, NJ: Prentice Hall, 1992), 563–565.

3. Jay Diamond and Gerald Pintel, *Retailing*, 6th ed. (Upper Saddle River, NJ: Prentice Hall, 1996), 83–84.

4. "Lowe's Restructures Its Store and Merchandising Organizations," *National Post*, August 30, 2011, FP5.

5. "Lowe's Restructures Its Store and Merchandising Organizations," *National Post*, August 30, 2011, FP5.

6. "Nike Redefines Its Regions amid Spending Pullback," *Globe and Mail*, March 21, 2009, B7.

7. Roger Martin, "Don't Ask, Don't Tell," *Globe and Mail*, July 22, 2012, A15.

8. Interview with Jamie Brown, CEO of Frantic Films.

9. Tom Randall, "Kindler Quits as Pfizer CEO before Special Meeting; Veterans to Take Over; Executives Frustrated with Management Style, Source Says," *National Post*, December 7, 2010, FP2.

10. Rick Spence, "It Pays to Flatten the Pyramid; Eschewing Old Hierarchies Can Foster Innovation," *National Post*, June 6, 2011, FP4.

11. Michael E. Raynor and Joseph L. Bower, "Lead from the Center," *Harvard Business Review*, May 2001, 93–102.

12. Bruce Horovitz, "Restoring the Golden-Arch Shine," *USA Today*, June 16, 1999, 3B.

13. *Hoover's Handbook of American Business 2006* (Austin: Hoover's Business Press, 2006); Brian Dumaine, "How I Delivered the Goods," *Fortune Small Business*, October, 2002.

14. Lee Hawkins, "Reversing 80 Years of History, GM Is Reining in Global Fiefs," *Wall Street Journal*, October 6, 2004, A1.

15. Donna Fenn, "The Buyers," *Inc.* (June 1996): 46–48+.

16. Mitchell Osak, "Customers Always Know Best; Customer Innovation Centres are Designed to Break Down Organizational and Functional Silos," *National Post*, September 7, 2010, FP5.

17. Interviews with Jamie Brown, CEO of Frantic Films.

18. Nelson Wyatt, "Bell Canada Plan Creates 3 Divisions," *The Winnipeg Free Press*, May 8, 2003, B7.

19. "Yahoo Adopts New Structure in Search for Revival Following Layoffs," *National Post*, April 11, 2012, FP5.

20. J. Galbraith, "Matrix Organization Designs: How to Combine Functional and Project Forms," *Business Horizons*, 1971, 29–40; H.F. Kolodny, "Evolution to a Matrix Organization," *Academy of Management Review* 4 (1979), 543–553.

21. Interview with Tom Ward, operations manager for Genstar Shipyards.

22. Diane Brady, "Martha Inc.," *BusinessWeek*, January 17, 2000, 62–66.

23. Miguel Helft, "Yahoo Chief Rearranges Managers Once Again," *New York Times*, February 27, 2009, B5.

24. Gail Edmondson, "Danone Hits Its Stride," *BusinessWeek*, February 1, 1999, 52–53.

25. Thomas A. Stewart, "See Jack. See Jack Run," *Fortune*, September 27, 1999, 124–127.

26. Wallace Immen, "The Power of Teamwork," *Globe and Mail*, October 15, 2010, B15.

27. James P. Sterba, "At the Met Opera, It's Not Over Till the Fat Man Folds," *Wall Street Journal*, January, 1998, 1, 6.

28. Jerald Greenberg and Robert A. Baron, *Behavior in Organizations: Understanding and Managing the Human*

Side of Work, 7th ed. (Upper Saddle River, NJ: Prentice Hall, 2000), 308–309.

29. Tyler Hamilton, "Welcome to the World Wide Grapevine," *Globe and Mail*, May 6, 2000, B1, B6.

CHAPTER 8

1. See Angelo S. DeNisi and Ricky W. Griffin, *Human Resource Management* (Boston: Houghton Mifflin, 2001) for a complete overview.
2. Grant Robertson, "Changing of the Guard," *Globe and Mail*, March 17, 2010, B1.
3. Patrick Brethour and Heather Scoffield, "Plenty of Work, Not Enough Bodies," *Globe and Mail*, August 21, 2006, B4.
4. Barrie McKenna, Labour Shortage Becoming 'Desperate'," *Globe and Mail*, February 8, 2012, B3; see also John Shmuel, "Labour Pains," *National Post*, February 14, 2011, FP1; see also Tavia Grant, "People Without Jobs, Jobs Without People," *Globe and Mail*, November 30, 2012, B2.
5. Todd Hirsch, "Labour Crunch Isn't What It's Cracked Up To Be," *Globe and Mail*, February 28, 2013, B2.
6. Elizabeth Church, "Store Owners Struggle with Staffing," *Globe and Mail*, November 25, 1996, B6.
7. Wallace Immen, "The Rise of the Virtual Job Fair," *Globe and Mail*, April 13, 2011, B16.
8. Diane Jermyn, "Internships Lead to Life-Changing Jobs," *Globe and Mail*, March 14, 2012, B16.
9. Christine Dobby, "Intern Nation," *National Post*, June 11, 2011, FP7.
10. Lauren Weber, "Your Resume vs. Oblivion," *Wall Street Journal*, January 24, 2012, B1.
11. Rachel Silverman, "No More Resumes, Say Some Firms," *Wall Street Journal*, January 24, 2012, B6.
12. Wallace Immen, "Prospective Hires Put to the Test," *Globe and Mail*, January 26, 2005, C1, C2.
13. Wallace Immen, "Prospective Hires Put to the Test," *Globe and Mail*, January 26, 2005, C1, C2.
14. Katie Rook, "Curveball Job Questions: How Not to Strike Out," *Globe and Mail*, September 3, 2005, B9.
15. Ogilvy Renault website, www.ogilvyrenault.com/en/; Emily Sternberg, Anouk Violette, William Hlibchuk, "Drug and Alcohol Testing by Employers in Canada—A Legal Issues Pulse-Check," May 28, 2008 [accessed July 2, 2010]; Canadian Human Rights Commission Policy on Alcohol and Drug Testing, June 2002, 1–16.
16. David Hutton, "Job Reference Chill Grows Icier," *Globe and Mail*, June 18, 2008, B1.
17. Kira Vermond, "Rolling Out the Welcome Mat," *Globe and Mail*, April 26, 2008, B19.
18. Wallace Immen, "Half of Workers Don't Fit In," *Globe and Mail*, October 22, 2008, C2.
19. Tony Wanless, "Picking Employees like a Matchmaker," *National Post*, December 27, 2011, FP8.
20. Bertrand Marotte, "From the Cockpit to the OR: CAE's Diversification," *Globe and Mail*, May 25, 2010, B3.
21. Jacqueline Nelson and Kasey Coholan, "Leaders in Leadership," *Canadian Business*, November 8, 2010, 61.
22. Wallace Immen, "Rookie Managers Left to Sink or Swim," *Globe and Mail*, April 2, 2011, B17.
23. Fiona MacFarlane, "Key to C-Suite May Just be a Hero; Male Sponsors Help Women Attain Executive Jobs," *National Post*, November 30, 2011, FP8; see also Mary Bitti, "From Mentors to Sponsors; Promoting Women," *National Post*, September 27, 2011, FP10.
24. Tavia Grant, "Weekend Workout: Reverse Mentoring," *Globe and Mail*, July 11, 2009, B14.
25. Eagle's Flight, http://www.eaglesflight.com [accessed July 23, 2013].
26. Kira Vermond, "Taking a Full-Circle Look at Work Reviews," *Globe and Mail*, November 24, 2007, B18.
27. Iain Marlow, Fixing the Dreaded Performance Review," *Globe and Mail*, July 15, 2011, B13.
28. Rachel Silverman, "Work Reviews Losing Steam," *Wall Street Journal*, December 19, 2011, B7.
29. Hugh Mackenzie, "Canada's CEO Elite 100," *Canadian Centre for Policy Alternatives*, January 2012.
30. Hugh Mackenzie, "Canada's CEO Elite 100," *Canadian Centre for Policy Alternatives*, January 2012.
31. Highest Paid CEOs, www.ca.finance.yahoo.com/news/highest-paid-ceos-174613134.
32. Boyd Erman, "Shareholders Win Voice on CEO Pay at 3 Big Banks," *Globe and Mail*, February 27, 2009, B1.
33. Joann Lublin, "Say on the Boss's Pay," *Wall Street Journal*, March 7, 2008, B1–B2.
34. Statistics Canada, www.statcan.gc.ca [accessed July 23, 2013].
35. "Plenty of Canadian Companies Offer Incentives but Few Track Their Effectiveness," *National Post*, November 10, 2010, FP14.
36. Andrew Willis, "Record Bonus Pool Building at Canada's Banks," *Globe and Mail*, June 2, 2010, B11.
37. Cathryn Atkinson, "The Total Package: Anatomy of a Great Place to Work," *Globe and Mail*, July 2, 2008, B6.
38. Jennifer Myers, "The Right Way to Reward," *Globe and Mail*, April 3, 2010, B13.
39. Canada's Economic Action Plan, http://actionplan.gc.ca/initiatives/eng/index.asp?mode=2&initiativeID=329.
40. J. Budak, "The Dark Side of Maternity Leave," *Canadian Business*, Vol. 84, 28–31.
41. Virginia Galt, "Companies, Unions, Expect Little Relief," *Globe and Mail*, September 15, 2004, B4.
42. Virginia Galt, "Gift of Time Pays off for Savvy Employers," *Globe and Mail*, December 28, 2004, B3.
43. Virginia Galt, "Gift of Time Pays off for Savvy Employers," *Globe and Mail*, December 28, 2004, B3.
44. Kamal Dib, "Diversity Works," *Canadian Business*, March 29, 2004, 53–54.
45. Catalyst website, www.catalyst.org/publication/ [accessed July 1, 2010].
46. Richard Blackwell and Brent Jang, "Top Court Sides with Airline Attendants," *Globe and Mail*, January 27, 2006, B1, B6.
47. Jennifer Peltz, "Fired NY Banker's Suit, and Suits, Raise Eyebrows," *Globe and Mail*, June 29, 2010, B5.
48. Bess Levin, "Citi Would Like to Make It Clear It Did Not Pay Debrahlee Lorenzana a Dime," http://dealbreaker.com/2012/05 [accessed July 24, 2013].
49. Brent Jang, "Air Canada Plans to End Forced Retirement at 60," *Globe and Mail*, January 28, 2012, B8.
50. CBC website, "Mandatory Retirement Fades in Canada," www.cbc.ca/canada/story/2009/08/20/mandatory-retirement-explainer523.html, August 20, 2009 [accessed July 1, 2010].
51. Omar El Akkad, "A Woman's Work May Never Be Done," *Globe and Mail*, March 28, 2006, B1, B4.

52. Michael Moss, "For Older Employees, On-the-Job Injuries Are More Often Deadly," *Wall Street Journal*, June 17, 1997, A1, A10.
53. Jill Mahoney, "Visible Majority by 2017," *Globe and Mail*, March 23, 2005, A1, A7.
54. Virginia Galt, "P & G Leverages Its Cultural Diversity," *Globe and Mail*, April 7, 2005, B1, B5.
55. Virginia Galt, "Western Union Remakes 'Canadian' Image," *Globe and Mail*, November 23, 2004, B1, B24.
56. "Commitment to Diversity," *National Post*, February 3, 2012, JV10.
57. Max Boisot, *Knowledge Assets* (Oxford: Oxford University Press, 1998).
58. Statistics Canada, www.statcan.ca.
59. Tavia Grant, "Financial Crisis Sparks More Demand for Temps at the Top," *Globe and Mail*, November 14, 2008, B16.
60. Citizenship and Immigration Canada website, www.cic.gc.ca/english/work/index.asp [accessed July 1, 2010].
61. Aaron Bernstein, "When Is a Temp Not a Temp?" *BusinessWeek*, December 7, 1998, 90–92.
62. David Lipsky and Clifford Donn, *Collective Bargaining in American Industry* (Lexington, MA: Lexington Books, 1981).
63. Statistics Canada, www.statcan.gc.ca/pub/75-001 [accessed May 3, 2012] (see Table 1); Melanie Trottman and Kris Maher, "Organized Labor Loses Members," *Wall Street Journal*, January 24, 2013, A6; UFCW Canada, www.ufcw.ca/index [accessed May 3, 2012].
64. Statistics Canada, www.statcan.gc.ca/pub/75001 [accessed May 3, 2012].
65. Statistics Canada, www.statcan.gc.ca/pub/75001 [accessed May 3, 2012].
66. Greg Keenan, "CAW Rewriting Playbook to Keep Factories Running," *Globe and Mail*, September 5, 2006, B3.
67. Jeff Gray, "Rocky Times Loom for Labour," *Globe and Mail*, January 7, 2012, B6.
68. Tony Van Alphen, "CAW working on Biggest Union Merger Ever," thestar.com, www.thestar.com/news/article/1103016 [accessed May 3, 2012].
69. Virginia Galt, "Worn-Out Middle Managers May Get Protection," *Globe and Mail*, January 3, 2005, B1, B8.
70. Greg Keenan, "CAW Seeks to Recoup Lost Membership," *Globe and Mail*, January 9, 2013, B5.
71. Marina Strauss, "Holt Workers Reject Creation of Union," *Globe and Mail*, June 30, 2012, B8; also Marina Strauss, "Loblaw Asian Chain in Labour Dispute," *Globe and Mail*, July 24, 2012, B6.
72. Paul McKie, "Goldcorp Workers Accept Offer, Dismantle Union," *Winnipeg Free Press*, April 22, 2000, A6.
73. "Tembec Ends Three-Month Strike," *National Post*, August 19, 2011, FP4.
74. Brent Jang, "Labour Board Calls Air Canada Stoppages Illegal," *Globe and Mail*, April 14, 2012, B7.
75. Brent Jang, "Rejected Deal Imposed on Air Canada Attendants," *Globe and Mail*, November 8, 2011, B9.
76. "Rio Tinto Alcan in Tentative Pact with Locked-Out Workers at Its Quebec Smelter," *National Post*, July 3, 2012, FP3.
77. Simon Houpt, "Canadian Press Asks for Conciliator," *Globe and Mail*, January 19, 2012, B10.
78. Scott Deveau, "Air Canada, Pilots Agree to Mediation," *National Post*, February 16, 2012, FP4.
79. Brent Jang, "Air Canada Moves to Appeal Arbitrator's Pension Ruling," *Globe and Mail*, October 24, 2011, B3.

CHAPTER 9

1. "Time is Money: 1 in 5 Canadians Late for Work at Least Once a Week," *National Post*, February 24, 2011, FP5.
2. "Bosses: Killing Them with Kindness Pays Off," *Globe and Mail*, October 8, 2008, C3.
3. Daniel Goleman, *Emotional Intelligence: Why It Can Matter More Than IQ* (New York: Bantam Books, 1995); Kenneth Law, Chi-Sum Wong, and Lynda Song, "The Construct and Criterion Validity of Emotional Intelligence and Its Potential Utility for Management Studies," *Journal of Applied Psychology* 89 no. 3 (2004): 78–90.
4. Daniel Goleman, "Leadership That Gets Results," *Harvard Business Review,* March–April 2000, 78–90.
5. Wallace Immen, "Emotional Smarts Sway Hiring Choices," *Globe and Mail*, August 24, 2011, B17.
6. "Half of Canadians Love Their Jobs," *Globe and Mail*, February 17, 2010, B20.
7. "Canadians Ranked No. 3 in Satisfaction with Their Current Employer," *National Post*, April 14, 2010, FP5.
8. Doris Burke, Corey Hajim, John Elliott, Jenny Mero, and Christopher Tkaczyk, "The Top Ten Companies for Leaders," *Fortune*, October 1, 2007, http://money.cnn.com/galleries/2007/fortune/0709/gallery.leaders_global_topten.fortune/index.html [accessed July 24, 2013].
9. Barbara Moses, "A Cruise with the Boss? A Box of Timbits? Time to Get Serious about Rewarding Employees," *Globe and Mail*, April 28, 2010, B16.
10. Frederick W. Taylor, *The Principles of Scientific Management* (New York: Harper and Brothers, 1911).
11. See Daniel Wren, *The History of Management Thought*, 5th ed. (New York: John Wiley & Sons, 2004).
12. Douglas McGregor, *The Human Side of Enterprise* (New York: McGraw-Hill, 1960).
13. Abraham Maslow, "A Theory of Human Motivation," *Psychological Review* (July 1943): 370–396.
14. Frederick Herzberg, Bernard Mausner, and Barbara Bloch Snydeman, *The Motivation to Work* (New York: Wiley, 1959).
15. Victor Vroom, *Work and Motivation* (New York: Wiley, 1964); Craig Pinder, *Work Motivation* (Glenview, IL: Scott, Foresman, 1984).
16. J. Stacy Adams, "Toward an Understanding of Inequity," *Journal of Abnormal and Social Psychology, Vol. 75*, Issue 5 (1963), 422–436.
17. Jeff Buckstein, "In Praise of Praise in the Workplace," *Globe and Mail*, June 15, 2005, C1, C5.
18. Deena Waisberg, "Tip of the Hat to Excellence; Employers get Creative with Rewards to Keep Top Performers," *National Post*, November 19, 2008, FP15.
19. For more information on some of the potential problems with goal setting, see Drake Bennett, "Do Goals Undermine Good Management?" *National Post*, March 24, 2009, FP10; Wallace Immen, "The Goal: To Set Goals That Really Can Be Met," *Globe and Mail*, March 20, 2009, B12.
20. Interviews with Sterling McLeod and Wayne Walker, senior vice-presidents of sales for Investors Group Financial Services.
21. Tavia Grant, "Workplace Democracy," *Globe and Mail*, May 30, 2009, B14.
22. Harvey Schachter, "Managing Without Managers," *Globe and Mail*, December 19, 2011, B5.

23. Brent Jang, "High-Flying WestJet Morale Gets Put to the Test," *Globe and Mail*, November 25, 2005, B3.

24. Virginia Galt, "Change Is a Good Thing When Everyone Is Involved," *Globe and Mail*, June 25, 2005, B11.

25. Tavia Grant, "Workplace Democracy," *Globe and Mail*, May 30, 2009, B14.

26. Robert Grant, "AES Corporation: Rewriting the Rules of Management," *Contemporary Strategy Analysis* (Hoboken, NJ: John Wiley & Sons, 2007), www.blackwellpublishing.com/grant/docs/17AES.pdf.

27. Patricia Kitchen, "Tap Your Employees," *Orlando Sentinel*, March 14, 2007, F1.

28. Mary Teresa Bitti, "The Power of Teamwork," *National Post*, December 18, 2009, FP12.

29. Tom Peters, *Liberation Management* (New York: Alfred Knopf, 1992), 238–239.

30. Charles Snow, Scott Snell, Sue Canney Davison, and Donald Hambrick, "Use Transnational Teams to Globalize Your Company," *Organizational Dynamics*, Spring 1996, 61.

31. Gregory Moorhead and Ricky W. Griffin, *Organizational Behavior*, 6th ed. (Boston: Houghton Mifflin, 2001), Chapter 7.

32. For a discussion of team effectiveness, see Nancy Langton and Stephen Robbins, *Organizational Behaviour*, 4th Canadian ed. (Toronto: Pearson Canada, 2006), 217–230.

33. Gregory Moorhead and Ricky W. Griffin, *Organizational Behavior*, 6th ed. (Boston: Houghton Mifflin, 2001), Chapter 7.

34. A.B. Drexler and R. Forrester, "Teamwork—Not Necessarily the Answer," *HR Magazine*, January 1998, 55–58.

35. Gregory Moorhead and Ricky W. Griffin, *Organizational Behavior*, 6th ed. (Boston: Houghton Mifflin, 2001), Chapter 7.

36. Ricky Griffin, *Task Design* (Glenview, IL: Scott, Foresman, 1982).

37. Richard J. Hackman and Greg Oldham, *Work Redesign* (Reading, MA: Addison-Wesley, 1980).

38. "Canadian Businesses World Leaders in Offering Work-From-Home Options," *National Post*, March 16, 2011, FP12.

39. Wallace Immen, "Most Firms Offer Flexible Work," *Globe and Mail*, July 2, 2011, B11.

40. Diane Jermyn, "Canada's Best Places to Work," *Globe and Mail*, October 7, 2011, E10; Gail Johnson, "Companies Who Cut the Cost of Education," *Globe and Mail*, December 8, 2011, B11.

41. Mary Gooderham, "Better Mom Becomes Better Manager," *Globe and Mail*, October 15, 2010, E6.

42. Diane Jermyn, "Canada's Best Places to Work," *Globe and Mail*, October 7, 2011, E10; Diane Jermyn, "Keeping Veteran Talent as Key Contributors," *Globe and Mail*, June 7, 2011, B14; Diane Jermyn, "The GTA's Top Employers for 2012," *Globe and Mail*, November 16, 2011, E4.

43. Mary Gooderham, "Where It's Not All About the Money," *Globe and Mail*, November 22, 2010, E2.

44. Jameson Berkow, "Workers of the World DISPERSE; Anything, Anywhere; Mobile Workers are Taking the Office With them in Greater Numbers," *National Post*, June 20, 2011, FP1.

45. "Looking Good in Green," *Maclean's*, May 9, 2011, 47.

46. Jameson Berkow, "Workers of the World DISPERSE; Anything, Anywhere; Mobile Workers are Taking the Office With them in Greater Numbers," *National Post*, June 20, 2011, FP1.

47. Joyce Rosenberg, "Out of Sight, On Your Mind: Learning to Trust Telecommuters," *Globe and Mail*, September 20, 2008, B19.

48. For example, Richard Branson, the founder of Virgin Group PLC, said that forcing workers to come to the office was a bad idea, but the mayor of New York City called telecommuting a dumb idea. An editorial in the *National Post* noted that both supporters and opponents of telecommuting actually have very little evidence on which to base their views. What is needed is systematic research to determine when telecommuting is effective and when it is not. See Omar El Akkad, "Branson Blasts Mayer's Telework Stand," *Globe and Mail*, March 6, 2013, B7; Omar El Akkad, "Telework or Teamwork? The Office Evolves," *Globe and Mail*, February 27, 2013, B1; "Yahoo right on Work; Past Management Allowed Inappropriate Telecommuting," *National Post*, March 6, 2013, FP11.

49. Rachel Silverman and Quentin Fottrell, "The Home Office in the Spotlight," *Wall Street Journal*, February 24, 2013, B6.

50. Diane Jermyn, "The 10 Best to Work for," *Globe and Mail*, September 30, 2010, B2; Cam Cole, "Flyers' Goalie Carousel is Norm; Job Sharing in Post-Season More Prevalent," *National Post*, June 1, 2010, B9.

51. John Kotter, "What Leaders Really Do," *Harvard Business Review*, December 2001: 85–94.

52. Copyright 2012 Pearson Canada Inc., Toronto, Ontario.

53. Ronald Heifetz and Marty Linsky, "A Survival Guide for Leaders," *Harvard Business Review*, June 2002: 65–74.

54. Frederick Reichheld, "Lead for Loyalty," *Harvard Business Review*, July–August, 2001: 76–83.

55. S.A. Kirkpatrick and E.A. Locke, "Leadership: Do Traits Matter?" *Academy of Management Executive*, May 1991: 48–60.

56. Daniel Goleman, "What Makes a Leader?" *Harvard Business Review*, November–December 1998: 93–99.

57. David Dorsey, "Andy Pearson Finds Love," *Fast Company*, August 2001, 78–86.

58. David A. Waldman and Francis J. Yammarino, "CEO Charismatic Leadership: Levels-of-Management and Levels-of-Analysis Effects," *Academy of Management Review*, Vol. 24 (1999), 266–285.

59. Ronald Ebert and Ricky Griffin, *Business Essentials*, 7th ed. (Upper Saddle River, NJ: Prentice Hall, 2009), 129.

60. Jane Howell and Boas Shamir, "The Role of Followers in the Charismatic Leadership Process: Relationships and Their Consequences," *Academy of Management Review*, January 2005, 96–112.

61. J. Richard Hackman and Ruth Wageman, "A Theory of Team Coaching," *Academy of Management Review*, April 2005: 269–287.

62. "How Women Lead," *Newsweek*, October 24, 2005, 46–70.

63. Madelaine Drohan, "What Makes a Canadian Manager?" *Globe and Mail*, February 25, 1997, B18.

64. Rebecca Walberg, "Canada's Management Dividend," *National Post*, November 17, 2009, FP14.

65. Sinclair Stewart, "Passed By at TD, CEO Hits Stride in New York," *Globe and Mail*, December 5, 2006, B1, B21; Zena Olijnyk, Mark Brown, Any Holloway, Calvin Leung, Alex Mlynek, Erin Pooley, Jeff Sanford, Andrew Wahl, and Thomas Watson, "Canada's Global Leaders," *Canadian Business*, March 8–April 10, 2005, 37–43.

66. Bryan Borzykowski, "Collaborating With a Far-Flung Team," *Globe and Mail*, January 18, 2012, B7.

CHAPTER 10

1. Neil Reynolds, "Technology Spurring a New Manufacturing Revolution," *Globe and Mail*, May 9, 2012, B2.
2. John Shinal, "3-D Printers Wave Their Magic Wands," *USA Today*, March 21, 2013, B1.
3. Susan Carey, "Airlines Lose the Winter Blahs," *Wall Street Journal*, February 29, 2012, B1.
4. Terry Hill, *Manufacturing Strategy*, 3rd edition (Boston: Irwin McGraw-Hill, 2000), Chapter 2–4; James A. Fitzsimmons, Mona J. Fitzsimmons, *Service Management: Operations Strategy, Information Technology*, 6th edition (Boston: Irwin McGraw-Hill, 2008), 46–48.
5. Susan Carey, "The Case of the Vanishing Airport Lines," *Wall Street Journal*, August 9, 2007, B1.
6. Christina Passariello, "Louis Vuitton Tries Modern Methods on Factory Lines," *Wall Street Journal*, October 9, 2006, A1, A15.
7. John Letzing, "Amazon Adds That Robotic Touch," *Wall Street Journal*, March 20, 2012, B1.
8. Rita Trichur, "Down on the Farm with Robo-Milker," *Globe and Mail*, March 17, 2011, B4.
9. Timothy Hay, "The Robots are Coming to Hospitals," *Wall Street Journal*, March 15, 2012, B12.
10. Neal Boudette, "Chrysler Gains Edge by Giving New Flexibility to Its Factories," *Wall Street Journal*, April 11, 2006, A1, A15.
11. Greg Keenan, "Ford's New Maxim: Flex Manufacturing," *Globe and Mail*, May 10, 2006, B3.
12. Lou Michel, "WNY's Trash, China's Treasure," *Buffalo News*, July 20, 2008.
13. Don Marshall, "Time for Just in Time," *PIM Review*, June 1991: 20–22; Gregg Stocker, "Quality Function Deployment: Listening to the Voice of the Customer," *APICS: The Performance Advantage*, September 1991, 44–48.
14. Lee J. Krajewski and Larry P. Ritzman, *Operations Management: Strategy and Analysis*, 6th ed. (Upper Saddle River, NJ: Prentice Hall, 2002), 153–154, 828–829; Robert S. Russell and Bernard W. Taylor III, *Operations Management*, 4th ed. (Upper Saddle River, NJ: Prentice Hall, 2003), 221–222, 593–595.
15. Robert S. Russell and Bernard W. Taylor III, *Operations Management*, 4th ed. (Upper Saddle River, NJ: Prentice Hall, 2003), 222–224.
16. "The Disney Institute," April 25, 2000, www.disney.go.com/DisneyWorld/DisneyInstitute/ProfessionalPrograms/DisneyDifference/index.html.
17. Marina Strauss, "Low Fills/High Stakes," *Globe and Mail*, May 12, 2010, B1.
18. Julian Beltrame, "Canada's Productivity on the Rise," *Globe and Mail*, March 14, 2012, B4.
19. Bart VanArk and Robert McGuckin, "International Comparisons of Labor Productivity and Per Capita Income," *Monthly Labor Review*, July 1999, 33–41.
20. Harvey Enchin, "Canada Urged to Stop Living Off Fat of the Land," *Globe and Mail*, October 25, 1991, B1, B6.
21. Barrie McKenna and Tavia Grant, "Canada's Productivity Trap," *Globe and Mail*, September 15, 2010, B1.
22. Alexandra Lopez-Pacheco, "Service Sector on Cusp of a Tech Revolution; Key Job Creator," *National Post*, November 16, 2010, FP14.
23. Jon Hilsenrath, "Behind Surging Productivity: The Service Sector Delivers," *Wall Street Journal*, November 7, 2003, A1, A8.
24. Peter Kennedy, "Canfor Goes High Tech to Cut Costs," *Globe and Mail*, July 29, 2000, 3.
25. Rachel Silverman, "Tracking Sensors Invade the Workplace," *Wall Street Journal*, March 7, 2013, B1.
26. Lee J. Krajewski and Larry P. Ritzman, *Operations Management: Strategy and Analysis*, 5th ed. (Reading, MA: Addison-Wesley, 1999), 229–230.
27. Bruce McDougall, "The Thinking Man's Assembly Line," *Canadian Business*, November 1991, 40.
28. Ted Wakefield, "No Pain, No Gain," *Canadian Business*, January 1993, 50–54.
29. Scott McCartney, "Ranking Airlines by Lost Bags, Canceled Flights," *Wall Street Journal*, January 5, 2012, D3.
30. Thomas Foster Jr., *Managing Quality: An Integrative Approach* (Upper Saddle River, NJ: Prentice Hall, 2001), 325–339.
31. Thomas Foster Jr., *Managing Quality: An Integrative Approach* (Upper Saddle River, NJ: Prentice Hall, 2001), 325–329.
32. James Evans and James Dean Jr., *Total Quality: Management, Organization, and Strategy*, 2nd ed. (Cincinnati, OH: South-Western, 2000), 230.
33. Margot Gibb-Clark, "Hospital Managers Gain Tool to Compare Notes," *Globe and Mail*, September 9, 1996, B9.
34. "Quality Customer Care," *National Post*, February 3, 2012, JV6.
35. Roberta S. Russell and Bernard W. Taylor III, *Operations Management,* 4th ed. (Upper Saddle River, NJ: Prentice Hall, 2003), 137–140.
36. Del Jones, "Baldrige Award Honors Record 7 Quality Winners," *USA Today*, November 26, 2003, B6.
37. Sunil Chopra and Peter Meindl, *Supply Chain Management: Strategy, Planning, and Operation*, 6th ed. (Upper Saddle River, NJ: Prentice Hall, 2001), 3–6; Lee J. Krajewski and Larry P. Ritzman, *Operations Management: Strategy and Analysis,* 5th ed. (Reading, MA: Addison-Wesley, 1999), Chapter 11; Roberta S. Russell and Bernard W. Taylor III, *Operations Management*, 4th ed. (Upper Saddle River, NJ: Prentice Hall, 2003), Chapter 7; Thomas Foster Jr., *Managing Quality: An Integrative Approach* (Upper Saddle River, NJ: Prentice Hall, 2001), Chapter 9.
38. Sunil Chopra and Peter Meindl, *Supply Chain Management: Strategy, Planning, and Operation*, 6th ed. (Upper Saddle River, NJ: Prentice Hall, 2001), Chapter 20.
39. Nick Rockel, "Keeping the Containers Moving," *Globe and Mail*, November 15, 2011, B15.
40. Joseph Sternberg, "Now Comes the Global Revolution in Services," *Wall Street Journal*, February 10, 2011, A17.

CHAPTER 11

1. Ronald Hilton, *Managerial Accounting*, 2nd ed. (New York: McGraw-Hill, 1994), 7.
2. David Milstead, "Accounting Issues Raise Big Red Flag Over Reborn GM," *Globe and Mail*, November 27, 2010, B12.
3. Tim Leech, "Mend our SOX; It Cost Billions, but Hasn't Made Statements More Reliable," *National Post*, October 19, 2011, FP15.
4. Chartered Accountants of Canada Website, http://www.cica.ca/about-cica/index.aspx [accessed March 22, 2013].
5. Based on The Bottom Line, April 2013 Issue, "Canada's Top 30 Accounting Firms".

6. CGAWebsite, http://www.cga-canada.org/en-ca/AboutCGACanada/Pages/AboutCGA-Canada.aspx [accessed March 22, 2013].
7. Certified Management Accountants of Canada website, www.cma-canada.org [accessed March 22, 2013].
8. The CICA Website, http://www.cica.ca/about-cica-and-the-profession/about-cpa-canada/index.aspx [accessed March 22, 2013].
9. Hollie Shaw, "Accounting's Big Bang Moment: Switch from GAAP," *National Post*, September 24, 2009, FP1.
10. Virginia Galt, "It's Crunch Time as Accounting Changes Loom," *Globe and Mail*, June 17, 2010, B10.
11. Al Rosen, "Cooking with IFRS," *Canadian Business*, July 20, 2009, 12.
12. Evolution of THE IFRS Foundation, http://www.ifrs.org/The-organisation/Documents/Who-We-Are-English-2013.pdf [accessed March 22, 2013].
13. David Milstead, "A Close Inspection of Shoppers' Revenue Accounting," *Globe and Mail*, May 17, 2010, B8.
14. Charles T. Horngren, Walter T. Harrison Jr., and Linda Smith Bamber, *Accounting*, 5th ed. (Upper Saddle River, NJ: Prentice Hall, 2002), 11–12, 39–41.
15. Charles T. Horngren, Walter T. Harrison Jr., and Linda Smith Bamber, *Accounting*, 5th ed. (Upper Saddle River, NJ: Prentice Hall, 2002), 17–20.
16. Billie Cunningham, Loren Nikolai, and John Bazley. *Accounting: Information for Business Decisions* (Fort Worth, TX: Dryden, 2000), 133–134.
17. Charles T. Horngren, Walter T. Harrison Jr., and Linda Smith Bamber, *Accounting*, 4th ed. (Upper Saddle River, NJ: Prentice Hall, 1999), 201–202.
18. *AICPA Website,* "Code of Professional Conduct," http://www.aicpa.org/research/standards/codeofconduct/pages/default.aspx.

SUPPLEMENT 4

1. "World's Fastest Internet," *Backbone Magazine*, November-December, 2012, 8.
2. CBC News Website, "Canadians No Longer the Biggest Web Addict, Report Shows," March 4, 2013 [accessed June 12, 2013].
3. Omar El Akkad, "Canadian Internet Usage Grows," *Globe and Mail*, May 11, 2010, B9.
4. Ian Marlow and Jacquie McNish, "Canada's Digital Divide," *Globe and Mail*, April 3, 2010, B1, B4.
5. Philip Kotler, Gary Armstrong, and Peggy H. Cunningham, *Principles of Marketing*, 6th Canadian ed. (Toronto: Pearson, 2005), 88.
6. Mike Lazaridis, "Because Someone Had to Stand Up for All Those Frustrated Engineers," Inc., April 2005, 98; "BlackBerry Subscribers Surge to over Three Million," May 9, 2005, www.blackberry.com/news/press/2005/pr-09_05_2005-01.shtml.
7. Michael Oliviera, "Canadian Retailers Lag Rivals in Online Selling," *Globe and Mail*, November 1, 2012, B1.
8. "Northrop Grumman Awards International Contracts for F-35 Joint Strike Fighter," Northrop Grumman News Release, September 29, 2005, www.irconnect.com/noc/pages/news_printer.html?=86963&print=1; Faith Keenan and Spencer E. Ante, "The New Teamwork," BusinessWeekOnline, February 18, 2002.
9. Laura Northrup, "Timbuk2 Really, Really Wants You to Be Happy with Their Bags," *Consumerist*, June 5,2009, at www.consumerist.com/5280357/timbuk2_really-really-wants-you-to-be. Emily Walzer, "Have It Your Way," *SGB, Vol. 38*, Issue 1 (January 2005), 42.
10. Google Annual Report, http://investor.google.com/pdf/2012_google_annual_report.pdf, 77 [accessed June 12, 2013]; David Milstead, "A Rocket, a Meteor—Or a One Trick Pony?" *Globe and Mail*, January, 29, 2010, B9.
11. Boyd Erman, "Online Brokerage Muscles In on the Road Show," *Globe and Mail*, March 29, 2010, B5.
12. 3D Systems, "3D Systems Helps Walter Reed Army Medical Center Rebuild Lives," July 6, 2005, www.3dsystems.com.
13. 3D Systems, "3D Systems Helps Walter Reed Army Medical Center Rebuild Lives," www.3dsystems.com/appsolutions/casestudies/walter_reed.asp; also Hannah Hickey, "Camera in a Pill Offers Cheaper, Easier Window on Your Insides," UWNews.org, January 24, 2008, http://uwnews.org/article.asp?articleid=39292.
14. "The Internet is Saving You Money," *Backbone Magazine*, March–April 2013, 8.
15. David LaGesse, "How to Turn Social Networking into a Job Offer," U.S. News & World Report, May 11, 2009, www.usnews.com/articles/business/careers/2009/05/11/how-to.
16. "ABN AMRO Mortgage Group Offers One Fee to Ford Motor Company Employees," *Mortgage Mag*, February 14, 2005, www.mortgagemag.com/n/502_003.htm; also "An Intranet's Life Cycle," morebusiness.com, June 16, 1999, www.morebusiness.com/getting_started/website/d928247851.brc.
17. Figure IT.2 is a modified version of diagrams on the BlackBerry website, Research In Motion Ltd., technical images, www.blackberry.com/images/technical/bes_exchange_arthitecture.gif.
18. Guy Dixon and Bert Archer, "Wifi in the Sky: Airlines Seek Web-based Revenue," *Globe and Mail*, June 7, 2013, B3.
19. Gayle Balfour, "The Wisdom of the Cloud," *Backbone Magazine*, May 2009, 16–20; SalesForce.com website, www.salesforce.com/cloudcomputing/ [accessed July 7, 2010].
20. Danny Bradbury, "Flying Cloudless," *Backbone Magazine*, December 2012, P26–30.
21. Nick Rockel, "Why Canada Lags in Cloud Computing," *Globe and Mail*, February 9, 2012, B4.
22. Jonathan Stoller, "It's Cool to Be Cold," *Globe and Mail*, December 20, 2012, B4.
23. IBM Website, http://www-01.ibm.com/software/data/bigdata/ [accessed June 12, 2103].
24. Gartner Website, http://www.gartner.com/it-glossary/big-data/ [accessed June 12, 2103].
25. Marina Strauss, "In Store Aisles, Dr. Dre Meets Big Data," *Globe and Mail*, March 5, 2013.
26. IT World, "How Has Big Data Demonstrated a Shift from Data Mining?" http://www.itworld.com/answers/topic/business-intelligence/question/how-has-big-data-demonstrated-shift-data-mining [accessed June 12th, 2103].
27. Kenneth C. Laudon and Jane P. Laudon, *Essentials of Management Information Systems*, 3rd ed. (Upper Saddle River, NJ: Prentice Hall, 1999), 383–388; E. Wainwright Martin, et al., *Managing Information Technology: What Managers Need to Know*, 3rd ed. (Upper Saddle River, NJ: Prentice-Hall, 1999), 225–227.

28. Phuong Tram, "Facebook and Privacy Invasions," Imprint Online, June 15, 2008, http://imprint.uwaterloo.ca/index.php?option=com_content&task=view&id=2570&Itemid=57; also Jacqui Cheng, "Canadian Group: Facebook a Minefield of Privacy Invasion," May 30, 2008, http://arstechnica.com/tech-policy/news/2008/05/canadian-group-files-complaint-over-facebook-privacy.ars; also "Cell Phones a Much Bigger Privacy Risk than Facebook," Fox News, February 20, 2009, www.foxnews.com/printer_friendly_story/0,3566,497544,00.html.

29. Danny Bradbury, "Predicting 2010," *Backbone Magazine*, March 2010, 23.

30. "Fraud Prevention," *Globe and Mail*, March 29, 2010, FP1.

31. Treasury Board of Canada Secretariat.

32. Siobhan Gorman, "The Cold War Goes Digital—and Corporate," *Globe and Mail*, January 14, 2010, B7.

33. Webopedia, www.webopedia.com/TERM/S/spyware.html.

CHAPTER 12

1. American Marketing Association, "Marketing Definitions" (December 1, 2010), at http://www.marketingpower.com.

2. Philip Kotler and Gary Armstrong, *Principles of Marketing*, 12th ed. (Upper Saddle River, NJ: Prentice Hall, 2008), 7.

3. "CRM (customer relationship management)," http://TechTarget.com [accessed December 8, 2010] at http://search-crm.techtarget.com/definition/CRM; "Customer Relationship Management," Wikipedia [accessed December 8, 2010] at http://en.wikipedia.org/wiki/Customer_relationship_management.

4. Poonam Khanna, "Hotel Chain Gets Personal with Customers," *Computing Canada*, April 8, 2005, 18.

5. "Fairmont Hotels & Resorts: Website Development and Enhanced CRM," *Accenture* [accessed December 8, 2010] at http://www.accenture.com/Global/Services/By_Industry/Travel/Client_Successes/FairmontCrm.htm.

6. Chris Umiastowski, "A Healthier Diet Can Nourish Your Portfolio," *Globe and Mail*, March 19, 2013, B15.

7. Shawn McCarthy and Greg Keenan, "Ottawa Demands Lower Auto Worker Costs," *Globe and Mail*, January 19, 2009, at http://v1business.theglobeandmail.com/servlet/story/RTGAM.20090119.wrautos19/BNStory/Business; McClatchy Newspapers, "Lemons into Lemonade," *Columbia Daily Tribune*, February 2, 2009, 7B.

8. Greg Keenan, "BMW Canada Seeks Top Luxury Spot," *Globe and Mail*, June 15, 2009, B5.

9. Marina Strauss, "Canadian Tire Targets the Price Sensitive," *Globe and Mail*, May 15, 2009, B4.

10. Eric Reguly, "Hard Time: Makers of Luxury Watches Clock a Slow Return to Sales Health," *Globe and Mail*, February 2, 2010, B1.

11. Steve Schifferes, "The Triumph of Lean Production," *BBC News*, February 27, 2007, at http://news.bbc.co.uk/2/hi/business/6346315stm.

12. Chris Isadore, "Sweet Spot: Luxury SUV's Are Hot," CNN/Money, www.cnnmoney.com, January 7, 2004.

13. Rasha Moutarda, "Gerontologists Go Beyond the Numbers," *Globe and Mail*, February 19, 2010, B9.

14. Aparita Bhandari, "Ethnic Marketing—It's More than Skin Deep," *Globe and Mail*, September 7, 2005, B3.

15. Canadian Media Directors Council, Media Digest, 2012, Ethnic Media, 16 (Toronto: Marketing, 2012), 84, http://www.yellowhouseevents.com/img/CMDC_images/CMDC_Digital_Ed_2012.pdf.

16. Marina Strauss, "Wal-Mart Expansion Eats Into Grocer Growth," *Globe and Mail*, April 25, 2013, B5; Bertrand Marotte, "Metro Forges into Ethnic Food Market with Stake in Adonis," *Globe and Mail*, October 27, 2011, B8.

17. "Financial Cards in Poland," *Euromonitor International*, (May 2008), at http://www.euromonitor.com/Consumer_Finance_in_Poland.

18. Tamara Audi, "Las Vegas Goes All Out to Attract Gay Travelers," *Wall Street Journal*, November 2, 2007, B1.

19. Philip Kotler, Gary Armstrong, Peggy Cunningham, *Principle of Marketing*, 7th edition, Pearson Education, 2008, 289–290.

20. Lauren Goldstein, "Dressing up an Old Brand," *Fortune*, November 9, 1998, 154–156.

21. Matt Phillips, "Pow! Romance! Comics Court Girls," *Wall Street Journal*, June 8, 2007, B1.

22. John Morton, "How to Spot the Really Important Prospects," *Business Marketing*, January 1990, 62–67.

23. Marina Strauss, "You, in the Yoga Pants, Metro Is Watching You," *Globe and Mail*, November 19, 2009, B1.

24. Susan Berfield, "Getting the Most Out of Every Shopper," *BusinessWeek*, February 9, 2009, 45.

25. Joseph Pereira, "Spying on the Sales Floor," *Wall Street Journal*, December 21, 2004, B1, B4.

26. Julie Jargon, "Kiwi Goes Beyond Shine in Effort to Step Up Sales," *Wall Street Journal*, December 20, 2007, B1.

27. Deborah Ball, Sarah Ellison, and Janet Adamy, "Probing Shoppers' Psyche," *Wall Street Journal*, October 28, 2004, B1, 8.

28. Peter Morton, "Marketing at Face Value," *National Post*, July 11, 2007, FP3

29. Emily Nelson, "P&G Checks Out Real Life," *Wall Street Journal*, May 17, 2001, B1, B4.

30. "2008 Brand Keys Customer Loyalty Engagement Index," (March 18, 2008) at http://www.brandkeys.com/awards/cli08.cfm.

31. AutoNorth website, "Toyota Canada Offers Free Scheduled Maintenance on All Models," January 6, 2010, www.autonorth.ca [accessed April 19, 2010].

32. Ibid.

33. Global News, Joel Eastwood, "New Database Will Allow Canadians To Track Government Spending," April 22, 2013, http://globalnews.ca/news/502224/new-database-will-allow-canadians-to-track-government-spending-data/ [accessed May 24, 2013].

34. Ben Austen, "Rock N' Roll Will Never Die," *Bloomberg Businessweek*, January 23–29, 2012, 74.

35. Ron Winslow, "Cholesterol Drug Advances," *Wall Street Journal*, November 18, 2010, B1–2.

36. "At P&G, The Innovation Well Runs Dry," *Bloomberg Businessweek*, September 10–16, 2012, 23-25.

37. Jeff Beer, "Oreo's Chinese Twist," *Canadian Business*, December 10, 2012, 66–67.

38. "BP's Brand Value Sinks with Oil Spill," *Columbia Daily Tribune*, September 16, 2010, accessed at http://www.columbiatribune.com/news/2010/sep/16/bps-brand-value-sinks-with-oil-spill/.

39. Millward Brown website, http://www.millwardbrown.com/BrandZ/Top_100_Global_Brands.aspx [accessed May 27, 2013].

40. Country Brand Index: 2013, http://www.futurebrand.com/images/uploads/studies/cbi/CBI_2012-Final.pdf [accessed May 27, 2013].

41. "Kellogg to Swallow P&G's Pringles for $2.7- Billion," *Globe and Mail*, February 16, 2012, B1.

42. Susan Krashinsky, "For Canada Goose, Sports Illustrated Swimsuit Edition is a Golden Egg," *Globe and Mail*, February 14, 2013, B3.

43. Judy Strauss, Adel El-Ansary, and Raymond Frost, *E-Marketing*, 5th ed. (Upper Saddle River, NJ: Prentice Hall, 2007); "Ten Corporate Blogs Worth Reading," February 19, 2009, at http://www.blogtrepreneuer.com/2009/02/19/ten-corporate-blogs-worth-reading/.

44. Marina Strauss, "Shoppers Sees Gold in Private Labels," *Globe and Mail*, January 3, 2005, B1–B2.

45. Courtland Bovee, John V. Thill, and George Dracopoulos, *Business in Action*, 2nd ed. (Don Mills, ON: Pearson Education, 2008), 332.

46. Marina Strauss, "(Re)Making a Name in No Name," *Globe and Mail*, March 21, 2009, B3.

47. Catherine McLean, "Why Canadian Brands Lose their Accents Abroad," *Globe and Mail*, January, 12, 2012, B11.

48. Cyndee Miller, "Little Relief Seen for New Product Failure Rate," *Marketing News*, June 21, 1993, 1; Nancy J. Kim, "Back to the Drawing Board," *The Bergen [New Jersey] Record*, December 4, 1994, B1, B4.

49. MSN website, Steve Mertl, "Buick LaCrosse's French Slang Meaning Latest Example of Pitfalls of Car Names," http://autos.ca.msn.com/news/canadian-press-automotive-news/article.aspxcp-documentid=22011666 [accessed April 25, 2010].

50. Susan Krashinsky, "A Top-Shelf Transformation," *Globe and Mail*, May 9, 2013, B4.

51. Deborah Ball, "The Perils of Packaging: Nestle Aims for Easier Openings," *Wall Street Journal*, November 17, 2005, B1, B5.

52. Stuart Elliott, "Tropicana Discovers Some Buyers Are Passionate about Packaging," *Wall Street Journal*, February 22, 2009.

CHAPTER 13

1. Greg Keenan, "Toyota's Discounts Ignite New Car War," *Globe and Mail*, March 4, 2010, B3.

2. "About Carbonite," at http://www.carbonite.com/en/about/company/our-story.

3. "Reverse Auction," *Encyclopedia of Management*, 2009, Encyclopedia.com. (January 16, 2011). http://www.encyclopedia.com/doc/1G2-3273100254.html; MediaBids.com, at http://www.mediabids.com/.

4. Coca-Cola Website, http://www.coca-colacompany.com/investors/ [accessed June 1, 2013].

5. Canadian Media Directors Council, *Media Digest, 2012-2013*, Net Advertising Volume by Medium, P13 (Toronto: Marketing, 2012), 8.

6. Canadian Media Directors Council, *Media Digest, 2012-2013*, Net Advertising Volume by Medium, P13 (Toronto: Marketing, 2012), 8.

7. Susan Krashinsky, "Papers Step Up in the Battle for Eyeballs," *Globe and Mail*, April 29, 2011, B8.

8. Canadian Media Directors Council, *Media Digest, 2011–2012*, Net Advertising Volume by Medium, P13 (Toronto: Marketing, 2013), 15; Susan Krashinsky, "Reports of TV's Death Greatly Exaggerated," *Globe and Mail*, April 13, 2010, B1.

9. Canadian Media Directors Council, *Media Digest, 2012-2013*, Net Advertising Volume by Medium, P13 (Toronto: Marketing, 2013), 8.

10. Alex Konrad, "Even With Record Prices, Expect a $10 Million Super Bowl Ad Soon," *Forbes*, February 2, 2013.

11. Susan Krashinsky, "Why Most Super Bowl Ads Get Stopped at the Border," *Globe and Mail*, February 3, 2012, B8.

12. Marina Strauss, "Super Bowl Clobbers the Grey Cup," *Globe and Mail*, January 26, 2008, B3.

13. Ronald Grover, "American Idol's Ads Infinitum," *Businessweek*, May 28, 2008, 38–39.

14. Canadian Media Directors Council, *Media Digest, 2012-2013*, Net Advertising Volume by Medium, P13 (Toronto: Marketing, 2013), 8.

15. Canadian Media Directors Council, *Media Digest, 2012-2013*, Net Advertising Volume by Medium, P13 (Toronto: Marketing, 2013), 8.

16. Canadian Media Directors Council, *Media Digest, 2012-2013*, Net Advertising Volume by Medium, P13 (Toronto: Marketing, 2013), 8.

17. Steve Ladurantaye, "Canadian Magazine Sales Slip in 2nd Half Of 2011," *Globe and Mail*, February 8, 2012, B11.

18. Canadian Media Directors Council, *Media Digest, 2012-2013*, Net Advertising Volume by Medium, P13 (Toronto: Marketing, 2013), 8.

19. "30 Second Spot: Dispatches from the World of Media and Advertising," *Globe and Mail*, October 31, 2008, B8.

20. Jason Magder, "iGotcha Grabs Attention," *Montreal Gazette*, October 3, 2011, A18.

21. Aaron O. Patrick, "Technology Boosts Outdoor Ads as Competition Becomes Fiercer," *Wall Street Journal*, August 23, 2006, A1, A10; Grant Robertson, "Growth in Internet Ads Outpaces All Others," *Globe and Mail*, June 23, 2006, B4; Canadian Media Directors Council, Media Digest, 2009–2010, Net Advertising Volume by Medium, P13 (Toronto: Marketing, 2009), 28, www.cmdc.ca/pdf/Media_Digest_2009.pdf.

22. Mike Blaney, "Word of Mouth Advertising," blog, www.themarketingguy.wordpress.com/2007/10/09/word-of-mouth-advertising.

23. Simon Houpt, "Tell a Friend: Companies Flock to Word-of-Mouth Marketing," *Globe and Mail*, April 16, 2010, B6.

24. Canadian Media Directors Council, *Media Digest, 2011–2012*, Net Advertising Volume by Medium, P13 (Toronto: Marketing, 2012), 12.

25. Susan Krashinski, "Advertisers Channel YouTube," *Globe and Mail*, March 29, 2013, B5.

26. Simon Houpt, "Super Bowl Marketers Are Changing Their Game," *Globe and Mail*, February 5, 2010, B5.

27. Susan Krashinsky, "TV Twitter Connection Takes Flight," *Globe and Mail*, April 26, 2013, B5.

28. P. Kotler, G. Armstrong, and P. Cunningham, *Principles of Marketing*, 6th Canadian ed. (Toronto: Pearson, 2005), 89–91.

29. Susan Krashinsky, "The Next Hot Marketer? You," *Globe and Mail*, February 8, 2013, B6.

30. Ronald Ebert and Ricky Griffin, *Business Essentials* (Upper Saddle River, NJ: Prentice Hall, 2009), 161.

31. Canadian Media Directors Council, *Media Digest, 2009–2010*, Internet and Mobile Media, P74 (Toronto: Marketing, 2009), 40, www.cmdc.ca/pdf/Media_Digest_2009.pdf.

32. Omar El Akkad, "Why Facebook Paid $1 Billion for Instagram," *Globe and Mail*, April 10, 2012, B18.

33. Sam Grobart, "Mobile Ads Are the Future, They're Also Lousy," *Bloomberg BusinessWeek*, November 5–11, 2012, P42.

34. Canadian Media Directors Council, *Media Digest, 2009–2010*, In-Game Advertising, P76 (Toronto: Marketing, 2009), 40, www.cmdc.ca/pdf/Media_Digest_2009.pdf.

35. Jeff Green, "The New Willy Loman Survives by Staying Home," *Bloomberg Business Week*, January 14–20, 2013, P17.

36. Simon Avery, "Do Not Call List Could Give Boost to Direct Mail," *Globe and Mail*, September 29, 2008, B3.

37. Hollie Shaw, "Do Not Call List a Ringing Success," *National Post*, March 13, 2009, FP12.

38. John Heinzl, "Beer Firms Rethink Giveaways," *Globe and Mail*, March 3, 2003, B1, B5.

39. Duncan Hood, "McDonald's Gets Shockingly Honest. I'm Lovin' It," *Canadian Business*, October 29, 2012, P4.

40. Bertrand Marotte, "Contraband Killing Convenience Stores," *Globe and Mail*, April 7, 2010, B9.

41. "Vending Machines: A Global Strategic Business Report," CompaniesAndMarkets.com: Market Report, September 1, 2010, at http://www.companiesandmarkets.com/Market-Report/vending-machines-a-global-strategic-business-report-companiesandmarkets.com.

42. AVON 2009 Annual Report, at http://phx.corporate-ir.net/phoenix.zhtml?c=90402&p=irol-irhome.

43. YAHOO! FINANCE, January 16, 2011, at http://finance.yahoo.com/q/is?annual&s=amzn.

44. "Marina Strauss, "Wal-Mart's Endless Aisle,'" *Globe and Mail*, December 5, 2011, B1.

45. Vito Pilieci, "Taxman Eyes Internet Sellers," *Winnipeg Free Press*, November 18, 2008, B5.

46. Bertrand Marotte, "Reeling in Fresh Customers," *Globe and Mail*, April 20, 2010, B3.

47. David Milstead, "Coke Gets Back into the Bottling Business," *Globe and Mail*, February 26, 2010, B10.

48. Michael Muchmore, "The Best Online Backup Services," *PC Magazine*, October 28, 2010, at http://www.pcmag.com/article2/0,2817,2288745.asp.

49. Mark Brown, "Target Becomes the Targeted," *Canadian Business*, April 29, 2013, 13–14.

CHAPTER 14

1. Steve Mertl, "Durability of Canada's Plastic Money Being Questioned," http://ca.news.yahoo.com/blogs/dailybrew/durability-canada-plastic-currency-questioned-201813438.html [accessed May 22, 2012].

2. Bank of Canada Banking and Financial Statistics, Series E1, Selected Monetary Aggregates, Dec 2012, S52.

3. RCMP Website, http://www.rcmp-grc.gc.ca/count-contre/cur-mon-2011-eng.htm [accessed May 12, 2012].

4. CBC News Website, "Is Canada's New $20 Bill Too 'Pornographic'? [accessed May 12, 2012].

5. *Bank of Canada Banking and Financial Statistics*, Series E1, Selected Monetary Aggregates, April 2009, S50.

6. Martin Hutchinson and Christopher Swann, "Dollars Flowing Fast, But Inflation Stands Pat," *Globe and Mail*, March 19, 2012, B9.

7. Tara Perkins, "Card Payment Players Clash over Code," *Globe and Mail*, January 18, 2010, B5.

8. Canadian Bankers Association, Credit Card Statistics, http://www.cba.ca/contents/files/statistics/stat_cc_db038_en.pdf [accessed May 12, 2012].

9. Boyd Erman, "Visa's IPO Taps into the World's Love of Plastic," *Globe and Mail*, February 26, 2008, B1, B6.

10. Canadian Bankers Association, Credit Card Statistics, http://www.cba.ca/contents/files/statistics/stat_cc_db038_en.pdf [accessed May 12, 2012].

11. Chris Sorensen, "Credit Card Tricks," *Maclean's*, July 11, 2011, P63.

12. *Bank of Canada Banking and Financial Statistics*, Series C1, Chartered Bank Assets, January 2013, S18.

13. Derek DeCloet, "As Canadian as... Banking?" *Canadian Business*, December 2011, 20.

14. Financial Post, Top 500 Rankings, http://www.financialpost.com/news/fp500/2011/index.html [accessed April 28, 2013].

15. Grant Robertson, "CIBC Joins Big Banks Profit Parade," *Globe and Mail*, March 9, 2012, B5.

16. Canadian Banker's Association Website, "The ABM Market in Canada," http://www.cba.ca/en/media-room/50-backgrounders-on-banking-issues/118-abm-market-in-canada [accessed January 18, 2013].

17. Tara Perkins and Grant Robertson, "The Bank Machine with a Personal Touch," *Globe and Mail*, June 3, 2010, B5.

18. Canadian Bankers Association, Debit Card Statistics, http://www.cba.ca/en/media-room/50-backgrounders-on-banking-issues/616-canadas-efficient-and-secure-payments-system [accessed May 15th, 2012].

19. "Statistics for Smart Cards," ePaynews.com, June 14, 2004, www.epaynews.com/statistics/scardstats.html.

20. Grant Robertson and Rita Trichur, "Banks Plot Mobile Payment Future," *Globe and Mail*, May 14, 2012, B1.

21. Rita Trichur and Grant Robertson, "CIBC, Rogers Launch Digital Wallet," *Globe and Mail*, May 16, 2012, B7.

22. "Mobile Wallets," *Globe and Mail*, November 8, 2012, MC3.

23. Grant Robertson and Tim Kaladze, "Banks Warn Volcker Rule Could Violate NAFTA," *Globe and Mail*, January 20, 2012, A1, B4.

24. Marina Strauss, "Need a Mortgage with Those Tools?" *Globe and Mail*, February 6, 2010, A1, A9.

25. CBC News Website, "Mortgage Rules to be Tightened Further by Ottawa," June 20, 2012, [accessed January 25th, 2013].

26. Tara Perkins, "They'll Even Plan Your Funeral," *Globe and Mail*, September 29, 2007, B4–B6.

27. Tara Perkins, "A Piece of Drywall Away from Being Part of the Branch," *Globe and Mail*, April 26, 2008, B6.

28. Business News Network website, "Ottawa Bans Insurance Sales on Bank Websites," May 27, 2010, www.bnn.ca/news/17916.html [accessed July 10, 2010].

29. William Robson, "Why Interest Rates Must Rise," *Canadian Business*, October 29, 2012, P30.

30. Barrie McKenna, "Envoy's Loonie Remarks Spark Krona Controversy," *Globe and Mail*, March 3, 2012, B5.

31. CTV News, http://www.ctvnews.ca/canada/mark-carney-named-bank-of-england-governor-1.1053945#ixzz2IekqZCH4 [accessed January 20, 2012].

32. Special Feature on Cooperatives, "A Force in the Canadian Banking System," *Globe and Mail*, May 15, 2012, CO 2.

33. Credit Union-Caisse Populaires, http://www.cucentral.ca/FactsFigures/top100-2Q12%2026-Sep-12.pdf, Septembre 2012 rankings.

34. Canadian Health Insurance Association website, https://www.clhia.ca/domino/html/clhia/clhia_lp4w_lnd_webstation.nsf/page/F85B39D8B2B428B185257824006528A4 [accessed May 23, 2012].

35. "Google VC Fund Looking for 'Young Companies with Awesome Potential,'" *National Post*, April 1, 2009, FP2.

36. Canada's Venture Capital and Private Equity Association website, http://www.cvca.ca/files/Resources/2011_VC_Data_Deck.pdf [accessed May 24, 2012].

37. David George-Cosh, "Lean Times for Tech Startups: VC's Offer Ideas on How to Kickstart the Industry," *National Post*, January 16, 2009, FP4; Stephen Hurwitz, "Misadventure Capitalism: A Byzantine Cross-Border Investment Regime Is Killing the Canadian Venture-Capital and Technology Industries," *National Post*, May 1, 2009, FP11.

38. "Air Canada Gets CAW Backing on Pension Request," *National Post*, October 25, 2012, B4.

39. Jeremy Torobin, "Dollar at Par: The New Normal," *Globe and Mail*, March 18, 2010, pp. B1, B6; Bank of Canada Website, http://www.bankofcanada.ca/cgi-bin/famecgi_fdps [accessed March 27, 2010].

40. LuAnn LaSalle, "Clearwater Eyes Productivity to Offset High Loonie," *Globe and Mail*, March 24, 2010, B1.

41. Gordon Pitts, "How Captain High Liner Beat the Dollar Odds," *Globe and Mail*, March 16, 2010, B1-B4.

42. *The Economist* website, Big Mac Index, May 23, 2012, http://www.economist.com/blogs/graphicdetail/2012/01/daily-chart-3 [accessed May 26, 2012.]

43. Robert J. Carbaugh, *International Economics*, 5th ed. (Cincinnati: South-Western, 1995), Chapter 11.

44. International Monetary Fund Website, http://www.imf.org/external/np/tre/activity/2012/010512.htm#tab1 [accessed May 23, 2012].

45. *EU Observer*, "IMF economists admit to 'errors' on austerity policy," http://euobserver.com/economic/118644 [accessed January 27, 2013].

46. Paul Bluestein, "The Inefficiency of International Financial Institutions," *Globe and Mail*, November 12, 2013. B4.

CHAPTER 15

1. Stefan Stern," The Rise of the Bean Counters," *National Post*, August 23, 2006, WK5.

2. Derek Sankey, "CFO Positions Demand Ever-Expanding Skill Set; Decision Makers," *National Post*, April 11, 2012, FP10.

3. Brent Jang, "CP Unveils Strategic Spending Plan," *Globe and Mail*, January 18, 2012, B9.

4. Hollie Shaw, "Walmart Canada to Invest $750 Million in Building Projects in 2012, *National Post*, February 8, 2012, FP4.

5. Barry Critchley, "Trading in Receivables," *National Post*, June 11, 2012, FP1.

6. Aaron Lucchetti, "As Housing Boomed, Moody's Opened Up," *Wall Street Journal*, April 11, 2008, A1, A15.

7. *Canadian Business*, Investor 500, Canada's Biggest Companies by Market Capitalization, 2012, 53.

8. Steve Ladurantaye, "Yellow Media Battles Debt Crunch," *Globe and Mail*, February 10, 2012, B1.

9. Virtual Brokers website, http://www.virtualbrokers.com/contents.aspx?page_id=2 [accessed June 1, 2012].

10. NASDAQ website, June 25, 2000, www.nasdaq.com/about/timeline.stm.

11. NASDAQ website, www.nasdaq.com [accessed May 29, 2010].

12. Richard Blackwell, "TSE 300 Shift Will Shrink Index," *Globe and Mail*, January 31, 2002, B17.

13. "Why Exchange-Traded Funds?" *Yahoo! Finance*, Exchange-Traded Funds Center, http://finance.yahoo.com/etf/education/02 [accessed June 1, 2012].

14. Janet McFarland, "OSC Rules Norshield Hedge Fund Misled Investors," *Globe and Mail*, March 9, 2010, B6.

15. Industry Canada website, www.ic.gc.ca [accessed May 31, 2010].

16. Norman M. Scarborough and Thomas W. Zimmerer, *Effective Small Business Management: An Entrepreneurial Approach*, 6th ed. (Upper Saddle River, NJ: Prentice Hall, 2000), 298–300.

17. Richard S. Boulton, Barry D. Libert, and Steve M. Samek, "Managing Risk in an Uncertain World," *Upside*, June 2000, 268–278.

18. Gordon Pitts and Bertrand Marotte, "Has Sabia Jumped from the Frying Pan into the Fire?" *Globe and Mail*, March 14, 2009, www.globeinvestor.com/servlet/story/GAM.20090314.RSABIA14/GIStory/.

19. Tara Perkins, "BMO Retreats to Its Low-Risk Roots," *Globe and Mail*, March 5, 2008, B5.

20. Joe Castaldo, "Bay Street Hurt by Talent Deficit," *Canadian Business*, December 9, 2009, 15.

21. Thomas P. Fitch, *Dictionary of Banking Terms*, 2nd ed. (Hauppauge, NY: Barron's, 1993), 531.

SUPPLEMENT 5

1. Mark S. Dorfman, *Introduction to Risk Management and Insurance*, 6th ed. (Upper Saddle River, NJ: Prentice Hall, 2000), Chapter 1.

2. Denyse O'Leary, "The Scams That Drive Up Premiums," *Globe and Mail*, May 2, 1995, B1; Denyse O'Leary, "Insurers United Against Fraud Face Serious Obstacles," *Globe and Mail*, May 2, 1995, B1.

3. Sinclair Stewart, "Sun Life's Insurance Policy: The Great Indian Middle Class," *Globe and Mail*, October 1, 2005, B1, B6.

4. Barbara Shecter, "Sun Life Limits Life Policies, Annuities; Poor Returns," *National Post*, December 13, 2011, FP1.

5. Yochi Dreazen, "As Iraq Terror Rises, Businessmen Find Niche in Life Insurance," *Wall Street Journal*, August 19, 2005, A1, A16.

6. Mark S. Dorfman, *Introduction to Risk Management and Insurance*, 6th ed. (Upper Saddle River, NJ: Prentice Hall, 2000), 420–421.

SOURCE NOTES

CHAPTER 1

The Mobile Phone Market: It's Competitive Out There!

Daisuke Wakabayashi, "Sony Stakes Recovery on New Smartphone," *Wall Street Journal*, March 2–3, 2013, B3; Ian Sherr, "Apple's $1 Billion Patent Award Cut," *Wall Street Journal*, March 2-3, 2013, B1; Will Connors, "Samsung Copies BlackBerry," *Wall Street Journal*, February 22, 2013, B5; Will Connors, Spencer Ante, and Thomas Gryta, "Finally a BlackBerry—But More Delays," *Wall Street Journal*, January 31, 2013, B1; C. Dobby and Anton Troianovski, "Huawei is now Third-Biggest Smartphone Seller," *Wall Street Journal*, January 28, 2013, B3; "RIM Speeds Up in Apps Race," *National Post*, January 23, 2013, FP1; "Samsung to Extend Lead in Phone Sales; 35 Percent Growth," *National Post*, January 5, 2013, FP13; Aries Poon, "Chief Plots HTC Comeback in 2013," *Wall Street Journal*, January 5-6, 2013, B3; Colum Murphy, "China's ZTE Targets iPhone," *Wall Street Journal*, December 29-30, 2012, B3; R. Vlastelica and P. Gupta, "Apple Shares Slide on Mobile Fears," *Globe and Mail*, December 6, 2012, B16; "Samsung Galaxy S3 Takes No. 1 Position in Smartphone Market," *National Post*, November 9, 2012, FP5; Omar El Akkad, "Samsung Smartphones Bite Apple," *Globe and Mail*, July 25, 2012, B1; Omar El Akkad, "Samsung Raises Stakes in Global Smartphone Battle," *Globe and Mail*, June 28, 2012, B1; Tarmo Virki, "Nokia to Cut 10,000 Jobs as Losses Widen; Shares Fall 16%; Q2 Cellphone Loss Larger Than Expected," *National Post*, June 15, 2012, FP6; Iain Marlow, "Samsung Claims Top Spot in Smartphone Shipments," *Globe and Mail*, April 28, 2012, B9; LuAnn LaSalle, "BlackBerry Maker Dialing Down?" *Winnipeg Free Press*, March 31, 2012, B4; Hui Neo, "Asian Mobile Giants Race to Catch Apple, Samsung; Rapid Smartphones," *National Post*, February 27, 2012, FP3; Christopher Lawton, "Nokia Takes Aim at High-End U.S. Market," *Wall Street Journal*, January 10, 2012, B5; Iain Marlow, "Trade Group Takes RIM to Court over BBM Name," *Globe and Mail*, December 23, 2011, B3; Iain Marlow, "RIM's Outlook Darkens with Delay of New Phone," *Globe and Mail*, December 16, 2011, B1; Iain Marlow, RIM Shares Hit Seven-Year Low," *Globe and Mail*, November 2, 2011, B3; Jameson Berkow, "Can Svelte Razr Recapture Sales for Motorola?; Aimed at Apple; Phonemaker Resurrects its Most Popular Brand," *National Post*, October 219, 2011, FP3; Carly Weeks, "The Dangers of a Smart Phone Free-for-All," *Globe and Mail*, September 1, 2011, B6; Iain Marlow, "Nokia Relinquishes Top Spot to Apple," *Globe and Mail*, July 22, 2011, B8; Henry Blodget, "RIM is Dead," *Canadian Business*, June 13, 2011, 30; Christopher Lawton and Amir Efrati, "Nokia's Latest Headache: Android," *Wall Street Journal*, June 2, 2011, B1; Eric Reguly, "New Crop of Rivals Hits Nokia Where It Hurts," *Globe and Mail*, June 1, 2011, B1; Christine Dobby, "RIM Market Share Plummets as Users Opt for Android Over BlackBerry," *National Post*, May 7, 2011, FP9; LuAnn LaSalle, "Consumers May Pass RIM Phones By, Analysts Say," *Winnipeg Free Press*, April 30, 2011, B10; Jacquie McNish, "Not a Great Week for RIM's Lazaridis," *Globe and Mail*, April 14, 2011, B8; David Berman, "RIM Can't Seem to Buy a Break," *Globe and Mail*, March 26, 2011, B7; "Android Dethrones BlackBerry as Top U.S. Smartphone Platform," *National Post*, March 8, 2011, FP6; Matt Hartley, "After Huge Profits, Jobs Trashes RIM; CEO's Rant Overshadows Technology Giant's Record Revenue and Earnings," *National Post*, October 19, 2010, FP1; LuAnn LaSalle, "BlackBerry's Out of Touch with Consumers: Analysts," *Winnipeg Free Press*, June 26, 2010, B8; "RIM Thumbs Its Way into the Top Five Mobile Handset Makers in First Quarter," *National Post*, May 1, 2010, FP5; "Research in Motion History," http://en.wikipedia.org/wiki/Research_In_Motion [accessed January 23, 2010]; "Timeline: The History of Research in Motion," http://forums.crackberry.com/f2/timeline-history-research-motion-7162/ [accessed January 23, 2010]; Grant Robertson, "Smart-Phone Application Scores Big," *Globe and Mail*, January 15, 2010, B4; "Android Mobile Phone a Challenge to Apple, RIM," *National Post*, December 15, 2009, FP5; Bob Willis, "Patent Lawsuit Against RIM Could See BlackBerry Ban in U.S. Market," *National Post*, December 4, 2009, FP4; "Klausner Technologies Sues Motorola, RIM Over Visual Voicemail Patents," *National Post*, November 24, 2009, FP5; "Nokia Plays Defence With Launch of New Gadget," *Globe and Mail*, August 25, 2009, B3.

Riversong: Innovative Canadian Guitars

Based on a case written by Christopher Ross, John Molson School of Business, Concordia University, Riversong Guitars, Vanier/BDC Case Competition 2013. "BDC's Young Entrepreneur Award Push Locals to Get Serious About Business, *Kelowna Capital News*, February 28, 2013; Danny Bradbury, "Lee's Music Puts Focus on Innovative Guitar Manufacturing with Riversong Guitars Venture," *Financial Post*, January 14, 2013.

The "China Effect" on Commodity Prices

Shirley Won, Why Demand for Palladium is Looking White Hot," *Globe and Mail*, March 7, 2011, B9; Carolyn Cui, "Chinese Cotton to Hoarding," *Wall Street Journal*, January 29-30, 2011, B1; Peter Koven, "Rare-Earth Share Bonanza; Increased Sharp as U.S. Seeks Secure Supply," *National Post*, October 19, 2010, FP4; Paul Waldie, "A Bigger Piece of the Pie: China's Appetite Drives Up Pecan Prices," *Globe and Mail*, October 19, 2010, B1.

Is Supply Management a Good Idea?

"Letters," *Canadian Business*, April 1, 2013, 8; Barrie McKenna, "Canada's Supply-Managed Stranglehold," *Globe and Mail*, March 23, 2013, B4; John Ivison, "Putting an End to Buy American; Trans-Pacific Talks a Chance to Slay Protectionism," *National Post*, March 4, 2013, A1; Graeme Hamilton, "Maple Syrup Cartel; Quebec's Syrup Monopoly Helped Spawn Smuggling, Prohibition Style," *National Post*, February 16, 2013, A6; Sophie Cousineau, "Trail of the Cross-Border Price Gap Leads to the Customs Department," *Globe and Mail*, February 9, 2013, B1; "Got Trade? A European Demand That We End Supply Management in Dairy and Poultry Would be a Blessing in Disguise," *National Post*, February 7, 2013, A12; Barrie McKenna, "Tough Tradeoffs are in the Cards for Canada-EU Free Trade," *Globe and Mail*, January 28, 2013, B1; Terence Corcoran, "Farm Stoppers," *National Post*, January 22, 2013, FP11; Ian Cumming, "Banned in Canada; Ontario Chobani Plant Still on Hold After a Year," *National Post*, January 9, 2013, FP11; Tim Shufelt, "The Great Canadian Maple Syrup Heist," *Canadian Business*, November 26, 2012, 52; Terence Corcoran, "Gerry Ritz's Soup Can Backdown," *National Post*, November 24, 2012, FP15; Andy Hoffman, "Japan's Entry Would Boost Trans-Pacific Trade Pact," *Globe and Mail*, November 12, 2013, B1; Kelly McParland, "More Holes Than Swiss Cheese in Smuggling Ring; Pizzerias Nabbed Sidestepping Dairy Tariffs," *National Post*, September 25, 2012, A6; Peter Foster, "War on Cheese," *National Post*, September 25, 2012, FP11; Paul Waldie, "OECD Praises End of Wheat Monopoly," *Globe and Mail*, September 2, 2012, A12.

CHAPTER 2

Evolving Models in Video Distribution: Netflix and Beyond

David Milstead, "Netflix Drama May Lack Happy Ending for Investors," *Globe and Mail*, September 6, 2012, B15; Samson Okalow, "Why Netflix Won't Conquer Canada," *Canadian Business*, February 1, 2013; "Blockbuster Closures: Dish Network To Shutter 300 Video Stores In U.S., Lay Off 3,000 Workers," *Huffington Post*, January 21, 2013; Jennifer Roberts, "Netflix Comes Roaring Back After Price-Hike Miscue," *Globe and Mail*, January 26, 2012, B7; Susan Krashinsky, "Astral Taking HBO Over the Top to Fend Off

Netflix Threat," *Globe and Mail*, December 14, 2011, B3; Marina Strauss and Iain Marlow, "Final Run For Blockbuster in Canada After Deals Rejected," *Globe and Mail*, September 1, 2011, B1; Sara Tibken, "Netflix Cancels Plan to Split DVD, Streaming Sites," *Globe and Mail*, October 11, 2011, B7; Susan Krashinsky, "A New Canadian Player on Hollywood TV Buying Spree," *Globe and Mail*, May 30, 2011, B12; Ronald Grover and Cliff Edwards, "Can Netflix Find Its Future by Abandoning the Past?" *BusinessWeek*, October 2, 2011, P32; David Milsted, "A Star is Reborn—As a Value Stock," *Globe and Mail*, November 3, 2011, B13; Susan Krashinsky, "Netflix Gets a Pass on Being Regulated—for Now," *Globe and Mail*, October 6, 2011, B5; Susan Krashinsky, "Netflix Offers a Mea Culpa—and a Defense," *Globe and Mail*, September 20, 2011, B4; Steve Laverdure, "For Blockbuster in Canada, The Closing Credits Roll," *Globe and Mail*, May 6, 2011, B1.

What Should We Do about R&D?

Barrie McKenna, "Missing in Action: A Canadian R&D Ecosystem," *Globe and Mail*, November 14, 2011, B1; Peter Foster, "Dim-Bulb R&D Policy," *National Post*, October 19, 2011, FP15; John Manley, "Centralize Ottawa's $5 B in R&D Funding," *National Post*, October 18, 2011, FP11; Barrie McKenna, "R&D Tax Scheme too Rich, Government Panel Finds," *Globe and Mail*, October 18, 2011, B1; Barrie McKenna, "A Golden Opportunity to Fix Our Broken R&D Model," *Globe and Mail*, October 17, 2011, B1.

Coalition Music: Entrepreneurial Spirit in the Entertainment Industry

Coalition Music Website, http://www.coalitionent.com/ [accessed May 1, 2013]; Canadian Independent Music Association, http://www.cimamusic.ca/Page.asp?PageID=122&ContentID=2602&SiteNodeID=66 [accessed May 1, 2013]; Music Managers Forum Canada, http://musicmanagersforum.ca/news/coalition-musics-artist-entrepreneur-program-discounted-for-mmf-members [accessed May 1, 2013]; Music Canada, http://www.musiccanada.com/newsitem.aspx?scid=63191 [accessed May 1, 2013].

Air Canada's Challenging Environment

SkyTrax World Airline Awards, 2011 Results, http://www.worldairlineawards.com/Awards_2012/namerica.htm [accessed February 3, 2013]; Frederico Tomescu, "Air Canada Eyes New Jets as Profit Outlook Brightens," *Financial Post*, December 6, 2012; Brent Jang, "Clouds Darken For Airlines," *Globe and Mail*, October 6, 2011, B1; Brent Jang, "Air Canada Pushes for Greater Transatlantic Traffic," *Globe and Mail*, December 18, 2009, B1; Slobodan Lekic, "Volcanic Ash Forces More Delays, Rerouting of Transatlantic Flights," *Globe and Mail*, May 9, 2010, B1; Robin Millard, "Volcanic Ash Cancels, Delays More Flights," *National Post*, May 9, 2010; Brent Jang, "Air Canada's Problems Pile Up," *Globe and Mail*, February 19, 2009, B1; CBC News website, "Volcanic Ash Costs Air Canada $20M over 5 Days," www.cbc.ca/world/story/2010/04/19/ash-cloud-airlines-cost.html, April 19, 2010; Air Canada Annual Report 2009, www.aircanada.com/en/about/investor/documents/2009_ar.pdf [accessed June 12, 2010].

CHAPTER 3

Chocolate: Paying The Price

"Slaves Feed World's Taste for Chocolate," *Knight Ridder News Service*, January 9, 2011; "Chocolate and Slavery: Child Labor in Cote d'Ivoire," *TED Case Studies, No. 664*, 2009; "Abolishing Child Labor on West African Cocoa Farms," SocialFunds.com, April 4, 2009; "Stop Child Labor: Cocoa Campaign" International Labour Rights Forum, 2008, April 3, 2010; Jennifer Alsever, "Fair Prices for Farmers: Simply Idea, Complex Reality," *New York Times*, March 19, 2006.

Some Frustrations in the Green Movement

Bjorn Lomborg, "Green Cars Have a Dirty Little Secret," *Wall Street Journal*, March 11, 2013, A15; Jeremy Cato, "It's Not Easy Buying Green," *Globe and Mail*, July 15, 2011, D1; Peter Foster, "The Coming Green Car Pileup," *National Post*, January 14, 2011, FP11; Veronique Dupont, "Consumer Interest in Green Cars Lags; Still Niche Market," *National Post*, January 12, 2011, FP3; Garry Marr, "We'll Go Green If the Price is Right," *National Post*, November 17, 2010, FP10; Peter Foster, "Yellow Brick Road to Green Serfdom," *National Post*, November 10, 2010, FP17; Sarah Schmidt, "Public 'Greenwashed' by Eco-Friendly Claims: Study," *Winnipeg Free Press*, October 26, 2010, A2.

Silicon Sisters: Gaming with a Social Twist

Based on a case written by Mary Charleson, Sprott-Shaw, Silicon Sisters Interactive, Vanier/BDC Case Competition 2010; Kate Taylor, "Outside the Boy Box: Women Are Embracing and Rethinking Video Games," *Globe and Mail*, September 6, 2012; Craig and Marc Kielburger, "What Are Some Kids' Video Games That Carry Positive Messages," August 6, 2012; Silicon Sisters Interactive Website, http://www.siliconsisters.ca/press.php [accessed April 20, 2013].

Should Whistle-Blowers Be Paid?

David Gauthier-Villars, "Renault Security Held in Spy Case," *Wall Street Journal*, March 12-13, 2011, B1; Edward Waitzer, "Should We Pay For Whistle-Blowing?" *National Post*, March 22, 2011, FP11; Dimitri Lascaris, "Speak Truth to Power," *National Post*, March 25, 2011, FP11; David Gauthier-Villars and Sebastian Moffett, "Renault to Yield in l'Affaire d'Espionnage," *Wall Street Journal*, March 10, 2011, B1.

The Problem of Consumer Skepticism

Jeremy Cato, "It's Not Easy Buying Green," *Globe and Mail*, July 15, 2011, D1; William Watson, "Green Except When It Costs," *National Post*, March 9, 2011, FP17; Lindsey Wiebe, "Logo La-La Land," *Winnipeg Free Press*, August 23, 2009, p. A7; Lindsey Wiebe, "Will Consumers Go For True 'Green' Products?," *Winnipeg Free Press*, August 2, 2009, (Books section), 6; Diane Katz, "The Grocery-Bag Dilemma: Is Paper or Plastic Greener?" *Winnipeg Free Press*, July 26, 2009, A11; Susan Krashninsky, "The Green Gap," *Globe and Mail*, July 17, 2009, B4; "Beyond the Green Marketing Mirage; GoodGuide Supplies Instant Information on a Host of Products," *National Post*, June 22, 2009, FP5; Terrence Belford, "Developers Blue Over Green Roofs," *Globe and Mail*, June 16, 2009, B10; David Ebner, "Coke Will Use The Olympics to Launch Its Latest Environmental Push, But Will a Generation That's Grown Wary of 'Greenwashing' Buy the PlantBottle?" *Globe and Mail*, June 10, 2009, B1; William Watson, "The Uses of Eco-OCD," *National Post*, May 30, 2009, FP19; Jennifer Wells, "How Recession Changed the Green Marketplace," *Globe and Mail*, April 20, 2009, B1; Konrad Yakabuski, "Green Dreams, Unplugged," *Globe and Mail*, April 4, 2009, F1; Lawrence Solomon, "Green Economics: It Just Doesn't Add Up," *National Post*, March 31, 2009, FP11; Alia McMullen, "Will Green Agenda Fade?; In Tough Times, Environmental Action May Lose Its Momentum," *National Post*, January 17, 2009, FP1; Joe Castaldo, "Green Counting," *Canadian Business*, October 13, 2008, 27.

CHAPTER 4

Internet Entrepreneurs: Moving Products Beyond the Rack

Becky Reuber, "Navigating the Shoals of Rapid Growth," *Globe and Mail*, April 15, 2011, B8; Boyd Erman, "Beyond the Rack Lands $12-Million Financing," *Globe and Mail*, July 12, 2010; "Flash Sale E-Tailer Beyond the Rack Expands Its Beauty Business by Adding Membership Base of BeautyStory.com," *Canadian Business*, July

5 2011, www.canadianbusiness.com/24772 [accessed September 27, 2011]; Jameson Berkow, "Montreal's Beyond the Rack Named North America's Fastest-Growing Online Retailer," *Financial Post*, June 24, 2011; Sramana Mitra, "The Promise of e-Commerce," *Forbes Magazine*, September 4, 2010; Beyond the Rack website, www.beyondtherack.com [accessed September 27, 2011]; Michael Krebs (CFO) provided statistics and information [accessed February 13, 2012]; Jerry Langton, "Did You Know This Shopping Website Is Canadian?" *Globe and Mail*, November 7, 2012.

Who Wants To Be a Teen Millionaire?

Amir Efrati, "Yahoo Snaps Up Teen-Created News App," *Globe and Mail*, March 26, 2013, B10; "Natural Curiosity Pays off for Yahoo's Teen Millionaire," *Globe and Mail*, March 27, 2013, B10; "Yahoo Buys Teen Developer's Bestselling App," CBC Website, March 26, 2013, http://www.cbc.ca/news/technology/story/2013/03/26/tech-yahoo.html [accessed April 26, 2013].

Building a Business, Planning a Better Meal

Entrepreneurship and New Ventures, Building a Business, Planning a Better Meal, Grace Gagliano, "Turning Meal Planning into a Business," BRADENTON.COM, August 19, 2010, at http://www.bradenton.com/2010/08/19/2515525/turning-meal-planning-into-a-business.html#ixzz0x3CL8WIj; http://www.grocerydash.com; Star-Ledger Wire Services, "Moms Combine Tech with Frugality to Save Money, Time at Supermarket," NJ.com, August 24, 2010, at http://www.nj.com/business/index.ssf/2010/08/moms_combine_tech_with_frugali.html; http://www.grocerydash.com.

Parasuco Jeans: The Story of a Born Entrepreneur

Patricia Gajo, "Jean-Ius," *Nuvo* magazine*,* Spring 2010, P72–73; Parasuco website*,* www.parasuco.com [accessed June 23, 2010]; Kristin Laird, "Parasuco's New Ad Campaign Is in Ice," *Marketing,* March 19, 2009; Eva Freide, "Flattery or Fakery," *Montreal Gazette,* July 22, 2008; Daniel Geiger, *Real Estate Weekly*, "Duane Reade Takes Deal for Parasuco Space," www.rew-online.com/news/story.aspx?id=907, March 26, 2010; Amy Verner, "Best Kept Denim Secret. The Hottest Brands are Canadian," *Globe and Mail*, September 24, 2011; Peter Kuitenbreur, "Signs of Life in A Slab of Concrete," *National Post*, January 24, 2012.

CHAPTER 5

Scotiabank: Canadian Bank or Global Player?

Grant Robertson, "Scotiabank's Patience Thins as China Weighs Guangzhou Deal," *Globe and Mail*, January 9, 2013, B1; Grant Robertson, "Scotiabank Sees Bright Future in South America," *Globe and Mail*, January 9, 2013, B1; Grant Robertson, "Shrinking Profit Margins Hit Scotiabank," *Globe and Mail*, May 30, 2012, B3; Grant Robertson, "Scotiabank Takes Stake in Chinese Bank," *Globe and Mail*, September 10, 2011, B9; Grant Robertson, "Scotiabank Finds a Pricier Merger Market," *Globe and Mail*, May 11, 2011, B4; Grant Robertson, "Canada's Banks Make Grade in World Standings," *Globe and Mail*, May 10, 2011, B4; Grant Robertson, "A Once Cautious Bank Takes a Bold Leap South," *Globe and Mail*, August 20, 2011, B6; Grant Robertson, "Scotiabank Profits Jump," *Globe and Mail*, August 30, 2011, B6; Steve Chase, "Scotiabank CEO Optimistic About Brazil Opportunities," *Globe and Mail*, August 9, 2011, B4; Steven Chase, "In Brazil, the Rise of the Mall," *Globe and Mail*, September 2, 2011, B1; Scotiabank Website, http://www.scotiabank.com/ca/en/0,,464,00.html [accessed April 27th, 2013].

The Neverending European Debt Crisis: The Divided Truth

Gabriele Steinhauser, Matthew Dalton, and Alkman Granitsas, "Cyprus Test Unity of Europe," *Wall Street Journal*, March 25, 2013, A1; Jonathan House and Christopher Bjork, "Spain Brings the Pain to Bank Investors," *Wall Street Journal*, March 25, 2013, C3; George Georgiopoulos, "Greece Dodges Debt Default as Bonds Swapped," *National Post*, March 9, 2012, FP1; Brian Blackstone, "ECB Sees No Losses on Athens Bond Buys," *Wall Street Journal*, February 22, 2012, A9; Stephen Fidler, "Greece Gets a Stay, with Trouble on the Way," *Wall Street Journal*, February 22, 2012, A8; Alkman Granitsas, Matina Stevis, and Nektaria Stamouli, "Greece Passes Sweeping Cuts," *Wall Street Journal*, February 13, 2012, A1; Trading Economics Website, http://www.tradingeconomics.com/germany/unemployment-rate [accessed April 27, 2013].

Connection That Matters: My World, My Choice!

Interview with Lianne Foti.

Tim Hortons' Slow US Expansion and the New Push towards the Middle East

Scott Anderson, "Tim Hortons to Go 'Upscale' in Expansion," *Globe and Mail*, March 6, 2010, B2; Jasmine Budak, "The Donut Offensive," *Canadian Business,* March 1, 2010, 36–38; Sunny Freeman, "Tim Hortons Rides Out Price Increases," *Globe and Mail*, February 26, 2010, B7; Simon Houpt, "Tim Hortons: At the Intersection of Commerce and Culture," *Globe and Mail*, March 6, 2010, B1; Susan Ma, "Tims Takes Manhattan," *Globe and Mail*, July 27, 2009, B3; Jason Kirby, "Tim's Takes on America," *Maclean's*, March 12, 2008, B3; Armina Ligaya, "What Fuels Tim Hortons Move into the Middle East," *Globe and Mail*, May 19, 2011, B11; James Cowan, "Why Can't Tim Horton's Find a CEO?," *Canadian Business,* March 19, 2012, 11; Tim Hortons website, http://www.timhortons.com/us/en/about/profile.html [accessed April 28, 2013].

CHAPTER 6

A Crisis for the 787 Dreamliner

Chris Cooper, "Rapping, Lectures: How Dreamliner Pilots are Passing the Time; Pilots of the Boeing 787s have been Grounded Along with the Planes," *National Post*, March 7, 2013, FP3; Andy Pasztor and Jon Ostrower, "Boeing Works to Redeem 787," *Wall Street Journal*, March 21, 2013, B3; Andy Pasztor and John Ostrower, "FAA Clears Boeing's Battery Fixes," *Wall Street Journal*, March 13, 2013, B3; Andy Pasztor, Monica Langley, and Jon Ostrower, "LaHood Still Has Questions on 787s," *Wall Street Journal*, March 7, 2013, B1; Andy Pasztor and John Ostrower, "Boeing, Battery Supplier at Odds over Fixes," *Wall Street Journal*, February 28, 2013, B4; Andy Pasztor, Yoree Koh, and Yoshio Takahashi, "Needed: Battery Expertise for Probe," *Wall Street Journal*, February 27, 2013, B8; Jon Ostrower, "FAA: 787 Can't Return Until Fire Risks Fixed," *Wall Street Journal*, February 23-24, 2013, B3; Monica Langley, "Chief of Embattled Boeing Steers Clear of the Spotlight," *Wall Street Journal*, February 22, 2013, A1; Andy Pasztor, Yoshio Takahashi, and Yoree Koh, "Dreamliner Probes Intensify," *Wall Street Journal*, January 22, 2013, B1.

Should You Say Goodbye to Traditional Land Lines?

Lucy Kellaway, "Requiem For the Land Line," *Globe and Mail*, February 13, 2013; Rita Trichur, "More People Hanging Up on Home Phones," *Globe and Mail*, April 2, 2012, B5; Chris Umiastowsky, "Hanging Up For Good on Ma Bell," *Globe and Mail*, September 26, 2011, P13; Brian Jackson, "Canadian Consumers Can Now Port Landline Numbers to Another VOIP Service," January 22, 2013, http://www.itbusiness.ca/news/canadians-can-now-port-landline-numbers-to-another-voip-service/19670 [accessed April 16, 2013].

Extending the Logic of Goal Setting

"Looking Good in Green," Maclean's, May 9, 2011, 47; Ford Aims for 25% of its Vehicles to be Electric or Hybrid by 2013," *National*

Post, June 10, 2011, FP4; Alexandra Lopez-Pacheco, "Planet-Friendly Offices," *National Post,* October 2, 2009, FP12; Rona Wins Kudos on Green Initiative," *Globe and Mail*, November 22, 2008, B7; John Murphy, "Honda CEO Vies for Green Mantle," *Wall Street Journal*, June 16, 2008, B1–B2; Sharda Prashad, "Good Green Goals," TheStar.com, April 22, 2007, www.thestar.com/printArticle/205855.

Will This Strategy Fly?

Eric Reguly, "Skies Getting Crowded in C Series Niche," *Globe and Mail*, June 21, 2011, B17; Greg Keenan, "Bombardier's Next Jet Faces New Hurdle: Cutthroat Prices," *Globe and Mail*, December 7, 2010, B1; Scott Deveau, "Build Larger CSeries, Bombardier Advised; Air Insight Report; Option of 150-Seat Version Could Steal Clients from Boeing," *National Post*, December 7, 2010, FP7; Bertrand Marotte, "Bombardier Sticks to Business-Jet Plan," *Globe and Mail*, December 3, 2010, B3; Greg Keenan, "Airbus Turns Up the Heat on Bombardier, Boeing," *Globe and Mail*, December 2, 2010, B3; Barry Critchley, "Bombardier Spices Up Orders for Indian Market; $390M Deal in Works," *National Post*, November 3, 2010, FP2; Bertrand Marotte, "Bombardier Plans Two New Business Jets," *Globe and Mail*, October 20, 2010, B5; Laura Cameron, "For Bombardier, A Case of Déjà Vu," *Canadian Business*, September 13, 2010, 28.

The Overtime Pay Controversy

Jeff Gray, "Overtime Ruling Not Expected to Spark Deluge of Cases," *Globe and Mail*, June 27, 2012, B4; Drew Hasselback, "Overtime at Issue in Class Rulings," *National Post*, June 27, 2012, FP14; "Class Actions Against Banks OK'd," *Winnipeg Free Press*, June 27, 2012, B4; Jeff Gray, "Overtime Lawsuits Hit a Snag," *Globe and Mail*, May 16, 2012, B9; Howard Levitt, "When Do Managers Punch the Clock?; How Employers Can Avoid Unwanted Overtime Payments," *National Post*, July 6, 2011, FP1; Jeff Gray, "Overtime Lawsuit Against Scotiabank Gets Green Light," *Globe and Mail*, June 7, 2011, B6; Daryl-Lynn Carlson, "Overtime a Laborious Issue," *National Post*, October 27, 2010, LP4; Jim Middlemiss, "Hurdle for Overtime Class-Action Suits," *National Post*, September 15, 2010, FP8; Barry Critchley, "Managers at Centre of CN Class Action; Overtime at Issue; Judge to Rule on Whether Supervisors are Management," *National Post*, August 18, 2010, FP2; Peter Taylor, "Suing by the Hour; Out-of-Touch Labour Legislation is Making Life Difficult for Employers and Hard-Working Employees Alike," *National Post*, December 9, 2009, FP15; "CIBC Staffers Seek OK for Overtime Group Suit," *Globe and Mail*, December 9, 2008, B10; Jim Middlemiss, "Lawsuit Seeks OT for Bankers; CIBC Targeted," *National Post*, October 29, 2008, FP1; Richard Blackwell, "KPMG to Pay Workers Overtime," *Globe and Mail*, February 20, 2008, B8; Virginia Galt, "Managers' Overtime Victory Short-Lived," *Globe and Mail*, April 20, 2007, B3.

CHAPTER 7

What Happened to the "Occupy Wall Street" Movement?

Gordon Crovitz, "Occupy Astro Turf," *Wall Street Journal*, January 30, 2012, A13; Omar El Akkad, "After the Campaign Put Out the Simple Twitter Hashtag #OccupyWallStreet, 'It Just Went Crazy'," *Globe and Mail*, December 22, 2011, A12; Kathryn Blaze Carlson, "Utopian Failure; Why The Occupy Movement Is Doomed: Huan Brains Crave Hierarchy," *National Post*, November 26, 2011, A10; Gary Mason, "Founders of Leadnow Strive to Build a Progressive Voice with Real Focus," *Globe and Mail*, November 26, 2011, A18; "Five Reasons Why Occupy Failed," *National Post*, November 19, 2011, A10; Gary Mason, "Sorry, Folks, But This Protest's in Danger of Fizzling Out," *Globe and Mail*, November 3, 2011, A19; "Rogue Senate Page Lends Her Support to the 99ers; Occupation Peaceful; Protesters in Ottawa, Montreal Camping Out In Downtown Parks," *National Post*, October 18, 2011, A8; Kim Mackrael, "Occupy Wall Street: Who They Are, What They Want," *Globe and Mail*, October 7, 2011, A23; Kelly McParland, "Confused Protesters March On; 'Movements' Don't Have Leaders or Clear Goals," *National Post*, October 4, 2011, A2.

Green Structures

Brenda Dalglish, "Up on the Roof, Green Takes Root," *Globe and Mail*, July 24, 2012, B7; Erica Kelly, "Banking's New Shade of Green," *Globe and Mail*, December 20, 2011, B8; Gail Johnson, "Easy To Be Green When Your Roof Saves You Money," *Globe and Mail*, November 15, 2011, B11; Martin Cash, "Terminal Case of Energy Efficiency," *Winnipeg Free Press*, October 29, 2011, B6; Shelley White, "Part Office Building, Part Power Plant," *Globe and Mail*, September 20, 2011, B10; "Green Buildings," *Canadian Business*, August 16–September 12, 2011, 55; Sarah Boesveld, "The Green Building Impact on Employees," *Globe and Mail*, October 19, 2010, B12; Jay Somerset, "A Building with an Energy All Its Own," *Globe and Mail*, November 11, 2008, B9.

Virtual Water Coolers: Encouraging Employee Engagement

Daina Lawrence, "Virtual Water Coolers and a Meeting of Minds," *Globe and Mail*, January 31, 2012, B14; Business Insider, "How to Create a Virtual Water Cooler for Your Company," March 6, 2013, http://www.businessinsider.com/how-to-create-a-virtual-water-cooler-for-your-company-2013-3 [accessed April 18, 2013]; "The Digital Water Cooler," *Globe and Mail*, September 21, 2012, http://www.theglobeandmail.com/globe-investor/personal-finance/financial-road-map/advmanulife/advmanulifearchives/the-digital-water-cooler/article4569745/ [accessed April 18, 2013]; Suzanne Bowness, "Telework or Teamwork? Yahoo and the Evolution of the Office," *Globe and Mail*, February 26, 2013.

Kodak's Troubling Moment

"The Business Picture/The End of An Era As Kodak Stops Making Cameras," *Globe and Mail*, February 10, 2012, B2; Kana Inagaki and Juro Osawa, "Fujifilm Thrived By Changing Focus," *Wall Street Journal*, January 20, 2012, B5; Mike Spector and Dana Mattioli, "Kodak: Tech Firms Hastened Slide," *Wall Street Journal*, January 20, 2012, B1; Ben Dobbin, "Restructuring Halts Kodak Stock's Freefall," *Globe and Mail*, January 11, 2012, B10; "Kodak Claims Apple Infringing on Four Patents Tied to Digital Images," *National Post*, January 11, 2012, FP12; Caroline Humer, "End of the Line for Film Group as Kodak Refocuses; Shares Jump 50%," *National Post*, January 11, 2012, FP12; Dana Mattioli, "Their Kodak Moments," *Wall Street Journal*, January 6, 2012, B1; www.wikipedia.org/wiki/Eastman_Kodak; "Eastman Kodak Shares Jump After General Counsel Named Co-President," *National Post*, December 24, 2011, FP9; "Kodak Eases Fears; Shares Soar 72%," *Globe and Mail*, October 24, 2011, B10.

CHAPTER 8

Hard Hits in Professional Sports

Susan Krashinsky, "NHL Lockout's Sour Taste Lingers," *Globe and Mail*, March 15, 2013, B6; Barrie McKenna, "Return of Hockey a Boon to Restaurants," *Globe and Mail*, January 24, 2013, B3; Mike Sielski, "NHL Races Back to Business," *Wall Street Journal*, January 7, 2013, B1; Ed Tait, "What's the Holdup?" *Winnipeg Free Press*, December 13, 2012, D1; R. Marowits, "NHL Lockout Causing Pain—and Gain—for Businesses," *Globe and Mail*, December 5, 2012, B6; Brian Mahoney, "Shorter Schedule Forces Brutal Stretches," *Globe and Mail*, December 7, 2011, S5; Barry Wilner and Howard Fendrich, "NFL, Players Bang Out 10-Year Deal," *Winnipeg Free Press*, July 26, 2011, D1; Barry Wilner, "Players Prepare for Chaos," *Winnipeg Free Press*, July 26, 2011, D4; Howard Fendrich, "NFL Labour Dispute Enters Overtime,

Winnipeg Free Press, July 23, 2011, C2; Barry Wilner, "Employees Hit Hardest If Players Don't Play," *Winnipeg Free Press*, June 14, 2011, C6; Dave Campbell, "No Indication of Significant Progress Toward New Agreement," *Winnipeg Free Press*, May 18, 2011, C2; "Business-Friendly Court Rules NFL Lockout Remains," *Winnipeg Free Press*, May 17, 2011, C2; Matthew Futterman, "NFL Owners Try Wedge," *Wall Street Journal*, March 18, 2011, B8; Matthew Futterman, "NFL Girds for fight, Says Loss Is Covered," *Wall Street Journal*, March 14, 2011, B1; Eric Lam, "NFL Lockout Not Threat To Broadcasters," *National Post*, September 14, 2010, FP8.

Green Careers

Derek Sankey, "Green Careers Available in Every Sector; Student Energy; Youth Meet to Find Sustainable Energy Future," *National Post*, November 7, 2012, FP11; "Looking Good in Green," *Maclean's*, May 9, 2011, 47; Katie Engelhart, "From the Bottom Up," *Canadian Business*, April 27–May 10, 2010, 60; Greg McMillan, "The Greening of the Jobscape," *Globe and Mail*, November 14, 2008, B7; Marjo Johne, "Show Us the Green, Workers Say," *Globe and Mail*, October 10, 2007, C1; "Creating Jobs by Going Green," www.premier.gov.on.ca/news/Product.asp?ProductID=1400.

Public Sector Unions

John Allemang, "Organized Labour is Fighting to Survive," *Globe and Mail*, March 24, 2012, F1; Catherine Swift, "Fighting the Union Mentality," *National Post*, August 6, 2011, FP17; Kris Maher, "Unions Push to Undo Ohio Law," *Wall Street Journal*, June 3, 2011, A5; Konrad Yakabuski, "Will Wisconsin's Chill on Labour Move North?," *Globe and Mail*, March 12, 2011, F1; Paul Vieira, "Public Spat; The Battle Boiling Over in Wisconsin Simmers in Canada," *National Post*, March 5, 2011, FP1; Terence Corcoran, "Why the Public Sector Is Hanging On for All It's Worth," *National Post*, March 5, 2011, A1; Howard Levitt, "Are Unions Losing their Purpose? Law Affords More Protection to Employees," *National Post*, July 8, 2009, FP12.

Behaviour-Based Interviewing

Cook, Geoff, "A Question of Evidence: The Behaviour-Based Interview," *Training Journal*, 2006, 61; Sarah Hood, "Hire Echelon," *Canadian Business*, June 7–June 20, 2004, 71; Celene Adams, "Interview Style Probes Past to Predict Future," *Globe and Mail*, April 29, 2002, B16 "Taking Questions to a Hire Level," *National Post*, March 23, 2001, C2; Barbara Simmons, "Be Ready for Tough 'Behaviour-Based' Interview", *Toronto Star*, December 16, 2000; Greg Crone, "The Right Questions Help Avoid Hiring Employees that are Clones of the Interviewer," *National Post*, October 27, 1999, C04; http://jobsearch.about.com/cs/interviews/a/behavioral.htm.

CHAPTER 9

Happiness and Satisfaction in the Workplace

"One in Two U.S. Employees Looking to Leave or Checked Out on the Job, Says *What's Working* Research," www.mercer.com/press-releases/1418665 [accessed January 3, 2012]; Derek Abma, "GenXers Least Happy At Work; Disappointment," *National Post*, November 30, 2011, FP10; Wallace Immen, "Study Highlights Generation Gap on Workplace Priorities," *Globe and Mail*, November 2, 2011, B19; Rajeev Peshawaria, "To Motivate Your Employees, You Need to Know What They Want," *Globe and Mail*, September 7, 2011, B19; "Not Happy At Work? You're Not Alone: One in Two Canadians Say They Would Leave," *National Post*, June 22, 2011, FP14; "Is Happiness Overrated?" *Wall Street Journal*, March 15, 2011, D1; Phyllis Korkki, "Don't Take a Job for the Paycheque Alone; Benefits of High Salary Ambiguous," *National Post*, November 17, 2010, FP9; Wallace Immen, "Meaning Means More than Money at Work: Poll," *Globe and Mail*, February 27, 2009, B14; Wallace Immen, "Boomers, Gen-Yers Agree: It's All About Respect," *Globe and Mail*, January 24, 2007, C1.

Tweet, Post: You're Fired

Tristin Hopper, "Human Rights Commission Dismisses Former Sportsnet Anchor's Claim Tying his Firing to Anti-Gay Remarks," *National Post*, April 16, 2013; Jeff Gray, "Think before You Tweet," *Globe and Mail*, May 25, 2011, B9; Fox News website, "Twitter Feed F-Word Gets Chrysler Employee Fired," http://www.foxnews.com/us/2011/03/10/f-word-appears-chryslers-twitter-feed/, March 11, 2011 [accessed January 4, 2012]; Scott Edmonds, "Car Dealership Employees Fired for Facebook Posts," Globe and Mail, December 9, 2010, B9; Charles Lewis, "Firing of Sportsnet Broadcaster After Gay Marriage Tweet Tests Religious Freedom, Free Speech," *National Post*, November 16, 2011.

Moving People to Move Movies

Ronald J. Ebert and Ricky W. Griffin, *Business Essentials*. Boston, MA: Pearson, 2013, p. 248. Used with permission.

Getting Employees Involved

R. Spence, "Harness Employee Power," *National Post*, June 25, 2012, FP4; "One in Two U.S. Employees Looking to Leave or Checked Out on the Job, Says *What's Working* Research," www.mercer.com/press-releases/1418665 [accessed January 3, 2012]; Marjo Johne, "Firing on All Cylinders with Social Media," *Globe and Mail*, October 21, 2011, B15; Wallace Immen, "Canadian Companies Warm to Social Media," *Globe and Mail*, June 10, 2011, B16; Darah Hansen, "New Age, New Problems; Social Media No. 1 Concern for Employers," *National Post*, June 8, 2011, FP11; Wallace Immen, "Feeling Unmotivated? HR Managers Say It's the Boss's Fault," *Globe and Mail*, March 23, 2011, B21; Richard Branson, "Don't Leave Employees on the Outside Looking In," *Canadian Business*, July 20–August 16, 2010, 13; Joe Castaldo, "How To Coax Ideas Out of a Sheepish Staff," *Canadian Business*, April 27–May 10, 2010, 80; Katie Engelhart, "From the Bottom Up," *Canadian Business*, April 27–May 10, 2010, 60; Leena Rao "I Love Rewards Raises $5.9 Million For Employee Rewards Program," TechCrunch website, retrieved May 7, 2009 from www.techcrunch.com/2009/05/07/i-love-rewards-raises-59-million-for-employee-rewards-program/; Chris Atchison, "Masters of One," *Profit, Vol. 28*, May 2009, Issue 2, 18; Ari Weinzweig, "Ask Inc: Tough Questions, Smart Answers," *Inc., Vol. 29*, December 2007, Issue 12, 84; Virginia Galt, "Ideas: Employees' Best-Kept Secrets," *Globe and Mail*, June 18, 2005, B11; Frederick A. Starke, Bruno Dyck, and Michael Mauws, "Coping with the Sudden Loss of an Indispensable Worker," *Journal of Applied Behavioural Science*, 39(2), 2003, 208–229; Timothy Aeppel, "On Factory Floors, Top Workers Hide Secrets to Success," *Wall Street Journal*, July 1, 2002, A1, A10; Timothy Aeppel, "Not All Workers Find Idea of Empowerment as Neat as It Sounds," *Wall Street Journal*, September 8, 1997, A1, A13.

CHAPTER 10

What's Happening to Manufacturing in Canada?

Greg Keenan, "Made (Smarter) in Canada: Inside a World-Beating Factory," *Globe and Mail*, March 2, 2013, B6; P. Cross, "Dutch Disease in Canada a Myth; Manufacturers Have Adapted to Higher Loonie," *National Post*, January 16, 2013, FP1; Greg Keenan, "GM to Slash Oshawa Line, Move Production to Tennessee," *Globe and Mail*, June 2, 2012, B4; Livio Di Matteo, "Everybody's Dutch; All G7 Nations Have Seen Manufacturing Declines," *National Post*, May 30, 2012, FP11; Greg Keenan, "Stage Set for Standoff with Unions, Auto Makers," *Globe and Mail*, April 17, 2012, B1; Barrie McKenna,

"Manufacturing Hard Hit, But It's Nowhere Near Dead," *Globe and Mail*, March 19, 2012, B1; Gordon Pitts, "In Alberta, Oil Sands Fuel a Factory Boom," *Globe and Mail*, March 6, 2012, B1; Greg Keenan, "Ten Years of High Loonie Takes Big Toll on Country's Factories," *Globe and Mail*, March 2, 2012, B1; Greg Keenan, "Indiana Beckons Factories Squeezed by Higher Costs," *Globe and Mail*, February 16, 2012, B1; Tavia Grant and Greg Keenan, "Factory Employment Hits a 35-Year Low as More Plants Close," *Globe and Mail*, November 5, 2011, B1; Jacquie McNish, "Maple Leaf's Big Move," *Globe and Mail*, October 20, 2011, B1; Kevin Carmichael, "From a Burst Bubble, a New Brand of Manufacturing Emerges in Ottawa," *Globe and Mail*, June 11, 2011, B11.

Producing Green Energy

Martin Hutchinson, "Solar Firm's Bankruptcy Shines Light on U.S. Policy," *Globe and Mail*, September 15, 2011, B12; Peter Foster, "Scorched by Solar," *National Post*, September 3, 2011, FP17; Neil Reynolds, "The German Irony: Will It Have to Import Nuclear Energy?" *Globe and Mail*, June 15, 2011, B2; Brian McKenna, "McGuinty's Green Energy 'Explosion' More of an Implosion," *Globe and Mail*, June 13, 2011, B2; Claudia Cattaneo, "Consumers Will Opt for Lowest Cost: Report," *National Post*, April 28, 2011, FP8; Lawrence Solomon, "Nuclear Power Extremes; The Problems with Nuclear Support from Both Right and Left," *National Post*, April 9, 2011, FP19; "The New Impossible Energy No-Fly Zone," May 17, 2011, FP11; Richard Blackwell, "Activists Lose Court Challenge Over Wind Power Turbines," *Globe and Mail*, March 4, 2011, B5; Todd Woody, "Solar Power Plans Spark Lawsuit Storm," *National Post*, February 25, 2011, FP3; Lawrence Solomon, "Green Collapse; Across the World, Unsustainable Subsidies for Wind and Solar Are Being Cut Back; Ontario Is Next," *National Post*, December 4, 2010, FP19; Lawrence Solomon, "Profitin' in the Wind; Billionaire Energy Tycoon T. Boone Pickens Has a Two-Step Plan to Cash In on Climate Change. Today," *National Post*, July 18, 2009, FP19; "Fossil Fuel Dependency to Continue for Rest of Century, Expert Says," *National Post*, July 16, 2009, FP4; Sigurd Lauge Pedersen, "Wind Power Works," *National Post*, May 12, 2009, FP13; Michael J. Trebilcock, "Wind Power is a Complete Disaster," *National Post*, April 9, 2009, FP13; Diane Francis, "Canada's Nuclear Power Play," *National Post*, October 25, 2008, FP2; Neil Reynolds, "Wind Turbine Marketers are Full of Hot Air," *Globe and Mail*, July 11, 2008, B2; Peter Moreira, "Irving Oil Looks to Make Waves with Tidal Power," *Globe and Mail*, May 27, 2008, B7; Rebecca Smith, "New Wave of Nuclear Plants Faces High Costs," *Wall Street Journal*, May 12, 2008, B1; Patrick Barta, "In Australia, a Wind-Powered Plant Makes Water from Ocean Fit to Drink," *Wall Street Journal*, March 11, 2008, A1; Lauren Etter, "Ethanol Craze Cools as Doubts Multiply," *Wall Street Journal*, November 28, 2007, A1; Patrick Barta, "Jatropha Plant Gains Steam in Global Race for Biofuels," *Wall Street Journal*, August 24, 2007, A1; Patrick Barta and Jane Spencer, "As Alternative Fuels Heat Up, Environmental Concerns Grow," *Wall Street Journal*, December 5, 2006, A1; Richard Blackwell, "In Ontario and Alberta, How Much Wind Power is too Much?" *Globe and Mail*, October 30, 2006, B1.

Supply Chain Disruptions

Noel Randewich, "Sales Hit Hard by Shortage of Hard Drives, Intel Says; Thai Flood Effect," *National Post*, December 13, 2011, FP11; "Honda Plants to Return to Normal Levels December 1," *National Post*, November 29, 2011, FP6; "Toyota Is Paralyzed by Thai Floods; Assembly Lines Halt," *National Post*, November 7, 2011, FP2; Scott Deveau, "Thailand Floods Hit Alliston Honda Plant; Parts Shortage," *National Post*, November 1, 2011, FP5; Barrie McKenna, "Supply Chain Disruptions from Japan Easing," *Globe and Mail*, June 2, 2011, B6; Scott Deveau, "Toyota Could Fall to No. 3 in Sales; Earnings 77%," *National Post*, May 12, 2011, FP1; Greg Keenan, "Toyota Slashes Sales Outlook," *Globe and Mail*, May 6, 2011, B1; Timothy Aeppel, "For Lean Factories, No Buffer," *Wall Street Journal*, April 29, 2011, B1; Anita Elash, "Plant Shutdown Sends Small Production Firms Scrambling," *Globe and Mail*, April 27, 2011, B7; "Ford to Idle Plants in Taiwan, China and South Africa in Wake of Parts Shortage," *National Post*, April 26,2011, FP3; Greg Keenan, "Toyota Extends Shutdowns at Plants in Canada, U.S.," *Globe and Mail*, April 20, 2011, B3; James Hookway and Aries Poon, "Crisis Tests Supply Chain's Weak Links," *Wall Street Journal*, March 18, 2011, A8; James Hookway and Wilawan Watcharasakwet, "Worries Rise over Disrupted Supplies," *Wall Street Journal*, March 17, 2011, A15; Omar El Akkad and Iain Marlow, "Global Tech Supply Chain to Face Shortages, Delays," *Globe and Mail*, March 16, 2011, B6.

Keeping the Quality High at Toyota

Jeff Bennett, "Lexus, Porsche Top Quality Survey," *Wall Street Journal*, February 14, 2013, B9; Chester Dawson, "Toyota Takes Sales Crown," *Wall Street Journal*, January 29, 2013, B1; H. Tabuchi and B. Vlasic, "Toyota Poised to Begin New Chapter: After a Lousy Past Few Years, Carmaker Fixes Quality Issues," *National Post,* January 3, 2013, FP2; Mike Ramsey, "Toyota in $1.1 Billion Gas-Pedal Settlement," *Wall Street Journal*, December 27, 2012, A1; "Toyota to Recall 2.77 Million Vehicles Worldwide to Fix Two Systems," *National Post*, November 15, 2012, FP9; "2012 Vehicle Dependability Study," www.autos.jdpower.com [accessed June 22, 2012]; "2012 Initial Quality Study," www.autos.jdpower.com [accessed June 22, 2012]; Richard Russell, "An Inconvenient Truth," *Globe and Mail*, July 22, 2011, D18; "U.S. Investigation of Toyota Finds No Electronic Flaws, Report Says," *National Post*, February 9, 2011, FP3; Chester Dawson and Hoshio Takahashi, "Toyota Set Push to Avoid Recalls," *Wall Street Journal*, February 24, 2011, B1; Alexis Leondis, "Honda, Ford Leap over Toyota in U.S. Customer Loyalty Rankings," *National Post*, May 14, 2010, FP4; Greg Keenan and John Gray, "Toyota Faces Class-Action Suits," *Business News Network*, www.bnn.ca/news/15452.html [accessed February 1, 2010]; Greg Keenan, "Toyota Executives Plan Media Blitz," *Globe and Mail*, February 1, 2010, B1; Greg Keenan, "Toyota Scrambles for Remedy as Recall Grows," *Globe and Mail*, January 30, 2010, B3; Paul Vieira, "Toyota Finds a Fix; Pedal Maker Speeds Up Output as Recall Grows," *National Post*, January 29, 2010, FP1; Greg Keenan, "As Toyota Stumbles, Rivals Eye Gains," *Globe and Mail*, January 29, 2010, B1; Greg Keenan, "Toyota Suspending Sales of Models Involved in Recall," *Globe and Mail*, January 27, 2010, B12; "Toyota Retains Quality Crown Over Ford, GM," *National Post*, June 23, 2009, FP12; John Lippert, Alan Ohnsman, and Kae Inoue, "Is Toyota the New GM? Founder's Grandson Thinks So," *Globe and Mail*, June 23, 2009, B15.

CHAPTER 11

Stolen Maple Syrup: Accounting for Missing Inventory

Brandon Borrell, "Sticky Gold," *Bloomberg Business Week*, January 4, 2013, 58–61; Tina Shufelt, "The Great Canadian Maple Syrup Heist," *Canadian Business*, November 26, 2012, 52–56; Anne Sutherland, "Vermont Firm Implicated in $20-Million Maple Syrup Heist From Quebec Warehouse," *Montreal Gazette*, February 8, 2013; Canadian Press, "Police Make Arrests in Massive Maple Syrup Heist," CTV News.ca, December 12, 2012; Graeme Hamilton, "The Maple Syrup Cartel: Quebec's Syrup Monopoly Helped Spawn Smuggling Prohibition Style," *National Post*, February 16, 2013; Bertrand Marotte, "Maple Syrup Delinquents Raided," Globe and Mail, April 18, 2013, B3.

Greener Accounting Practices

Ken Garen, "Are You Ready to Prosper?" *The Practical Accountant*, June 2008, SR29; Jeff Sanford, "The Next Pension Crisis," *Canadian*

Business, 80, 14, August 2007, 62–63; Dom Serafini, "Regulations Are the Consumers' Best Friends," *Intermedia*, July 2004, 32, 2, ABI/INFORM Global database, 23.

How Will Twitter Turn Tweets into Treasure?

MarketWatch.com (WSJ), "As Twitter Turns 7, IPO Billions Beckon," http://blogs.marketwatch.com/thetell/2013/03/21/as-twitter-turns-7-ipo-billions-beckon/ [accessed March 23, 2013]; Erick Schonfeld, "Costolo: Twitter Now Has 190 Million Users Tweeting 65 Million Times a Day," *TechCrunch*, June 8, 2010 at http://techcrunch.com/2010/06/08/twitter-190-millionusers/; Kate Kaye, "Tracking 'Promoted Trends': Twitter Draws Diverse Advertisers," *ClickZ*, March 2, 2011, at http://www.clickz.com/clickz/news/2030238/tracking-promotedtrends-twitter-draws-diverse-advertisers.

Untangling an Accounting Mess at Bankrupt Nortel

Janet McFarland and Richard Blackwell, "Three Former Nortel Executives Found Not Guilty of Fraud," *Globe and Mail*, January 14, 2013, B1; Peg Brickley, "Nortel Reaches Pact with U.S. Retirees," *Globe and Mail*, January 3, 2013, B3; Janet McFarland, "Claims of Fraud 'Preposterous,'" *Globe and Mail*, January 20, 2012, B1; "Nortel Timeline: March 2004 to March 2006," *National Post*, January 14, 2012, FP5; "Nortel Timeline: April 2006 to January 2012," *National Post*, January 14, 2012, FP6; Theresa Tedesco, "Nortel Ghost Still Haunts Nation," *National Post*, January 14, 2012, FP4; Jamie Sturgeon, "Crown, Defence Square Off; Former CEO Dunn Accused of Fraud," *National Post*, January 13, 2012, FP1.

CHAPTER 12

New Product Development Strategies & the Power of Brand Equity

Marc Hacking, "When Competitors Team Up," *Globe and Mail*, January 24, 2012, B11; Ian Sherr, "Auto Makers Debut 'Intelligent' Car Systems," *Globe and Mail*, January 13, 2012, B8; Magna International Website, Vehicle Content, www.magna.com/about-magna/our-customers/vehiclecontent [accessed April 28th, 2012]; Courtland Bovee, John Thill and George Dracopoulos, "Magna International," *Business in Action*, Pearson Education, 2009, 228.

Green Products and Services

"Coke Improves Green Credentials by Making Bottles from Plant-Based Plastics," *Globe and Mail*, December 16, 2011, B7; Robert Matas, "B.C. Forecasts Boom Market for Clean-Energy Vehicles," *Globe and Mail*, November 17, 2011, S3; Leslie Guevarra, "How Con-Way Delivers Greener Trucking; Sustainability," *National Post*, September 13, 2011, FP7; Richard Russell, "Rolling in the Green," *Globe and Mail*, August 12, 2011, D20; "Ford Management Looks to Green Technology to Give Brand a Market Edge," *National Post*, June 14, 2011, FP9; Brent Jang, "CN Touts the Green Advantage of Rail Shipments," *Globe and Mail*, April 28, 2011, B3; "PepsiCo to Begin Testing New Plant-Based Bottle Next Year," *National Post*, March 16, 2011, FP6; Bertrand Marotte, "A Green Twist on a Private Comfort," *Globe and Mail*, March 4, 2011, B5.

Marketing to the Boomers

Patricia Lovett-Reid, "Boomers a Booming Investment; Industries for Aging Population Poised to Benefit," *National Post*, September 10, 2011, FP10; Gerry Marr, "Aging Boomers to Fuel Housing Needs by 2030; Study finds 80% of Demand to Arise from Seniors," *National Post*, September 9, 2011, FP3; Michael Dolan, "Baby Boomer Fears Cast Pall over Markets; Fewer Investors; Aging Population an Ominous Sign for Stocks," *National Post*, September 8, 2011, FP8; Ellen Byron, "How to Market to an Aging Boomer: Flattery, Subterfuge and Euphemism," *Wall Street Journal*, February 5–6, 2011, A1.

Retailers Are Tracking Your Every Move

Tim Kiladze, "Who's Watching Whom," *Report on Business*, February 2013, 12–13; Marina Strauss, "In Store Aisles, Dr. Dre Meets Big Data," *Globe and Mail*, March 5, 2013, B20; Anton Troianovski, "New WiFi Pitch: Tracking Shoppers," *Globe and Mail*, June 19, 2012, B9; Marina Strauss, "Retailers Revamp With a High-Tech Makeover," *Globe and Mail*, February 21, 2012, B3; "Big Brother Arrives at a Store near You," *Bloomberg Businessweek*, December 19–25, 2011, 41–42; Susan Krashinsky, "Ads That Reach Out to the Passing Pedestrian," *Globe and Mail*, February 28, 2012, B3; Bryan Borzykowski, "Are Checkout Counters Headed for Extinction?" *Globe and Mail*, February 22, 2013, B12.

Lululemon: Proven Model, New Targets, and Emerging Threats

Lululemon website, www.lululemon.com [accessed May 28, 2013]; Marina Strauss, "Lululemon Backs Off Supplier Blame," *Globe and Mail*, March 22, 2013, B3; Original vs. Knockoff," *Canadian Business*, January, 2013, P25; Richard Warnica, "Lulu For Him," *Canadian Business*, April 15, 2013, 50–53; Marina Strauss, "Lululemon Finds Peace Despite Copycats," *Globe and Mail*, December 3, 2012, B2; "In Search of Lululemon's Retailing Karma," *Canadian Business*, September 2011, 24; "Lululemon Shares Fall as Prospects Disappoint," *CBC News*, June 2, 2012; Marina Strauss, "Lululemon Stretches to Balance Expansion against Profit," *Globe and Mail*, June 7, 2012; Marina Strauss, "Lululemon Rides out Recession in Quality Fashion," *Globe and Mail*, March 29, 2010, B1; Marina Strauss, "Lululemon Ramps Up Plans to Hit the Net," *Globe and Mail*, March 27, 2009, B8; Sunny Freeman, "Lululemon Targeting 45 Markets for Showroom Openings to Create Brand Buzz," *Canadian Business*, March 25, 2010; Sunny Freeman, "Ask the Legends: Chip Wilson," *Profit*, March 2010; *Canadian Business* website [accessed April 22, 2010]; Marina Strauss, "New Mantra Pays Off for Lululemon," *Globe and Mail*, December 10, 2009, B2; Marina Strauss, "Lululemon's Plan for Lean Times," *Globe and Mail*, March 28, 2009, B3.

CHAPTER 13

Promoting a Successful Yogurt Craze

Susan Krashinsky, "In the War for Healthy Eating, Greek Yogurt Takes Palates by Storm," *Globe and Mail*, March 16th, 2012, B5; Chris Nuttall-Smith, "Greek Yogurt Put to the Taste Test," *Globe and Mail*, March 20, 2012; Leslie Beck, "Greek Yogurt Is All the Rage—But Is It Good for Me?" *Globe and Mail*, August 3, 2011; Terence Corcoran, "Canada's Big Fat Chobani Greek Yogurt Drama," *Financial Post*, April 2, 2012; Dominique Vidalon and Noelle Mennella, "Danone Plays Catch-Up in Greek Yogurt Race," *Edmonton Journal*, April 7, 2012; Richard Blackwell, "Milking the Yogurt Market," *Globe and Mail*, October 22, 2012, B10.

A "Helping Hand" for Professional Inspiration: wowOwow!

Meghan Casserly and Jenna Goudreau, "Top 100 Websites for Women," Forbes.com, June 23, 2010, at http://www.forbes.com/2010/06/23/100-best-womens-blogs-forbes-woman-time-websites.html; "Wowowow.com Gives a Voice to Mature Women," TimesOnline, April 6, 2008, at http://technology.timesonline.co.uk/tol/news/tech_and_web/the_web/article3662890.ece; Stephanie Rosenbloom, "Boldface in Cyberspace: It's a Woman's Domain," *The New York Times*, March 6, 2008, at http://www.nytimes.com/2008/03/06/fashion/06WOW.html; Geraldine Baum, "It's Web 101 for This Experienced Intern," *Los Angeles Times*: Article

Collections, March 6, 2009, at http://articles.latimes.com/2009/mar/06/nation/na-senior-intern6; Asa Aarons, "'On the Job' Training Takes on New Meaning," NY1.com, March 23, 2009, at http://www.ny1.com/? ArID=96052.

The "Gamification" of Promotions

Simon Houpt, "It's All Fun and Games—Until Someone Bonds with a Brand," *Globe and Mail*, January 7, 2011, B1; Donna Hoffman and Marek Fodor, "Measuring ROI of Social Media Marketing; It Requires New Measurements That Begin with Tracking Customers' Investments," *National Post*, November 23, 2010, FP11; Jordan Timm, "Jerry Bears, Doobage and the Invention of Social Networking," *Canadian Business*, September 13, 2010, 74; Jordan Timm, "Amber Mac's New Rules of Engagement," *Canadian Business*, September 13, 2010, 55; "Social Media," http://en.wikipedia.org/wiki/Social_Media [accessed on April 27, 2011]; Lyndsie Bourgon, "Reaping Social Media Rewards," *Canadian Business*, July 20–August 16, 2010, 19.

The Keystone XL Pipeline

Shawn McCarthy, "New Keystone Route Skirts No-Go Zones," *Globe and Mail*, April 20, 2012, B3; Lee-Anne Goodman, "Celebs Join Pipeline Battle," *Winnipeg Free Press*, November 7, 2011, A14; Tom Ford, "U.S. Environmental Politics Threaten Our Prosperity," *Winnipeg Free Press*, November 7, 2011, A13; Shawn McCarthy, "State Department E-Mails Trigger Allegations of Bias," *Globe and Mail*, September 23, 2011, B9; "Activists Plan 'Civil Disobedience' in Ottawa to Protest Keystone XL Pipeline," *National Post*, August 26, 2011, FP5; Sheldon Alberts, "Aftermath of a Spill; Enbridge Cleanup Grades Well, but Pipeline Fears Remain," *National Post*, July 23, 2011, FP3; Peter Foster, "Franken Pipeline," *National Post*, June 17, 2011, FP11; Nathan VanderKlippe, "Aging Pipes," *Globe and Mail*, February 19, 2011, B6.

Transforming the Real Estate Distribution Model

Tara Perkins, "Percentage Change: The Commission Game," *Globe and Mail*, May 25, 2013, B6–B7; Steve Ladurantaye, "Upstart Property Website Pries Open Industry Data Vault," *Globe and Mail*, October 26, 2011, B1; Steve Ladurantaye, "Realtor Group Set to Open Online Trove of Real Estate Information," *Globe and Mail*, July 21, 2011, B1; Sunny Freeman, "Real Estate Board Resists Mandated Fair-Competition Rules," *Winnipeg Free Press*, July 9, 2011, B9; Garry Marr, "New Toronto Real Estate Board Policy Will Let Consumers Browse MLS Data," *National Post*, June 25, 2011, FP17; Steve Ladurantaye, "Real Estate Industry, Competition Bureau Lock Horns Again," *Globe and Mail*, May 28, 2011, B1; Steve Ladurantaye, "Competition Bureau Asked to Settle New Fight over MLS Listings," *Globe and Mail*, May 2, 2011, B1; Grant Robinson and Tara Perkins, "What Your Broker Doesn't Want You To Know," *Globe and Mail*, December 22, 2010, B4; Michael McCullough, "Estate Sale," *Canadian Business*, November 9–22, 2010, 55; Peter Foster, "CREA Cartel Not Broken Yet," *National Post*, October 26, 2010, FP11; Steve Ladurantaye, "The Deal That Ended a Year-Long Real Estate Battle," *Globe and Mail*, October 26, 2010, B4; Jonathan Ratner, "New Deal May Alter Buying of Homes," *Winnipeg Free Press*, October 25, 2010, B6; Steve Ladurantaye, "Realtors Ratify Deal to Give Consumers Wider Choice on Services," *Globe and Mail*, October 25, 2010, B4; "CREA Won Nothing in MLS Deal, Lawyer Says," *National Post*, October 19, 2010, FP6; Patricia Lovett-Reid, "Your Options in the Brave New Real Estate World; The Era of 5% Commissions May Soon Become a Distant Memory," *National Post*, October 16, 2010, FP10; Murray McNeill, "A Real Estate Revolution," *Winnipeg Free Press*, October 15, 2010, B6; Steve Ladurantaye, "Do-It-Yourselfers Are Shaking Up an Industry; Real Estate Agents Are Fighting Back," *The Globe and Mail*, May 20, 2010, B1; "How an Epic Battle Began," *National Post*, May 1, 2010, FP1; "Plans Shake Pillars of Real Estate; Proposals from Both Sides Would Overhaul Industry," *National Post*, February 12, 2010, FP1; Steve Ladurantaye, "The Battle to Unlock the Housing Market," *Globe and Mail*, January 30, 2010, B1.

CHAPTER 14

Beware of the Credit-Card Trap!

Roma Luciw, "Young and Prey to Debt," *Globe and Mail*, November 8, 2011, L1; Rob Carrick, "Borrowing to Pay for Your Wedding," *Globe and Mail*, May 1, 2012, B1; Canadian Bankers Association, http://www.cba.ca/en/media-room/50-backgrounders-on-banking-issues/626-canadas-banks-made-of-canada [accessed Jan 24, 2013]; Dianne Nice, "Credit Card Crackdown May Cost Consumers," *Globe and Mail*, August 30, 2010, CBC Website, "Card Costs: Who Pays What to Whom," Dec 17, 2010, http://www.cbc.ca/news/story/2009/04/16/f-cardfees.html [accessed May 27, 2012].

Say Hello to Your Digital Wallet

Tim Shufelt, "Death of the Wallet," *Canadian Business*, February, 18, 2013, P66; Matt O'Grady, "The End of Cash is Coming Soon—Like it or Not," *Canadian Business*, March 19, 2012, P54–55; John Greenwood, "Digital Wallet Promises Big Payday for Banks and Retailers," October 16, 2012; Grant Robertson and Rita Trichur, "Banks Plot Mobile Payment Future," *Globe and Mail*, May 14, 2012, B1; ComScore Website, http://www.comscore.com/Insights/Presentations_and_Whitepapers/2012/2013_Digital_Wallets_and_Payments [accessed January 27th, 2013]; "Mobile Wallets," *Globe and Mail*, November 8, 2012, MC3.

Canadian Banks: On the Edge of a Mortgage Crisis?

"How Low Will House Prices Go?," *Canadian Business*, February 18, 2013, 52–54; Tara Perkins, "Housing Market Cools but Does Not Freeze," *Globe and Mail*, October 16, 2013, B14; Richard Blackwell and Grant Robertson, "Mortgage Wars May Prompt More People to Buy," *Globe and Mail*, March 9, 2012, B3; Peter Shawn Taylor, "Mortgages for Free," *Canadian Business*, April 2, 2012, 28; Matthew McLearn, "Putting Out the Fire," *Canadian Business*, May 14, 2012, 38–42; Rob Carrick, "Ready to Be Bold? Sell the House and Rent," *Globe and Mail*, May 1, 2012, B11; Rob Carrick, "Goodbye to Three Irritating Bank Practices," *Globe and Mail*, March 6, 2012, B14; Richard Blackwell and Tara Perkins, "Mortgage Wars Combatants Losing Taste for Blood," *Globe and Mail*, March 24, 2012, B1; Special Report, "The Housing Market Will Crash," *Canadian Business*, February 20, 2012, 26–28.

CHAPTER 15

Hoarding Cash: Good or Bad Idea?

Brady Yauch, "Is Carney Right to Ask Businesses to Spend?" *Business News Network*, August 8, 2012, http://www.bnn.ca/News/2012/8/24; Stephen Fidler, "Firms' Cash Hoarding Stunts Europe," *Wall Street Journal*, March 24–25, 2012, A10; David Parkinson, "The Myth of Canada's Cash Mountain," *Globe and Mail*, March 24, 2012, B10; "U.S. Firms Hoarding Large Cash Stockpiles; $1.2T Saved After Bad Credit Crisis Memories," *National Post*, March 15, 2012, FP6; Simon Avery, "Teck Keen to Put Its Cash to Work," *Globe and Mail*, November 8, 2011, p. B16; Tim Kiladze, "Cash-Hoarding Firms Look Smart Now," *Globe and Mail*, September 27, 2011, B15; Simon Avery, "Billions in the Vault, But Not Much Bang," *Globe and Mail*, August 19, 2011, B10; Greg Keenan, "'Fortress Balance Sheets' Breed a New Kind of Crisis," *Globe and Mail*, August 10, 2011, B1; Paul Wiseman, "Strong Corporate Stats, Lingering U.S. Joblessness," *Winnipeg Free Press*, July 23, 2011, B16; David Parkinson, "Shareholders'

Lament: Mountains of Cash, Miserly Payouts," *Globe and Mail*, July 16, 2011, B15; Kevin Carmichael, "Caution Keeps Cash-Rich U.S. Employers from Hiring," *Globe and Mail*, July 9, 2011, B1; Alan Reynolds, "The Myth of Corporate Cash Hoarding," *Wall Street Journal*, February 23, 2011, A17.

Short Selling: Herbalife and Sino-Forest

Juliet Chung, "Einhorn: Bet against Herbalife Profitable," *Wall Street Journal*, January 24, 2013, C3; Juliet Chung, "Showdown over Herbalife Spotlights New Wall Street," *Wall Street Journal*, January 10, 2012, A1; Andy Hoffman and Jeff Gray, "Sino-Forest Files for Bankruptcy Protection," *Globe and Mail*, March 31, 2012, B4; Terence Corcoran, "Sino Kiss-Off Comes Too Late; Woes Take Down Forest of Global Reputations," *National Post*, June 22, 2011, FP1; Peter Koven, "Paulson Dumps Sino Stake; Shares Down 14.4% Before Hedge Fund's Sale Revealed," *National Post*, June 21, 2011, FP1; Peter Koven, "Block Questions Sino-Forest Documents; Shares Slip 4.5%; Did Related Firm Sell Sino-Forest Timber Rights?" *National Post*, June 18, 2011, FP4; Peter Koven and David Pett, "Sino Call Fails to Convince; Stock Plunges Further 32% as CEO Tries to Explain Arcane Business Strategy," *National Post*, June 15, 2011, FP1; Jonathan Chevreau, "Investor ED Flags; Due Diligence is Critical, As Tale of Sino-Forest Shows," *National Post*, June 11, 2011, FP9; David Pett and John Shmuel, "Muddy Waters Research 'Craps'; Dundee Blasts Attacker of Sino-Forest," *National Post*, June 8, 2011, FP1; David Pett and John Shmuel, "Sino-Forest Falls 20.6% After Short Seller's Report; Muddy Waters," *National Post*, June 3, 2011, FP7.

The Next Frontier, Mobile Investing

Tara Perkins, "Trading (Slowly) Goes Mobile," *Globe and Mail*, May 24, 2011, B17; Rob Carrick, "Have Your Say on the Best Money Blogs," *Globe and Mail*, May 3, 2011, B19; "Poll: How Likely Are You to Conduct Investing on a Mobile Device?" http://www.theglobeandmail.com/globe-investor/2011-online-broker-rankings/poll-how-likely-are-you-to-conduct-investing-on-a-mobile-device/article2236011/ [accessed January 5, 2012]; Rob Carrick, Mathew Ingram, Howard Lindzon, Boyd Erman, David Berman and Andrew Willis, "Best of Blogs," http://www.theglobeandmail.com/report-on-business/best-of-the-blogs/article683468/page2/ [accessed January 5, 2012].

Crowdfunding for Entrepreneurs

Zachary Gubler, "Inventive Funding Deserves Creative Regulation," *Wall Street Journal*, February 1, 2013, A13; A. Cortese, "CircleUp Helps Small Consumer Goods Firms Round Up Money; An Alternative to Tapping Credit Cards," *National Post*, January 28, 2013, FP7; M. Medley, "Words from their Sponsors; Authors Cash In on Crowd-Sourced Funding Sites such as Kickstarter and Indiegogo," *National Post*, January 9, 2013, B5; Q. Casey, "It Takes a Crowd; Olympians Go Online to Finance Training," *National Post*, December 31, 2012, FP1; J. McFarland, "OSC Weighs 'Crowdfunding' Against Risk of Fraud," *Globe and Mail*, December 15, 2012, B6; C. Dobby, "Ontario to Back Startup Crowdfunding; Fraud Warning," *National Post*, November 30, 2012, FP5; Q. Casey, "Crowd Money," *National Post*, October 22, 2012, FP1; B. Critchley, "Crowd Funds Close the Gap," *National Post*, September 20, 2012, FP2; K. Carmichael, "Facebook Generation Takes On the Regulators," *Globe and Mail*, August 23, 2012, B7; D. Indiviglo, "The Foolishness of Crowds," *Globe and Mail*, March 22, 2012, B11.

Growing Up Social: Graduating to an IPO

Evelyn Rusli, "LinkedIn Rallies While Its Web Peers Lose Luster," *Wall Street Journal*, February 28, 2013, B1; Evelyn Rusli and John Letzing, "Groupon Lands with a Thud," *Wall Street Journal*, February 28, 2013, B2; Evelyn Rusli, "Facebook Shares Rally Above $30," *Wall Street Journal*, January 10, 2013, B4; Nivedita Bhattacharjee and Alexei Oreskovic, "Groupon Fights for Its Life as Daily Deals Fade," *Business News Network*, November 12, 2012, http://www.bnn.ca/News/2012/11/12; Fabrice Taylor, "Facebook's Hidden Costs," *Globe and Mail*, May 29, 2012, B9; Andrew Ackerman, "No Violations Found in Facebook IPO," *Globe and Mail*, May 31, 2012, B8; Douglas MacMillan "How Mark Zuckerberg Jacked the Valley," *Canadian Business*, May 21–27, 2012, 61–67; "The Facebook Hype Meter," *Canadian Business*, June 11, 2012, 74; Lynn Cowan, "Groupon IPO Cheers Companies Waiting in the Wings," *Globe and Mail*, November 5, 2011, B6; David Milstead, "As Groupon Shares Soar, it's Time to Discount the Frenzy," *Globe and Mail*, November 8, 2011, B15; Fabrice Taylor, "Stop and Let It Pop," *Canadian Business*, June 2012, 20; Omar El Akkad and Paul Waldie, "Work Experience: LinkedIn Founder Net Worth: Billions," *Globe and Mail*, May 10, 2011, B1, B6; David Parkinson, "As Facebook Falls Flat, LinkedIn Adds Friends," *Globe and Mail*, May 30, 2012, B14.

NAME AND ORGANIZATION INDEX

C

D

E

F

G

H

I

J

K

N

O

P

Q

R

S

T

U

V

W

X

Y

Z

SUBJECT INDEX

boldface page number indicates definition; *f* indicates figure; *t* indicates table

C

E

F

G

H

I

N

O

Q

R

S

T

Y

Z